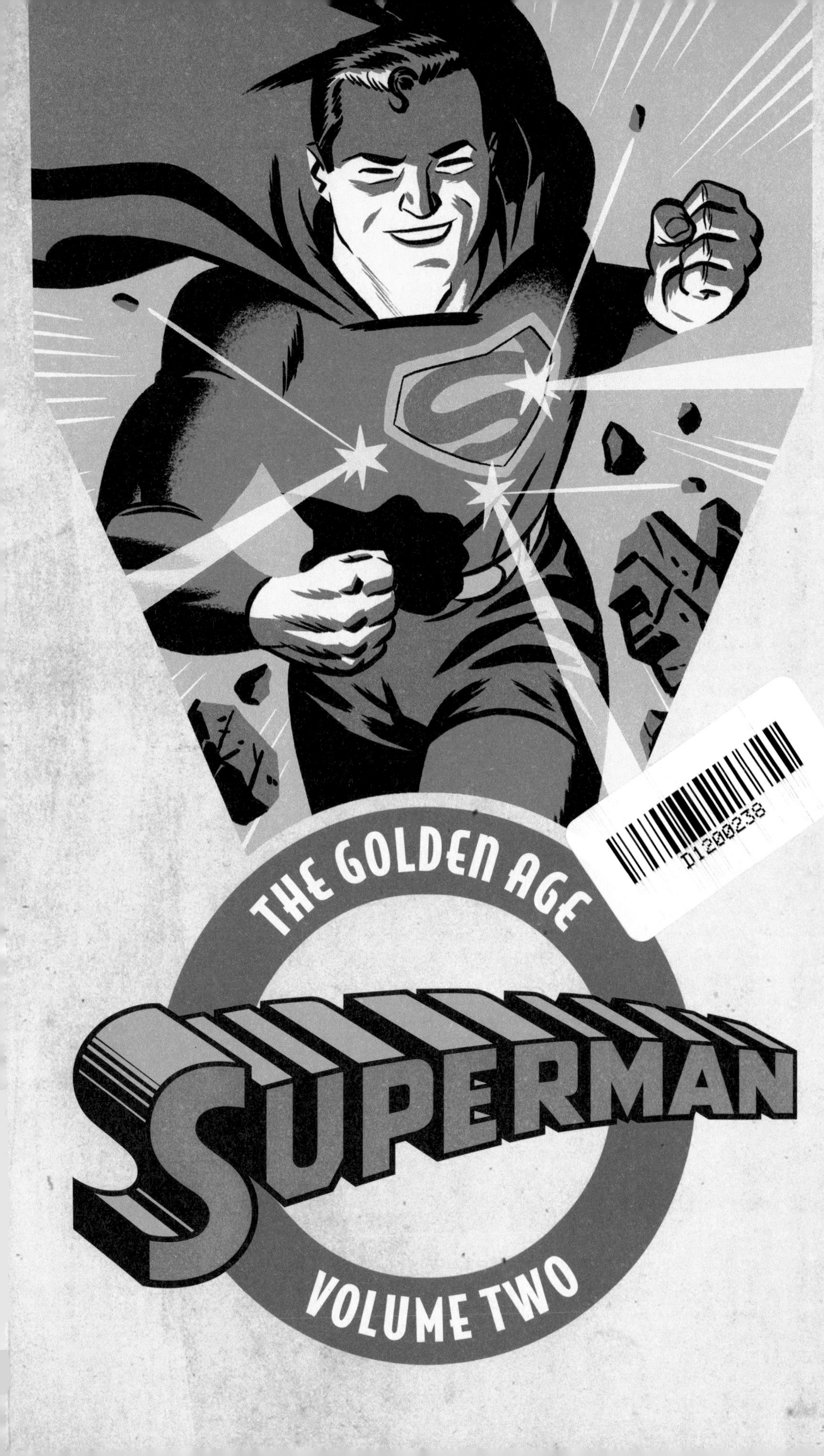

THE GOLDEN AGE
SUPERMAN
VOLUME TWO

JERRY SIEGEL
WRITER

JOE SHUSTER
JACK BURNLEY
WAYNE BORING
ARTISTS

MICHAEL CHO
COVER ARTIST

SUPERMAN created by **JERRY SIEGEL** and **JOE SHUSTER**.
By special arrangement with the Jerry Siegel family.

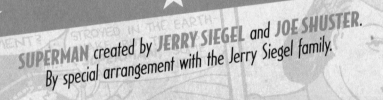

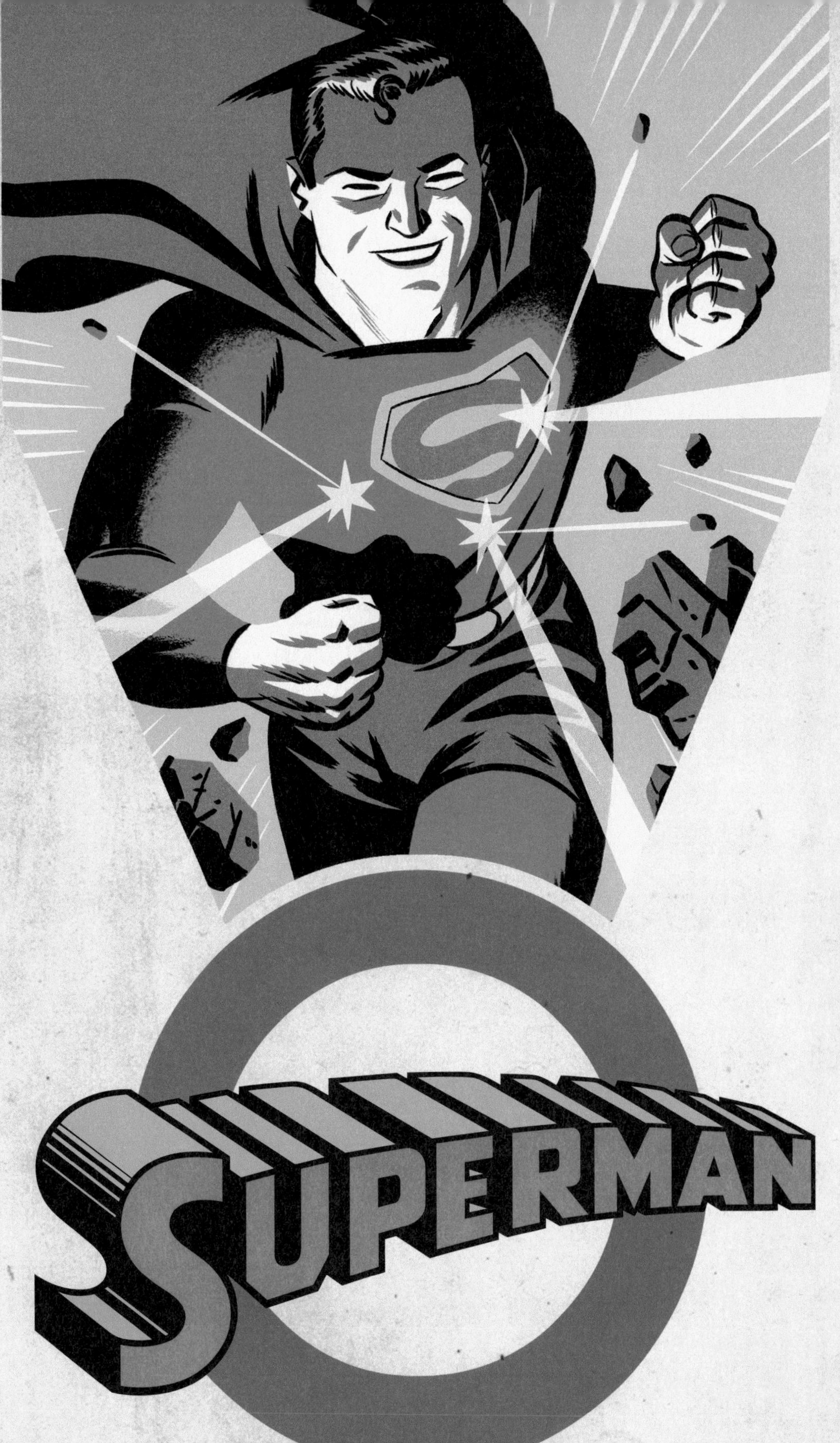
SUPERMAN

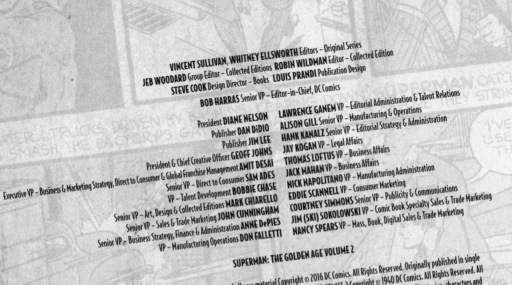

VINCENT SULLIVAN, WHITNEY ELLSWORTH Editors – Original Series
JEB WOODARD Group Editor – Collected Editions **ROBIN WILDMAN** Editor – Collected Edition
STEVE COOK Design Director – Books **LOUIS PRANDI** Publication Design

BOB HARRAS Senior VP – Editor-in-Chief, DC Comics

President **DIANE NELSON**
Publisher **DAN DiDIO**
Publisher **JIM LEE**
President & Chief Creative Officer **GEOFF JOHNS**
Executive VP – Business & Marketing Strategy, Direct to Consumer & Global Franchise Management **AMIT DESAI**
Senior VP – Direct to Consumer **SAM ADES**
VP – Talent Development **BOBBIE CHASE**
Senior VP – Art, Design & Collected Editions **MARK CHIARELLO**
Senior VP – Sales & Trade Marketing **JOHN CUNNINGHAM**
Senior VP – Business Strategy, Finance & Administration **ANNE DePIES**
VP – Manufacturing Operations **DON FALLETTI**

LAWRENCE GANEM VP – Editorial Administration & Talent Relations
ALISON GILL Senior VP – Manufacturing & Operations
HANK KANALZ Senior VP – Editorial Strategy & Administration
JAY KOGAN VP – Legal Affairs
THOMAS LOFTUS VP – Business Affairs
JACK MAHAN VP – Business Affairs
NICK NAPOLITANO VP – Manufacturing Administration
EDDIE SCANNELL VP – Consumer Marketing
COURTNEY SIMMONS Senior VP – Publicity & Communications
JIM (SKI) SOKOLOWSKI VP – Comic Book Specialty Sales & Trade Marketing
NANCY SPEARS VP – Mass, Book, Digital Sales & Trade Marketing

SUPERMAN: THE GOLDEN AGE VOLUME 2

DC Comics, 2900 West Alameda Ave., Burbank, CA 91505
Printed by LSC Communications, Salem, VA, USA. 10/28/16. First Printing.
ISBN: 978-1-4012-6530-4

Library of Congress Cataloging-in-Publication Data is Available.

MIX
Paper from responsible sources
FSC® C132124
www.fsc.org

All stories by **JERRY SIEGEL** and all art by **JOE SHUSTER** except where noted.

*These titles were originally untitled and are titled here for reader convenience.

DC strives to be as thorough as possible in its effort to determine creators' identities from all available sources.
This process is not perfect, and as a result, some attributions may be incomplete or wrongly assigned.

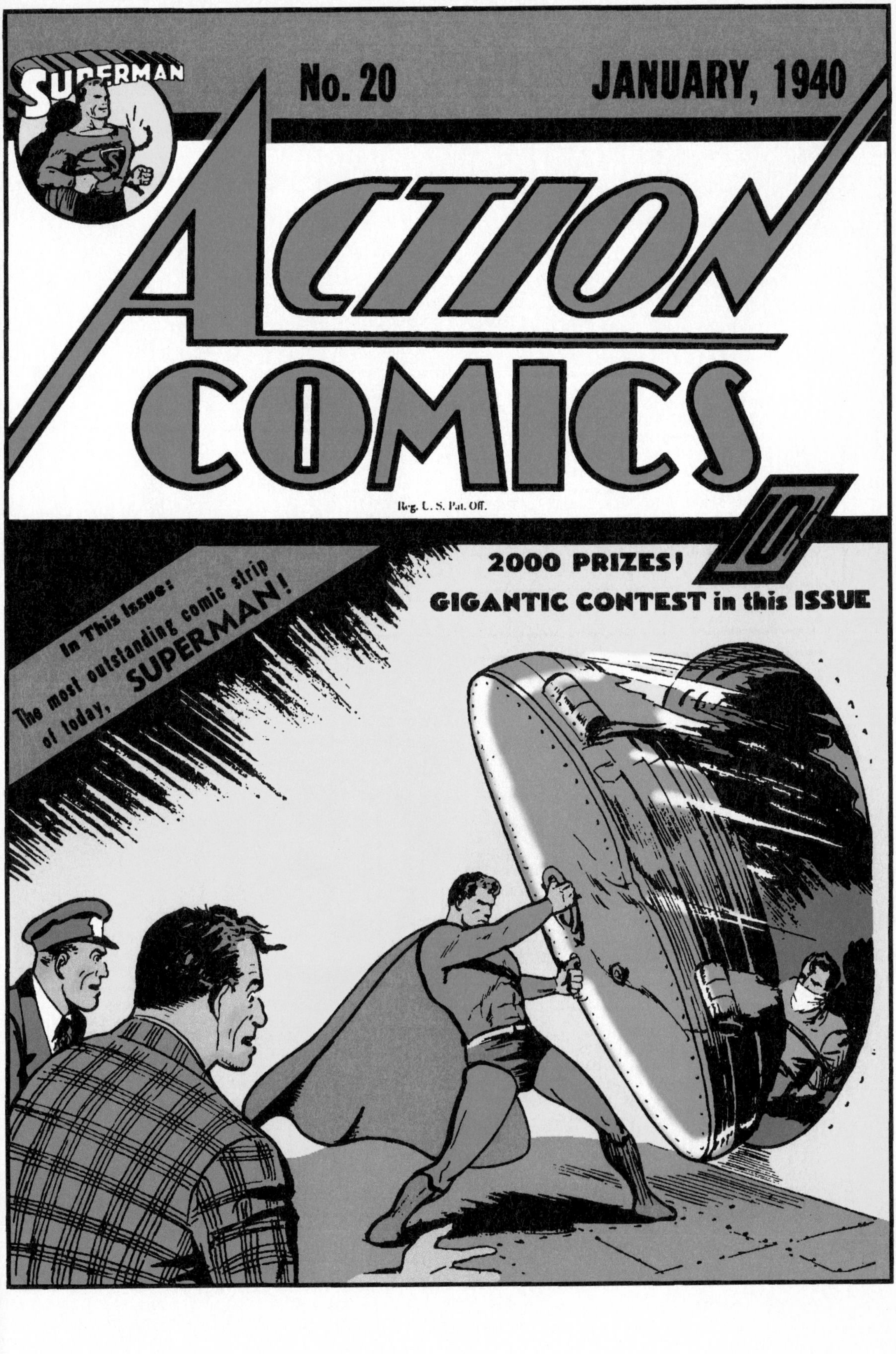
SUPERMAN
No. 20
JANUARY, 1940
ACTION COMICS
Reg. U. S. Pat. Off.
2000 PRIZES!
GIGANTIC CONTEST in this ISSUE
In This Issue:
The most outstanding comic strip of today, SUPERMAN!

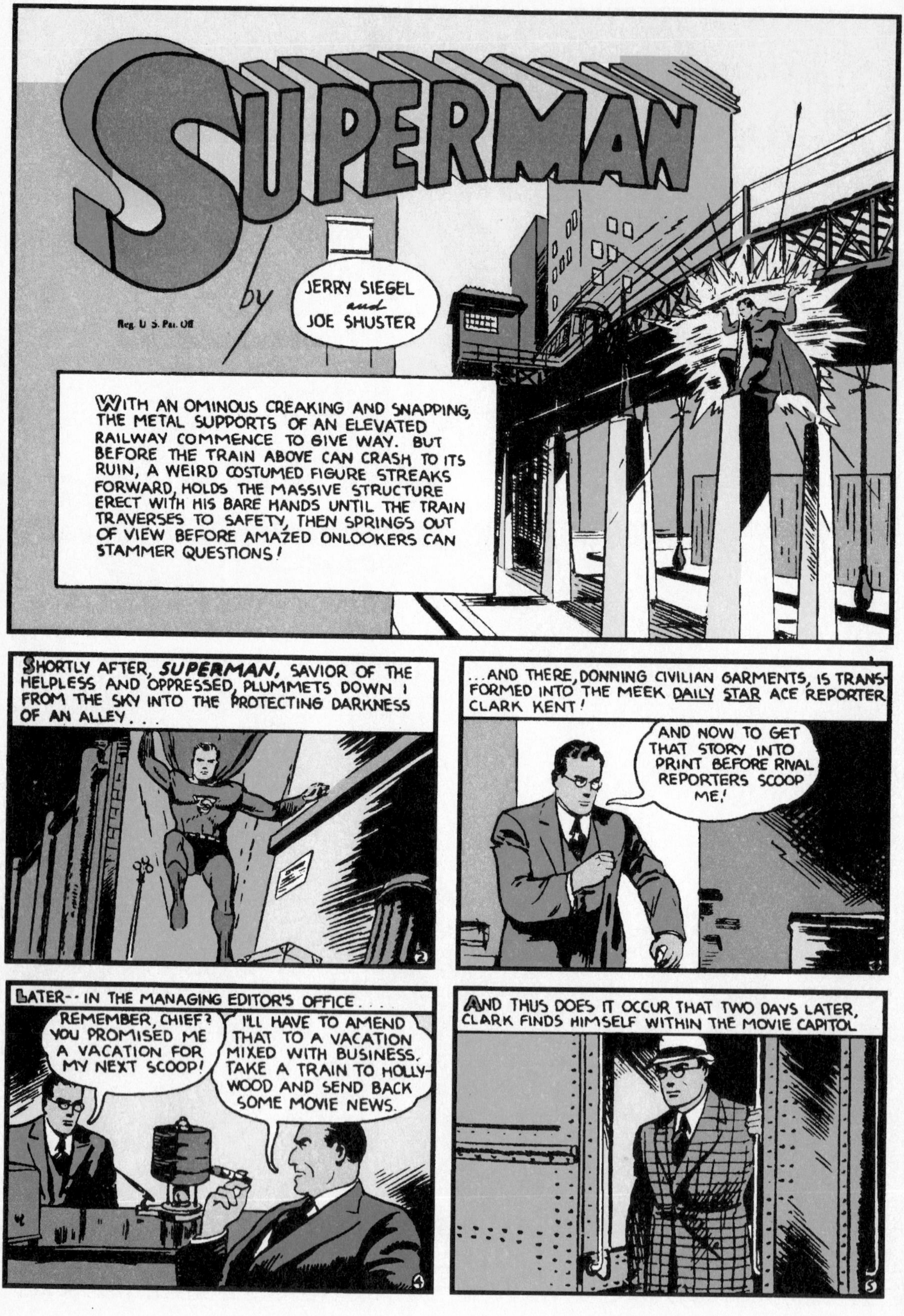
SUPERMAN
Reg. U. S. Pat. Off
by
JERRY SIEGEL and JOE SHUSTER
WITH AN OMINOUS CREAKING AND SNAPPING, THE METAL SUPPORTS OF AN ELEVATED RAILWAY COMMENCE TO GIVE WAY. BUT BEFORE THE TRAIN ABOVE CAN CRASH TO ITS RUIN, A WEIRD COSTUMED FIGURE STREAKS FORWARD, HOLDS THE MASSIVE STRUCTURE ERECT WITH HIS BARE HANDS UNTIL THE TRAIN TRAVERSES TO SAFETY, THEN SPRINGS OUT OF VIEW BEFORE AMAZED ONLOOKERS CAN STAMMER QUESTIONS!
SHORTLY AFTER, SUPERMAN, SAVIOR OF THE HELPLESS AND OPPRESSED, PLUMMETS DOWN FROM THE SKY INTO THE PROTECTING DARKNESS OF AN ALLEY...
...AND THERE, DONNING CIVILIAN GARMENTS, IS TRANSFORMED INTO THE MEEK DAILY STAR ACE REPORTER CLARK KENT!
AND NOW TO GET THAT STORY INTO PRINT BEFORE RIVAL REPORTERS SCOOP ME!
LATER-- IN THE MANAGING EDITOR'S OFFICE...
REMEMBER, CHIEF? YOU PROMISED ME A VACATION FOR MY NEXT SCOOP!
I'LL HAVE TO AMEND THAT TO A VACATION MIXED WITH BUSINESS. TAKE A TRAIN TO HOLLYWOOD AND SEND BACK SOME MOVIE NEWS.
AND THUS DOES IT OCCUR THAT TWO DAYS LATER, CLARK FINDS HIMSELF WITHIN THE MOVIE CAPITOL

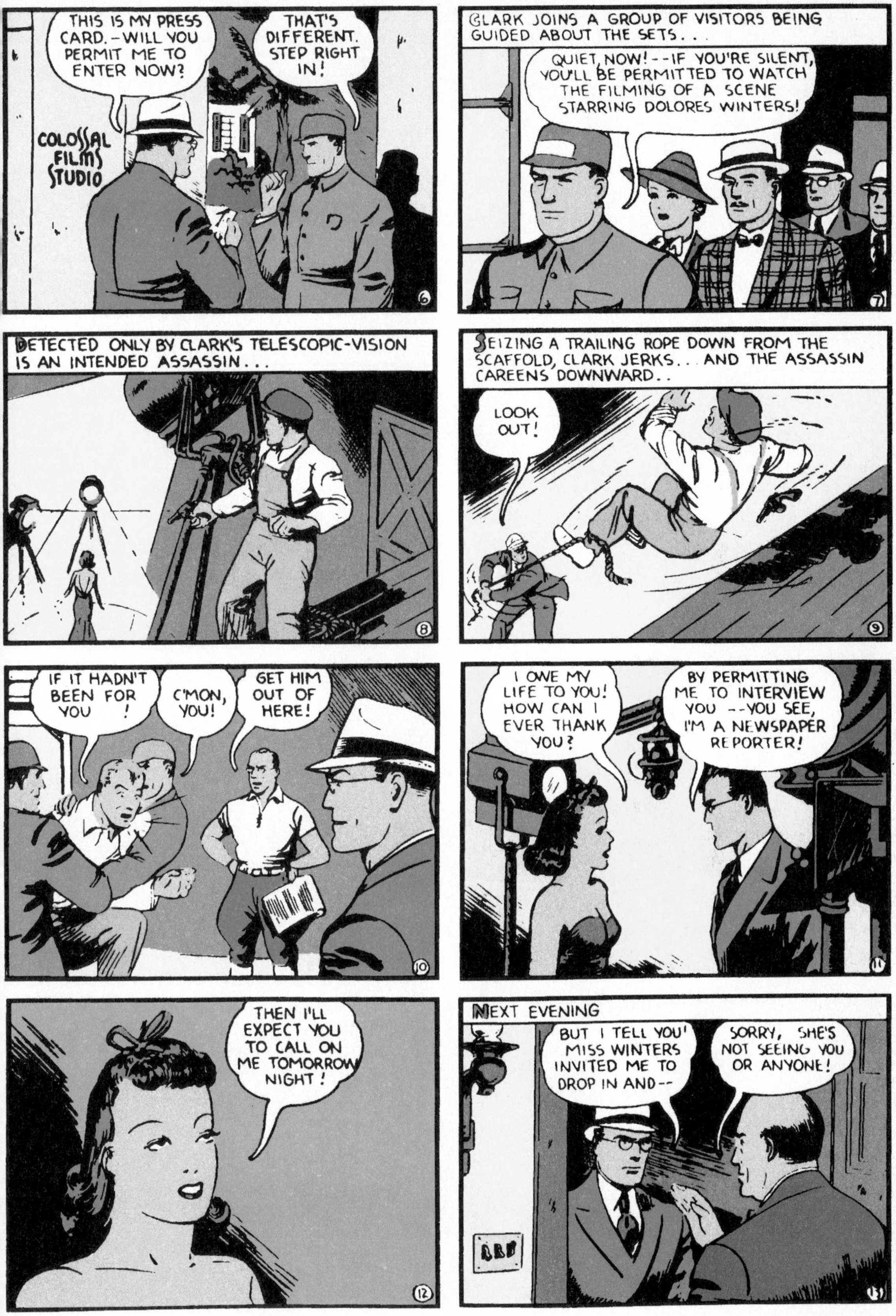
THIS IS MY PRESS CARD.–WILL YOU PERMIT ME TO ENTER NOW?
THAT'S DIFFERENT. STEP RIGHT IN!
COLOSSAL FILMS STUDIO
CLARK JOINS A GROUP OF VISITORS BEING GUIDED ABOUT THE SETS...
QUIET, NOW!--IF YOU'RE SILENT, YOU'LL BE PERMITTED TO WATCH THE FILMING OF A SCENE STARRING DOLORES WINTERS!
DETECTED ONLY BY CLARK'S TELESCOPIC-VISION IS AN INTENDED ASSASSIN...
SEIZING A TRAILING ROPE DOWN FROM THE SCAFFOLD, CLARK JERKS... AND THE ASSASSIN CAREENS DOWNWARD..
LOOK OUT!
IF IT HADN'T BEEN FOR YOU !
C'MON, YOU!
GET HIM OUT OF HERE!
I OWE MY LIFE TO YOU! HOW CAN I EVER THANK YOU?
BY PERMITTING ME TO INTERVIEW YOU --YOU SEE, I'M A NEWSPAPER REPORTER!
THEN I'LL EXPECT YOU TO CALL ON ME TOMORROW NIGHT!
NEXT EVENING
BUT I TELL YOU! MISS WINTERS INVITED ME TO DROP IN AND--
SORRY, SHE'S NOT SEEING YOU OR ANYONE!

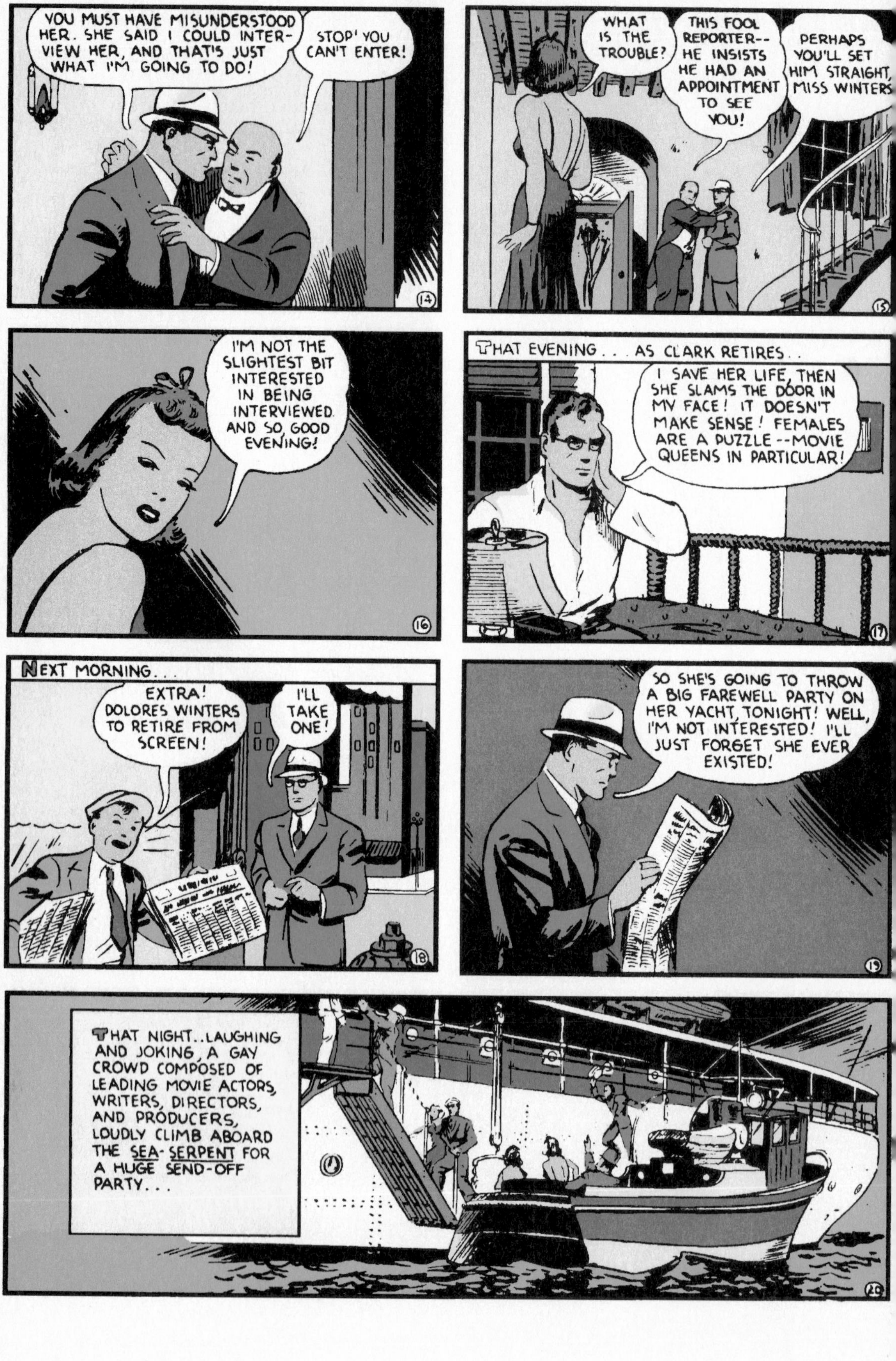
YOU MUST HAVE MISUNDERSTOOD HER. SHE SAID I COULD INTERVIEW HER, AND THAT'S JUST WHAT I'M GOING TO DO!
STOP! YOU CAN'T ENTER!
14
WHAT IS THE TROUBLE?
THIS FOOL REPORTER-- HE INSISTS HE HAD AN APPOINTMENT TO SEE YOU!
PERHAPS YOU'LL SET HIM STRAIGHT, MISS WINTERS
15
I'M NOT THE SLIGHTEST BIT INTERESTED IN BEING INTERVIEWED. AND SO, GOOD EVENING!
16
THAT EVENING . . . AS CLARK RETIRES . .
I SAVE HER LIFE, THEN SHE SLAMS THE DOOR IN MY FACE! IT DOESN'T MAKE SENSE! FEMALES ARE A PUZZLE--MOVIE QUEENS IN PARTICULAR!
17
NEXT MORNING . . .
EXTRA! DOLORES WINTERS TO RETIRE FROM SCREEN!
I'LL TAKE ONE!
18
SO SHE'S GOING TO THROW A BIG FAREWELL PARTY ON HER YACHT, TONIGHT! WELL, I'M NOT INTERESTED! I'LL JUST FORGET SHE EVER EXISTED!
19
THAT NIGHT..LAUGHING AND JOKING, A GAY CROWD COMPOSED OF LEADING MOVIE ACTORS, WRITERS, DIRECTORS, AND PRODUCERS, LOUDLY CLIMB ABOARD THE SEA-SERPENT FOR A HUGE SEND-OFF PARTY . . .
20

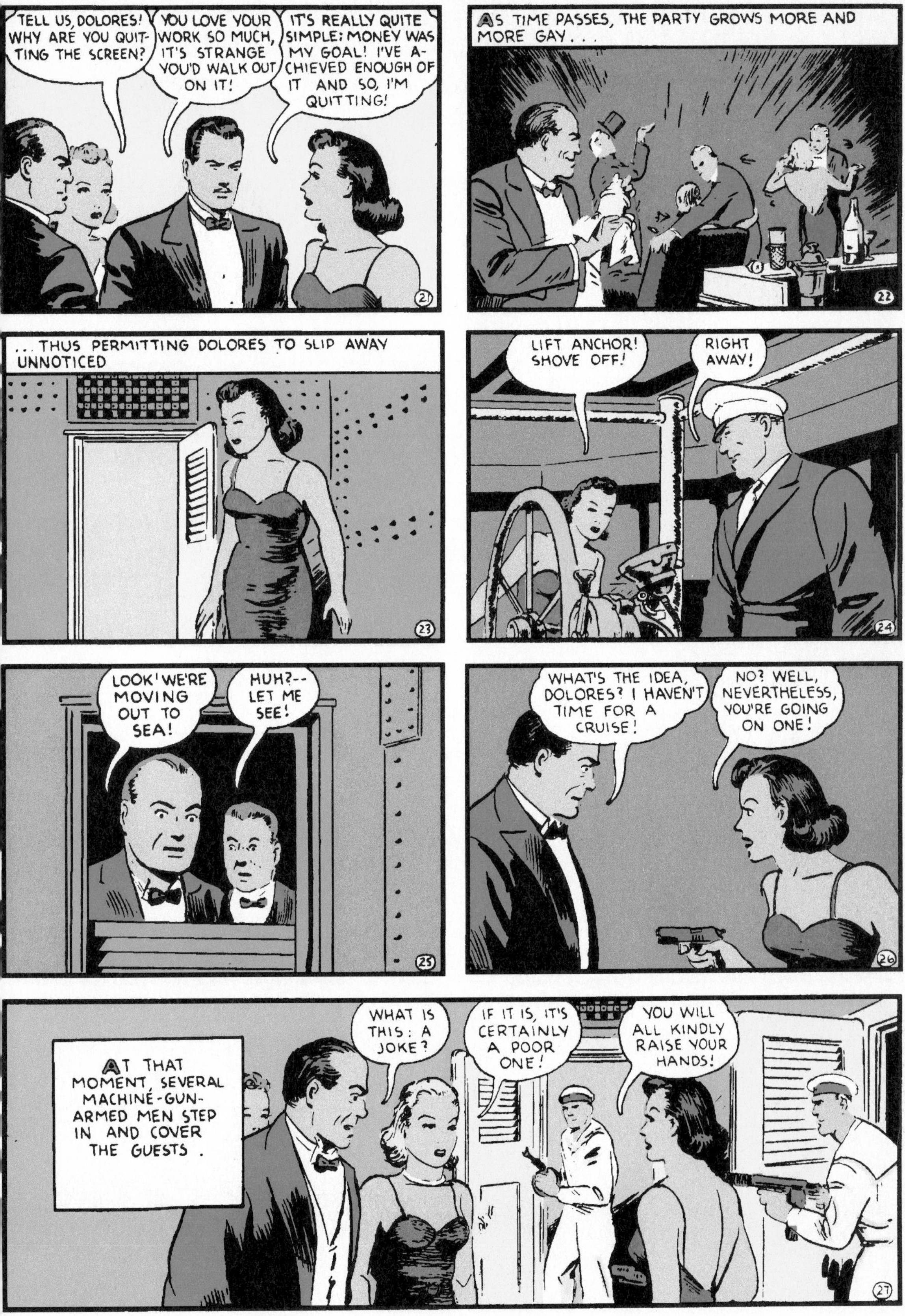
TELL US, DOLORES! WHY ARE YOU QUIT-TING THE SCREEN?
YOU LOVE YOUR WORK SO MUCH, IT'S STRANGE YOU'D WALK OUT ON IT!
IT'S REALLY QUITE SIMPLE: MONEY WAS MY GOAL! I'VE A-CHIEVED ENOUGH OF IT AND SO, I'M QUITTING!
21
AS TIME PASSES, THE PARTY GROWS MORE AND MORE GAY . . .
22
. . . THUS PERMITTING DOLORES TO SLIP AWAY UNNOTICED
23
LIFT ANCHOR! SHOVE OFF!
RIGHT AWAY!
24
LOOK! WE'RE MOVING OUT TO SEA!
HUH?-- LET ME SEE!
25
WHAT'S THE IDEA, DOLORES? I HAVEN'T TIME FOR A CRUISE!
NO? WELL, NEVERTHELESS, YOU'RE GOING ON ONE!
26
AT THAT MOMENT, SEVERAL MACHINE-GUN-ARMED MEN STEP IN AND COVER THE GUESTS .
WHAT IS THIS: A JOKE?
IF IT IS, IT'S CERTAINLY A POOR ONE!
YOU WILL ALL KINDLY RAISE YOUR HANDS!
27

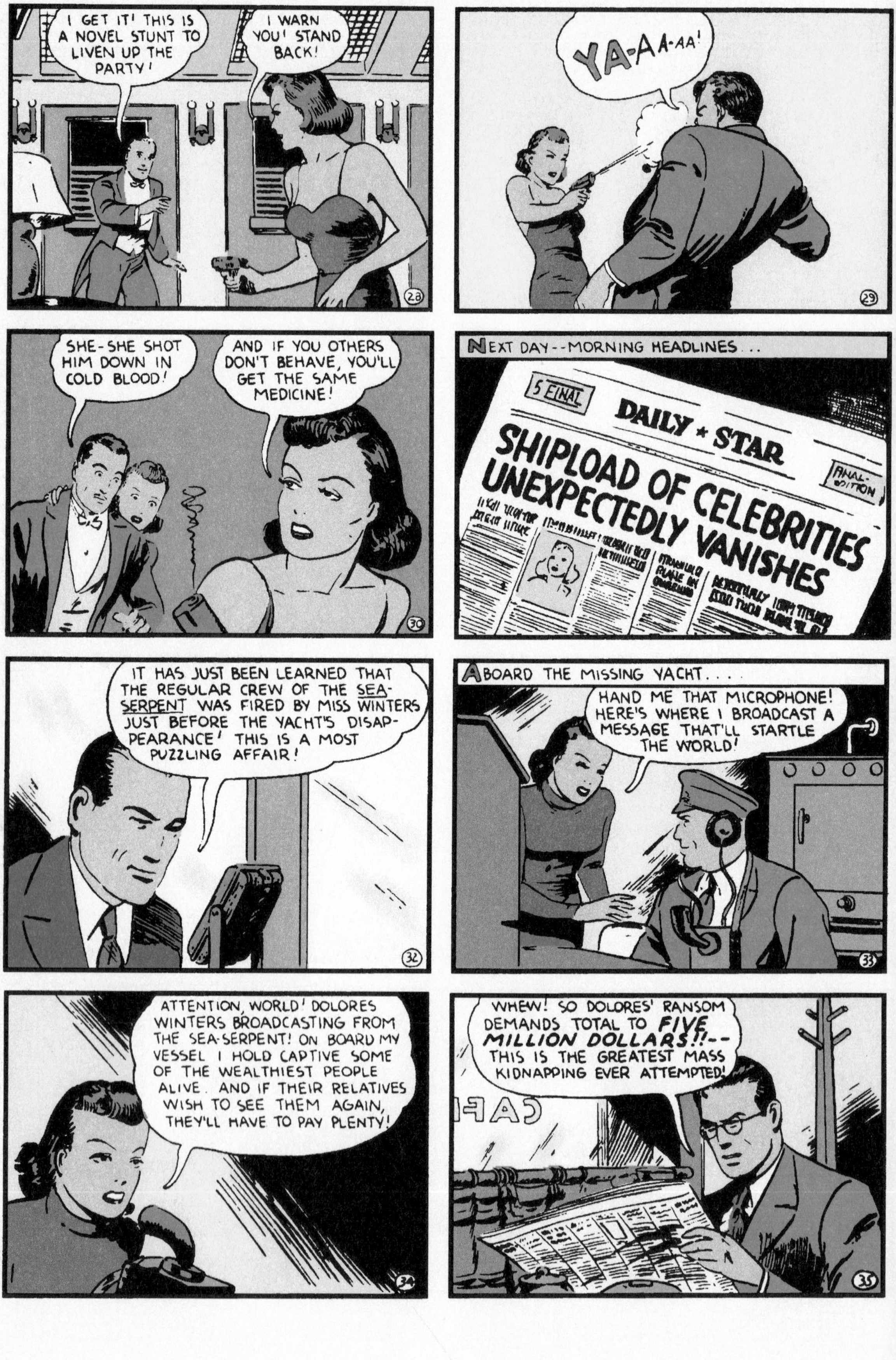
I GET IT! THIS IS A NOVEL STUNT TO LIVEN UP THE PARTY!
I WARN YOU! STAND BACK!
YA-AA-AA!
SHE-SHE SHOT HIM DOWN IN COLD BLOOD!
AND IF YOU OTHERS DON'T BEHAVE, YOU'LL GET THE SAME MEDICINE!
NEXT DAY--MORNING HEADLINES...
5 FINAL
DAILY ★ STAR
FINAL EDITION
SHIPLOAD OF CELEBRITIES UNEXPECTEDLY VANISHES
IT HAS JUST BEEN LEARNED THAT THE REGULAR CREW OF THE SEA-SERPENT WAS FIRED BY MISS WINTERS JUST BEFORE THE YACHT'S DISAPPEARANCE! THIS IS A MOST PUZZLING AFFAIR!
ABOARD THE MISSING YACHT....
HAND ME THAT MICROPHONE! HERE'S WHERE I BROADCAST A MESSAGE THAT'LL STARTLE THE WORLD!
ATTENTION, WORLD! DOLORES WINTERS BROADCASTING FROM THE SEA-SERPENT! ON BOARD MY VESSEL I HOLD CAPTIVE SOME OF THE WEALTHIEST PEOPLE ALIVE. AND IF THEIR RELATIVES WISH TO SEE THEM AGAIN, THEY'LL HAVE TO PAY PLENTY!
WHEW! SO DOLORES' RANSOM DEMANDS TOTAL TO FIVE MILLION DOLLARS!!-- THIS IS THE GREATEST MASS KIDNAPPING EVER ATTEMPTED!

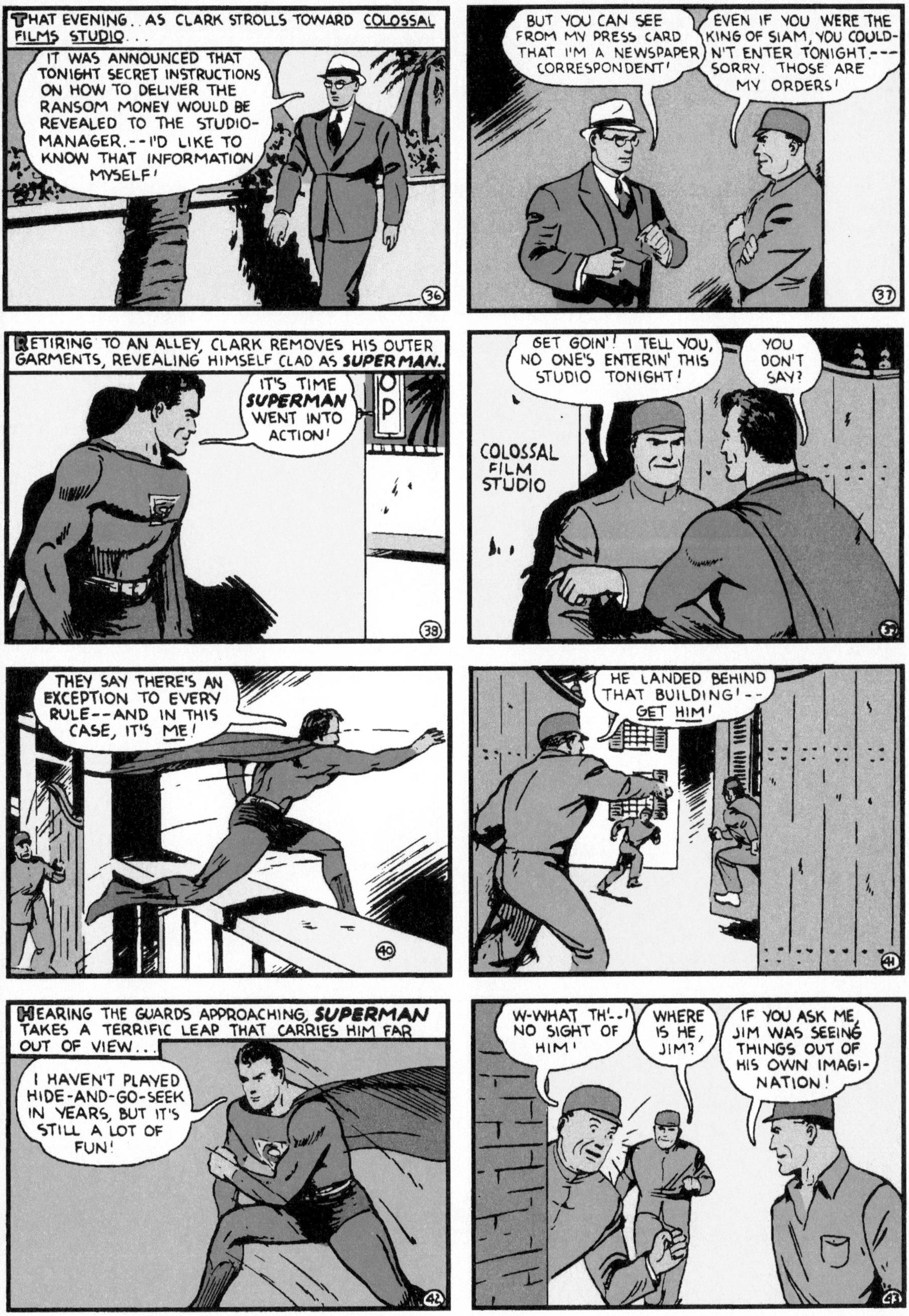
THAT EVENING.. AS CLARK STROLLS TOWARD COLOSSAL FILMS STUDIO...
IT WAS ANNOUNCED THAT TONIGHT SECRET INSTRUCTIONS ON HOW TO DELIVER THE RANSOM MONEY WOULD BE REVEALED TO THE STUDIO-MANAGER.--I'D LIKE TO KNOW THAT INFORMATION MYSELF!
36
BUT YOU CAN SEE FROM MY PRESS CARD THAT I'M A NEWSPAPER CORRESPONDENT!
EVEN IF YOU WERE THE KING OF SIAM, YOU COULDN'T ENTER TONIGHT.--- SORRY. THOSE ARE MY ORDERS!
37
RETIRING TO AN ALLEY, CLARK REMOVES HIS OUTER GARMENTS, REVEALING HIMSELF CLAD AS SUPERMAN..
IT'S TIME SUPERMAN WENT INTO ACTION!
38
GET GOIN'! I TELL YOU, NO ONE'S ENTERIN' THIS STUDIO TONIGHT!
YOU DON'T SAY?
COLOSSAL FILM STUDIO
THEY SAY THERE'S AN EXCEPTION TO EVERY RULE--AND IN THIS CASE, IT'S ME!
40
HE LANDED BEHIND THAT BUILDING!-- GET HIM!
41
HEARING THE GUARDS APPROACHING, SUPERMAN TAKES A TERRIFIC LEAP THAT CARRIES HIM FAR OUT OF VIEW..
I HAVEN'T PLAYED HIDE-AND-GO-SEEK IN YEARS, BUT IT'S STILL A LOT OF FUN!
42
W-WHAT TH'--! NO SIGHT OF HIM!
WHERE IS HE, JIM?
IF YOU ASK ME, JIM WAS SEEING THINGS OUT OF HIS OWN IMAGINATION!

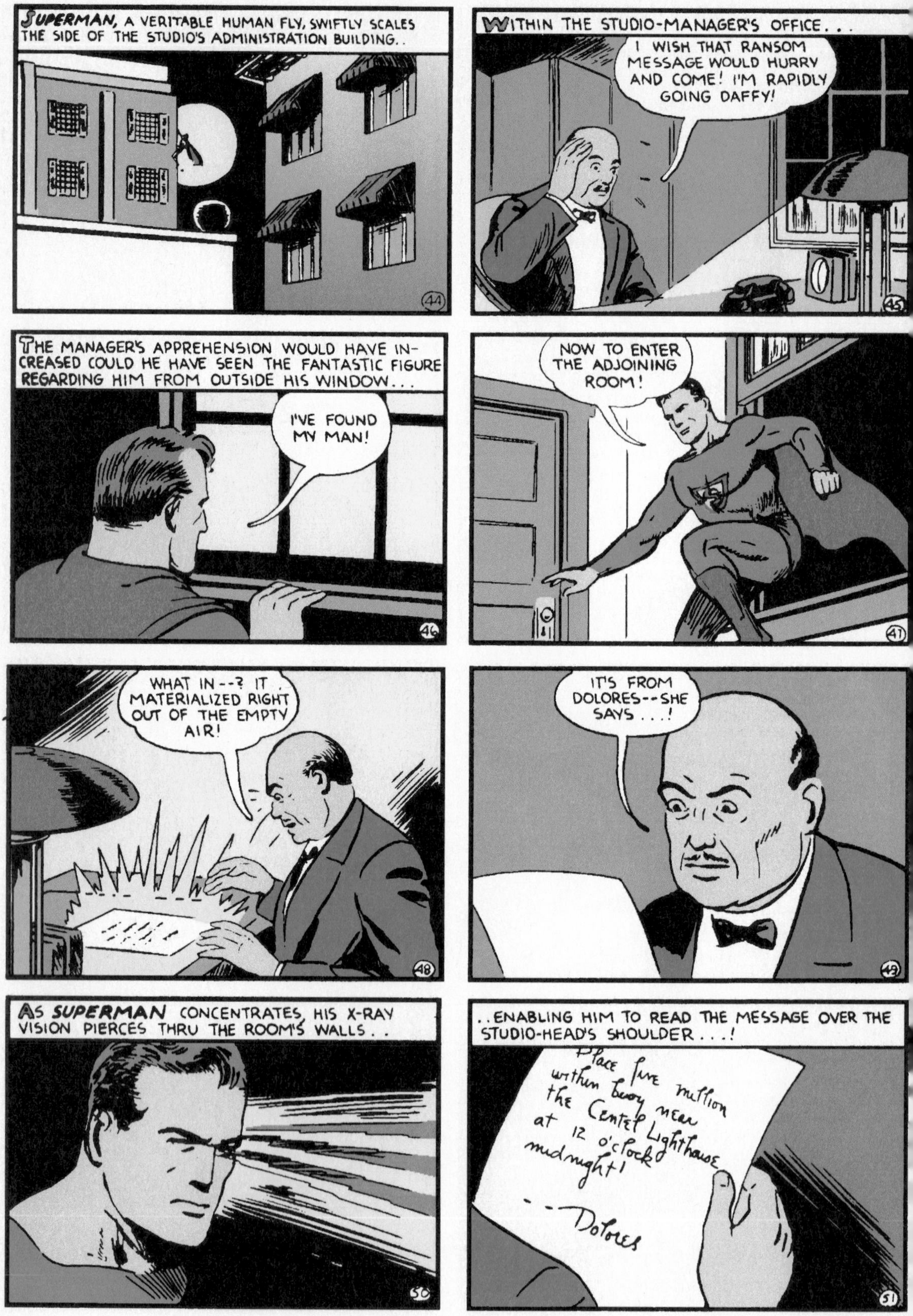
SUPERMAN, A VERITABLE HUMAN FLY, SWIFTLY SCALES THE SIDE OF THE STUDIO'S ADMINISTRATION BUILDING..
WITHIN THE STUDIO-MANAGER'S OFFICE...
I WISH THAT RANSOM MESSAGE WOULD HURRY AND COME! I'M RAPIDLY GOING DAFFY!
THE MANAGER'S APPREHENSION WOULD HAVE INCREASED COULD HE HAVE SEEN THE FANTASTIC FIGURE REGARDING HIM FROM OUTSIDE HIS WINDOW...
I'VE FOUND MY MAN!
NOW TO ENTER THE ADJOINING ROOM!
WHAT IN--? IT MATERIALIZED RIGHT OUT OF THE EMPTY AIR!
IT'S FROM DOLORES--SHE SAYS...!
AS SUPERMAN CONCENTRATES, HIS X-RAY VISION PIERCES THRU THE ROOM'S WALLS..
..ENABLING HIM TO READ THE MESSAGE OVER THE STUDIO-HEAD'S SHOULDER...!
Place five million
within buoy near
the Center Lighthouse
at 12 o'clock
midnight!
--Dolores

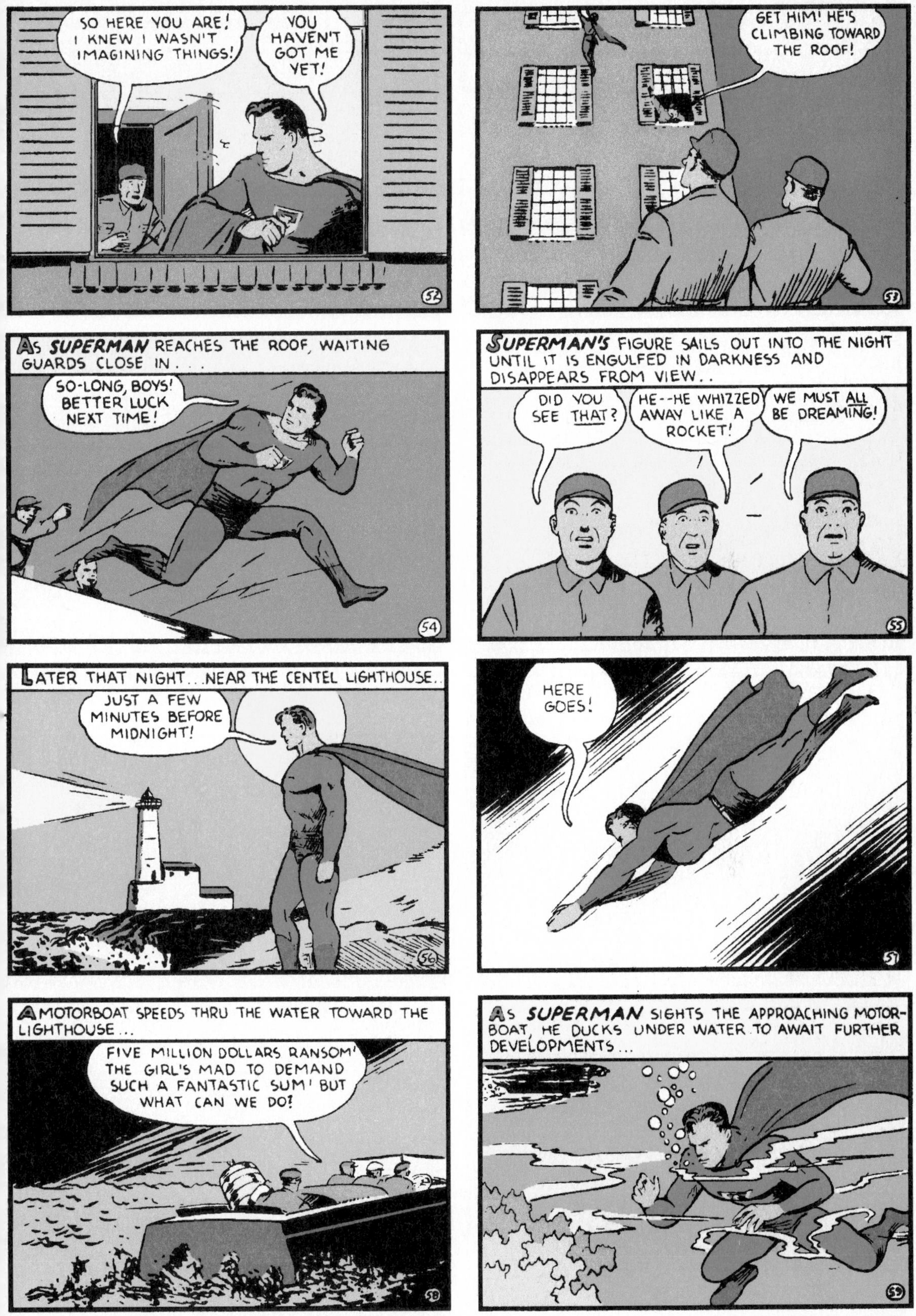
SO HERE YOU ARE! I KNEW I WASN'T IMAGINING THINGS!
YOU HAVEN'T GOT ME YET!
GET HIM! HE'S CLIMBING TOWARD THE ROOF!
AS SUPERMAN REACHES THE ROOF, WAITING GUARDS CLOSE IN. . .
SO-LONG, BOYS! BETTER LUCK NEXT TIME!
SUPERMAN'S FIGURE SAILS OUT INTO THE NIGHT UNTIL IT IS ENGULFED IN DARKNESS AND DISAPPEARS FROM VIEW. .
DID YOU SEE THAT?
HE--HE WHIZZED AWAY LIKE A ROCKET!
WE MUST ALL BE DREAMING!
LATER THAT NIGHT...NEAR THE CENTEL LIGHTHOUSE..
JUST A FEW MINUTES BEFORE MIDNIGHT!
HERE GOES!
A MOTORBOAT SPEEDS THRU THE WATER TOWARD THE LIGHTHOUSE...
FIVE MILLION DOLLARS RANSOM! THE GIRL'S MAD TO DEMAND SUCH A FANTASTIC SUM! BUT WHAT CAN WE DO?
AS SUPERMAN SIGHTS THE APPROACHING MOTOR-BOAT, HE DUCKS UNDER WATER TO AWAIT FURTHER DEVELOPMENTS...

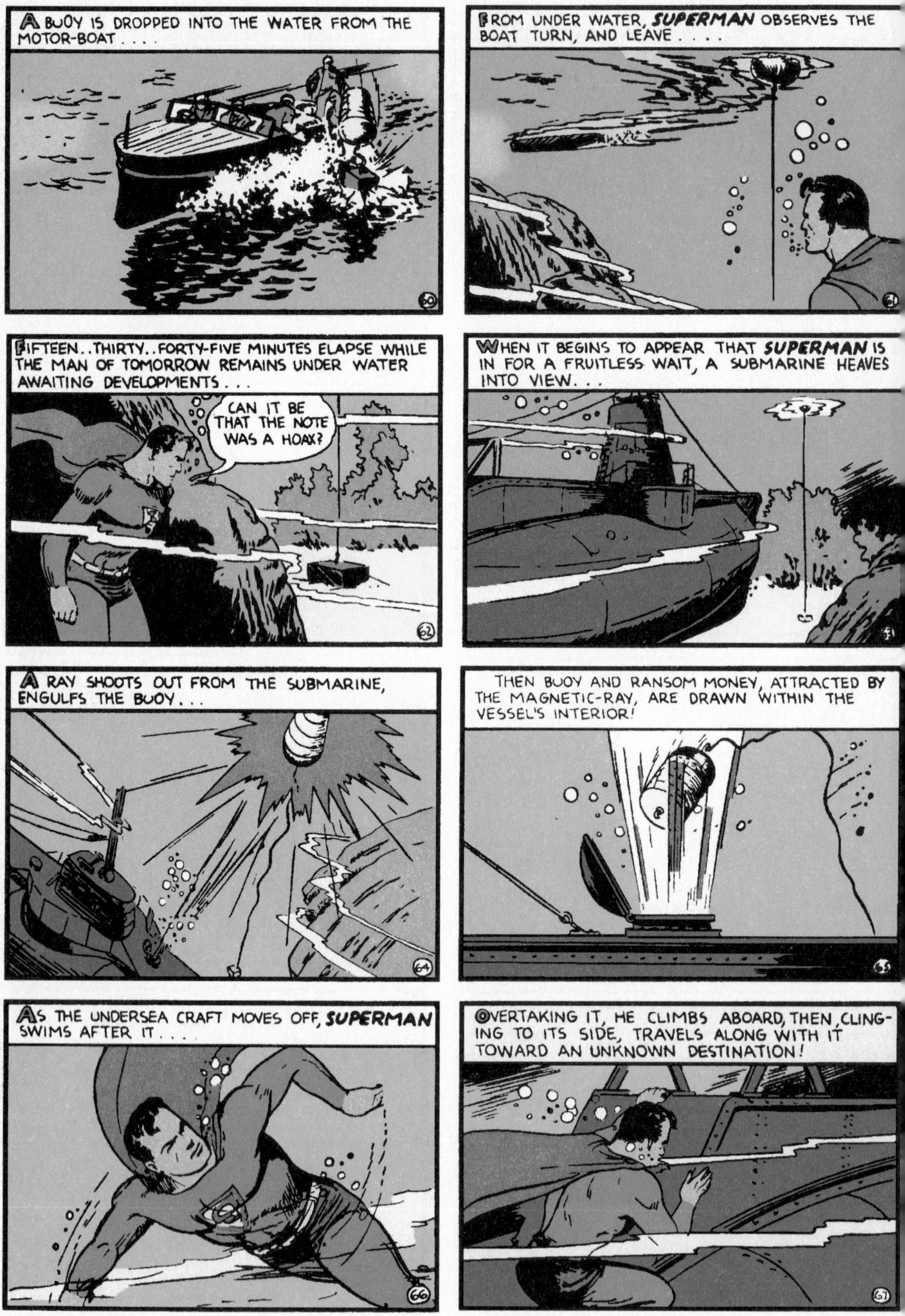
A BUOY IS DROPPED INTO THE WATER FROM THE MOTOR-BOAT . . . .
FROM UNDER WATER, SUPERMAN OBSERVES THE BOAT TURN, AND LEAVE . . . .
FIFTEEN..THIRTY..FORTY-FIVE MINUTES ELAPSE WHILE THE MAN OF TOMORROW REMAINS UNDER WATER AWAITING DEVELOPMENTS . . .
CAN IT BE THAT THE NOTE WAS A HOAX?
WHEN IT BEGINS TO APPEAR THAT SUPERMAN IS IN FOR A FRUITLESS WAIT, A SUBMARINE HEAVES INTO VIEW. . .
A RAY SHOOTS OUT FROM THE SUBMARINE, ENGULFS THE BUOY . . .
THEN BUOY AND RANSOM MONEY, ATTRACTED BY THE MAGNETIC-RAY, ARE DRAWN WITHIN THE VESSEL'S INTERIOR!
AS THE UNDERSEA CRAFT MOVES OFF, SUPERMAN SWIMS AFTER IT . . .
OVERTAKING IT, HE CLIMBS ABOARD, THEN, CLINGING TO ITS SIDE, TRAVELS ALONG WITH IT TOWARD AN UNKNOWN DESTINATION!

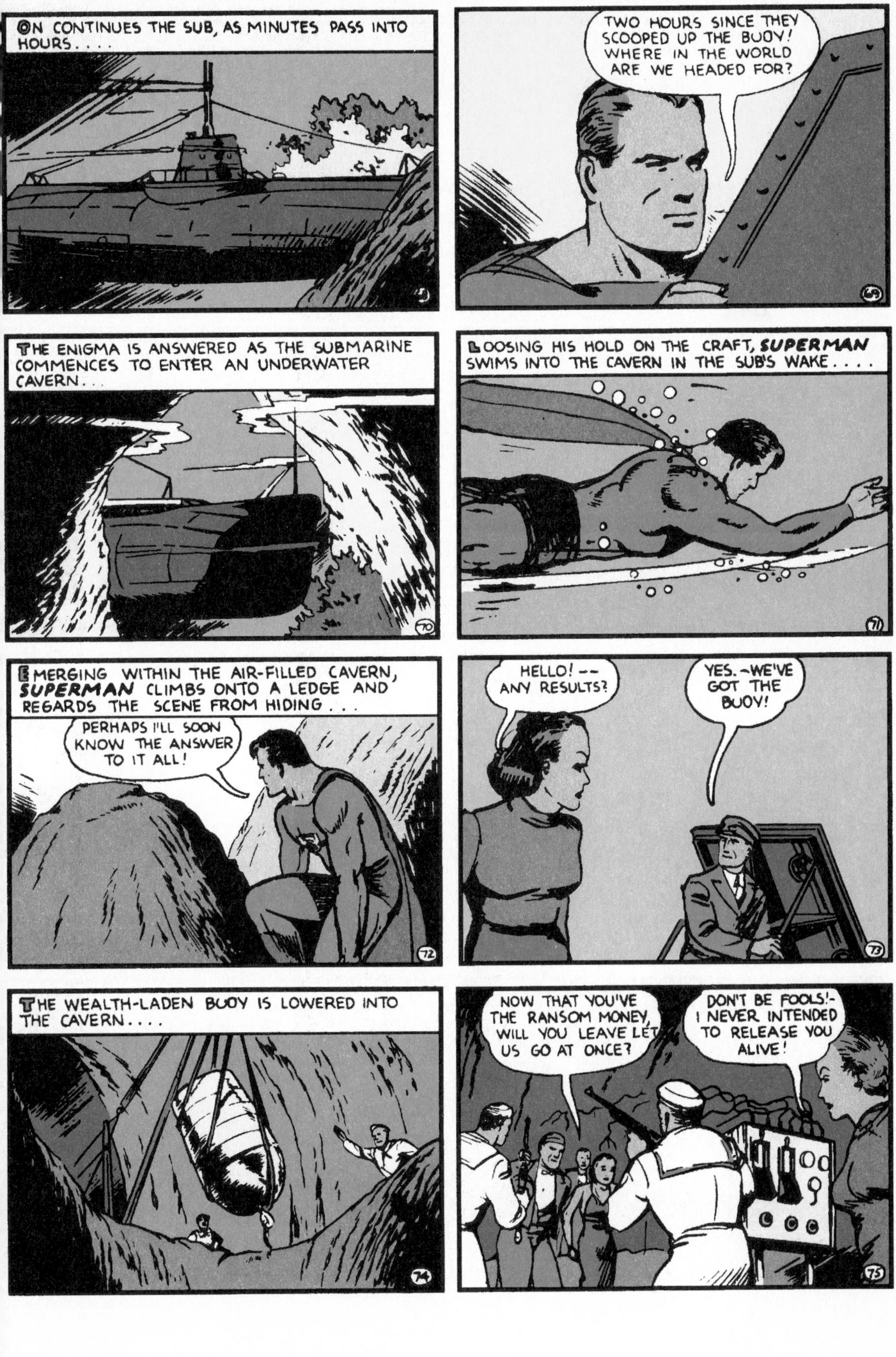
ON CONTINUES THE SUB, AS MINUTES PASS INTO HOURS....
TWO HOURS SINCE THEY SCOOPED UP THE BUOY! WHERE IN THE WORLD ARE WE HEADED FOR?
THE ENIGMA IS ANSWERED AS THE SUBMARINE COMMENCES TO ENTER AN UNDERWATER CAVERN...
LOOSING HIS HOLD ON THE CRAFT, SUPERMAN SWIMS INTO THE CAVERN IN THE SUB'S WAKE....
EMERGING WITHIN THE AIR-FILLED CAVERN, SUPERMAN CLIMBS ONTO A LEDGE AND REGARDS THE SCENE FROM HIDING...
PERHAPS I'LL SOON KNOW THE ANSWER TO IT ALL!
HELLO! -- ANY RESULTS?
YES.-WE'VE GOT THE BUOY!
THE WEALTH-LADEN BUOY IS LOWERED INTO THE CAVERN....
NOW THAT YOU'VE THE RANSOM MONEY, WILL YOU LEAVE LET US GO AT ONCE?
DON'T BE FOOLS!- I NEVER INTENDED TO RELEASE YOU ALIVE!

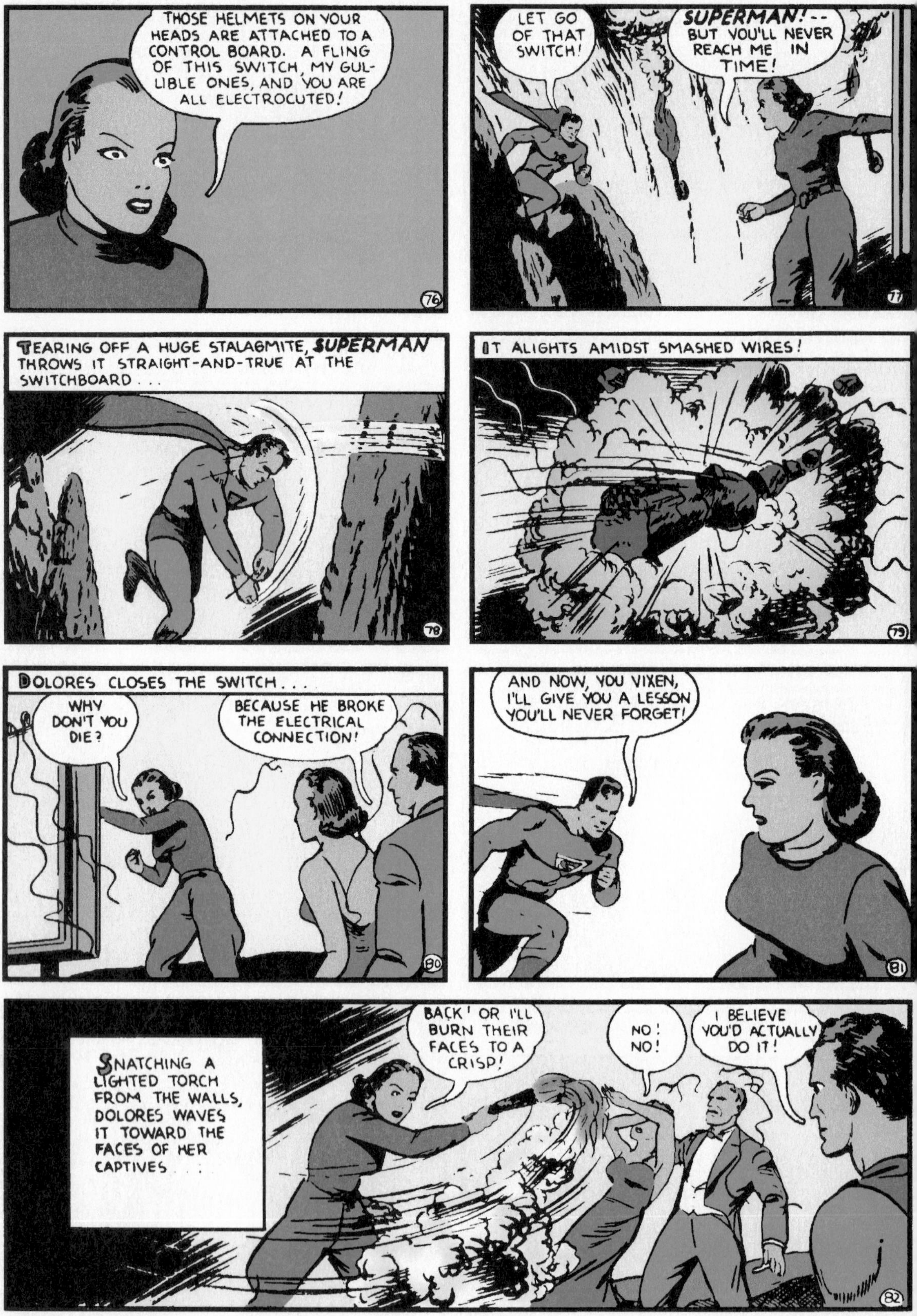
THOSE HELMETS ON YOUR HEADS ARE ATTACHED TO A CONTROL BOARD. A FLING OF THIS SWITCH, MY GULLIBLE ONES, AND YOU ARE ALL ELECTROCUTED!
76
LET GO OF THAT SWITCH!
SUPERMAN!-- BUT YOU'LL NEVER REACH ME IN TIME!
77
TEARING OFF A HUGE STALAGMITE, SUPERMAN THROWS IT STRAIGHT-AND-TRUE AT THE SWITCHBOARD . . .
78
IT ALIGHTS AMIDST SMASHED WIRES!
79
DOLORES CLOSES THE SWITCH . . .
WHY DON'T YOU DIE?
BECAUSE HE BROKE THE ELECTRICAL CONNECTION!
80
AND NOW, YOU VIXEN, I'LL GIVE YOU A LESSON YOU'LL NEVER FORGET!
81
SNATCHING A LIGHTED TORCH FROM THE WALLS, DOLORES WAVES IT TOWARD THE FACES OF HER CAPTIVES . . .
BACK! OR I'LL BURN THEIR FACES TO A CRISP!
NO! NO!
I BELIEVE YOU'D ACTUALLY DO IT!
82

SUPERMAN HAS A SUDDEN BURST OF INTUITION...

THOSE EVIL BLAZING EYES... THERE'S ONLY ONE PERSON ON THIS EARTH WHO COULD POSSESS THEM...! ULTRA!

YOU ARE INDEED PERCEPTIVE, SUPERMAN! YOU THOUGHT YOU HAD KILLED ME IN OUR LAST ENCOUNTER, DIDN'T YOU? BUT LOOK--AS YOU CAN SEE, I'M VERY MUCH ALIVE!

BUT-- I SAW YOU DIE, MYSELF!

MY ASSISTANTS, FINDING MY BODY, REVIVED ME VIA ADRENALIN. HOWEVER, IT WAS CLEAR THAT MY RECOVERY COULD BE ONLY TEMPORARY.

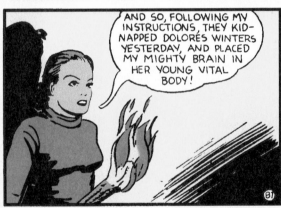

AND SO, FOLLOWING MY INSTRUCTIONS, THEY KIDNAPPED DOLORES WINTERS YESTERDAY, AND PLACED MY MIGHTY BRAIN IN HER YOUNG VITAL BODY!

IT APPEARS THAT WE'RE DEADLOCKED!

EITHER YOU LEAVE, OR I'LL SCORCH THE CAPTIVES, AT ONCE!

ABRUPTLY, SUPERMAN SUMMONS ALL THE POWER IN HIS POWERFUL LUNGS, AND BLOWS OUT THE TORCH FROM WHERE HE STANDS..

YOU BLEW IT OUT!

AND HERE'S WHERE I END YOUR FIENDISH CAREER OF CRIME!

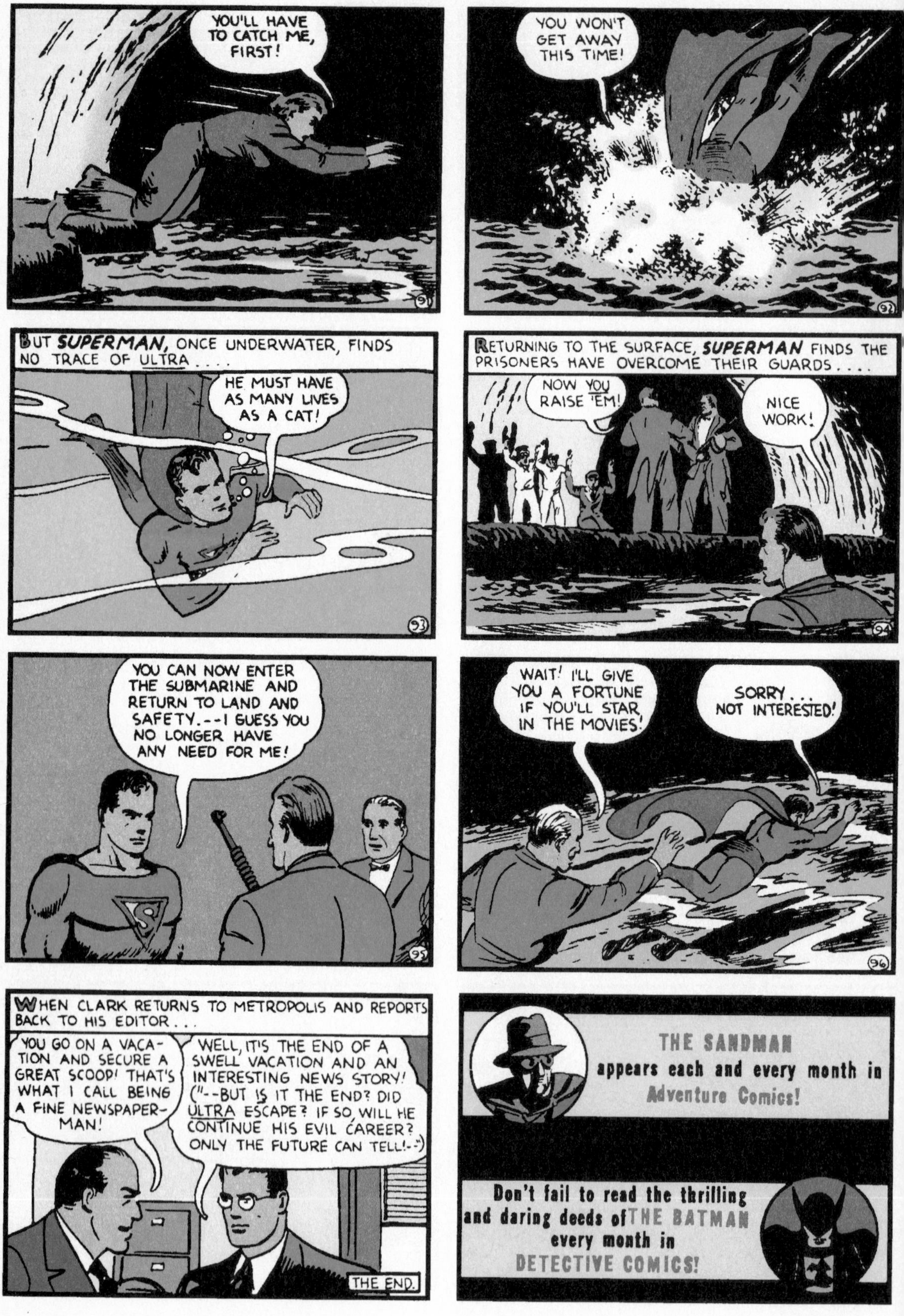
YOU'LL HAVE TO CATCH ME, FIRST!
YOU WON'T GET AWAY THIS TIME!
BUT SUPERMAN, ONCE UNDERWATER, FINDS NO TRACE OF ULTRA . . . .
HE MUST HAVE AS MANY LIVES AS A CAT!
RETURNING TO THE SURFACE, SUPERMAN FINDS THE PRISONERS HAVE OVERCOME THEIR GUARDS . . . .
NOW YOU RAISE 'EM!
NICE WORK!
YOU CAN NOW ENTER THE SUBMARINE AND RETURN TO LAND AND SAFETY.--I GUESS YOU NO LONGER HAVE ANY NEED FOR ME!
WAIT! I'LL GIVE YOU A FORTUNE IF YOU'LL STAR IN THE MOVIES!
SORRY... NOT INTERESTED!
WHEN CLARK RETURNS TO METROPOLIS AND REPORTS BACK TO HIS EDITOR . . .
YOU GO ON A VACATION AND SECURE A GREAT SCOOP! THAT'S WHAT I CALL BEING A FINE NEWSPAPER-MAN!
WELL, IT'S THE END OF A SWELL VACATION AND AN INTERESTING NEWS STORY! ("--BUT IS IT THE END? DID ULTRA ESCAPE? IF SO, WILL HE CONTINUE HIS EVIL CAREER? ONLY THE FUTURE CAN TELL!--")
THE END.
THE SANDMAN appears each and every month in Adventure Comics!
Don't fail to read the thrilling and daring deeds of THE BATMAN every month in DETECTIVE COMICS!

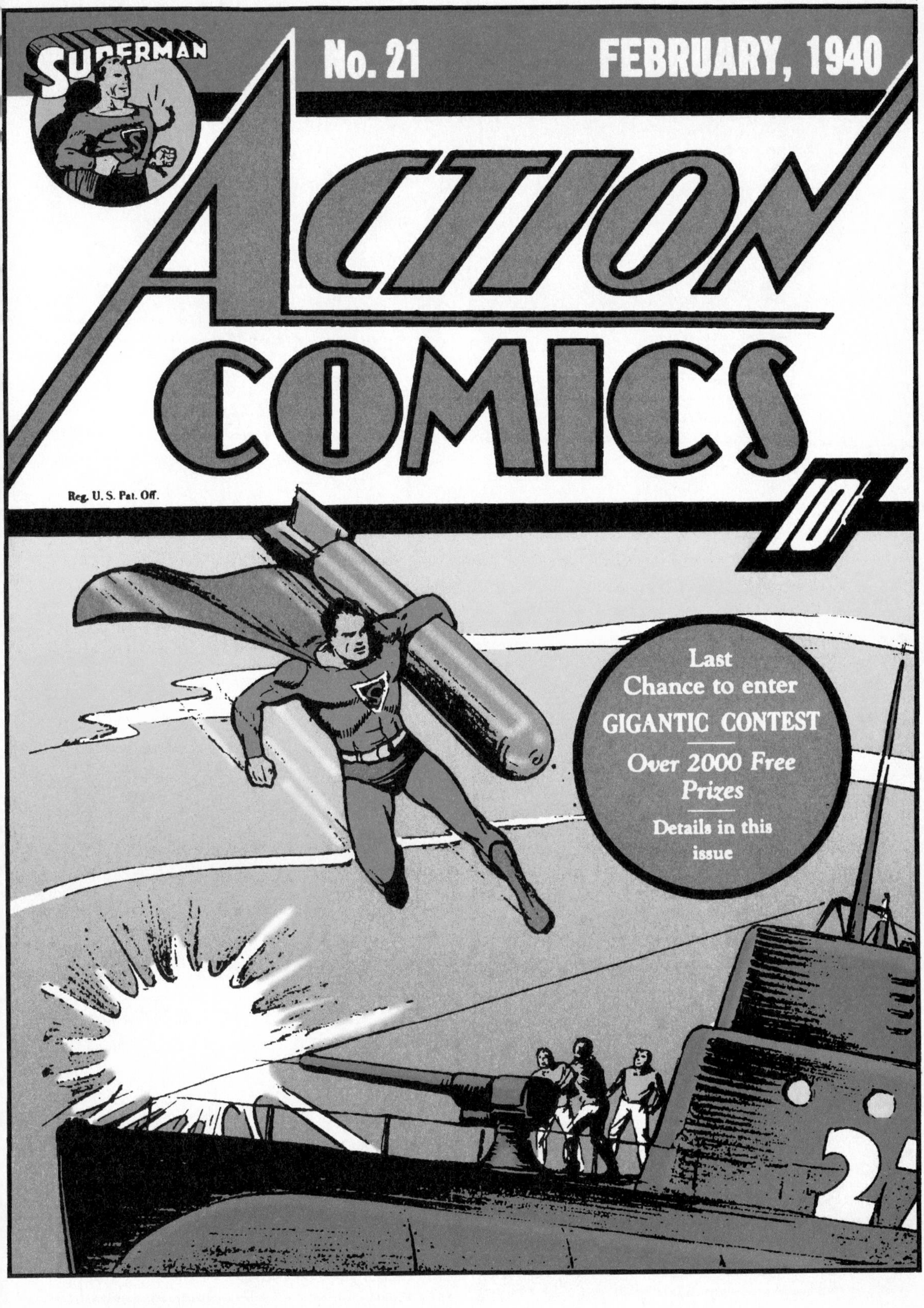
SUPERMAN
No. 21
FEBRUARY, 1940
ACTION COMICS
Reg. U. S. Pat. Off.
10¢
Last
Chance to enter
GIGANTIC CONTEST
Over 2000 Free
Prizes
Details in this
issue

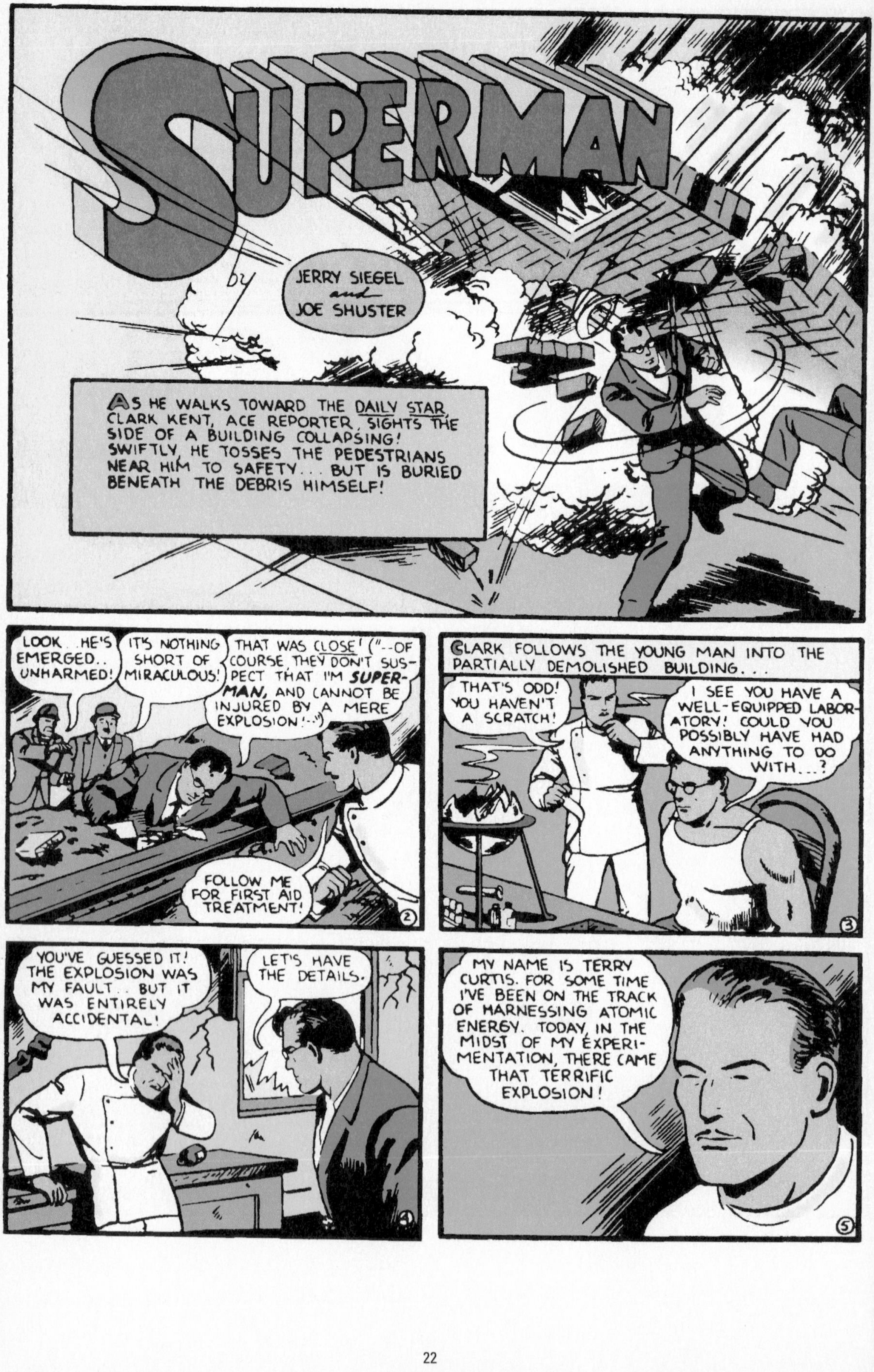
SUPERMAN
by
JERRY SIEGEL and JOE SHUSTER
AS HE WALKS TOWARD THE DAILY STAR, CLARK KENT, ACE REPORTER, SIGHTS THE SIDE OF A BUILDING COLLAPSING! SWIFTLY, HE TOSSES THE PEDESTRIANS NEAR HIM TO SAFETY... BUT IS BURIED BENEATH THE DEBRIS HIMSELF!
LOOK.. HE'S EMERGED.. UNHARMED!
IT'S NOTHING SHORT OF MIRACULOUS!
THAT WAS CLOSE! ("--OF COURSE, THEY DON'T SUSPECT THAT I'M SUPERMAN, AND CANNOT BE INJURED BY A MERE EXPLOSION!--")
FOLLOW ME FOR FIRST AID TREATMENT!
2
CLARK FOLLOWS THE YOUNG MAN INTO THE PARTIALLY DEMOLISHED BUILDING...
THAT'S ODD! YOU HAVEN'T A SCRATCH!
I SEE YOU HAVE A WELL-EQUIPPED LABORATORY! COULD YOU POSSIBLY HAVE HAD ANYTHING TO DO WITH...?
3
YOU'VE GUESSED IT! THE EXPLOSION WAS MY FAULT.. BUT IT WAS ENTIRELY ACCIDENTAL!
LET'S HAVE THE DETAILS.
4
MY NAME IS TERRY CURTIS. FOR SOME TIME I'VE BEEN ON THE TRACK OF HARNESSING ATOMIC ENERGY. TODAY, IN THE MIDST OF MY EXPERIMENTATION, THERE CAME THAT TERRIFIC EXPLOSION!
5

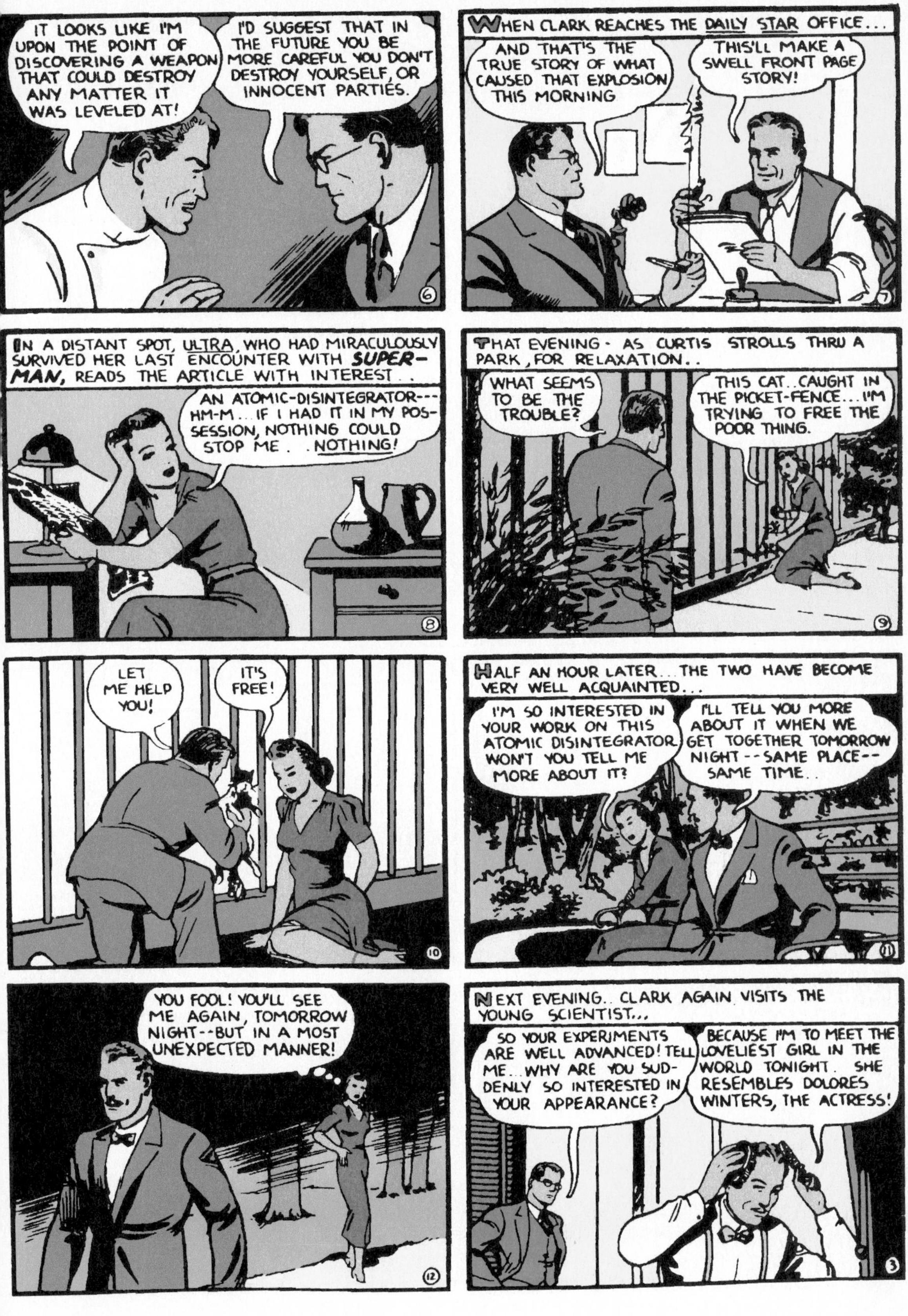
IT LOOKS LIKE I'M UPON THE POINT OF DISCOVERING A WEAPON THAT COULD DESTROY ANY MATTER IT WAS LEVELED AT!
I'D SUGGEST THAT IN THE FUTURE YOU BE MORE CAREFUL YOU DON'T DESTROY YOURSELF, OR INNOCENT PARTIES.
WHEN CLARK REACHES THE DAILY STAR OFFICE...
AND THAT'S THE TRUE STORY OF WHAT CAUSED THAT EXPLOSION THIS MORNING
THIS'LL MAKE A SWELL FRONT PAGE STORY!
IN A DISTANT SPOT, ULTRA, WHO HAD MIRACULOUSLY SURVIVED HER LAST ENCOUNTER WITH SUPERMAN, READS THE ARTICLE WITH INTEREST..
AN ATOMIC-DISINTEGRATOR--- HM-M... IF I HAD IT IN MY POSSESSION, NOTHING COULD STOP ME. . NOTHING!
THAT EVENING - AS CURTIS STROLLS THRU A PARK, FOR RELAXATION..
WHAT SEEMS TO BE THE TROUBLE?
THIS CAT.. CAUGHT IN THE PICKET-FENCE... I'M TRYING TO FREE THE POOR THING.
LET ME HELP YOU!
IT'S FREE!
HALF AN HOUR LATER... THE TWO HAVE BECOME VERY WELL ACQUAINTED...
I'M SO INTERESTED IN YOUR WORK ON THIS ATOMIC DISINTEGRATOR. WON'T YOU TELL ME MORE ABOUT IT?
I'LL TELL YOU MORE ABOUT IT WHEN WE GET TOGETHER TOMORROW NIGHT -- SAME PLACE -- SAME TIME..
YOU FOOL! YOU'LL SEE ME AGAIN, TOMORROW NIGHT--BUT IN A MOST UNEXPECTED MANNER!
NEXT EVENING.. CLARK AGAIN VISITS THE YOUNG SCIENTIST...
SO YOUR EXPERIMENTS ARE WELL ADVANCED! TELL ME... WHY ARE YOU SUDDENLY SO INTERESTED IN YOUR APPEARANCE?
BECAUSE I'M TO MEET THE LOVELIEST GIRL IN THE WORLD TONIGHT. SHE RESEMBLES DOLORES WINTERS, THE ACTRESS!

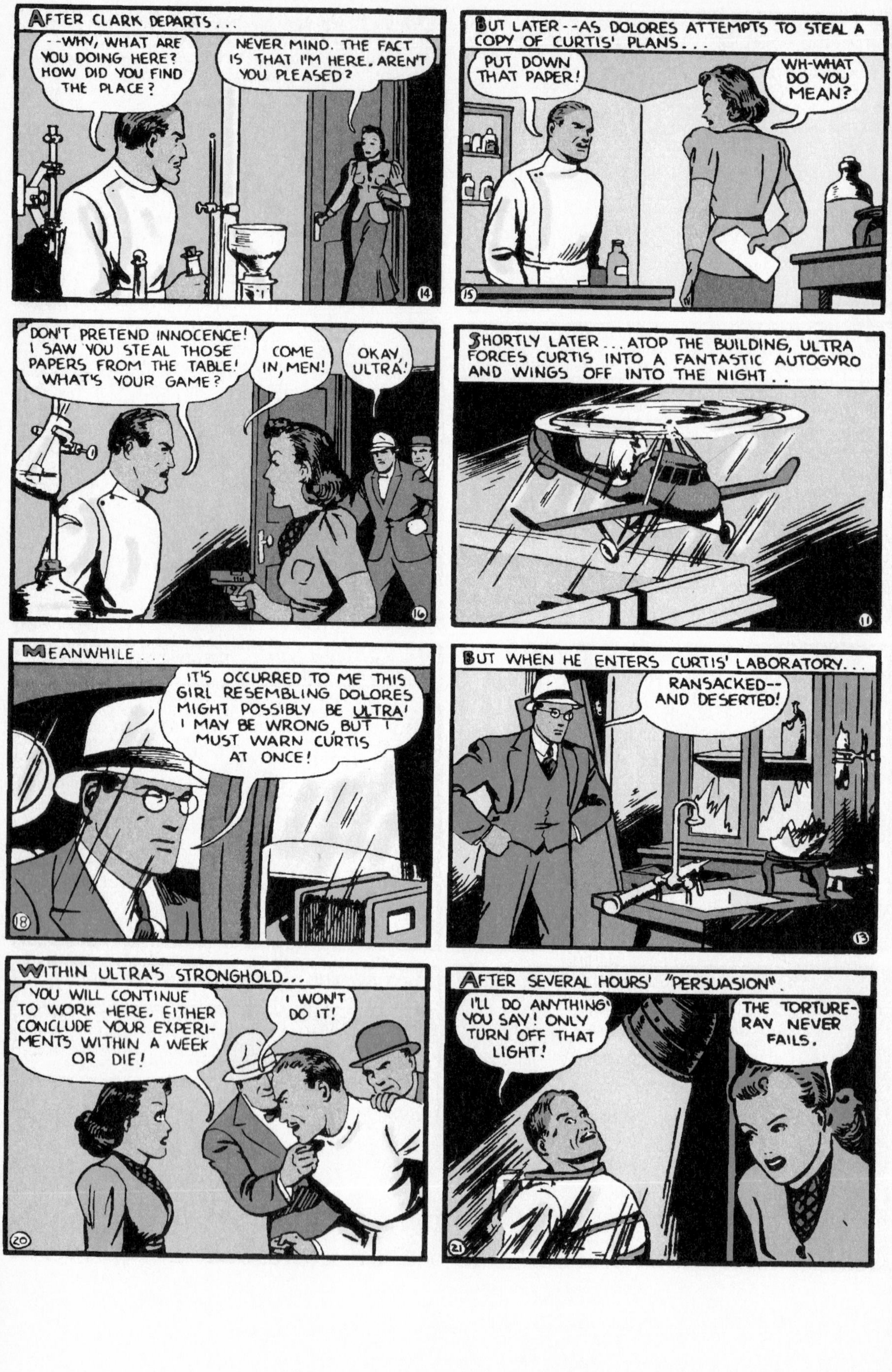

AFTER CLARK DEPARTS...
--WHY, WHAT ARE YOU DOING HERE? HOW DID YOU FIND THE PLACE?
NEVER MIND. THE FACT IS THAT I'M HERE. AREN'T YOU PLEASED?
14
BUT LATER--AS DOLORES ATTEMPTS TO STEAL A COPY OF CURTIS' PLANS...
PUT DOWN THAT PAPER!
WH-WHAT DO YOU MEAN?
15
DON'T PRETEND INNOCENCE! I SAW YOU STEAL THOSE PAPERS FROM THE TABLE! WHAT'S YOUR GAME?
COME IN, MEN!
OKAY, ULTRA!
16
SHORTLY LATER... ATOP THE BUILDING, ULTRA FORCES CURTIS INTO A FANTASTIC AUTOGYRO AND WINGS OFF INTO THE NIGHT..
11
MEANWHILE...
IT'S OCCURRED TO ME THIS GIRL RESEMBLING DOLORES MIGHT POSSIBLY BE ULTRA! I MAY BE WRONG, BUT I MUST WARN CURTIS AT ONCE!
18
BUT WHEN HE ENTERS CURTIS' LABORATORY...
RANSACKED--AND DESERTED!
13
WITHIN ULTRA'S STRONGHOLD...
YOU WILL CONTINUE TO WORK HERE. EITHER CONCLUDE YOUR EXPERIMENTS WITHIN A WEEK OR DIE!
I WON'T DO IT!
20
AFTER SEVERAL HOURS' "PERSUASION".
I'LL DO ANYTHING YOU SAY! ONLY TURN OFF THAT LIGHT!
THE TORTURE-RAY NEVER FAILS.
21

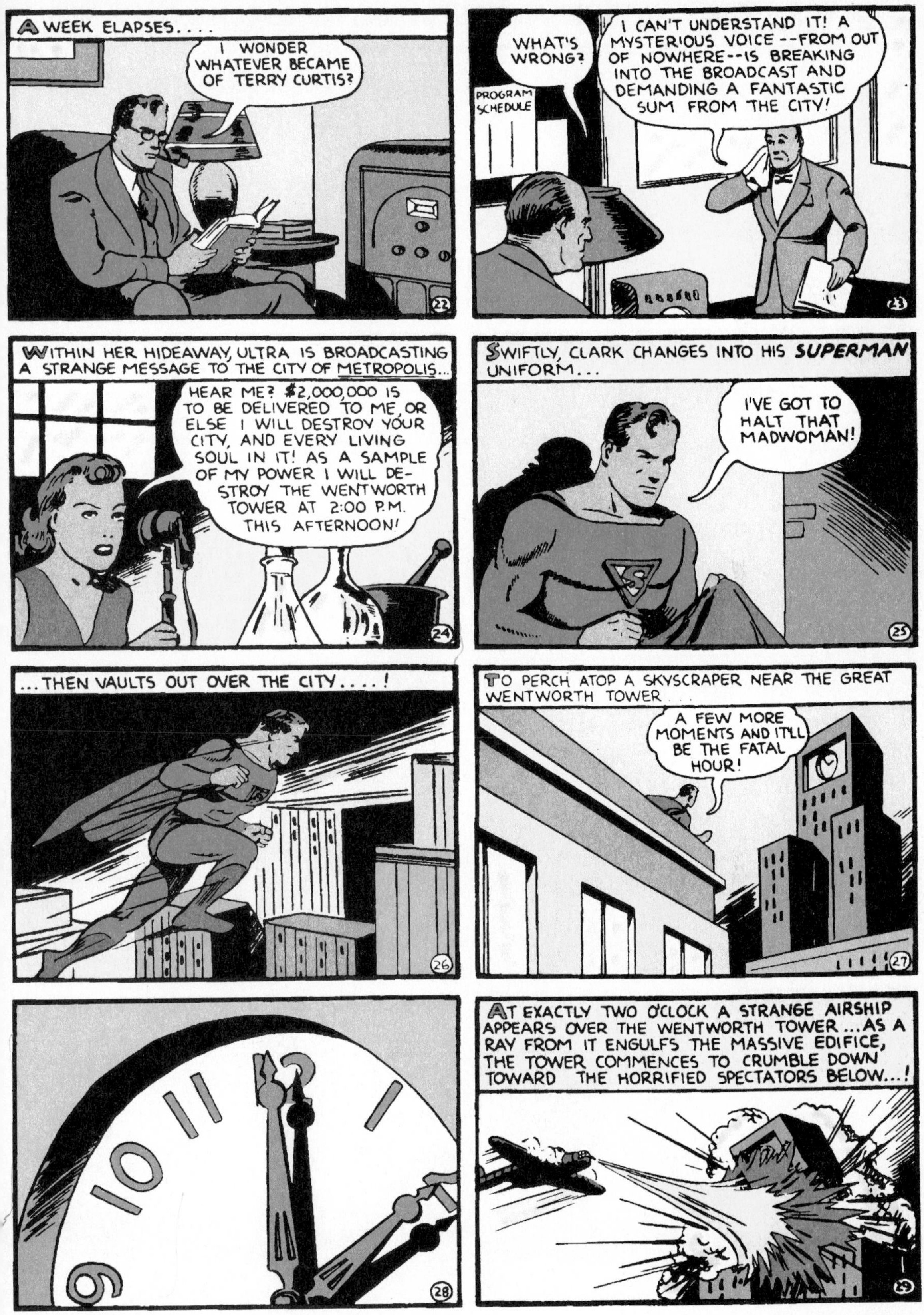
A WEEK ELAPSES....
I WONDER WHATEVER BECAME OF TERRY CURTIS?
PROGRAM SCHEDULE
WHAT'S WRONG?
I CAN'T UNDERSTAND IT! A MYSTERIOUS VOICE--FROM OUT OF NOWHERE--IS BREAKING INTO THE BROADCAST AND DEMANDING A FANTASTIC SUM FROM THE CITY!
WITHIN HER HIDEAWAY, ULTRA IS BROADCASTING A STRANGE MESSAGE TO THE CITY OF METROPOLIS...
HEAR ME? $2,000,000 IS TO BE DELIVERED TO ME, OR ELSE I WILL DESTROY YOUR CITY, AND EVERY LIVING SOUL IN IT! AS A SAMPLE OF MY POWER I WILL DESTROY THE WENTWORTH TOWER AT 2:00 P.M. THIS AFTERNOON!
SWIFTLY, CLARK CHANGES INTO HIS SUPERMAN UNIFORM...
I'VE GOT TO HALT THAT MADWOMAN!
...THEN VAULTS OUT OVER THE CITY....!
TO PERCH ATOP A SKYSCRAPER NEAR THE GREAT WENTWORTH TOWER...
A FEW MORE MOMENTS AND IT'LL BE THE FATAL HOUR!
AT EXACTLY TWO O'CLOCK A STRANGE AIRSHIP APPEARS OVER THE WENTWORTH TOWER...AS A RAY FROM IT ENGULFS THE MASSIVE EDIFICE, THE TOWER COMMENCES TO CRUMBLE DOWN TOWARD THE HORRIFIED SPECTATORS BELOW...!

DOWN STREAKS **SUPERMAN'S** FIGURE TOWARD THE FAR-DISTANT STREET.

STRIKING THE EARTH, HE SEIZES THE HUGE BULK OF THE TOWER AND HOLDS IT ERECT WHILE THE TERRIFIED SPECTATORS SURGE BACK...!

ONLY WHEN THE STREETS ARE CLEARED DOES **SUPERMAN** PERMIT THE MIGHTY TOWER TO COLLAPSE!

A TERRIFIC LEAP LAUNCHES THE MAN OF TOMORROW UP INTO THE SKY IN PURSUIT OF THE FANTASTIC AIR-VESSEL---

I'LL OVERTAKE THEM IN A FEW SECONDS!

WITHIN THE SKY-SHIP...

SOMEONE PURSUING US--- IT'S SUPERMAN!

I'LL GIVE HIM A TASTE OF THE DISINTEGRATOR!

OUT STABS THE DESTRUCTIVE RAY TOWARD **SUPERMAN'S** FIGURE. BUT THE MAN OF STEEL TWISTS ASIDE, ELUDING IT...

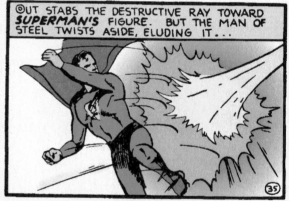

AS **SUPERMAN** STRIKES EARTH, HE SEES THE VESSEL SWOOPING DOWN TOWARD HIM, DISINTEGRATOR AIMED DIRECTLY AT HIM...

OH-OH!

SEIZING A HUGE BOULDER, **SUPERMAN** HURLS IT UP INTO THE AIR SO THAT IT SMASHES INTO THE DISINTEGRATOR, DESTROYING IT...

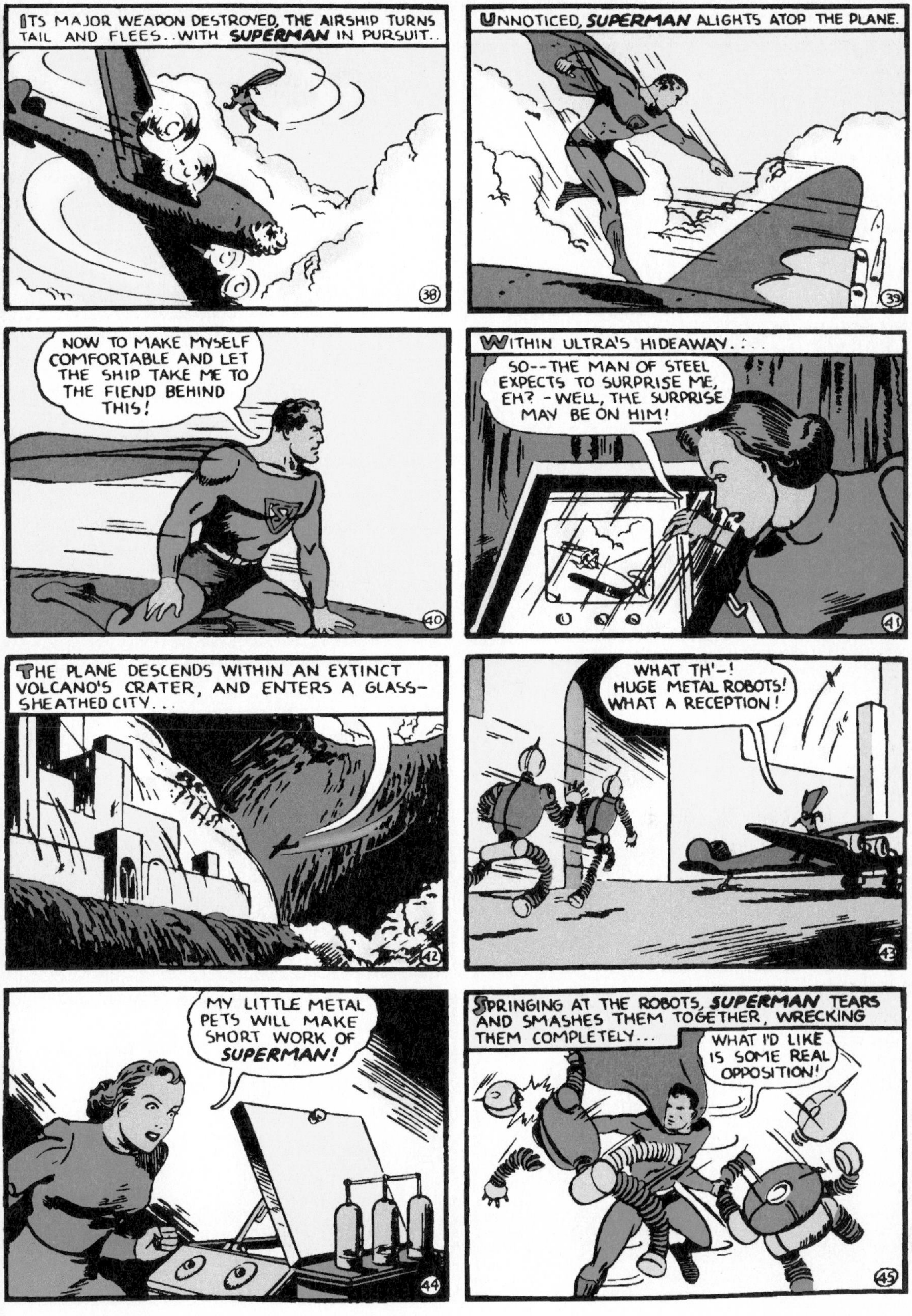
ITS MAJOR WEAPON DESTROYED, THE AIRSHIP TURNS TAIL AND FLEES..WITH SUPERMAN IN PURSUIT..
38
UNNOTICED, SUPERMAN ALIGHTS ATOP THE PLANE.
39
NOW TO MAKE MYSELF COMFORTABLE AND LET THE SHIP TAKE ME TO THE FIEND BEHIND THIS!
40
WITHIN ULTRA'S HIDEAWAY....
SO--THE MAN OF STEEL EXPECTS TO SURPRISE ME, EH? -WELL, THE SURPRISE MAY BE ON HIM!
41
THE PLANE DESCENDS WITHIN AN EXTINCT VOLCANO'S CRATER, AND ENTERS A GLASS-SHEATHED CITY...
42
WHAT TH'-! HUGE METAL ROBOTS! WHAT A RECEPTION!
43
MY LITTLE METAL PETS WILL MAKE SHORT WORK OF SUPERMAN!
44
SPRINGING AT THE ROBOTS, SUPERMAN TEARS AND SMASHES THEM TOGETHER, WRECKING THEM COMPLETELY...
WHAT I'D LIKE IS SOME REAL OPPOSITION!
45

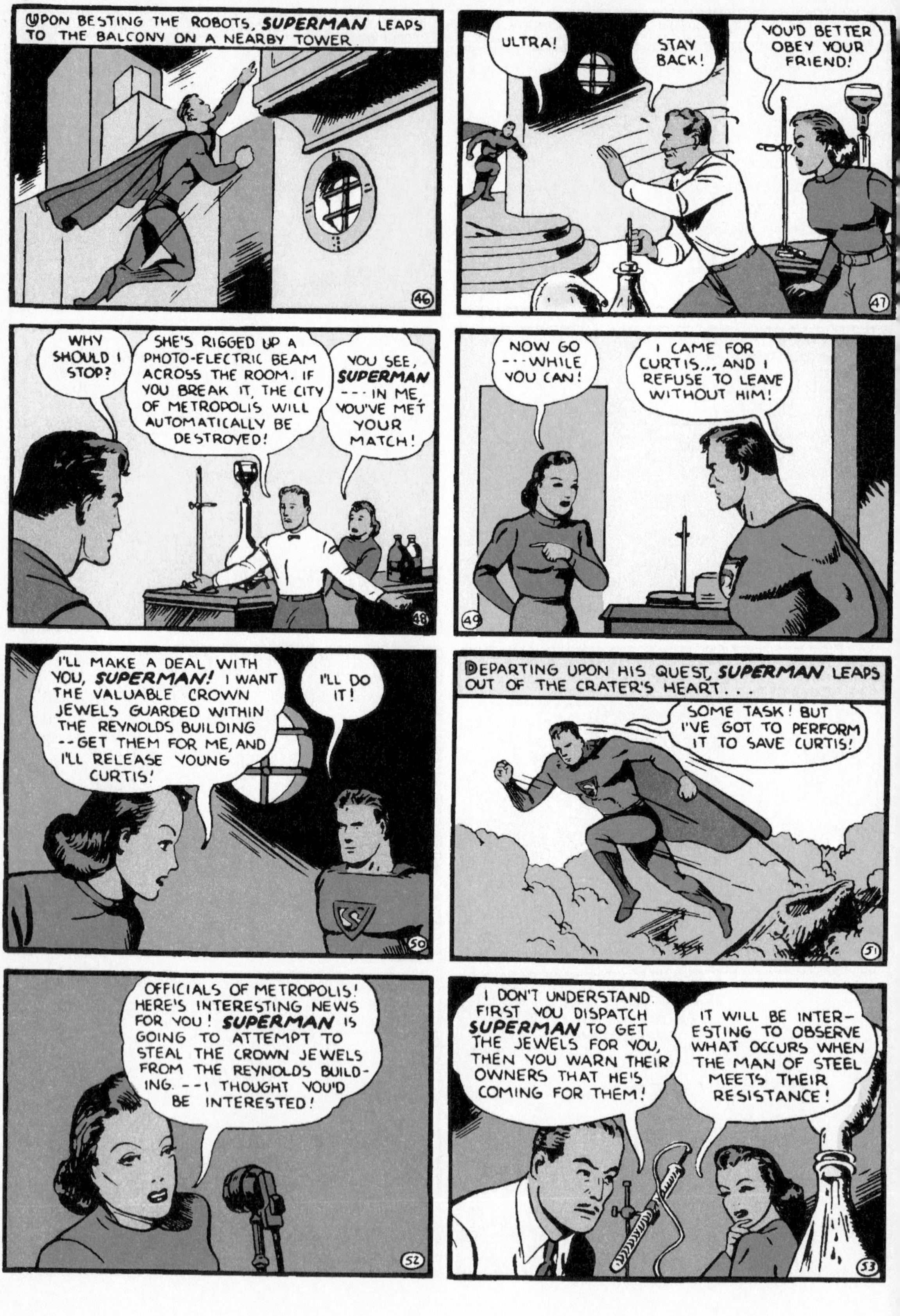
UPON BESTING THE ROBOTS, SUPERMAN LEAPS TO THE BALCONY ON A NEARBY TOWER
46
ULTRA!
STAY BACK!
YOU'D BETTER OBEY YOUR FRIEND!
47
WHY SHOULD I STOP?
SHE'S RIGGED UP A PHOTO-ELECTRIC BEAM ACROSS THE ROOM. IF YOU BREAK IT, THE CITY OF METROPOLIS WILL AUTOMATICALLY BE DESTROYED!
YOU SEE, SUPERMAN --- IN ME, YOU'VE MET YOUR MATCH!
48
NOW GO --- WHILE YOU CAN!
I CAME FOR CURTIS... AND I REFUSE TO LEAVE WITHOUT HIM!
49
I'LL MAKE A DEAL WITH YOU, SUPERMAN! I WANT THE VALUABLE CROWN JEWELS GUARDED WITHIN THE REYNOLDS BUILDING --GET THEM FOR ME, AND I'LL RELEASE YOUNG CURTIS!
I'LL DO IT!
50
DEPARTING UPON HIS QUEST, SUPERMAN LEAPS OUT OF THE CRATER'S HEART...
SOME TASK! BUT I'VE GOT TO PERFORM IT TO SAVE CURTIS!
51
OFFICIALS OF METROPOLIS! HERE'S INTERESTING NEWS FOR YOU! SUPERMAN IS GOING TO ATTEMPT TO STEAL THE CROWN JEWELS FROM THE REYNOLDS BUILDING. --I THOUGHT YOU'D BE INTERESTED!
52
I DON'T UNDERSTAND. FIRST YOU DISPATCH SUPERMAN TO GET THE JEWELS FOR YOU, THEN YOU WARN THEIR OWNERS THAT HE'S COMING FOR THEM!
IT WILL BE INTERESTING TO OBSERVE WHAT OCCURS WHEN THE MAN OF STEEL MEETS THEIR RESISTANCE!
53

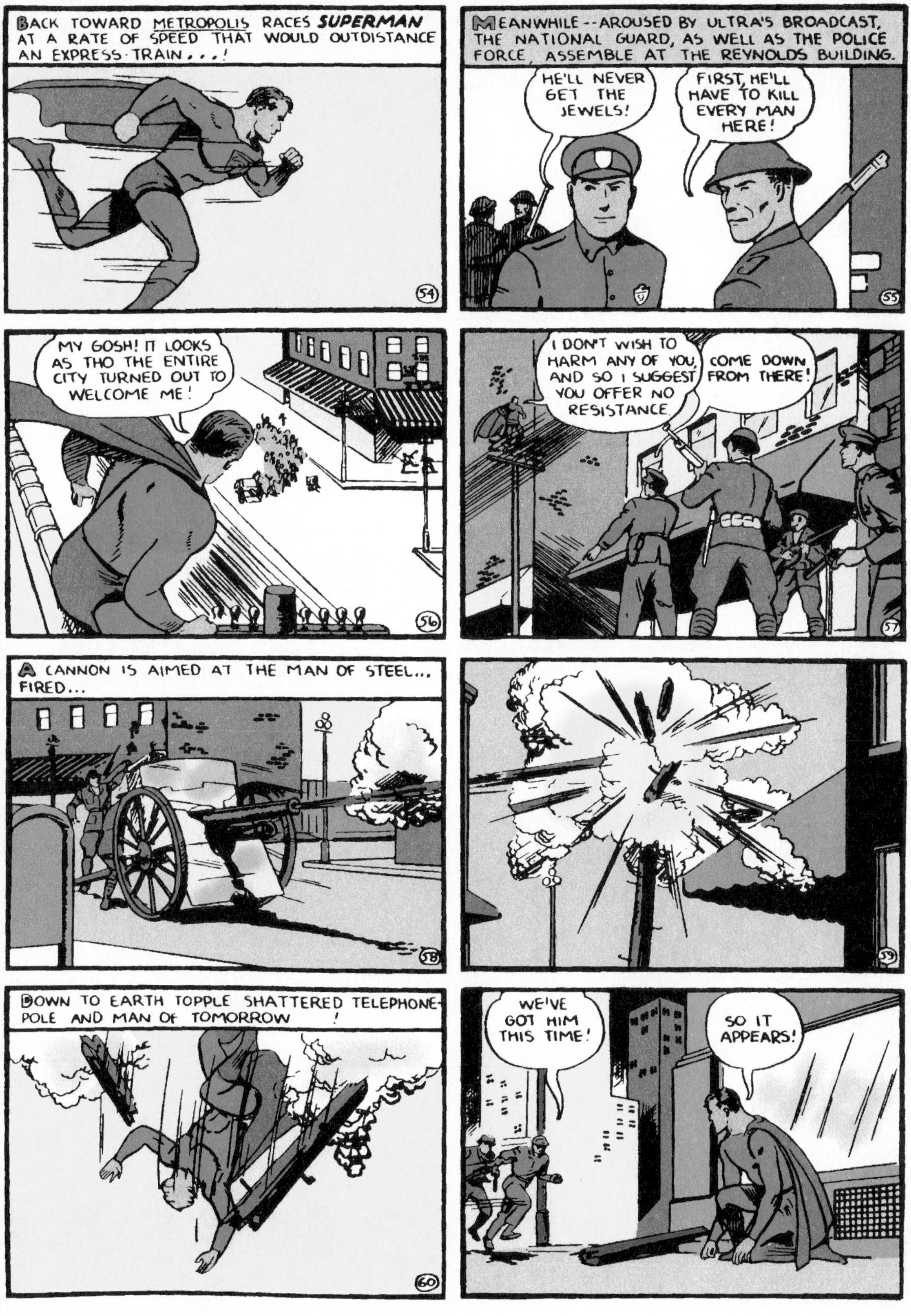
BACK TOWARD METROPOLIS RACES SUPERMAN AT A RATE OF SPEED THAT WOULD OUTDISTANCE AN EXPRESS-TRAIN...!
54
MEANWHILE--AROUSED BY ULTRA'S BROADCAST, THE NATIONAL GUARD, AS WELL AS THE POLICE FORCE, ASSEMBLE AT THE REYNOLDS BUILDING.
HE'LL NEVER GET THE JEWELS!
FIRST, HE'LL HAVE TO KILL EVERY MAN HERE!
55
MY GOSH! IT LOOKS AS THO THE ENTIRE CITY TURNED OUT TO WELCOME ME!
56
I DON'T WISH TO HARM ANY OF YOU, AND SO I SUGGEST YOU OFFER NO RESISTANCE.
COME DOWN FROM THERE!
57
A CANNON IS AIMED AT THE MAN OF STEEL... FIRED...
58
59
DOWN TO EARTH TOPPLE SHATTERED TELEPHONE-POLE AND MAN OF TOMORROW!
60
WE'VE GOT HIM THIS TIME!
SO IT APPEARS!

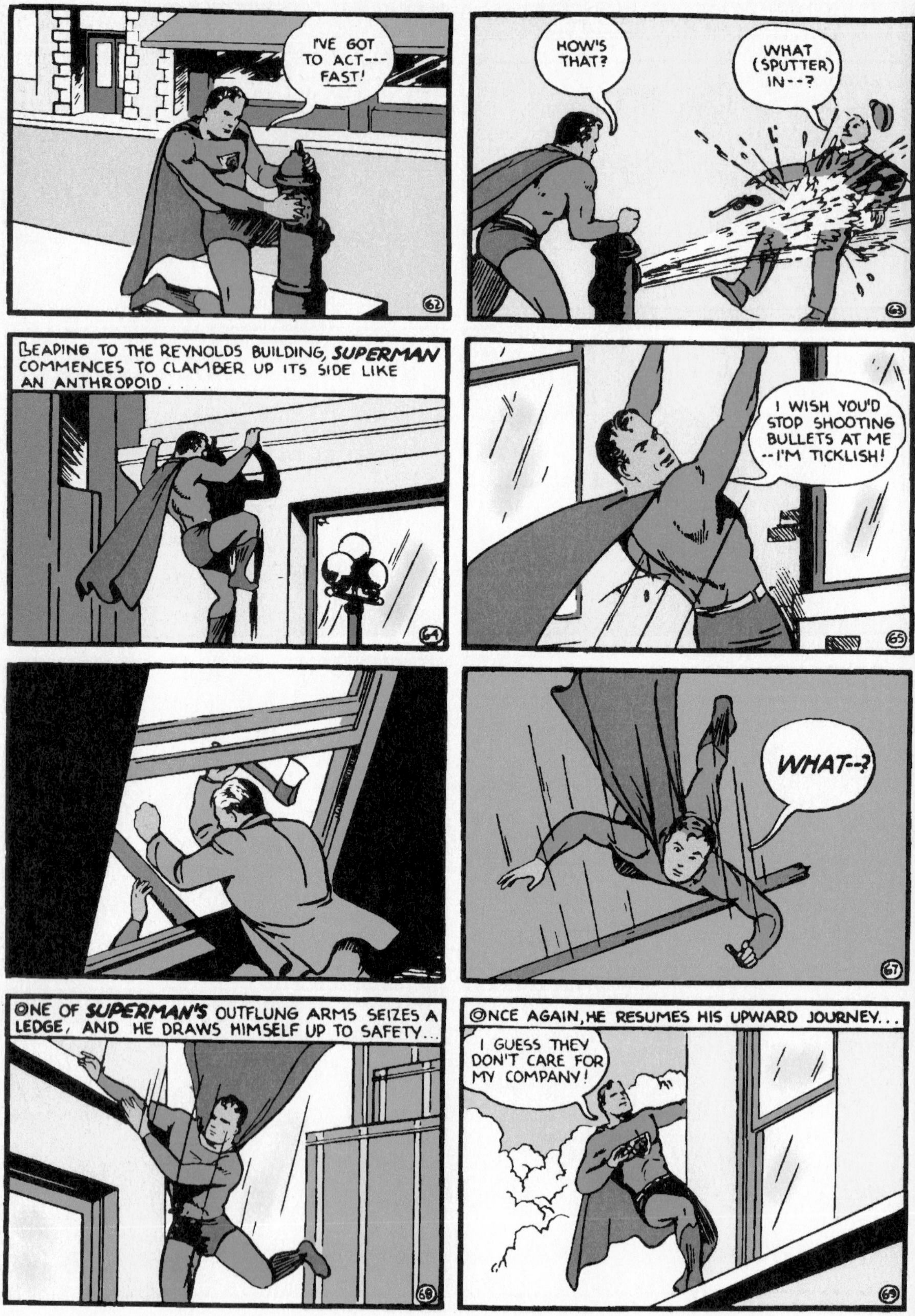
I'VE GOT TO ACT--- FAST!
HOW'S THAT?
WHAT (SPUTTER) IN--?
LEAPING TO THE REYNOLDS BUILDING, SUPERMAN COMMENCES TO CLAMBER UP ITS SIDE LIKE AN ANTHROPOID . . .
I WISH YOU'D STOP SHOOTING BULLETS AT ME --I'M TICKLISH!
WHAT--?
ONE OF SUPERMAN'S OUTFLUNG ARMS SEIZES A LEDGE, AND HE DRAWS HIMSELF UP TO SAFETY...
ONCE AGAIN, HE RESUMES HIS UPWARD JOURNEY...
I GUESS THEY DON'T CARE FOR MY COMPANY!

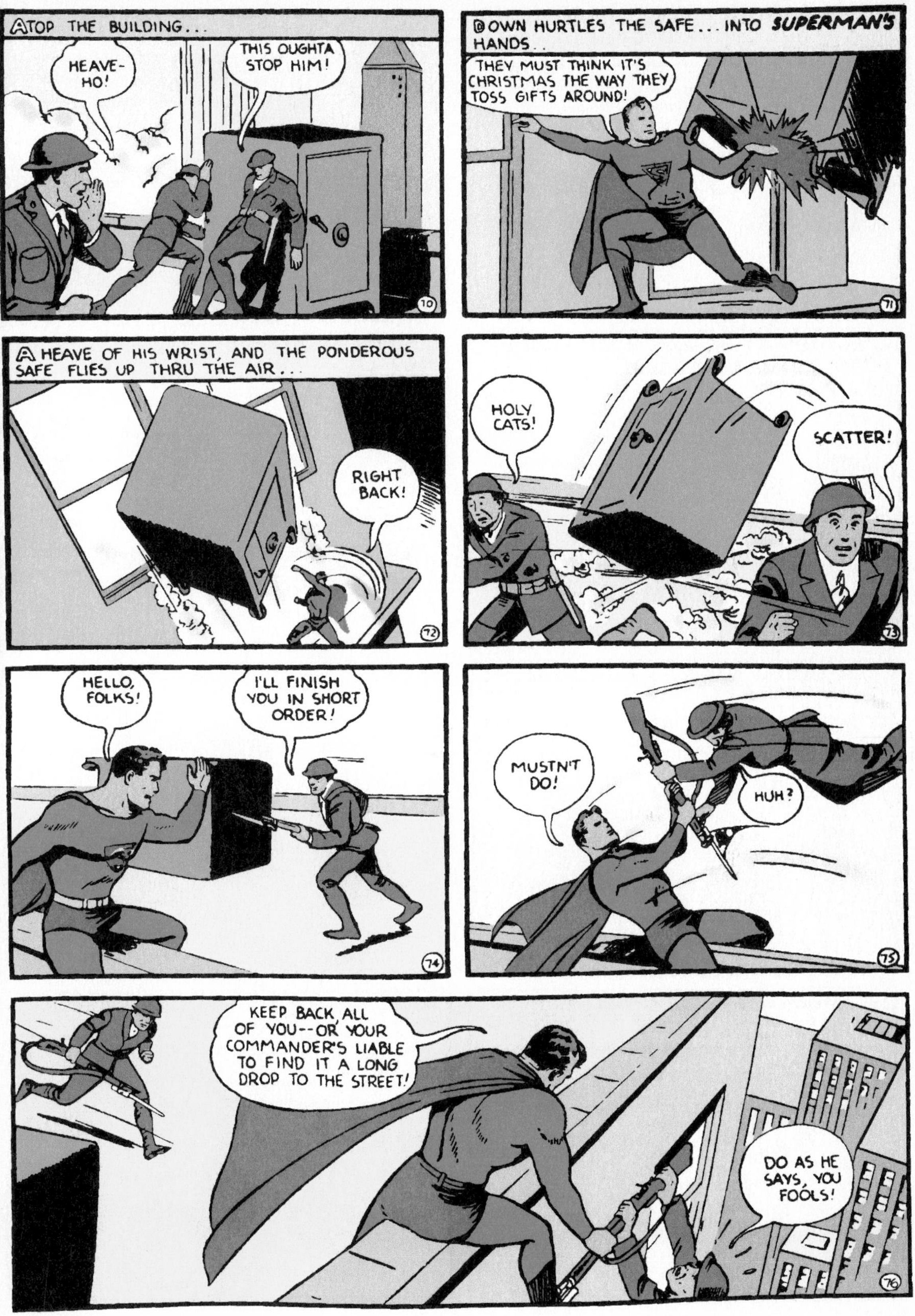
ATOP THE BUILDING...
HEAVE-HO!
THIS OUGHTA STOP HIM!
DOWN HURTLES THE SAFE... INTO SUPERMAN'S HANDS..
THEY MUST THINK IT'S CHRISTMAS THE WAY THEY TOSS GIFTS AROUND!
A HEAVE OF HIS WRIST, AND THE PONDEROUS SAFE FLIES UP THRU THE AIR...
RIGHT BACK!
HOLY CATS!
SCATTER!
HELLO, FOLKS!
I'LL FINISH YOU IN SHORT ORDER!
MUSTN'T DO!
HUH?
KEEP BACK, ALL OF YOU--OR YOUR COMMANDER'S LIABLE TO FIND IT A LONG DROP TO THE STREET!
DO AS HE SAYS, YOU FOOLS!

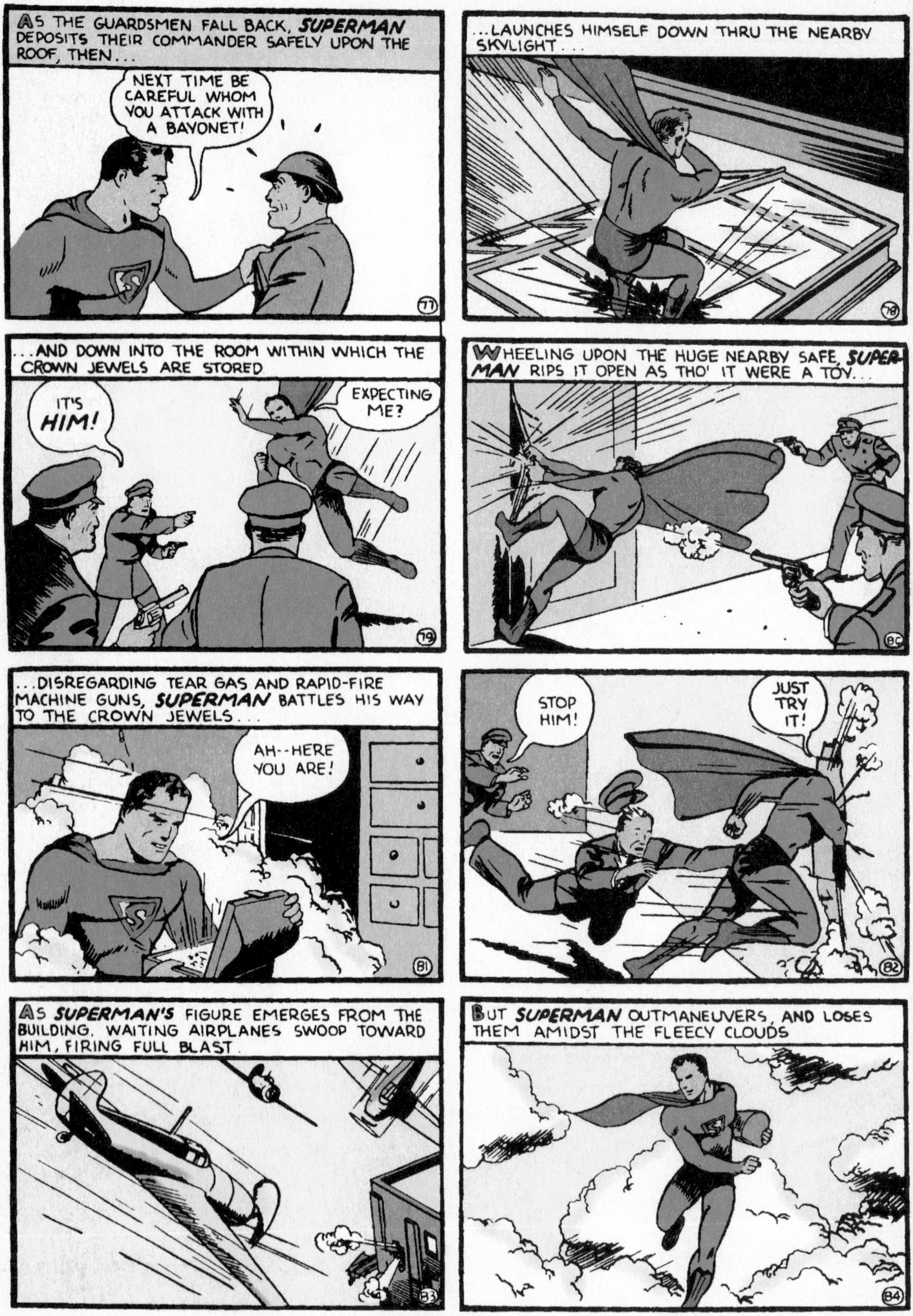
AS THE GUARDSMEN FALL BACK, SUPERMAN DEPOSITS THEIR COMMANDER SAFELY UPON THE ROOF, THEN...
NEXT TIME BE CAREFUL WHOM YOU ATTACK WITH A BAYONET!
...LAUNCHES HIMSELF DOWN THRU THE NEARBY SKYLIGHT...
...AND DOWN INTO THE ROOM WITHIN WHICH THE CROWN JEWELS ARE STORED
IT'S HIM!
EXPECTING ME?
WHEELING UPON THE HUGE NEARBY SAFE, SUPERMAN RIPS IT OPEN AS THO' IT WERE A TOY...
...DISREGARDING TEAR GAS AND RAPID-FIRE MACHINE GUNS, SUPERMAN BATTLES HIS WAY TO THE CROWN JEWELS...
AH--HERE YOU ARE!
STOP HIM!
JUST TRY IT!
AS SUPERMAN'S FIGURE EMERGES FROM THE BUILDING, WAITING AIRPLANES SWOOP TOWARD HIM, FIRING FULL BLAST.
BUT SUPERMAN OUTMANEUVERS, AND LOSES THEM AMIDST THE FLEECY CLOUDS

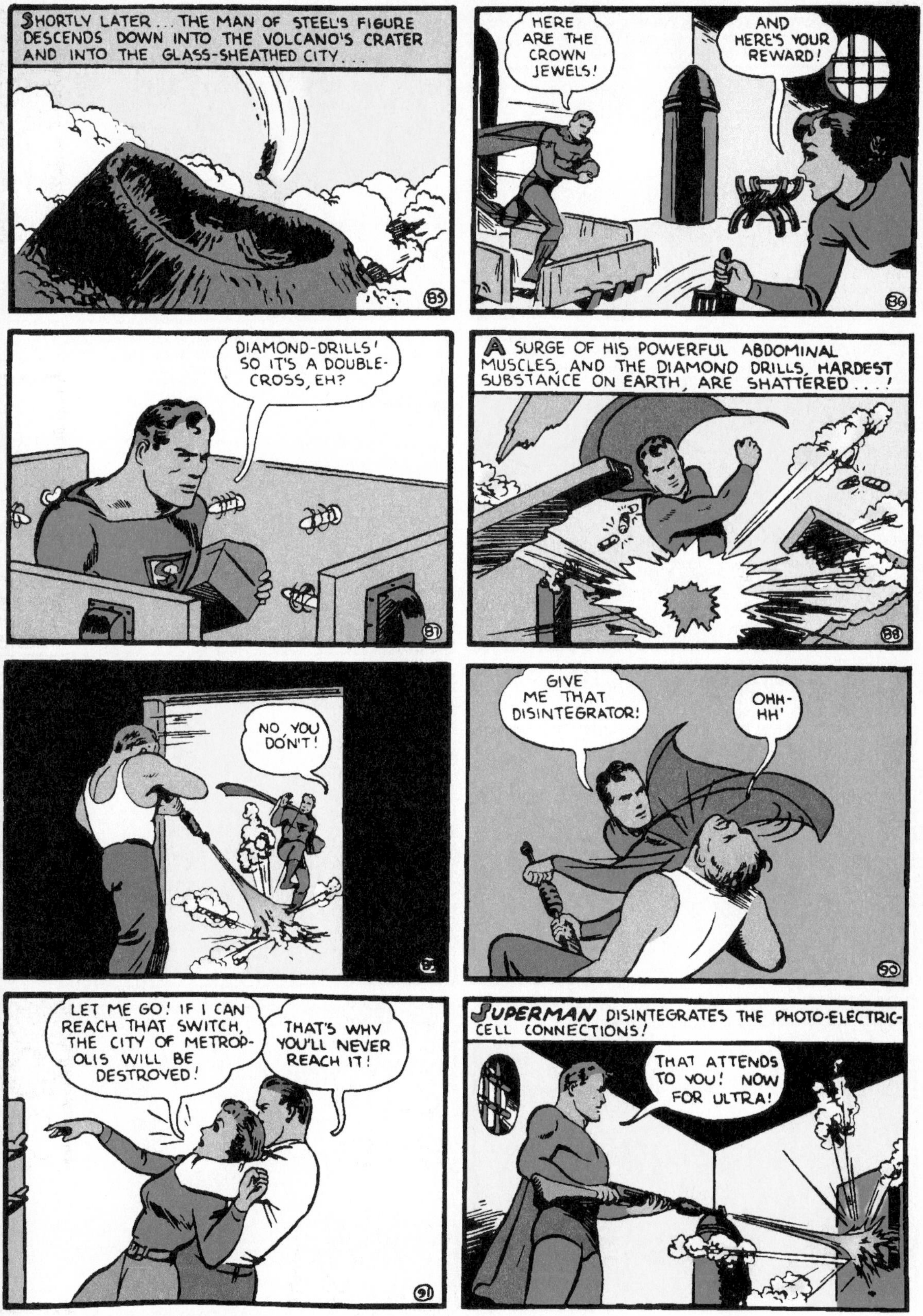
SHORTLY LATER... THE MAN OF STEEL'S FIGURE DESCENDS DOWN INTO THE VOLCANO'S CRATER AND INTO THE GLASS-SHEATHED CITY...
HERE ARE THE CROWN JEWELS!
AND HERE'S YOUR REWARD!
DIAMOND-DRILLS! SO IT'S A DOUBLE-CROSS, EH?
A SURGE OF HIS POWERFUL ABDOMINAL MUSCLES, AND THE DIAMOND DRILLS, HARDEST SUBSTANCE ON EARTH, ARE SHATTERED...!
NO, YOU DON'T!
GIVE ME THAT DISINTEGRATOR!
OHH-HH'
LET ME GO! IF I CAN REACH THAT SWITCH, THE CITY OF METROP-OLIS WILL BE DESTROYED!
THAT'S WHY YOU'LL NEVER REACH IT!
SUPERMAN DISINTEGRATES THE PHOTO-ELECTRIC-CELL CONNECTIONS!
THAT ATTENDS TO YOU! NOW FOR ULTRA!

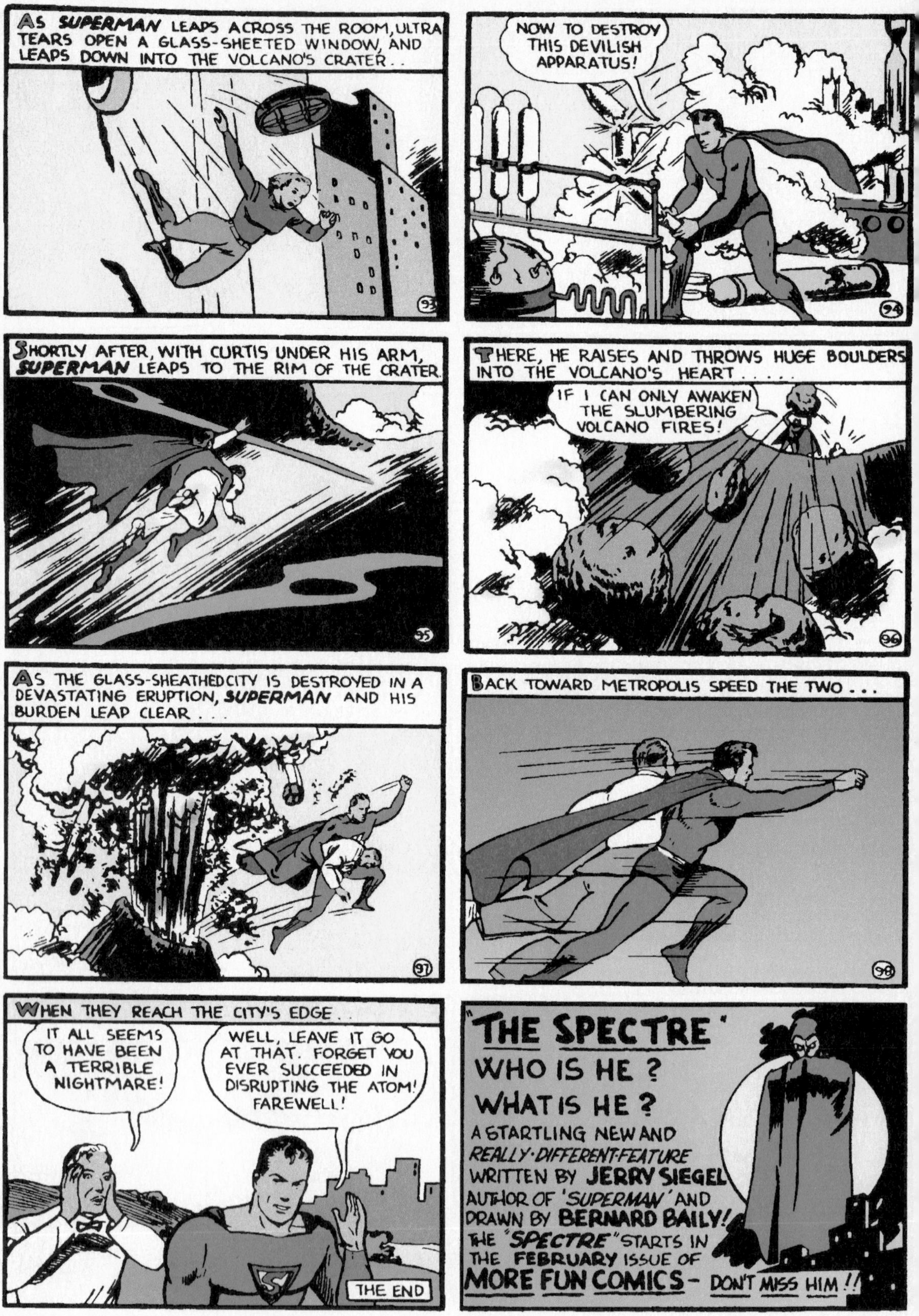
AS SUPERMAN LEAPS ACROSS THE ROOM, ULTRA TEARS OPEN A GLASS-SHEETED WINDOW, AND LEAPS DOWN INTO THE VOLCANO'S CRATER . .
NOW TO DESTROY THIS DEVILISH APPARATUS!
SHORTLY AFTER, WITH CURTIS UNDER HIS ARM, SUPERMAN LEAPS TO THE RIM OF THE CRATER.
THERE, HE RAISES AND THROWS HUGE BOULDERS INTO THE VOLCANO'S HEART . . . .
IF I CAN ONLY AWAKEN THE SLUMBERING VOLCANO FIRES!
AS THE GLASS-SHEATHED CITY IS DESTROYED IN A DEVASTATING ERUPTION, SUPERMAN AND HIS BURDEN LEAP CLEAR . . .
BACK TOWARD METROPOLIS SPEED THE TWO . . .
WHEN THEY REACH THE CITY'S EDGE . .
IT ALL SEEMS TO HAVE BEEN A TERRIBLE NIGHTMARE!
WELL, LEAVE IT GO AT THAT. FORGET YOU EVER SUCCEEDED IN DISRUPTING THE ATOM! FAREWELL!
THE END
"THE SPECTRE"
WHO IS HE ?
WHAT IS HE ?
A STARTLING NEW AND REALLY-DIFFERENT-FEATURE WRITTEN BY JERRY SIEGEL AUTHOR OF 'SUPERMAN' AND DRAWN BY BERNARD BAILY!
THE "SPECTRE" STARTS IN THE FEBRUARY ISSUE OF MORE FUN COMICS - DON'T MISS HIM!!

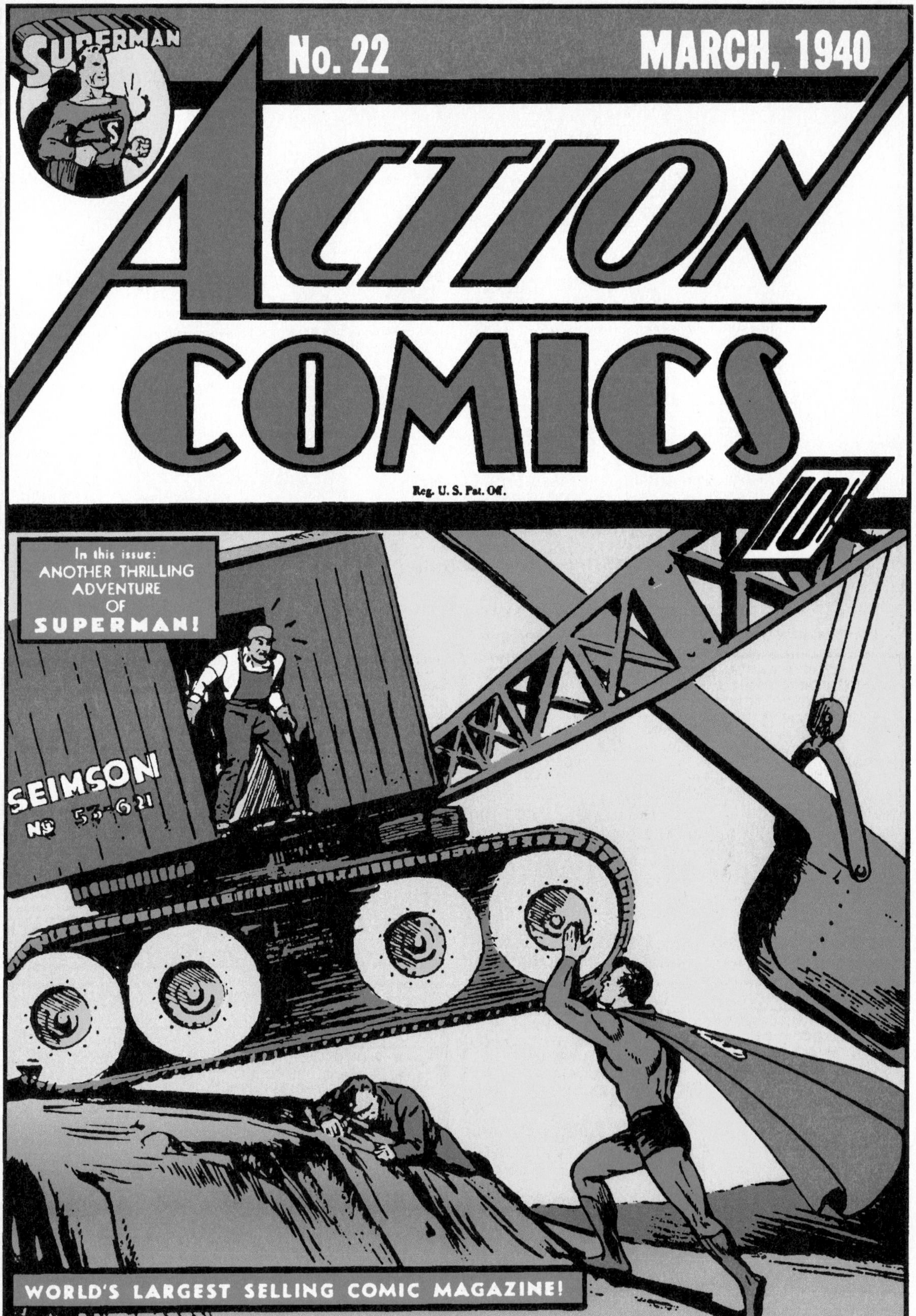
SUPERMAN
No. 22
MARCH, 1940
ACTION COMICS
Reg. U. S. Pat. Off.
10¢
In this issue:
ANOTHER THRILLING
ADVENTURE
OF
SUPERMAN!
SEIMSON
WORLD'S LARGEST SELLING COMIC MAGAZINE!

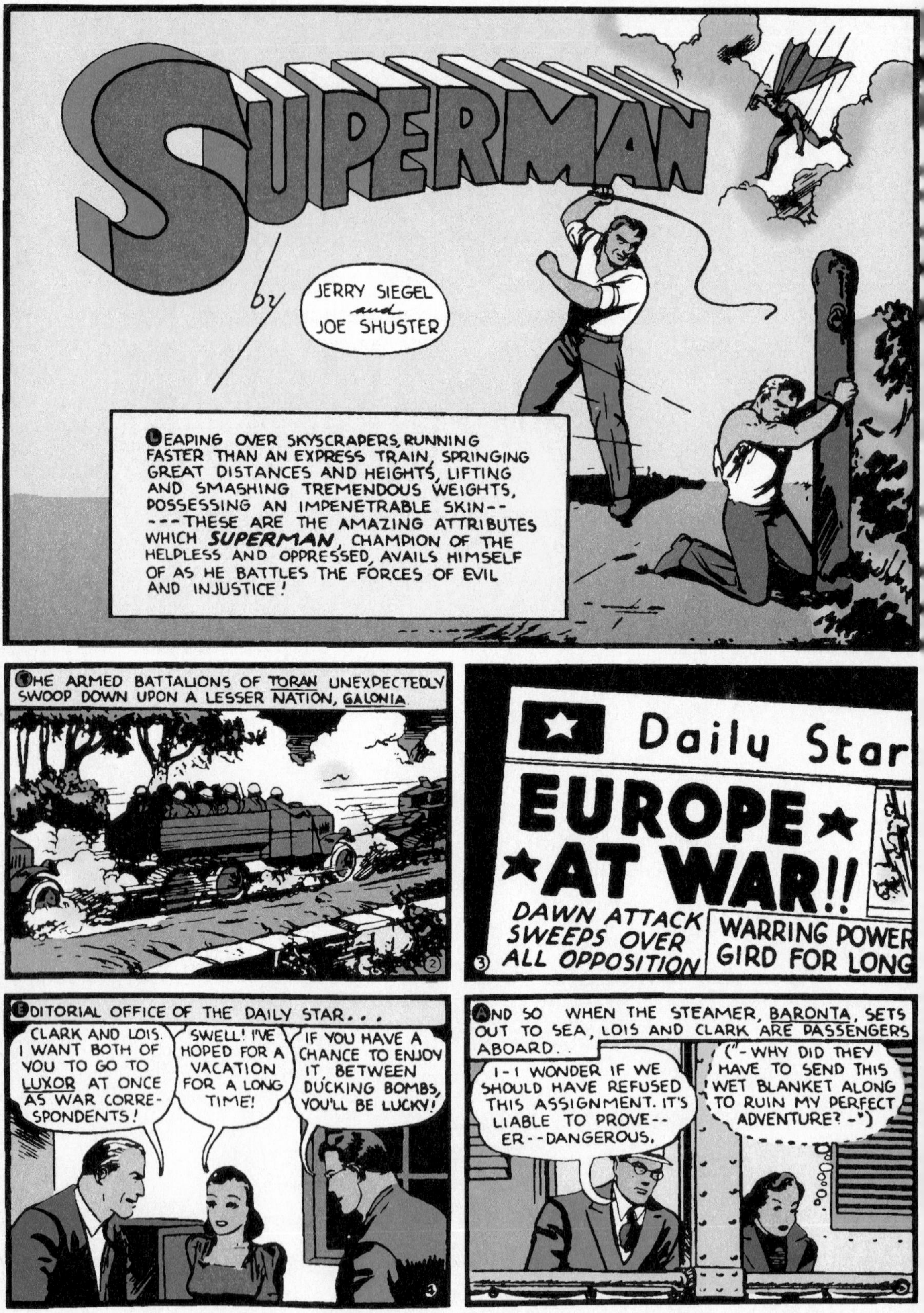
SUPERMAN
by JERRY SIEGEL and JOE SHUSTER
LEAPING OVER SKYSCRAPERS, RUNNING FASTER THAN AN EXPRESS TRAIN, SPRINGING GREAT DISTANCES AND HEIGHTS, LIFTING AND SMASHING TREMENDOUS WEIGHTS, POSSESSING AN IMPENETRABLE SKIN-- ---THESE ARE THE AMAZING ATTRIBUTES WHICH SUPERMAN, CHAMPION OF THE HELPLESS AND OPPRESSED, AVAILS HIMSELF OF AS HE BATTLES THE FORCES OF EVIL AND INJUSTICE!
THE ARMED BATTALIONS OF TORAN UNEXPECTEDLY SWOOP DOWN UPON A LESSER NATION, GALONIA.
Daily Star
EUROPE AT WAR!!
DAWN ATTACK SWEEPS OVER ALL OPPOSITION
WARRING POWER GIRD FOR LONG
EDITORIAL OFFICE OF THE DAILY STAR...
CLARK AND LOIS. I WANT BOTH OF YOU TO GO TO LUXOR AT ONCE AS WAR CORRESPONDENTS!
SWELL! I'VE HOPED FOR A VACATION FOR A LONG TIME!
IF YOU HAVE A CHANCE TO ENJOY IT, BETWEEN DUCKING BOMBS, YOU'LL BE LUCKY!
AND SO WHEN THE STEAMER, BARONTA, SETS OUT TO SEA, LOIS AND CLARK ARE PASSENGERS ABOARD.
I-I WONDER IF WE SHOULD HAVE REFUSED THIS ASSIGNMENT. IT'S LIABLE TO PROVE-- ER--DANGEROUS.
("-WHY DID THEY HAVE TO SEND THIS WET BLANKET ALONG TO RUIN MY PERFECT ADVENTURE? -")

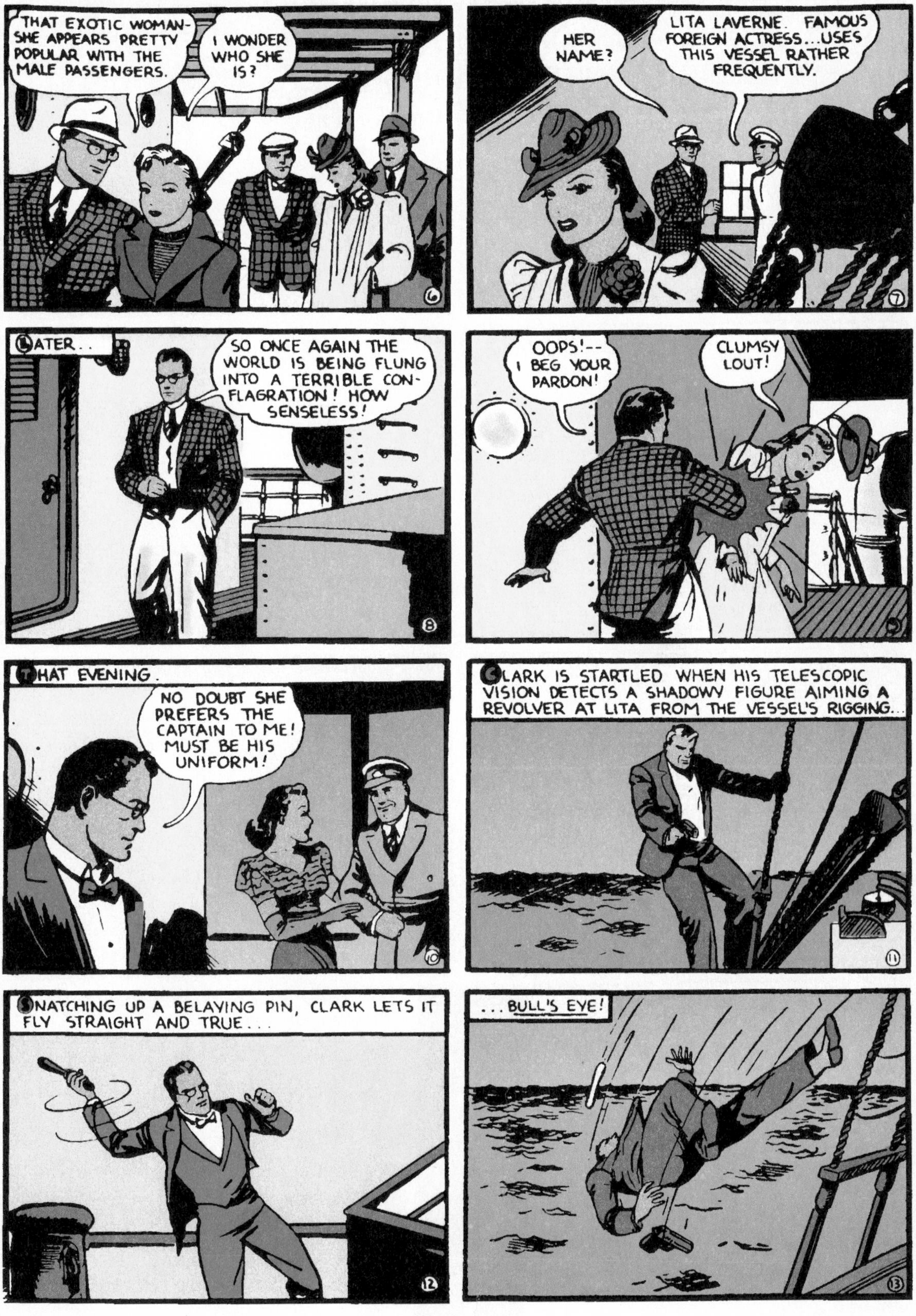
THAT EXOTIC WOMAN-SHE APPEARS PRETTY POPULAR WITH THE MALE PASSENGERS.
I WONDER WHO SHE IS?
HER NAME?
LITA LAVERNE. FAMOUS FOREIGN ACTRESS...USES THIS VESSEL RATHER FREQUENTLY.
LATER..
SO ONCE AGAIN THE WORLD IS BEING FLUNG INTO A TERRIBLE CON-FLAGRATION! HOW SENSELESS!
OOPS!-- I BEG YOUR PARDON!
CLUMSY LOUT!
THAT EVENING.
NO DOUBT SHE PREFERS THE CAPTAIN TO ME! MUST BE HIS UNIFORM!
CLARK IS STARTLED WHEN HIS TELESCOPIC VISION DETECTS A SHADOWY FIGURE AIMING A REVOLVER AT LITA FROM THE VESSEL'S RIGGING...
SNATCHING UP A BELAVING PIN, CLARK LETS IT FLY STRAIGHT AND TRUE...
...BULL'S EYE!

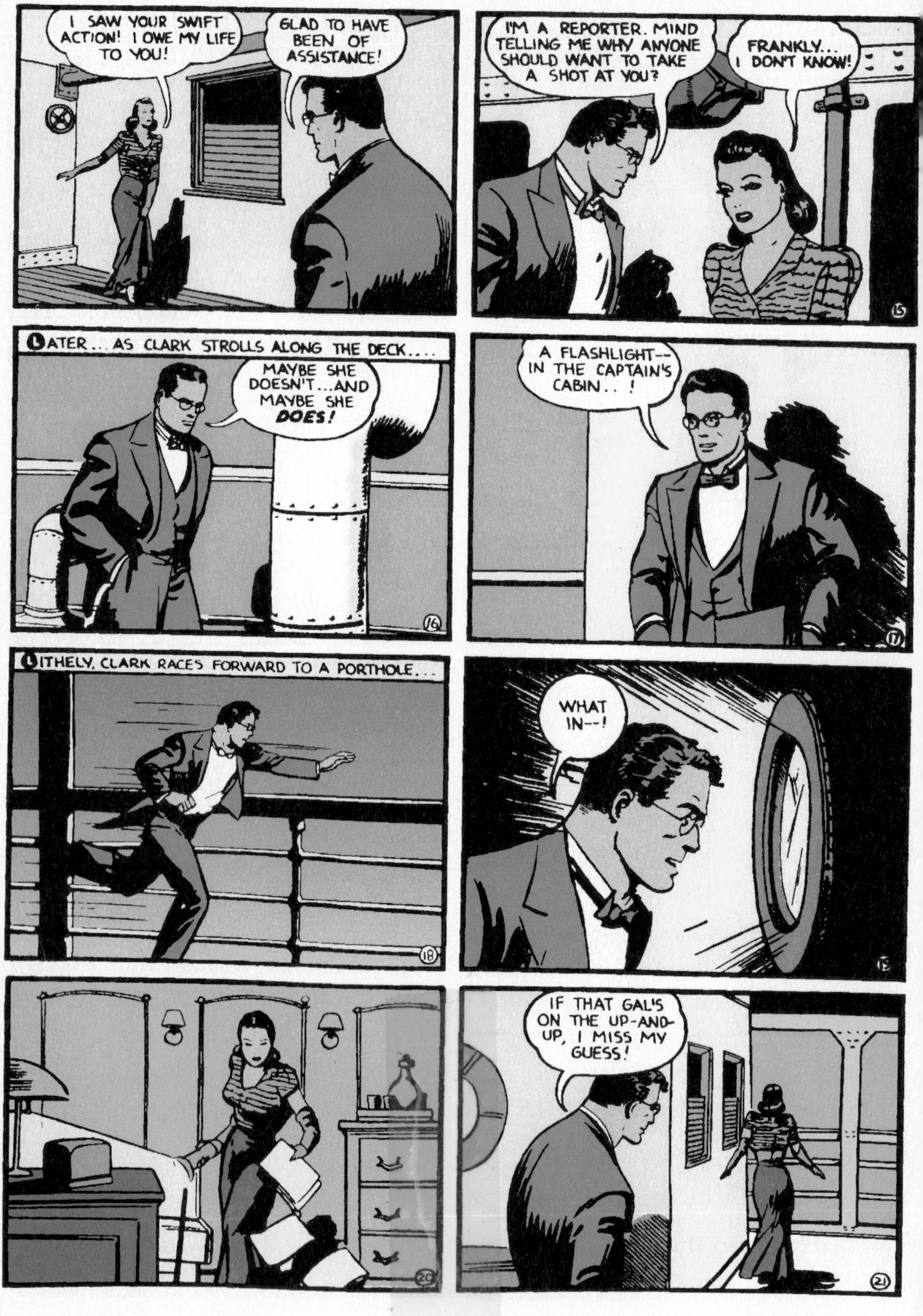

I SAW YOUR SWIFT ACTION! I OWE MY LIFE TO YOU!
GLAD TO HAVE BEEN OF ASSISTANCE!
I'M A REPORTER. MIND TELLING ME WHY ANYONE SHOULD WANT TO TAKE A SHOT AT YOU?
FRANKLY... I DON'T KNOW!
LATER... AS CLARK STROLLS ALONG THE DECK....
MAYBE SHE DOESN'T...AND MAYBE SHE DOES!
A FLASHLIGHT-- IN THE CAPTAIN'S CABIN..!
LITHELY, CLARK RACES FORWARD TO A PORTHOLE...
WHAT IN--!
IF THAT GAL'S ON THE UP-AND-UP, I MISS MY GUESS!

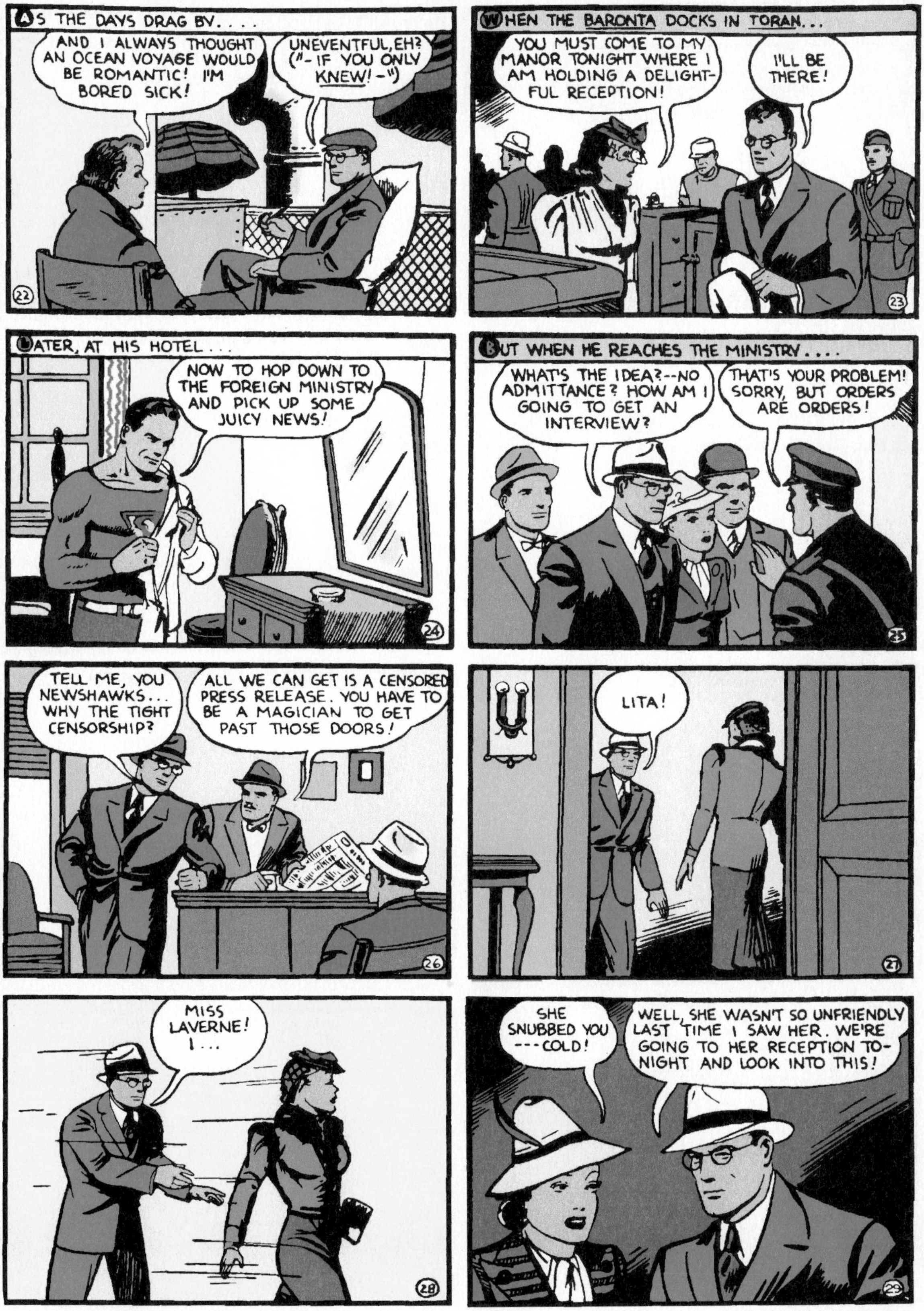
AS THE DAYS DRAG BY. . . .
AND I ALWAYS THOUGHT AN OCEAN VOYAGE WOULD BE ROMANTIC! I'M BORED SICK!
UNEVENTFUL, EH? ("- IF YOU ONLY KNEW! -")
22
WHEN THE BARONTA DOCKS IN TORAN...
YOU MUST COME TO MY MANOR TONIGHT WHERE I AM HOLDING A DELIGHTFUL RECEPTION!
I'LL BE THERE!
23
LATER, AT HIS HOTEL . . .
NOW TO HOP DOWN TO THE FOREIGN MINISTRY AND PICK UP SOME JUICY NEWS!
24
BUT WHEN HE REACHES THE MINISTRY . . . .
WHAT'S THE IDEA?--NO ADMITTANCE? HOW AM I GOING TO GET AN INTERVIEW?
THAT'S YOUR PROBLEM! SORRY, BUT ORDERS ARE ORDERS!
25
TELL ME, YOU NEWSHAWKS... WHY THE TIGHT CENSORSHIP?
ALL WE CAN GET IS A CENSORED PRESS RELEASE. YOU HAVE TO BE A MAGICIAN TO GET PAST THOSE DOORS!
26
LITA!
27
MISS LAVERNE! I...
28
SHE SNUBBED YOU ---COLD!
WELL, SHE WASN'T SO UNFRIENDLY LAST TIME I SAW HER. WE'RE GOING TO HER RECEPTION TONIGHT AND LOOK INTO THIS!
29

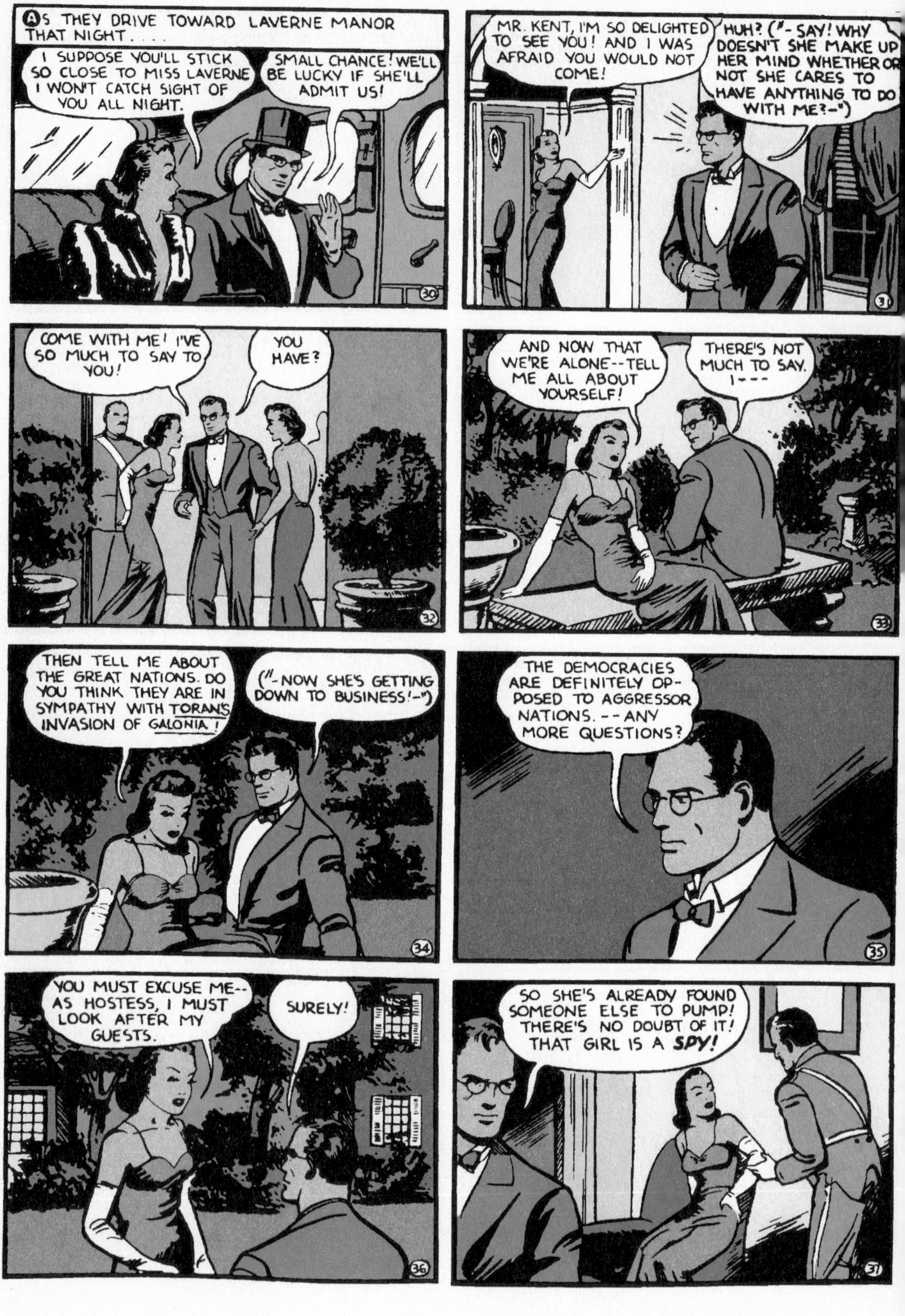
AS THEY DRIVE TOWARD LAVERNE MANOR THAT NIGHT. . . .
I SUPPOSE YOU'LL STICK SO CLOSE TO MISS LAVERNE I WON'T CATCH SIGHT OF YOU ALL NIGHT.
SMALL CHANCE! WE'LL BE LUCKY IF SHE'LL ADMIT US!
MR. KENT, I'M SO DELIGHTED TO SEE YOU! AND I WAS AFRAID YOU WOULD NOT COME!
HUH? ("- SAY! WHY DOESN'T SHE MAKE UP HER MIND WHETHER OR NOT SHE CARES TO HAVE ANYTHING TO DO WITH ME?-")
COME WITH ME! I'VE SO MUCH TO SAY TO YOU!
YOU HAVE?
AND NOW THAT WE'RE ALONE--TELL ME ALL ABOUT YOURSELF!
THERE'S NOT MUCH TO SAY. I---
THEN TELL ME ABOUT THE GREAT NATIONS. DO YOU THINK THEY ARE IN SYMPATHY WITH TORAN'S INVASION OF GALONIA!
("- NOW SHE'S GETTING DOWN TO BUSINESS!-")
THE DEMOCRACIES ARE DEFINITELY OPPOSED TO AGGRESSOR NATIONS. --ANY MORE QUESTIONS?
YOU MUST EXCUSE ME--AS HOSTESS, I MUST LOOK AFTER MY GUESTS.
SURELY!
SO SHE'S ALREADY FOUND SOMEONE ELSE TO PUMP! THERE'S NO DOUBT OF IT! THAT GIRL IS A SPY!

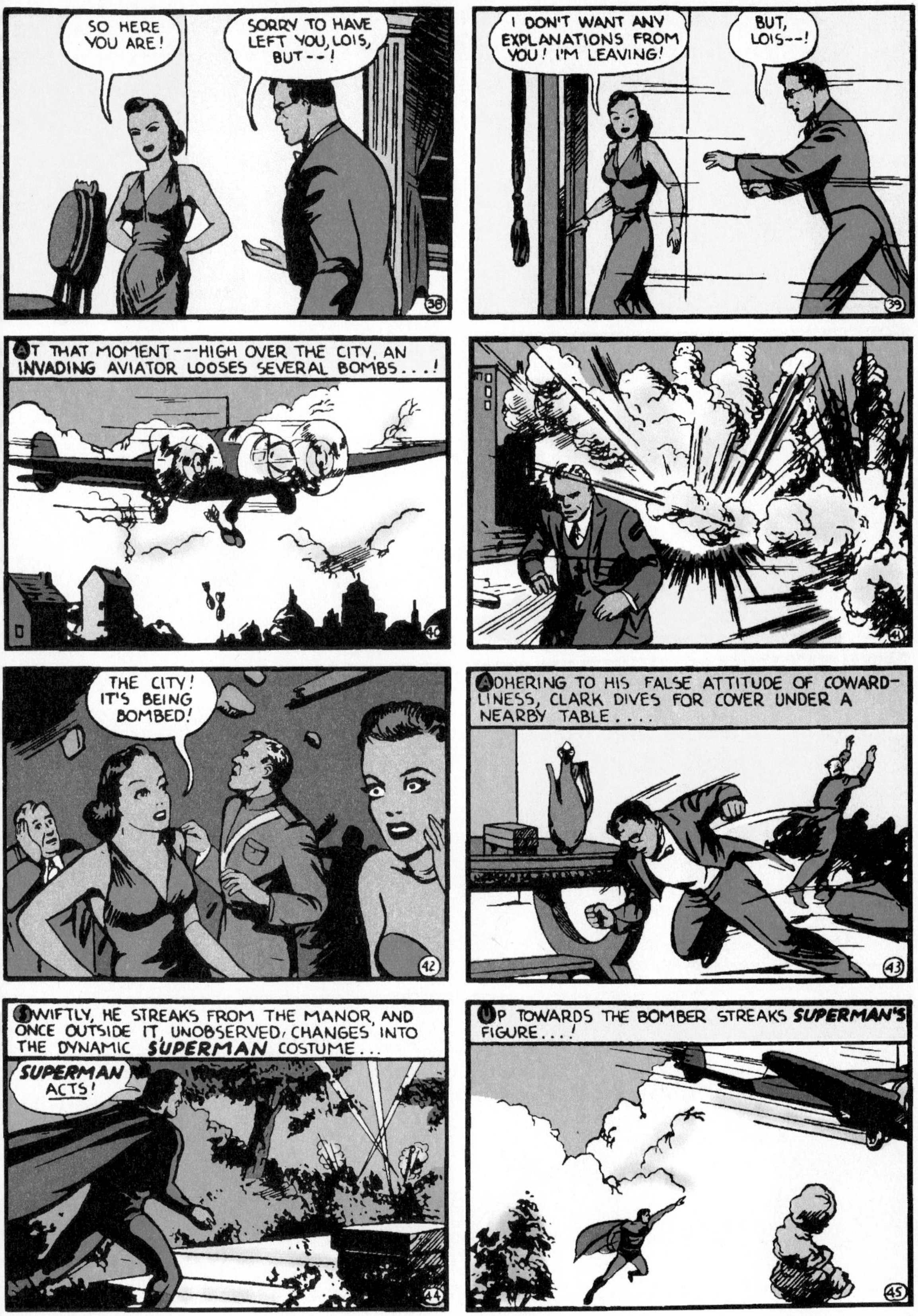
SO HERE YOU ARE!
SORRY TO HAVE LEFT YOU, LOIS, BUT--!
I DON'T WANT ANY EXPLANATIONS FROM YOU! I'M LEAVING!
BUT, LOIS--!
AT THAT MOMENT---HIGH OVER THE CITY, AN INVADING AVIATOR LOOSES SEVERAL BOMBS...!
THE CITY! IT'S BEING BOMBED!
ADHERING TO HIS FALSE ATTITUDE OF COWARDLINESS, CLARK DIVES FOR COVER UNDER A NEARBY TABLE....
SWIFTLY, HE STREAKS FROM THE MANOR, AND ONCE OUTSIDE IT, UNOBSERVED, CHANGES INTO THE DYNAMIC SUPERMAN COSTUME...
SUPERMAN ACTS!
UP TOWARDS THE BOMBER STREAKS SUPERMAN'S FIGURE...!

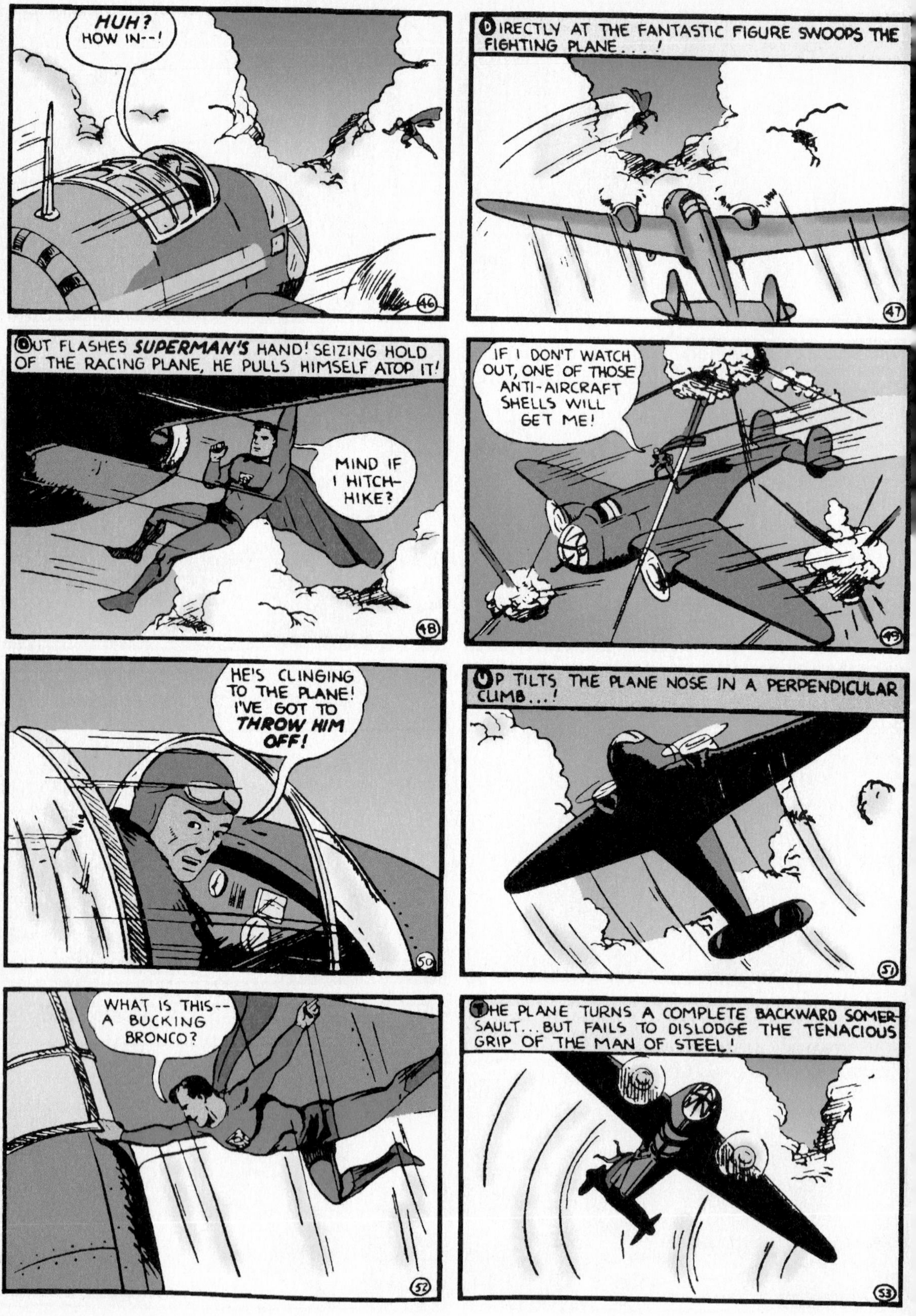
HUH? HOW IN--!
DIRECTLY AT THE FANTASTIC FIGURE SWOOPS THE FIGHTING PLANE...!
OUT FLASHES SUPERMAN'S HAND! SEIZING HOLD OF THE RACING PLANE, HE PULLS HIMSELF ATOP IT!
MIND IF I HITCH-HIKE?
IF I DON'T WATCH OUT, ONE OF THOSE ANTI-AIRCRAFT SHELLS WILL GET ME!
HE'S CLINGING TO THE PLANE! I'VE GOT TO THROW HIM OFF!
UP TILTS THE PLANE NOSE IN A PERPENDICULAR CLIMB...!
WHAT IS THIS-- A BUCKING BRONCO?
THE PLANE TURNS A COMPLETE BACKWARD SOMER-SAULT...BUT FAILS TO DISLODGE THE TENACIOUS GRIP OF THE MAN OF STEEL!

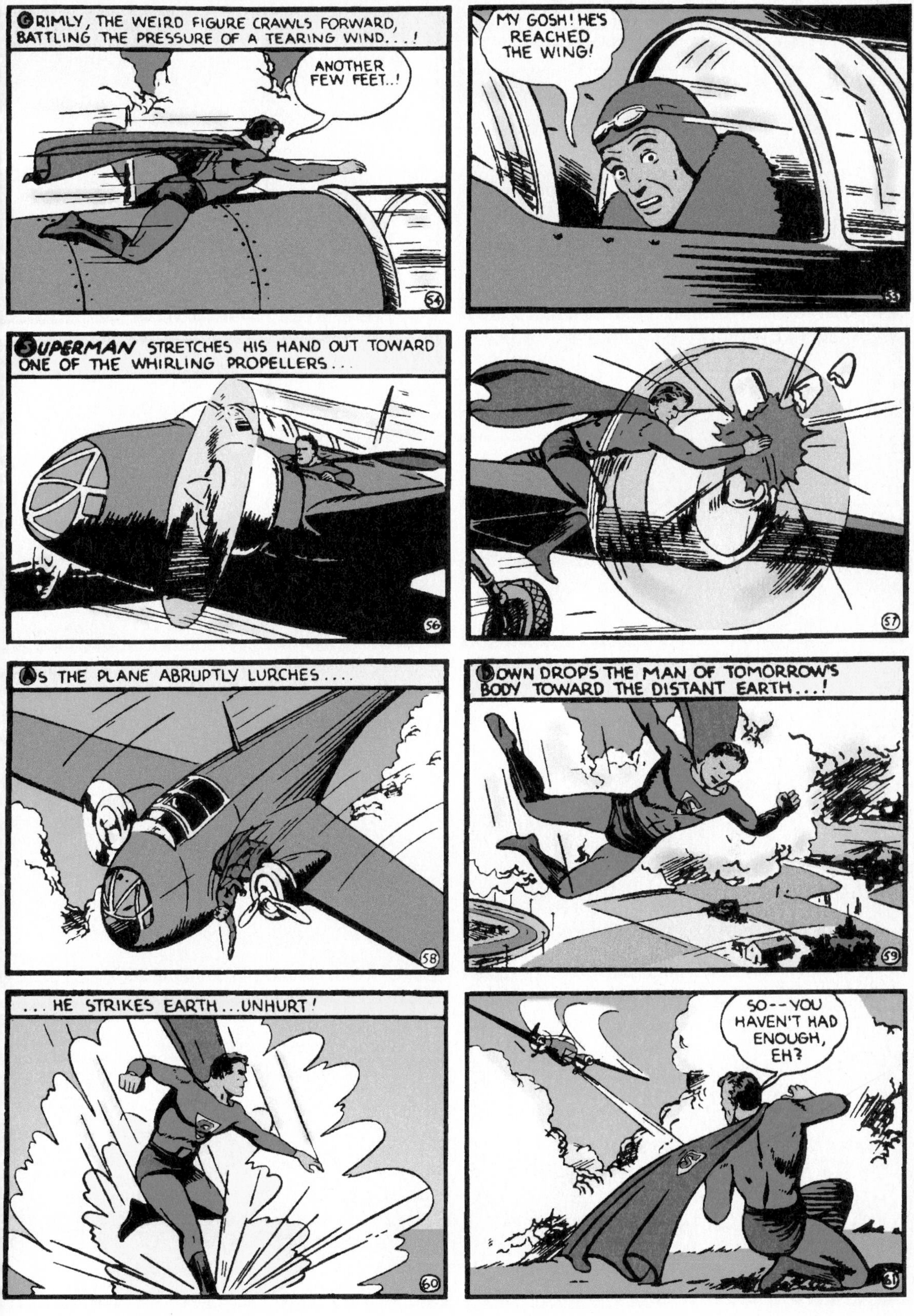
GRIMLY, THE WEIRD FIGURE CRAWLS FORWARD, BATTLING THE PRESSURE OF A TEARING WIND...!
ANOTHER FEW FEET..!
MY GOSH! HE'S REACHED THE WING!
SUPERMAN STRETCHES HIS HAND OUT TOWARD ONE OF THE WHIRLING PROPELLERS...
AS THE PLANE ABRUPTLY LURCHES....
DOWN DROPS THE MAN OF TOMORROW'S BODY TOWARD THE DISTANT EARTH...!
...HE STRIKES EARTH...UNHURT!
SO--YOU HAVEN'T HAD ENOUGH, EH?

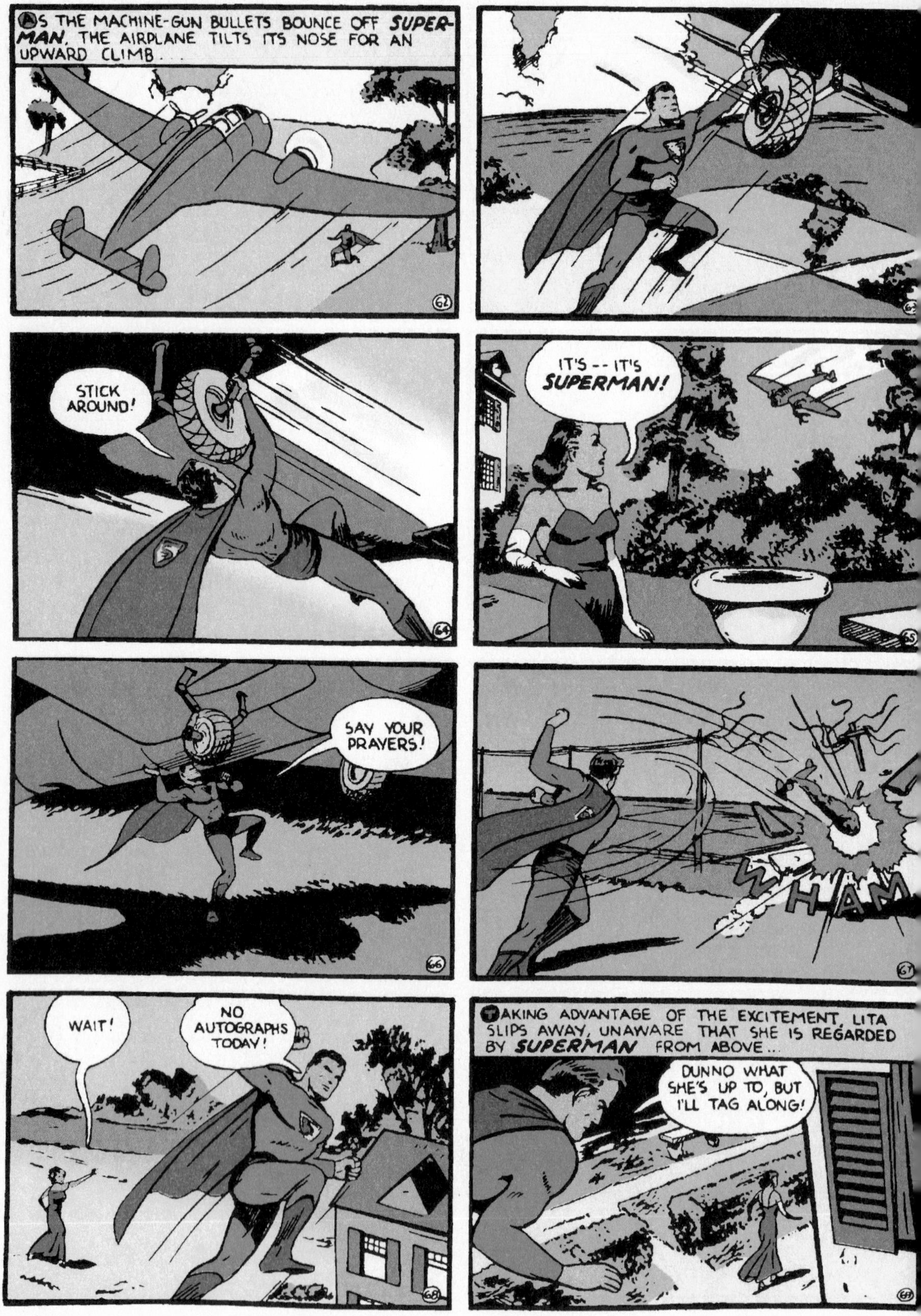
AS THE MACHINE-GUN BULLETS BOUNCE OFF SUPERMAN, THE AIRPLANE TILTS ITS NOSE FOR AN UPWARD CLIMB...
STICK AROUND!
IT'S -- IT'S SUPERMAN!
SAY YOUR PRAYERS!
WHAM
WAIT!
NO AUTOGRAPHS TODAY!
TAKING ADVANTAGE OF THE EXCITEMENT, LITA SLIPS AWAY, UNAWARE THAT SHE IS REGARDED BY SUPERMAN FROM ABOVE...
DUNNO WHAT SHE'S UP TO, BUT I'LL TAG ALONG!

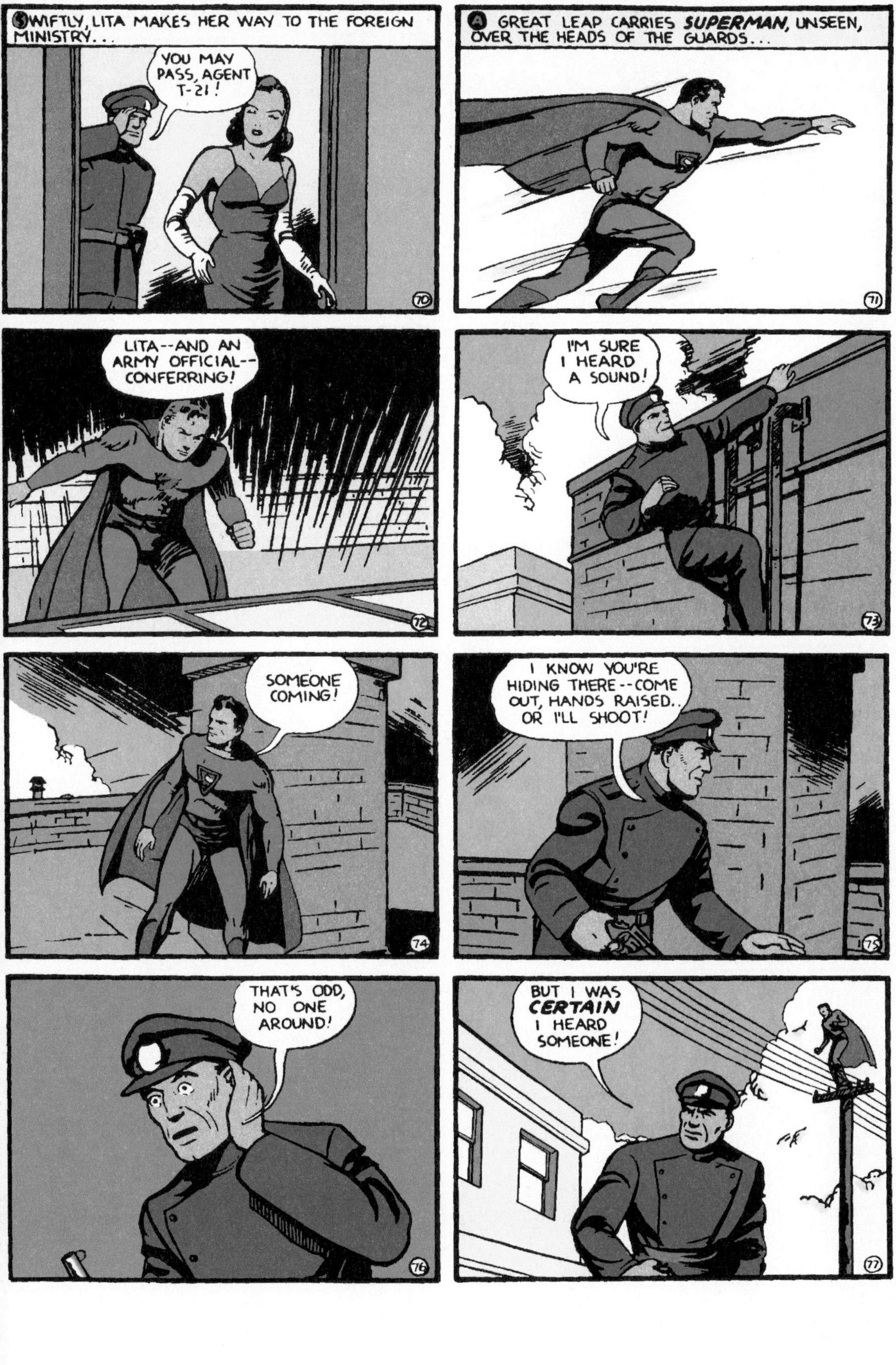
SWIFTLY, LITA MAKES HER WAY TO THE FOREIGN MINISTRY...
YOU MAY PASS, AGENT T-21!
70
A GREAT LEAP CARRIES SUPERMAN, UNSEEN, OVER THE HEADS OF THE GUARDS...
71
LITA--AND AN ARMY OFFICIAL--CONFERRING!
72
I'M SURE I HEARD A SOUND!
73
SOMEONE COMING!
74
I KNOW YOU'RE HIDING THERE--COME OUT, HANDS RAISED.. OR I'LL SHOOT!
75
THAT'S ODD, NO ONE AROUND!
76
BUT I WAS CERTAIN I HEARD SOMEONE!
77

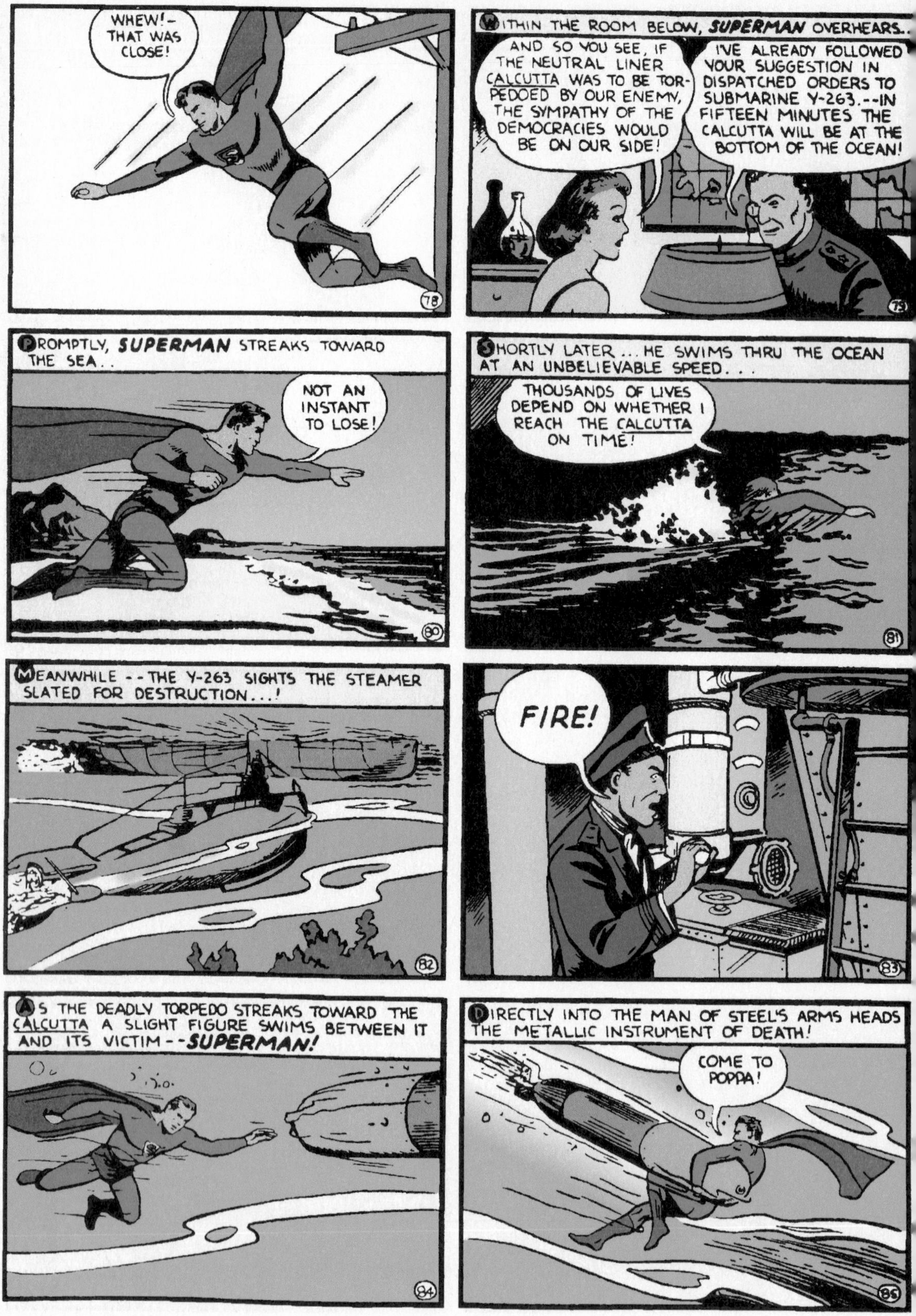
WHEW!-THAT WAS CLOSE!
WITHIN THE ROOM BELOW, SUPERMAN OVERHEARS..
AND SO YOU SEE, IF THE NEUTRAL LINER CALCUTTA WAS TO BE TORPEDOED BY OUR ENEMY, THE SYMPATHY OF THE DEMOCRACIES WOULD BE ON OUR SIDE!
I'VE ALREADY FOLLOWED YOUR SUGGESTION IN DISPATCHED ORDERS TO SUBMARINE Y-263.--IN FIFTEEN MINUTES THE CALCUTTA WILL BE AT THE BOTTOM OF THE OCEAN!
PROMPTLY, SUPERMAN STREAKS TOWARD THE SEA..
NOT AN INSTANT TO LOSE!
SHORTLY LATER... HE SWIMS THRU THE OCEAN AT AN UNBELIEVABLE SPEED..
THOUSANDS OF LIVES DEPEND ON WHETHER I REACH THE CALCUTTA ON TIME!
MEANWHILE--THE Y-263 SIGHTS THE STEAMER SLATED FOR DESTRUCTION...!
FIRE!
AS THE DEADLY TORPEDO STREAKS TOWARD THE CALCUTTA A SLIGHT FIGURE SWIMS BETWEEN IT AND ITS VICTIM--SUPERMAN!
DIRECTLY INTO THE MAN OF STEEL'S ARMS HEADS THE METALLIC INSTRUMENT OF DEATH!
COME TO POPPA!

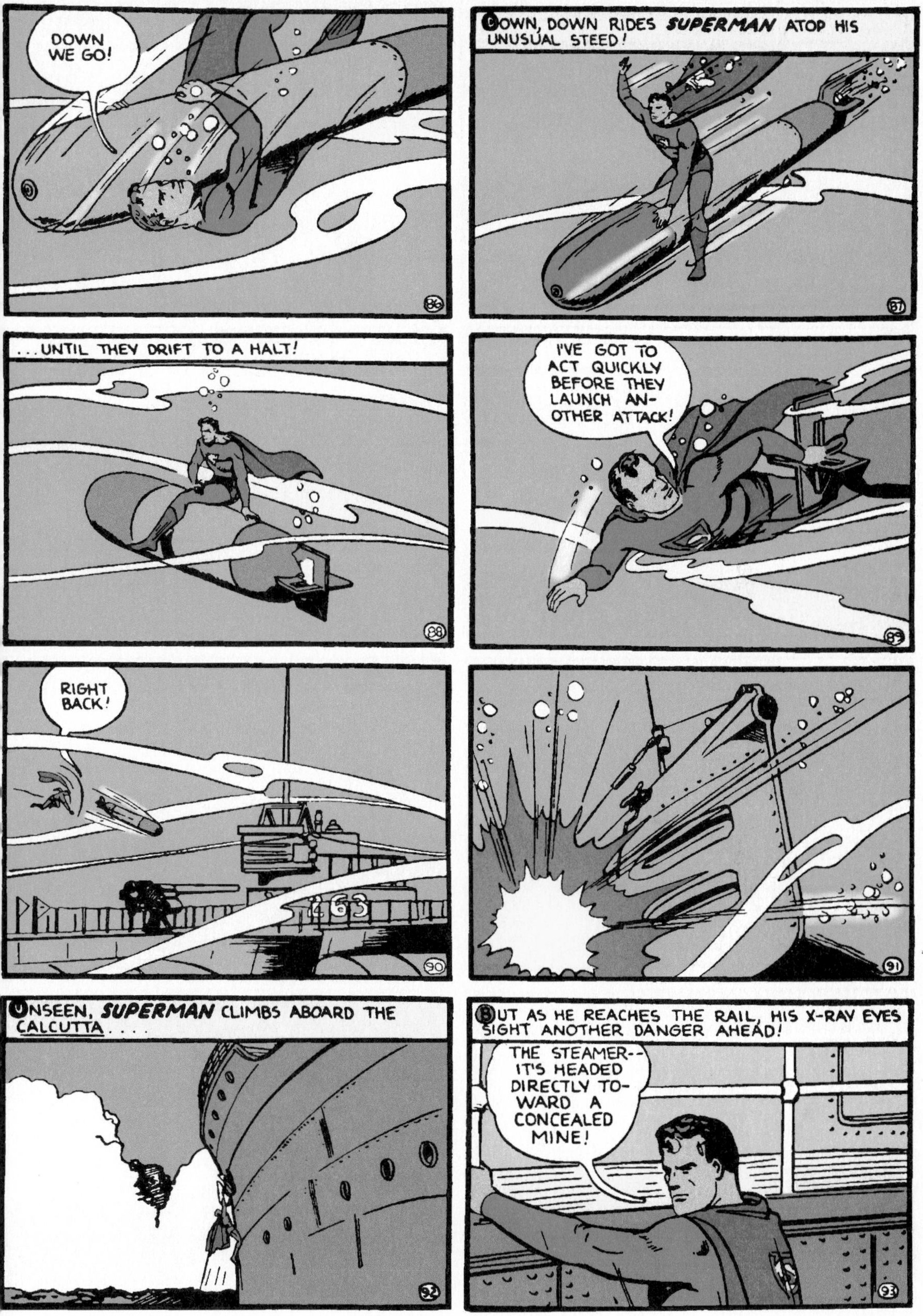
DOWN WE GO!
DOWN, DOWN RIDES SUPERMAN ATOP HIS UNUSUAL STEED!
...UNTIL THEY DRIFT TO A HALT!
I'VE GOT TO ACT QUICKLY BEFORE THEY LAUNCH AN-OTHER ATTACK!
RIGHT BACK!
UNSEEN, SUPERMAN CLIMBS ABOARD THE CALCUTTA....
BUT AS HE REACHES THE RAIL, HIS X-RAY EYES SIGHT ANOTHER DANGER AHEAD!
THE STEAMER--IT'S HEADED DIRECTLY TO-WARD A CONCEALED MINE!

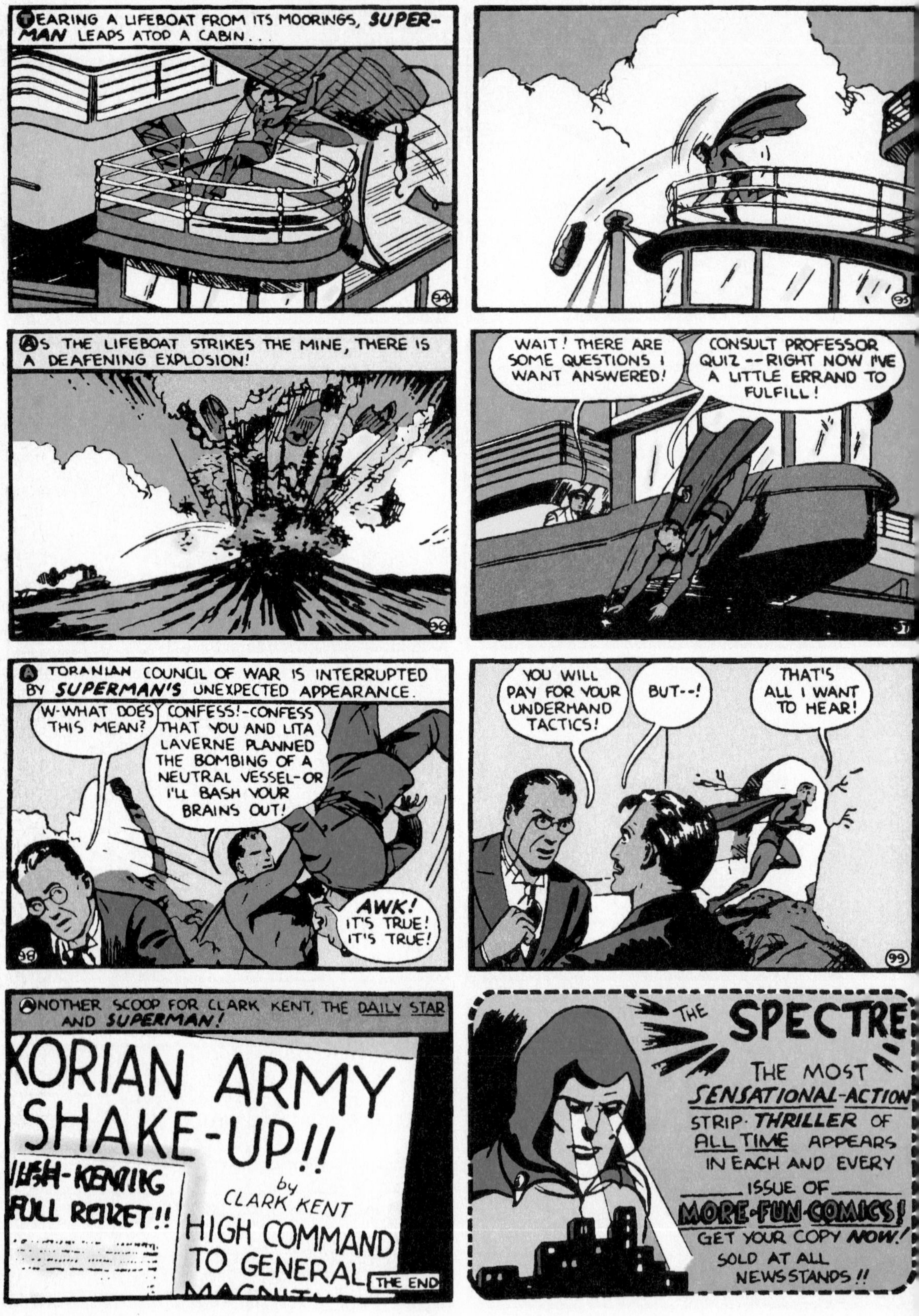
TEARING A LIFEBOAT FROM ITS MOORINGS, SUPERMAN LEAPS ATOP A CABIN...
AS THE LIFEBOAT STRIKES THE MINE, THERE IS A DEAFENING EXPLOSION!
WAIT! THERE ARE SOME QUESTIONS I WANT ANSWERED!
CONSULT PROFESSOR QUIZ -- RIGHT NOW I'VE A LITTLE ERRAND TO FULFILL!
A TORANIAN COUNCIL OF WAR IS INTERRUPTED BY SUPERMAN'S UNEXPECTED APPEARANCE.
W-WHAT DOES THIS MEAN?
CONFESS!-CONFESS THAT YOU AND LITA LAVERNE PLANNED THE BOMBING OF A NEUTRAL VESSEL-OR I'LL BASH YOUR BRAINS OUT!
AWK! IT'S TRUE! IT'S TRUE!
YOU WILL PAY FOR YOUR UNDERHAND TACTICS!
BUT--!
THAT'S ALL I WANT TO HEAR!
ANOTHER SCOOP FOR CLARK KENT, THE DAILY STAR AND SUPERMAN!
KORIAN ARMY SHAKE-UP!!
by CLARK KENT
HIGH COMMAND TO GENERAL
THE END
THE SPECTRE
THE MOST SENSATIONAL-ACTION STRIP-THRILLER OF ALL TIME APPEARS IN EACH AND EVERY ISSUE OF MORE-FUN-COMICS!
GET YOUR COPY NOW! SOLD AT ALL NEWSSTANDS!!

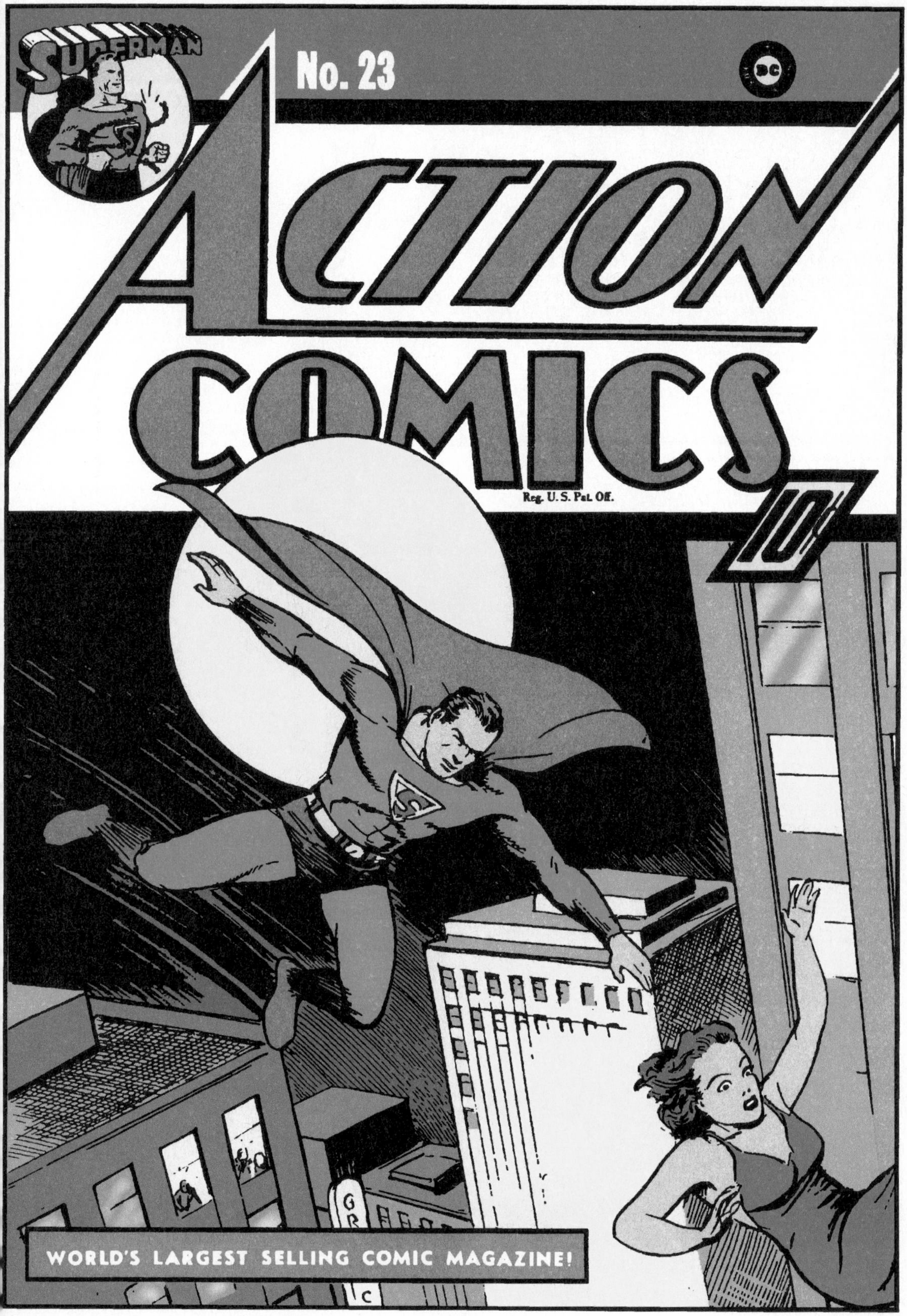
SUPERMAN
No. 23
DC
ACTION COMICS
Reg. U.S. Pat. Off.
10¢
WORLD'S LARGEST SELLING COMIC MAGAZINE!

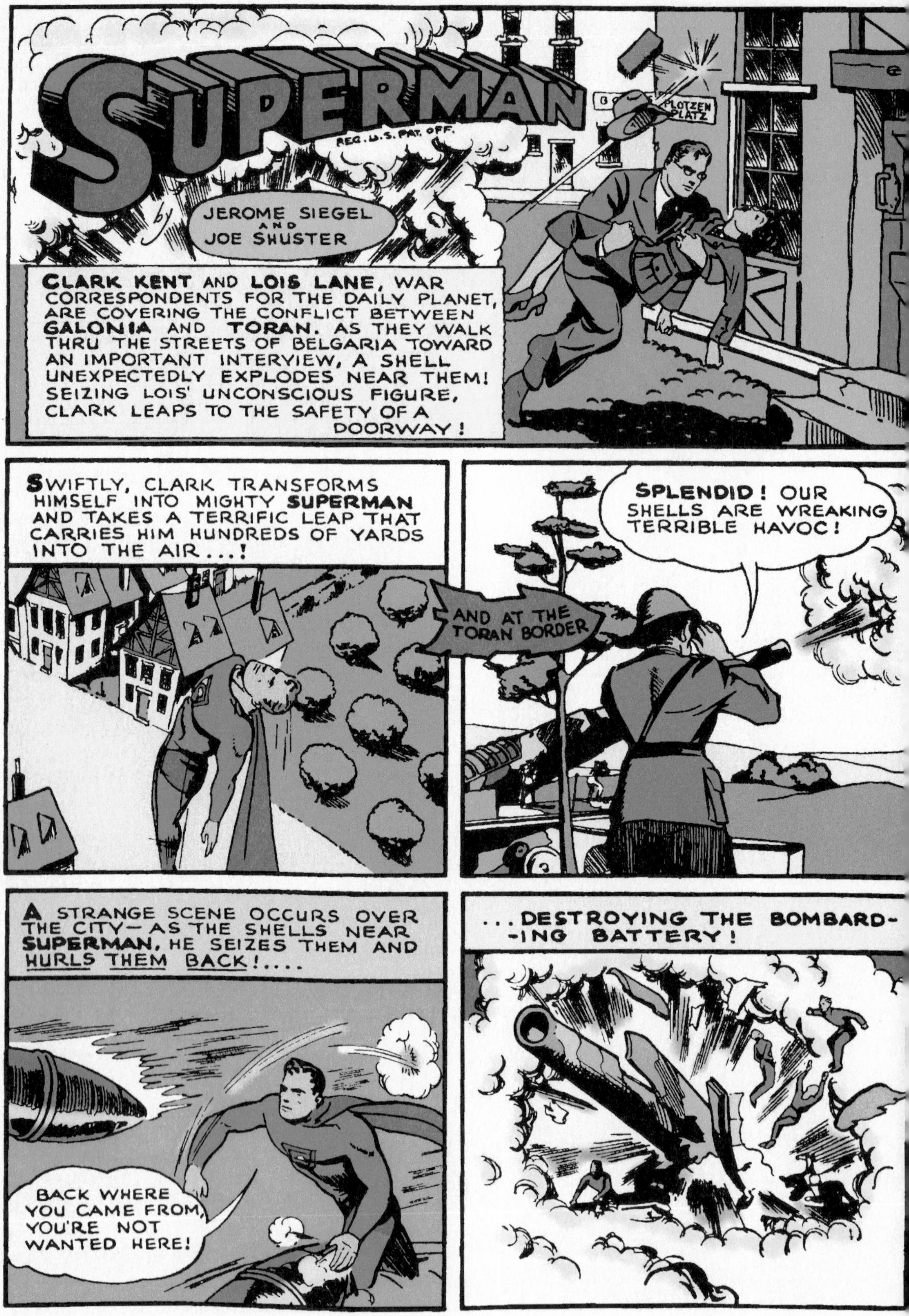
SUPERMAN
REG. U.S. PAT. OFF.
by JEROME SIEGEL AND JOE SHUSTER
PLOTZEN PLATZ
CLARK KENT AND LOIS LANE, WAR CORRESPONDENTS FOR THE DAILY PLANET, ARE COVERING THE CONFLICT BETWEEN GALONIA AND TORAN. AS THEY WALK THRU THE STREETS OF BELGARIA TOWARD AN IMPORTANT INTERVIEW, A SHELL UNEXPECTEDLY EXPLODES NEAR THEM! SEIZING LOIS' UNCONSCIOUS FIGURE, CLARK LEAPS TO THE SAFETY OF A DOORWAY!
SWIFTLY, CLARK TRANSFORMS HIMSELF INTO MIGHTY SUPERMAN AND TAKES A TERRIFIC LEAP THAT CARRIES HIM HUNDREDS OF YARDS INTO THE AIR...!
AND AT THE TORAN BORDER
SPLENDID! OUR SHELLS ARE WREAKING TERRIBLE HAVOC!
A STRANGE SCENE OCCURS OVER THE CITY—AS THE SHELLS NEAR SUPERMAN, HE SEIZES THEM AND HURLS THEM BACK!....
BACK WHERE YOU CAME FROM, YOU'RE NOT WANTED HERE!
...DESTROYING THE BOMBARD--ING BATTERY!

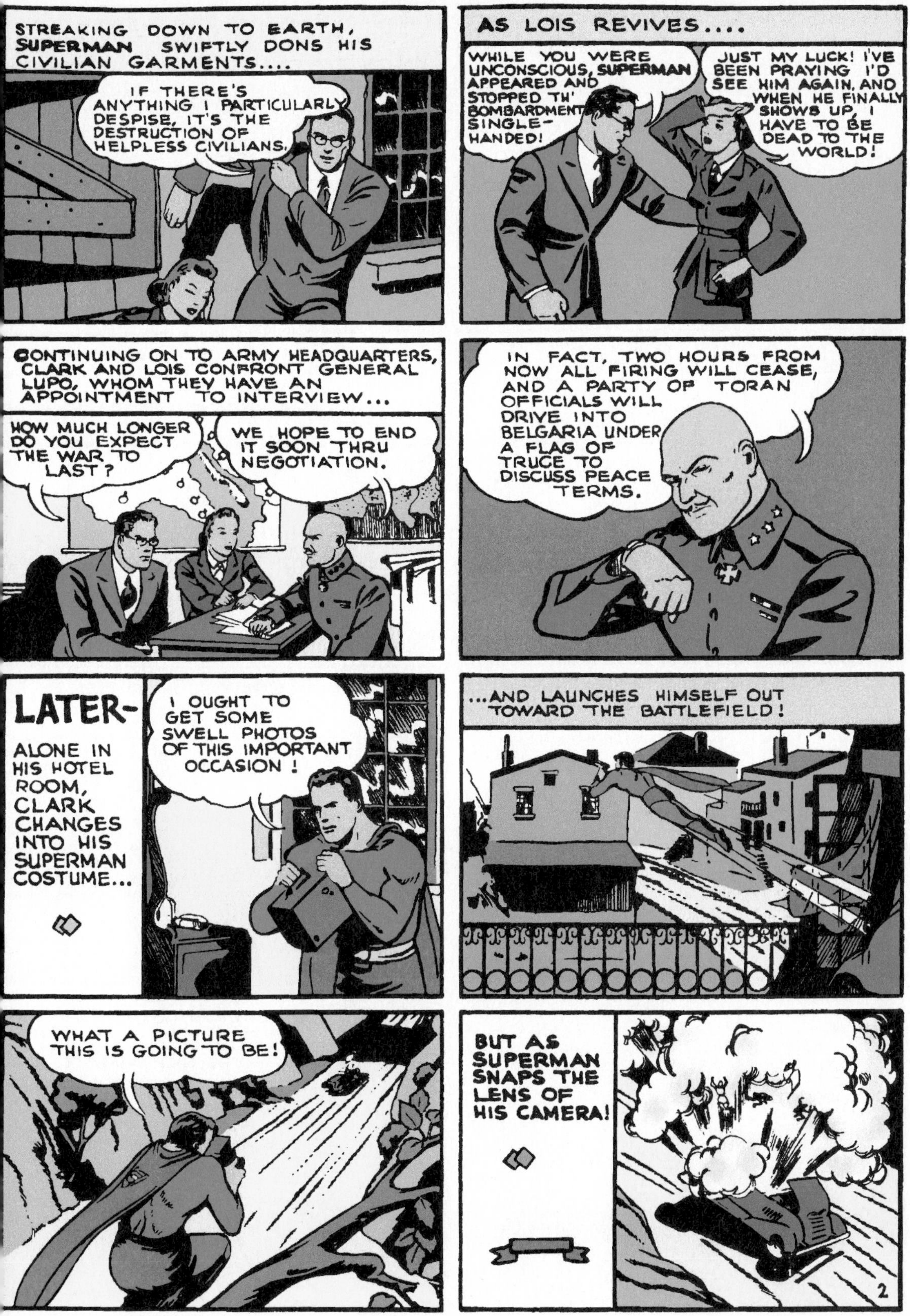
STREAKING DOWN TO EARTH, SUPERMAN SWIFTLY DONS HIS CIVILIAN GARMENTS....
IF THERE'S ANYTHING I PARTICULARLY DESPISE, IT'S THE DESTRUCTION OF HELPLESS CIVILIANS.
AS LOIS REVIVES....
WHILE YOU WERE UNCONSCIOUS, SUPERMAN APPEARED AND STOPPED TH' BOMBARDMENT SINGLE-HANDED!
JUST MY LUCK! I'VE BEEN PRAYING I'D SEE HIM AGAIN, AND WHEN HE FINALLY SHOWS UP, I HAVE TO BE DEAD TO THE WORLD!
CONTINUING ON TO ARMY HEADQUARTERS, CLARK AND LOIS CONFRONT GENERAL LUPO, WHOM THEY HAVE AN APPOINTMENT TO INTERVIEW...
HOW MUCH LONGER DO YOU EXPECT THE WAR TO LAST?
WE HOPE TO END IT SOON THRU NEGOTIATION.
IN FACT, TWO HOURS FROM NOW ALL FIRING WILL CEASE, AND A PARTY OF TORAN OFFICIALS WILL DRIVE INTO BELGARIA UNDER A FLAG OF TRUCE TO DISCUSS PEACE TERMS.
LATER-
ALONE IN HIS HOTEL ROOM, CLARK CHANGES INTO HIS SUPERMAN COSTUME...
I OUGHT TO GET SOME SWELL PHOTOS OF THIS IMPORTANT OCCASION!
...AND LAUNCHES HIMSELF OUT TOWARD THE BATTLEFIELD!
WHAT A PICTURE THIS IS GOING TO BE!
BUT AS SUPERMAN SNAPS THE LENS OF HIS CAMERA!
2

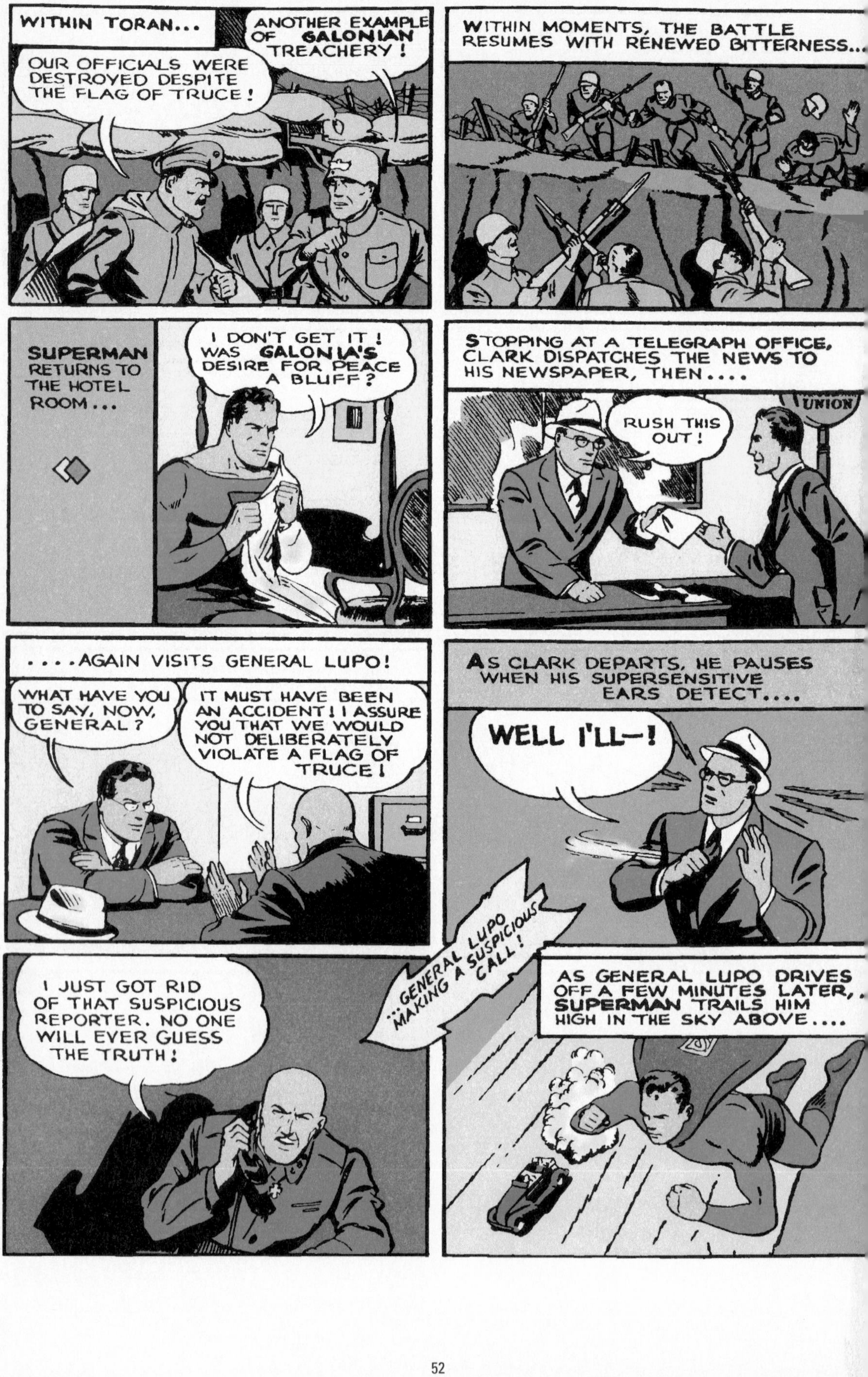
WITHIN TORAN...
OUR OFFICIALS WERE DESTROYED DESPITE THE FLAG OF TRUCE!
ANOTHER EXAMPLE OF GALONIAN TREACHERY!
WITHIN MOMENTS, THE BATTLE RESUMES WITH RENEWED BITTERNESS...
SUPERMAN RETURNS TO THE HOTEL ROOM...
I DON'T GET IT! WAS GALONIA'S DESIRE FOR PEACE A BLUFF?
STOPPING AT A TELEGRAPH OFFICE, CLARK DISPATCHES THE NEWS TO HIS NEWSPAPER, THEN....
UNION
RUSH THIS OUT!
....AGAIN VISITS GENERAL LUPO!
WHAT HAVE YOU TO SAY, NOW, GENERAL?
IT MUST HAVE BEEN AN ACCIDENT! I ASSURE YOU THAT WE WOULD NOT DELIBERATELY VIOLATE A FLAG OF TRUCE!
AS CLARK DEPARTS, HE PAUSES WHEN HIS SUPERSENSITIVE EARS DETECT....
WELL I'LL—!
...GENERAL LUPO MAKING A SUSPICIOUS CALL!
I JUST GOT RID OF THAT SUSPICIOUS REPORTER. NO ONE WILL EVER GUESS THE TRUTH!
AS GENERAL LUPO DRIVES OFF A FEW MINUTES LATER, SUPERMAN TRAILS HIM HIGH IN THE SKY ABOVE....

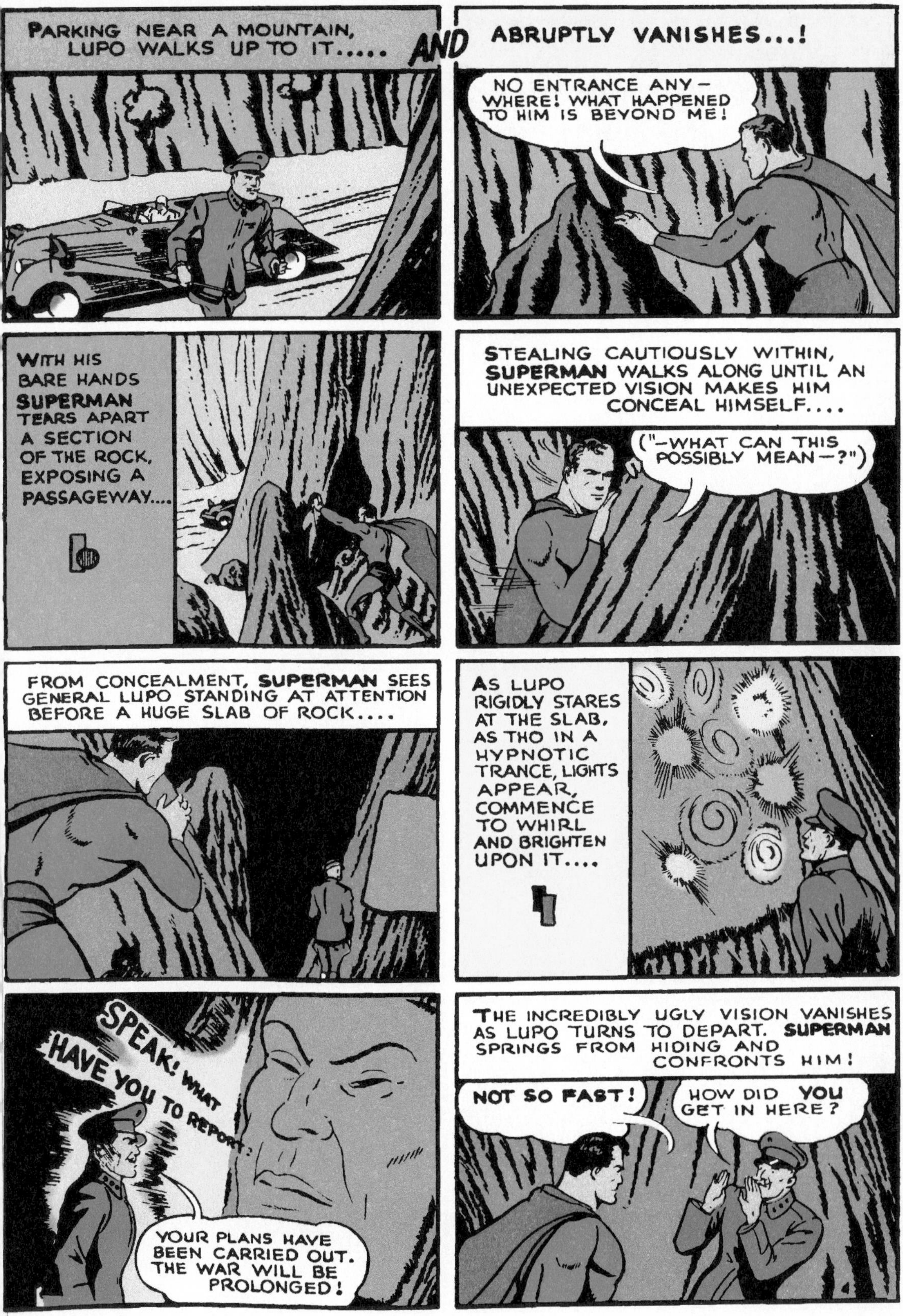
PARKING NEAR A MOUNTAIN, LUPO WALKS UP TO IT.....
AND
ABRUPTLY VANISHES...!
NO ENTRANCE ANY-WHERE! WHAT HAPPENED TO HIM IS BEYOND ME!
WITH HIS BARE HANDS SUPERMAN TEARS APART A SECTION OF THE ROCK, EXPOSING A PASSAGEWAY....
STEALING CAUTIOUSLY WITHIN, SUPERMAN WALKS ALONG UNTIL AN UNEXPECTED VISION MAKES HIM CONCEAL HIMSELF....
("-WHAT CAN THIS POSSIBLY MEAN-?")
FROM CONCEALMENT, SUPERMAN SEES GENERAL LUPO STANDING AT ATTENTION BEFORE A HUGE SLAB OF ROCK....
AS LUPO RIGIDLY STARES AT THE SLAB, AS THO IN A HYPNOTIC TRANCE, LIGHTS APPEAR, COMMENCE TO WHIRL AND BRIGHTEN UPON IT....
SPEAK! WHAT HAVE YOU TO REPORT?
YOUR PLANS HAVE BEEN CARRIED OUT. THE WAR WILL BE PROLONGED!
THE INCREDIBLY UGLY VISION VANISHES AS LUPO TURNS TO DEPART. SUPERMAN SPRINGS FROM HIDING AND CONFRONTS HIM!
NOT SO FAST!
HOW DID YOU GET IN HERE?

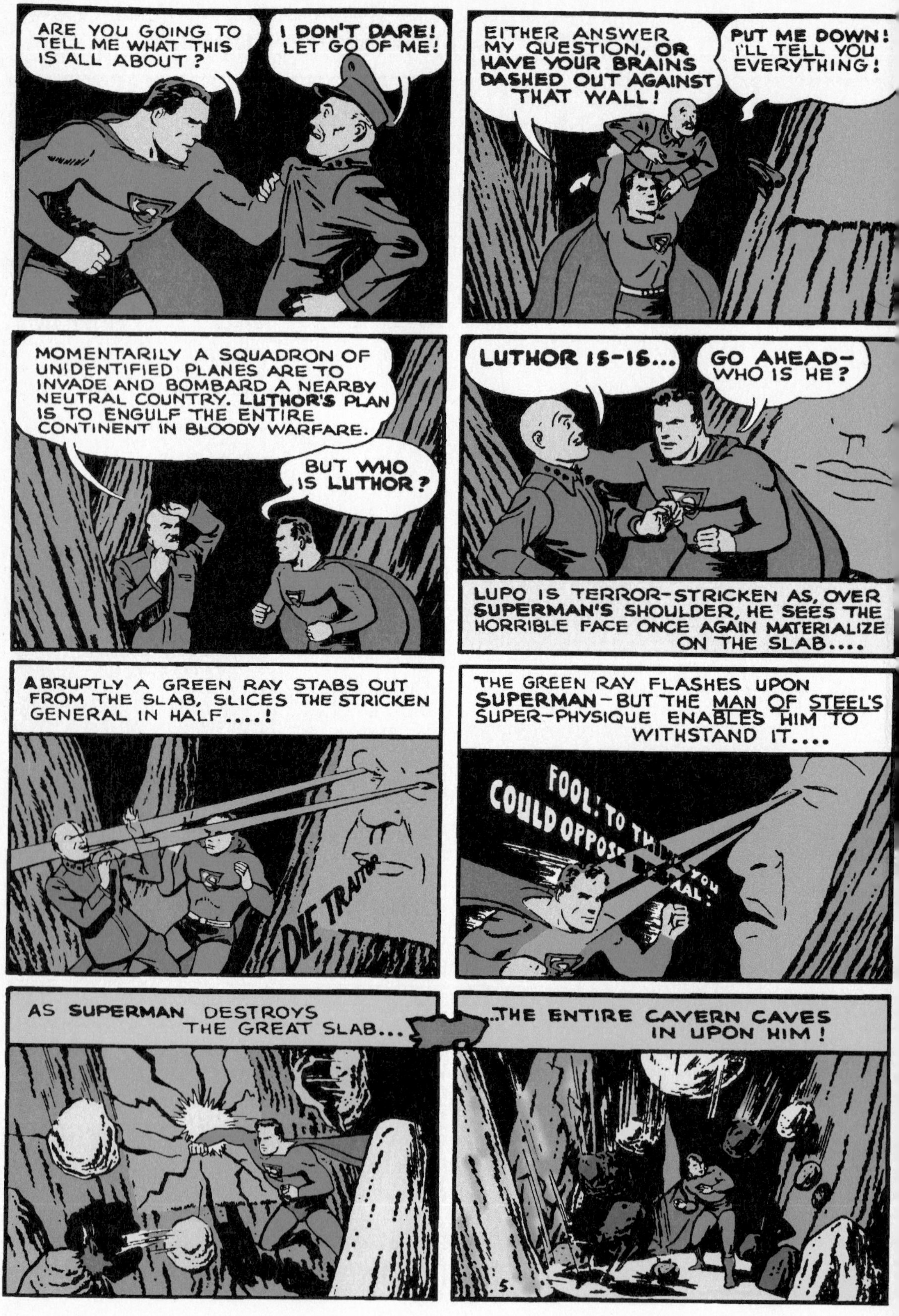
ARE YOU GOING TO TELL ME WHAT THIS IS ALL ABOUT ?
I DON'T DARE! LET GO OF ME!
EITHER ANSWER MY QUESTION, OR HAVE YOUR BRAINS DASHED OUT AGAINST THAT WALL!
PUT ME DOWN! I'LL TELL YOU EVERYTHING!
MOMENTARILY A SQUADRON OF UNIDENTIFIED PLANES ARE TO INVADE AND BOMBARD A NEARBY NEUTRAL COUNTRY. LUTHOR'S PLAN IS TO ENGULF THE ENTIRE CONTINENT IN BLOODY WARFARE.
BUT WHO IS LUTHOR?
LUTHOR IS-IS...
GO AHEAD- WHO IS HE?
LUPO IS TERROR-STRICKEN AS, OVER SUPERMAN'S SHOULDER, HE SEES THE HORRIBLE FACE ONCE AGAIN MATERIALIZE ON THE SLAB....
ABRUPTLY A GREEN RAY STABS OUT FROM THE SLAB, SLICES THE STRICKEN GENERAL IN HALF....!
DIE TRAITOR
THE GREEN RAY FLASHES UPON SUPERMAN—BUT THE MAN OF STEEL'S SUPER-PHYSIQUE ENABLES HIM TO WITHSTAND IT....
AS SUPERMAN DESTROYS THE GREAT SLAB...
...THE ENTIRE CAVERN CAVES IN UPON HIM!
5.

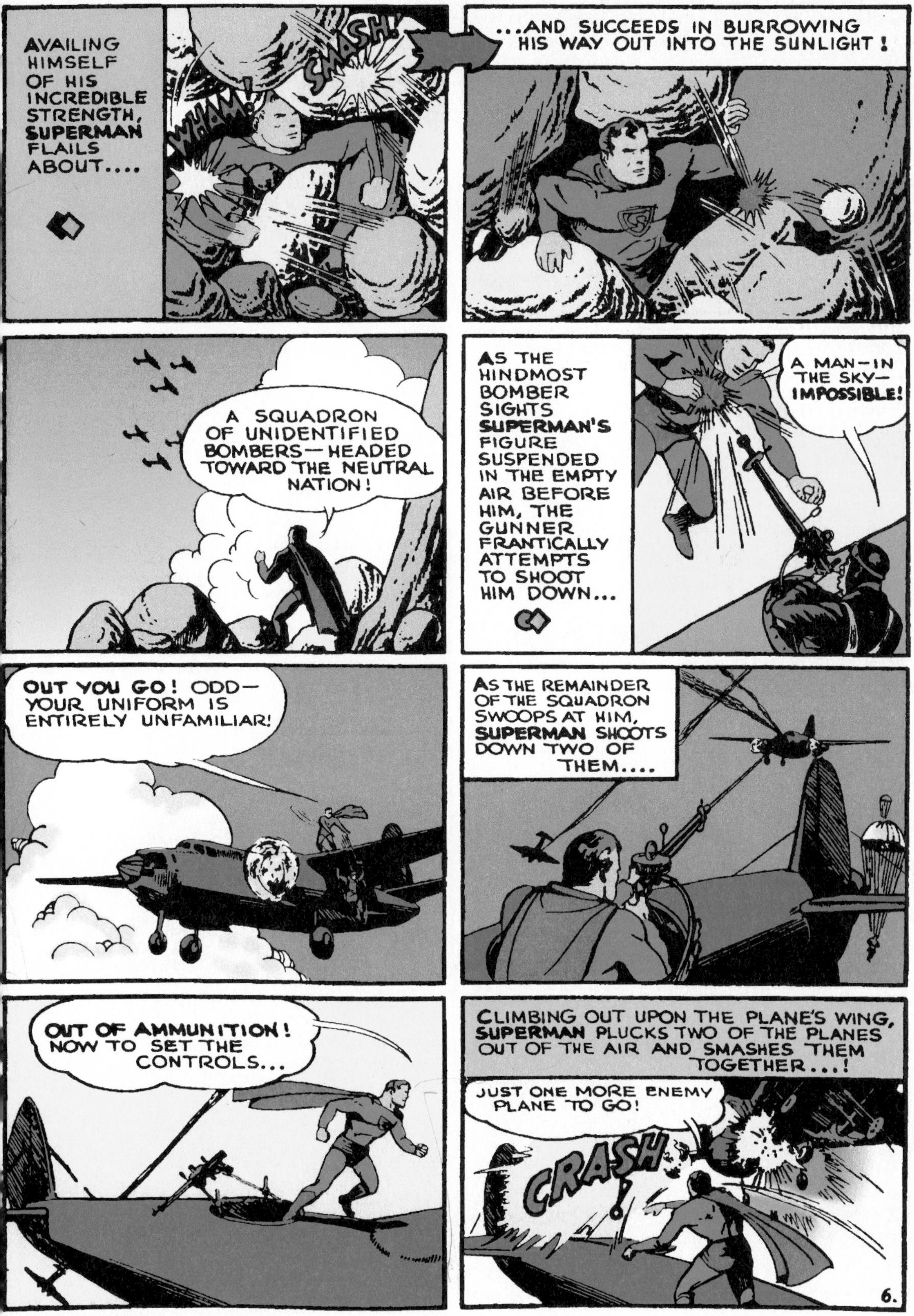
AVAILING HIMSELF OF HIS INCREDIBLE STRENGTH, SUPERMAN FLAILS ABOUT....
WHAM!
SMASH!
...AND SUCCEEDS IN BURROWING HIS WAY OUT INTO THE SUNLIGHT!
A SQUADRON OF UNIDENTIFIED BOMBERS—HEADED TOWARD THE NEUTRAL NATION!
AS THE HINDMOST BOMBER SIGHTS SUPERMAN'S FIGURE SUSPENDED IN THE EMPTY AIR BEFORE HIM, THE GUNNER FRANTICALLY ATTEMPTS TO SHOOT HIM DOWN...
A MAN—IN THE SKY—IMPOSSIBLE!
OUT YOU GO! ODD—YOUR UNIFORM IS ENTIRELY UNFAMILIAR!
AS THE REMAINDER OF THE SQUADRON SWOOPS AT HIM, SUPERMAN SHOOTS DOWN TWO OF THEM....
OUT OF AMMUNITION! NOW TO SET THE CONTROLS...
CLIMBING OUT UPON THE PLANE'S WING, SUPERMAN PLUCKS TWO OF THE PLANES OUT OF THE AIR AND SMASHES THEM TOGETHER...!
JUST ONE MORE ENEMY PLANE TO GO!
CRASH!
6.

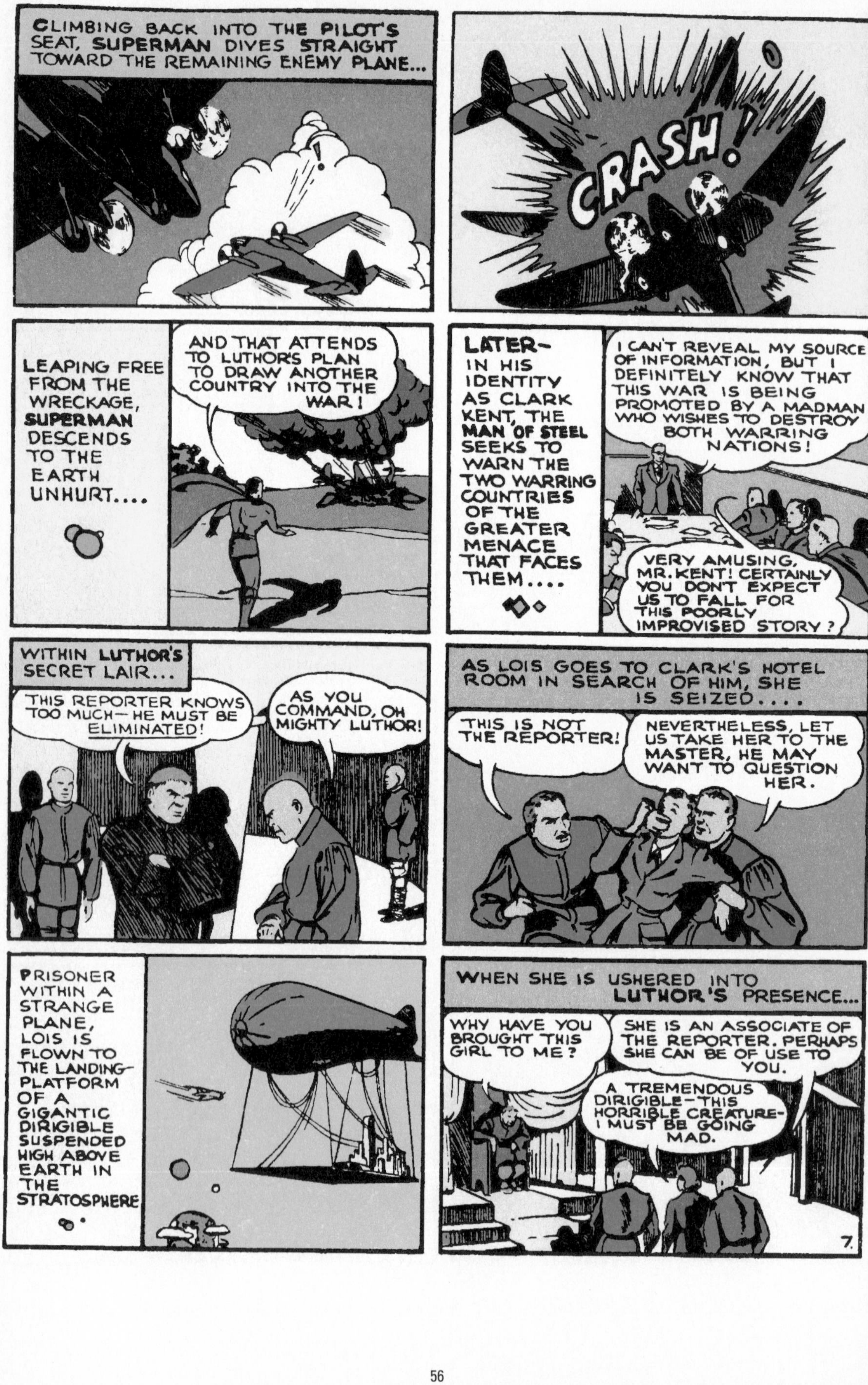
CLIMBING BACK INTO THE PILOT'S SEAT, SUPERMAN DIVES STRAIGHT TOWARD THE REMAINING ENEMY PLANE...
CRASH!
LEAPING FREE FROM THE WRECKAGE, SUPERMAN DESCENDS TO THE EARTH UNHURT....
AND THAT ATTENDS TO LUTHOR'S PLAN TO DRAW ANOTHER COUNTRY INTO THE WAR!
LATER– IN HIS IDENTITY AS CLARK KENT, THE MAN OF STEEL SEEKS TO WARN THE TWO WARRING COUNTRIES OF THE GREATER MENACE THAT FACES THEM....
I CAN'T REVEAL MY SOURCE OF INFORMATION, BUT I DEFINITELY KNOW THAT THIS WAR IS BEING PROMOTED BY A MADMAN WHO WISHES TO DESTROY BOTH WARRING NATIONS!
VERY AMUSING, MR. KENT! CERTAINLY YOU DON'T EXPECT US TO FALL FOR THIS POORLY IMPROVISED STORY?
WITHIN LUTHOR'S SECRET LAIR...
THIS REPORTER KNOWS TOO MUCH– HE MUST BE ELIMINATED!
AS YOU COMMAND, OH MIGHTY LUTHOR!
AS LOIS GOES TO CLARK'S HOTEL ROOM IN SEARCH OF HIM, SHE IS SEIZED....
THIS IS NOT THE REPORTER!
NEVERTHELESS, LET US TAKE HER TO THE MASTER, HE MAY WANT TO QUESTION HER.
PRISONER WITHIN A STRANGE PLANE, LOIS IS FLOWN TO THE LANDING-PLATFORM OF A GIGANTIC DIRIGIBLE SUSPENDED HIGH ABOVE EARTH IN THE STRATOSPHERE
WHEN SHE IS USHERED INTO LUTHOR'S PRESENCE...
WHY HAVE YOU BROUGHT THIS GIRL TO ME?
SHE IS AN ASSOCIATE OF THE REPORTER. PERHAPS SHE CAN BE OF USE TO YOU.
A TREMENDOUS DIRIGIBLE– THIS HORRIBLE CREATURE– I MUST BE GOING MAD.
7.

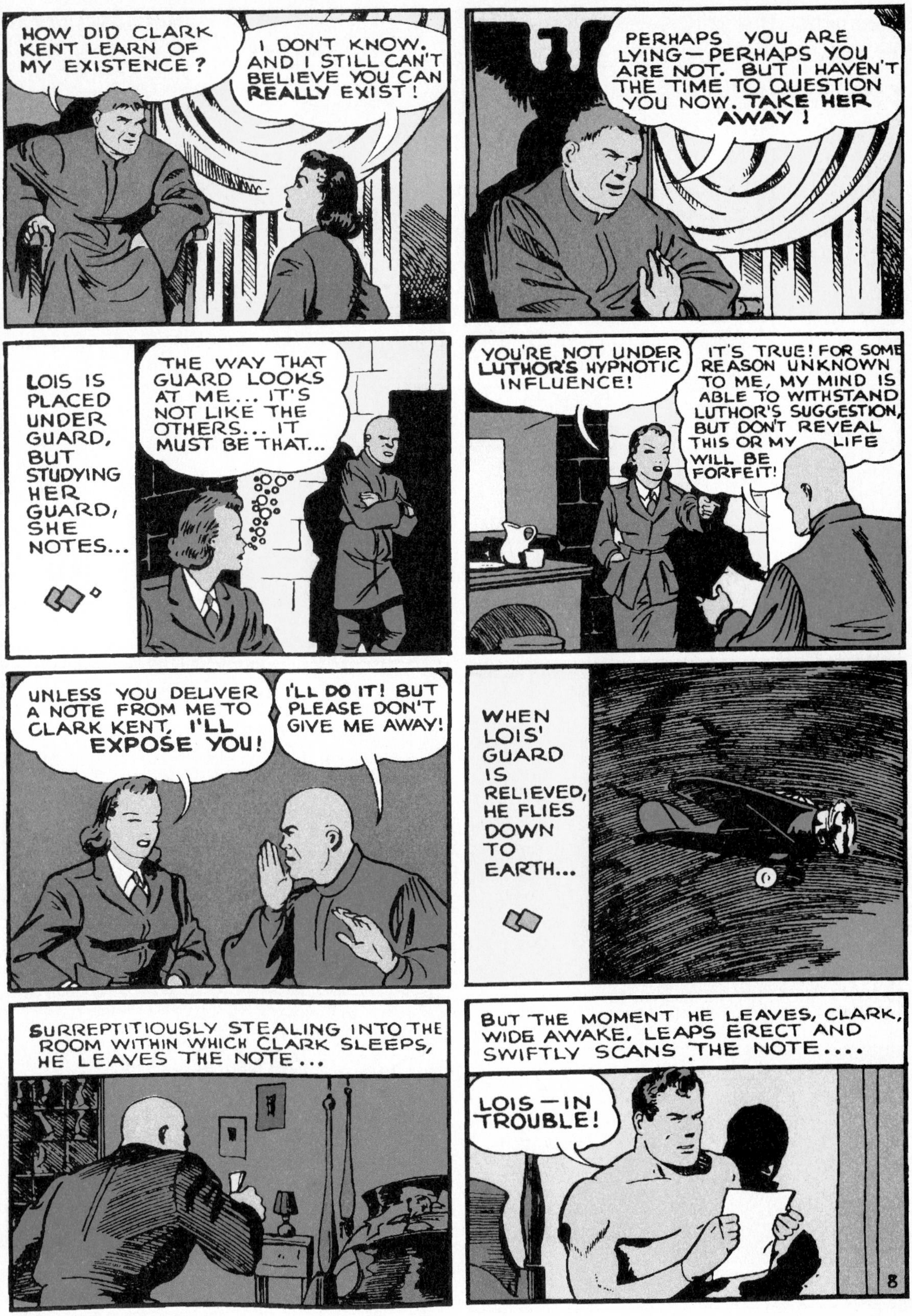
HOW DID CLARK KENT LEARN OF MY EXISTENCE?
I DON'T KNOW. AND I STILL CAN'T BELIEVE YOU CAN REALLY EXIST!
PERHAPS YOU ARE LYING—PERHAPS YOU ARE NOT. BUT I HAVEN'T THE TIME TO QUESTION YOU NOW. TAKE HER AWAY!
LOIS IS PLACED UNDER GUARD, BUT STUDYING HER GUARD, SHE NOTES...
THE WAY THAT GUARD LOOKS AT ME... IT'S NOT LIKE THE OTHERS... IT MUST BE THAT...
YOU'RE NOT UNDER LUTHOR'S HYPNOTIC INFLUENCE!
IT'S TRUE! FOR SOME REASON UNKNOWN TO ME, MY MIND IS ABLE TO WITHSTAND LUTHOR'S SUGGESTION, BUT DON'T REVEAL THIS OR MY LIFE WILL BE FORFEIT!
UNLESS YOU DELIVER A NOTE FROM ME TO CLARK KENT, I'LL EXPOSE YOU!
I'LL DO IT! BUT PLEASE DON'T GIVE ME AWAY!
WHEN LOIS' GUARD IS RELIEVED, HE FLIES DOWN TO EARTH...
SURREPTITIOUSLY STEALING INTO THE ROOM WITHIN WHICH CLARK SLEEPS, HE LEAVES THE NOTE...
BUT THE MOMENT HE LEAVES, CLARK, WIDE AWAKE, LEAPS ERECT AND SWIFTLY SCANS THE NOTE....
LOIS—IN TROUBLE!
8

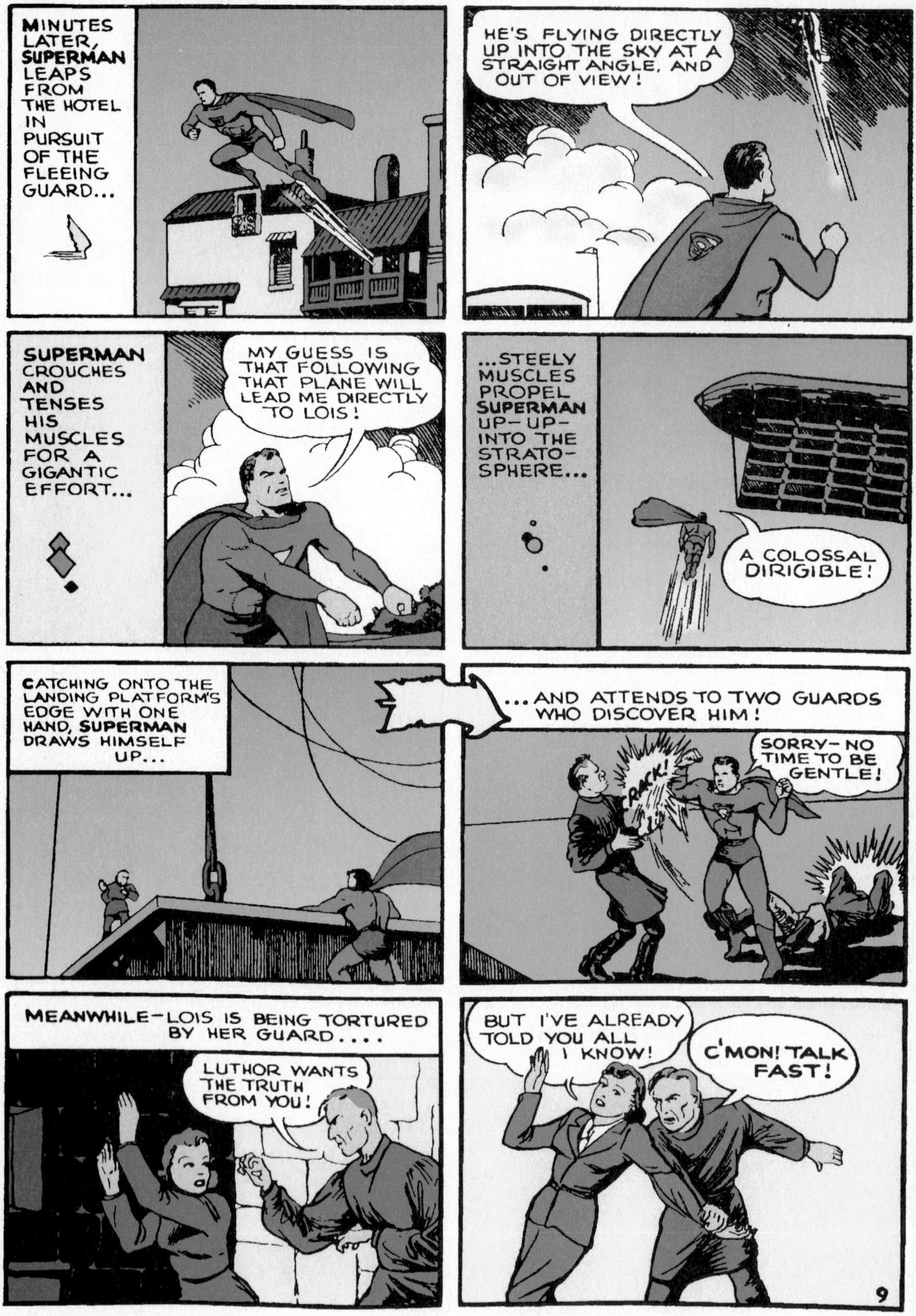
MINUTES LATER, SUPERMAN LEAPS FROM THE HOTEL IN PURSUIT OF THE FLEEING GUARD...
HE'S FLYING DIRECTLY UP INTO THE SKY AT A STRAIGHT ANGLE, AND OUT OF VIEW!
SUPERMAN CROUCHES AND TENSES HIS MUSCLES FOR A GIGANTIC EFFORT...
MY GUESS IS THAT FOLLOWING THAT PLANE WILL LEAD ME DIRECTLY TO LOIS!
...STEELY MUSCLES PROPEL SUPERMAN UP-UP-INTO THE STRATO-SPHERE...
A COLOSSAL DIRIGIBLE!
CATCHING ONTO THE LANDING PLATFORM'S EDGE WITH ONE HAND, SUPERMAN DRAWS HIMSELF UP...
...AND ATTENDS TO TWO GUARDS WHO DISCOVER HIM!
SORRY-NO TIME TO BE GENTLE!
RACK!
MEANWHILE-LOIS IS BEING TORTURED BY HER GUARD....
LUTHOR WANTS THE TRUTH FROM YOU!
BUT I'VE ALREADY TOLD YOU ALL I KNOW!
C'MON! TALK FAST!
9

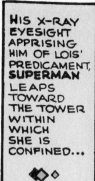

HIS X-RAY EYESIGHT APPRISING HIM OF LOIS' PREDICAMENT, **SUPERMAN** LEAPS TOWARD THE TOWER WITHIN WHICH SHE IS CONFINED...

I'LL ATTEND TO THAT BRUTE IN SHORT ORDER.

SUPERMAN!

HOW'S THAT!

QUICK! TAKE MY ARM— WE'VE GOT TO GET OUT OF HERE!

I'D ADVISE YOU NOT TO LEAVE!

I DON'T FEAR YOU— YOU CAN'T HARM ME!

BUT THE GIRL— SHE IS NOT INVULNERABLE! EITHER SUBMIT OR SHE DIES!

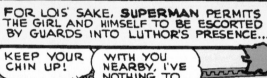

FOR LOIS' SAKE, **SUPERMAN** PERMITS THE GIRL AND HIMSELF TO BE ESCORTED BY GUARDS INTO LUTHOR'S PRESENCE...

KEEP YOUR CHIN UP!

WITH YOU NEARBY, I'VE NOTHING TO FEAR!

WHAT SORT OF CREATURE ARE YOU?

JUST AN ORDINARY MAN— BUT WITH TH' BRAIN OF A SUPER-GENIUS! WITH SCIENTIFIC MIRACLES AT MY FINGERTIPS, I'M PREPARING TO MAKE MYSELF SUPREME MASTER OF TH' WORLD!

MY PLAN? TO SEND THE NATIONS OF THE EARTH AT EACH OTHER'S THROATS, SO THAT WHEN THEY ARE SUFFICIENTLY WEAKENED, I CAN STEP IN AND ASSUME CHARGE!

THE ONLY THING YOU SHOULD STEP INTO IS A STRAIGHT-JACKET!

ACCEDING TO LUTHOR'S DEMANDS, **SUPERMAN** PERMITS HIMSELF TO BE CHAINED TO THE WALL WHILE FOUR GREEN RAYS BORE STEADILY AT HIM....

VERY INTERESTING, HOW STRONG YOUR SKIN IS — BUT I GUARANTEE YOU THAT FIVE MINUTES UNDER THOSE RAYS WILL RESULT IN YOUR ANNIHILATION.

10

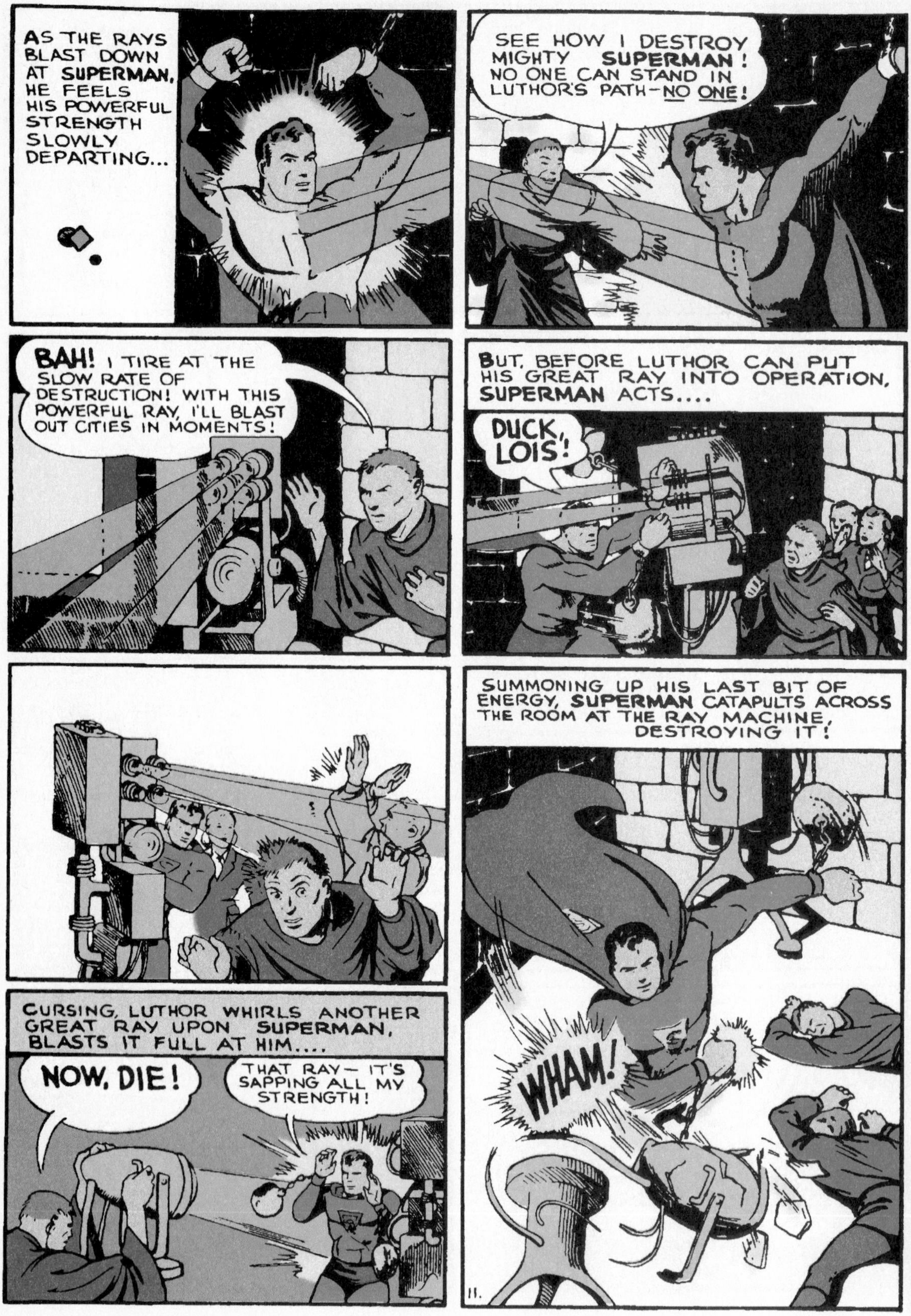
AS THE RAYS BLAST DOWN AT SUPERMAN, HE FEELS HIS POWERFUL STRENGTH SLOWLY DEPARTING...
SEE HOW I DESTROY MIGHTY SUPERMAN! NO ONE CAN STAND IN LUTHOR'S PATH-NO ONE!
BAH! I TIRE AT THE SLOW RATE OF DESTRUCTION! WITH THIS POWERFUL RAY, I'LL BLAST OUT CITIES IN MOMENTS!
BUT, BEFORE LUTHOR CAN PUT HIS GREAT RAY INTO OPERATION, SUPERMAN ACTS....
DUCK, LOIS!
CURSING, LUTHOR WHIRLS ANOTHER GREAT RAY UPON SUPERMAN, BLASTS IT FULL AT HIM....
NOW, DIE!
THAT RAY- IT'S SAPPING ALL MY STRENGTH!
SUMMONING UP HIS LAST BIT OF ENERGY, SUPERMAN CATAPULTS ACROSS THE ROOM AT THE RAY MACHINE, DESTROYING IT!
WHAM!
11.

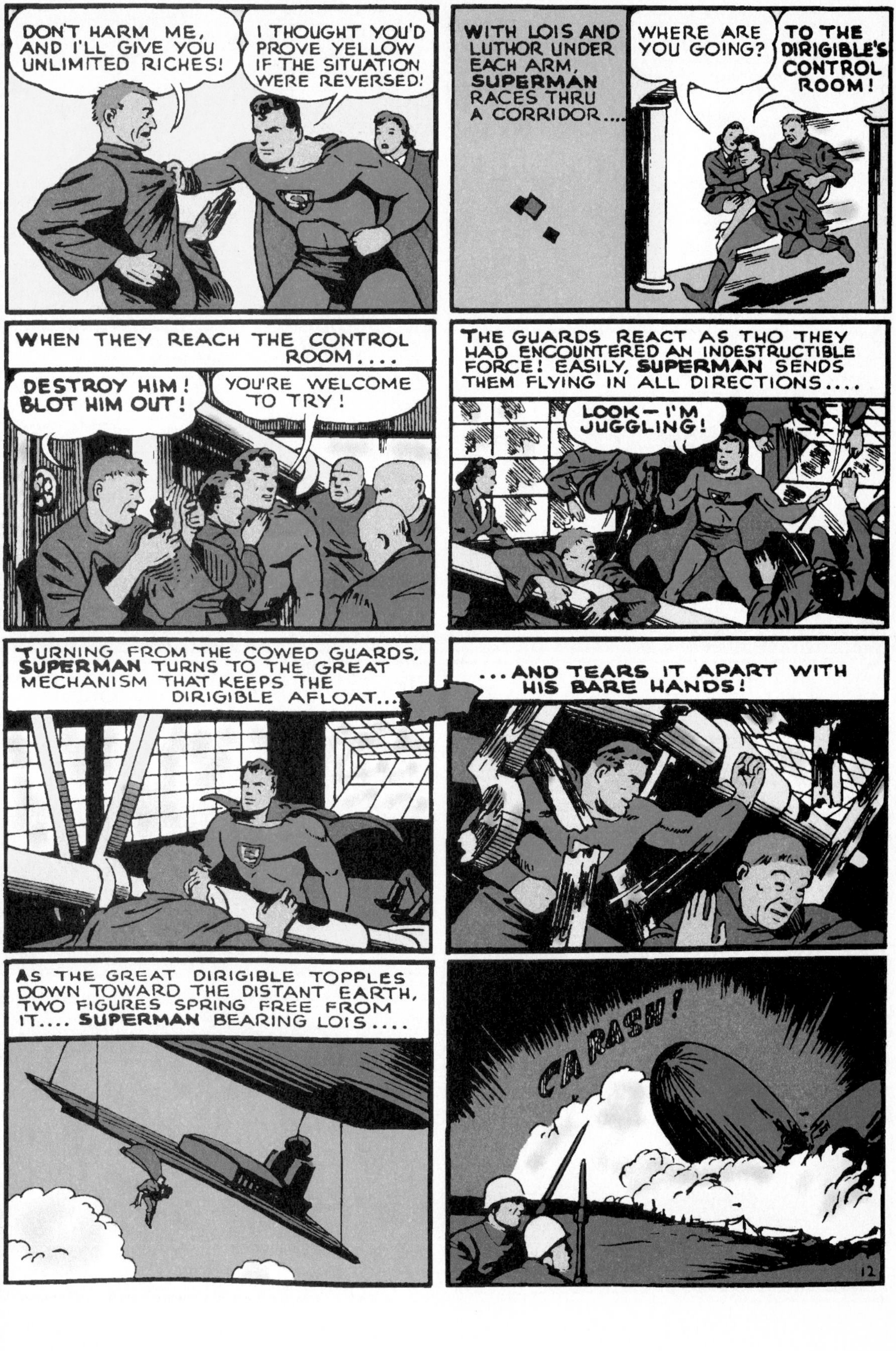
DON'T HARM ME, AND I'LL GIVE YOU UNLIMITED RICHES!
I THOUGHT YOU'D PROVE YELLOW IF THE SITUATION WERE REVERSED!
WITH LOIS AND LUTHOR UNDER EACH ARM, SUPERMAN RACES THRU A CORRIDOR....
WHERE ARE YOU GOING?
TO THE DIRIGIBLE'S CONTROL ROOM!
WHEN THEY REACH THE CONTROL ROOM....
DESTROY HIM! BLOT HIM OUT!
YOU'RE WELCOME TO TRY!
THE GUARDS REACT AS THO THEY HAD ENCOUNTERED AN INDESTRUCTIBLE FORCE! EASILY, SUPERMAN SENDS THEM FLYING IN ALL DIRECTIONS....
LOOK—I'M JUGGLING!
TURNING FROM THE COWED GUARDS, SUPERMAN TURNS TO THE GREAT MECHANISM THAT KEEPS THE DIRIGIBLE AFLOAT...
...AND TEARS IT APART WITH HIS BARE HANDS!
AS THE GREAT DIRIGIBLE TOPPLES DOWN TOWARD THE DISTANT EARTH, TWO FIGURES SPRING FREE FROM IT.... SUPERMAN BEARING LOIS....
CA RASH!
12

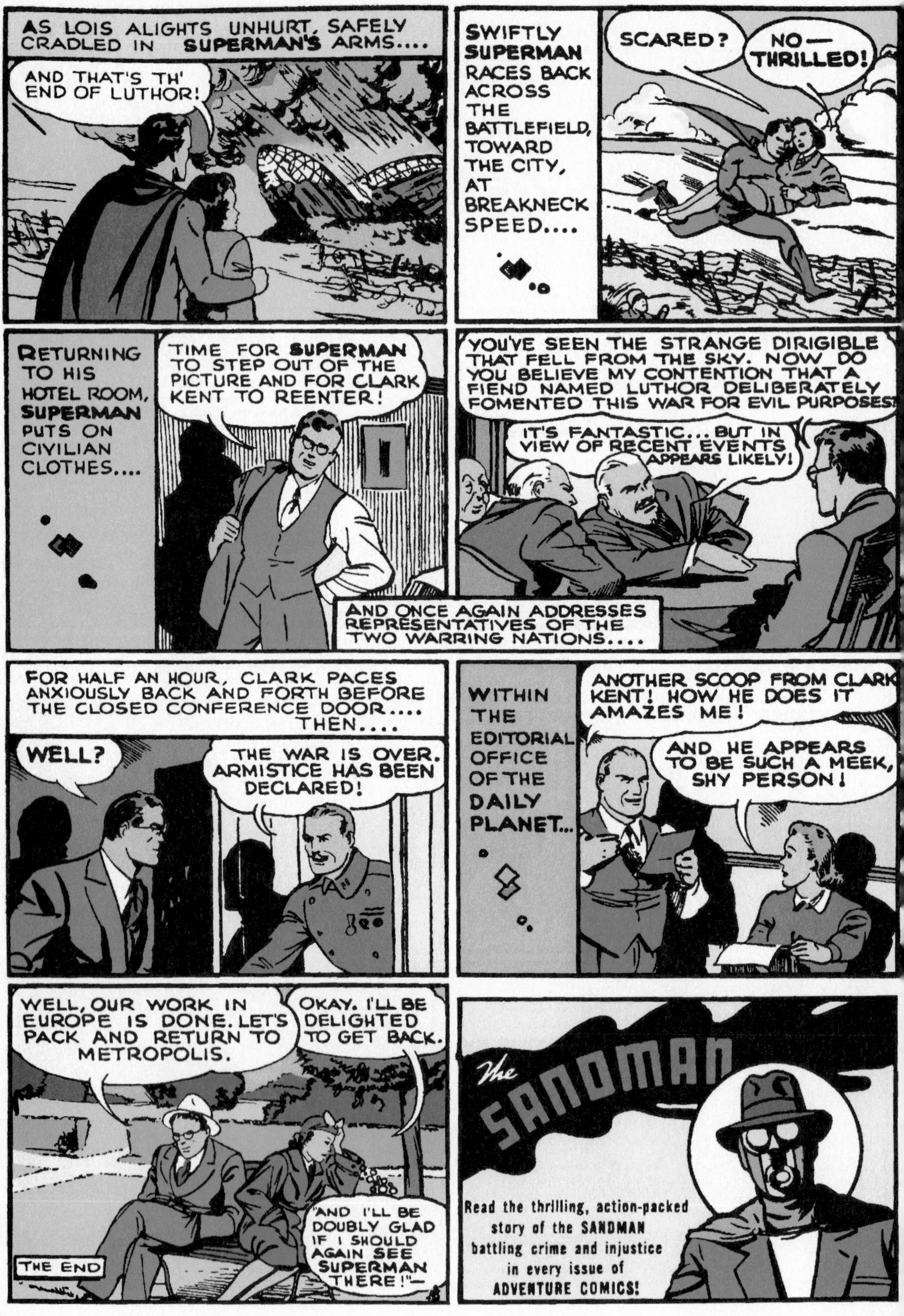
AS LOIS ALIGHTS UNHURT, SAFELY CRADLED IN SUPERMAN'S ARMS....
AND THAT'S TH' END OF LUTHOR!
SWIFTLY SUPERMAN RACES BACK ACROSS THE BATTLEFIELD, TOWARD THE CITY, AT BREAKNECK SPEED....
SCARED?
NO— THRILLED!
RETURNING TO HIS HOTEL ROOM, SUPERMAN PUTS ON CIVILIAN CLOTHES....
TIME FOR SUPERMAN TO STEP OUT OF THE PICTURE AND FOR CLARK KENT TO REENTER!
YOU'VE SEEN THE STRANGE DIRIGIBLE THAT FELL FROM THE SKY. NOW DO YOU BELIEVE MY CONTENTION THAT A FIEND NAMED LUTHOR DELIBERATELY FOMENTED THIS WAR FOR EVIL PURPOSES?
IT'S FANTASTIC... BUT IN VIEW OF RECENT EVENTS APPEARS LIKELY!
AND ONCE AGAIN ADDRESSES REPRESENTATIVES OF THE TWO WARRING NATIONS....
FOR HALF AN HOUR, CLARK PACES ANXIOUSLY BACK AND FORTH BEFORE THE CLOSED CONFERENCE DOOR.... THEN....
WELL?
THE WAR IS OVER. ARMISTICE HAS BEEN DECLARED!
WITHIN THE EDITORIAL OFFICE OF THE DAILY PLANET...
ANOTHER SCOOP FROM CLARK KENT! HOW HE DOES IT AMAZES ME!
AND HE APPEARS TO BE SUCH A MEEK, SHY PERSON!
WELL, OUR WORK IN EUROPE IS DONE. LET'S PACK AND RETURN TO METROPOLIS.
OKAY. I'LL BE DELIGHTED TO GET BACK.
"AND I'LL BE DOUBLY GLAD IF I SHOULD AGAIN SEE SUPERMAN THERE!"—
THE END
The SANDMAN
Read the thrilling, action-packed story of the SANDMAN battling crime and injustice in every issue of ADVENTURE COMICS!

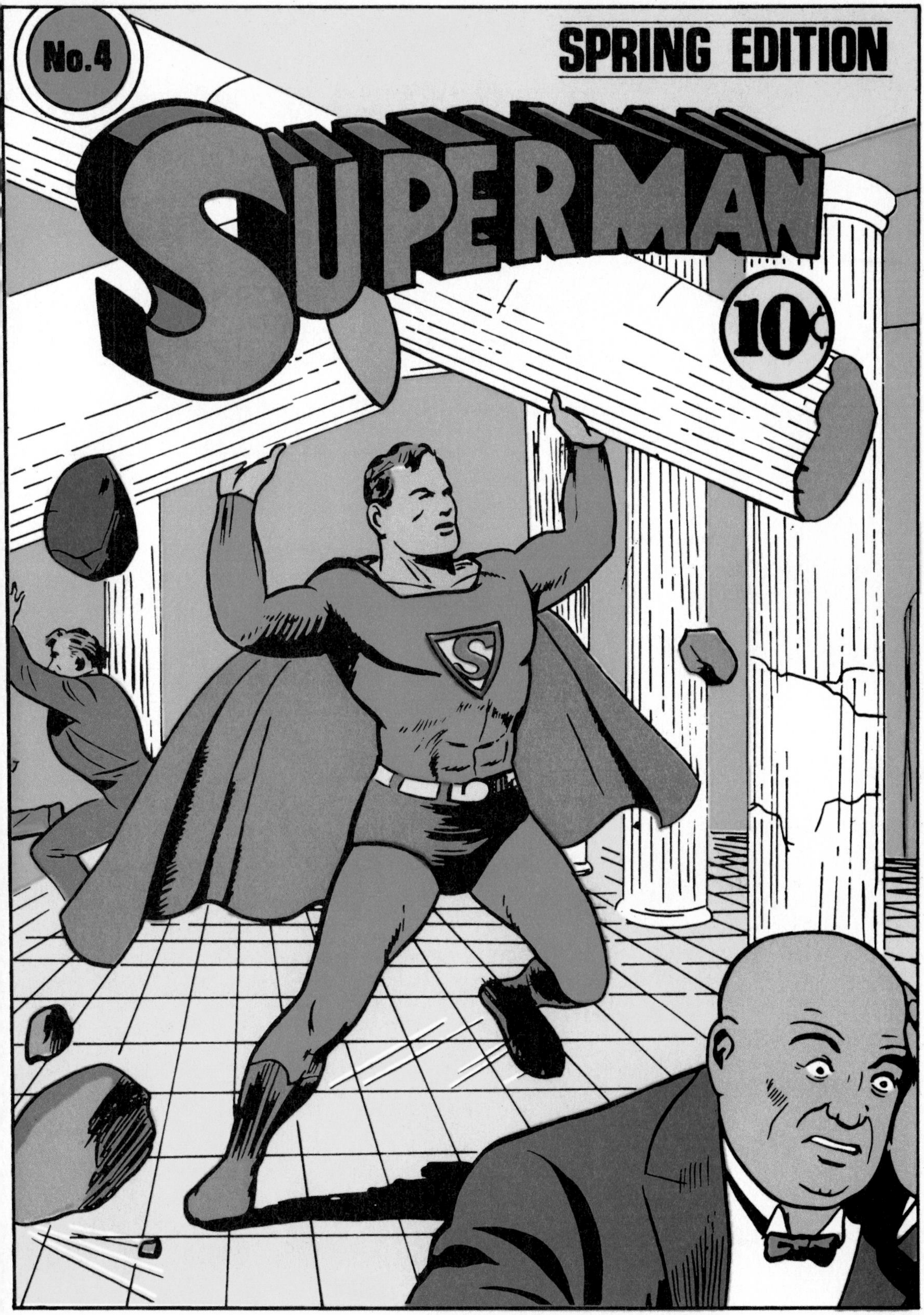
No.4
SPRING EDITION
SUPERMAN
10¢

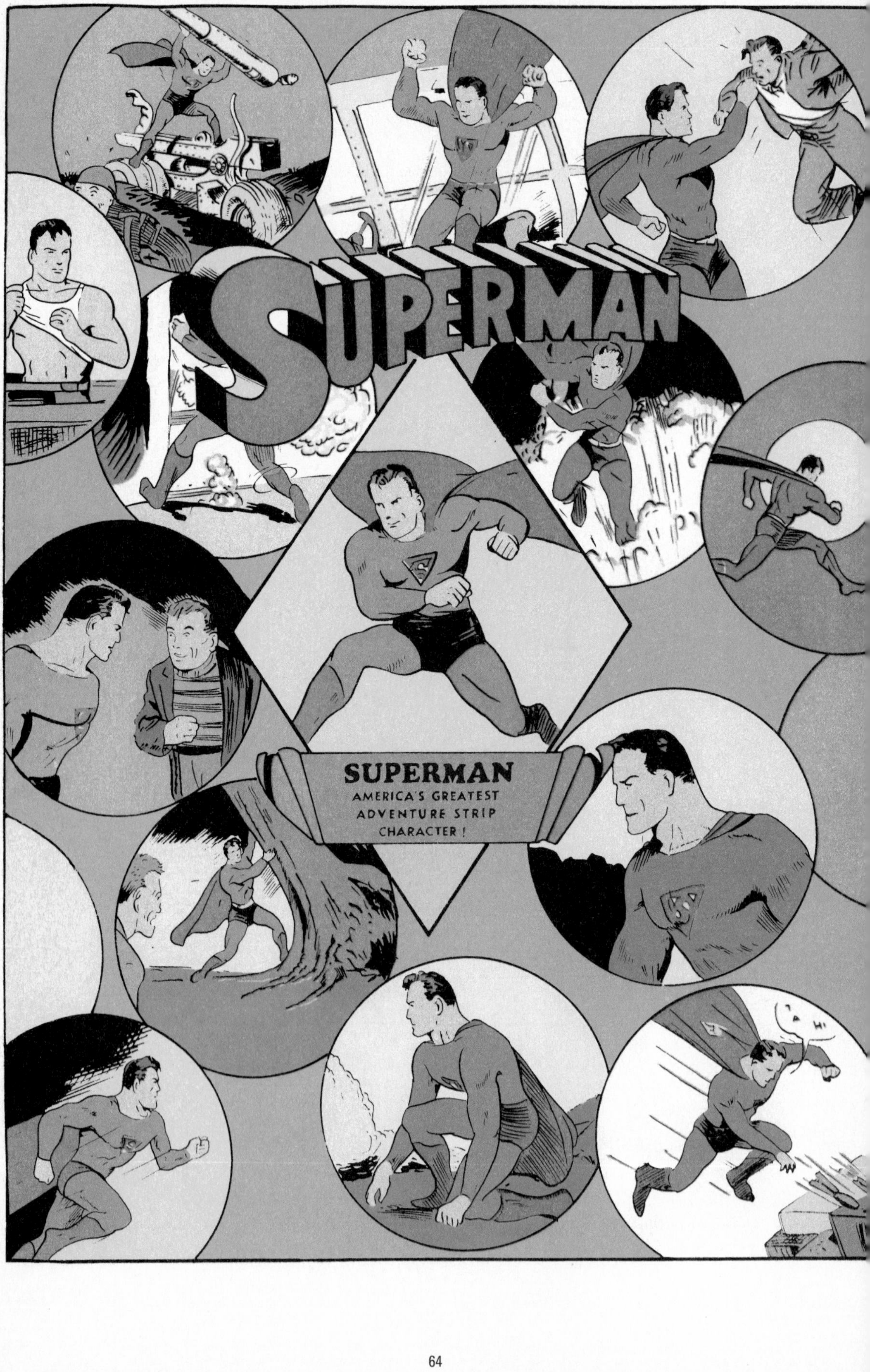
SUPERMAN
SUPERMAN
AMERICA'S GREATEST
ADVENTURE STRIP
CHARACTER!

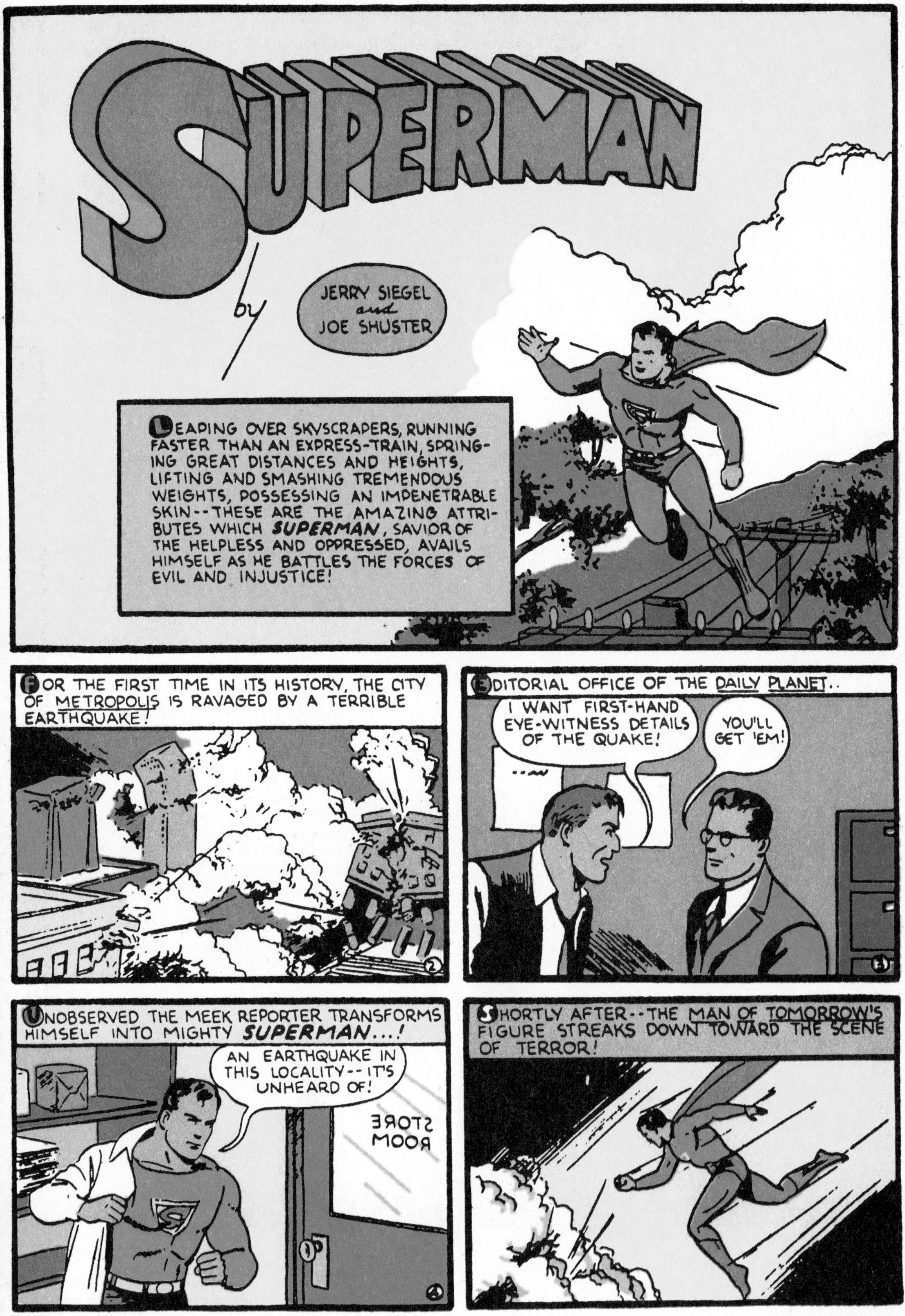
SUPERMAN
by
JERRY SIEGEL and JOE SHUSTER
LEAPING OVER SKYSCRAPERS, RUNNING FASTER THAN AN EXPRESS-TRAIN, SPRINGING GREAT DISTANCES AND HEIGHTS, LIFTING AND SMASHING TREMENDOUS WEIGHTS, POSSESSING AN IMPENETRABLE SKIN--THESE ARE THE AMAZING ATTRIBUTES WHICH SUPERMAN, SAVIOR OF THE HELPLESS AND OPPRESSED, AVAILS HIMSELF AS HE BATTLES THE FORCES OF EVIL AND INJUSTICE!
FOR THE FIRST TIME IN ITS HISTORY, THE CITY OF METROPOLIS IS RAVAGED BY A TERRIBLE EARTHQUAKE!
EDITORIAL OFFICE OF THE DAILY PLANET..
I WANT FIRST-HAND EYE-WITNESS DETAILS OF THE QUAKE!
YOU'LL GET 'EM!
UNOBSERVED THE MEEK REPORTER TRANSFORMS HIMSELF INTO MIGHTY SUPERMAN...!
AN EARTHQUAKE IN THIS LOCALITY--IT'S UNHEARD OF!
STORE ROOM
SHORTLY AFTER--THE MAN OF TOMORROW'S FIGURE STREAKS DOWN TOWARD THE SCENE OF TERROR!

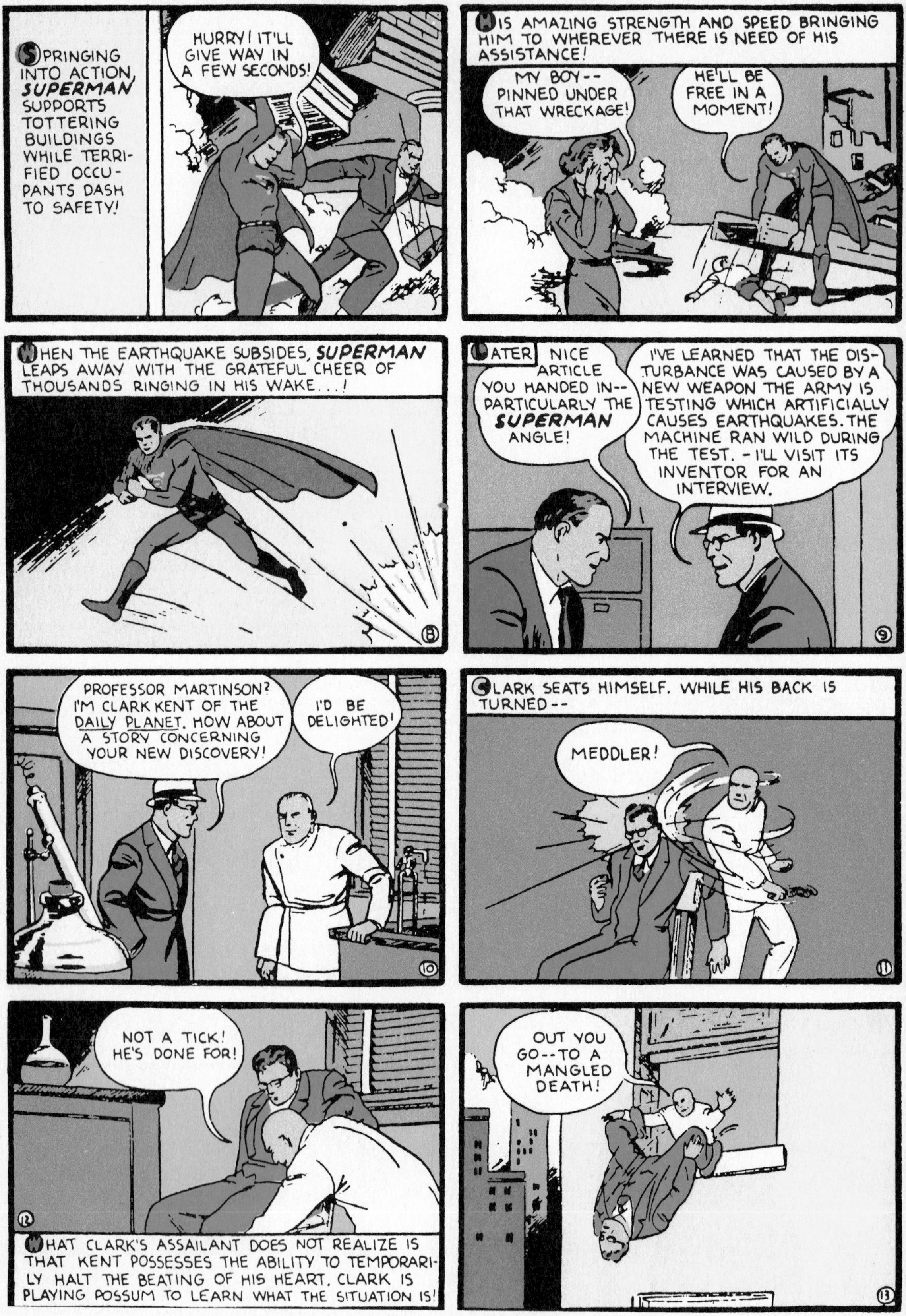

SPRINGING INTO ACTION, SUPERMAN SUPPORTS TOTTERING BUILDINGS WHILE TERRIFIED OCCUPANTS DASH TO SAFETY!
HURRY! IT'LL GIVE WAY IN A FEW SECONDS!
HIS AMAZING STRENGTH AND SPEED BRINGING HIM TO WHEREVER THERE IS NEED OF HIS ASSISTANCE!
MY BOY-- PINNED UNDER THAT WRECKAGE!
HE'LL BE FREE IN A MOMENT!
WHEN THE EARTHQUAKE SUBSIDES, SUPERMAN LEAPS AWAY WITH THE GRATEFUL CHEER OF THOUSANDS RINGING IN HIS WAKE...!
LATER
NICE ARTICLE YOU HANDED IN-- PARTICULARLY THE SUPERMAN ANGLE!
I'VE LEARNED THAT THE DISTURBANCE WAS CAUSED BY A NEW WEAPON THE ARMY IS TESTING WHICH ARTIFICIALLY CAUSES EARTHQUAKES. THE MACHINE RAN WILD DURING THE TEST. - I'LL VISIT ITS INVENTOR FOR AN INTERVIEW.
PROFESSOR MARTINSON? I'M CLARK KENT OF THE DAILY PLANET. HOW ABOUT A STORY CONCERNING YOUR NEW DISCOVERY!
I'D BE DELIGHTED!
CLARK SEATS HIMSELF. WHILE HIS BACK IS TURNED--
MEDDLER!
NOT A TICK! HE'S DONE FOR!
WHAT CLARK'S ASSAILANT DOES NOT REALIZE IS THAT KENT POSSESSES THE ABILITY TO TEMPORARILY HALT THE BEATING OF HIS HEART. CLARK IS PLAYING POSSUM TO LEARN WHAT THE SITUATION IS!
OUT YOU GO--TO A MANGLED DEATH!

DOWN HURTLES THE REPORTER'S FIGURE--!

ABRUPTLY--OUT FLASHES ONE OF HIS HANDS, CLUTCHING THE SIDE OF THE SKYSCRAPER IN A STEELY GRIP, HALTING HIS PLUNGE!

TIME OUT!

IT TAKES BUT A FEW SECONDS TO REMOVE HIS OUTER GARMENTS .... THEN HE COMMENCES TO CLIMB SWIFTLY BACK TOWARD THE LABORATORY ---- AS SUPERMAN!

NOW IT'S *MY* TURN!

WITHIN THE LABORATORY---

A SNOOPING REPORTER INTERFERED WHILE I WAS GOING THRU THE PROFESSOR'S DESK. BUT I DISPOSED OF HIM!

SPLENDID! BUT IT'S UNFORTUNATE YOU COULDN'T FIND THE PLANS WE SEEK!

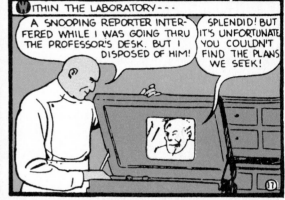

AT A DISTANT SPOT...

("-SUPERMAN EAVESDROPPING! I'LL ATTEND TO HIM!-")

SHORTLY AFTER--A WEIRD PLANE APPEARS IN THE SKY AND RELEASES A DEADLY BOMB DOWN TOWARD THE MAN OF STEEL'S FIGURE...

THIS HAS GOT TO STOP BEFORE BOMBS FALL ON INNOCENT PEOPLE IN THE STREET!

A FLIP OF *SUPERMAN'S* WRIST, AND THE BOMB HURTLES BACK TO ITS SOURCE, DESTROYING THE PLANE!

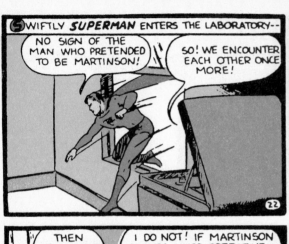

SWIFTLY *SUPERMAN* ENTERS THE LABORATORY--

NO SIGN OF THE MAN WHO PRETENDED TO BE MARTINSON!

SO! WE ENCOUNTER EACH OTHER ONCE MORE!

22

LUTHOR! THE MAD SCIENTIST WHO PLOTS TO DOMINATE THE EARTH!

PERMIT ME TO INTRODUCE PROFESSOR MARTINSON-- A RETICENT INDIVIDUAL WHO REFUSES TO REVEAL TO ME THE DETAILS OF HIS DISCOVERY!

23

THEN YOU ADMIT FAILURE!

I DO NOT! IF MARTINSON PROVES UNCO-OPERATIVE, I MAY BE MORE FORTUNATE WITH THE ARMY ITSELF!

24

I WONDER WHAT LUTHOR HAS UP HIS SLEEVE? I'M SURE HE'S ABOUT TO SPRING SOMETHING!

25

THAT EVENING--WITHIN THE ARMY CAMP, *SUPERMAN* SEES ONE OF THE INVENTION'S GUARDS ATTACK THE OTHER.

THAT WAS SIMPLE!

26

AS THE REMAINING GUARD SIGNALS WITH A FLASH-LIGHT, AN AUTOGYRO DESCENDS TO THE BUILDING'S ROOF.

27

BUT WHILE THE CONSPIRATORS ATTEMPT TO STEAL THE INVENTION, AN UNEXPECTED INTRUDER INTERFERES.

HEY!

OW-WW!

MUSN'T STEAL! IT'S NOT NICE!

28

GET BACK TO LUTHOR! AND WARN HIM TO ABANDON HIS ATTEMPTS TO GET THIS INVENTION!

WE'LL TELL HIM -- ONLY DON'T HARM US!

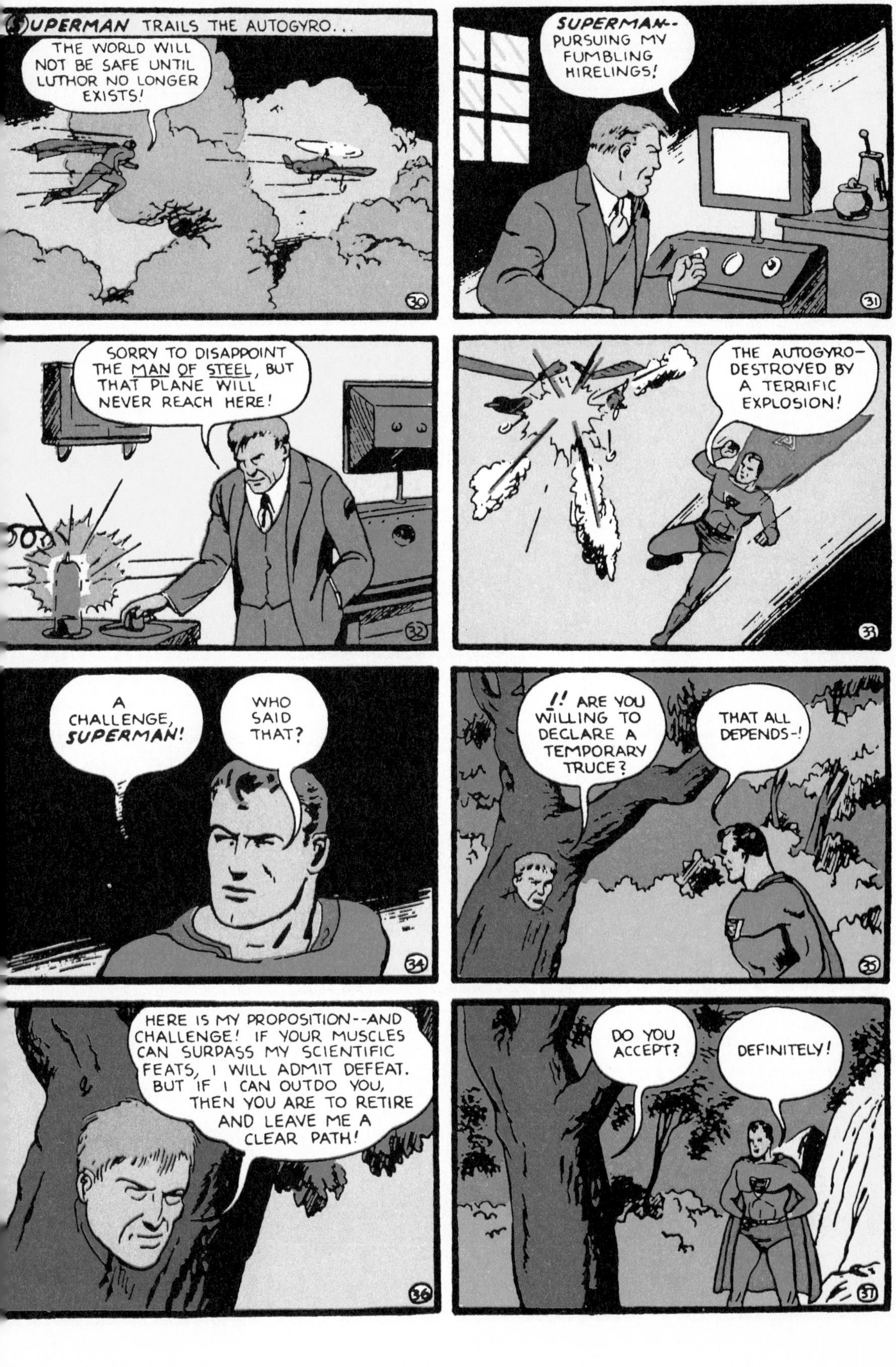
SUPERMAN TRAILS THE AUTOGYRO...
THE WORLD WILL NOT BE SAFE UNTIL LUTHOR NO LONGER EXISTS!
30
SUPERMAN-- PURSUING MY FUMBLING HIRELINGS!
31
SORRY TO DISAPPOINT THE MAN OF STEEL, BUT THAT PLANE WILL NEVER REACH HERE!
32
THE AUTOGYRO- DESTROYED BY A TERRIFIC EXPLOSION!
33
A CHALLENGE, SUPERMAN!
WHO SAID THAT?
34
!! ARE YOU WILLING TO DECLARE A TEMPORARY TRUCE?
THAT ALL DEPENDS-!
35
HERE IS MY PROPOSITION--AND CHALLENGE! IF YOUR MUSCLES CAN SURPASS MY SCIENTIFIC FEATS, I WILL ADMIT DEFEAT. BUT IF I CAN OUTDO YOU, THEN YOU ARE TO RETIRE AND LEAVE ME A CLEAR PATH!
36
DO YOU ACCEPT?
DEFINITELY!
37

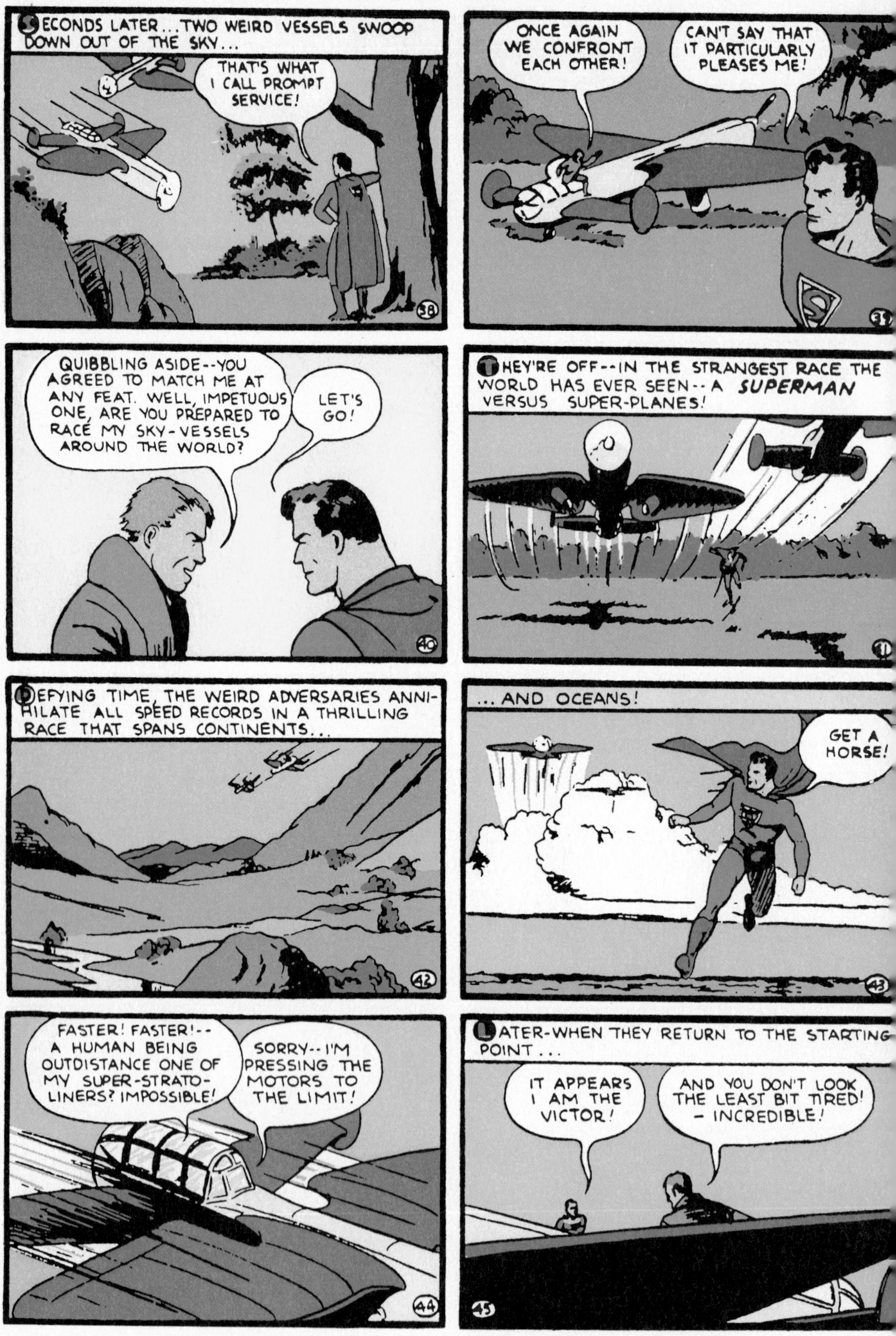
SECONDS LATER...TWO WEIRD VESSELS SWOOP DOWN OUT OF THE SKY...
THAT'S WHAT I CALL PROMPT SERVICE!
38
ONCE AGAIN WE CONFRONT EACH OTHER!
CAN'T SAY THAT IT PARTICULARLY PLEASES ME!
QUIBBLING ASIDE--YOU AGREED TO MATCH ME AT ANY FEAT. WELL, IMPETUOUS ONE, ARE YOU PREPARED TO RACE MY SKY-VESSELS AROUND THE WORLD?
LET'S GO!
40
THEY'RE OFF--IN THE STRANGEST RACE THE WORLD HAS EVER SEEN--A SUPERMAN VERSUS SUPER-PLANES!
DEFYING TIME, THE WEIRD ADVERSARIES ANNIHILATE ALL SPEED RECORDS IN A THRILLING RACE THAT SPANS CONTINENTS...
42
...AND OCEANS!
GET A HORSE!
FASTER! FASTER!--A HUMAN BEING OUTDISTANCE ONE OF MY SUPER-STRATO-LINERS? IMPOSSIBLE!
SORRY--I'M PRESSING THE MOTORS TO THE LIMIT!
44
LATER-WHEN THEY RETURN TO THE STARTING POINT...
IT APPEARS I AM THE VICTOR!
AND YOU DON'T LOOK THE LEAST BIT TIRED! - INCREDIBLE!
45

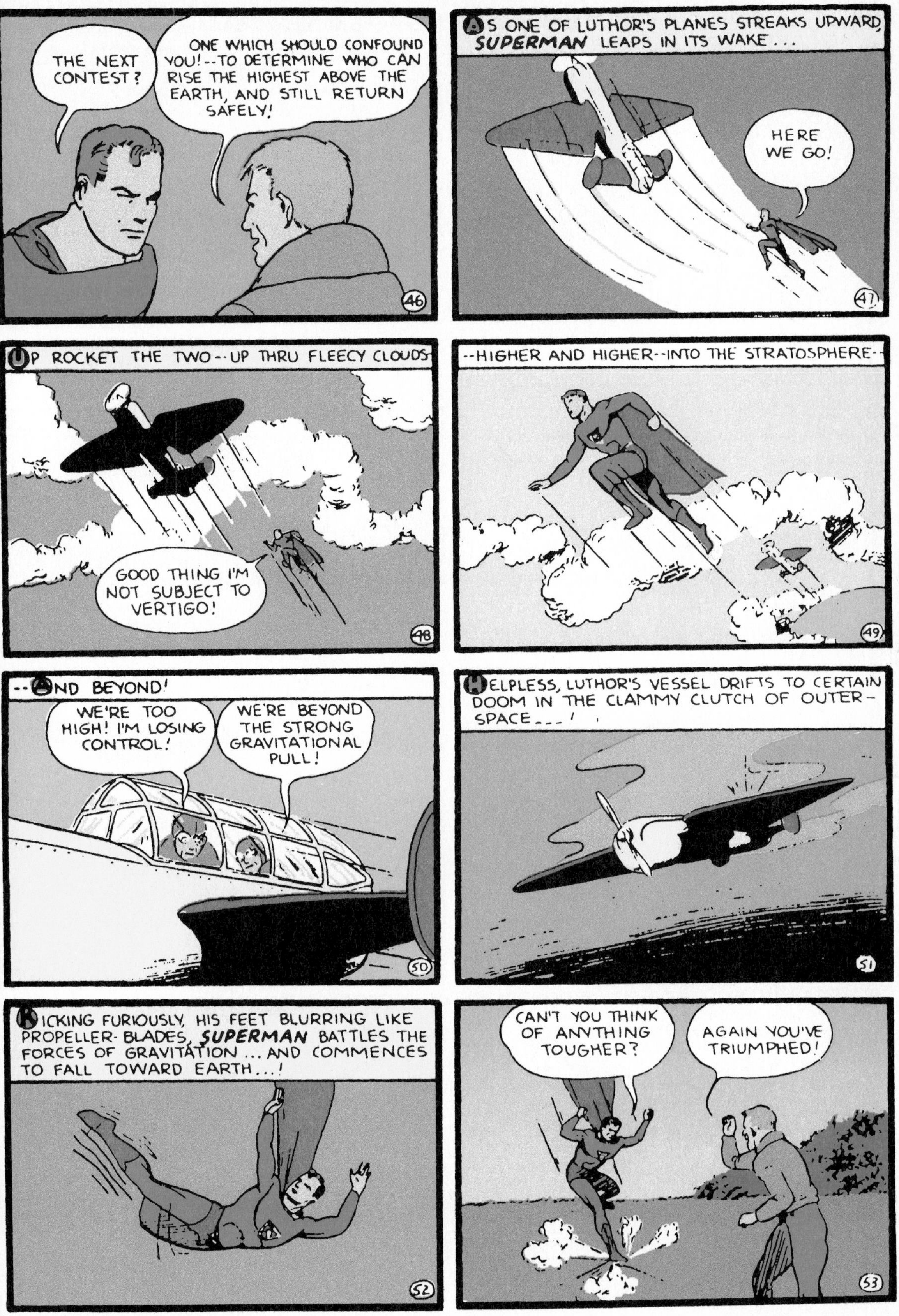
THE NEXT CONTEST?
ONE WHICH SHOULD CONFOUND YOU!--TO DETERMINE WHO CAN RISE THE HIGHEST ABOVE THE EARTH, AND STILL RETURN SAFELY!
46
AS ONE OF LUTHOR'S PLANES STREAKS UPWARD, SUPERMAN LEAPS IN ITS WAKE...
HERE WE GO!
47
UP ROCKET THE TWO--UP THRU FLEECY CLOUDS-
GOOD THING I'M NOT SUBJECT TO VERTIGO!
48
--HIGHER AND HIGHER--INTO THE STRATOSPHERE--
49
--AND BEYOND!
WE'RE TOO HIGH! I'M LOSING CONTROL!
WE'RE BEYOND THE STRONG GRAVITATIONAL PULL!
50
HELPLESS, LUTHOR'S VESSEL DRIFTS TO CERTAIN DOOM IN THE CLAMMY CLUTCH OF OUTER-SPACE---!
51
KICKING FURIOUSLY, HIS FEET BLURRING LIKE PROPELLER-BLADES, SUPERMAN BATTLES THE FORCES OF GRAVITATION ... AND COMMENCES TO FALL TOWARD EARTH...!
52
CAN'T YOU THINK OF ANYTHING TOUGHER?
AGAIN YOU'VE TRIUMPHED!
53

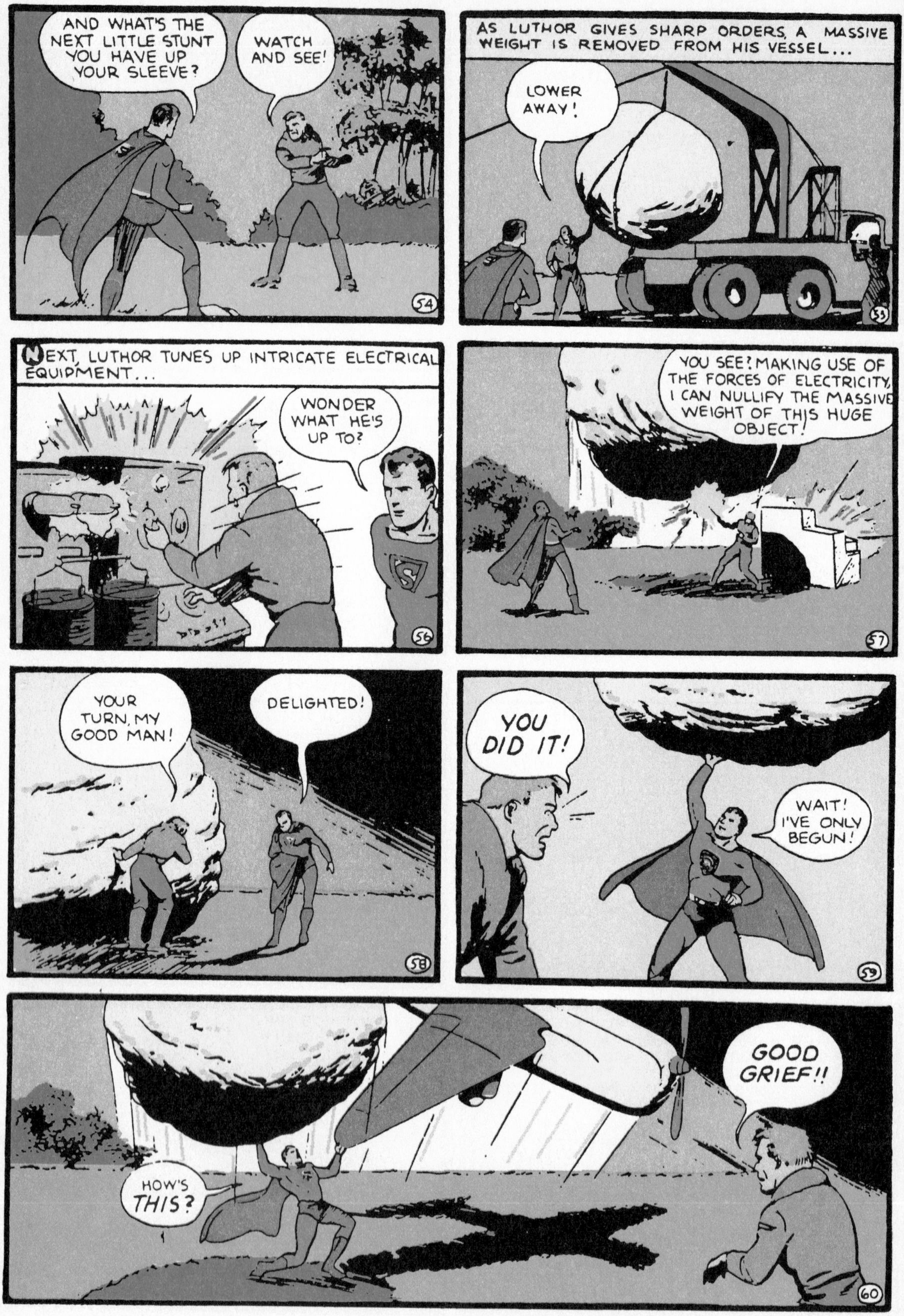

AND WHAT'S THE NEXT LITTLE STUNT YOU HAVE UP YOUR SLEEVE?
WATCH AND SEE!
AS LUTHOR GIVES SHARP ORDERS, A MASSIVE WEIGHT IS REMOVED FROM HIS VESSEL...
LOWER AWAY!
NEXT, LUTHOR TUNES UP INTRICATE ELECTRICAL EQUIPMENT...
WONDER WHAT HE'S UP TO?
YOU SEE? MAKING USE OF THE FORCES OF ELECTRICITY, I CAN NULLIFY THE MASSIVE WEIGHT OF THIS HUGE OBJECT!
YOUR TURN, MY GOOD MAN!
DELIGHTED!
YOU DID IT!
WAIT! I'VE ONLY BEGUN!
GOOD GRIEF!!
HOW'S THIS?

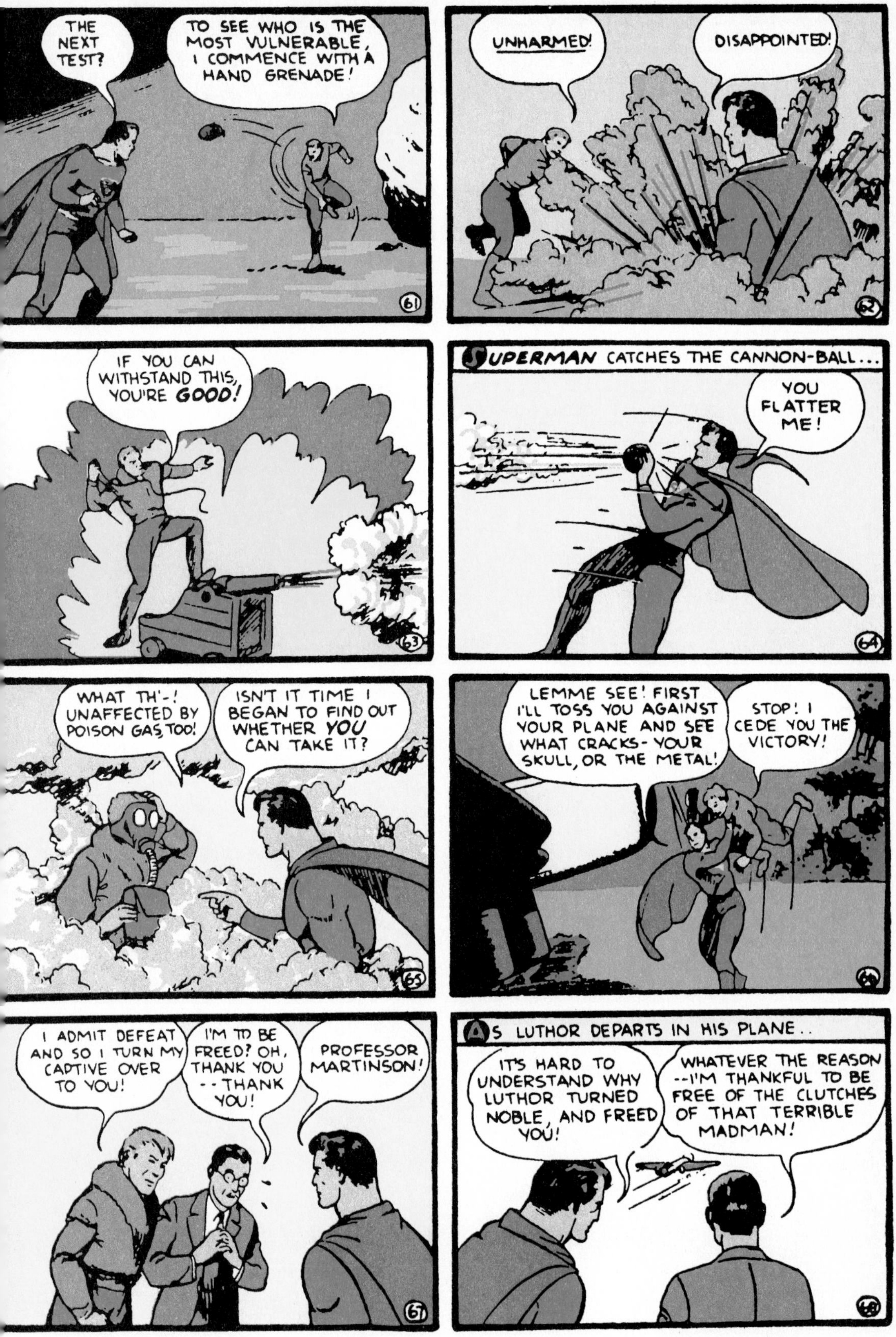
THE NEXT TEST?
TO SEE WHO IS THE MOST VULNERABLE, I COMMENCE WITH A HAND GRENADE!
UNHARMED!
DISAPPOINTED!
IF YOU CAN WITHSTAND THIS, YOU'RE GOOD!
SUPERMAN CATCHES THE CANNON-BALL...
YOU FLATTER ME!
WHAT TH'-! UNAFFECTED BY POISON GAS, TOO!
ISN'T IT TIME I BEGAN TO FIND OUT WHETHER YOU CAN TAKE IT?
LEMME SEE! FIRST I'LL TOSS YOU AGAINST YOUR PLANE AND SEE WHAT CRACKS- YOUR SKULL, OR THE METAL!
STOP! I CEDE YOU THE VICTORY!
I ADMIT DEFEAT AND SO I TURN MY CAPTIVE OVER TO YOU!
I'M TO BE FREED? OH, THANK YOU --THANK YOU!
PROFESSOR MARTINSON!
AS LUTHOR DEPARTS IN HIS PLANE..
IT'S HARD TO UNDERSTAND WHY LUTHOR TURNED NOBLE, AND FREED YOU!
WHATEVER THE REASON --I'M THANKFUL TO BE FREE OF THE CLUTCHES OF THAT TERRIBLE MADMAN!

Seizing Martinson, *SUPERMAN* leaps back toward the city...

I--I MUST BE DREAMING!

WITH YOUR EYES WIDE OPEN?

Later--within Martinson's laboratory...

SOMETIMES I'M SORRY I EVER INVENTED THE THING!

ATTENTION! *NEWS FLASH!*

QUIET-- LISTEN!

STARTLING NEWS HAS JUST COME OVER THE WIRE! THE ARMY'S MYSTERIOUS NEW WEAPON HAS BEEN STOLEN! EVERY EFFORT IS BEING MADE TO APPREHEND THE THIEVES!

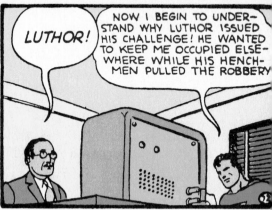

LUTHOR!

NOW I BEGIN TO UNDERSTAND WHY LUTHOR ISSUED HIS CHALLENGE! HE WANTED TO KEEP ME OCCUPIED ELSEWHERE WHILE HIS HENCHMEN PULLED THE ROBBERY

IF THE INVENTION COULD ONLY BE DESTROYED! IT'S SO COMPLEX THAT NO ONE BUT MYSELF COULD BUILD ANOTHER!

FELLA-YOU'VE GIVEN ME AN IDEA!

TELL ME, QUICK! DO YOU HAVE ANY IDEA WHERE LUTHOR HELD YOU DURING YOUR CAPTIVITY?

I'M CERTAIN IT WAS IN SATAN'S CANYON!

ANOTHER NEWS FLASH! A PORTION OF THE CITY WAS JUST SHAKEN BY AN EARTHQUAKE. A MYSTERIOUS CHARACTER NAMED *LUTHOR* DEMANDS THE CITY'S SURRENDER!

WAIT!

CAN'T! --NOT NOW!

I'VE GOT TO ATTEND TO LUTHOR--AND FAST!

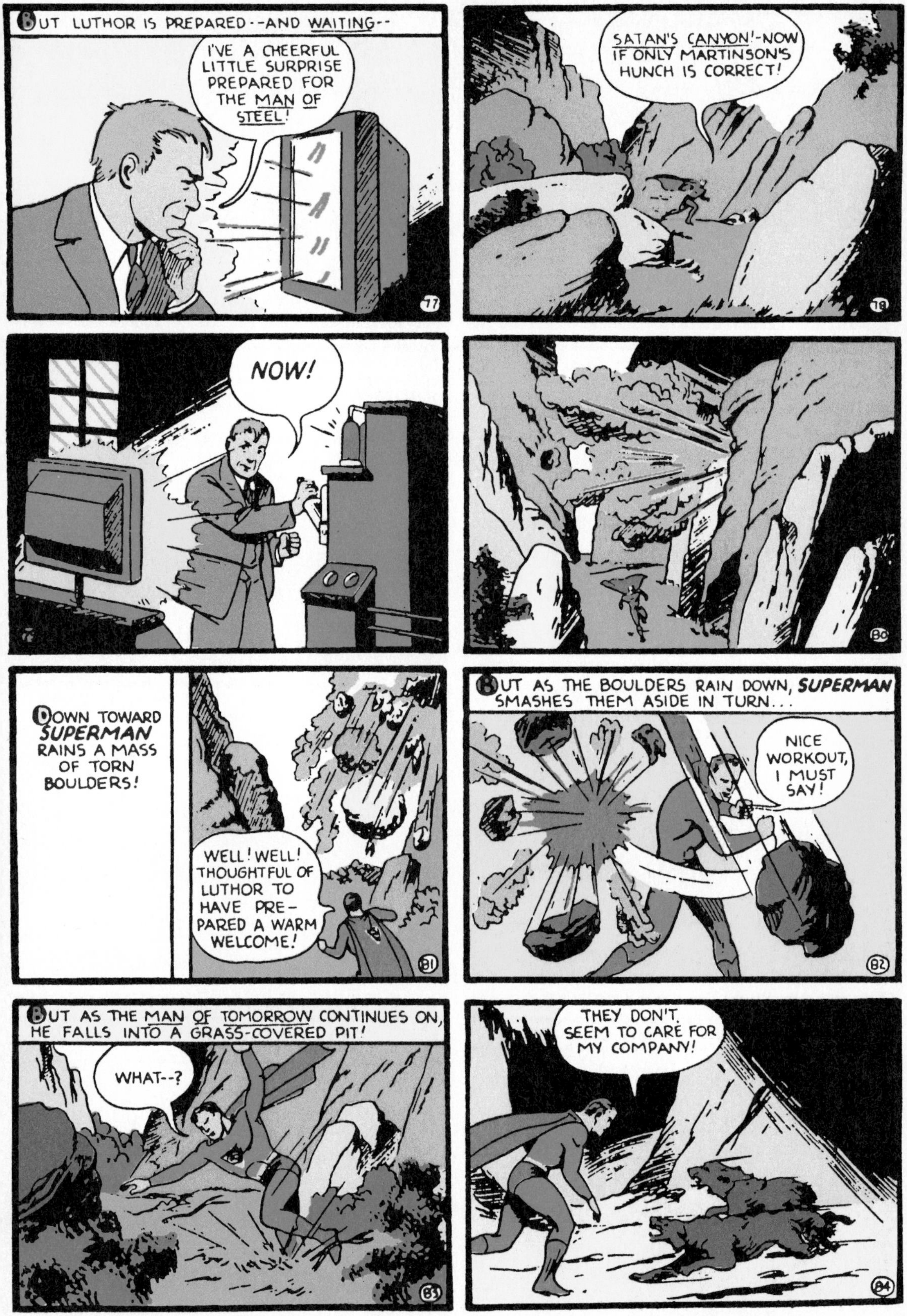
BUT LUTHOR IS PREPARED--AND WAITING--
I'VE A CHEERFUL LITTLE SURPRISE PREPARED FOR THE MAN OF STEEL!
77
SATAN'S CANYON!-NOW IF ONLY MARTINSON'S HUNCH IS CORRECT!
78
NOW!
79
80
DOWN TOWARD SUPERMAN RAINS A MASS OF TORN BOULDERS!
WELL! WELL! THOUGHTFUL OF LUTHOR TO HAVE PRE-PARED A WARM WELCOME!
81
BUT AS THE BOULDERS RAIN DOWN, SUPERMAN SMASHES THEM ASIDE IN TURN...
NICE WORKOUT, I MUST SAY!
82
BUT AS THE MAN OF TOMORROW CONTINUES ON, HE FALLS INTO A GRASS-COVERED PIT!
WHAT--?
83
THEY DON'T SEEM TO CARE FOR MY COMPANY!
84

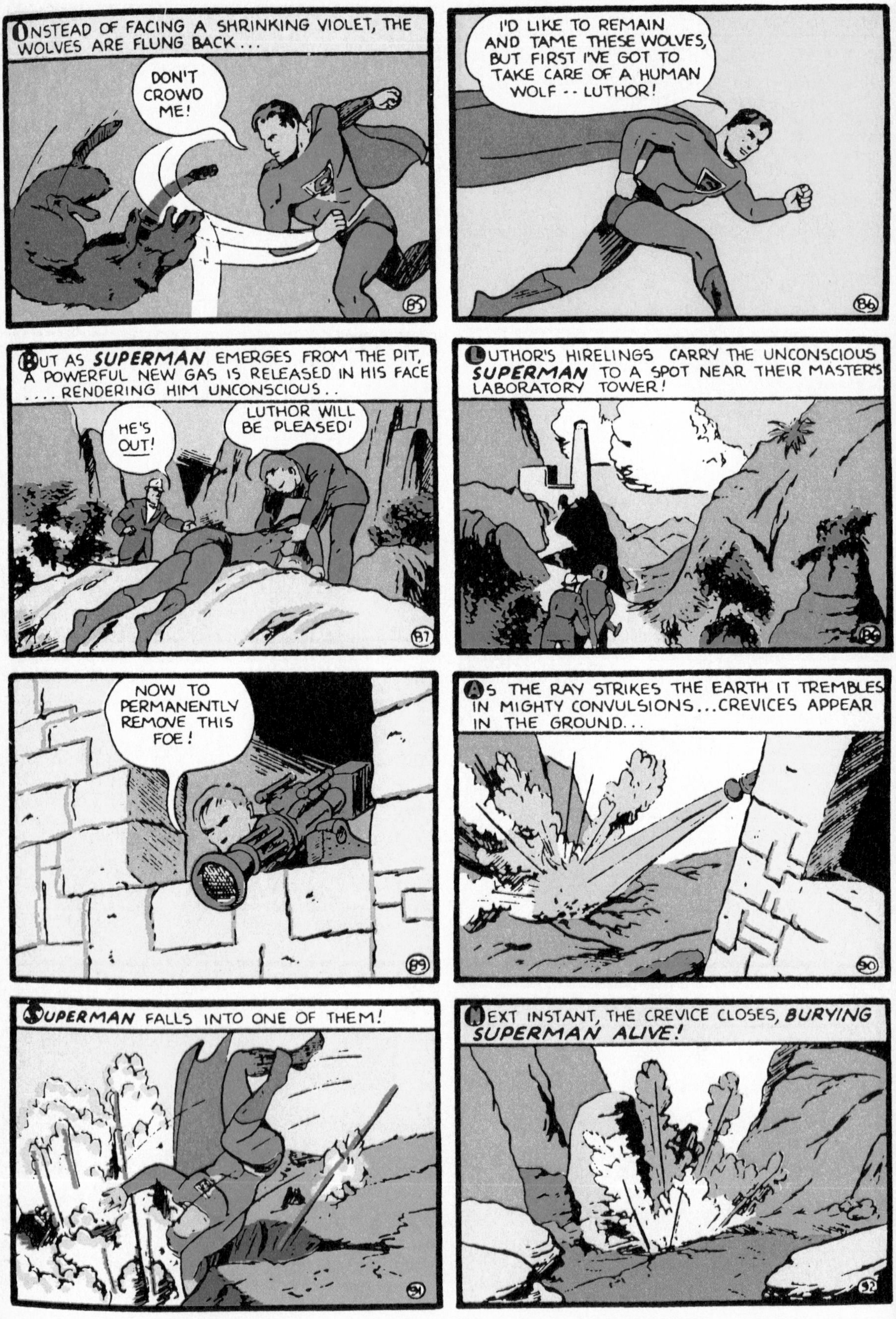
INSTEAD OF FACING A SHRINKING VIOLET, THE WOLVES ARE FLUNG BACK...
DON'T CROWD ME!
I'D LIKE TO REMAIN AND TAME THESE WOLVES, BUT FIRST I'VE GOT TO TAKE CARE OF A HUMAN WOLF -- LUTHOR!
BUT AS SUPERMAN EMERGES FROM THE PIT, A POWERFUL NEW GAS IS RELEASED IN HIS FACE .... RENDERING HIM UNCONSCIOUS..
HE'S OUT!
LUTHOR WILL BE PLEASED!
LUTHOR'S HIRELINGS CARRY THE UNCONSCIOUS SUPERMAN TO A SPOT NEAR THEIR MASTER'S LABORATORY TOWER!
NOW TO PERMANENTLY REMOVE THIS FOE!
AS THE RAY STRIKES THE EARTH IT TREMBLES IN MIGHTY CONVULSIONS...CREVICES APPEAR IN THE GROUND...
SUPERMAN FALLS INTO ONE OF THEM!
NEXT INSTANT, THE CREVICE CLOSES, BURYING SUPERMAN ALIVE!

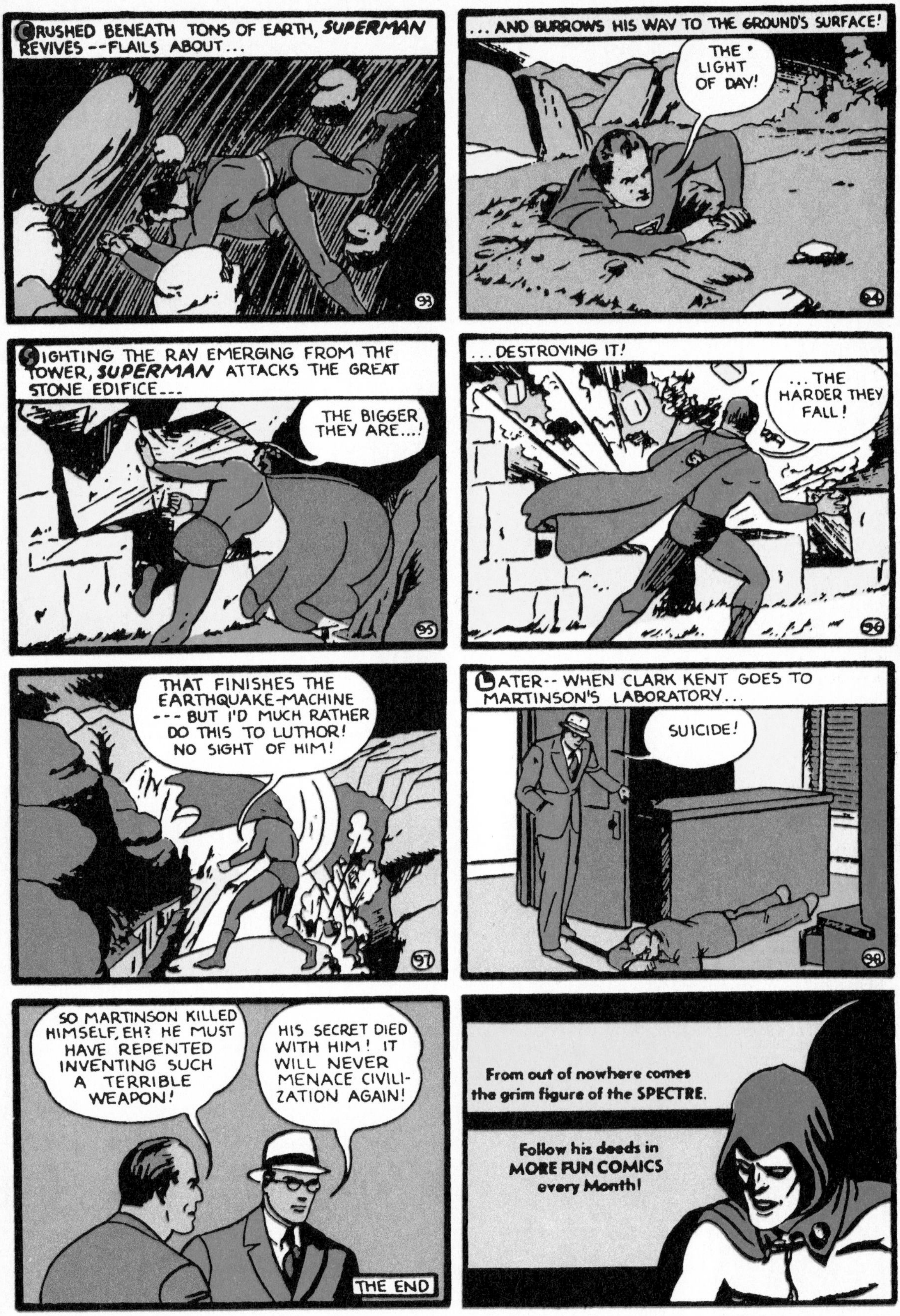
CRUSHED BENEATH TONS OF EARTH, SUPERMAN REVIVES --FLAILS ABOUT...
...AND BURROWS HIS WAY TO THE GROUND'S SURFACE!
THE LIGHT OF DAY!
SIGHTING THE RAY EMERGING FROM THE TOWER, SUPERMAN ATTACKS THE GREAT STONE EDIFICE---
THE BIGGER THEY ARE...!
...DESTROYING IT!
...THE HARDER THEY FALL!
THAT FINISHES THE EARTHQUAKE-MACHINE --- BUT I'D MUCH RATHER DO THIS TO LUTHOR! NO SIGHT OF HIM!
LATER-- WHEN CLARK KENT GOES TO MARTINSON'S LABORATORY...
SUICIDE!
SO MARTINSON KILLED HIMSELF, EH? HE MUST HAVE REPENTED INVENTING SUCH A TERRIBLE WEAPON!
HIS SECRET DIED WITH HIM! IT WILL NEVER MENACE CIVILIZATION AGAIN!
THE END
From out of nowhere comes the grim figure of the SPECTRE.
Follow his deeds in MORE FUN COMICS every Month!

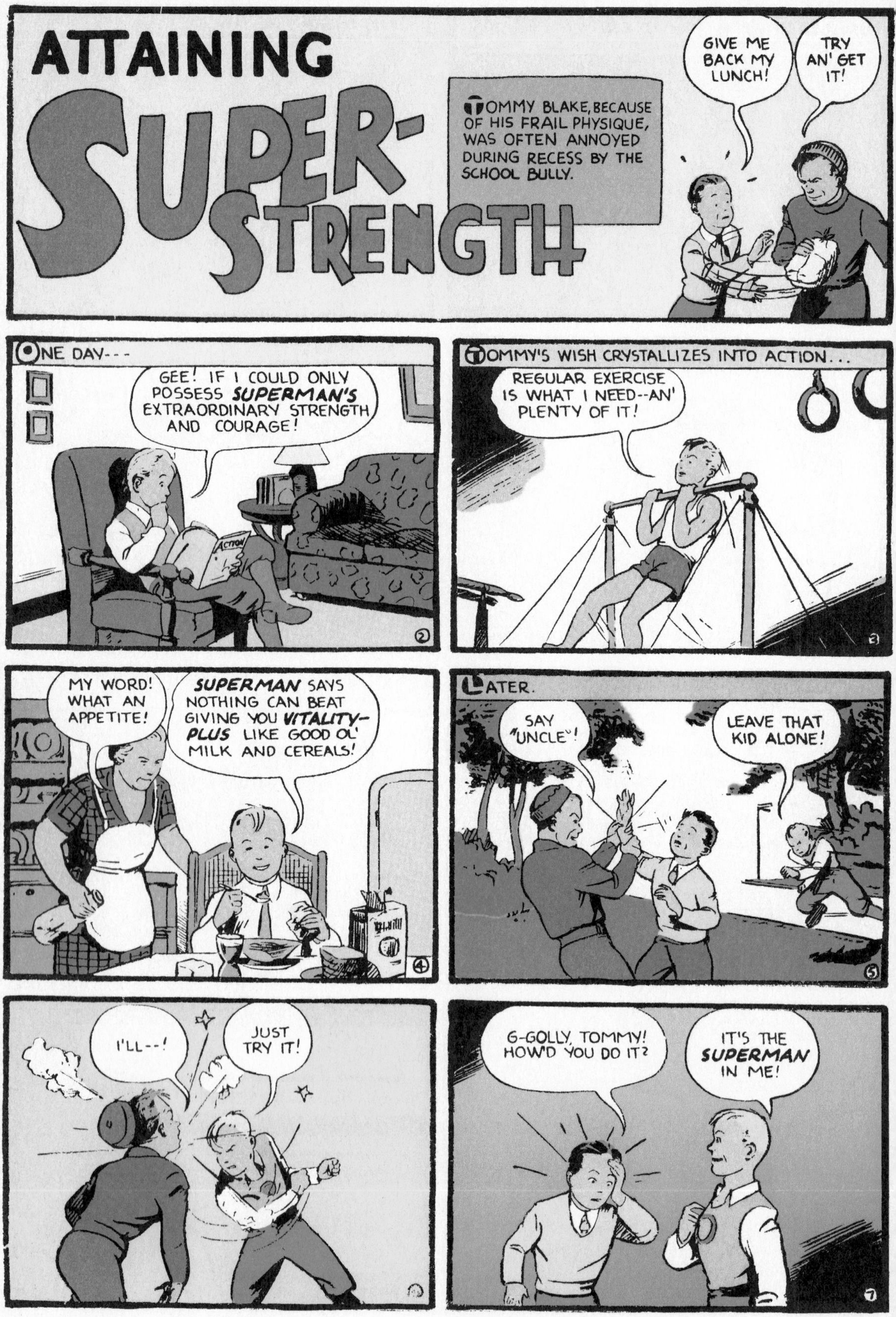
ATTAINING SUPER-STRENGTH
TOMMY BLAKE, BECAUSE OF HIS FRAIL PHYSIQUE, WAS OFTEN ANNOYED DURING RECESS BY THE SCHOOL BULLY.
GIVE ME BACK MY LUNCH!
TRY AN' GET IT!
ONE DAY---
GEE! IF I COULD ONLY POSSESS SUPERMAN'S EXTRAORDINARY STRENGTH AND COURAGE!
ACTION
TOMMY'S WISH CRYSTALLIZES INTO ACTION...
REGULAR EXERCISE IS WHAT I NEED--AN' PLENTY OF IT!
MY WORD! WHAT AN APPETITE!
SUPERMAN SAYS NOTHING CAN BEAT GIVING YOU VITALITY-PLUS LIKE GOOD OL' MILK AND CEREALS!
LATER.
SAY "UNCLE"!
LEAVE THAT KID ALONE!
I'LL--!
JUST TRY IT!
G-GOLLY, TOMMY! HOW'D YOU DO IT?
IT'S THE SUPERMAN IN ME!

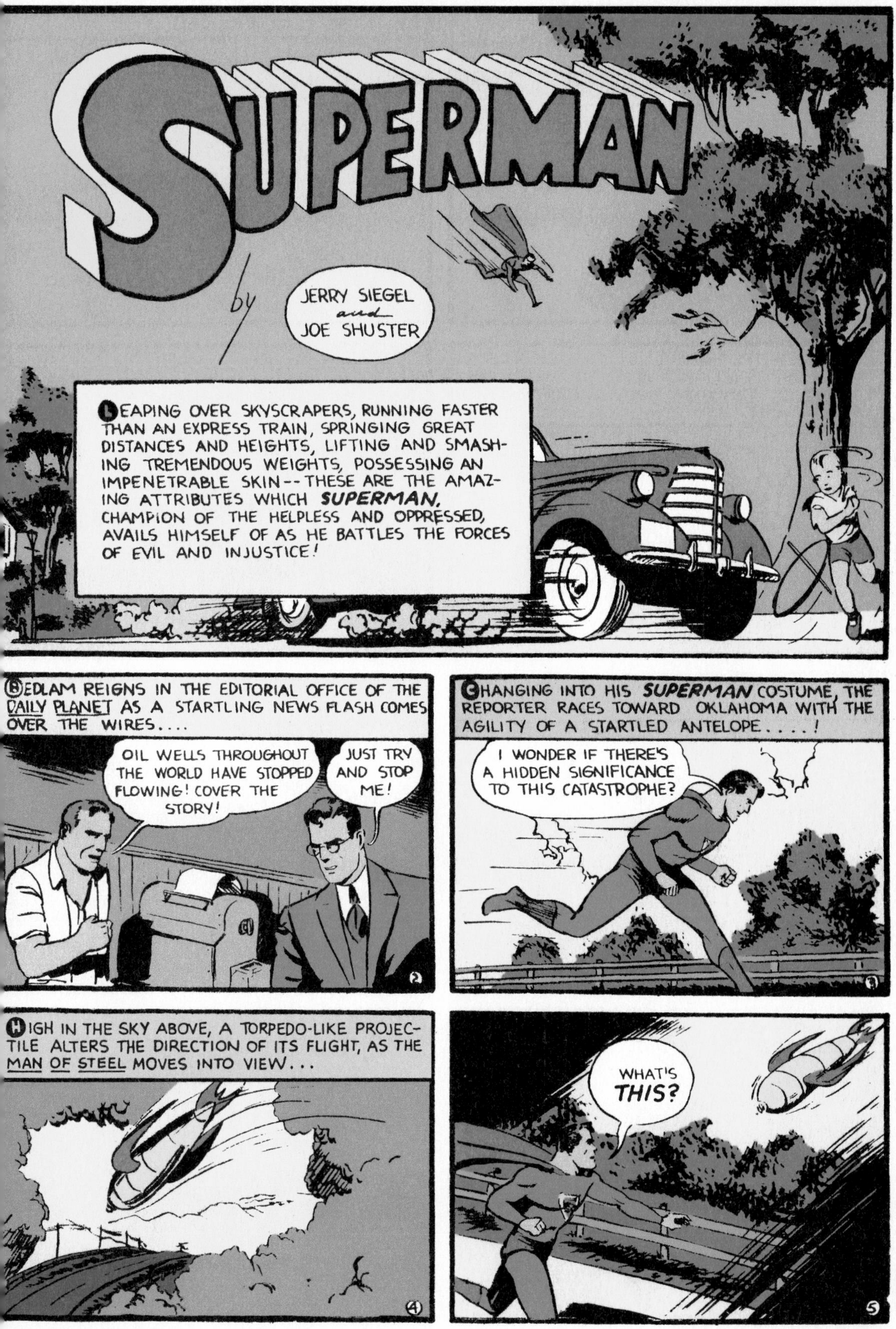
SUPERMAN
by
JERRY SIEGEL
and
JOE SHUSTER
LEAPING OVER SKYSCRAPERS, RUNNING FASTER THAN AN EXPRESS TRAIN, SPRINGING GREAT DISTANCES AND HEIGHTS, LIFTING AND SMASHING TREMENDOUS WEIGHTS, POSSESSING AN IMPENETRABLE SKIN--THESE ARE THE AMAZING ATTRIBUTES WHICH SUPERMAN, CHAMPION OF THE HELPLESS AND OPPRESSED, AVAILS HIMSELF OF AS HE BATTLES THE FORCES OF EVIL AND INJUSTICE!
BEDLAM REIGNS IN THE EDITORIAL OFFICE OF THE DAILY PLANET AS A STARTLING NEWS FLASH COMES OVER THE WIRES....
OIL WELLS THROUGHOUT THE WORLD HAVE STOPPED FLOWING! COVER THE STORY!
JUST TRY AND STOP ME!
CHANGING INTO HIS SUPERMAN COSTUME, THE REPORTER RACES TOWARD OKLAHOMA WITH THE AGILITY OF A STARTLED ANTELOPE....!
I WONDER IF THERE'S A HIDDEN SIGNIFICANCE TO THIS CATASTROPHE?
HIGH IN THE SKY ABOVE, A TORPEDO-LIKE PROJECTILE ALTERS THE DIRECTION OF ITS FLIGHT, AS THE MAN OF STEEL MOVES INTO VIEW...
WHAT'S THIS?

SWIFTER THAN LIGHT, **SUPERMAN** SEEKS TO DODGE THE PROJECTILE, BUT IT FOLLOWS HIS EVERY MOVEMENT!

IT SEEMS TO HAVE ALMOST HUMAN INTELLIGENCE!

AN ALERT LEAP, AND....

GOT YOU!

UP ROCKETS THE PROJECTILE...EXECUTES A SERIES OF MAD GYRATIONS CALCULATED TO THROW OFF THE <u>MAN</u> OF <u>TOMORROW</u>, BUT **SUPERMAN** GRIMLY HANGS ON...!

THIS IS BETTER THAN THE <u>COASTER</u> AT CONEY ISLAND!

RADIO-CONTROLLED! WELL, LET'S SEE WHAT TEARING A FEW WIRES WILL DO ABOUT THAT!

INSTANTLY, THE SKY-TORPEDO PLUMMETS TOWARD EARTH!

NEXT STOP...THE GRAVEYARD!

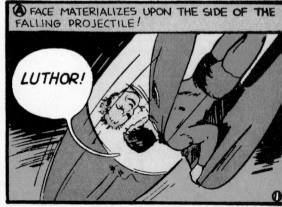

A FACE MATERIALIZES UPON THE SIDE OF THE FALLING PROJECTILE!

LUTHOR!

I WARN YOU, **SUPERMAN**--KEEP CLEAR OF THE OIL-WELL MYSTERY-- OR DIE!

SORRY...I CHOOSE TO MEDDLE IN THE OIL WELL AFFAIR... AND I REFUSE TO DIE!

AS THE PROJECTILE STRIKES THE GROUND...

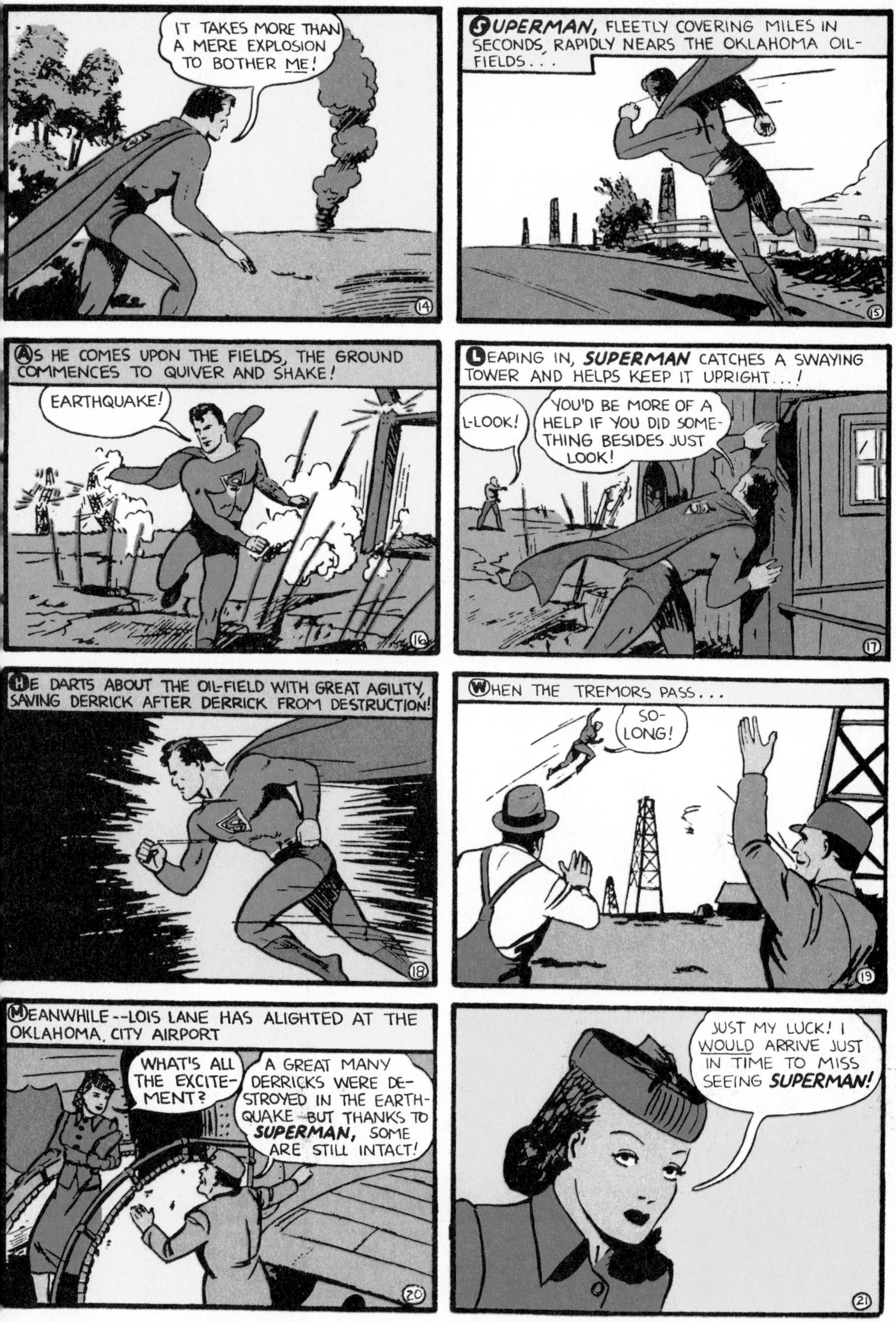
IT TAKES MORE THAN A MERE EXPLOSION TO BOTHER ME!
SUPERMAN, FLEETLY COVERING MILES IN SECONDS, RAPIDLY NEARS THE OKLAHOMA OIL-FIELDS...
AS HE COMES UPON THE FIELDS, THE GROUND COMMENCES TO QUIVER AND SHAKE!
EARTHQUAKE!
LEAPING IN, SUPERMAN CATCHES A SWAYING TOWER AND HELPS KEEP IT UPRIGHT...!
L-LOOK!
YOU'D BE MORE OF A HELP IF YOU DID SOMETHING BESIDES JUST LOOK!
HE DARTS ABOUT THE OIL-FIELD WITH GREAT AGILITY, SAVING DERRICK AFTER DERRICK FROM DESTRUCTION!
WHEN THE TREMORS PASS...
SO-LONG!
MEANWHILE--LOIS LANE HAS ALIGHTED AT THE OKLAHOMA CITY AIRPORT
WHAT'S ALL THE EXCITEMENT?
A GREAT MANY DERRICKS WERE DESTROYED IN THE EARTHQUAKE BUT THANKS TO SUPERMAN, SOME ARE STILL INTACT!
JUST MY LUCK! I WOULD ARRIVE JUST IN TIME TO MISS SEEING SUPERMAN!

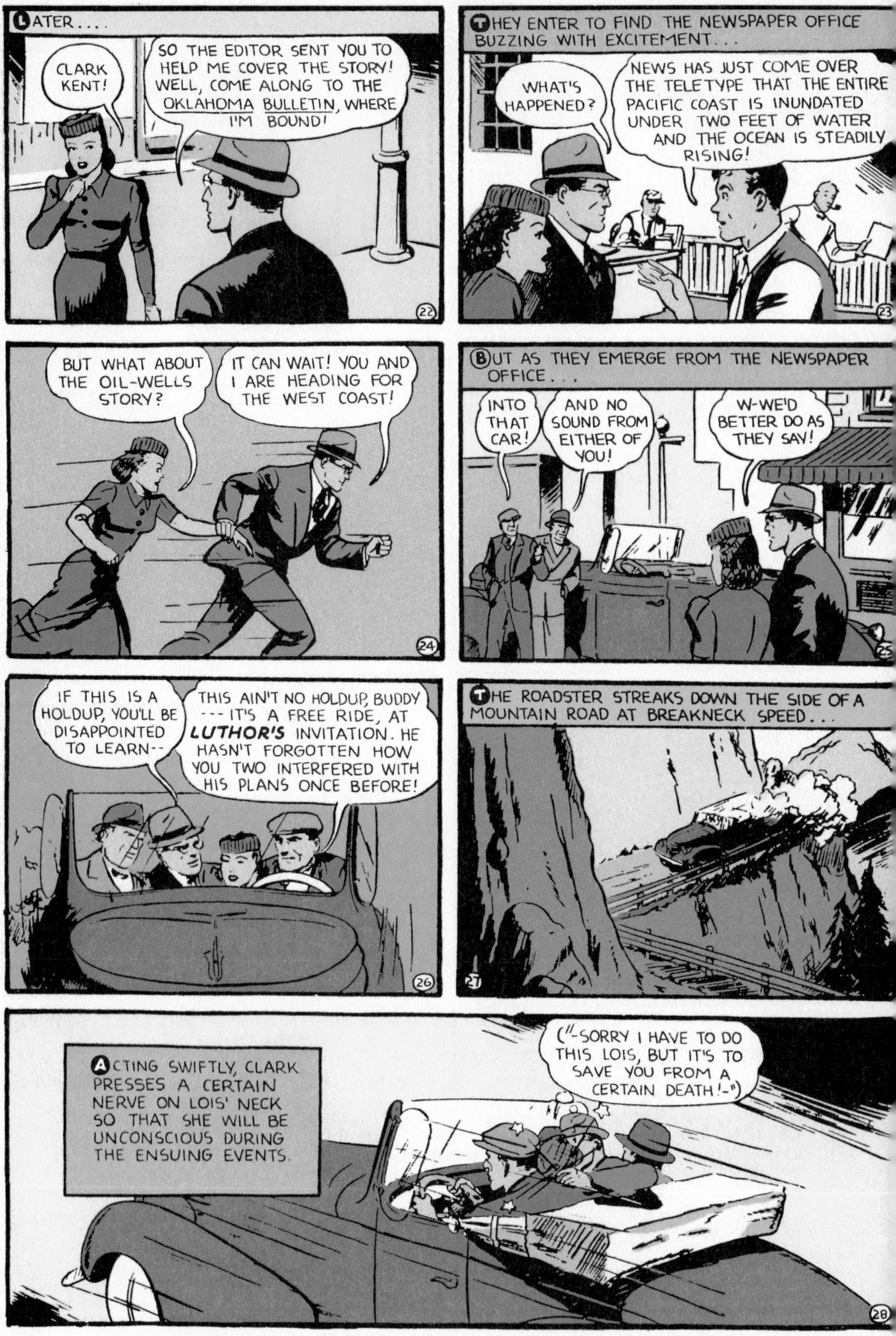
LATER....
CLARK KENT!
SO THE EDITOR SENT YOU TO HELP ME COVER THE STORY! WELL, COME ALONG TO THE OKLAHOMA BULLETIN, WHERE I'M BOUND!
THEY ENTER TO FIND THE NEWSPAPER OFFICE BUZZING WITH EXCITEMENT...
WHAT'S HAPPENED?
NEWS HAS JUST COME OVER THE TELETYPE THAT THE ENTIRE PACIFIC COAST IS INUNDATED UNDER TWO FEET OF WATER AND THE OCEAN IS STEADILY RISING!
BUT WHAT ABOUT THE OIL-WELLS STORY?
IT CAN WAIT! YOU AND I ARE HEADING FOR THE WEST COAST!
BUT AS THEY EMERGE FROM THE NEWSPAPER OFFICE...
INTO THAT CAR!
AND NO SOUND FROM EITHER OF YOU!
W-WE'D BETTER DO AS THEY SAY!
IF THIS IS A HOLDUP, YOU'LL BE DISAPPOINTED TO LEARN--
THIS AIN'T NO HOLDUP, BUDDY --- IT'S A FREE RIDE, AT LUTHOR'S INVITATION. HE HASN'T FORGOTTEN HOW YOU TWO INTERFERED WITH HIS PLANS ONCE BEFORE!
THE ROADSTER STREAKS DOWN THE SIDE OF A MOUNTAIN ROAD AT BREAKNECK SPEED...
ACTING SWIFTLY, CLARK PRESSES A CERTAIN NERVE ON LOIS' NECK SO THAT SHE WILL BE UNCONSCIOUS DURING THE ENSUING EVENTS.
("-SORRY I HAVE TO DO THIS LOIS, BUT IT'S TO SAVE YOU FROM A CERTAIN DEATH!-")

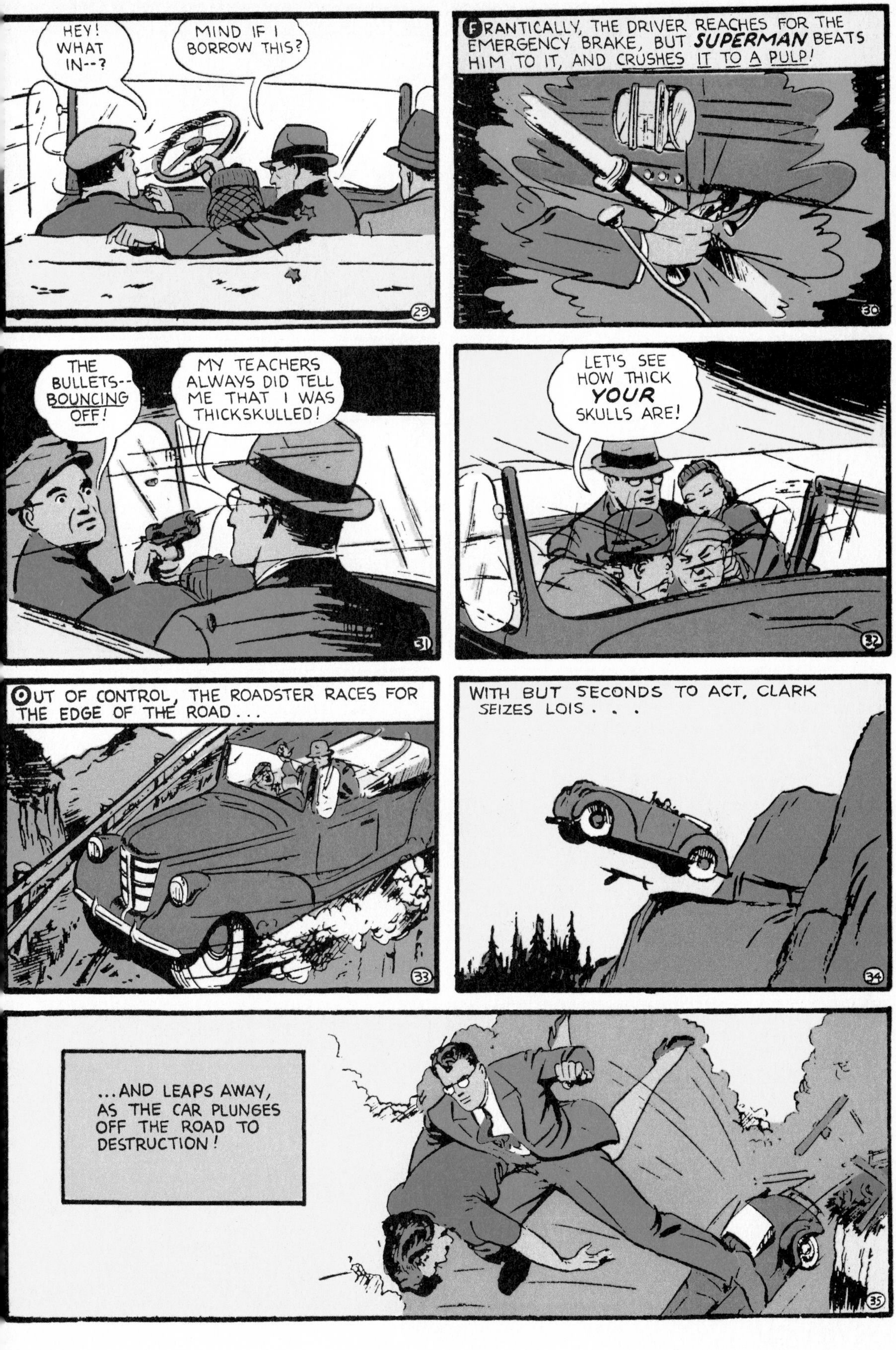
HEY! WHAT IN--?
MIND IF I BORROW THIS?
29
FRANTICALLY, THE DRIVER REACHES FOR THE EMERGENCY BRAKE, BUT SUPERMAN BEATS HIM TO IT, AND CRUSHES IT TO A PULP!
30
THE BULLETS-- BOUNCING OFF!
MY TEACHERS ALWAYS DID TELL ME THAT I WAS THICKSKULLED!
31
LET'S SEE HOW THICK YOUR SKULLS ARE!
32
OUT OF CONTROL, THE ROADSTER RACES FOR THE EDGE OF THE ROAD...
33
WITH BUT SECONDS TO ACT, CLARK SEIZES LOIS . . .
34
...AND LEAPS AWAY, AS THE CAR PLUNGES OFF THE ROAD TO DESTRUCTION!
35

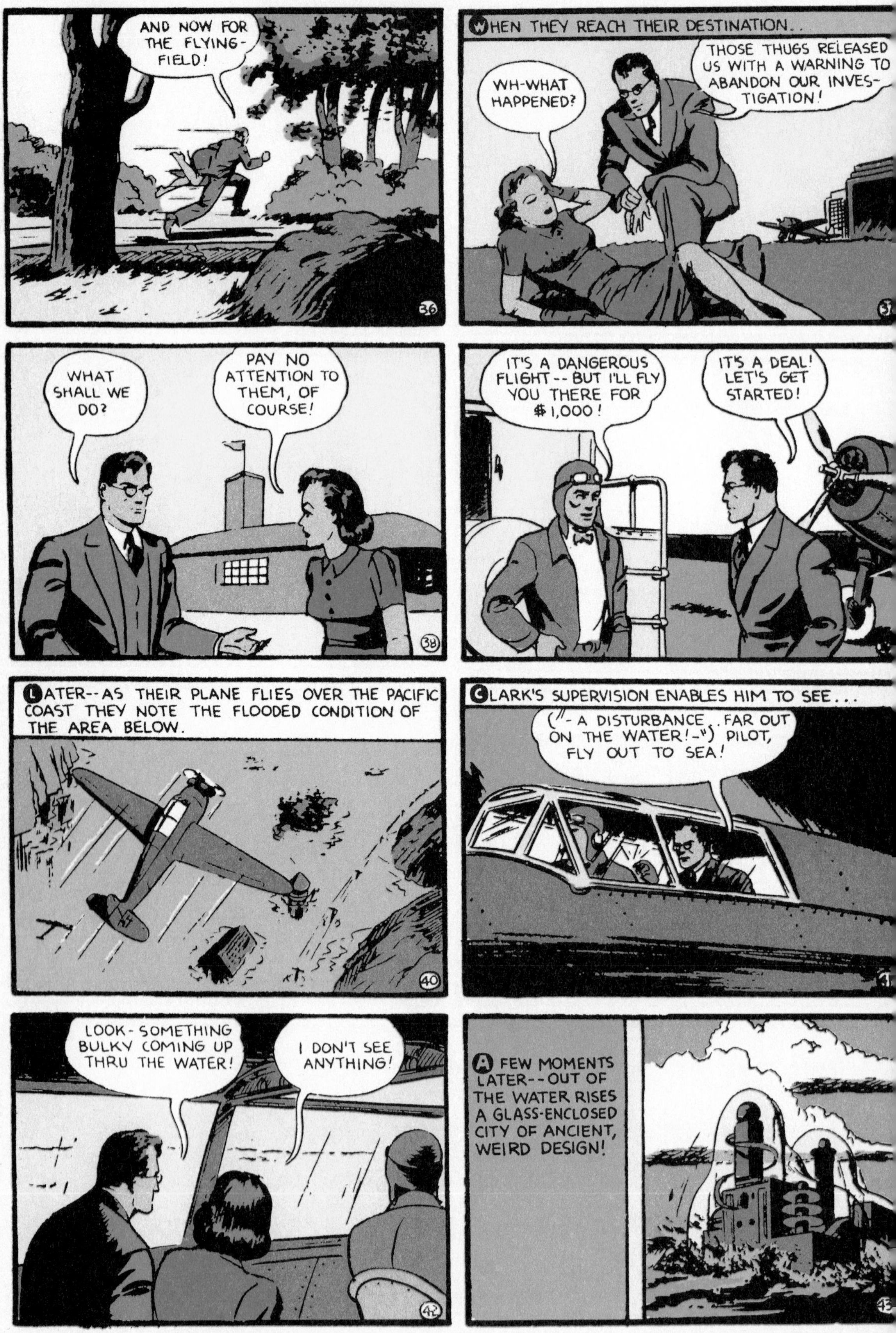
AND NOW FOR THE FLYING-FIELD!
36
WHEN THEY REACH THEIR DESTINATION..
WH-WHAT HAPPENED?
THOSE THUGS RELEASED US WITH A WARNING TO ABANDON OUR INVES-TIGATION!
WHAT SHALL WE DO?
PAY NO ATTENTION TO THEM, OF COURSE!
38
IT'S A DANGEROUS FLIGHT -- BUT I'LL FLY YOU THERE FOR $1,000!
IT'S A DEAL! LET'S GET STARTED!
LATER--AS THEIR PLANE FLIES OVER THE PACIFIC COAST THEY NOTE THE FLOODED CONDITION OF THE AREA BELOW.
40
CLARK'S SUPERVISION ENABLES HIM TO SEE...
("- A DISTURBANCE.. FAR OUT ON THE WATER!-") PILOT, FLY OUT TO SEA!
LOOK- SOMETHING BULKY COMING UP THRU THE WATER!
I DON'T SEE ANYTHING!
42
A FEW MOMENTS LATER--OUT OF THE WATER RISES A GLASS-ENCLOSED CITY OF ANCIENT, WEIRD DESIGN!
43

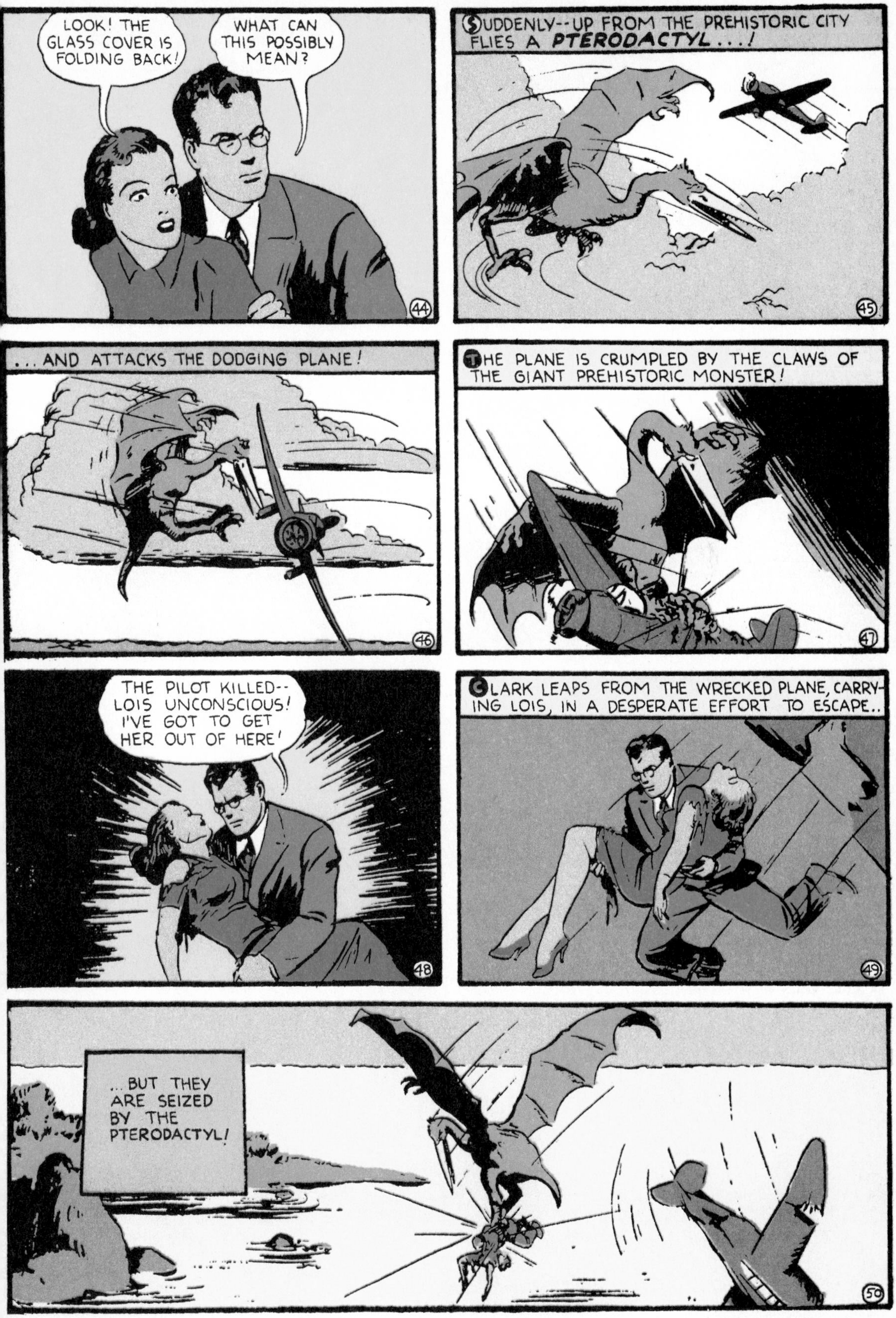
LOOK! THE GLASS COVER IS FOLDING BACK!
WHAT CAN THIS POSSIBLY MEAN?
SUDDENLY--UP FROM THE PREHISTORIC CITY FLIES A PTERODACTYL...!
...AND ATTACKS THE DODGING PLANE!
THE PLANE IS CRUMPLED BY THE CLAWS OF THE GIANT PREHISTORIC MONSTER!
THE PILOT KILLED--LOIS UNCONSCIOUS! I'VE GOT TO GET HER OUT OF HERE!
CLARK LEAPS FROM THE WRECKED PLANE, CARRYING LOIS, IN A DESPERATE EFFORT TO ESCAPE..
...BUT THEY ARE SEIZED BY THE PTERODACTYL!

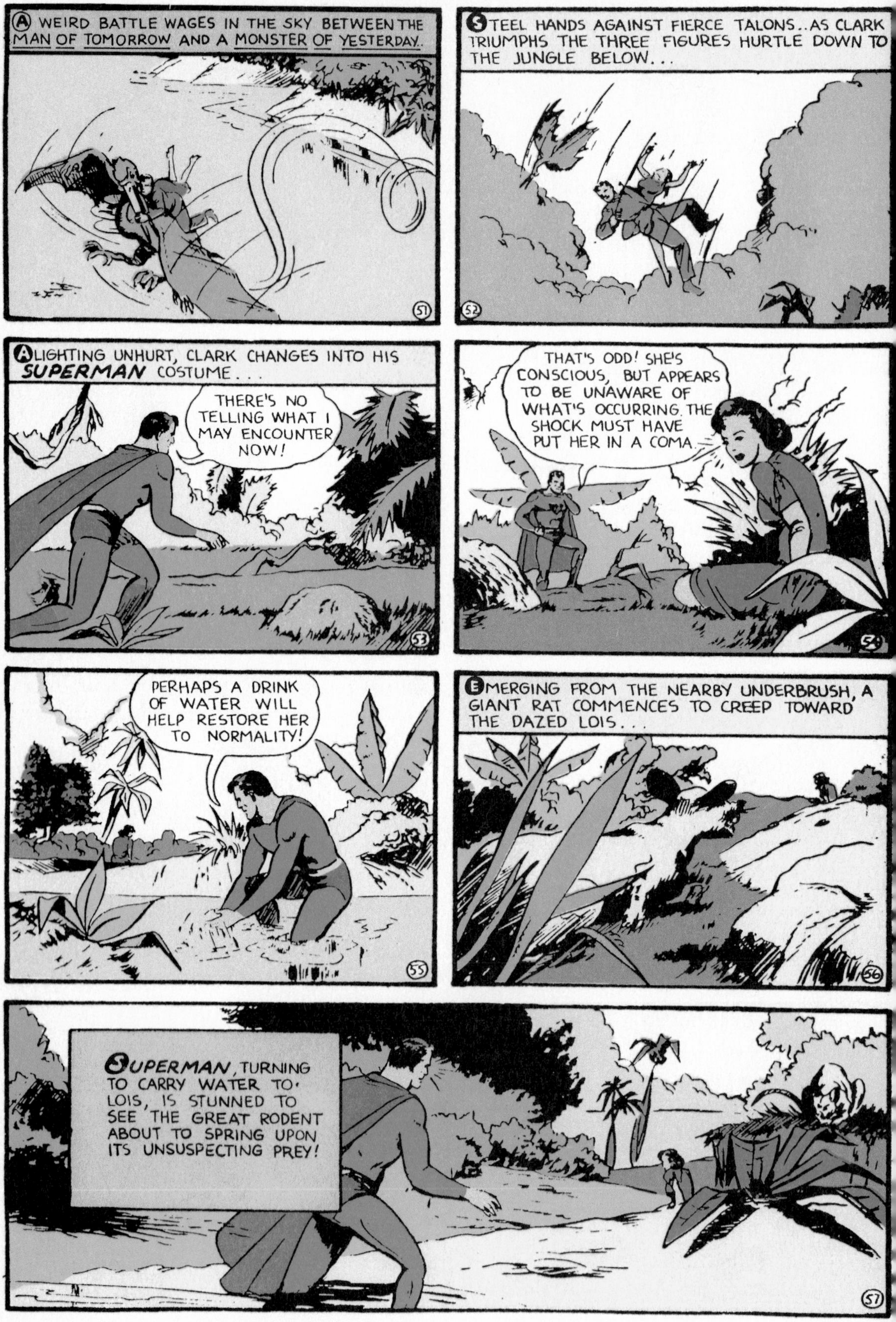
A WEIRD BATTLE WAGES IN THE SKY BETWEEN THE MAN OF TOMORROW AND A MONSTER OF YESTERDAY.
51
STEEL HANDS AGAINST FIERCE TALONS..AS CLARK TRIUMPHS THE THREE FIGURES HURTLE DOWN TO THE JUNGLE BELOW...
52
ALIGHTING UNHURT, CLARK CHANGES INTO HIS SUPERMAN COSTUME...
THERE'S NO TELLING WHAT I MAY ENCOUNTER NOW!
53
THAT'S ODD! SHE'S CONSCIOUS, BUT APPEARS TO BE UNAWARE OF WHAT'S OCCURRING. THE SHOCK MUST HAVE PUT HER IN A COMA.
54
PERHAPS A DRINK OF WATER WILL HELP RESTORE HER TO NORMALITY!
55
EMERGING FROM THE NEARBY UNDERBRUSH, A GIANT RAT COMMENCES TO CREEP TOWARD THE DAZED LOIS...
56
SUPERMAN, TURNING TO CARRY WATER TO LOIS, IS STUNNED TO SEE THE GREAT RODENT ABOUT TO SPRING UPON ITS UNSUSPECTING PREY!
57

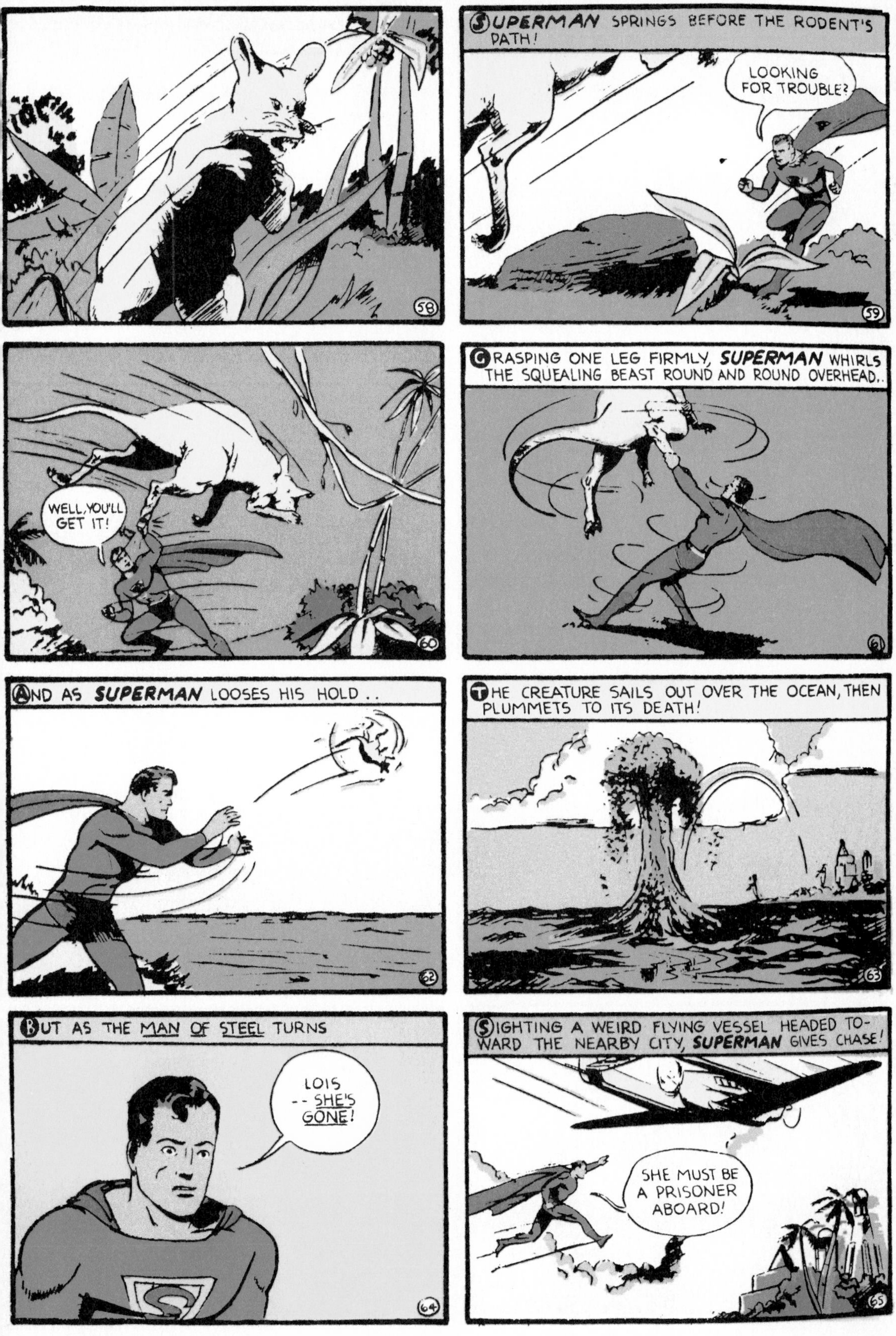
SUPERMAN SPRINGS BEFORE THE RODENT'S PATH!
LOOKING FOR TROUBLE?
WELL, YOU'LL GET IT!
GRASPING ONE LEG FIRMLY, SUPERMAN WHIRLS THE SQUEALING BEAST ROUND AND ROUND OVERHEAD..
AND AS SUPERMAN LOOSES HIS HOLD..
THE CREATURE SAILS OUT OVER THE OCEAN, THEN PLUMMETS TO ITS DEATH!
BUT AS THE MAN OF STEEL TURNS
LOIS -- SHE'S GONE!
SIGHTING A WEIRD FLYING VESSEL HEADED TOWARD THE NEARBY CITY, SUPERMAN GIVES CHASE!
SHE MUST BE A PRISONER ABOARD!

As SUPERMAN NEARS THE CITY..

SUPERMAN! OFFER NO RESISTANCE--OR MISS LANE WILL BE DESTROYED!

LUTHOR'S VOICE!

66

FOR LOIS' SAKE, SUPERMAN STANDS PASSIVELY BY AS SHE LEAVES THE WEIRD VESSEL..

SO, MAN OF STEEL--WE MEET AGAIN!

SO-- IT'S YOU AGAIN, LUTHOR! AND AS EVIL AS USUAL!

67

I DON'T CARE WHAT HAPPENS TO ME-BUT IF YOU HARM THAT GIRL--

ON THE CONTRARY, I WILL HAVE HER TREATED SO THAT HER SENSES RETURN--TAKE HER TO THE GREEN LABORATORY, MEN!

68

SUPERMAN ACCOMPANIES LUTHOR IN A TOUR OF THE CITY...

HOW DID YOU CREATE THIS WEIRD CITY?

IT WAS CREATED YEARS AGO--- I MERELY SALVAGED IT. WHAT YOU ARE WALKING UPON, IS A REMNANT OF THE SUNKEN CONTINENT, PACIFO!

YOU'LL ADMIT IT WAS A MIRACULOUS ACHIEVEMENT! WORKING UNDERWATER, I RAISED A GLASSOLITE-DOME OVER THE CITY, DRAINED OUT THE WATER, THEN RAISED THE CITY TO THE SURFACE OF THE OCEAN.

THEN IT WAS THIS TITANIC UNDERWATER UPHEAVAL THAT CAUSED THE OCEAN TO OVERFLOW! ...AND IT WAS YOU WHO TAPPED THE OIL-WELLS AND STOLE THE OIL FOR YOUR EVIL PURPOSES!

70

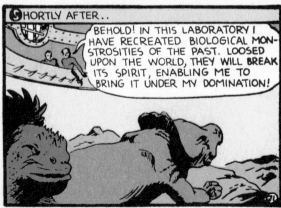

SHORTLY AFTER..

BEHOLD! IN THIS LABORATORY I HAVE RECREATED BIOLOGICAL MONSTROSITIES OF THE PAST. LOOSED UPON THE WORLD, THEY WILL BREAK ITS SPIRIT, ENABLING ME TO BRING IT UNDER MY DOMINATION!

71

BUT SURELY YOU WOULDN'T REALLY PERPETRATE SUCH AN INHUMAN CRIME ---!

IF YOU GIVE ME YOUR ASSISTANCE, I WILL BE INCLINED TO BE MORE MERCIFUL WITH THE WORLD, OTHERWISE...! WELL, WHAT IS YOUR DECISION?

72

GIVE ME A FEW MOMENTS! I MUST THINK-- THINK ...!

73

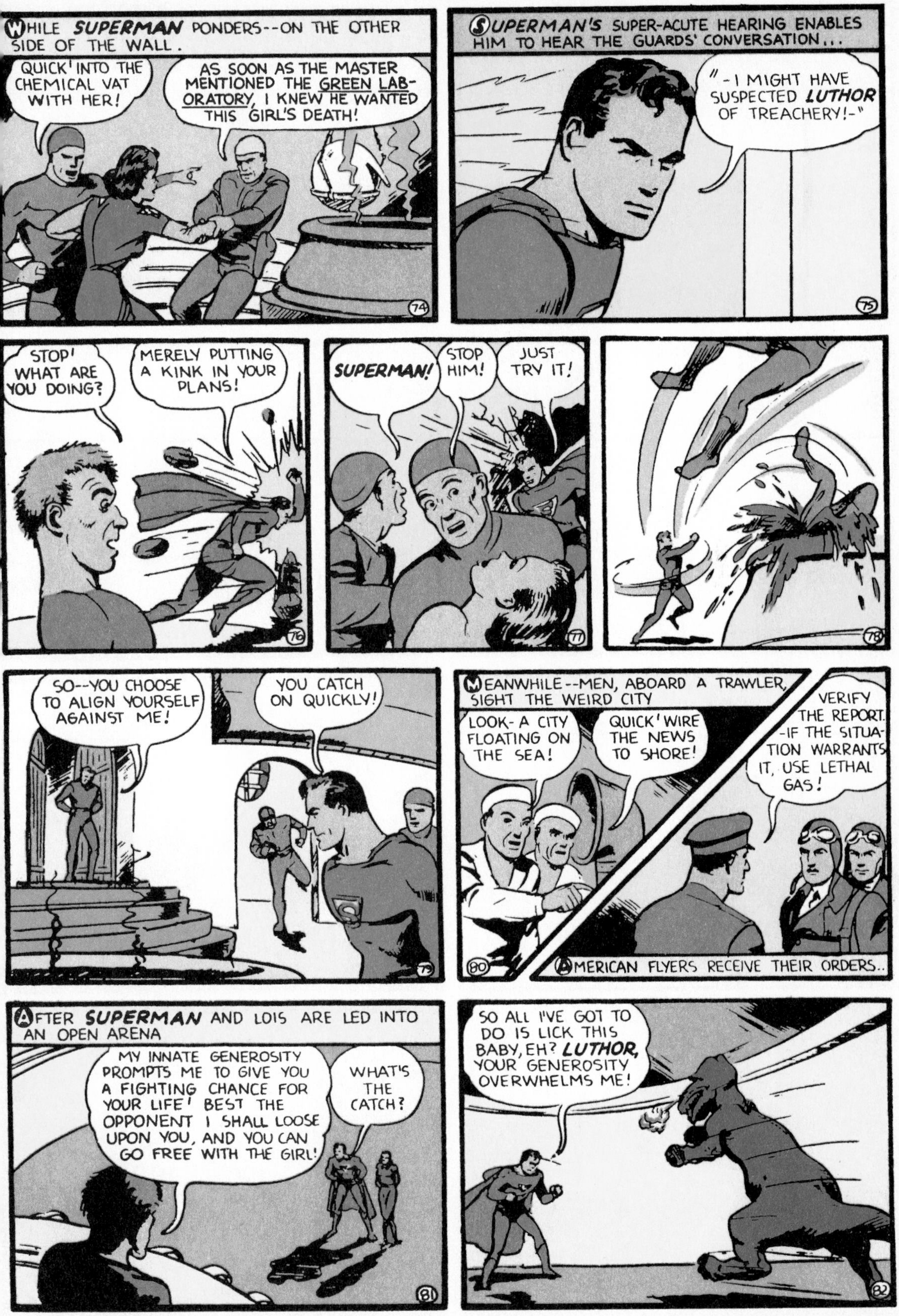
WHILE SUPERMAN PONDERS--ON THE OTHER SIDE OF THE WALL.
QUICK! INTO THE CHEMICAL VAT WITH HER!
AS SOON AS THE MASTER MENTIONED THE GREEN LABORATORY, I KNEW HE WANTED THIS GIRL'S DEATH!
SUPERMAN'S SUPER-ACUTE HEARING ENABLES HIM TO HEAR THE GUARDS' CONVERSATION...
"-I MIGHT HAVE SUSPECTED LUTHOR OF TREACHERY!-"
STOP! WHAT ARE YOU DOING?
MERELY PUTTING A KINK IN YOUR PLANS!
SUPERMAN!
STOP HIM!
JUST TRY IT!
SO--YOU CHOOSE TO ALIGN YOURSELF AGAINST ME!
YOU CATCH ON QUICKLY!
MEANWHILE--MEN, ABOARD A TRAWLER, SIGHT THE WEIRD CITY
LOOK- A CITY FLOATING ON THE SEA!
QUICK! WIRE THE NEWS TO SHORE!
AMERICAN FLYERS RECEIVE THEIR ORDERS..
VERIFY THE REPORT. -IF THE SITUATION WARRANTS IT, USE LETHAL GAS!
AFTER SUPERMAN AND LOIS ARE LED INTO AN OPEN ARENA
MY INNATE GENEROSITY PROMPTS ME TO GIVE YOU A FIGHTING CHANCE FOR YOUR LIFE! BEST THE OPPONENT I SHALL LOOSE UPON YOU, AND YOU CAN GO FREE WITH THE GIRL!
WHAT'S THE CATCH?
SO ALL I'VE GOT TO DO IS LICK THIS BABY, EH? LUTHOR, YOUR GENEROSITY OVERWHELMS ME!

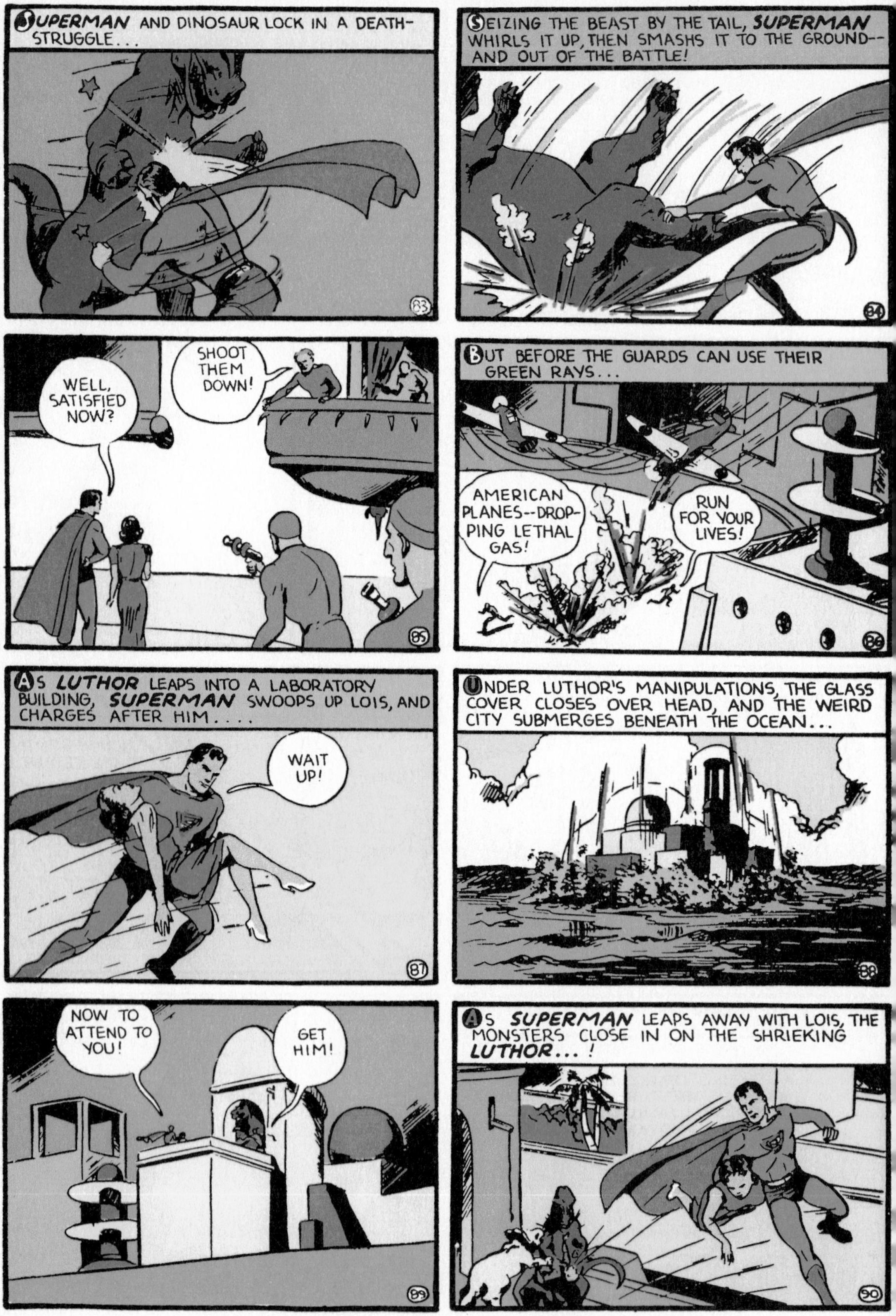
SUPERMAN AND DINOSAUR LOCK IN A DEATH-STRUGGLE...
SEIZING THE BEAST BY THE TAIL, SUPERMAN WHIRLS IT UP, THEN SMASHS IT TO THE GROUND--AND OUT OF THE BATTLE!
WELL, SATISFIED NOW?
SHOOT THEM DOWN!
BUT BEFORE THE GUARDS CAN USE THEIR GREEN RAYS...
AMERICAN PLANES--DROPPING LETHAL GAS!
RUN FOR YOUR LIVES!
AS LUTHOR LEAPS INTO A LABORATORY BUILDING, SUPERMAN SWOOPS UP LOIS, AND CHARGES AFTER HIM....
WAIT UP!
UNDER LUTHOR'S MANIPULATIONS, THE GLASS COVER CLOSES OVER HEAD, AND THE WEIRD CITY SUBMERGES BENEATH THE OCEAN...
NOW TO ATTEND TO YOU!
GET HIM!
AS SUPERMAN LEAPS AWAY WITH LOIS, THE MONSTERS CLOSE IN ON THE SHRIEKING LUTHOR... !

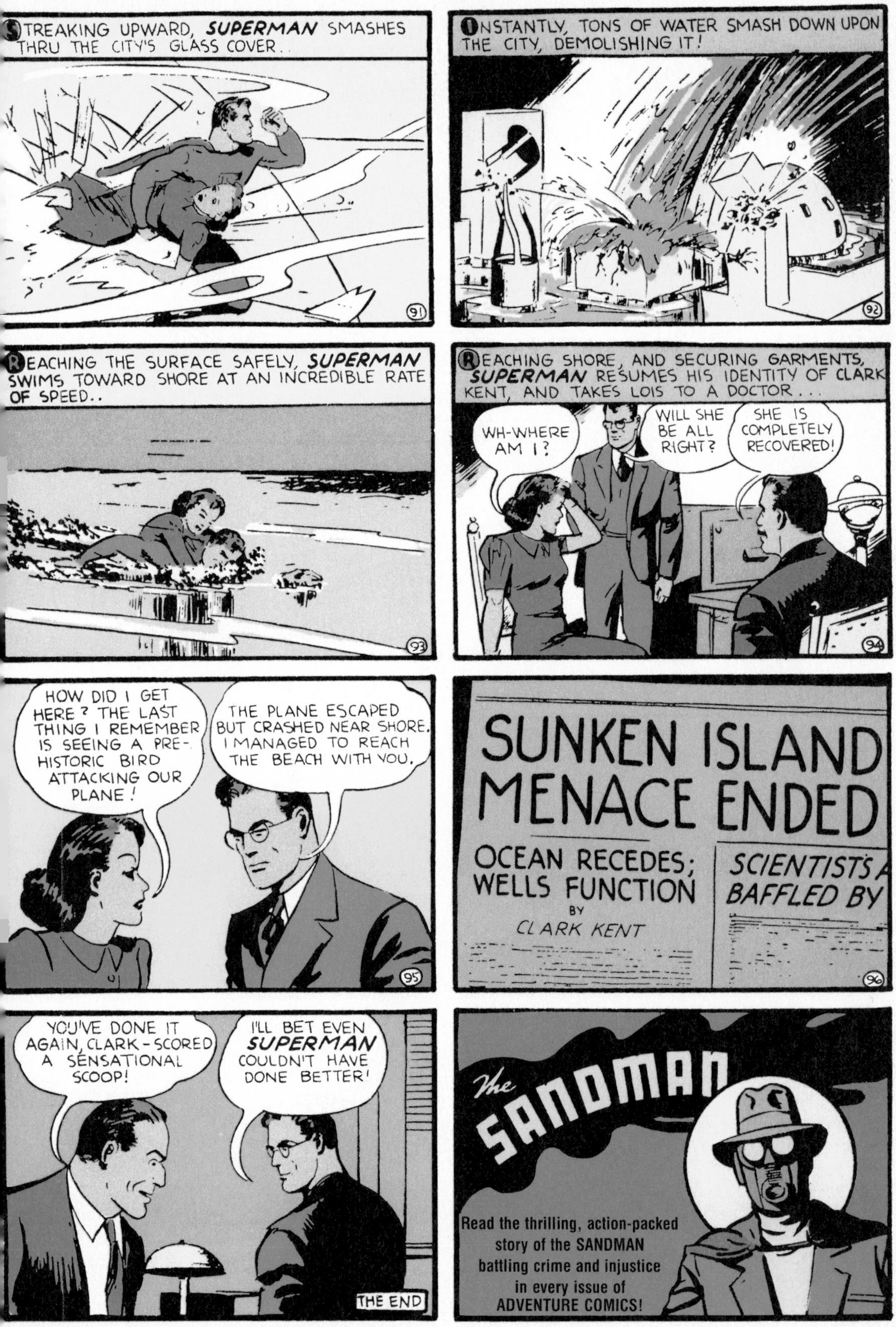
STREAKING UPWARD, SUPERMAN SMASHES THRU THE CITY'S GLASS COVER..
91
INSTANTLY, TONS OF WATER SMASH DOWN UPON THE CITY, DEMOLISHING IT!
92
REACHING THE SURFACE SAFELY, SUPERMAN SWIMS TOWARD SHORE AT AN INCREDIBLE RATE OF SPEED..
93
REACHING SHORE, AND SECURING GARMENTS, SUPERMAN RESUMES HIS IDENTITY OF CLARK KENT, AND TAKES LOIS TO A DOCTOR...
WH-WHERE AM I?
WILL SHE BE ALL RIGHT?
SHE IS COMPLETELY RECOVERED!
94
HOW DID I GET HERE? THE LAST THING I REMEMBER IS SEEING A PRE-HISTORIC BIRD ATTACKING OUR PLANE!
THE PLANE ESCAPED BUT CRASHED NEAR SHORE. I MANAGED TO REACH THE BEACH WITH YOU.
95
SUNKEN ISLAND MENACE ENDED
OCEAN RECEDES; WELLS FUNCTION
BY
CLARK KENT
SCIENTISTS
BAFFLED BY
96
YOU'VE DONE IT AGAIN, CLARK-SCORED A SENSATIONAL SCOOP!
I'LL BET EVEN SUPERMAN COULDN'T HAVE DONE BETTER!
THE END
The SANDMAN
Read the thrilling, action-packed story of the SANDMAN battling crime and injustice in every issue of ADVENTURE COMICS!

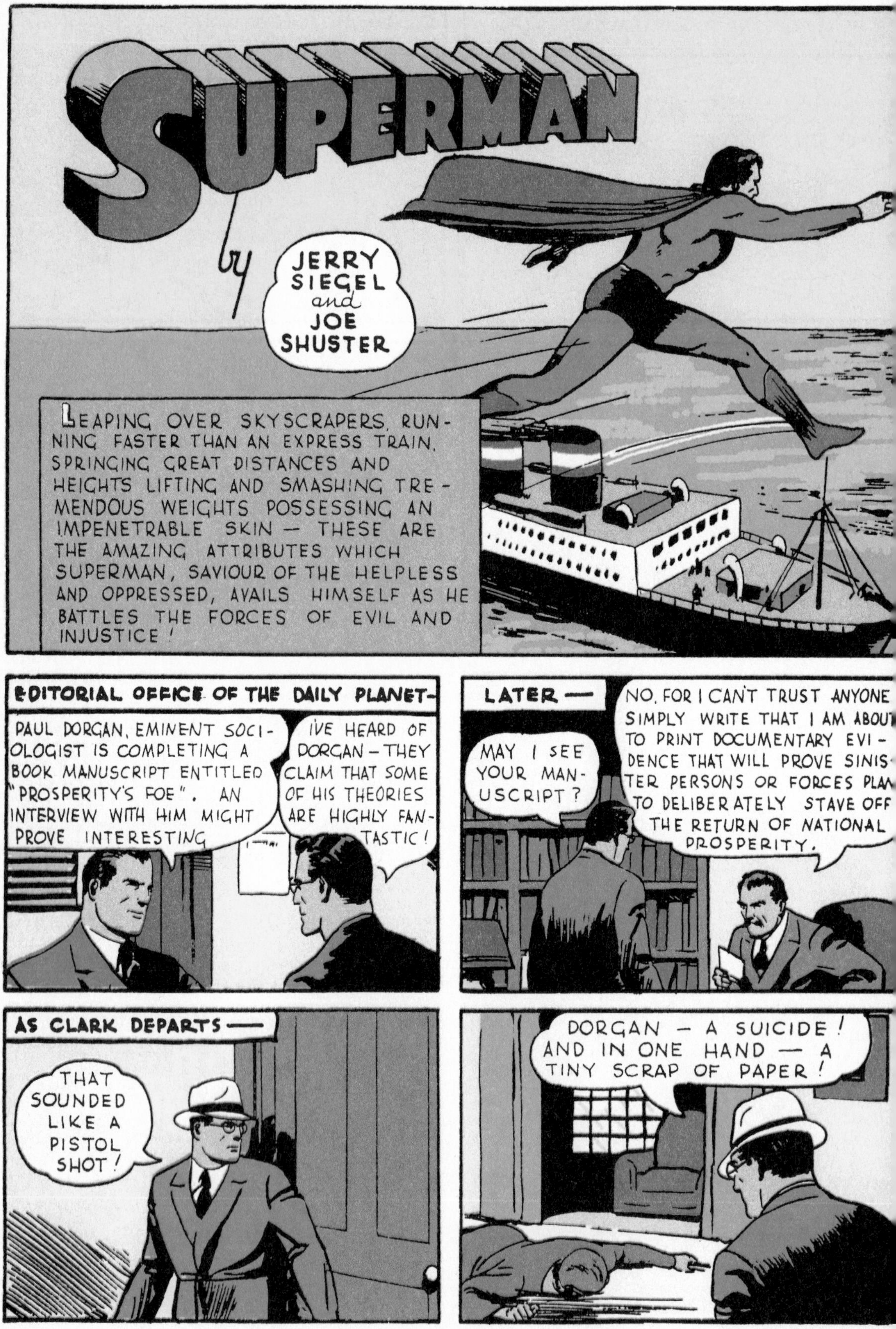
SUPERMAN
by JERRY SIEGEL and JOE SHUSTER
LEAPING OVER SKYSCRAPERS, RUNNING FASTER THAN AN EXPRESS TRAIN, SPRINGING GREAT DISTANCES AND HEIGHTS LIFTING AND SMASHING TREMENDOUS WEIGHTS POSSESSING AN IMPENETRABLE SKIN — THESE ARE THE AMAZING ATTRIBUTES WHICH SUPERMAN, SAVIOUR OF THE HELPLESS AND OPPRESSED, AVAILS HIMSELF AS HE BATTLES THE FORCES OF EVIL AND INJUSTICE!
EDITORIAL OFFICE OF THE DAILY PLANET—
PAUL DORGAN, EMINENT SOCIOLOGIST IS COMPLETING A BOOK MANUSCRIPT ENTITLED "PROSPERITY'S FOE". AN INTERVIEW WITH HIM MIGHT PROVE INTERESTING
I'VE HEARD OF DORGAN — THEY CLAIM THAT SOME OF HIS THEORIES ARE HIGHLY FANTASTIC!
LATER —
MAY I SEE YOUR MANUSCRIPT?
NO, FOR I CAN'T TRUST ANYONE SIMPLY WRITE THAT I AM ABOUT TO PRINT DOCUMENTARY EVIDENCE THAT WILL PROVE SINISTER PERSONS OR FORCES PLAN TO DELIBERATELY STAVE OFF THE RETURN OF NATIONAL PROSPERITY.
AS CLARK DEPARTS —
THAT SOUNDED LIKE A PISTOL SHOT!
DORGAN — A SUICIDE! AND IN ONE HAND — A TINY SCRAP OF PAPER!

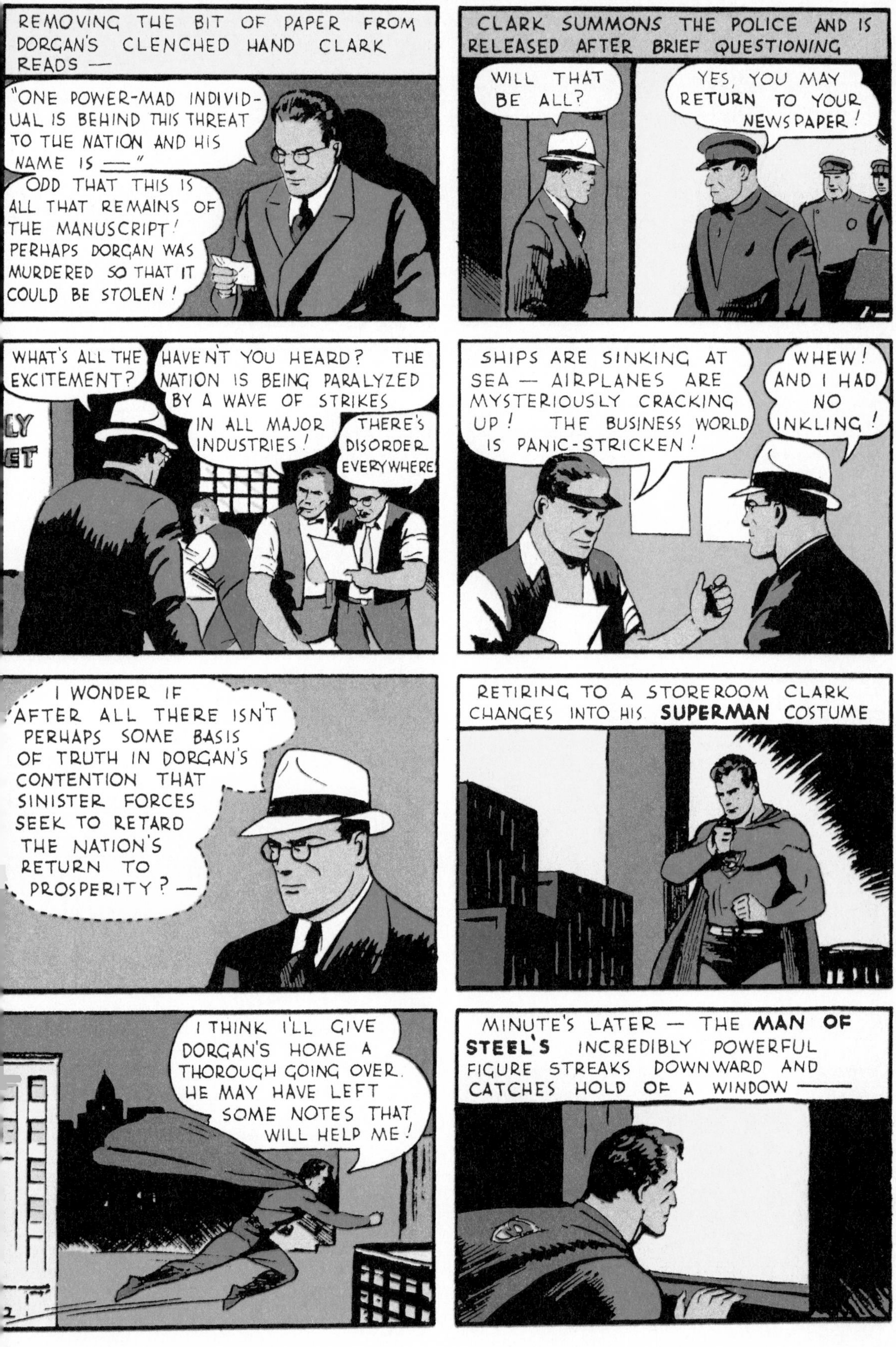
REMOVING THE BIT OF PAPER FROM DORGAN'S CLENCHED HAND CLARK READS —
"ONE POWER-MAD INDIVIDUAL IS BEHIND THIS THREAT TO THE NATION AND HIS NAME IS —"
ODD THAT THIS IS ALL THAT REMAINS OF THE MANUSCRIPT! PERHAPS DORGAN WAS MURDERED SO THAT IT COULD BE STOLEN!
CLARK SUMMONS THE POLICE AND IS RELEASED AFTER BRIEF QUESTIONING
WILL THAT BE ALL?
YES, YOU MAY RETURN TO YOUR NEWSPAPER!
WHAT'S ALL THE EXCITEMENT?
HAVEN'T YOU HEARD? THE NATION IS BEING PARALYZED BY A WAVE OF STRIKES IN ALL MAJOR INDUSTRIES!
THERE'S DISORDER EVERYWHERE!
SHIPS ARE SINKING AT SEA — AIRPLANES ARE MYSTERIOUSLY CRACKING UP! THE BUSINESS WORLD IS PANIC-STRICKEN!
WHEW! AND I HAD NO INKLING!
I WONDER IF AFTER ALL THERE ISN'T PERHAPS SOME BASIS OF TRUTH IN DORGAN'S CONTENTION THAT SINISTER FORCES SEEK TO RETARD THE NATION'S RETURN TO PROSPERITY? —
RETIRING TO A STOREROOM CLARK CHANGES INTO HIS SUPERMAN COSTUME
I THINK I'LL GIVE DORGAN'S HOME A THOROUGH GOING OVER. HE MAY HAVE LEFT SOME NOTES THAT WILL HELP ME!
MINUTE'S LATER — THE MAN OF STEEL'S INCREDIBLY POWERFUL FIGURE STREAKS DOWNWARD AND CATCHES HOLD OF A WINDOW —

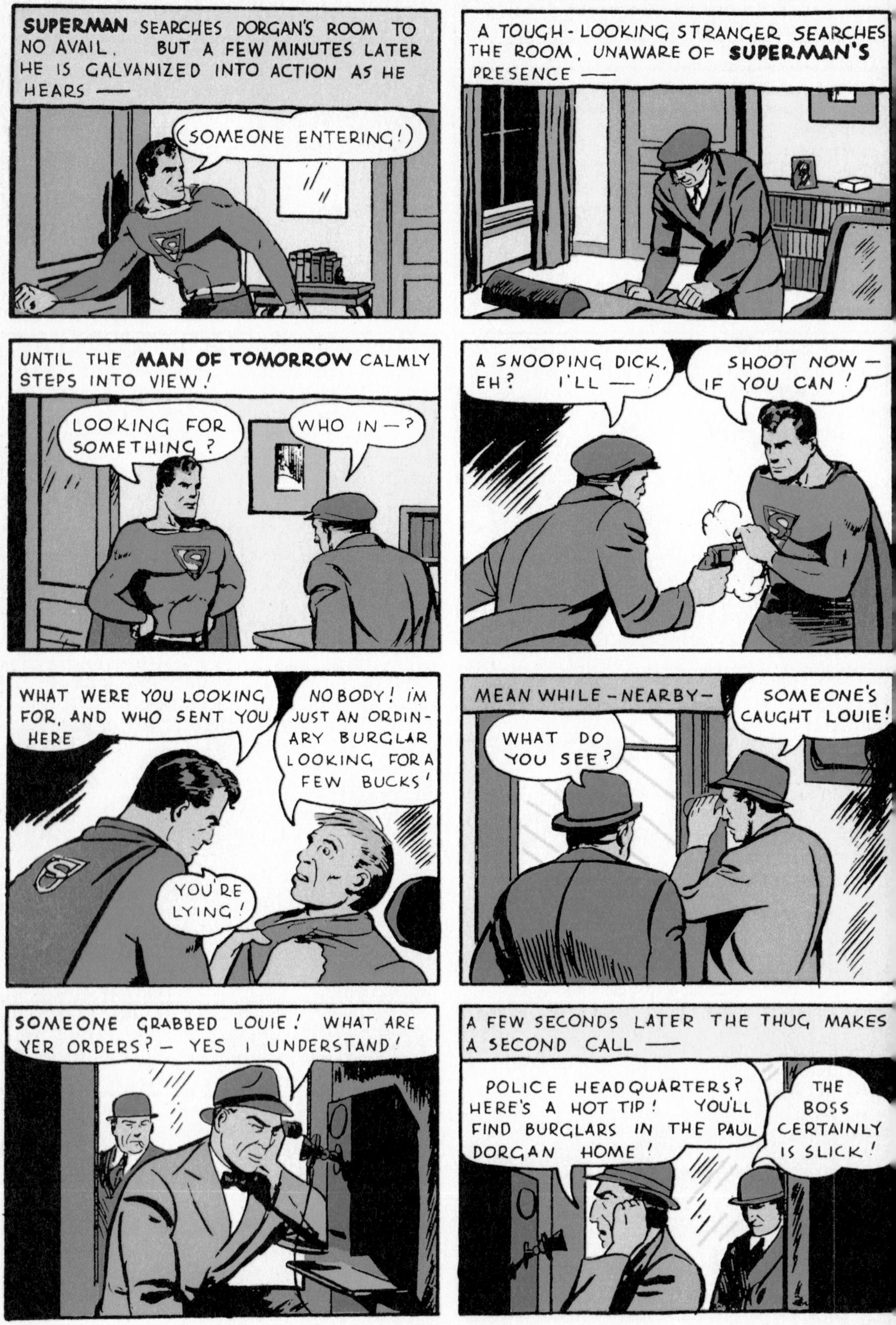
SUPERMAN SEARCHES DORGAN'S ROOM TO NO AVAIL. BUT A FEW MINUTES LATER HE IS GALVANIZED INTO ACTION AS HE HEARS —
(SOMEONE ENTERING!)
A TOUGH-LOOKING STRANGER SEARCHES THE ROOM, UNAWARE OF SUPERMAN'S PRESENCE —
UNTIL THE MAN OF TOMORROW CALMLY STEPS INTO VIEW!
LOOKING FOR SOMETHING?
WHO IN—?
A SNOOPING DICK, EH? I'LL —!
SHOOT NOW — IF YOU CAN!
WHAT WERE YOU LOOKING FOR, AND WHO SENT YOU HERE
NOBODY! I'M JUST AN ORDINARY BURGLAR LOOKING FOR A FEW BUCKS!
YOU'RE LYING!
MEANWHILE - NEARBY -
WHAT DO YOU SEE?
SOMEONE'S CAUGHT LOUIE!
SOMEONE GRABBED LOUIE! WHAT ARE YER ORDERS? — YES I UNDERSTAND!
A FEW SECONDS LATER THE THUG MAKES A SECOND CALL —
POLICE HEADQUARTERS? HERE'S A HOT TIP! YOU'LL FIND BURGLARS IN THE PAUL DORGAN HOME!
THE BOSS CERTAINLY IS SLICK!

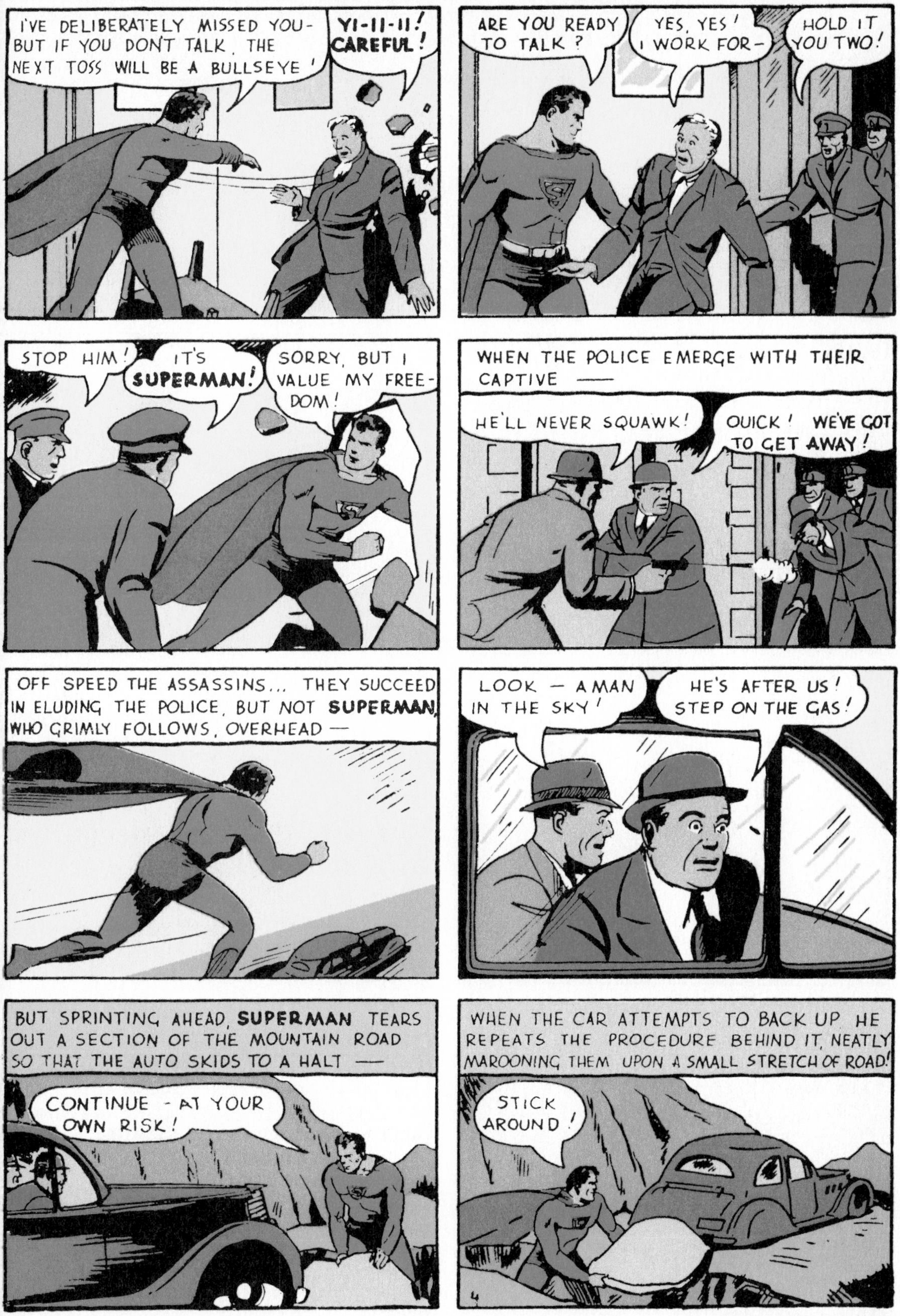
I'VE DELIBERATELY MISSED YOU- BUT IF YOU DON'T TALK, THE NEXT TOSS WILL BE A BULLSEYE!
YI-II-II! CAREFUL!
ARE YOU READY TO TALK?
YES, YES! I WORK FOR-
HOLD IT YOU TWO!
STOP HIM!
IT'S SUPERMAN!
SORRY, BUT I VALUE MY FREE-DOM!
WHEN THE POLICE EMERGE WITH THEIR CAPTIVE ——
HE'LL NEVER SQUAWK!
QUICK! WE'VE GOT TO GET AWAY!
OFF SPEED THE ASSASSINS... THEY SUCCEED IN ELUDING THE POLICE, BUT NOT SUPERMAN, WHO GRIMLY FOLLOWS, OVERHEAD —
LOOK — A MAN IN THE SKY!
HE'S AFTER US! STEP ON THE GAS!
BUT SPRINTING AHEAD, SUPERMAN TEARS OUT A SECTION OF THE MOUNTAIN ROAD SO THAT THE AUTO SKIDS TO A HALT —
CONTINUE - AT YOUR OWN RISK!
WHEN THE CAR ATTEMPTS TO BACK UP HE REPEATS THE PROCEDURE BEHIND IT, NEATLY MAROONING THEM UPON A SMALL STRETCH OF ROAD!
STICK AROUND!

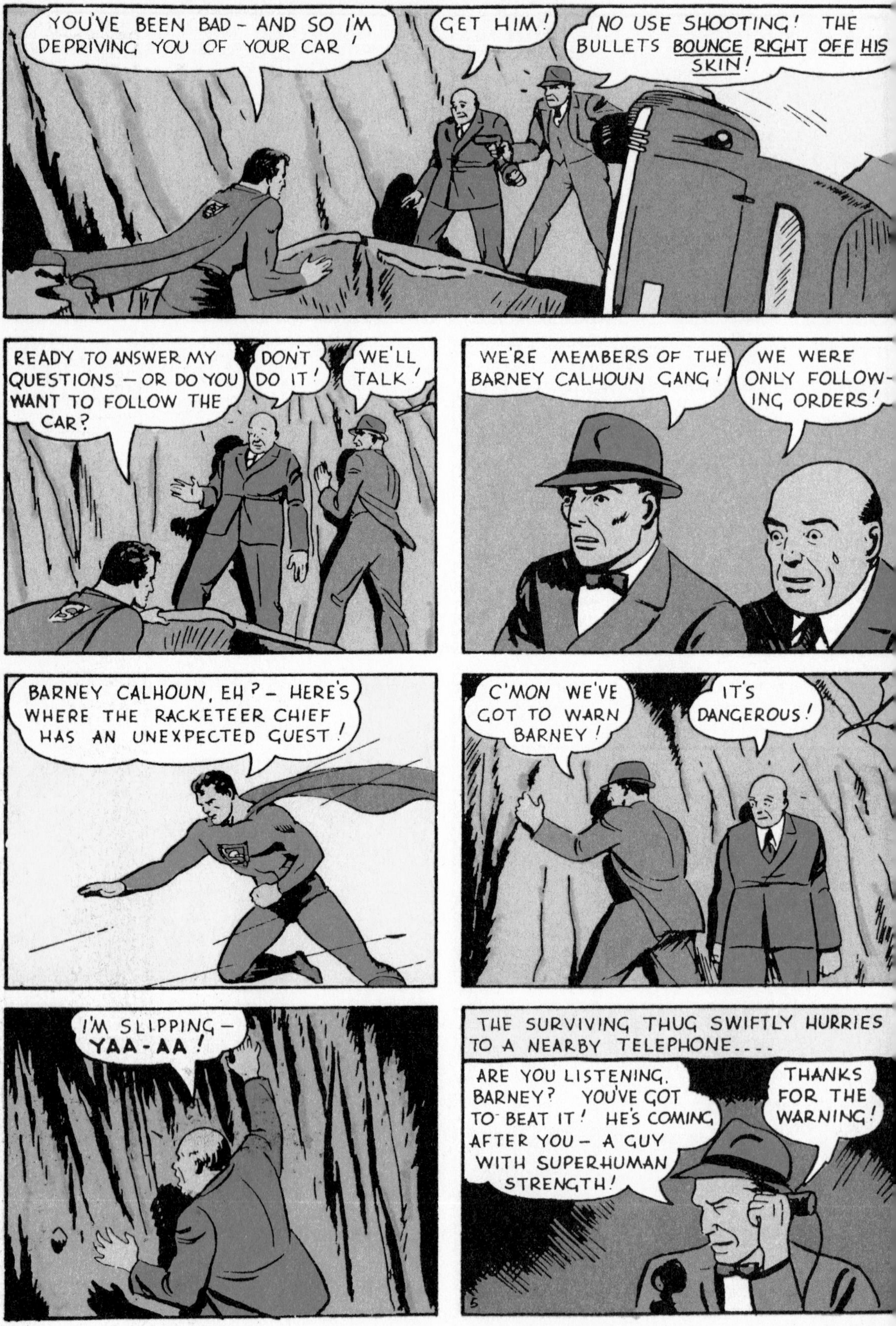
YOU'VE BEEN BAD - AND SO I'M DEPRIVING YOU OF YOUR CAR!
GET HIM!
NO USE SHOOTING! THE BULLETS BOUNCE RIGHT OFF HIS SKIN!
READY TO ANSWER MY QUESTIONS - OR DO YOU WANT TO FOLLOW THE CAR?
DON'T DO IT!
WE'LL TALK!
WE'RE MEMBERS OF THE BARNEY CALHOUN GANG!
WE WERE ONLY FOLLOWING ORDERS!
BARNEY CALHOUN, EH? - HERE'S WHERE THE RACKETEER CHIEF HAS AN UNEXPECTED GUEST!
C'MON WE'VE GOT TO WARN BARNEY!
IT'S DANGEROUS!
I'M SLIPPING - YAA-AA!
THE SURVIVING THUG SWIFTLY HURRIES TO A NEARBY TELEPHONE....
ARE YOU LISTENING, BARNEY? YOU'VE GOT TO BEAT IT! HE'S COMING AFTER YOU - A GUY WITH SUPERHUMAN STRENGTH!
THANKS FOR THE WARNING!
5

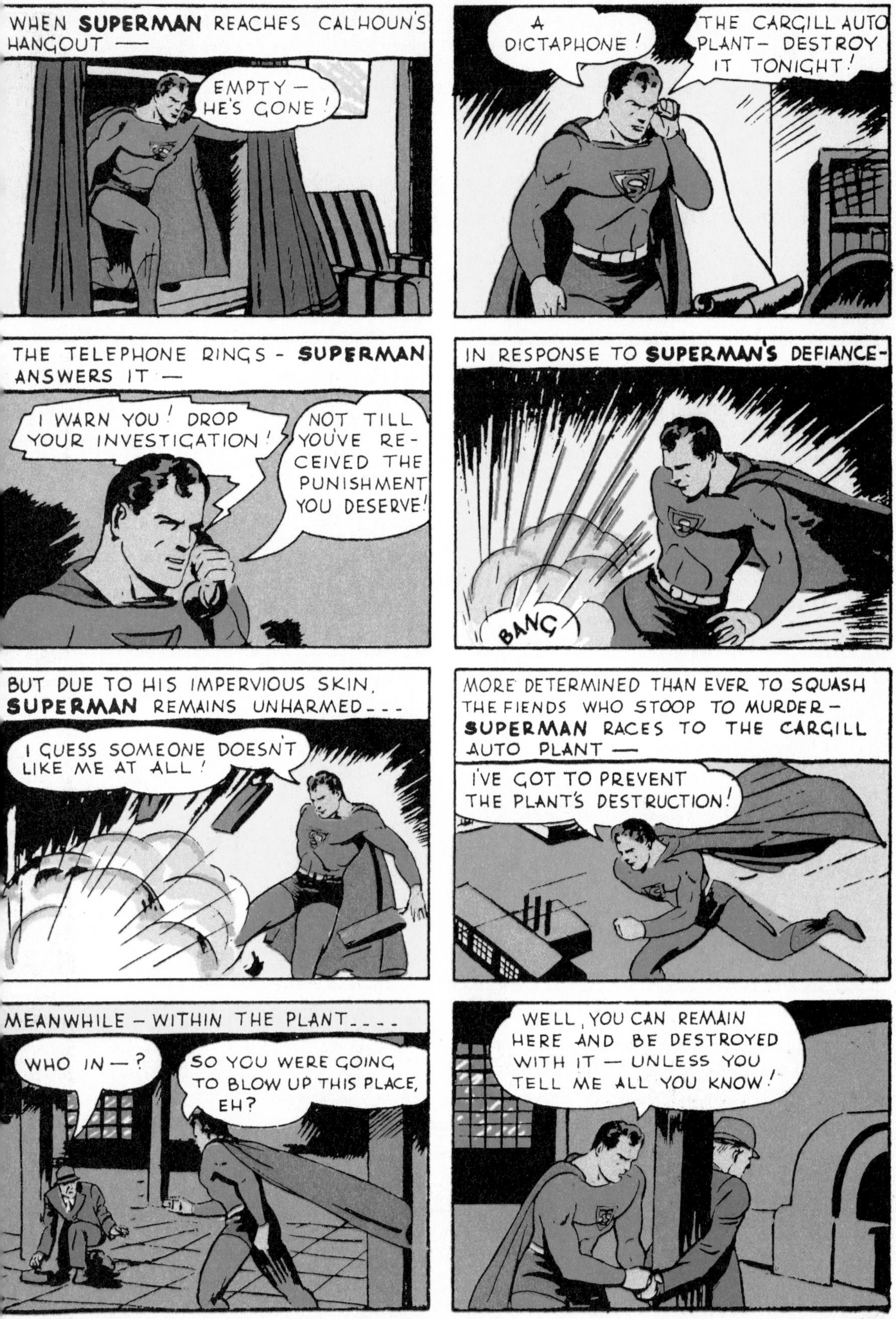
WHEN SUPERMAN REACHES CALHOUN'S HANGOUT —
EMPTY — HE'S GONE!
A DICTAPHONE!
THE CARGILL AUTO PLANT— DESTROY IT TONIGHT!
THE TELEPHONE RINGS - SUPERMAN ANSWERS IT —
I WARN YOU! DROP YOUR INVESTIGATION!
NOT TILL YOU'VE RECEIVED THE PUNISHMENT YOU DESERVE!
IN RESPONSE TO SUPERMAN'S DEFIANCE-
BANG
BUT DUE TO HIS IMPERVIOUS SKIN, SUPERMAN REMAINS UNHARMED---
I GUESS SOMEONE DOESN'T LIKE ME AT ALL!
MORE DETERMINED THAN EVER TO SQUASH THE FIENDS WHO STOOP TO MURDER— SUPERMAN RACES TO THE CARGILL AUTO PLANT —
I'VE GOT TO PREVENT THE PLANT'S DESTRUCTION!
MEANWHILE — WITHIN THE PLANT----
WHO IN—?
SO YOU WERE GOING TO BLOW UP THIS PLACE, EH?
WELL, YOU CAN REMAIN HERE AND BE DESTROYED WITH IT — UNLESS YOU TELL ME ALL YOU KNOW!

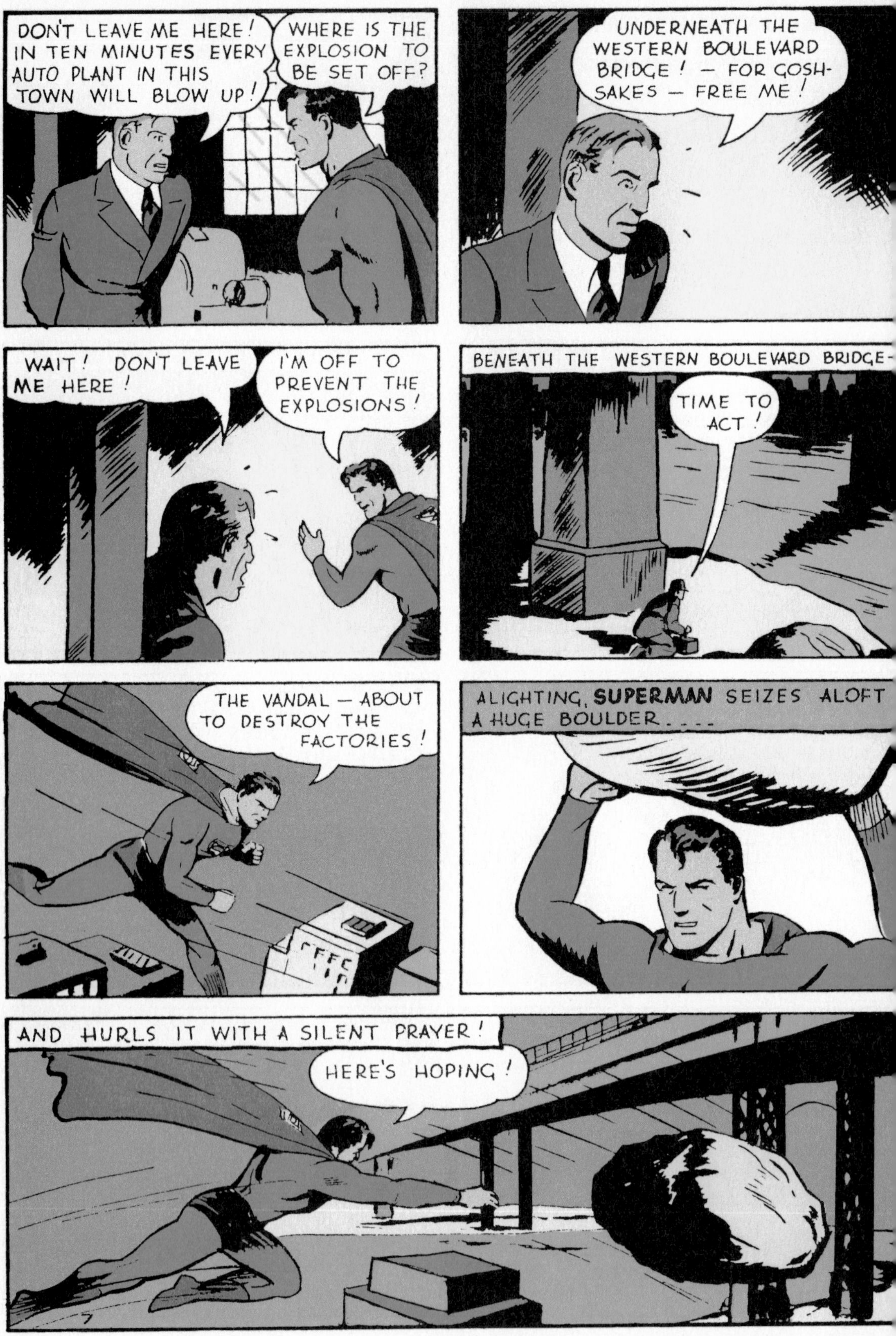
DON'T LEAVE ME HERE! IN TEN MINUTES EVERY AUTO PLANT IN THIS TOWN WILL BLOW UP!
WHERE IS THE EXPLOSION TO BE SET OFF?
UNDERNEATH THE WESTERN BOULEVARD BRIDGE! — FOR GOSH-SAKES — FREE ME!
WAIT! DON'T LEAVE ME HERE!
I'M OFF TO PREVENT THE EXPLOSIONS!
BENEATH THE WESTERN BOULEVARD BRIDGE-
TIME TO ACT!
THE VANDAL — ABOUT TO DESTROY THE FACTORIES!
ALIGHTING, SUPERMAN SEIZES ALOFT A HUGE BOULDER....
AND HURLS IT WITH A SILENT PRAYER!
HERE'S HOPING!

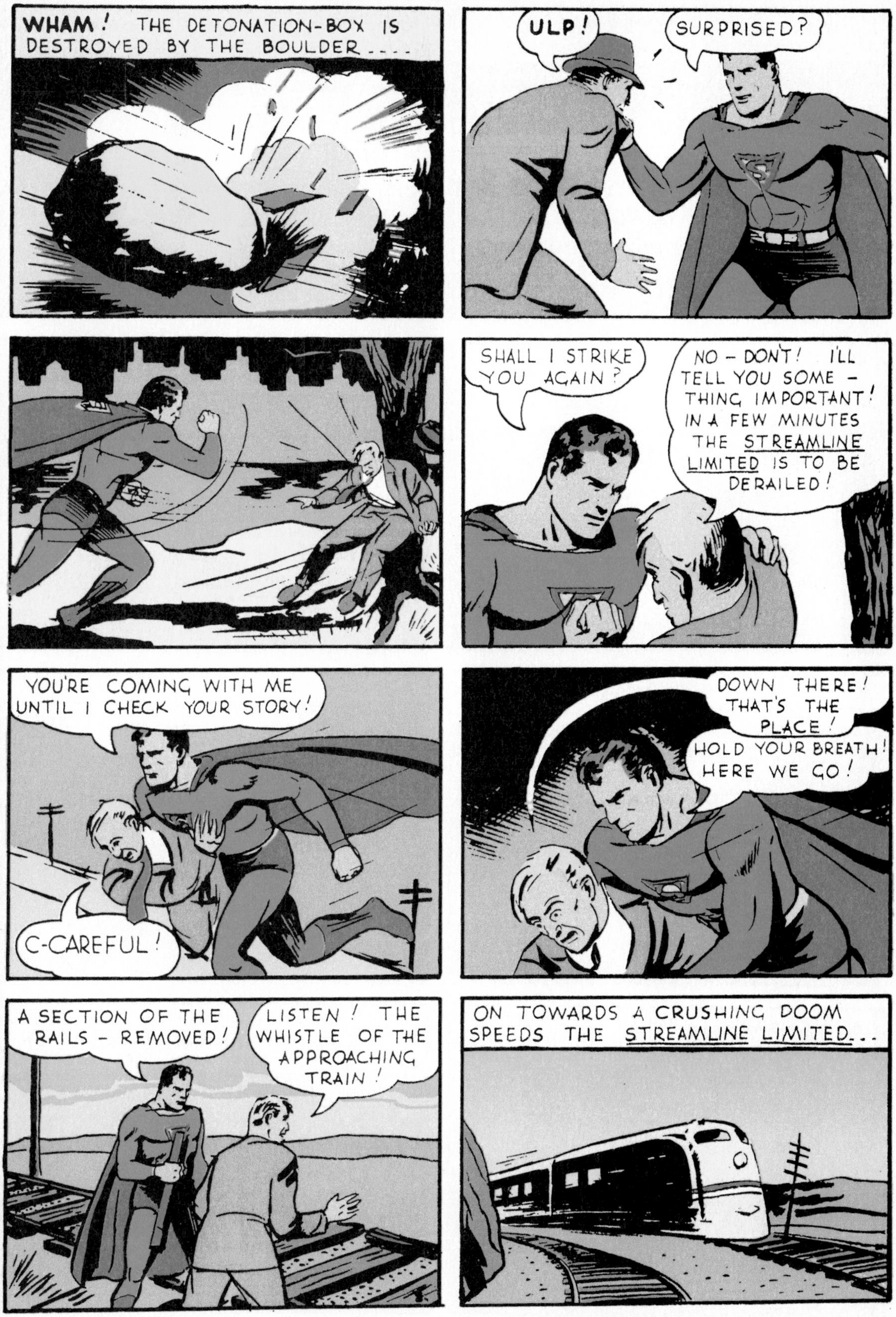
WHAM! THE DETONATION-BOX IS DESTROYED BY THE BOULDER....
ULP!
SURPRISED?
SHALL I STRIKE YOU AGAIN?
NO - DON'T! I'LL TELL YOU SOME - THING IMPORTANT! IN A FEW MINUTES THE STREAMLINE LIMITED IS TO BE DERAILED!
YOU'RE COMING WITH ME UNTIL I CHECK YOUR STORY!
C-CAREFUL!
DOWN THERE! THAT'S THE PLACE!
HOLD YOUR BREATH! HERE WE GO!
A SECTION OF THE RAILS - REMOVED!
LISTEN! THE WHISTLE OF THE APPROACHING TRAIN!
ON TOWARDS A CRUSHING DOOM SPEEDS THE STREAMLINE LIMITED...

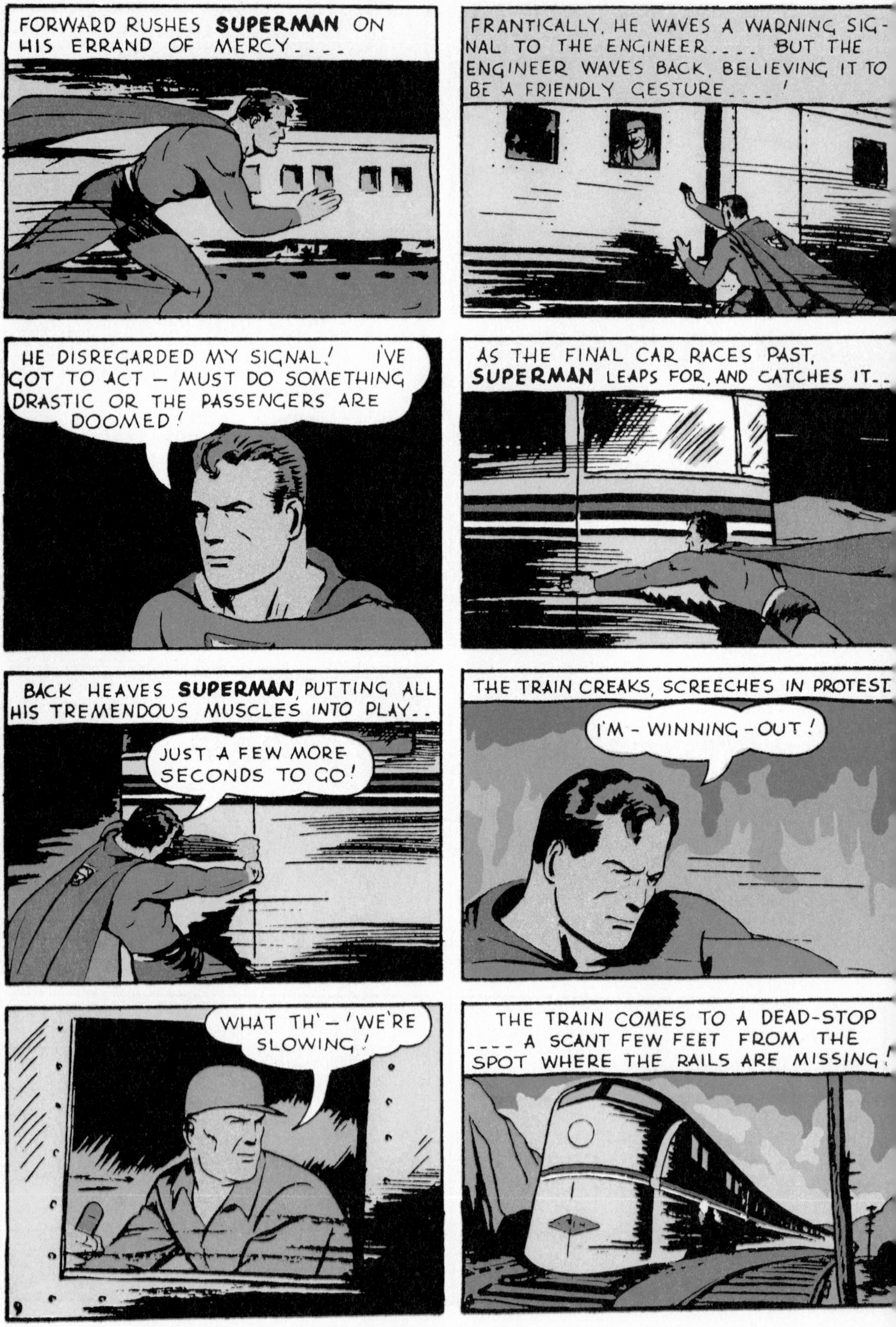
FORWARD RUSHES SUPERMAN ON HIS ERRAND OF MERCY....
FRANTICALLY, HE WAVES A WARNING SIGNAL TO THE ENGINEER.... BUT THE ENGINEER WAVES BACK, BELIEVING IT TO BE A FRIENDLY GESTURE....!
HE DISREGARDED MY SIGNAL! I'VE GOT TO ACT — MUST DO SOMETHING DRASTIC OR THE PASSENGERS ARE DOOMED!
AS THE FINAL CAR RACES PAST, SUPERMAN LEAPS FOR, AND CATCHES IT..
BACK HEAVES SUPERMAN, PUTTING ALL HIS TREMENDOUS MUSCLES INTO PLAY..
JUST A FEW MORE SECONDS TO GO!
THE TRAIN CREAKS, SCREECHES IN PROTEST.
I'M - WINNING - OUT!
WHAT TH'—'WE'RE SLOWING!
THE TRAIN COMES TO A DEAD-STOP .... A SCANT FEW FEET FROM THE SPOT WHERE THE RAILS ARE MISSING!

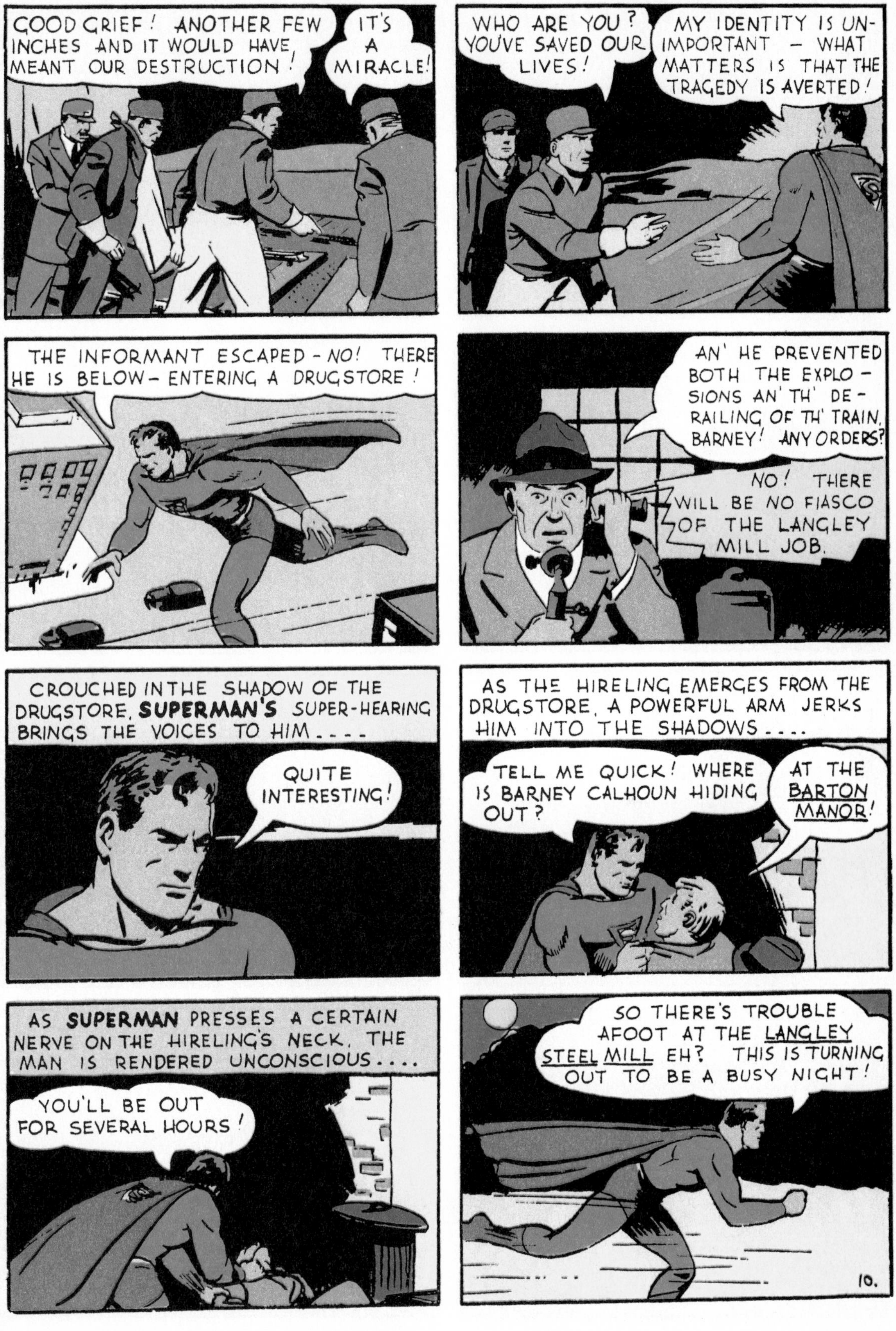
GOOD GRIEF! ANOTHER FEW INCHES AND IT WOULD HAVE MEANT OUR DESTRUCTION!
IT'S A MIRACLE!
WHO ARE YOU? YOU'VE SAVED OUR LIVES!
MY IDENTITY IS UN-IMPORTANT – WHAT MATTERS IS THAT THE TRAGEDY IS AVERTED!
THE INFORMANT ESCAPED - NO! THERE HE IS BELOW - ENTERING A DRUGSTORE!
AN' HE PREVENTED BOTH THE EXPLO-SIONS AN' TH' DE-RAILING OF TH' TRAIN, BARNEY! ANY ORDERS?
NO! THERE WILL BE NO FIASCO OF THE LANGLEY MILL JOB.
CROUCHED IN THE SHADOW OF THE DRUGSTORE, SUPERMAN'S SUPER-HEARING BRINGS THE VOICES TO HIM....
QUITE INTERESTING!
AS THE HIRELING EMERGES FROM THE DRUGSTORE, A POWERFUL ARM JERKS HIM INTO THE SHADOWS....
TELL ME QUICK! WHERE IS BARNEY CALHOUN HIDING OUT?
AT THE BARTON MANOR!
AS SUPERMAN PRESSES A CERTAIN NERVE ON THE HIRELING'S NECK, THE MAN IS RENDERED UNCONSCIOUS....
YOU'LL BE OUT FOR SEVERAL HOURS!
SO THERE'S TROUBLE AFOOT AT THE LANGLEY STEEL MILL EH? THIS IS TURNING OUT TO BE A BUSY NIGHT!
10.

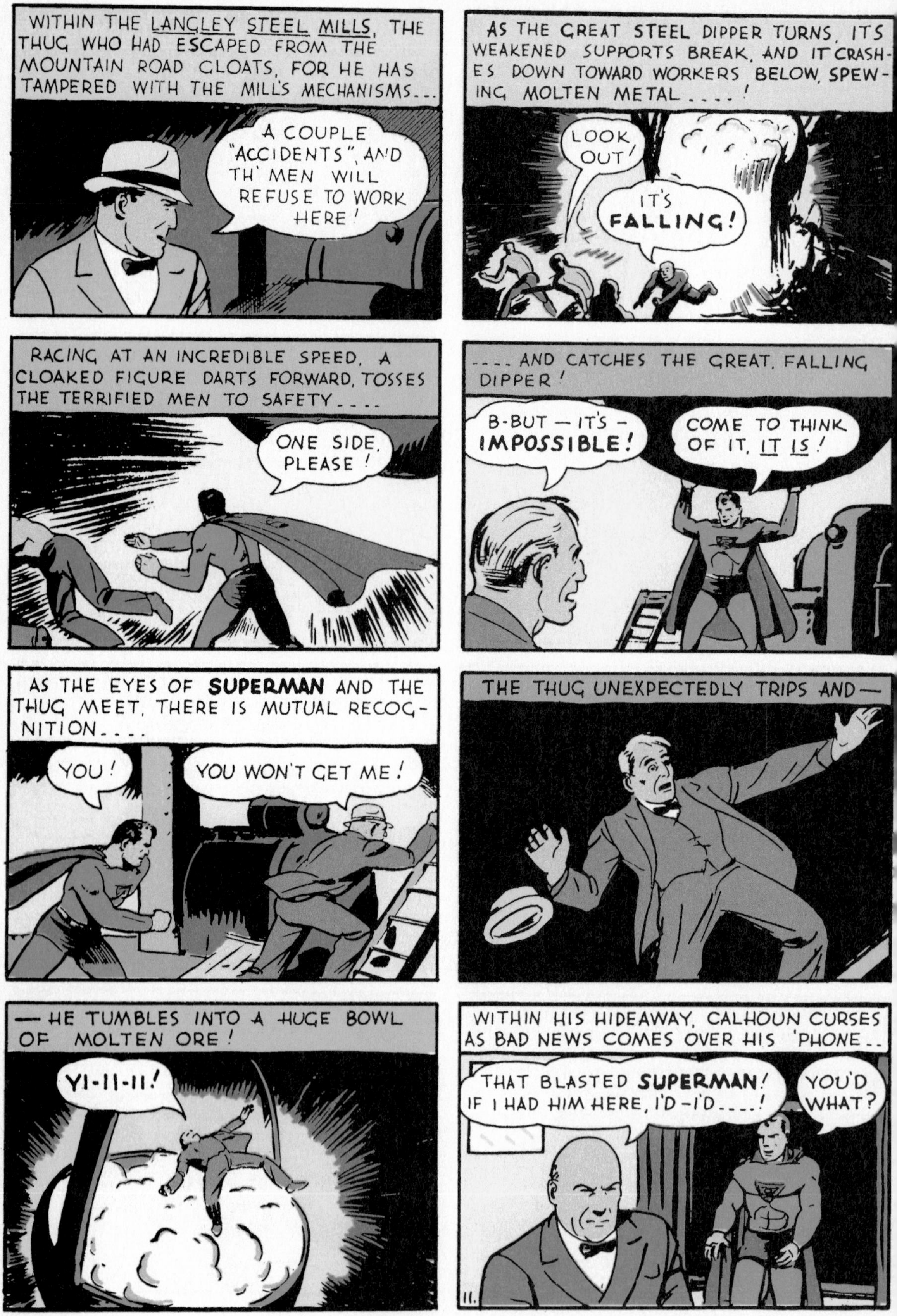
WITHIN THE LANGLEY STEEL MILLS, THE THUG WHO HAD ESCAPED FROM THE MOUNTAIN ROAD GLOATS, FOR HE HAS TAMPERED WITH THE MILL'S MECHANISMS...
A COUPLE "ACCIDENTS", AND TH' MEN WILL REFUSE TO WORK HERE!
AS THE GREAT STEEL DIPPER TURNS, ITS WEAKENED SUPPORTS BREAK, AND IT CRASHES DOWN TOWARD WORKERS BELOW, SPEWING MOLTEN METAL....!
LOOK OUT!
IT'S FALLING!
RACING AT AN INCREDIBLE SPEED, A CLOAKED FIGURE DARTS FORWARD, TOSSES THE TERRIFIED MEN TO SAFETY....
ONE SIDE, PLEASE!
....AND CATCHES THE GREAT, FALLING DIPPER!
B-BUT — IT'S — IMPOSSIBLE!
COME TO THINK OF IT, IT IS!
AS THE EYES OF SUPERMAN AND THE THUG MEET, THERE IS MUTUAL RECOGNITION....
YOU!
YOU WON'T GET ME!
THE THUG UNEXPECTEDLY TRIPS AND—
—HE TUMBLES INTO A HUGE BOWL OF MOLTEN ORE!
YI-II-II!
WITHIN HIS HIDEAWAY, CALHOUN CURSES AS BAD NEWS COMES OVER HIS 'PHONE..
THAT BLASTED SUPERMAN! IF I HAD HIM HERE, I'D-I'D....!
YOU'D WHAT?
11.

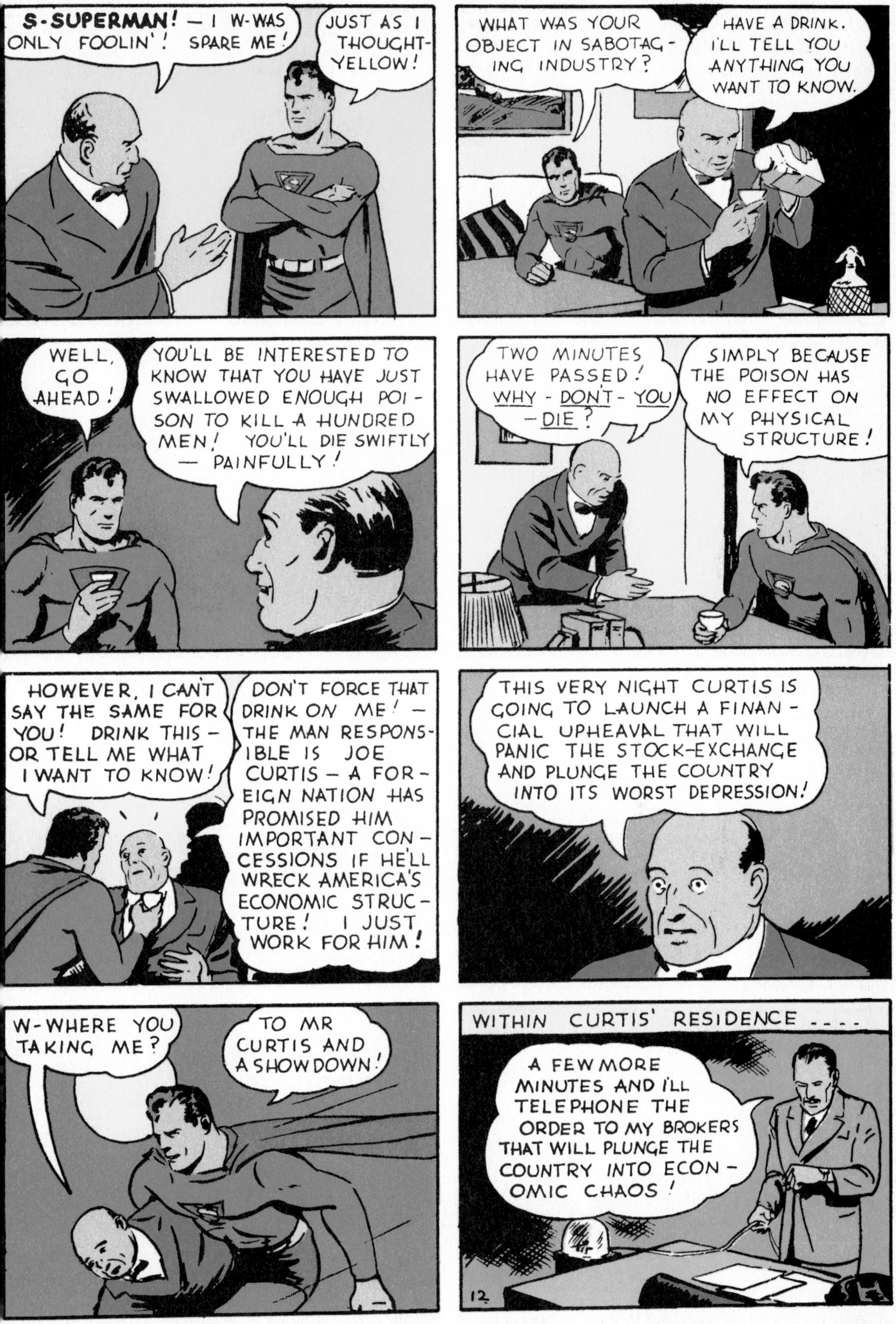
S-SUPERMAN! — I W-WAS ONLY FOOLIN'! SPARE ME!
JUST AS I THOUGHT-YELLOW!
WHAT WAS YOUR OBJECT IN SABOTAGING INDUSTRY?
HAVE A DRINK. I'LL TELL YOU ANYTHING YOU WANT TO KNOW.
WELL, GO AHEAD!
YOU'LL BE INTERESTED TO KNOW THAT YOU HAVE JUST SWALLOWED ENOUGH POISON TO KILL A HUNDRED MEN! YOU'LL DIE SWIFTLY — PAINFULLY!
TWO MINUTES HAVE PASSED! WHY - DON'T - YOU - DIE?
SIMPLY BECAUSE THE POISON HAS NO EFFECT ON MY PHYSICAL STRUCTURE!
HOWEVER, I CAN'T SAY THE SAME FOR YOU! DRINK THIS — OR TELL ME WHAT I WANT TO KNOW!
DON'T FORCE THAT DRINK ON ME! — THE MAN RESPONSIBLE IS JOE CURTIS — A FOREIGN NATION HAS PROMISED HIM IMPORTANT CONCESSIONS IF HE'LL WRECK AMERICA'S ECONOMIC STRUCTURE! I JUST WORK FOR HIM!
THIS VERY NIGHT CURTIS IS GOING TO LAUNCH A FINANCIAL UPHEAVAL THAT WILL PANIC THE STOCK-EXCHANGE AND PLUNGE THE COUNTRY INTO ITS WORST DEPRESSION!
W-WHERE YOU TAKING ME?
TO MR CURTIS AND A SHOWDOWN!
WITHIN CURTIS' RESIDENCE ....
A FEW MORE MINUTES AND I'LL TELEPHONE THE ORDER TO MY BROKERS THAT WILL PLUNGE THE COUNTRY INTO ECONOMIC CHAOS!
12

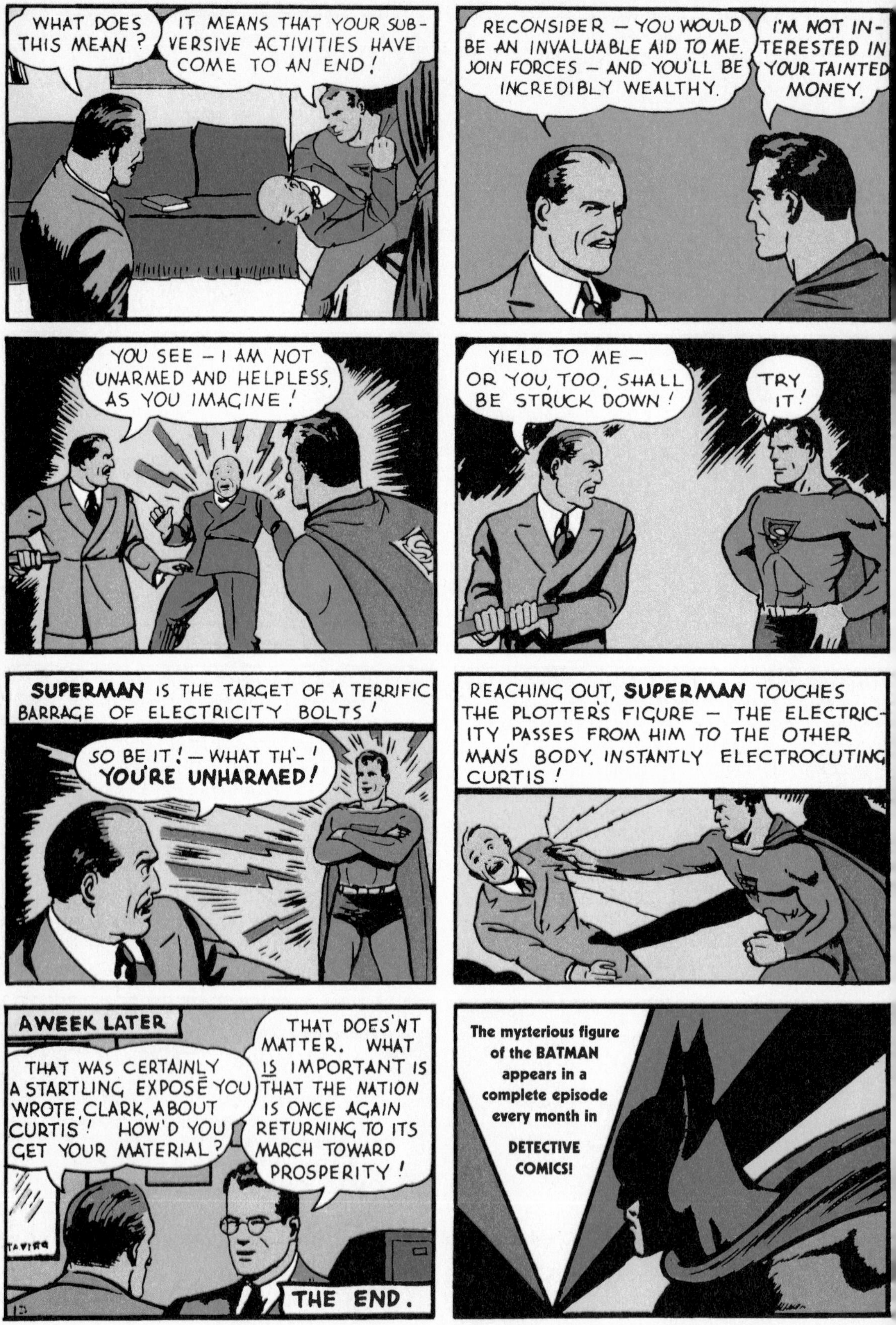
WHAT DOES THIS MEAN ?
IT MEANS THAT YOUR SUB-VERSIVE ACTIVITIES HAVE COME TO AN END !
RECONSIDER — YOU WOULD BE AN INVALUABLE AID TO ME. JOIN FORCES — AND YOU'LL BE INCREDIBLY WEALTHY.
I'M NOT IN-TERESTED IN YOUR TAINTED MONEY.
YOU SEE — I AM NOT UNARMED AND HELPLESS, AS YOU IMAGINE !
YIELD TO ME — OR YOU, TOO, SHALL BE STRUCK DOWN !
TRY IT !
SUPERMAN IS THE TARGET OF A TERRIFIC BARRAGE OF ELECTRICITY BOLTS !
SO BE IT ! — WHAT TH'- ! YOU'RE UNHARMED !
REACHING OUT, SUPERMAN TOUCHES THE PLOTTER'S FIGURE — THE ELECTRIC-ITY PASSES FROM HIM TO THE OTHER MAN'S BODY, INSTANTLY ELECTROCUTING CURTIS !
A WEEK LATER
THAT WAS CERTAINLY A STARTLING EXPOSÉ YOU WROTE, CLARK, ABOUT CURTIS ! HOW'D YOU GET YOUR MATERIAL ?
THAT DOES'NT MATTER. WHAT IS IMPORTANT IS THAT THE NATION IS ONCE AGAIN RETURNING TO ITS MARCH TOWARD PROSPERITY !
THE END.
The mysterious figure of the BATMAN appears in a complete episode every month in
DETECTIVE COMICS!

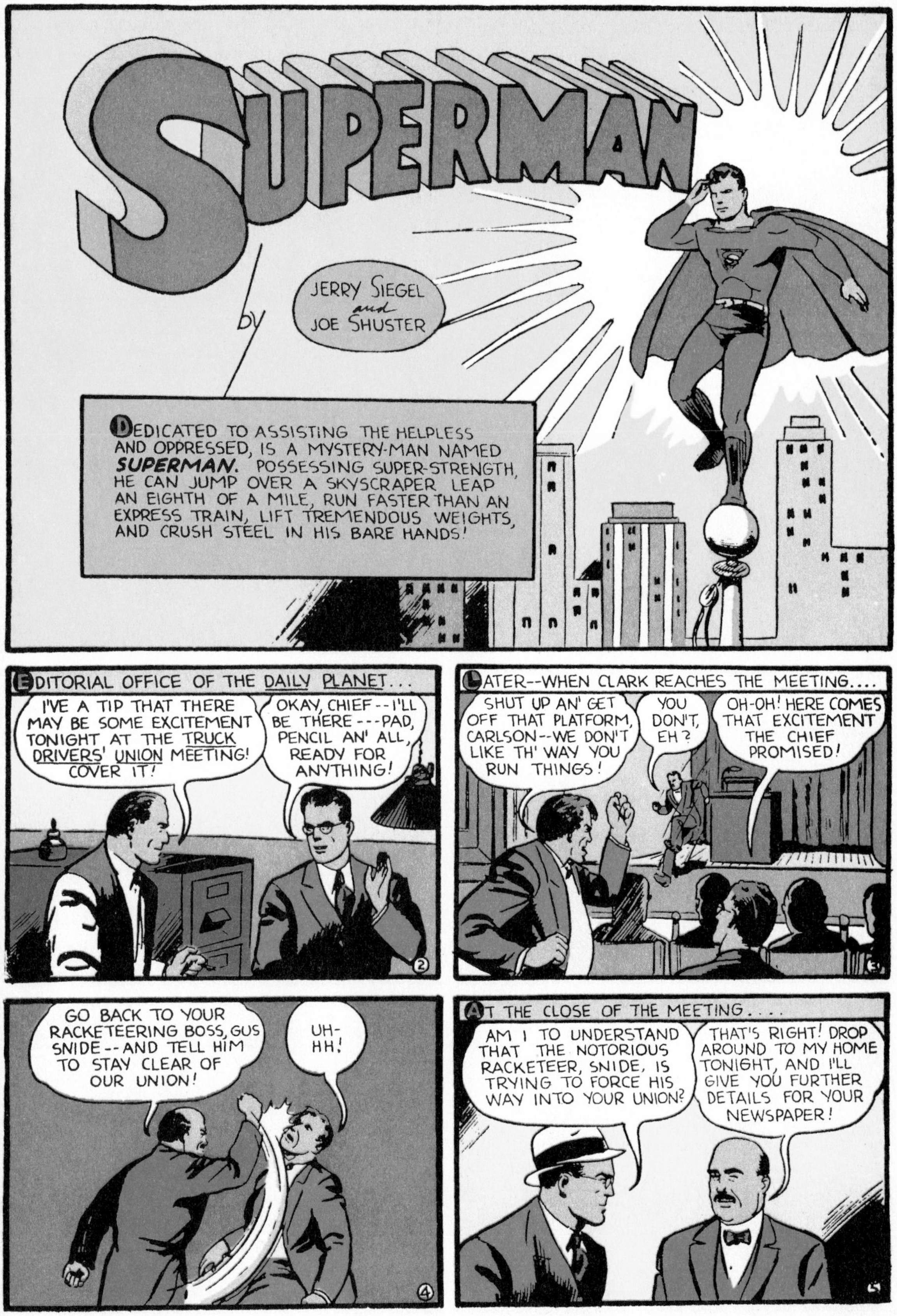
SUPERMAN
by
JERRY SIEGEL
and
JOE SHUSTER
DEDICATED TO ASSISTING THE HELPLESS AND OPPRESSED, IS A MYSTERY-MAN NAMED SUPERMAN. POSSESSING SUPER-STRENGTH, HE CAN JUMP OVER A SKYSCRAPER LEAP AN EIGHTH OF A MILE, RUN FASTER THAN AN EXPRESS TRAIN, LIFT TREMENDOUS WEIGHTS, AND CRUSH STEEL IN HIS BARE HANDS!
EDITORIAL OFFICE OF THE DAILY PLANET...
I'VE A TIP THAT THERE MAY BE SOME EXCITEMENT TONIGHT AT THE TRUCK DRIVERS' UNION MEETING! COVER IT!
OKAY, CHIEF -- I'LL BE THERE --- PAD, PENCIL AN' ALL, READY FOR ANYTHING!
2
LATER--WHEN CLARK REACHES THE MEETING....
SHUT UP AN' GET OFF THAT PLATFORM, CARLSON--WE DON'T LIKE TH' WAY YOU RUN THINGS!
YOU DON'T, EH?
OH-OH! HERE COMES THAT EXCITEMENT THE CHIEF PROMISED!
3
GO BACK TO YOUR RACKETEERING BOSS, GUS SNIDE--AND TELL HIM TO STAY CLEAR OF OUR UNION!
UH-HH!
4
AT THE CLOSE OF THE MEETING...
AM I TO UNDERSTAND THAT THE NOTORIOUS RACKETEER, SNIDE, IS TRYING TO FORCE HIS WAY INTO YOUR UNION?
THAT'S RIGHT! DROP AROUND TO MY HOME TONIGHT, AND I'LL GIVE YOU FURTHER DETAILS FOR YOUR NEWSPAPER!
5

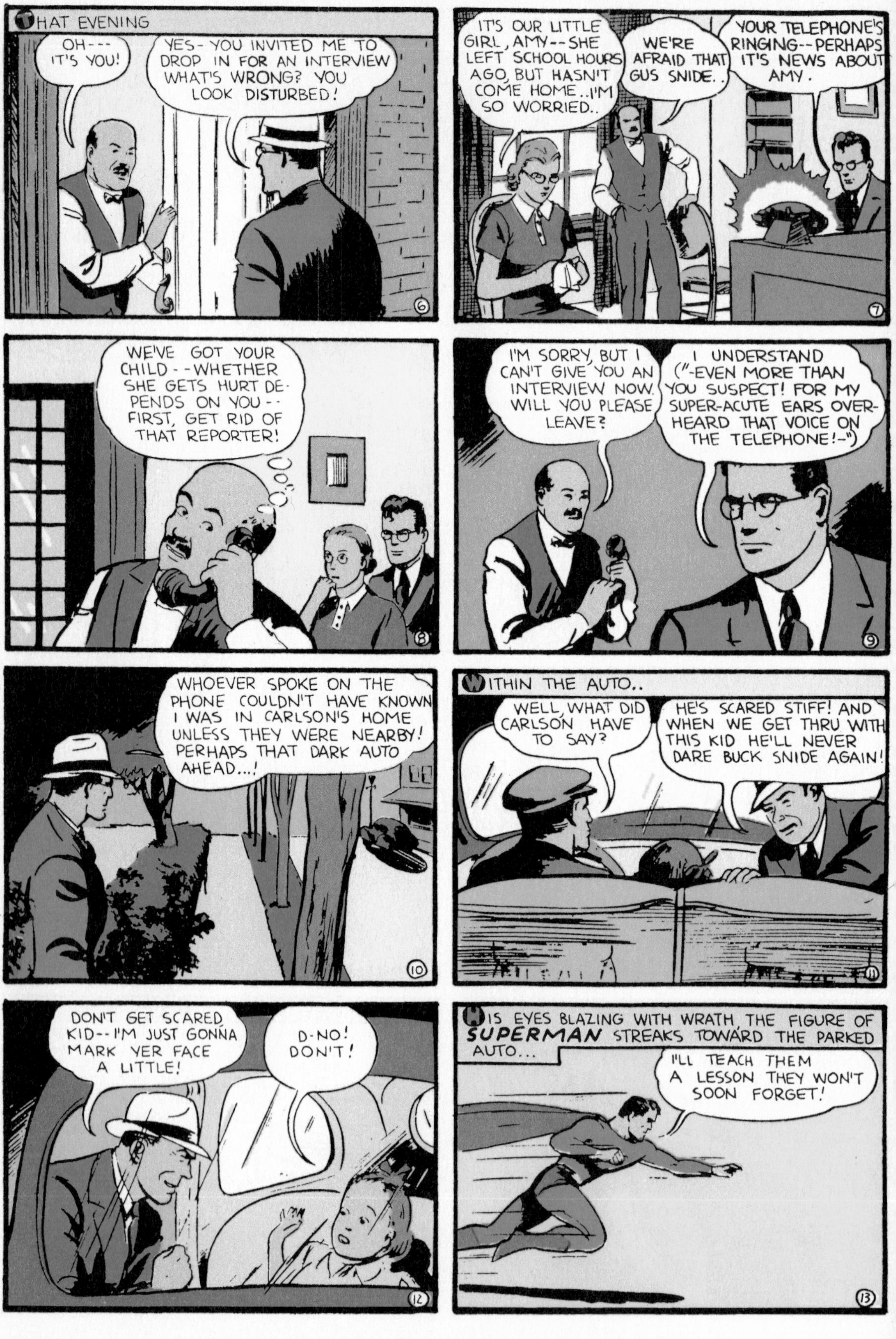
THAT EVENING
OH--- IT'S YOU!
YES- YOU INVITED ME TO DROP IN FOR AN INTERVIEW WHAT'S WRONG? YOU LOOK DISTURBED!
IT'S OUR LITTLE GIRL, AMY--SHE LEFT SCHOOL HOURS AGO, BUT HASN'T COME HOME..I'M SO WORRIED..
WE'RE AFRAID THAT GUS SNIDE..
YOUR TELEPHONE'S RINGING--PERHAPS IT'S NEWS ABOUT AMY.
WE'VE GOT YOUR CHILD--WHETHER SHE GETS HURT DEPENDS ON YOU--FIRST, GET RID OF THAT REPORTER!
I'M SORRY, BUT I CAN'T GIVE YOU AN INTERVIEW NOW. WILL YOU PLEASE LEAVE?
I UNDERSTAND ("-EVEN MORE THAN YOU SUSPECT! FOR MY SUPER-ACUTE EARS OVERHEARD THAT VOICE ON THE TELEPHONE!-")
WHOEVER SPOKE ON THE PHONE COULDN'T HAVE KNOWN I WAS IN CARLSON'S HOME UNLESS THEY WERE NEARBY! PERHAPS THAT DARK AUTO AHEAD...!
WITHIN THE AUTO..
WELL, WHAT DID CARLSON HAVE TO SAY?
HE'S SCARED STIFF! AND WHEN WE GET THRU WITH THIS KID HE'LL NEVER DARE BUCK SNIDE AGAIN!
DON'T GET SCARED KID--I'M JUST GONNA MARK YER FACE A LITTLE!
D-NO! DON'T!
HIS EYES BLAZING WITH WRATH, THE FIGURE OF SUPERMAN STREAKS TOWARD THE PARKED AUTO...
I'LL TEACH THEM A LESSON THEY WON'T SOON FORGET!

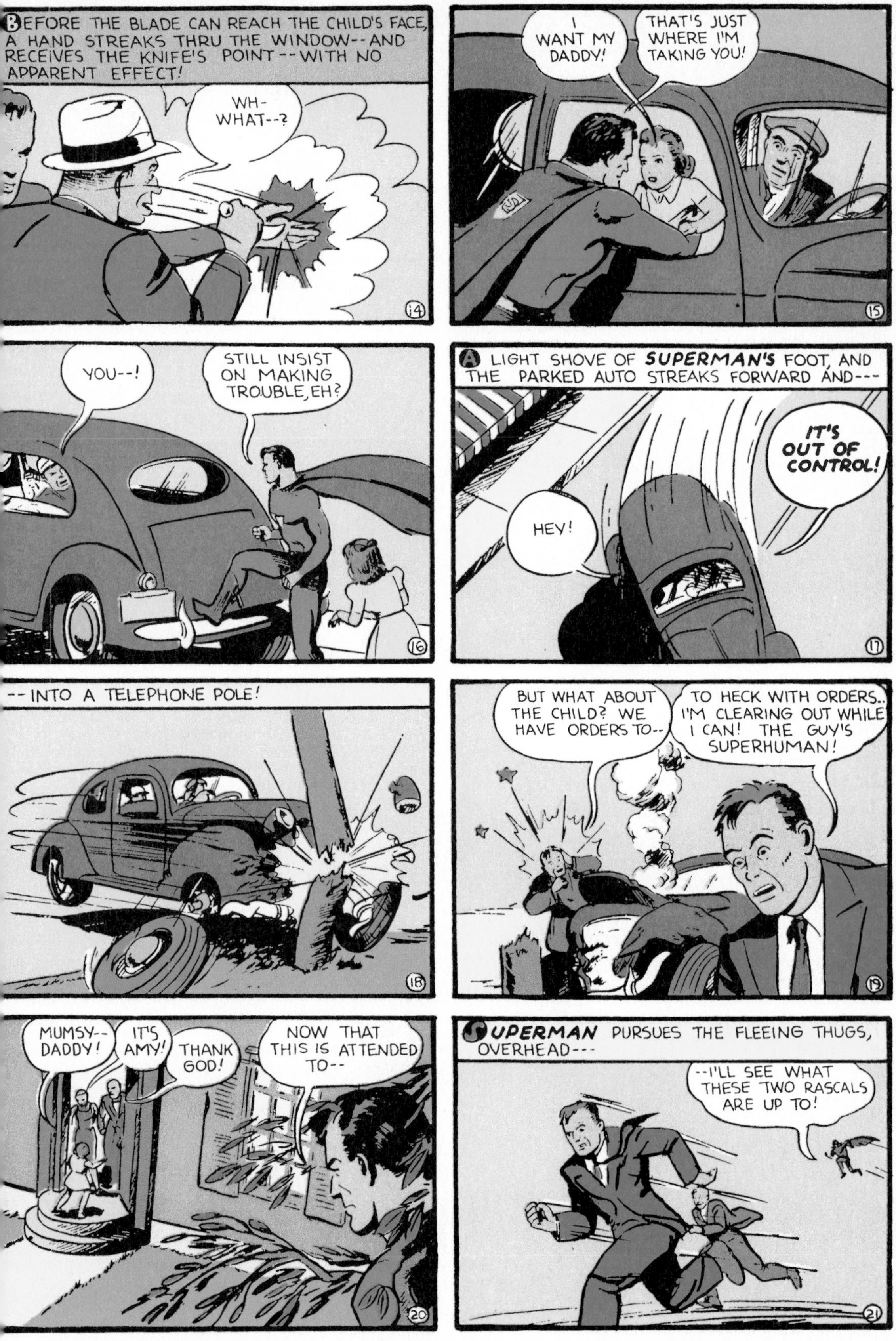
BEFORE THE BLADE CAN REACH THE CHILD'S FACE, A HAND STREAKS THRU THE WINDOW--AND RECEIVES THE KNIFE'S POINT--WITH NO APPARENT EFFECT!
WH-WHAT--?
14
I WANT MY DADDY!
THAT'S JUST WHERE I'M TAKING YOU!
15
YOU--!
STILL INSIST ON MAKING TROUBLE, EH?
16
A LIGHT SHOVE OF SUPERMAN'S FOOT, AND THE PARKED AUTO STREAKS FORWARD AND---
IT'S OUT OF CONTROL!
HEY!
17
--INTO A TELEPHONE POLE!
18
BUT WHAT ABOUT THE CHILD? WE HAVE ORDERS TO--
TO HECK WITH ORDERS.. I'M CLEARING OUT WHILE I CAN! THE GUY'S SUPERHUMAN!
19
MUMSY--DADDY!
IT'S AMY!
THANK GOD!
NOW THAT THIS IS ATTENDED TO--
20
SUPERMAN PURSUES THE FLEEING THUGS, OVERHEAD---
--I'LL SEE WHAT THESE TWO RASCALS ARE UP TO!
21

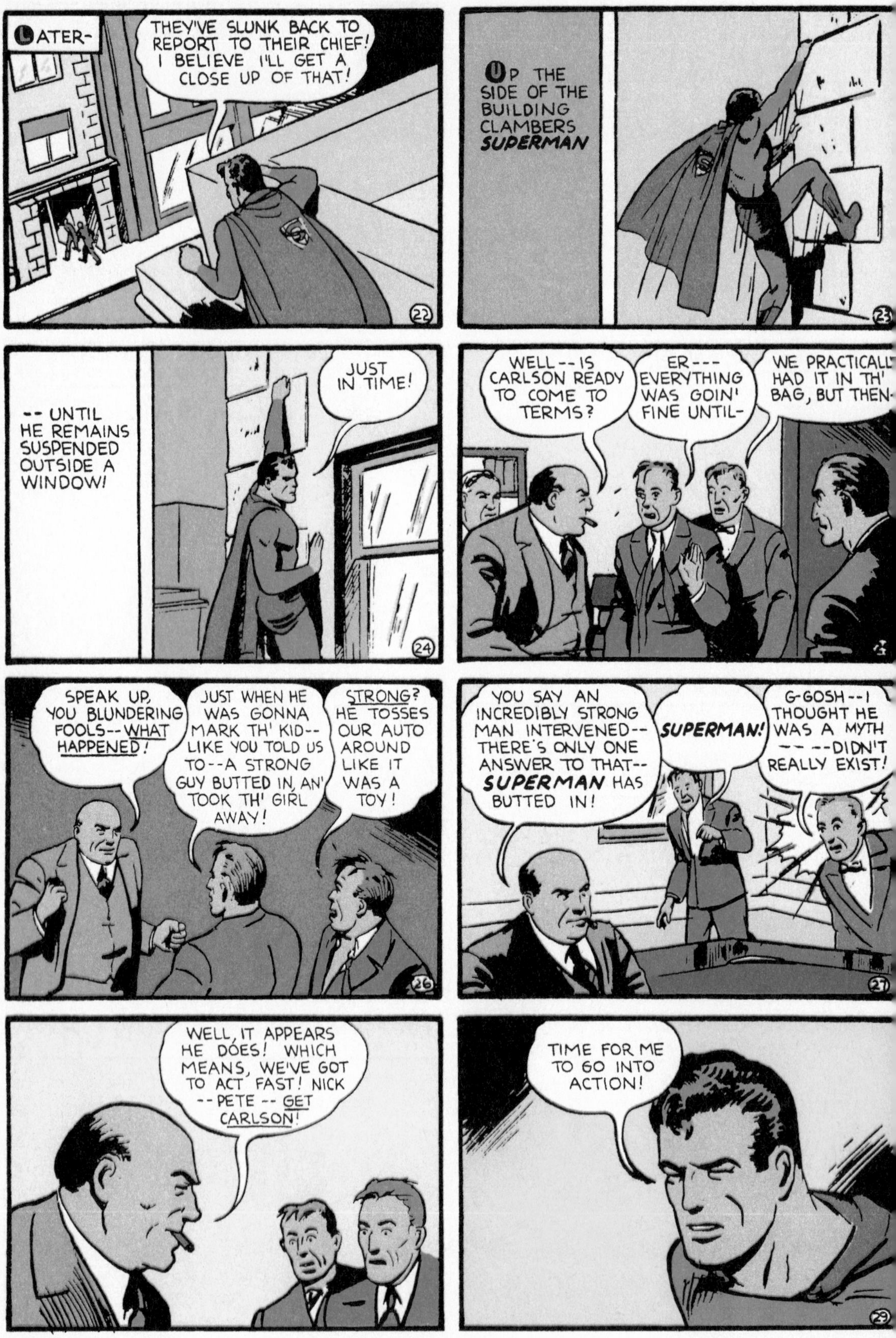
LATER-
THEY'VE SLUNK BACK TO REPORT TO THEIR CHIEF! I BELIEVE I'LL GET A CLOSE UP OF THAT!
UP THE SIDE OF THE BUILDING CLAMBERS SUPERMAN
-- UNTIL HE REMAINS SUSPENDED OUTSIDE A WINDOW!
JUST IN TIME!
WELL -- IS CARLSON READY TO COME TO TERMS?
ER--- EVERYTHING WAS GOIN' FINE UNTIL-
WE PRACTICALL HAD IT IN TH' BAG, BUT THEN-
SPEAK UP, YOU BLUNDERING FOOLS-- WHAT HAPPENED!
JUST WHEN HE WAS GONNA MARK TH' KID-- LIKE YOU TOLD US TO--A STRONG GUY BUTTED IN, AN' TOOK TH' GIRL AWAY!
STRONG? HE TOSSES OUR AUTO AROUND LIKE IT WAS A TOY!
YOU SAY AN INCREDIBLY STRONG MAN INTERVENED-- THERE'S ONLY ONE ANSWER TO THAT-- SUPERMAN HAS BUTTED IN!
SUPERMAN!
G-GOSH--I THOUGHT HE WAS A MYTH -- --DIDN'T REALLY EXIST!
WELL, IT APPEARS HE DOES! WHICH MEANS, WE'VE GOT TO ACT FAST! NICK --PETE -- GET CARLSON!
TIME FOR ME TO GO INTO ACTION!

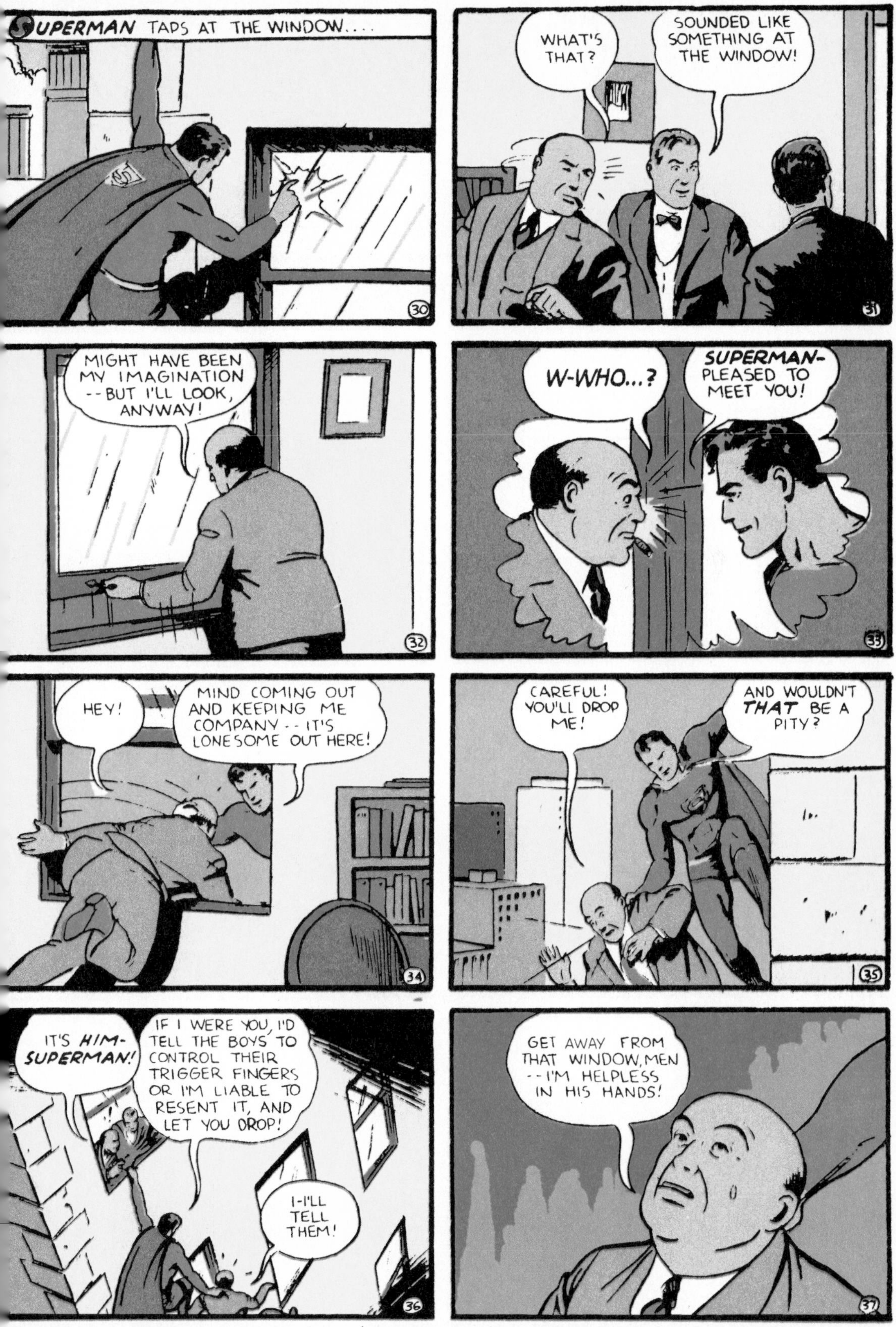
SUPERMAN TAPS AT THE WINDOW....
WHAT'S THAT?
SOUNDED LIKE SOMETHING AT THE WINDOW!
MIGHT HAVE BEEN MY IMAGINATION --BUT I'LL LOOK, ANYWAY!
W-WHO...?
SUPERMAN- PLEASED TO MEET YOU!
HEY!
MIND COMING OUT AND KEEPING ME COMPANY--IT'S LONESOME OUT HERE!
CAREFUL! YOU'LL DROP ME!
AND WOULDN'T THAT BE A PITY?
IT'S HIM- SUPERMAN!
IF I WERE YOU, I'D TELL THE BOYS TO CONTROL THEIR TRIGGER FINGERS OR I'M LIABLE TO RESENT IT, AND LET YOU DROP!
I-I'LL TELL THEM!
GET AWAY FROM THAT WINDOW, MEN --I'M HELPLESS IN HIS HANDS!

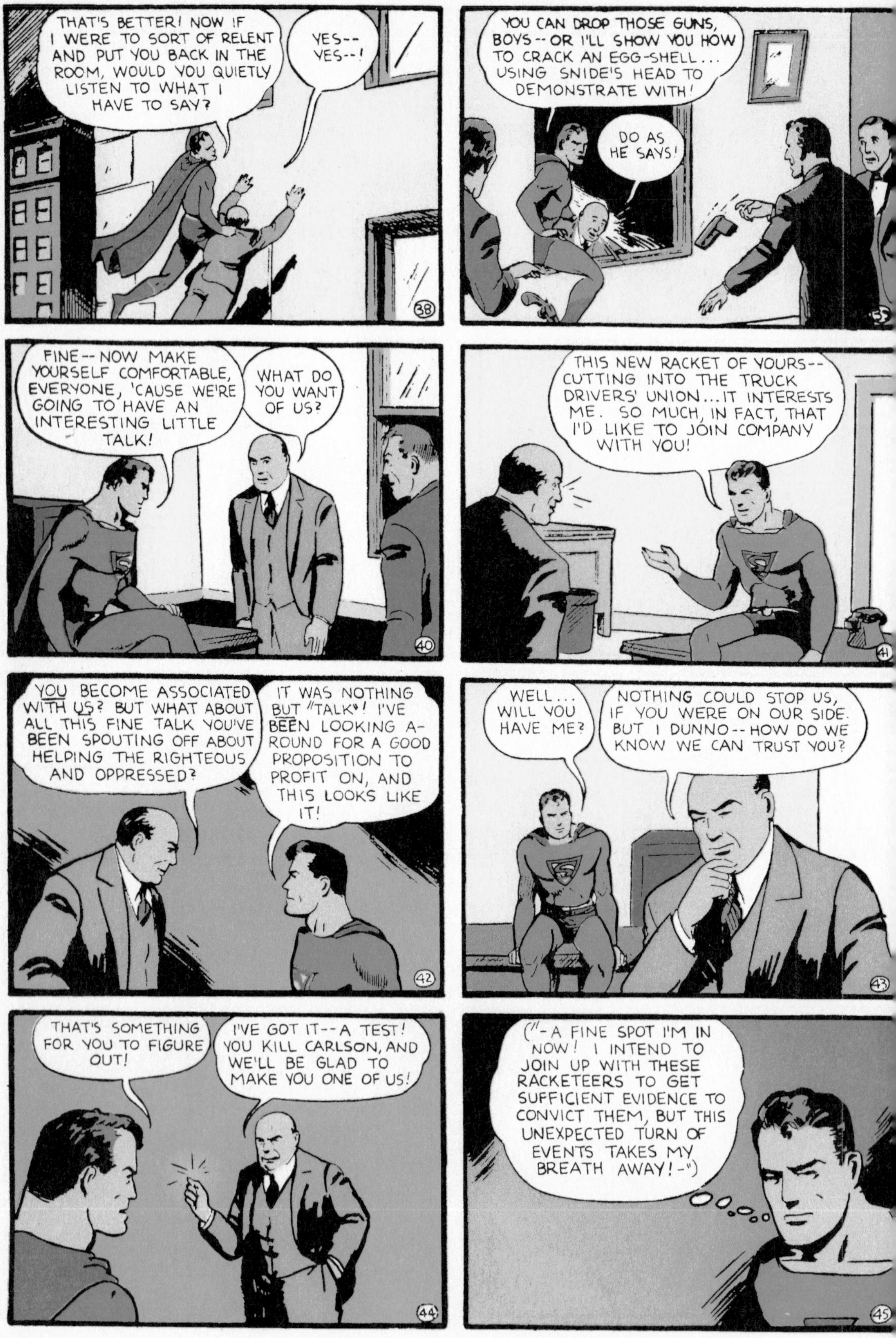
THAT'S BETTER! NOW IF I WERE TO SORT OF RELENT AND PUT YOU BACK IN THE ROOM, WOULD YOU QUIETLY LISTEN TO WHAT I HAVE TO SAY?
YES-- YES--!
YOU CAN DROP THOSE GUNS, BOYS -- OR I'LL SHOW YOU HOW TO CRACK AN EGG-SHELL... USING SNIDE'S HEAD TO DEMONSTRATE WITH!
DO AS HE SAYS!
FINE-- NOW MAKE YOURSELF COMFORTABLE, EVERYONE, 'CAUSE WE'RE GOING TO HAVE AN INTERESTING LITTLE TALK!
WHAT DO YOU WANT OF US?
THIS NEW RACKET OF YOURS-- CUTTING INTO THE TRUCK DRIVERS' UNION... IT INTERESTS ME. SO MUCH, IN FACT, THAT I'D LIKE TO JOIN COMPANY WITH YOU!
YOU BECOME ASSOCIATED WITH US? BUT WHAT ABOUT ALL THIS FINE TALK YOU'VE BEEN SPOUTING OFF ABOUT HELPING THE RIGHTEOUS AND OPPRESSED?
IT WAS NOTHING BUT "TALK"! I'VE BEEN LOOKING A-ROUND FOR A GOOD PROPOSITION TO PROFIT ON, AND THIS LOOKS LIKE IT!
WELL... WILL YOU HAVE ME?
NOTHING COULD STOP US, IF YOU WERE ON OUR SIDE. BUT I DUNNO-- HOW DO WE KNOW WE CAN TRUST YOU?
THAT'S SOMETHING FOR YOU TO FIGURE OUT!
I'VE GOT IT-- A TEST! YOU KILL CARLSON, AND WE'LL BE GLAD TO MAKE YOU ONE OF US!
("-A FINE SPOT I'M IN NOW! I INTEND TO JOIN UP WITH THESE RACKETEERS TO GET SUFFICIENT EVIDENCE TO CONVICT THEM, BUT THIS UNEXPECTED TURN OF EVENTS TAKES MY BREATH AWAY!-")

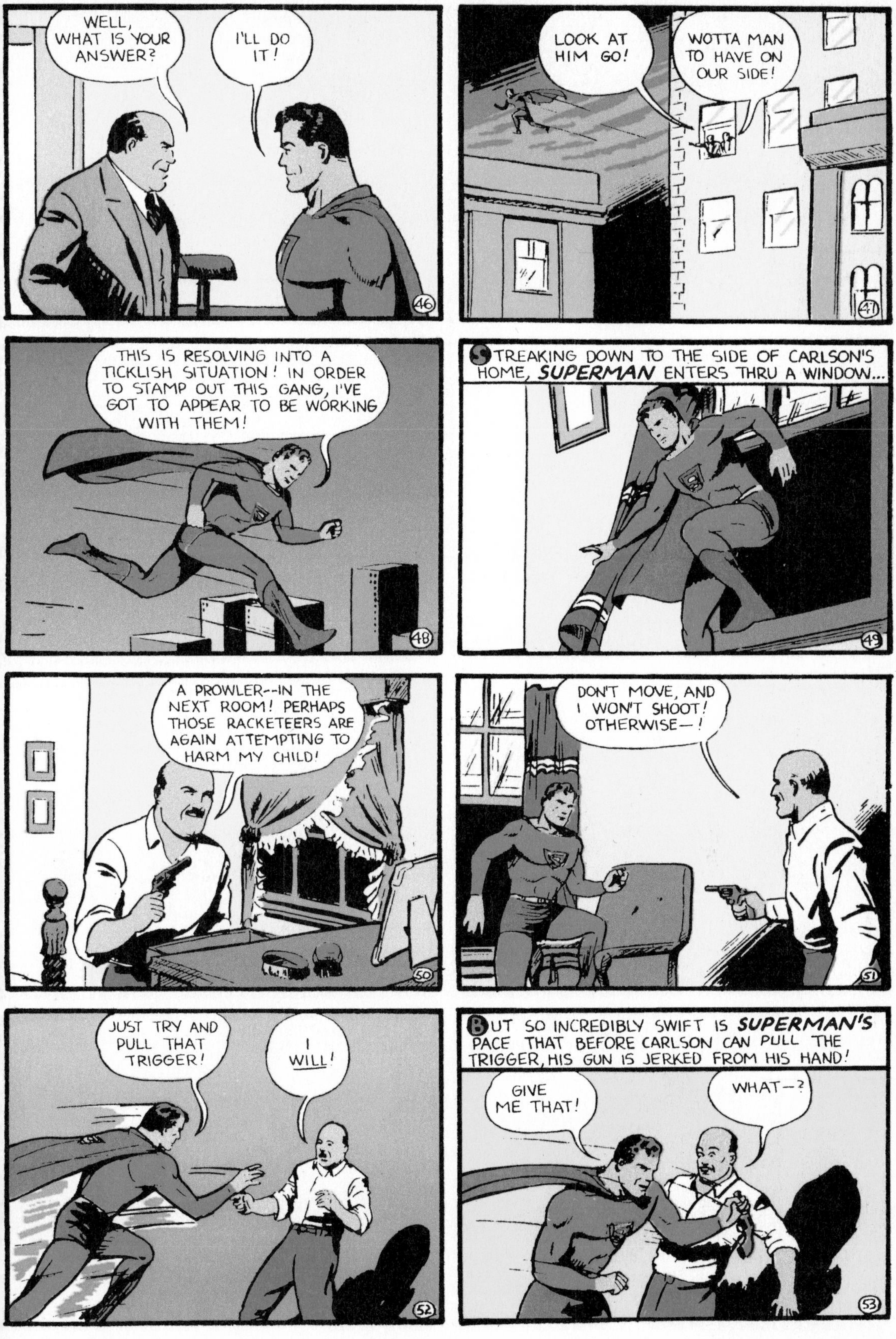

WELL, WHAT IS YOUR ANSWER?
I'LL DO IT!
46
LOOK AT HIM GO!
WOTTA MAN TO HAVE ON OUR SIDE!
47
THIS IS RESOLVING INTO A TICKLISH SITUATION! IN ORDER TO STAMP OUT THIS GANG, I'VE GOT TO APPEAR TO BE WORKING WITH THEM!
48
STREAKING DOWN TO THE SIDE OF CARLSON'S HOME, SUPERMAN ENTERS THRU A WINDOW...
49
A PROWLER--IN THE NEXT ROOM! PERHAPS THOSE RACKETEERS ARE AGAIN ATTEMPTING TO HARM MY CHILD!
50
DON'T MOVE, AND I WON'T SHOOT! OTHERWISE—!
51
JUST TRY AND PULL THAT TRIGGER!
I WILL!
52
BUT SO INCREDIBLY SWIFT IS SUPERMAN'S PACE THAT BEFORE CARLSON CAN PULL THE TRIGGER, HIS GUN IS JERKED FROM HIS HAND!
GIVE ME THAT!
WHAT—?
53

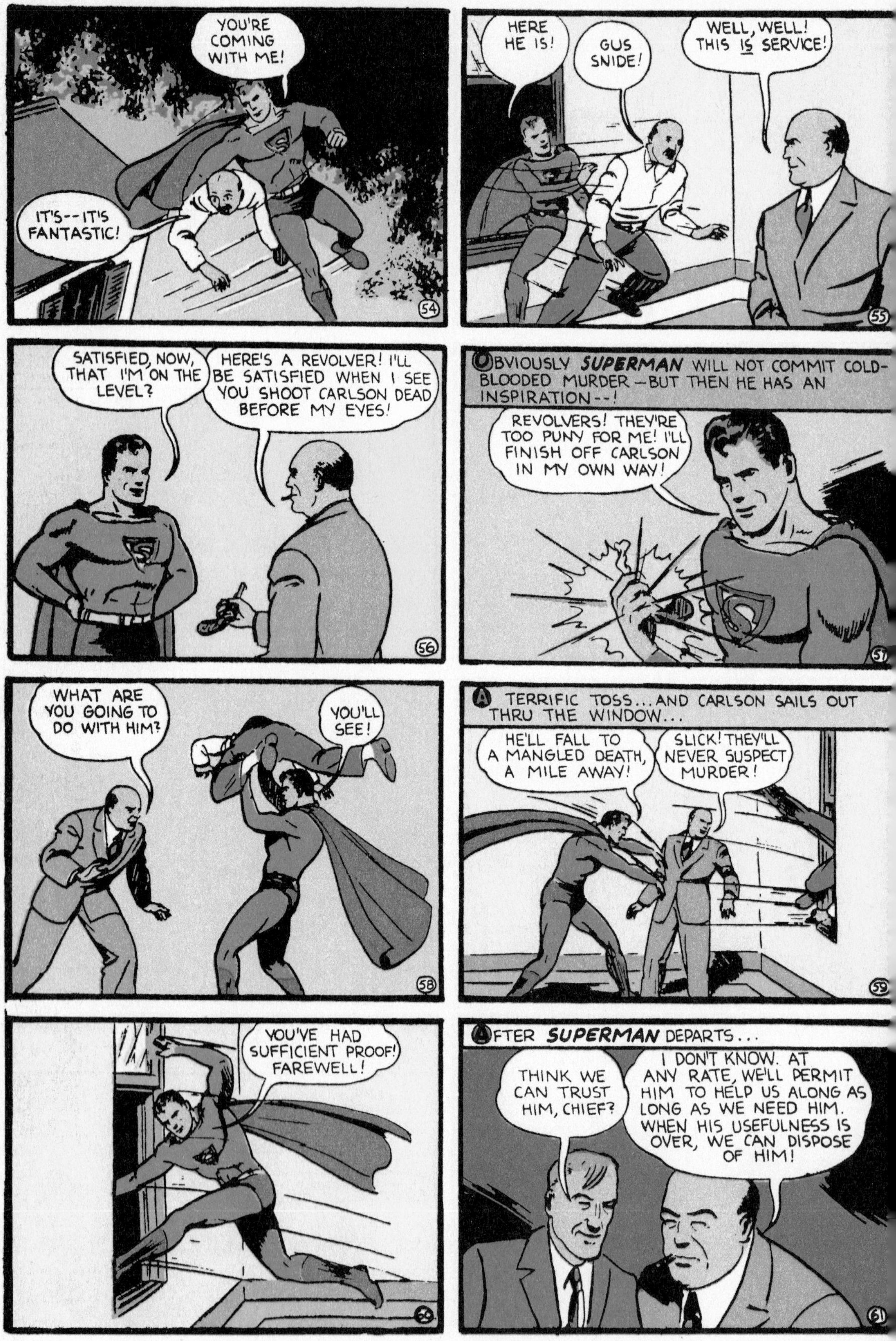
YOU'RE COMING WITH ME!
IT'S--IT'S FANTASTIC!
HERE HE IS!
GUS SNIDE!
WELL, WELL! THIS IS SERVICE!
SATISFIED, NOW, THAT I'M ON THE LEVEL?
HERE'S A REVOLVER! I'LL BE SATISFIED WHEN I SEE YOU SHOOT CARLSON DEAD BEFORE MY EYES!
OBVIOUSLY SUPERMAN WILL NOT COMMIT COLD-BLOODED MURDER—BUT THEN HE HAS AN INSPIRATION--!
REVOLVERS! THEY'RE TOO PUNY FOR ME! I'LL FINISH OFF CARLSON IN MY OWN WAY!
WHAT ARE YOU GOING TO DO WITH HIM?
YOU'LL SEE!
A TERRIFIC TOSS...AND CARLSON SAILS OUT THRU THE WINDOW...
HE'LL FALL TO A MANGLED DEATH, A MILE AWAY!
SLICK! THEY'LL NEVER SUSPECT MURDER!
YOU'VE HAD SUFFICIENT PROOF! FAREWELL!
AFTER SUPERMAN DEPARTS...
THINK WE CAN TRUST HIM, CHIEF?
I DON'T KNOW. AT ANY RATE, WE'LL PERMIT HIM TO HELP US ALONG AS LONG AS WE NEED HIM. WHEN HIS USEFULNESS IS OVER, WE CAN DISPOSE OF HIM!

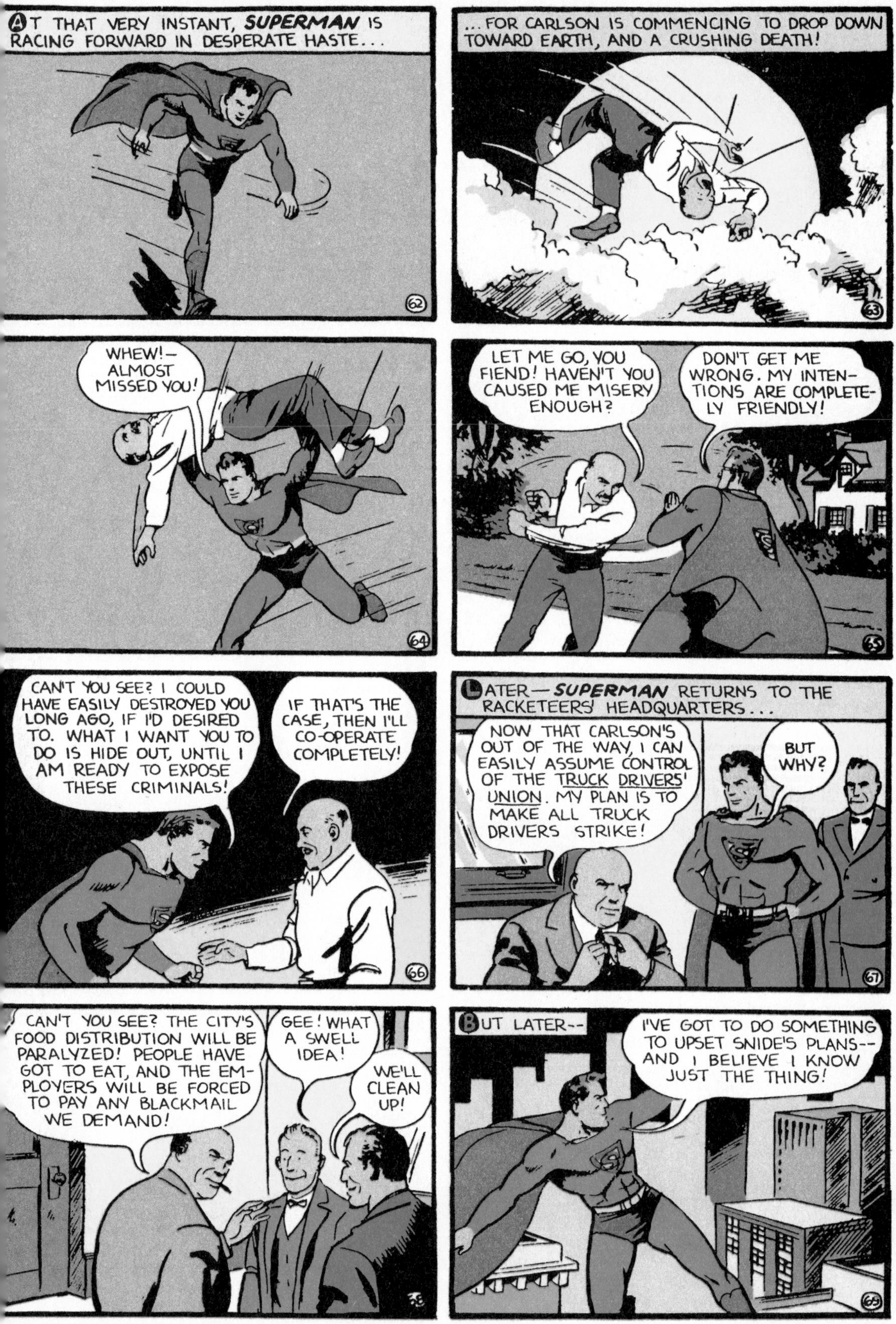
AT THAT VERY INSTANT, SUPERMAN IS RACING FORWARD IN DESPERATE HASTE...
62
...FOR CARLSON IS COMMENCING TO DROP DOWN TOWARD EARTH, AND A CRUSHING DEATH!
63
WHEW!— ALMOST MISSED YOU!
64
LET ME GO, YOU FIEND! HAVEN'T YOU CAUSED ME MISERY ENOUGH?
DON'T GET ME WRONG. MY INTENTIONS ARE COMPLETELY FRIENDLY!
65
CAN'T YOU SEE? I COULD HAVE EASILY DESTROYED YOU LONG AGO, IF I'D DESIRED TO. WHAT I WANT YOU TO DO IS HIDE OUT, UNTIL I AM READY TO EXPOSE THESE CRIMINALS!
IF THAT'S THE CASE, THEN I'LL CO-OPERATE COMPLETELY!
66
LATER—SUPERMAN RETURNS TO THE RACKETEERS' HEADQUARTERS...
NOW THAT CARLSON'S OUT OF THE WAY, I CAN EASILY ASSUME CONTROL OF THE TRUCK DRIVERS' UNION. MY PLAN IS TO MAKE ALL TRUCK DRIVERS STRIKE!
BUT WHY?
67
CAN'T YOU SEE? THE CITY'S FOOD DISTRIBUTION WILL BE PARALYZED! PEOPLE HAVE GOT TO EAT, AND THE EMPLOYERS WILL BE FORCED TO PAY ANY BLACKMAIL WE DEMAND!
GEE! WHAT A SWELL IDEA!
WE'LL CLEAN UP!
68
BUT LATER--
I'VE GOT TO DO SOMETHING TO UPSET SNIDE'S PLANS-- AND I BELIEVE I KNOW JUST THE THING!
69

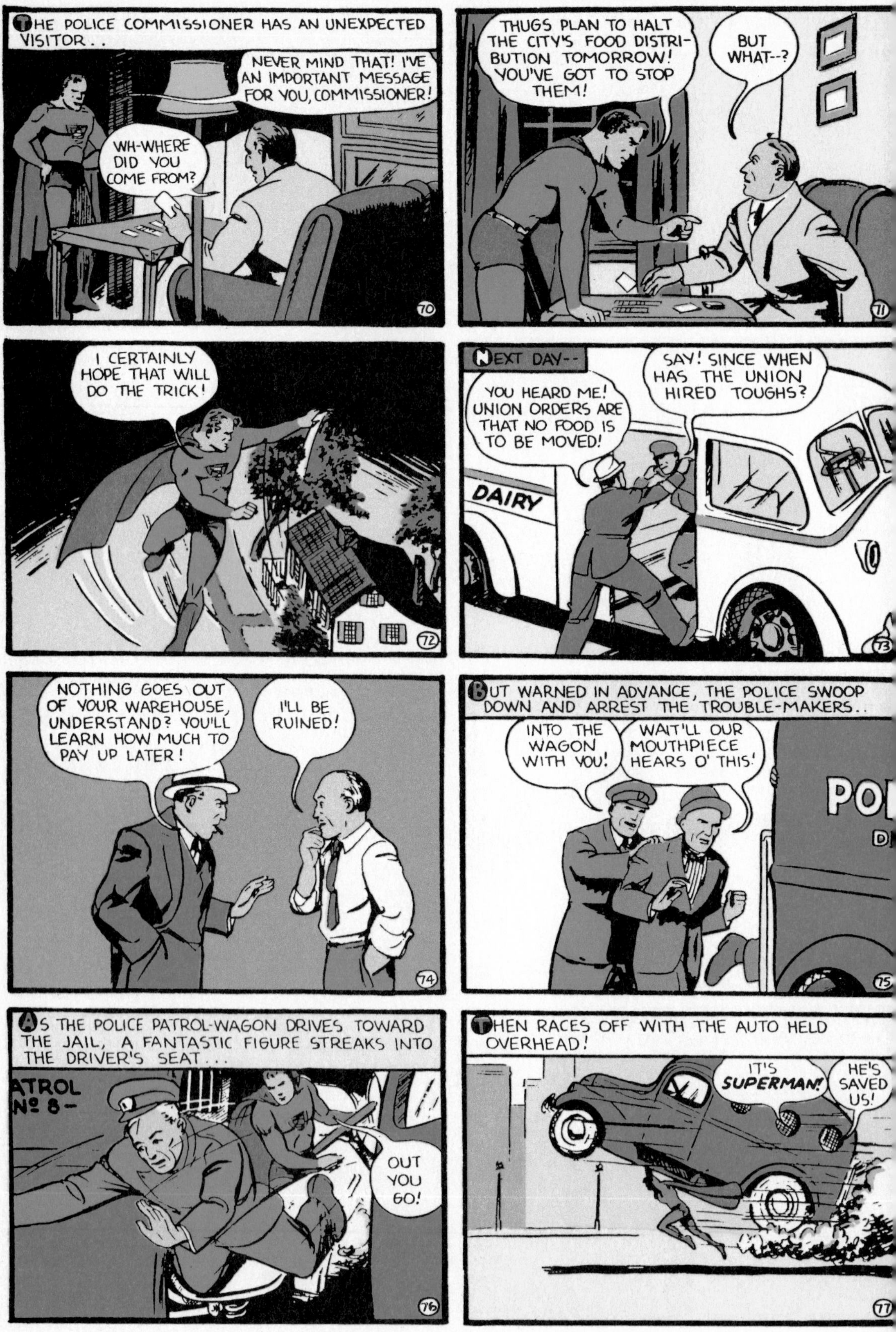
THE POLICE COMMISSIONER HAS AN UNEXPECTED VISITOR . .
NEVER MIND THAT! I'VE AN IMPORTANT MESSAGE FOR YOU, COMMISSIONER!
WH-WHERE DID YOU COME FROM?
70
THUGS PLAN TO HALT THE CITY'S FOOD DISTRIBUTION TOMORROW! YOU'VE GOT TO STOP THEM!
BUT WHAT--?
71
I CERTAINLY HOPE THAT WILL DO THE TRICK!
72
NEXT DAY--
SAY! SINCE WHEN HAS THE UNION HIRED TOUGHS?
YOU HEARD ME! UNION ORDERS ARE THAT NO FOOD IS TO BE MOVED!
DAIRY
73
NOTHING GOES OUT OF YOUR WAREHOUSE, UNDERSTAND? YOU'LL LEARN HOW MUCH TO PAY UP LATER!
I'LL BE RUINED!
74
BUT WARNED IN ADVANCE, THE POLICE SWOOP DOWN AND ARREST THE TROUBLE-MAKERS . .
INTO THE WAGON WITH YOU!
WAIT'LL OUR MOUTHPIECE HEARS O' THIS!
75
AS THE POLICE PATROL-WAGON DRIVES TOWARD THE JAIL, A FANTASTIC FIGURE STREAKS INTO THE DRIVER'S SEAT . . .
ATROL
Nº 8 -
OUT YOU GO!
76
THEN RACES OFF WITH THE AUTO HELD OVERHEAD!
IT'S SUPERMAN!
HE'S SAVED US!
77

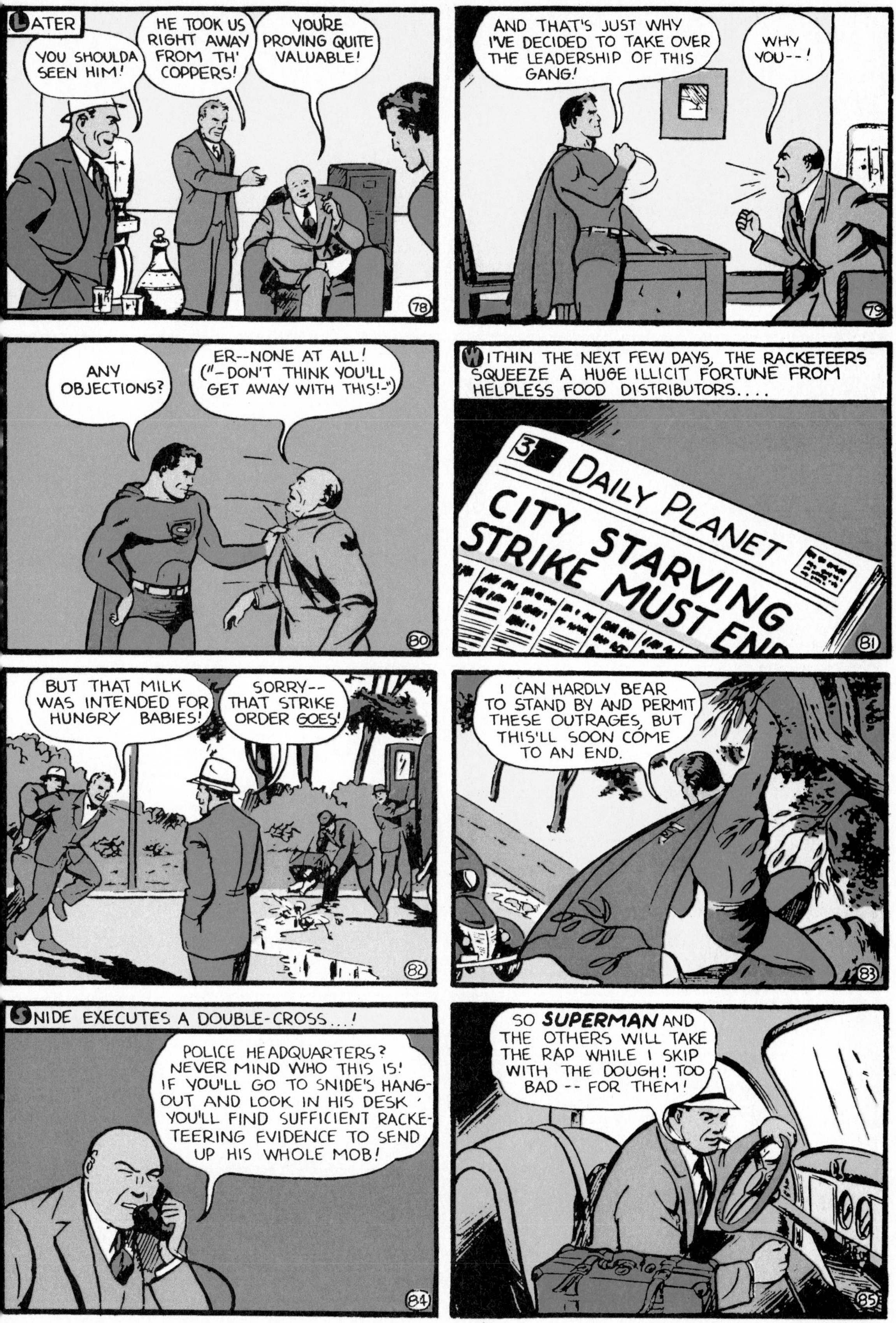
LATER
YOU SHOULDA SEEN HIM!
HE TOOK US RIGHT AWAY FROM TH' COPPERS!
YOU'RE PROVING QUITE VALUABLE!
78
AND THAT'S JUST WHY I'VE DECIDED TO TAKE OVER THE LEADERSHIP OF THIS GANG!
WHY YOU--!
79
ANY OBJECTIONS?
ER--NONE AT ALL! ("-DON'T THINK YOU'LL GET AWAY WITH THIS!-")
80
WITHIN THE NEXT FEW DAYS, THE RACKETEERS SQUEEZE A HUGE ILLICIT FORTUNE FROM HELPLESS FOOD DISTRIBUTORS....
DAILY PLANET
CITY STARVING
STRIKE MUST END
81
BUT THAT MILK WAS INTENDED FOR HUNGRY BABIES!
SORRY-- THAT STRIKE ORDER GOES!
82
I CAN HARDLY BEAR TO STAND BY AND PERMIT THESE OUTRAGES, BUT THIS'LL SOON COME TO AN END.
83
SNIDE EXECUTES A DOUBLE-CROSS...!
POLICE HEADQUARTERS? NEVER MIND WHO THIS IS! IF YOU'LL GO TO SNIDE'S HANG-OUT AND LOOK IN HIS DESK YOU'LL FIND SUFFICIENT RACKETEERING EVIDENCE TO SEND UP HIS WHOLE MOB!
84
SO SUPERMAN AND THE OTHERS WILL TAKE THE RAP WHILE I SKIP WITH THE DOUGH! TOO BAD -- FOR THEM!
85

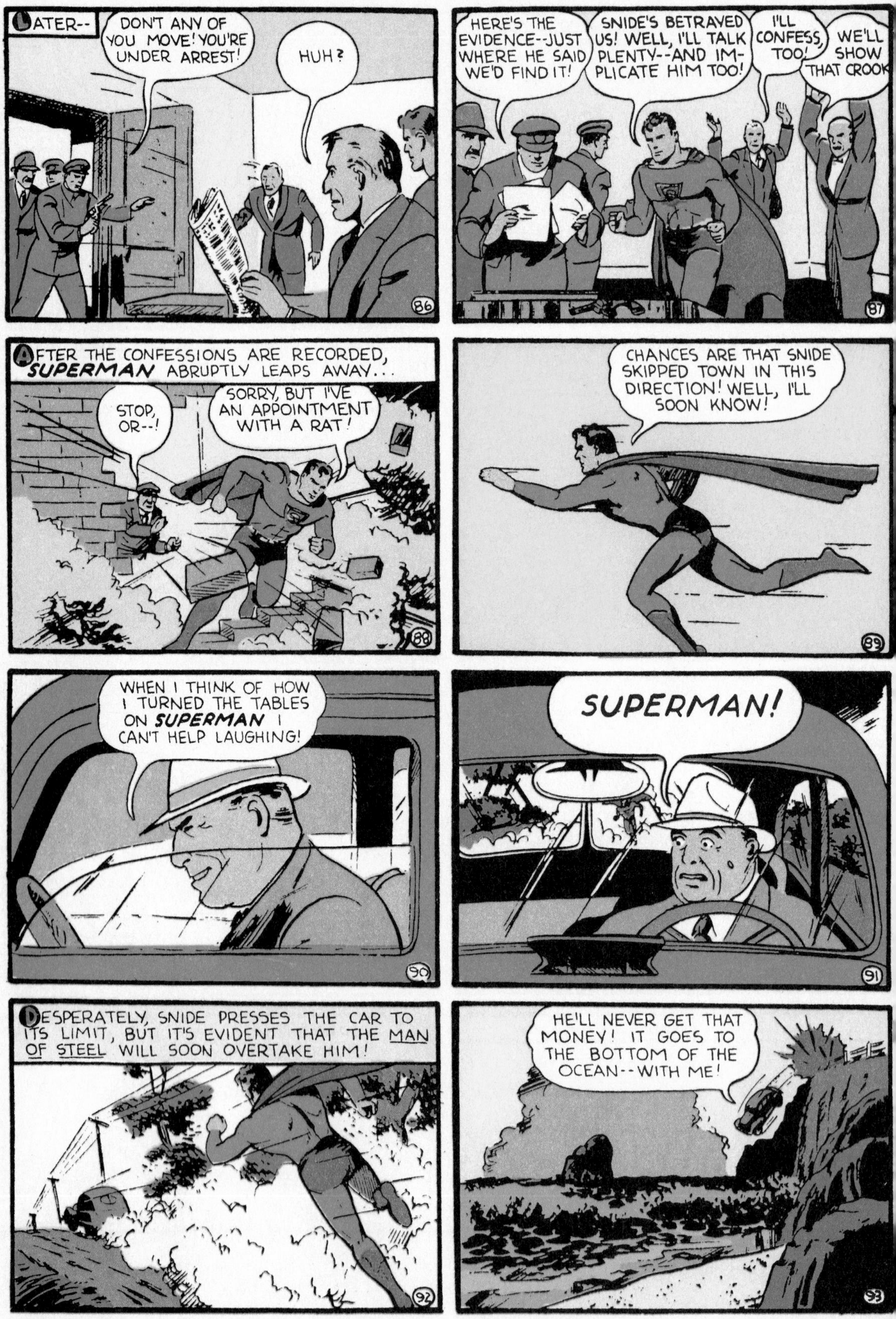
LATER--
DON'T ANY OF YOU MOVE! YOU'RE UNDER ARREST!
HUH?
HERE'S THE EVIDENCE--JUST WHERE HE SAID WE'D FIND IT!
SNIDE'S BETRAYED US! WELL, I'LL TALK PLENTY--AND IMPLICATE HIM TOO!
I'LL CONFESS, TOO!
WE'LL SHOW THAT CROOK
AFTER THE CONFESSIONS ARE RECORDED, SUPERMAN ABRUPTLY LEAPS AWAY...
STOP, OR--!
SORRY, BUT I'VE AN APPOINTMENT WITH A RAT!
CHANCES ARE THAT SNIDE SKIPPED TOWN IN THIS DIRECTION! WELL, I'LL SOON KNOW!
WHEN I THINK OF HOW I TURNED THE TABLES ON SUPERMAN I CAN'T HELP LAUGHING!
SUPERMAN!
DESPERATELY, SNIDE PRESSES THE CAR TO ITS LIMIT, BUT IT'S EVIDENT THAT THE MAN OF STEEL WILL SOON OVERTAKE HIM!
HE'LL NEVER GET THAT MONEY! IT GOES TO THE BOTTOM OF THE OCEAN--WITH ME!

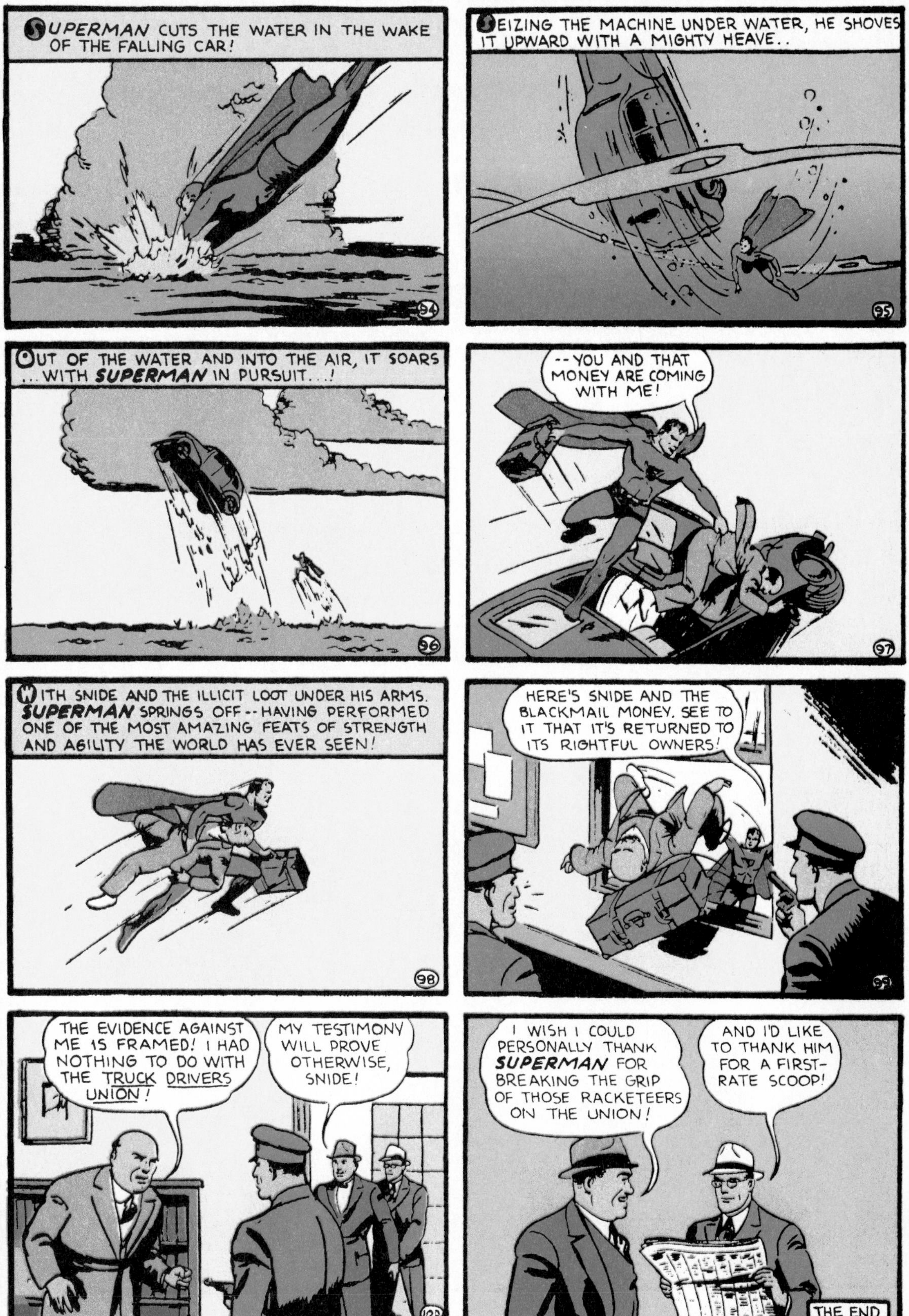
SUPERMAN CUTS THE WATER IN THE WAKE OF THE FALLING CAR!
SEIZING THE MACHINE UNDER WATER, HE SHOVES IT UPWARD WITH A MIGHTY HEAVE..
OUT OF THE WATER AND INTO THE AIR, IT SOARS ...WITH SUPERMAN IN PURSUIT...!
--YOU AND THAT MONEY ARE COMING WITH ME!
WITH SNIDE AND THE ILLICIT LOOT UNDER HIS ARMS, SUPERMAN SPRINGS OFF--HAVING PERFORMED ONE OF THE MOST AMAZING FEATS OF STRENGTH AND AGILITY THE WORLD HAS EVER SEEN!
HERE'S SNIDE AND THE BLACKMAIL MONEY. SEE TO IT THAT IT'S RETURNED TO ITS RIGHTFUL OWNERS!
THE EVIDENCE AGAINST ME IS FRAMED! I HAD NOTHING TO DO WITH THE TRUCK DRIVERS UNION!
MY TESTIMONY WILL PROVE OTHERWISE, SNIDE!
I WISH I COULD PERSONALLY THANK SUPERMAN FOR BREAKING THE GRIP OF THOSE RACKETEERS ON THE UNION!
AND I'D LIKE TO THANK HIM FOR A FIRST-RATE SCOOP!
THE END

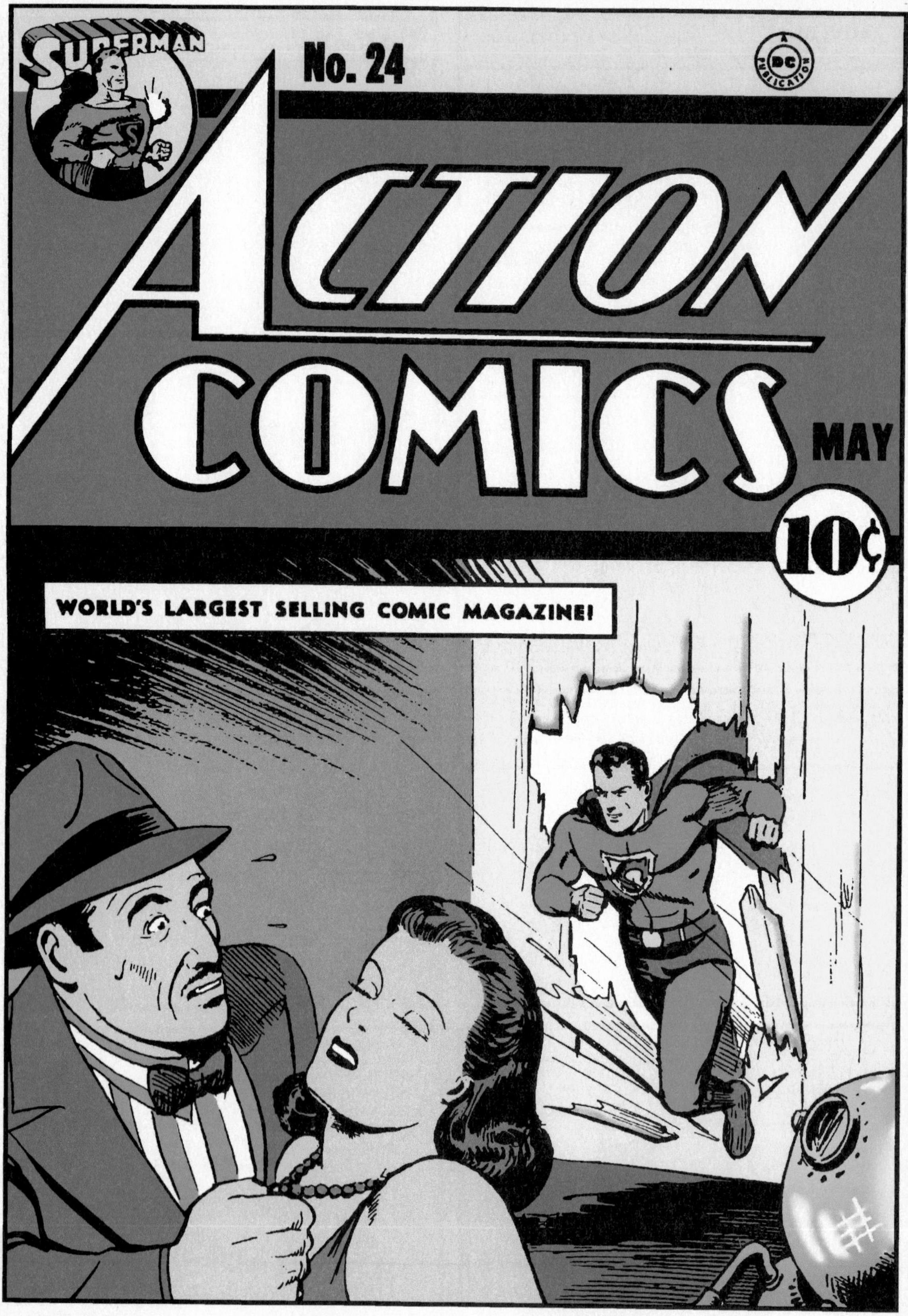
SUPERMAN
No. 24
A DC PUBLICATION
ACTION COMICS
MAY
10¢
WORLD'S LARGEST SELLING COMIC MAGAZINE!

SUPERMAN

by JERRY SIEGEL and JOE SHUSTER

LEAPING OVER SKYSCRAPERS, RUNNING FASTER THAN AN EXPRESS TRAIN, SPRINGING GREAT DISTANCES AND HEIGHTS, LIFTING AND SMASHING TREMENDOUS WEIGHTS, POSSESSING AN IMPENETRABLE SKIN--- THESE ARE THE AMAZING ATTRIBUTES WHICH *SUPERMAN*, SAVIOR OF THE HELP- LESS AND OPPRESSED, AVAILS HIMSELF OF AS HE BATTLES THE FORCES OF EVIL AND INJUSTICE!

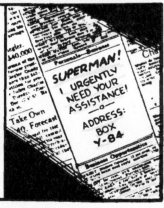

WITHIN THE PAGES OF EVERY METROPO- LIS NEWSPAPER THERE APPEARS A STARTLING ADVERTISEMENT...

SUPERMAN! I URGENTLY NEED YOUR ASSISTANCE! —o— ADDRESS: BOX Y-84

I'LL BET THERE'S A HUMDINGER OF A STORY BEHIND THAT AD!

I SHOULD SAY THERE IS! IT WAS PLACED BY ONE OF THE WEALTHIEST MEN IN THIS TOWN: RUFUS CARNAHAN, A RETIRED INDUSTRIALIST. HURRY DOWN TO HIS PLACE AND TRY TO DIG UP SOME- THING IN TIME FOR THE AFTERNOON EDITION!

③

LATER, WHEN CLARK REACHES THE HUGE CARNAHAN MANSION...

YOUR BUSINESS, SIR? MR CARNAHAN IS RATHER INDISPOSED AND CANNOT SEE EVERYONE!

WELL, HE'LL SEE ME. I'M A REPORTER FROM THE *DAILY PLANET*. I CAME ABOUT...

④

- AND STAY OUT! NO REPORTERS WANTED!

CORDIAL CUSS, AREN'T YOU?

⑤

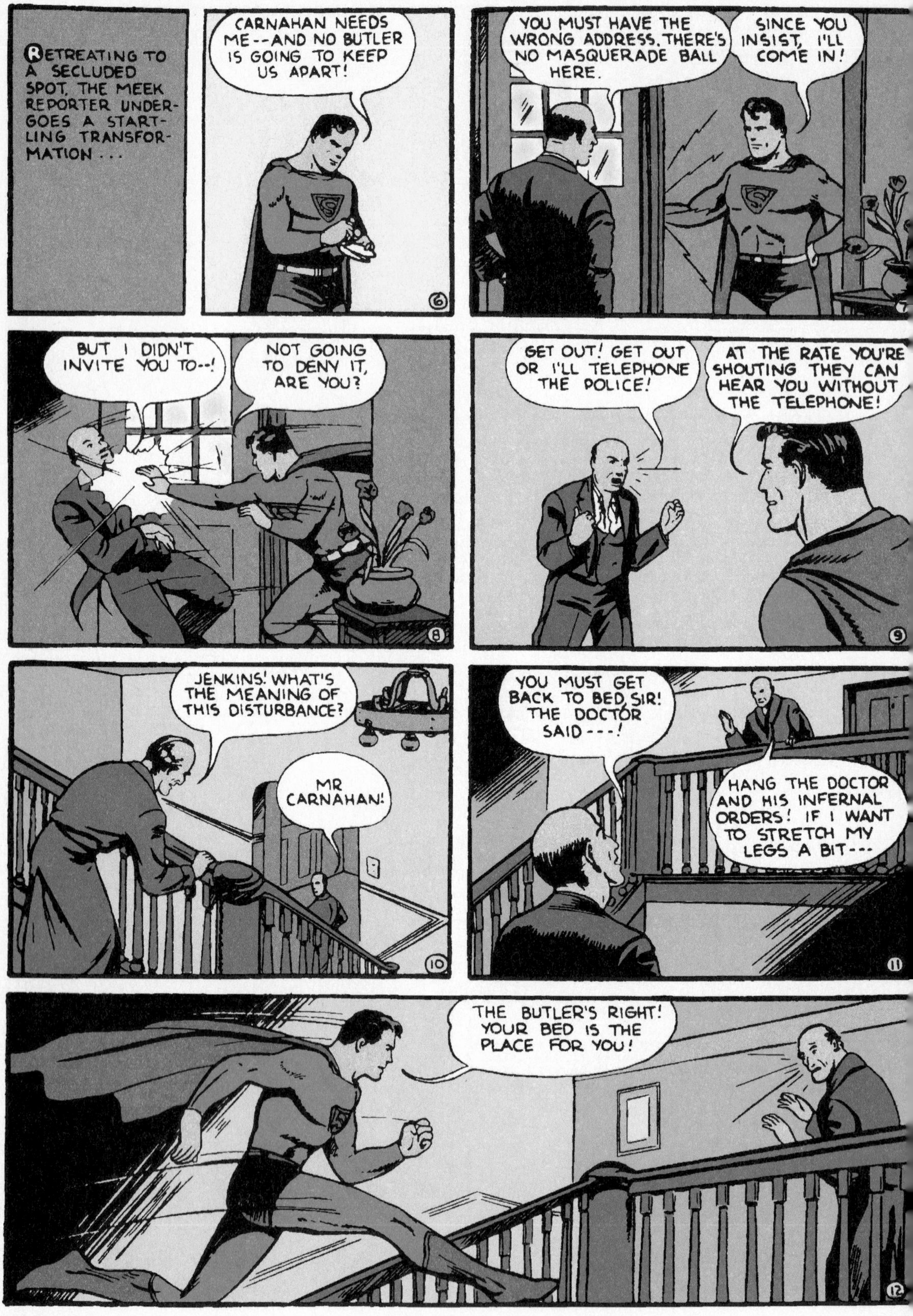
RETREATING TO A SECLUDED SPOT, THE MEEK REPORTER UNDERGOES A STARTLING TRANSFORMATION . . .
CARNAHAN NEEDS ME--AND NO BUTLER IS GOING TO KEEP US APART!
6
YOU MUST HAVE THE WRONG ADDRESS. THERE'S NO MASQUERADE BALL HERE.
SINCE YOU INSIST, I'LL COME IN!
7
BUT I DIDN'T INVITE YOU TO--!
NOT GOING TO DENY IT, ARE YOU?
8
GET OUT! GET OUT OR I'LL TELEPHONE THE POLICE!
AT THE RATE YOU'RE SHOUTING THEY CAN HEAR YOU WITHOUT THE TELEPHONE!
9
JENKINS! WHAT'S THE MEANING OF THIS DISTURBANCE?
MR CARNAHAN!
10
YOU MUST GET BACK TO BED, SIR! THE DOCTOR SAID---!
HANG THE DOCTOR AND HIS INFERNAL ORDERS! IF I WANT TO STRETCH MY LEGS A BIT---
11
THE BUTLER'S RIGHT! YOUR BED IS THE PLACE FOR YOU!
12

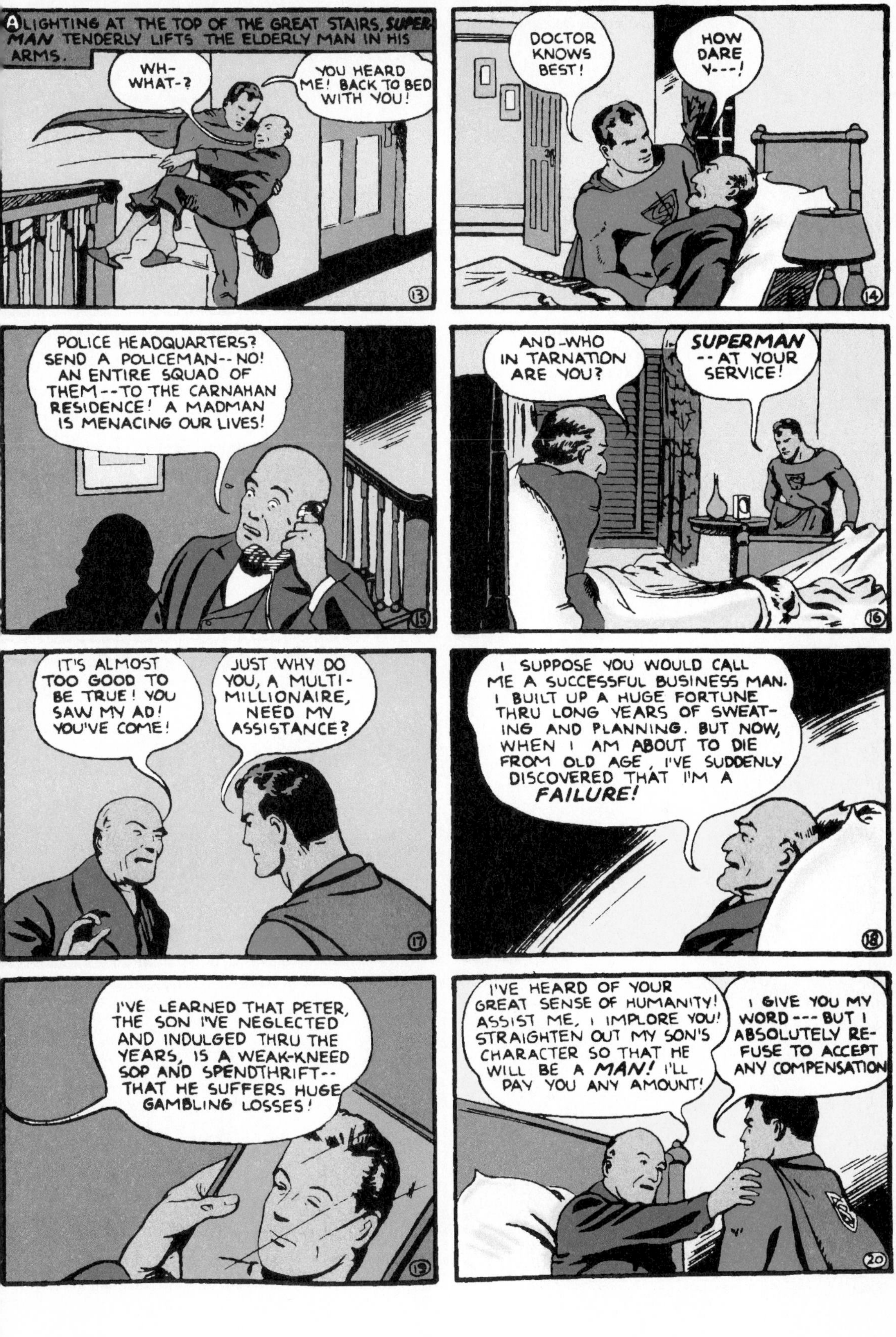
A LIGHTING AT THE TOP OF THE GREAT STAIRS, SUPERMAN TENDERLY LIFTS THE ELDERLY MAN IN HIS ARMS.
WH- WHAT-?
YOU HEARD ME! BACK TO BED WITH YOU!
13
DOCTOR KNOWS BEST!
HOW DARE Y---!
14
POLICE HEADQUARTERS? SEND A POLICEMAN--NO! AN ENTIRE SQUAD OF THEM--TO THE CARNAHAN RESIDENCE! A MADMAN IS MENACING OUR LIVES!
15
AND-WHO IN TARNATION ARE YOU?
SUPERMAN --AT YOUR SERVICE!
16
IT'S ALMOST TOO GOOD TO BE TRUE! YOU SAW MY AD! YOU'VE COME!
JUST WHY DO YOU, A MULTI-MILLIONAIRE, NEED MY ASSISTANCE?
17
I SUPPOSE YOU WOULD CALL ME A SUCCESSFUL BUSINESS MAN. I BUILT UP A HUGE FORTUNE THRU LONG YEARS OF SWEATING AND PLANNING. BUT NOW, WHEN I AM ABOUT TO DIE FROM OLD AGE, I'VE SUDDENLY DISCOVERED THAT I'M A FAILURE!
18
I'VE LEARNED THAT PETER, THE SON I'VE NEGLECTED AND INDULGED THRU THE YEARS, IS A WEAK-KNEED SOP AND SPENDTHRIFT--THAT HE SUFFERS HUGE GAMBLING LOSSES!
19
I'VE HEARD OF YOUR GREAT SENSE OF HUMANITY! ASSIST ME, I IMPLORE YOU! STRAIGHTEN OUT MY SON'S CHARACTER SO THAT HE WILL BE A MAN! I'LL PAY YOU ANY AMOUNT!
I GIVE YOU MY WORD---BUT I ABSOLUTELY REFUSE TO ACCEPT ANY COMPENSATION
20

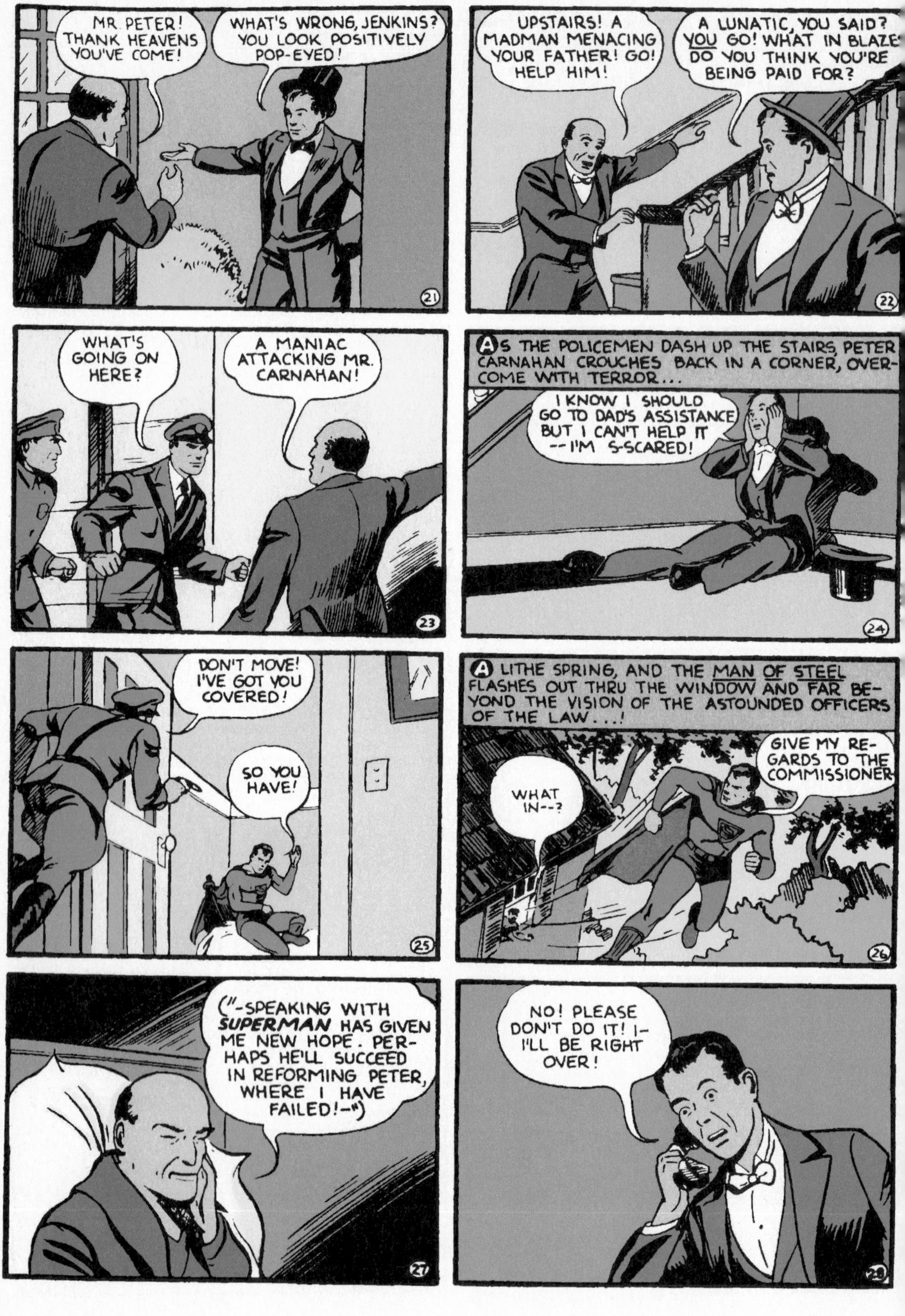
MR. PETER! THANK HEAVENS YOU'VE COME!
WHAT'S WRONG, JENKINS? YOU LOOK POSITIVELY POP-EYED!
21
UPSTAIRS! A MADMAN MENACING YOUR FATHER! GO! HELP HIM!
A LUNATIC, YOU SAID? YOU GO! WHAT IN BLAZE DO YOU THINK YOU'RE BEING PAID FOR?
22
WHAT'S GOING ON HERE?
A MANIAC ATTACKING MR. CARNAHAN!
23
AS THE POLICEMEN DASH UP THE STAIRS, PETER CARNAHAN CROUCHES BACK IN A CORNER, OVER-COME WITH TERROR...
I KNOW I SHOULD GO TO DAD'S ASSISTANCE BUT I CAN'T HELP IT --I'M S-SCARED!
24
DON'T MOVE! I'VE GOT YOU COVERED!
SO YOU HAVE!
25
A LITHE SPRING, AND THE MAN OF STEEL FLASHES OUT THRU THE WINDOW AND FAR BE-YOND THE VISION OF THE ASTOUNDED OFFICERS OF THE LAW...!
WHAT IN--?
GIVE MY RE-GARDS TO THE COMMISSIONER
26
("-SPEAKING WITH SUPERMAN HAS GIVEN ME NEW HOPE. PER-HAPS HE'LL SUCCEED IN REFORMING PETER, WHERE I HAVE FAILED!-")
27
NO! PLEASE DON'T DO IT! I-I'LL BE RIGHT OVER!
28

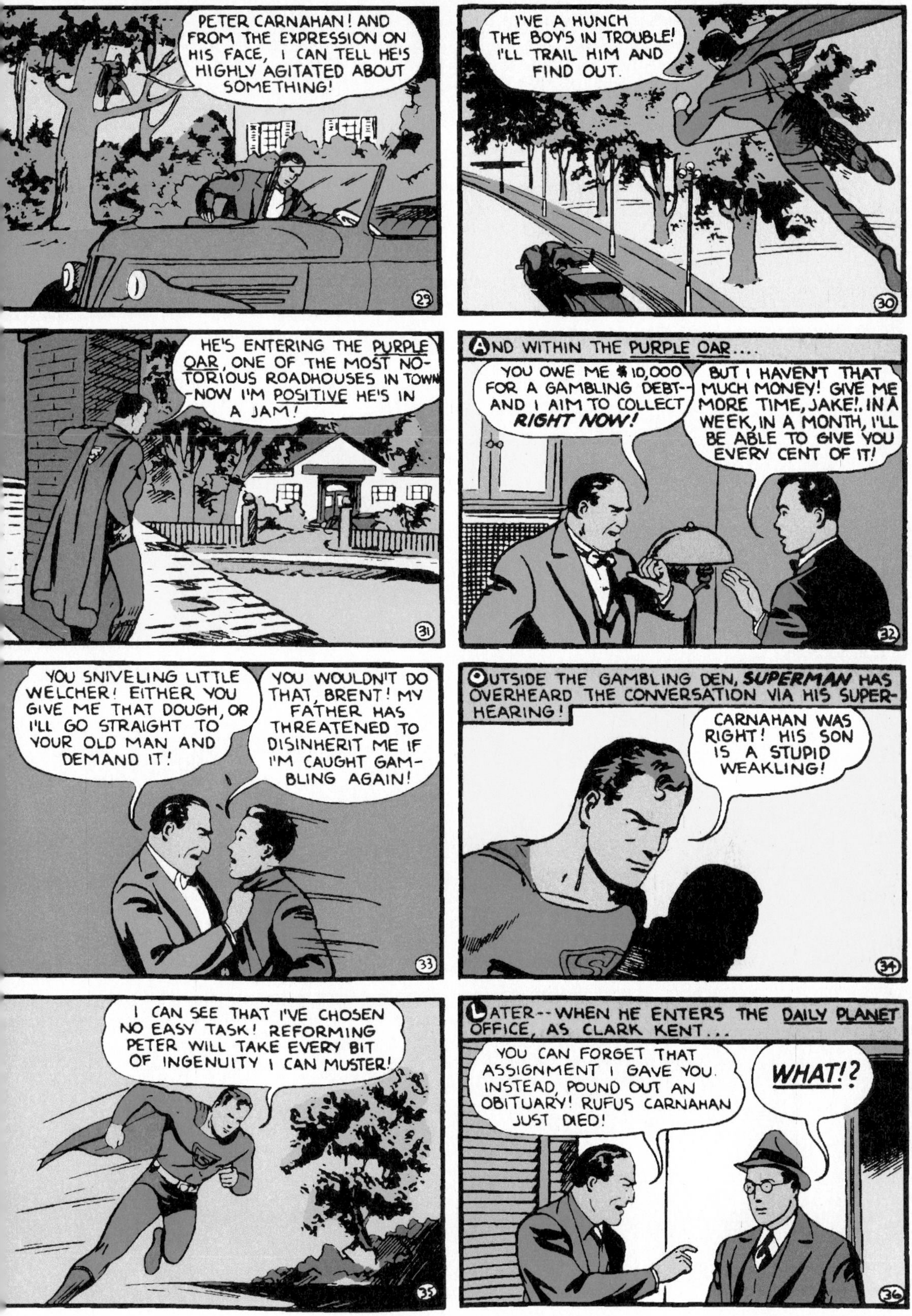
PETER CARNAHAN! AND FROM THE EXPRESSION ON HIS FACE, I CAN TELL HE'S HIGHLY AGITATED ABOUT SOMETHING!
I'VE A HUNCH THE BOY'S IN TROUBLE! I'LL TRAIL HIM AND FIND OUT.
HE'S ENTERING THE PURPLE OAR, ONE OF THE MOST NOTORIOUS ROADHOUSES IN TOWN --NOW I'M POSITIVE HE'S IN A JAM!
AND WITHIN THE PURPLE OAR....
YOU OWE ME $10,000 FOR A GAMBLING DEBT--AND I AIM TO COLLECT RIGHT NOW!
BUT I HAVEN'T THAT MUCH MONEY! GIVE ME MORE TIME, JAKE!. IN A WEEK, IN A MONTH, I'LL BE ABLE TO GIVE YOU EVERY CENT OF IT!
YOU SNIVELING LITTLE WELCHER! EITHER YOU GIVE ME THAT DOUGH, OR I'LL GO STRAIGHT TO YOUR OLD MAN AND DEMAND IT!
YOU WOULDN'T DO THAT, BRENT! MY FATHER HAS THREATENED TO DISINHERIT ME IF I'M CAUGHT GAMBLING AGAIN!
OUTSIDE THE GAMBLING DEN, SUPERMAN HAS OVERHEARD THE CONVERSATION VIA HIS SUPER-HEARING!
CARNAHAN WAS RIGHT! HIS SON IS A STUPID WEAKLING!
I CAN SEE THAT I'VE CHOSEN NO EASY TASK! REFORMING PETER WILL TAKE EVERY BIT OF INGENUITY I CAN MUSTER!
LATER--WHEN HE ENTERS THE DAILY PLANET OFFICE, AS CLARK KENT...
YOU CAN FORGET THAT ASSIGNMENT I GAVE YOU. INSTEAD, POUND OUT AN OBITUARY! RUFUS CARNAHAN JUST DIED!
WHAT!?

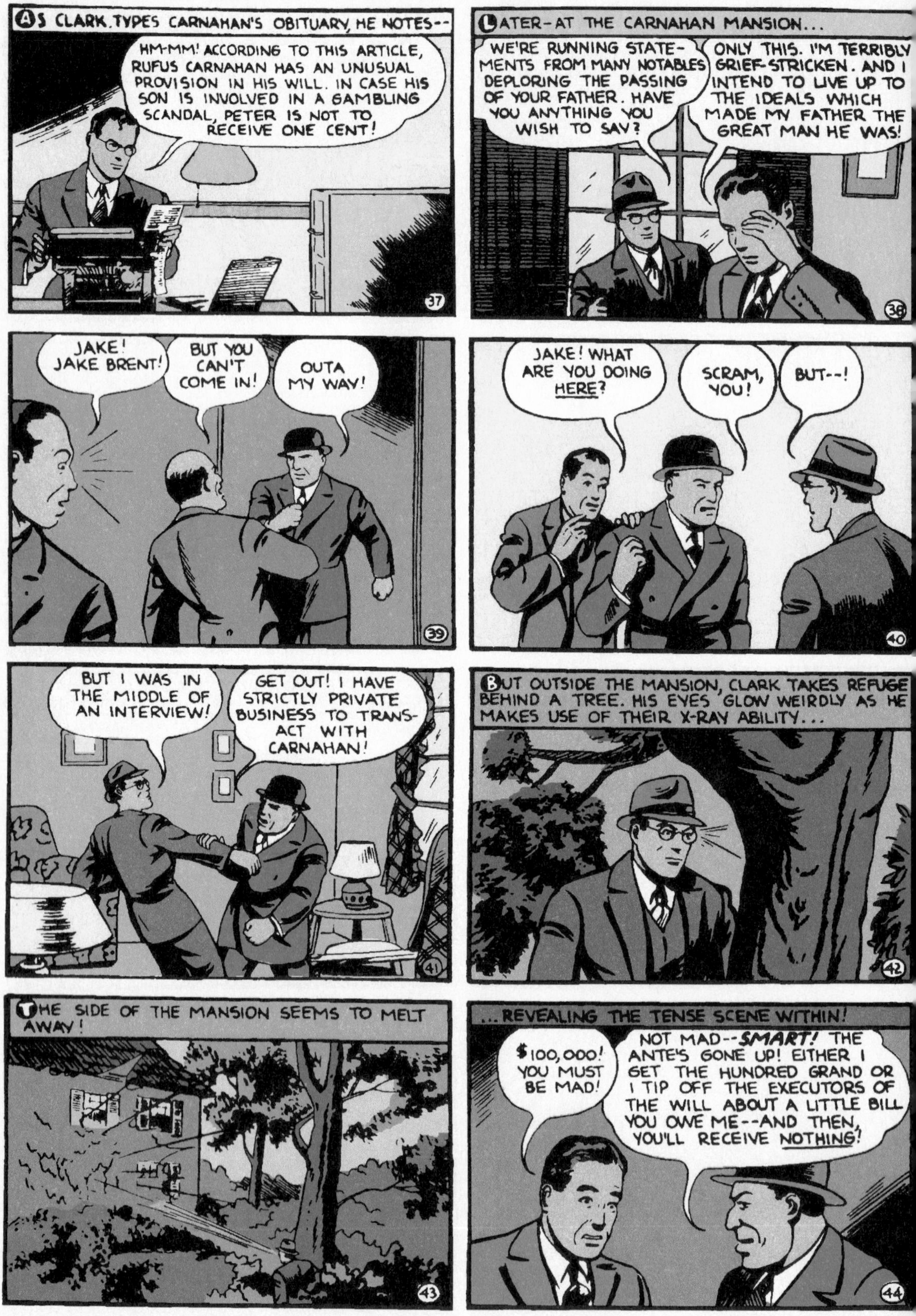
AS CLARK TYPES CARNAHAN'S OBITUARY, HE NOTES--
HM-MM! ACCORDING TO THIS ARTICLE, RUFUS CARNAHAN HAS AN UNUSUAL PROVISION IN HIS WILL. IN CASE HIS SON IS INVOLVED IN A GAMBLING SCANDAL, PETER IS NOT TO RECEIVE ONE CENT!
37
LATER-AT THE CARNAHAN MANSION...
WE'RE RUNNING STATEMENTS FROM MANY NOTABLES DEPLORING THE PASSING OF YOUR FATHER. HAVE YOU ANYTHING YOU WISH TO SAY?
ONLY THIS. I'M TERRIBLY GRIEF-STRICKEN. AND I INTEND TO LIVE UP TO THE IDEALS WHICH MADE MY FATHER THE GREAT MAN HE WAS!
38
JAKE! JAKE BRENT!
BUT YOU CAN'T COME IN!
OUTA MY WAY!
39
JAKE! WHAT ARE YOU DOING HERE?
SCRAM, YOU!
BUT--!
40
BUT I WAS IN THE MIDDLE OF AN INTERVIEW!
GET OUT! I HAVE STRICTLY PRIVATE BUSINESS TO TRANSACT WITH CARNAHAN!
41
BUT OUTSIDE THE MANSION, CLARK TAKES REFUGE BEHIND A TREE. HIS EYES GLOW WEIRDLY AS HE MAKES USE OF THEIR X-RAY ABILITY...
42
THE SIDE OF THE MANSION SEEMS TO MELT AWAY!
43
...REVEALING THE TENSE SCENE WITHIN!
$100,000! YOU MUST BE MAD!
NOT MAD--SMART! THE ANTE'S GONE UP! EITHER I GET THE HUNDRED GRAND OR I TIP OFF THE EXECUTORS OF THE WILL ABOUT A LITTLE BILL YOU OWE ME--AND THEN, YOU'LL RECEIVE NOTHING!
44

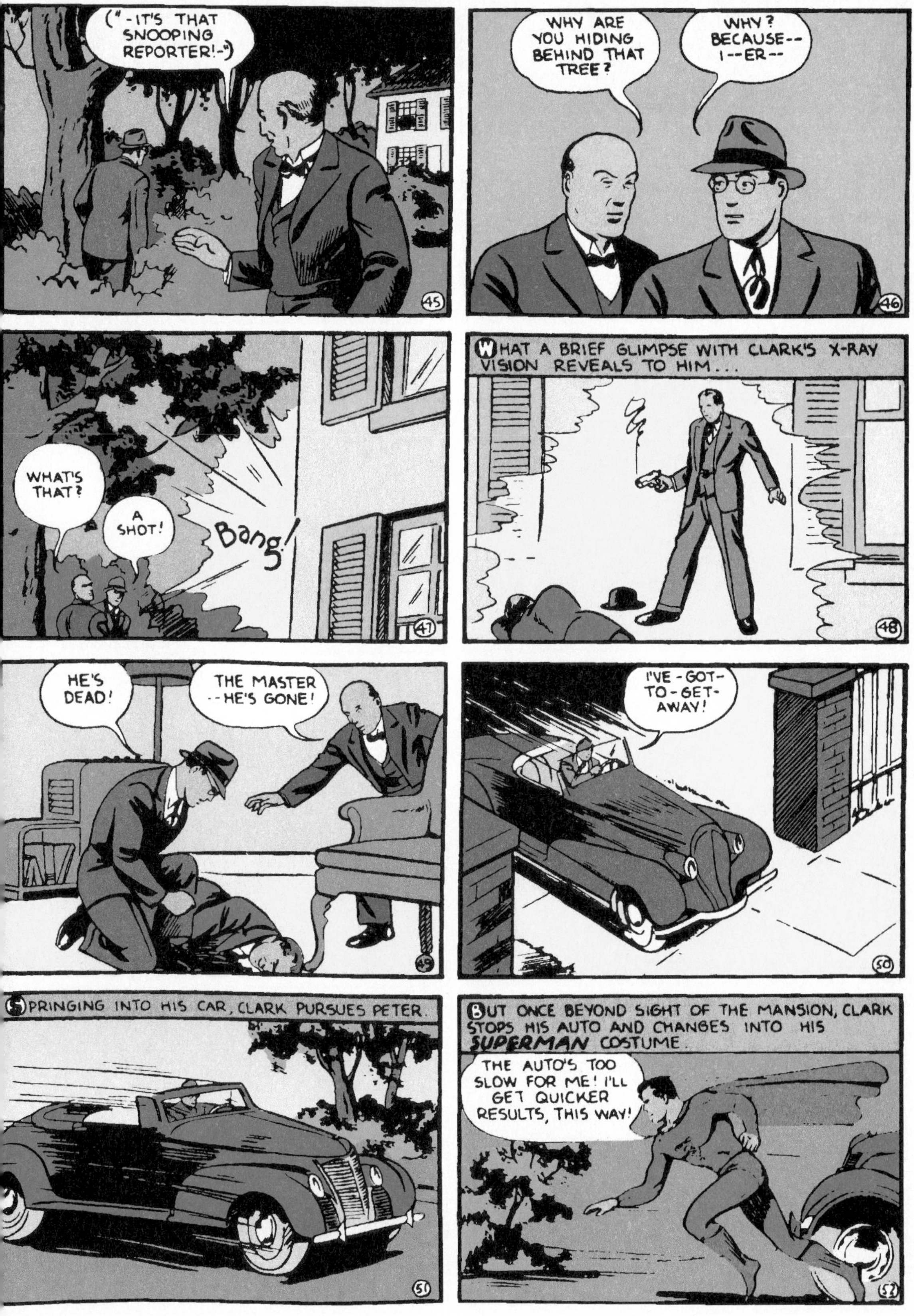
("-IT'S THAT SNOOPING REPORTER!-")
WHY ARE YOU HIDING BEHIND THAT TREE?
WHY? BECAUSE-- I--ER--
WHAT'S THAT?
A SHOT!
Bang!
WHAT A BRIEF GLIMPSE WITH CLARK'S X-RAY VISION REVEALS TO HIM...
HE'S DEAD!
THE MASTER --HE'S GONE!
I'VE-GOT-TO-GET-AWAY!
SPRINGING INTO HIS CAR, CLARK PURSUES PETER.
BUT ONCE BEYOND SIGHT OF THE MANSION, CLARK STOPS HIS AUTO AND CHANGES INTO HIS SUPERMAN COSTUME.
THE AUTO'S TOO SLOW FOR ME! I'LL GET QUICKER RESULTS, THIS WAY!

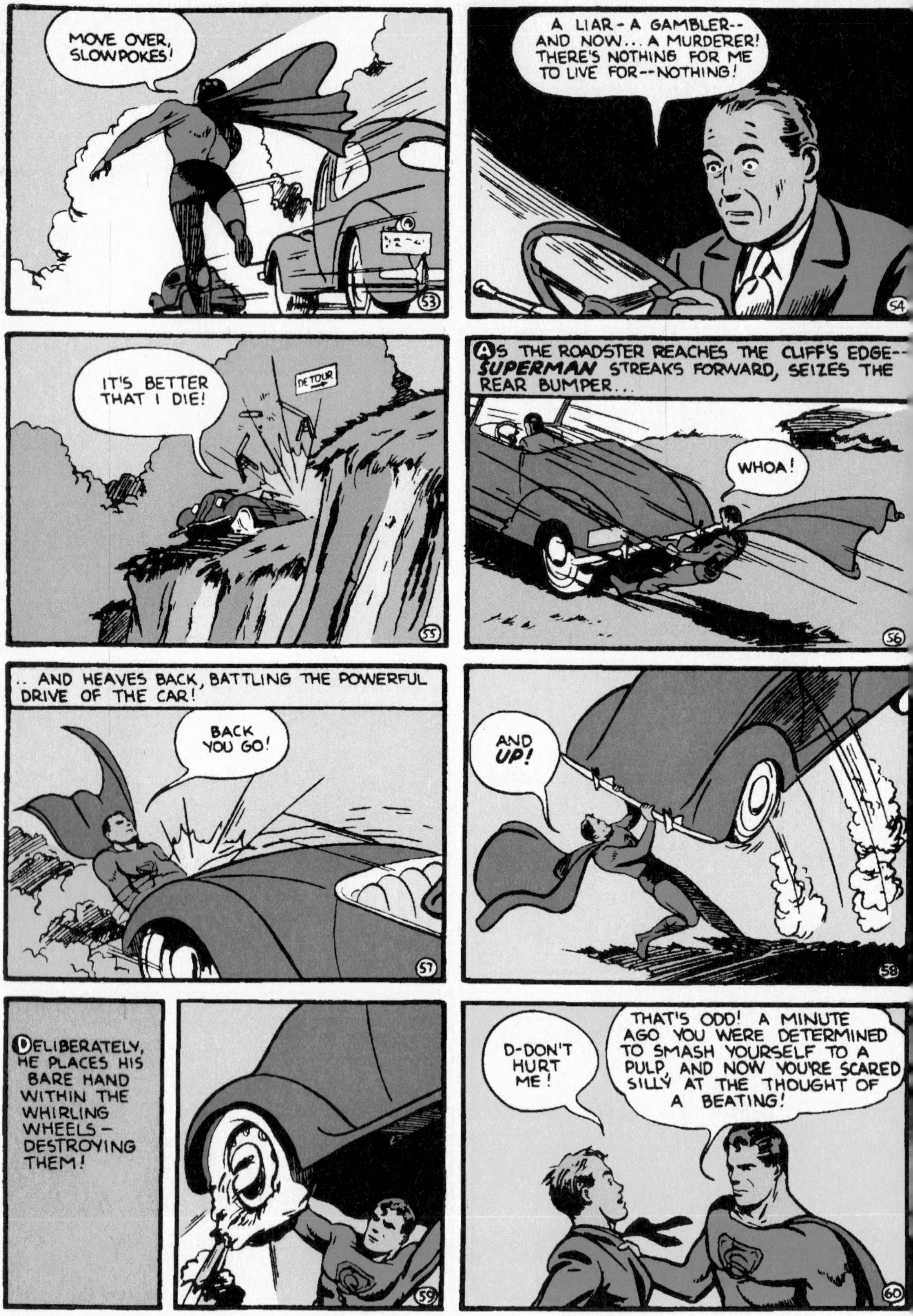
MOVE OVER, SLOWPOKES!
A LIAR - A GAMBLER-- AND NOW... A MURDERER! THERE'S NOTHING FOR ME TO LIVE FOR--NOTHING!
IT'S BETTER THAT I DIE!
DETOUR
AS THE ROADSTER REACHES THE CLIFF'S EDGE-- SUPERMAN STREAKS FORWARD, SEIZES THE REAR BUMPER...
WHOA!
.. AND HEAVES BACK, BATTLING THE POWERFUL DRIVE OF THE CAR!
BACK YOU GO!
AND UP!
DELIBERATELY, HE PLACES HIS BARE HAND WITHIN THE WHIRLING WHEELS— DESTROYING THEM!
D-DON'T HURT ME!
THAT'S ODD! A MINUTE AGO YOU WERE DETERMINED TO SMASH YOURSELF TO A PULP, AND NOW YOU'RE SCARED SILLY AT THE THOUGHT OF A BEATING!

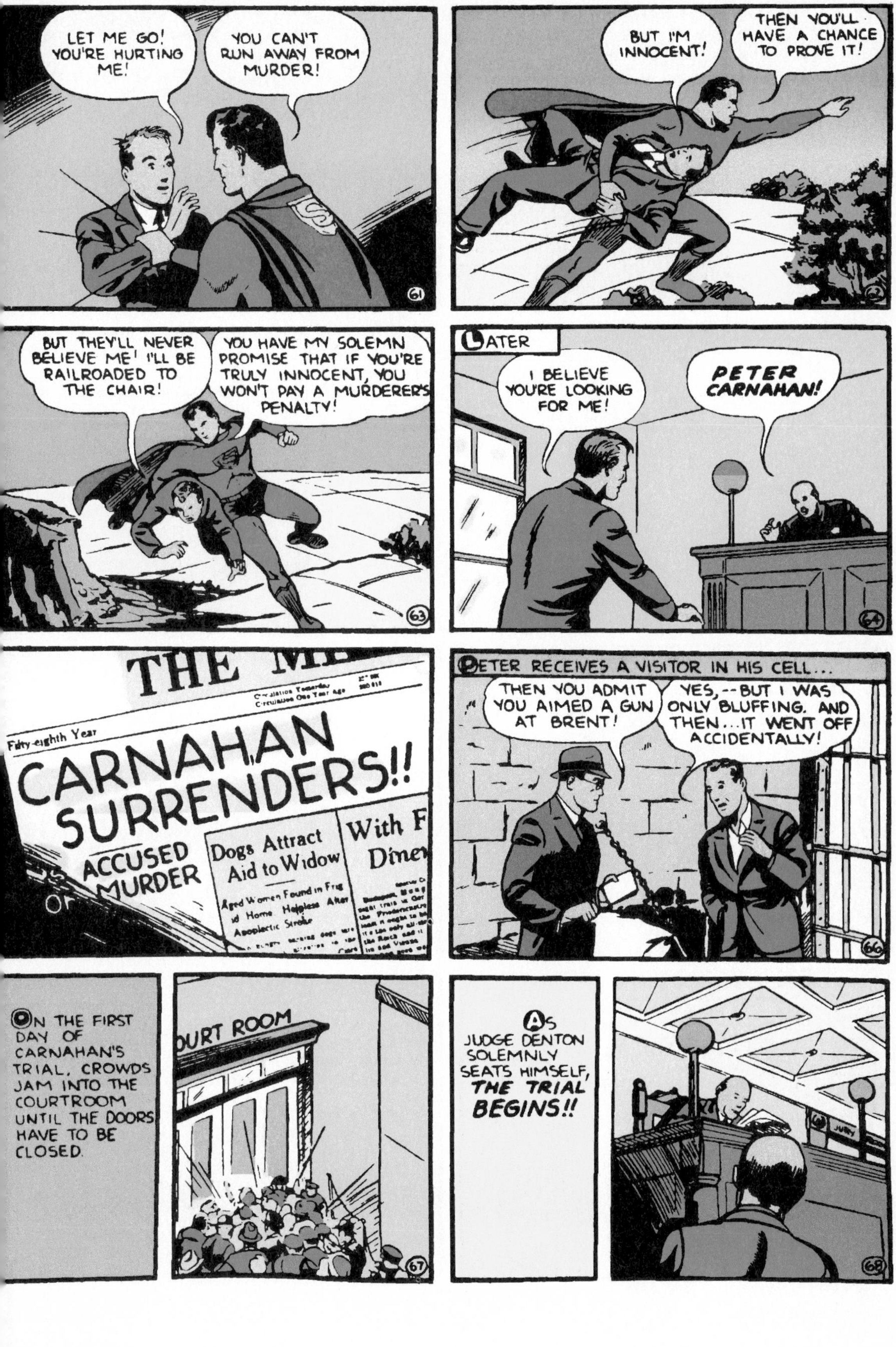
LET ME GO! YOU'RE HURTING ME!
YOU CAN'T RUN AWAY FROM MURDER!
BUT I'M INNOCENT!
THEN YOU'LL HAVE A CHANCE TO PROVE IT!
BUT THEY'LL NEVER BELIEVE ME! I'LL BE RAILROADED TO THE CHAIR!
YOU HAVE MY SOLEMN PROMISE THAT IF YOU'RE TRULY INNOCENT, YOU WON'T PAY A MURDERER'S PENALTY!
LATER
I BELIEVE YOU'RE LOOKING FOR ME!
PETER CARNAHAN!
THE
Fifty-eighth Year
CARNAHAN SURRENDERS!!
ACCUSED
MURDER
Dogs Attract Aid to Widow
PETER RECEIVES A VISITOR IN HIS CELL...
THEN YOU ADMIT YOU AIMED A GUN AT BRENT!
YES,--BUT I WAS ONLY BLUFFING. AND THEN...IT WENT OFF ACCIDENTALLY!
ON THE FIRST DAY OF CARNAHAN'S TRIAL, CROWDS JAM INTO THE COURTROOM UNTIL THE DOORS HAVE TO BE CLOSED.
OURT ROOM
AS JUDGE DENTON SOLEMNLY SEATS HIMSELF, THE TRIAL BEGINS!!
JURY

THE DISTRICT ATTORNEY MAKES HIS OPENING ADDRESS TO THE JURY

IT IS TRUE THAT THE VICTIM WAS NOT AN ASSET TO SOCIETY, BUT THE FACT REMAINS THAT THE ACCUSED SHOT HIM DOWN IN COLD BLOOD AND WE MUST SEE TO IT THAT HE PAYS THE SUPREME PENALTY!

IS IT TRUE THAT WHEN YOU LEFT THE ROOM PETER CARNAHAN AND JAKE BRENT WERE ALONE TOGETHER AND THAT WHEN YOU RETURNED, BRENT WAS SHOT DEAD AND YOUR MASTER GONE?

YES.

SHORTLY AFTER YOU FOUND BRENT SLAIN DID YOU SEE YOUNG CARNAHAN FLEE FROM THE SCENE OF THE CRIME?

YES, I DID!

DID YOU OWE THE DECEASED BRENT A GAMBLING DEBT?

YES, BUT--!

DOES YOUR FATHER'S WILL PROVIDE THAT IF YOU ARE INVOLVED IN ANY GAMBLING ESCAPADE, YOU ARE TO RECEIVE NO PART OF THE MILLIONS HE LEFT BEHIND HIM?

THAT'S TRUE... ONLY TOO TRUE!

DID BRENT THREATEN TO EXPOSE YOUR GAMBLING DEBT TO HIM IF YOU FAILED TO PAY HIM A HUGE SUM?

YES. HE TRIED TO BLACKMAIL ME. HE...

ISN'T IT A FACT THAT YOU DELIBERATELY SHOT DOWN JAKE BRENT TO SHUT HIS MOUTH?

NO! NO! NO!

AND SEVERAL DAYS LATER...!

WE, THE MEMBERS OF THE JURY, FIND THE ACCUSED-- *GUILTY*, OF MURDER IN THE FIRST DEGREE!

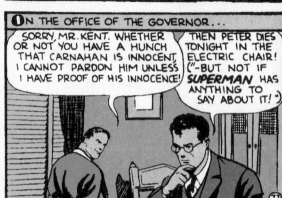

IN THE OFFICE OF THE GOVERNOR...

SORRY, MR. KENT. WHETHER OR NOT YOU HAVE A HUNCH THAT CARNAHAN IS INNOCENT, I CANNOT PARDON HIM UNLESS I HAVE PROOF OF HIS INNOCENCE!

THEN PETER DIES TONIGHT IN THE ELECTRIC CHAIR! ("-BUT NOT IF *SUPERMAN* HAS ANYTHING TO SAY ABOUT IT!")

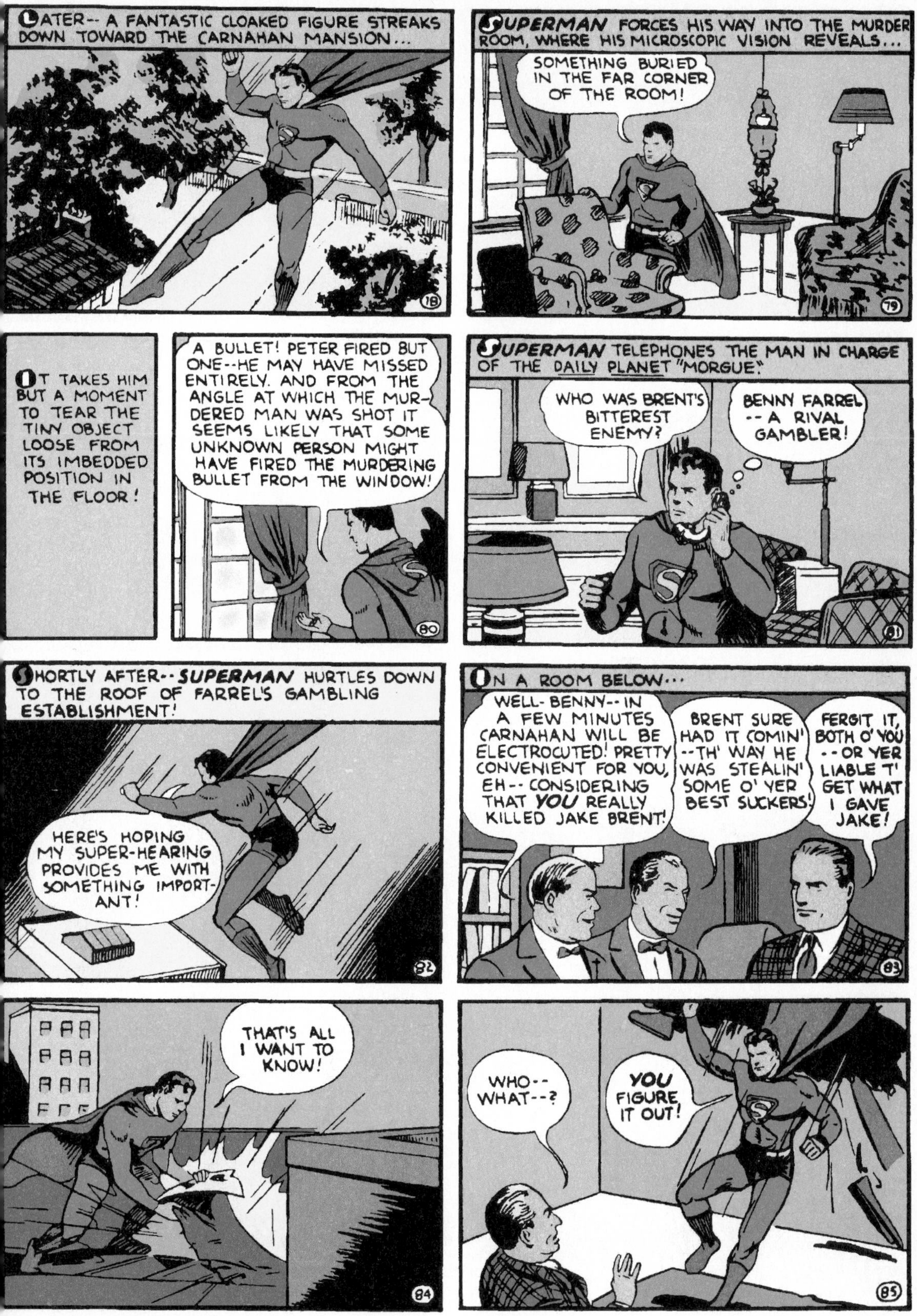
LATER-- A FANTASTIC CLOAKED FIGURE STREAKS DOWN TOWARD THE CARNAHAN MANSION...
SUPERMAN FORCES HIS WAY INTO THE MURDER ROOM, WHERE HIS MICROSCOPIC VISION REVEALS...
SOMETHING BURIED IN THE FAR CORNER OF THE ROOM!
IT TAKES HIM BUT A MOMENT TO TEAR THE TINY OBJECT LOOSE FROM ITS IMBEDDED POSITION IN THE FLOOR!
A BULLET! PETER FIRED BUT ONE--HE MAY HAVE MISSED ENTIRELY. AND FROM THE ANGLE AT WHICH THE MURDERED MAN WAS SHOT IT SEEMS LIKELY THAT SOME UNKNOWN PERSON MIGHT HAVE FIRED THE MURDERING BULLET FROM THE WINDOW!
SUPERMAN TELEPHONES THE MAN IN CHARGE OF THE DAILY PLANET "MORGUE."
WHO WAS BRENT'S BITTEREST ENEMY?
BENNY FARREL --A RIVAL GAMBLER!
SHORTLY AFTER--SUPERMAN HURTLES DOWN TO THE ROOF OF FARREL'S GAMBLING ESTABLISHMENT!
HERE'S HOPING MY SUPER-HEARING PROVIDES ME WITH SOMETHING IMPORTANT!
IN A ROOM BELOW...
WELL-BENNY--IN A FEW MINUTES CARNAHAN WILL BE ELECTROCUTED! PRETTY CONVENIENT FOR YOU, EH--CONSIDERING THAT YOU REALLY KILLED JAKE BRENT!
BRENT SURE HAD IT COMIN' --TH' WAY HE WAS STEALIN' SOME O' YER BEST SUCKERS!
FERGIT IT, BOTH O' YOU --OR YER LIABLE T' GET WHAT I GAVE JAKE!
THAT'S ALL I WANT TO KNOW!
WHO-- WHAT--?
YOU FIGURE IT OUT!

Panel 86:
WHAT DO YOU WANT?

YOU--TO PAY FOR YOUR CRIME!

Panel 87:
KEEP AWAY, BLAST YOU!

Panel 88:
BUT THE BULLETS BOUNCE OFF SUPERMAN'S SUPER-TOUGH SKIN, AND...

OUCH! MY WRIST!

THOSE BULLETS OF YOURS SEEM TO PREFER YOUR COMPANY! BENNY, YOU'RE COMING WITH ME TO CONFESS THAT YOU IN-STEAD OF CARNAHAN SHOULD BE ELECTROCUTED!

Panel 89:
THERE ARE ONLY TEN MINUTES TO GO BEFORE THE FALL-GUY GETS IT. YOU'LL NEVER MAKE IT IN TIME!

WE'LL SEE ABOUT THAT!

Panel 90:
AT THAT VERY MOMENT.. REPORTERS FROM THE VARIOUS NEWSPAPERS FILE INTO THE EXECUTION-CHAMBER...

I'M GETTING USED TO THESE EXECUTIONS FINALLY! WHERE'S CLARK KENT?

HE PROBABLY IS TOO SCARED TO SHOW UP!

Panel 91:
SPRINGING AWAY FROM THE GAMBLING ESTAB-LISHMENT WITH FARREL UNDER HIS ARM, SUPERMAN RACES AT BREAKNECK SPEED AGAINST TIME..

Panel 93:
AND SIMULTANEOUSLY PETER IS LED DOWN THE GLOOMY BLUE-LIT CORRIDOR TOWARD THE EXECUTION-CHAMBER...

BUT I'M INNOCENT, I TELL YOU --- INNOCENT!

SO THEY ALL SAY!

PEACE, MY SON!

Panel 94:
...STRAPPED INTO THE ELECTRIC CHAIR!...

PLEASE DON'T DO THIS TO ME! DON'T! I BEG OF YOU, DON'T! I DIDN'T KILL BRENT! I--!

THE EXECUTIONER REACHES FOR THE SWITCH!

WHAT CAN SUPER-MAN POSSIBLY DO TO SAVE PETER NOW?

ONTO THE POWER-HOUSE WHICH SUPPLIES ELECTRICITY TO METROPOLIS AND THE PRISON STREAKS THE MAN OF TOMORROW!

WITH A BURST OF AMAZING STRENGTH, HE RIPS AN INTEGRAL PIECE FROM THE DYNAMO...

I HATE TO BE DESTRUCTIVE--BUT THE SITUATION DEMANDS IT!

WITHIN THE ELECTROCUTION-CHAMBER...

THE LIGHTS--THEY'RE OUT!

NO ELECTRICITY--WE'LL HAVE TO POSTPONE THE ELECTROCUTION!

LATER--AT THE GOVERNOR'S HOME...

GO AHEAD--CONFESS, OR I'LL SHAKE YOUR TEETH LOOSE!

MAKE HIM STOP! I DID IT! I CONFESS I KILLED JAKE!

THIS IS MOST IRREGULAR!

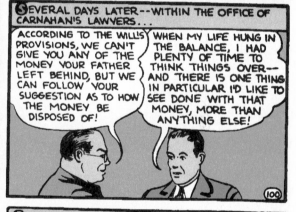

YOU HEARD ME! THIS IS THE GOVERNOR!--CARNAHAN IS PARDONED!

NO NEED FOR ME TO HANG AROUND ANY FURTHER. SO-LONG!

SEVERAL DAYS LATER--WITHIN THE OFFICE OF CARNAHAN'S LAWYERS...

ACCORDING TO THE WILL'S PROVISIONS, WE CAN'T GIVE YOU ANY OF THE MONEY YOUR FATHER LEFT BEHIND, BUT WE CAN FOLLOW YOUR SUGGESTION AS TO HOW THE MONEY BE DISPOSED OF!

WHEN MY LIFE HUNG IN THE BALANCE, I HAD PLENTY OF TIME TO THINK THINGS OVER--AND THERE IS ONE THING IN PARTICULAR I'D LIKE TO SEE DONE WITH THAT MONEY, MORE THAN ANYTHING ELSE!

I'D LIKE TO ESTABLISH A HOME FOR WAYWARD UNDERPRIVILEGED YOUTHS-SEE THAT THEY DON'T SUCCUMB TO THE PITFALLS I FACED! AND I WOULD LIKE NOTHING BETTER THAN TO DIRECT IT!

SIX MONTHS LATER--

CONGRATULATIONS, PETER! YOU'VE ACCOMPLISHED MIRACLES IN GUIDING THE CHARACTER OF YOUR CHARGES!

THANK YOU! I'M TRYING HARD TO ATONE FOR THE MESS I MADE OF MY LIFE. I ONLY REGRET THAT I COULDN'T HAVE MADE MY FATHER PROUD OF ME WHILE HE LIVED!

RUFUS CARNAHAN HOME FOR YOUTH

THE END

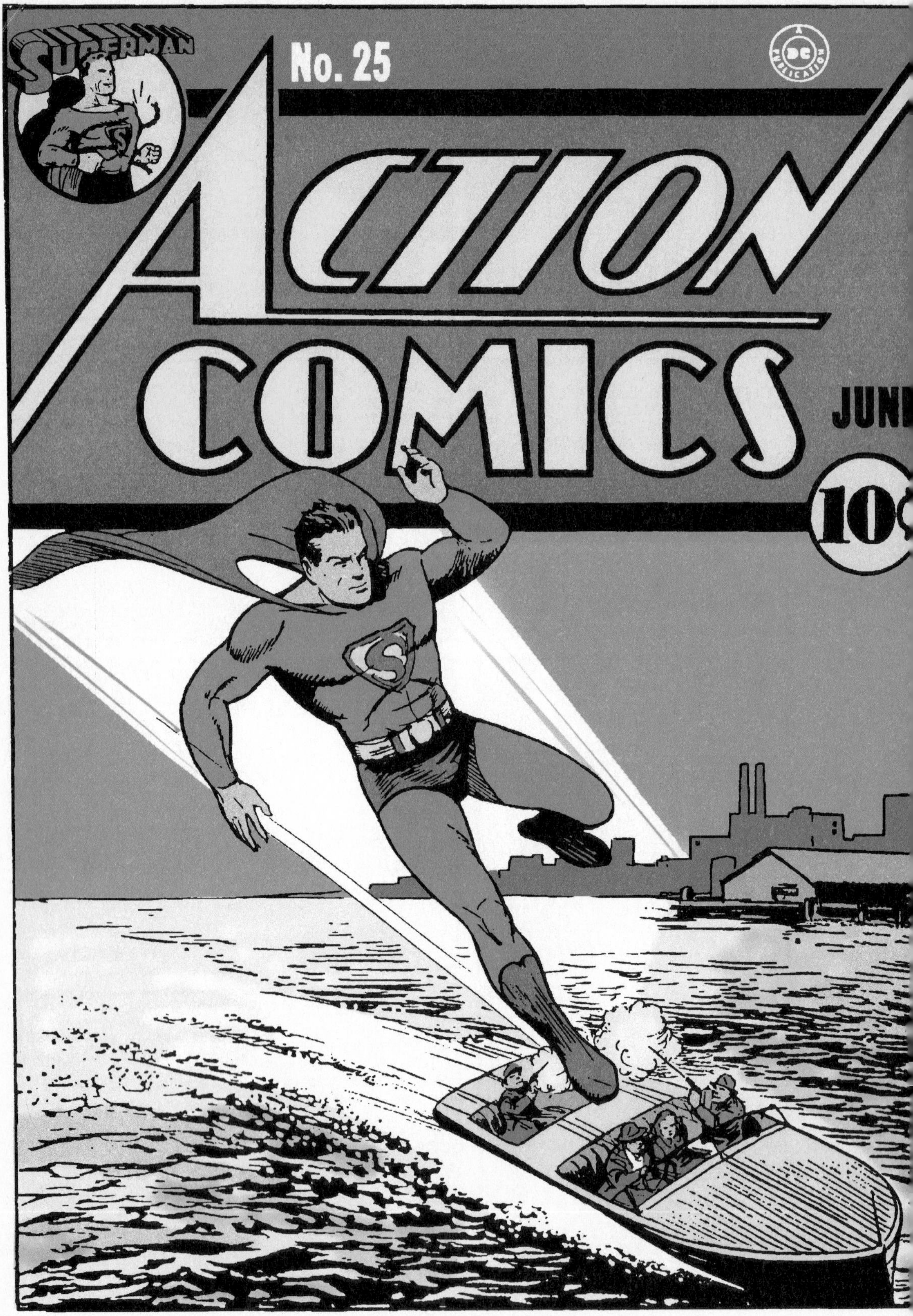
SUPERMAN
No. 25
A DC PUBLICATION
ACTION COMICS
JUN
10¢

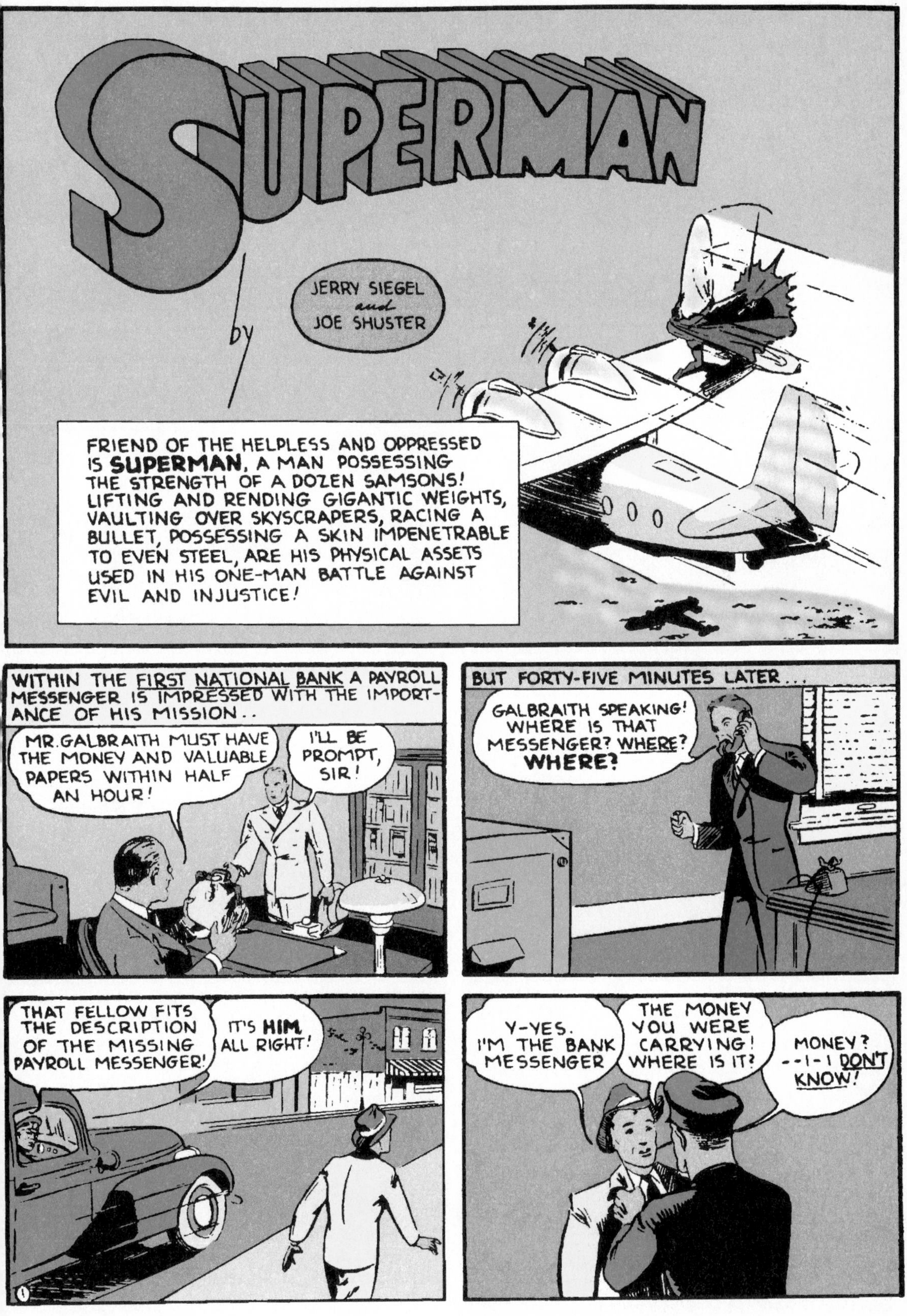
SUPERMAN
by
JERRY SIEGEL and JOE SHUSTER
FRIEND OF THE HELPLESS AND OPPRESSED IS SUPERMAN, A MAN POSSESSING THE STRENGTH OF A DOZEN SAMSONS! LIFTING AND RENDING GIGANTIC WEIGHTS, VAULTING OVER SKYSCRAPERS, RACING A BULLET, POSSESSING A SKIN IMPENETRABLE TO EVEN STEEL, ARE HIS PHYSICAL ASSETS USED IN HIS ONE-MAN BATTLE AGAINST EVIL AND INJUSTICE!
WITHIN THE FIRST NATIONAL BANK A PAYROLL MESSENGER IS IMPRESSED WITH THE IMPORTANCE OF HIS MISSION..
MR. GALBRAITH MUST HAVE THE MONEY AND VALUABLE PAPERS WITHIN HALF AN HOUR!
I'LL BE PROMPT, SIR!
BUT FORTY-FIVE MINUTES LATER...
GALBRAITH SPEAKING! WHERE IS THAT MESSENGER? WHERE? WHERE?
THAT FELLOW FITS THE DESCRIPTION OF THE MISSING PAYROLL MESSENGER!
IT'S HIM ALL RIGHT!
Y-YES. I'M THE BANK MESSENGER
THE MONEY YOU WERE CARRYING! WHERE IS IT?
MONEY? --I-I DON'T KNOW!

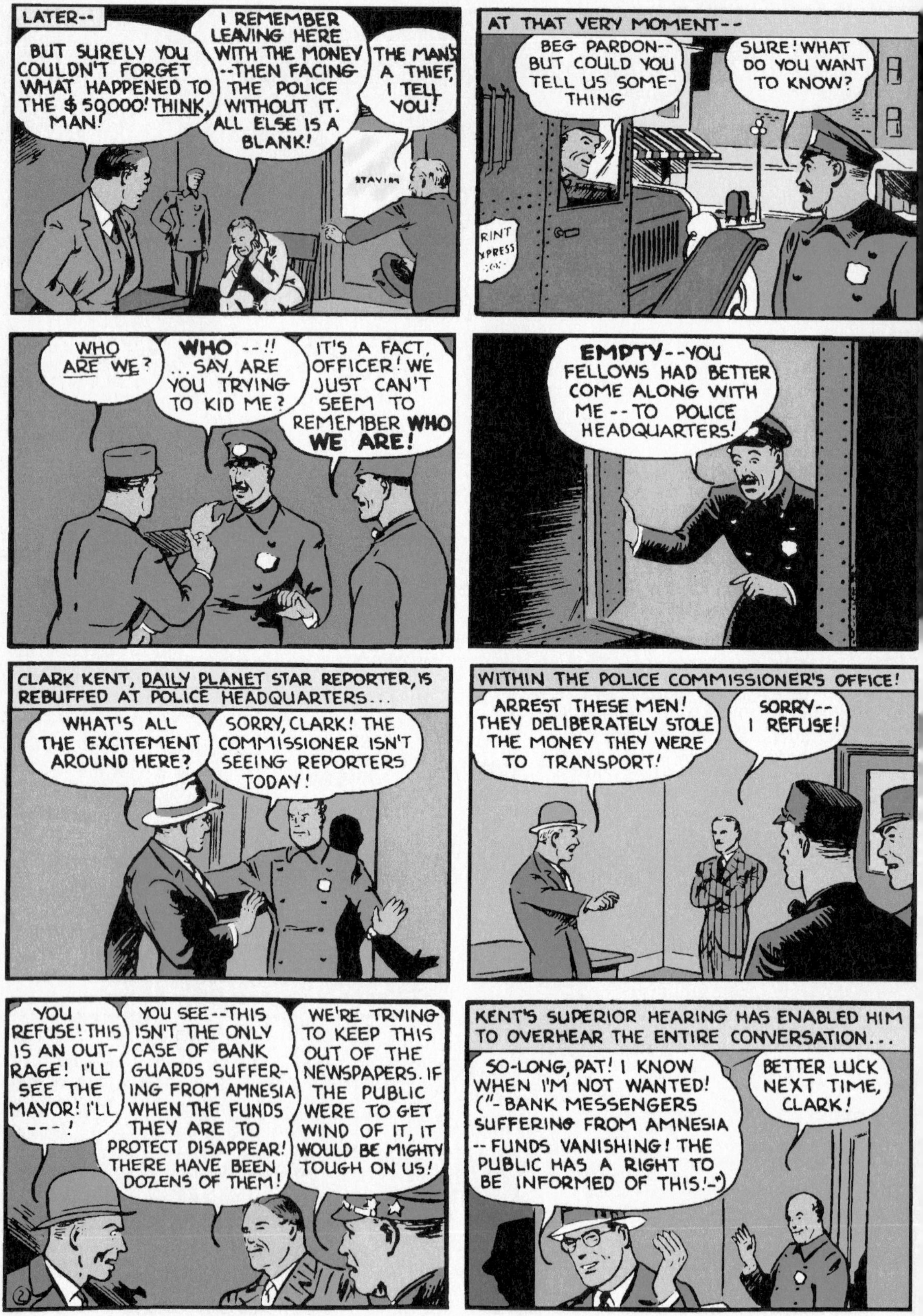
LATER--
BUT SURELY YOU COULDN'T FORGET WHAT HAPPENED TO THE $50000! THINK, MAN!
I REMEMBER LEAVING HERE WITH THE MONEY --THEN FACING THE POLICE WITHOUT IT. ALL ELSE IS A BLANK!
THE MAN'S A THIEF, I TELL YOU!
AT THAT VERY MOMENT--
BEG PARDON-- BUT COULD YOU TELL US SOMETHING
SURE! WHAT DO YOU WANT TO KNOW?
WHO ARE WE?
WHO--!! ...SAY, ARE YOU TRYING TO KID ME?
IT'S A FACT, OFFICER! WE JUST CAN'T SEEM TO REMEMBER WHO WE ARE!
EMPTY--YOU FELLOWS HAD BETTER COME ALONG WITH ME--TO POLICE HEADQUARTERS!
CLARK KENT, DAILY PLANET STAR REPORTER, IS REBUFFED AT POLICE HEADQUARTERS...
WHAT'S ALL THE EXCITEMENT AROUND HERE?
SORRY, CLARK! THE COMMISSIONER ISN'T SEEING REPORTERS TODAY!
WITHIN THE POLICE COMMISSIONER'S OFFICE!
ARREST THESE MEN! THEY DELIBERATELY STOLE THE MONEY THEY WERE TO TRANSPORT!
SORRY-- I REFUSE!
YOU REFUSE! THIS IS AN OUTRAGE! I'LL SEE THE MAYOR! I'LL ---!
YOU SEE--THIS ISN'T THE ONLY CASE OF BANK GUARDS SUFFERING FROM AMNESIA WHEN THE FUNDS THEY ARE TO PROTECT DISAPPEAR! THERE HAVE BEEN DOZENS OF THEM!
WE'RE TRYING TO KEEP THIS OUT OF THE NEWSPAPERS. IF THE PUBLIC WERE TO GET WIND OF IT, IT WOULD BE MIGHTY TOUGH ON US!
2
KENT'S SUPERIOR HEARING HAS ENABLED HIM TO OVERHEAR THE ENTIRE CONVERSATION...
SO-LONG, PAT! I KNOW WHEN I'M NOT WANTED! ("-BANK MESSENGERS SUFFERING FROM AMNESIA --FUNDS VANISHING! THE PUBLIC HAS A RIGHT TO BE INFORMED OF THIS!-")
BETTER LUCK NEXT TIME, CLARK!

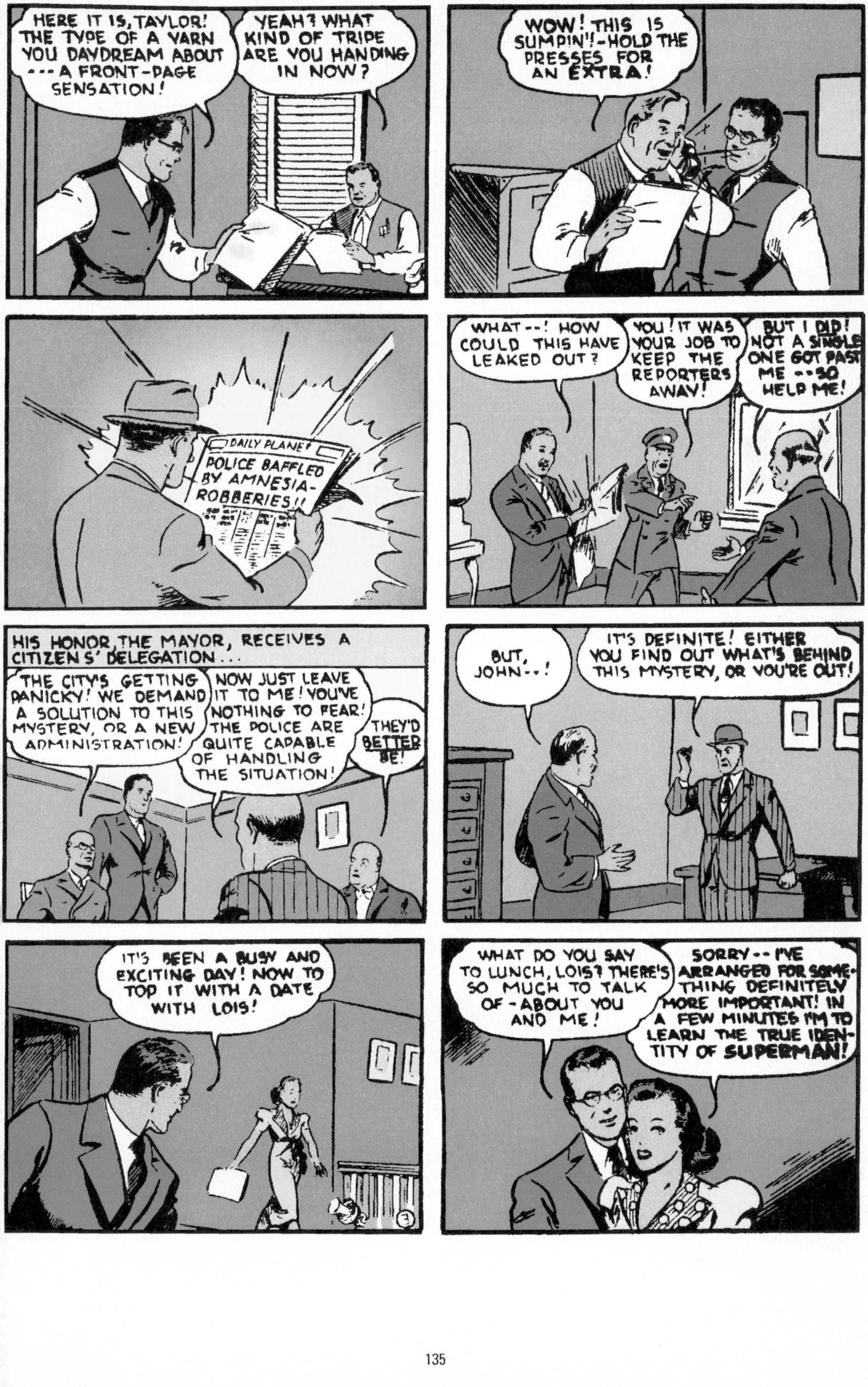
HERE IT IS, TAYLOR! THE TYPE OF A YARN YOU DAYDREAM ABOUT ---A FRONT-PAGE SENSATION!
YEAH? WHAT KIND OF TRIPE ARE YOU HANDING IN NOW?
WOW! THIS IS SUMPIN'!-HOLD THE PRESSES FOR AN EXTRA!
DAILY PLANET
POLICE BAFFLED BY AMNESIA-ROBBERIES!!
WHAT--! HOW COULD THIS HAVE LEAKED OUT?
YOU! IT WAS YOUR JOB TO KEEP THE REPORTERS AWAY!
BUT I DID! NOT A SINGLE ONE GOT PAST ME --SO HELP ME!
HIS HONOR, THE MAYOR, RECEIVES A CITIZENS' DELEGATION...
THE CITY'S GETTING PANICKY! WE DEMAND A SOLUTION TO THIS MYSTERY, OR A NEW ADMINISTRATION!
NOW JUST LEAVE IT TO ME! YOU'VE NOTHING TO FEAR! THE POLICE ARE QUITE CAPABLE OF HANDLING THE SITUATION!
THEY'D BETTER BE!
BUT, JOHN--!
IT'S DEFINITE! EITHER YOU FIND OUT WHAT'S BEHIND THIS MYSTERY, OR YOU'RE OUT!
IT'S BEEN A BUSY AND EXCITING DAY! NOW TO TOP IT WITH A DATE WITH LOIS!
WHAT DO YOU SAY TO LUNCH, LOIS? THERE'S SO MUCH TO TALK OF-ABOUT YOU AND ME!
SORRY--I'VE ARRANGED FOR SOME-THING DEFINITELY MORE IMPORTANT! IN A FEW MINUTES I'M TO LEARN THE TRUE IDEN-TITY OF SUPERMAN!

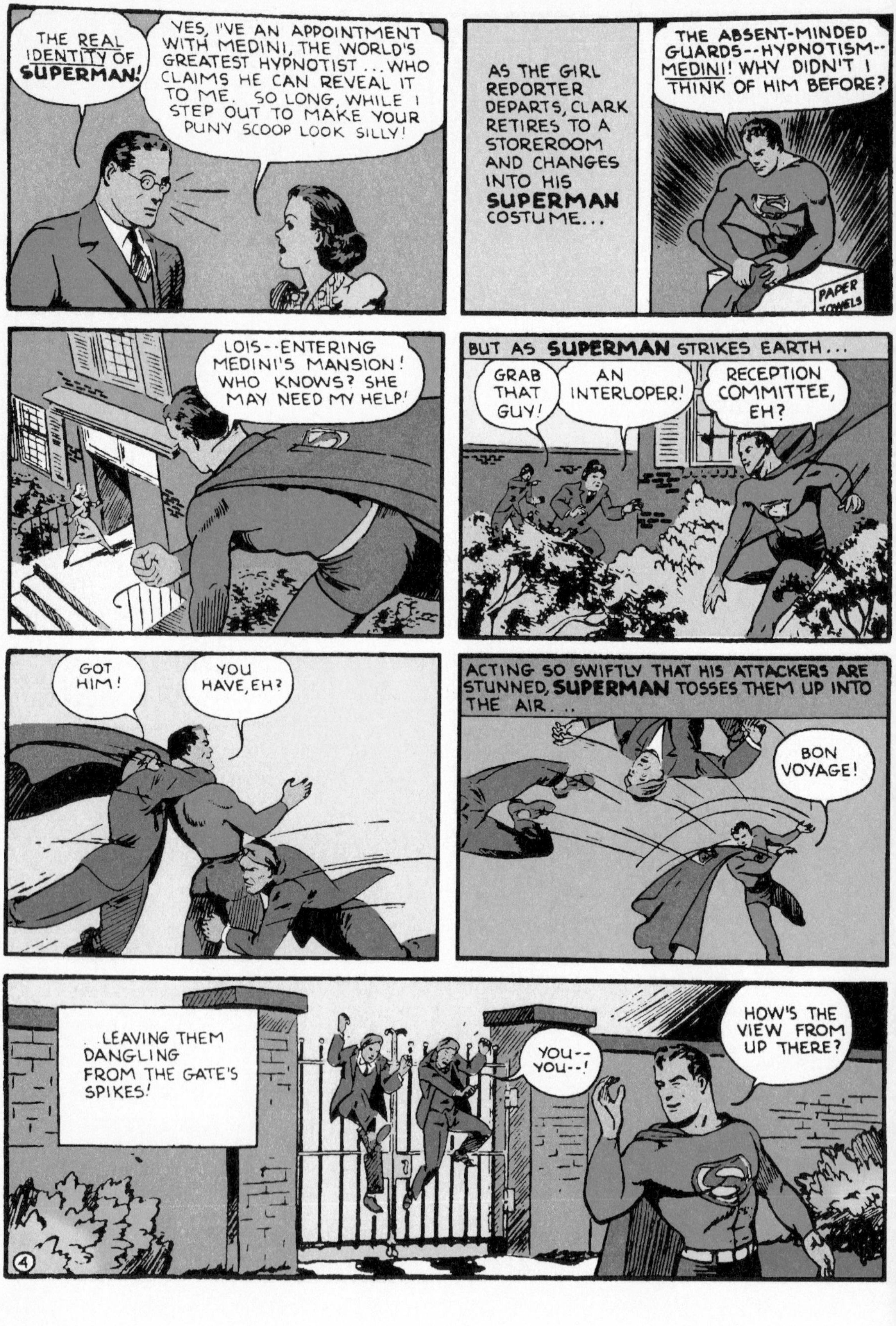

THE REAL IDENTITY OF SUPERMAN!
YES, I'VE AN APPOINTMENT WITH MEDINI, THE WORLD'S GREATEST HYPNOTIST ... WHO CLAIMS HE CAN REVEAL IT TO ME. SO LONG, WHILE I STEP OUT TO MAKE YOUR PUNY SCOOP LOOK SILLY!
AS THE GIRL REPORTER DEPARTS, CLARK RETIRES TO A STOREROOM AND CHANGES INTO HIS SUPERMAN COSTUME...
THE ABSENT-MINDED GUARDS--HYPNOTISM--MEDINI! WHY DIDN'T I THINK OF HIM BEFORE?
PAPER TOWELS
LOIS--ENTERING MEDINI'S MANSION! WHO KNOWS? SHE MAY NEED MY HELP!
BUT AS SUPERMAN STRIKES EARTH...
GRAB THAT GUY!
AN INTERLOPER!
RECEPTION COMMITTEE, EH?
GOT HIM!
YOU HAVE, EH?
ACTING SO SWIFTLY THAT HIS ATTACKERS ARE STUNNED, SUPERMAN TOSSES THEM UP INTO THE AIR...
BON VOYAGE!
...LEAVING THEM DANGLING FROM THE GATE'S SPIKES!
YOU--YOU--!
HOW'S THE VIEW FROM UP THERE?
4

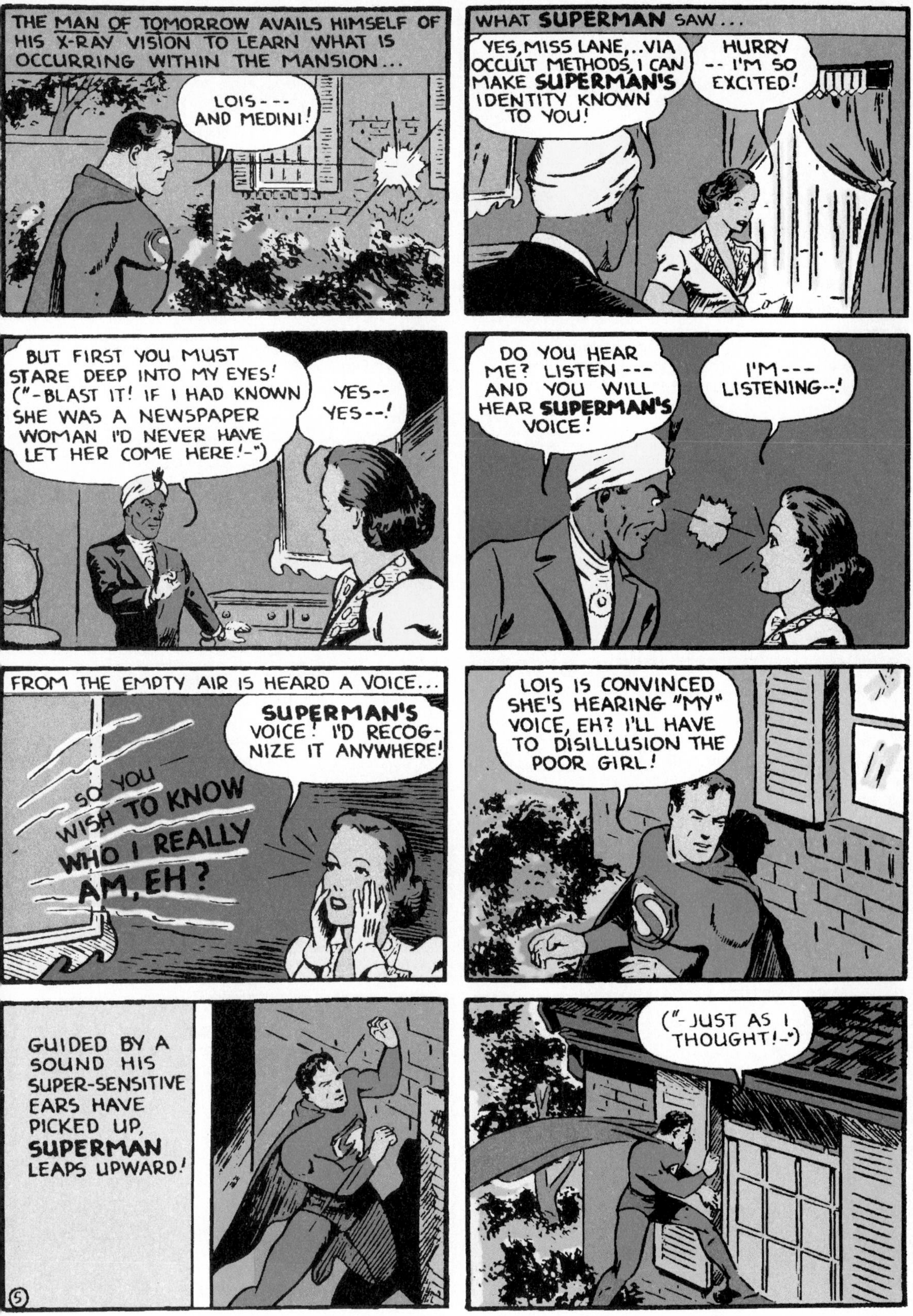
THE MAN OF TOMORROW AVAILS HIMSELF OF HIS X-RAY VISION TO LEARN WHAT IS OCCURRING WITHIN THE MANSION...
LOIS--- AND MEDINI!
WHAT SUPERMAN SAW...
YES, MISS LANE,..VIA OCCULT METHODS, I CAN MAKE SUPERMAN'S IDENTITY KNOWN TO YOU!
HURRY -- I'M SO EXCITED!
BUT FIRST YOU MUST STARE DEEP INTO MY EYES! ("-BLAST IT! IF I HAD KNOWN SHE WAS A NEWSPAPER WOMAN I'D NEVER HAVE LET HER COME HERE!-")
YES-- YES--!
DO YOU HEAR ME? LISTEN --- AND YOU WILL HEAR SUPERMAN'S VOICE!
I'M--- LISTENING--!
FROM THE EMPTY AIR IS HEARD A VOICE...
SO YOU WISH TO KNOW WHO I REALLY AM, EH?
SUPERMAN'S VOICE! I'D RECOGNIZE IT ANYWHERE!
LOIS IS CONVINCED SHE'S HEARING "MY" VOICE, EH? I'LL HAVE TO DISILLUSION THE POOR GIRL!
GUIDED BY A SOUND HIS SUPER-SENSITIVE EARS HAVE PICKED UP, SUPERMAN LEAPS UPWARD!
5
("-JUST AS I THOUGHT!-")

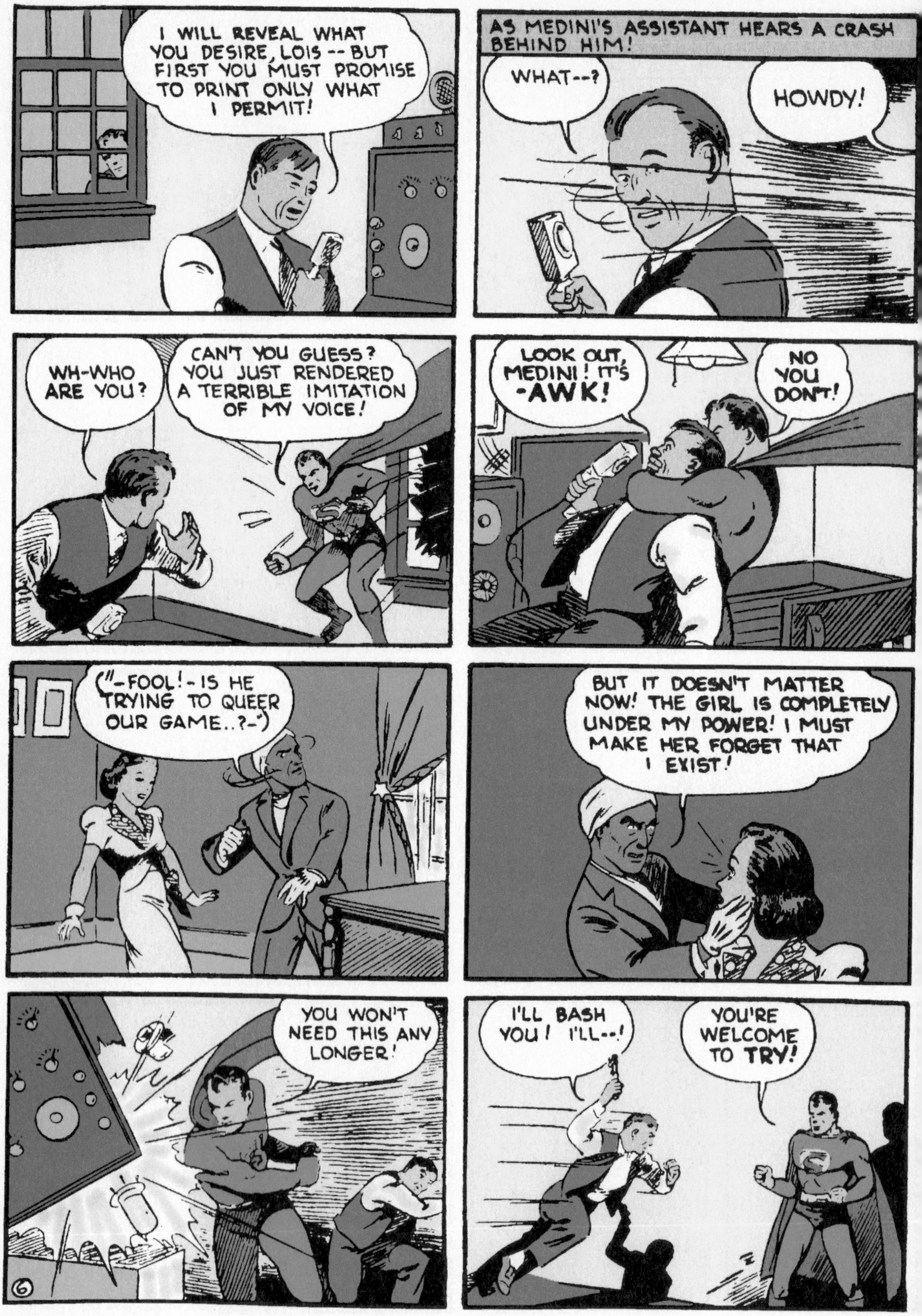
I WILL REVEAL WHAT YOU DESIRE, LOIS -- BUT FIRST YOU MUST PROMISE TO PRINT ONLY WHAT I PERMIT!
AS MEDINI'S ASSISTANT HEARS A CRASH BEHIND HIM!
WHAT--?
HOWDY!
WH-WHO ARE YOU?
CAN'T YOU GUESS? YOU JUST RENDERED A TERRIBLE IMITATION OF MY VOICE!
LOOK OUT, MEDINI! IT'S -AWK!
NO YOU DON'T!
("-FOOL!- IS HE TRYING TO QUEER OUR GAME..?-")
BUT IT DOESN'T MATTER NOW! THE GIRL IS COMPLETELY UNDER MY POWER! I MUST MAKE HER FORGET THAT I EXIST!
YOU WON'T NEED THIS ANY LONGER!
6
I'LL BASH YOU! I'LL--!
YOU'RE WELCOME TO TRY!

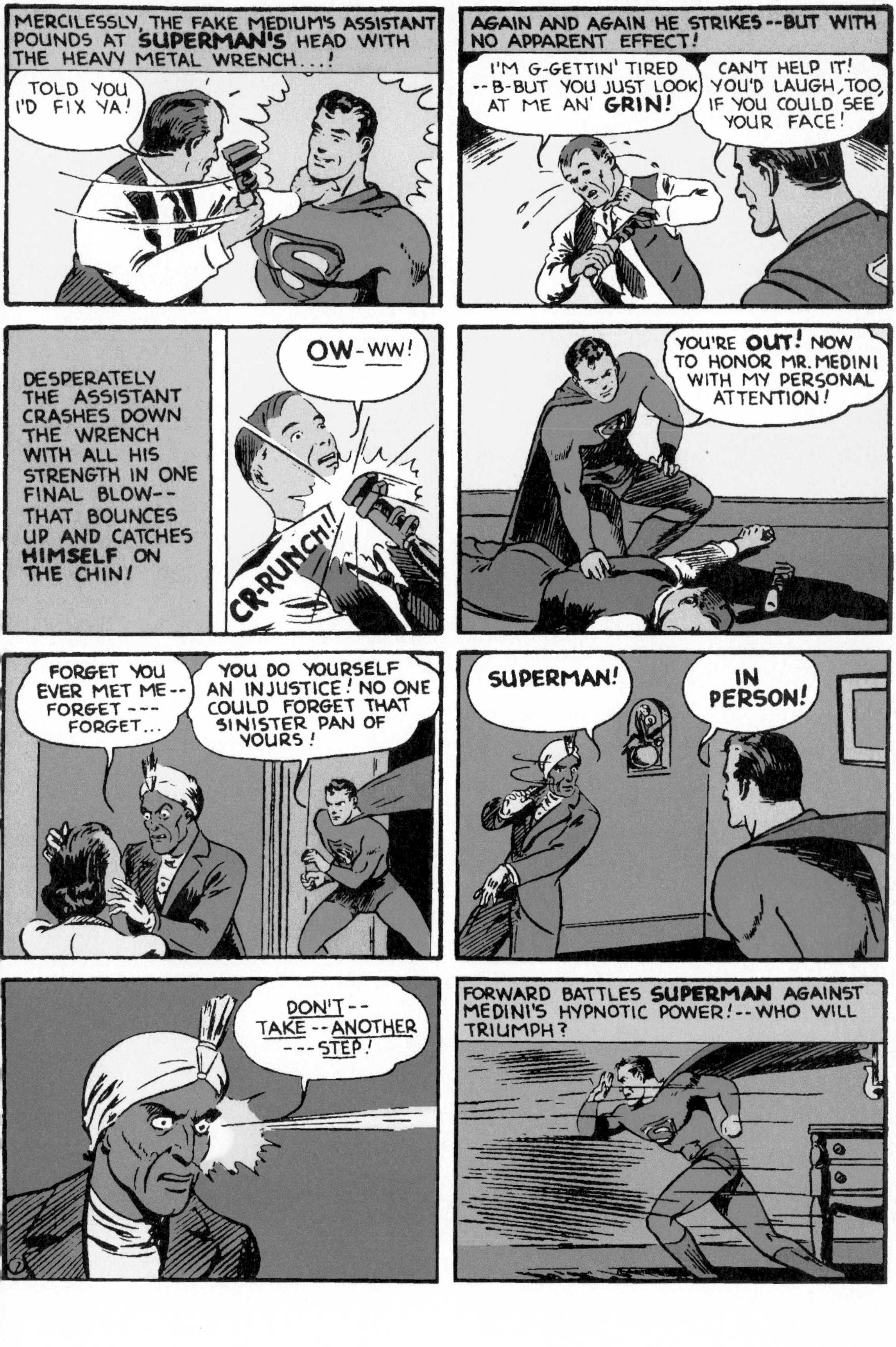
MERCILESSLY, THE FAKE MEDIUM'S ASSISTANT POUNDS AT SUPERMAN'S HEAD WITH THE HEAVY METAL WRENCH...!
TOLD YOU I'D FIX YA!
AGAIN AND AGAIN HE STRIKES--BUT WITH NO APPARENT EFFECT!
I'M G-GETTIN' TIRED --B-BUT YOU JUST LOOK AT ME AN' GRIN!
CAN'T HELP IT! YOU'D LAUGH, TOO, IF YOU COULD SEE YOUR FACE!
DESPERATELY THE ASSISTANT CRASHES DOWN THE WRENCH WITH ALL HIS STRENGTH IN ONE FINAL BLOW-- THAT BOUNCES UP AND CATCHES HIMSELF ON THE CHIN!
OW-WW!
CR-RUNCH!!
YOU'RE OUT! NOW TO HONOR MR. MEDINI WITH MY PERSONAL ATTENTION!
FORGET YOU EVER MET ME-- FORGET --- FORGET...
YOU DO YOURSELF AN INJUSTICE! NO ONE COULD FORGET THAT SINISTER PAN OF YOURS!
SUPERMAN!
IN PERSON!
DON'T-- TAKE--ANOTHER ---STEP!
FORWARD BATTLES SUPERMAN AGAINST MEDINI'S HYPNOTIC POWER!--WHO WILL TRIUMPH?

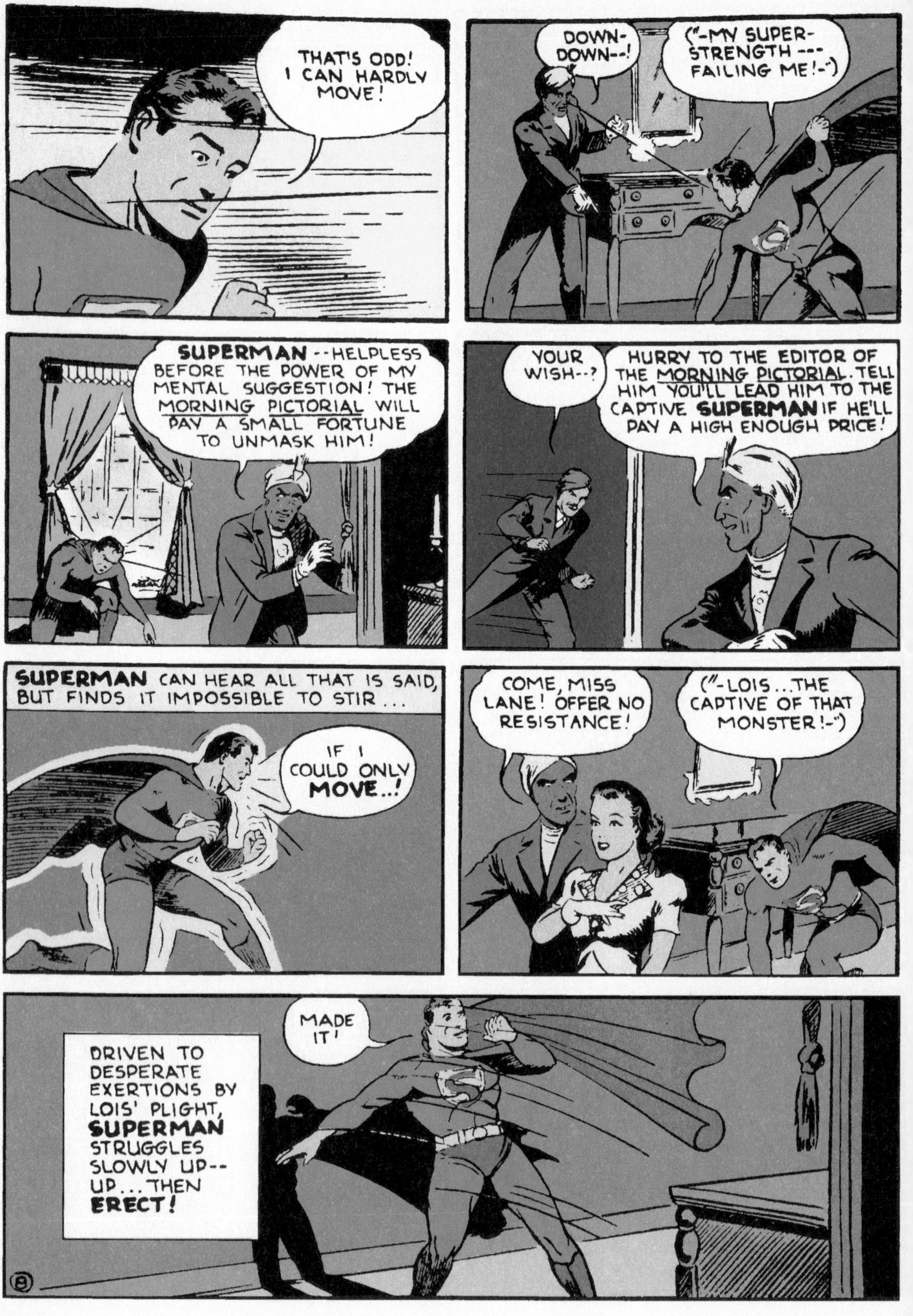
THAT'S ODD! I CAN HARDLY MOVE!
DOWN-DOWN--!
("-MY SUPER-STRENGTH --- FAILING ME!-")
SUPERMAN --HELPLESS BEFORE THE POWER OF MY MENTAL SUGGESTION! THE MORNING PICTORIAL WILL PAY A SMALL FORTUNE TO UNMASK HIM!
YOUR WISH--?
HURRY TO THE EDITOR OF THE MORNING PICTORIAL. TELL HIM YOU'LL LEAD HIM TO THE CAPTIVE SUPERMAN IF HE'LL PAY A HIGH ENOUGH PRICE!
SUPERMAN CAN HEAR ALL THAT IS SAID, BUT FINDS IT IMPOSSIBLE TO STIR...
IF I COULD ONLY MOVE..!
COME, MISS LANE! OFFER NO RESISTANCE!
("-LOIS...THE CAPTIVE OF THAT MONSTER!-")
DRIVEN TO DESPERATE EXERTIONS BY LOIS' PLIGHT, SUPERMAN STRUGGLES SLOWLY UP--UP...THEN ERECT!
MADE IT!
8

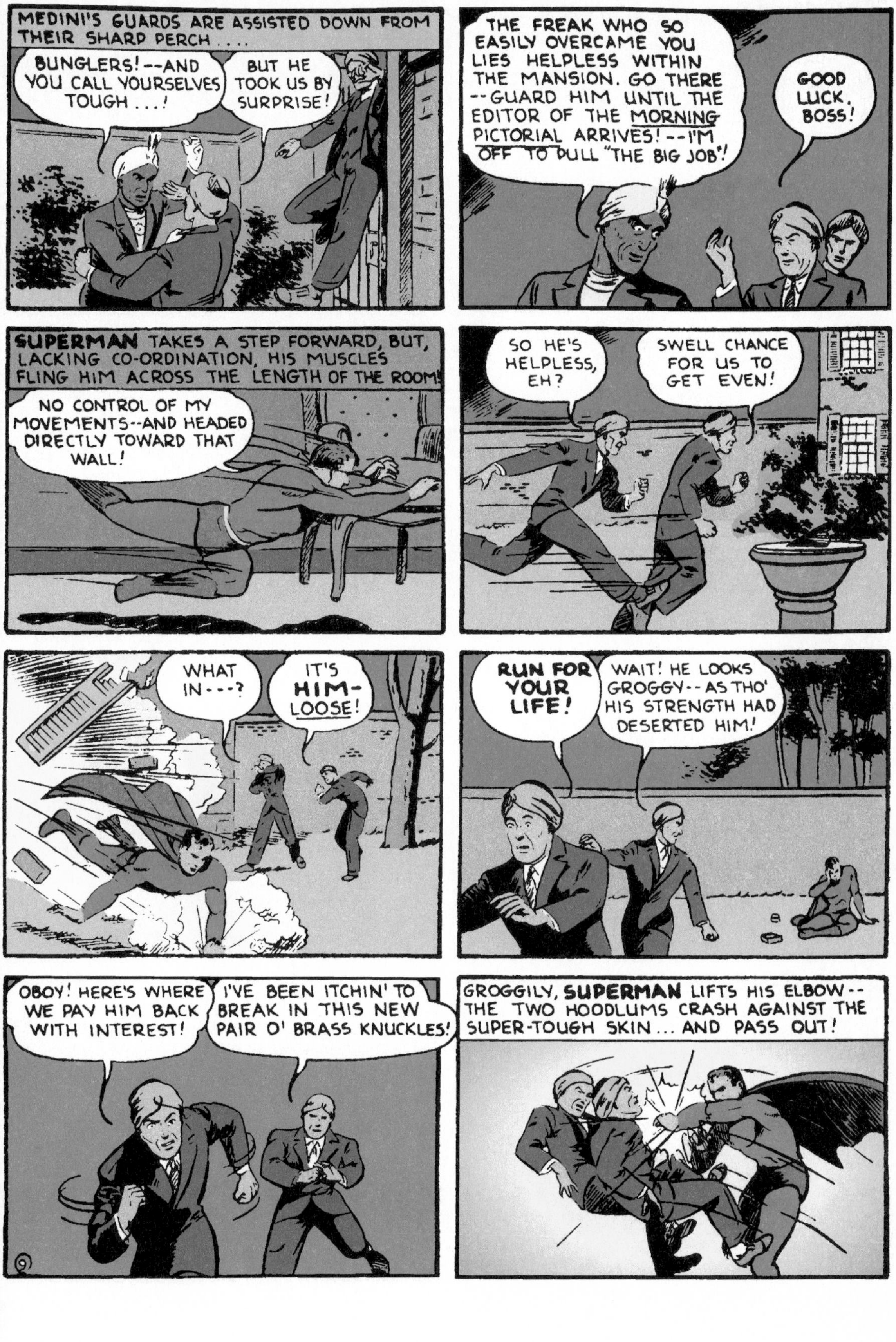
MEDINI'S GUARDS ARE ASSISTED DOWN FROM THEIR SHARP PERCH....
BUNGLERS!--AND YOU CALL YOURSELVES TOUGH...!
BUT HE TOOK US BY SURPRISE!
THE FREAK WHO SO EASILY OVERCAME YOU LIES HELPLESS WITHIN THE MANSION. GO THERE --GUARD HIM UNTIL THE EDITOR OF THE MORNING PICTORIAL ARRIVES!--I'M OFF TO PULL "THE BIG JOB"!
GOOD LUCK, BOSS!
SUPERMAN TAKES A STEP FORWARD, BUT, LACKING CO-ORDINATION, HIS MUSCLES FLING HIM ACROSS THE LENGTH OF THE ROOM!
NO CONTROL OF MY MOVEMENTS--AND HEADED DIRECTLY TOWARD THAT WALL!
SO HE'S HELPLESS, EH?
SWELL CHANCE FOR US TO GET EVEN!
WHAT IN---?
IT'S HIM-LOOSE!
RUN FOR YOUR LIFE!
WAIT! HE LOOKS GROGGY--AS THO' HIS STRENGTH HAD DESERTED HIM!
OBOY! HERE'S WHERE WE PAY HIM BACK WITH INTEREST!
I'VE BEEN ITCHIN' TO BREAK IN THIS NEW PAIR O' BRASS KNUCKLES!
GROGGILY, SUPERMAN LIFTS HIS ELBOW--THE TWO HOODLUMS CRASH AGAINST THE SUPER-TOUGH SKIN... AND PASS OUT!

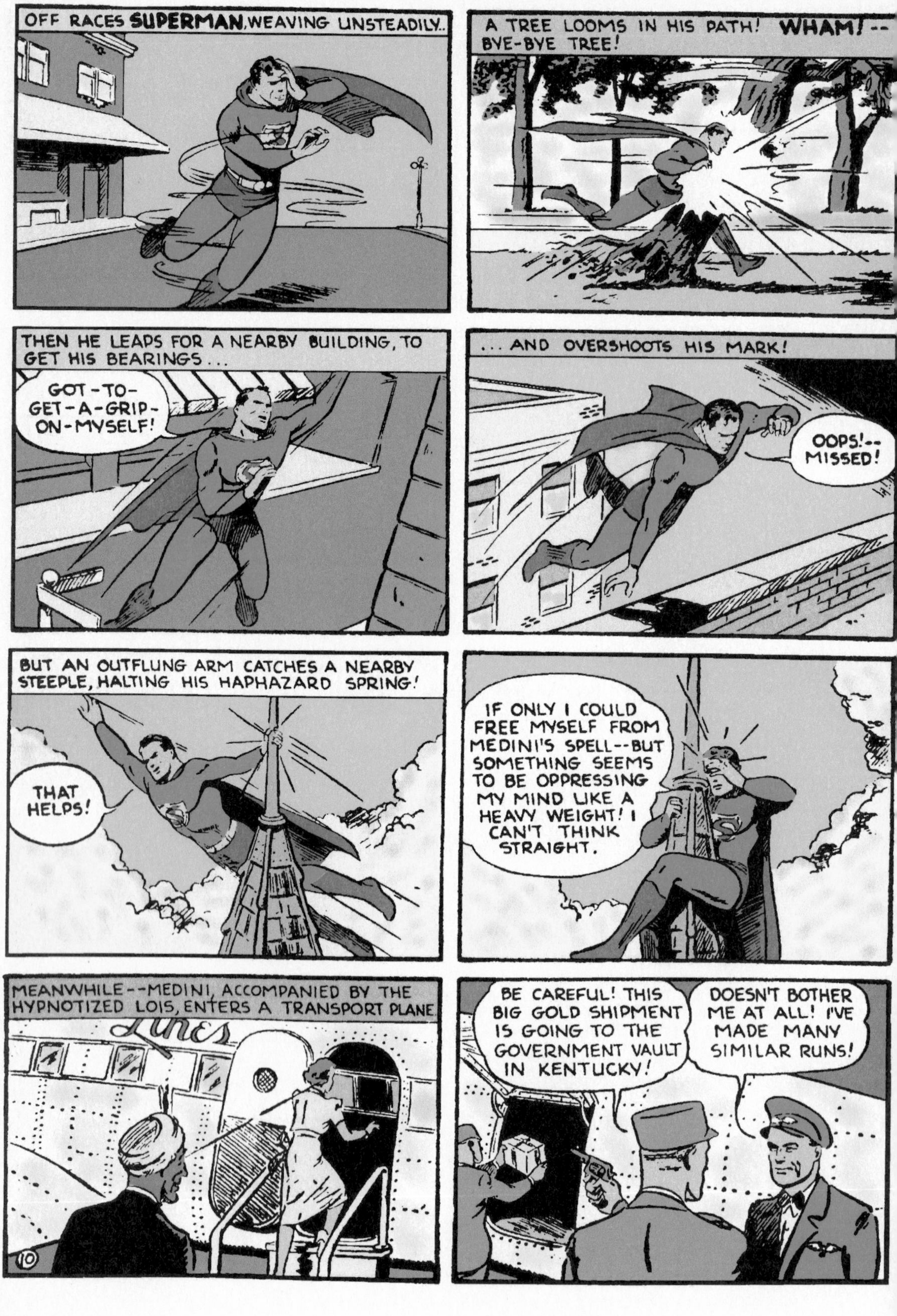
OFF RACES SUPERMAN, WEAVING UNSTEADILY..
A TREE LOOMS IN HIS PATH! WHAM!-- BYE-BYE TREE!
THEN HE LEAPS FOR A NEARBY BUILDING, TO GET HIS BEARINGS...
GOT-TO-GET-A-GRIP-ON-MYSELF!
...AND OVERSHOOTS HIS MARK!
OOPS!--MISSED!
BUT AN OUTFLUNG ARM CATCHES A NEARBY STEEPLE, HALTING HIS HAPHAZARD SPRING!
THAT HELPS!
IF ONLY I COULD FREE MYSELF FROM MEDINI'S SPELL--BUT SOMETHING SEEMS TO BE OPPRESSING MY MIND LIKE A HEAVY WEIGHT! I CAN'T THINK STRAIGHT.
MEANWHILE--MEDINI, ACCOMPANIED BY THE HYPNOTIZED LOIS, ENTERS A TRANSPORT PLANE.
10
BE CAREFUL! THIS BIG GOLD SHIPMENT IS GOING TO THE GOVERNMENT VAULT IN KENTUCKY!
DOESN'T BOTHER ME AT ALL! I'VE MADE MANY SIMILAR RUNS!

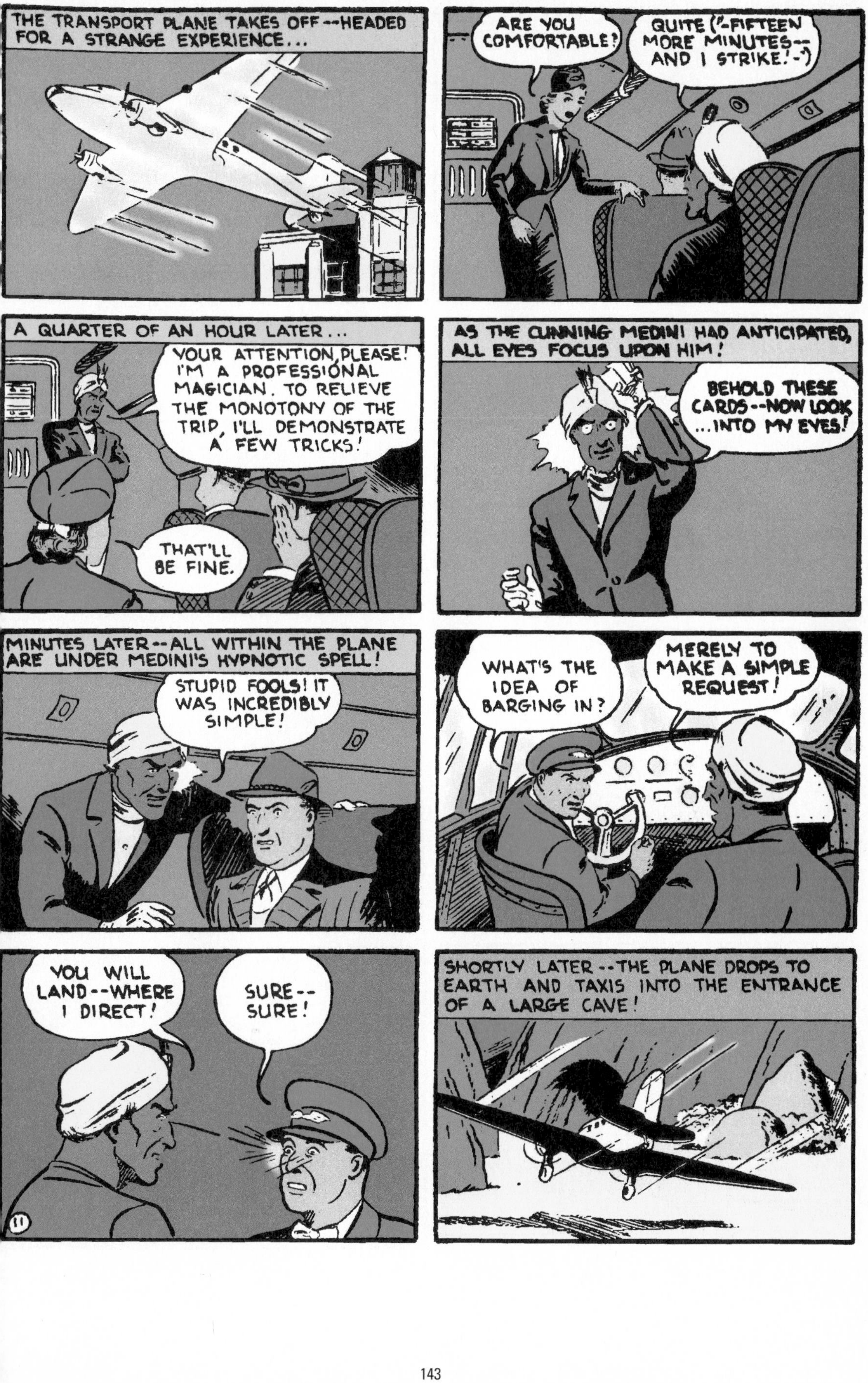
THE TRANSPORT PLANE TAKES OFF--HEADED FOR A STRANGE EXPERIENCE...
ARE YOU COMFORTABLE?
QUITE ("-FIFTEEN MORE MINUTES--AND I STRIKE!-")
A QUARTER OF AN HOUR LATER...
YOUR ATTENTION, PLEASE! I'M A PROFESSIONAL MAGICIAN. TO RELIEVE THE MONOTONY OF THE TRIP, I'LL DEMONSTRATE A FEW TRICKS!
THAT'LL BE FINE.
AS THE CUNNING MEDINI HAD ANTICIPATED, ALL EYES FOCUS UPON HIM!
BEHOLD THESE CARDS--NOW LOOK ...INTO MY EYES!
MINUTES LATER--ALL WITHIN THE PLANE ARE UNDER MEDINI'S HYPNOTIC SPELL!
STUPID FOOLS! IT WAS INCREDIBLY SIMPLE!
WHAT'S THE IDEA OF BARGING IN?
MERELY TO MAKE A SIMPLE REQUEST!
YOU WILL LAND--WHERE I DIRECT!
SURE--SURE!
11
SHORTLY LATER--THE PLANE DROPS TO EARTH AND TAXIS INTO THE ENTRANCE OF A LARGE CAVE!

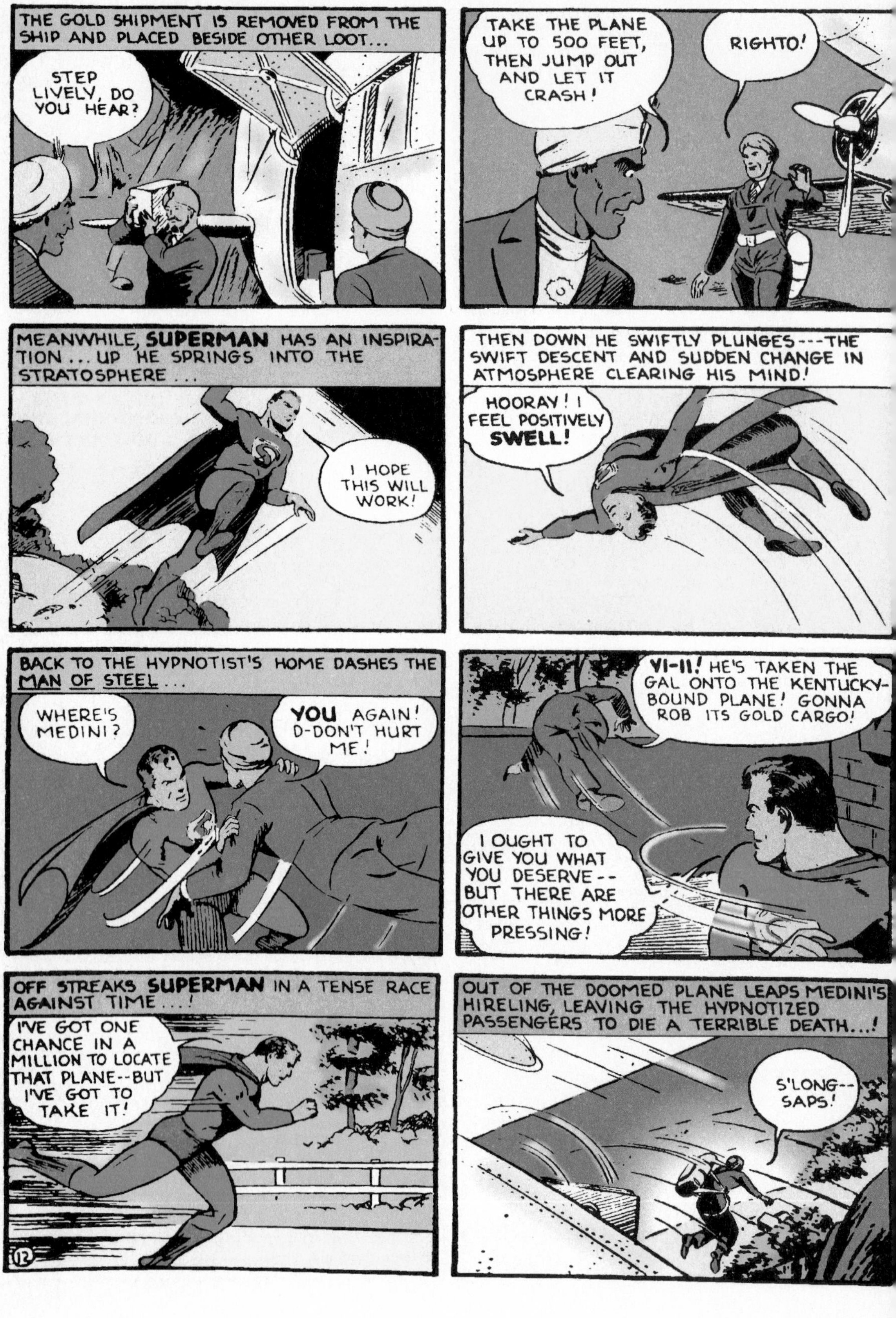
THE GOLD SHIPMENT IS REMOVED FROM THE SHIP AND PLACED BESIDE OTHER LOOT...
STEP LIVELY, DO YOU HEAR?
TAKE THE PLANE UP TO 500 FEET, THEN JUMP OUT AND LET IT CRASH!
RIGHTO!
MEANWHILE, SUPERMAN HAS AN INSPIRATION... UP HE SPRINGS INTO THE STRATOSPHERE...
I HOPE THIS WILL WORK!
THEN DOWN HE SWIFTLY PLUNGES---THE SWIFT DESCENT AND SUDDEN CHANGE IN ATMOSPHERE CLEARING HIS MIND!
HOORAY! I FEEL POSITIVELY SWELL!
BACK TO THE HYPNOTIST'S HOME DASHES THE MAN OF STEEL...
WHERE'S MEDINI?
YOU AGAIN! D-DON'T HURT ME!
YI-II! HE'S TAKEN THE GAL ONTO THE KENTUCKY-BOUND PLANE! GONNA ROB ITS GOLD CARGO!
I OUGHT TO GIVE YOU WHAT YOU DESERVE--BUT THERE ARE OTHER THINGS MORE PRESSING!
OFF STREAKS SUPERMAN IN A TENSE RACE AGAINST TIME...!
I'VE GOT ONE CHANCE IN A MILLION TO LOCATE THAT PLANE--BUT I'VE GOT TO TAKE IT!
12
OUT OF THE DOOMED PLANE LEAPS MEDINI'S HIRELING, LEAVING THE HYPNOTIZED PASSENGERS TO DIE A TERRIBLE DEATH...!
S'LONG--SAPS!

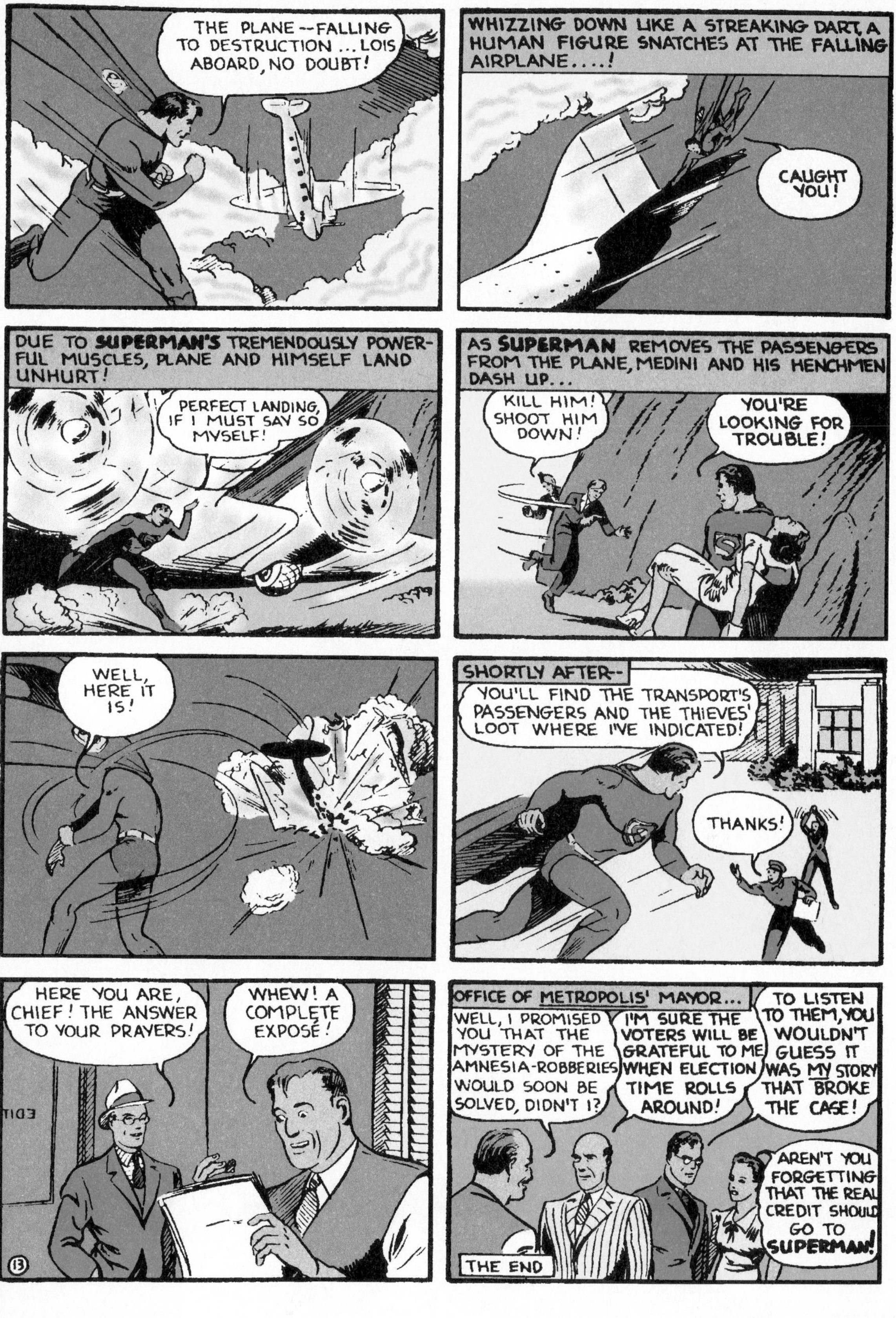
THE PLANE--FALLING TO DESTRUCTION ... LOIS ABOARD, NO DOUBT!
WHIZZING DOWN LIKE A STREAKING DART, A HUMAN FIGURE SNATCHES AT THE FALLING AIRPLANE....!
CAUGHT YOU!
DUE TO SUPERMAN'S TREMENDOUSLY POWERFUL MUSCLES, PLANE AND HIMSELF LAND UNHURT!
PERFECT LANDING, IF I MUST SAY SO MYSELF!
AS SUPERMAN REMOVES THE PASSENGERS FROM THE PLANE, MEDINI AND HIS HENCHMEN DASH UP...
KILL HIM! SHOOT HIM DOWN!
YOU'RE LOOKING FOR TROUBLE!
WELL, HERE IT IS!
SHORTLY AFTER--
YOU'LL FIND THE TRANSPORT'S PASSENGERS AND THE THIEVES' LOOT WHERE I'VE INDICATED!
THANKS!
HERE YOU ARE, CHIEF! THE ANSWER TO YOUR PRAYERS!
WHEW! A COMPLETE EXPOSÉ!
13
OFFICE OF METROPOLIS' MAYOR...
WELL, I PROMISED YOU THAT THE MYSTERY OF THE AMNESIA-ROBBERIES WOULD SOON BE SOLVED, DIDN'T I?
I'M SURE THE VOTERS WILL BE GRATEFUL TO ME WHEN ELECTION TIME ROLLS AROUND!
TO LISTEN TO THEM, YOU WOULDN'T GUESS IT WAS MY STORY THAT BROKE THE CASE!
AREN'T YOU FORGETTING THAT THE REAL CREDIT SHOULD GO TO SUPERMAN!
THE END

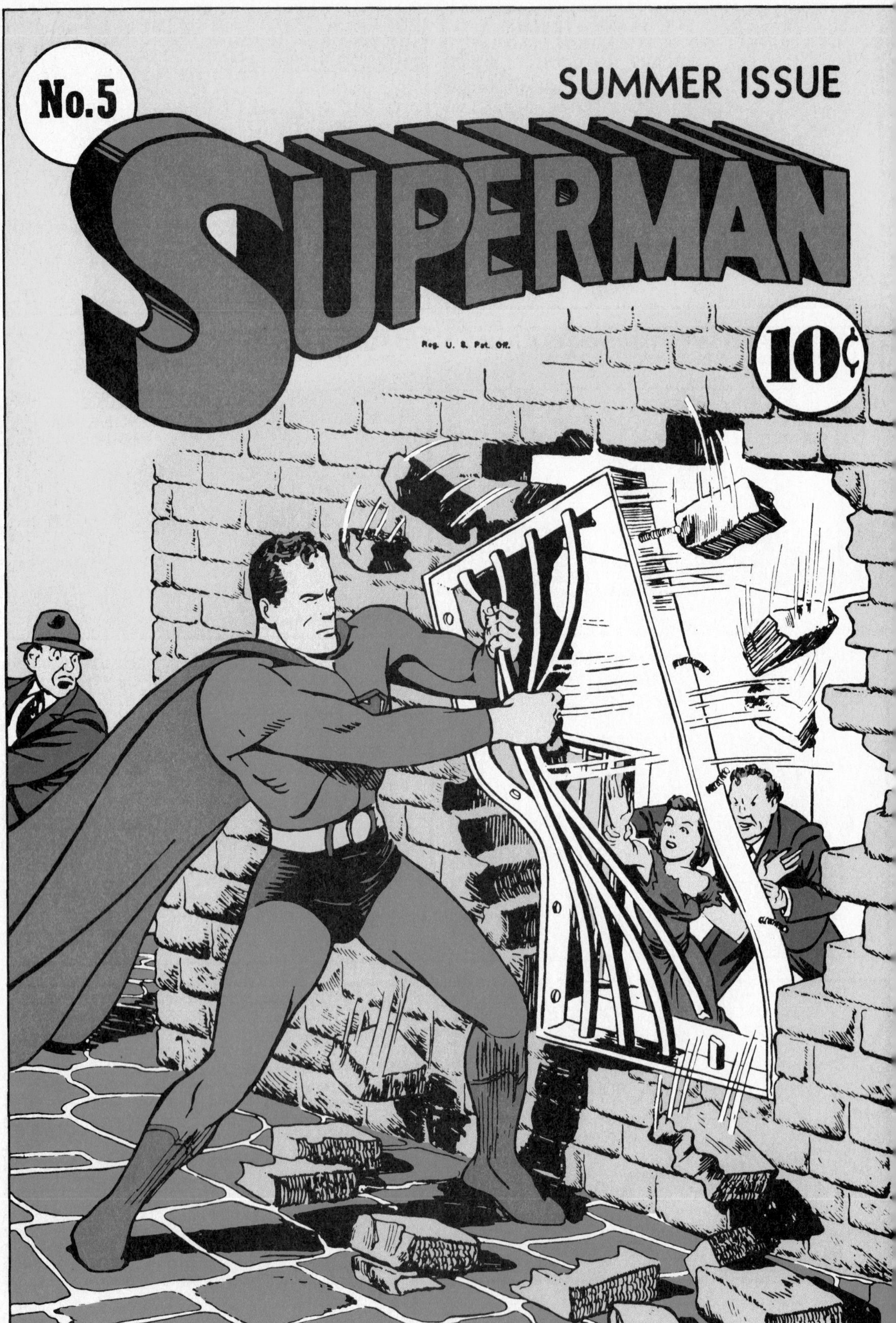
No.5
SUMMER ISSUE
SUPERMAN
Reg. U. S. Pat. Off.
10¢

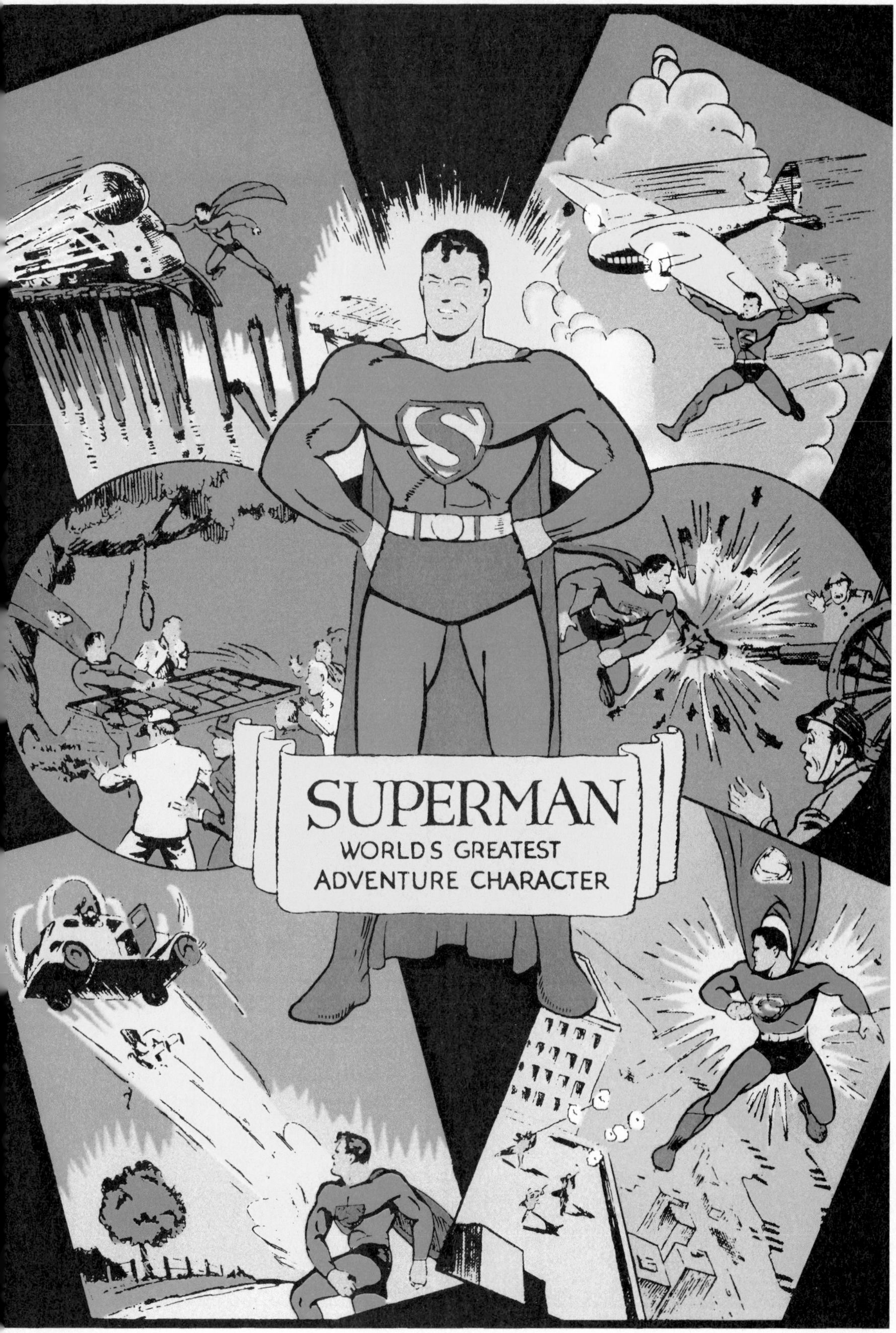
SUPERMAN
WORLD S GREATEST
ADVENTURE CHARACTER

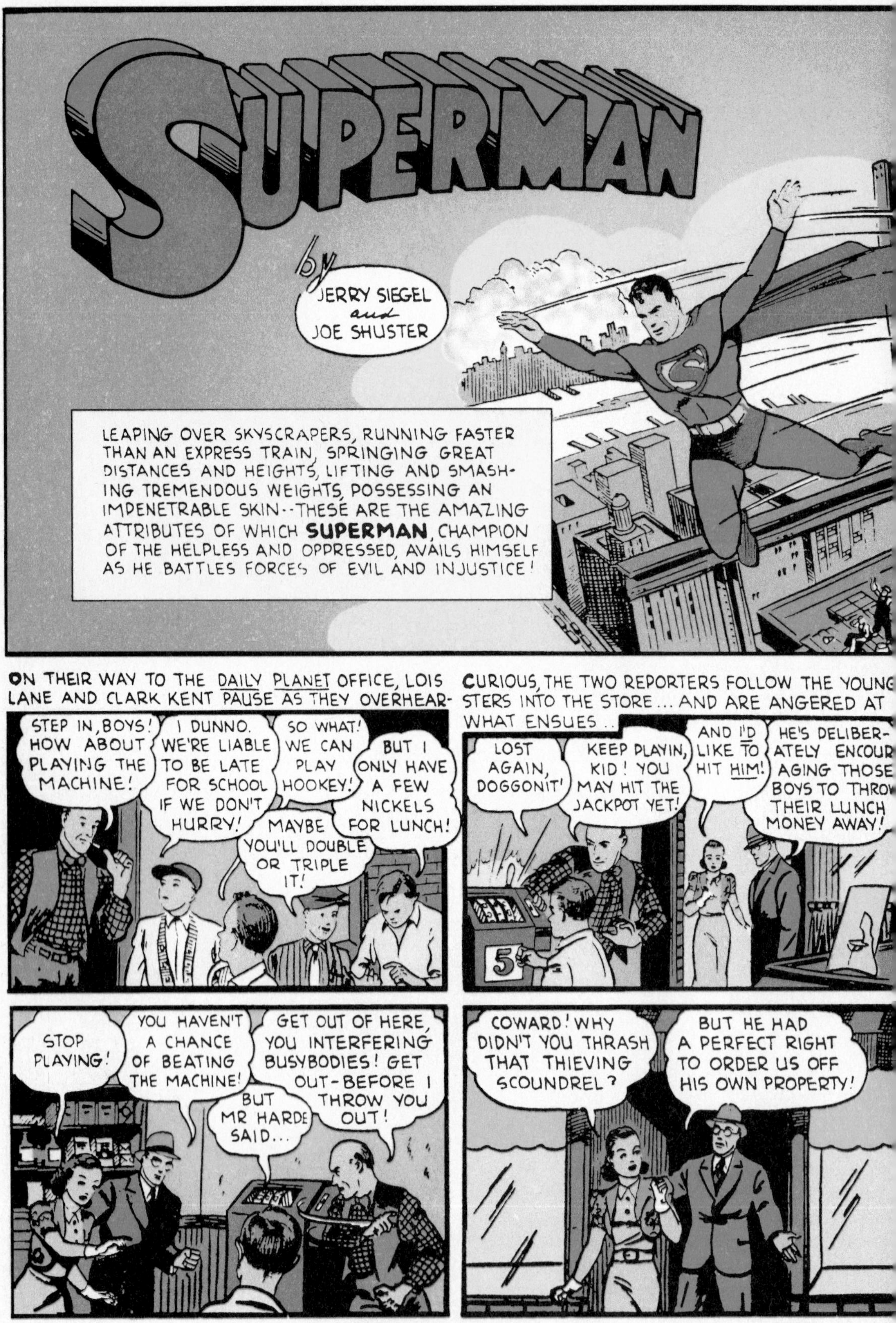
SUPERMAN
by
JERRY SIEGEL and JOE SHUSTER
LEAPING OVER SKYSCRAPERS, RUNNING FASTER THAN AN EXPRESS TRAIN, SPRINGING GREAT DISTANCES AND HEIGHTS, LIFTING AND SMASHING TREMENDOUS WEIGHTS, POSSESSING AN IMPENETRABLE SKIN--THESE ARE THE AMAZING ATTRIBUTES OF WHICH SUPERMAN, CHAMPION OF THE HELPLESS AND OPPRESSED, AVAILS HIMSELF AS HE BATTLES FORCES OF EVIL AND INJUSTICE!
ON THEIR WAY TO THE DAILY PLANET OFFICE, LOIS LANE AND CLARK KENT PAUSE AS THEY OVERHEAR-
STEP IN, BOYS! HOW ABOUT PLAYING THE MACHINE!
I DUNNO. WE'RE LIABLE TO BE LATE FOR SCHOOL IF WE DON'T HURRY!
SO WHAT! WE CAN PLAY HOOKEY!
BUT I ONLY HAVE A FEW NICKELS FOR LUNCH!
MAYBE YOU'LL DOUBLE OR TRIPLE IT!
CURIOUS, THE TWO REPORTERS FOLLOW THE YOUNGSTERS INTO THE STORE... AND ARE ANGERED AT WHAT ENSUES..
LOST AGAIN, DOGGONIT!
KEEP PLAYIN, KID! YOU MAY HIT THE JACKPOT YET!
AND I'D LIKE TO HIT HIM!
HE'S DELIBERATELY ENCOURAGING THOSE BOYS TO THROW THEIR LUNCH MONEY AWAY!
STOP PLAYING!
YOU HAVEN'T A CHANCE OF BEATING THE MACHINE!
GET OUT OF HERE, YOU INTERFERING BUSYBODIES! GET OUT-BEFORE I THROW YOU OUT!
BUT MR HARDE SAID...
COWARD! WHY DIDN'T YOU THRASH THAT THIEVING SCOUNDREL?
BUT HE HAD A PERFECT RIGHT TO ORDER US OFF HIS OWN PROPERTY!

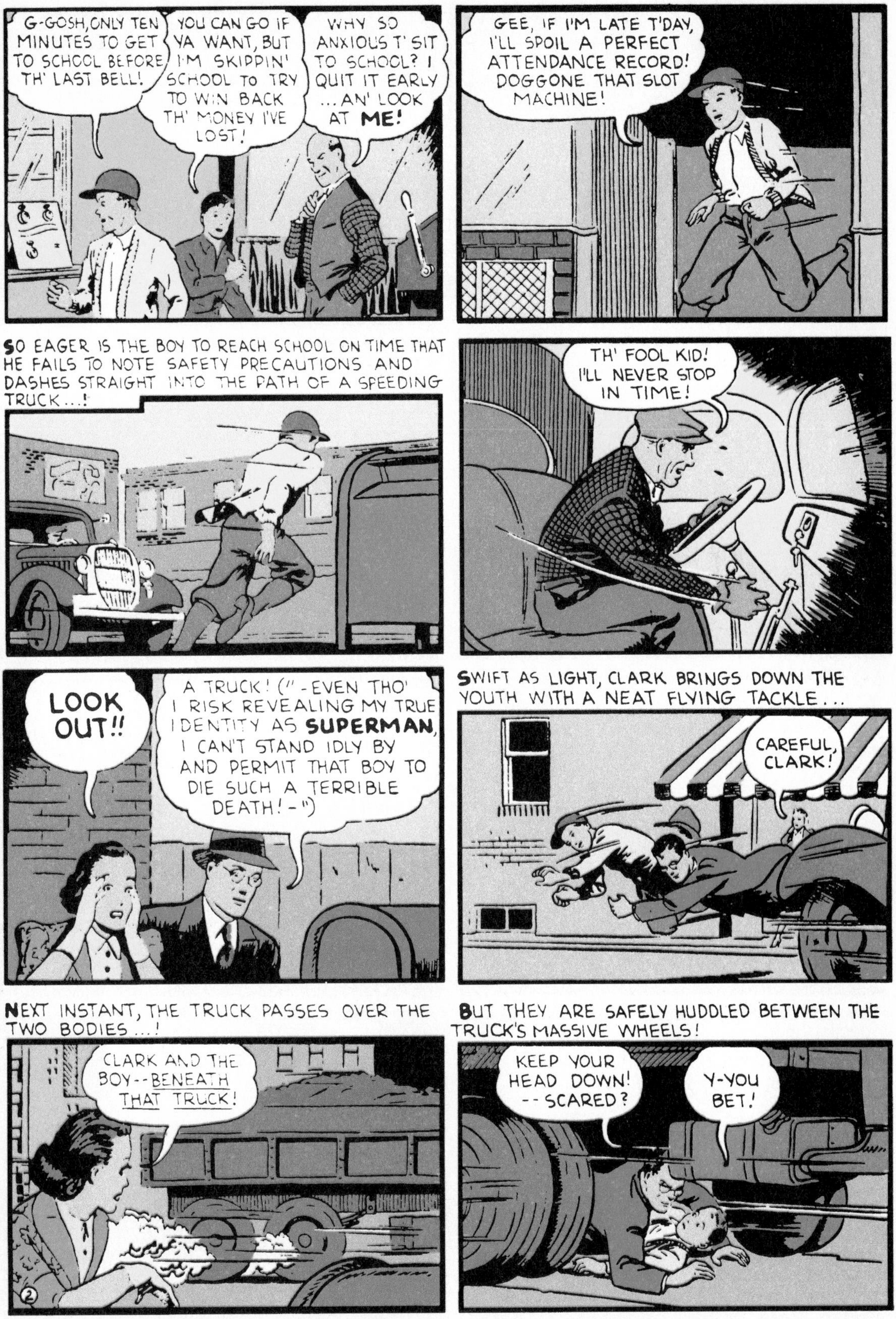
G-GOSH, ONLY TEN MINUTES TO GET TO SCHOOL BEFORE TH' LAST BELL!
YOU CAN GO IF YA WANT, BUT I'M SKIPPIN' SCHOOL TO TRY TO WIN BACK TH' MONEY I'VE LOST!
WHY SO ANXIOUS T' SIT TO SCHOOL? I QUIT IT EARLY ...AN' LOOK AT ME!
GEE, IF I'M LATE T'DAY, I'LL SPOIL A PERFECT ATTENDANCE RECORD! DOGGONE THAT SLOT MACHINE!
SO EAGER IS THE BOY TO REACH SCHOOL ON TIME THAT HE FAILS TO NOTE SAFETY PRECAUTIONS AND DASHES STRAIGHT INTO THE PATH OF A SPEEDING TRUCK...!
TH' FOOL KID! I'LL NEVER STOP IN TIME!
LOOK OUT!!
A TRUCK! ("-EVEN THO' I RISK REVEALING MY TRUE IDENTITY AS SUPERMAN, I CAN'T STAND IDLY BY AND PERMIT THAT BOY TO DIE SUCH A TERRIBLE DEATH!-")
SWIFT AS LIGHT, CLARK BRINGS DOWN THE YOUTH WITH A NEAT FLYING TACKLE...
CAREFUL, CLARK!
NEXT INSTANT, THE TRUCK PASSES OVER THE TWO BODIES...!
CLARK AND THE BOY--BENEATH THAT TRUCK!
2
BUT THEY ARE SAFELY HUDDLED BETWEEN THE TRUCK'S MASSIVE WHEELS!
KEEP YOUR HEAD DOWN! --SCARED?
Y-YOU BET!

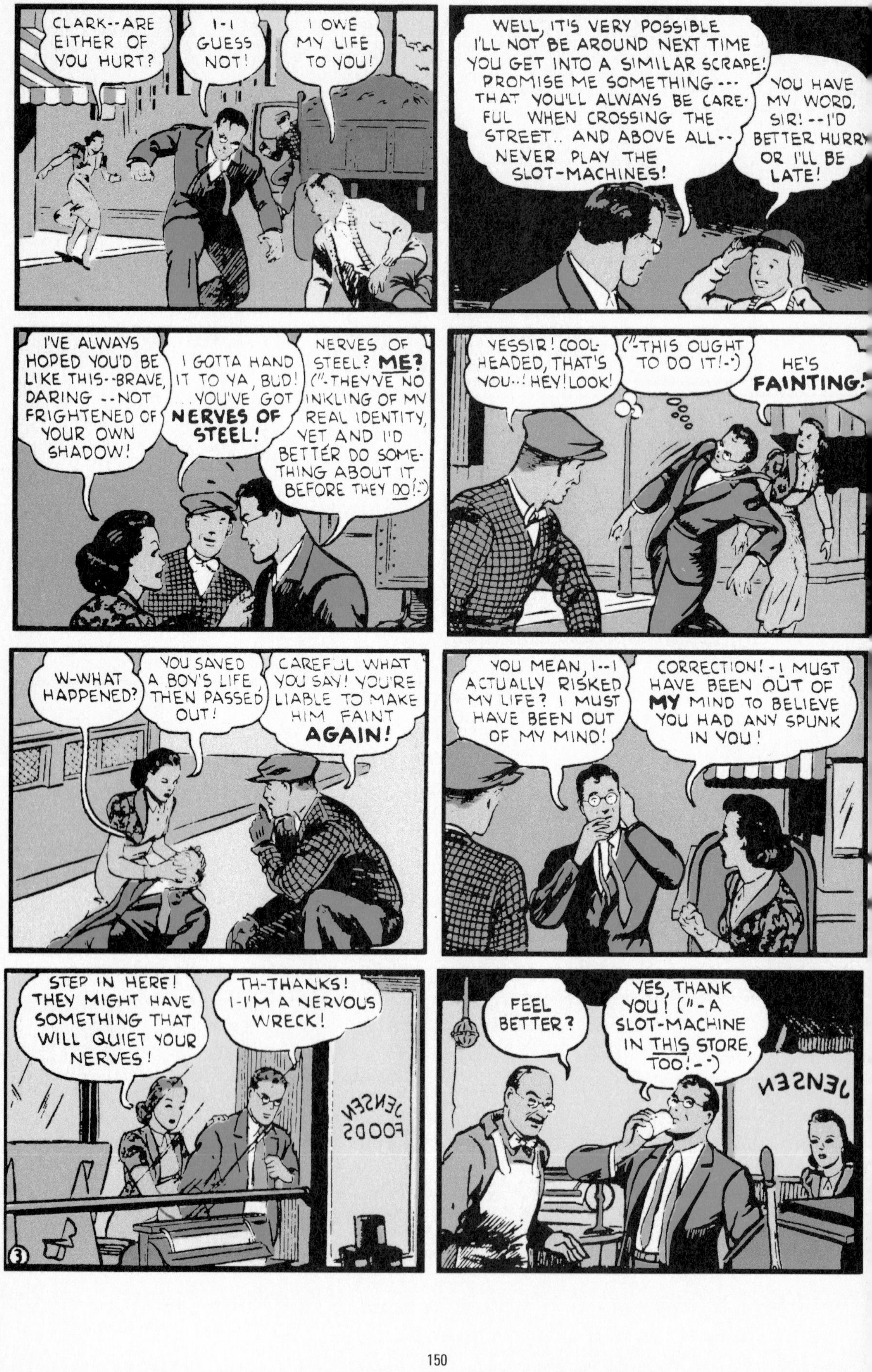
CLARK--ARE EITHER OF YOU HURT?
I-I GUESS NOT!
I OWE MY LIFE TO YOU!
WELL, IT'S VERY POSSIBLE I'LL NOT BE AROUND NEXT TIME YOU GET INTO A SIMILAR SCRAPE! PROMISE ME SOMETHING--- THAT YOU'LL ALWAYS BE CARE-FUL WHEN CROSSING THE STREET.. AND ABOVE ALL-- NEVER PLAY THE SLOT-MACHINES!
YOU HAVE MY WORD, SIR! --I'D BETTER HURRY OR I'LL BE LATE!
I'VE ALWAYS HOPED YOU'D BE LIKE THIS--BRAVE, DARING --NOT FRIGHTENED OF YOUR OWN SHADOW!
I GOTTA HAND IT TO YA, BUD! ...YOU'VE GOT **NERVES OF STEEL!**
NERVES OF STEEL? **ME?** ("-THEY'VE NO INKLING OF MY REAL IDENTITY, YET AND I'D BETTER DO SOMETHING ABOUT IT, BEFORE THEY DO!-")
YESSIR! COOL-HEADED, THAT'S YOU..! HEY! LOOK!
("-THIS OUGHT TO DO IT!-")
HE'S **FAINTING!**
W-WHAT HAPPENED?
YOU SAVED A BOY'S LIFE THEN PASSED OUT!
CAREFUL WHAT YOU SAY! YOU'RE LIABLE TO MAKE HIM FAINT **AGAIN!**
YOU MEAN, I--I ACTUALLY RISKED MY LIFE? I MUST HAVE BEEN OUT OF MY MIND!
CORRECTION! -I MUST HAVE BEEN OUT OF **MY** MIND TO BELIEVE YOU HAD ANY SPUNK IN YOU!
STEP IN HERE! THEY MIGHT HAVE SOMETHING THAT WILL QUIET YOUR NERVES!
TH-THANKS! I-I'M A NERVOUS WRECK!
JENSEN FOODS
3
FEEL BETTER?
YES, THANK YOU! ("-A SLOT-MACHINE IN THIS STORE, TOO!-")
JENSEN

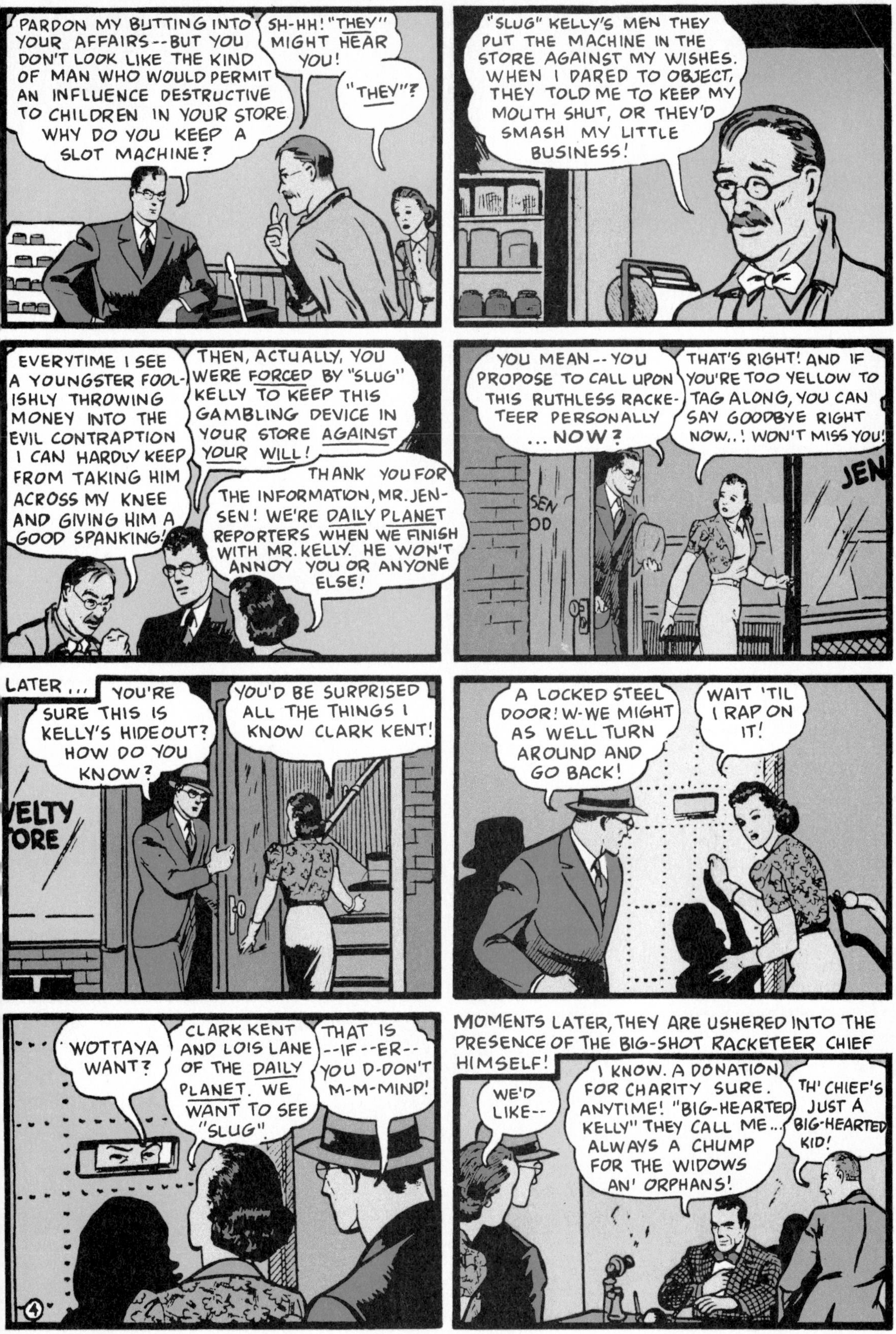
PARDON MY BUTTING INTO YOUR AFFAIRS--BUT YOU DON'T LOOK LIKE THE KIND OF MAN WHO WOULD PERMIT AN INFLUENCE DESTRUCTIVE TO CHILDREN IN YOUR STORE WHY DO YOU KEEP A SLOT MACHINE?
SH-HH! "THEY" MIGHT HEAR YOU!
"THEY"?
"SLUG" KELLY'S MEN THEY PUT THE MACHINE IN THE STORE AGAINST MY WISHES. WHEN I DARED TO OBJECT, THEY TOLD ME TO KEEP MY MOUTH SHUT, OR THEY'D SMASH MY LITTLE BUSINESS!
EVERYTIME I SEE A YOUNGSTER FOOLISHLY THROWING MONEY INTO THE EVIL CONTRAPTION I CAN HARDLY KEEP FROM TAKING HIM ACROSS MY KNEE AND GIVING HIM A GOOD SPANKING!
THEN, ACTUALLY, YOU WERE FORCED BY "SLUG" KELLY TO KEEP THIS GAMBLING DEVICE IN YOUR STORE AGAINST YOUR WILL!
THANK YOU FOR THE INFORMATION, MR. JENSEN! WE'RE DAILY PLANET REPORTERS WHEN WE FINISH WITH MR. KELLY. HE WON'T ANNOY YOU OR ANYONE ELSE!
YOU MEAN--YOU PROPOSE TO CALL UPON THIS RUTHLESS RACKETEER PERSONALLY ...NOW?
THAT'S RIGHT! AND IF YOU'RE TOO YELLOW TO TAG ALONG, YOU CAN SAY GOODBYE RIGHT NOW..! WON'T MISS YOU!
JEN
LATER...
YOU'RE SURE THIS IS KELLY'S HIDEOUT? HOW DO YOU KNOW?
YOU'D BE SURPRISED ALL THE THINGS I KNOW CLARK KENT!
ELTY
ORE
A LOCKED STEEL DOOR! W-WE MIGHT AS WELL TURN AROUND AND GO BACK!
WAIT 'TIL I RAP ON IT!
WOTTAYA WANT?
CLARK KENT AND LOIS LANE OF THE DAILY PLANET. WE WANT TO SEE "SLUG".
THAT IS --IF--ER-- YOU D-DON'T M-M-MIND!
4
MOMENTS LATER, THEY ARE USHERED INTO THE PRESENCE OF THE BIG-SHOT RACKETEER CHIEF HIMSELF!
WE'D LIKE--
I KNOW. A DONATION FOR CHARITY SURE. ANYTIME! "BIG-HEARTED KELLY" THEY CALL ME... ALWAYS A CHUMP FOR THE WIDOWS AN' ORPHANS!
TH' CHIEF'S JUST A BIG-HEARTED KID!

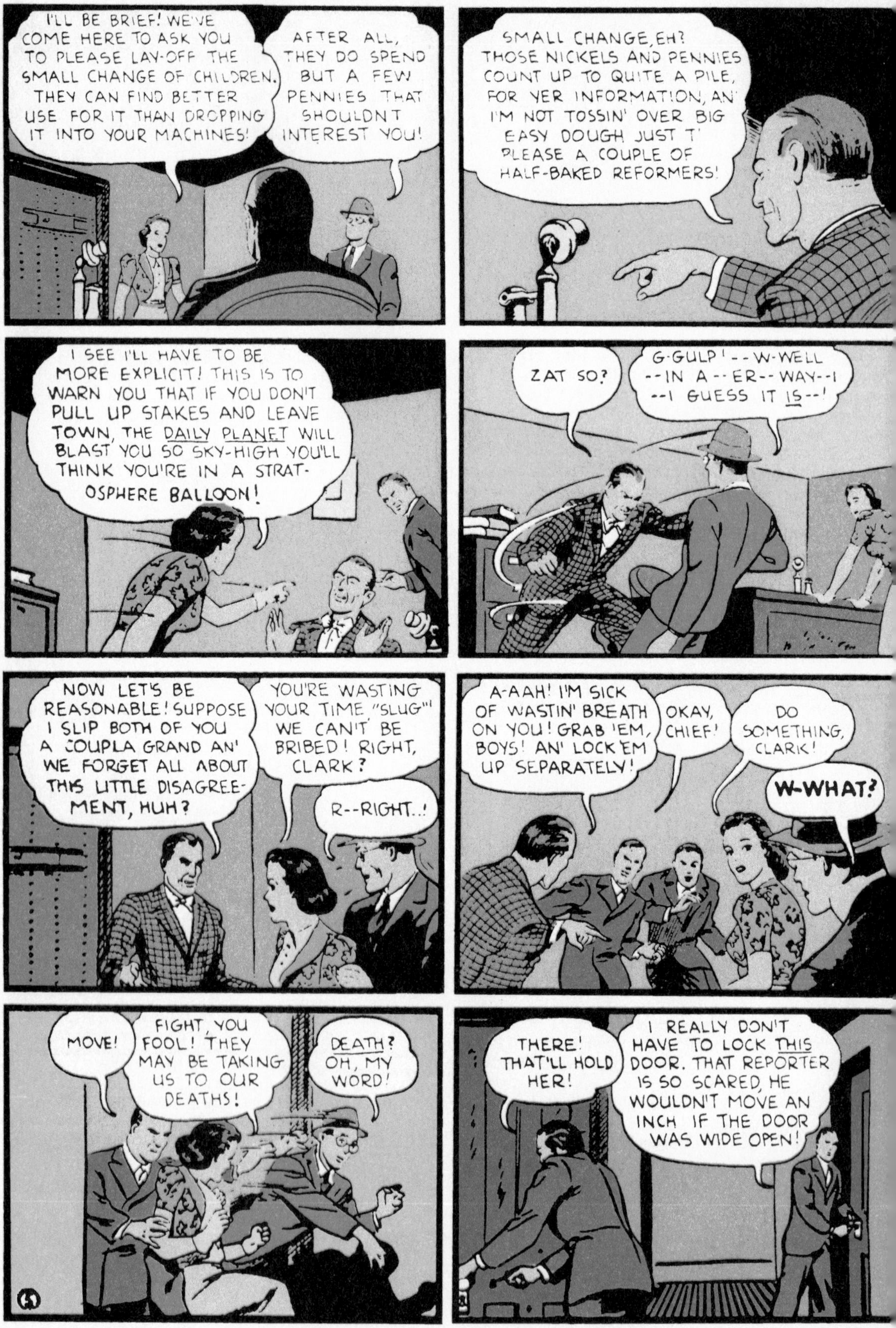
I'LL BE BRIEF! WE'VE COME HERE TO ASK YOU TO PLEASE LAY-OFF THE SMALL CHANGE OF CHILDREN. THEY CAN FIND BETTER USE FOR IT THAN DROPPING IT INTO YOUR MACHINES!
AFTER ALL, THEY DO SPEND BUT A FEW PENNIES THAT SHOULDN'T INTEREST YOU!
SMALL CHANGE, EH? THOSE NICKELS AND PENNIES COUNT UP TO QUITE A PILE, FOR YER INFORMATION, AN' I'M NOT TOSSIN' OVER BIG EASY DOUGH JUST T' PLEASE A COUPLE OF HALF-BAKED REFORMERS!
I SEE I'LL HAVE TO BE MORE EXPLICIT! THIS IS TO WARN YOU THAT IF YOU DON'T PULL UP STAKES AND LEAVE TOWN, THE DAILY PLANET WILL BLAST YOU SO SKY-HIGH YOU'LL THINK YOU'RE IN A STRAT-OSPHERE BALLOON!
ZAT SO?
G-GULP! --W-WELL --IN A--ER--WAY--I --I GUESS IT IS--!
NOW LET'S BE REASONABLE! SUPPOSE I SLIP BOTH OF YOU A COUPLA GRAND AN' WE FORGET ALL ABOUT THIS LITTLE DISAGREE-MENT, HUH?
YOU'RE WASTING YOUR TIME "SLUG"! WE CAN'T BE BRIBED! RIGHT, CLARK?
R--RIGHT..!
A-AAH! I'M SICK OF WASTIN' BREATH ON YOU! GRAB 'EM, BOYS! AN' LOCK 'EM UP SEPARATELY!
OKAY, CHIEF!
DO SOMETHING, CLARK!
W-WHAT?
MOVE!
FIGHT, YOU FOOL! THEY MAY BE TAKING US TO OUR DEATHS!
DEATH? OH, MY WORD!
THERE! THAT'LL HOLD HER!
I REALLY DON'T HAVE TO LOCK THIS DOOR. THAT REPORTER IS SO SCARED, HE WOULDN'T MOVE AN INCH IF THE DOOR WAS WIDE OPEN!

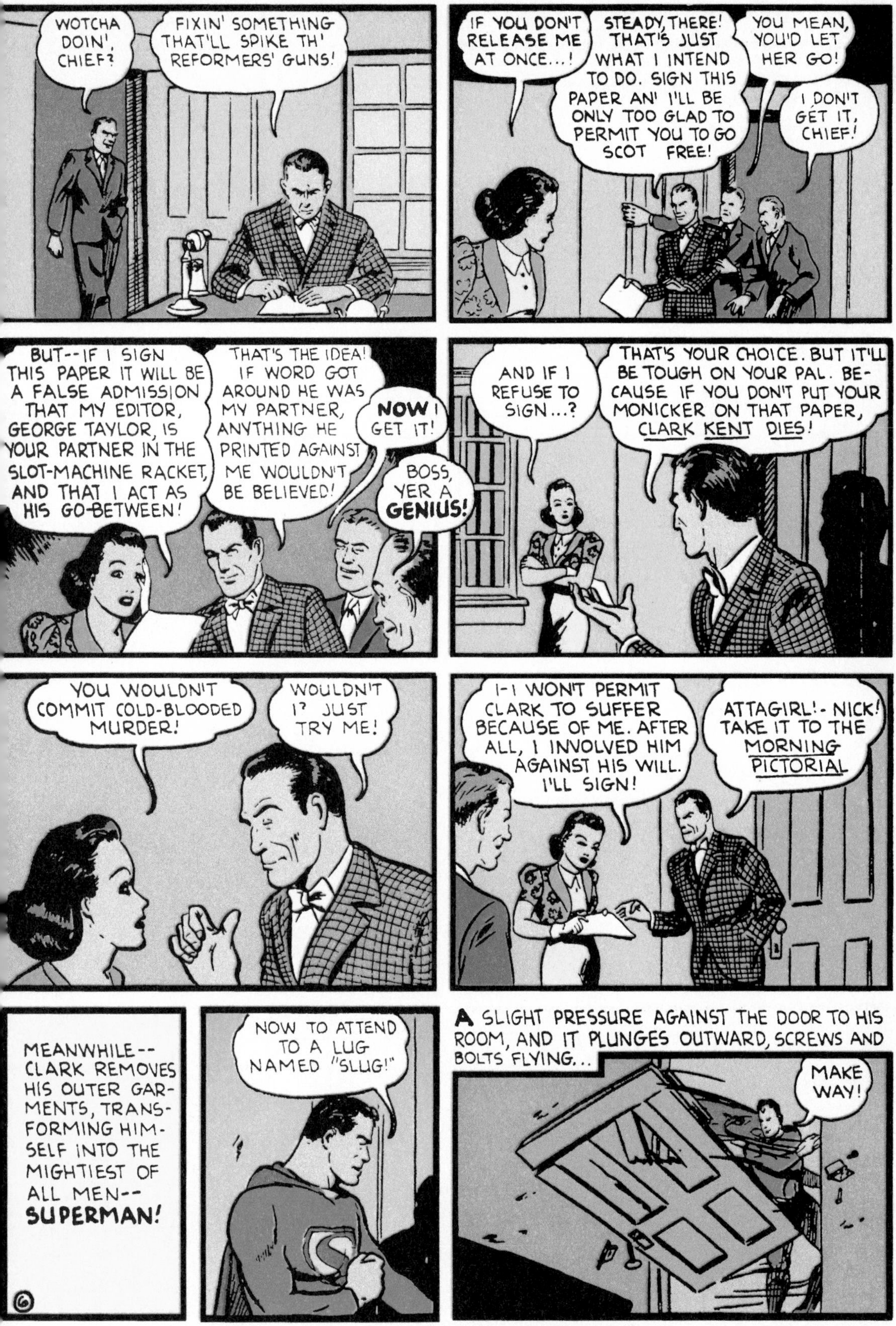
WOTCHA DOIN', CHIEF?
FIXIN' SOMETHING THAT'LL SPIKE TH' REFORMERS' GUNS!
IF YOU DON'T RELEASE ME AT ONCE...!
STEADY, THERE! THAT'S JUST WHAT I INTEND TO DO. SIGN THIS PAPER AN' I'LL BE ONLY TOO GLAD TO PERMIT YOU TO GO SCOT FREE!
YOU MEAN, YOU'D LET HER GO!
I DON'T GET IT, CHIEF!
BUT--IF I SIGN THIS PAPER IT WILL BE A FALSE ADMISSION THAT MY EDITOR, GEORGE TAYLOR, IS YOUR PARTNER IN THE SLOT-MACHINE RACKET, AND THAT I ACT AS HIS GO-BETWEEN!
THAT'S THE IDEA! IF WORD GOT AROUND HE WAS MY PARTNER, ANYTHING HE PRINTED AGAINST ME WOULDN'T BE BELIEVED!
NOW I GET IT!
BOSS, YER A GENIUS!
AND IF I REFUSE TO SIGN...?
THAT'S YOUR CHOICE. BUT IT'LL BE TOUGH ON YOUR PAL. BECAUSE IF YOU DON'T PUT YOUR MONICKER ON THAT PAPER, CLARK KENT DIES!
YOU WOULDN'T COMMIT COLD-BLOODED MURDER!
WOULDN'T I? JUST TRY ME!
I-I WON'T PERMIT CLARK TO SUFFER BECAUSE OF ME. AFTER ALL, I INVOLVED HIM AGAINST HIS WILL. I'LL SIGN!
ATTAGIRL!- NICK! TAKE IT TO THE MORNING PICTORIAL
MEANWHILE-- CLARK REMOVES HIS OUTER GARMENTS, TRANSFORMING HIMSELF INTO THE MIGHTIEST OF ALL MEN-- SUPERMAN!
6
NOW TO ATTEND TO A LUG NAMED "SLUG!"
A SLIGHT PRESSURE AGAINST THE DOOR TO HIS ROOM, AND IT PLUNGES OUTWARD, SCREWS AND BOLTS FLYING...
MAKE WAY!

SWIFTLY, **SUPERMAN** CATCHES THE DOOR BEFORE IT CAN STRIKE THE FLOOR...

MUSTN'T MAKE ANY MORE NOISE THAN I CAN HELP--YET!

OFF ALONG THE HALLWAY HE HURRIES..

I'M ON MY WAY!

SUDDENLY..

WHAT--!

OOPS!

AS THE HOODLUM FIRES AT HIM, THE <u>MAN OF STEEL</u> SLAPS BACK THE BULLET SO THAT IT STRIKES THE GUN FROM THE GUNMAN'S HAND!

HEY--!

JUST LIKE HANDBALL!

OH-BOY! DOZENS OF SLOT-MACHINES!

THIS END UP!

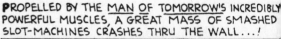

FUN, EH?

PROPELLED BY THE <u>MAN OF TOMORROW'S</u> INCREDIBLY POWERFUL MUSCLES, A GREAT MASS OF SMASHED SLOT-MACHINES CRASHES THRU THE WALL...!

⑦

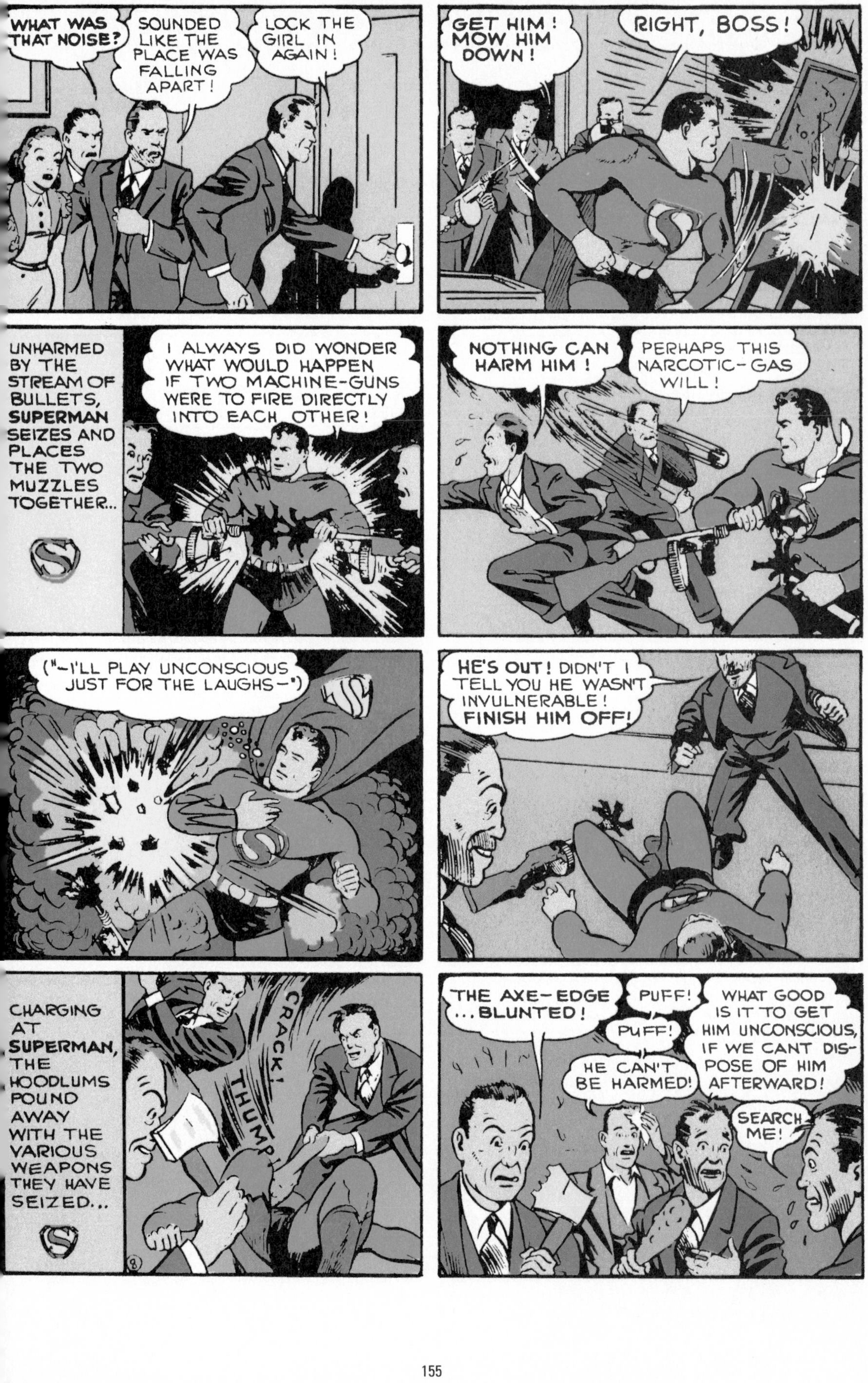
WHAT WAS THAT NOISE?
SOUNDED LIKE THE PLACE WAS FALLING APART!
LOCK THE GIRL IN AGAIN!
GET HIM! MOW HIM DOWN!
RIGHT, BOSS!
UNHARMED BY THE STREAM OF BULLETS, SUPERMAN SEIZES AND PLACES THE TWO MUZZLES TOGETHER...
I ALWAYS DID WONDER WHAT WOULD HAPPEN IF TWO MACHINE-GUNS WERE TO FIRE DIRECTLY INTO EACH OTHER!
NOTHING CAN HARM HIM!
PERHAPS THIS NARCOTIC-GAS WILL!
("-I'LL PLAY UNCONSCIOUS JUST FOR THE LAUGHS-")
HE'S OUT! DIDN'T I TELL YOU HE WASN'T INVULNERABLE! FINISH HIM OFF!
CHARGING AT SUPERMAN, THE HOODLUMS POUND AWAY WITH THE VARIOUS WEAPONS THEY HAVE SEIZED...
CRACK!
THUMP!
THE AXE-EDGE ...BLUNTED!
PUFF!
PUFF!
HE CAN'T BE HARMED!
WHAT GOOD IS IT TO GET HIM UNCONSCIOUS, IF WE CANT DISPOSE OF HIM AFTERWARD!
SEARCH ME!

THE CHEMICAL FLUID FROM THIS FIRE-EXTINGUISHER WILL BLIND HIM!

HURRY! HE'S REVIVING!

KEEP AWAY! I'LL BLIND YOU! I'LL—!

GIVE ME THAT!

THANKS FOR THE MISSILE!

LIGHTING FIRE-BRANDS, THE THUGS BRANDISH THEM AT SUPERMAN....

THAT'S RIGHT! FIRE WILL GET HIM!

YOU HOPE!

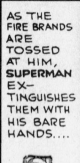

AS THE FIRE BRANDS ARE TOSSED AT HIM, SUPERMAN EXTINGUISHES THEM WITH HIS BARE HANDS....

WANT TO JUGGLE, EH?

LET'S RUN FOR IT!

THE GUY AIN'T HUMAN!

WHEW! SLAMMED THE STEEL DOOR SHUT IN HIS FACE JUST IN TIME!

SAFE AT LAST!

THE STEEL DOOR-SHAKING!

HE'S ATTACKING ON THE OTHER SIDE! —BACK!

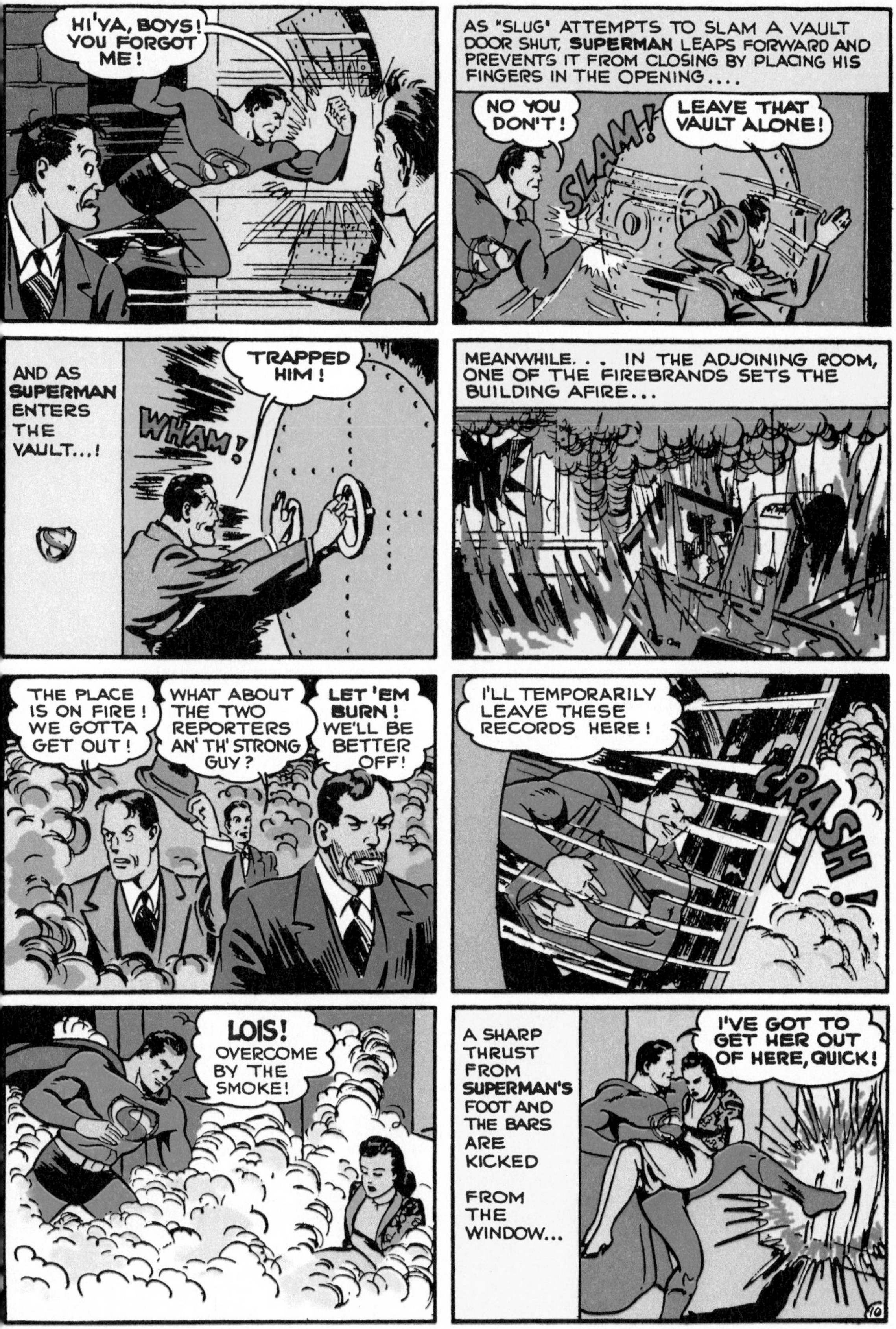
HI'YA, BOYS! YOU FORGOT ME!
AS "SLUG" ATTEMPTS TO SLAM A VAULT DOOR SHUT, SUPERMAN LEAPS FORWARD AND PREVENTS IT FROM CLOSING BY PLACING HIS FINGERS IN THE OPENING....
NO YOU DON'T!
SLAM!
LEAVE THAT VAULT ALONE!
AND AS SUPERMAN ENTERS THE VAULT...!
TRAPPED HIM!
WHAM!
MEANWHILE. . . IN THE ADJOINING ROOM, ONE OF THE FIREBRANDS SETS THE BUILDING AFIRE...
THE PLACE IS ON FIRE! WE GOTTA GET OUT!
WHAT ABOUT THE TWO REPORTERS AN' TH' STRONG GUY?
LET 'EM BURN! WE'LL BE BETTER OFF!
I'LL TEMPORARILY LEAVE THESE RECORDS HERE!
CRASH!
LOIS! OVERCOME BY THE SMOKE!
A SHARP THRUST FROM SUPERMAN'S FOOT AND THE BARS ARE KICKED FROM THE WINDOW...
I'VE GOT TO GET HER OUT OF HERE, QUICK!
10

DOWN TOWARD EARTH LEAPS THE MAN OF STEEL WITH HIS PRECIOUS BURDEN

WH-WHERE AM I?

ON YOUR WAY TO TERRA FIRMA, MY DEAR!

BUT WHAT OF CLARK?

I'M ON MY WAY BACK TO RESCUE HIM!

SHORTLY AFTER.

SUPERMAN GUIDED ME OUT— BUT WHAT ARE THESE LEDGER BOOKS HE GAVE ME?

"SLUG'S" SECRET RECORDS!

MEANWHILE— — — IN THE EDITORIAL OFFICE OF THE DAILY PLANET...

HAVE YOU SEEN THE MORNING PICTORIAL'S EXTRA?

WHAT IN BLAZES—?

MORNING PICTORIAL

PLANET EDITOR AND REPORTER IN LEAGUE WITH RACKETEER

REPORTERS SIGNED STORY SENT TO MORNING PICTORIAL

NO DOUBT OF THE SIGNATURE ON THAT STATEMENT! IT'S LOIS'! BUT WHY SHOULD SHE—?

I CAN EXPLAIN, CHIEF!

"SLUG" FORCED ME TO SIGN THAT PAPER AGAINST MY WILL! HE THINKS THAT YOU'LL NOW BE HANDICAPPED IN A FIGHT AGAINST HIM!

HE THINKS SO, EH? WELL, WITH THE AID OF HIS SECRET RECORDS, WE'LL SETTLE MR. KELLY'S HASH!

("ONE QUICK GLANCE AND MY PHOTOGRAPHIC MEMORY WILL ENABLE ME TO REMEMBER ALL THESE NAMES AND ADDRESSES!")

SLIPPING AWAY INTO A STOREROOM, CLARK ONCE AGAIN CHANGES INTO HIS SUPERMAN COSTUME...

NOW TO VISIT THE VARIOUS STORES WHERE "SLUG" PLACED HIS SLOT MACHINES!

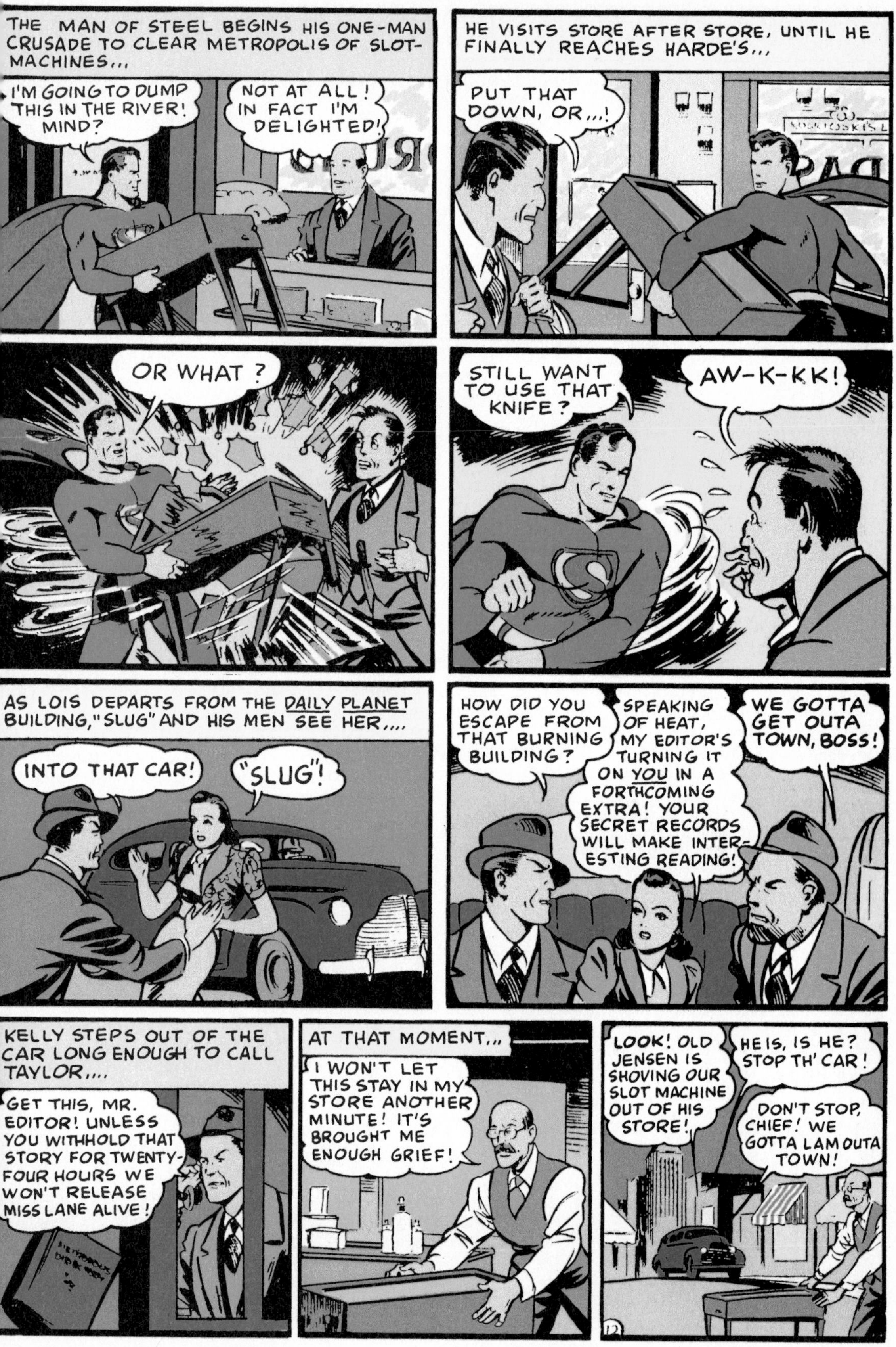
THE MAN OF STEEL BEGINS HIS ONE-MAN CRUSADE TO CLEAR METROPOLIS OF SLOT-MACHINES...
I'M GOING TO DUMP THIS IN THE RIVER! MIND?
NOT AT ALL! IN FACT I'M DELIGHTED!
HE VISITS STORE AFTER STORE, UNTIL HE FINALLY REACHES HARDE'S...
PUT THAT DOWN, OR...!
OR WHAT?
STILL WANT TO USE THAT KNIFE?
AW-K-KK!
AS LOIS DEPARTS FROM THE DAILY PLANET BUILDING, "SLUG" AND HIS MEN SEE HER....
INTO THAT CAR!
"SLUG"!
HOW DID YOU ESCAPE FROM THAT BURNING BUILDING?
SPEAKING OF HEAT, MY EDITOR'S TURNING IT ON YOU IN A FORTHCOMING EXTRA! YOUR SECRET RECORDS WILL MAKE INTERESTING READING!
WE GOTTA GET OUTA TOWN, BOSS!
KELLY STEPS OUT OF THE CAR LONG ENOUGH TO CALL TAYLOR....
GET THIS, MR. EDITOR! UNLESS YOU WITHHOLD THAT STORY FOR TWENTY-FOUR HOURS WE WON'T RELEASE MISS LANE ALIVE!
AT THAT MOMENT...
I WON'T LET THIS STAY IN MY STORE ANOTHER MINUTE! IT'S BROUGHT ME ENOUGH GRIEF!
LOOK! OLD JENSEN IS SHOVING OUR SLOT MACHINE OUT OF HIS STORE!
HE IS, IS HE? STOP TH' CAR!
DON'T STOP, CHIEF! WE GOTTA LAM OUTA TOWN!
12

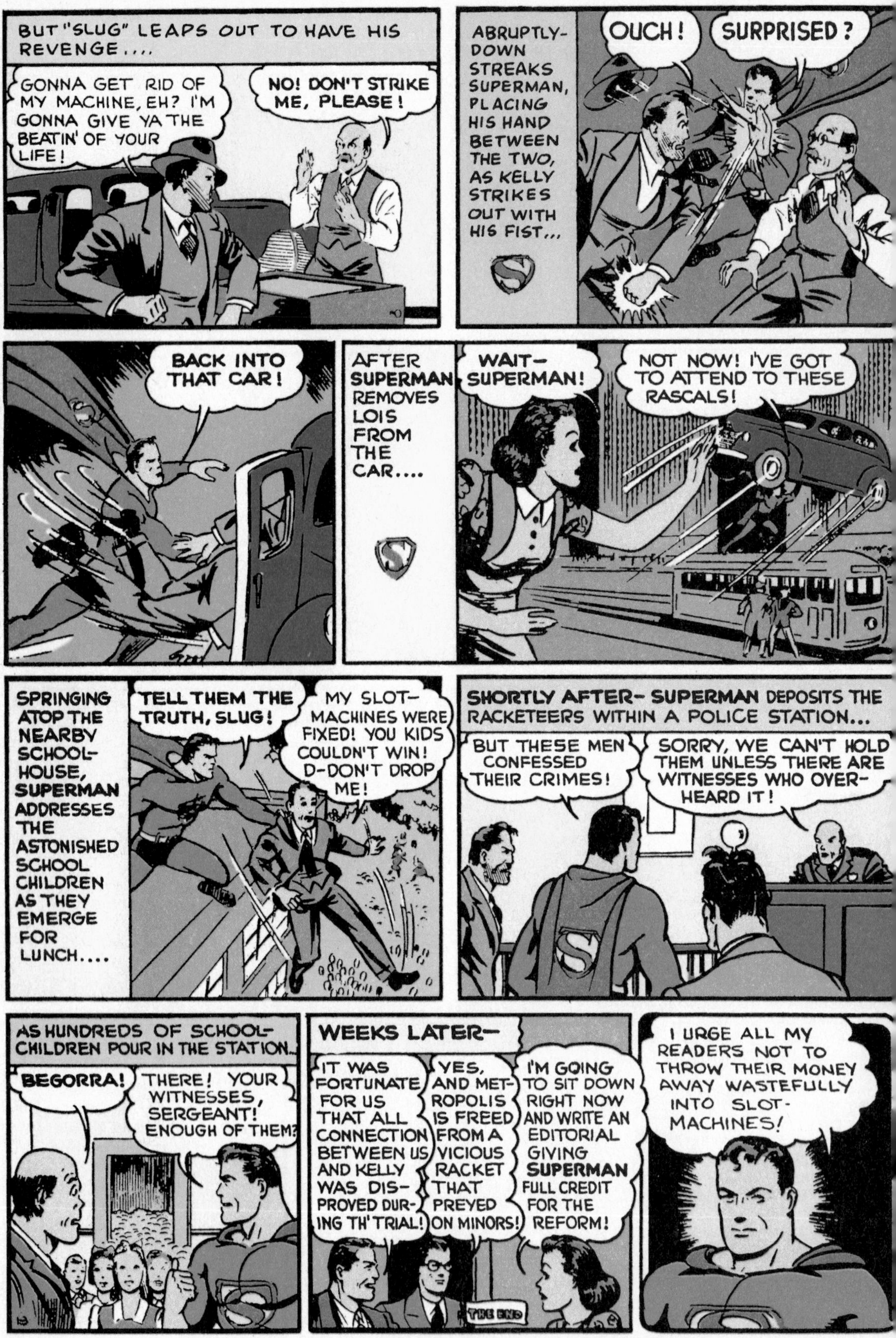

BUT "SLUG" LEAPS OUT TO HAVE HIS REVENGE....
GONNA GET RID OF MY MACHINE, EH? I'M GONNA GIVE YA THE BEATIN' OF YOUR LIFE!
NO! DON'T STRIKE ME, PLEASE!
ABRUPTLY- DOWN STREAKS SUPERMAN, PLACING HIS HAND BETWEEN THE TWO, AS KELLY STRIKES OUT WITH HIS FIST...
OUCH!
SURPRISED?
BACK INTO THAT CAR!
AFTER SUPERMAN REMOVES LOIS FROM THE CAR....
WAIT- SUPERMAN!
NOT NOW! I'VE GOT TO ATTEND TO THESE RASCALS!
SPRINGING ATOP THE NEARBY SCHOOL-HOUSE, SUPERMAN ADDRESSES THE ASTONISHED SCHOOL CHILDREN AS THEY EMERGE FOR LUNCH....
TELL THEM THE TRUTH, SLUG!
MY SLOT-MACHINES WERE FIXED! YOU KIDS COULDN'T WIN! D-DON'T DROP ME!
SHORTLY AFTER- SUPERMAN DEPOSITS THE RACKETEERS WITHIN A POLICE STATION...
BUT THESE MEN CONFESSED THEIR CRIMES!
SORRY, WE CAN'T HOLD THEM UNLESS THERE ARE WITNESSES WHO OVER-HEARD IT!
AS HUNDREDS OF SCHOOL-CHILDREN POUR IN THE STATION...
BEGORRA!
THERE! YOUR WITNESSES, SERGEANT! ENOUGH OF THEM?
WEEKS LATER-
IT WAS FORTUNATE FOR US THAT ALL CONNECTION BETWEEN US AND KELLY WAS DIS-PROVED DUR-ING TH' TRIAL!
YES, AND MET-ROPOLIS IS FREED FROM A VICIOUS RACKET THAT PREYED ON MINORS!
I'M GOING TO SIT DOWN RIGHT NOW AND WRITE AN EDITORIAL GIVING SUPERMAN FULL CREDIT FOR THE REFORM!
THE END
I URGE ALL MY READERS NOT TO THROW THEIR MONEY AWAY WASTEFULLY INTO SLOT-MACHINES!

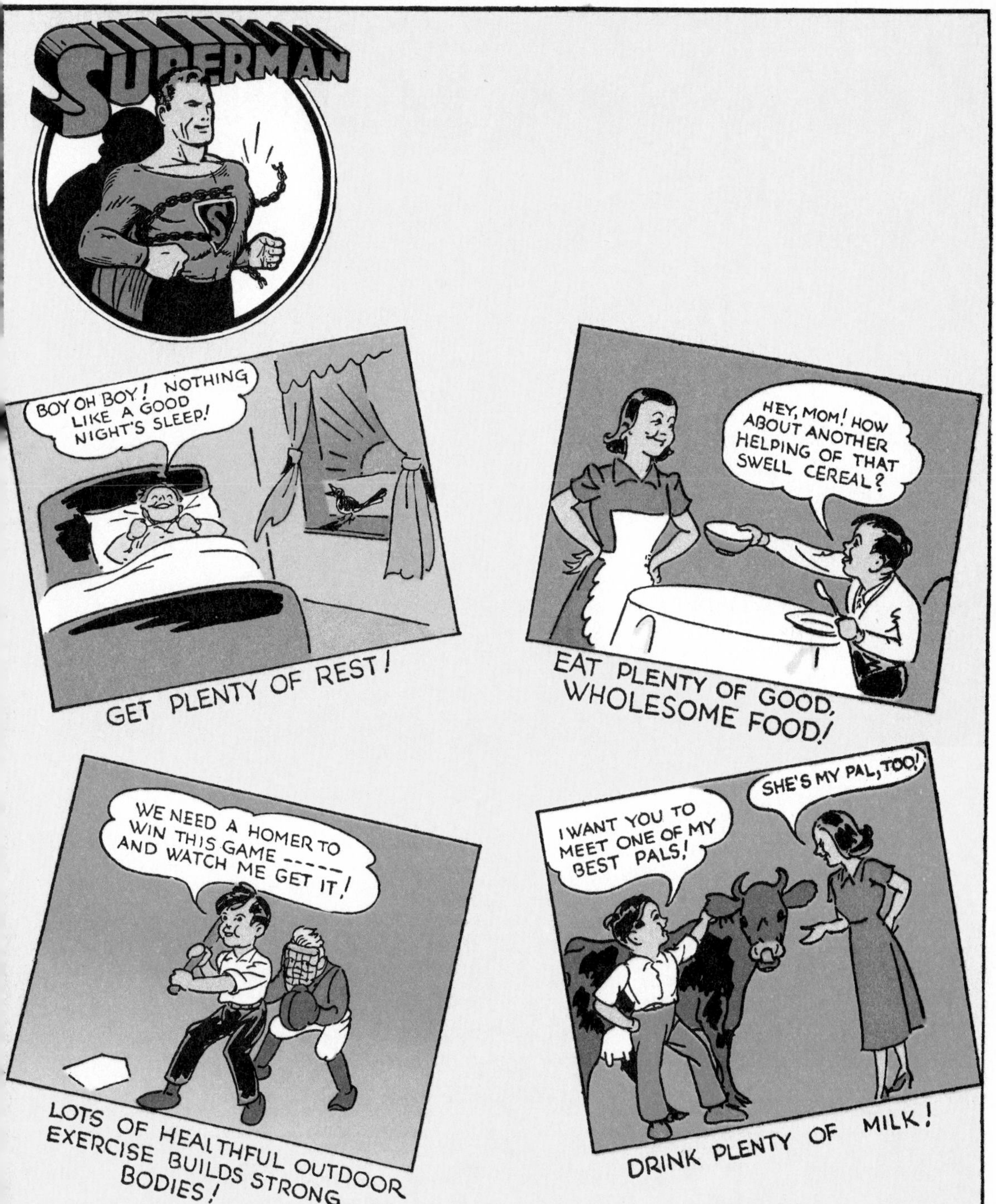
SUPERMAN
BOY OH BOY! NOTHING LIKE A GOOD NIGHT'S SLEEP!
GET PLENTY OF REST!
HEY, MOM! HOW ABOUT ANOTHER HELPING OF THAT SWELL CEREAL?
EAT PLENTY OF GOOD, WHOLESOME FOOD!
WE NEED A HOMER TO WIN THIS GAME ----- AND WATCH ME GET IT!
LOTS OF HEALTHFUL OUTDOOR EXERCISE BUILDS STRONG BODIES!
I WANT YOU TO MEET ONE OF MY BEST PALS!
SHE'S MY PAL, TOO!
DRINK PLENTY OF MILK!

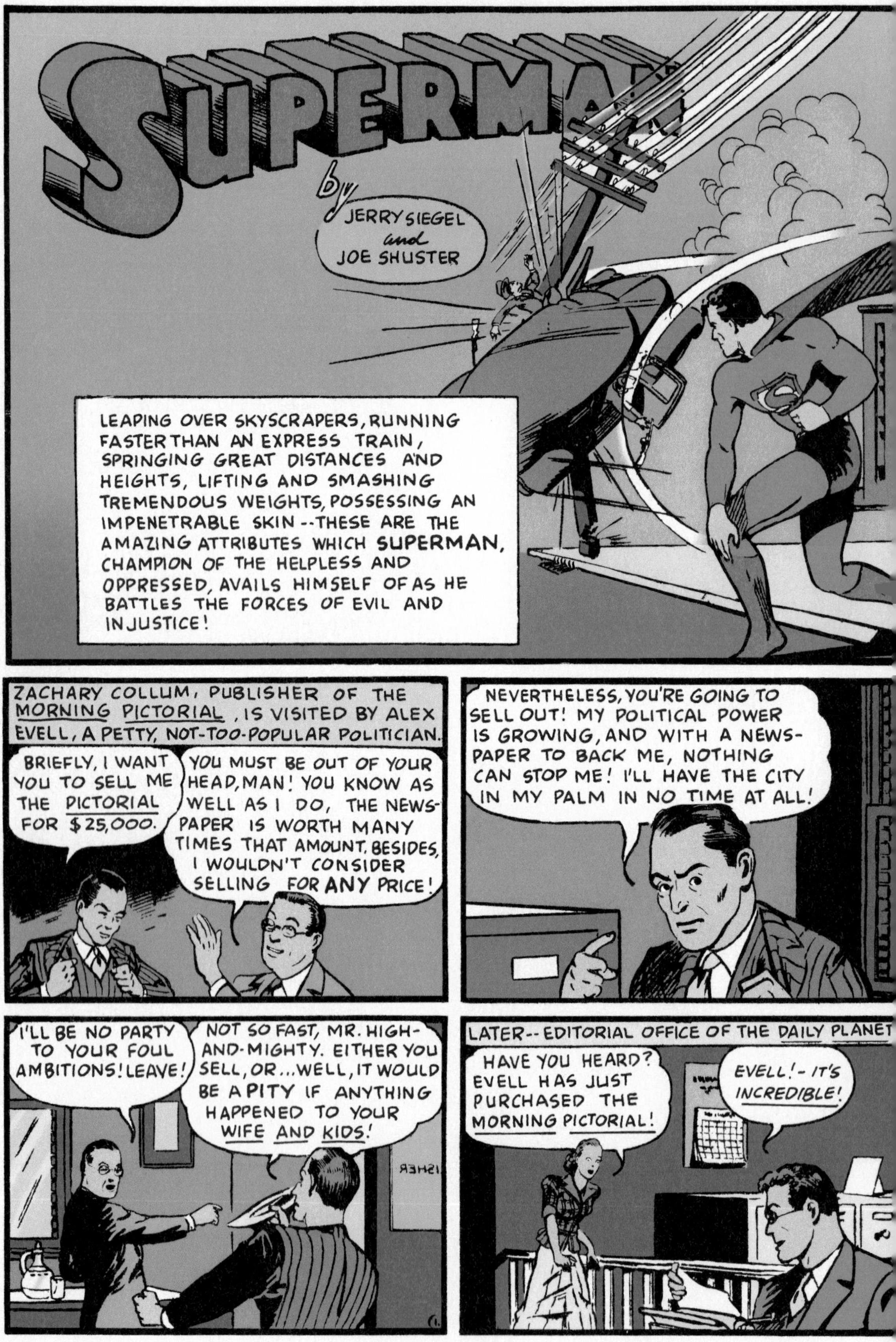
SUPERMAN
by JERRY SIEGEL and JOE SHUSTER
LEAPING OVER SKYSCRAPERS, RUNNING FASTER THAN AN EXPRESS TRAIN, SPRINGING GREAT DISTANCES AND HEIGHTS, LIFTING AND SMASHING TREMENDOUS WEIGHTS, POSSESSING AN IMPENETRABLE SKIN --THESE ARE THE AMAZING ATTRIBUTES WHICH SUPERMAN, CHAMPION OF THE HELPLESS AND OPPRESSED, AVAILS HIMSELF OF AS HE BATTLES THE FORCES OF EVIL AND INJUSTICE!
ZACHARY COLLUM, PUBLISHER OF THE MORNING PICTORIAL, IS VISITED BY ALEX EVELL, A PETTY, NOT-TOO-POPULAR POLITICIAN.
BRIEFLY, I WANT YOU TO SELL ME THE PICTORIAL FOR $25,000.
YOU MUST BE OUT OF YOUR HEAD, MAN! YOU KNOW AS WELL AS I DO, THE NEWSPAPER IS WORTH MANY TIMES THAT AMOUNT. BESIDES, I WOULDN'T CONSIDER SELLING FOR ANY PRICE!
NEVERTHELESS, YOU'RE GOING TO SELL OUT! MY POLITICAL POWER IS GROWING, AND WITH A NEWSPAPER TO BACK ME, NOTHING CAN STOP ME! I'LL HAVE THE CITY IN MY PALM IN NO TIME AT ALL!
I'LL BE NO PARTY TO YOUR FOUL AMBITIONS! LEAVE!
NOT SO FAST, MR. HIGH-AND-MIGHTY. EITHER YOU SELL, OR...WELL, IT WOULD BE A PITY IF ANYTHING HAPPENED TO YOUR WIFE AND KIDS!
LATER--EDITORIAL OFFICE OF THE DAILY PLANET
HAVE YOU HEARD? EVELL HAS JUST PURCHASED THE MORNING PICTORIAL!
EVELL!- IT'S INCREDIBLE!

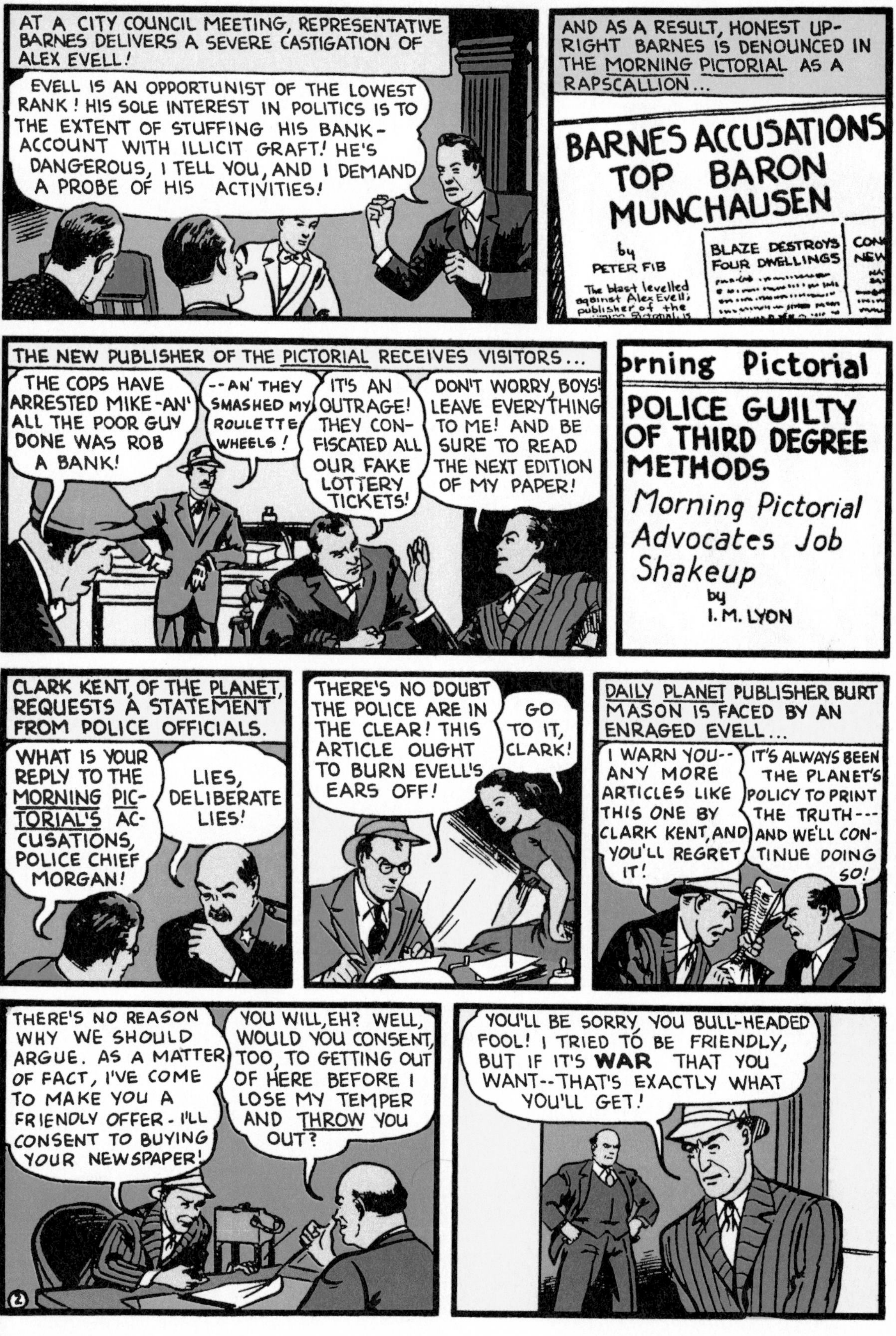
AT A CITY COUNCIL MEETING, REPRESENTATIVE BARNES DELIVERS A SEVERE CASTIGATION OF ALEX EVELL!
EVELL IS AN OPPORTUNIST OF THE LOWEST RANK! HIS SOLE INTEREST IN POLITICS IS TO THE EXTENT OF STUFFING HIS BANK-ACCOUNT WITH ILLICIT GRAFT! HE'S DANGEROUS, I TELL YOU, AND I DEMAND A PROBE OF HIS ACTIVITIES!
AND AS A RESULT, HONEST UPRIGHT BARNES IS DENOUNCED IN THE MORNING PICTORIAL AS A RAPSCALLION...
BARNES ACCUSATIONS TOP BARON MUNCHAUSEN
by PETER FIB
The blast levelled against Alex Evell, publisher of the
BLAZE DESTROYS FOUR DWELLINGS
THE NEW PUBLISHER OF THE PICTORIAL RECEIVES VISITORS...
THE COPS HAVE ARRESTED MIKE-AN' ALL THE POOR GUY DONE WAS ROB A BANK!
--AN' THEY SMASHED MY ROULETTE WHEELS!
IT'S AN OUTRAGE! THEY CONFISCATED ALL OUR FAKE LOTTERY TICKETS!
DON'T WORRY, BOYS! LEAVE EVERYTHING TO ME! AND BE SURE TO READ THE NEXT EDITION OF MY PAPER!
orning Pictorial
POLICE GUILTY OF THIRD DEGREE METHODS
Morning Pictorial Advocates Job Shakeup
by I. M. LYON
CLARK KENT, OF THE PLANET, REQUESTS A STATEMENT FROM POLICE OFFICIALS.
WHAT IS YOUR REPLY TO THE MORNING PICTORIAL'S ACCUSATIONS, POLICE CHIEF MORGAN!
LIES, DELIBERATE LIES!
THERE'S NO DOUBT THE POLICE ARE IN THE CLEAR! THIS ARTICLE OUGHT TO BURN EVELL'S EARS OFF!
GO TO IT, CLARK!
DAILY PLANET PUBLISHER BURT MASON IS FACED BY AN ENRAGED EVELL...
I WARN YOU--ANY MORE ARTICLES LIKE THIS ONE BY CLARK KENT, AND YOU'LL REGRET IT!
IT'S ALWAYS BEEN THE PLANET'S POLICY TO PRINT THE TRUTH---AND WE'LL CONTINUE DOING SO!
THERE'S NO REASON WHY WE SHOULD ARGUE. AS A MATTER OF FACT, I'VE COME TO MAKE YOU A FRIENDLY OFFER - I'LL CONSENT TO BUYING YOUR NEWSPAPER!
YOU WILL, EH? WELL, WOULD YOU CONSENT, TOO, TO GETTING OUT OF HERE BEFORE I LOSE MY TEMPER AND THROW YOU OUT?
2
YOU'LL BE SORRY, YOU BULL-HEADED FOOL! I TRIED TO BE FRIENDLY, BUT IF IT'S WAR THAT YOU WANT--THAT'S EXACTLY WHAT YOU'LL GET!

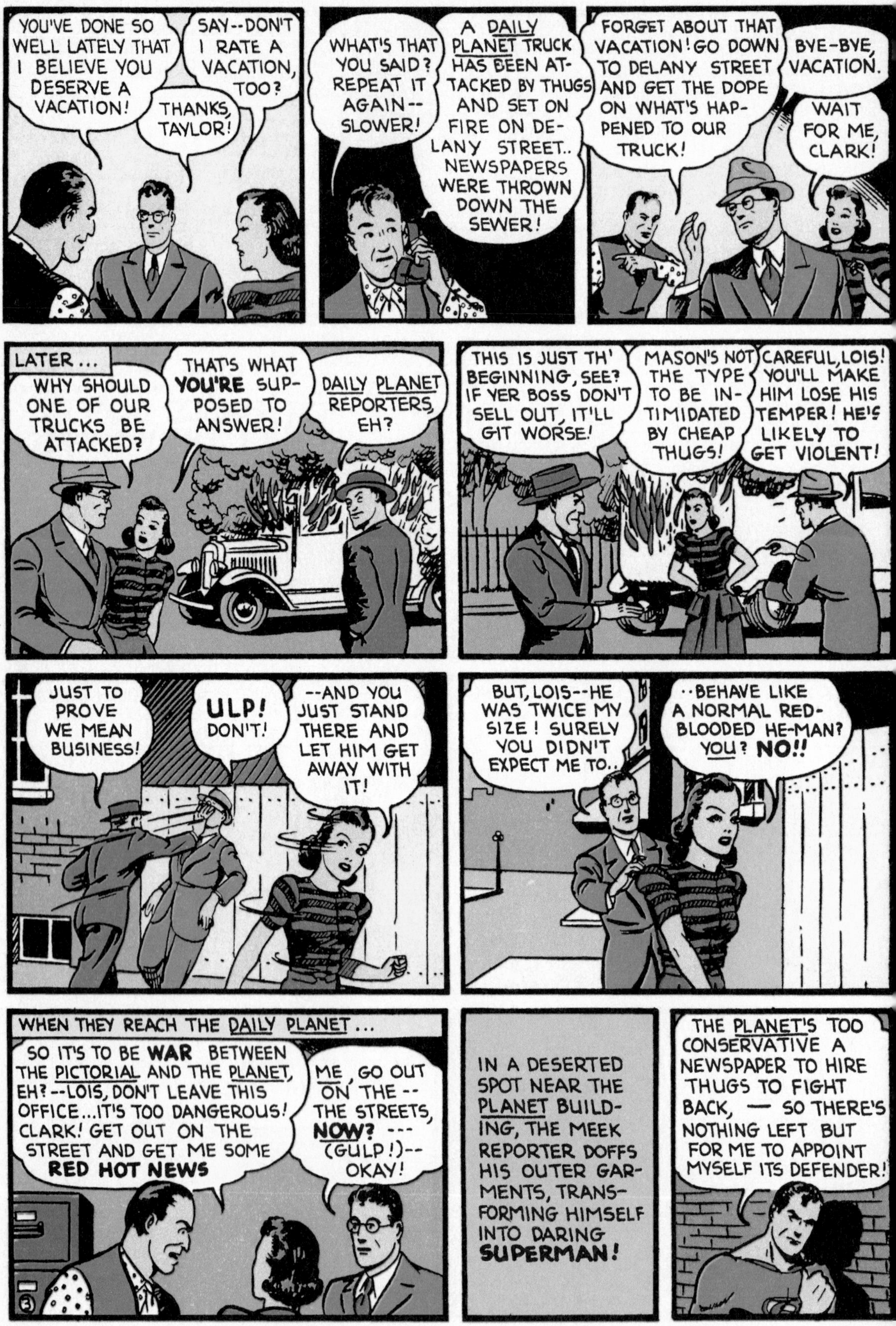
YOU'VE DONE SO WELL LATELY THAT I BELIEVE YOU DESERVE A VACATION!
SAY--DON'T I RATE A VACATION, TOO?
THANKS, TAYLOR!
WHAT'S THAT YOU SAID? REPEAT IT AGAIN-- SLOWER!
A DAILY PLANET TRUCK HAS BEEN ATTACKED BY THUGS AND SET ON FIRE ON DELANY STREET.. NEWSPAPERS WERE THROWN DOWN THE SEWER!
FORGET ABOUT THAT VACATION! GO DOWN TO DELANY STREET AND GET THE DOPE ON WHAT'S HAPPENED TO OUR TRUCK!
BYE-BYE, VACATION.
WAIT FOR ME, CLARK!
LATER...
WHY SHOULD ONE OF OUR TRUCKS BE ATTACKED?
THAT'S WHAT YOU'RE SUPPOSED TO ANSWER!
DAILY PLANET REPORTERS, EH?
THIS IS JUST TH' BEGINNING, SEE? IF YER BOSS DON'T SELL OUT, IT'LL GIT WORSE!
MASON'S NOT THE TYPE TO BE INTIMIDATED BY CHEAP THUGS!
CAREFUL, LOIS! YOU'LL MAKE HIM LOSE HIS TEMPER! HE'S LIKELY TO GET VIOLENT!
JUST TO PROVE WE MEAN BUSINESS!
ULP! DON'T!
--AND YOU JUST STAND THERE AND LET HIM GET AWAY WITH IT!
BUT, LOIS--HE WAS TWICE MY SIZE! SURELY YOU DIDN'T EXPECT ME TO..
..BEHAVE LIKE A NORMAL RED-BLOODED HE-MAN? YOU? NO!!
WHEN THEY REACH THE DAILY PLANET...
SO IT'S TO BE WAR BETWEEN THE PICTORIAL AND THE PLANET, EH? --LOIS, DON'T LEAVE THIS OFFICE...IT'S TOO DANGEROUS! CLARK! GET OUT ON THE STREET AND GET ME SOME RED HOT NEWS
ME, GO OUT ON THE -- THE STREETS, NOW? --- (GULP!)-- OKAY!
IN A DESERTED SPOT NEAR THE PLANET BUILDING, THE MEEK REPORTER DOFFS HIS OUTER GARMENTS, TRANSFORMING HIMSELF INTO DARING SUPERMAN!
THE PLANET'S TOO CONSERVATIVE A NEWSPAPER TO HIRE THUGS TO FIGHT BACK, — SO THERE'S NOTHING LEFT BUT FOR ME TO APPOINT MYSELF ITS DEFENDER!
3

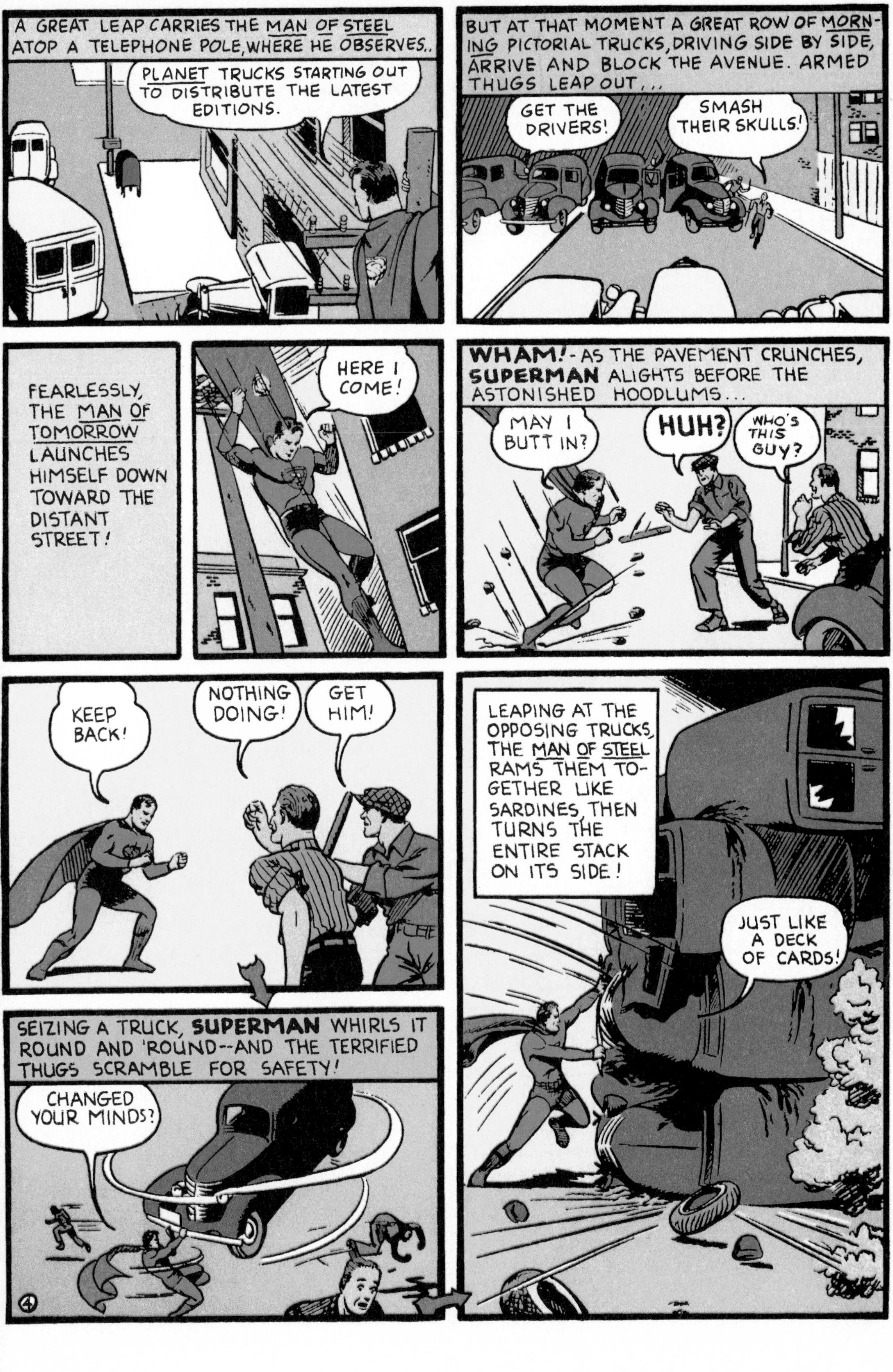
A GREAT LEAP CARRIES THE MAN OF STEEL ATOP A TELEPHONE POLE, WHERE HE OBSERVES..
PLANET TRUCKS STARTING OUT TO DISTRIBUTE THE LATEST EDITIONS.
BUT AT THAT MOMENT A GREAT ROW OF MORNING PICTORIAL TRUCKS, DRIVING SIDE BY SIDE, ARRIVE AND BLOCK THE AVENUE. ARMED THUGS LEAP OUT...
GET THE DRIVERS!
SMASH THEIR SKULLS!
FEARLESSLY, THE MAN OF TOMORROW LAUNCHES HIMSELF DOWN TOWARD THE DISTANT STREET!
HERE I COME!
WHAM! - AS THE PAVEMENT CRUNCHES, SUPERMAN ALIGHTS BEFORE THE ASTONISHED HOODLUMS...
MAY I BUTT IN?
HUH?
WHO'S THIS GUY?
KEEP BACK!
NOTHING DOING!
GET HIM!
SEIZING A TRUCK, SUPERMAN WHIRLS IT ROUND AND 'ROUND--AND THE TERRIFIED THUGS SCRAMBLE FOR SAFETY!
CHANGED YOUR MINDS?
4
LEAPING AT THE OPPOSING TRUCKS, THE MAN OF STEEL RAMS THEM TOGETHER LIKE SARDINES, THEN TURNS THE ENTIRE STACK ON ITS SIDE!
JUST LIKE A DECK OF CARDS!

AS THE DAILY PLANET TRUCKS PROCEED, A GREAT TANK-LIKE TRUCK STREAKS TOWARD THEM...

BUT LEAPING IN WITH SUPER-SPEED, **SUPERMAN** SEIZES THE TRUCK'S BUMPER...

UP...

...AND **OVER!**

WHIRLING, **SUPERMAN** SIGHTS A MOB OF HOODLUMS ATTEMPTING TO OVERTURN A DAILY PLANET TRUCK....

THERE SHE GOES!

SPRINGING FORWARD, THE MAN OF TOMORROW CATCHES THE TOPPLING TRUCK....

GOTCHA!

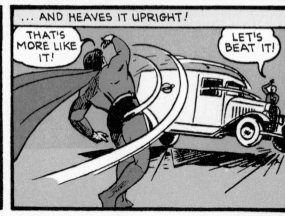

...AND HEAVES IT UPRIGHT!

THAT'S MORE LIKE IT!

LET'S BEAT IT!

AS THE THUGS LEAP INTO THE TRUCK AND SPEED AWAY, **SUPERMAN** RACES AFTER THEM...

HEY! WAIT FOR ME!

OVERTAKING IT, HE LIFTS IT OVERHEAD, THEN SPRINGS UPWARD...

HOLD TIGHT, BOYS; WE'RE GOING FOR A RIDE!

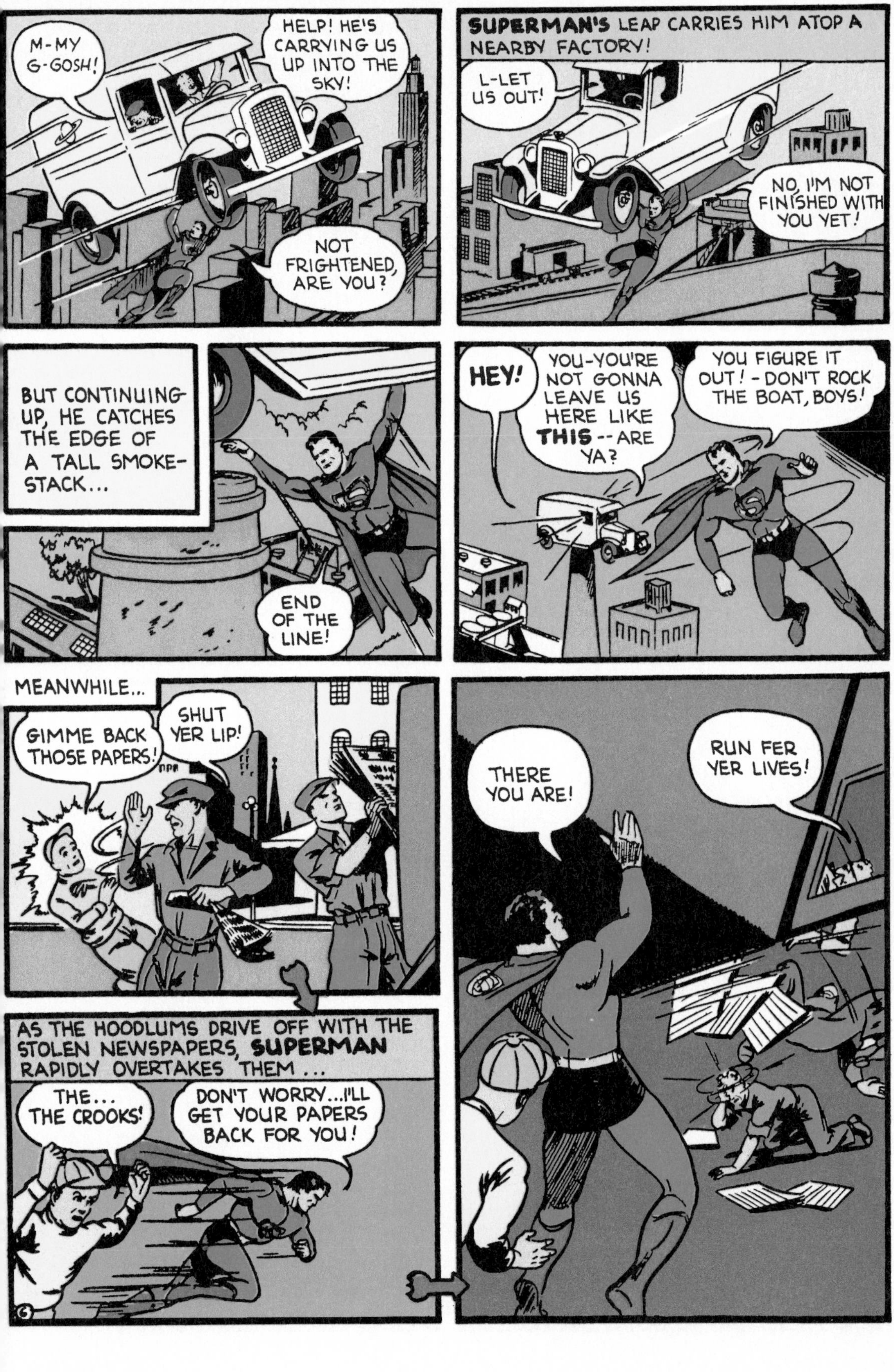
M-MY G-GOSH!
HELP! HE'S CARRYING US UP INTO THE SKY!
NOT FRIGHTENED, ARE YOU?
SUPERMAN'S LEAP CARRIES HIM ATOP A NEARBY FACTORY!
L-LET US OUT!
NO, I'M NOT FINISHED WITH YOU YET!
BUT CONTINUING UP, HE CATCHES THE EDGE OF A TALL SMOKE-STACK...
END OF THE LINE!
HEY!
YOU-YOU'RE NOT GONNA LEAVE US HERE LIKE THIS--ARE YA?
YOU FIGURE IT OUT! - DON'T ROCK THE BOAT, BOYS!
MEANWHILE...
GIMME BACK THOSE PAPERS!
SHUT YER LIP!
AS THE HOODLUMS DRIVE OFF WITH THE STOLEN NEWSPAPERS, SUPERMAN RAPIDLY OVERTAKES THEM...
THE... THE CROOKS!
DON'T WORRY...I'LL GET YOUR PAPERS BACK FOR YOU!
6
THERE YOU ARE!
RUN FER YER LIVES!

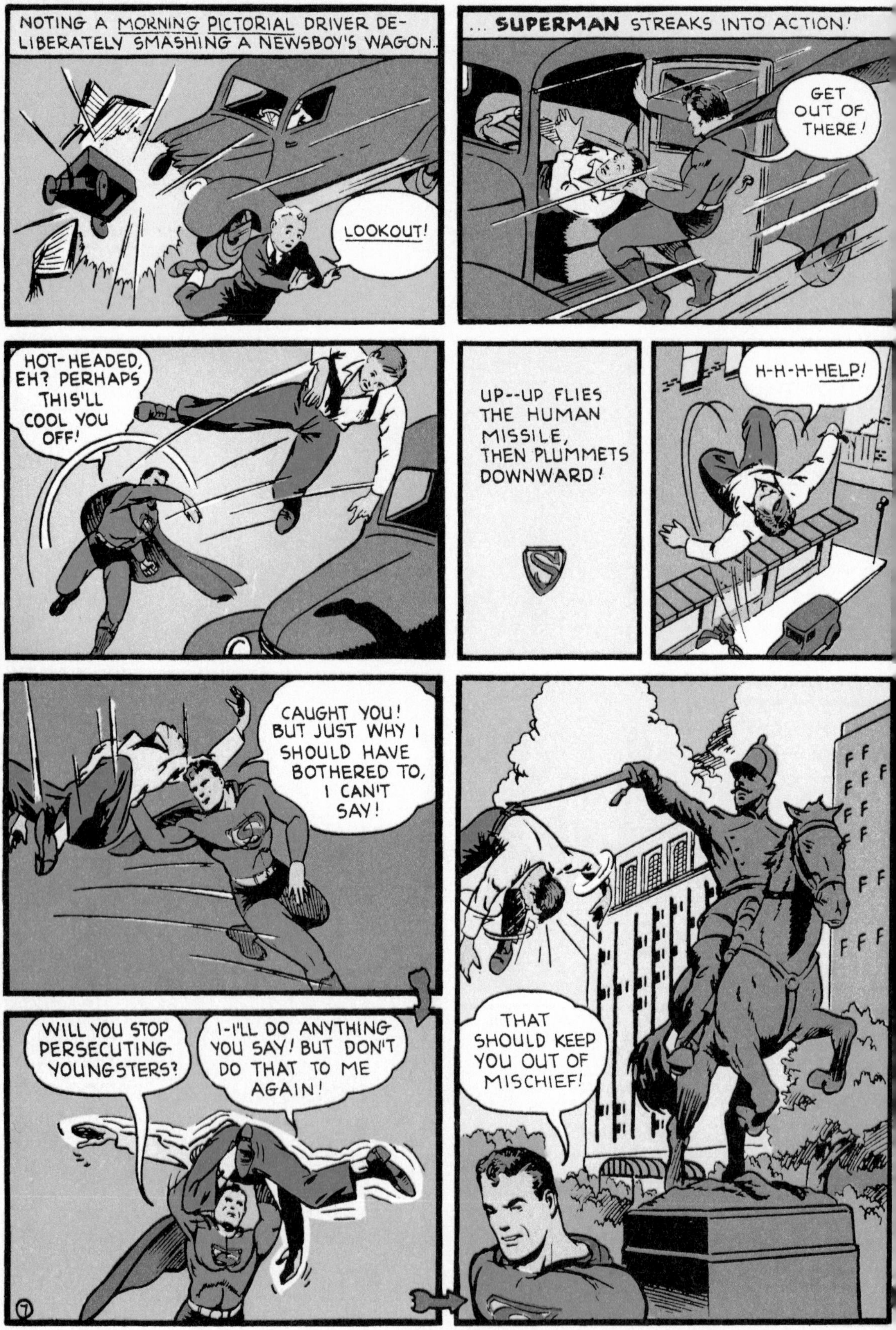
NOTING A MORNING PICTORIAL DRIVER DE-LIBERATELY SMASHING A NEWSBOY'S WAGON..
LOOKOUT!
... SUPERMAN STREAKS INTO ACTION!
GET OUT OF THERE!
HOT-HEADED, EH? PERHAPS THIS'LL COOL YOU OFF!
UP--UP FLIES THE HUMAN MISSILE, THEN PLUMMETS DOWNWARD!
H-H-H-HELP!
CAUGHT YOU! BUT JUST WHY I SHOULD HAVE BOTHERED TO, I CAN'T SAY!
WILL YOU STOP PERSECUTING YOUNGSTERS?
I-I'LL DO ANYTHING YOU SAY! BUT DON'T DO THAT TO ME AGAIN!
7
THAT SHOULD KEEP YOU OUT OF MISCHIEF!

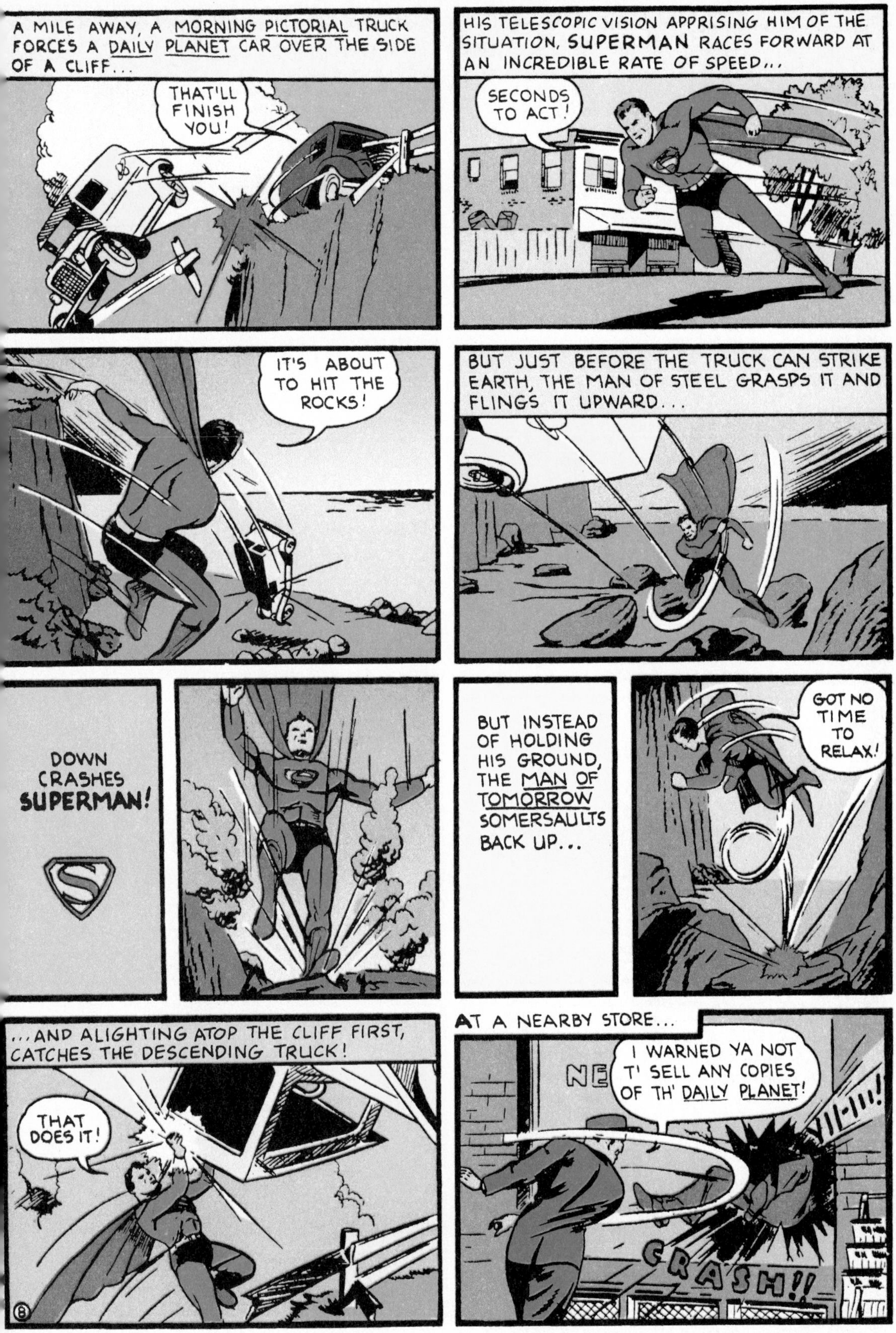

A MILE AWAY, A MORNING PICTORIAL TRUCK FORCES A DAILY PLANET CAR OVER THE SIDE OF A CLIFF...
THAT'LL FINISH YOU!
HIS TELESCOPIC VISION APPRISING HIM OF THE SITUATION, SUPERMAN RACES FORWARD AT AN INCREDIBLE RATE OF SPEED...
SECONDS TO ACT!
IT'S ABOUT TO HIT THE ROCKS!
BUT JUST BEFORE THE TRUCK CAN STRIKE EARTH, THE MAN OF STEEL GRASPS IT AND FLINGS IT UPWARD...
DOWN CRASHES SUPERMAN!
BUT INSTEAD OF HOLDING HIS GROUND, THE MAN OF TOMORROW SOMERSAULTS BACK UP...
GOT NO TIME TO RELAX!
...AND ALIGHTING ATOP THE CLIFF FIRST, CATCHES THE DESCENDING TRUCK!
THAT DOES IT!
8
AT A NEARBY STORE...
I WARNED YA NOT T' SELL ANY COPIES OF TH' DAILY PLANET!
NE
YII-III!
CRASH!!

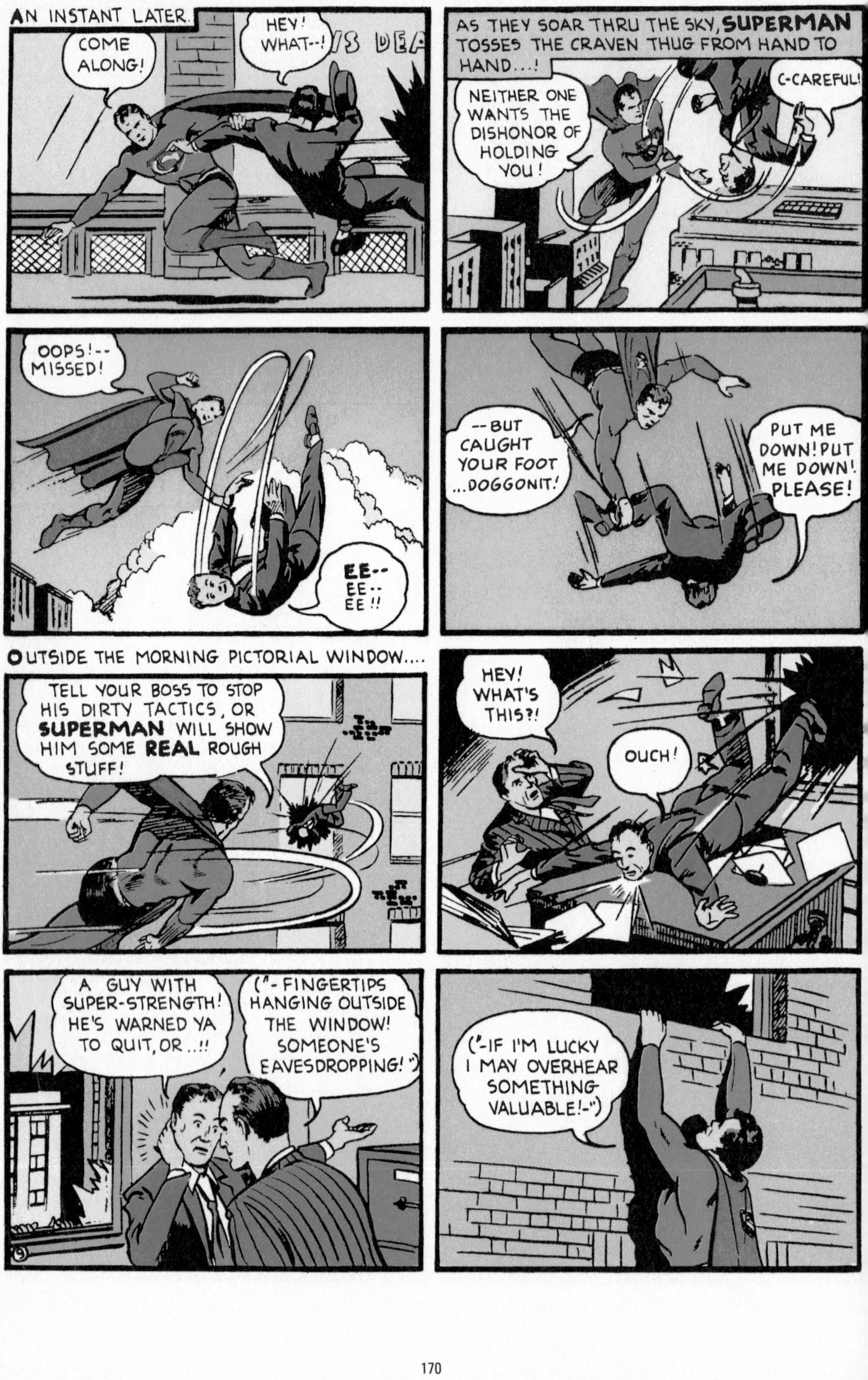
AN INSTANT LATER.
COME ALONG!
HEY! WHAT--!
AS THEY SOAR THRU THE SKY, SUPERMAN TOSSES THE CRAVEN THUG FROM HAND TO HAND...!
NEITHER ONE WANTS THE DISHONOR OF HOLDING YOU!
C-CAREFUL!
OOPS!-- MISSED!
EE-- EE-- EE!!
--BUT CAUGHT YOUR FOOT ...DOGGONIT!
PUT ME DOWN! PUT ME DOWN! PLEASE!
OUTSIDE THE MORNING PICTORIAL WINDOW....
TELL YOUR BOSS TO STOP HIS DIRTY TACTICS, OR SUPERMAN WILL SHOW HIM SOME REAL ROUGH STUFF!
HEY! WHAT'S THIS?!
OUCH!
A GUY WITH SUPER-STRENGTH! HE'S WARNED YA TO QUIT, OR..!!
("-FINGERTIPS HANGING OUTSIDE THE WINDOW! SOMEONE'S EAVESDROPPING!")
("-IF I'M LUCKY I MAY OVERHEAR SOMETHING VALUABLE!-")

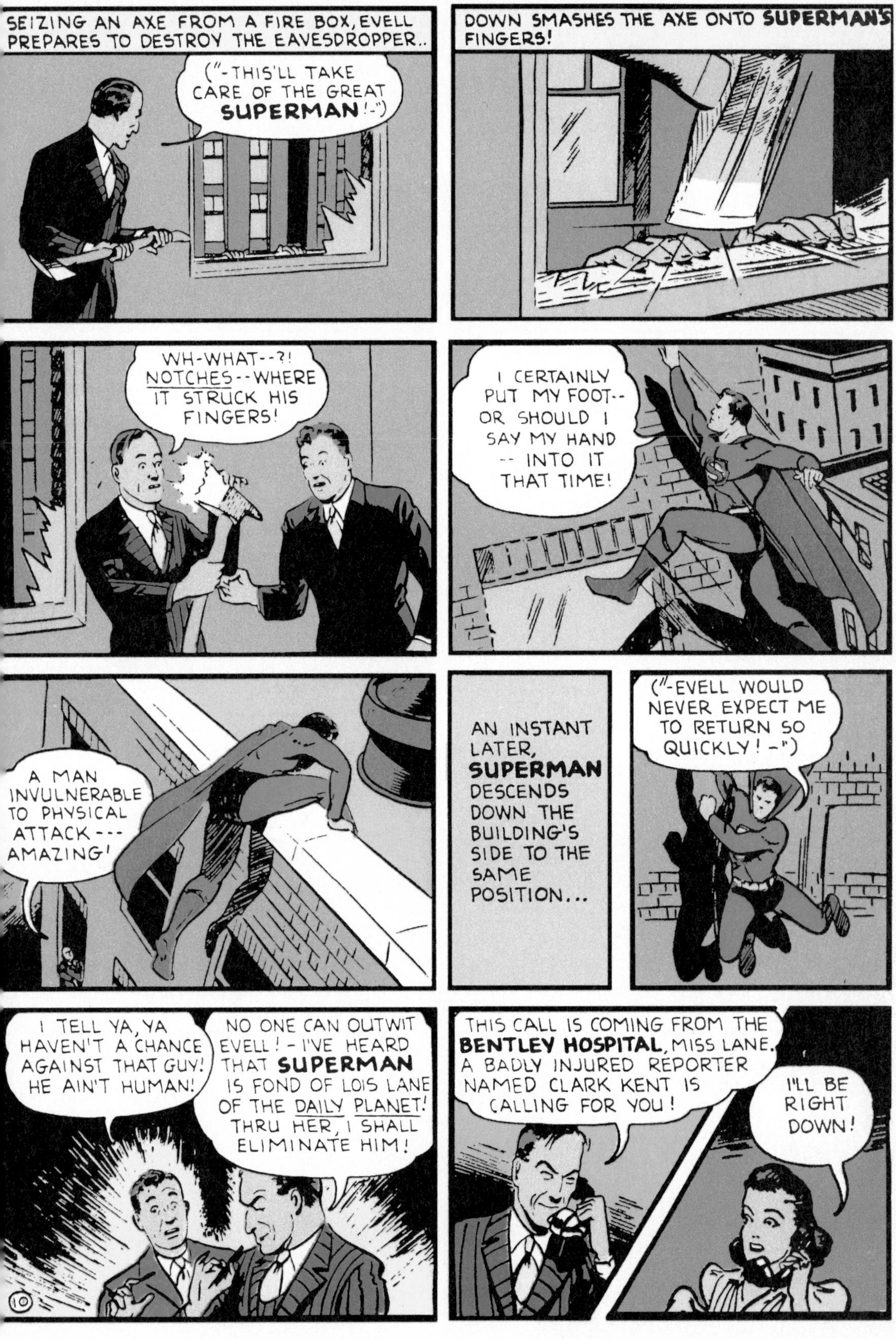

SEIZING AN AXE FROM A FIRE BOX, EVELL PREPARES TO DESTROY THE EAVESDROPPER..
("-THIS'LL TAKE CARE OF THE GREAT SUPERMAN!-")
DOWN SMASHES THE AXE ONTO SUPERMAN'S FINGERS!
WH-WHAT--?! NOTCHES--WHERE IT STRUCK HIS FINGERS!
I CERTAINLY PUT MY FOOT--OR SHOULD I SAY MY HAND -- INTO IT THAT TIME!
A MAN INVULNERABLE TO PHYSICAL ATTACK--- AMAZING!
AN INSTANT LATER, SUPERMAN DESCENDS DOWN THE BUILDING'S SIDE TO THE SAME POSITION...
("-EVELL WOULD NEVER EXPECT ME TO RETURN SO QUICKLY!-")
I TELL YA, YA HAVEN'T A CHANCE AGAINST THAT GUY! HE AIN'T HUMAN!
NO ONE CAN OUTWIT EVELL! - I'VE HEARD THAT SUPERMAN IS FOND OF LOIS LANE OF THE DAILY PLANET! THRU HER, I SHALL ELIMINATE HIM!
10
THIS CALL IS COMING FROM THE BENTLEY HOSPITAL, MISS LANE. A BADLY INJURED REPORTER NAMED CLARK KENT IS CALLING FOR YOU!
I'LL BE RIGHT DOWN!

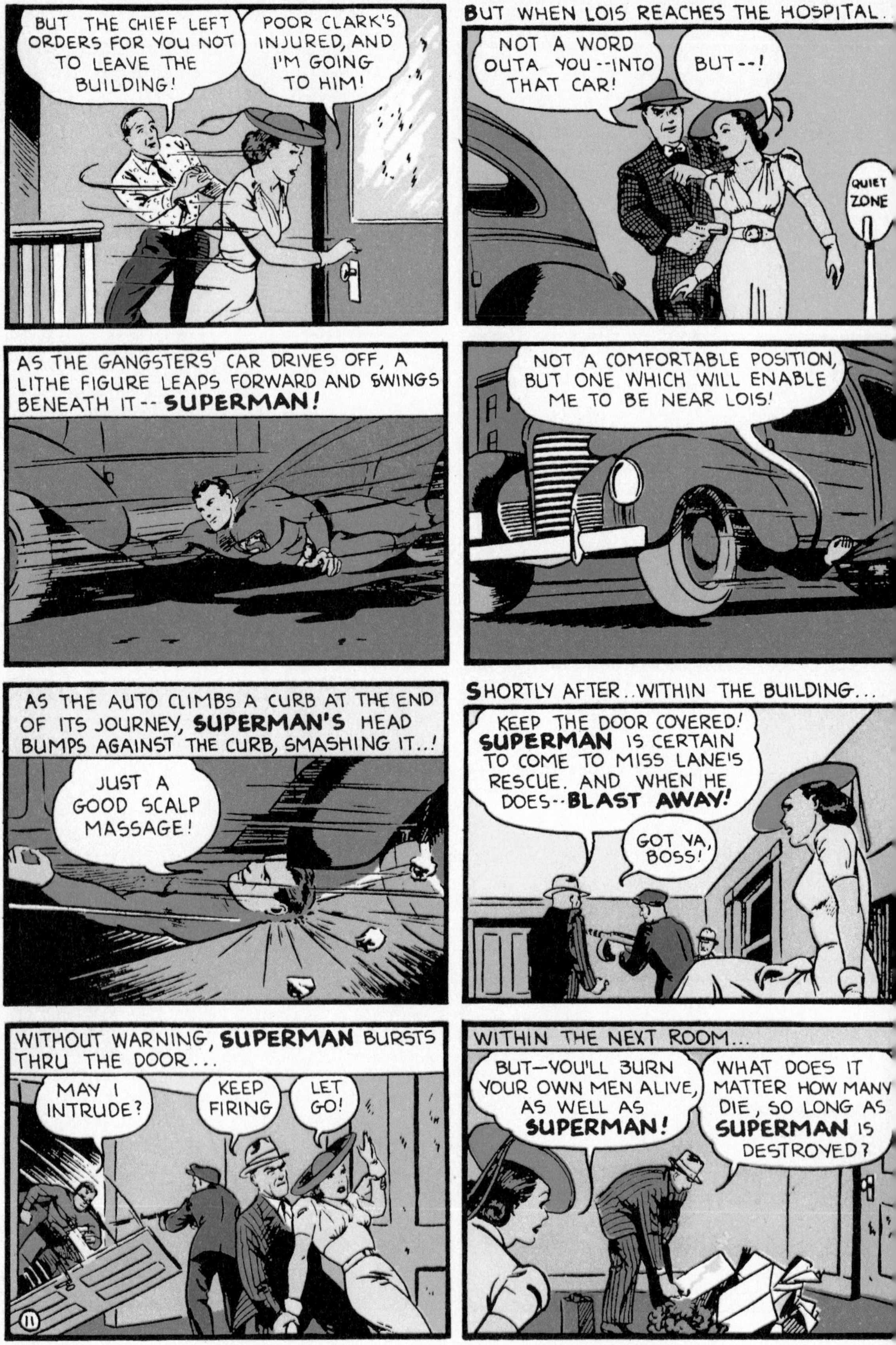
BUT THE CHIEF LEFT ORDERS FOR YOU NOT TO LEAVE THE BUILDING!
POOR CLARK'S INJURED, AND I'M GOING TO HIM!
BUT WHEN LOIS REACHES THE HOSPITAL.
NOT A WORD OUTA YOU--INTO THAT CAR!
BUT--!
QUIET ZONE
AS THE GANGSTERS' CAR DRIVES OFF, A LITHE FIGURE LEAPS FORWARD AND SWINGS BENEATH IT-- SUPERMAN!
NOT A COMFORTABLE POSITION, BUT ONE WHICH WILL ENABLE ME TO BE NEAR LOIS!
AS THE AUTO CLIMBS A CURB AT THE END OF ITS JOURNEY, SUPERMAN'S HEAD BUMPS AGAINST THE CURB, SMASHING IT..!
JUST A GOOD SCALP MASSAGE!
SHORTLY AFTER..WITHIN THE BUILDING...
KEEP THE DOOR COVERED! SUPERMAN IS CERTAIN TO COME TO MISS LANE'S RESCUE. AND WHEN HE DOES--BLAST AWAY!
GOT YA, BOSS!
WITHOUT WARNING, SUPERMAN BURSTS THRU THE DOOR...
MAY I INTRUDE?
KEEP FIRING
LET GO!
11
WITHIN THE NEXT ROOM...
BUT—YOU'LL BURN YOUR OWN MEN ALIVE, AS WELL AS SUPERMAN!
WHAT DOES IT MATTER HOW MANY DIE, SO LONG AS SUPERMAN IS DESTROYED?

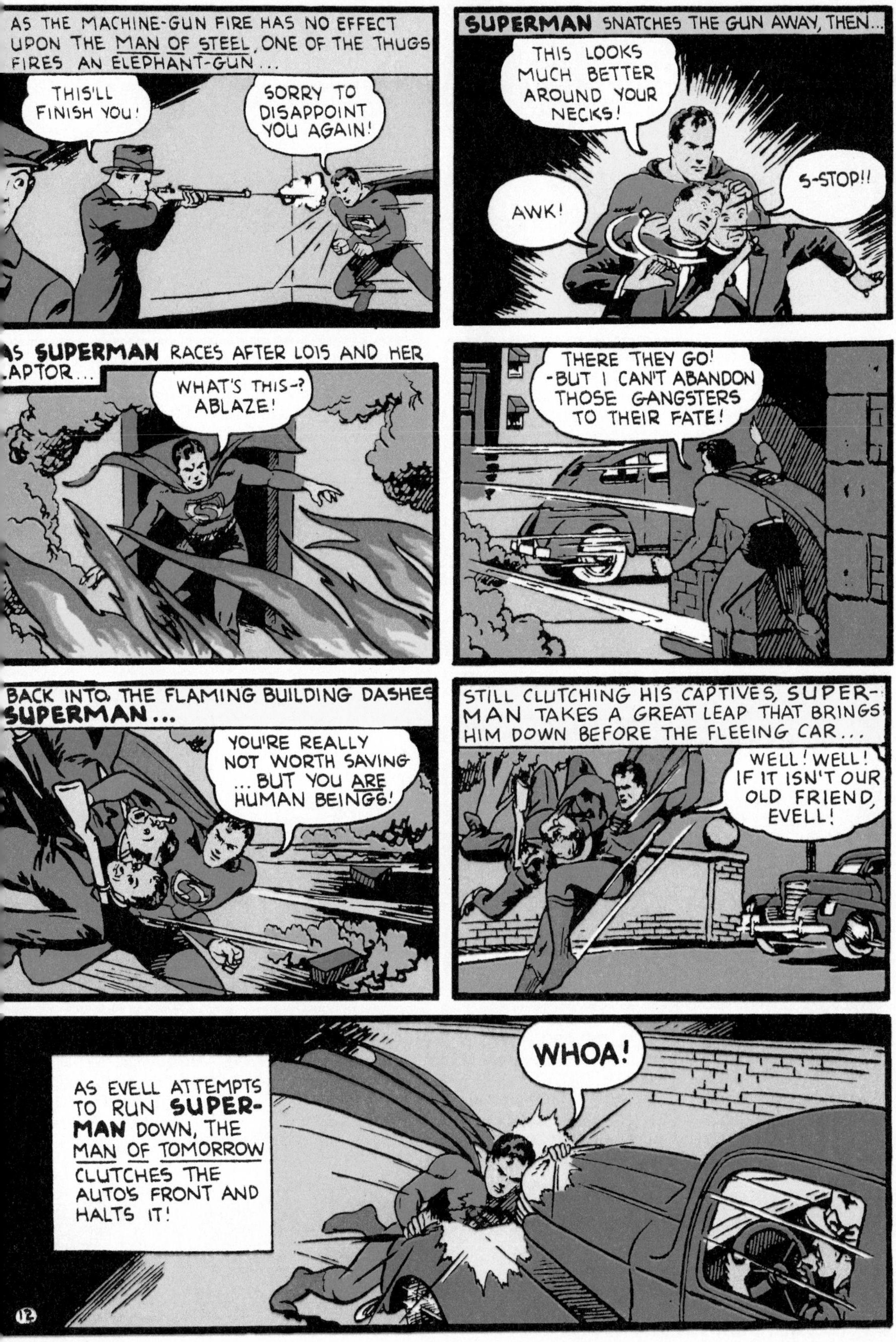

AS THE MACHINE-GUN FIRE HAS NO EFFECT UPON THE MAN OF STEEL, ONE OF THE THUGS FIRES AN ELEPHANT-GUN...
THIS'LL FINISH YOU!
SORRY TO DISAPPOINT YOU AGAIN!
SUPERMAN SNATCHES THE GUN AWAY, THEN...
THIS LOOKS MUCH BETTER AROUND YOUR NECKS!
AWK!
S-STOP!!
AS SUPERMAN RACES AFTER LOIS AND HER CAPTOR...
WHAT'S THIS-? ABLAZE!
THERE THEY GO! -BUT I CAN'T ABANDON THOSE GANGSTERS TO THEIR FATE!
BACK INTO THE FLAMING BUILDING DASHES SUPERMAN...
YOU'RE REALLY NOT WORTH SAVING ...BUT YOU ARE HUMAN BEINGS!
STILL CLUTCHING HIS CAPTIVES, SUPERMAN TAKES A GREAT LEAP THAT BRINGS HIM DOWN BEFORE THE FLEEING CAR...
WELL! WELL! IF IT ISN'T OUR OLD FRIEND, EVELL!
AS EVELL ATTEMPTS TO RUN SUPERMAN DOWN, THE MAN OF TOMORROW CLUTCHES THE AUTO'S FRONT AND HALTS IT!
WHOA!
12

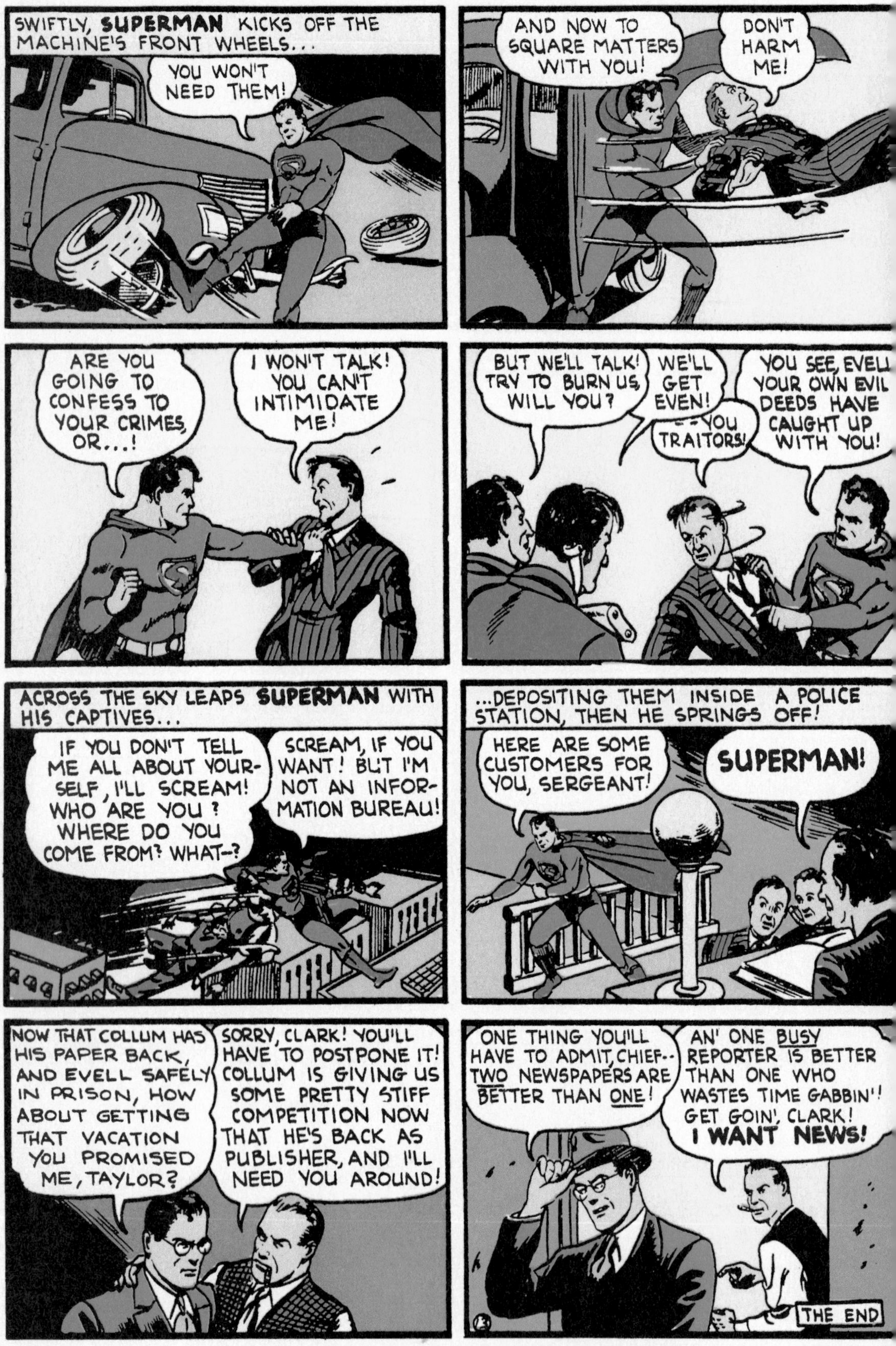
SWIFTLY, SUPERMAN KICKS OFF THE MACHINE'S FRONT WHEELS...
YOU WON'T NEED THEM!
AND NOW TO SQUARE MATTERS WITH YOU!
DON'T HARM ME!
ARE YOU GOING TO CONFESS TO YOUR CRIMES, OR...!
I WON'T TALK! YOU CAN'T INTIMIDATE ME!
BUT WE'LL TALK! TRY TO BURN US, WILL YOU?
WE'LL GET EVEN!
--YOU TRAITORS!
YOU SEE, EVELL YOUR OWN EVIL DEEDS HAVE CAUGHT UP WITH YOU!
ACROSS THE SKY LEAPS SUPERMAN WITH HIS CAPTIVES...
IF YOU DON'T TELL ME ALL ABOUT YOURSELF, I'LL SCREAM! WHO ARE YOU? WHERE DO YOU COME FROM? WHAT--?
SCREAM, IF YOU WANT! BUT I'M NOT AN INFORMATION BUREAU!
...DEPOSITING THEM INSIDE A POLICE STATION, THEN HE SPRINGS OFF!
HERE ARE SOME CUSTOMERS FOR YOU, SERGEANT!
SUPERMAN!
NOW THAT COLLUM HAS HIS PAPER BACK, AND EVELL SAFELY IN PRISON, HOW ABOUT GETTING THAT VACATION YOU PROMISED ME, TAYLOR?
SORRY, CLARK! YOU'LL HAVE TO POSTPONE IT! COLLUM IS GIVING US SOME PRETTY STIFF COMPETITION NOW THAT HE'S BACK AS PUBLISHER, AND I'LL NEED YOU AROUND!
ONE THING YOU'LL HAVE TO ADMIT, CHIEF--TWO NEWSPAPERS ARE BETTER THAN ONE!
AN' ONE BUSY REPORTER IS BETTER THAN ONE WHO WASTES TIME GABBIN'! GET GOIN', CLARK! I WANT NEWS!
THE END

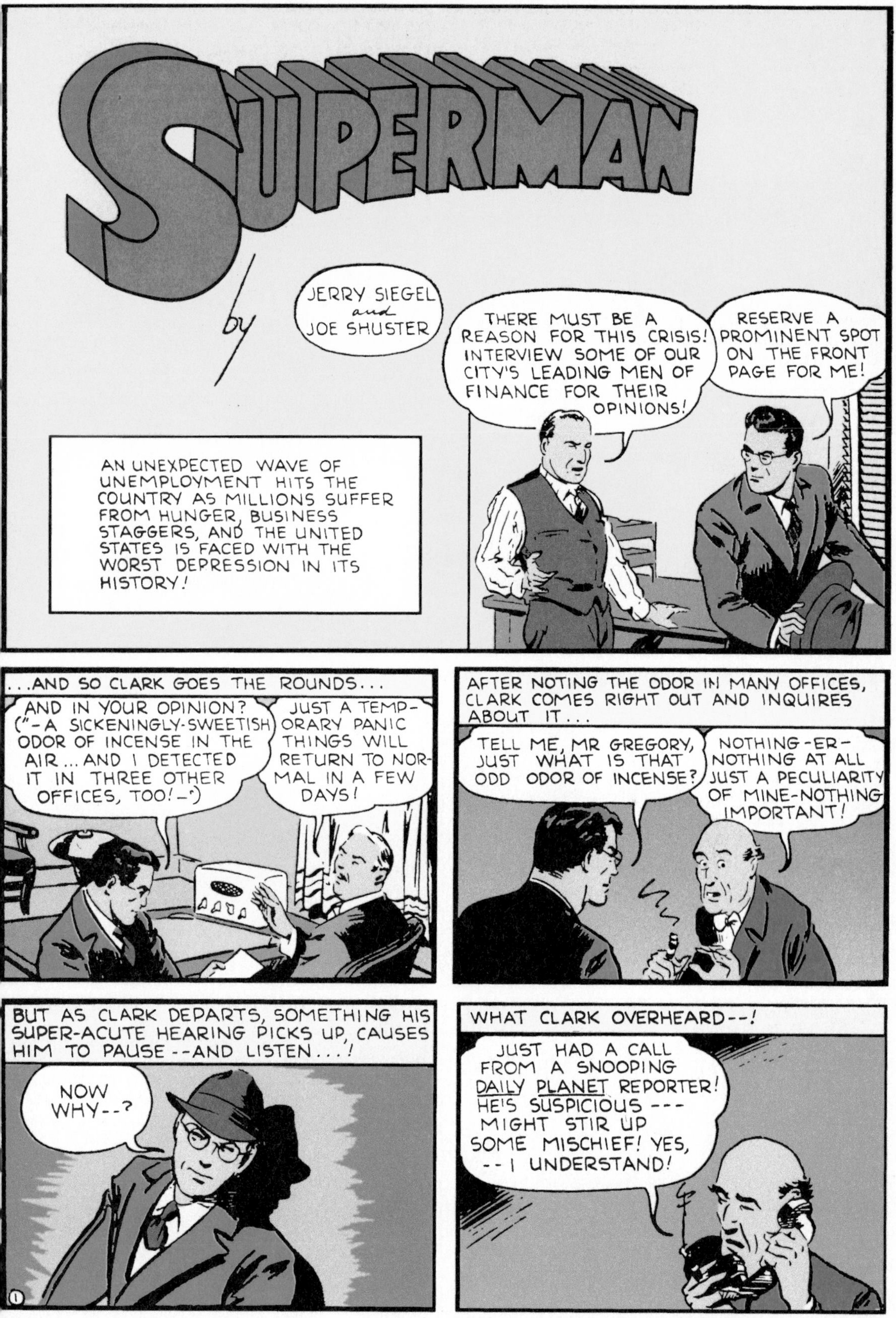
SUPERMAN
by
JERRY SIEGEL and JOE SHUSTER
AN UNEXPECTED WAVE OF UNEMPLOYMENT HITS THE COUNTRY AS MILLIONS SUFFER FROM HUNGER, BUSINESS STAGGERS, AND THE UNITED STATES IS FACED WITH THE WORST DEPRESSION IN ITS HISTORY!
THERE MUST BE A REASON FOR THIS CRISIS! INTERVIEW SOME OF OUR CITY'S LEADING MEN OF FINANCE FOR THEIR OPINIONS!
RESERVE A PROMINENT SPOT ON THE FRONT PAGE FOR ME!
...AND SO CLARK GOES THE ROUNDS...
AND IN YOUR OPINION? ("-A SICKENINGLY-SWEETISH ODOR OF INCENSE IN THE AIR... AND I DETECTED IT IN THREE OTHER OFFICES, TOO!-")
JUST A TEMPORARY PANIC THINGS WILL RETURN TO NORMAL IN A FEW DAYS!
AFTER NOTING THE ODOR IN MANY OFFICES, CLARK COMES RIGHT OUT AND INQUIRES ABOUT IT...
TELL ME, MR GREGORY, JUST WHAT IS THAT ODD ODOR OF INCENSE?
NOTHING-ER-NOTHING AT ALL JUST A PECULIARITY OF MINE-NOTHING IMPORTANT!
BUT AS CLARK DEPARTS, SOMETHING HIS SUPER-ACUTE HEARING PICKS UP, CAUSES HIM TO PAUSE--AND LISTEN...!
NOW WHY--?
WHAT CLARK OVERHEARD--!
JUST HAD A CALL FROM A SNOOPING DAILY PLANET REPORTER! HE'S SUSPICIOUS --- MIGHT STIR UP SOME MISCHIEF! YES, -- I UNDERSTAND!
1

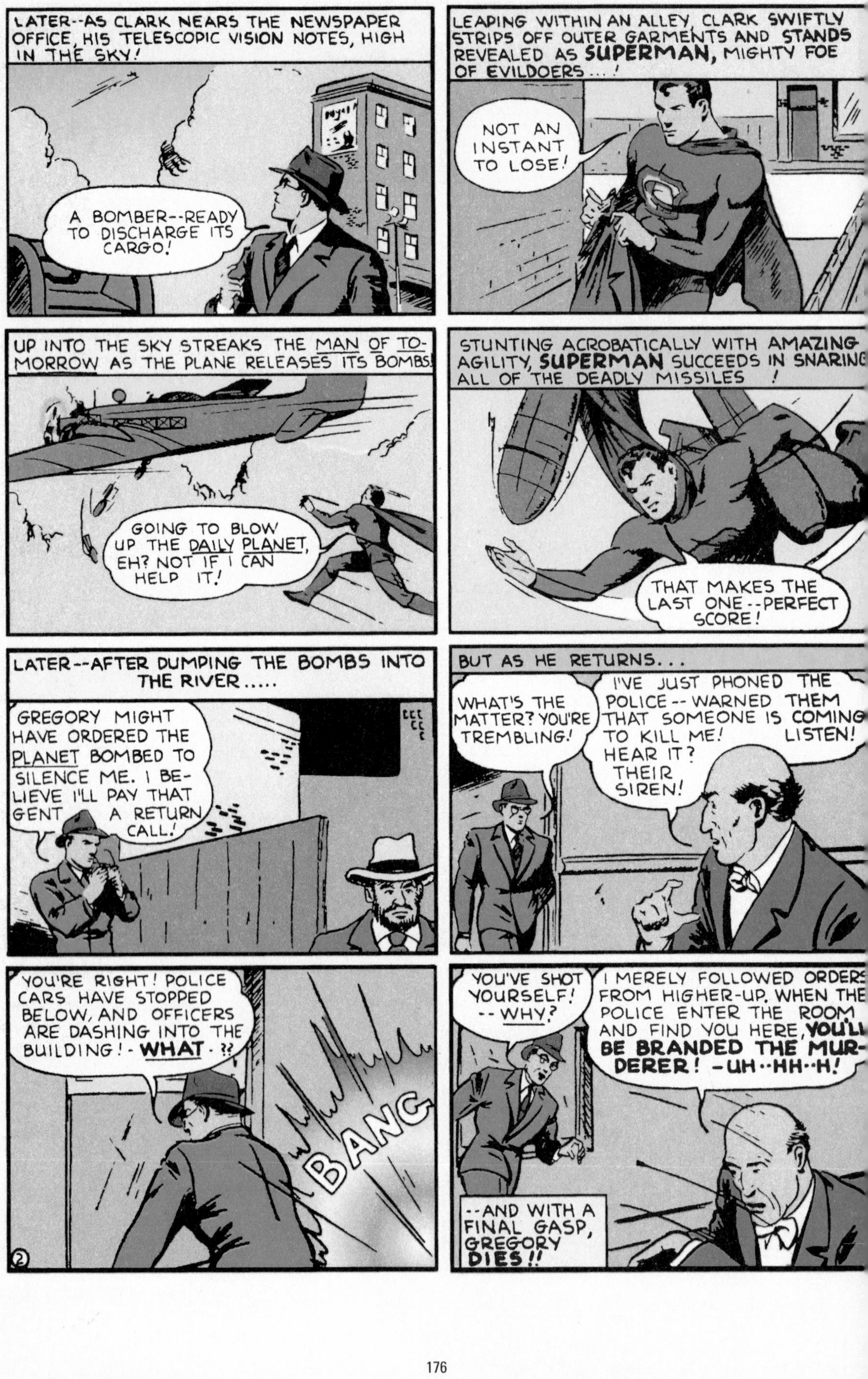
LATER--AS CLARK NEARS THE NEWSPAPER OFFICE, HIS TELESCOPIC VISION NOTES, HIGH IN THE SKY!
A BOMBER--READY TO DISCHARGE ITS CARGO!
LEAPING WITHIN AN ALLEY, CLARK SWIFTLY STRIPS OFF OUTER GARMENTS AND STANDS REVEALED AS SUPERMAN, MIGHTY FOE OF EVILDOERS...!
NOT AN INSTANT TO LOSE!
UP INTO THE SKY STREAKS THE MAN OF TO-MORROW AS THE PLANE RELEASES ITS BOMBS!
GOING TO BLOW UP THE DAILY PLANET, EH? NOT IF I CAN HELP IT!
STUNTING ACROBATICALLY WITH AMAZING AGILITY, SUPERMAN SUCCEEDS IN SNARING ALL OF THE DEADLY MISSILES !
THAT MAKES THE LAST ONE--PERFECT SCORE!
LATER--AFTER DUMPING THE BOMBS INTO THE RIVER.....
GREGORY MIGHT HAVE ORDERED THE PLANET BOMBED TO SILENCE ME. I BE-LIEVE I'LL PAY THAT GENT A RETURN CALL!
BUT AS HE RETURNS...
WHAT'S THE MATTER? YOU'RE TREMBLING!
I'VE JUST PHONED THE POLICE--WARNED THEM THAT SOMEONE IS COMING TO KILL ME! LISTEN! HEAR IT? THEIR SIREN!
YOU'RE RIGHT! POLICE CARS HAVE STOPPED BELOW, AND OFFICERS ARE DASHING INTO THE BUILDING! - WHAT - ??
BANG
2
YOU'VE SHOT YOURSELF! --WHY?
I MERELY FOLLOWED ORDERS FROM HIGHER-UP. WHEN THE POLICE ENTER THE ROOM AND FIND YOU HERE, YOU'LL BE BRANDED THE MUR-DERER! -UH--HH--H!
--AND WITH A FINAL GASP, GREGORY DIES!!

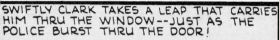

Panel 1:

SWIFTLY CLARK TAKES A LEAP THAT CARRIES HIM THRU THE WINDOW--JUST AS THE POLICE BURST THRU THE DOOR!

TOUGH ON THE PLOTTERS' PLANS, BUT I REFUSE TO REMAIN HERE AND BE THE FALL-GUY!

Panel 2:

CLARK ALIGHTS ATOP A NEARBY BUILDING!

WAS THAT A CLOSE CALL!

Panel 3:

WALKING DOWN THRU THE BUILDING, CLARK SHORTLY AFTER EMERGES ON THE STREET.

S'MATTER, PAT?

JUST ANOTHER MURDER, KENT! I GUESS IT'S OKAY FOR YOU TO ENTER!

Panel 4:

IT CERTAINLY DOESN'T TAKE YOU REPORTERS LONG TO SCENT A STORY!

JUST THE BLOODHOUND IN ME! AND WHO KNOWS, I MAY EVEN SOLVE THE CRIME FOR YOU!

SMALL CHANCE 'O THAT! THIS IS A MURDER WITHOUT A CLUE--AN' IF YOU CAN FIND THE KILLER, YOU'D HAVE TO BE A SUPERMAN!

Panel 5:

YOU'LL NEVER FIND THE MURDERER, SERGEANT-- BECAUSE THIS MAN KILLED HIMSELF! NOTE THE ANGLE AT WHICH THE BULLET ENTERED HIS SKULL!

BY GEORGE! HE'S RIGHT-- IT'S SUICIDE!

Panel 6:

CLARK TELEPHONES HIS STORY TO A RE-WRITE MAN AT THE OFFICE...

READY? ALL RIGHT! -- HERE'S THE DOPE!

Panel 7:

DETERMINING TO REVISIT ANOTHER OFFICE WITHIN WHICH HE HAD DETECTED THE INCENSE, CLARK RETURNS TO THE OFFICE OF BORDEN MOSELY, RUTHLESS FINANCIAL GIANT.

AN' WHERE DO YA THINK YER GOIN'?

IN, MY GOOD MAN, TO SEE MR. MOSELY --IN--

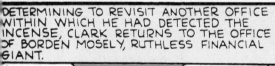

RECEPTIONIST

Panel 8:

OUT! MOSELY AIN'T IN TO NO REPORTERS, SEE?

I-- SEE--!

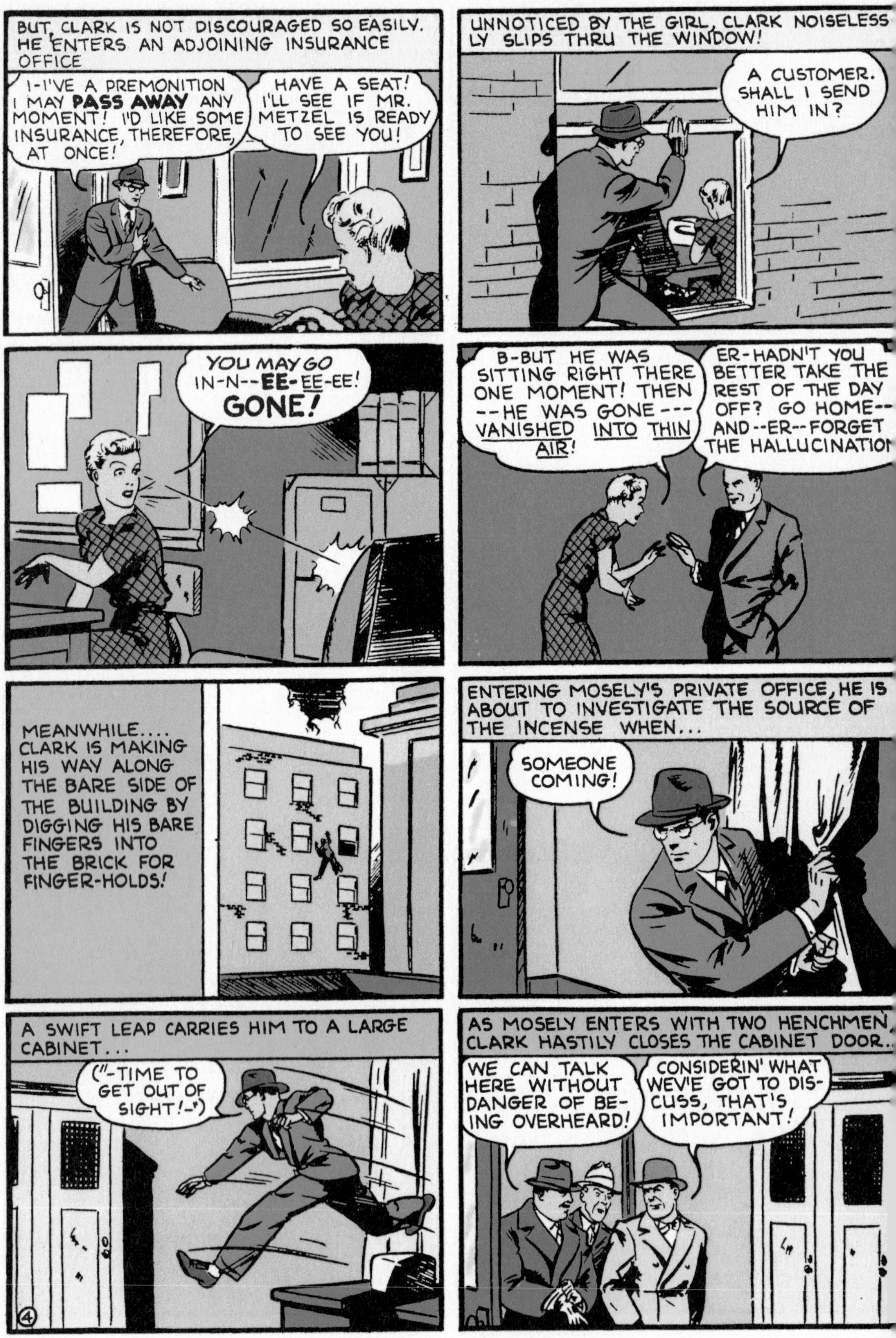
BUT, CLARK IS NOT DISCOURAGED SO EASILY. HE ENTERS AN ADJOINING INSURANCE OFFICE
I-I'VE A PREMONITION I MAY **PASS AWAY** ANY MOMENT! I'D LIKE SOME INSURANCE, THEREFORE, AT ONCE!
HAVE A SEAT! I'LL SEE IF MR. METZEL IS READY TO SEE YOU!
UNNOTICED BY THE GIRL, CLARK NOISELESSLY SLIPS THRU THE WINDOW!
A CUSTOMER. SHALL I SEND HIM IN?
YOU MAY GO IN-N--EE-EE-EE! GONE!
B-BUT HE WAS SITTING RIGHT THERE ONE MOMENT! THEN --HE WAS GONE--- VANISHED INTO THIN AIR!
ER-HADN'T YOU BETTER TAKE THE REST OF THE DAY OFF? GO HOME-- AND--ER--FORGET THE HALLUCINATION
MEANWHILE.... CLARK IS MAKING HIS WAY ALONG THE BARE SIDE OF THE BUILDING BY DIGGING HIS BARE FINGERS INTO THE BRICK FOR FINGER-HOLDS!
ENTERING MOSELY'S PRIVATE OFFICE, HE IS ABOUT TO INVESTIGATE THE SOURCE OF THE INCENSE WHEN...
SOMEONE COMING!
A SWIFT LEAP CARRIES HIM TO A LARGE CABINET...
("-TIME TO GET OUT OF SIGHT!-")
4
AS MOSELY ENTERS WITH TWO HENCHMEN, CLARK HASTILY CLOSES THE CABINET DOOR..
WE CAN TALK HERE WITHOUT DANGER OF BEING OVERHEARD!
CONSIDERIN' WHAT WEV'E GOT TO DISCUSS, THAT'S IMPORTANT!

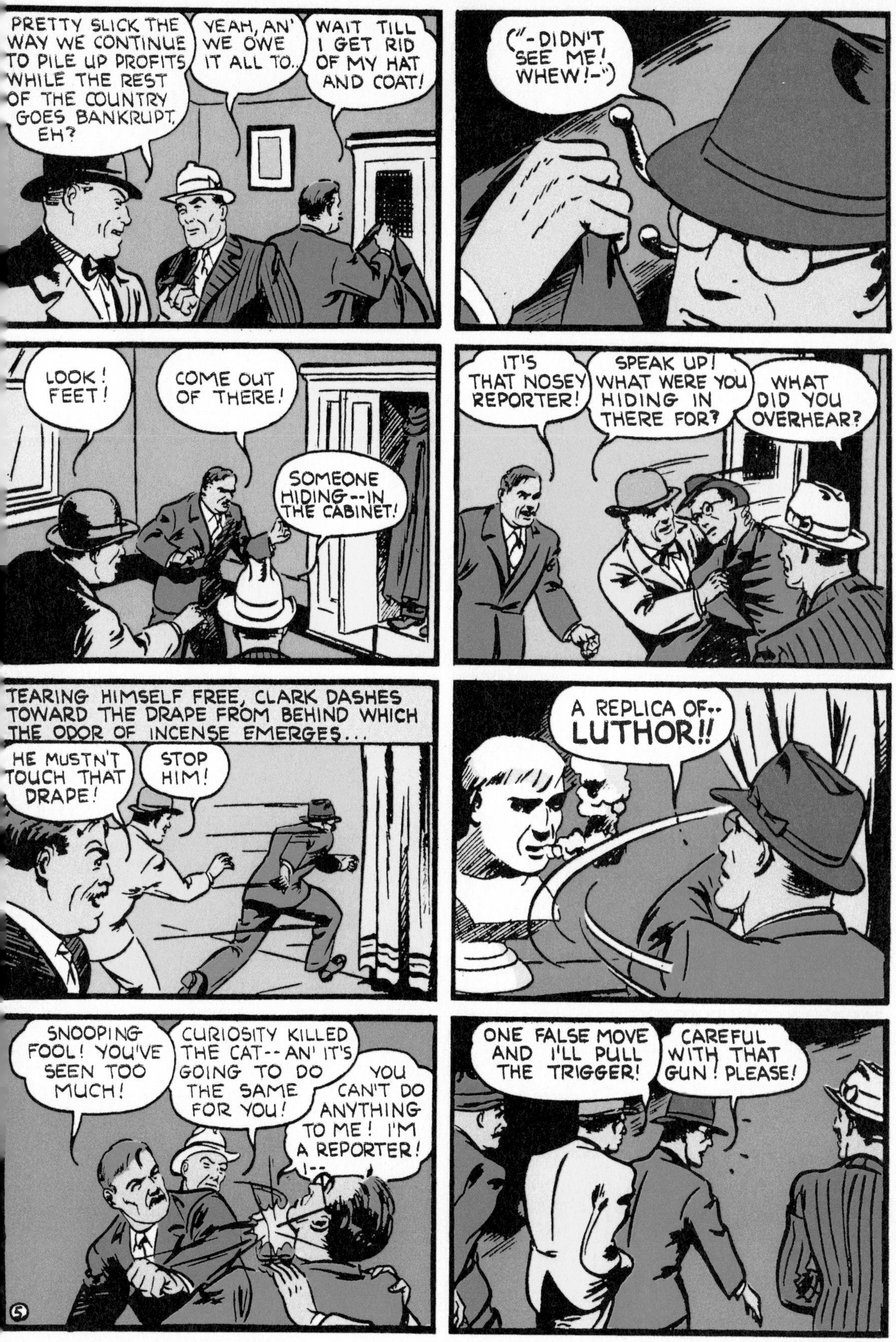
PRETTY SLICK THE WAY WE CONTINUE TO PILE UP PROFITS WHILE THE REST OF THE COUNTRY GOES BANKRUPT, EH?
YEAH, AN' WE OWE IT ALL TO..
WAIT TILL I GET RID OF MY HAT AND COAT!
("-DIDN'T SEE ME! WHEW!-")
LOOK! FEET!
COME OUT OF THERE!
SOMEONE HIDING--IN THE CABINET!
IT'S THAT NOSEY REPORTER!
SPEAK UP! WHAT WERE YOU HIDING IN THERE FOR?
WHAT DID YOU OVERHEAR?
TEARING HIMSELF FREE, CLARK DASHES TOWARD THE DRAPE FROM BEHIND WHICH THE ODOR OF INCENSE EMERGES...
HE MUSTN'T TOUCH THAT DRAPE!
STOP HIM!
A REPLICA OF-- LUTHOR!!
SNOOPING FOOL! YOU'VE SEEN TOO MUCH!
CURIOSITY KILLED THE CAT--AN' IT'S GOING TO DO THE SAME FOR YOU!
YOU CAN'T DO ANYTHING TO ME! I'M A REPORTER! I--
5
ONE FALSE MOVE AND I'LL PULL THE TRIGGER!
CAREFUL WITH THAT GUN! PLEASE!

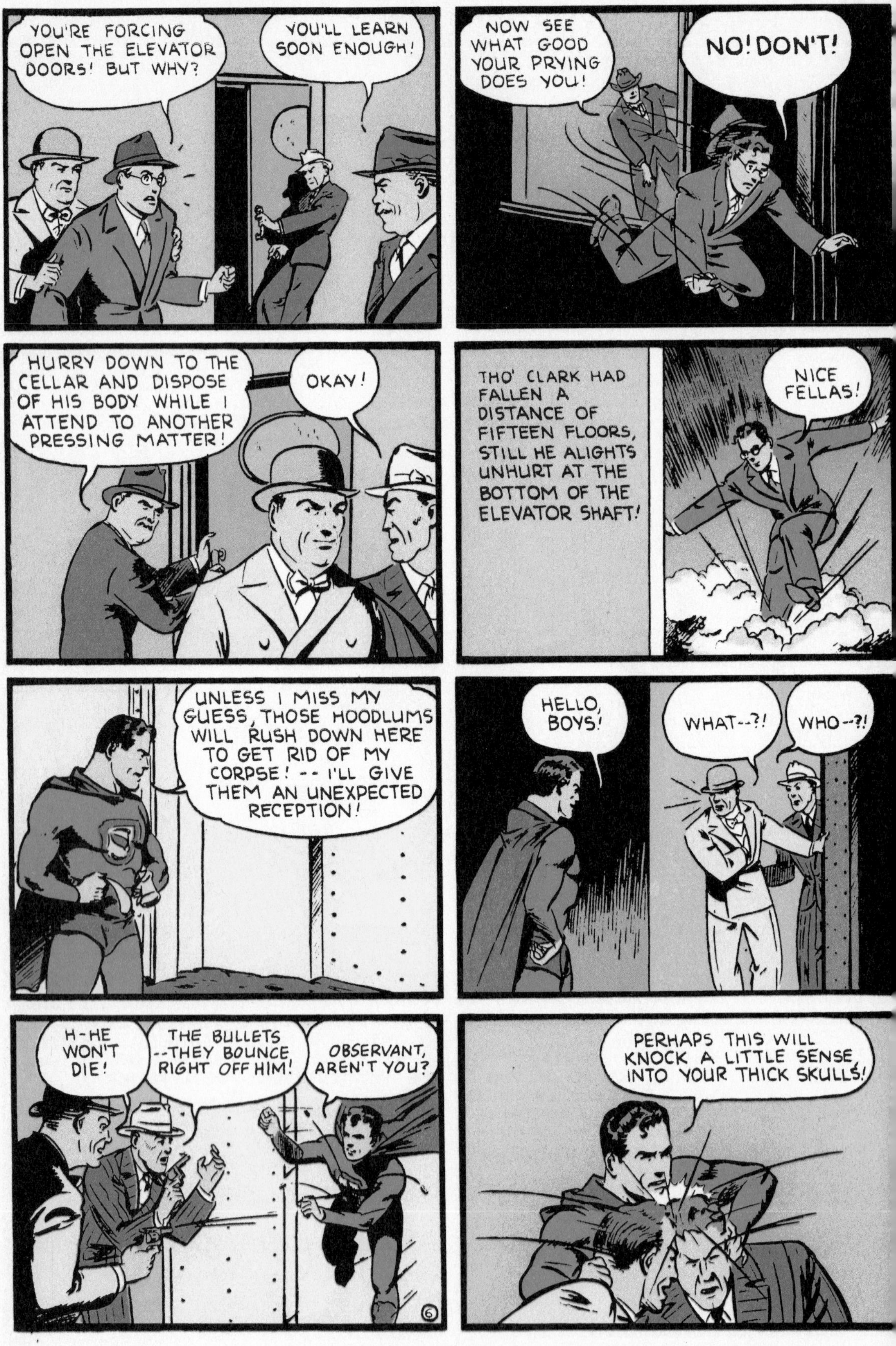
YOU'RE FORCING OPEN THE ELEVATOR DOORS! BUT WHY?
YOU'LL LEARN SOON ENOUGH!
NOW SEE WHAT GOOD YOUR PRYING DOES YOU!
NO! DON'T!
HURRY DOWN TO THE CELLAR AND DISPOSE OF HIS BODY WHILE I ATTEND TO ANOTHER PRESSING MATTER!
OKAY!
THO' CLARK HAD FALLEN A DISTANCE OF FIFTEEN FLOORS, STILL HE ALIGHTS UNHURT AT THE BOTTOM OF THE ELEVATOR SHAFT!
NICE FELLAS!
UNLESS I MISS MY GUESS, THOSE HOODLUMS WILL RUSH DOWN HERE TO GET RID OF MY CORPSE! -- I'LL GIVE THEM AN UNEXPECTED RECEPTION!
HELLO, BOYS!
WHAT--?!
WHO--?!
H-HE WON'T DIE!
THE BULLETS --THEY BOUNCE RIGHT OFF HIM!
OBSERVANT, AREN'T YOU?
6
PERHAPS THIS WILL KNOCK A LITTLE SENSE INTO YOUR THICK SKULLS!

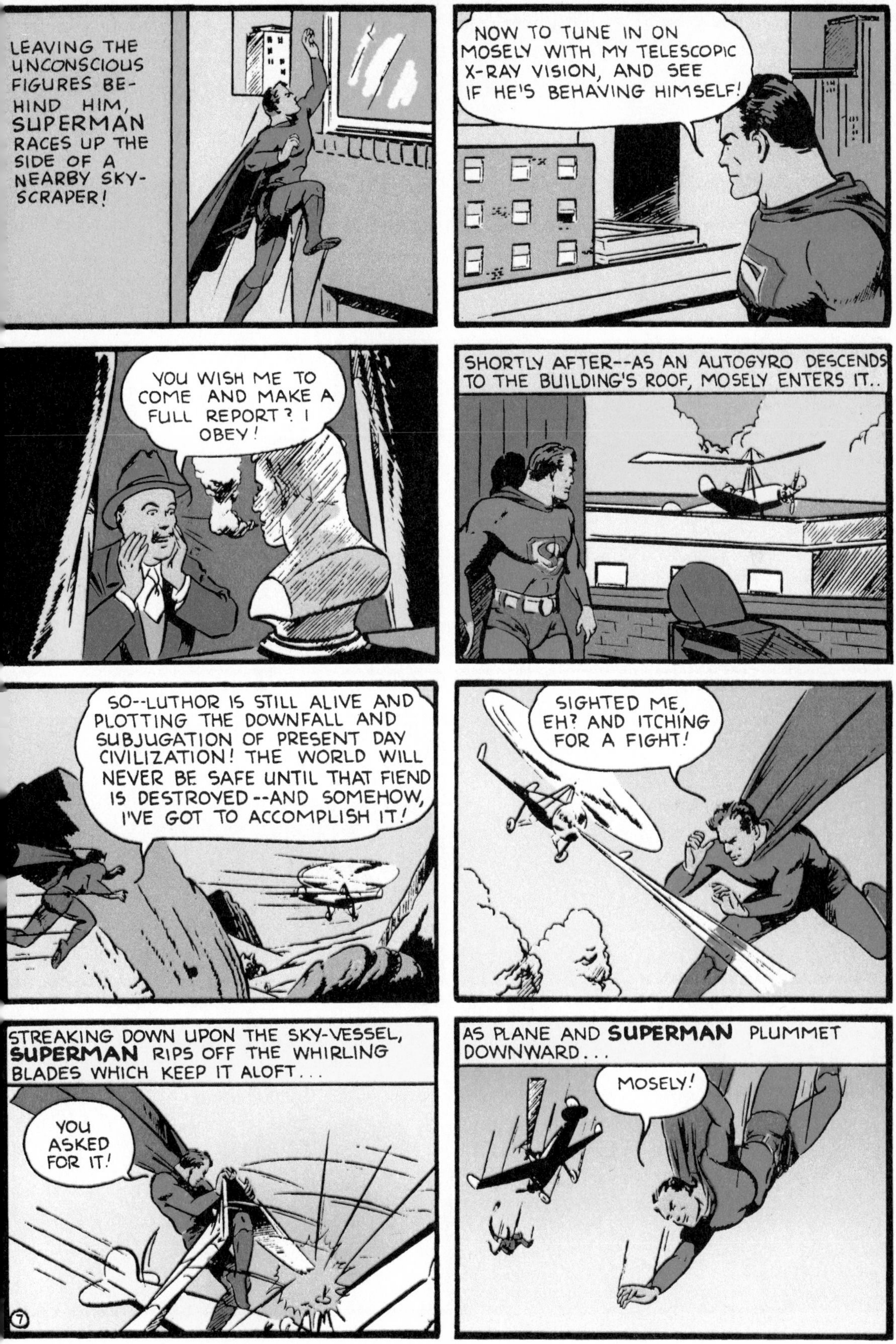
LEAVING THE UNCONSCIOUS FIGURES BEHIND HIM, SUPERMAN RACES UP THE SIDE OF A NEARBY SKY-SCRAPER!
NOW TO TUNE IN ON MOSELY WITH MY TELESCOPIC X-RAY VISION, AND SEE IF HE'S BEHAVING HIMSELF!
YOU WISH ME TO COME AND MAKE A FULL REPORT? I OBEY!
SHORTLY AFTER--AS AN AUTOGYRO DESCENDS TO THE BUILDING'S ROOF, MOSELY ENTERS IT..
SO--LUTHOR IS STILL ALIVE AND PLOTTING THE DOWNFALL AND SUBJUGATION OF PRESENT DAY CIVILIZATION! THE WORLD WILL NEVER BE SAFE UNTIL THAT FIEND IS DESTROYED--AND SOMEHOW, I'VE GOT TO ACCOMPLISH IT!
SIGHTED ME, EH? AND ITCHING FOR A FIGHT!
STREAKING DOWN UPON THE SKY-VESSEL, SUPERMAN RIPS OFF THE WHIRLING BLADES WHICH KEEP IT ALOFT...
YOU ASKED FOR IT!
7
AS PLANE AND SUPERMAN PLUMMET DOWNWARD...
MOSELY!

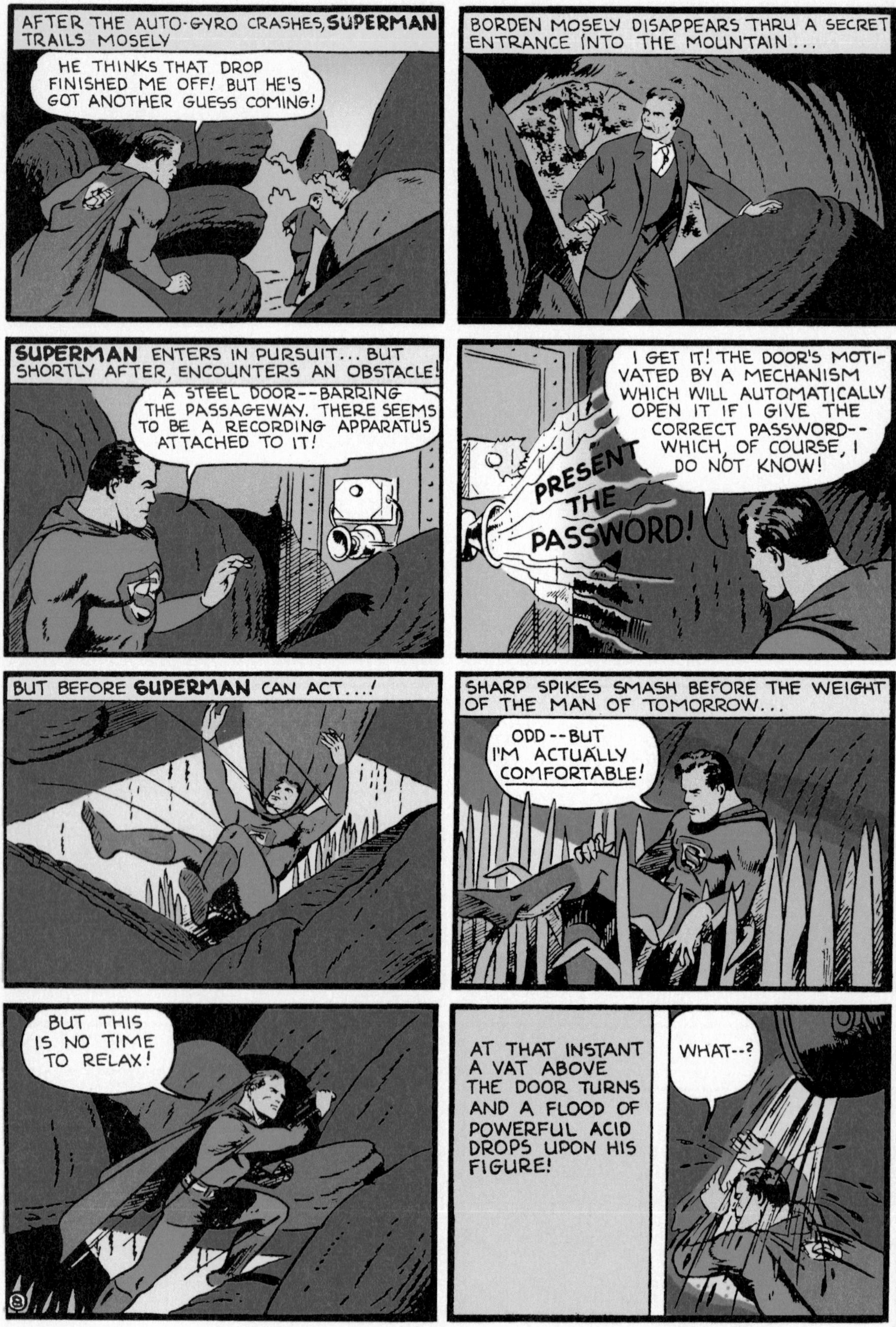
AFTER THE AUTO-GYRO CRASHES, SUPERMAN TRAILS MOSELY
HE THINKS THAT DROP FINISHED ME OFF! BUT HE'S GOT ANOTHER GUESS COMING!
BORDEN MOSELY DISAPPEARS THRU A SECRET ENTRANCE INTO THE MOUNTAIN...
SUPERMAN ENTERS IN PURSUIT... BUT SHORTLY AFTER, ENCOUNTERS AN OBSTACLE!
A STEEL DOOR--BARRING THE PASSAGEWAY. THERE SEEMS TO BE A RECORDING APPARATUS ATTACHED TO IT!
PRESENT THE PASSWORD!
I GET IT! THE DOOR'S MOTIVATED BY A MECHANISM WHICH WILL AUTOMATICALLY OPEN IT IF I GIVE THE CORRECT PASSWORD--WHICH, OF COURSE, I DO NOT KNOW!
BUT BEFORE SUPERMAN CAN ACT....!
SHARP SPIKES SMASH BEFORE THE WEIGHT OF THE MAN OF TOMORROW...
ODD--BUT I'M ACTUALLY COMFORTABLE!
BUT THIS IS NO TIME TO RELAX!
AT THAT INSTANT A VAT ABOVE THE DOOR TURNS AND A FLOOD OF POWERFUL ACID DROPS UPON HIS FIGURE!
WHAT--?

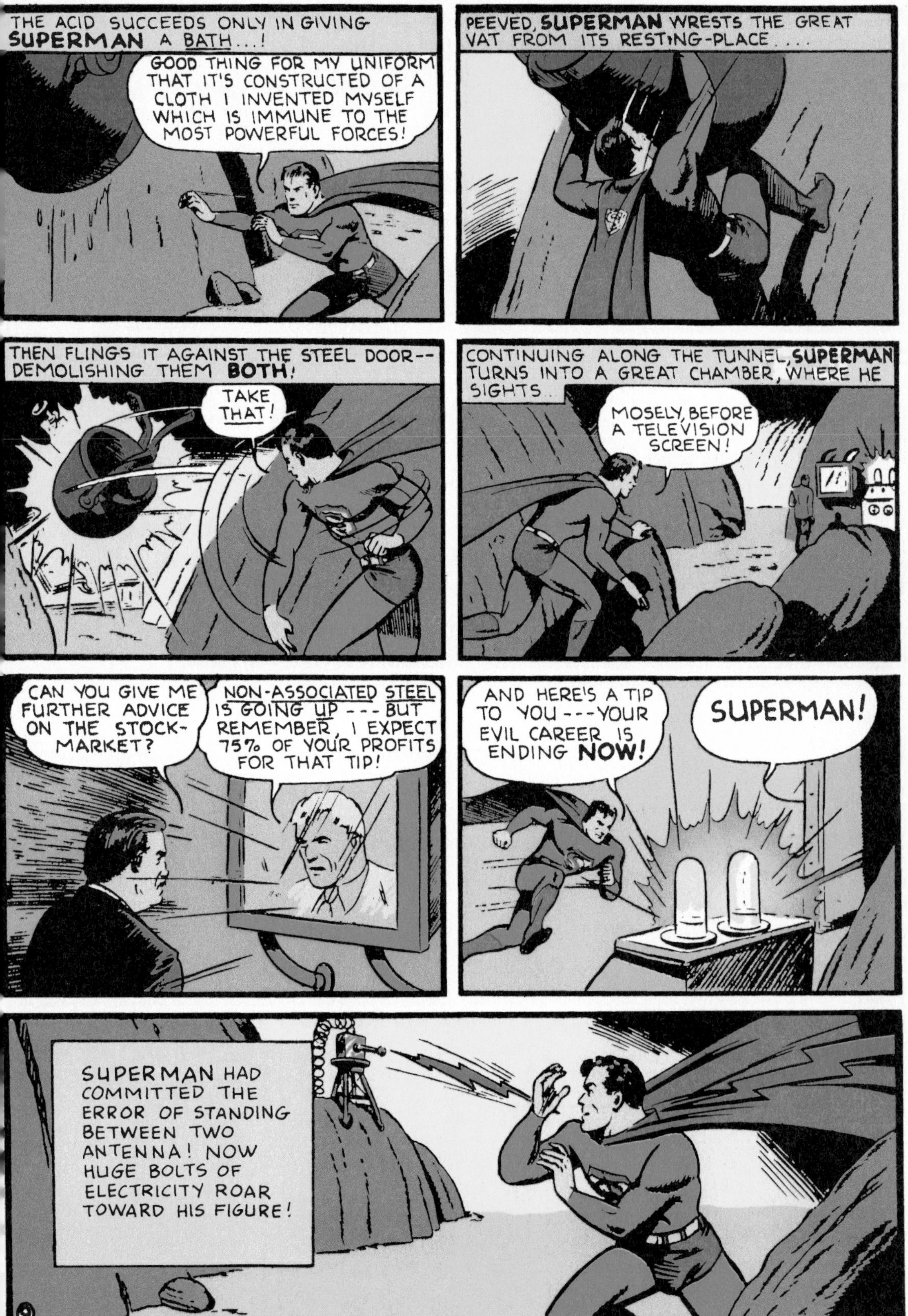
THE ACID SUCCEEDS ONLY IN GIVING SUPERMAN A BATH...!
GOOD THING FOR MY UNIFORM THAT IT'S CONSTRUCTED OF A CLOTH I INVENTED MYSELF WHICH IS IMMUNE TO THE MOST POWERFUL FORCES!
PEEVED, SUPERMAN WRESTS THE GREAT VAT FROM ITS RESTING-PLACE....
THEN FLINGS IT AGAINST THE STEEL DOOR-- DEMOLISHING THEM BOTH!
TAKE THAT!
CONTINUING ALONG THE TUNNEL, SUPERMAN TURNS INTO A GREAT CHAMBER, WHERE HE SIGHTS..
MOSELY, BEFORE A TELEVISION SCREEN!
CAN YOU GIVE ME FURTHER ADVICE ON THE STOCK-MARKET?
NON-ASSOCIATED STEEL IS GOING UP --- BUT REMEMBER, I EXPECT 75% OF YOUR PROFITS FOR THAT TIP!
AND HERE'S A TIP TO YOU ---YOUR EVIL CAREER IS ENDING NOW!
SUPERMAN!
SUPERMAN HAD COMMITTED THE ERROR OF STANDING BETWEEN TWO ANTENNA! NOW HUGE BOLTS OF ELECTRICITY ROAR TOWARD HIS FIGURE!

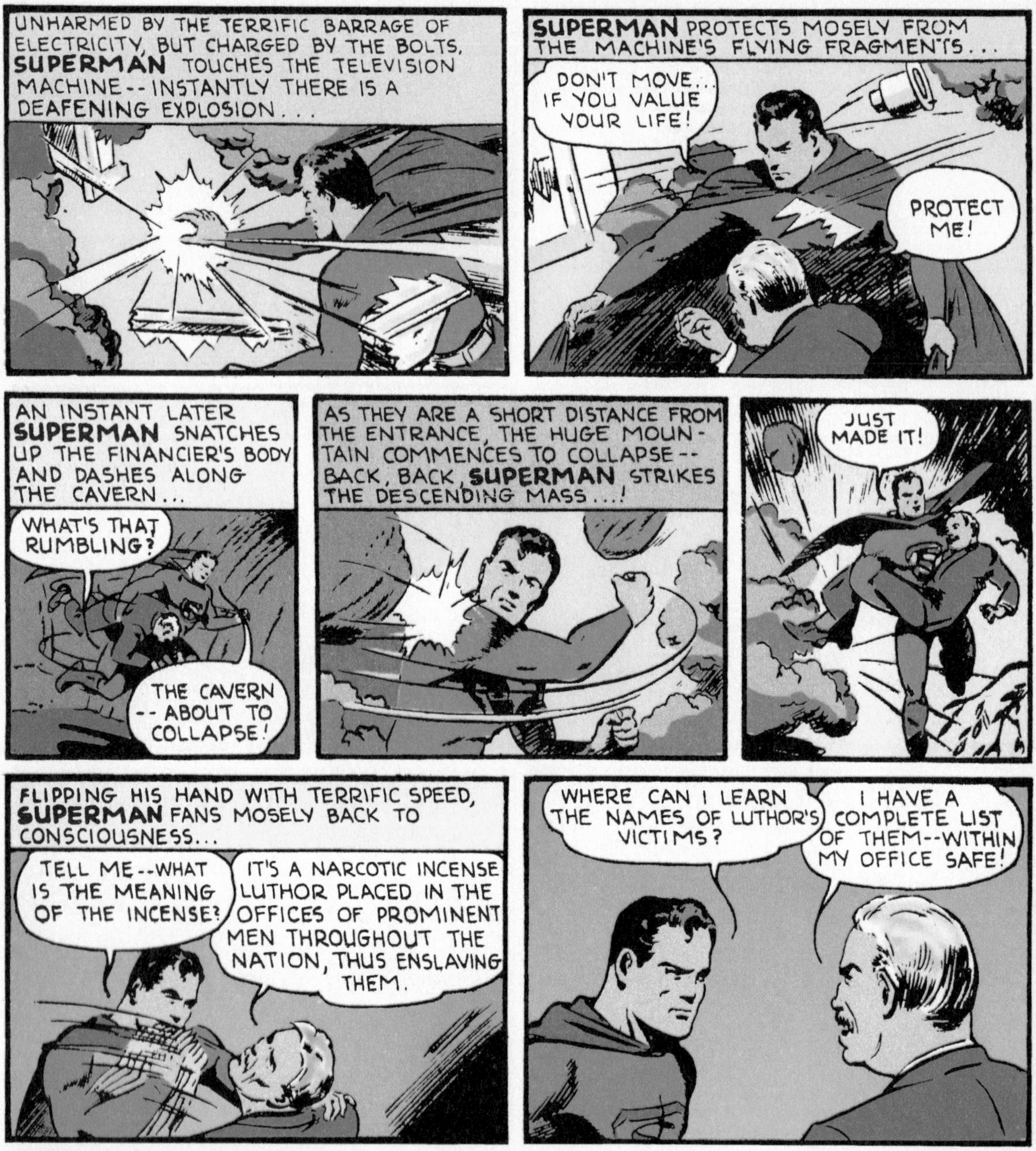
UNHARMED BY THE TERRIFIC BARRAGE OF ELECTRICITY, BUT CHARGED BY THE BOLTS, SUPERMAN TOUCHES THE TELEVISION MACHINE--INSTANTLY THERE IS A DEAFENING EXPLOSION...
SUPERMAN PROTECTS MOSELY FROM THE MACHINE'S FLYING FRAGMENTS...
DON'T MOVE... IF YOU VALUE YOUR LIFE!
PROTECT ME!
AN INSTANT LATER SUPERMAN SNATCHES UP THE FINANCIER'S BODY AND DASHES ALONG THE CAVERN...
WHAT'S THAT RUMBLING?
THE CAVERN --ABOUT TO COLLAPSE!
AS THEY ARE A SHORT DISTANCE FROM THE ENTRANCE, THE HUGE MOUNTAIN COMMENCES TO COLLAPSE--BACK, BACK, SUPERMAN STRIKES THE DESCENDING MASS...!
JUST MADE IT!
FLIPPING HIS HAND WITH TERRIFIC SPEED, SUPERMAN FANS MOSELY BACK TO CONSCIOUSNESS...
TELL ME--WHAT IS THE MEANING OF THE INCENSE?
IT'S A NARCOTIC INCENSE LUTHOR PLACED IN THE OFFICES OF PROMINENT MEN THROUGHOUT THE NATION, THUS ENSLAVING THEM.
WHERE CAN I LEARN THE NAMES OF LUTHOR'S VICTIMS?
I HAVE A COMPLETE LIST OF THEM--WITHIN MY OFFICE SAFE!
SHORTLY AFTER--SUPERMAN STREAKS DOWN TO THE WINDOW SILL OF THE FINANCIER'S OFFICE, CLUTCHING MOSELY UNDER HIS ARM..
YOU'D BETTER BE TELLING THE TRUTH!
I AM! I AM!
10
THERE! IT'S OPEN!
I'LL KNOW IN A FEW MINUTES WHETHER YOU'RE LYING!
SUFFOCATE, BLAST YOU!
MOSELY

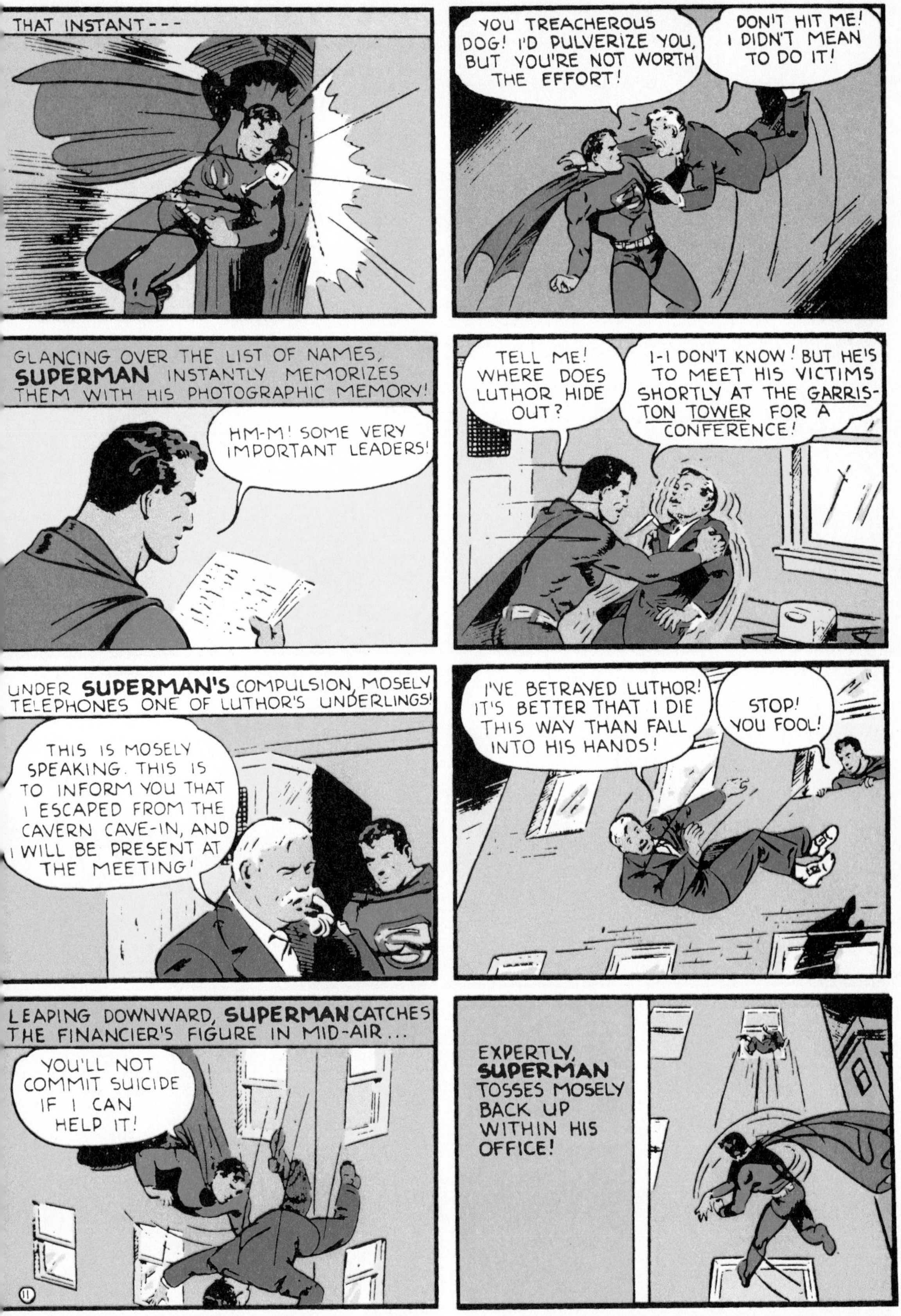
THAT INSTANT---
YOU TREACHEROUS DOG! I'D PULVERIZE YOU, BUT YOU'RE NOT WORTH THE EFFORT!
DON'T HIT ME! I DIDN'T MEAN TO DO IT!
GLANCING OVER THE LIST OF NAMES, SUPERMAN INSTANTLY MEMORIZES THEM WITH HIS PHOTOGRAPHIC MEMORY!
HM-M! SOME VERY IMPORTANT LEADERS!
TELL ME! WHERE DOES LUTHOR HIDE OUT?
I-I DON'T KNOW! BUT HE'S TO MEET HIS VICTIMS SHORTLY AT THE GARRISTON TOWER FOR A CONFERENCE!
UNDER SUPERMAN'S COMPULSION, MOSELY TELEPHONES ONE OF LUTHOR'S UNDERLINGS!
THIS IS MOSELY SPEAKING. THIS IS TO INFORM YOU THAT I ESCAPED FROM THE CAVERN CAVE-IN, AND I WILL BE PRESENT AT THE MEETING!
I'VE BETRAYED LUTHOR! IT'S BETTER THAT I DIE THIS WAY THAN FALL INTO HIS HANDS!
STOP! YOU FOOL!
LEAPING DOWNWARD, SUPERMAN CATCHES THE FINANCIER'S FIGURE IN MID-AIR...
YOU'LL NOT COMMIT SUICIDE IF I CAN HELP IT!
11
EXPERTLY, SUPERMAN TOSSES MOSELY BACK UP WITHIN HIS OFFICE!

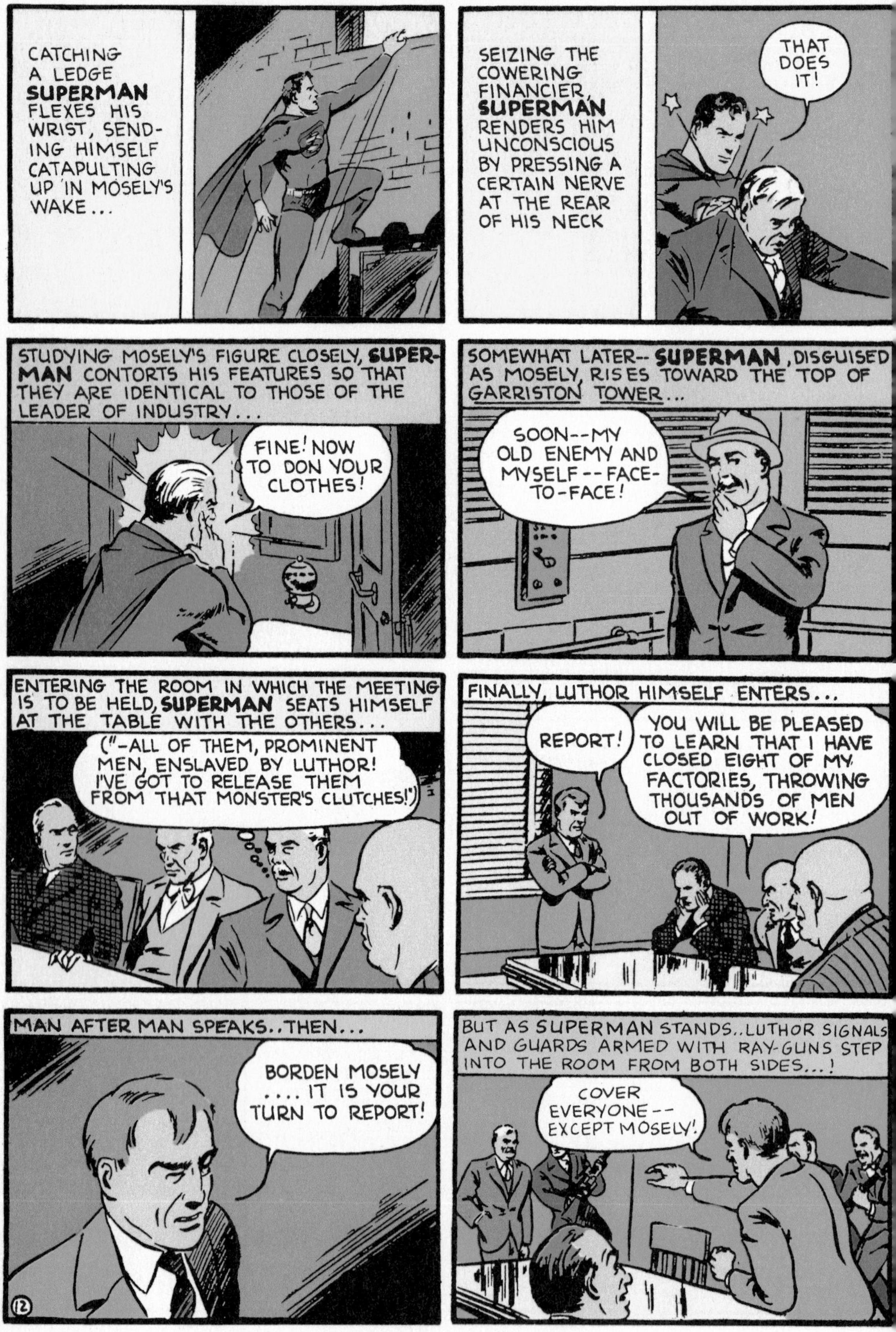
CATCHING A LEDGE SUPERMAN FLEXES HIS WRIST, SENDING HIMSELF CATAPULTING UP IN MOSELY'S WAKE...
SEIZING THE COWERING FINANCIER, SUPERMAN RENDERS HIM UNCONSCIOUS BY PRESSING A CERTAIN NERVE AT THE REAR OF HIS NECK
THAT DOES IT!
STUDYING MOSELY'S FIGURE CLOSELY, SUPERMAN CONTORTS HIS FEATURES SO THAT THEY ARE IDENTICAL TO THOSE OF THE LEADER OF INDUSTRY...
FINE! NOW TO DON YOUR CLOTHES!
SOMEWHAT LATER-- SUPERMAN, DISGUISED AS MOSELY, RISES TOWARD THE TOP OF GARRISTON TOWER...
SOON--MY OLD ENEMY AND MYSELF--FACE-TO-FACE!
ENTERING THE ROOM IN WHICH THE MEETING IS TO BE HELD, SUPERMAN SEATS HIMSELF AT THE TABLE WITH THE OTHERS...
("-ALL OF THEM, PROMINENT MEN, ENSLAVED BY LUTHOR! I'VE GOT TO RELEASE THEM FROM THAT MONSTER'S CLUTCHES!")
FINALLY, LUTHOR HIMSELF ENTERS...
REPORT!
YOU WILL BE PLEASED TO LEARN THAT I HAVE CLOSED EIGHT OF MY FACTORIES, THROWING THOUSANDS OF MEN OUT OF WORK!
MAN AFTER MAN SPEAKS..THEN...
BORDEN MOSELY .... IT IS YOUR TURN TO REPORT!
12
BUT AS SUPERMAN STANDS..LUTHOR SIGNALS AND GUARDS ARMED WITH RAY-GUNS STEP INTO THE ROOM FROM BOTH SIDES...!
COVER EVERYONE-- EXCEPT MOSELY!

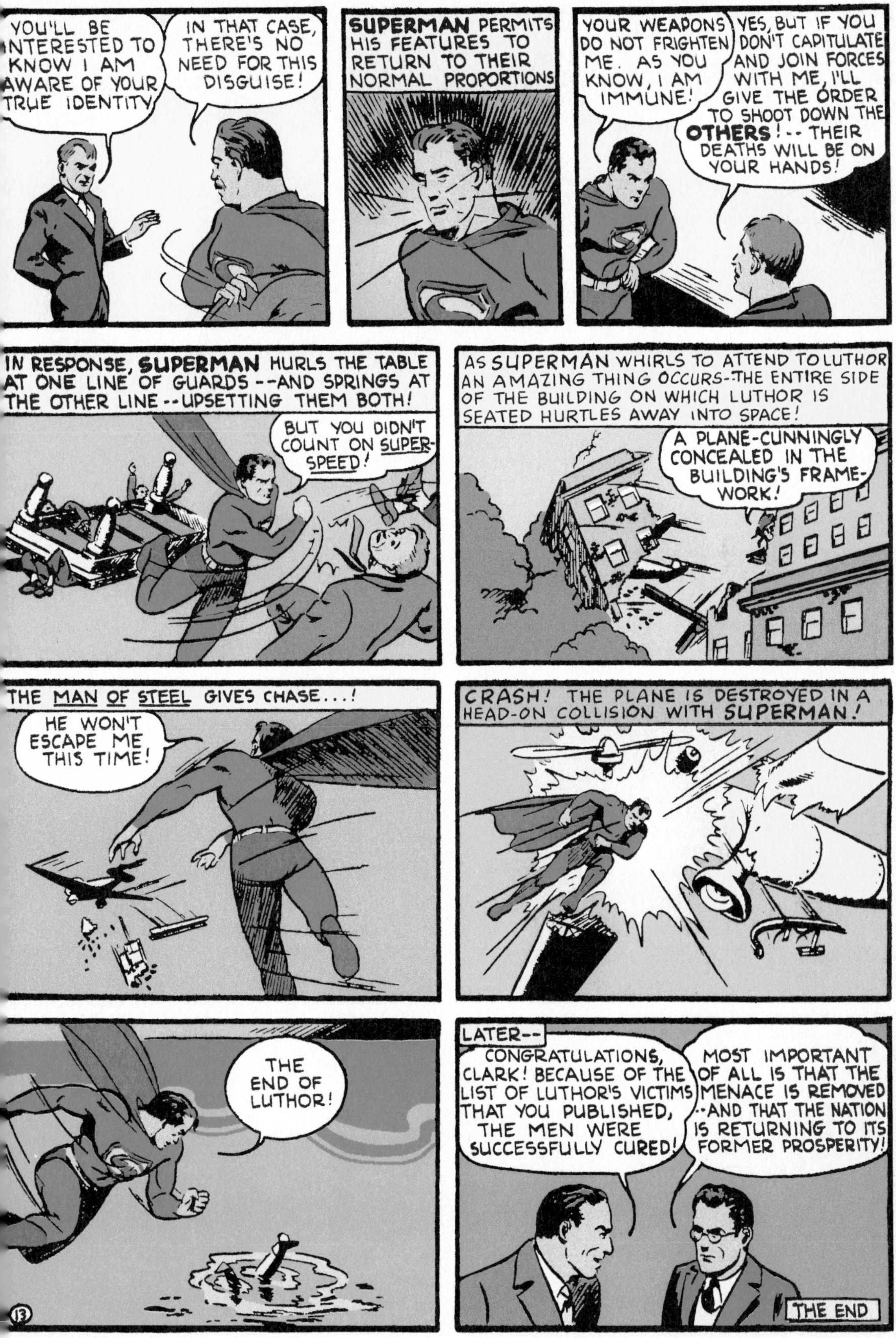
YOU'LL BE INTERESTED TO KNOW I AM AWARE OF YOUR TRUE IDENTITY
IN THAT CASE, THERE'S NO NEED FOR THIS DISGUISE!
SUPERMAN PERMITS HIS FEATURES TO RETURN TO THEIR NORMAL PROPORTIONS
YOUR WEAPONS DO NOT FRIGHTEN ME. AS YOU KNOW, I AM IMMUNE!
YES, BUT IF YOU DON'T CAPITULATE AND JOIN FORCES WITH ME, I'LL GIVE THE ORDER TO SHOOT DOWN THE OTHERS! -- THEIR DEATHS WILL BE ON YOUR HANDS!
IN RESPONSE, SUPERMAN HURLS THE TABLE AT ONE LINE OF GUARDS --AND SPRINGS AT THE OTHER LINE -- UPSETTING THEM BOTH!
BUT YOU DIDN'T COUNT ON SUPER-SPEED!
AS SUPERMAN WHIRLS TO ATTEND TO LUTHOR AN AMAZING THING OCCURS- THE ENTIRE SIDE OF THE BUILDING ON WHICH LUTHOR IS SEATED HURTLES AWAY INTO SPACE!
A PLANE-CUNNINGLY CONCEALED IN THE BUILDING'S FRAME-WORK!
THE MAN OF STEEL GIVES CHASE...!
HE WON'T ESCAPE ME THIS TIME!
CRASH! THE PLANE IS DESTROYED IN A HEAD-ON COLLISION WITH SUPERMAN!
THE END OF LUTHOR!
13
LATER--
CONGRATULATIONS, CLARK! BECAUSE OF THE LIST OF LUTHOR'S VICTIMS THAT YOU PUBLISHED, THE MEN WERE SUCCESSFULLY CURED!
MOST IMPORTANT OF ALL IS THAT THE MENACE IS REMOVED --AND THAT THE NATION IS RETURNING TO ITS FORMER PROSPERITY!
THE END

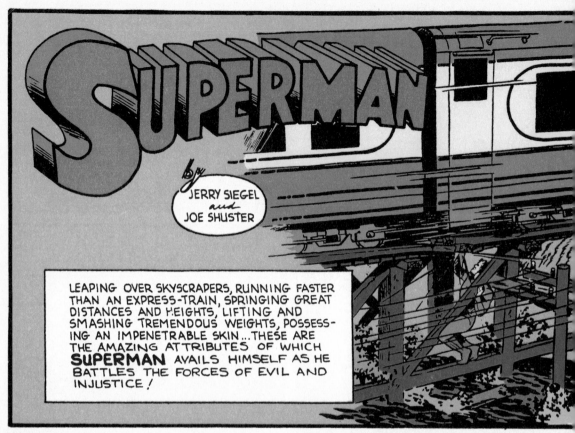

SUPERMAN

by JERRY SIEGEL and JOE SHUSTER

LEAPING OVER SKYSCRAPERS, RUNNING FASTER THAN AN EXPRESS-TRAIN, SPRINGING GREAT DISTANCES AND HEIGHTS, LIFTING AND SMASHING TREMENDOUS WEIGHTS, POSSESSING AN IMPENETRABLE SKIN...THESE ARE THE AMAZING ATTRIBUTES OF WHICH **SUPERMAN** AVAILS HIMSELF AS HE BATTLES THE FORCES OF EVIL AND INJUSTICE!

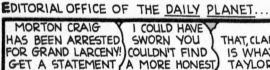

EDITORIAL OFFICE OF THE _DAILY PLANET_...

MORTON CRAIG HAS BEEN ARRESTED FOR GRAND LARCENY! GET A STATEMENT FROM HIM!

I COULD HAVE SWORN YOU COULDN'T FIND A MORE HONEST MAN THAN CRAIG! WONDER WHAT CAME OVER HIM?

THAT, CLARK, IS WHAT TAYLOR WANTS **YOU** TO FIND OUT!

BUT WHEN CLARK REACHES THE CITY JAIL...

BUT SURELY YOU MUST HAVE SOME JUSTIFICATION FOR YOUR ACT! WHAT DROVE YOU TO IT?

I'M NOT SAYING ANYTHING, I TELL YOU!

IF THERE'S ANYTHING I CAN DO--

YOU CAN! GET ME DR. BREN! I FEEL TERRIBLY RUN DOWN! HE'LL KNOW WHAT TO DO!

LATER...

I'LL HAVE TO ASK YOU WHAT YOU ARE GOING TO DO TO THE PRISONER, DR. BREN!

CRAIG SUFFERS FROM ANEMIA. AN INJECTION WILL HELP.- NOW, IF YOU'LL LEAVE US ALONE...

I'LL GO! IT'S PLAIN I WON'T GET ANY INFORMATION FROM CRAIG!

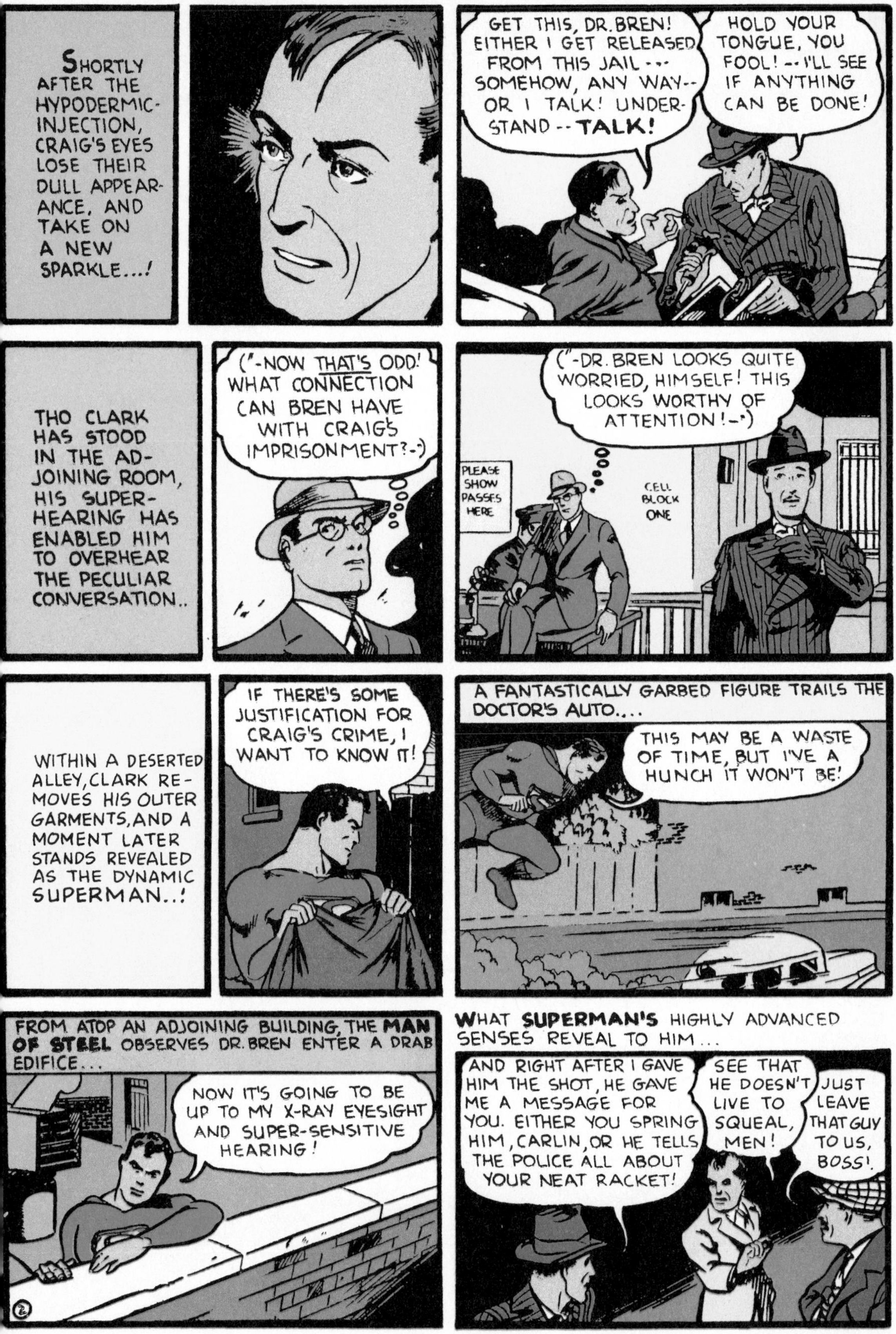
SHORTLY AFTER THE HYPODERMIC-INJECTION, CRAIG'S EYES LOSE THEIR DULL APPEARANCE, AND TAKE ON A NEW SPARKLE...!
GET THIS, DR. BREN! EITHER I GET RELEASED FROM THIS JAIL --- SOMEHOW, ANY WAY-- OR I TALK! UNDERSTAND -- TALK!
HOLD YOUR TONGUE, YOU FOOL! -- I'LL SEE IF ANYTHING CAN BE DONE!
THO CLARK HAS STOOD IN THE ADJOINING ROOM, HIS SUPER-HEARING HAS ENABLED HIM TO OVERHEAR THE PECULIAR CONVERSATION..
("-NOW THAT'S ODD! WHAT CONNECTION CAN BREN HAVE WITH CRAIG'S IMPRISONMENT?-")
("-DR. BREN LOOKS QUITE WORRIED, HIMSELF! THIS LOOKS WORTHY OF ATTENTION!-")
PLEASE SHOW PASSES HERE
CELL BLOCK ONE
WITHIN A DESERTED ALLEY, CLARK REMOVES HIS OUTER GARMENTS, AND A MOMENT LATER STANDS REVEALED AS THE DYNAMIC SUPERMAN..!
IF THERE'S SOME JUSTIFICATION FOR CRAIG'S CRIME, I WANT TO KNOW IT!
A FANTASTICALLY GARBED FIGURE TRAILS THE DOCTOR'S AUTO....
THIS MAY BE A WASTE OF TIME, BUT I'VE A HUNCH IT WON'T BE!
FROM ATOP AN ADJOINING BUILDING, THE MAN OF STEEL OBSERVES DR. BREN ENTER A DRAB EDIFICE...
NOW IT'S GOING TO BE UP TO MY X-RAY EYESIGHT AND SUPER-SENSITIVE HEARING!
2
WHAT SUPERMAN'S HIGHLY ADVANCED SENSES REVEAL TO HIM...
AND RIGHT AFTER I GAVE HIM THE SHOT, HE GAVE ME A MESSAGE FOR YOU. EITHER YOU SPRING HIM, CARLIN, OR HE TELLS THE POLICE ALL ABOUT YOUR NEAT RACKET!
SEE THAT HE DOESN'T LIVE TO SQUEAL, MEN!
JUST LEAVE THAT GUY TO US, BOSS!

(-AND JUST LEAVE THEM TO ME!--)

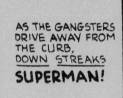

AS THE GANGSTERS DRIVE AWAY FROM THE CURB, DOWN STREAKS **SUPERMAN!**

NOW TO THROW A HITCH INTO THEIR SMUG PLANS!

ALIGHTING BEHIND THE AUTO, THE MAN OF TOMORROW GIVES IT A TERRIFIC SHOVE...

MIND CHANGING YOUR COURSE?

...SO THAT IT HURTLES INTO A TRAFFIC LIGHT STAND!

HEY! WHO YOU TRYIN' TO KILL?

BUT--!

NONE OF YOUR LIP! DRIVE TO THE STATION! YOU'RE UNDER ARREST-- ALL OF YOU!

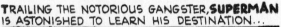

AND A FEW MOMENTS LATER

CARLIN, GOING OUT! WONDER WHAT HE'S UP TO?

TRAILING THE NOTORIOUS GANGSTER, **SUPERMAN** IS ASTONISHED TO LEARN HIS DESTINATION...

--THE LABORATORY OF PROFESSOR CARL GRINSTEAD ..ONE OF THE WORLD'S MOST ACCOMPLISHED CHEMISTS!

I'LL HAVE TO WAIT FOR THE GUARD TO LOOK THE OTHER WAY. PERHAPS THIS WILL HELP!

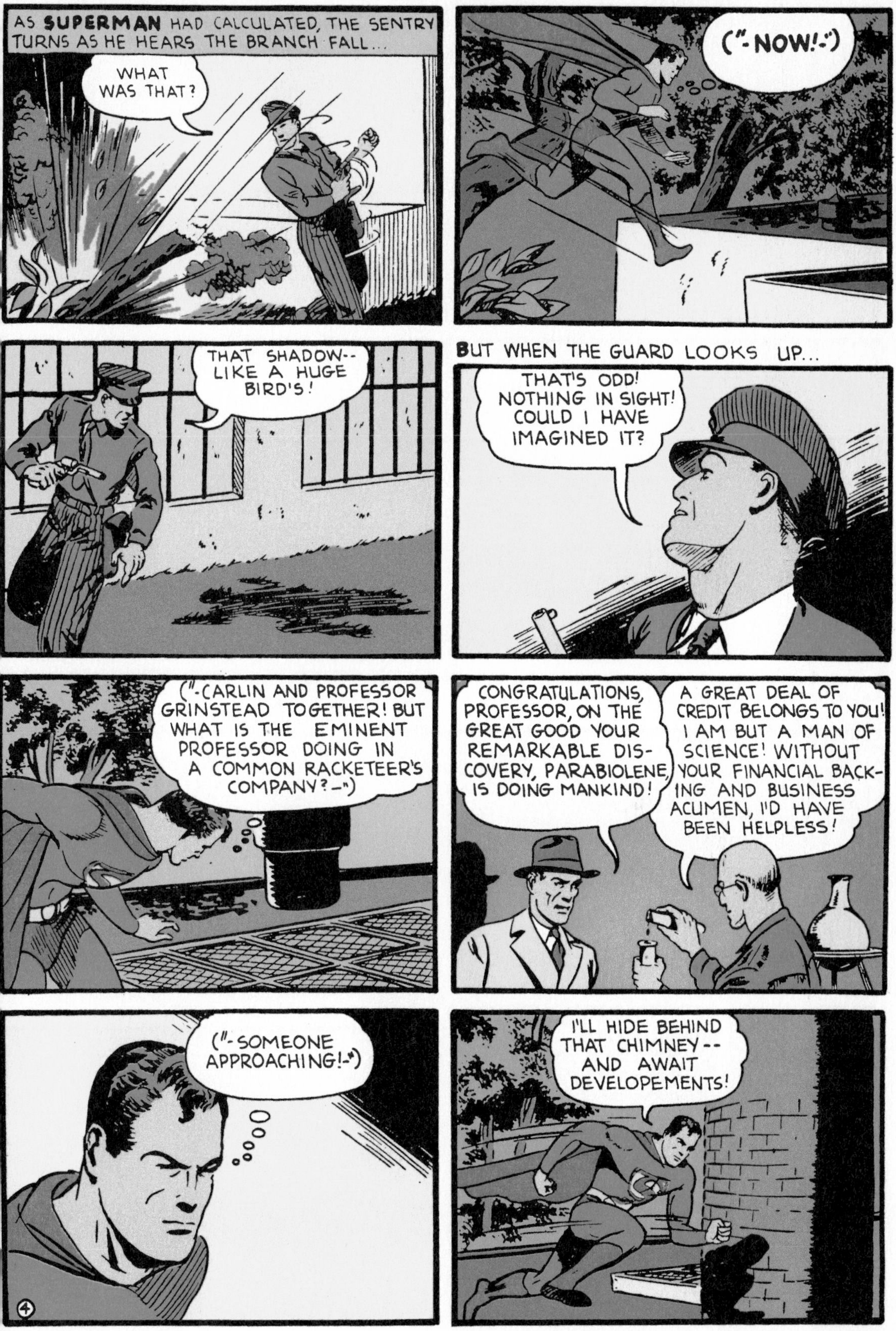
AS SUPERMAN HAD CALCULATED, THE SENTRY TURNS AS HE HEARS THE BRANCH FALL...
WHAT WAS THAT?
("-NOW!-")
THAT SHADOW-- LIKE A HUGE BIRD'S!
BUT WHEN THE GUARD LOOKS UP...
THAT'S ODD! NOTHING IN SIGHT! COULD I HAVE IMAGINED IT?
("-CARLIN AND PROFESSOR GRINSTEAD TOGETHER! BUT WHAT IS THE EMINENT PROFESSOR DOING IN A COMMON RACKETEER'S COMPANY?-")
CONGRATULATIONS, PROFESSOR, ON THE GREAT GOOD YOUR REMARKABLE DIS-COVERY, PARABIOLENE, IS DOING MANKIND!
A GREAT DEAL OF CREDIT BELONGS TO YOU! I AM BUT A MAN OF SCIENCE! WITHOUT YOUR FINANCIAL BACK-ING AND BUSINESS ACUMEN, I'D HAVE BEEN HELPLESS!
("-SOMEONE APPROACHING!-")
I'LL HIDE BEHIND THAT CHIMNEY-- AND AWAIT DEVELOPEMENTS!
4

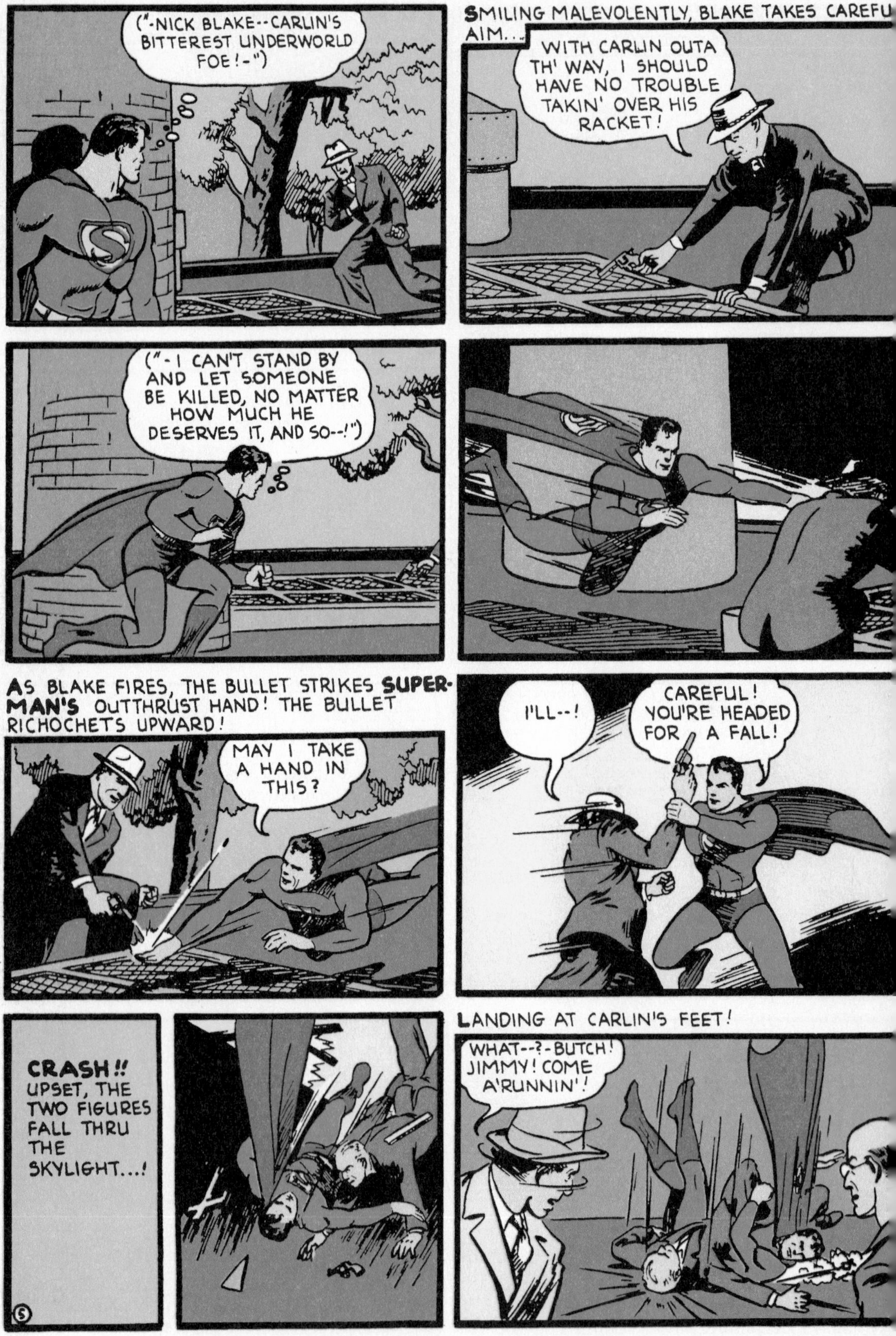
("-NICK BLAKE--CARLIN'S BITTEREST UNDERWORLD FOE!-")
SMILING MALEVOLENTLY, BLAKE TAKES CAREFU
AIM...
WITH CARLIN OUTA TH' WAY, I SHOULD HAVE NO TROUBLE TAKIN' OVER HIS RACKET!
("-I CAN'T STAND BY AND LET SOMEONE BE KILLED, NO MATTER HOW MUCH HE DESERVES IT, AND SO--!")
AS BLAKE FIRES, THE BULLET STRIKES SUPERMAN'S OUTTHRUST HAND! THE BULLET RICHOCHETS UPWARD!
MAY I TAKE A HAND IN THIS?
I'LL--!
CAREFUL! YOU'RE HEADED FOR A FALL!
CRASH!! UPSET, THE TWO FIGURES FALL THRU THE SKYLIGHT...!
5
LANDING AT CARLIN'S FEET!
WHAT--?-BUTCH! JIMMY! COME A'RUNNIN'!

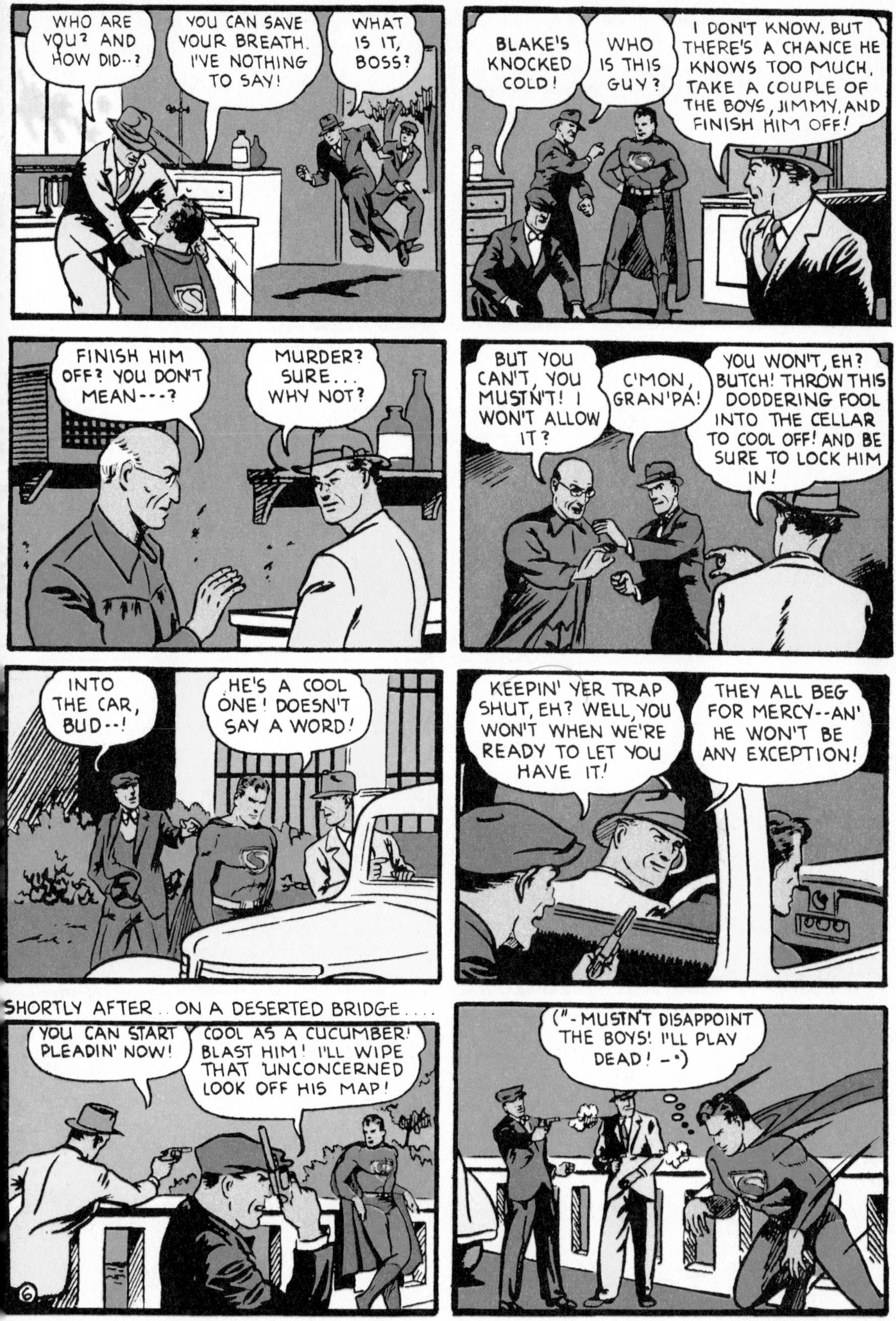
WHO ARE YOU? AND HOW DID--?
YOU CAN SAVE YOUR BREATH. I'VE NOTHING TO SAY!
WHAT IS IT, BOSS?
BLAKE'S KNOCKED COLD!
WHO IS THIS GUY?
I DON'T KNOW. BUT THERE'S A CHANCE HE KNOWS TOO MUCH. TAKE A COUPLE OF THE BOYS, JIMMY, AND FINISH HIM OFF!
FINISH HIM OFF? YOU DON'T MEAN---?
MURDER? SURE... WHY NOT?
BUT YOU CAN'T, YOU MUSTN'T! I WON'T ALLOW IT?
C'MON, GRAN'PA!
YOU WON'T, EH? BUTCH! THROW THIS DODDERING FOOL INTO THE CELLAR TO COOL OFF! AND BE SURE TO LOCK HIM IN!
INTO THE CAR, BUD--!
HE'S A COOL ONE! DOESN'T SAY A WORD!
KEEPIN' YER TRAP SHUT, EH? WELL, YOU WON'T WHEN WE'RE READY TO LET YOU HAVE IT!
THEY ALL BEG FOR MERCY--AN' HE WON'T BE ANY EXCEPTION!
SHORTLY AFTER... ON A DESERTED BRIDGE....
YOU CAN START PLEADIN' NOW!
COOL AS A CUCUMBER! BLAST HIM! I'LL WIPE THAT UNCONCERNED LOOK OFF HIS MAP!
6
("-MUSTN'T DISAPPOINT THE BOYS! I'LL PLAY DEAD! -")

LIFTING THE **MAN OF TOMORROW'S** BODY, THE HOODLUMS TOSS IT OVER THE BRIDGE'S SIDE SO THAT IT TOPPLES DOWN INTO THE RIVER...

SHOOT IF HE RISES!

NO SIGHT OF HIM! HE'S FINISHED FOR GOOD!

BUT THE MUSCLE MEN WOULD HAVE BEEN SURPRISED IF THEY COULD HAVE WITNESSED A STRANGE SCENE AT THE BOTTOM OF THE RIVER..

("-THEY'RE TURNING - LEAVING! I GUESS IT'LL BE OKAY TO EMERGE NOW! -")

AS THE GANGSTERS' CAR DRIVES OFF, A DRIPPING FIGURE EMERGES FROM THE RIVER!

LEAVING WITHOUT ME!

CATCHING THE AUTO'S REAR BUMPER IN A NEAT FLYING TACKLE....

CAN'T LET THEM DO THAT!

...THE **MAN OF STEEL** SWINGS BENEATH THE CAR'S BODY!

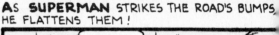

NOT COMFORTABLE ...BUT IT'LL DO!

GOSH, THIS ROAD IS BUMPY!

QUIT COMPLAININ'!

AS **SUPERMAN** STRIKES THE ROAD'S BUMPS, HE FLATTENS THEM!

TOOK THAT ONE WITH ME!

⑦

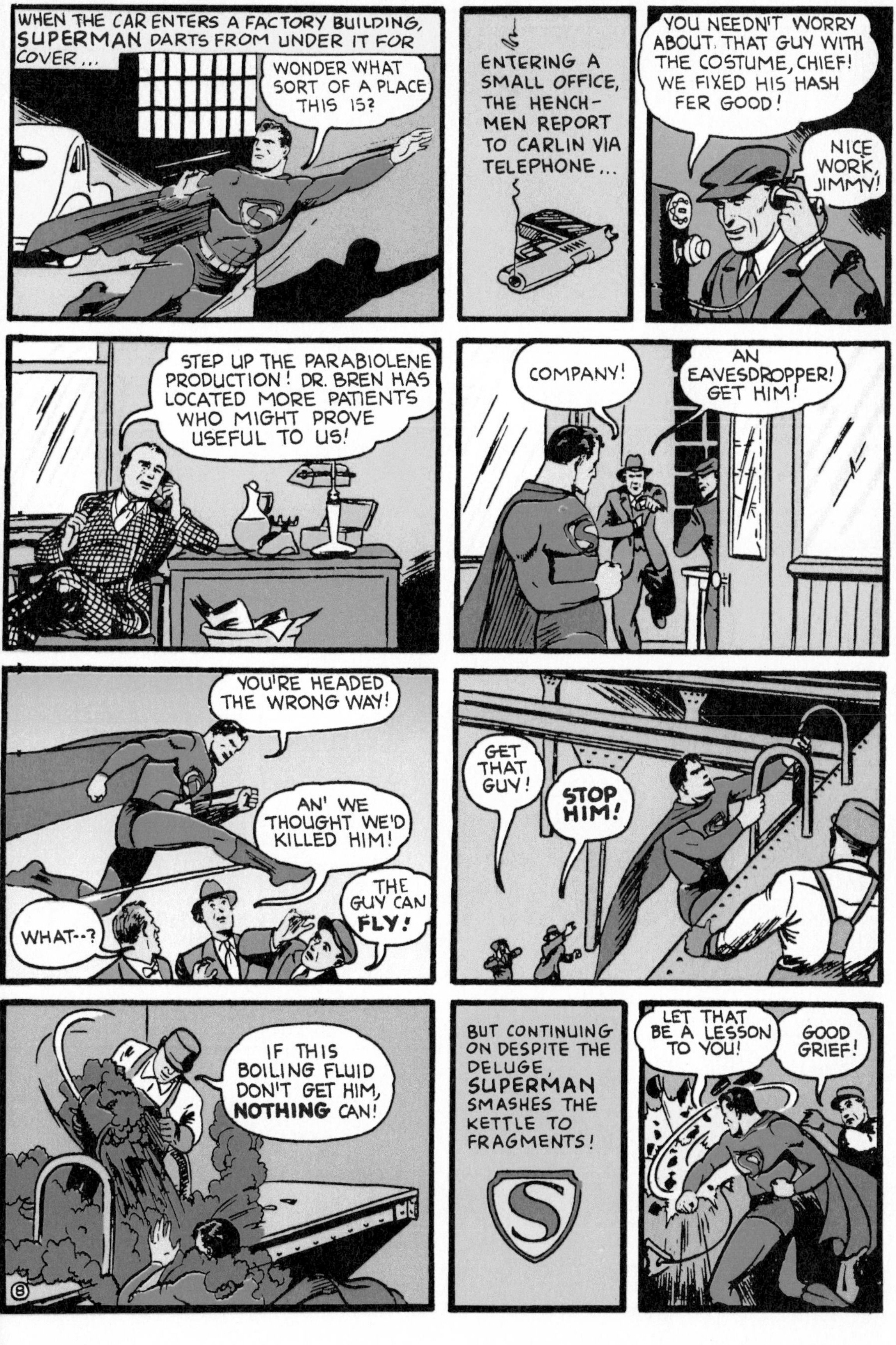
WHEN THE CAR ENTERS A FACTORY BUILDING, SUPERMAN DARTS FROM UNDER IT FOR COVER...
WONDER WHAT SORT OF A PLACE THIS IS?
ENTERING A SMALL OFFICE, THE HENCH-MEN REPORT TO CARLIN VIA TELEPHONE...
YOU NEEDN'T WORRY ABOUT THAT GUY WITH THE COSTUME, CHIEF! WE FIXED HIS HASH FER GOOD!
NICE WORK, JIMMY!
STEP UP THE PARABIOLENE PRODUCTION! DR. BREN HAS LOCATED MORE PATIENTS WHO MIGHT PROVE USEFUL TO US!
COMPANY!
AN EAVESDROPPER! GET HIM!
YOU'RE HEADED THE WRONG WAY!
AN' WE THOUGHT WE'D KILLED HIM!
WHAT--?
THE GUY CAN FLY!
GET THAT GUY!
STOP HIM!
IF THIS BOILING FLUID DON'T GET HIM, NOTHING CAN!
8
BUT CONTINUING ON DESPITE THE DELUGE, SUPERMAN SMASHES THE KETTLE TO FRAGMENTS!
LET THAT BE A LESSON TO YOU!
GOOD GRIEF!

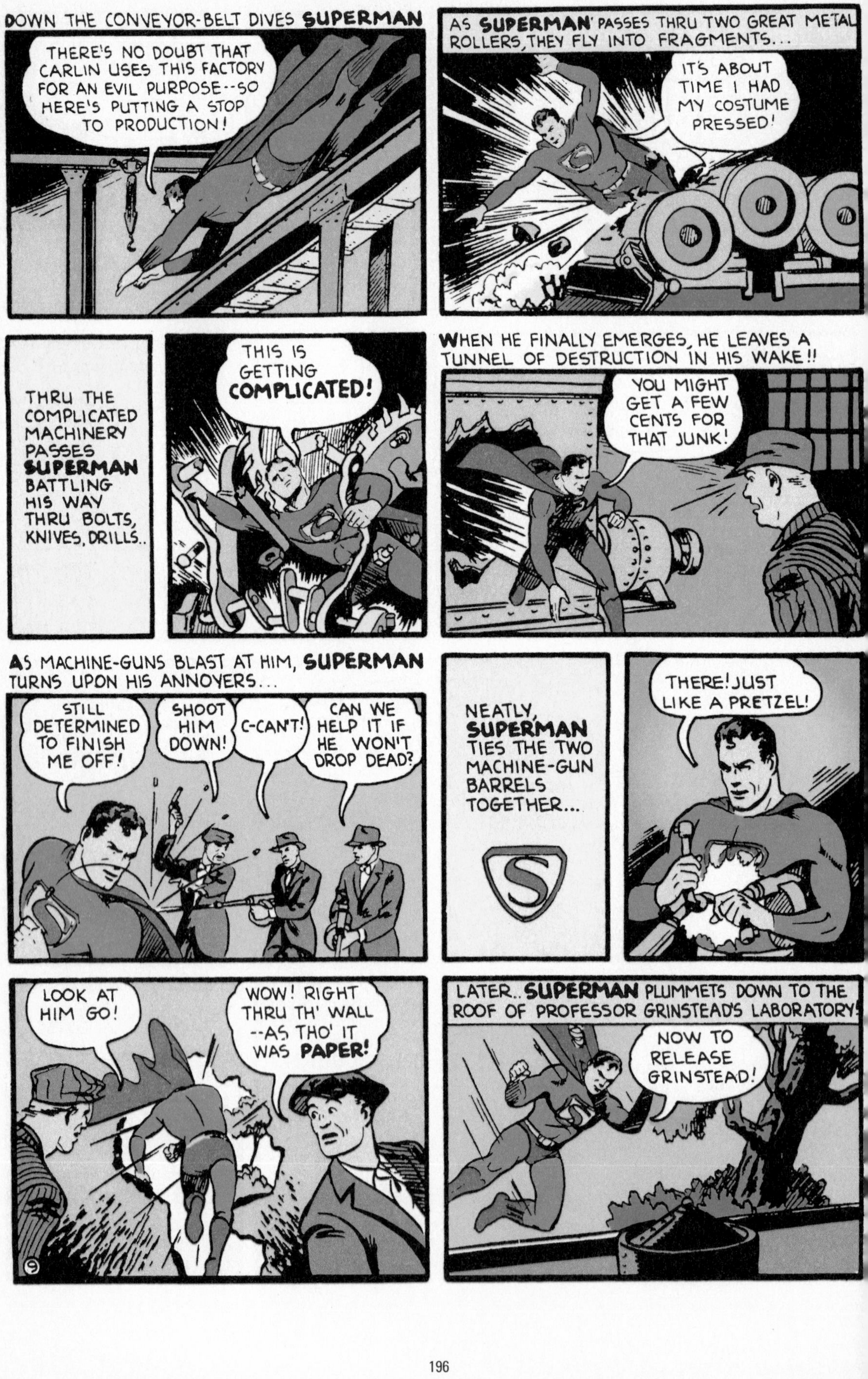
DOWN THE CONVEYOR-BELT DIVES SUPERMAN
THERE'S NO DOUBT THAT CARLIN USES THIS FACTORY FOR AN EVIL PURPOSE--SO HERE'S PUTTING A STOP TO PRODUCTION!
AS SUPERMAN PASSES THRU TWO GREAT METAL ROLLERS, THEY FLY INTO FRAGMENTS...
IT'S ABOUT TIME I HAD MY COSTUME PRESSED!
THRU THE COMPLICATED MACHINERY PASSES SUPERMAN BATTLING HIS WAY THRU BOLTS, KNIVES, DRILLS..
THIS IS GETTING COMPLICATED!
WHEN HE FINALLY EMERGES, HE LEAVES A TUNNEL OF DESTRUCTION IN HIS WAKE!!
YOU MIGHT GET A FEW CENTS FOR THAT JUNK!
AS MACHINE-GUNS BLAST AT HIM, SUPERMAN TURNS UPON HIS ANNOYERS...
STILL DETERMINED TO FINISH ME OFF!
SHOOT HIM DOWN!
C-CAN'T!
CAN WE HELP IT IF HE WON'T DROP DEAD?
NEATLY, SUPERMAN TIES THE TWO MACHINE-GUN BARRELS TOGETHER...
THERE! JUST LIKE A PRETZEL!
LOOK AT HIM GO!
WOW! RIGHT THRU TH' WALL --AS THO' IT WAS PAPER!
LATER.. SUPERMAN PLUMMETS DOWN TO THE ROOF OF PROFESSOR GRINSTEAD'S LABORATORY!
NOW TO RELEASE GRINSTEAD!

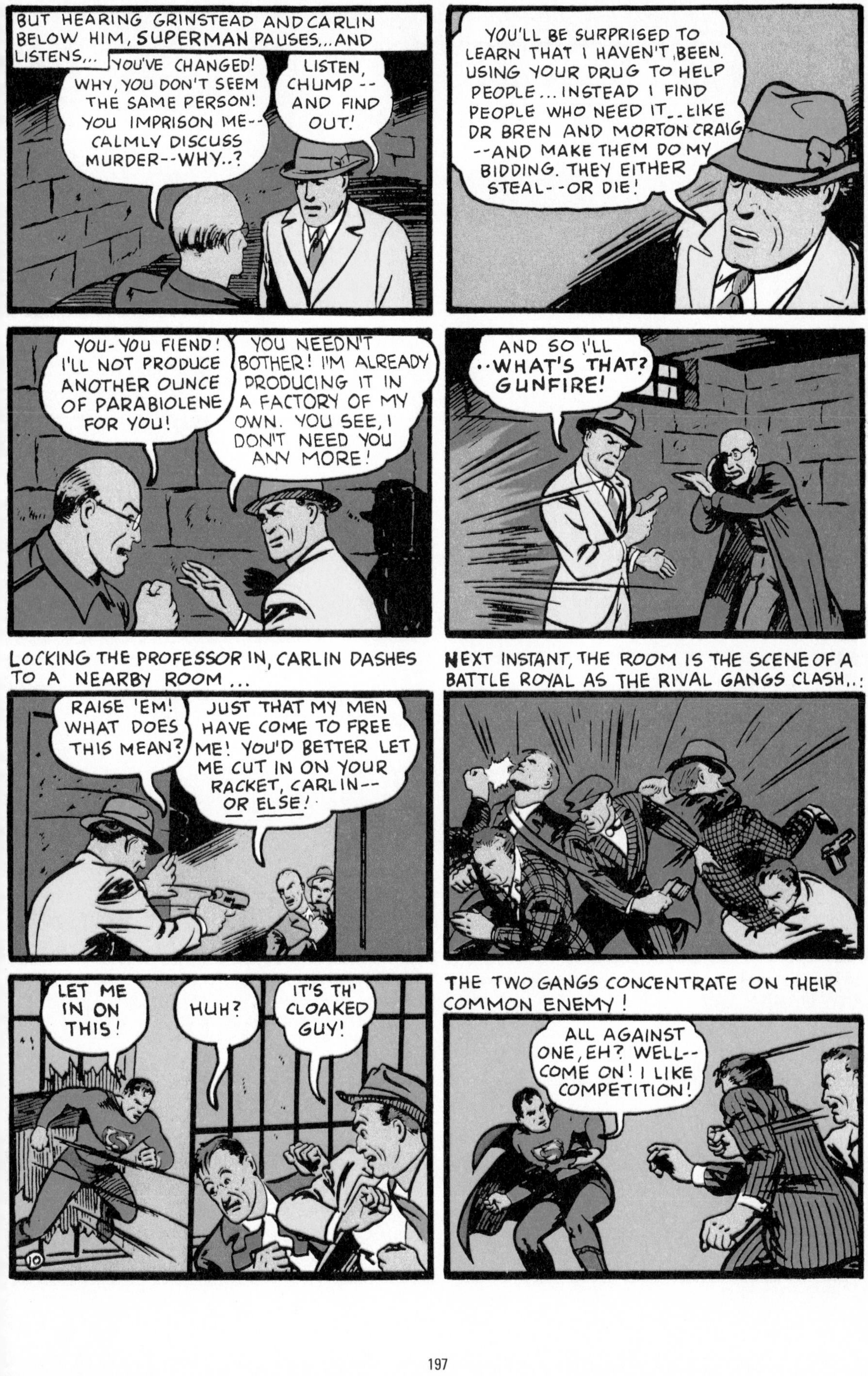
BUT HEARING GRINSTEAD AND CARLIN BELOW HIM, SUPERMAN PAUSES,.. AND LISTENS,..
YOU'VE CHANGED! WHY, YOU DON'T SEEM THE SAME PERSON! YOU IMPRISON ME-- CALMLY DISCUSS MURDER--WHY..?
LISTEN, CHUMP -- AND FIND OUT!
YOU'LL BE SURPRISED TO LEARN THAT I HAVEN'T BEEN USING YOUR DRUG TO HELP PEOPLE... INSTEAD I FIND PEOPLE WHO NEED IT.. LIKE DR BREN AND MORTON CRAIG --AND MAKE THEM DO MY BIDDING. THEY EITHER STEAL--OR DIE!
YOU-YOU FIEND! I'LL NOT PRODUCE ANOTHER OUNCE OF PARABIOLENE FOR YOU!
YOU NEEDN'T BOTHER! I'M ALREADY PRODUCING IT IN A FACTORY OF MY OWN. YOU SEE, I DON'T NEED YOU ANY MORE!
AND SO I'LL ..WHAT'S THAT? GUNFIRE!
LOCKING THE PROFESSOR IN, CARLIN DASHES TO A NEARBY ROOM...
RAISE 'EM! WHAT DOES THIS MEAN?
JUST THAT MY MEN HAVE COME TO FREE ME! YOU'D BETTER LET ME CUT IN ON YOUR RACKET, CARLIN-- OR ELSE!
NEXT INSTANT, THE ROOM IS THE SCENE OF A BATTLE ROYAL AS THE RIVAL GANGS CLASH,..
LET ME IN ON THIS!
HUH?
IT'S TH' CLOAKED GUY!
10
THE TWO GANGS CONCENTRATE ON THEIR COMMON ENEMY!
ALL AGAINST ONE, EH? WELL-- COME ON! I LIKE COMPETITION!

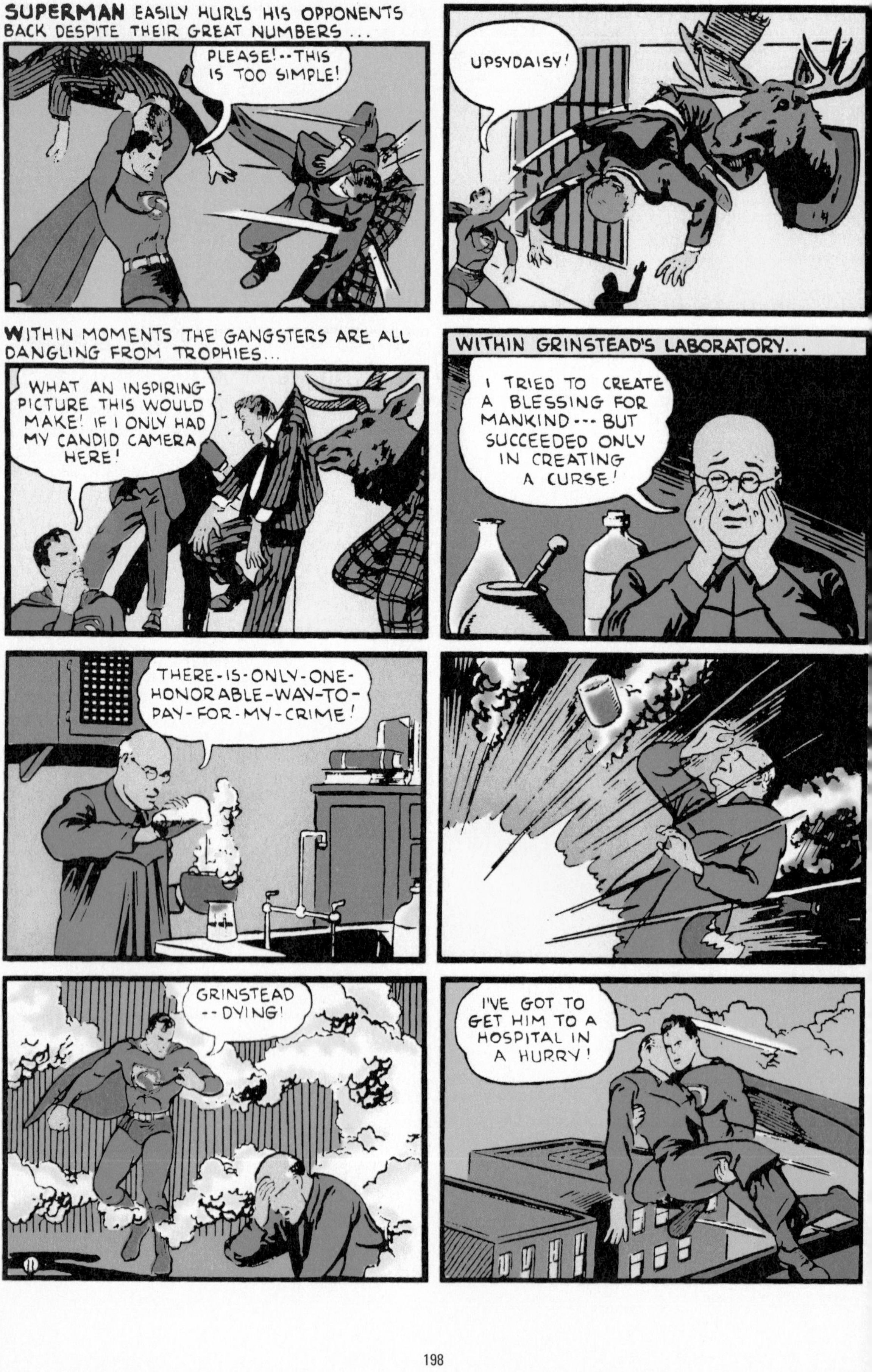
SUPERMAN EASILY HURLS HIS OPPONENTS BACK DESPITE THEIR GREAT NUMBERS . . .
PLEASE! --THIS IS TOO SIMPLE!
UPSYDAISY!
WITHIN MOMENTS THE GANGSTERS ARE ALL DANGLING FROM TROPHIES . . .
WHAT AN INSPIRING PICTURE THIS WOULD MAKE! IF I ONLY HAD MY CANDID CAMERA HERE!
WITHIN GRINSTEAD'S LABORATORY . . .
I TRIED TO CREATE A BLESSING FOR MANKIND --- BUT SUCCEEDED ONLY IN CREATING A CURSE!
THERE-IS-ONLY-ONE-HONORABLE-WAY-TO-PAY-FOR-MY-CRIME!
GRINSTEAD --DYING!
I'VE GOT TO GET HIM TO A HOSPITAL IN A HURRY!

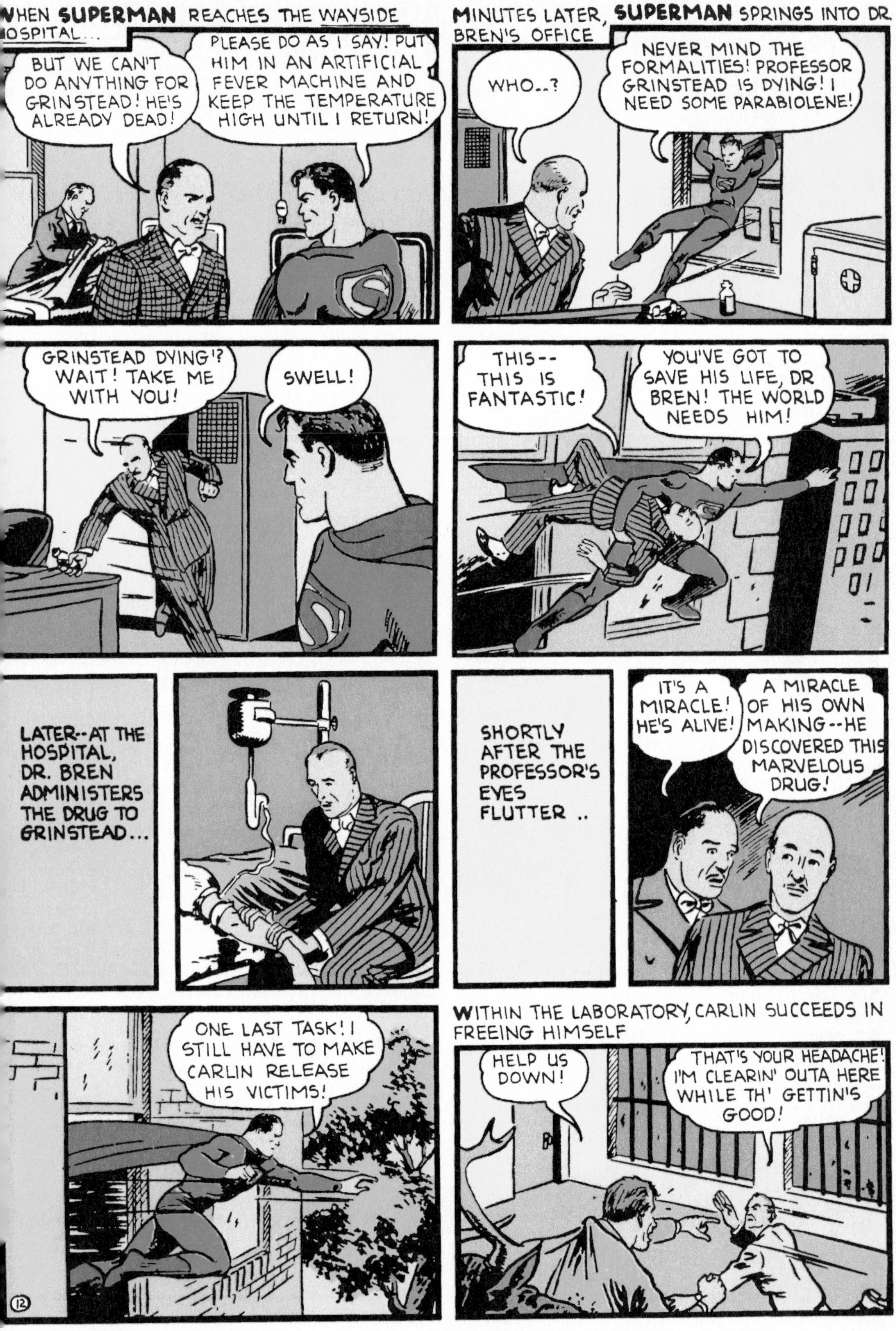
WHEN SUPERMAN REACHES THE WAYSIDE HOSPITAL...
BUT WE CAN'T DO ANYTHING FOR GRINSTEAD! HE'S ALREADY DEAD!
PLEASE DO AS I SAY! PUT HIM IN AN ARTIFICIAL FEVER MACHINE AND KEEP THE TEMPERATURE HIGH UNTIL I RETURN!
MINUTES LATER, SUPERMAN SPRINGS INTO DR. BREN'S OFFICE
WHO..?
NEVER MIND THE FORMALITIES! PROFESSOR GRINSTEAD IS DYING! I NEED SOME PARABIOLENE!
GRINSTEAD DYING'? WAIT! TAKE ME WITH YOU!
SWELL!
THIS-- THIS IS FANTASTIC!
YOU'VE GOT TO SAVE HIS LIFE, DR BREN! THE WORLD NEEDS HIM!
LATER--AT THE HOSPITAL, DR. BREN ADMINISTERS THE DRUG TO GRINSTEAD...
SHORTLY AFTER THE PROFESSOR'S EYES FLUTTER ..
IT'S A MIRACLE! HE'S ALIVE!
A MIRACLE OF HIS OWN MAKING--HE DISCOVERED THIS MARVELOUS DRUG!
ONE LAST TASK! I STILL HAVE TO MAKE CARLIN RELEASE HIS VICTIMS!
12
WITHIN THE LABORATORY, CARLIN SUCCEEDS IN FREEING HIMSELF
HELP US DOWN!
THAT'S YOUR HEADACHE! I'M CLEARIN' OUTA HERE WHILE TH' GETTIN'S GOOD!

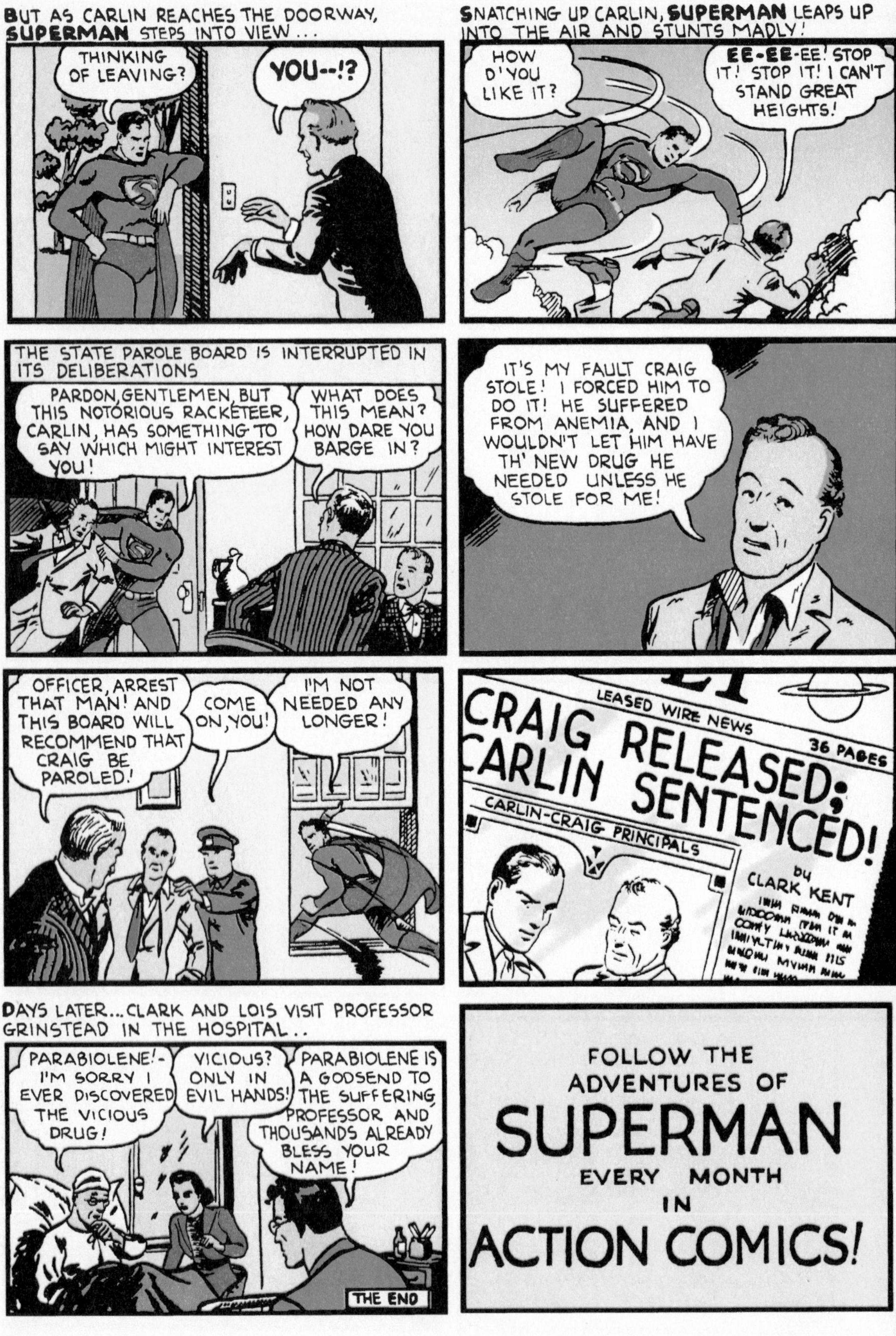
BUT AS CARLIN REACHES THE DOORWAY, SUPERMAN STEPS INTO VIEW...
THINKING OF LEAVING?
YOU--!?
SNATCHING UP CARLIN, SUPERMAN LEAPS UP INTO THE AIR AND STUNTS MADLY!
HOW D'YOU LIKE IT?
EE-EE-EE! STOP IT! STOP IT! I CAN'T STAND GREAT HEIGHTS!
THE STATE PAROLE BOARD IS INTERRUPTED IN ITS DELIBERATIONS
PARDON, GENTLEMEN, BUT THIS NOTORIOUS RACKETEER, CARLIN, HAS SOMETHING TO SAY WHICH MIGHT INTEREST YOU!
WHAT DOES THIS MEAN? HOW DARE YOU BARGE IN?
IT'S MY FAULT CRAIG STOLE! I FORCED HIM TO DO IT! HE SUFFERED FROM ANEMIA, AND I WOULDN'T LET HIM HAVE TH' NEW DRUG HE NEEDED UNLESS HE STOLE FOR ME!
OFFICER, ARREST THAT MAN! AND THIS BOARD WILL RECOMMEND THAT CRAIG BE PAROLED!
COME ON, YOU!
I'M NOT NEEDED ANY LONGER!
LEASED WIRE NEWS
36 PAGES
CRAIG RELEASED; CARLIN SENTENCED!
CARLIN-CRAIG PRINCIPALS
by CLARK KENT
DAYS LATER... CLARK AND LOIS VISIT PROFESSOR GRINSTEAD IN THE HOSPITAL..
PARABIOLENE! - I'M SORRY I EVER DISCOVERED THE VICIOUS DRUG!
VICIOUS? ONLY IN EVIL HANDS!
PARABIOLENE IS A GODSEND TO THE SUFFERING, PROFESSOR AND THOUSANDS ALREADY BLESS YOUR NAME!
THE END
FOLLOW THE ADVENTURES OF SUPERMAN EVERY MONTH IN ACTION COMICS!

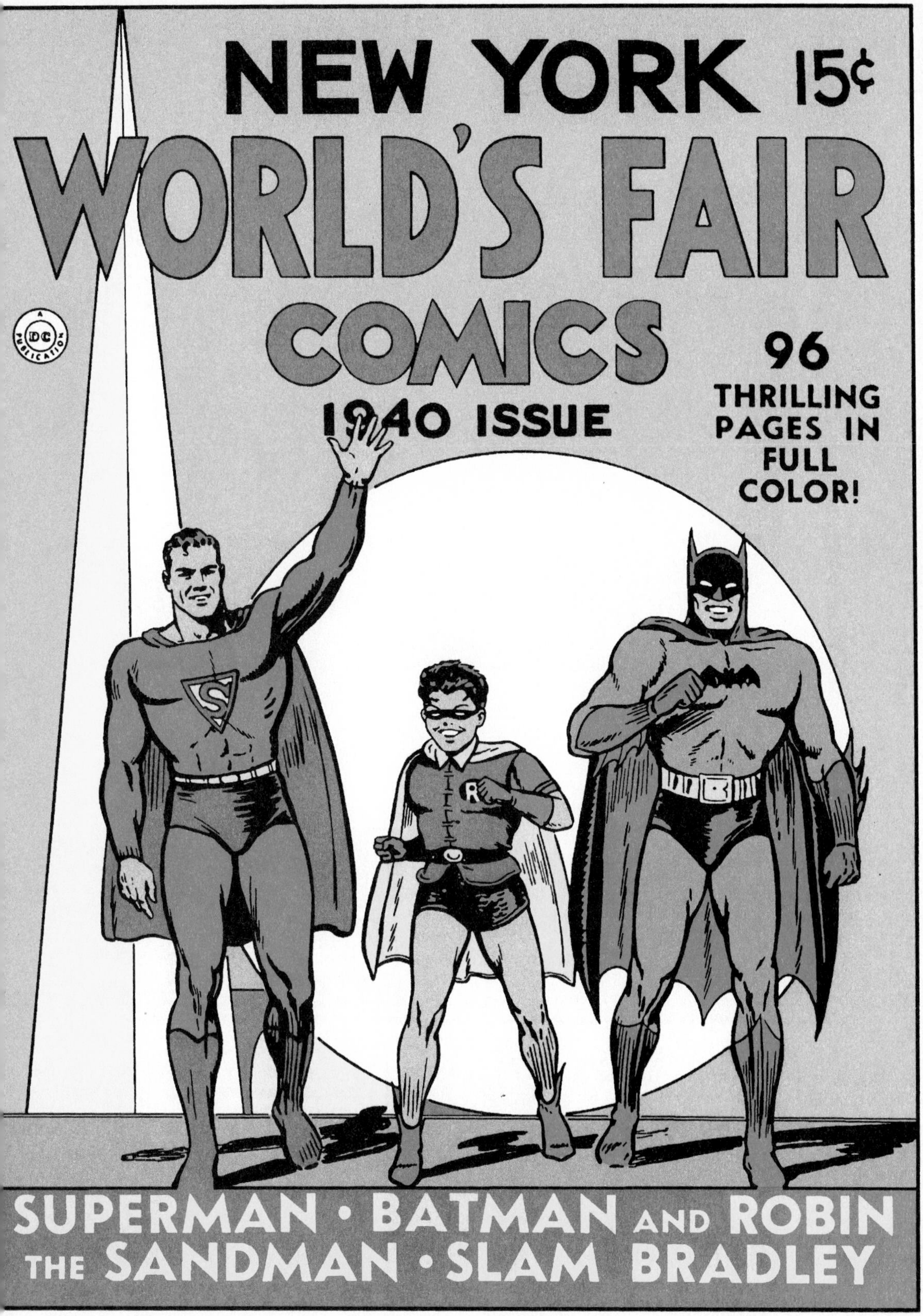
NEW YORK
15¢
WORLD'S FAIR
COMICS
A DC PUBLICATION
1940 ISSUE
96
THRILLING
PAGES IN
FULL
COLOR!
SUPERMAN • BATMAN AND ROBIN
THE SANDMAN • SLAM BRADLEY

SUPERMAN

by Jerry Siegel and Joe Shuster

SUPERMAN, DYNAMIC FOE OF CRIME AND INJUSTICE, USES HIS AMAZING SPEED AND STRENGTH TO DEFEAT THE SINISTER PLANS OF A MASTER JEWEL THIEF AND HIS GANG IN A THRILLING ADVENTURE THAT BEGINS UNEXPECTEDLY WHEN CLARK KENT AND LOIS LANE PAY A VISIT TO THE NEW YORK **WORLD'S FAIR!**

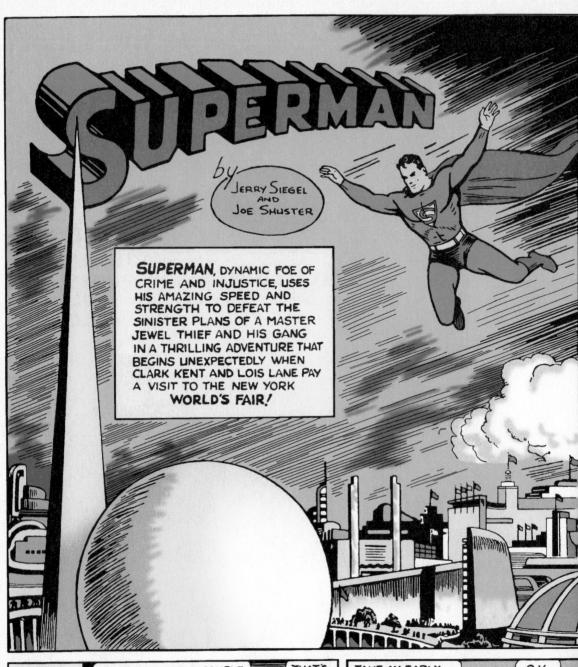

CLARK KENT, MEEK *DAILY PLANET* REPORTER IS CALLED INTO EDITOR TAYLOR'S OFFICE!

CLARK, I WANT A COUPLE OF FEATURE STORIES ON THE N.Y. WORLD'S FAIR, AND I'M GIVING THE ASSIGNMENTS TO YOU AND LOIS LANE!

THAT'S SWELL!

TAKE AN EARLY PLANE FOR N.Y. TOMORROW MORNING- YOU'LL GET THERE IN TIME TO SPEND THE AFTERNOON AND EVENING AT THE FAIR!

O.K., CHIEF!

CLARK, DELIGHTED AT THE PROSPECT OF GOING TO THE FAIR WITH LOIS, RUSHES OUT TO TELL HER THE NEWS!

ISN'T THAT GREAT, LOIS? WE'LL COVER THIS ASSIGNMENT TOGETHER! TAYLOR WANTS YOU TO GIVE THE FEMININE SLANT ON THE FAIR!

I DON'T SEE WHY TAYLOR HAD TO SEND CLARK ALONG—I COULD HANDLE THE STORY WITHOUT HIS HELP! ANYWAY, THIS WILL GIVE ME A CHANCE TO SHOW HIM UP!

NEXT MORNING, A PLANE LEAVES METROPOLIS BOUND FOR NEW YORK WITH CLARK AND LOIS ABOARD!

THIS SEEMS MORE LIKE A HOLIDAY TRIP THAN AN ACTUAL WORKING ASSIGNMENT, LOIS!

HERE WE ARE AT LA GUARDIA FIELD!

A CAB WILL GET US TO THE FAIR IN A JIFFY!

A FEW MINUTES LATER, THEY ARRIVE AT THE FAIR!

ISN'T IT MARVELOUS?

THE FAIR IS BETTER THAN EVER, THIS YEAR!

CLARK AND LOIS ENJOY EVERY MINUTE OF THEIR VISIT, AS THEY GO THROUGH MANY OF THE FAIR'S COLORFUL BUILDINGS··

THERE CERTAINLY ARE A LOT OF FASCINATING SIGHTS AND EXHIBITS FOR US TO WRITE ABOUT

YES-- AND I READ THAT ONE OF THE WORLD'S LARGEST PRECIOUS JEWELS, THE FAMOUS MADRAS EMERALD, HAS JUST ARRIVED FROM INDIA AND WILL BE PRESENTED FOR EXHIBITION HERE AT THE HOUSE OF JEWELS, TONIGHT AT 8 O'CLOCK!

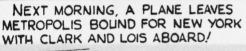

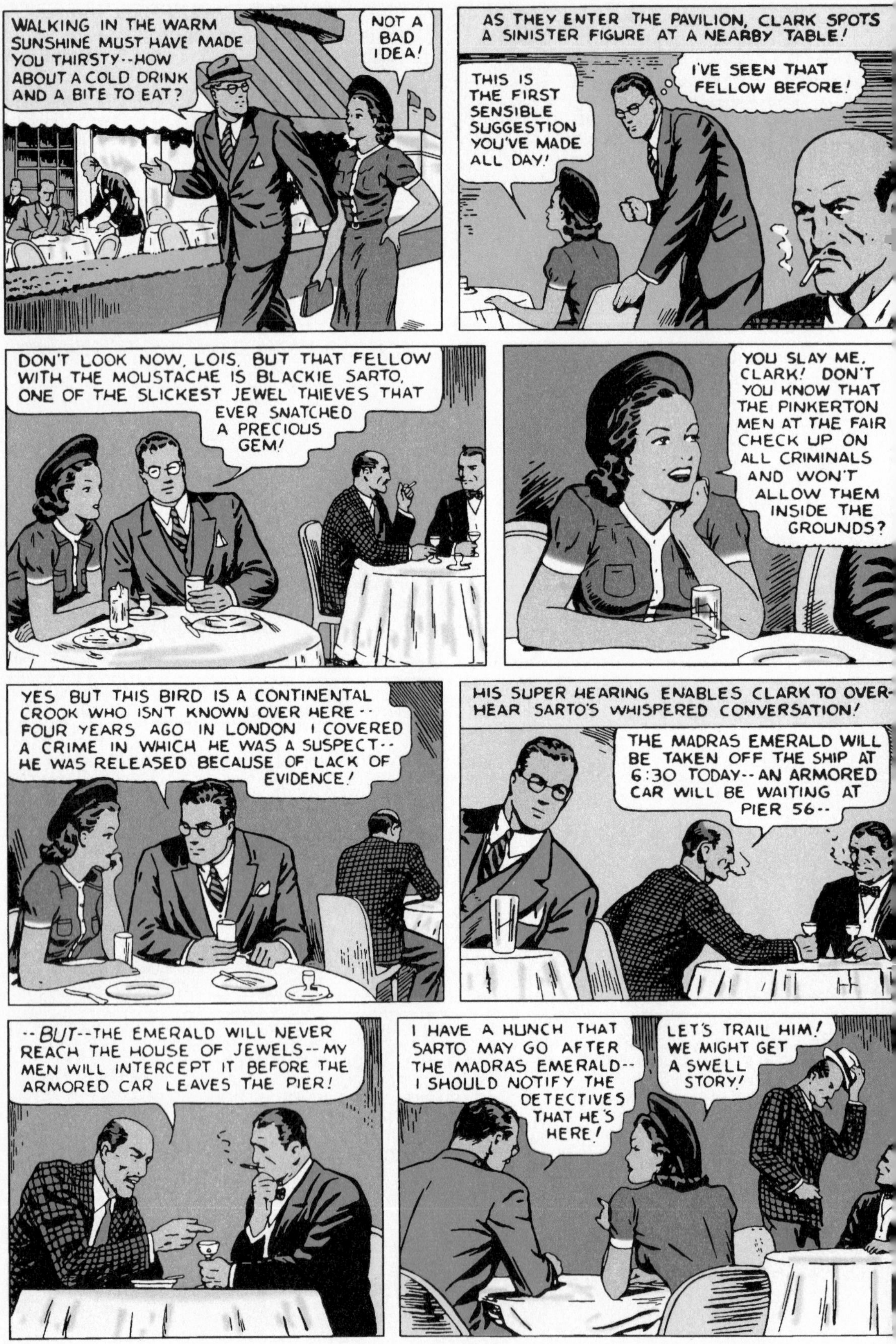
WALKING IN THE WARM SUNSHINE MUST HAVE MADE YOU THIRSTY--HOW ABOUT A COLD DRINK AND A BITE TO EAT?
NOT A BAD IDEA!
AS THEY ENTER THE PAVILION, CLARK SPOTS A SINISTER FIGURE AT A NEARBY TABLE!
THIS IS THE FIRST SENSIBLE SUGGESTION YOU'VE MADE ALL DAY!
I'VE SEEN THAT FELLOW BEFORE!
DON'T LOOK NOW, LOIS, BUT THAT FELLOW WITH THE MOUSTACHE IS BLACKIE SARTO, ONE OF THE SLICKEST JEWEL THIEVES THAT EVER SNATCHED A PRECIOUS GEM!
YOU SLAY ME, CLARK! DON'T YOU KNOW THAT THE PINKERTON MEN AT THE FAIR CHECK UP ON ALL CRIMINALS AND WON'T ALLOW THEM INSIDE THE GROUNDS?
YES BUT THIS BIRD IS A CONTINENTAL CROOK WHO ISN'T KNOWN OVER HERE-- FOUR YEARS AGO IN LONDON I COVERED A CRIME IN WHICH HE WAS A SUSPECT-- HE WAS RELEASED BECAUSE OF LACK OF EVIDENCE!
HIS SUPER HEARING ENABLES CLARK TO OVER-HEAR SARTO'S WHISPERED CONVERSATION!
THE MADRAS EMERALD WILL BE TAKEN OFF THE SHIP AT 6:30 TODAY--AN ARMORED CAR WILL BE WAITING AT PIER 56--
--BUT--THE EMERALD WILL NEVER REACH THE HOUSE OF JEWELS--MY MEN WILL INTERCEPT IT BEFORE THE ARMORED CAR LEAVES THE PIER!
I HAVE A HUNCH THAT SARTO MAY GO AFTER THE MADRAS EMERALD-- I SHOULD NOTIFY THE DETECTIVES THAT HE'S HERE!
LET'S TRAIL HIM! WE MIGHT GET A SWELL STORY!

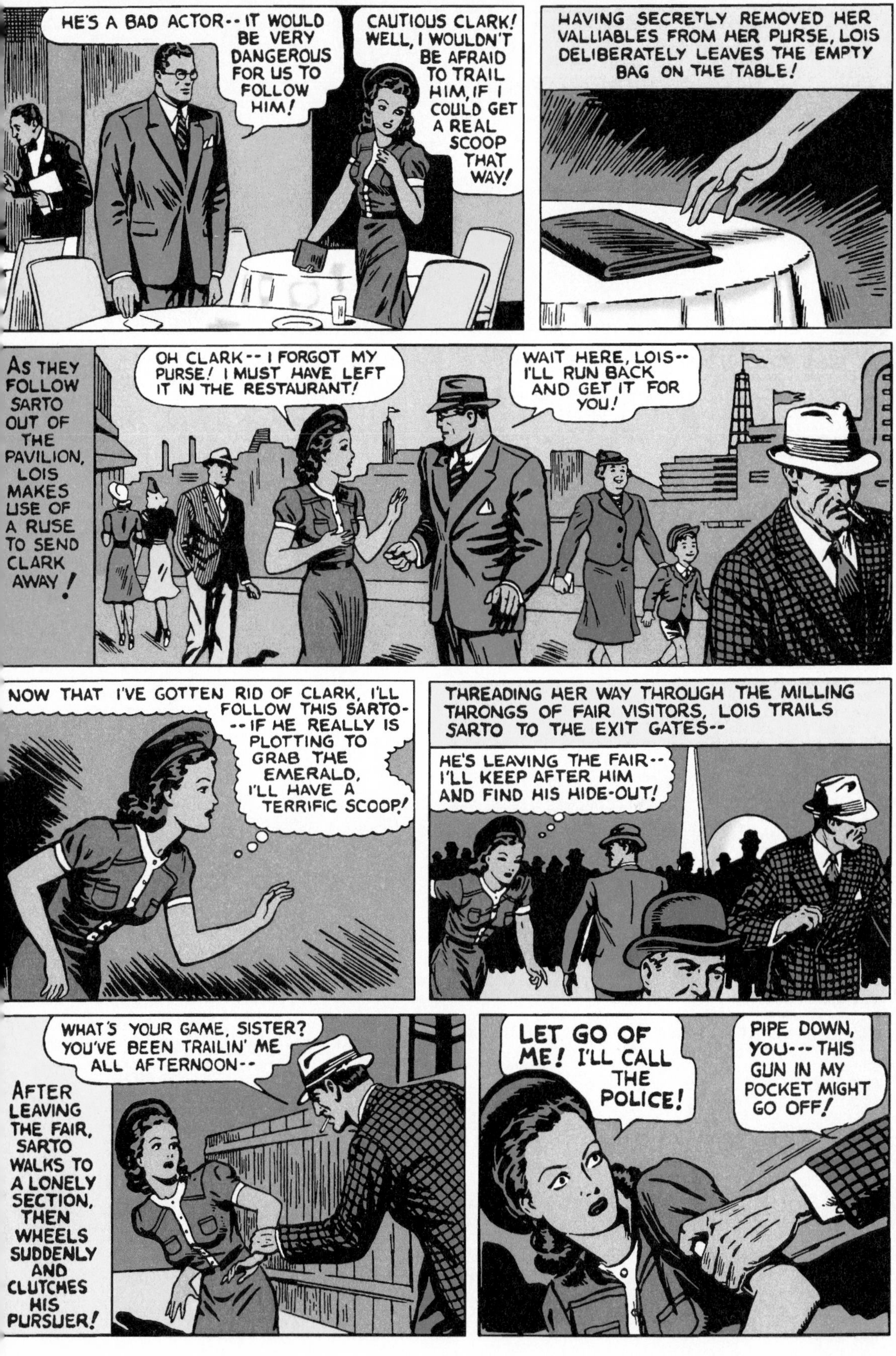
HE'S A BAD ACTOR-- IT WOULD BE VERY DANGEROUS FOR US TO FOLLOW HIM!
CAUTIOUS CLARK! WELL, I WOULDN'T BE AFRAID TO TRAIL HIM, IF I COULD GET A REAL SCOOP THAT WAY!
HAVING SECRETLY REMOVED HER VALLIABLES FROM HER PURSE, LOIS DELIBERATELY LEAVES THE EMPTY BAG ON THE TABLE!
AS THEY FOLLOW SARTO OUT OF THE PAVILION, LOIS MAKES USE OF A RUSE TO SEND CLARK AWAY!
OH CLARK-- I FORGOT MY PURSE! I MUST HAVE LEFT IT IN THE RESTAURANT!
WAIT HERE, LOIS-- I'LL RUN BACK AND GET IT FOR YOU!
NOW THAT I'VE GOTTEN RID OF CLARK, I'LL FOLLOW THIS SARTO--IF HE REALLY IS PLOTTING TO GRAB THE EMERALD, I'LL HAVE A TERRIFIC SCOOP!
THREADING HER WAY THROUGH THE MILLING THRONGS OF FAIR VISITORS, LOIS TRAILS SARTO TO THE EXIT GATES--
HE'S LEAVING THE FAIR-- I'LL KEEP AFTER HIM AND FIND HIS HIDE-OUT!
AFTER LEAVING THE FAIR, SARTO WALKS TO A LONELY SECTION, THEN WHEELS SUDDENLY AND CLUTCHES HIS PURSUER!
WHAT'S YOUR GAME, SISTER? YOU'VE BEEN TRAILIN' ME ALL AFTERNOON--
LET GO OF ME! I'LL CALL THE POLICE!
PIPE DOWN, YOU--- THIS GUN IN MY POCKET MIGHT GO OFF!

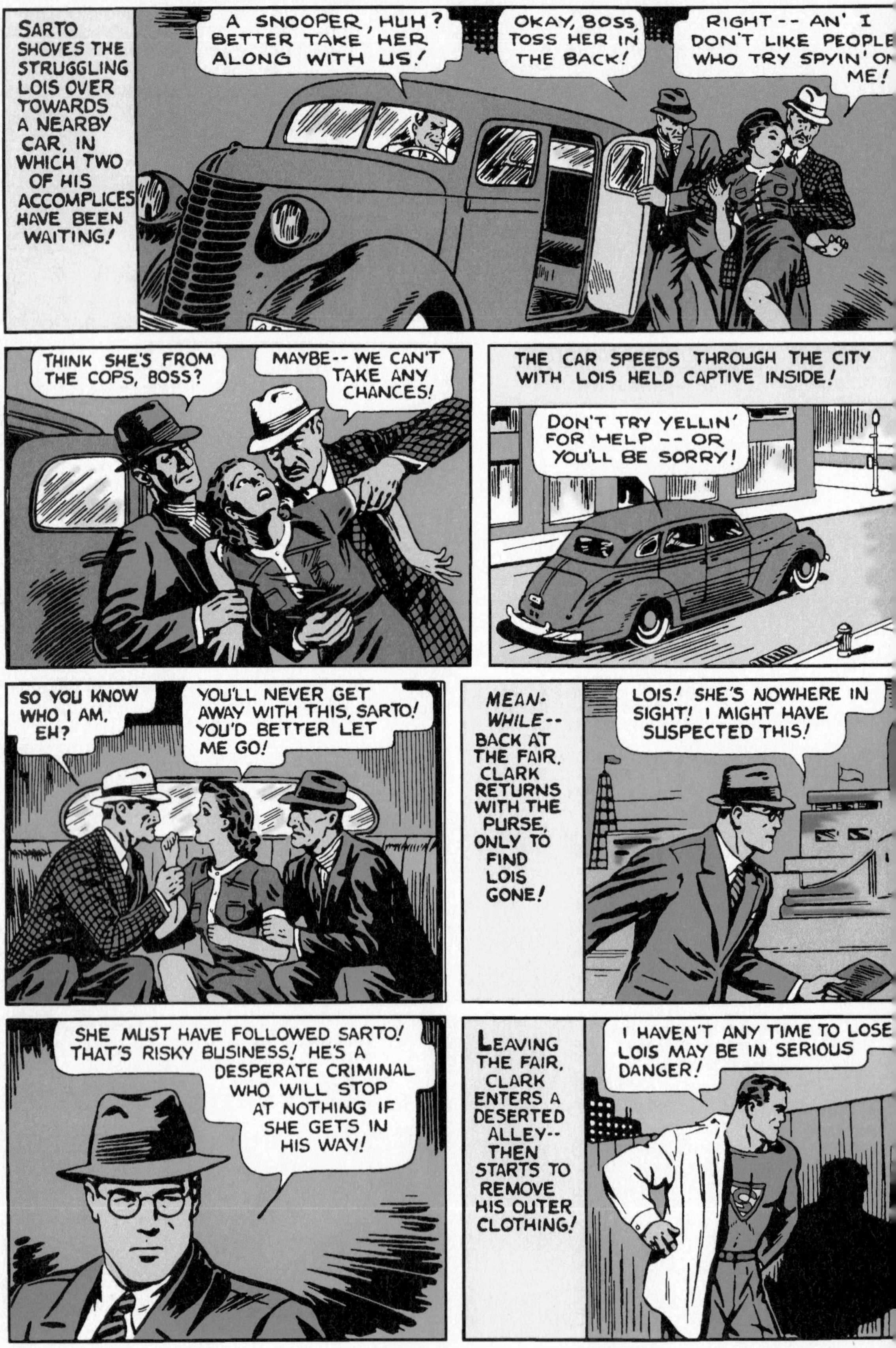
SARTO SHOVES THE STRUGGLING LOIS OVER TOWARDS A NEARBY CAR, IN WHICH TWO OF HIS ACCOMPLICES HAVE BEEN WAITING!
A SNOOPER, HUH? BETTER TAKE HER ALONG WITH US!
OKAY, BOSS, TOSS HER IN THE BACK!
RIGHT -- AN' I DON'T LIKE PEOPLE WHO TRY SPYIN' ON ME!
THINK SHE'S FROM THE COPS, BOSS?
MAYBE -- WE CAN'T TAKE ANY CHANCES!
THE CAR SPEEDS THROUGH THE CITY WITH LOIS HELD CAPTIVE INSIDE!
DON'T TRY YELLIN' FOR HELP -- OR YOU'LL BE SORRY!
SO YOU KNOW WHO I AM, EH?
YOU'LL NEVER GET AWAY WITH THIS, SARTO! YOU'D BETTER LET ME GO!
MEAN-WHILE -- BACK AT THE FAIR, CLARK RETURNS WITH THE PURSE, ONLY TO FIND LOIS GONE!
LOIS! SHE'S NOWHERE IN SIGHT! I MIGHT HAVE SUSPECTED THIS!
SHE MUST HAVE FOLLOWED SARTO! THAT'S RISKY BUSINESS! HE'S A DESPERATE CRIMINAL WHO WILL STOP AT NOTHING IF SHE GETS IN HIS WAY!
LEAVING THE FAIR, CLARK ENTERS A DESERTED ALLEY -- THEN STARTS TO REMOVE HIS OUTER CLOTHING!
I HAVEN'T ANY TIME TO LOSE -- LOIS MAY BE IN SERIOUS DANGER!

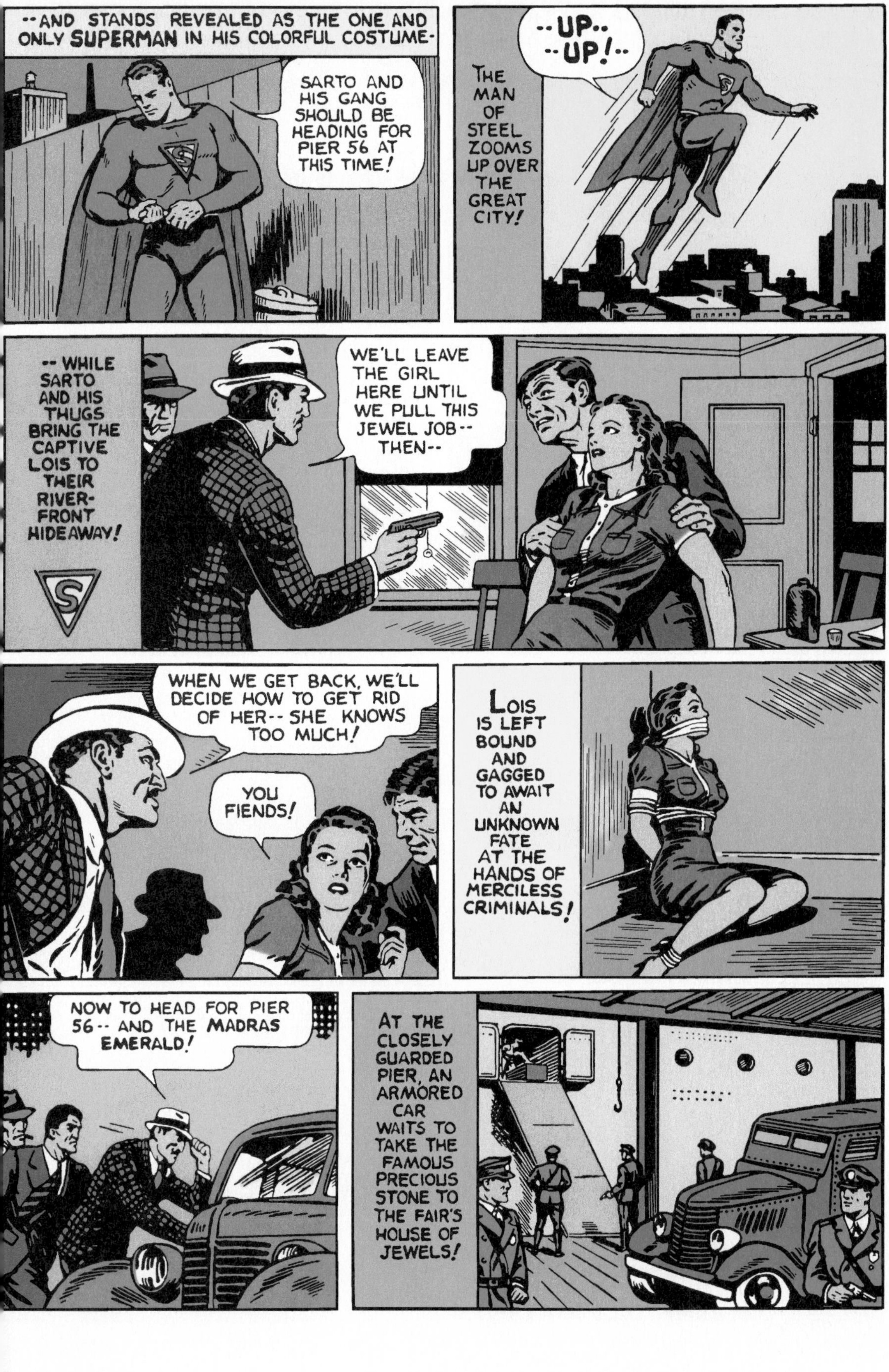

--AND STANDS REVEALED AS THE ONE AND ONLY SUPERMAN IN HIS COLORFUL COSTUME-
SARTO AND HIS GANG SHOULD BE HEADING FOR PIER 56 AT THIS TIME!
--UP-- --UP!--
THE MAN OF STEEL ZOOMS UP OVER THE GREAT CITY!
-- WHILE SARTO AND HIS THUGS BRING THE CAPTIVE LOIS TO THEIR RIVER-FRONT HIDEAWAY!
WE'LL LEAVE THE GIRL HERE UNTIL WE PULL THIS JEWEL JOB -- THEN--
WHEN WE GET BACK, WE'LL DECIDE HOW TO GET RID OF HER-- SHE KNOWS TOO MUCH!
YOU FIENDS!
LOIS IS LEFT BOUND AND GAGGED TO AWAIT AN UNKNOWN FATE AT THE HANDS OF MERCILESS CRIMINALS!
NOW TO HEAD FOR PIER 56-- AND THE MADRAS EMERALD!
AT THE CLOSELY GUARDED PIER, AN ARMORED CAR WAITS TO TAKE THE FAMOUS PRECIOUS STONE TO THE FAIR'S HOUSE OF JEWELS!

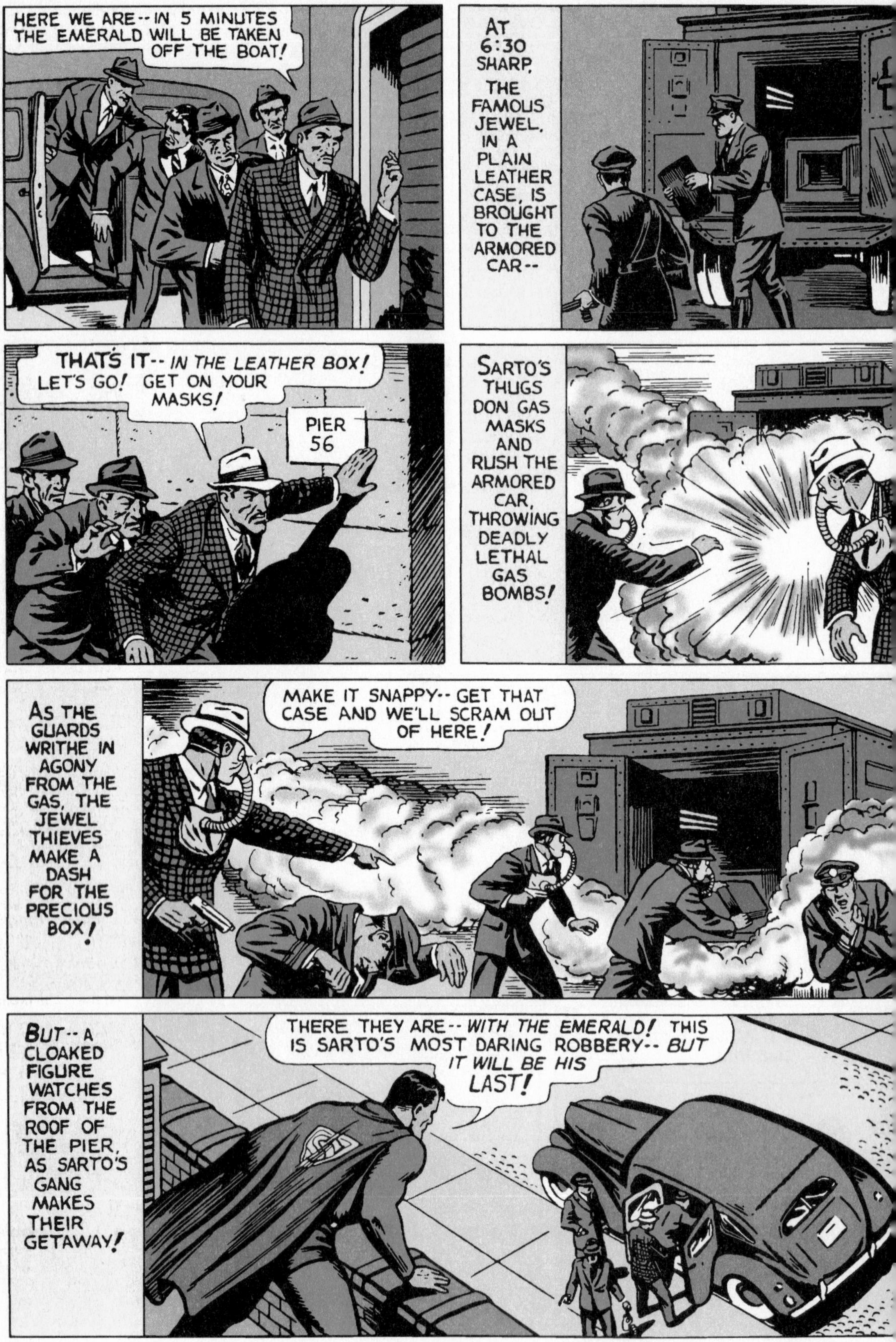

HERE WE ARE--IN 5 MINUTES THE EMERALD WILL BE TAKEN OFF THE BOAT!
AT 6:30 SHARP, THE FAMOUS JEWEL, IN A PLAIN LEATHER CASE, IS BROUGHT TO THE ARMORED CAR--
THAT'S IT--IN THE LEATHER BOX! LET'S GO! GET ON YOUR MASKS!
PIER 56
SARTO'S THUGS DON GAS MASKS AND RUSH THE ARMORED CAR, THROWING DEADLY LETHAL GAS BOMBS!
AS THE GUARDS WRITHE IN AGONY FROM THE GAS, THE JEWEL THIEVES MAKE A DASH FOR THE PRECIOUS BOX!
MAKE IT SNAPPY--GET THAT CASE AND WE'LL SCRAM OUT OF HERE!
BUT--A CLOAKED FIGURE WATCHES FROM THE ROOF OF THE PIER, AS SARTO'S GANG MAKES THEIR GETAWAY!
THERE THEY ARE--WITH THE EMERALD! THIS IS SARTO'S MOST DARING ROBBERY--BUT IT WILL BE HIS LAST!

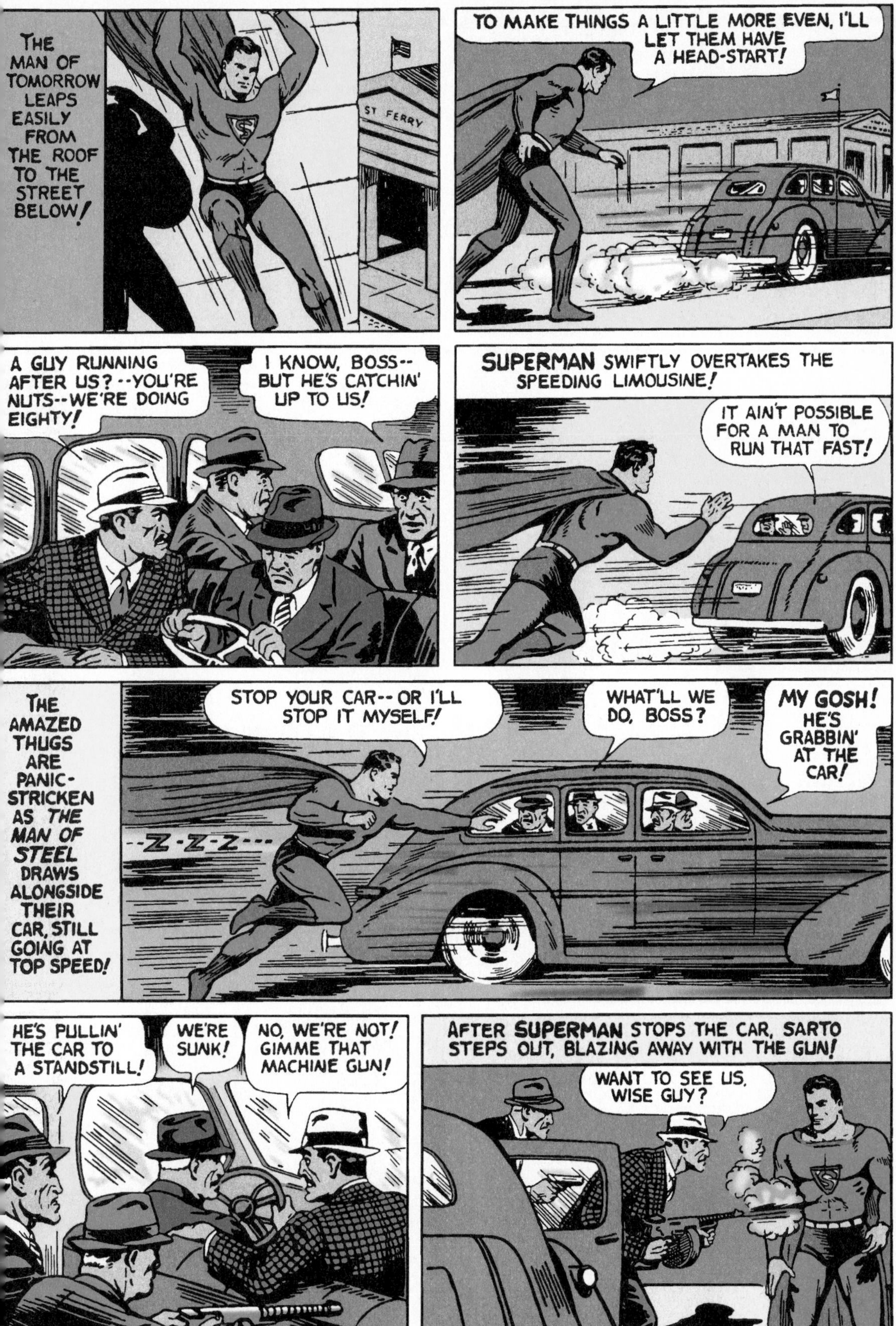

THE MAN OF TOMORROW LEAPS EASILY FROM THE ROOF TO THE STREET BELOW!
ST FERRY
TO MAKE THINGS A LITTLE MORE EVEN, I'LL LET THEM HAVE A HEAD-START!
A GUY RUNNING AFTER US? --YOU'RE NUTS--WE'RE DOING EIGHTY!
I KNOW, BOSS--BUT HE'S CATCHIN' UP TO US!
SUPERMAN SWIFTLY OVERTAKES THE SPEEDING LIMOUSINE!
IT AIN'T POSSIBLE FOR A MAN TO RUN THAT FAST!
THE AMAZED THUGS ARE PANIC-STRICKEN AS THE MAN OF STEEL DRAWS ALONGSIDE THEIR CAR, STILL GOING AT TOP SPEED!
STOP YOUR CAR--OR I'LL STOP IT MYSELF!
WHAT'LL WE DO, BOSS?
MY GOSH! HE'S GRABBIN' AT THE CAR!
--Z-Z-Z---
HE'S PULLIN' THE CAR TO A STANDSTILL!
WE'RE SUNK!
NO, WE'RE NOT! GIMME THAT MACHINE GUN!
AFTER SUPERMAN STOPS THE CAR, SARTO STEPS OUT, BLAZING AWAY WITH THE GUN!
WANT TO SEE US, WISE GUY?

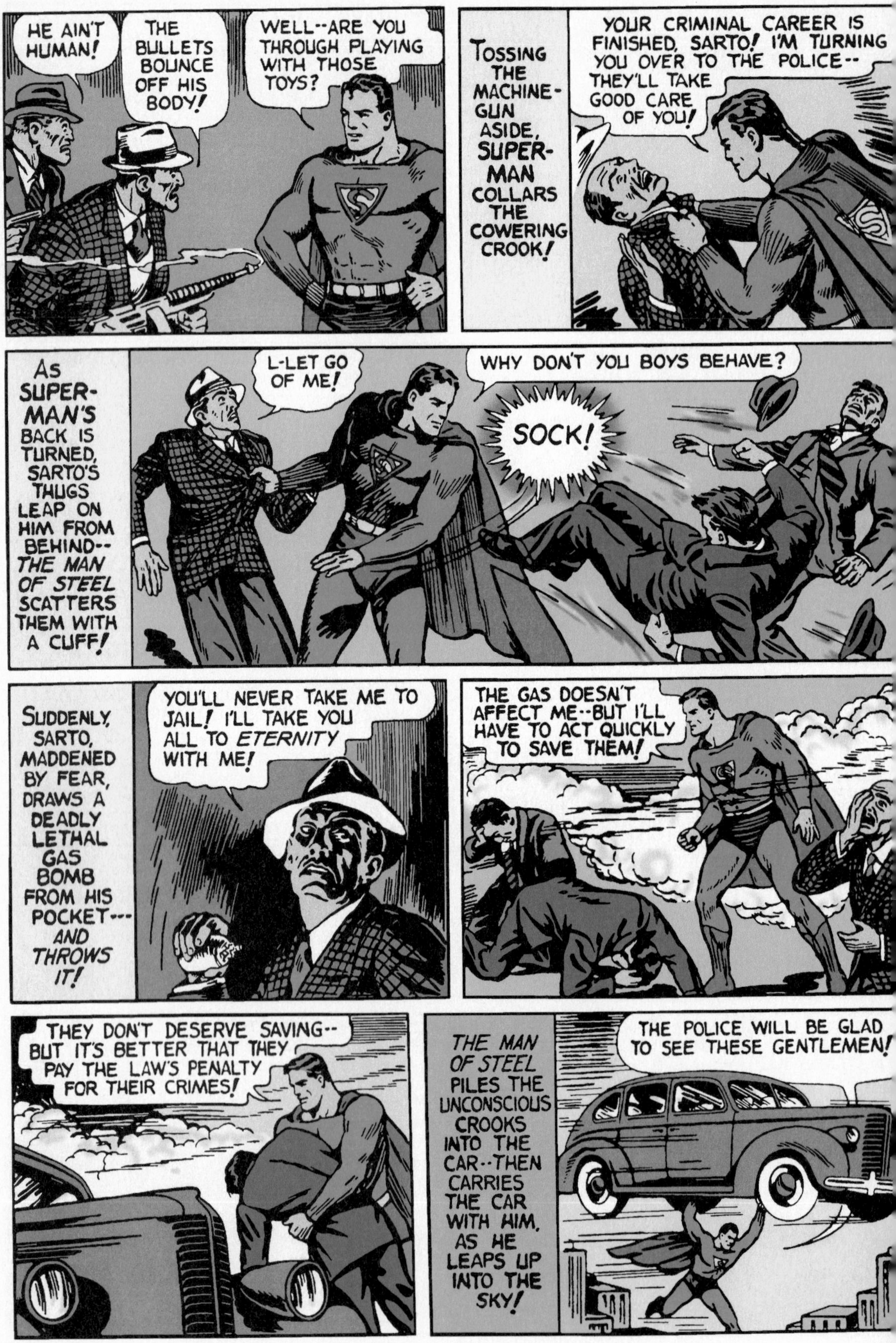
HE AIN'T HUMAN!
THE BULLETS BOUNCE OFF HIS BODY!
WELL--ARE YOU THROUGH PLAYING WITH THOSE TOYS?
TOSSING THE MACHINE-GUN ASIDE, SUPERMAN COLLARS THE COWERING CROOK!
YOUR CRIMINAL CAREER IS FINISHED, SARTO! I'M TURNING YOU OVER TO THE POLICE--THEY'LL TAKE GOOD CARE OF YOU!
AS SUPERMAN'S BACK IS TURNED, SARTO'S THUGS LEAP ON HIM FROM BEHIND--THE MAN OF STEEL SCATTERS THEM WITH A CUFF!
L-LET GO OF ME!
WHY DON'T YOU BOYS BEHAVE?
SOCK!
SUDDENLY, SARTO, MADDENED BY FEAR, DRAWS A DEADLY LETHAL GAS BOMB FROM HIS POCKET---AND THROWS IT!
YOU'LL NEVER TAKE ME TO JAIL! I'LL TAKE YOU ALL TO ETERNITY WITH ME!
THE GAS DOESN'T AFFECT ME--BUT I'LL HAVE TO ACT QUICKLY TO SAVE THEM!
THEY DON'T DESERVE SAVING--BUT IT'S BETTER THAT THEY PAY THE LAW'S PENALTY FOR THEIR CRIMES!
THE MAN OF STEEL PILES THE UNCONSCIOUS CROOKS INTO THE CAR--THEN CARRIES THE CAR WITH HIM, AS HE LEAPS UP INTO THE SKY!
THE POLICE WILL BE GLAD TO SEE THESE GENTLEMEN!

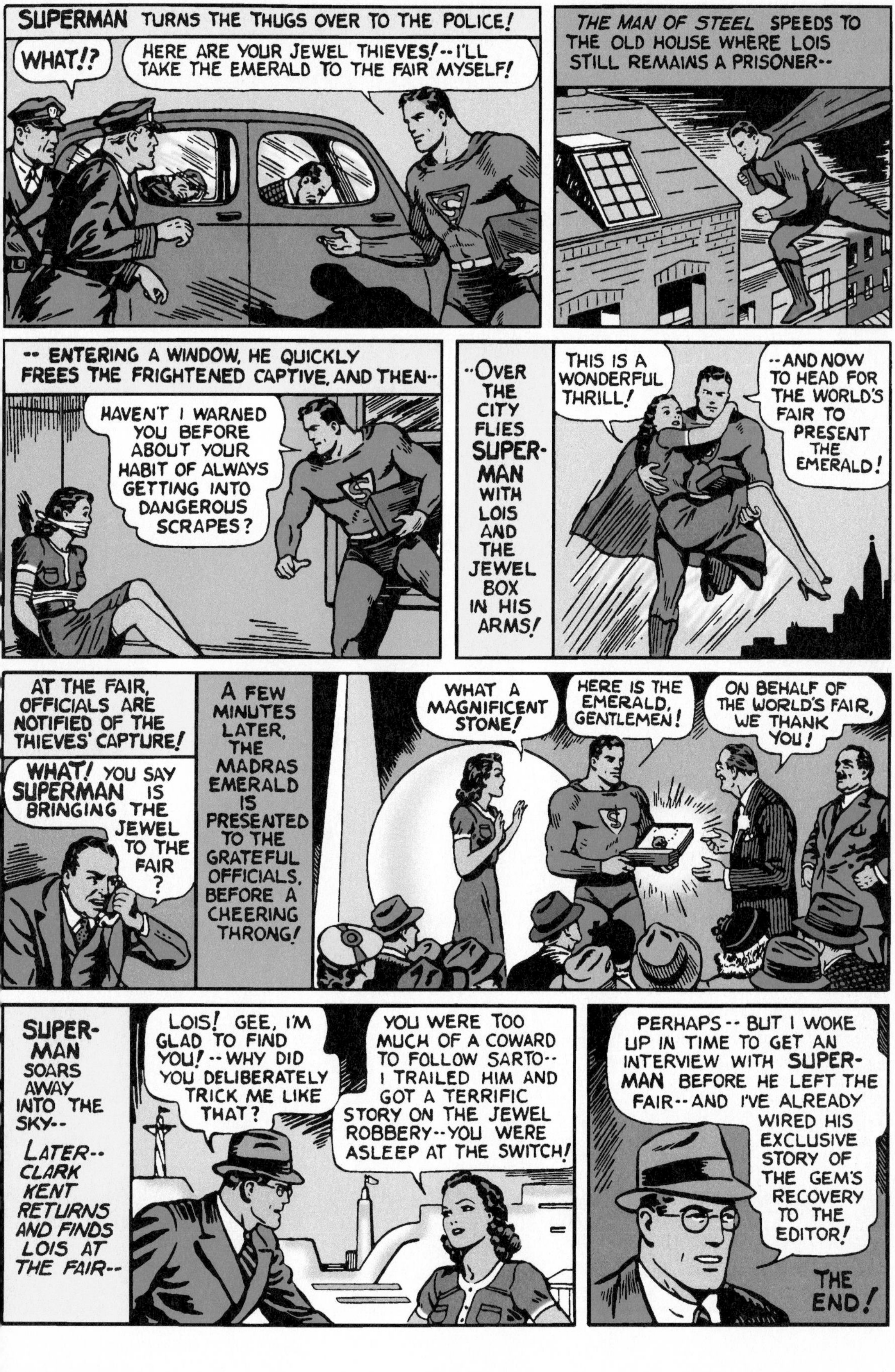
SUPERMAN TURNS THE THUGS OVER TO THE POLICE!
WHAT!?
HERE ARE YOUR JEWEL THIEVES! --I'LL TAKE THE EMERALD TO THE FAIR MYSELF!
THE MAN OF STEEL SPEEDS TO THE OLD HOUSE WHERE LOIS STILL REMAINS A PRISONER--
-- ENTERING A WINDOW, HE QUICKLY FREES THE FRIGHTENED CAPTIVE, AND THEN--
HAVEN'T I WARNED YOU BEFORE ABOUT YOUR HABIT OF ALWAYS GETTING INTO DANGEROUS SCRAPES?
..OVER THE CITY FLIES SUPERMAN WITH LOIS AND THE JEWEL BOX IN HIS ARMS!
THIS IS A WONDERFUL THRILL!
--AND NOW TO HEAD FOR THE WORLD'S FAIR TO PRESENT THE EMERALD!
AT THE FAIR, OFFICIALS ARE NOTIFIED OF THE THIEVES' CAPTURE!
WHAT! YOU SAY SUPERMAN IS BRINGING THE JEWEL TO THE FAIR?
A FEW MINUTES LATER, THE MADRAS EMERALD IS PRESENTED TO THE GRATEFUL OFFICIALS, BEFORE A CHEERING THRONG!
WHAT A MAGNIFICENT STONE!
HERE IS THE EMERALD, GENTLEMEN!
ON BEHALF OF THE WORLD'S FAIR, WE THANK YOU!
SUPERMAN SOARS AWAY INTO THE SKY--
LATER--CLARK KENT RETURNS AND FINDS LOIS AT THE FAIR--
LOIS! GEE, I'M GLAD TO FIND YOU! --WHY DID YOU DELIBERATELY TRICK ME LIKE THAT?
YOU WERE TOO MUCH OF A COWARD TO FOLLOW SARTO-- I TRAILED HIM AND GOT A TERRIFIC STORY ON THE JEWEL ROBBERY--YOU WERE ASLEEP AT THE SWITCH!
PERHAPS-- BUT I WOKE UP IN TIME TO GET AN INTERVIEW WITH SUPERMAN BEFORE HE LEFT THE FAIR--AND I'VE ALREADY WIRED HIS EXCLUSIVE STORY OF THE GEM'S RECOVERY TO THE EDITOR!
THE END!

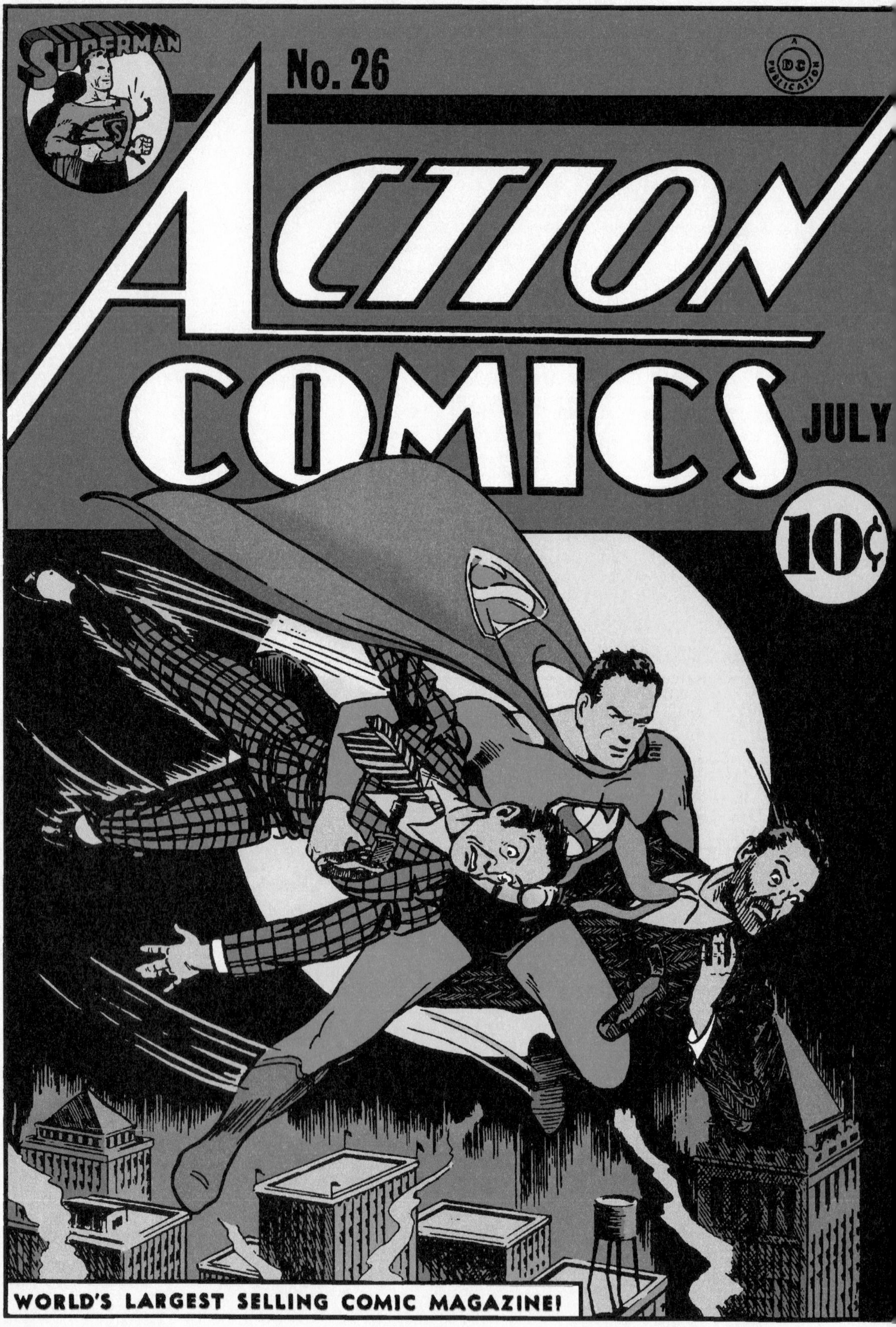
SUPERMAN
No. 26
A DC PUBLICATION
ACTION COMICS
JULY
10¢
WORLD'S LARGEST SELLING COMIC MAGAZINE!

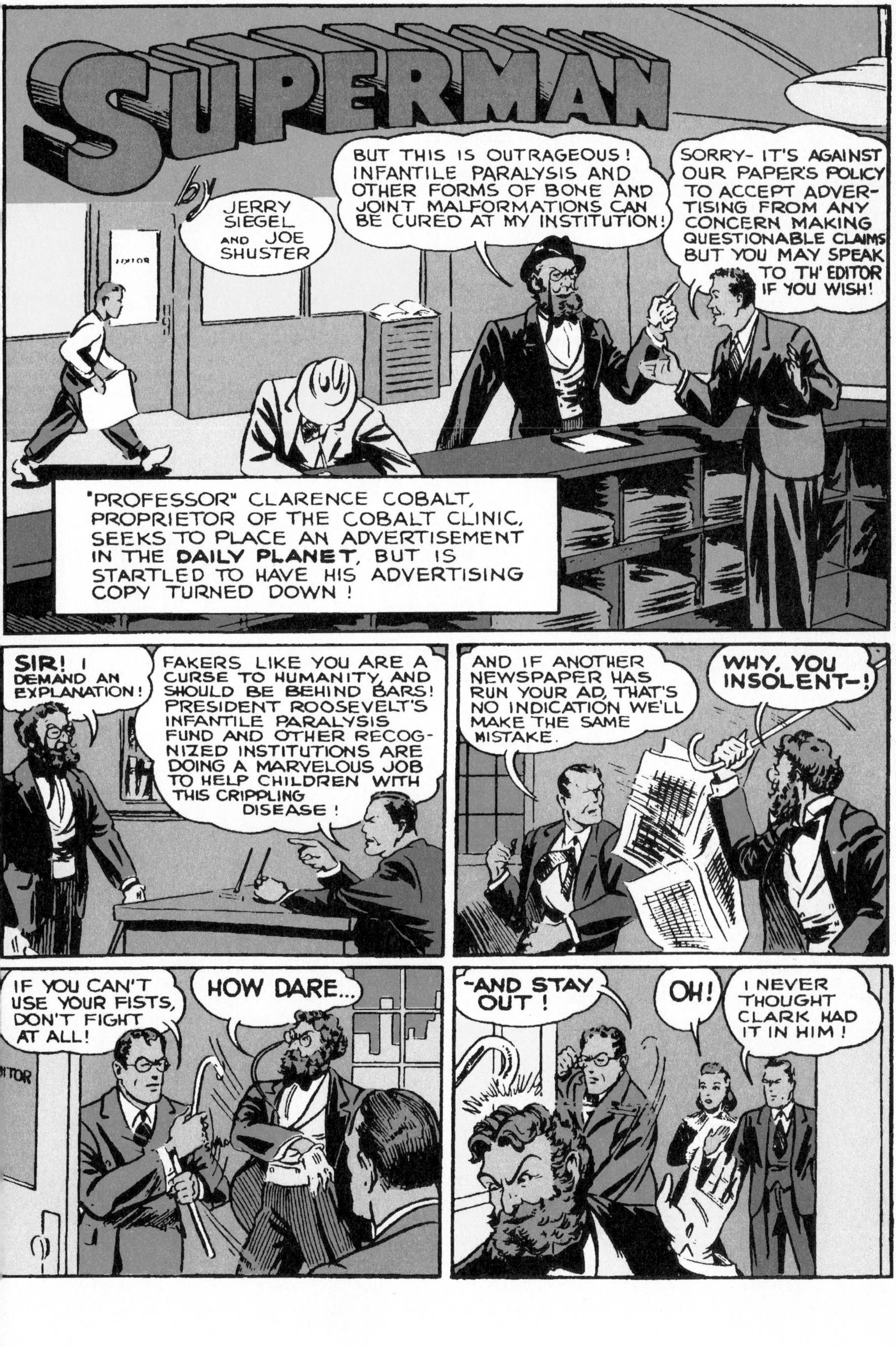
SUPERMAN
by
JERRY SIEGEL AND JOE SHUSTER
BUT THIS IS OUTRAGEOUS! INFANTILE PARALYSIS AND OTHER FORMS OF BONE AND JOINT MALFORMATIONS CAN BE CURED AT MY INSTITUTION!
SORRY- IT'S AGAINST OUR PAPER'S POLICY TO ACCEPT ADVERTISING FROM ANY CONCERN MAKING QUESTIONABLE CLAIMS BUT YOU MAY SPEAK TO TH' EDITOR IF YOU WISH!
"PROFESSOR" CLARENCE COBALT, PROPRIETOR OF THE COBALT CLINIC, SEEKS TO PLACE AN ADVERTISEMENT IN THE DAILY PLANET, BUT IS STARTLED TO HAVE HIS ADVERTISING COPY TURNED DOWN!
SIR! I DEMAND AN EXPLANATION!
FAKERS LIKE YOU ARE A CURSE TO HUMANITY, AND SHOULD BE BEHIND BARS! PRESIDENT ROOSEVELT'S INFANTILE PARALYSIS FUND AND OTHER RECOGNIZED INSTITUTIONS ARE DOING A MARVELOUS JOB TO HELP CHILDREN WITH THIS CRIPPLING DISEASE!
AND IF ANOTHER NEWSPAPER HAS RUN YOUR AD, THAT'S NO INDICATION WE'LL MAKE THE SAME MISTAKE.
WHY, YOU INSOLENT-!
IF YOU CAN'T USE YOUR FISTS, DON'T FIGHT AT ALL!
HOW DARE...
-AND STAY OUT!
OH!
I NEVER THOUGHT CLARK HAD IT IN HIM!

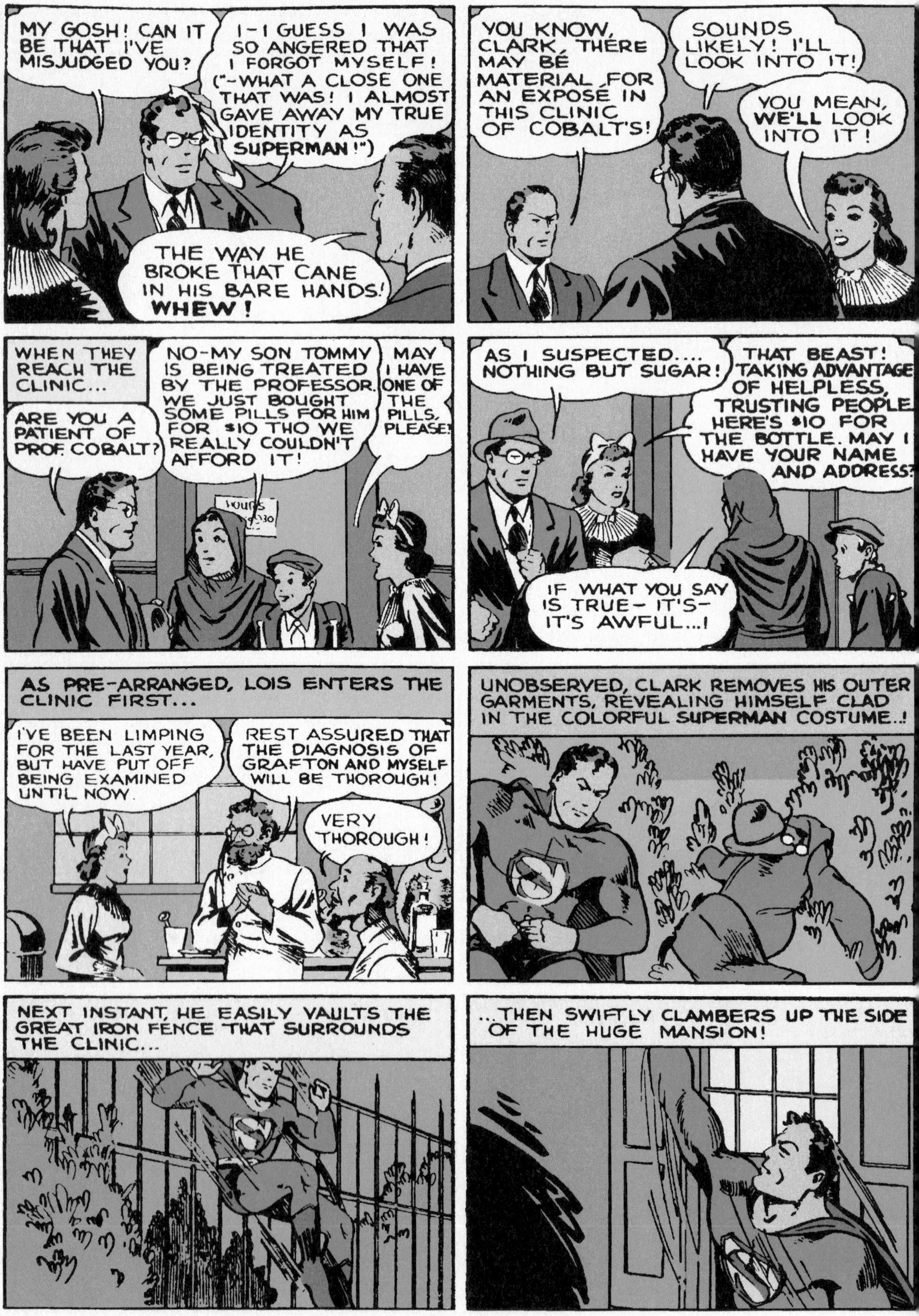
MY GOSH! CAN IT BE THAT I'VE MISJUDGED YOU?
I-I GUESS I WAS SO ANGERED THAT I FORGOT MYSELF! ("-WHAT A CLOSE ONE THAT WAS! I ALMOST GAVE AWAY MY TRUE IDENTITY AS SUPERMAN!")
THE WAY HE BROKE THAT CANE IN HIS BARE HANDS! WHEW!
YOU KNOW, CLARK, THERE MAY BE MATERIAL FOR AN EXPOSÉ IN THIS CLINIC OF COBALT'S!
SOUNDS LIKELY! I'LL LOOK INTO IT!
YOU MEAN, WE'LL LOOK INTO IT!
WHEN THEY REACH THE CLINIC...
ARE YOU A PATIENT OF PROF. COBALT?
NO-MY SON TOMMY IS BEING TREATED BY THE PROFESSOR. WE JUST BOUGHT SOME PILLS FOR HIM FOR $10 THO WE REALLY COULDN'T AFFORD IT!
MAY I HAVE ONE OF THE PILLS, PLEASE!
AS I SUSPECTED.... NOTHING BUT SUGAR!
THAT BEAST! TAKING ADVANTAGE OF HELPLESS, TRUSTING PEOPLE. HERE'S $10 FOR THE BOTTLE. MAY I HAVE YOUR NAME AND ADDRESS?
IF WHAT YOU SAY IS TRUE- IT'S- IT'S AWFUL...!
AS PRE-ARRANGED, LOIS ENTERS THE CLINIC FIRST...
I'VE BEEN LIMPING FOR THE LAST YEAR, BUT HAVE PUT OFF BEING EXAMINED UNTIL NOW.
REST ASSURED THAT THE DIAGNOSIS OF GRAFTON AND MYSELF WILL BE THOROUGH!
VERY THOROUGH!
UNOBSERVED, CLARK REMOVES HIS OUTER GARMENTS, REVEALING HIMSELF CLAD IN THE COLORFUL SUPERMAN COSTUME..!
NEXT INSTANT, HE EASILY VAULTS THE GREAT IRON FENCE THAT SURROUNDS THE CLINIC...
...THEN SWIFTLY CLAMBERS UP THE SIDE OF THE HUGE MANSION!

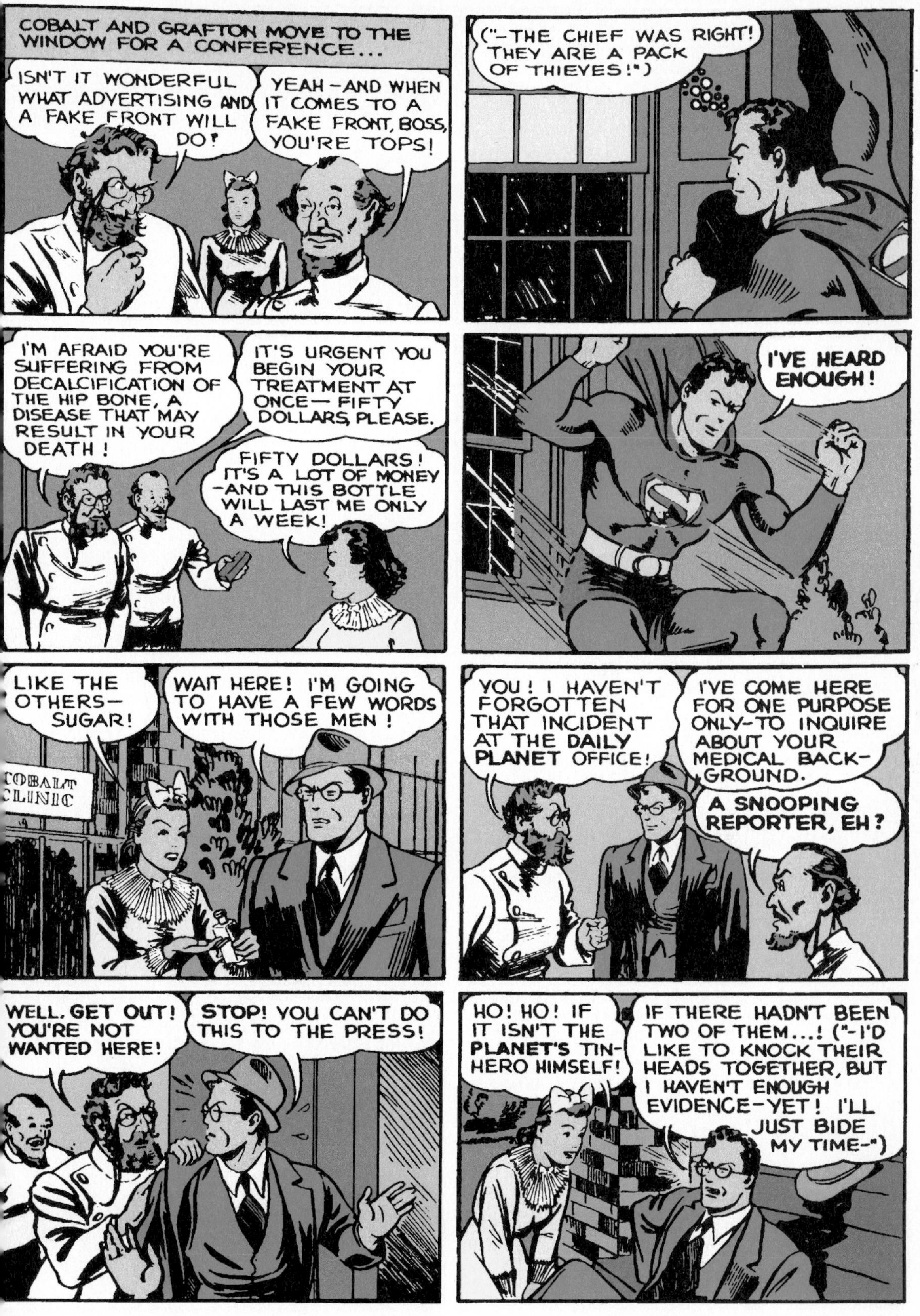

COBALT AND GRAFTON MOVE TO THE WINDOW FOR A CONFERENCE...
ISN'T IT WONDERFUL WHAT ADVERTISING AND A FAKE FRONT WILL DO?
YEAH -AND WHEN IT COMES TO A FAKE FRONT, BOSS, YOU'RE TOPS!
("-THE CHIEF WAS RIGHT! THEY ARE A PACK OF THIEVES!")
I'M AFRAID YOU'RE SUFFERING FROM DECALCIFICATION OF THE HIP BONE, A DISEASE THAT MAY RESULT IN YOUR DEATH!
IT'S URGENT YOU BEGIN YOUR TREATMENT AT ONCE— FIFTY DOLLARS, PLEASE.
FIFTY DOLLARS! IT'S A LOT OF MONEY -AND THIS BOTTLE WILL LAST ME ONLY A WEEK!
I'VE HEARD ENOUGH!
LIKE THE OTHERS— SUGAR!
WAIT HERE! I'M GOING TO HAVE A FEW WORDS WITH THOSE MEN!
COBALT CLINIC
YOU! I HAVEN'T FORGOTTEN THAT INCIDENT AT THE DAILY PLANET OFFICE!
I'VE COME HERE FOR ONE PURPOSE ONLY-TO INQUIRE ABOUT YOUR MEDICAL BACK-GROUND.
A SNOOPING REPORTER, EH?
WELL, GET OUT! YOU'RE NOT WANTED HERE!
STOP! YOU CAN'T DO THIS TO THE PRESS!
HO! HO! IF IT ISN'T THE PLANET'S TIN-HERO HIMSELF!
IF THERE HADN'T BEEN TWO OF THEM...! ("-I'D LIKE TO KNOCK THEIR HEADS TOGETHER, BUT I HAVEN'T ENOUGH EVIDENCE-YET! I'LL JUST BIDE MY TIME-")

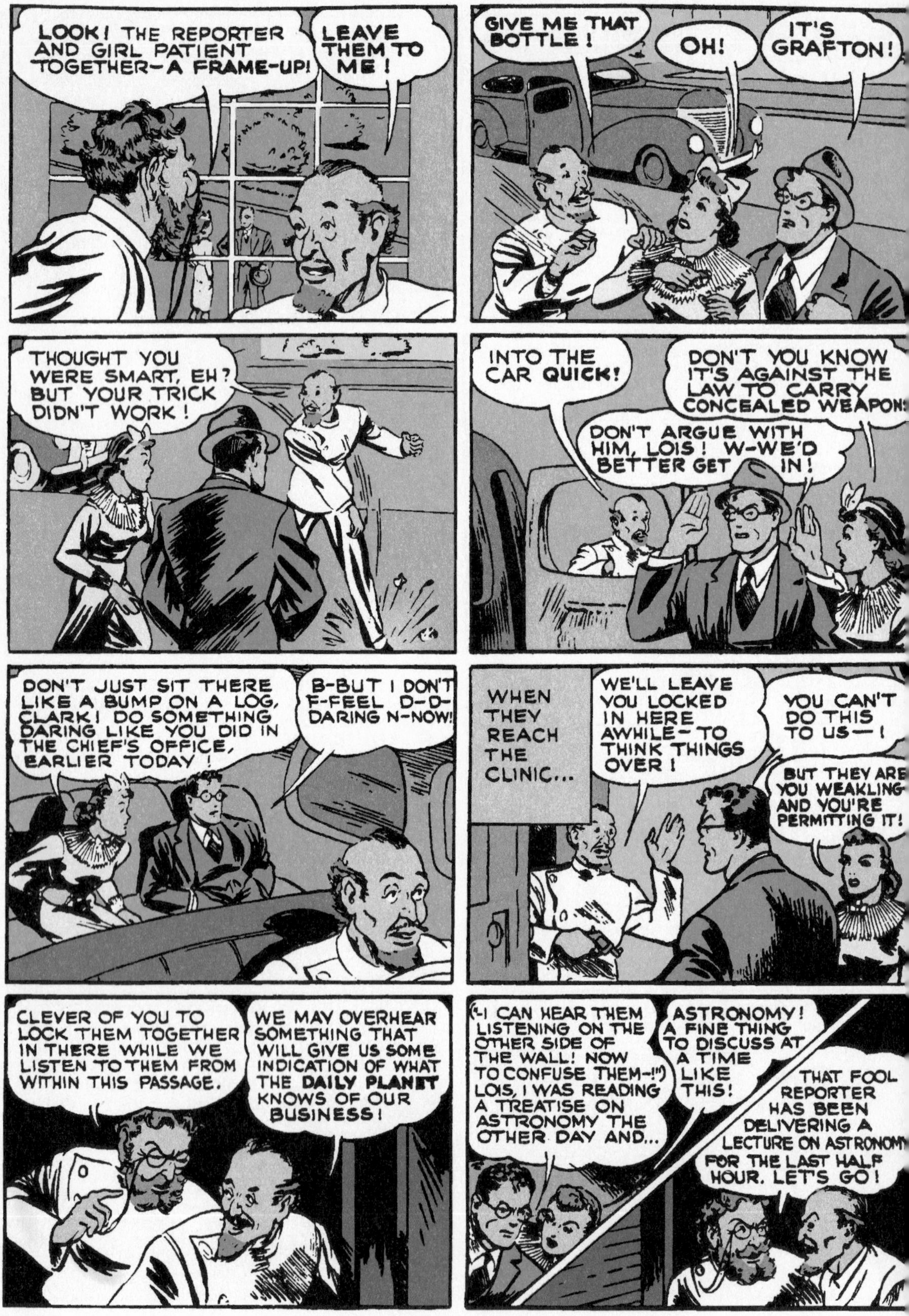
LOOK! THE REPORTER AND GIRL PATIENT TOGETHER—A FRAME-UP!
LEAVE THEM TO ME!
GIVE ME THAT BOTTLE!
OH!
IT'S GRAFTON!
THOUGHT YOU WERE SMART, EH? BUT YOUR TRICK DIDN'T WORK!
INTO THE CAR QUICK!
DON'T YOU KNOW IT'S AGAINST THE LAW TO CARRY CONCEALED WEAPONS
DON'T ARGUE WITH HIM, LOIS! W-WE'D BETTER GET IN!
DON'T JUST SIT THERE LIKE A BUMP ON A LOG, CLARK! DO SOMETHING DARING LIKE YOU DID IN THE CHIEF'S OFFICE, EARLIER TODAY!
B-BUT I DON'T F-FEEL D-D-DARING N-NOW!
WHEN THEY REACH THE CLINIC...
WE'LL LEAVE YOU LOCKED IN HERE AWHILE—TO THINK THINGS OVER!
YOU CAN'T DO THIS TO US—!
BUT THEY ARE YOU WEAKLING AND YOU'RE PERMITTING IT!
CLEVER OF YOU TO LOCK THEM TOGETHER IN THERE WHILE WE LISTEN TO THEM FROM WITHIN THIS PASSAGE.
WE MAY OVERHEAR SOMETHING THAT WILL GIVE US SOME INDICATION OF WHAT THE DAILY PLANET KNOWS OF OUR BUSINESS!
("I CAN HEAR THEM LISTENING ON THE OTHER SIDE OF THE WALL! NOW TO CONFUSE THEM-!") LOIS, I WAS READING A TREATISE ON ASTRONOMY THE OTHER DAY AND...
ASTRONOMY! A FINE THING TO DISCUSS AT A TIME LIKE THIS!
THAT FOOL REPORTER HAS BEEN DELIVERING A LECTURE ON ASTRONOMY FOR THE LAST HALF HOUR. LET'S GO!

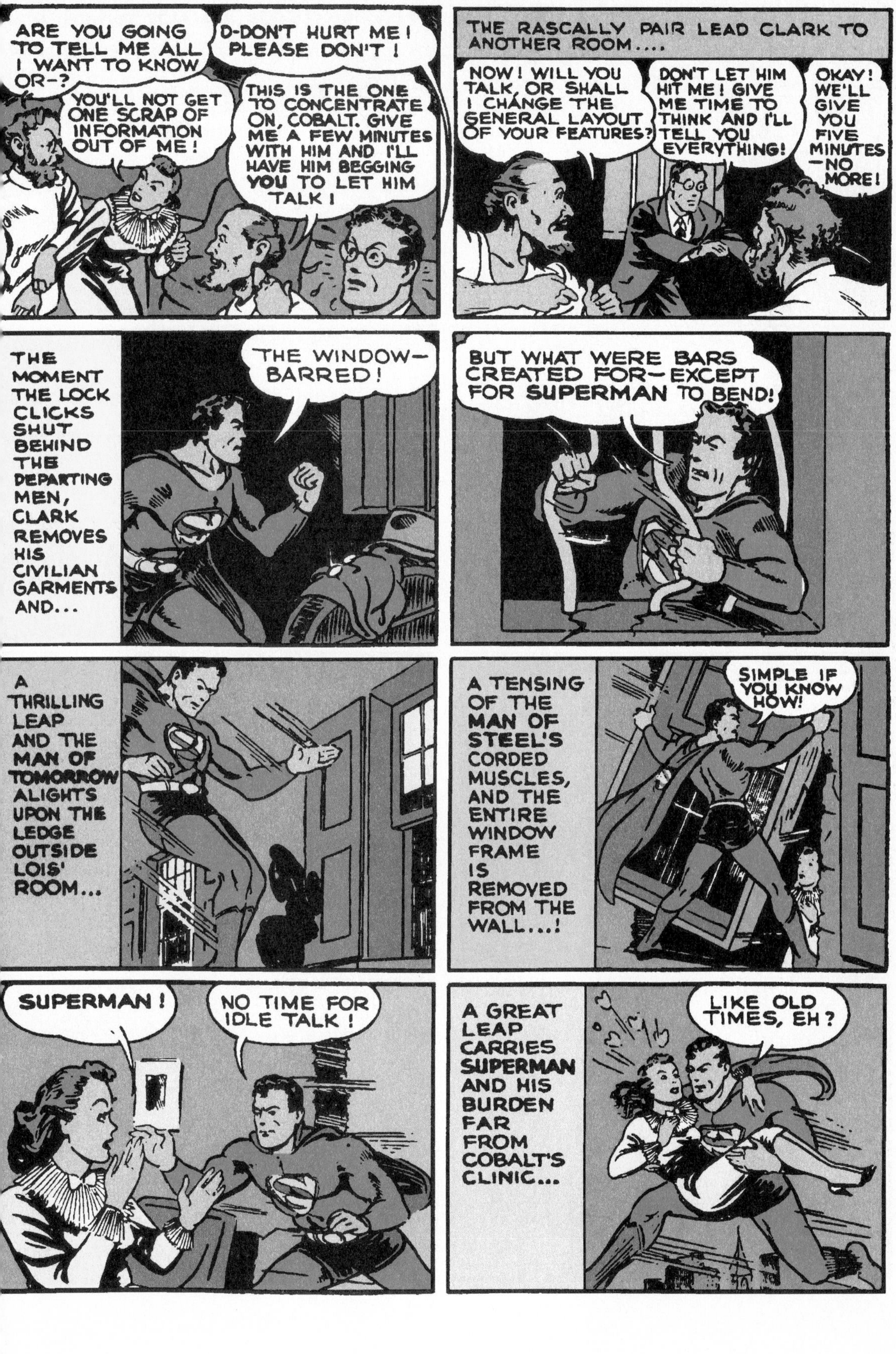
ARE YOU GOING TO TELL ME ALL I WANT TO KNOW OR–?
D-DON'T HURT ME! PLEASE DON'T!
YOU'LL NOT GET ONE SCRAP OF INFORMATION OUT OF ME!
THIS IS THE ONE TO CONCENTRATE ON, COBALT. GIVE ME A FEW MINUTES WITH HIM AND I'LL HAVE HIM BEGGING YOU TO LET HIM TALK!
THE RASCALLY PAIR LEAD CLARK TO ANOTHER ROOM....
NOW! WILL YOU TALK, OR SHALL I CHANGE THE GENERAL LAYOUT OF YOUR FEATURES?
DON'T LET HIM HIT ME! GIVE ME TIME TO THINK AND I'LL TELL YOU EVERYTHING!
OKAY! WE'LL GIVE YOU FIVE MINUTES –NO MORE!
THE MOMENT THE LOCK CLICKS SHUT BEHIND THE DEPARTING MEN, CLARK REMOVES HIS CIVILIAN GARMENTS AND...
THE WINDOW– BARRED!
BUT WHAT WERE BARS CREATED FOR– EXCEPT FOR SUPERMAN TO BEND!
A THRILLING LEAP AND THE MAN OF TOMORROW ALIGHTS UPON THE LEDGE OUTSIDE LOIS' ROOM...
A TENSING OF THE MAN OF STEEL'S CORDED MUSCLES, AND THE ENTIRE WINDOW FRAME IS REMOVED FROM THE WALL...!
SIMPLE IF YOU KNOW HOW!
SUPERMAN!
NO TIME FOR IDLE TALK!
A GREAT LEAP CARRIES SUPERMAN AND HIS BURDEN FAR FROM COBALT'S CLINIC...
LIKE OLD TIMES, EH?

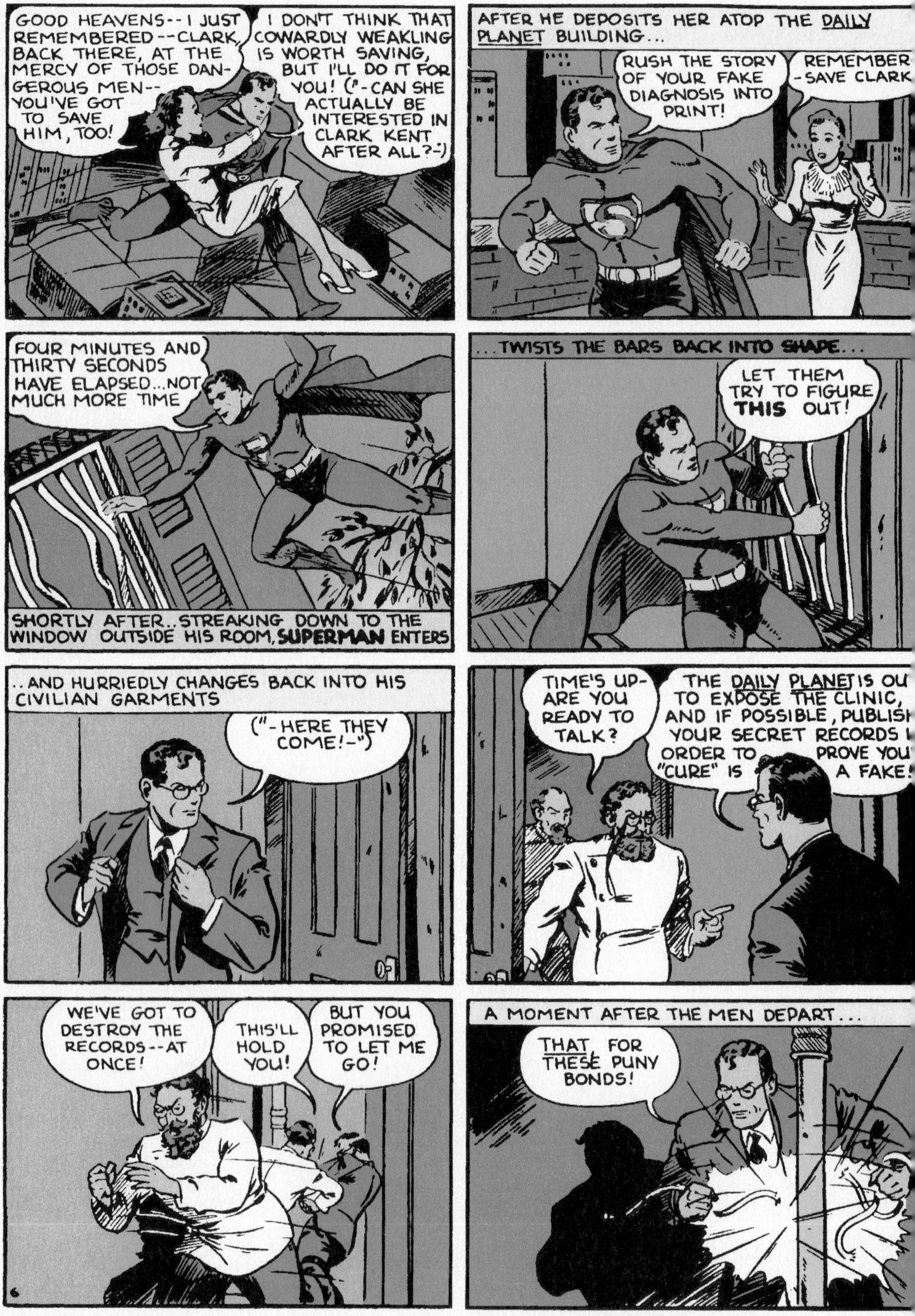
GOOD HEAVENS--I JUST REMEMBERED--CLARK, BACK THERE, AT THE MERCY OF THOSE DANGEROUS MEN--YOU'VE GOT TO SAVE HIM, TOO!
I DON'T THINK THAT COWARDLY WEAKLING IS WORTH SAVING, BUT I'LL DO IT FOR YOU! ("-CAN SHE ACTUALLY BE INTERESTED IN CLARK KENT AFTER ALL?-")
AFTER HE DEPOSITS HER ATOP THE DAILY PLANET BUILDING...
RUSH THE STORY OF YOUR FAKE DIAGNOSIS INTO PRINT!
REMEMBER -SAVE CLARK
FOUR MINUTES AND THIRTY SECONDS HAVE ELAPSED...NOT MUCH MORE TIME
SHORTLY AFTER..STREAKING DOWN TO THE WINDOW OUTSIDE HIS ROOM, SUPERMAN ENTERS
...TWISTS THE BARS BACK INTO SHAPE...
LET THEM TRY TO FIGURE THIS OUT!
..AND HURRIEDLY CHANGES BACK INTO HIS CIVILIAN GARMENTS
("-HERE THEY COME!-")
TIME'S UP-ARE YOU READY TO TALK?
THE DAILY PLANET IS OU TO EXPOSE THE CLINIC, AND IF POSSIBLE, PUBLIS YOUR SECRET RECORDS ORDER TO PROVE YOU "CURE" IS A FAKE!
WE'VE GOT TO DESTROY THE RECORDS--AT ONCE!
THIS'LL HOLD YOU!
BUT YOU PROMISED TO LET ME GO!
A MOMENT AFTER THE MEN DEPART...
THAT, FOR THESE PUNY BONDS!

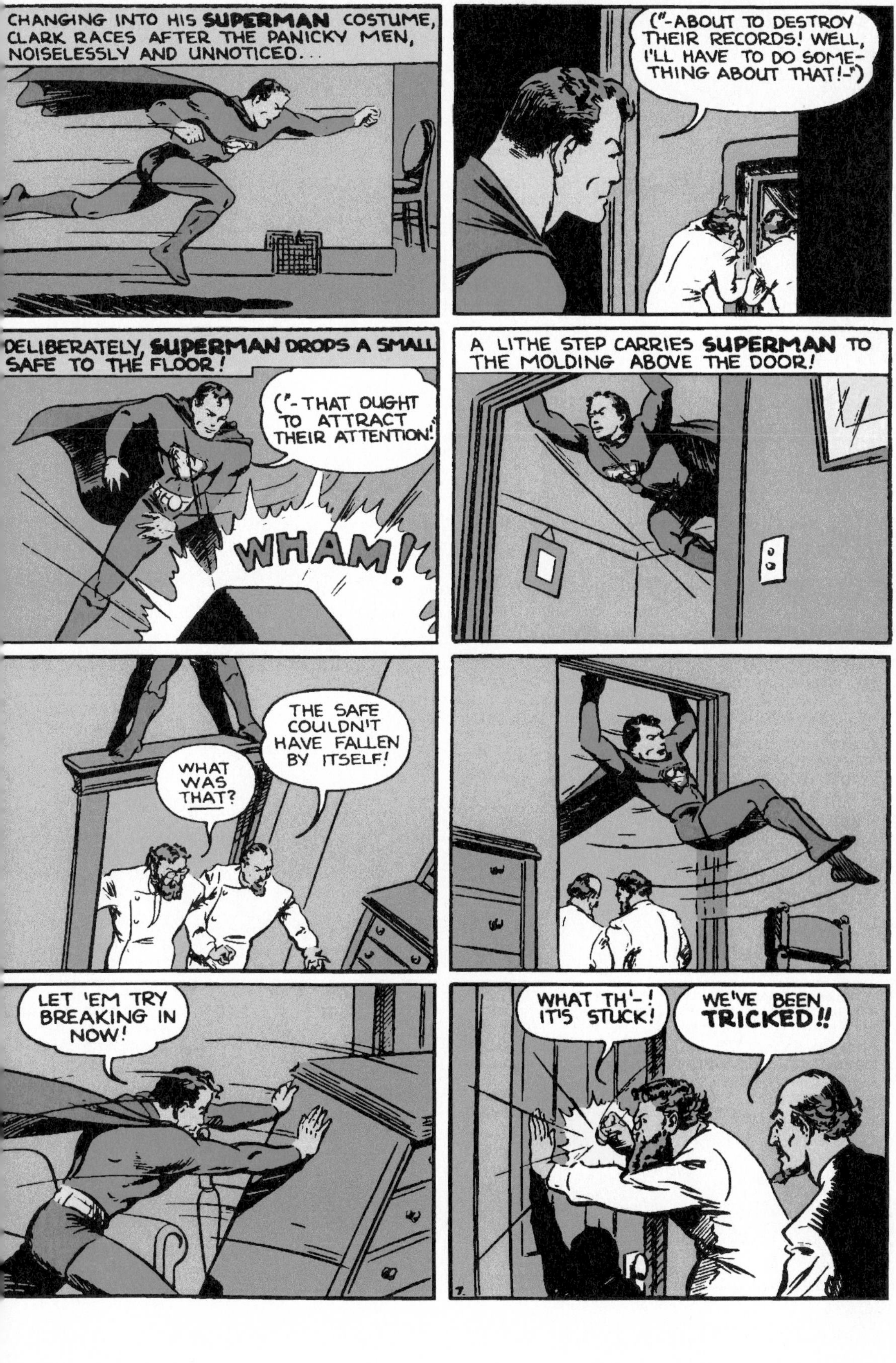

CHANGING INTO HIS SUPERMAN COSTUME, CLARK RACES AFTER THE PANICKY MEN, NOISELESSLY AND UNNOTICED...
("-ABOUT TO DESTROY THEIR RECORDS! WELL, I'LL HAVE TO DO SOMETHING ABOUT THAT!-")
DELIBERATELY, SUPERMAN DROPS A SMALL SAFE TO THE FLOOR!
("-THAT OUGHT TO ATTRACT THEIR ATTENTION!-")
WHAM!
A LITHE STEP CARRIES SUPERMAN TO THE MOLDING ABOVE THE DOOR!
THE SAFE COULDN'T HAVE FALLEN BY ITSELF!
WHAT WAS THAT?
LET 'EM TRY BREAKING IN NOW!
WHAT TH'-! IT'S STUCK!
WE'VE BEEN TRICKED!!
7.

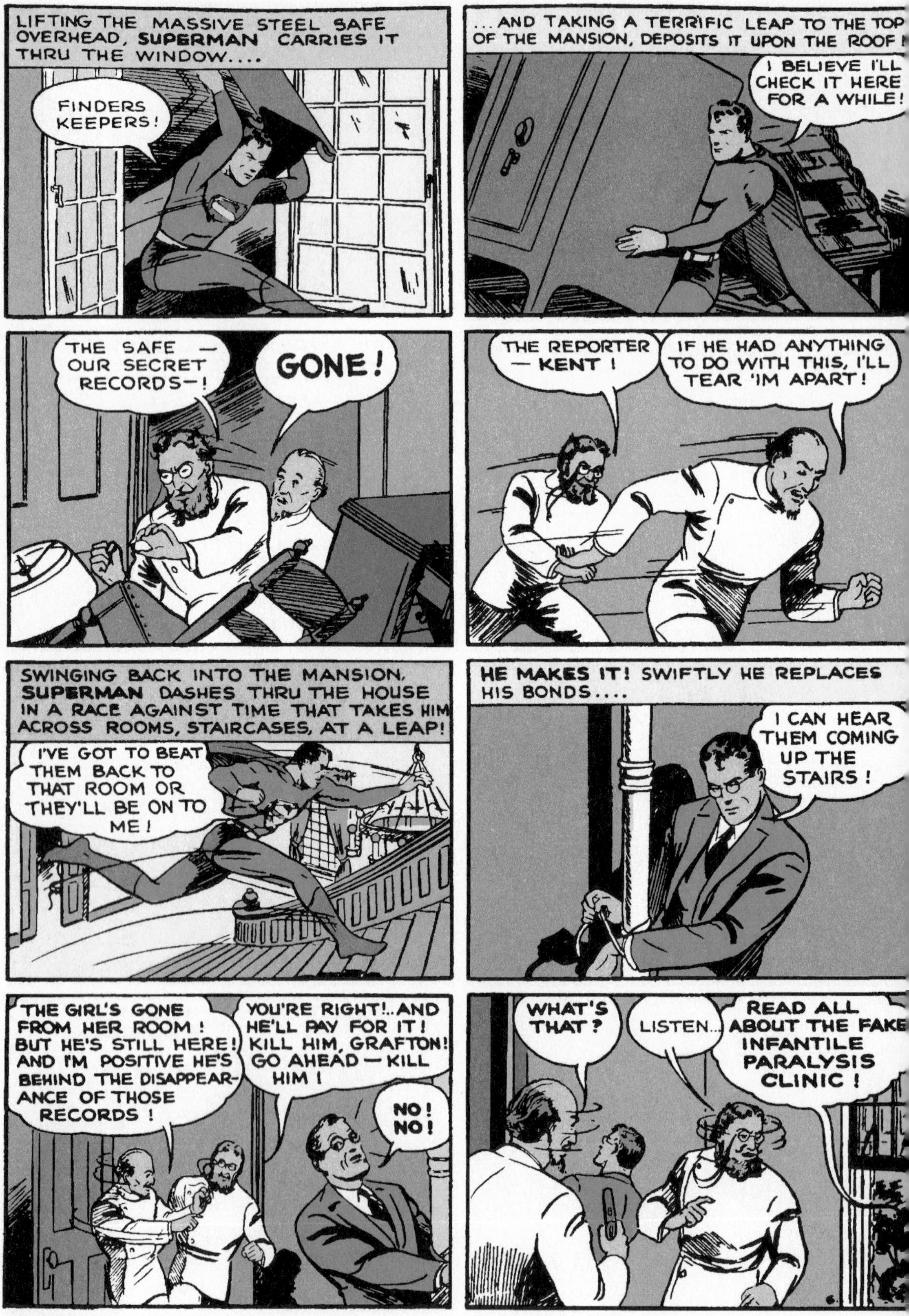
LIFTING THE MASSIVE STEEL SAFE OVERHEAD, SUPERMAN CARRIES IT THRU THE WINDOW....
FINDERS KEEPERS!
...AND TAKING A TERRIFIC LEAP TO THE TOP OF THE MANSION, DEPOSITS IT UPON THE ROOF!
I BELIEVE I'LL CHECK IT HERE FOR A WHILE!
THE SAFE — OUR SECRET RECORDS—!
GONE!
THE REPORTER — KENT!
IF HE HAD ANYTHING TO DO WITH THIS, I'LL TEAR 'IM APART!
SWINGING BACK INTO THE MANSION, SUPERMAN DASHES THRU THE HOUSE IN A RACE AGAINST TIME THAT TAKES HIM ACROSS ROOMS, STAIRCASES, AT A LEAP!
I'VE GOT TO BEAT THEM BACK TO THAT ROOM OR THEY'LL BE ON TO ME!
HE MAKES IT! SWIFTLY HE REPLACES HIS BONDS....
I CAN HEAR THEM COMING UP THE STAIRS!
THE GIRL'S GONE FROM HER ROOM! BUT HE'S STILL HERE! AND I'M POSITIVE HE'S BEHIND THE DISAPPEARANCE OF THOSE RECORDS!
YOU'RE RIGHT!..AND HE'LL PAY FOR IT! KILL HIM, GRAFTON! GO AHEAD — KILL HIM!
NO! NO!
WHAT'S THAT?
LISTEN...
READ ALL ABOUT THE FAKE INFANTILE PARALYSIS CLINIC!

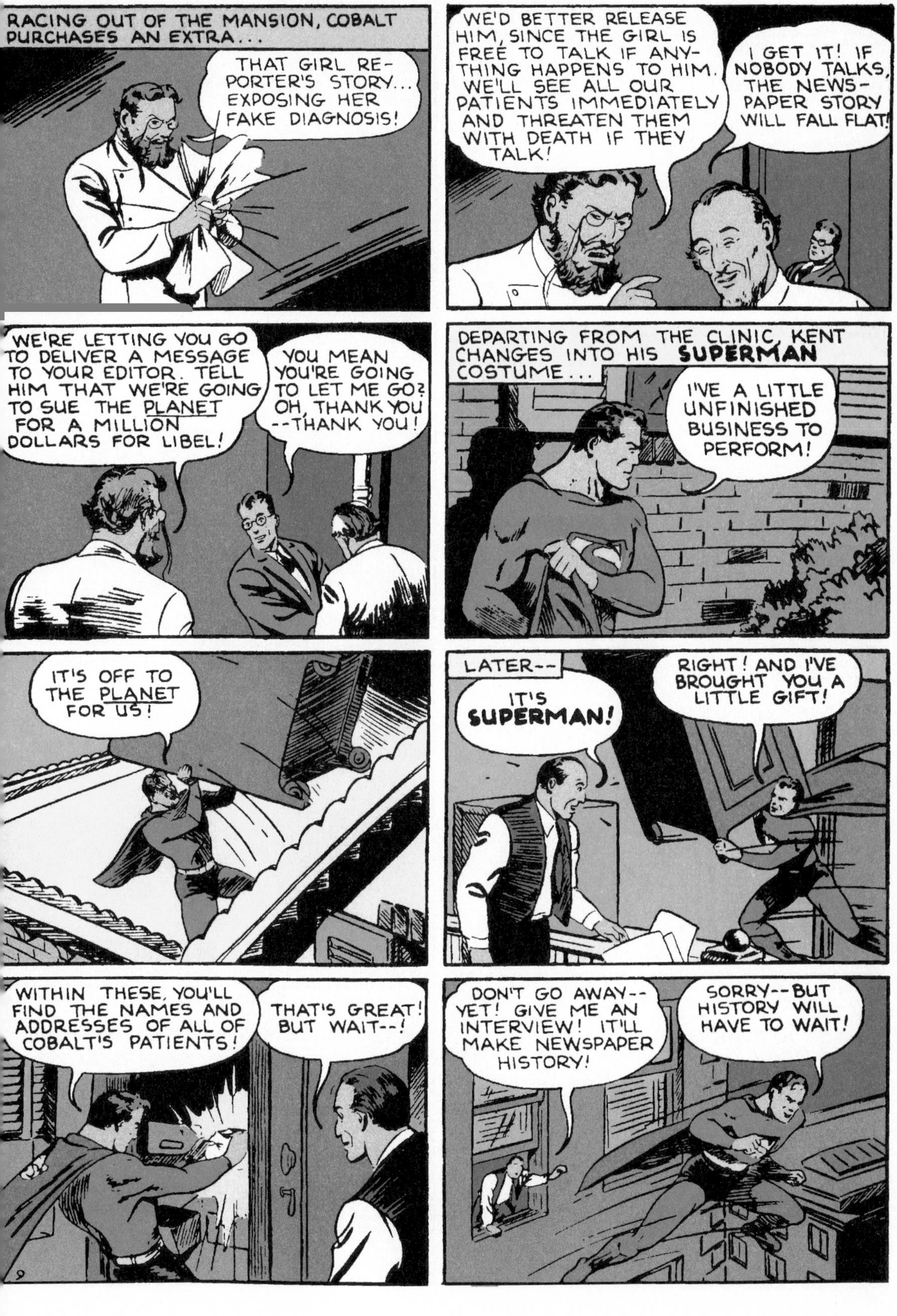
RACING OUT OF THE MANSION, COBALT PURCHASES AN EXTRA...
THAT GIRL REPORTER'S STORY... EXPOSING HER FAKE DIAGNOSIS!
WE'D BETTER RELEASE HIM, SINCE THE GIRL IS FREE TO TALK IF ANYTHING HAPPENS TO HIM. WE'LL SEE ALL OUR PATIENTS IMMEDIATELY AND THREATEN THEM WITH DEATH IF THEY TALK!
I GET IT! IF NOBODY TALKS, THE NEWSPAPER STORY WILL FALL FLAT!
WE'RE LETTING YOU GO TO DELIVER A MESSAGE TO YOUR EDITOR. TELL HIM THAT WE'RE GOING TO SUE THE PLANET FOR A MILLION DOLLARS FOR LIBEL!
YOU MEAN YOU'RE GOING TO LET ME GO? OH, THANK YOU --THANK YOU!
DEPARTING FROM THE CLINIC, KENT CHANGES INTO HIS SUPERMAN COSTUME...
I'VE A LITTLE UNFINISHED BUSINESS TO PERFORM!
IT'S OFF TO THE PLANET FOR US!
LATER--
IT'S SUPERMAN!
RIGHT! AND I'VE BROUGHT YOU A LITTLE GIFT!
WITHIN THESE, YOU'LL FIND THE NAMES AND ADDRESSES OF ALL OF COBALT'S PATIENTS!
THAT'S GREAT! BUT WAIT--!
DON'T GO AWAY--YET! GIVE ME AN INTERVIEW! IT'LL MAKE NEWSPAPER HISTORY!
SORRY--BUT HISTORY WILL HAVE TO WAIT!

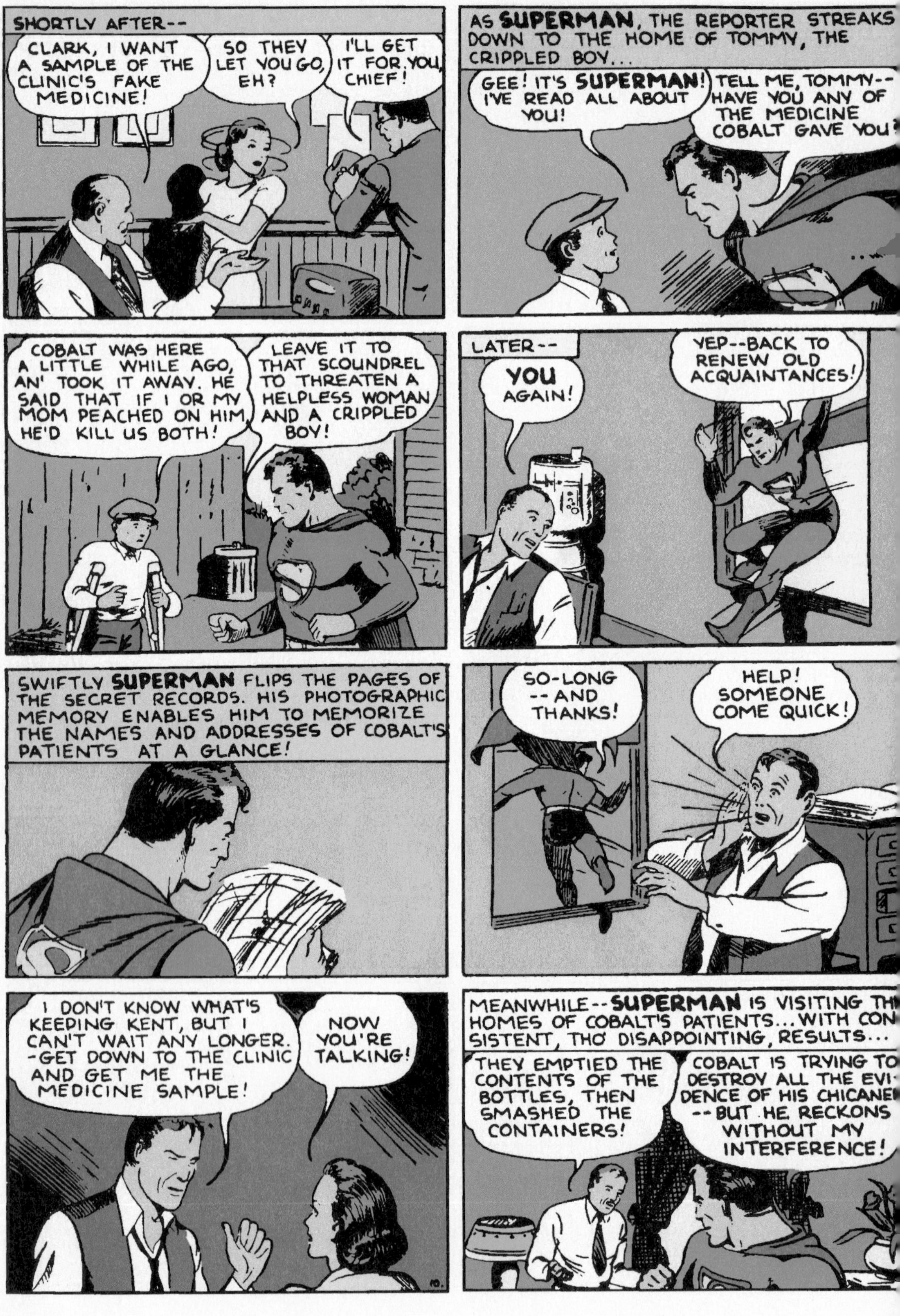

SHORTLY AFTER--
CLARK, I WANT A SAMPLE OF THE CLINIC'S FAKE MEDICINE!
SO THEY LET YOU GO, EH?
I'LL GET IT FOR YOU, CHIEF!
AS SUPERMAN, THE REPORTER STREAKS DOWN TO THE HOME OF TOMMY, THE CRIPPLED BOY...
GEE! IT'S SUPERMAN! I'VE READ ALL ABOUT YOU!
TELL ME, TOMMY-- HAVE YOU ANY OF THE MEDICINE COBALT GAVE YOU?
COBALT WAS HERE A LITTLE WHILE AGO, AN' TOOK IT AWAY. HE SAID THAT IF I OR MY MOM PEACHED ON HIM, HE'D KILL US BOTH!
LEAVE IT TO THAT SCOUNDREL TO THREATEN A HELPLESS WOMAN AND A CRIPPLED BOY!
LATER--
YOU AGAIN!
YEP--BACK TO RENEW OLD ACQUAINTANCES!
SWIFTLY SUPERMAN FLIPS THE PAGES OF THE SECRET RECORDS. HIS PHOTOGRAPHIC MEMORY ENABLES HIM TO MEMORIZE THE NAMES AND ADDRESSES OF COBALT'S PATIENTS AT A GLANCE!
SO-LONG --AND THANKS!
HELP! SOMEONE COME QUICK!
I DON'T KNOW WHAT'S KEEPING KENT, BUT I CAN'T WAIT ANY LONGER. -GET DOWN TO THE CLINIC AND GET ME THE MEDICINE SAMPLE!
NOW YOU'RE TALKING!
MEANWHILE--SUPERMAN IS VISITING THE HOMES OF COBALT'S PATIENTS...WITH CONSISTENT, THO' DISAPPOINTING, RESULTS...
THEY EMPTIED THE CONTENTS OF THE BOTTLES, THEN SMASHED THE CONTAINERS!
COBALT IS TRYING TO DESTROY ALL THE EVIDENCE OF HIS CHICANERY --BUT HE RECKONS WITHOUT MY INTERFERENCE!

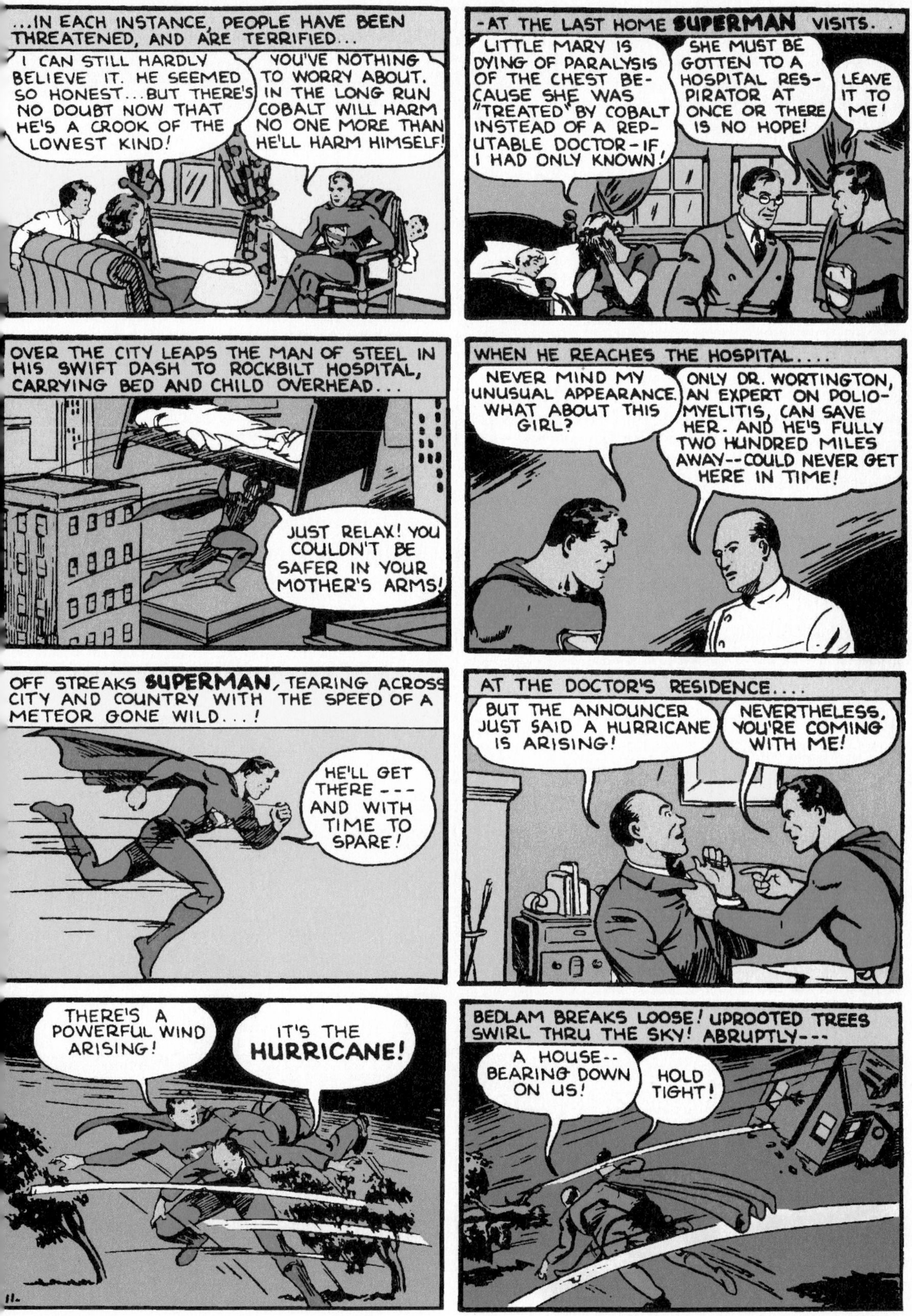
...IN EACH INSTANCE, PEOPLE HAVE BEEN THREATENED, AND ARE TERRIFIED...
I CAN STILL HARDLY BELIEVE IT. HE SEEMED SO HONEST...BUT THERE'S NO DOUBT NOW THAT HE'S A CROOK OF THE LOWEST KIND!
YOU'VE NOTHING TO WORRY ABOUT. IN THE LONG RUN COBALT WILL HARM NO ONE MORE THAN HE'LL HARM HIMSELF!
-AT THE LAST HOME SUPERMAN VISITS. .
LITTLE MARY IS DYING OF PARALYSIS OF THE CHEST BECAUSE SHE WAS "TREATED" BY COBALT INSTEAD OF A REPUTABLE DOCTOR-IF I HAD ONLY KNOWN!
SHE MUST BE GOTTEN TO A HOSPITAL RESPIRATOR AT ONCE OR THERE IS NO HOPE!
LEAVE IT TO ME!
OVER THE CITY LEAPS THE MAN OF STEEL IN HIS SWIFT DASH TO ROCKBILT HOSPITAL, CARRYING BED AND CHILD OVERHEAD...
JUST RELAX! YOU COULDN'T BE SAFER IN YOUR MOTHER'S ARMS!
WHEN HE REACHES THE HOSPITAL....
NEVER MIND MY UNUSUAL APPEARANCE. WHAT ABOUT THIS GIRL?
ONLY DR. WORTINGTON, AN EXPERT ON POLIOMYELITIS, CAN SAVE HER. AND HE'S FULLY TWO HUNDRED MILES AWAY--COULD NEVER GET HERE IN TIME!
OFF STREAKS SUPERMAN, TEARING ACROSS CITY AND COUNTRY WITH THE SPEED OF A METEOR GONE WILD...!
HE'LL GET THERE--- AND WITH TIME TO SPARE!
AT THE DOCTOR'S RESIDENCE....
BUT THE ANNOUNCER JUST SAID A HURRICANE IS ARISING!
NEVERTHELESS, YOU'RE COMING WITH ME!
THERE'S A POWERFUL WIND ARISING!
IT'S THE HURRICANE!
BEDLAM BREAKS LOOSE! UPROOTED TREES SWIRL THRU THE SKY! ABRUPTLY---
A HOUSE-- BEARING DOWN ON US!
HOLD TIGHT!

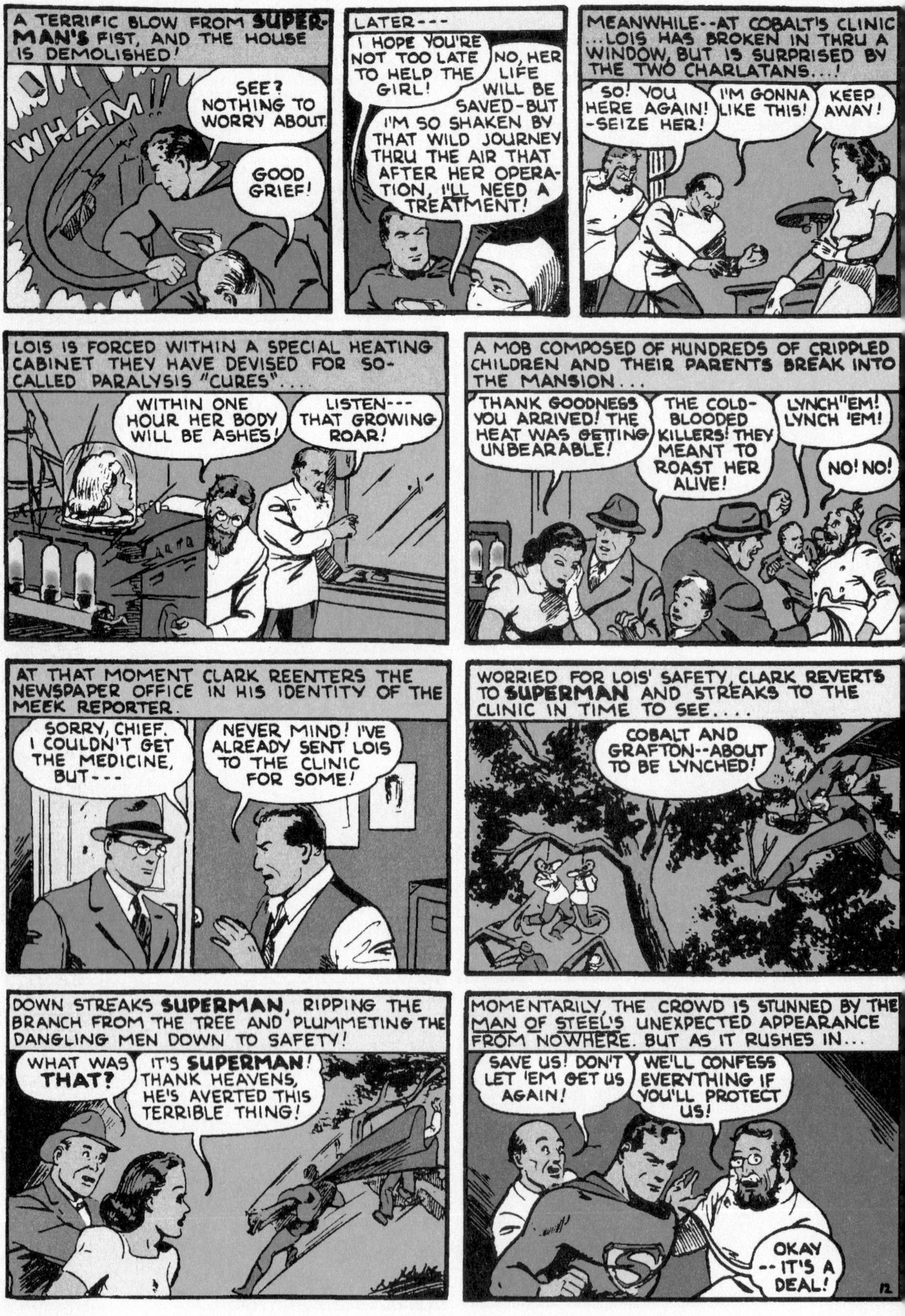
A TERRIFIC BLOW FROM SUPERMAN'S FIST, AND THE HOUSE IS DEMOLISHED!
WHAM!!
SEE? NOTHING TO WORRY ABOUT.
GOOD GRIEF!
LATER---
I HOPE YOU'RE NOT TOO LATE TO HELP THE GIRL!
NO, HER LIFE WILL BE SAVED-BUT I'M SO SHAKEN BY THAT WILD JOURNEY THRU THE AIR THAT AFTER HER OPERATION, I'LL NEED A TREATMENT!
MEANWHILE--AT COBALT'S CLINIC ...LOIS HAS BROKEN IN THRU A WINDOW, BUT IS SURPRISED BY THE TWO CHARLATANS...!
SO! YOU HERE AGAIN! -SEIZE HER!
I'M GONNA LIKE THIS!
KEEP AWAY!
LOIS IS FORCED WITHIN A SPECIAL HEATING CABINET THEY HAVE DEVISED FOR SO-CALLED PARALYSIS "CURES"...
WITHIN ONE HOUR HER BODY WILL BE ASHES!
LISTEN--- THAT GROWING ROAR!
A MOB COMPOSED OF HUNDREDS OF CRIPPLED CHILDREN AND THEIR PARENTS BREAK INTO THE MANSION...
THANK GOODNESS YOU ARRIVED! THE HEAT WAS GETTING UNBEARABLE!
THE COLD-BLOODED KILLERS! THEY MEANT TO ROAST HER ALIVE!
LYNCH 'EM! LYNCH 'EM!
NO! NO!
AT THAT MOMENT CLARK REENTERS THE NEWSPAPER OFFICE IN HIS IDENTITY OF THE MEEK REPORTER.
SORRY, CHIEF. I COULDN'T GET THE MEDICINE, BUT---
NEVER MIND! I'VE ALREADY SENT LOIS TO THE CLINIC FOR SOME!
WORRIED FOR LOIS' SAFETY, CLARK REVERTS TO SUPERMAN AND STREAKS TO THE CLINIC IN TIME TO SEE....
COBALT AND GRAFTON--ABOUT TO BE LYNCHED!
DOWN STREAKS SUPERMAN, RIPPING THE BRANCH FROM THE TREE AND PLUMMETING THE DANGLING MEN DOWN TO SAFETY!
WHAT WAS THAT?
IT'S SUPERMAN! THANK HEAVENS, HE'S AVERTED THIS TERRIBLE THING!
MOMENTARILY, THE CROWD IS STUNNED BY THE MAN OF STEEL'S UNEXPECTED APPEARANCE FROM NOWHERE. BUT AS IT RUSHES IN...
SAVE US! DON'T LET 'EM GET US AGAIN!
WE'LL CONFESS EVERYTHING IF YOU'LL PROTECT US!
OKAY --IT'S A DEAL!
12

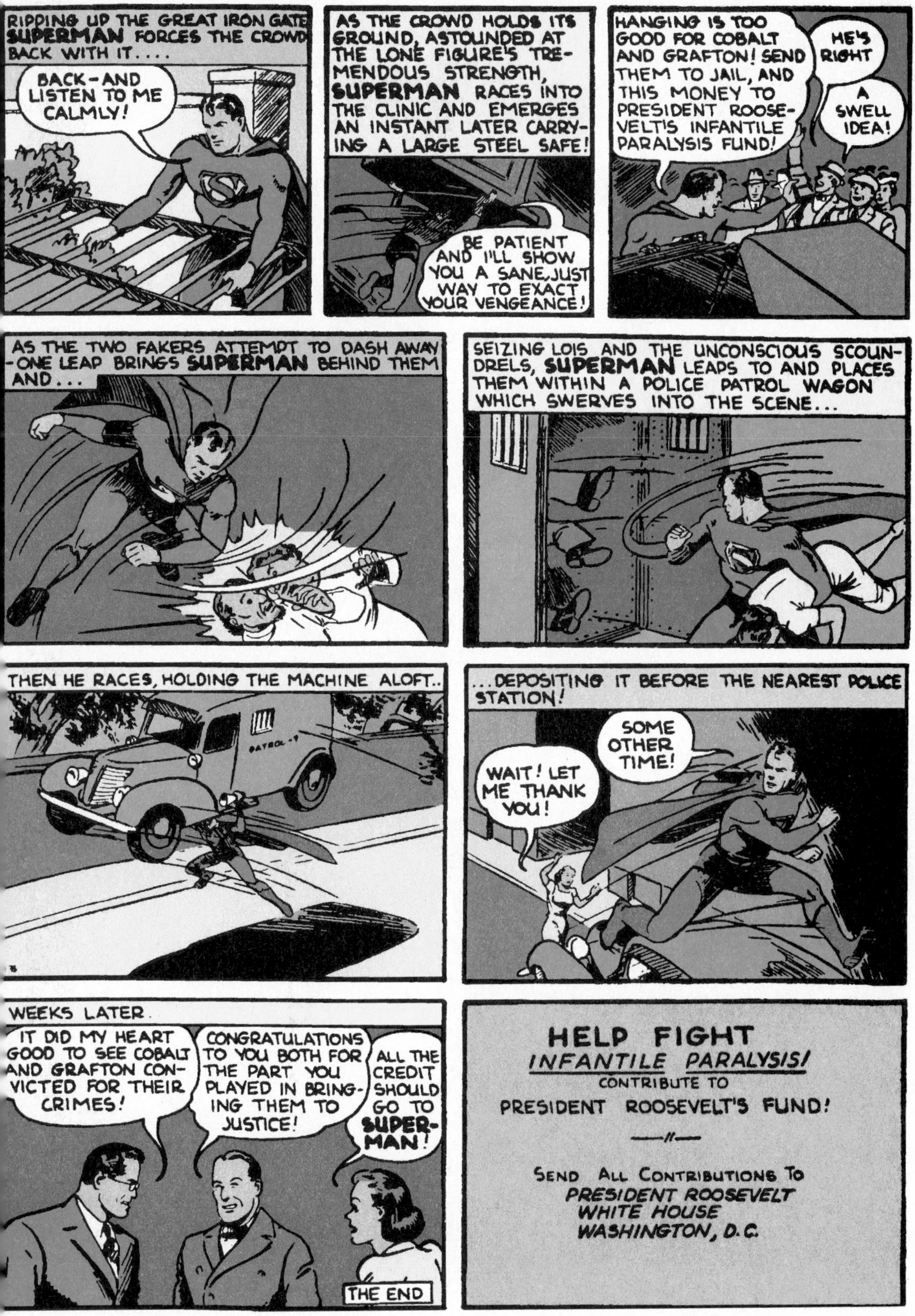
RIPPING UP THE GREAT IRON GATE SUPERMAN FORCES THE CROWD BACK WITH IT....
BACK—AND LISTEN TO ME CALMLY!
AS THE CROWD HOLDS ITS GROUND, ASTOUNDED AT THE LONE FIGURE'S TREMENDOUS STRENGTH, SUPERMAN RACES INTO THE CLINIC AND EMERGES AN INSTANT LATER CARRYING A LARGE STEEL SAFE!
BE PATIENT AND I'LL SHOW YOU A SANE, JUST WAY TO EXACT YOUR VENGEANCE!
HANGING IS TOO GOOD FOR COBALT AND GRAFTON! SEND THEM TO JAIL, AND THIS MONEY TO PRESIDENT ROOSEVELT'S INFANTILE PARALYSIS FUND!
HE'S RIGHT
A SWELL IDEA!
AS THE TWO FAKERS ATTEMPT TO DASH AWAY - ONE LEAP BRINGS SUPERMAN BEHIND THEM AND...
SEIZING LOIS AND THE UNCONSCIOUS SCOUNDRELS, SUPERMAN LEAPS TO AND PLACES THEM WITHIN A POLICE PATROL WAGON WHICH SWERVES INTO THE SCENE...
THEN HE RACES, HOLDING THE MACHINE ALOFT..
PATROL-7
...DEPOSITING IT BEFORE THE NEAREST POLICE STATION!
WAIT! LET ME THANK YOU!
SOME OTHER TIME!
WEEKS LATER.
IT DID MY HEART GOOD TO SEE COBALT AND GRAFTON CONVICTED FOR THEIR CRIMES!
CONGRATULATIONS TO YOU BOTH FOR THE PART YOU PLAYED IN BRINGING THEM TO JUSTICE!
ALL THE CREDIT SHOULD GO TO SUPERMAN!
THE END
HELP FIGHT
INFANTILE PARALYSIS!
CONTRIBUTE TO
PRESIDENT ROOSEVELT'S FUND!
SEND ALL CONTRIBUTIONS TO
PRESIDENT ROOSEVELT
WHITE HOUSE
WASHINGTON, D.C.

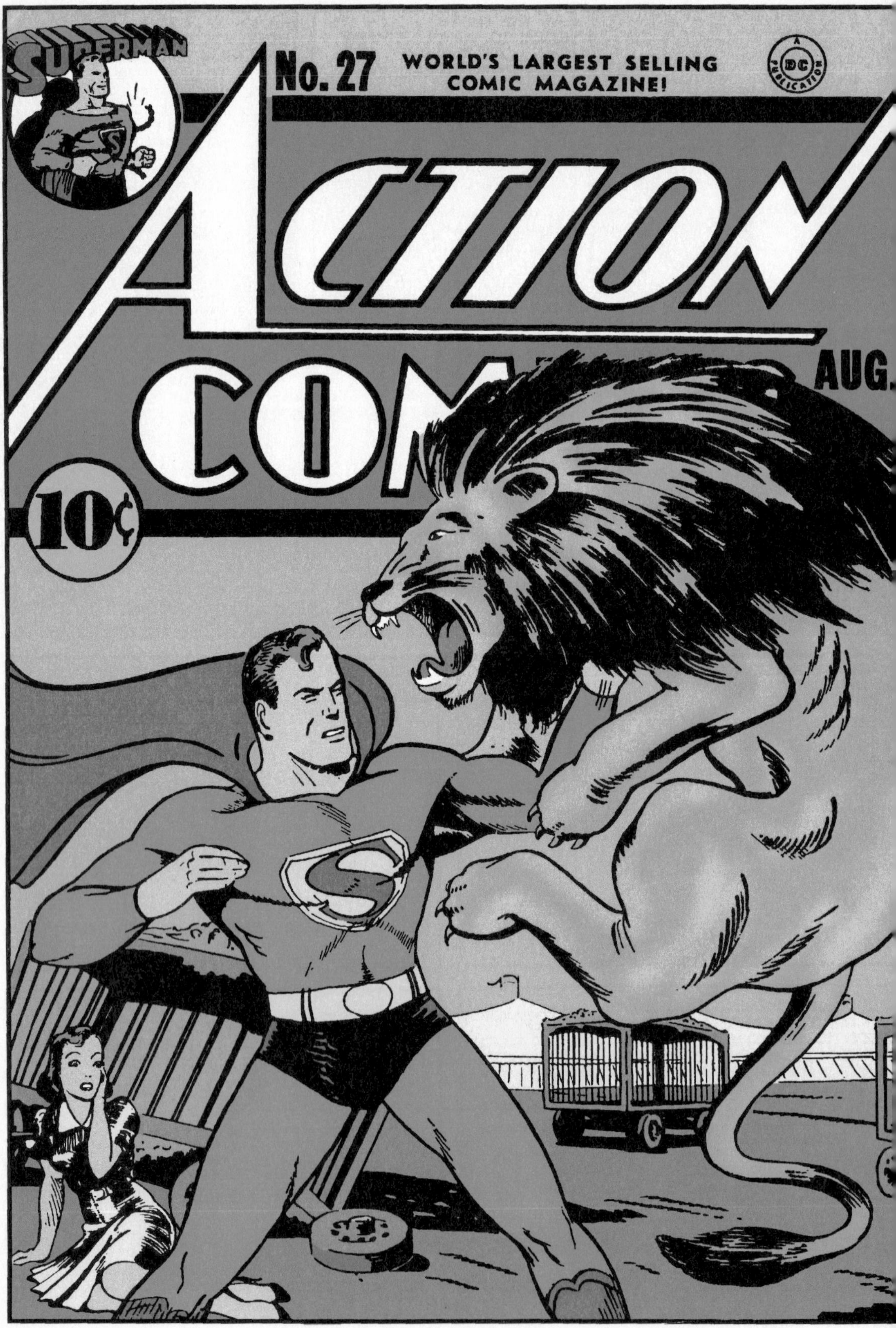
SUPERMAN
No. 27
WORLD'S LARGEST SELLING
COMIC MAGAZINE!
A DC PUBLICATION
ACTION
COM
AUG.
10¢

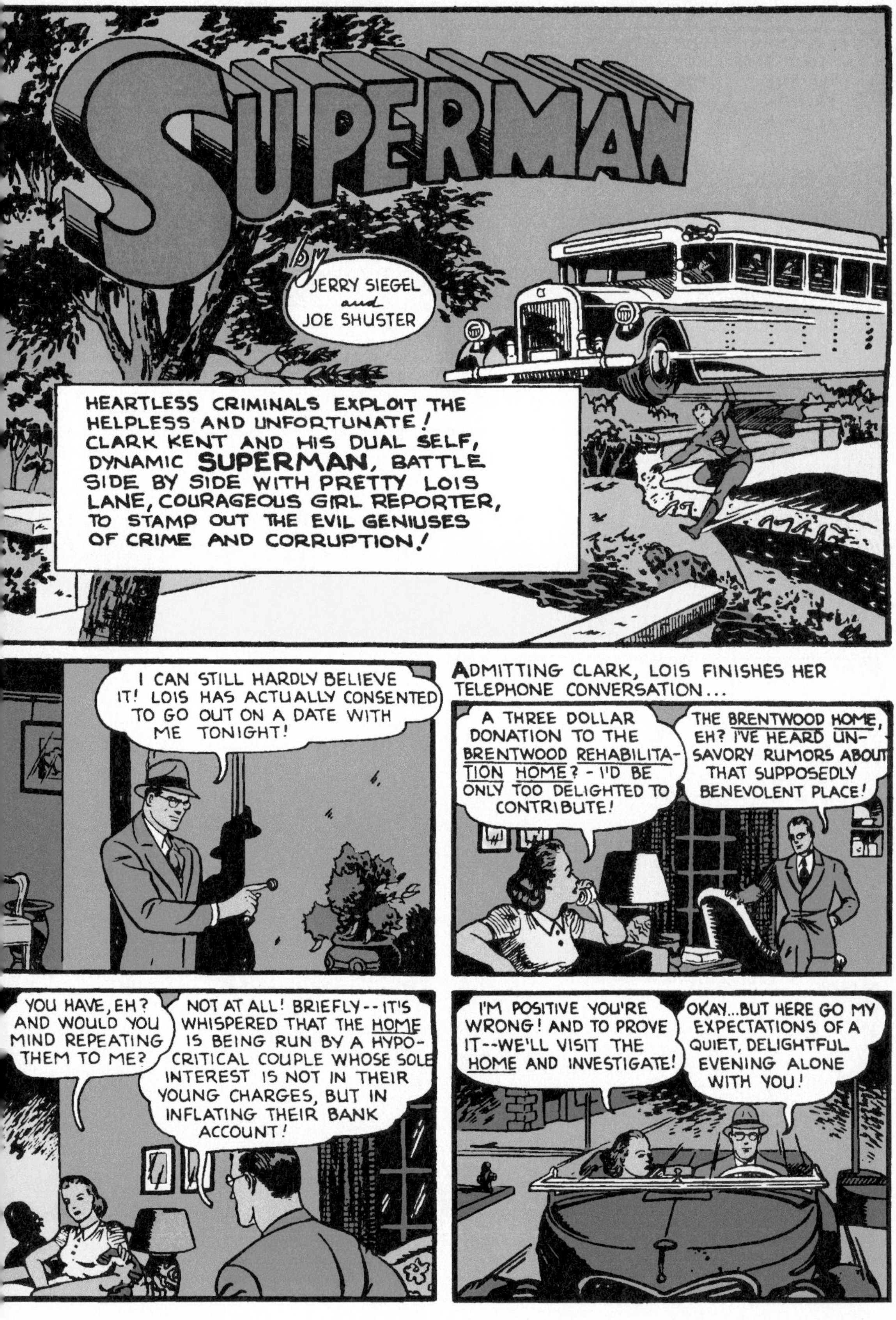
SUPERMAN
by
JERRY SIEGEL and JOE SHUSTER
HEARTLESS CRIMINALS EXPLOIT THE HELPLESS AND UNFORTUNATE! CLARK KENT AND HIS DUAL SELF, DYNAMIC SUPERMAN, BATTLE SIDE BY SIDE WITH PRETTY LOIS LANE, COURAGEOUS GIRL REPORTER, TO STAMP OUT THE EVIL GENIUSES OF CRIME AND CORRUPTION!
I CAN STILL HARDLY BELIEVE IT! LOIS HAS ACTUALLY CONSENTED TO GO OUT ON A DATE WITH ME TONIGHT!
ADMITTING CLARK, LOIS FINISHES HER TELEPHONE CONVERSATION...
A THREE DOLLAR DONATION TO THE BRENTWOOD REHABILITATION HOME? - I'D BE ONLY TOO DELIGHTED TO CONTRIBUTE!
THE BRENTWOOD HOME, EH? I'VE HEARD UNSAVORY RUMORS ABOUT THAT SUPPOSEDLY BENEVOLENT PLACE!
YOU HAVE, EH? AND WOULD YOU MIND REPEATING THEM TO ME?
NOT AT ALL! BRIEFLY--IT'S WHISPERED THAT THE HOME IS BEING RUN BY A HYPOCRITICAL COUPLE WHOSE SOLE INTEREST IS NOT IN THEIR YOUNG CHARGES, BUT IN INFLATING THEIR BANK ACCOUNT!
I'M POSITIVE YOU'RE WRONG! AND TO PROVE IT--WE'LL VISIT THE HOME AND INVESTIGATE!
OKAY...BUT HERE GO MY EXPECTATIONS OF A QUIET, DELIGHTFUL EVENING ALONE WITH YOU!

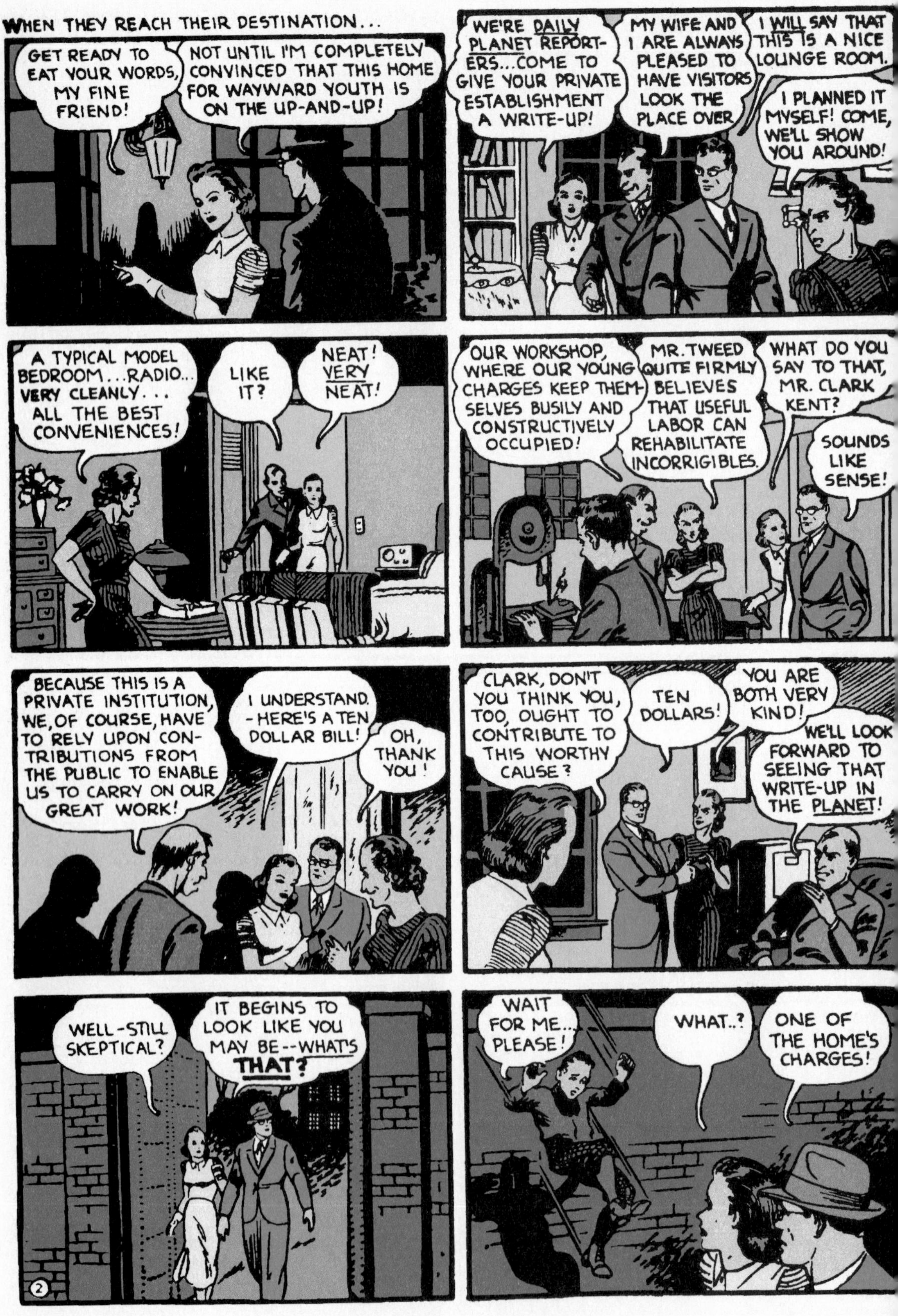
WHEN THEY REACH THEIR DESTINATION...
GET READY TO EAT YOUR WORDS, MY FINE FRIEND!
NOT UNTIL I'M COMPLETELY CONVINCED THAT THIS HOME FOR WAYWARD YOUTH IS ON THE UP-AND-UP!
WE'RE DAILY PLANET REPORTERS...COME TO GIVE YOUR PRIVATE ESTABLISHMENT A WRITE-UP!
MY WIFE AND I ARE ALWAYS PLEASED TO HAVE VISITORS LOOK THE PLACE OVER
I WILL SAY THAT THIS IS A NICE LOUNGE ROOM.
I PLANNED IT MYSELF! COME, WE'LL SHOW YOU AROUND!
A TYPICAL MODEL BEDROOM...RADIO... VERY CLEANLY... ALL THE BEST CONVENIENCES!
LIKE IT?
NEAT! VERY NEAT!
OUR WORKSHOP, WHERE OUR YOUNG CHARGES KEEP THEMSELVES BUSILY AND CONSTRUCTIVELY OCCUPIED!
MR. TWEED QUITE FIRMLY BELIEVES THAT USEFUL LABOR CAN REHABILITATE INCORRIGIBLES.
WHAT DO YOU SAY TO THAT, MR. CLARK KENT?
SOUNDS LIKE SENSE!
BECAUSE THIS IS A PRIVATE INSTITUTION, WE, OF COURSE, HAVE TO RELY UPON CONTRIBUTIONS FROM THE PUBLIC TO ENABLE US TO CARRY ON OUR GREAT WORK!
I UNDERSTAND. - HERE'S A TEN DOLLAR BILL!
OH, THANK YOU!
CLARK, DON'T YOU THINK YOU, TOO, OUGHT TO CONTRIBUTE TO THIS WORTHY CAUSE?
TEN DOLLARS!
YOU ARE BOTH VERY KIND!
WE'LL LOOK FORWARD TO SEEING THAT WRITE-UP IN THE PLANET!
WELL-STILL SKEPTICAL?
IT BEGINS TO LOOK LIKE YOU MAY BE--WHAT'S THAT?
2
WAIT FOR ME... PLEASE!
WHAT..?
ONE OF THE HOME'S CHARGES!

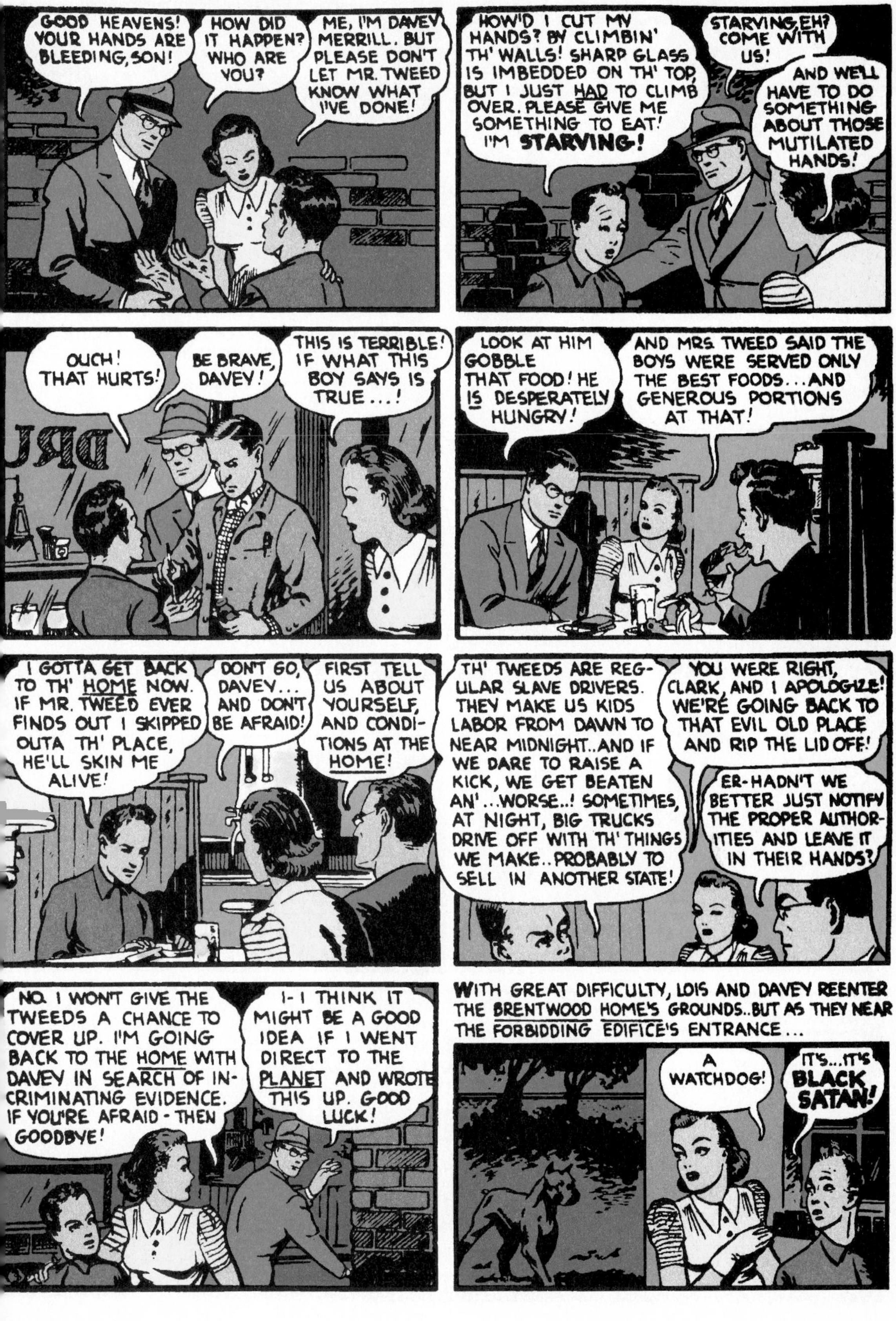
GOOD HEAVENS! YOUR HANDS ARE BLEEDING, SON!
HOW DID IT HAPPEN? WHO ARE YOU?
ME, I'M DAVEY MERRILL. BUT PLEASE DON'T LET MR. TWEED KNOW WHAT I'VE DONE!
HOW'D I CUT MY HANDS? BY CLIMBIN' TH' WALLS! SHARP GLASS IS IMBEDDED ON TH' TOP, BUT I JUST HAD TO CLIMB OVER. PLEASE GIVE ME SOMETHING TO EAT! I'M STARVING!
STARVING, EH? COME WITH US!
AND WE'LL HAVE TO DO SOMETHING ABOUT THOSE MUTILATED HANDS!
OUCH! THAT HURTS!
BE BRAVE, DAVEY!
THIS IS TERRIBLE! IF WHAT THIS BOY SAYS IS TRUE...!
LOOK AT HIM GOBBLE THAT FOOD! HE IS DESPERATELY HUNGRY!
AND MRS. TWEED SAID THE BOYS WERE SERVED ONLY THE BEST FOODS...AND GENEROUS PORTIONS AT THAT!
I GOTTA GET BACK TO TH' HOME NOW. IF MR. TWEED EVER FINDS OUT I SKIPPED OUTA TH' PLACE, HE'LL SKIN ME ALIVE!
DON'T GO, DAVEY... AND DON'T BE AFRAID!
FIRST TELL US ABOUT YOURSELF, AND CONDITIONS AT THE HOME!
TH' TWEEDS ARE REGULAR SLAVE DRIVERS. THEY MAKE US KIDS LABOR FROM DAWN TO NEAR MIDNIGHT..AND IF WE DARE TO RAISE A KICK, WE GET BEATEN AN'...WORSE..! SOMETIMES, AT NIGHT, BIG TRUCKS DRIVE OFF WITH TH' THINGS WE MAKE..PROBABLY TO SELL IN ANOTHER STATE!
YOU WERE RIGHT, CLARK, AND I APOLOGIZE! WE'RE GOING BACK TO THAT EVIL OLD PLACE AND RIP THE LID OFF!
ER-HADN'T WE BETTER JUST NOTIFY THE PROPER AUTHORITIES AND LEAVE IT IN THEIR HANDS?
NO. I WON'T GIVE THE TWEEDS A CHANCE TO COVER UP. I'M GOING BACK TO THE HOME WITH DAVEY IN SEARCH OF INCRIMINATING EVIDENCE. IF YOU'RE AFRAID - THEN GOODBYE!
I-I THINK IT MIGHT BE A GOOD IDEA IF I WENT DIRECT TO THE PLANET AND WROTE THIS UP. GOOD LUCK!
WITH GREAT DIFFICULTY, LOIS AND DAVEY REENTER THE BRENTWOOD HOME'S GROUNDS..BUT AS THEY NEAR THE FORBIDDING EDIFICE'S ENTRANCE...
A WATCHDOG!
IT'S...IT'S BLACK SATAN!

BLACK SATAN? I SHOULDA WARNED YA! THEY LEAVE HIM LOOSE SO WE WON'T DARE LEAVE TH' HOME! IF HE CATCHES US WE'RE GONERS!

HURRY! HURRY!

IF I CAN ONLY FIND THAT SKELETON KEY!

IF THIS FAILS TO WORK--!

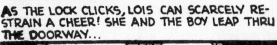

AS THE LOCK CLICKS, LOIS CAN SCARCELY RESTRAIN A CHEER! SHE AND THE BOY LEAP THRU THE DOORWAY...

HE'D HAVE HAD US IN ANOTHER SECOND!

SLAM TH' DOOR!

JUST IN TIME!

WHEW!

BLACK SATAN BARKING! THERE'S SOMETHING WRONG!

THE TWO INTRUDERS TIPTOE THRU THE DARKENED HOME..

SEE! THIS IS WHERE WE REALLY SLEEP!

CRAMMED TOGETHER LIKE CATTLE!--YOU CAN RETIRE, DAVEY, WHILE I CONTINUE TO LOOK FOR EVIDENCE!

THE TWEEDS MUST TERRIFY THEIR YOUNG CHARGES SO THOROUGHLY THAT THEY DON'T TALK EVEN AFTER THEY LEAVE THE HOME!

M-MRS. TWEED!

DAVEY MERRILL! WHAT ARE YOU DOING OUT OF YOUR BED--AND FULLY CLAD?

④

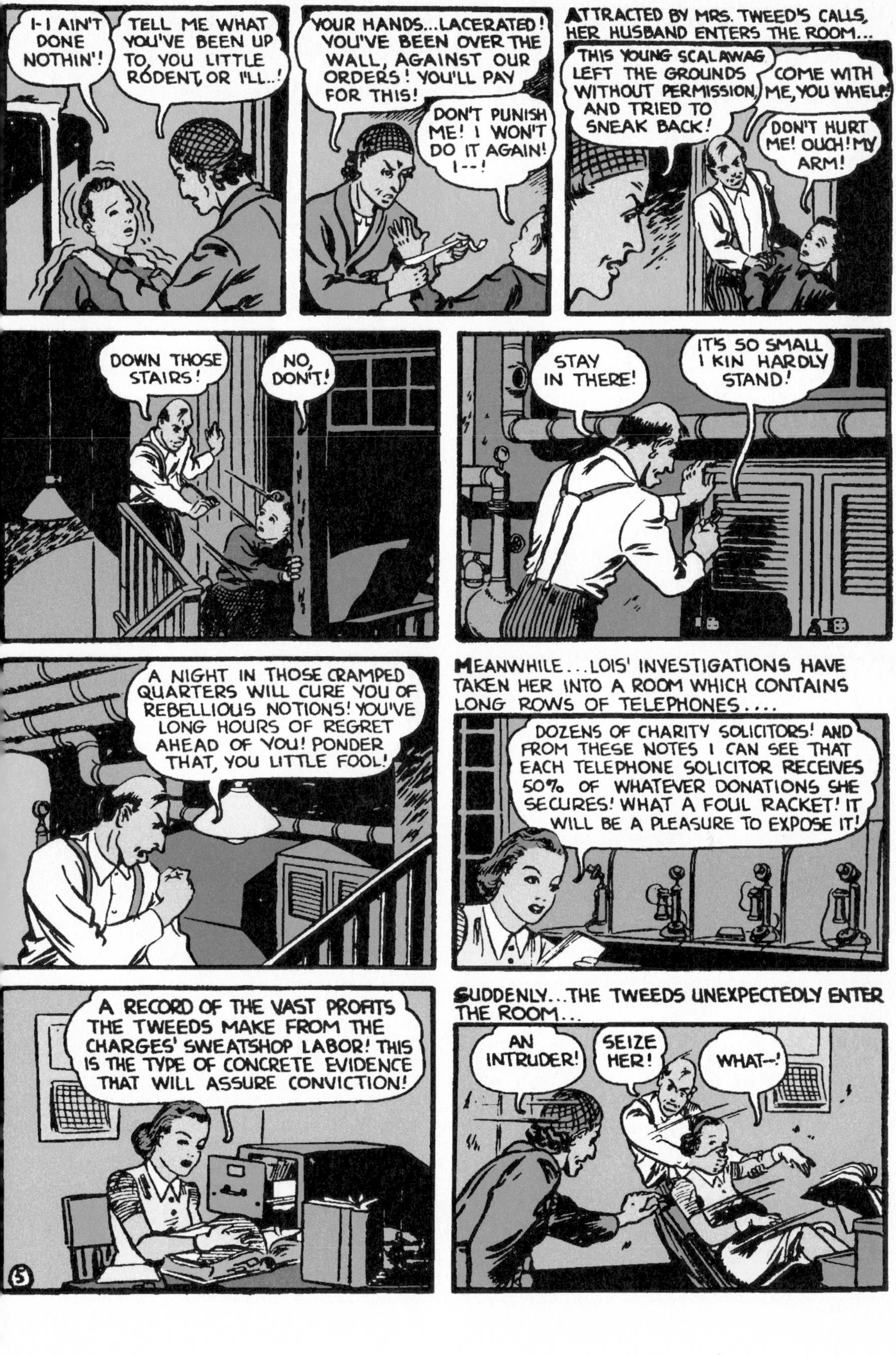

I-I AIN'T DONE NOTHIN'!
TELL ME WHAT YOU'VE BEEN UP TO, YOU LITTLE RODENT, OR I'LL...!
YOUR HANDS...LACERATED! YOU'VE BEEN OVER THE WALL, AGAINST OUR ORDERS! YOU'LL PAY FOR THIS!
DON'T PUNISH ME! I WON'T DO IT AGAIN! I--!
ATTRACTED BY MRS. TWEED'S CALLS, HER HUSBAND ENTERS THE ROOM...
THIS YOUNG SCALAWAG LEFT THE GROUNDS WITHOUT PERMISSION, AND TRIED TO SNEAK BACK!
COME WITH ME, YOU WHELP!
DON'T HURT ME! OUCH! MY ARM!
DOWN THOSE STAIRS!
NO, DON'T!
STAY IN THERE!
IT'S SO SMALL I KIN HARDLY STAND!
A NIGHT IN THOSE CRAMPED QUARTERS WILL CURE YOU OF REBELLIOUS NOTIONS! YOU'VE LONG HOURS OF REGRET AHEAD OF YOU! PONDER THAT, YOU LITTLE FOOL!
MEANWHILE...LOIS' INVESTIGATIONS HAVE TAKEN HER INTO A ROOM WHICH CONTAINS LONG ROWS OF TELEPHONES....
DOZENS OF CHARITY SOLICITORS! AND FROM THESE NOTES I CAN SEE THAT EACH TELEPHONE SOLICITOR RECEIVES 50% OF WHATEVER DONATIONS SHE SECURES! WHAT A FOUL RACKET! IT WILL BE A PLEASURE TO EXPOSE IT!
A RECORD OF THE VAST PROFITS THE TWEEDS MAKE FROM THE CHARGES' SWEATSHOP LABOR! THIS IS THE TYPE OF CONCRETE EVIDENCE THAT WILL ASSURE CONVICTION!
5
SUDDENLY...THE TWEEDS UNEXPECTEDLY ENTER THE ROOM...
AN INTRUDER!
SEIZE HER!
WHAT--!

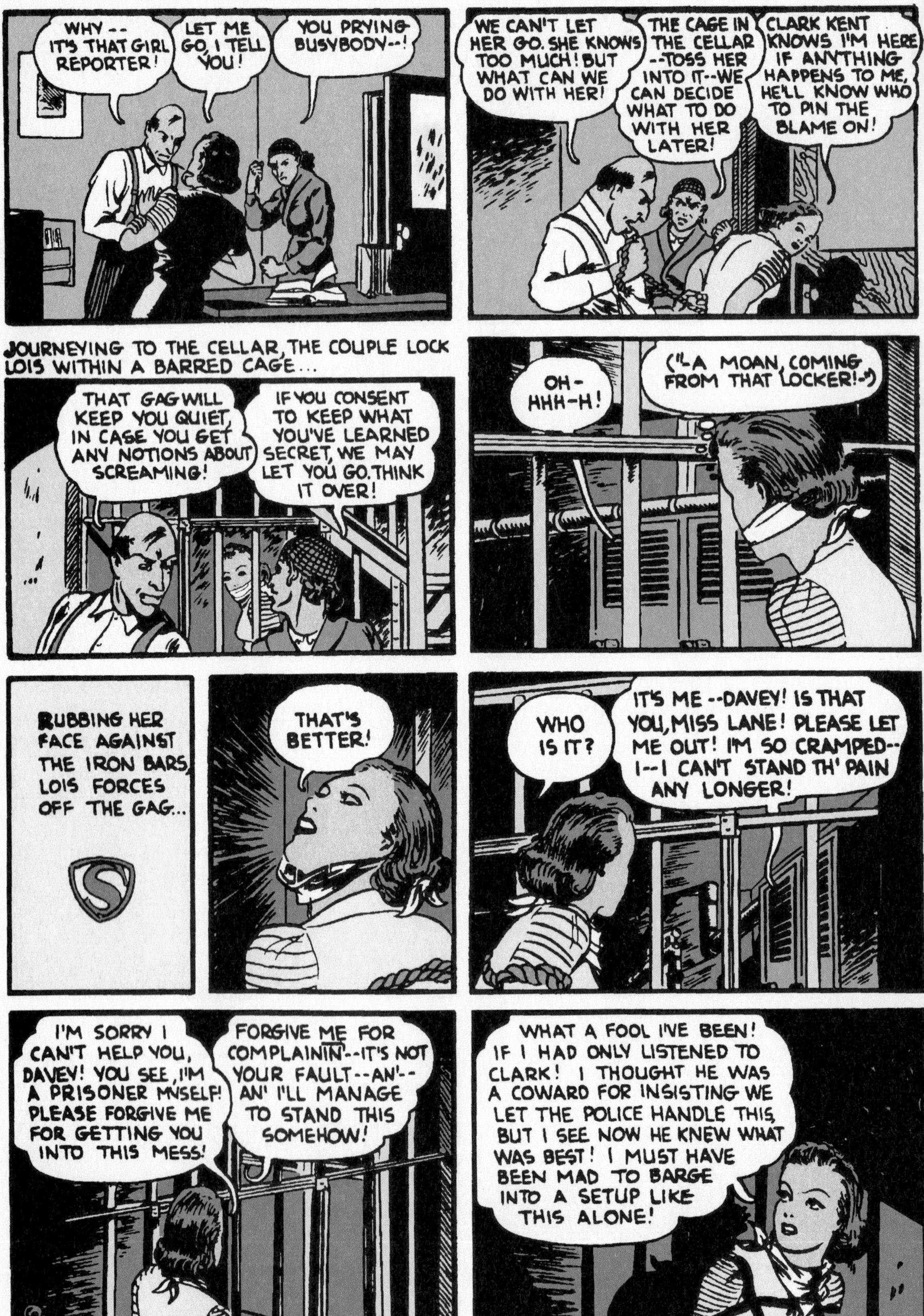
WHY -- IT'S THAT GIRL REPORTER!
LET ME GO, I TELL YOU!
YOU PRYING BUSYBODY--!
WE CAN'T LET HER GO. SHE KNOWS TOO MUCH! BUT WHAT CAN WE DO WITH HER!
THE CAGE IN THE CELLAR --TOSS HER INTO IT--WE CAN DECIDE WHAT TO DO WITH HER LATER!
CLARK KENT KNOWS I'M HERE IF ANYTHING HAPPENS TO ME, HE'LL KNOW WHO TO PIN THE BLAME ON!
JOURNEYING TO THE CELLAR, THE COUPLE LOCK LOIS WITHIN A BARRED CAGE...
THAT GAG WILL KEEP YOU QUIET, IN CASE YOU GET ANY NOTIONS ABOUT SCREAMING!
IF YOU CONSENT TO KEEP WHAT YOU'VE LEARNED SECRET, WE MAY LET YOU GO. THINK IT OVER!
OH-HHH-H!
("A MOAN, COMING FROM THAT LOCKER!-")
RUBBING HER FACE AGAINST THE IRON BARS, LOIS FORCES OFF THE GAG...
THAT'S BETTER!
WHO IS IT?
IT'S ME --DAVEY! IS THAT YOU, MISS LANE! PLEASE LET ME OUT! I'M SO CRAMPED-- I--I CAN'T STAND TH' PAIN ANY LONGER!
I'M SORRY I CAN'T HELP YOU, DAVEY! YOU SEE, I'M A PRISONER MYSELF! PLEASE FORGIVE ME FOR GETTING YOU INTO THIS MESS!
FORGIVE ME FOR COMPLAININ'--IT'S NOT YOUR FAULT--AN'-- AN' I'LL MANAGE TO STAND THIS SOMEHOW!
WHAT A FOOL I'VE BEEN! IF I HAD ONLY LISTENED TO CLARK! I THOUGHT HE WAS A COWARD FOR INSISTING WE LET THE POLICE HANDLE THIS, BUT I SEE NOW HE KNEW WHAT WAS BEST! I MUST HAVE BEEN MAD TO BARGE INTO A SETUP LIKE THIS ALONE!

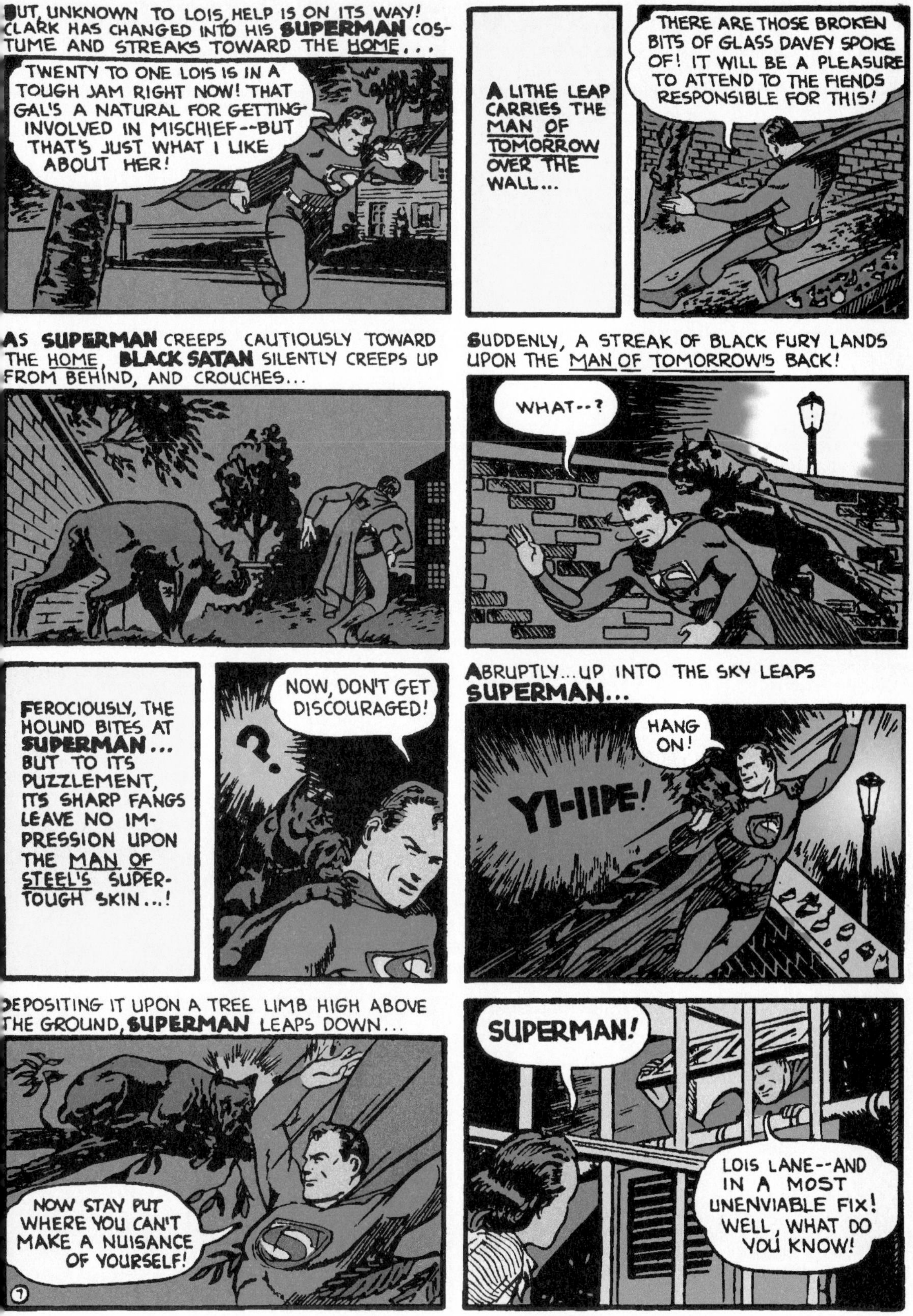
BUT, UNKNOWN TO LOIS, HELP IS ON ITS WAY! CLARK HAS CHANGED INTO HIS SUPERMAN COSTUME AND STREAKS TOWARD THE HOME...
TWENTY TO ONE LOIS IS IN A TOUGH JAM RIGHT NOW! THAT GAL'S A NATURAL FOR GETTING INVOLVED IN MISCHIEF--BUT THAT'S JUST WHAT I LIKE ABOUT HER!
A LITHE LEAP CARRIES THE MAN OF TOMORROW OVER THE WALL...
THERE ARE THOSE BROKEN BITS OF GLASS DAVEY SPOKE OF! IT WILL BE A PLEASURE TO ATTEND TO THE FIENDS RESPONSIBLE FOR THIS!
AS SUPERMAN CREEPS CAUTIOUSLY TOWARD THE HOME, BLACK SATAN SILENTLY CREEPS UP FROM BEHIND, AND CROUCHES...
SUDDENLY, A STREAK OF BLACK FURY LANDS UPON THE MAN OF TOMORROW'S BACK!
WHAT--?
FEROCIOUSLY, THE HOUND BITES AT SUPERMAN... BUT TO ITS PUZZLEMENT, ITS SHARP FANGS LEAVE NO IMPRESSION UPON THE MAN OF STEEL'S SUPER-TOUGH SKIN...!
NOW, DON'T GET DISCOURAGED!
?
ABRUPTLY...UP INTO THE SKY LEAPS SUPERMAN...
HANG ON!
YI-IIPE!
DEPOSITING IT UPON A TREE LIMB HIGH ABOVE THE GROUND, SUPERMAN LEAPS DOWN...
NOW STAY PUT WHERE YOU CAN'T MAKE A NUISANCE OF YOURSELF!
7
SUPERMAN!
LOIS LANE--AND IN A MOST UNENVIABLE FIX! WELL, WHAT DO YOU KNOW!

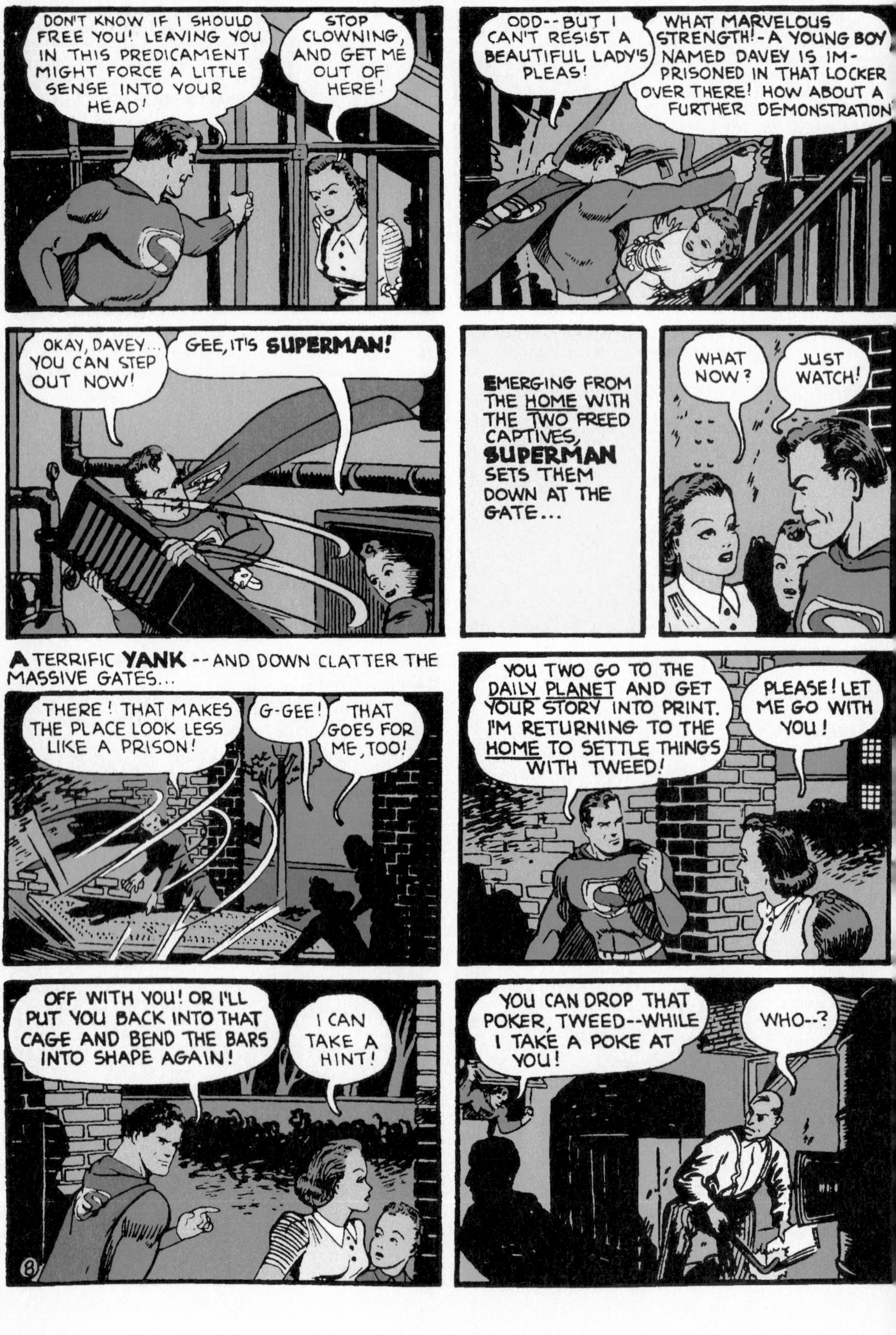
DON'T KNOW IF I SHOULD FREE YOU! LEAVING YOU IN THIS PREDICAMENT MIGHT FORCE A LITTLE SENSE INTO YOUR HEAD!
STOP CLOWNING, AND GET ME OUT OF HERE!
ODD--BUT I CAN'T RESIST A BEAUTIFUL LADY'S PLEAS!
WHAT MARVELOUS STRENGTH!-A YOUNG BOY NAMED DAVEY IS IMPRISONED IN THAT LOCKER OVER THERE! HOW ABOUT A FURTHER DEMONSTRATION
OKAY, DAVEY... YOU CAN STEP OUT NOW!
GEE, IT'S SUPERMAN!
EMERGING FROM THE HOME WITH THE TWO FREED CAPTIVES, SUPERMAN SETS THEM DOWN AT THE GATE...
WHAT NOW?
JUST WATCH!
A TERRIFIC YANK --AND DOWN CLATTER THE MASSIVE GATES...
THERE! THAT MAKES THE PLACE LOOK LESS LIKE A PRISON!
G-GEE!
THAT GOES FOR ME, TOO!
YOU TWO GO TO THE DAILY PLANET AND GET YOUR STORY INTO PRINT. I'M RETURNING TO THE HOME TO SETTLE THINGS WITH TWEED!
PLEASE! LET ME GO WITH YOU!
OFF WITH YOU! OR I'LL PUT YOU BACK INTO THAT CAGE AND BEND THE BARS INTO SHAPE AGAIN!
I CAN TAKE A HINT!
8
YOU CAN DROP THAT POKER, TWEED--WHILE I TAKE A POKE AT YOU!
WHO--?

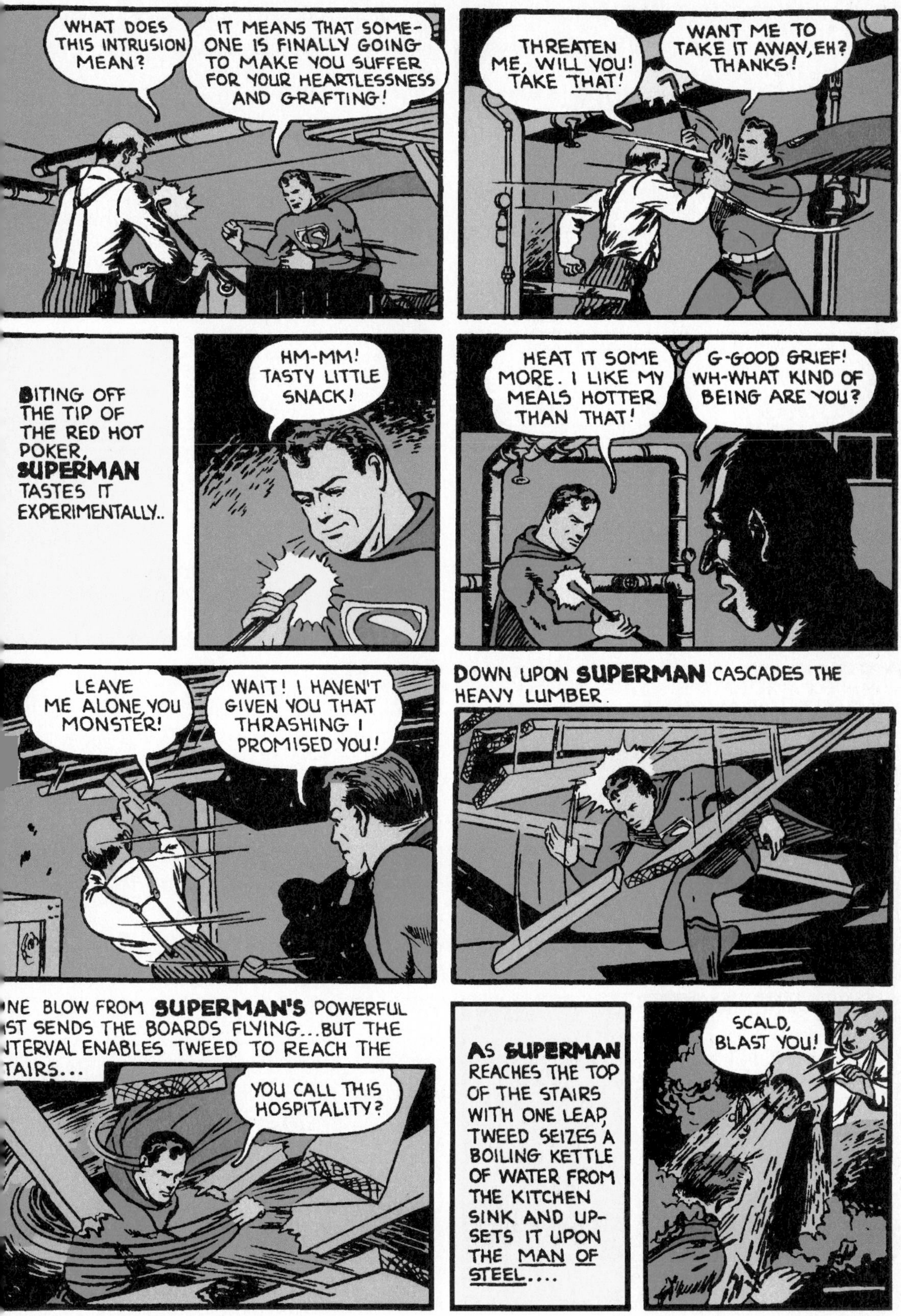
WHAT DOES THIS INTRUSION MEAN?
IT MEANS THAT SOME-ONE IS FINALLY GOING TO MAKE YOU SUFFER FOR YOUR HEARTLESSNESS AND GRAFTING!
THREATEN ME, WILL YOU! TAKE THAT!
WANT ME TO TAKE IT AWAY, EH? THANKS!
BITING OFF THE TIP OF THE RED HOT POKER, SUPERMAN TASTES IT EXPERIMENTALLY..
HM-MM! TASTY LITTLE SNACK!
HEAT IT SOME MORE. I LIKE MY MEALS HOTTER THAN THAT!
G-GOOD GRIEF! WH-WHAT KIND OF BEING ARE YOU?
LEAVE ME ALONE, YOU MONSTER!
WAIT! I HAVEN'T GIVEN YOU THAT THRASHING I PROMISED YOU!
DOWN UPON SUPERMAN CASCADES THE HEAVY LUMBER.
NE BLOW FROM SUPERMAN'S POWERFUL IST SENDS THE BOARDS FLYING...BUT THE NTERVAL ENABLES TWEED TO REACH THE TAIRS...
YOU CALL THIS HOSPITALITY?
AS SUPERMAN REACHES THE TOP OF THE STAIRS WITH ONE LEAP, TWEED SEIZES A BOILING KETTLE OF WATER FROM THE KITCHEN SINK AND UP-SETS IT UPON THE MAN OF STEEL....
SCALD, BLAST YOU!

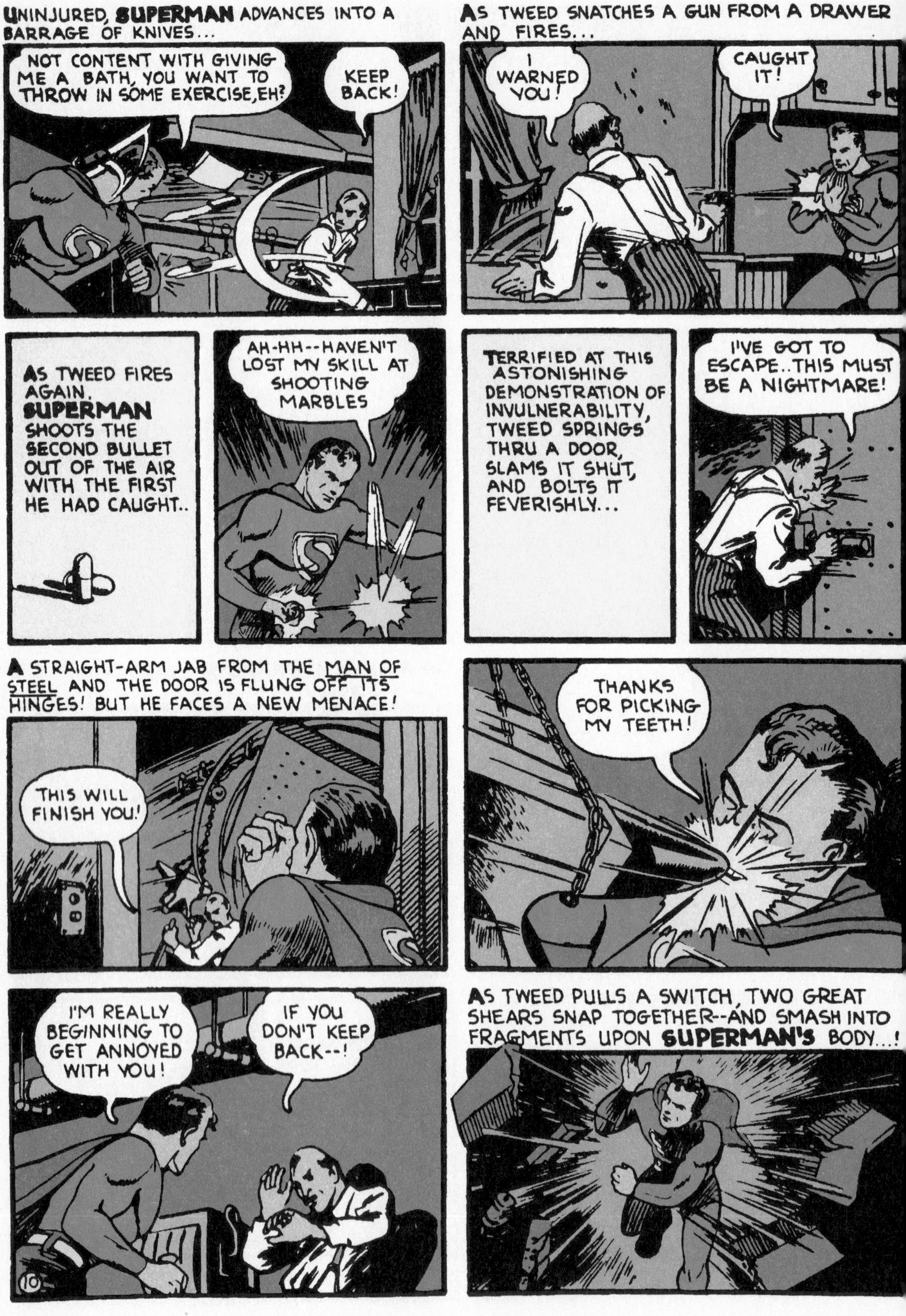
UNINJURED, SUPERMAN ADVANCES INTO A BARRAGE OF KNIVES...
NOT CONTENT WITH GIVING ME A BATH, YOU WANT TO THROW IN SOME EXERCISE, EH?
KEEP BACK!
AS TWEED SNATCHES A GUN FROM A DRAWER AND FIRES...
I WARNED YOU!
CAUGHT IT!
AS TWEED FIRES AGAIN, SUPERMAN SHOOTS THE SECOND BULLET OUT OF THE AIR WITH THE FIRST HE HAD CAUGHT..
AH-HH--HAVEN'T LOST MY SKILL AT SHOOTING MARBLES
TERRIFIED AT THIS ASTONISHING DEMONSTRATION OF INVULNERABILITY, TWEED SPRINGS THRU A DOOR, SLAMS IT SHUT, AND BOLTS IT FEVERISHLY...
I'VE GOT TO ESCAPE..THIS MUST BE A NIGHTMARE!
A STRAIGHT-ARM JAB FROM THE MAN OF STEEL AND THE DOOR IS FLUNG OFF ITS HINGES! BUT HE FACES A NEW MENACE!
THIS WILL FINISH YOU!
THANKS FOR PICKING MY TEETH!
I'M REALLY BEGINNING TO GET ANNOYED WITH YOU!
IF YOU DON'T KEEP BACK--!
10
AS TWEED PULLS A SWITCH, TWO GREAT SHEARS SNAP TOGETHER--AND SMASH INTO FRAGMENTS UPON SUPERMAN'S BODY...!

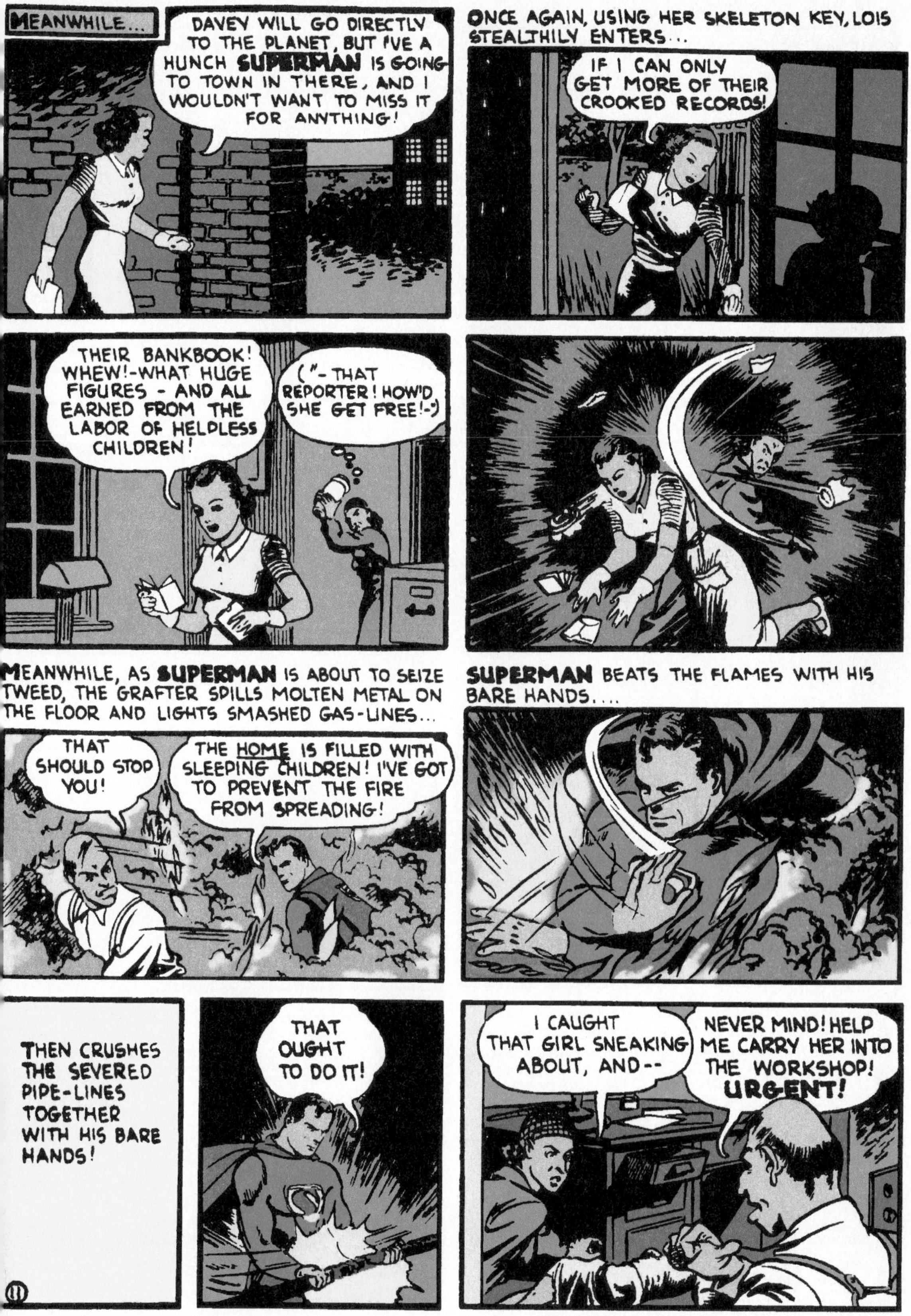

MEANWHILE...
DAVEY WILL GO DIRECTLY TO THE PLANET, BUT I'VE A HUNCH SUPERMAN IS GOING TO TOWN IN THERE, AND I WOULDN'T WANT TO MISS IT FOR ANYTHING!
ONCE AGAIN, USING HER SKELETON KEY, LOIS STEALTHILY ENTERS...
IF I CAN ONLY GET MORE OF THEIR CROOKED RECORDS!
THEIR BANKBOOK! WHEW!-WHAT HUGE FIGURES - AND ALL EARNED FROM THE LABOR OF HELPLESS CHILDREN!
("-THAT REPORTER! HOW'D SHE GET FREE!-")
MEANWHILE, AS SUPERMAN IS ABOUT TO SEIZE TWEED, THE GRAFTER SPILLS MOLTEN METAL ON THE FLOOR AND LIGHTS SMASHED GAS-LINES...
THAT SHOULD STOP YOU!
THE HOME IS FILLED WITH SLEEPING CHILDREN! I'VE GOT TO PREVENT THE FIRE FROM SPREADING!
SUPERMAN BEATS THE FLAMES WITH HIS BARE HANDS....
THEN CRUSHES THE SEVERED PIPE-LINES TOGETHER WITH HIS BARE HANDS!
11
THAT OUGHT TO DO IT!
I CAUGHT THAT GIRL SNEAKING ABOUT, AND--
NEVER MIND! HELP ME CARRY HER INTO THE WORKSHOP! URGENT!

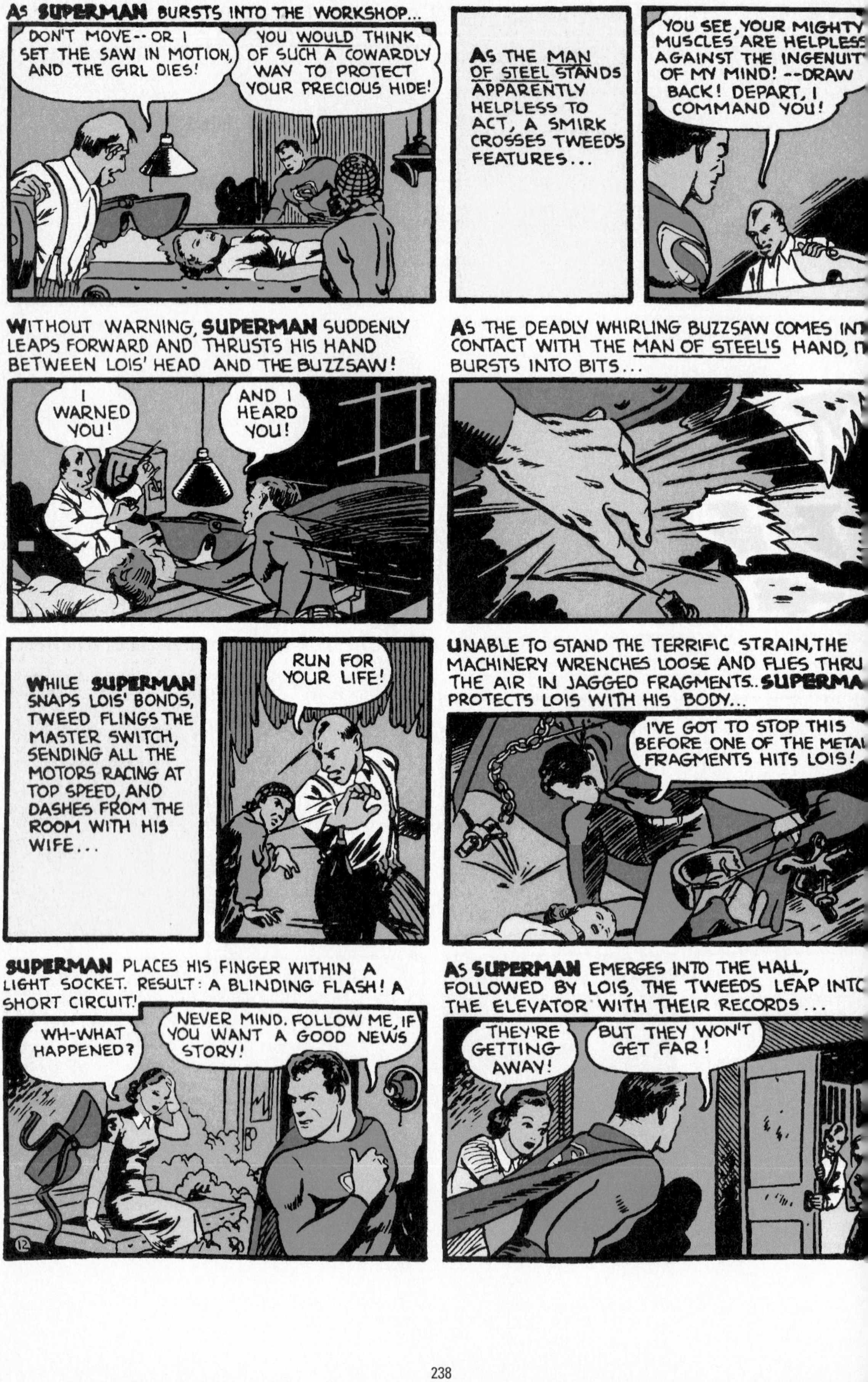

AS SUPERMAN BURSTS INTO THE WORKSHOP...
DON'T MOVE--OR I SET THE SAW IN MOTION, AND THE GIRL DIES!
YOU WOULD THINK OF SUCH A COWARDLY WAY TO PROTECT YOUR PRECIOUS HIDE!
AS THE MAN OF STEEL STANDS APPARENTLY HELPLESS TO ACT, A SMIRK CROSSES TWEED'S FEATURES...
YOU SEE, YOUR MIGHTY MUSCLES ARE HELPLES AGAINST THE INGENUIT OF MY MIND! --DRAW BACK! DEPART, I COMMAND YOU!
WITHOUT WARNING, SUPERMAN SUDDENLY LEAPS FORWARD AND THRUSTS HIS HAND BETWEEN LOIS' HEAD AND THE BUZZSAW!
I WARNED YOU!
AND I HEARD YOU!
AS THE DEADLY WHIRLING BUZZSAW COMES IN CONTACT WITH THE MAN OF STEEL'S HAND, I BURSTS INTO BITS...
WHILE SUPERMAN SNAPS LOIS' BONDS, TWEED FLINGS THE MASTER SWITCH, SENDING ALL THE MOTORS RACING AT TOP SPEED, AND DASHES FROM THE ROOM WITH HIS WIFE...
RUN FOR YOUR LIFE!
UNABLE TO STAND THE TERRIFIC STRAIN, THE MACHINERY WRENCHES LOOSE AND FLIES THRU THE AIR IN JAGGED FRAGMENTS.. SUPERMA PROTECTS LOIS WITH HIS BODY...
I'VE GOT TO STOP THIS BEFORE ONE OF THE META FRAGMENTS HITS LOIS!
SUPERMAN PLACES HIS FINGER WITHIN A LIGHT SOCKET. RESULT: A BLINDING FLASH! A SHORT CIRCUIT!
WH-WHAT HAPPENED?
NEVER MIND. FOLLOW ME, IF YOU WANT A GOOD NEWS STORY!
12
AS SUPERMAN EMERGES INTO THE HALL, FOLLOWED BY LOIS, THE TWEEDS LEAP INTO THE ELEVATOR WITH THEIR RECORDS...
THEY'RE GETTING AWAY!
BUT THEY WON'T GET FAR!

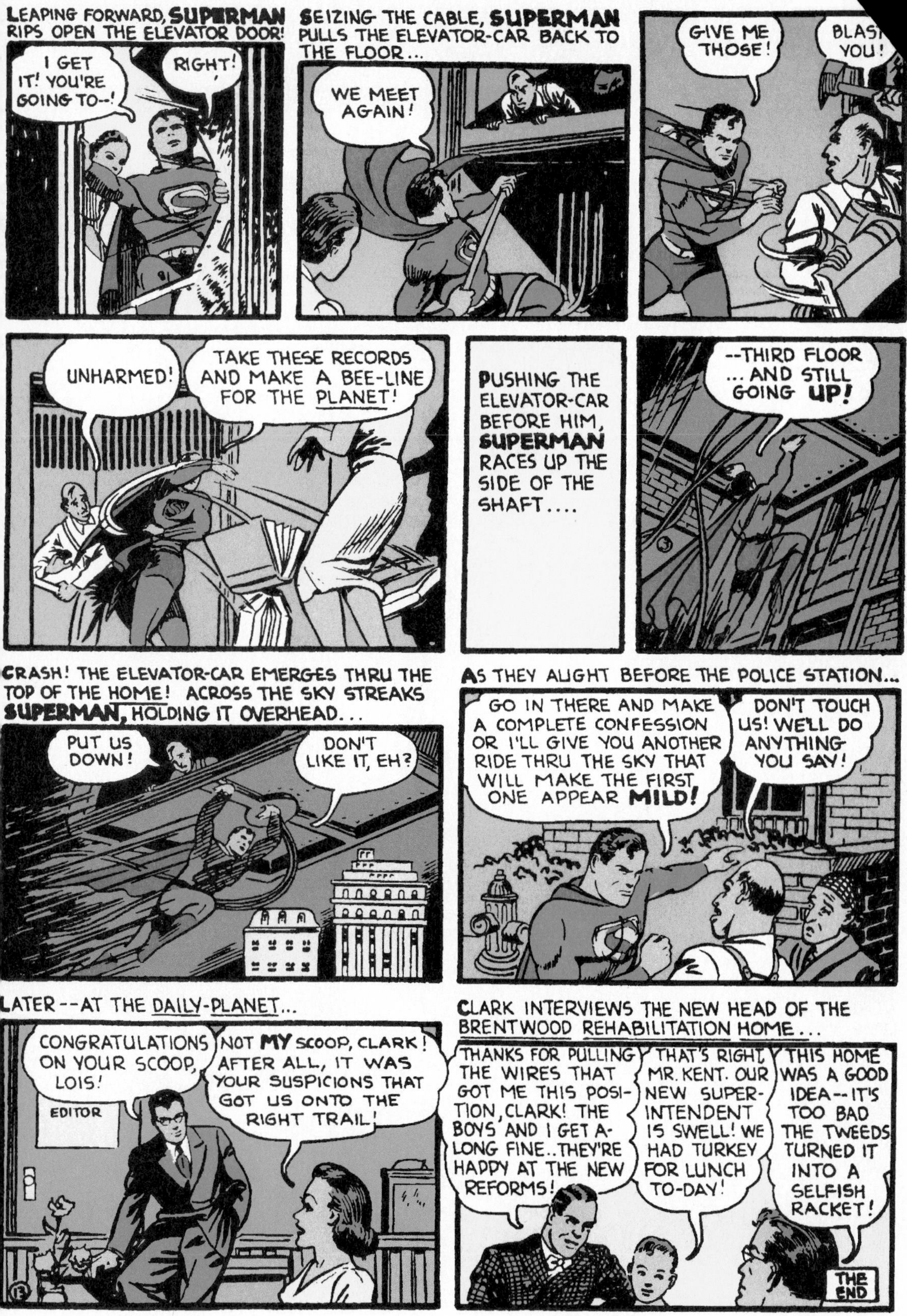
LEAPING FORWARD, SUPERMAN RIPS OPEN THE ELEVATOR DOOR!
I GET IT! YOU'RE GOING TO--!
RIGHT!
SEIZING THE CABLE, SUPERMAN PULLS THE ELEVATOR-CAR BACK TO THE FLOOR...
WE MEET AGAIN!
GIVE ME THOSE!
BLAS YOU!
UNHARMED!
TAKE THESE RECORDS AND MAKE A BEE-LINE FOR THE PLANET!
PUSHING THE ELEVATOR-CAR BEFORE HIM, SUPERMAN RACES UP THE SIDE OF THE SHAFT....
--THIRD FLOOR ... AND STILL GOING UP!
CRASH! THE ELEVATOR-CAR EMERGES THRU THE TOP OF THE HOME! ACROSS THE SKY STREAKS SUPERMAN, HOLDING IT OVERHEAD...
PUT US DOWN!
DON'T LIKE IT, EH?
AS THEY ALIGHT BEFORE THE POLICE STATION...
GO IN THERE AND MAKE A COMPLETE CONFESSION OR I'LL GIVE YOU ANOTHER RIDE THRU THE SKY THAT WILL MAKE THE FIRST ONE APPEAR MILD!
DON'T TOUCH US! WE'LL DO ANYTHING YOU SAY!
LATER--AT THE DAILY-PLANET...
CONGRATULATIONS ON YOUR SCOOP, LOIS!
NOT MY SCOOP, CLARK! AFTER ALL, IT WAS YOUR SUSPICIONS THAT GOT US ONTO THE RIGHT TRAIL!
EDITOR
CLARK INTERVIEWS THE NEW HEAD OF THE BRENTWOOD REHABILITATION HOME...
THANKS FOR PULLING THE WIRES THAT GOT ME THIS POSITION, CLARK! THE BOYS AND I GET ALONG FINE..THEY'RE HAPPY AT THE NEW REFORMS!
THAT'S RIGHT, MR. KENT. OUR NEW SUPERINTENDENT IS SWELL! WE HAD TURKEY FOR LUNCH TO-DAY!
THIS HOME WAS A GOOD IDEA--IT'S TOO BAD THE TWEEDS TURNED IT INTO A SELFISH RACKET!
THE END

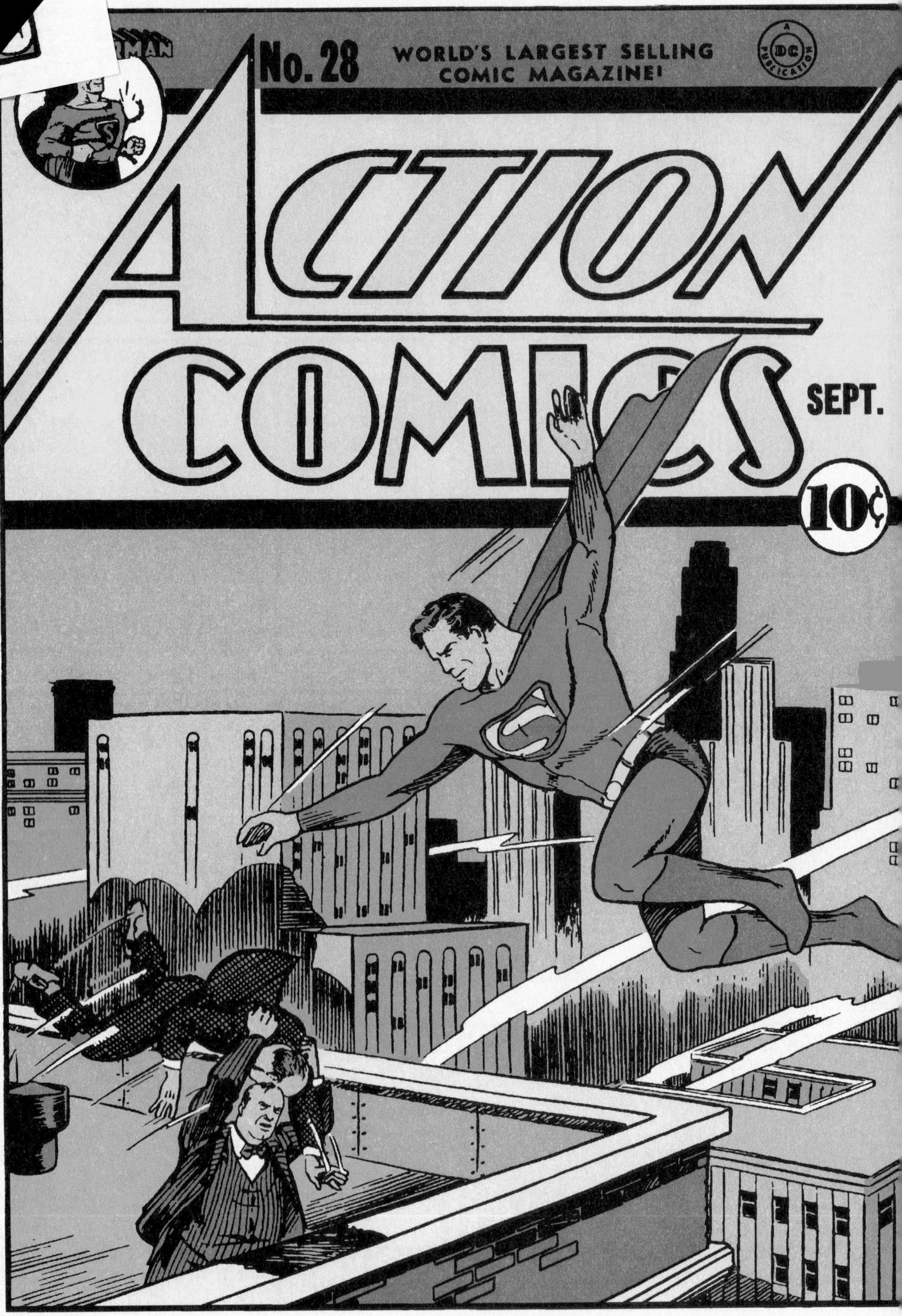
No. 28
WORLD'S LARGEST SELLING
COMIC MAGAZINE!
A DC PUBLICATION
ACTION
COMICS
SEPT.
10¢

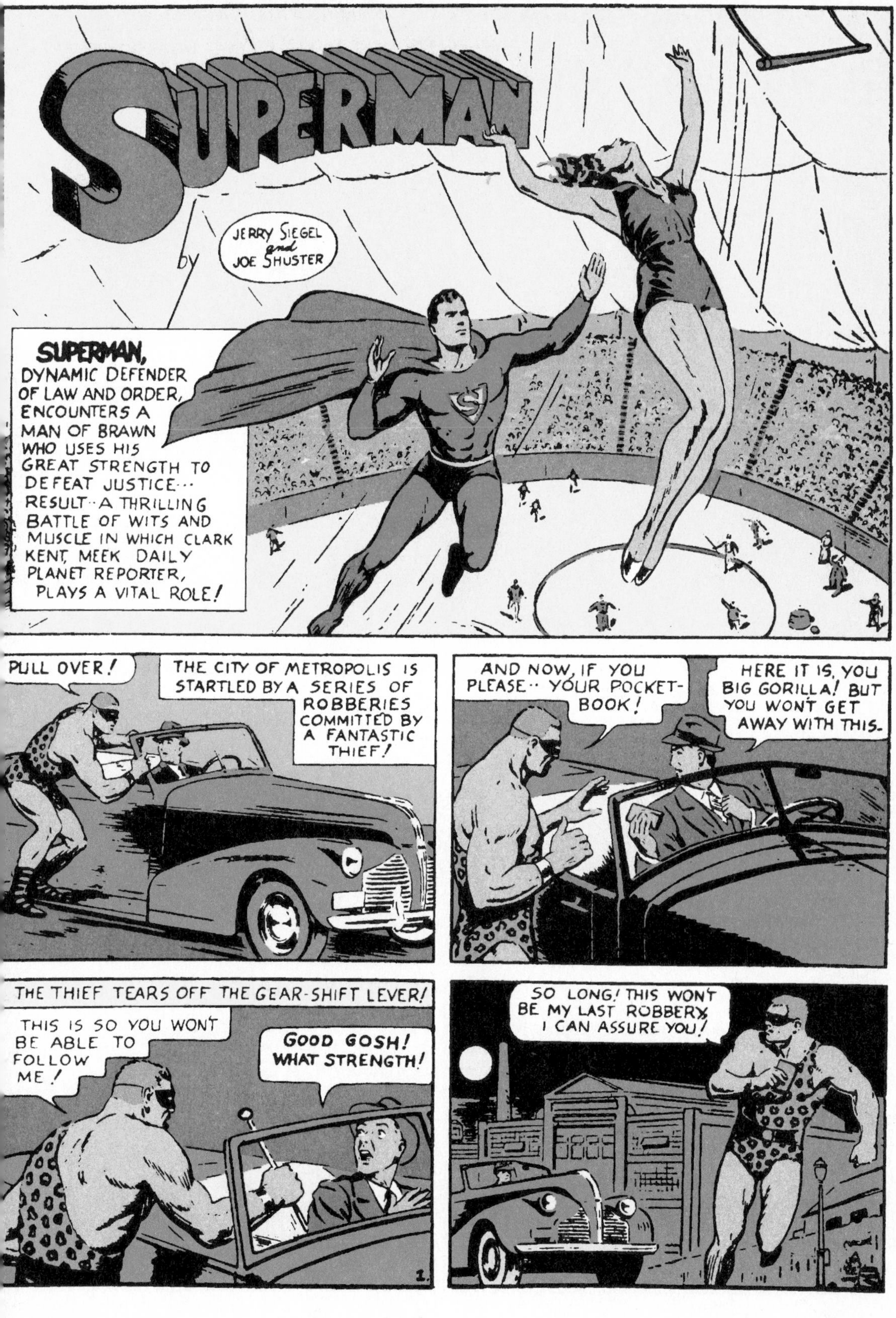
SUPERMAN
by JERRY SIEGEL and JOE SHUSTER
SUPERMAN, DYNAMIC DEFENDER OF LAW AND ORDER, ENCOUNTERS A MAN OF BRAWN WHO USES HIS GREAT STRENGTH TO DEFEAT JUSTICE... RESULT.. A THRILLING BATTLE OF WITS AND MUSCLE IN WHICH CLARK KENT, MEEK DAILY PLANET REPORTER, PLAYS A VITAL ROLE!
PULL OVER!
THE CITY OF METROPOLIS IS STARTLED BY A SERIES OF ROBBERIES COMMITTED BY A FANTASTIC THIEF!
AND NOW, IF YOU PLEASE.. YOUR POCKET-BOOK!
HERE IT IS, YOU BIG GORILLA! BUT YOU WON'T GET AWAY WITH THIS.
THE THIEF TEARS OFF THE GEAR-SHIFT LEVER!
THIS IS SO YOU WON'T BE ABLE TO FOLLOW ME!
GOOD GOSH! WHAT STRENGTH!
1.
SO LONG! THIS WON'T BE MY LAST ROBBERY, I CAN ASSURE YOU!

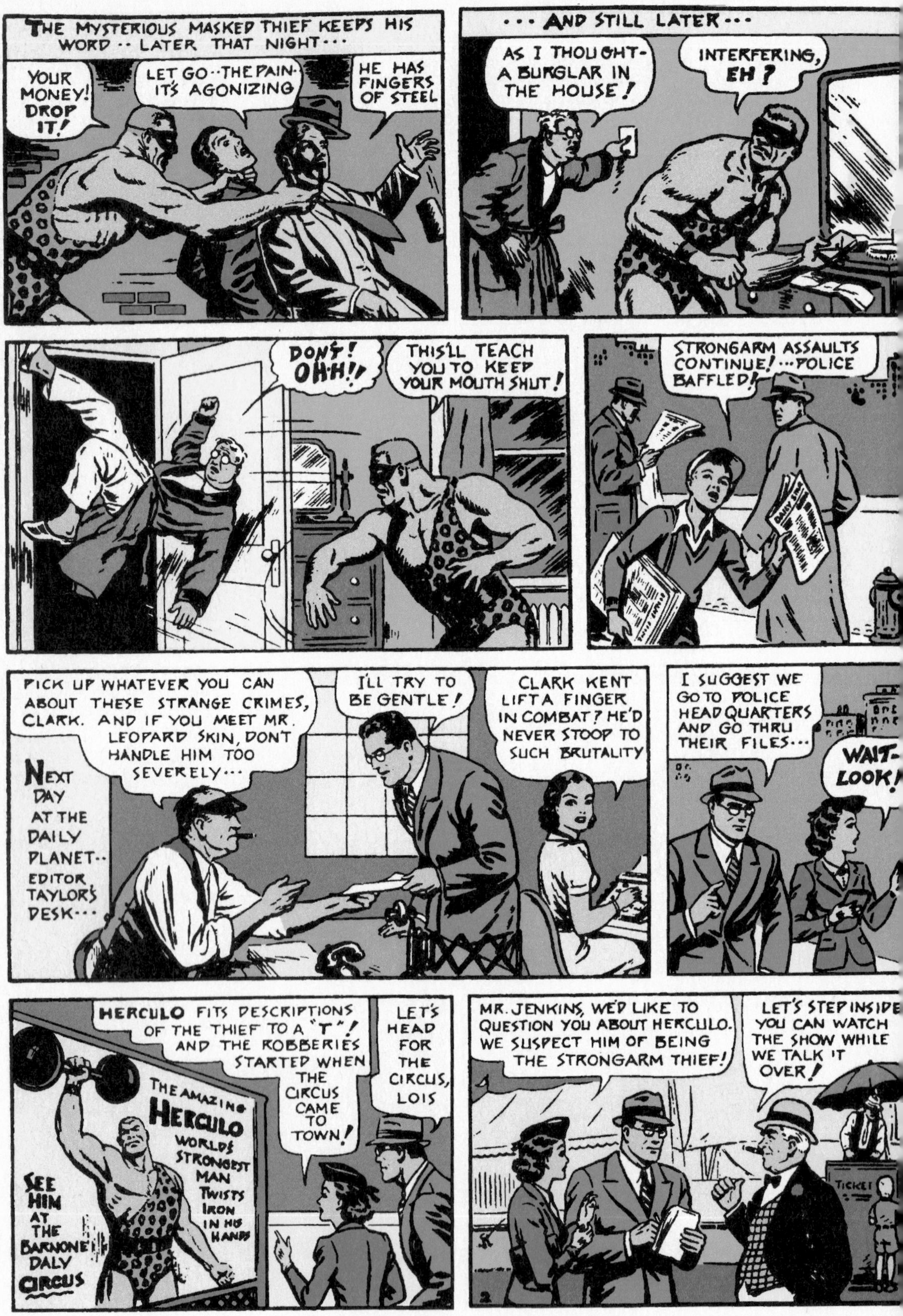

THE MYSTERIOUS MASKED THIEF KEEPS HIS WORD -- LATER THAT NIGHT ---
YOUR MONEY! DROP IT!
LET GO -- THE PAIN -- IT'S AGONIZING
HE HAS FINGERS OF STEEL
--- AND STILL LATER ---
AS I THOUGHT - A BURGLAR IN THE HOUSE!
INTERFERING, EH?
DON'T! OH-H!!
THIS'LL TEACH YOU TO KEEP YOUR MOUTH SHUT!
STRONGARM ASSAULTS CONTINUE! ... POLICE BAFFLED!
NEXT DAY AT THE DAILY PLANET -- EDITOR TAYLOR'S DESK ---
PICK UP WHATEVER YOU CAN ABOUT THESE STRANGE CRIMES, CLARK. AND IF YOU MEET MR. LEOPARD SKIN, DON'T HANDLE HIM TOO SEVERELY ---
I'LL TRY TO BE GENTLE!
CLARK KENT LIFT A FINGER IN COMBAT? HE'D NEVER STOOP TO SUCH BRUTALITY
I SUGGEST WE GO TO POLICE HEADQUARTERS AND GO THRU THEIR FILES ---
WAIT - LOOK!
THE AMAZING HERCULO WORLD'S STRONGEST MAN TWISTS IRON IN HIS HANDS
SEE HIM AT THE BARNONE' DALY CIRCUS
HERCULO FITS DESCRIPTIONS OF THE THIEF TO A "T"! AND THE ROBBERIES STARTED WHEN THE CIRCUS CAME TO TOWN!
LET'S HEAD FOR THE CIRCUS, LOIS
MR. JENKINS, WE'D LIKE TO QUESTION YOU ABOUT HERCULO. WE SUSPECT HIM OF BEING THE STRONGARM THIEF!
LET'S STEP INSIDE YOU CAN WATCH THE SHOW WHILE WE TALK IT OVER!

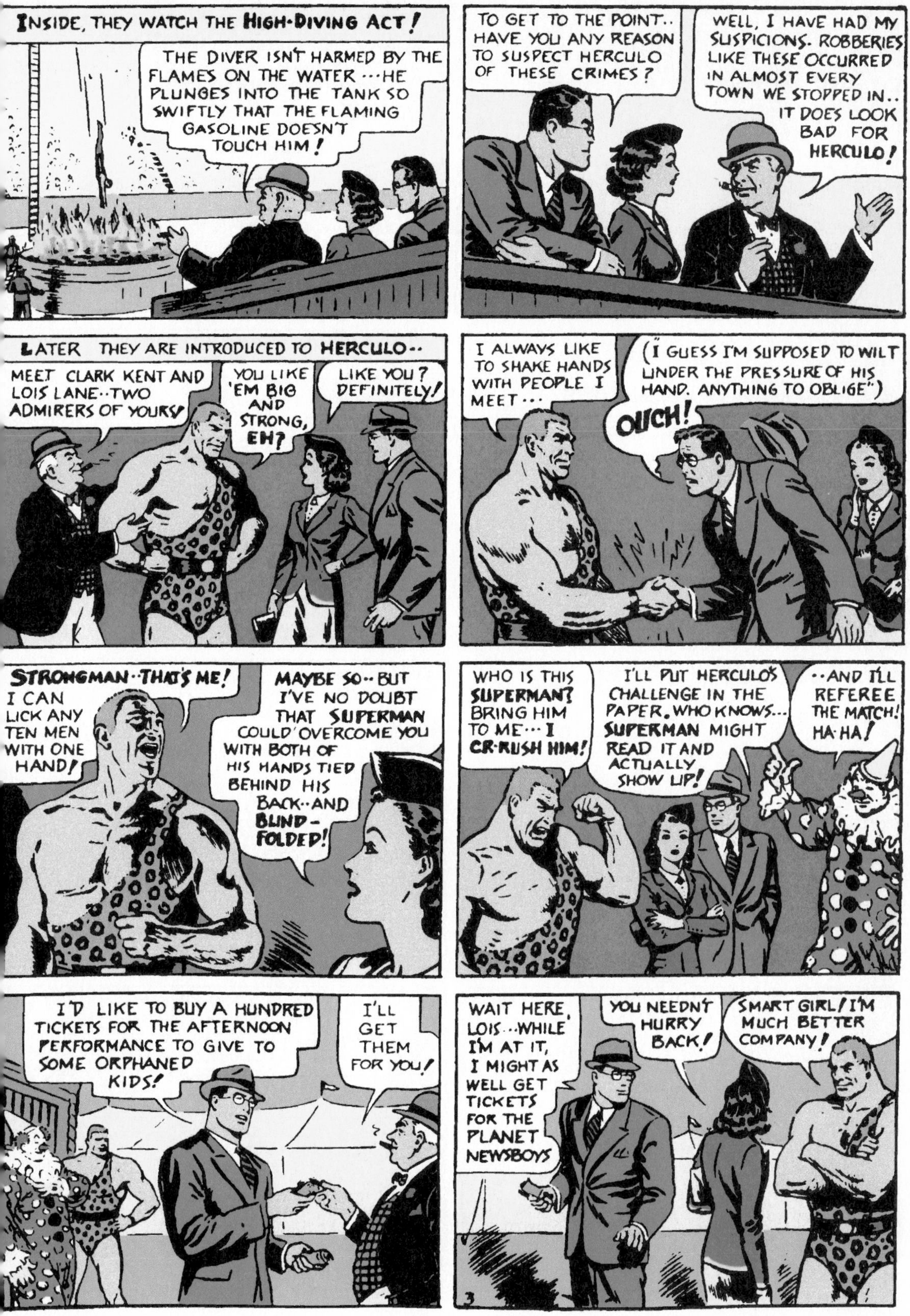
INSIDE, THEY WATCH THE HIGH-DIVING ACT!
THE DIVER ISN'T HARMED BY THE FLAMES ON THE WATER ... HE PLUNGES INTO THE TANK SO SWIFTLY THAT THE FLAMING GASOLINE DOESN'T TOUCH HIM!
TO GET TO THE POINT.. HAVE YOU ANY REASON TO SUSPECT HERCULO OF THESE CRIMES?
WELL, I HAVE HAD MY SUSPICIONS. ROBBERIES LIKE THESE OCCURRED IN ALMOST EVERY TOWN WE STOPPED IN.. IT DOES LOOK BAD FOR HERCULO!
LATER THEY ARE INTRODUCED TO HERCULO..
MEET CLARK KENT AND LOIS LANE..TWO ADMIRERS OF YOURS!
YOU LIKE 'EM BIG AND STRONG, EH?
LIKE YOU? DEFINITELY!
I ALWAYS LIKE TO SHAKE HANDS WITH PEOPLE I MEET...
("I GUESS I'M SUPPOSED TO WILT UNDER THE PRESSURE OF HIS HAND. ANYTHING TO OBLIGE")
OUCH!
STRONGMAN..THAT'S ME! I CAN LICK ANY TEN MEN WITH ONE HAND!
MAYBE SO.. BUT I'VE NO DOUBT THAT SUPERMAN COULD OVERCOME YOU WITH BOTH OF HIS HANDS TIED BEHIND HIS BACK..AND BLIND-FOLDED!
WHO IS THIS SUPERMAN? BRING HIM TO ME... I CR-RUSH HIM!
I'LL PUT HERCULO'S CHALLENGE IN THE PAPER. WHO KNOWS... SUPERMAN MIGHT READ IT AND ACTUALLY SHOW UP!
..AND I'LL REFEREE THE MATCH! HA-HA!
I'D LIKE TO BUY A HUNDRED TICKETS FOR THE AFTERNOON PERFORMANCE TO GIVE TO SOME ORPHANED KIDS!
I'LL GET THEM FOR YOU!
WAIT HERE, LOIS...WHILE I'M AT IT, I MIGHT AS WELL GET TICKETS FOR THE PLANET NEWSBOYS
YOU NEEDN'T HURRY BACK!
SMART GIRL! I'M MUCH BETTER COMPANY!
3

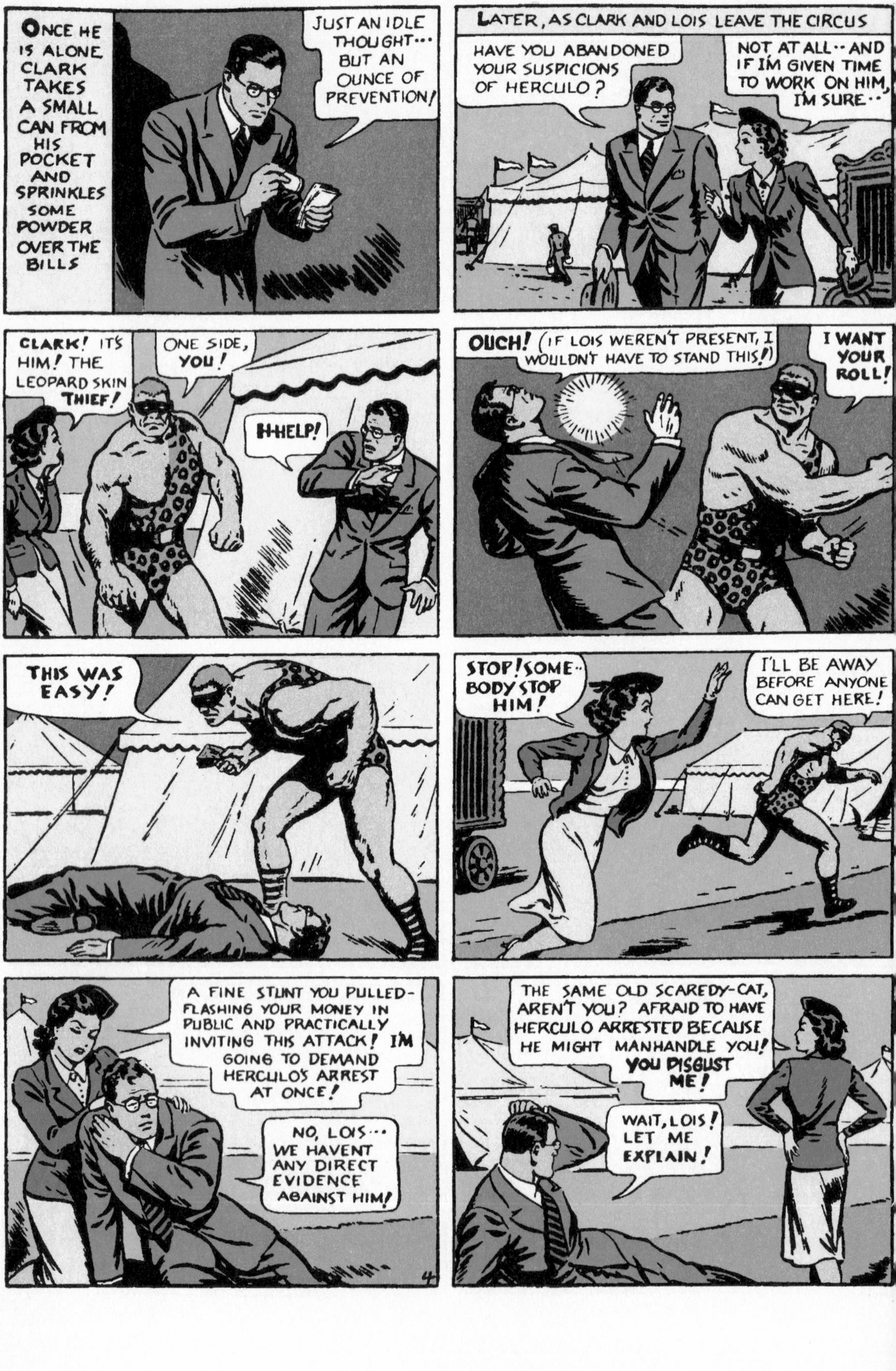
ONCE HE IS ALONE CLARK TAKES A SMALL CAN FROM HIS POCKET AND SPRINKLES SOME POWDER OVER THE BILLS
JUST AN IDLE THOUGHT··· BUT AN OUNCE OF PREVENTION!
LATER, AS CLARK AND LOIS LEAVE THE CIRCUS
HAVE YOU ABANDONED YOUR SUSPICIONS OF HERCULO?
NOT AT ALL·· AND IF I'M GIVEN TIME TO WORK ON HIM, I'M SURE··
CLARK! IT'S HIM! THE LEOPARD SKIN THIEF!
ONE SIDE, YOU!
H-HELP!
OUCH! (IF LOIS WEREN'T PRESENT, I WOULDN'T HAVE TO STAND THIS!)
I WANT YOUR ROLL!
THIS WAS EASY!
STOP! SOME-BODY STOP HIM!
I'LL BE AWAY BEFORE ANYONE CAN GET HERE!
A FINE STUNT YOU PULLED- FLASHING YOUR MONEY IN PUBLIC AND PRACTICALLY INVITING THIS ATTACK! I'M GOING TO DEMAND HERCULO'S ARREST AT ONCE!
NO, LOIS··· WE HAVENT ANY DIRECT EVIDENCE AGAINST HIM!
THE SAME OLD SCAREDY-CAT, AREN'T YOU? AFRAID TO HAVE HERCULO ARRESTED BECAUSE HE MIGHT MANHANDLE YOU! YOU DISGUST ME!
WAIT, LOIS! LET ME EXPLAIN!

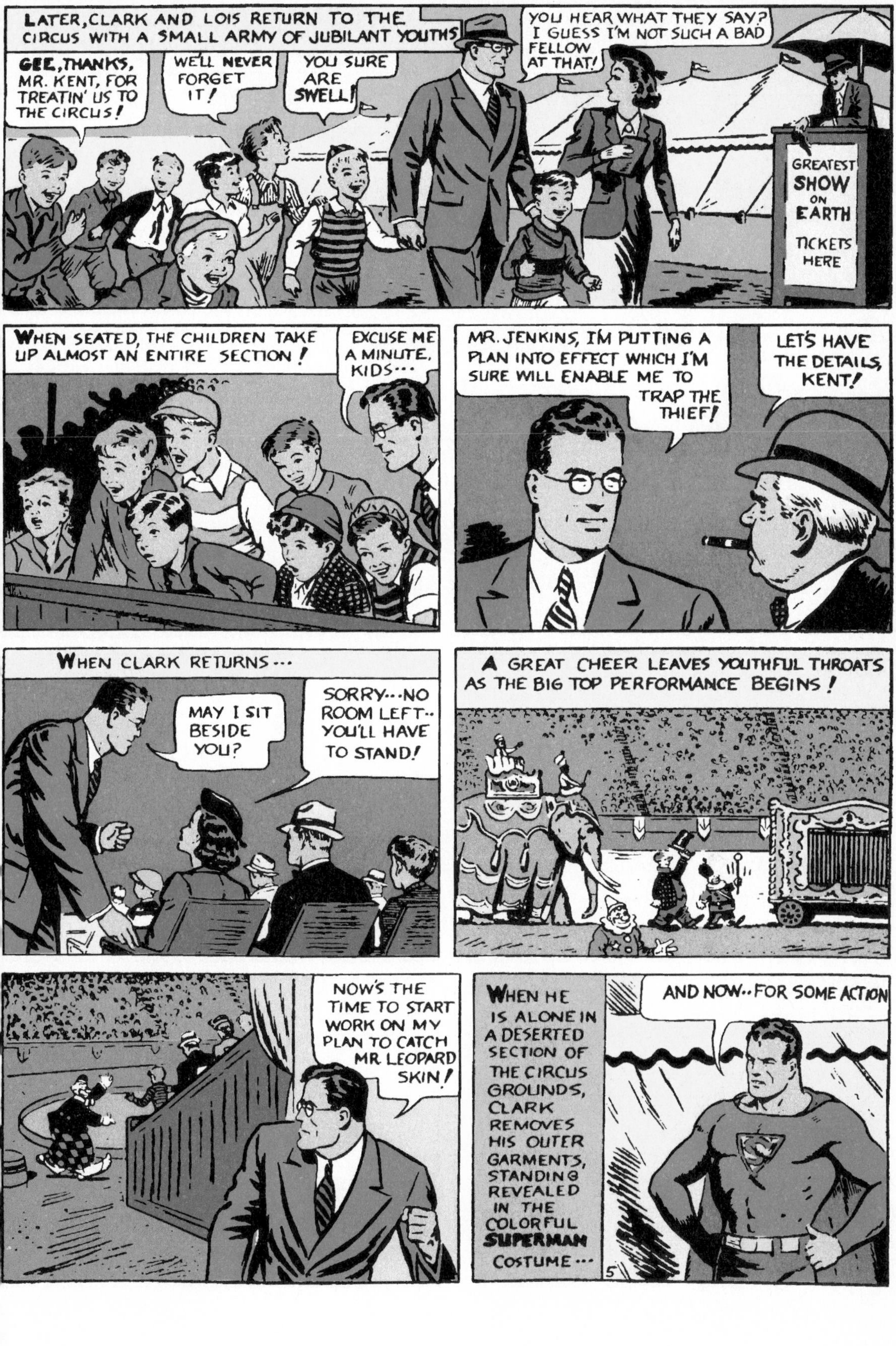
LATER, CLARK AND LOIS RETURN TO THE CIRCUS WITH A SMALL ARMY OF JUBILANT YOUTHS
GEE, THANKS, MR. KENT, FOR TREATIN' US TO THE CIRCUS!
WE'LL NEVER FORGET IT!
YOU SURE ARE SWELL!
YOU HEAR WHAT THEY SAY? I GUESS I'M NOT SUCH A BAD FELLOW AT THAT!
GREATEST SHOW ON EARTH
TICKETS HERE
WHEN SEATED, THE CHILDREN TAKE UP ALMOST AN ENTIRE SECTION!
EXCUSE ME A MINUTE, KIDS···
MR. JENKINS, I'M PUTTING A PLAN INTO EFFECT WHICH I'M SURE WILL ENABLE ME TO TRAP THE THIEF!
LET'S HAVE THE DETAILS, KENT!
WHEN CLARK RETURNS···
MAY I SIT BESIDE YOU?
SORRY···NO ROOM LEFT·· YOU'LL HAVE TO STAND!
A GREAT CHEER LEAVES YOUTHFUL THROATS AS THE BIG TOP PERFORMANCE BEGINS!
NOW'S THE TIME TO START WORK ON MY PLAN TO CATCH MR LEOPARD SKIN!
WHEN HE IS ALONE IN A DESERTED SECTION OF THE CIRCUS GROUNDS, CLARK REMOVES HIS OUTER GARMENTS, STANDING REVEALED IN THE COLORFUL SUPERMAN COSTUME···
AND NOW··FOR SOME ACTION
5

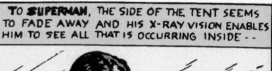

CAUTIOUSLY THE MAN OF TOMORROW STEALS TOWARD THE PERFORMERS' DRESSING TENT!

IF HERCULO IS THE MAN I WANT, I'LL SOON KNOW!

TO SUPERMAN, THE SIDE OF THE TENT SEEMS TO FADE AWAY AND HIS X-RAY VISION ENABLES HIM TO SEE ALL THAT IS OCCURRING INSIDE --

BETTER STEP ON IT, HERCULO.... WE GO ON IN TEN MINUTES

BAH! I TAKE MY TIME!

"A SHADOW ON THE TENT! SOMEONE WATCHING FROM THE OTHER SIDE!"

HERCULO TAKES A ROUND-ABOUT PATH THAT TAKES HIM BEHIND THE MAN OF STEEL. SILENTLY HE CREEPS FORWARD!--

ANOTHER SECOND AND I'LL HAVE HIM!

GOT YOU!

YOU HAVE, EH?

GUESS AGAIN!

UGHH!

WHAT'S THE IDEA OF SPYING ON US?

YOU CHALLENGED ME TO AN ENCOUNTER! WELL, HERE I AM!

SUPERMAN!

6

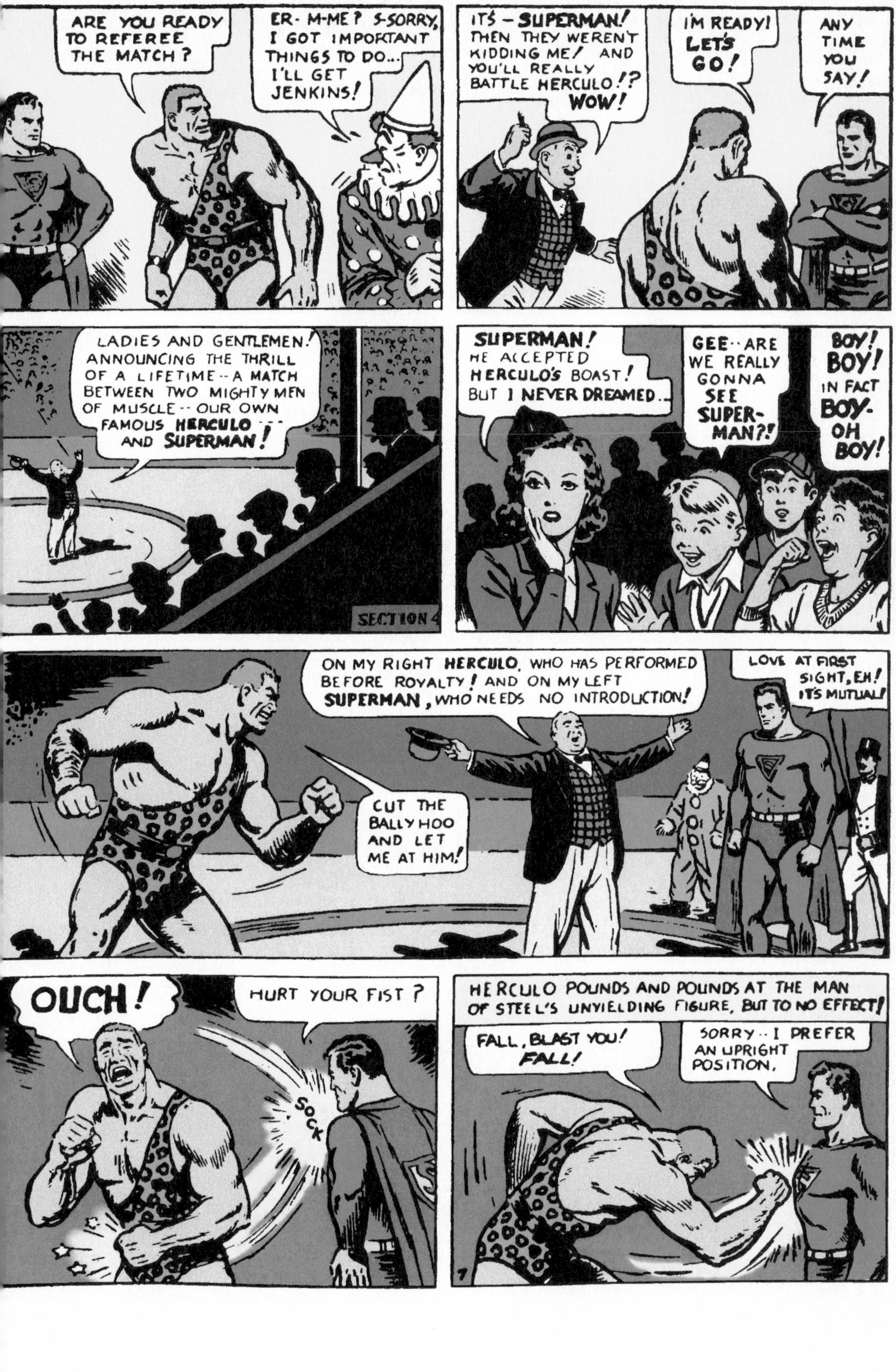
ARE YOU READY TO REFEREE THE MATCH?
ER- M-ME? S-SORRY, I GOT IMPORTANT THINGS TO DO... I'LL GET JENKINS!
IT'S -- SUPERMAN! THEN THEY WEREN'T KIDDING ME! AND YOU'LL REALLY BATTLE HERCULO!? WOW!
I'M READY! LET'S GO!
ANY TIME YOU SAY!
LADIES AND GENTLEMEN! ANNOUNCING THE THRILL OF A LIFETIME -- A MATCH BETWEEN TWO MIGHTY MEN OF MUSCLE -- OUR OWN FAMOUS HERCULO --- AND SUPERMAN!
SECTION 4
SUPERMAN! HE ACCEPTED HERCULO'S BOAST! BUT I NEVER DREAMED...
GEE.. ARE WE REALLY GONNA SEE SUPER-MAN?!
BOY! BOY! IN FACT BOY-OH BOY!
ON MY RIGHT HERCULO, WHO HAS PERFORMED BEFORE ROYALTY! AND ON MY LEFT SUPERMAN, WHO NEEDS NO INTRODUCTION!
LOVE AT FIRST SIGHT, EH! IT'S MUTUAL!
CUT THE BALLYHOO AND LET ME AT HIM!
OUCH!
HURT YOUR FIST?
SOCK
HERCULO POUNDS AND POUNDS AT THE MAN OF STEEL'S UNYIELDING FIGURE, BUT TO NO EFFECT!
FALL, BLAST YOU! FALL!
SORRY.. I PREFER AN UPRIGHT POSITION.

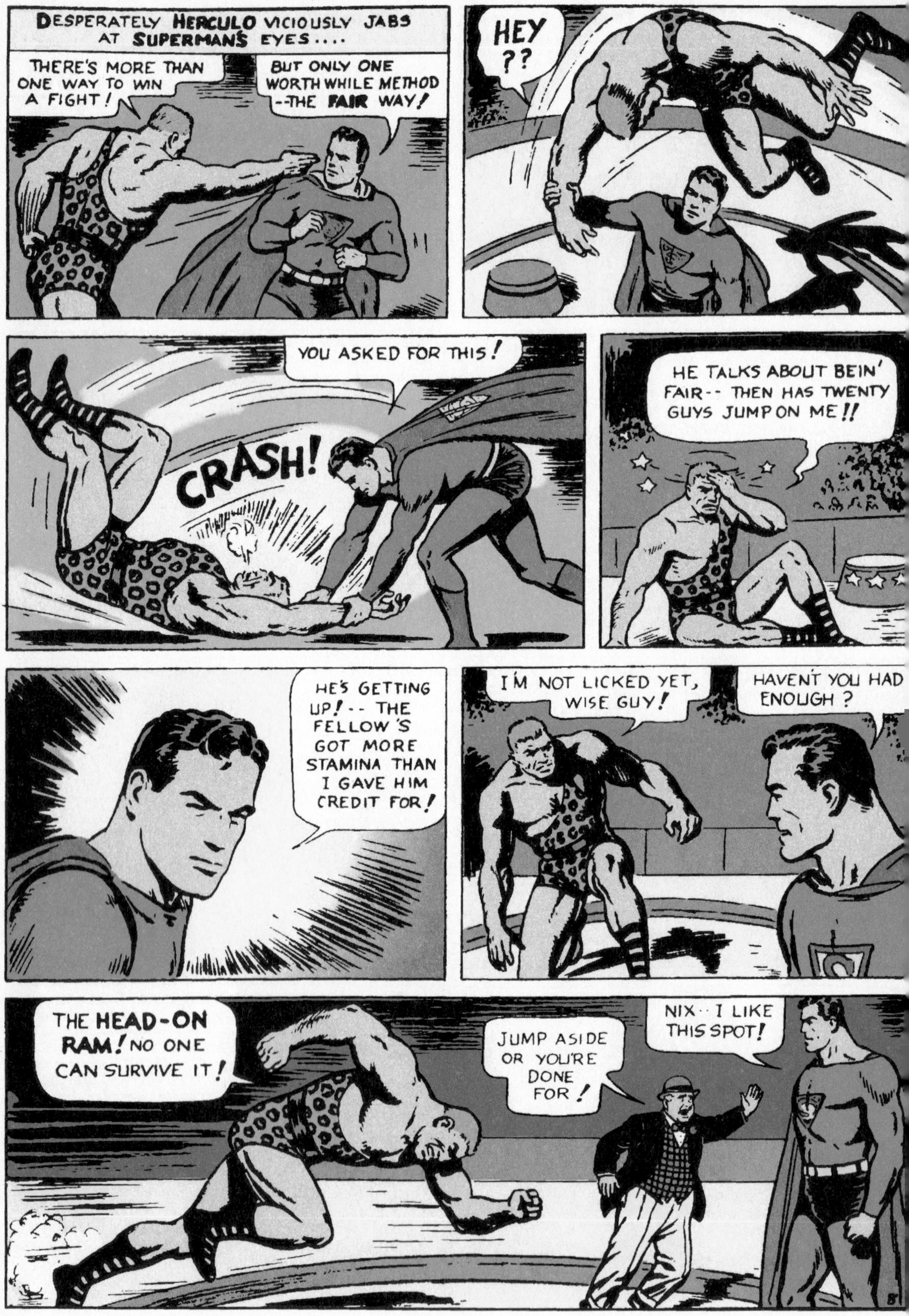
DESPERATELY HERCULO VICIOUSLY JABS AT SUPERMAN'S EYES....
THERE'S MORE THAN ONE WAY TO WIN A FIGHT!
BUT ONLY ONE WORTH WHILE METHOD --THE FAIR WAY!
HEY ??
YOU ASKED FOR THIS!
CRASH!
HE TALKS ABOUT BEIN' FAIR-- THEN HAS TWENTY GUYS JUMP ON ME!!
HE'S GETTING UP!-- THE FELLOW'S GOT MORE STAMINA THAN I GAVE HIM CREDIT FOR!
I'M NOT LICKED YET, WISE GUY!
HAVEN'T YOU HAD ENOUGH ?
THE HEAD-ON RAM! NO ONE CAN SURVIVE IT!
JUMP ASIDE OR YOU'RE DONE FOR!
NIX-- I LIKE THIS SPOT!

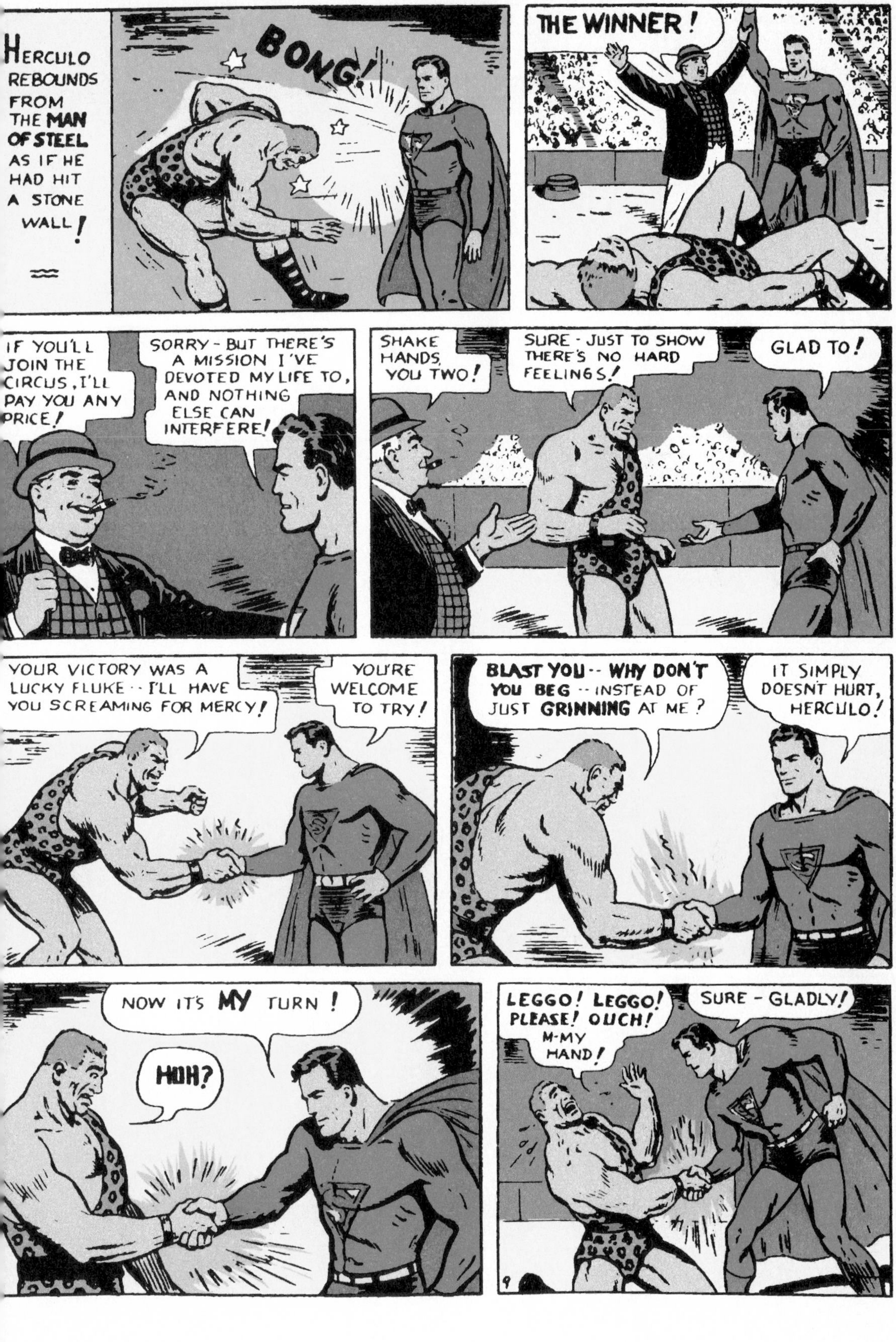
HERCULO REBOUNDS FROM THE MAN OF STEEL AS IF HE HAD HIT A STONE WALL!
BONG!
THE WINNER!
IF YOU'LL JOIN THE CIRCUS, I'LL PAY YOU ANY PRICE!
SORRY - BUT THERE'S A MISSION I'VE DEVOTED MY LIFE TO, AND NOTHING ELSE CAN INTERFERE!
SHAKE HANDS, YOU TWO!
SURE - JUST TO SHOW THERE'S NO HARD FEELINGS!
GLAD TO!
YOUR VICTORY WAS A LUCKY FLUKE -- I'LL HAVE YOU SCREAMING FOR MERCY!
YOU'RE WELCOME TO TRY!
BLAST YOU -- WHY DON'T YOU BEG -- INSTEAD OF JUST GRINNING AT ME?
IT SIMPLY DOESN'T HURT, HERCULO!
NOW IT'S MY TURN!
HUH?
LEGGO! LEGGO! PLEASE! OUCH! M-MY HAND!
SURE - GLADLY!
9

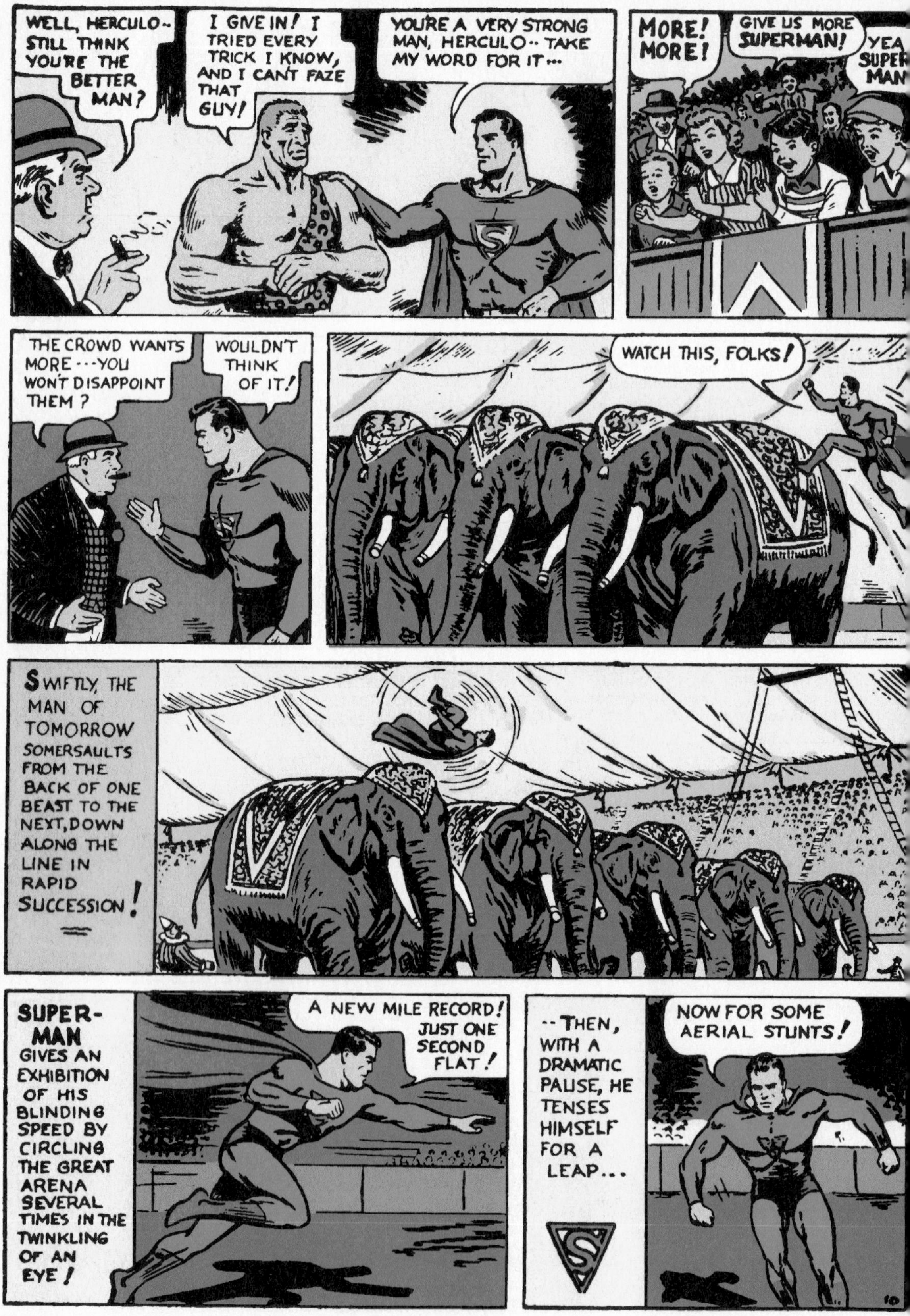
WELL, HERCULO--
STILL THINK
YOU'RE THE
BETTER
MAN?
I GIVE IN! I
TRIED EVERY
TRICK I KNOW,
AND I CAN'T FAZE
THAT
GUY!
YOU'RE A VERY STRONG
MAN, HERCULO-- TAKE
MY WORD FOR IT---
MORE!
MORE!
GIVE US MORE
SUPERMAN!
THE CROWD WANTS
MORE---YOU
WON'T DISAPPOINT
THEM?
WOULDN'T
THINK
OF IT!
WATCH THIS, FOLKS!
SWIFTLY, THE
MAN OF
TOMORROW
SOMERSAULTS
FROM THE
BACK OF ONE
BEAST TO THE
NEXT, DOWN
ALONG THE
LINE IN
RAPID
SUCCESSION!
SUPER-
MAN
GIVES AN
EXHIBITION
OF HIS
BLINDING
SPEED BY
CIRCLING
THE GREAT
ARENA
SEVERAL
TIMES IN THE
TWINKLING
OF AN
EYE!
A NEW MILE RECORD!
JUST ONE
SECOND
FLAT!
--THEN,
WITH A
DRAMATIC
PAUSE, HE
TENSES
HIMSELF
FOR A
LEAP...
NOW FOR SOME
AERIAL STUNTS!
10

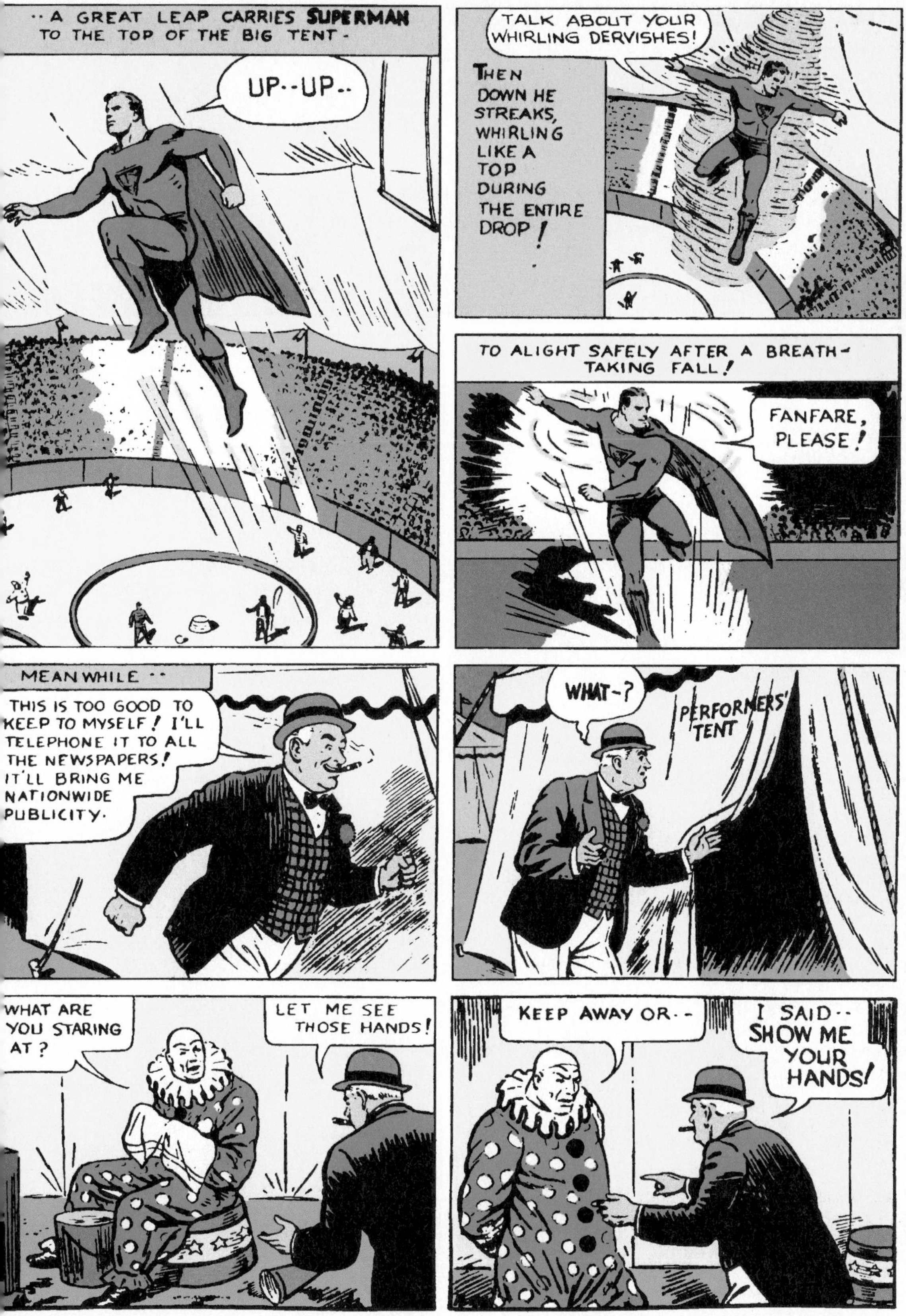
..A GREAT LEAP CARRIES SUPERMAN TO THE TOP OF THE BIG TENT-
UP--UP--
TALK ABOUT YOUR WHIRLING DERVISHES!
THEN DOWN HE STREAKS, WHIRLING LIKE A TOP DURING THE ENTIRE DROP!
TO ALIGHT SAFELY AFTER A BREATH-TAKING FALL!
FANFARE, PLEASE!
MEANWHILE --
THIS IS TOO GOOD TO KEEP TO MYSELF! I'LL TELEPHONE IT TO ALL THE NEWSPAPERS! IT'LL BRING ME NATIONWIDE PUBLICITY.
WHAT-?
PERFORMERS' TENT
WHAT ARE YOU STARING AT?
LET ME SEE THOSE HANDS!
KEEP AWAY OR--
I SAID-- SHOW ME YOUR HANDS!

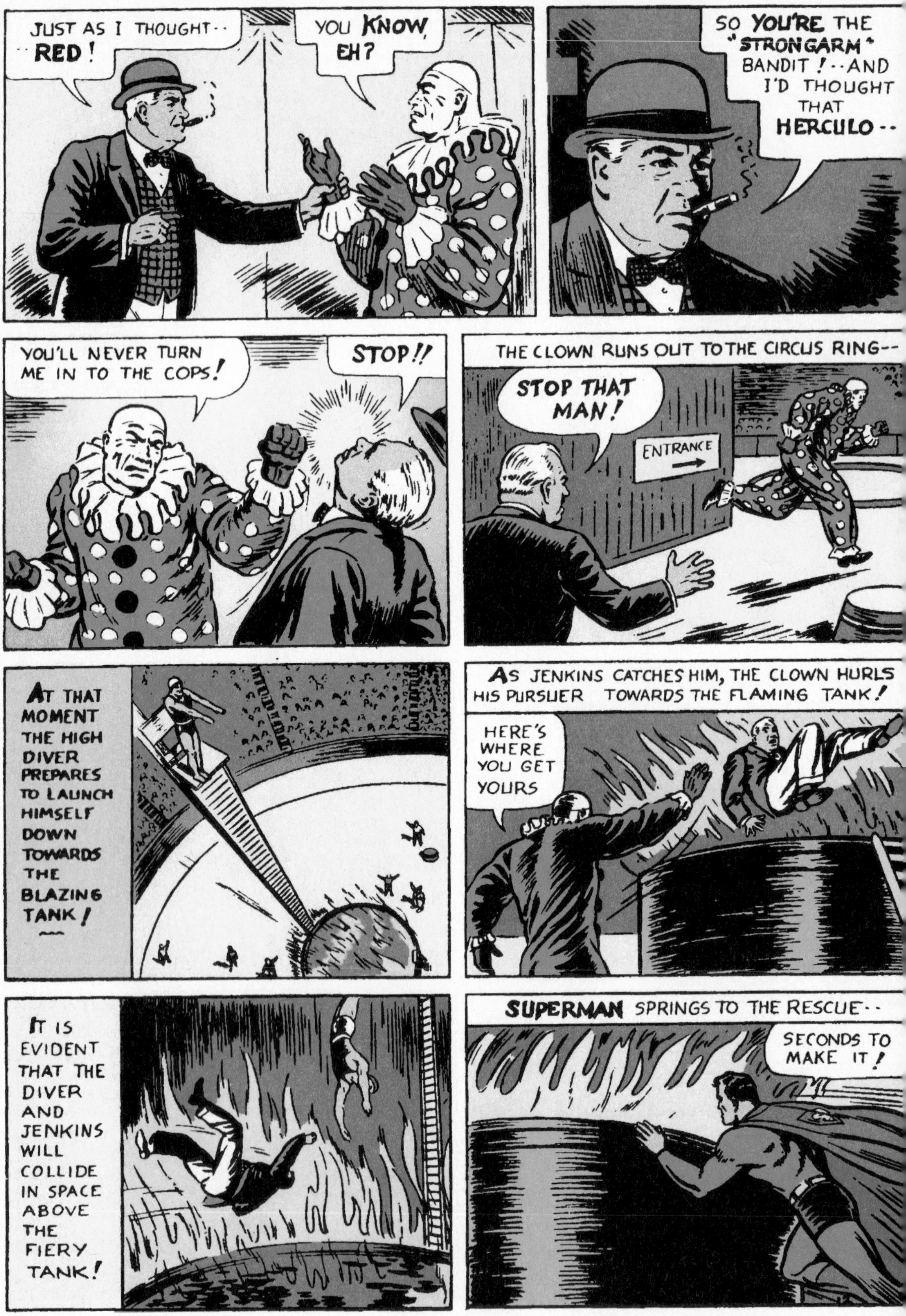

JUST AS I THOUGHT-- --RED!
YOU KNOW, EH?
SO YOU'RE THE "STRONGARM" BANDIT!--AND I'D THOUGHT THAT HERCULO--
YOU'LL NEVER TURN ME IN TO THE COPS!
STOP!!
THE CLOWN RUNS OUT TO THE CIRCUS RING--
STOP THAT MAN!
ENTRANCE
AT THAT MOMENT THE HIGH DIVER PREPARES TO LAUNCH HIMSELF DOWN TOWARDS THE BLAZING TANK! --
AS JENKINS CATCHES HIM, THE CLOWN HURLS HIS PURSUER TOWARDS THE FLAMING TANK!
HERE'S WHERE YOU GET YOURS
IT IS EVIDENT THAT THE DIVER AND JENKINS WILL COLLIDE IN SPACE ABOVE THE FIERY TANK!
SUPERMAN SPRINGS TO THE RESCUE--
SECONDS TO MAKE IT!

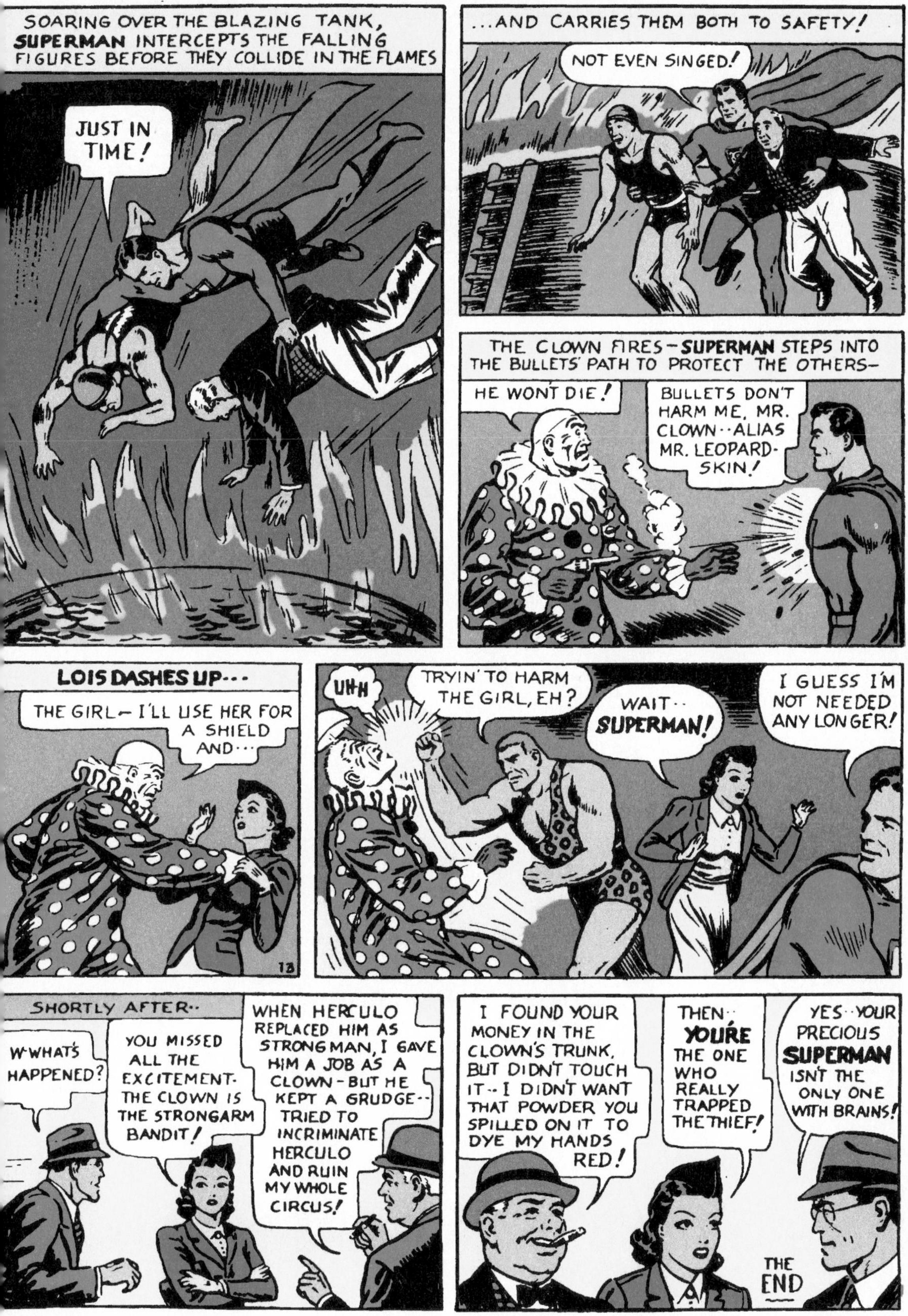
SOARING OVER THE BLAZING TANK, SUPERMAN INTERCEPTS THE FALLING FIGURES BEFORE THEY COLLIDE IN THE FLAMES
JUST IN TIME!
...AND CARRIES THEM BOTH TO SAFETY!
NOT EVEN SINGED!
THE CLOWN FIRES—SUPERMAN STEPS INTO THE BULLETS' PATH TO PROTECT THE OTHERS—
HE WON'T DIE!
BULLETS DON'T HARM ME, MR. CLOWN--ALIAS MR. LEOPARD-SKIN!
LOIS DASHES UP---
THE GIRL—I'LL USE HER FOR A SHIELD AND---
13
UHH
TRYIN' TO HARM THE GIRL, EH?
WAIT-- SUPERMAN!
I GUESS I'M NOT NEEDED ANY LONGER!
SHORTLY AFTER--
W-WHAT'S HAPPENED?
YOU MISSED ALL THE EXCITEMENT-THE CLOWN IS THE STRONGARM BANDIT!
WHEN HERCULO REPLACED HIM AS STRONGMAN, I GAVE HIM A JOB AS A CLOWN-BUT HE KEPT A GRUDGE--TRIED TO INCRIMINATE HERCULO AND RUIN MY WHOLE CIRCUS!
I FOUND YOUR MONEY IN THE CLOWN'S TRUNK, BUT DIDN'T TOUCH IT--I DIDN'T WANT THAT POWDER YOU SPILLED ON IT TO DYE MY HANDS RED!
THEN-- YOU'RE THE ONE WHO REALLY TRAPPED THE THIEF!
YES--YOUR PRECIOUS SUPERMAN ISN'T THE ONLY ONE WITH BRAINS!
THE END

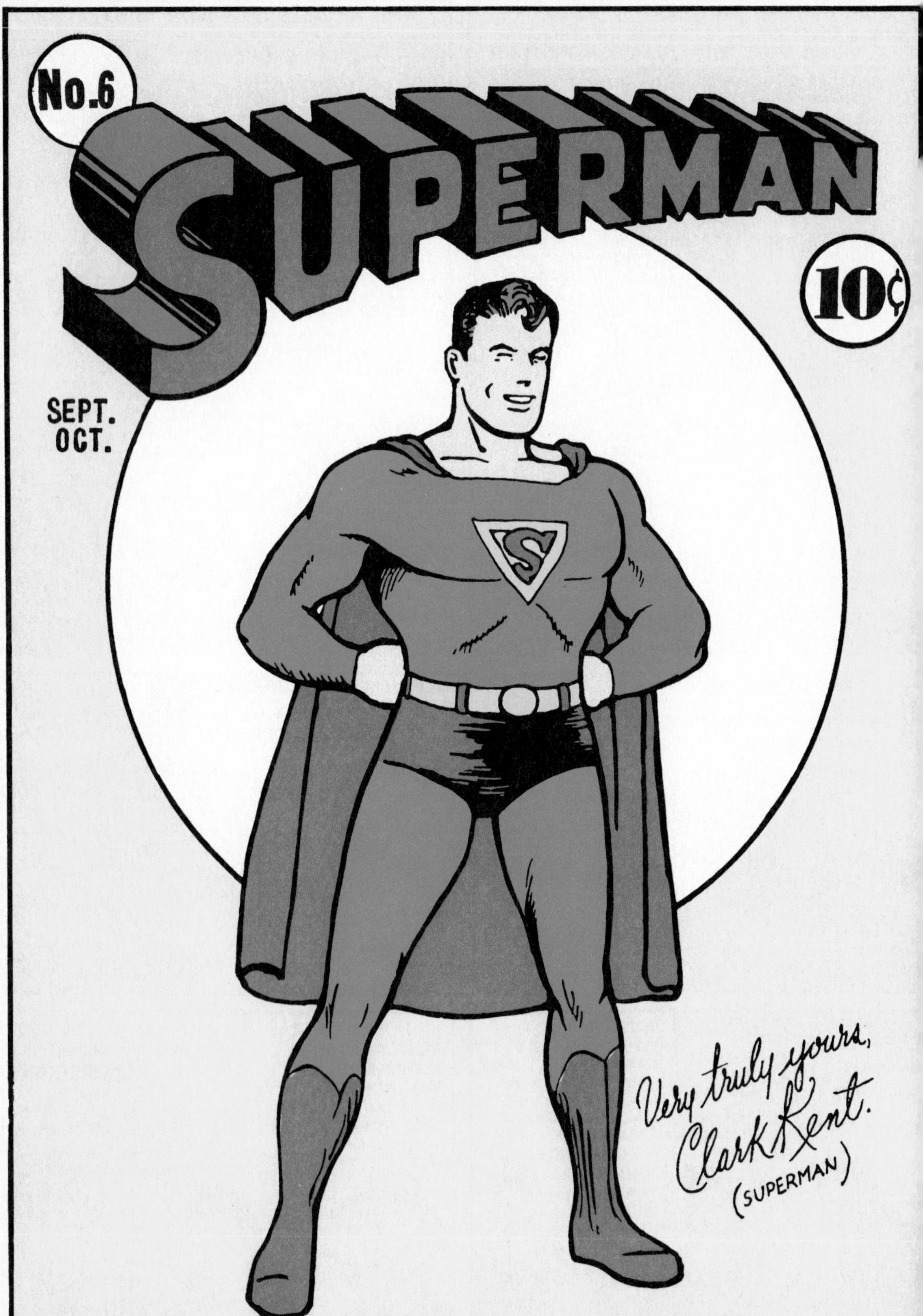
No.6
SUPERMAN
10¢
SEPT.
OCT.
Very truly yours,
Clark Kent.
(SUPERMAN)

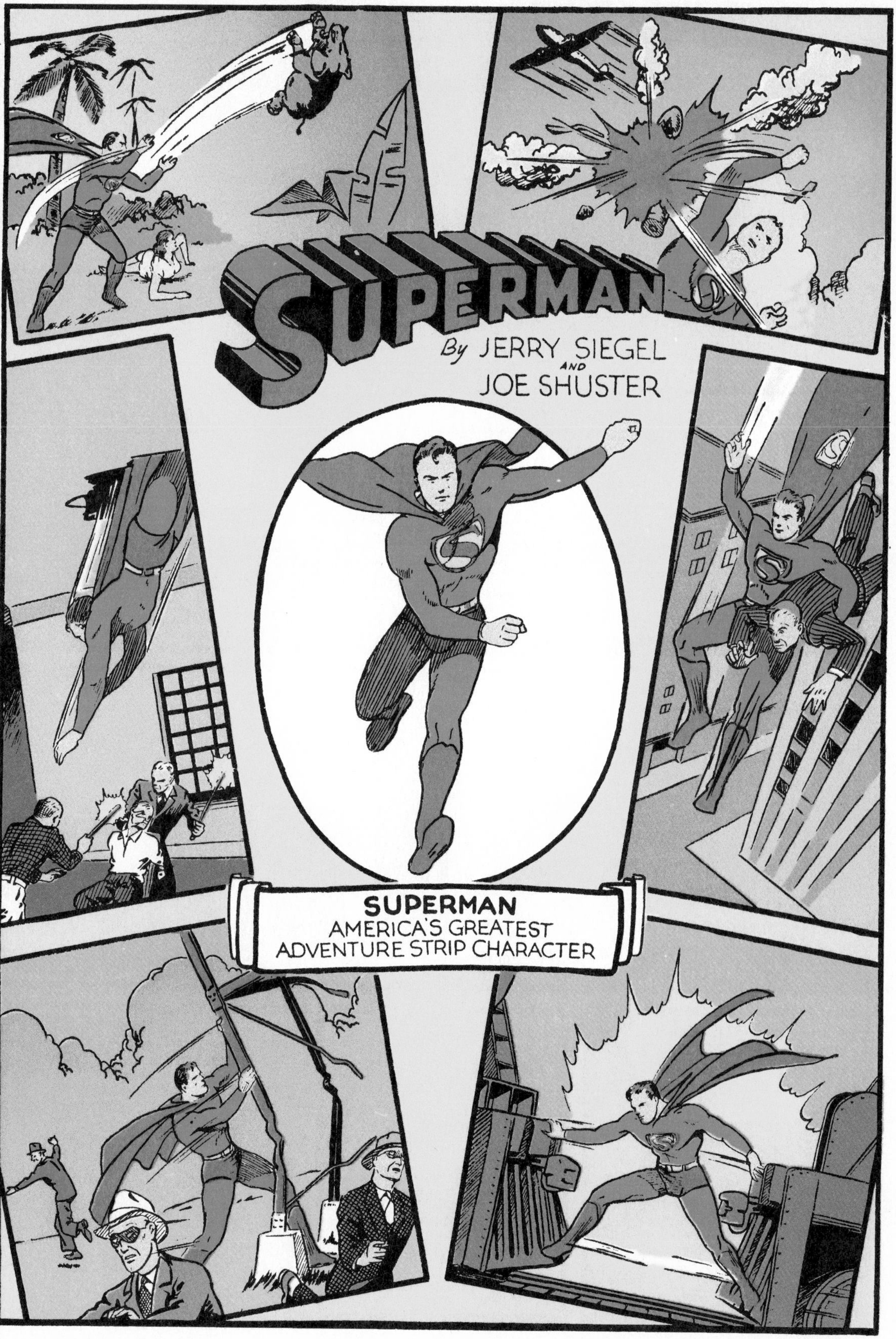
SUPERMAN
By JERRY SIEGEL AND JOE SHUSTER
SUPERMAN
AMERICA'S GREATEST
ADVENTURE STRIP CHARACTER

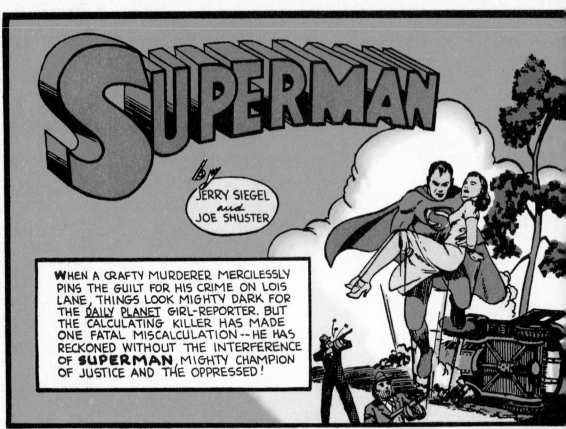

SUPERMAN

By JERRY SIEGEL *and* JOE SHUSTER

WHEN A CRAFTY MURDERER MERCILESSLY PINS THE GUILT FOR HIS CRIME ON LOIS LANE, THINGS LOOK MIGHTY DARK FOR THE DAILY PLANET GIRL-REPORTER. BUT THE CALCULATING KILLER HAS MADE ONE FATAL MISCALCULATION -- HE HAS RECKONED WITHOUT THE INTERFERENCE OF SUPERMAN, MIGHTY CHAMPION OF JUSTICE AND THE OPPRESSED!

EDITORIAL ROOM OF THE DAILY PLANET, METROPOLIS' LEADING NEWSPAPER...

WHAT A DAY! NOT ONE BIT OF INTERESTING NEWS STIRRING!

ARE YOU FORGETTING, MY ESTEEMED FELLOW JOURNALIST, THAT WHEN THERE'S NOTHING IMPORTANT TO WRITE ABOUT, A GOOD REPORTER SALLIES FORTH AND DIGS UP A STORY, SOMEWHERE, SOMEHOW?

NORVAL, THE JEWEL COLLECTOR, SHOULD MAKE GOOD COPY! HE KEEPS PRICELESS GEMS IN HIS OWN HOME...AND HAS RIGGED UP FANTASTIC DEVICES TO PROTECT THEM!

NO ONE ANSWERS... AND THE DOOR IS OPEN. I'LL WALK RIGHT IN!

BUT AS LOIS ENTERS --SHE IS SUDDENLY SEIZED FROM BEHIND -- A CHLOROFORM SOAKED CLOTH IS PRESSED AGAINST HER NOSTRILS, UNTIL HER STRUGGLES LESSEN AND SHE DROPS OFF INTO UNCONSCIOUSNESS!

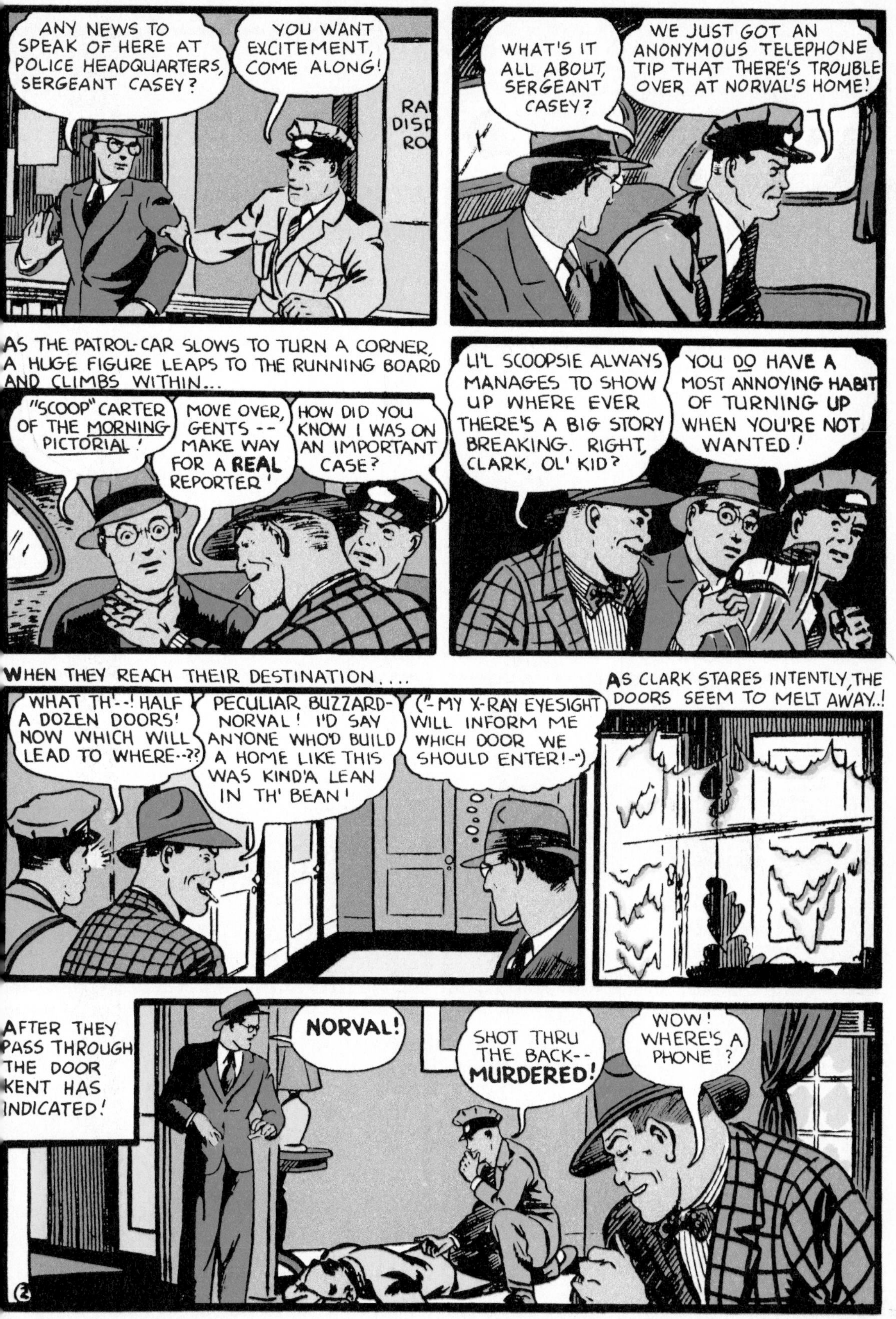
ANY NEWS TO SPEAK OF HERE AT POLICE HEADQUARTERS, SERGEANT CASEY?
YOU WANT EXCITEMENT, COME ALONG!
WHAT'S IT ALL ABOUT, SERGEANT CASEY?
WE JUST GOT AN ANONYMOUS TELEPHONE TIP THAT THERE'S TROUBLE OVER AT NORVAL'S HOME!
AS THE PATROL-CAR SLOWS TO TURN A CORNER, A HUGE FIGURE LEAPS TO THE RUNNING BOARD AND CLIMBS WITHIN...
"SCOOP" CARTER OF THE MORNING PICTORIAL!
MOVE OVER, GENTS -- MAKE WAY FOR A REAL REPORTER!
HOW DID YOU KNOW I WAS ON AN IMPORTANT CASE?
LI'L SCOOPSIE ALWAYS MANAGES TO SHOW UP WHERE EVER THERE'S A BIG STORY BREAKING. RIGHT, CLARK, OL' KID?
YOU DO HAVE A MOST ANNOYING HABIT OF TURNING UP WHEN YOU'RE NOT WANTED!
WHEN THEY REACH THEIR DESTINATION....
WHAT TH'--! HALF A DOZEN DOORS! NOW WHICH WILL LEAD TO WHERE--??
PECULIAR BUZZARD-NORVAL! I'D SAY ANYONE WHO'D BUILD A HOME LIKE THIS WAS KIND'A LEAN IN TH' BEAN!
("-MY X-RAY EYESIGHT WILL INFORM ME WHICH DOOR WE SHOULD ENTER!-")
AS CLARK STARES INTENTLY, THE DOORS SEEM TO MELT AWAY..!
AFTER THEY PASS THROUGH THE DOOR KENT HAS INDICATED!
NORVAL!
SHOT THRU THE BACK--MURDERED!
WOW! WHERE'S A PHONE?
2

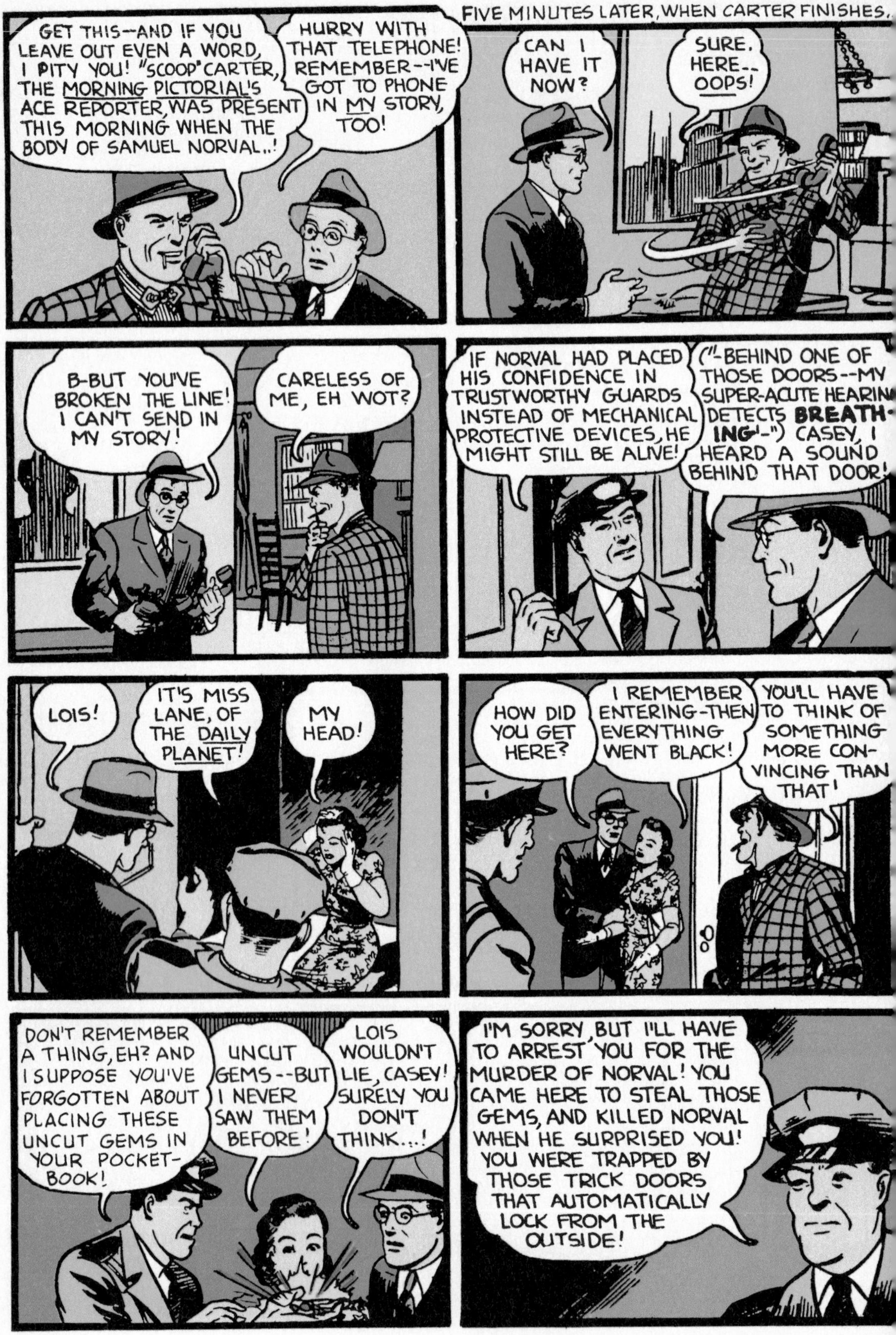
GET THIS--AND IF YOU LEAVE OUT EVEN A WORD, I PITY YOU! "SCOOP" CARTER, THE MORNING PICTORIAL'S ACE REPORTER, WAS PRESENT THIS MORNING WHEN THE BODY OF SAMUEL NORVAL..!
HURRY WITH THAT TELEPHONE! REMEMBER--I'VE GOT TO PHONE IN MY STORY, TOO!
FIVE MINUTES LATER, WHEN CARTER FINISHES.
CAN I HAVE IT NOW?
SURE. HERE-- OOPS!
B-BUT YOU'VE BROKEN THE LINE! I CAN'T SEND IN MY STORY!
CARELESS OF ME, EH WOT?
IF NORVAL HAD PLACED HIS CONFIDENCE IN TRUSTWORTHY GUARDS INSTEAD OF MECHANICAL PROTECTIVE DEVICES, HE MIGHT STILL BE ALIVE!
("-BEHIND ONE OF THOSE DOORS--MY SUPER-ACUTE HEARING DETECTS BREATH-ING!-") CASEY, I HEARD A SOUND BEHIND THAT DOOR!
LOIS!
IT'S MISS LANE, OF THE DAILY PLANET!
MY HEAD!
HOW DID YOU GET HERE?
I REMEMBER ENTERING-THEN EVERYTHING WENT BLACK!
YOU'LL HAVE TO THINK OF SOMETHING MORE CON-VINCING THAN THAT!
DON'T REMEMBER A THING, EH? AND I SUPPOSE YOU'VE FORGOTTEN ABOUT PLACING THESE UNCUT GEMS IN YOUR POCKET-BOOK!
UNCUT GEMS--BUT I NEVER SAW THEM BEFORE!
LOIS WOULDN'T LIE, CASEY! SURELY YOU DON'T THINK...!
I'M SORRY, BUT I'LL HAVE TO ARREST YOU FOR THE MURDER OF NORVAL! YOU CAME HERE TO STEAL THOSE GEMS, AND KILLED NORVAL WHEN HE SURPRISED YOU! YOU WERE TRAPPED BY THOSE TRICK DOORS THAT AUTOMATICALLY LOCK FROM THE OUTSIDE!

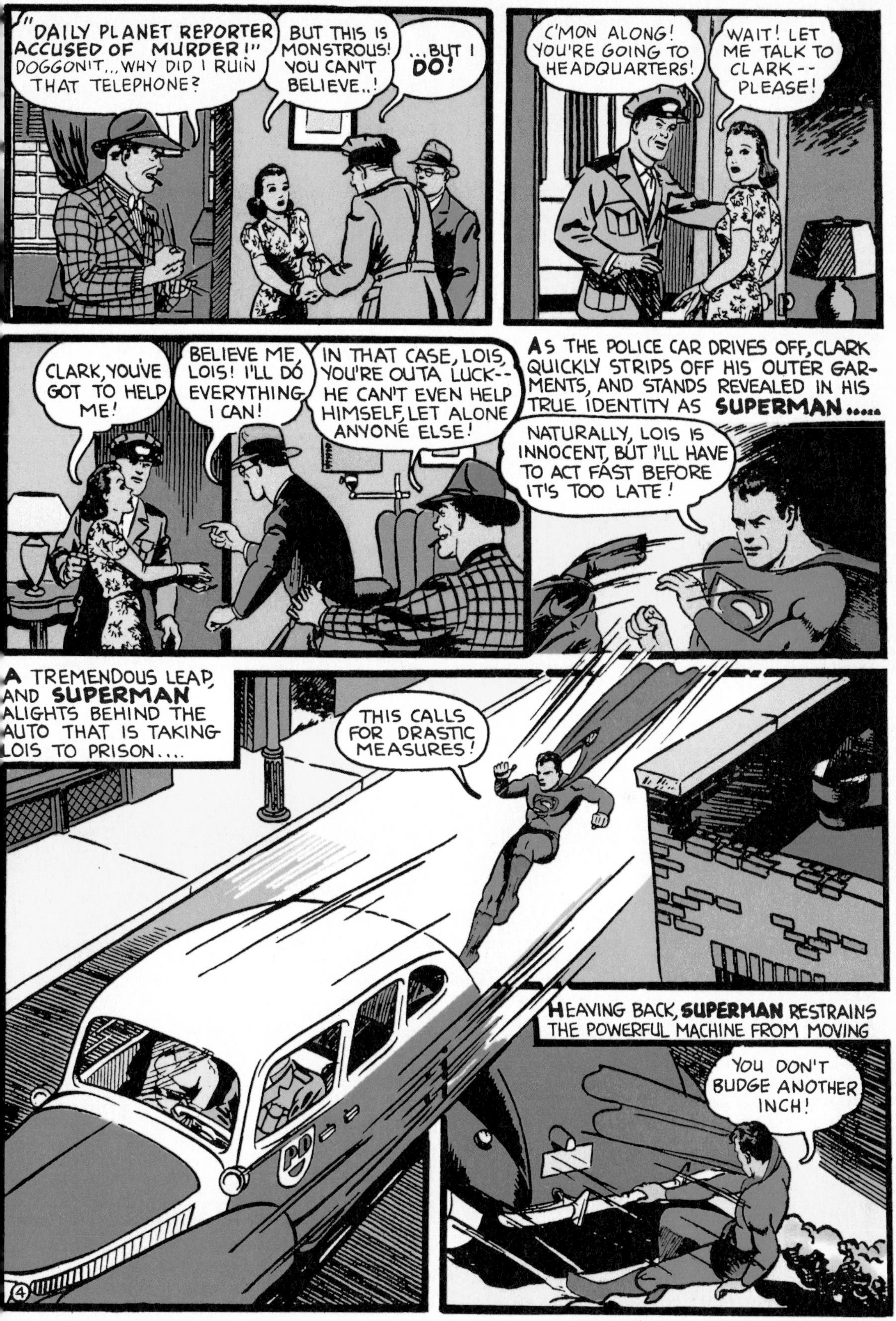
"DAILY PLANET REPORTER ACCUSED OF MURDER!" DOGGONIT... WHY DID I RUIN THAT TELEPHONE?
BUT THIS IS MONSTROUS! YOU CAN'T BELIEVE..!
...BUT I DO!
C'MON ALONG! YOU'RE GOING TO HEADQUARTERS!
WAIT! LET ME TALK TO CLARK-- PLEASE!
CLARK, YOU'VE GOT TO HELP ME!
BELIEVE ME, LOIS! I'LL DO EVERYTHING I CAN!
IN THAT CASE, LOIS, YOU'RE OUTA LUCK-- HE CAN'T EVEN HELP HIMSELF, LET ALONE ANYONE ELSE!
AS THE POLICE CAR DRIVES OFF, CLARK QUICKLY STRIPS OFF HIS OUTER GARMENTS, AND STANDS REVEALED IN HIS TRUE IDENTITY AS SUPERMAN.....
NATURALLY, LOIS IS INNOCENT, BUT I'LL HAVE TO ACT FAST BEFORE IT'S TOO LATE!
A TREMENDOUS LEAP, AND SUPERMAN ALIGHTS BEHIND THE AUTO THAT IS TAKING LOIS TO PRISON....
THIS CALLS FOR DRASTIC MEASURES!
HEAVING BACK, SUPERMAN RESTRAINS THE POWERFUL MACHINE FROM MOVING
YOU DON'T BUDGE ANOTHER INCH!
4

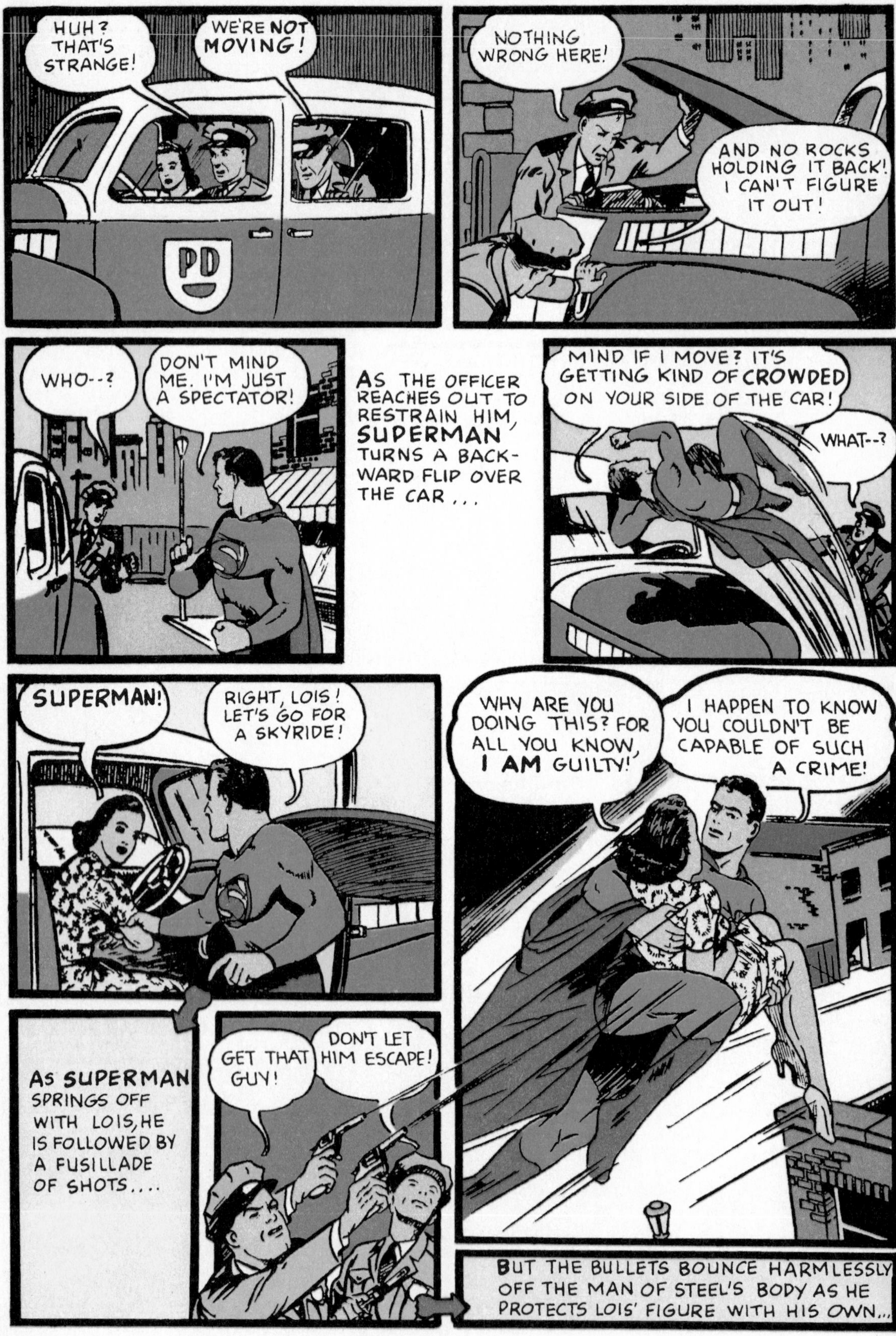
HUH? THAT'S STRANGE!
WE'RE NOT MOVING!
NOTHING WRONG HERE!
AND NO ROCKS HOLDING IT BACK! I CAN'T FIGURE IT OUT!
WHO--?
DON'T MIND ME. I'M JUST A SPECTATOR!
AS THE OFFICER REACHES OUT TO RESTRAIN HIM, SUPERMAN TURNS A BACKWARD FLIP OVER THE CAR...
MIND IF I MOVE? IT'S GETTING KIND OF CROWDED ON YOUR SIDE OF THE CAR!
WHAT--?
SUPERMAN!
RIGHT, LOIS! LET'S GO FOR A SKYRIDE!
WHY ARE YOU DOING THIS? FOR ALL YOU KNOW, I AM GUILTY!
I HAPPEN TO KNOW YOU COULDN'T BE CAPABLE OF SUCH A CRIME!
AS SUPERMAN SPRINGS OFF WITH LOIS, HE IS FOLLOWED BY A FUSILLADE OF SHOTS....
GET THAT GUY!
DON'T LET HIM ESCAPE!
BUT THE BULLETS BOUNCE HARMLESSLY OFF THE MAN OF STEEL'S BODY AS HE PROTECTS LOIS' FIGURE WITH HIS OWN...

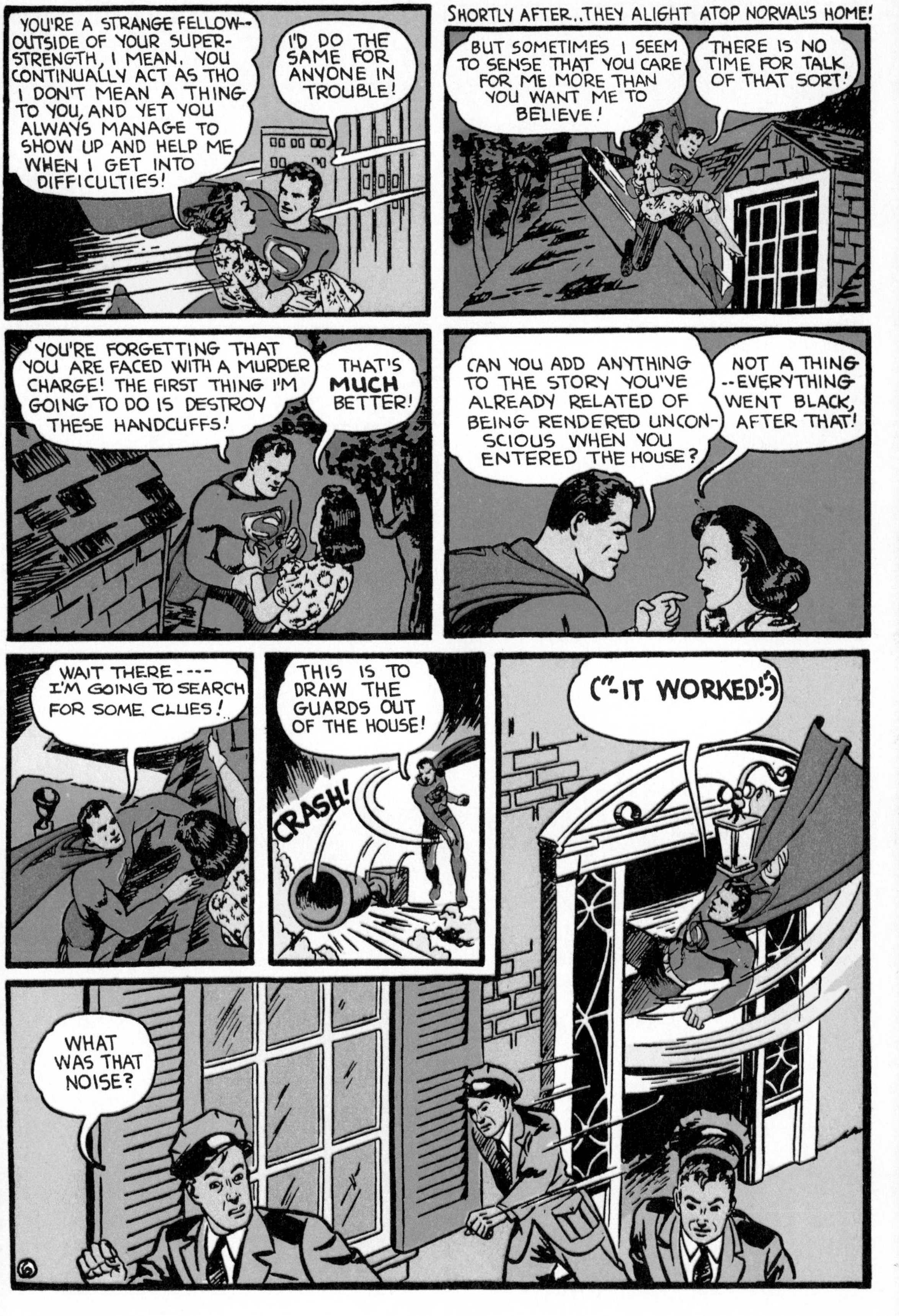
YOU'RE A STRANGE FELLOW--OUTSIDE OF YOUR SUPER-STRENGTH, I MEAN. YOU CONTINUALLY ACT AS THO I DON'T MEAN A THING TO YOU, AND YET YOU ALWAYS MANAGE TO SHOW UP AND HELP ME WHEN I GET INTO DIFFICULTIES!
I'D DO THE SAME FOR ANYONE IN TROUBLE!
SHORTLY AFTER..THEY ALIGHT ATOP NORVAL'S HOME!
BUT SOMETIMES I SEEM TO SENSE THAT YOU CARE FOR ME MORE THAN YOU WANT ME TO BELIEVE!
THERE IS NO TIME FOR TALK OF THAT SORT!
YOU'RE FORGETTING THAT YOU ARE FACED WITH A MURDER CHARGE! THE FIRST THING I'M GOING TO DO IS DESTROY THESE HANDCUFFS!
THAT'S MUCH BETTER!
CAN YOU ADD ANYTHING TO THE STORY YOU'VE ALREADY RELATED OF BEING RENDERED UNCONSCIOUS WHEN YOU ENTERED THE HOUSE?
NOT A THING --EVERYTHING WENT BLACK, AFTER THAT!
WAIT THERE---- I'M GOING TO SEARCH FOR SOME CLUES!
THIS IS TO DRAW THE GUARDS OUT OF THE HOUSE!
CRASH!
("-IT WORKED!")
WHAT WAS THAT NOISE?
6

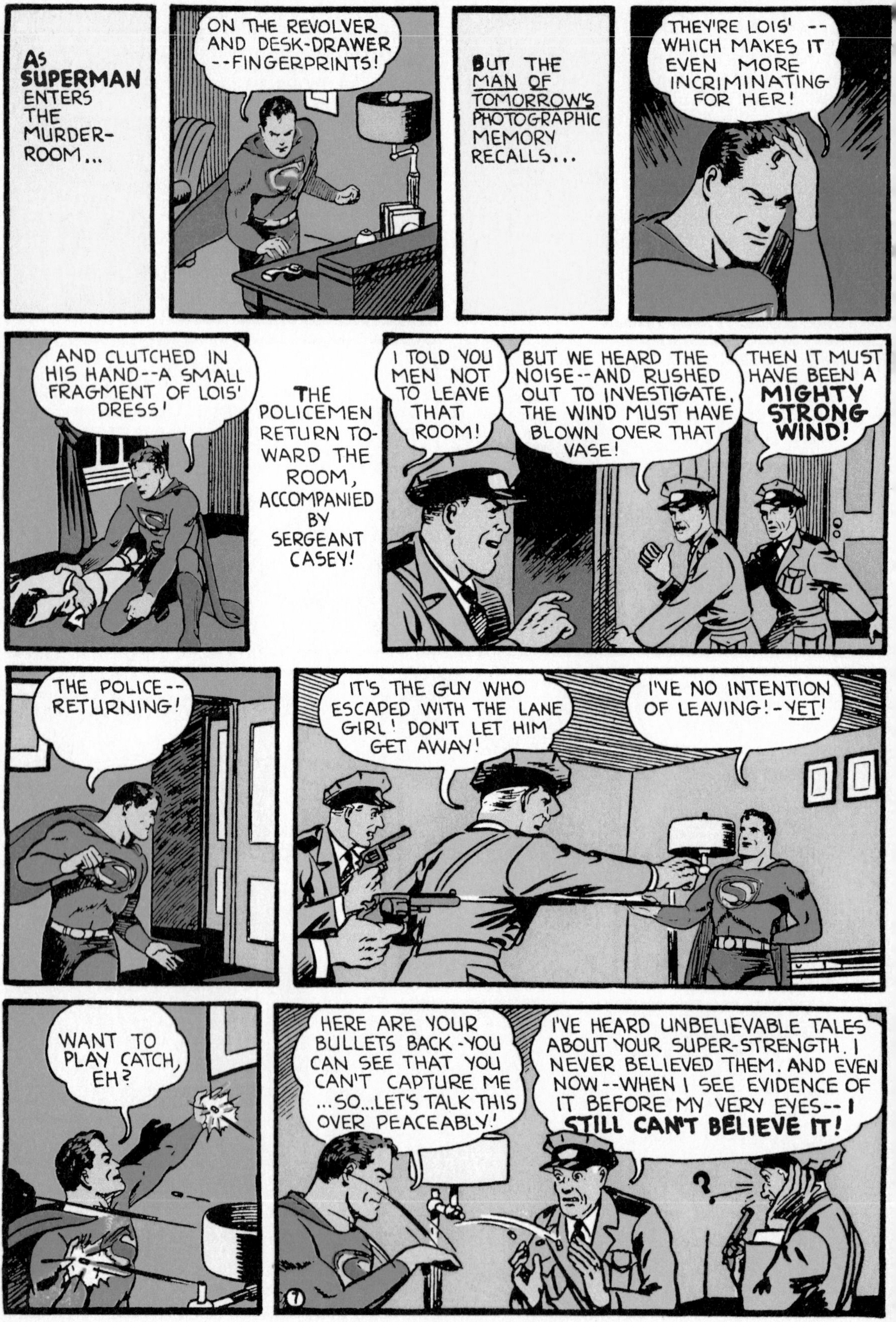

AS SUPERMAN ENTERS THE MURDER-ROOM...
ON THE REVOLVER AND DESK-DRAWER --FINGERPRINTS!
BUT THE MAN OF TOMORROW'S PHOTOGRAPHIC MEMORY RECALLS...
THEY'RE LOIS' -- WHICH MAKES IT EVEN MORE INCRIMINATING FOR HER!
AND CLUTCHED IN HIS HAND--A SMALL FRAGMENT OF LOIS' DRESS!
THE POLICEMEN RETURN TOWARD THE ROOM, ACCOMPANIED BY SERGEANT CASEY!
I TOLD YOU MEN NOT TO LEAVE THAT ROOM!
BUT WE HEARD THE NOISE--AND RUSHED OUT TO INVESTIGATE. THE WIND MUST HAVE BLOWN OVER THAT VASE!
THEN IT MUST HAVE BEEN A MIGHTY STRONG WIND!
THE POLICE--RETURNING!
IT'S THE GUY WHO ESCAPED WITH THE LANE GIRL! DON'T LET HIM GET AWAY!
I'VE NO INTENTION OF LEAVING!-YET!
WANT TO PLAY CATCH, EH?
HERE ARE YOUR BULLETS BACK-YOU CAN SEE THAT YOU CAN'T CAPTURE ME ...SO...LET'S TALK THIS OVER PEACEABLY!
I'VE HEARD UNBELIEVABLE TALES ABOUT YOUR SUPER-STRENGTH. I NEVER BELIEVED THEM. AND EVEN NOW--WHEN I SEE EVIDENCE OF IT BEFORE MY VERY EYES--I STILL CAN'T BELIEVE IT!
?
7

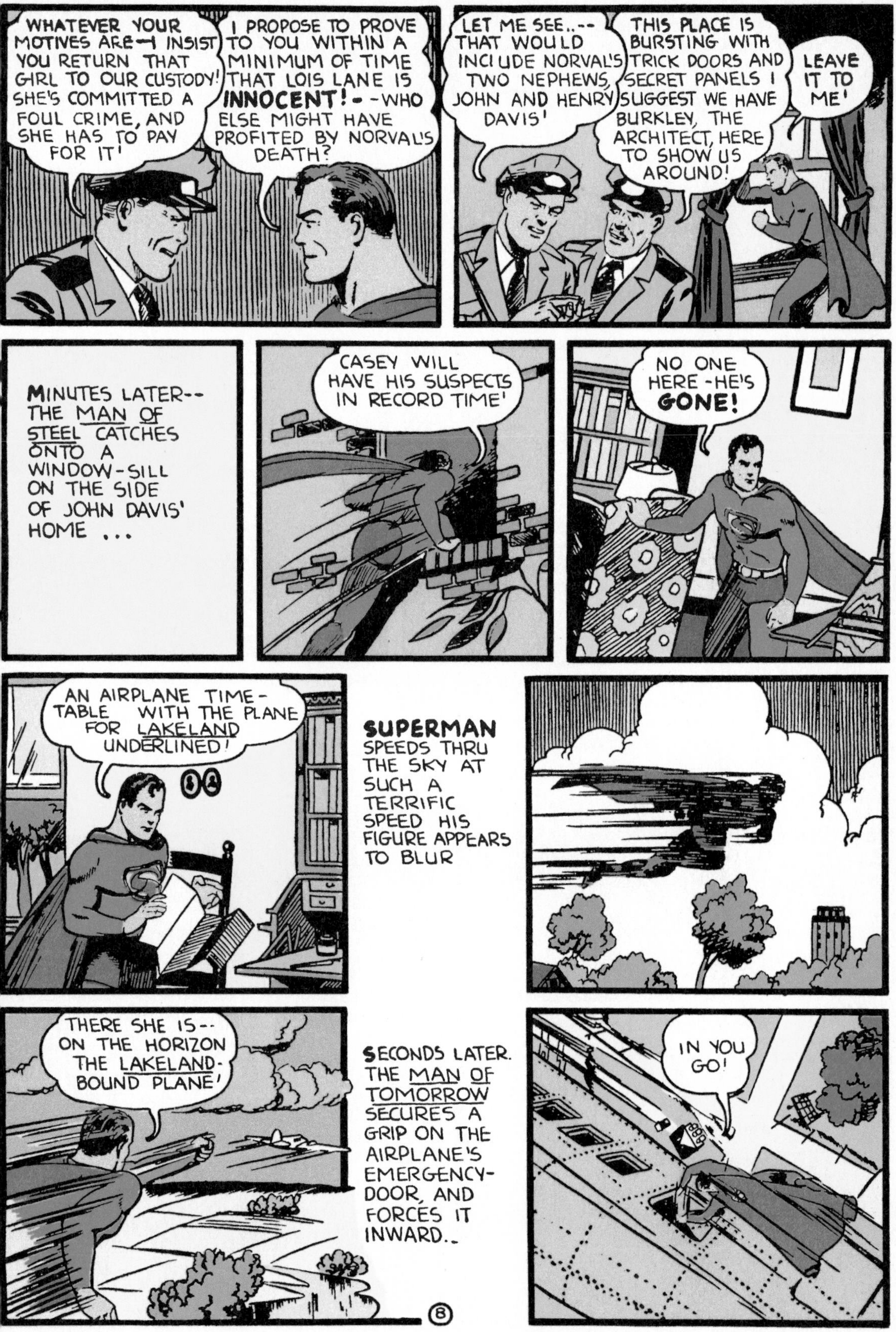
WHATEVER YOUR MOTIVES ARE—I INSIST YOU RETURN THAT GIRL TO OUR CUSTODY! SHE'S COMMITTED A FOUL CRIME, AND SHE HAS TO PAY FOR IT!
I PROPOSE TO PROVE TO YOU WITHIN A MINIMUM OF TIME THAT LOIS LANE IS INNOCENT!--WHO ELSE MIGHT HAVE PROFITED BY NORVAL'S DEATH?
LET ME SEE..--THAT WOULD INCLUDE NORVAL'S TWO NEPHEWS, JOHN AND HENRY DAVIS!
THIS PLACE IS BURSTING WITH TRICK DOORS AND SECRET PANELS I SUGGEST WE HAVE BURKLEY, THE ARCHITECT, HERE TO SHOW US AROUND!
LEAVE IT TO ME!
MINUTES LATER--THE MAN OF STEEL CATCHES ONTO A WINDOW-SILL ON THE SIDE OF JOHN DAVIS' HOME ...
CASEY WILL HAVE HIS SUSPECTS IN RECORD TIME!
NO ONE HERE-HE'S GONE!
AN AIRPLANE TIME-TABLE WITH THE PLANE FOR LAKELAND UNDERLINED!
SUPERMAN SPEEDS THRU THE SKY AT SUCH A TERRIFIC SPEED HIS FIGURE APPEARS TO BLUR
THERE SHE IS--ON THE HORIZON THE LAKELAND-BOUND PLANE!
SECONDS LATER. THE MAN OF TOMORROW SECURES A GRIP ON THE AIRPLANE'S EMERGENCY-DOOR, AND FORCES IT INWARD..
IN YOU GO!
8

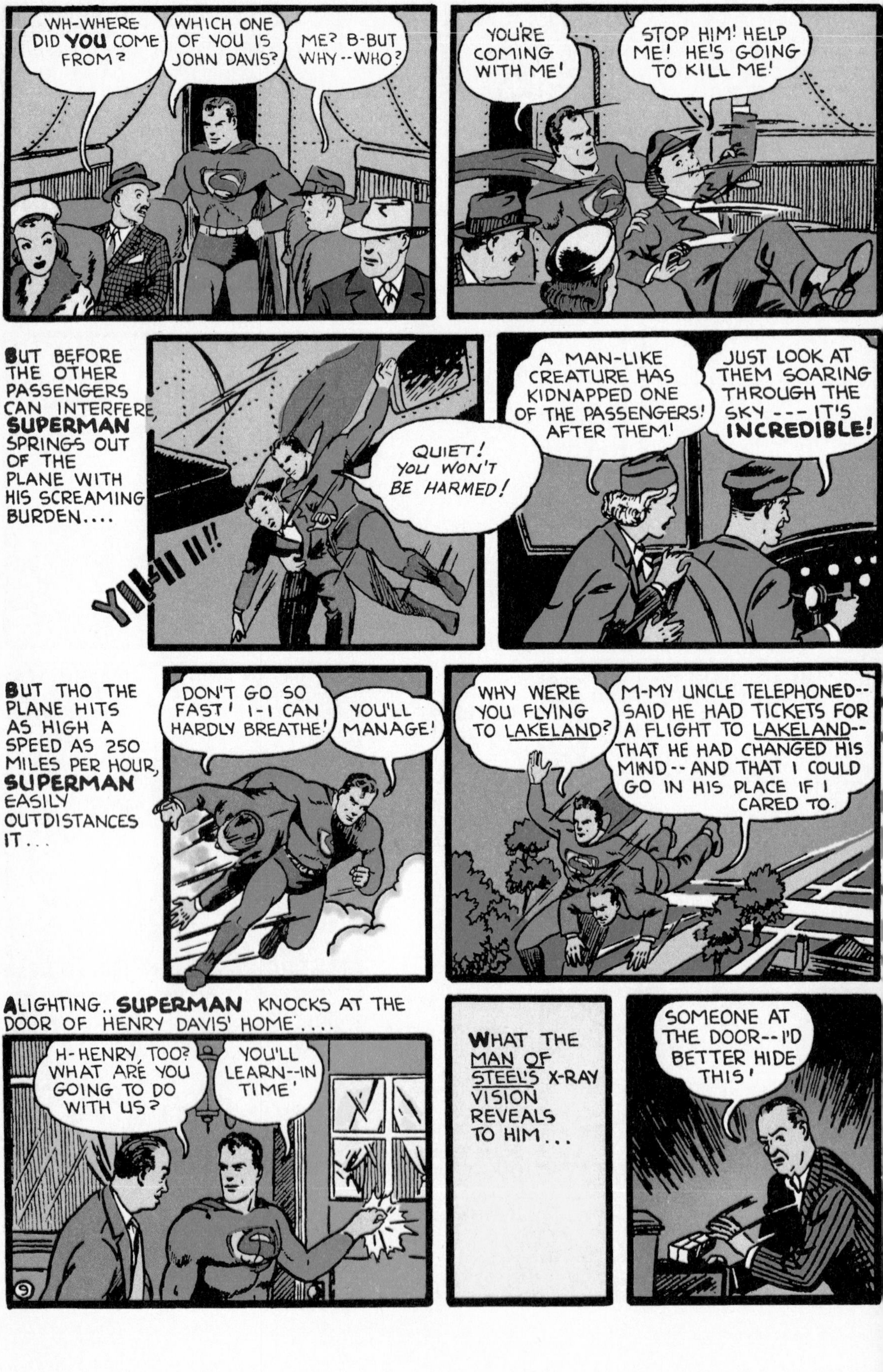
WH-WHERE DID YOU COME FROM?
WHICH ONE OF YOU IS JOHN DAVIS?
ME? B-BUT WHY--WHO?
YOU'RE COMING WITH ME!
STOP HIM! HELP ME! HE'S GOING TO KILL ME!
BUT BEFORE THE OTHER PASSENGERS CAN INTERFERE, SUPERMAN SPRINGS OUT OF THE PLANE WITH HIS SCREAMING BURDEN....
QUIET! YOU WON'T BE HARMED!
YIII-II II!!
A MAN-LIKE CREATURE HAS KIDNAPPED ONE OF THE PASSENGERS! AFTER THEM!
JUST LOOK AT THEM SOARING THROUGH THE SKY --- IT'S INCREDIBLE!
BUT THO THE PLANE HITS AS HIGH A SPEED AS 250 MILES PER HOUR, SUPERMAN EASILY OUTDISTANCES IT...
DON'T GO SO FAST! I-I CAN HARDLY BREATHE!
YOU'LL MANAGE!
WHY WERE YOU FLYING TO LAKELAND?
M-MY UNCLE TELEPHONED--SAID HE HAD TICKETS FOR A FLIGHT TO LAKELAND--THAT HE HAD CHANGED HIS MIND--AND THAT I COULD GO IN HIS PLACE IF I CARED TO.
ALIGHTING.. SUPERMAN KNOCKS AT THE DOOR OF HENRY DAVIS' HOME....
H-HENRY, TOO? WHAT ARE YOU GOING TO DO WITH US?
YOU'LL LEARN--IN TIME!
9
WHAT THE MAN OF STEEL'S X-RAY VISION REVEALS TO HIM...
SOMEONE AT THE DOOR--I'D BETTER HIDE THIS!

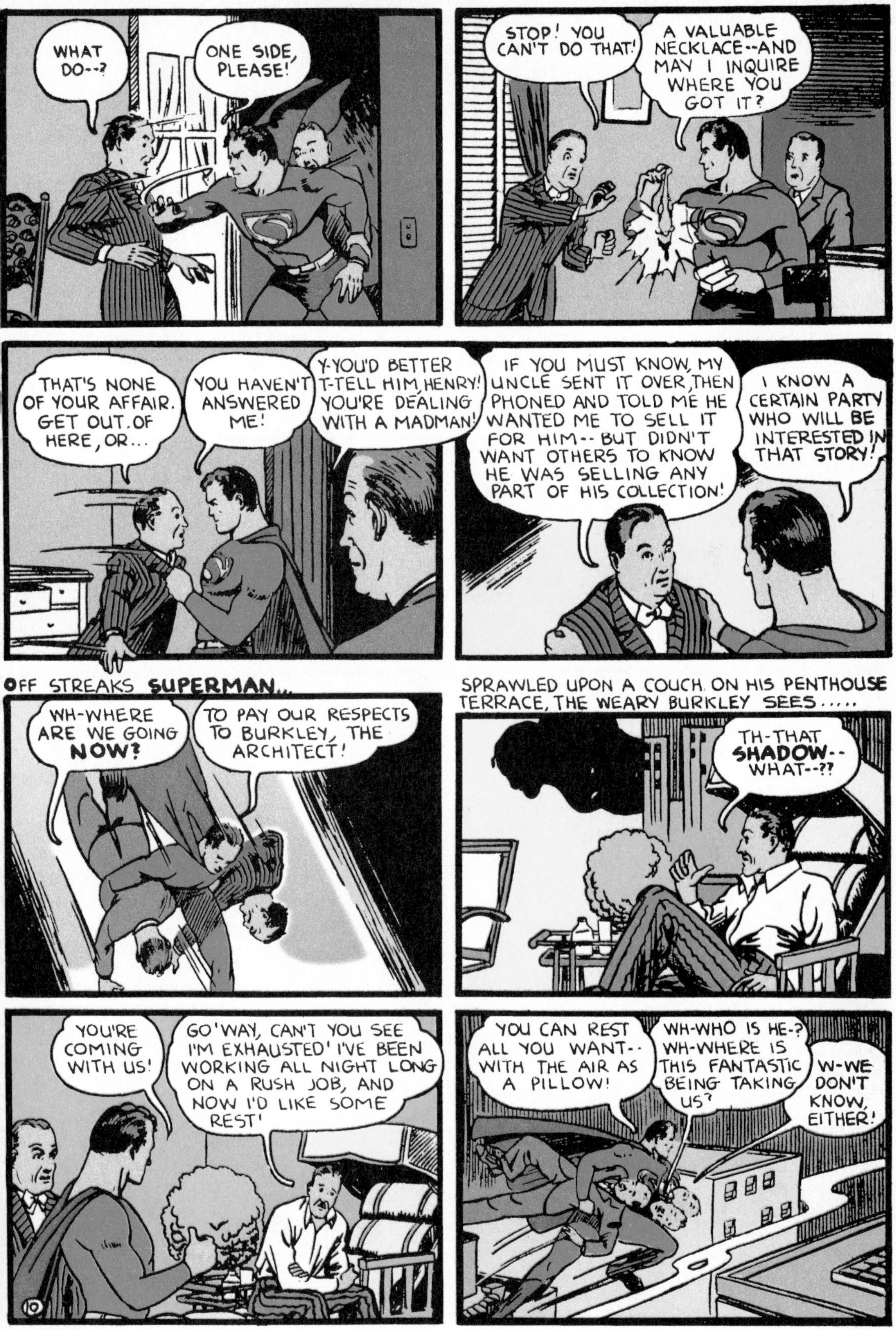

WHAT DO--?
ONE SIDE, PLEASE!
STOP! YOU CAN'T DO THAT!
A VALUABLE NECKLACE--AND MAY I INQUIRE WHERE YOU GOT IT?
THAT'S NONE OF YOUR AFFAIR. GET OUT OF HERE, OR...
YOU HAVEN'T ANSWERED ME!
Y-YOU'D BETTER T-TELL HIM, HENRY! YOU'RE DEALING WITH A MADMAN!
IF YOU MUST KNOW, MY UNCLE SENT IT OVER, THEN PHONED AND TOLD ME HE WANTED ME TO SELL IT FOR HIM-- BUT DIDN'T WANT OTHERS TO KNOW HE WAS SELLING ANY PART OF HIS COLLECTION!
I KNOW A CERTAIN PARTY WHO WILL BE INTERESTED IN THAT STORY!
OFF STREAKS SUPERMAN...
WH-WHERE ARE WE GOING NOW?
TO PAY OUR RESPECTS TO BURKLEY, THE ARCHITECT!
SPRAWLED UPON A COUCH ON HIS PENTHOUSE TERRACE, THE WEARY BURKLEY SEES.....
TH-THAT SHADOW-- WHAT--??
YOU'RE COMING WITH US!
GO'WAY, CAN'T YOU SEE I'M EXHAUSTED! I'VE BEEN WORKING ALL NIGHT LONG ON A RUSH JOB, AND NOW I'D LIKE SOME REST!
10
YOU CAN REST ALL YOU WANT-- WITH THE AIR AS A PILLOW!
WH-WHO IS HE-? WH-WHERE IS THIS FANTASTIC BEING TAKING US?
W-WE DON'T KNOW, EITHER!

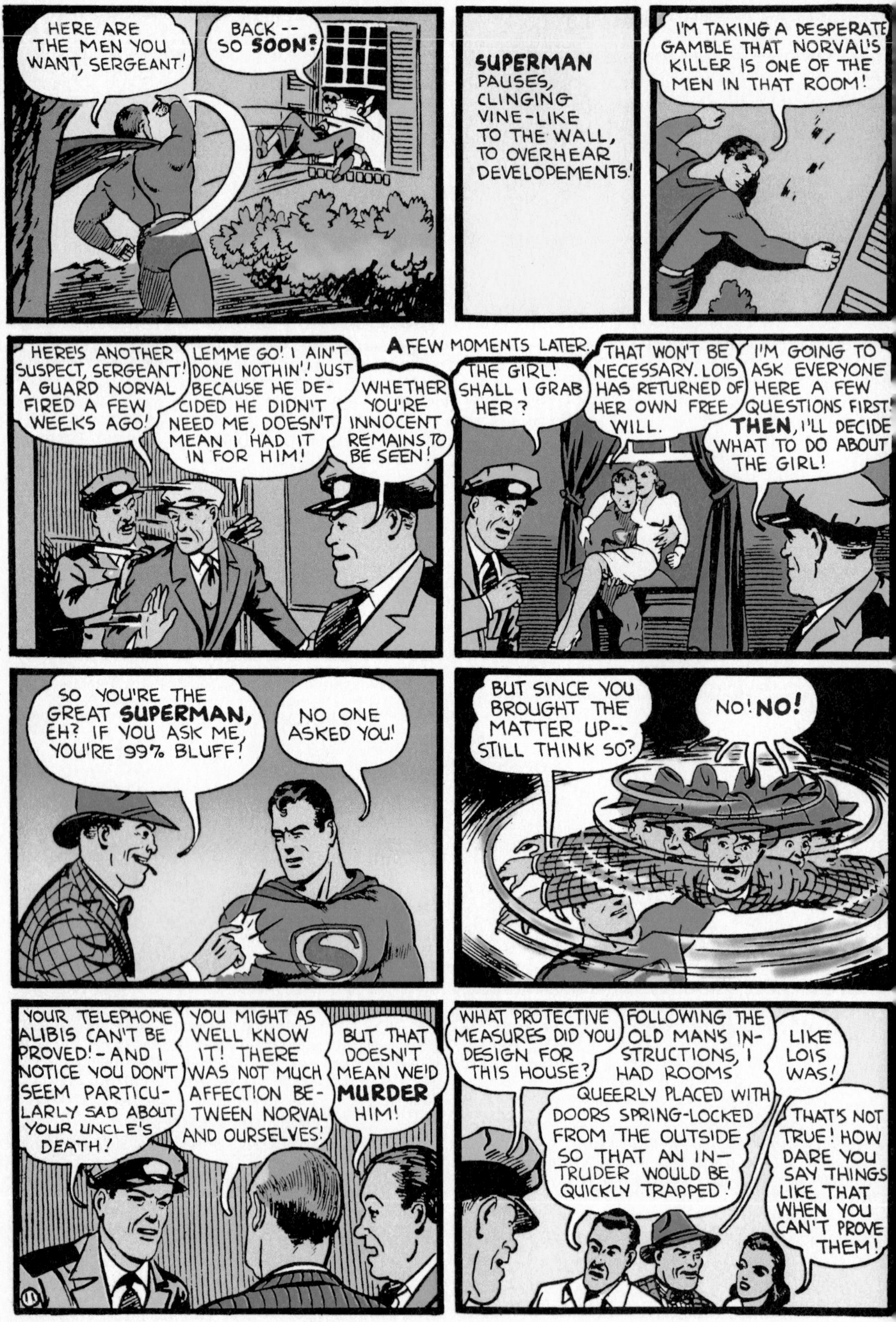
HERE ARE THE MEN YOU WANT, SERGEANT!
BACK -- SO **SOON**?
SUPERMAN PAUSES, CLINGING VINE-LIKE TO THE WALL, TO OVERHEAR DEVELOPEMENTS!
I'M TAKING A DESPERATE GAMBLE THAT NORVAL'S KILLER IS ONE OF THE MEN IN THAT ROOM!
HERE'S ANOTHER SUSPECT, SERGEANT! A GUARD NORVAL FIRED A FEW WEEKS AGO!
LEMME GO! I AIN'T DONE NOTHIN'! JUST BECAUSE HE DECIDED HE DIDN'T NEED ME, DOESN'T MEAN I HAD IT IN FOR HIM!
WHETHER YOU'RE INNOCENT REMAINS TO BE SEEN!
A FEW MOMENTS LATER..
THE GIRL! SHALL I GRAB HER?
THAT WON'T BE NECESSARY. LOIS HAS RETURNED OF HER OWN FREE WILL.
I'M GOING TO ASK EVERYONE HERE A FEW QUESTIONS FIRST! **THEN**, I'LL DECIDE WHAT TO DO ABOUT THE GIRL!
SO YOU'RE THE GREAT **SUPERMAN**, EH? IF YOU ASK ME, YOU'RE 99% BLUFF!
NO ONE ASKED YOU!
BUT SINCE YOU BROUGHT THE MATTER UP-- STILL THINK SO?
NO! **NO!**
YOUR TELEPHONE ALIBIS CAN'T BE PROVED! - AND I NOTICE YOU DON'T SEEM PARTICULARLY SAD ABOUT YOUR UNCLE'S DEATH!
YOU MIGHT AS WELL KNOW IT! THERE WAS NOT MUCH AFFECTION BETWEEN NORVAL AND OURSELVES!
BUT THAT DOESN'T MEAN WE'D **MURDER** HIM!
WHAT PROTECTIVE MEASURES DID YOU DESIGN FOR THIS HOUSE?
FOLLOWING THE OLD MAN'S INSTRUCTIONS, I HAD ROOMS QUEERLY PLACED WITH DOORS SPRING-LOCKED FROM THE OUTSIDE SO THAT AN INTRUDER WOULD BE QUICKLY TRAPPED!
LIKE LOIS WAS!
THAT'S NOT TRUE! HOW DARE YOU SAY THINGS LIKE THAT WHEN YOU CAN'T PROVE THEM!

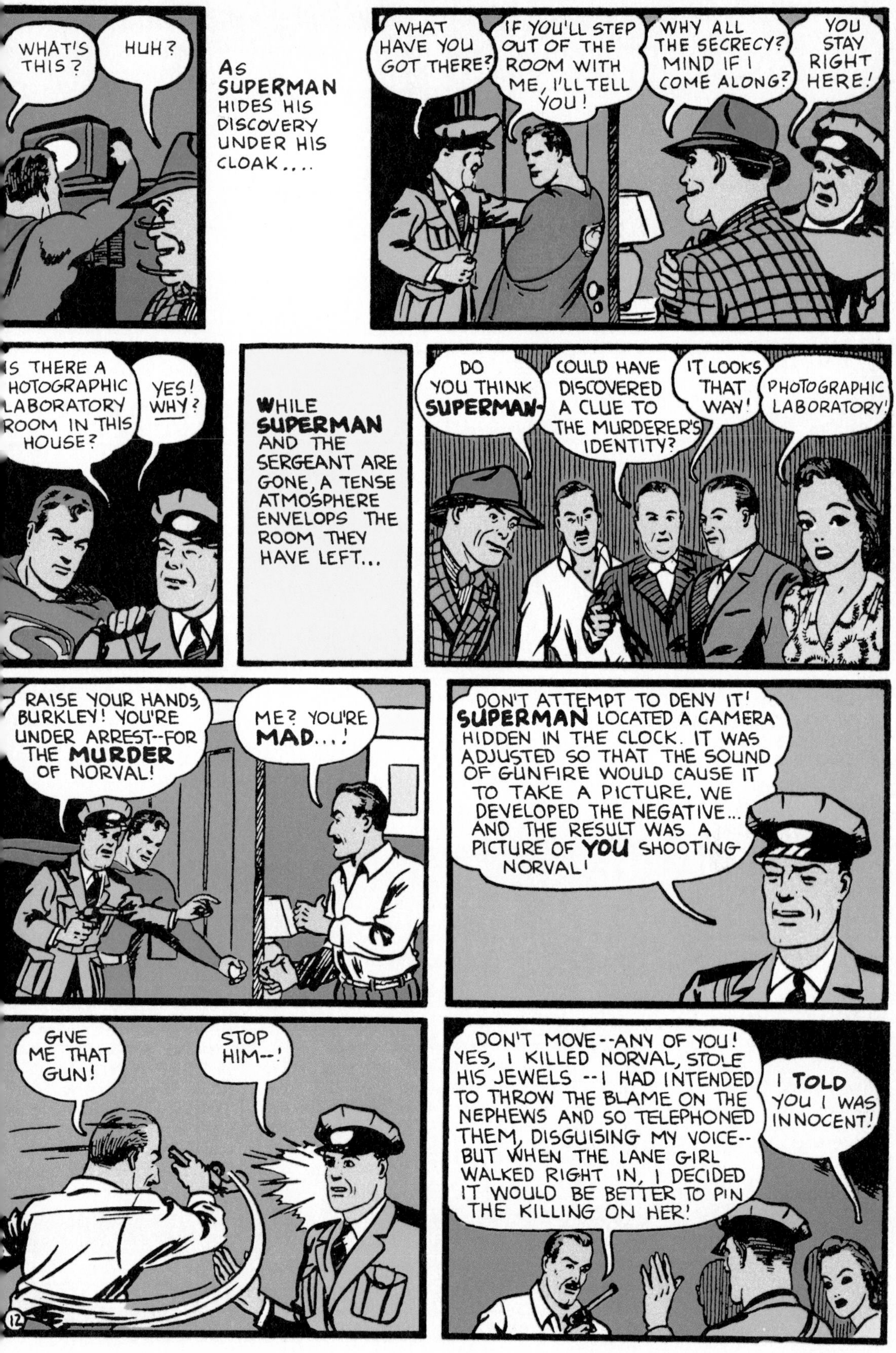

WHAT'S THIS?
HUH?
AS SUPERMAN HIDES HIS DISCOVERY UNDER HIS CLOAK....
WHAT HAVE YOU GOT THERE?
IF YOU'LL STEP OUT OF THE ROOM WITH ME, I'LL TELL YOU!
WHY ALL THE SECRECY? MIND IF I COME ALONG?
YOU STAY RIGHT HERE!
IS THERE A PHOTOGRAPHIC LABORATORY ROOM IN THIS HOUSE?
YES! WHY?
WHILE SUPERMAN AND THE SERGEANT ARE GONE, A TENSE ATMOSPHERE ENVELOPS THE ROOM THEY HAVE LEFT...
DO YOU THINK SUPERMAN-
COULD HAVE DISCOVERED A CLUE TO THE MURDERER'S IDENTITY?
IT LOOKS THAT WAY!
PHOTOGRAPHIC LABORATORY!
RAISE YOUR HANDS, BURKLEY! YOU'RE UNDER ARREST--FOR THE MURDER OF NORVAL!
ME? YOU'RE MAD...!
DON'T ATTEMPT TO DENY IT! SUPERMAN LOCATED A CAMERA HIDDEN IN THE CLOCK. IT WAS ADJUSTED SO THAT THE SOUND OF GUNFIRE WOULD CAUSE IT TO TAKE A PICTURE. WE DEVELOPED THE NEGATIVE... AND THE RESULT WAS A PICTURE OF YOU SHOOTING NORVAL!
GIVE ME THAT GUN!
STOP HIM--!
12
DON'T MOVE--ANY OF YOU! YES, I KILLED NORVAL, STOLE HIS JEWELS --I HAD INTENDED TO THROW THE BLAME ON THE NEPHEWS AND SO TELEPHONED THEM, DISGUISING MY VOICE--BUT WHEN THE LANE GIRL WALKED RIGHT IN, I DECIDED IT WOULD BE BETTER TO PIN THE KILLING ON HER!
I TOLD YOU I WAS INNOCENT!

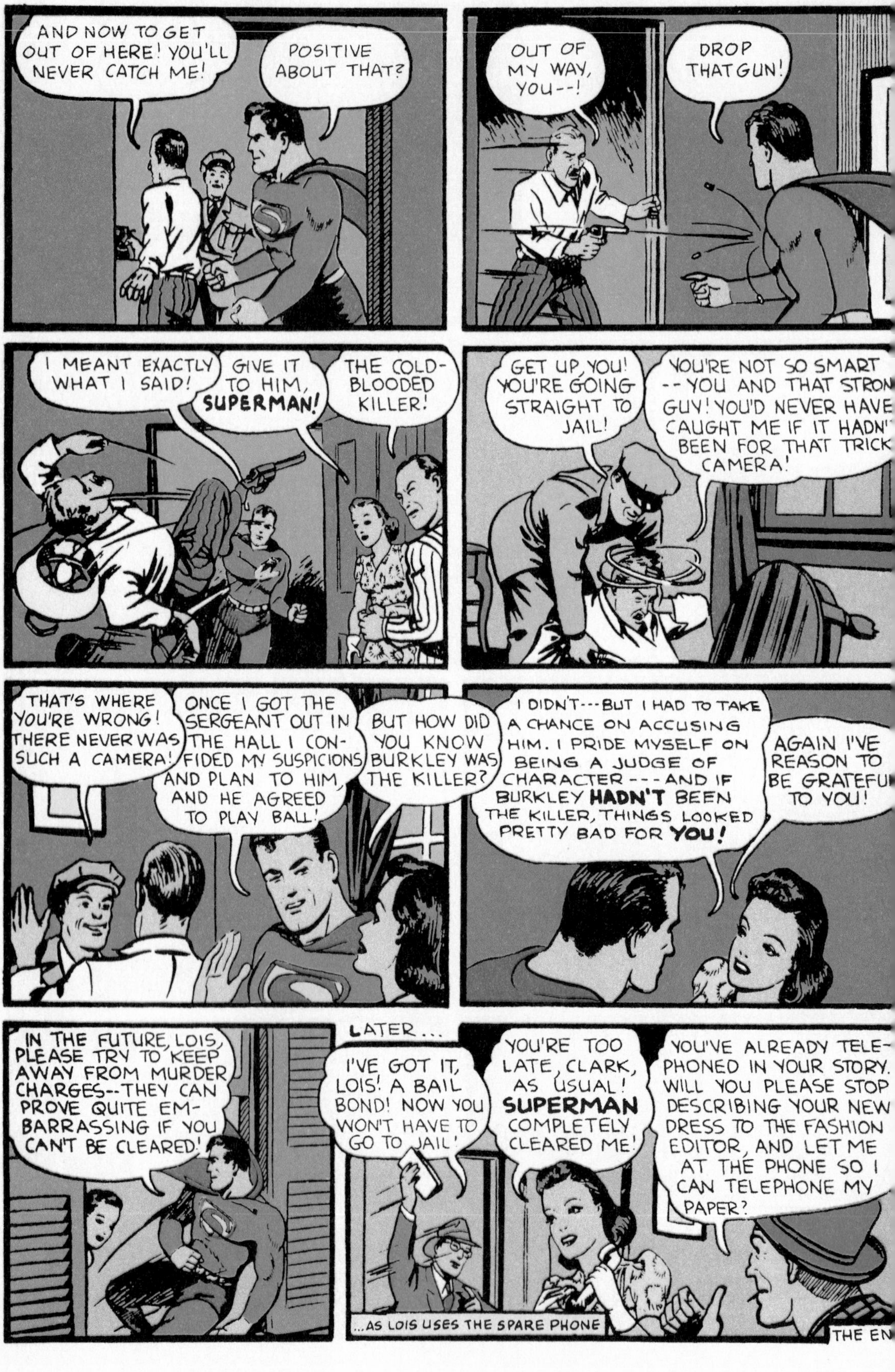
AND NOW TO GET OUT OF HERE! YOU'LL NEVER CATCH ME!
POSITIVE ABOUT THAT?
OUT OF MY WAY, YOU--!
DROP THAT GUN!
I MEANT EXACTLY WHAT I SAID!
GIVE IT TO HIM, SUPERMAN!
THE COLD-BLOODED KILLER!
GET UP, YOU! YOU'RE GOING STRAIGHT TO JAIL!
YOU'RE NOT SO SMART --YOU AND THAT STRON GUY! YOU'D NEVER HAVE CAUGHT ME IF IT HADN' BEEN FOR THAT TRICK CAMERA!
THAT'S WHERE YOU'RE WRONG! THERE NEVER WAS SUCH A CAMERA!
ONCE I GOT THE SERGEANT OUT IN THE HALL I CONFIDED MY SUSPICIONS AND PLAN TO HIM, AND HE AGREED TO PLAY BALL!
BUT HOW DID YOU KNOW BURKLEY WAS THE KILLER?
I DIDN'T---BUT I HAD TO TAKE A CHANCE ON ACCUSING HIM. I PRIDE MYSELF ON BEING A JUDGE OF CHARACTER---AND IF BURKLEY HADN'T BEEN THE KILLER, THINGS LOOKED PRETTY BAD FOR YOU!
AGAIN I'VE REASON TO BE GRATEFU TO YOU!
IN THE FUTURE, LOIS, PLEASE TRY TO KEEP AWAY FROM MURDER CHARGES--THEY CAN PROVE QUITE EMBARRASSING IF YOU CAN'T BE CLEARED!
LATER...
I'VE GOT IT, LOIS! A BAIL BOND! NOW YOU WON'T HAVE TO GO TO JAIL!
YOU'RE TOO LATE, CLARK, AS USUAL! SUPERMAN COMPLETELY CLEARED ME!
YOU'VE ALREADY TELEPHONED IN YOUR STORY. WILL YOU PLEASE STOP DESCRIBING YOUR NEW DRESS TO THE FASHION EDITOR, AND LET ME AT THE PHONE SO I CAN TELEPHONE MY PAPER?
...AS LOIS USES THE SPARE PHONE
THE EN

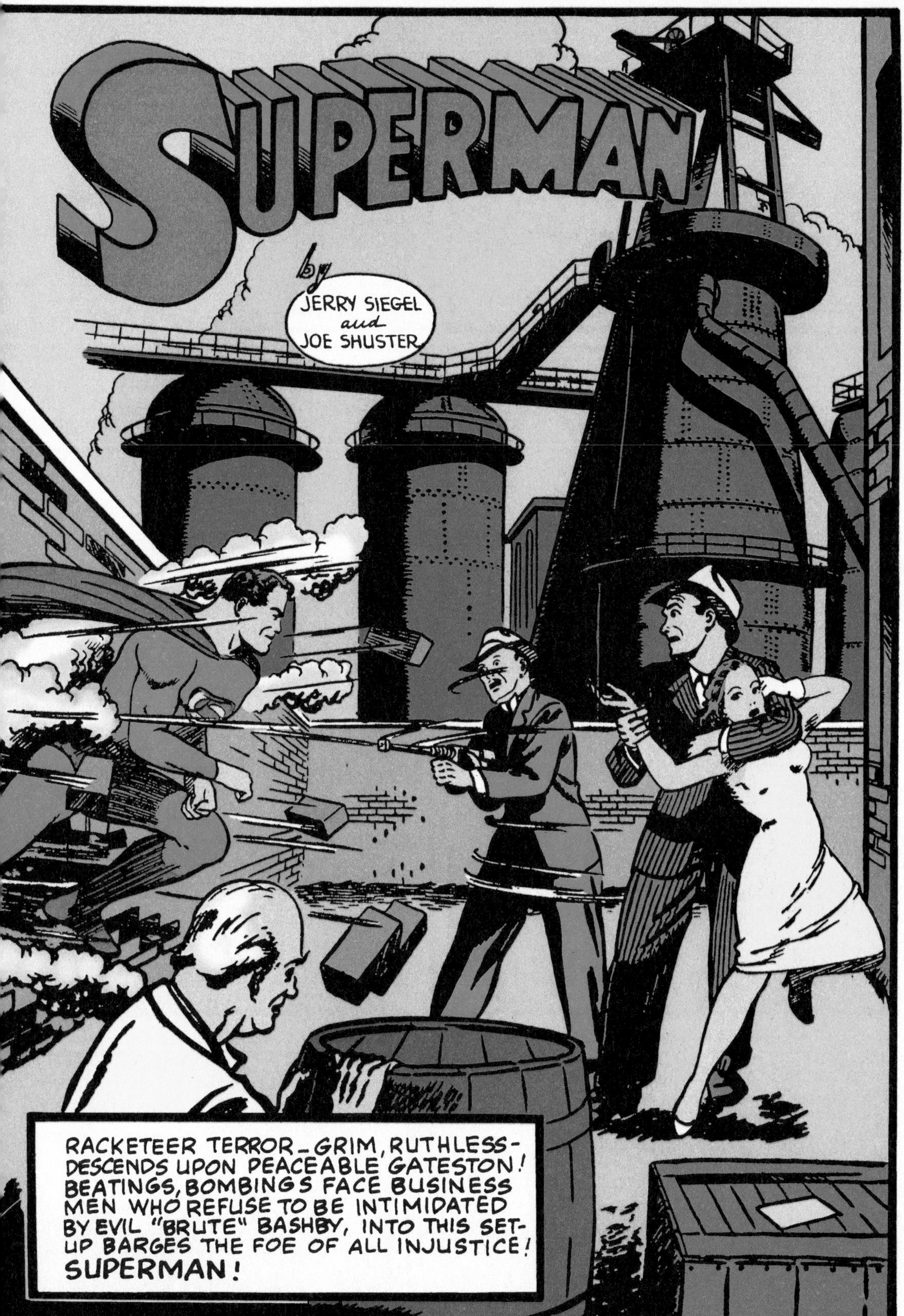
SUPERMAN
by
JERRY SIEGEL
and
JOE SHUSTER
RACKETEER TERROR – GRIM, RUTHLESS – DESCENDS UPON PEACEABLE GATESTON! BEATINGS, BOMBINGS FACE BUSINESS MEN WHO REFUSE TO BE INTIMIDATED BY EVIL "BRUTE" BASHBY, INTO THIS SET-UP BARGES THE FOE OF ALL INJUSTICE! SUPERMAN!

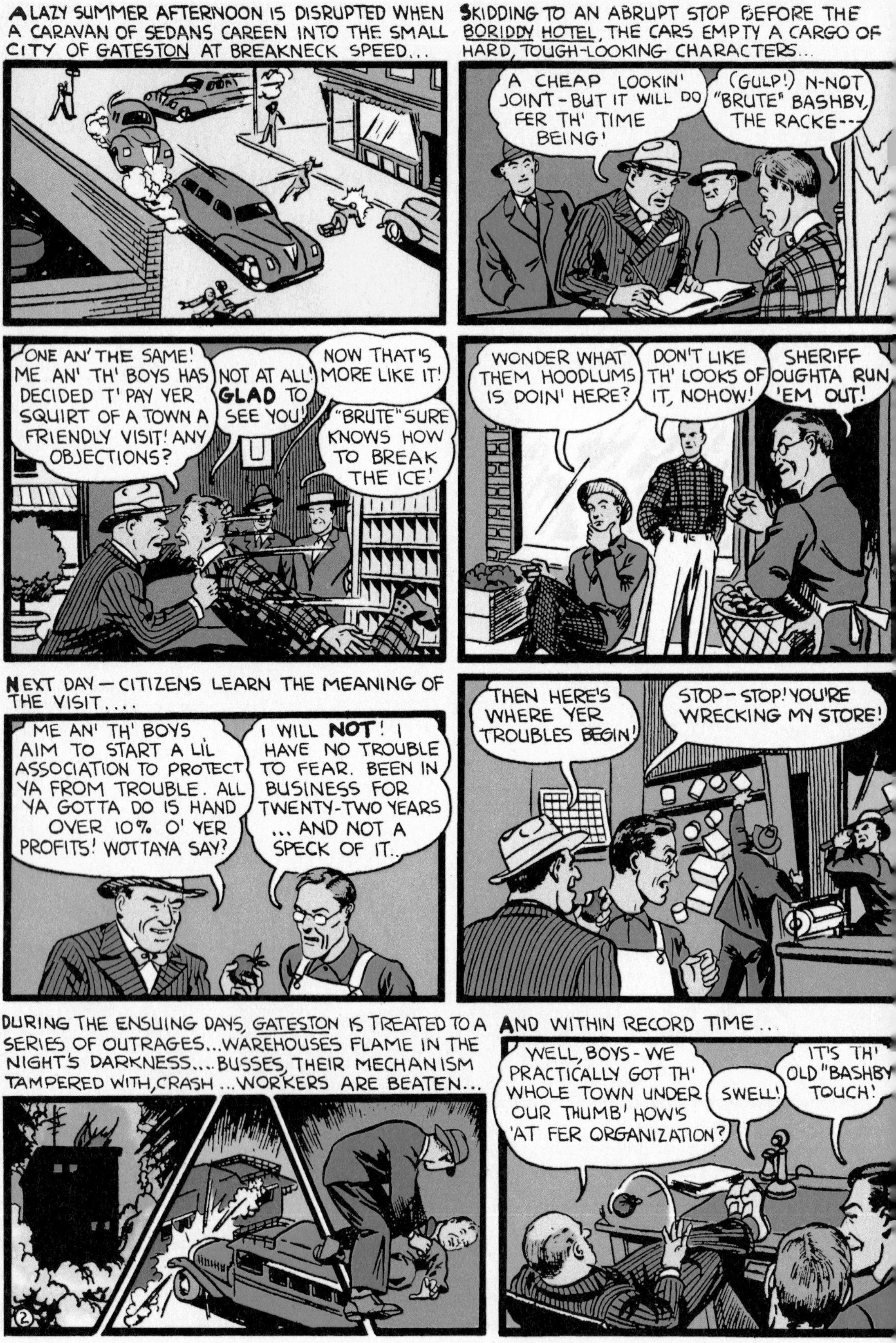
A LAZY SUMMER AFTERNOON IS DISRUPTED WHEN A CARAVAN OF SEDANS CAREEN INTO THE SMALL CITY OF GATESTON AT BREAKNECK SPEED...
SKIDDING TO AN ABRUPT STOP BEFORE THE BORIDDY HOTEL, THE CARS EMPTY A CARGO OF HARD, TOUGH-LOOKING CHARACTERS...
A CHEAP LOOKIN' JOINT - BUT IT WILL DO FER TH' TIME BEING!
(GULP!) N-NOT "BRUTE" BASHBY, THE RACKE---
ONE AN' THE SAME! ME AN' TH' BOYS HAS DECIDED T' PAY YER SQUIRT OF A TOWN A FRIENDLY VISIT! ANY OBJECTIONS?
NOT AT ALL! GLAD TO SEE YOU!
NOW THAT'S MORE LIKE IT!
"BRUTE" SURE KNOWS HOW TO BREAK THE ICE!
WONDER WHAT THEM HOODLUMS IS DOIN' HERE?
DON'T LIKE TH' LOOKS OF IT, NOHOW!
SHERIFF OUGHTA RUN 'EM OUT!
NEXT DAY — CITIZENS LEARN THE MEANING OF THE VISIT....
ME AN' TH' BOYS AIM TO START A LIL ASSOCIATION TO PROTECT YA FROM TROUBLE. ALL YA GOTTA DO IS HAND OVER 10% O' YER PROFITS! WOTTAYA SAY?
I WILL NOT! I HAVE NO TROUBLE TO FEAR. BEEN IN BUSINESS FOR TWENTY-TWO YEARS ... AND NOT A SPECK OF IT..
THEN HERE'S WHERE YER TROUBLES BEGIN!
STOP — STOP! YOU'RE WRECKING MY STORE!
DURING THE ENSUING DAYS, GATESTON IS TREATED TO A SERIES OF OUTRAGES... WAREHOUSES FLAME IN THE NIGHT'S DARKNESS.... BUSSES, THEIR MECHANISM TAMPERED WITH, CRASH ... WORKERS ARE BEATEN...
2
AND WITHIN RECORD TIME...
WELL, BOYS - WE PRACTICALLY GOT TH' WHOLE TOWN UNDER OUR THUMB! HOW'S 'AT FER ORGANIZATION?
SWELL!
IT'S TH' OLD "BASHBY TOUCH!"

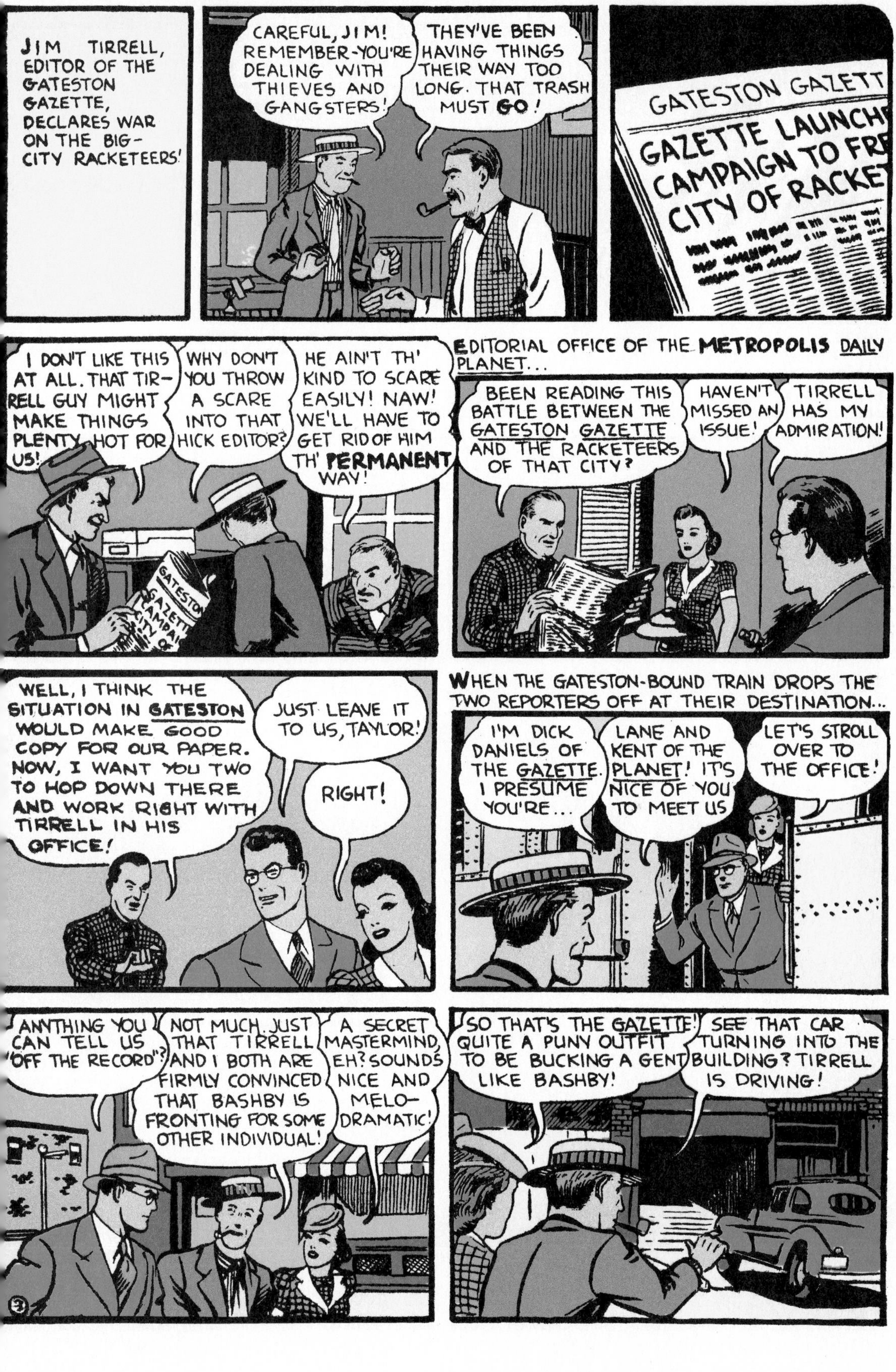
JIM TIRRELL, EDITOR OF THE GATESTON GAZETTE, DECLARES WAR ON THE BIG-CITY RACKETEERS!
CAREFUL, JIM! REMEMBER-YOU'RE DEALING WITH THIEVES AND GANGSTERS!
THEY'VE BEEN HAVING THINGS THEIR WAY TOO LONG. THAT TRASH MUST GO!
GATESTON GAZETT
GAZETTE LAUNCH
CAMPAIGN TO FR
CITY OF RACKET
I DON'T LIKE THIS AT ALL. THAT TIRRELL GUY MIGHT MAKE THINGS PLENTY HOT FOR US!
WHY DON'T YOU THROW A SCARE INTO THAT HICK EDITOR?
HE AIN'T TH' KIND TO SCARE EASILY! NAW! WE'LL HAVE TO GET RID OF HIM TH' PERMANENT WAY!
EDITORIAL OFFICE OF THE METROPOLIS DAILY PLANET...
BEEN READING THIS BATTLE BETWEEN THE GATESTON GAZETTE AND THE RACKETEERS OF THAT CITY?
HAVEN'T MISSED AN ISSUE!
TIRRELL HAS MY ADMIRATION!
WELL, I THINK THE SITUATION IN GATESTON WOULD MAKE GOOD COPY FOR OUR PAPER. NOW, I WANT YOU TWO TO HOP DOWN THERE AND WORK RIGHT WITH TIRRELL IN HIS OFFICE!
JUST LEAVE IT TO US, TAYLOR!
RIGHT!
WHEN THE GATESTON-BOUND TRAIN DROPS THE TWO REPORTERS OFF AT THEIR DESTINATION...
I'M DICK DANIELS OF THE GAZETTE. I PRESUME YOU'RE...
LANE AND KENT OF THE PLANET! IT'S NICE OF YOU TO MEET US
LET'S STROLL OVER TO THE OFFICE!
ANYTHING YOU CAN TELL US "OFF THE RECORD"?
NOT MUCH. JUST THAT TIRRELL AND I BOTH ARE FIRMLY CONVINCED THAT BASHBY IS FRONTING FOR SOME OTHER INDIVIDUAL!
A SECRET MASTERMIND, EH? SOUNDS NICE AND MELO-DRAMATIC!
SO THAT'S THE GAZETTE! QUITE A PUNY OUTFIT TO BE BUCKING A GENT LIKE BASHBY!
SEE THAT CAR TURNING INTO THE BUILDING? TIRRELL IS DRIVING!

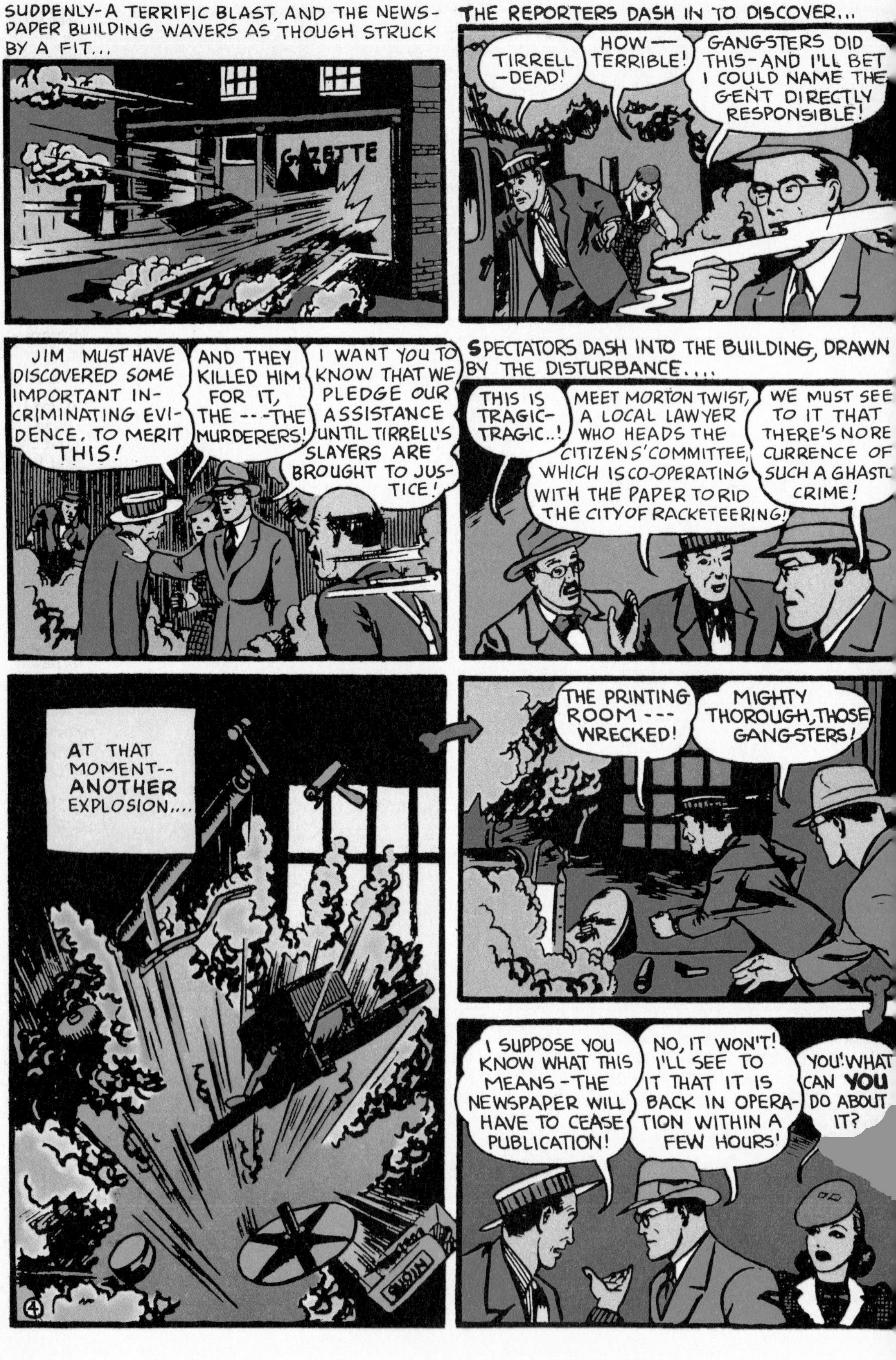

SUDDENLY-A TERRIFIC BLAST, AND THE NEWSPAPER BUILDING WAVERS AS THOUGH STRUCK BY A FIT...
GAZETTE
THE REPORTERS DASH IN TO DISCOVER...
TIRRELL -DEAD!
HOW— TERRIBLE!
GANGSTERS DID THIS-AND I'LL BET I COULD NAME THE GENT DIRECTLY RESPONSIBLE!
JIM MUST HAVE DISCOVERED SOME IMPORTANT INCRIMINATING EVIDENCE, TO MERIT THIS!
AND THEY KILLED HIM FOR IT, THE---THE MURDERERS!
I WANT YOU TO KNOW THAT WE PLEDGE OUR ASSISTANCE UNTIL TIRRELL'S SLAYERS ARE BROUGHT TO JUSTICE!
SPECTATORS DASH INTO THE BUILDING, DRAWN BY THE DISTURBANCE....
THIS IS TRAGIC-TRAGIC..!
MEET MORTON TWIST, A LOCAL LAWYER WHO HEADS THE CITIZENS' COMMITTEE, WHICH IS CO-OPERATING WITH THE PAPER TO RID THE CITY OF RACKETEERING!
WE MUST SEE TO IT THAT THERE'S NO RECURRENCE OF SUCH A GHASTL CRIME!
AT THAT MOMENT--ANOTHER EXPLOSION....
THE PRINTING ROOM--- WRECKED!
MIGHTY THOROUGH, THOSE GANGSTERS!
I SUPPOSE YOU KNOW WHAT THIS MEANS-THE NEWSPAPER WILL HAVE TO CEASE PUBLICATION!
NO, IT WON'T! I'LL SEE TO IT THAT IT IS BACK IN OPERATION WITHIN A FEW HOURS!
YOU! WHAT CAN YOU DO ABOUT IT?

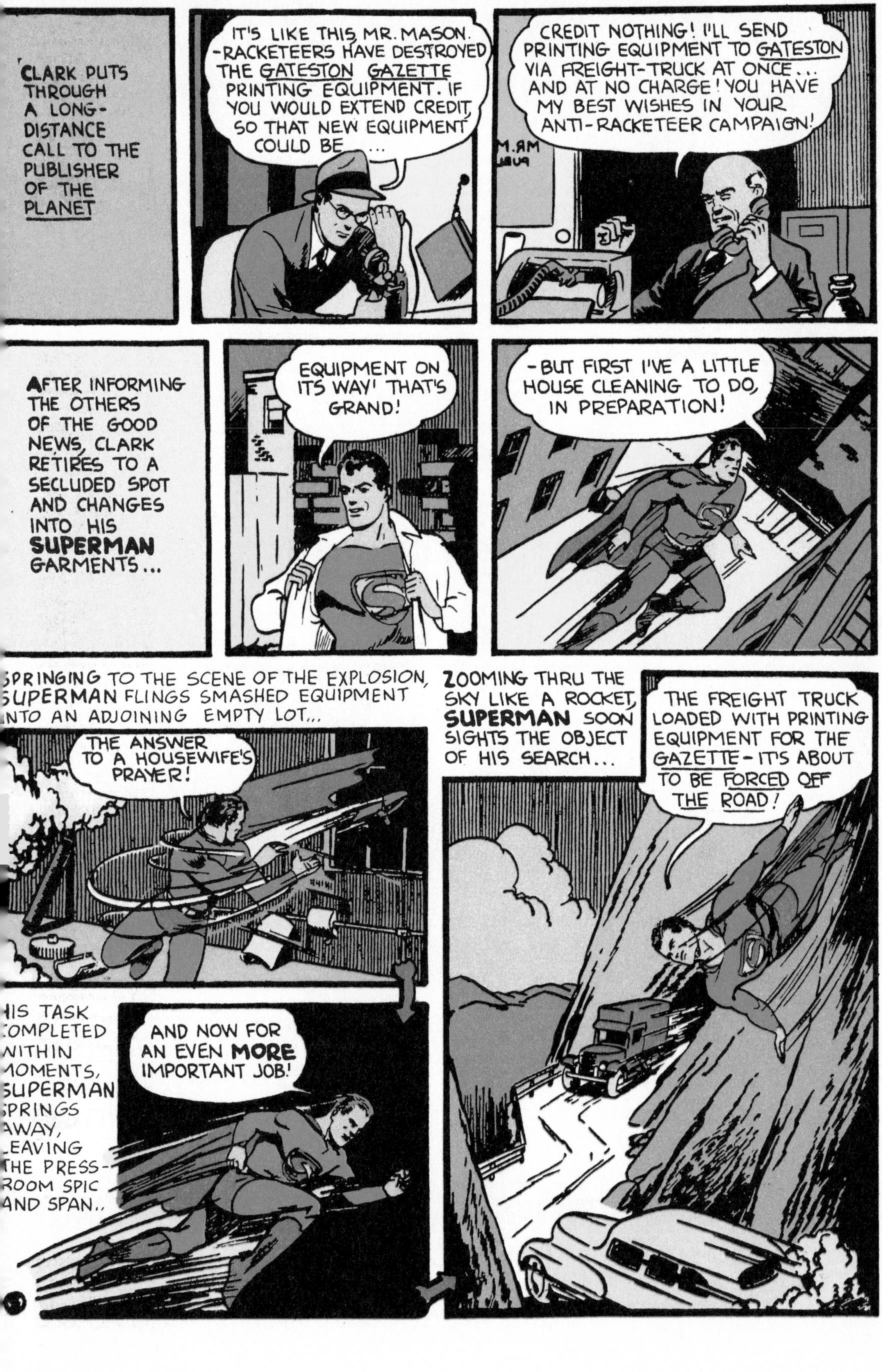
CLARK PUTS THROUGH A LONG-DISTANCE CALL TO THE PUBLISHER OF THE PLANET
IT'S LIKE THIS, MR. MASON. -RACKETEERS HAVE DESTROYED THE GATESTON GAZETTE PRINTING EQUIPMENT. IF YOU WOULD EXTEND CREDIT, SO THAT NEW EQUIPMENT COULD BE ...
CREDIT NOTHING! I'LL SEND PRINTING EQUIPMENT TO GATESTON VIA FREIGHT-TRUCK AT ONCE... AND AT NO CHARGE! YOU HAVE MY BEST WISHES IN YOUR ANTI-RACKETEER CAMPAIGN!
AFTER INFORMING THE OTHERS OF THE GOOD NEWS, CLARK RETIRES TO A SECLUDED SPOT AND CHANGES INTO HIS SUPERMAN GARMENTS...
EQUIPMENT ON ITS WAY! THAT'S GRAND!
-BUT FIRST I'VE A LITTLE HOUSE CLEANING TO DO, IN PREPARATION!
SPRINGING TO THE SCENE OF THE EXPLOSION, SUPERMAN FLINGS SMASHED EQUIPMENT INTO AN ADJOINING EMPTY LOT...
THE ANSWER TO A HOUSEWIFE'S PRAYER!
HIS TASK COMPLETED WITHIN MOMENTS, SUPERMAN SPRINGS AWAY, LEAVING THE PRESS-ROOM SPIC AND SPAN..
AND NOW FOR AN EVEN MORE IMPORTANT JOB!
ZOOMING THRU THE SKY LIKE A ROCKET, SUPERMAN SOON SIGHTS THE OBJECT OF HIS SEARCH...
THE FREIGHT TRUCK LOADED WITH PRINTING EQUIPMENT FOR THE GAZETTE - IT'S ABOUT TO BE FORCED OFF THE ROAD!

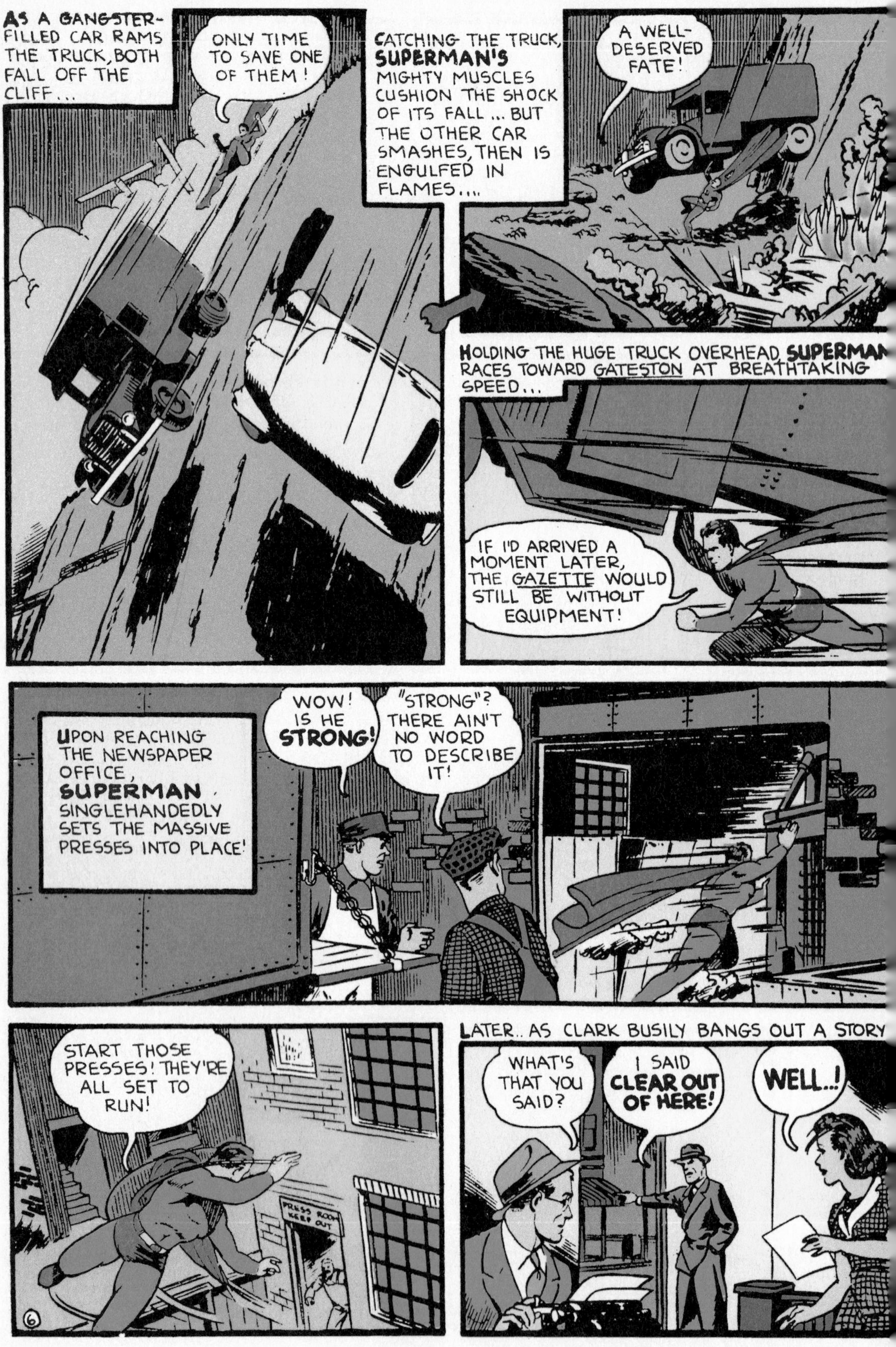
AS A GANGSTER-FILLED CAR RAMS THE TRUCK, BOTH FALL OFF THE CLIFF...
ONLY TIME TO SAVE ONE OF THEM!
CATCHING THE TRUCK, SUPERMAN'S MIGHTY MUSCLES CUSHION THE SHOCK OF ITS FALL ... BUT THE OTHER CAR SMASHES, THEN IS ENGULFED IN FLAMES....
A WELL-DESERVED FATE!
HOLDING THE HUGE TRUCK OVERHEAD, SUPERMAN RACES TOWARD GATESTON AT BREATHTAKING SPEED...
IF I'D ARRIVED A MOMENT LATER, THE GAZETTE WOULD STILL BE WITHOUT EQUIPMENT!
UPON REACHING THE NEWSPAPER OFFICE, SUPERMAN SINGLEHANDEDLY SETS THE MASSIVE PRESSES INTO PLACE!
WOW! IS HE STRONG!
"STRONG"? THERE AIN'T NO WORD TO DESCRIBE IT!
START THOSE PRESSES! THEY'RE ALL SET TO RUN!
PRESS ROOM KEEP OUT
6
LATER.. AS CLARK BUSILY BANGS OUT A STORY
WHAT'S THAT YOU SAID?
I SAID CLEAR OUT OF HERE!
WELL..!

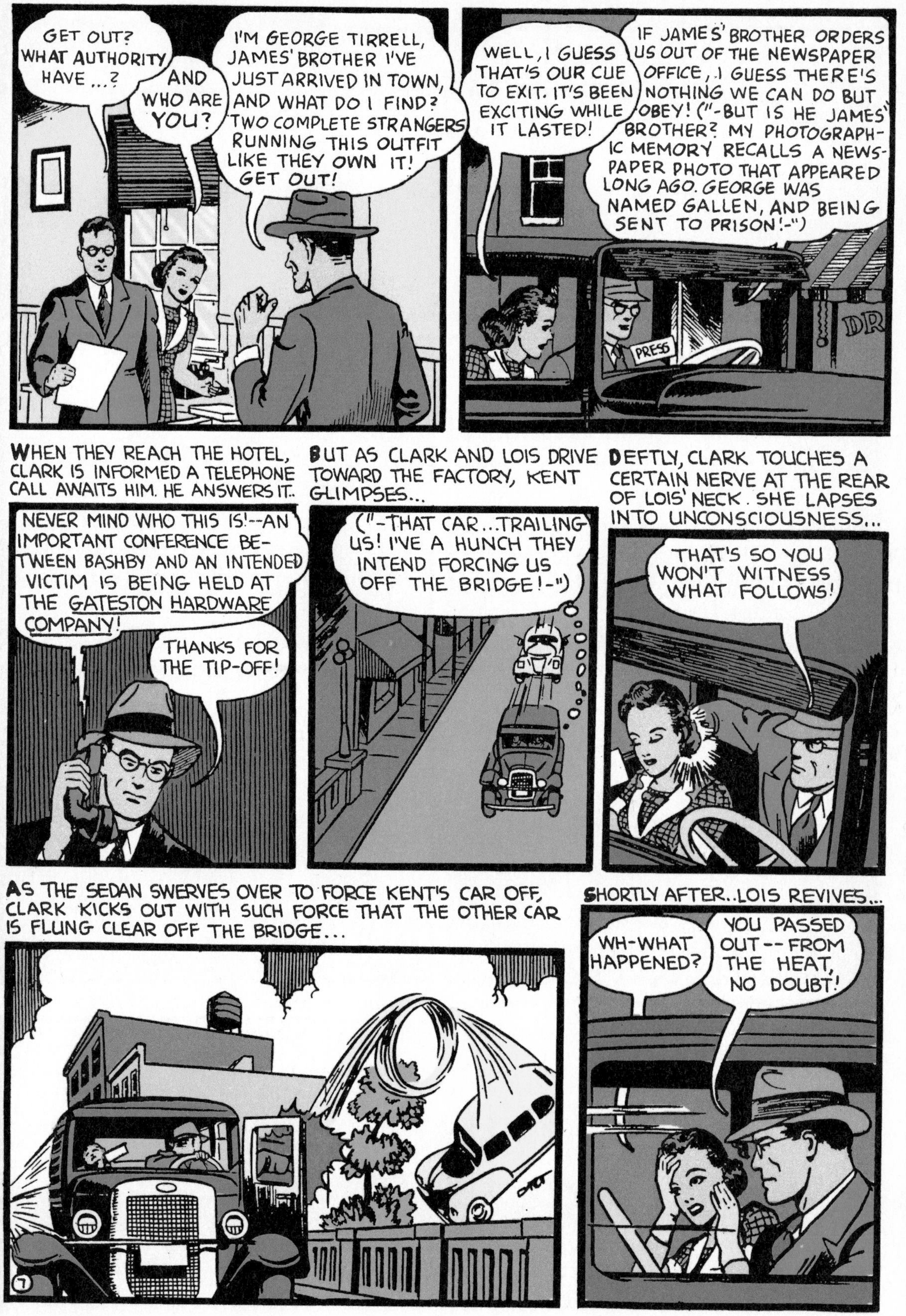
GET OUT? WHAT AUTHORITY HAVE ...?
AND WHO ARE YOU?
I'M GEORGE TIRRELL, JAMES' BROTHER I'VE JUST ARRIVED IN TOWN, AND WHAT DO I FIND? TWO COMPLETE STRANGERS RUNNING THIS OUTFIT LIKE THEY OWN IT! GET OUT!
WELL, I GUESS THAT'S OUR CUE TO EXIT. IT'S BEEN EXCITING WHILE IT LASTED!
IF JAMES' BROTHER ORDERS US OUT OF THE NEWSPAPER OFFICE, I GUESS THERE'S NOTHING WE CAN DO BUT OBEY! ("-BUT IS HE JAMES' BROTHER? MY PHOTOGRAPHIC MEMORY RECALLS A NEWSPAPER PHOTO THAT APPEARED LONG AGO. GEORGE WAS NAMED GALLEN, AND BEING SENT TO PRISON!-")
PRESS
DR
WHEN THEY REACH THE HOTEL, CLARK IS INFORMED A TELEPHONE CALL AWAITS HIM. HE ANSWERS IT..
NEVER MIND WHO THIS IS!--AN IMPORTANT CONFERENCE BETWEEN BASHBY AND AN INTENDED VICTIM IS BEING HELD AT THE GATESTON HARDWARE COMPANY!
THANKS FOR THE TIP-OFF!
BUT AS CLARK AND LOIS DRIVE TOWARD THE FACTORY, KENT GLIMPSES...
("-THAT CAR...TRAILING US! I'VE A HUNCH THEY INTEND FORCING US OFF THE BRIDGE!-")
DEFTLY, CLARK TOUCHES A CERTAIN NERVE AT THE REAR OF LOIS' NECK. SHE LAPSES INTO UNCONSCIOUSNESS...
THAT'S SO YOU WON'T WITNESS WHAT FOLLOWS!
AS THE SEDAN SWERVES OVER TO FORCE KENT'S CAR OFF, CLARK KICKS OUT WITH SUCH FORCE THAT THE OTHER CAR IS FLUNG CLEAR OFF THE BRIDGE...
7
SHORTLY AFTER..LOIS REVIVES...
WH-WHAT HAPPENED?
YOU PASSED OUT -- FROM THE HEAT, NO DOUBT!

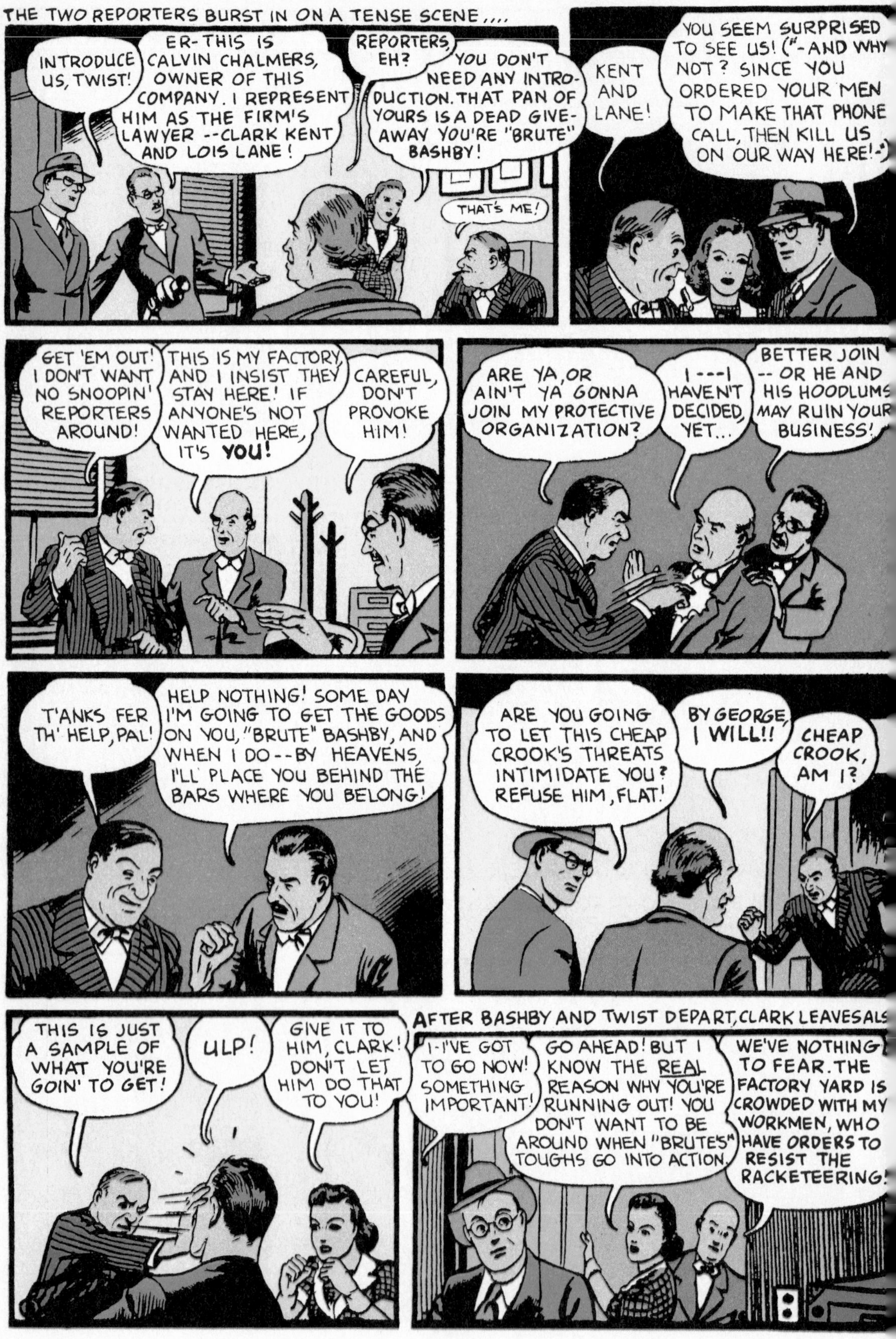
THE TWO REPORTERS BURST IN ON A TENSE SCENE ....
INTRODUCE US, TWIST!
ER-THIS IS CALVIN CHALMERS, OWNER OF THIS COMPANY. I REPRESENT HIM AS THE FIRM'S LAWYER --CLARK KENT AND LOIS LANE!
REPORTERS, EH?
YOU DON'T NEED ANY INTRODUCTION. THAT PAN OF YOURS IS A DEAD GIVE-AWAY YOU'RE "BRUTE" BASHBY!
THAT'S ME!
KENT AND LANE!
YOU SEEM SURPRISED TO SEE US! ("-AND WHY NOT? SINCE YOU ORDERED YOUR MEN TO MAKE THAT PHONE CALL, THEN KILL US ON OUR WAY HERE!")
GET 'EM OUT! I DON'T WANT NO SNOOPIN' REPORTERS AROUND!
THIS IS MY FACTORY AND I INSIST THEY STAY HERE! IF ANYONE'S NOT WANTED HERE, IT'S YOU!
CAREFUL, DON'T PROVOKE HIM!
ARE YA, OR AIN'T YA GONNA JOIN MY PROTECTIVE ORGANIZATION?
I---I HAVEN'T DECIDED, YET...
BETTER JOIN -- OR HE AND HIS HOODLUMS MAY RUIN YOUR BUSINESS!
T'ANKS FER TH' HELP, PAL!
HELP NOTHING! SOME DAY I'M GOING TO GET THE GOODS ON YOU, "BRUTE" BASHBY, AND WHEN I DO--BY HEAVENS, I'LL PLACE YOU BEHIND THE BARS WHERE YOU BELONG!
ARE YOU GOING TO LET THIS CHEAP CROOK'S THREATS INTIMIDATE YOU? REFUSE HIM, FLAT!
BY GEORGE, I WILL!!
CHEAP CROOK, AM I?
THIS IS JUST A SAMPLE OF WHAT YOU'RE GOIN' TO GET!
ULP!
GIVE IT TO HIM, CLARK! DON'T LET HIM DO THAT TO YOU!
AFTER BASHBY AND TWIST DEPART, CLARK LEAVES ALS
I-I'VE GOT TO GO NOW! SOMETHING IMPORTANT!
GO AHEAD! BUT I KNOW THE REAL REASON WHY YOU'RE RUNNING OUT! YOU DON'T WANT TO BE AROUND WHEN "BRUTE'S" TOUGHS GO INTO ACTION.
WE'VE NOTHING TO FEAR. THE FACTORY YARD IS CROWDED WITH MY WORKMEN, WHO HAVE ORDERS TO RESIST THE RACKETEERING!

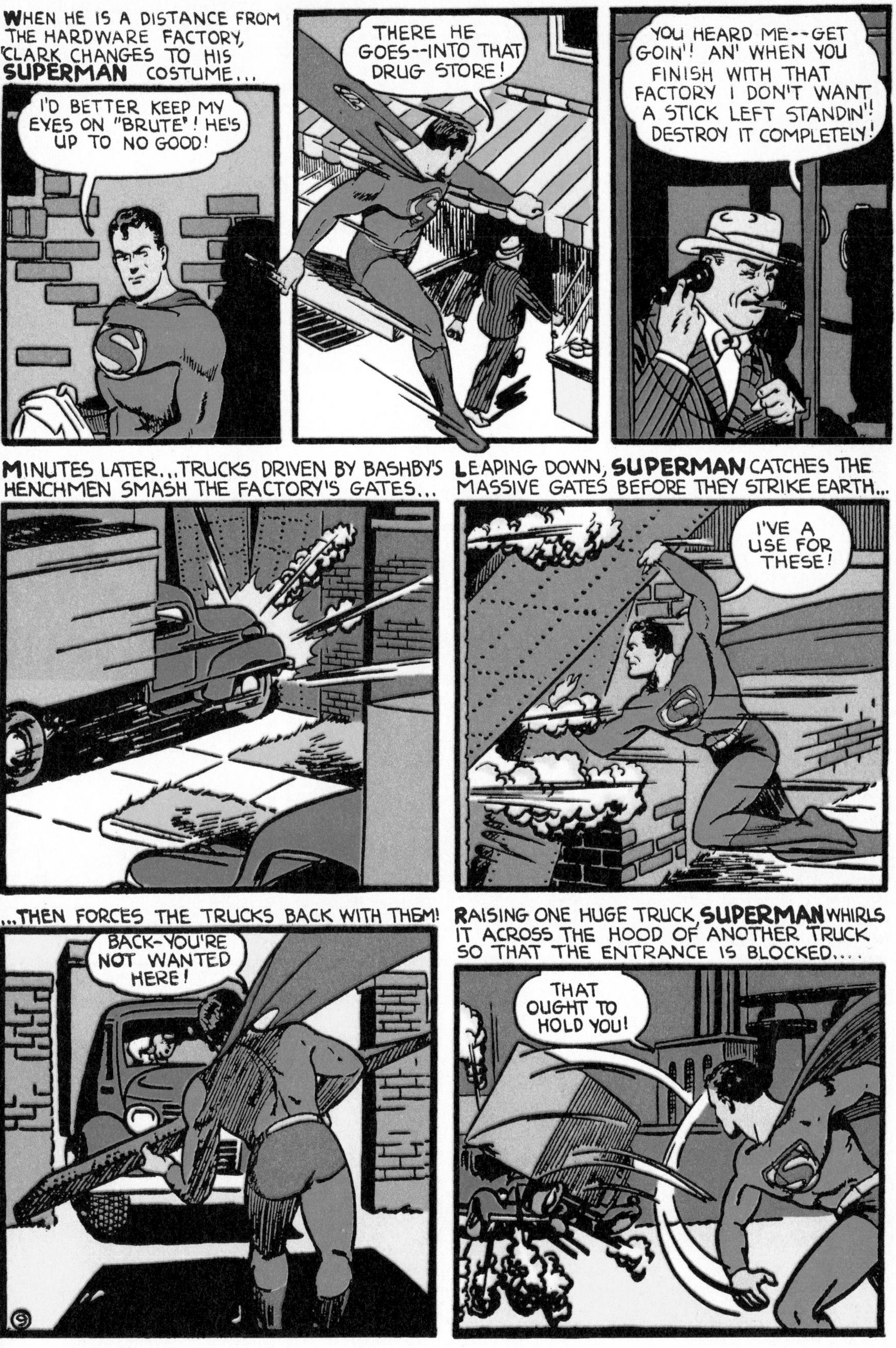
WHEN HE IS A DISTANCE FROM THE HARDWARE FACTORY, CLARK CHANGES TO HIS SUPERMAN COSTUME...
I'D BETTER KEEP MY EYES ON "BRUTE"! HE'S UP TO NO GOOD!
THERE HE GOES--INTO THAT DRUG STORE!
YOU HEARD ME--GET GOIN'! AN' WHEN YOU FINISH WITH THAT FACTORY I DON'T WANT A STICK LEFT STANDIN'! DESTROY IT COMPLETELY!
MINUTES LATER...TRUCKS DRIVEN BY BASHBY'S HENCHMEN SMASH THE FACTORY'S GATES...
LEAPING DOWN, SUPERMAN CATCHES THE MASSIVE GATES BEFORE THEY STRIKE EARTH...
I'VE A USE FOR THESE!
...THEN FORCES THE TRUCKS BACK WITH THEM!
BACK-YOU'RE NOT WANTED HERE!
RAISING ONE HUGE TRUCK, SUPERMAN WHIRLS IT ACROSS THE HOOD OF ANOTHER TRUCK SO THAT THE ENTRANCE IS BLOCKED....
THAT OUGHT TO HOLD YOU!

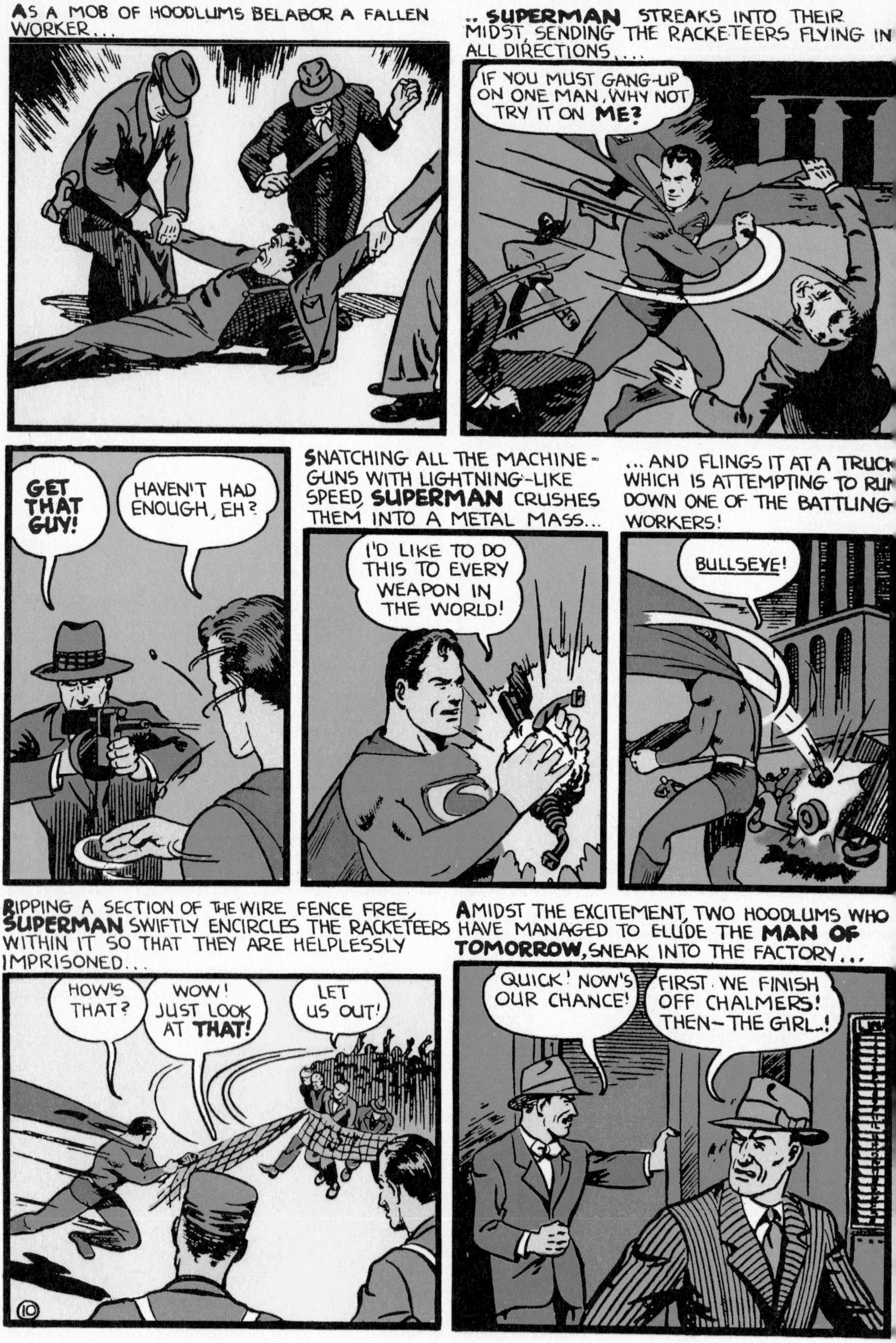
AS A MOB OF HOODLUMS BELABOR A FALLEN WORKER...
.. SUPERMAN STREAKS INTO THEIR MIDST, SENDING THE RACKETEERS FLYING IN ALL DIRECTIONS....
IF YOU MUST GANG-UP ON ONE MAN, WHY NOT TRY IT ON ME?
GET THAT GUY!
HAVEN'T HAD ENOUGH, EH?
SNATCHING ALL THE MACHINE-GUNS WITH LIGHTNING-LIKE SPEED, SUPERMAN CRUSHES THEM INTO A METAL MASS...
I'D LIKE TO DO THIS TO EVERY WEAPON IN THE WORLD!
... AND FLINGS IT AT A TRUCK WHICH IS ATTEMPTING TO RUN DOWN ONE OF THE BATTLING WORKERS!
BULLSEYE!
RIPPING A SECTION OF THE WIRE FENCE FREE, SUPERMAN SWIFTLY ENCIRCLES THE RACKETEERS WITHIN IT SO THAT THEY ARE HELPLESSLY IMPRISONED...
HOW'S THAT?
WOW! JUST LOOK AT THAT!
LET US OUT!
10
AMIDST THE EXCITEMENT, TWO HOODLUMS WHO HAVE MANAGED TO ELUDE THE MAN OF TOMORROW, SNEAK INTO THE FACTORY...
QUICK! NOW'S OUR CHANCE!
FIRST WE FINISH OFF CHALMERS! THEN—THE GIRL..!

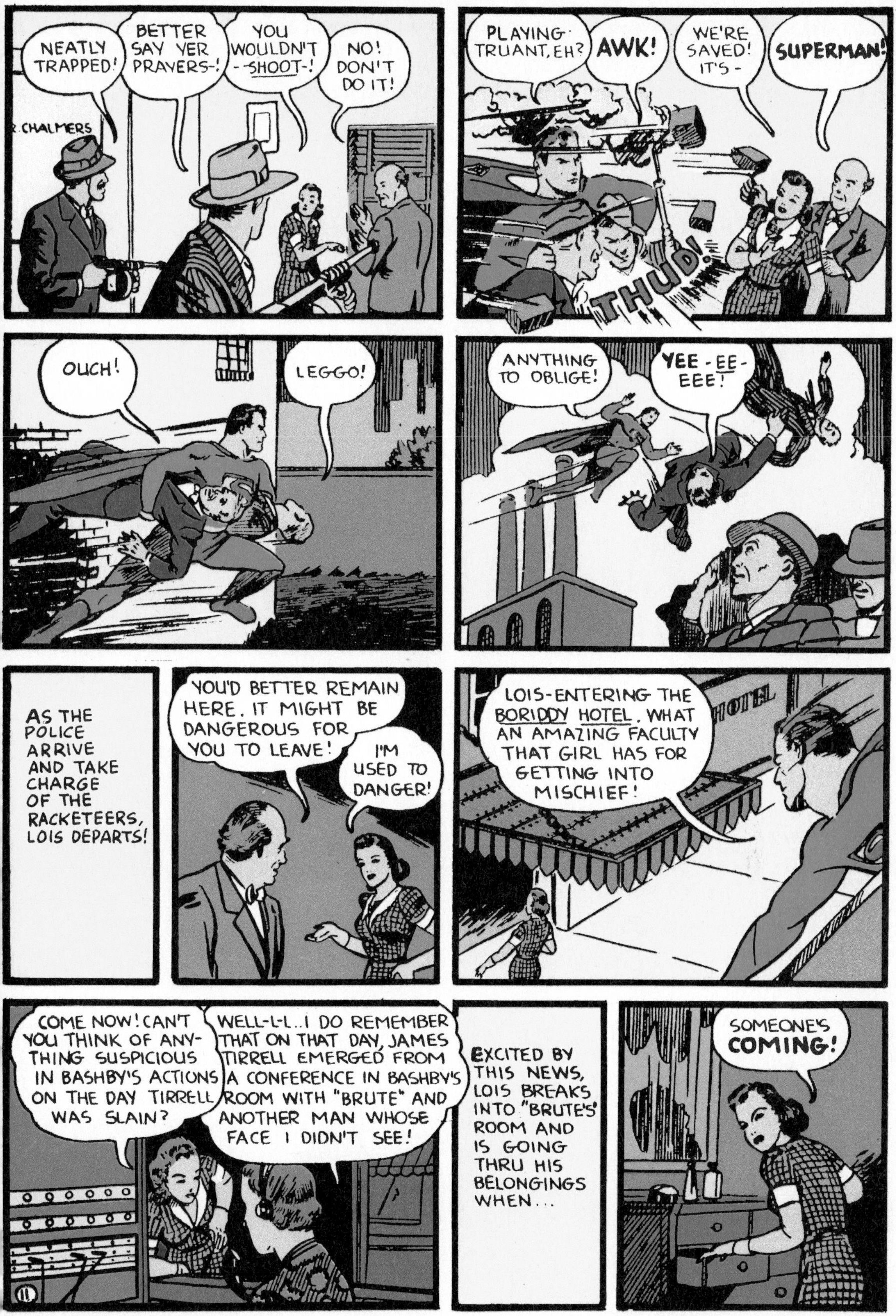
NEATLY TRAPPED!
BETTER SAY YER PRAYERS-!
YOU WOULDN'T --SHOOT-!
NO! DON'T DO IT!
R. CHALMERS
PLAYING TRUANT, EH?
AWK!
WE'RE SAVED! IT'S -
SUPERMAN!
THUD!
OUCH!
LEGGO!
ANYTHING TO OBLIGE!
YEE-EE-EEE!
AS THE POLICE ARRIVE AND TAKE CHARGE OF THE RACKETEERS, LOIS DEPARTS!
YOU'D BETTER REMAIN HERE. IT MIGHT BE DANGEROUS FOR YOU TO LEAVE!
I'M USED TO DANGER!
LOIS-ENTERING THE BORIDDY HOTEL. WHAT AN AMAZING FACULTY THAT GIRL HAS FOR GETTING INTO MISCHIEF!
HOTEL
COME NOW! CAN'T YOU THINK OF ANYTHING SUSPICIOUS IN BASHBY'S ACTIONS ON THE DAY TIRRELL WAS SLAIN?
WELL-L-L..I DO REMEMBER THAT ON THAT DAY, JAMES TIRRELL EMERGED FROM A CONFERENCE IN BASHBY'S ROOM WITH "BRUTE" AND ANOTHER MAN WHOSE FACE I DIDN'T SEE!
11
EXCITED BY THIS NEWS, LOIS BREAKS INTO "BRUTE'S" ROOM AND IS GOING THRU HIS BELONGINGS WHEN...
SOMEONE'S COMING!

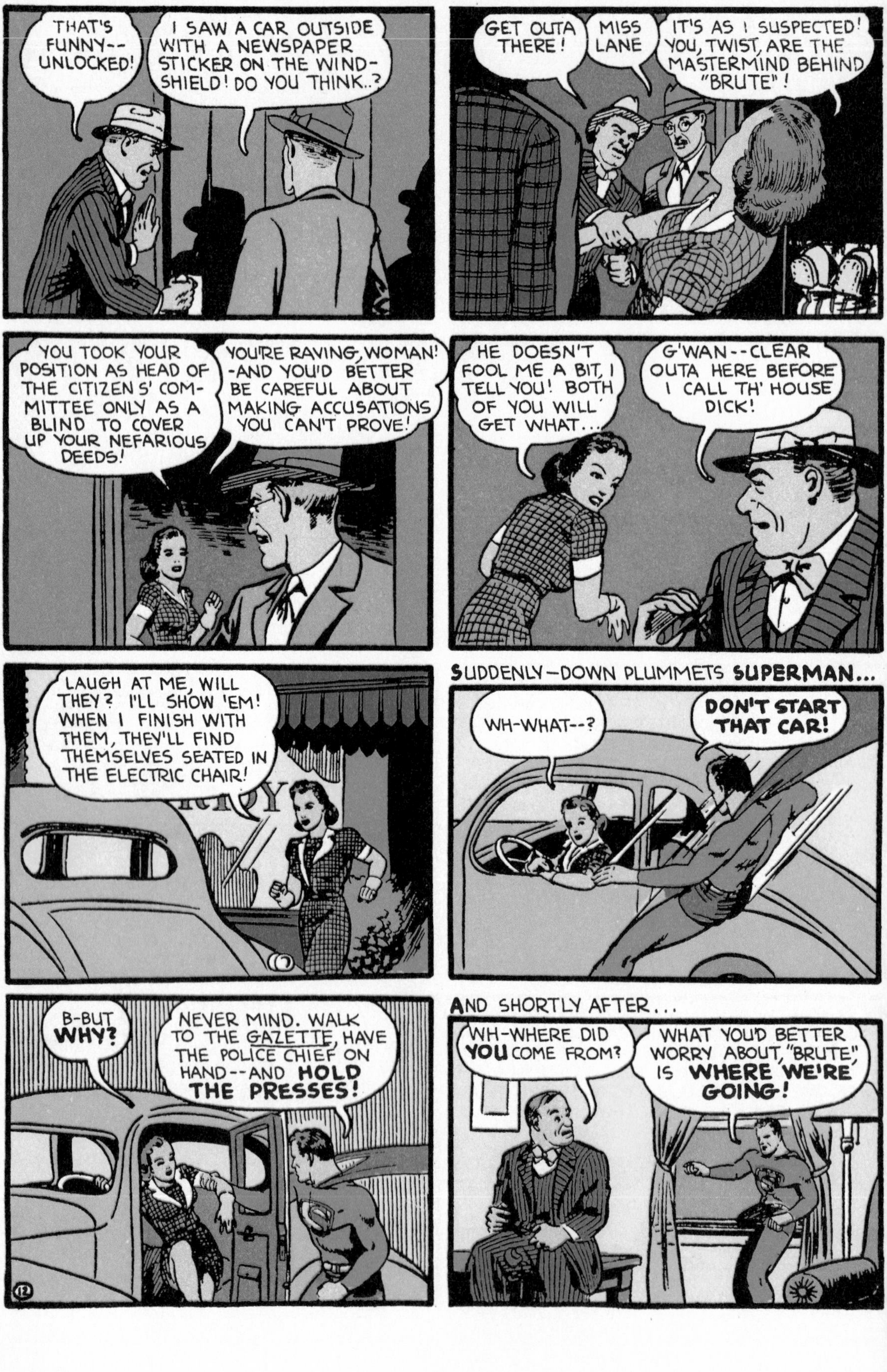
THAT'S FUNNY-- UNLOCKED!
I SAW A CAR OUTSIDE WITH A NEWSPAPER STICKER ON THE WIND-SHIELD! DO YOU THINK..?
GET OUTA THERE!
MISS LANE
IT'S AS I SUSPECTED! YOU, TWIST, ARE THE MASTERMIND BEHIND "BRUTE"!
YOU TOOK YOUR POSITION AS HEAD OF THE CITIZEN S' COM-MITTEE ONLY AS A BLIND TO COVER UP YOUR NEFARIOUS DEEDS!
YOU'RE RAVING, WOMAN! -AND YOU'D BETTER BE CAREFUL ABOUT MAKING ACCUSATIONS YOU CAN'T PROVE!
HE DOESN'T FOOL ME A BIT, I TELL YOU! BOTH OF YOU WILL GET WHAT...
G'WAN--CLEAR OUTA HERE BEFORE I CALL TH' HOUSE DICK!
LAUGH AT ME, WILL THEY? I'LL SHOW 'EM! WHEN I FINISH WITH THEM, THEY'LL FIND THEMSELVES SEATED IN THE ELECTRIC CHAIR!
SUDDENLY—DOWN PLUMMETS SUPERMAN...
WH-WHAT--?
DON'T START THAT CAR!
B-BUT WHY?
NEVER MIND. WALK TO THE GAZETTE, HAVE THE POLICE CHIEF ON HAND--AND HOLD THE PRESSES!
12
AND SHORTLY AFTER...
WH-WHERE DID YOU COME FROM?
WHAT YOU'D BETTER WORRY ABOUT, "BRUTE," IS WHERE WE'RE GOING!

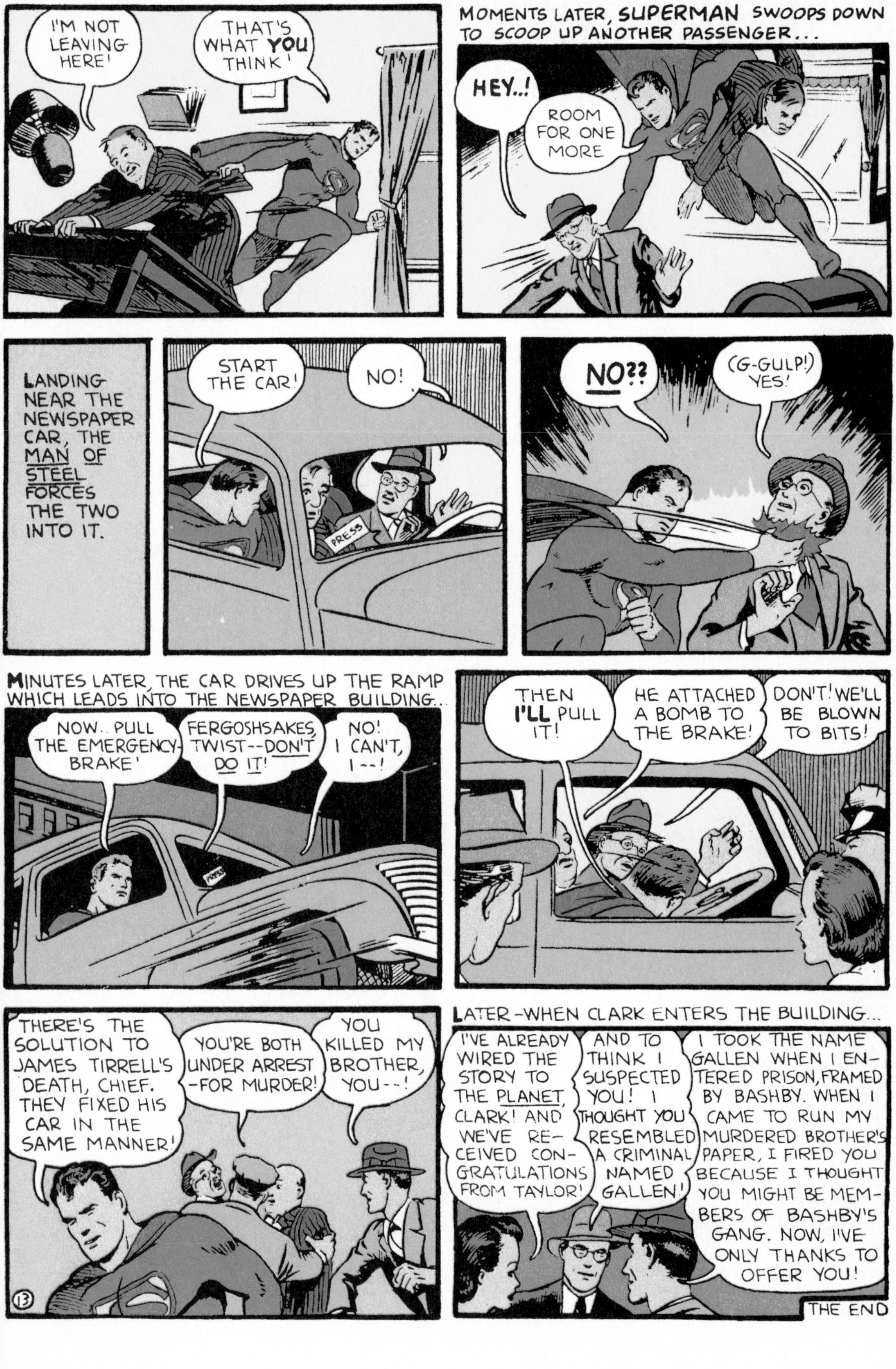
I'M NOT LEAVING HERE!
THAT'S WHAT YOU THINK!
MOMENTS LATER, SUPERMAN SWOOPS DOWN TO SCOOP UP ANOTHER PASSENGER...
HEY..!
ROOM FOR ONE MORE
LANDING NEAR THE NEWSPAPER CAR, THE MAN OF STEEL FORCES THE TWO INTO IT.
START THE CAR!
NO!
PRESS
NO??
(G-GULP!) YES!
MINUTES LATER, THE CAR DRIVES UP THE RAMP WHICH LEADS INTO THE NEWSPAPER BUILDING...
NOW.. PULL THE EMERGENCY-BRAKE!
FERGOSHSAKES, TWIST--DON'T DO IT!
NO! I CAN'T, I--!
PRESS
THEN I'LL PULL IT!
HE ATTACHED A BOMB TO THE BRAKE!
DON'T! WE'LL BE BLOWN TO BITS!
THERE'S THE SOLUTION TO JAMES TIRRELL'S DEATH, CHIEF. THEY FIXED HIS CAR IN THE SAME MANNER!
YOU'RE BOTH UNDER ARREST -FOR MURDER!
YOU KILLED MY BROTHER, YOU--!
13
LATER-WHEN CLARK ENTERS THE BUILDING...
I'VE ALREADY WIRED THE STORY TO THE PLANET, CLARK! AND WE'VE RECEIVED CONGRATULATIONS FROM TAYLOR!
AND TO THINK I SUSPECTED YOU! I THOUGHT YOU RESEMBLED A CRIMINAL NAMED GALLEN!
I TOOK THE NAME GALLEN WHEN I ENTERED PRISON, FRAMED BY BASHBY. WHEN I CAME TO RUN MY MURDERED BROTHER'S PAPER, I FIRED YOU BECAUSE I THOUGHT YOU MIGHT BE MEMBERS OF BASHBY'S GANG. NOW, I'VE ONLY THANKS TO OFFER YOU!
THE END

SUPER STRENGTH

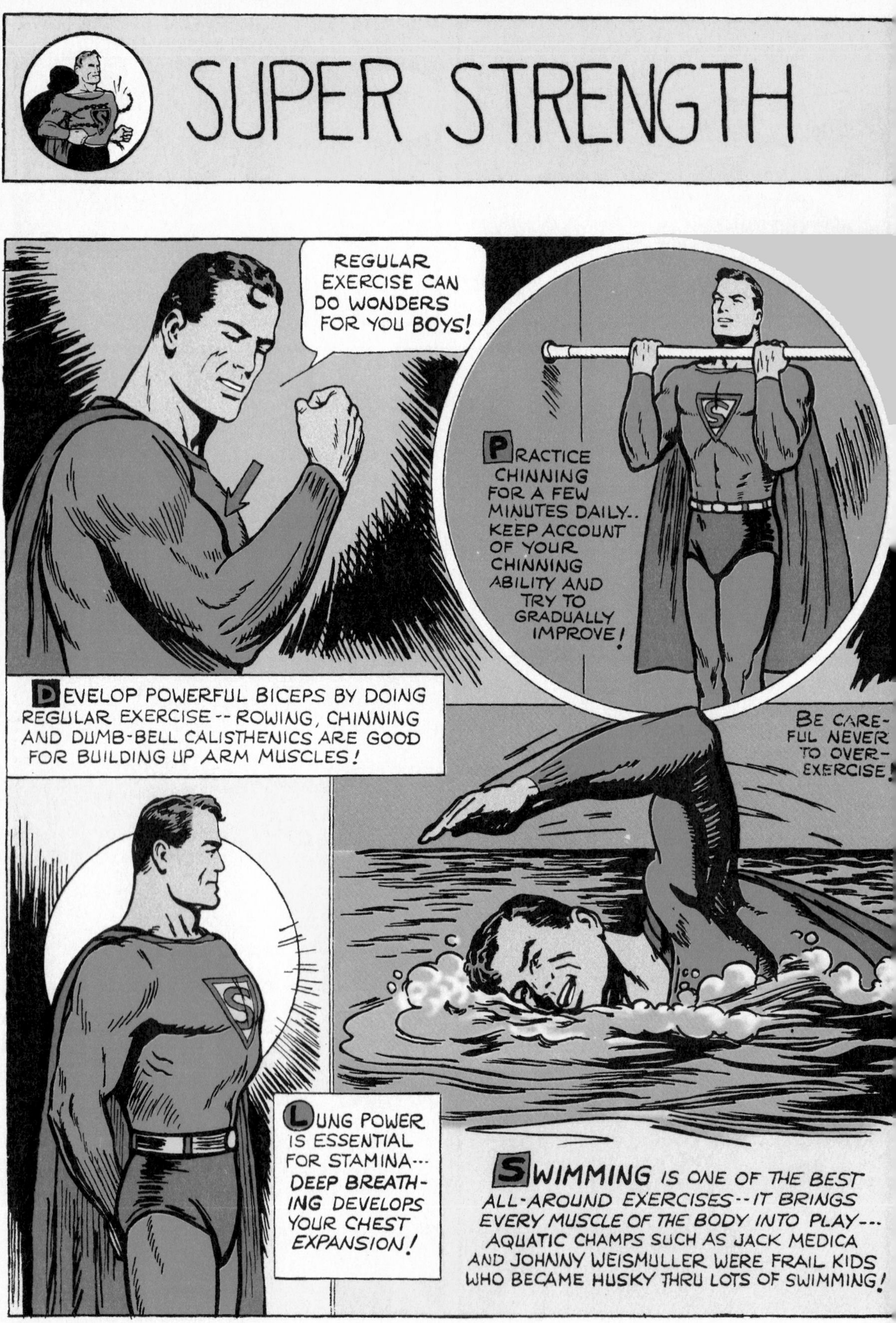
REGULAR EXERCISE CAN DO WONDERS FOR YOU BOYS!
PRACTICE CHINNING FOR A FEW MINUTES DAILY.. KEEP ACCOUNT OF YOUR CHINNING ABILITY AND TRY TO GRADUALLY IMPROVE!
DEVELOP POWERFUL BICEPS BY DOING REGULAR EXERCISE -- ROWING, CHINNING AND DUMB-BELL CALISTHENICS ARE GOOD FOR BUILDING UP ARM MUSCLES!
BE CAREFUL NEVER TO OVER-EXERCISE!
LUNG POWER IS ESSENTIAL FOR STAMINA--- DEEP BREATHING DEVELOPS YOUR CHEST EXPANSION!
SWIMMING IS ONE OF THE BEST ALL-AROUND EXERCISES -- IT BRINGS EVERY MUSCLE OF THE BODY INTO PLAY--- AQUATIC CHAMPS SUCH AS JACK MEDICA AND JOHNNY WEISMULLER WERE FRAIL KIDS WHO BECAME HUSKY THRU LOTS OF SWIMMING!

SUPERMAN

by

Jerry Siegel and Joe Shuster

TERROR STALKS SAN CALUMA, A SMALL SOUTH AMERICAN COUNTRY, AS IT IS RAVAGED BY EARTHQUAKE AND TORNADO....

WHEN NATURE'S FURY EBBS, THE POPULACE IS LEFT IN MISERABLE CIRCUMSTANCES--DEATH, DISEASE AND HUNGER STALK THE LAND...

IN THE UNITED STATES, SYMPATHY IS DEMONSTRATED IN A PRACTICAL MANNER...

DONATIONS FOR THE SUFFERING CITIZENS OF SAN CALUMA HAVE BEEN GRATIFYING! IMMEDIATE AID AND SUPPLIES WILL BE RUSHED!

OFFICE OF GEORGE TAYLOR, EDITOR OF METROPOLIS' CRUSADING NEWSPAPER, THE DAILY PLANET..

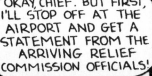

CLARK, I WANT YOU TO COVER THE DEPARTURE OF THE RELIEF SHIP FOR SAN CALUMA!

OKAY, CHIEF. BUT FIRST, I'LL STOP OFF AT THE AIRPORT AND GET A STATEMENT FROM THE ARRIVING RELIEF COMMISSION OFFICIALS!

MEANWHILE--IN THE PLANE CARRYING THE OFFICIALS TO THE FLYING FIELD...

("-ANOTHER MOMENT, AND THE TIME TO STRIKE WILL HAVE ARRIVED!-")

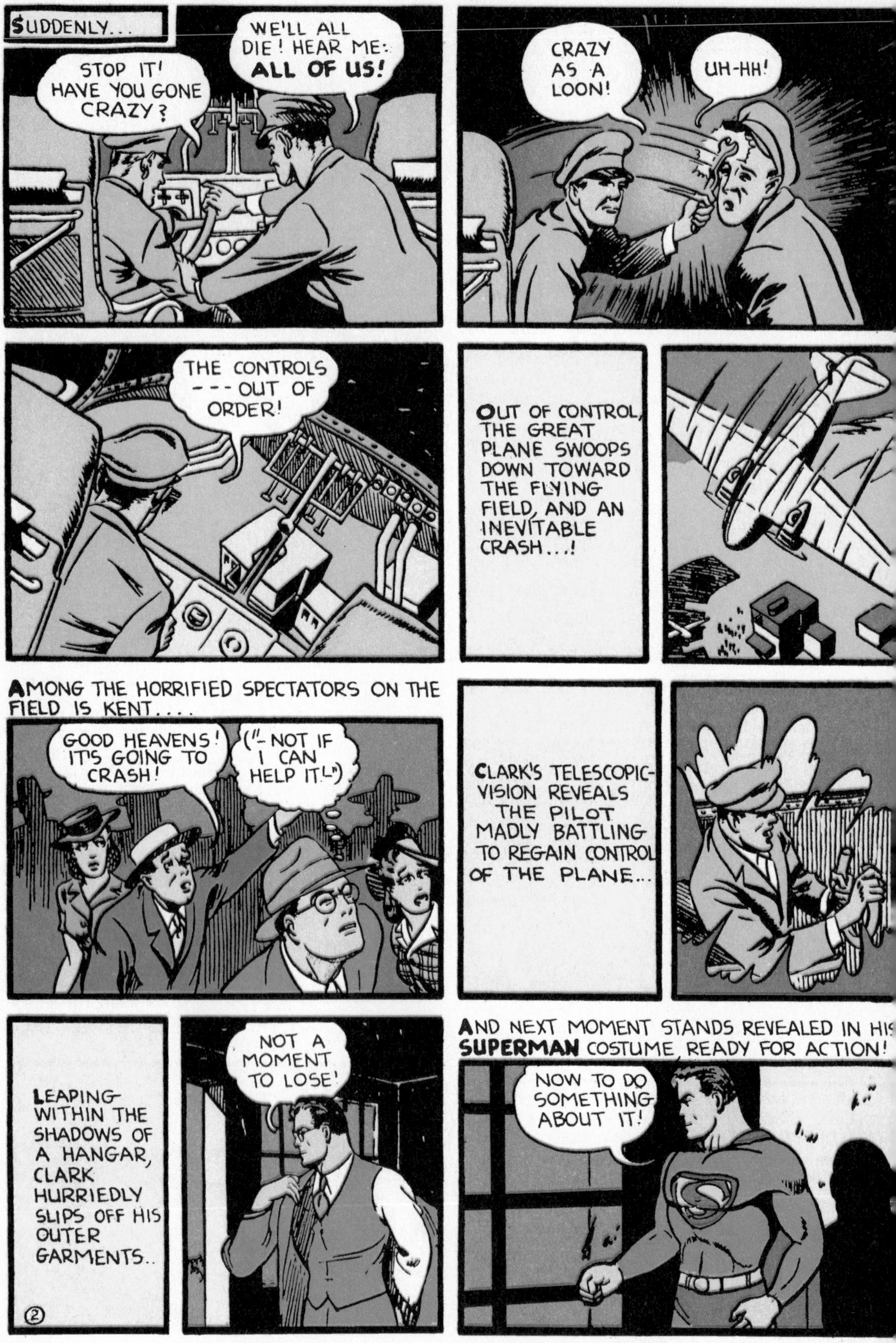
SUDDENLY...
STOP IT! HAVE YOU GONE CRAZY?
WE'LL ALL DIE! HEAR ME: ALL OF US!
CRAZY AS A LOON!
UH-HH!
THE CONTROLS --- OUT OF ORDER!
OUT OF CONTROL, THE GREAT PLANE SWOOPS DOWN TOWARD THE FLYING FIELD, AND AN INEVITABLE CRASH...!
AMONG THE HORRIFIED SPECTATORS ON THE FIELD IS KENT....
GOOD HEAVENS! IT'S GOING TO CRASH!
("-NOT IF I CAN HELP IT!")
CLARK'S TELESCOPIC-VISION REVEALS THE PILOT MADLY BATTLING TO REGAIN CONTROL OF THE PLANE...
LEAPING WITHIN THE SHADOWS OF A HANGAR, CLARK HURRIEDLY SLIPS OFF HIS OUTER GARMENTS..
2
NOT A MOMENT TO LOSE!
AND NEXT MOMENT STANDS REVEALED IN HIS SUPERMAN COSTUME, READY FOR ACTION!
NOW TO DO SOMETHING ABOUT IT!

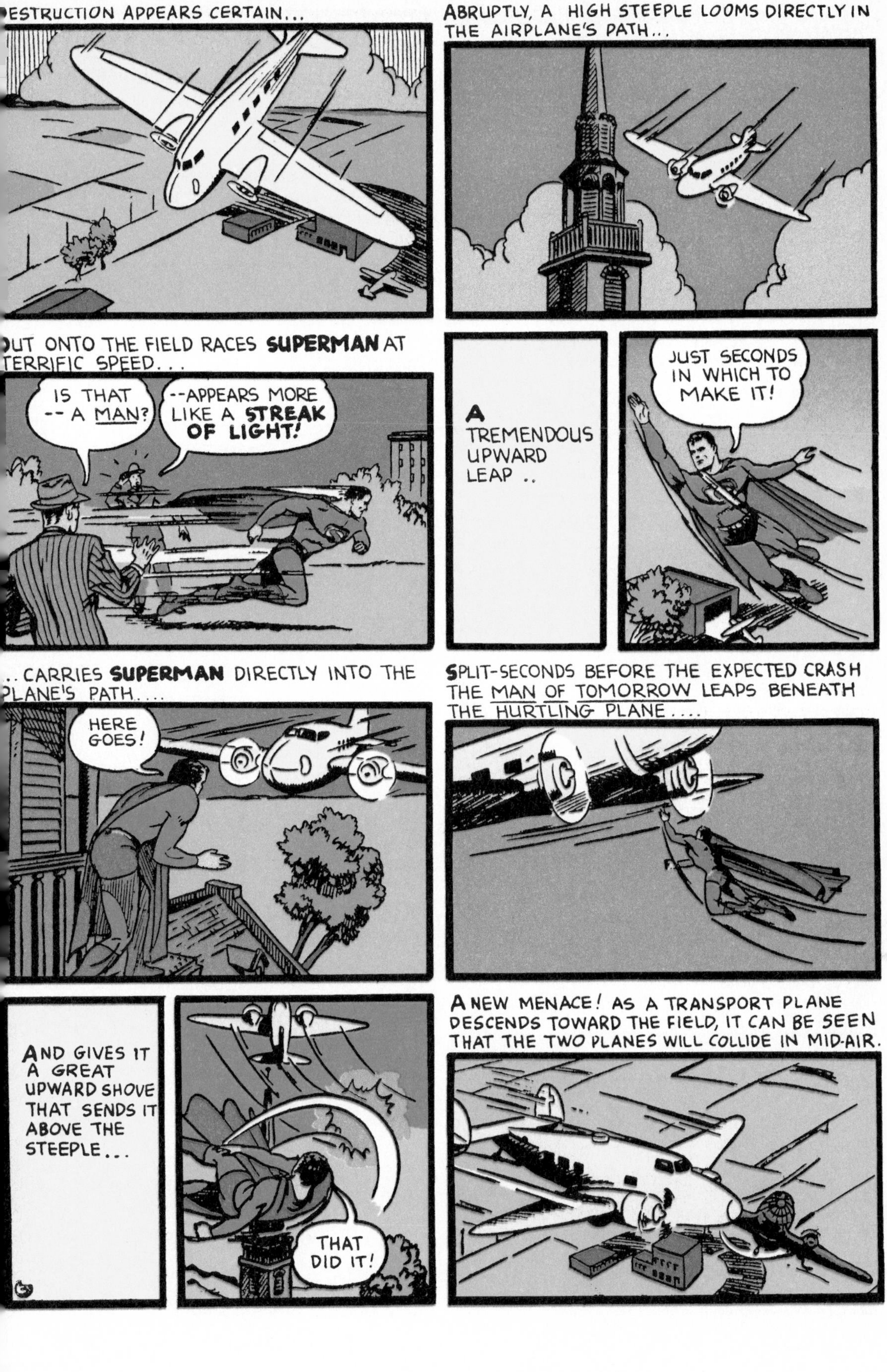
ESTRUCTION APPEARS CERTAIN...
ABRUPTLY, A HIGH STEEPLE LOOMS DIRECTLY IN THE AIRPLANE'S PATH...
UT ONTO THE FIELD RACES SUPERMAN AT TERRIFIC SPEED...
IS THAT -- A MAN?
--APPEARS MORE LIKE A STREAK OF LIGHT!
A TREMENDOUS UPWARD LEAP ..
JUST SECONDS IN WHICH TO MAKE IT!
.. CARRIES SUPERMAN DIRECTLY INTO THE PLANE'S PATH....
HERE GOES!
SPLIT-SECONDS BEFORE THE EXPECTED CRASH THE MAN OF TOMORROW LEAPS BENEATH THE HURTLING PLANE....
AND GIVES IT A GREAT UPWARD SHOVE THAT SENDS IT ABOVE THE STEEPLE...
THAT DID IT!
A NEW MENACE! AS A TRANSPORT PLANE DESCENDS TOWARD THE FIELD, IT CAN BE SEEN THAT THE TWO PLANES WILL COLLIDE IN MID-AIR.

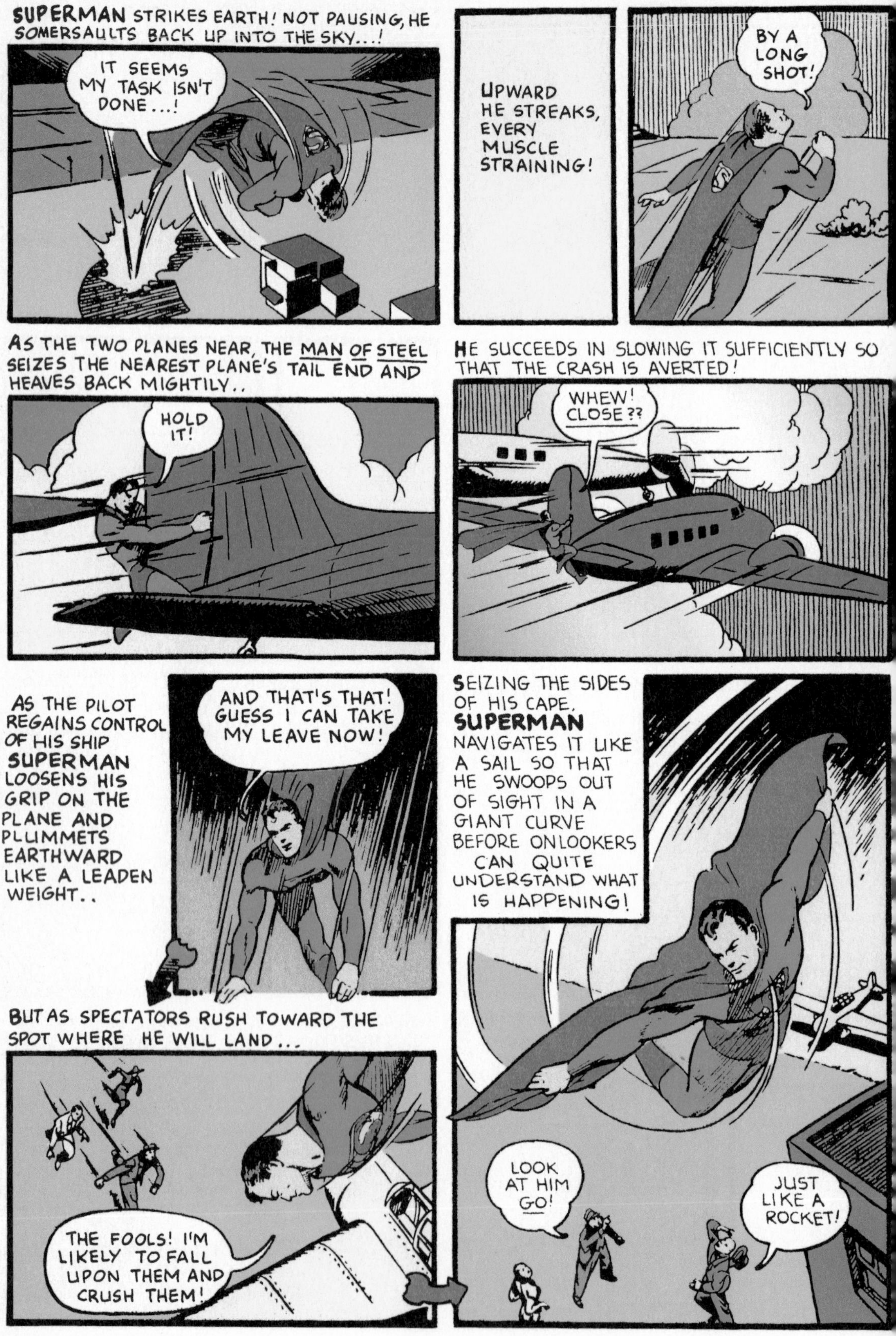
SUPERMAN STRIKES EARTH! NOT PAUSING, HE SOMERSAULTS BACK UP INTO THE SKY...!
IT SEEMS MY TASK ISN'T DONE...!
UPWARD HE STREAKS, EVERY MUSCLE STRAINING!
BY A LONG SHOT!
AS THE TWO PLANES NEAR, THE MAN OF STEEL SEIZES THE NEAREST PLANE'S TAIL END AND HEAVES BACK MIGHTILY..
HOLD IT!
HE SUCCEEDS IN SLOWING IT SUFFICIENTLY SO THAT THE CRASH IS AVERTED!
WHEW! CLOSE??
AS THE PILOT REGAINS CONTROL OF HIS SHIP SUPERMAN LOOSENS HIS GRIP ON THE PLANE AND PLUMMETS EARTHWARD LIKE A LEADEN WEIGHT..
AND THAT'S THAT! GUESS I CAN TAKE MY LEAVE NOW!
BUT AS SPECTATORS RUSH TOWARD THE SPOT WHERE HE WILL LAND...
THE FOOLS! I'M LIKELY TO FALL UPON THEM AND CRUSH THEM!
SEIZING THE SIDES OF HIS CAPE, SUPERMAN NAVIGATES IT LIKE A SAIL SO THAT HE SWOOPS OUT OF SIGHT IN A GIANT CURVE BEFORE ONLOOKERS CAN QUITE UNDERSTAND WHAT IS HAPPENING!
LOOK AT HIM GO!
JUST LIKE A ROCKET!

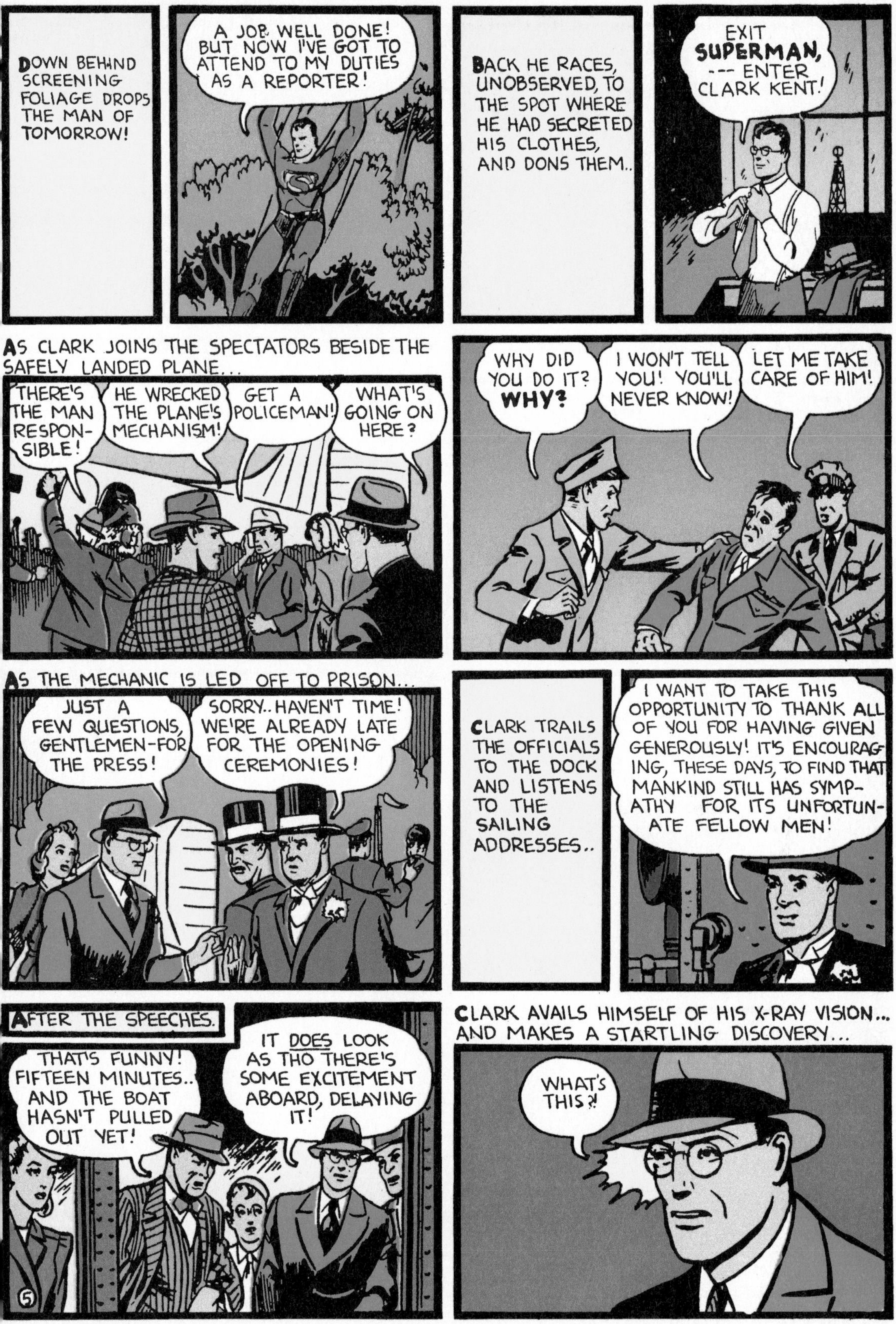
DOWN BEHIND SCREENING FOLIAGE DROPS THE MAN OF TOMORROW!
A JOB WELL DONE! BUT NOW I'VE GOT TO ATTEND TO MY DUTIES AS A REPORTER!
BACK HE RACES, UNOBSERVED, TO THE SPOT WHERE HE HAD SECRETED HIS CLOTHES, AND DONS THEM..
EXIT SUPERMAN, --- ENTER CLARK KENT!
AS CLARK JOINS THE SPECTATORS BESIDE THE SAFELY LANDED PLANE...
THERE'S THE MAN RESPON-SIBLE!
HE WRECKED THE PLANE'S MECHANISM!
GET A POLICEMAN!
WHAT'S GOING ON HERE?
WHY DID YOU DO IT? WHY?
I WON'T TELL YOU! YOU'LL NEVER KNOW!
LET ME TAKE CARE OF HIM!
AS THE MECHANIC IS LED OFF TO PRISON...
JUST A FEW QUESTIONS, GENTLEMEN-FOR THE PRESS!
SORRY.. HAVEN'T TIME! WE'RE ALREADY LATE FOR THE OPENING CEREMONIES!
CLARK TRAILS THE OFFICIALS TO THE DOCK AND LISTENS TO THE SAILING ADDRESSES..
I WANT TO TAKE THIS OPPORTUNITY TO THANK ALL OF YOU FOR HAVING GIVEN GENEROUSLY! IT'S ENCOURAG-ING, THESE DAYS, TO FIND THAT MANKIND STILL HAS SYMP-ATHY FOR ITS UNFORTUN-ATE FELLOW MEN!
AFTER THE SPEECHES.
THAT'S FUNNY! FIFTEEN MINUTES.. AND THE BOAT HASN'T PULLED OUT YET!
IT DOES LOOK AS THO THERE'S SOME EXCITEMENT ABOARD, DELAYING IT!
5
CLARK AVAILS HIMSELF OF HIS X-RAY VISION... AND MAKES A STARTLING DISCOVERY...
WHAT'S THIS?!

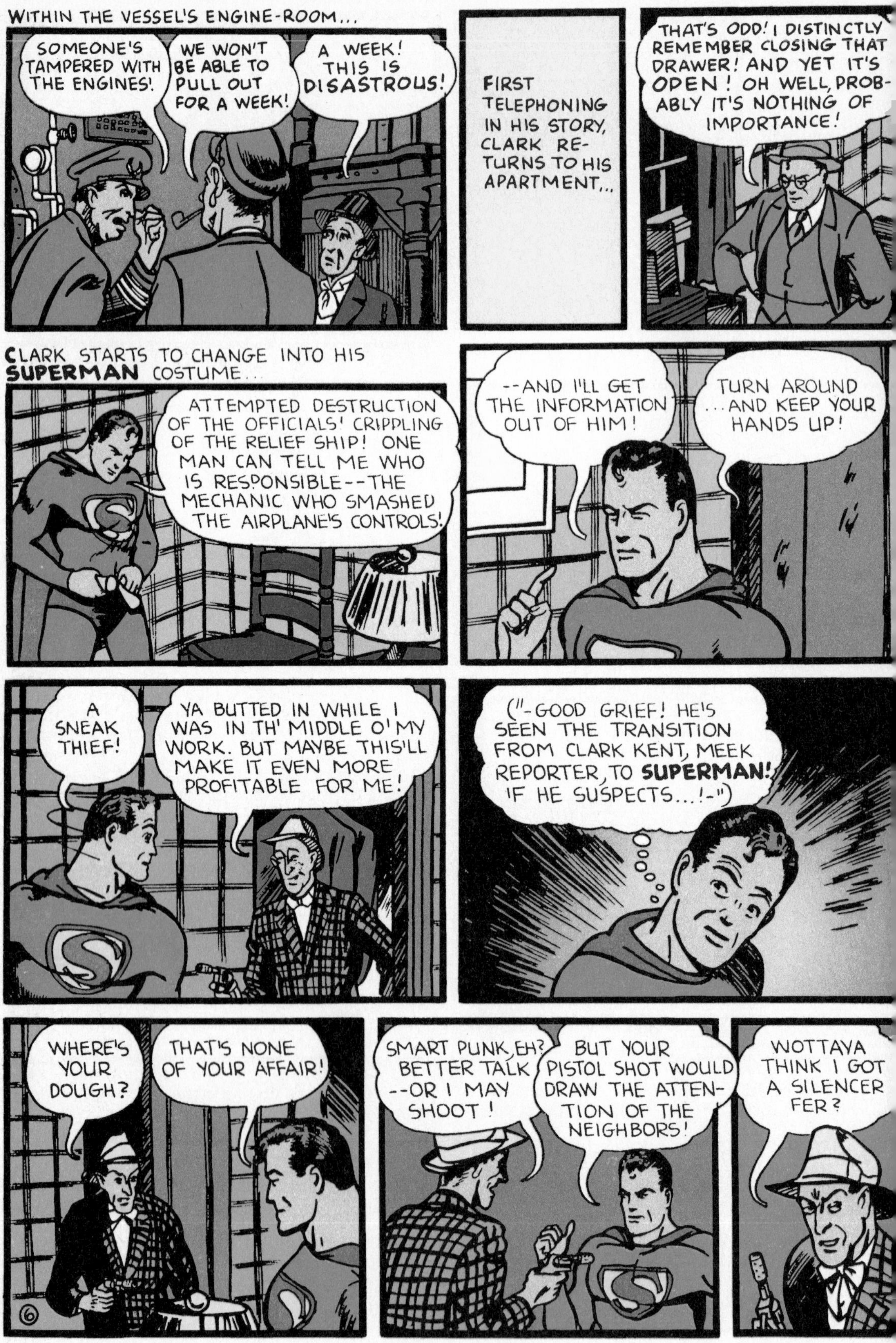
WITHIN THE VESSEL'S ENGINE-ROOM...
SOMEONE'S TAMPERED WITH THE ENGINES!
WE WON'T BE ABLE TO PULL OUT FOR A WEEK!
A WEEK! THIS IS DISASTROUS!
FIRST TELEPHONING IN HIS STORY, CLARK RETURNS TO HIS APARTMENT...
THAT'S ODD! I DISTINCTLY REMEMBER CLOSING THAT DRAWER! AND YET IT'S OPEN! OH WELL, PROBABLY IT'S NOTHING OF IMPORTANCE!
CLARK STARTS TO CHANGE INTO HIS SUPERMAN COSTUME...
ATTEMPTED DESTRUCTION OF THE OFFICIALS' CRIPPLING OF THE RELIEF SHIP! ONE MAN CAN TELL ME WHO IS RESPONSIBLE--THE MECHANIC WHO SMASHED THE AIRPLANE'S CONTROLS!
--AND I'LL GET THE INFORMATION OUT OF HIM!
TURN AROUND ...AND KEEP YOUR HANDS UP!
A SNEAK THIEF!
YA BUTTED IN WHILE I WAS IN TH' MIDDLE O' MY WORK. BUT MAYBE THIS'LL MAKE IT EVEN MORE PROFITABLE FOR ME!
("-GOOD GRIEF! HE'S SEEN THE TRANSITION FROM CLARK KENT, MEEK REPORTER, TO SUPERMAN! IF HE SUSPECTS...!-")
WHERE'S YOUR DOUGH?
THAT'S NONE OF YOUR AFFAIR!
6
SMART PUNK, EH? BETTER TALK --OR I MAY SHOOT!
BUT YOUR PISTOL SHOT WOULD DRAW THE ATTENTION OF THE NEIGHBORS!
WOTTAYA THINK I GOT A SILENCER FER?

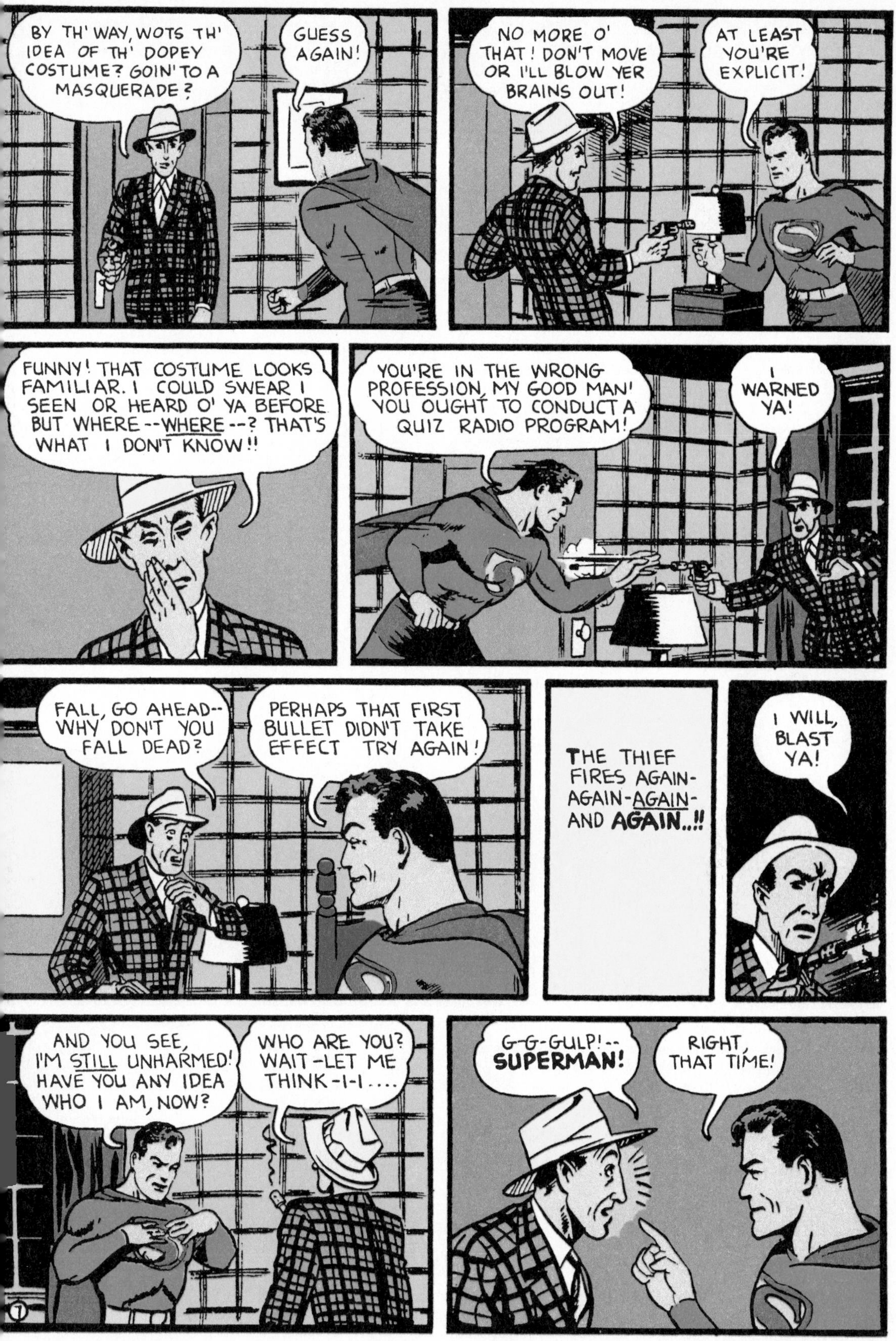
BY TH' WAY, WOTS TH' IDEA OF TH' DOPEY COSTUME? GOIN' TO A MASQUERADE?
GUESS AGAIN!
NO MORE O' THAT! DON'T MOVE OR I'LL BLOW YER BRAINS OUT!
AT LEAST YOU'RE EXPLICIT!
FUNNY! THAT COSTUME LOOKS FAMILIAR. I COULD SWEAR I SEEN OR HEARD O' YA BEFORE BUT WHERE--WHERE--? THAT'S WHAT I DON'T KNOW!!
YOU'RE IN THE WRONG PROFESSION, MY GOOD MAN! YOU OUGHT TO CONDUCT A QUIZ RADIO PROGRAM!
I WARNED YA!
FALL, GO AHEAD--WHY DON'T YOU FALL DEAD?
PERHAPS THAT FIRST BULLET DIDN'T TAKE EFFECT TRY AGAIN!
THE THIEF FIRES AGAIN-AGAIN-AGAIN-AND AGAIN..!!
I WILL, BLAST YA!
AND YOU SEE, I'M STILL UNHARMED! HAVE YOU ANY IDEA WHO I AM, NOW?
WHO ARE YOU? WAIT-LET ME THINK-I-I....
7
G-G-GULP!--SUPERMAN!
RIGHT, THAT TIME!

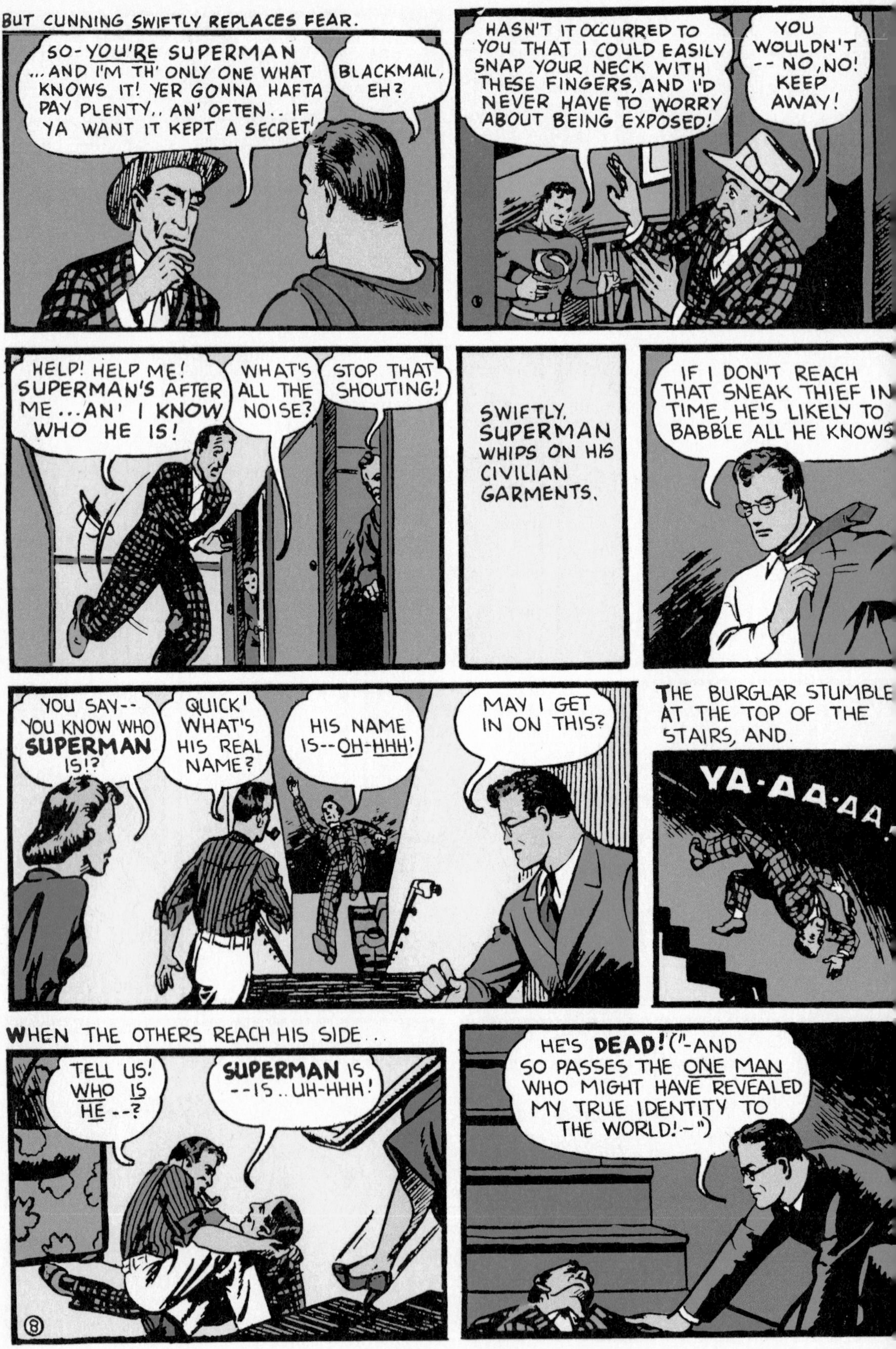

BUT CUNNING SWIFTLY REPLACES FEAR.
SO-YOU'RE SUPERMAN ...AND I'M TH' ONLY ONE WHAT KNOWS IT! YER GONNA HAFTA PAY PLENTY.. AN' OFTEN.. IF YA WANT IT KEPT A SECRET!
BLACKMAIL, EH?
HASN'T IT OCCURRED TO YOU THAT I COULD EASILY SNAP YOUR NECK WITH THESE FINGERS, AND I'D NEVER HAVE TO WORRY ABOUT BEING EXPOSED!
YOU WOULDN'T -- NO, NO! KEEP AWAY!
HELP! HELP ME! SUPERMAN'S AFTER ME... AN' I KNOW WHO HE IS!
WHAT'S ALL THE NOISE?
STOP THAT SHOUTING!
SWIFTLY, SUPERMAN WHIPS ON HIS CIVILIAN GARMENTS.
IF I DON'T REACH THAT SNEAK THIEF IN TIME, HE'S LIKELY TO BABBLE ALL HE KNOWS
YOU SAY-- YOU KNOW WHO SUPERMAN IS!?
QUICK! WHAT'S HIS REAL NAME?
HIS NAME IS--OH-HHH!
MAY I GET IN ON THIS?
THE BURGLAR STUMBLE AT THE TOP OF THE STAIRS, AND.
YA-AA-AA-
WHEN THE OTHERS REACH HIS SIDE..
TELL US! WHO IS HE --?
SUPERMAN IS --IS.. UH-HHH!
8
HE'S DEAD! ("-AND SO PASSES THE ONE MAN WHO MIGHT HAVE REVEALED MY TRUE IDENTITY TO THE WORLD!-")

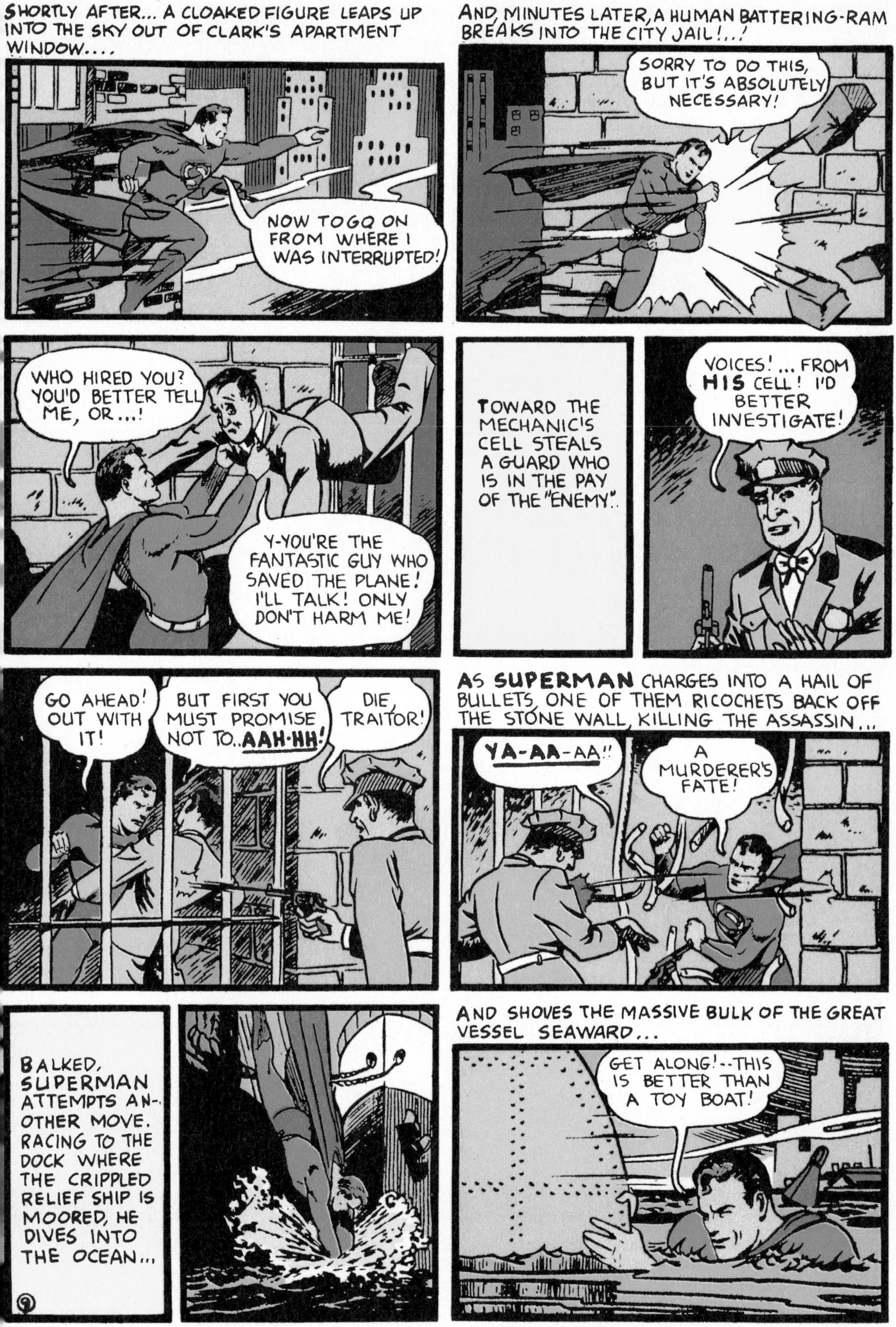
SHORTLY AFTER... A CLOAKED FIGURE LEAPS UP INTO THE SKY OUT OF CLARK'S APARTMENT WINDOW....
NOW TO GO ON FROM WHERE I WAS INTERRUPTED!
AND, MINUTES LATER, A HUMAN BATTERING-RAM BREAKS INTO THE CITY JAIL!..!
SORRY TO DO THIS, BUT IT'S ABSOLUTELY NECESSARY!
WHO HIRED YOU? YOU'D BETTER TELL ME, OR...!
Y-YOU'RE THE FANTASTIC GUY WHO SAVED THE PLANE! I'LL TALK! ONLY DON'T HARM ME!
TOWARD THE MECHANIC'S CELL STEALS A GUARD WHO IS IN THE PAY OF THE "ENEMY".
VOICES! ... FROM HIS CELL! I'D BETTER INVESTIGATE!
GO AHEAD! OUT WITH IT!
BUT FIRST YOU MUST PROMISE NOT TO..AAH-HH!
DIE, TRAITOR!
AS SUPERMAN CHARGES INTO A HAIL OF BULLETS, ONE OF THEM RICOCHETS BACK OFF THE STONE WALL, KILLING THE ASSASSIN...
YA-AA-AA!!
A MURDERER'S FATE!
BALKED, SUPERMAN ATTEMPTS AN-OTHER MOVE. RACING TO THE DOCK WHERE THE CRIPPLED RELIEF SHIP IS MOORED, HE DIVES INTO THE OCEAN...
AND SHOVES THE MASSIVE BULK OF THE GREAT VESSEL SEAWARD...
GET ALONG!--THIS IS BETTER THAN A TOY BOAT!

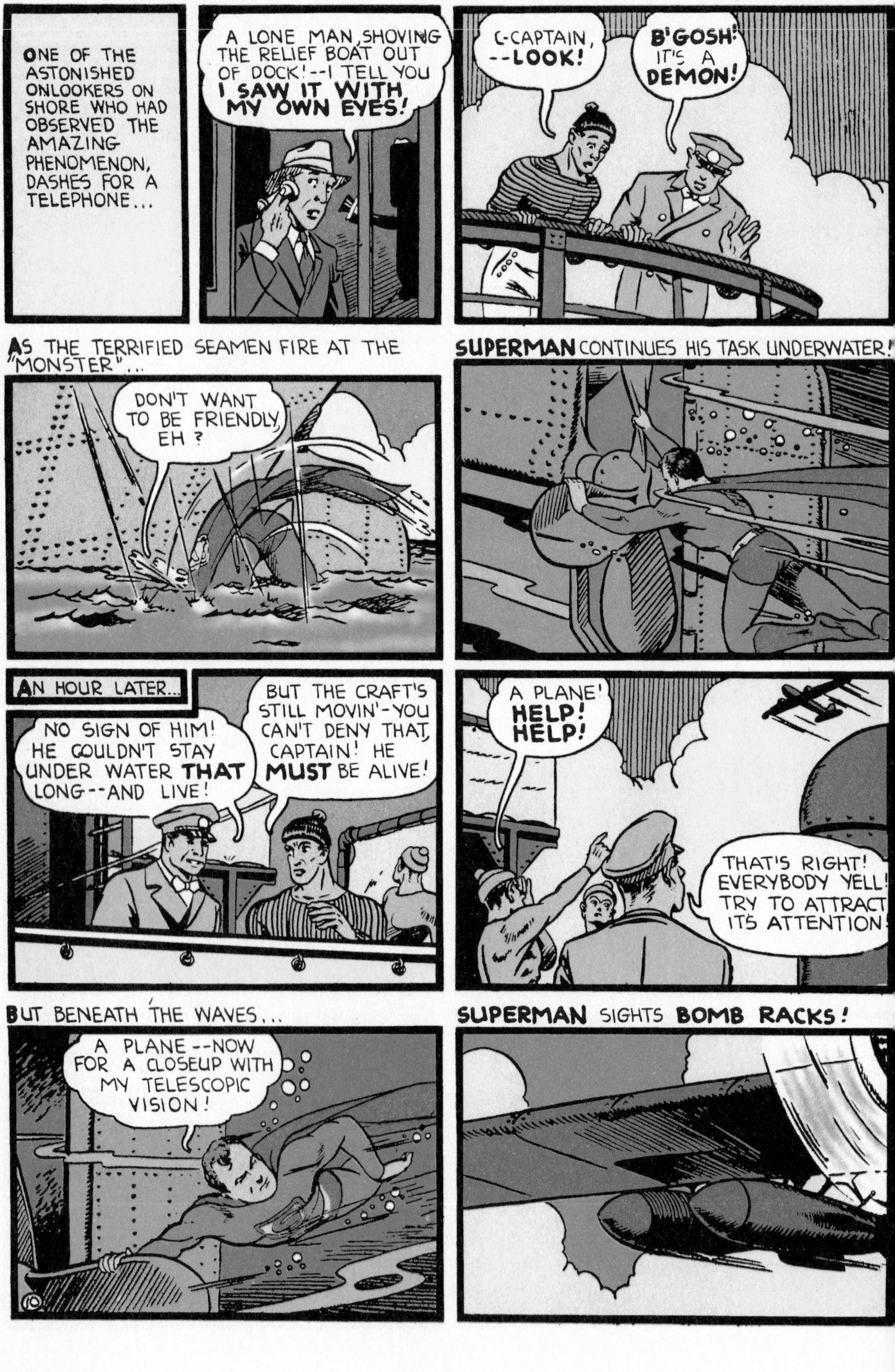

ONE OF THE ASTONISHED ONLOOKERS ON SHORE WHO HAD OBSERVED THE AMAZING PHENOMENON, DASHES FOR A TELEPHONE...
A LONE MAN, SHOVING THE RELIEF BOAT OUT OF DOCK!--I TELL YOU I SAW IT WITH MY OWN EYES!
C-CAPTAIN, --LOOK!
B'GOSH! IT'S A DEMON!
AS THE TERRIFIED SEAMEN FIRE AT THE "MONSTER"...
DON'T WANT TO BE FRIENDLY, EH ?
SUPERMAN CONTINUES HIS TASK UNDERWATER!
AN HOUR LATER...
NO SIGN OF HIM! HE COULDN'T STAY UNDER WATER THAT LONG--AND LIVE!
BUT THE CRAFT'S STILL MOVIN'-YOU CAN'T DENY THAT, CAPTAIN! HE MUST BE ALIVE!
A PLANE! HELP! HELP!
THAT'S RIGHT! EVERYBODY YELL! TRY TO ATTRACT IT'S ATTENTION!
BUT BENEATH THE WAVES...
A PLANE--NOW FOR A CLOSEUP WITH MY TELESCOPIC VISION!
10
SUPERMAN SIGHTS BOMB RACKS!

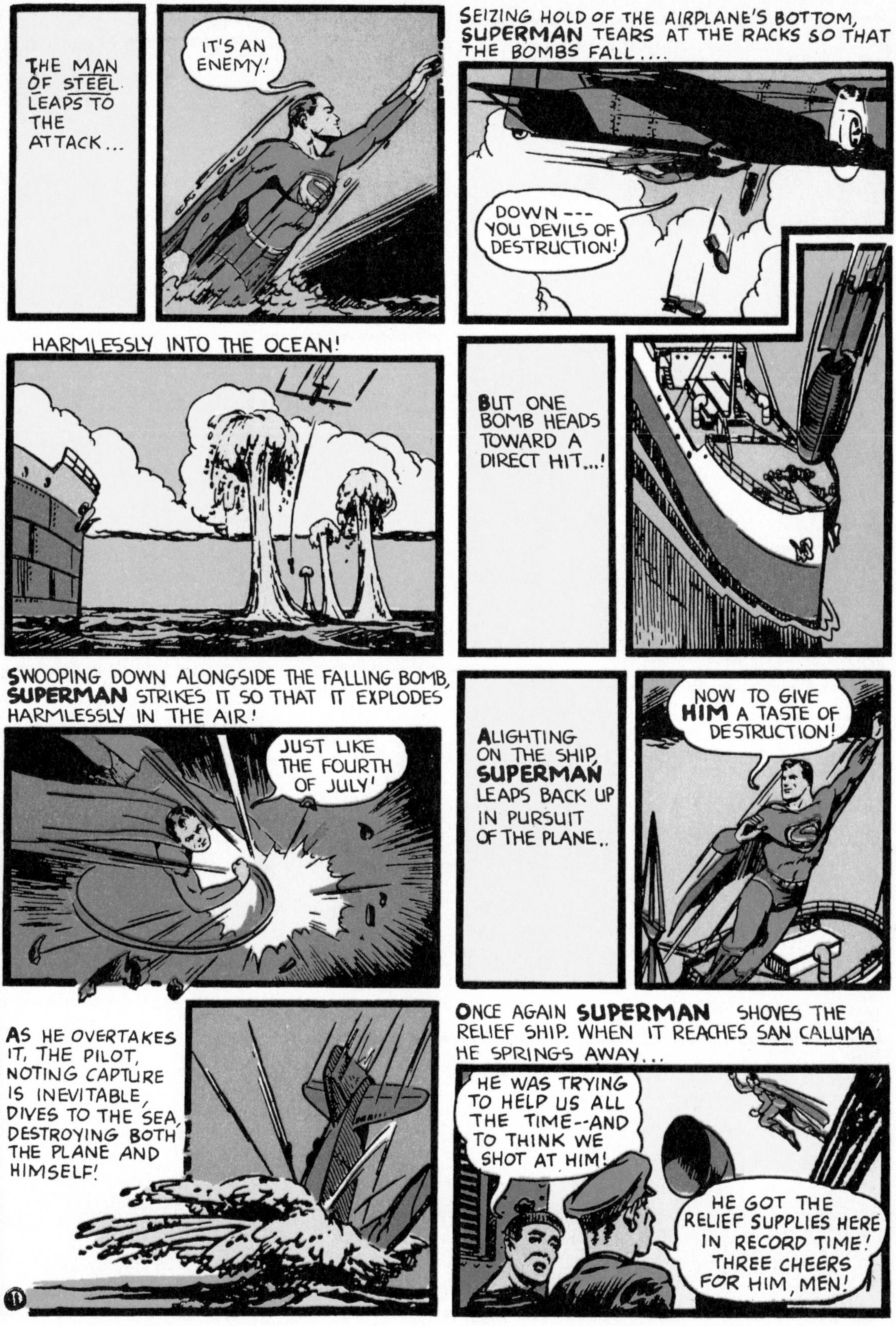
THE MAN OF STEEL LEAPS TO THE ATTACK...
IT'S AN ENEMY!
SEIZING HOLD OF THE AIRPLANE'S BOTTOM, SUPERMAN TEARS AT THE RACKS SO THAT THE BOMBS FALL....
DOWN--- YOU DEVILS OF DESTRUCTION!
HARMLESSLY INTO THE OCEAN!
BUT ONE BOMB HEADS TOWARD A DIRECT HIT...!
SWOOPING DOWN ALONGSIDE THE FALLING BOMB, SUPERMAN STRIKES IT SO THAT IT EXPLODES HARMLESSLY IN THE AIR!
JUST LIKE THE FOURTH OF JULY!
ALIGHTING ON THE SHIP, SUPERMAN LEAPS BACK UP IN PURSUIT OF THE PLANE..
NOW TO GIVE HIM A TASTE OF DESTRUCTION!
AS HE OVERTAKES IT, THE PILOT, NOTING CAPTURE IS INEVITABLE, DIVES TO THE SEA, DESTROYING BOTH THE PLANE AND HIMSELF!
ONCE AGAIN SUPERMAN SHOVES THE RELIEF SHIP. WHEN IT REACHES SAN CALUMA HE SPRINGS AWAY...
HE WAS TRYING TO HELP US ALL THE TIME--AND TO THINK WE SHOT AT HIM!
HE GOT THE RELIEF SUPPLIES HERE IN RECORD TIME! THREE CHEERS FOR HIM, MEN!

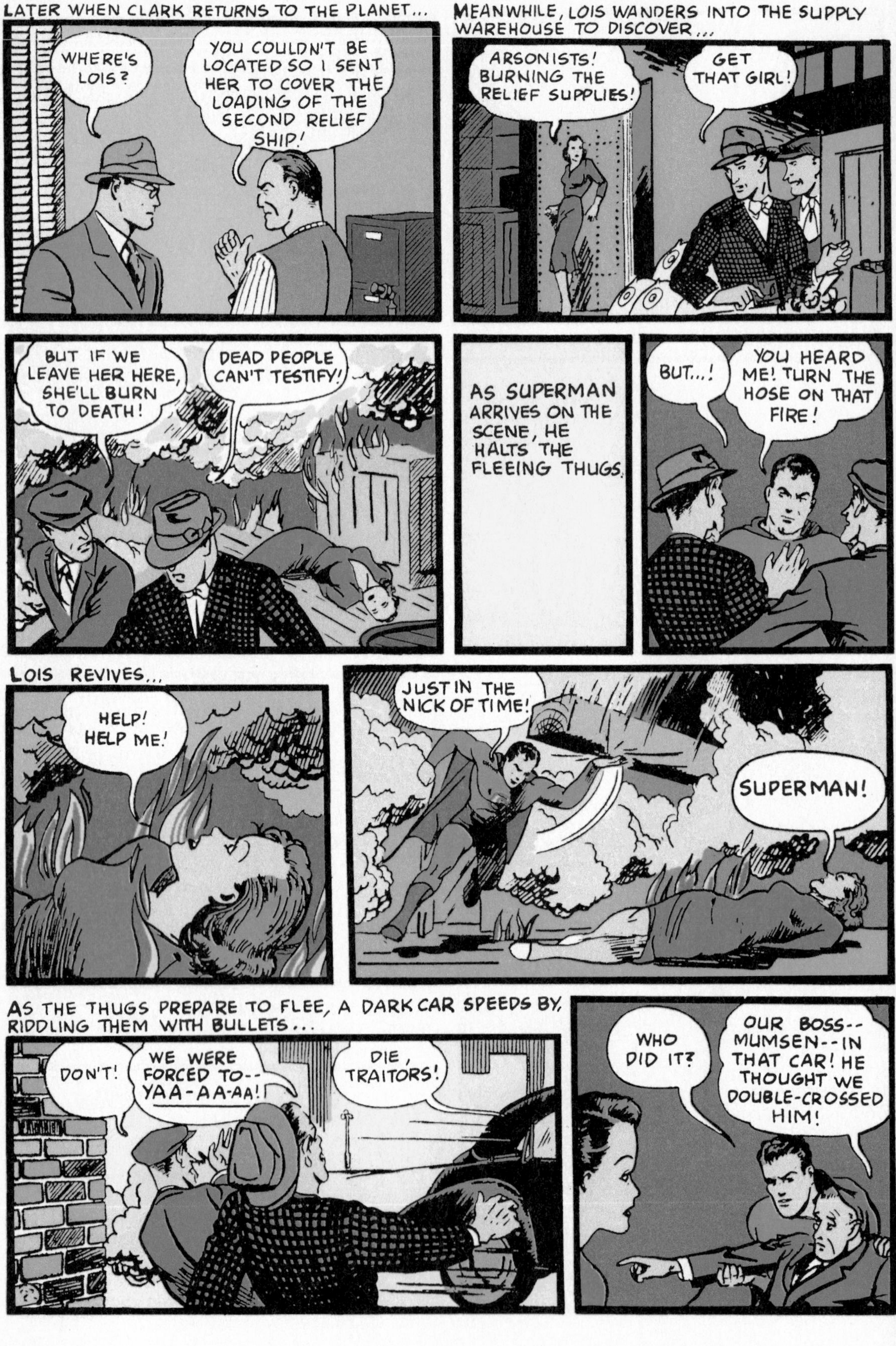
LATER WHEN CLARK RETURNS TO THE PLANET...
WHERE'S LOIS?
YOU COULDN'T BE LOCATED SO I SENT HER TO COVER THE LOADING OF THE SECOND RELIEF SHIP!
MEANWHILE, LOIS WANDERS INTO THE SUPPLY WAREHOUSE TO DISCOVER...
ARSONISTS! BURNING THE RELIEF SUPPLIES!
GET THAT GIRL!
BUT IF WE LEAVE HER HERE, SHE'LL BURN TO DEATH!
DEAD PEOPLE CAN'T TESTIFY!
AS SUPERMAN ARRIVES ON THE SCENE, HE HALTS THE FLEEING THUGS.
BUT...!
YOU HEARD ME! TURN THE HOSE ON THAT FIRE!
LOIS REVIVES...
HELP! HELP ME!
JUST IN THE NICK OF TIME!
SUPERMAN!
AS THE THUGS PREPARE TO FLEE, A DARK CAR SPEEDS BY, RIDDLING THEM WITH BULLETS...
DON'T!
WE WERE FORCED TO--YAA-AA-AA!
DIE, TRAITORS!
WHO DID IT?
OUR BOSS--MUMSEN--IN THAT CAR! HE THOUGHT WE DOUBLE-CROSSED HIM!

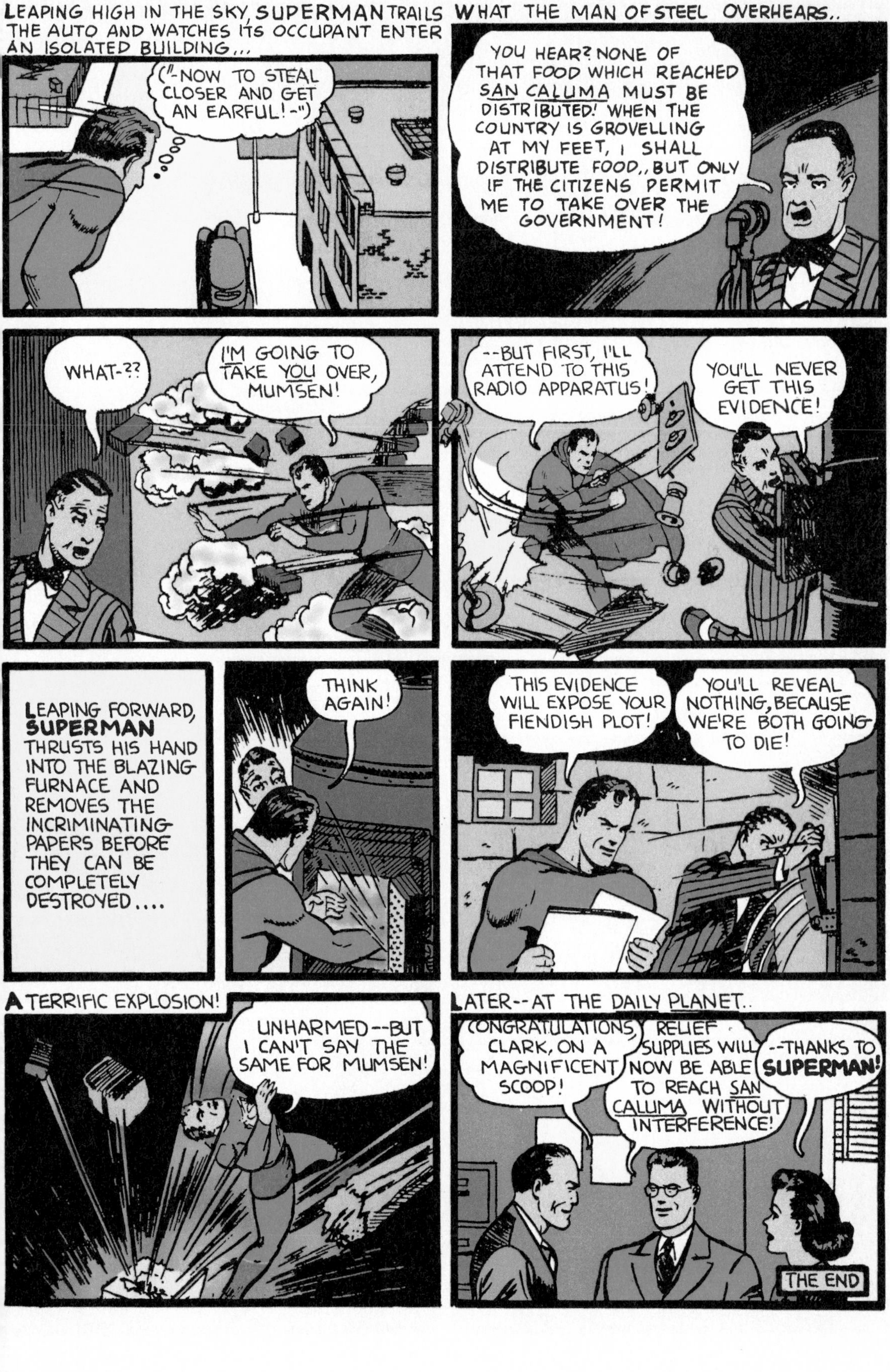
LEAPING HIGH IN THE SKY, SUPERMAN TRAILS THE AUTO AND WATCHES ITS OCCUPANT ENTER AN ISOLATED BUILDING...
("--NOW TO STEAL CLOSER AND GET AN EARFUL!--")
WHAT THE MAN OF STEEL OVERHEARS..
YOU HEAR? NONE OF THAT FOOD WHICH REACHED SAN CALUMA MUST BE DISTRIBUTED! WHEN THE COUNTRY IS GROVELLING AT MY FEET, I SHALL DISTRIBUTE FOOD,, BUT ONLY IF THE CITIZENS PERMIT ME TO TAKE OVER THE GOVERNMENT!
WHAT-??
I'M GOING TO TAKE YOU OVER, MUMSEN!
--BUT FIRST, I'LL ATTEND TO THIS RADIO APPARATUS!
YOU'LL NEVER GET THIS EVIDENCE!
LEAPING FORWARD, SUPERMAN THRUSTS HIS HAND INTO THE BLAZING FURNACE AND REMOVES THE INCRIMINATING PAPERS BEFORE THEY CAN BE COMPLETELY DESTROYED....
THINK AGAIN!
THIS EVIDENCE WILL EXPOSE YOUR FIENDISH PLOT!
YOU'LL REVEAL NOTHING, BECAUSE WE'RE BOTH GOING TO DIE!
A TERRIFIC EXPLOSION!
UNHARMED--BUT I CAN'T SAY THE SAME FOR MUMSEN!
LATER--AT THE DAILY PLANET..
CONGRATULATIONS, CLARK, ON A MAGNIFICENT SCOOP!
RELIEF SUPPLIES WILL NOW BE ABLE TO REACH SAN CALUMA WITHOUT INTERFERENCE!
--THANKS TO SUPERMAN!
THE END

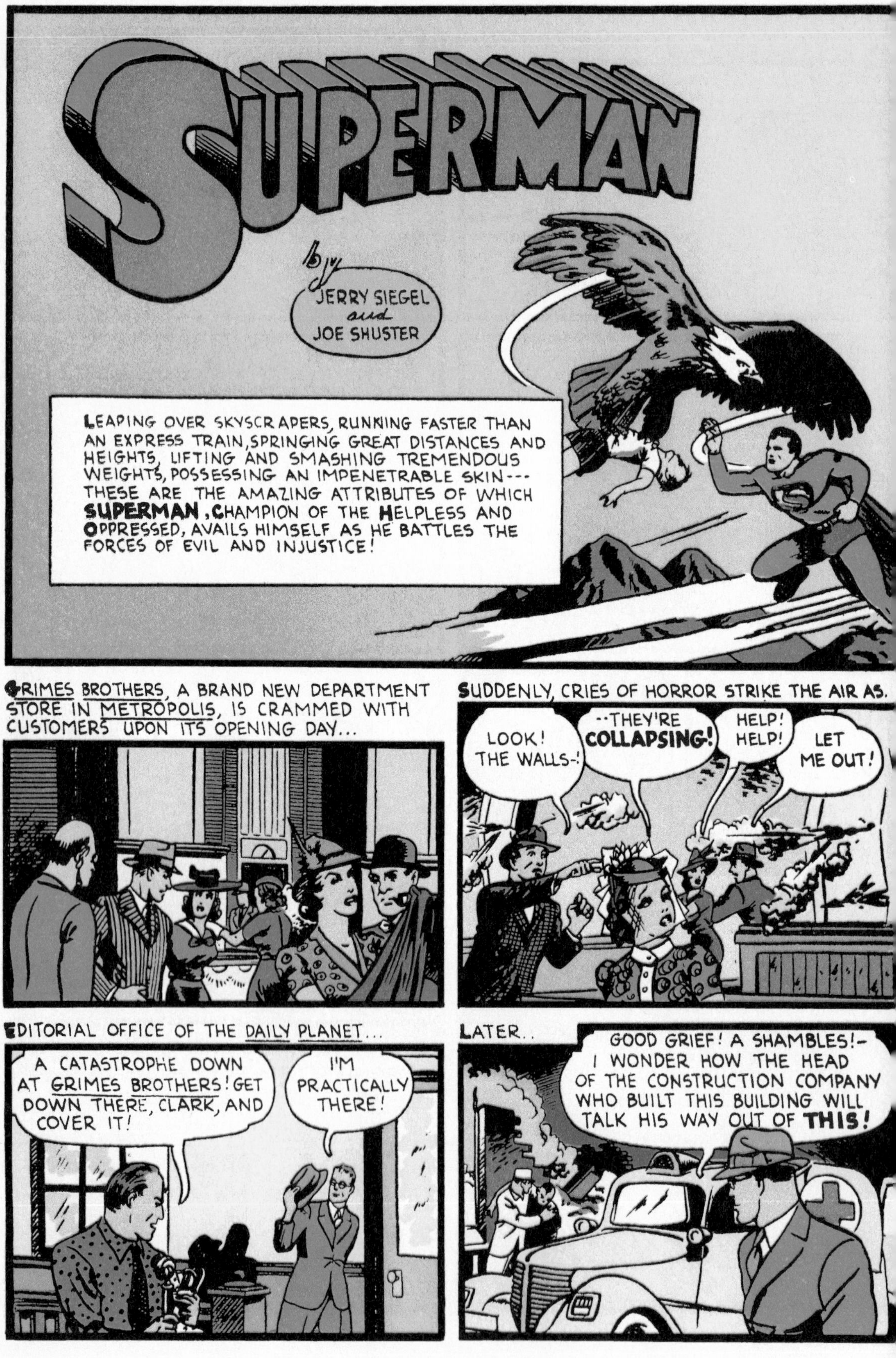
SUPERMAN
by JERRY SIEGEL and JOE SHUSTER
LEAPING OVER SKYSCRAPERS, RUNNING FASTER THAN AN EXPRESS TRAIN, SPRINGING GREAT DISTANCES AND HEIGHTS, LIFTING AND SMASHING TREMENDOUS WEIGHTS, POSSESSING AN IMPENETRABLE SKIN--- THESE ARE THE AMAZING ATTRIBUTES OF WHICH SUPERMAN, CHAMPION OF THE HELPLESS AND OPPRESSED, AVAILS HIMSELF AS HE BATTLES THE FORCES OF EVIL AND INJUSTICE!
GRIMES BROTHERS, A BRAND NEW DEPARTMENT STORE IN METROPOLIS, IS CRAMMED WITH CUSTOMERS UPON ITS OPENING DAY...
SUDDENLY, CRIES OF HORROR STRIKE THE AIR AS.
LOOK! THE WALLS-!
--THEY'RE COLLAPSING!
HELP! HELP!
LET ME OUT!
EDITORIAL OFFICE OF THE DAILY PLANET...
A CATASTROPHE DOWN AT GRIMES BROTHERS! GET DOWN THERE, CLARK, AND COVER IT!
I'M PRACTICALLY THERE!
LATER..
GOOD GRIEF! A SHAMBLES!- I WONDER HOW THE HEAD OF THE CONSTRUCTION COMPANY WHO BUILT THIS BUILDING WILL TALK HIS WAY OUT OF THIS!

WHEN CLARK REACHES THE OFFICE BUILDING IN WHICH IS LOCATED THE <u>GLOBE</u> CONSTRUCTION COMPANY'S OFFICES...

OOPS! BEG YOUR PARDON!

401 - 415 ⇨
⇦ 416 - 430

WAS HE IN A HURRY!

THE OFFICE DOOR'S AJAR! MIGHT JUST AS WELL WALK RIGHT IN AND MAKE MYSELF AT HOME!

GLOBE CONSTRUCTION CO.

A CORPSE! -NO DOUBT, THE HEAD OF THE FIRM!

RAISE YOUR HANDS--- AND TURN!

SERGEANT CLANCY! WHEW! FOR A MINUTE I THOUGHT THE MURDERER MIGHT HAVE RETURNED!

<u>MURDERER?</u> ODD, KENT, HOW YOU MANAGE TO SHOW UP AT THE SCENE OF CRIMES BEFORE WE DO..ALMOST AS THO' YOU WERE INVOLVED!

GLOBE CONSTRU

AND FOR YOUR FURTHER INFORMATION, MY DEAR AMATEUR SNOOPER, THIS BIRD WASN'T MURDERED. IT'S PLAIN TO SEE HE COMMITTED SUICIDE!

BUT CLARK KNOWS BETTER, FOR HIS MICROSCOPIC-VISION NOTES...

("-FINGER MARKS ON THE CORPSE'S THROAT! HE WAS CHOKED BEFORE HE WAS SHOT! AND THERE'S ONE FINGERPRINT MISSING ON THE RIGHT HAND, INDICATING THAT THE KILLER HAS ONLY FOUR FINGERS ON HIS RIGHT HAND!-")

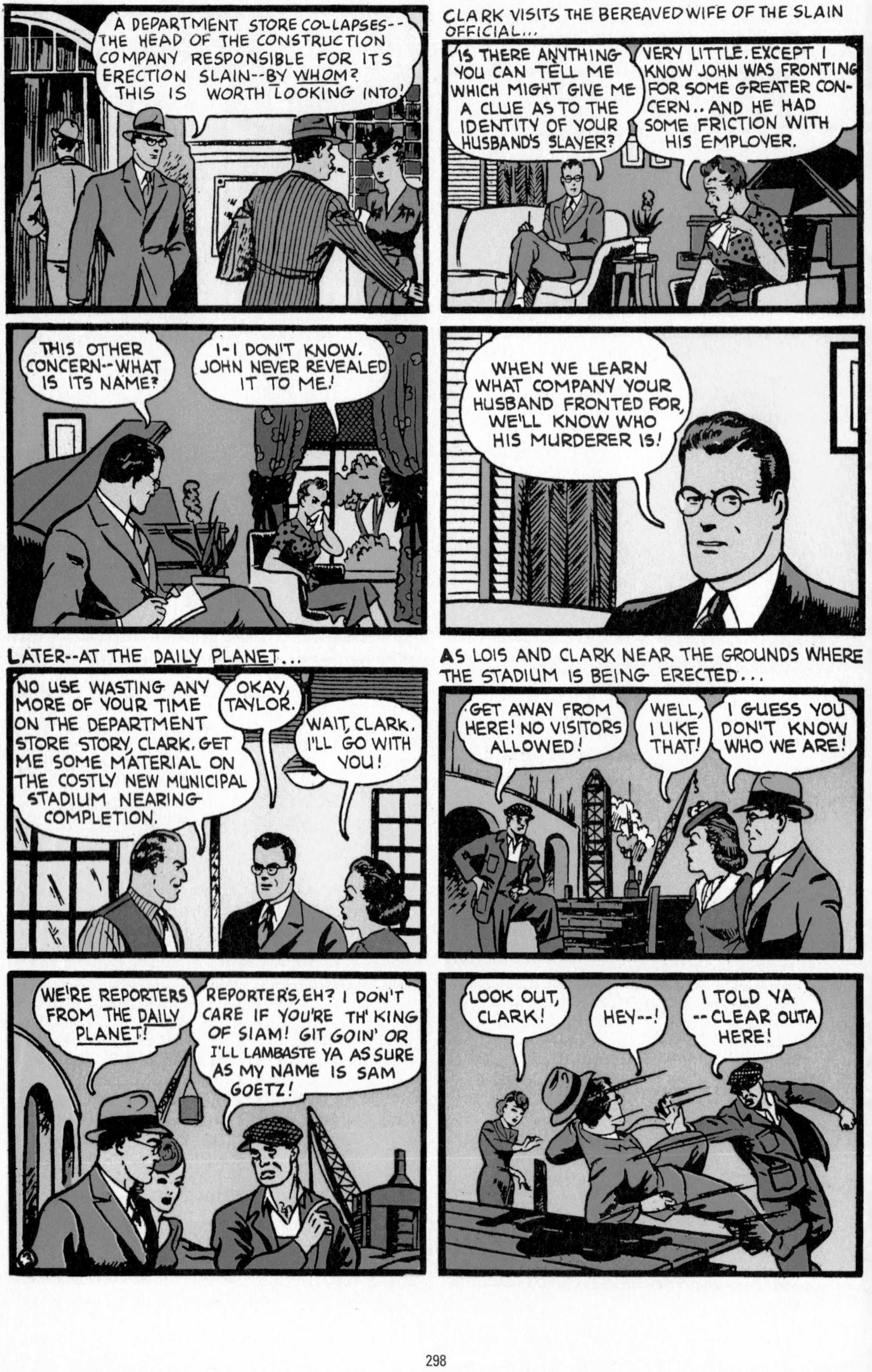
A DEPARTMENT STORE COLLAPSES-- THE HEAD OF THE CONSTRUCTION COMPANY RESPONSIBLE FOR ITS ERECTION SLAIN--BY WHOM? THIS IS WORTH LOOKING INTO!
CLARK VISITS THE BEREAVED WIFE OF THE SLAIN OFFICIAL...
IS THERE ANYTHING YOU CAN TELL ME WHICH MIGHT GIVE ME A CLUE AS TO THE IDENTITY OF YOUR HUSBAND'S SLAYER?
VERY LITTLE. EXCEPT I KNOW JOHN WAS FRONTING FOR SOME GREATER CONCERN.. AND HE HAD SOME FRICTION WITH HIS EMPLOYER.
THIS OTHER CONCERN--WHAT IS ITS NAME?
I-I DON'T KNOW. JOHN NEVER REVEALED IT TO ME!
WHEN WE LEARN WHAT COMPANY YOUR HUSBAND FRONTED FOR, WE'LL KNOW WHO HIS MURDERER IS!
LATER--AT THE DAILY PLANET...
NO USE WASTING ANY MORE OF YOUR TIME ON THE DEPARTMENT STORE STORY, CLARK. GET ME SOME MATERIAL ON THE COSTLY NEW MUNICIPAL STADIUM NEARING COMPLETION.
OKAY, TAYLOR.
WAIT, CLARK. I'LL GO WITH YOU!
AS LOIS AND CLARK NEAR THE GROUNDS WHERE THE STADIUM IS BEING ERECTED...
GET AWAY FROM HERE! NO VISITORS ALLOWED!
WELL, I LIKE THAT!
I GUESS YOU DON'T KNOW WHO WE ARE!
WE'RE REPORTERS FROM THE DAILY PLANET!
REPORTER'S, EH? I DON'T CARE IF YOU'RE TH' KING OF SIAM! GIT GOIN' OR I'LL LAMBASTE YA AS SURE AS MY NAME IS SAM GOETZ!
LOOK OUT, CLARK!
HEY--!
I TOLD YA --CLEAR OUTA HERE!

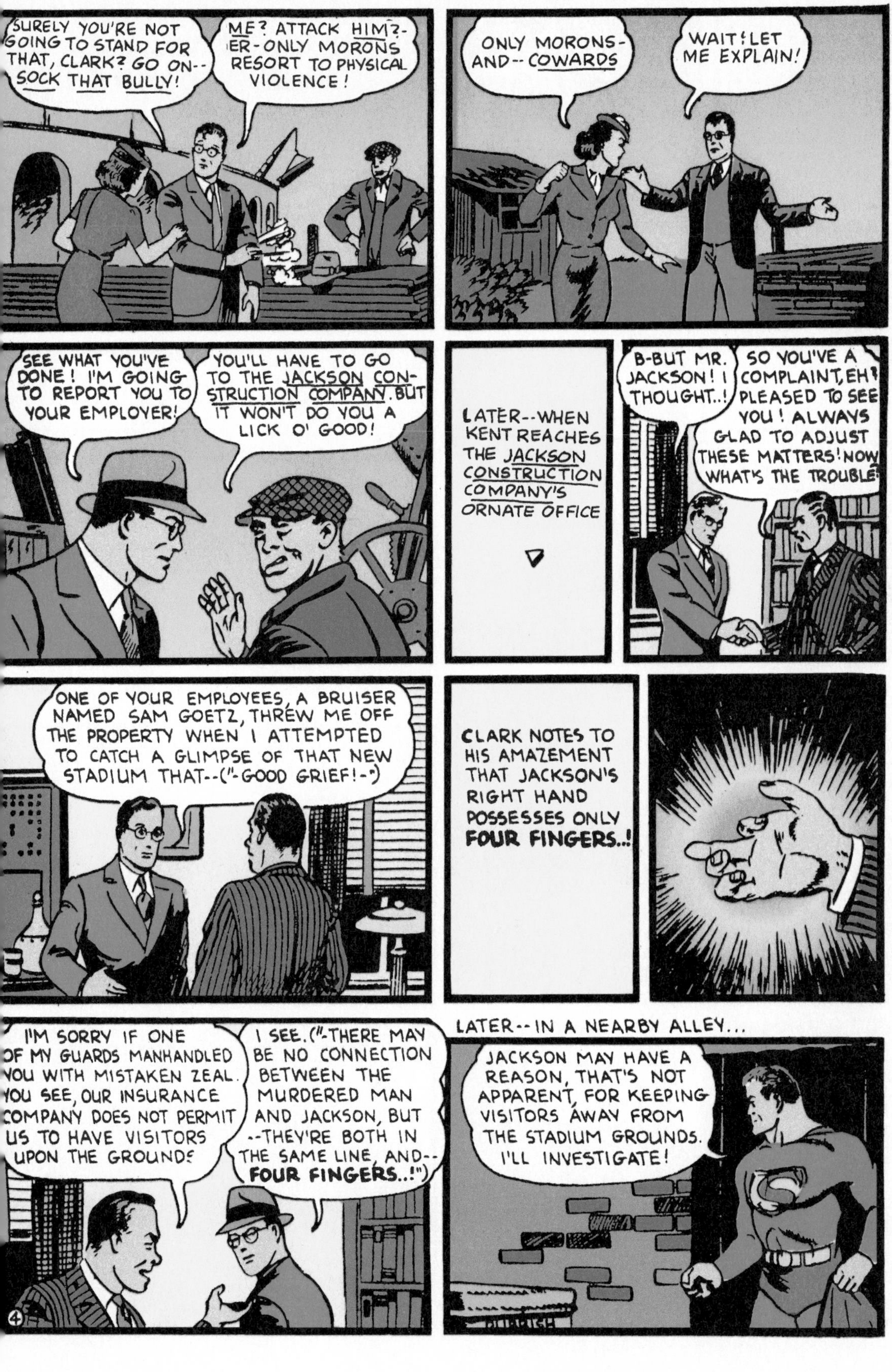
SURELY YOU'RE NOT GOING TO STAND FOR THAT, CLARK? GO ON--SOCK THAT BULLY!
ME? ATTACK HIM?-ER-ONLY MORONS RESORT TO PHYSICAL VIOLENCE!
ONLY MORONS-AND--COWARDS
WAIT! LET ME EXPLAIN!
SEE WHAT YOU'VE DONE! I'M GOING TO REPORT YOU TO YOUR EMPLOYER!
YOU'LL HAVE TO GO TO THE JACKSON CONSTRUCTION COMPANY. BUT IT WON'T DO YOU A LICK O' GOOD!
LATER--WHEN KENT REACHES THE JACKSON CONSTRUCTION COMPANY'S ORNATE OFFICE
B-BUT MR. JACKSON! I THOUGHT..!
SO YOU'VE A COMPLAINT, EH? PLEASED TO SEE YOU! ALWAYS GLAD TO ADJUST THESE MATTERS! NOW WHAT'S THE TROUBLE?
ONE OF YOUR EMPLOYEES, A BRUISER NAMED SAM GOETZ, THREW ME OFF THE PROPERTY WHEN I ATTEMPTED TO CATCH A GLIMPSE OF THAT NEW STADIUM THAT--("-GOOD GRIEF!-")
CLARK NOTES TO HIS AMAZEMENT THAT JACKSON'S RIGHT HAND POSSESSES ONLY FOUR FINGERS..!
I'M SORRY IF ONE OF MY GUARDS MANHANDLED YOU WITH MISTAKEN ZEAL. YOU SEE, OUR INSURANCE COMPANY DOES NOT PERMIT US TO HAVE VISITORS UPON THE GROUNDS
I SEE. ("-THERE MAY BE NO CONNECTION BETWEEN THE MURDERED MAN AND JACKSON, BUT --THEY'RE BOTH IN THE SAME LINE, AND--FOUR FINGERS..!")
4
LATER--IN A NEARBY ALLEY...
JACKSON MAY HAVE A REASON, THAT'S NOT APPARENT, FOR KEEPING VISITORS AWAY FROM THE STADIUM GROUNDS. I'LL INVESTIGATE!

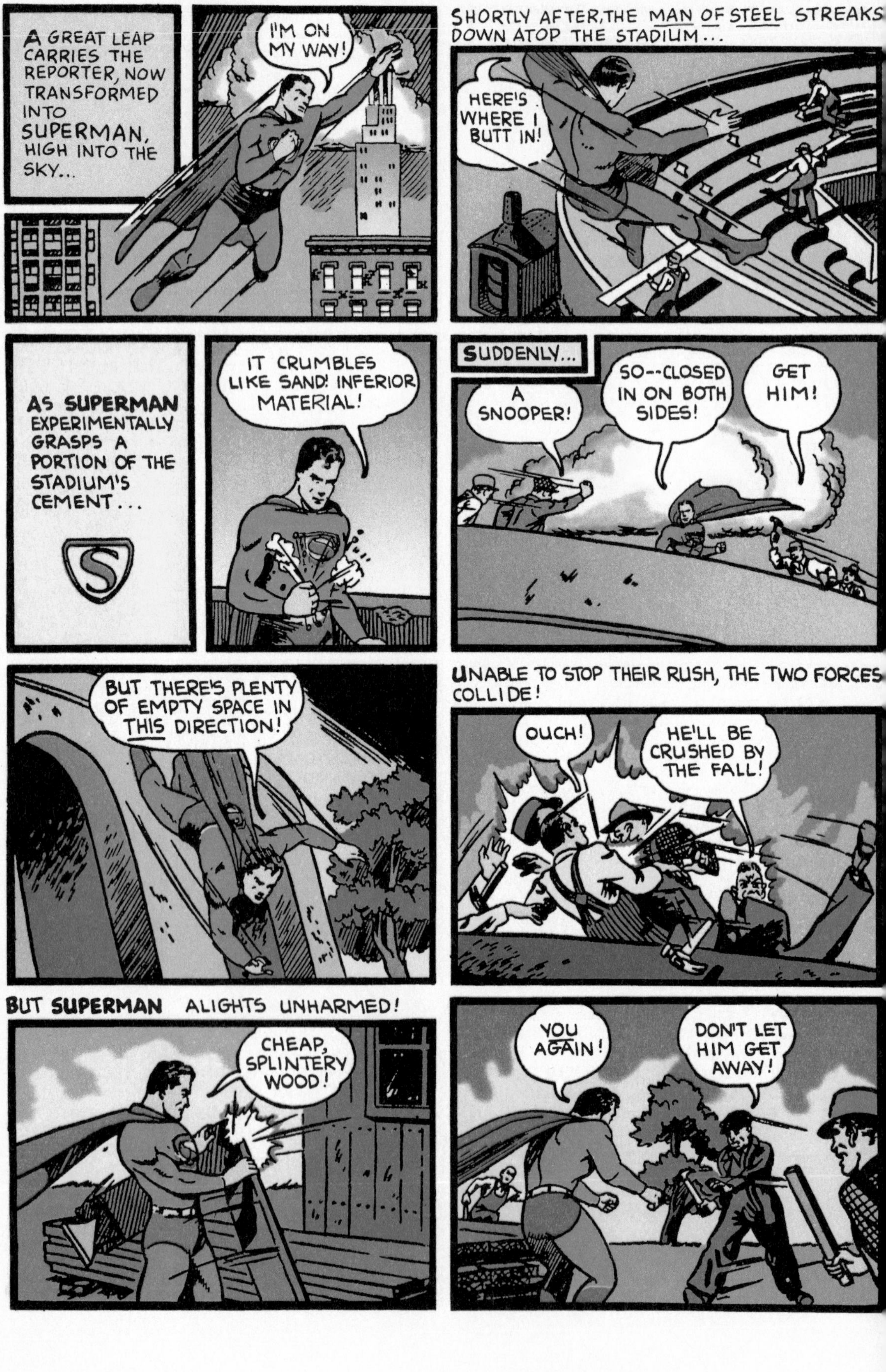
A GREAT LEAP CARRIES THE REPORTER, NOW TRANSFORMED INTO SUPERMAN, HIGH INTO THE SKY...
I'M ON MY WAY!
SHORTLY AFTER, THE MAN OF STEEL STREAKS DOWN ATOP THE STADIUM...
HERE'S WHERE I BUTT IN!
AS SUPERMAN EXPERIMENTALLY GRASPS A PORTION OF THE STADIUM'S CEMENT...
IT CRUMBLES LIKE SAND! INFERIOR MATERIAL!
SUDDENLY...
A SNOOPER!
SO--CLOSED IN ON BOTH SIDES!
GET HIM!
BUT THERE'S PLENTY OF EMPTY SPACE IN THIS DIRECTION!
UNABLE TO STOP THEIR RUSH, THE TWO FORCES COLLIDE!
OUCH!
HE'LL BE CRUSHED BY THE FALL!
BUT SUPERMAN ALIGHTS UNHARMED!
CHEAP, SPLINTERY WOOD!
YOU AGAIN!
DON'T LET HIM GET AWAY!

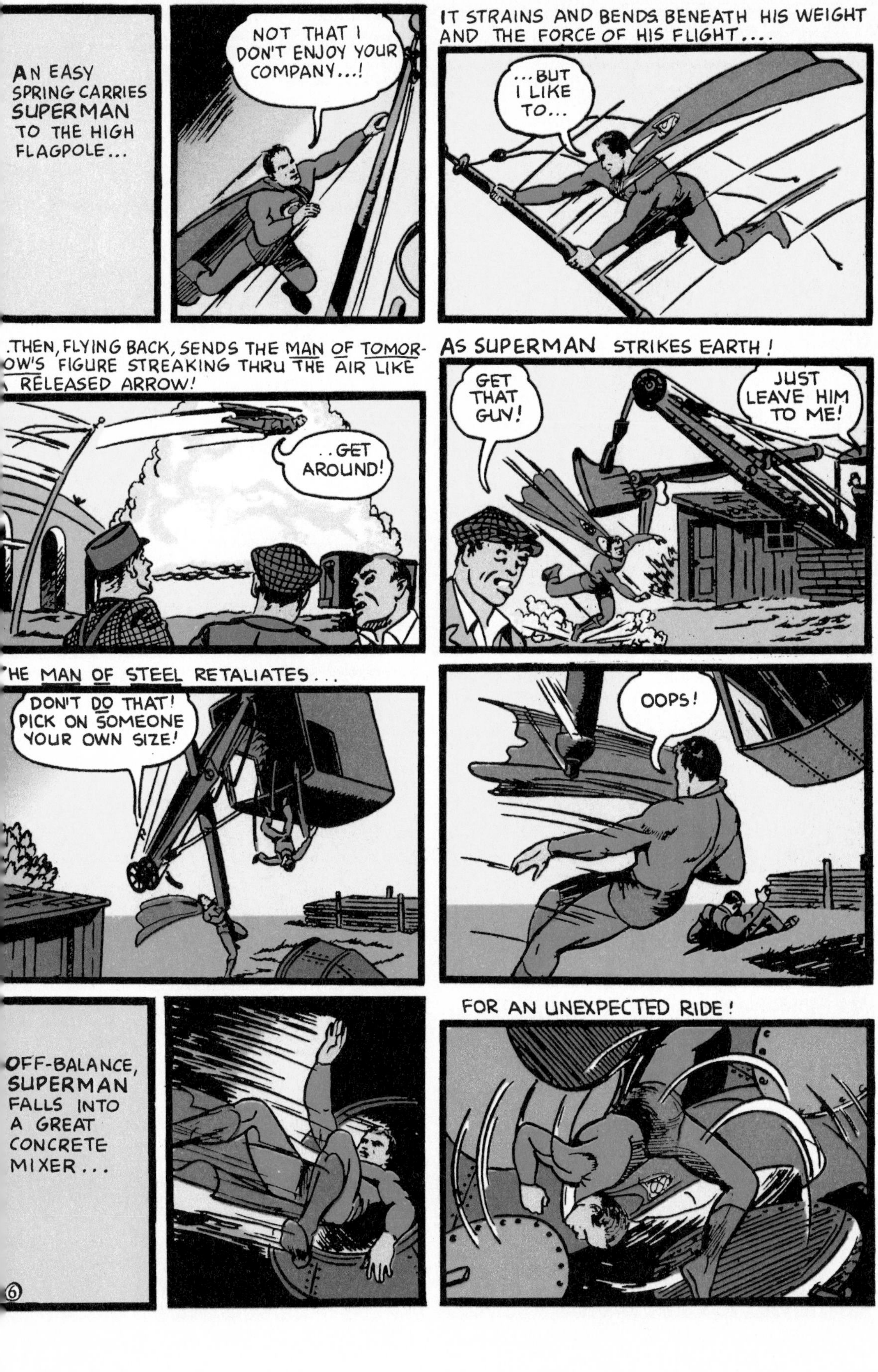
AN EASY SPRING CARRIES SUPERMAN TO THE HIGH FLAGPOLE...
NOT THAT I DON'T ENJOY YOUR COMPANY...!
IT STRAINS AND BENDS BENEATH HIS WEIGHT AND THE FORCE OF HIS FLIGHT....
...BUT I LIKE TO...
.THEN, FLYING BACK, SENDS THE MAN OF TOMOR-OW'S FIGURE STREAKING THRU THE AIR LIKE RELEASED ARROW!
..GET AROUND!
AS SUPERMAN STRIKES EARTH!
GET THAT GUY!
JUST LEAVE HIM TO ME!
HE MAN OF STEEL RETALIATES...
DON'T DO THAT! PICK ON SOMEONE YOUR OWN SIZE!
OOPS!
OFF-BALANCE, SUPERMAN FALLS INTO A GREAT CONCRETE MIXER...
6
FOR AN UNEXPECTED RIDE!

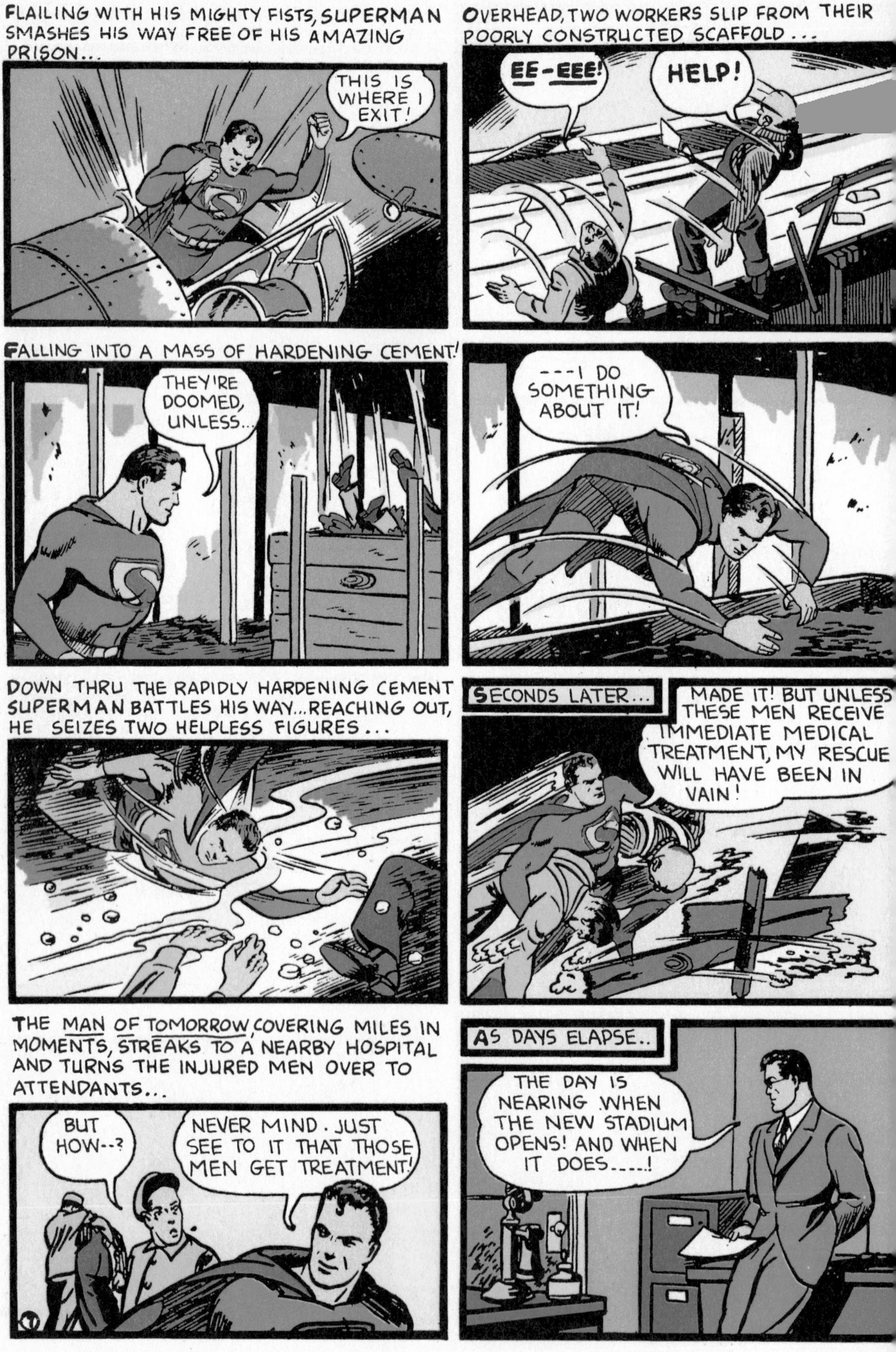
FLAILING WITH HIS MIGHTY FISTS, SUPERMAN SMASHES HIS WAY FREE OF HIS AMAZING PRISON...
THIS IS WHERE I EXIT!
OVERHEAD, TWO WORKERS SLIP FROM THEIR POORLY CONSTRUCTED SCAFFOLD...
EE-EEE!
HELP!
FALLING INTO A MASS OF HARDENING CEMENT!
THEY'RE DOOMED, UNLESS...
---I DO SOMETHING ABOUT IT!
DOWN THRU THE RAPIDLY HARDENING CEMENT SUPERMAN BATTLES HIS WAY...REACHING OUT, HE SEIZES TWO HELPLESS FIGURES...
SECONDS LATER...
MADE IT! BUT UNLESS THESE MEN RECEIVE IMMEDIATE MEDICAL TREATMENT, MY RESCUE WILL HAVE BEEN IN VAIN!
THE MAN OF TOMORROW, COVERING MILES IN MOMENTS, STREAKS TO A NEARBY HOSPITAL AND TURNS THE INJURED MEN OVER TO ATTENDANTS...
BUT HOW--?
NEVER MIND. JUST SEE TO IT THAT THOSE MEN GET TREATMENT!
AS DAYS ELAPSE..
THE DAY IS NEARING WHEN THE NEW STADIUM OPENS! AND WHEN IT DOES.....!

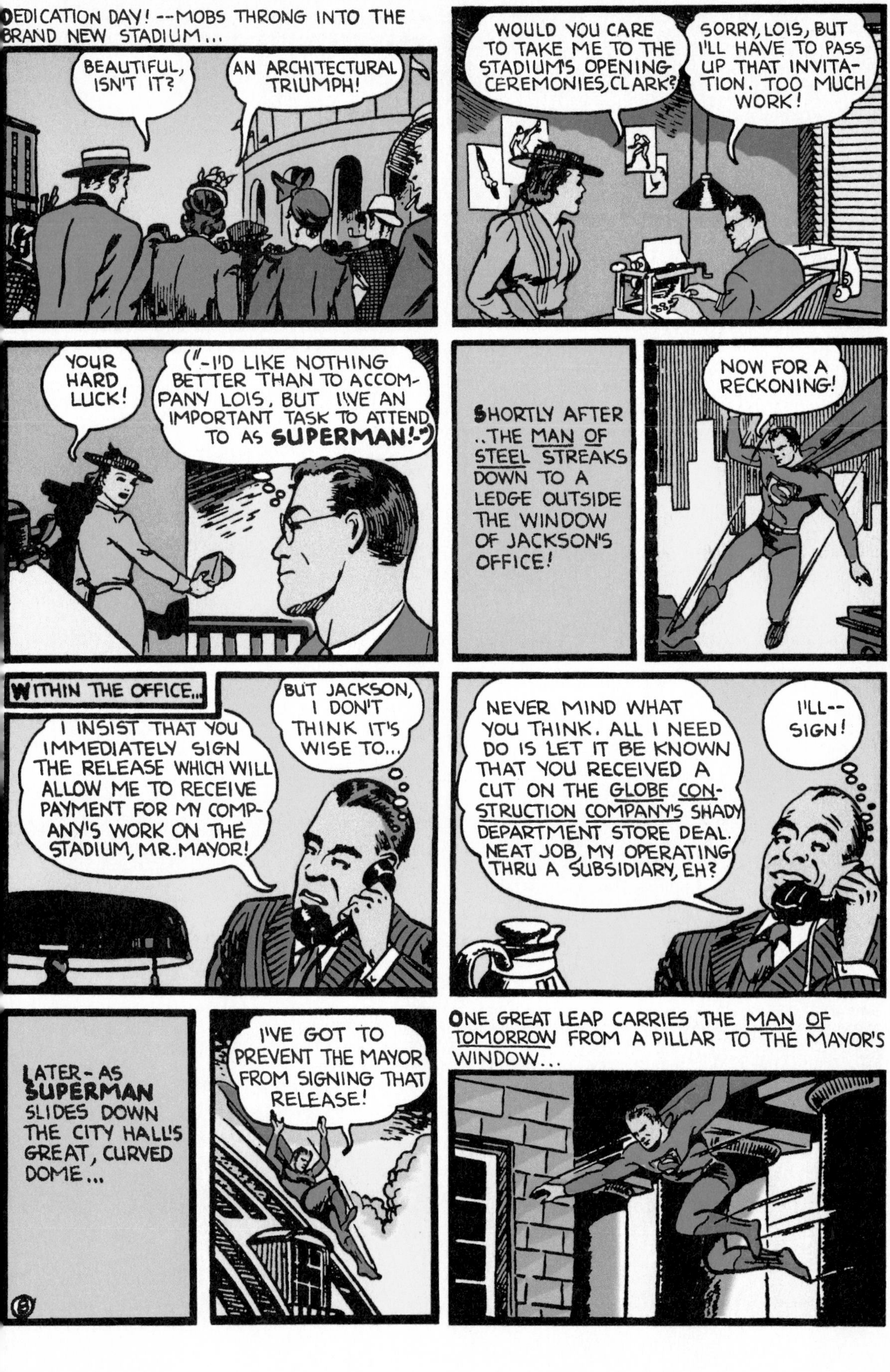
DEDICATION DAY! --MOBS THRONG INTO THE BRAND NEW STADIUM...
BEAUTIFUL, ISN'T IT?
AN ARCHITECTURAL TRIUMPH!
WOULD YOU CARE TO TAKE ME TO THE STADIUM'S OPENING CEREMONIES, CLARK?
SORRY, LOIS, BUT I'LL HAVE TO PASS UP THAT INVITATION. TOO MUCH WORK!
YOUR HARD LUCK!
("-I'D LIKE NOTHING BETTER THAN TO ACCOMPANY LOIS, BUT I'VE AN IMPORTANT TASK TO ATTEND TO AS SUPERMAN!-")
SHORTLY AFTER ..THE MAN OF STEEL STREAKS DOWN TO A LEDGE OUTSIDE THE WINDOW OF JACKSON'S OFFICE!
NOW FOR A RECKONING!
WITHIN THE OFFICE..
I INSIST THAT YOU IMMEDIATELY SIGN THE RELEASE WHICH WILL ALLOW ME TO RECEIVE PAYMENT FOR MY COMPANY'S WORK ON THE STADIUM, MR. MAYOR!
BUT JACKSON, I DON'T THINK IT'S WISE TO...
NEVER MIND WHAT YOU THINK. ALL I NEED DO IS LET IT BE KNOWN THAT YOU RECEIVED A CUT ON THE GLOBE CONSTRUCTION COMPANY'S SHADY DEPARTMENT STORE DEAL. NEAT JOB, MY OPERATING THRU A SUBSIDIARY, EH?
I'LL-- SIGN!
LATER-AS SUPERMAN SLIDES DOWN THE CITY HALL'S GREAT, CURVED DOME...
I'VE GOT TO PREVENT THE MAYOR FROM SIGNING THAT RELEASE!
ONE GREAT LEAP CARRIES THE MAN OF TOMORROW FROM A PILLAR TO THE MAYOR'S WINDOW...

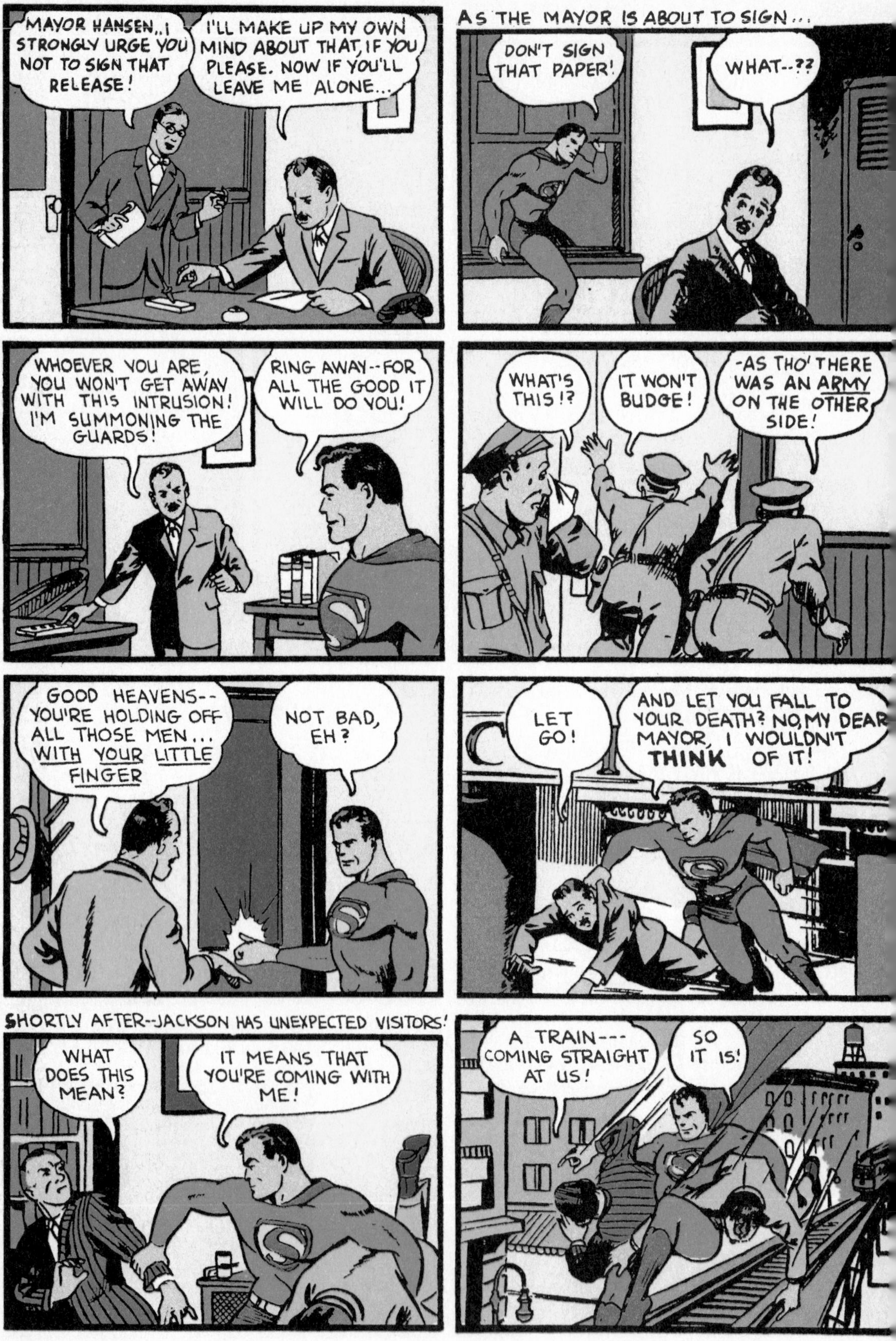
MAYOR HANSEN..I STRONGLY URGE YOU NOT TO SIGN THAT RELEASE!
I'LL MAKE UP MY OWN MIND ABOUT THAT, IF YOU PLEASE. NOW IF YOU'LL LEAVE ME ALONE...
AS THE MAYOR IS ABOUT TO SIGN...
DON'T SIGN THAT PAPER!
WHAT--??
WHOEVER YOU ARE, YOU WON'T GET AWAY WITH THIS INTRUSION! I'M SUMMONING THE GUARDS!
RING AWAY--FOR ALL THE GOOD IT WILL DO YOU!
WHAT'S THIS!?
IT WON'T BUDGE!
-AS THO' THERE WAS AN ARMY ON THE OTHER SIDE!
GOOD HEAVENS--YOU'RE HOLDING OFF ALL THOSE MEN... WITH YOUR LITTLE FINGER
NOT BAD, EH?
LET GO!
AND LET YOU FALL TO YOUR DEATH? NO, MY DEAR MAYOR, I WOULDN'T THINK OF IT!
SHORTLY AFTER--JACKSON HAS UNEXPECTED VISITORS!
WHAT DOES THIS MEAN?
IT MEANS THAT YOU'RE COMING WITH ME!
A TRAIN--- COMING STRAIGHT AT US!
SO IT IS!

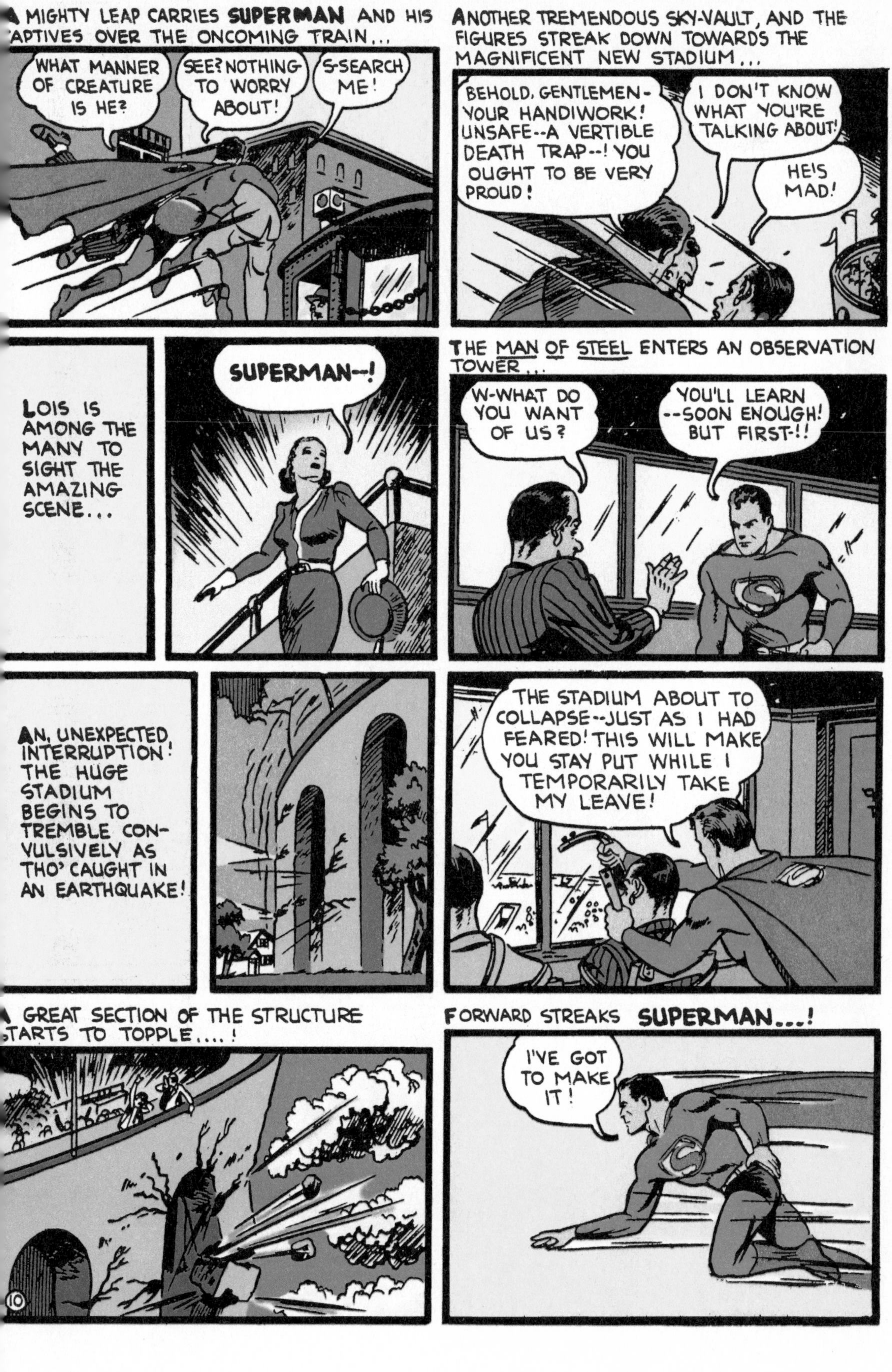
A MIGHTY LEAP CARRIES SUPERMAN AND HIS
APTIVES OVER THE ONCOMING TRAIN...
WHAT MANNER OF CREATURE IS HE?
SEE? NOTHING TO WORRY ABOUT!
S-SEARCH ME!
ANOTHER TREMENDOUS SKY-VAULT, AND THE FIGURES STREAK DOWN TOWARDS THE MAGNIFICENT NEW STADIUM...
BEHOLD, GENTLEMEN- YOUR HANDIWORK! UNSAFE--A VERTIBLE DEATH TRAP--! YOU OUGHT TO BE VERY PROUD!
I DON'T KNOW WHAT YOU'RE TALKING ABOUT!
HE'S MAD!
LOIS IS AMONG THE MANY TO SIGHT THE AMAZING SCENE...
SUPERMAN--!
THE MAN OF STEEL ENTERS AN OBSERVATION TOWER...
W-WHAT DO YOU WANT OF US?
YOU'LL LEARN --SOON ENOUGH! BUT FIRST-!!
AN UNEXPECTED INTERRUPTION! THE HUGE STADIUM BEGINS TO TREMBLE CONVULSIVELY AS THO' CAUGHT IN AN EARTHQUAKE!
THE STADIUM ABOUT TO COLLAPSE--JUST AS I HAD FEARED! THIS WILL MAKE YOU STAY PUT WHILE I TEMPORARILY TAKE MY LEAVE!
GREAT SECTION OF THE STRUCTURE
TARTS TO TOPPLE....!
10
FORWARD STREAKS SUPERMAN...!
I'VE GOT TO MAKE IT!

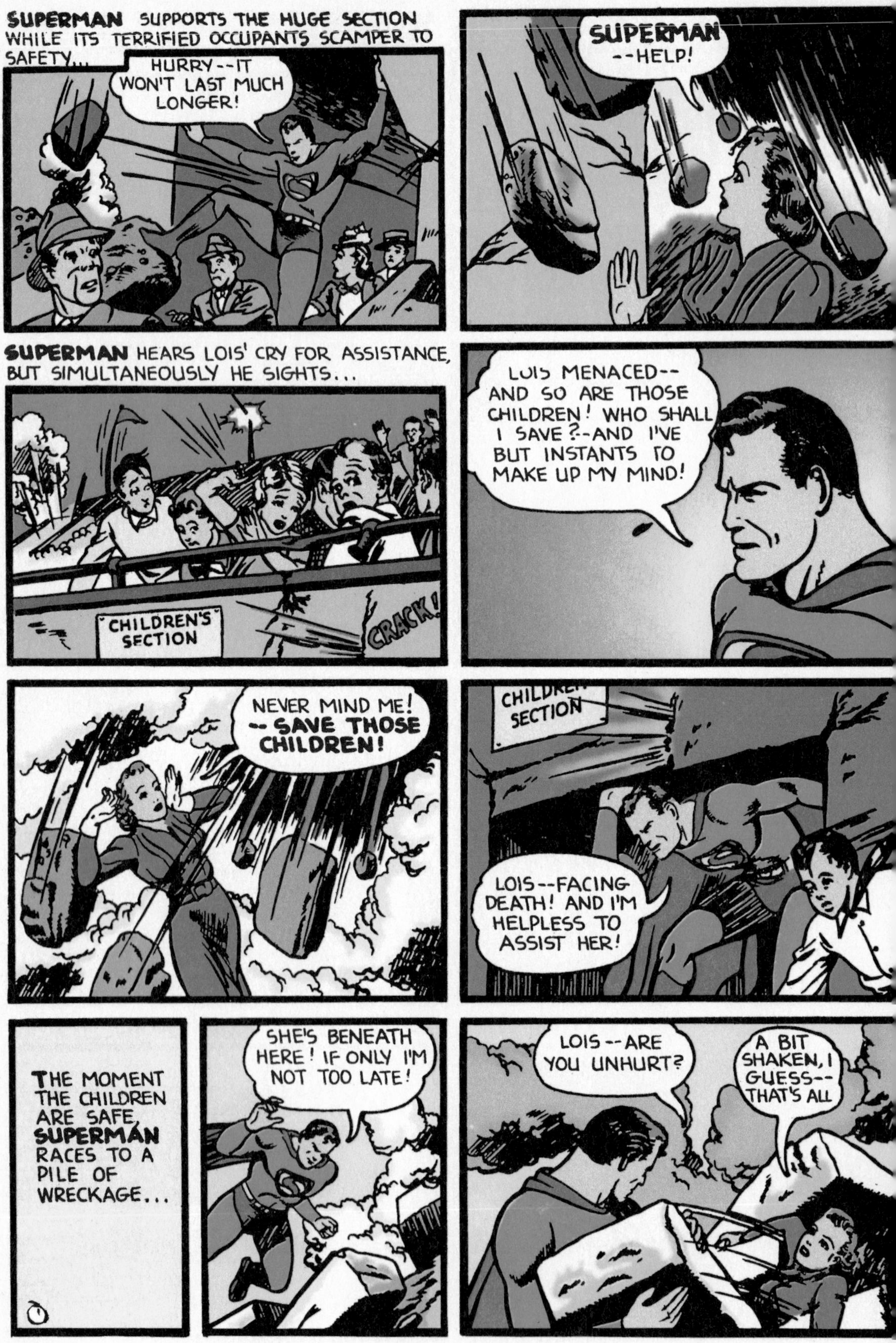
SUPERMAN SUPPORTS THE HUGE SECTION WHILE ITS TERRIFIED OCCUPANTS SCAMPER TO SAFETY...
HURRY--IT WON'T LAST MUCH LONGER!
SUPERMAN --HELP!
SUPERMAN HEARS LOIS' CRY FOR ASSISTANCE, BUT SIMULTANEOUSLY HE SIGHTS...
"CHILDREN'S SECTION"
CRACK!
LOIS MENACED--AND SO ARE THOSE CHILDREN! WHO SHALL I SAVE?--AND I'VE BUT INSTANTS TO MAKE UP MY MIND!
NEVER MIND ME! --SAVE THOSE CHILDREN!
SECTION
LOIS--FACING DEATH! AND I'M HELPLESS TO ASSIST HER!
THE MOMENT THE CHILDREN ARE SAFE, SUPERMAN RACES TO A PILE OF WRECKAGE...
SHE'S BENEATH HERE! IF ONLY I'M NOT TOO LATE!
LOIS--ARE YOU UNHURT?
A BIT SHAKEN, I GUESS--THAT'S ALL

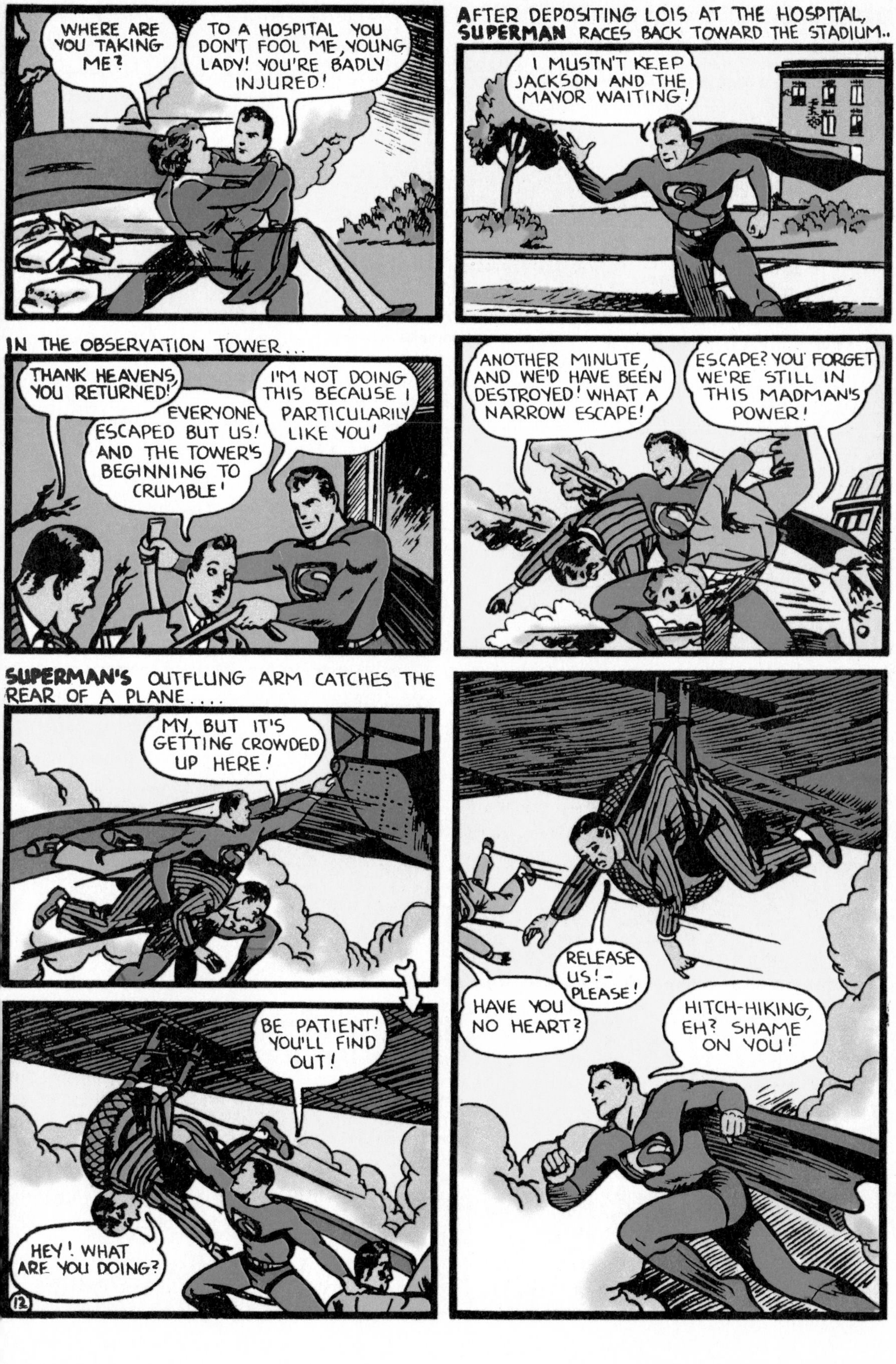
WHERE ARE YOU TAKING ME?
TO A HOSPITAL YOU DON'T FOOL ME, YOUNG LADY! YOU'RE BADLY INJURED!
AFTER DEPOSITING LOIS AT THE HOSPITAL, SUPERMAN RACES BACK TOWARD THE STADIUM..
I MUSTN'T KEEP JACKSON AND THE MAYOR WAITING!
IN THE OBSERVATION TOWER...
THANK HEAVENS, YOU RETURNED!
EVERYONE ESCAPED BUT US! AND THE TOWER'S BEGINNING TO CRUMBLE!
I'M NOT DOING THIS BECAUSE I PARTICULARILY LIKE YOU!
ANOTHER MINUTE, AND WE'D HAVE BEEN DESTROYED! WHAT A NARROW ESCAPE!
ESCAPE? YOU FORGET WE'RE STILL IN THIS MADMAN'S POWER!
SUPERMAN'S OUTFLUNG ARM CATCHES THE REAR OF A PLANE....
MY, BUT IT'S GETTING CROWDED UP HERE!
BE PATIENT! YOU'LL FIND OUT!
HEY! WHAT ARE YOU DOING?
12
RELEASE US! - PLEASE!
HAVE YOU NO HEART?
HITCH-HIKING, EH? SHAME ON YOU!

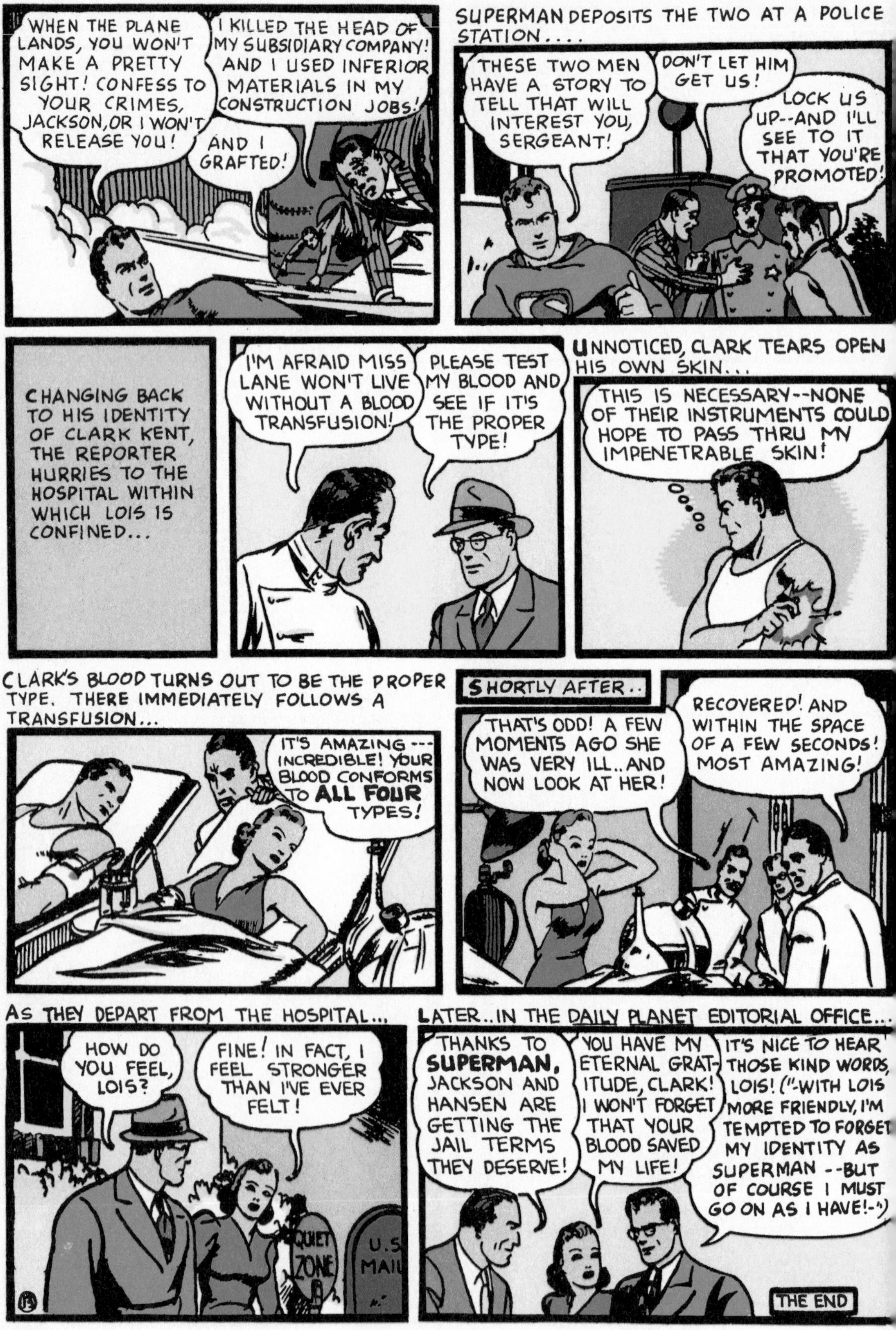

WHEN THE PLANE LANDS, YOU WON'T MAKE A PRETTY SIGHT! CONFESS TO YOUR CRIMES, JACKSON, OR I WON'T RELEASE YOU!
I KILLED THE HEAD OF MY SUBSIDIARY COMPANY! AND I USED INFERIOR MATERIALS IN MY CONSTRUCTION JOBS!
AND I GRAFTED!
SUPERMAN DEPOSITS THE TWO AT A POLICE STATION....
THESE TWO MEN HAVE A STORY TO TELL THAT WILL INTEREST YOU, SERGEANT!
DON'T LET HIM GET US!
LOCK US UP--AND I'LL SEE TO IT THAT YOU'RE PROMOTED!
CHANGING BACK TO HIS IDENTITY OF CLARK KENT, THE REPORTER HURRIES TO THE HOSPITAL WITHIN WHICH LOIS IS CONFINED...
I'M AFRAID MISS LANE WON'T LIVE WITHOUT A BLOOD TRANSFUSION!
PLEASE TEST MY BLOOD AND SEE IF IT'S THE PROPER TYPE!
UNNOTICED, CLARK TEARS OPEN HIS OWN SKIN...
THIS IS NECESSARY--NONE OF THEIR INSTRUMENTS COULD HOPE TO PASS THRU MY IMPENETRABLE SKIN!
CLARK'S BLOOD TURNS OUT TO BE THE PROPER TYPE. THERE IMMEDIATELY FOLLOWS A TRANSFUSION...
IT'S AMAZING---INCREDIBLE! YOUR BLOOD CONFORMS TO ALL FOUR TYPES!
SHORTLY AFTER..
THAT'S ODD! A FEW MOMENTS AGO SHE WAS VERY ILL.. AND NOW LOOK AT HER!
RECOVERED! AND WITHIN THE SPACE OF A FEW SECONDS! MOST AMAZING!
AS THEY DEPART FROM THE HOSPITAL...
HOW DO YOU FEEL, LOIS?
FINE! IN FACT, I FEEL STRONGER THAN I'VE EVER FELT!
QUIET ZONE
U.S. MAIL
LATER..IN THE DAILY PLANET EDITORIAL OFFICE...
THANKS TO SUPERMAN, JACKSON AND HANSEN ARE GETTING THE JAIL TERMS THEY DESERVE!
YOU HAVE MY ETERNAL GRATITUDE, CLARK! I WON'T FORGET THAT YOUR BLOOD SAVED MY LIFE!
IT'S NICE TO HEAR THOSE KIND WORDS, LOIS! ("-WITH LOIS MORE FRIENDLY, I'M TEMPTED TO FORGET MY IDENTITY AS SUPERMAN --BUT OF COURSE I MUST GO ON AS I HAVE!-")
THE END

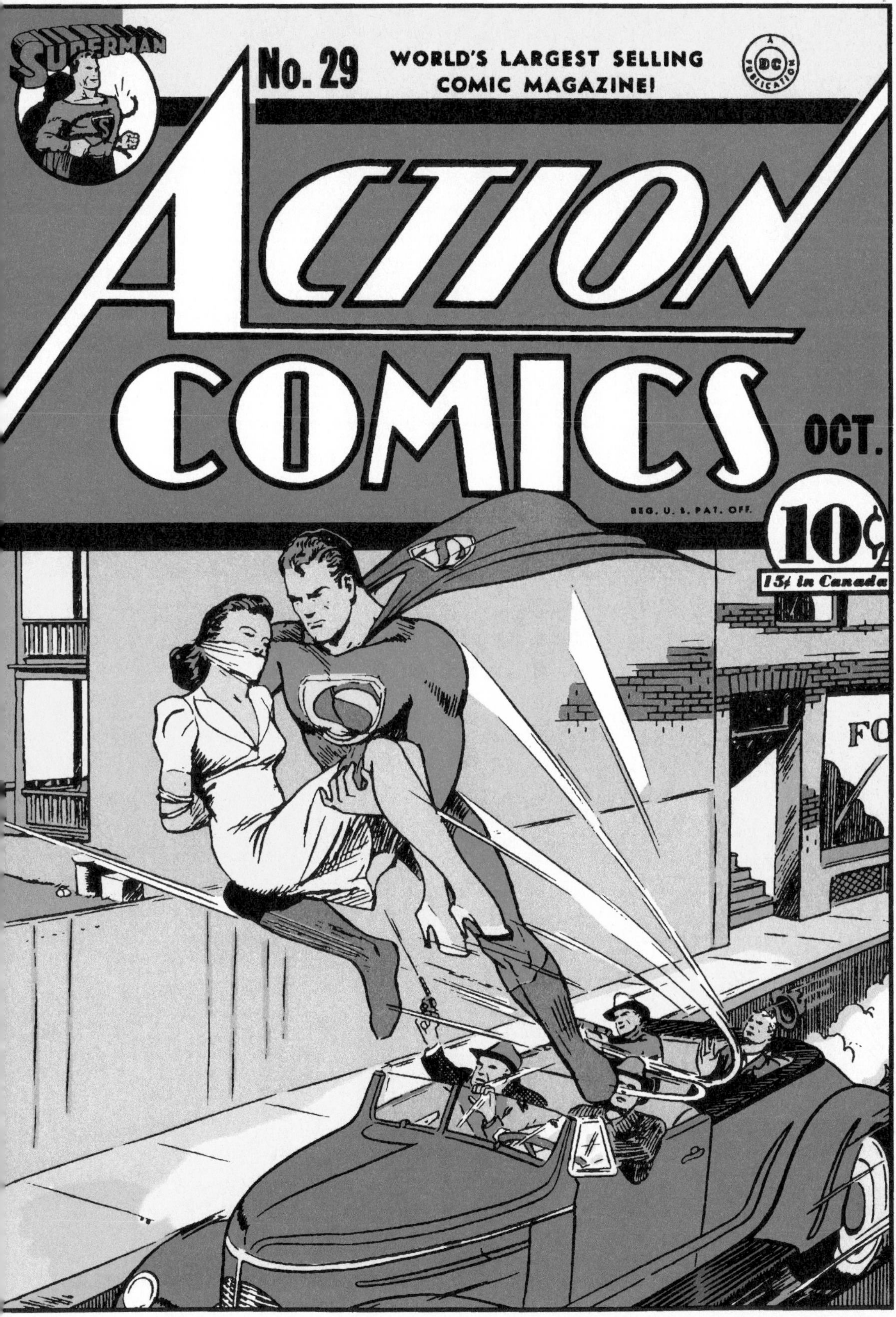
SUPERMAN
No. 29
WORLD'S LARGEST SELLING
COMIC MAGAZINE!
A DC PUBLICATION
ACTION
COMICS
OCT.
REG. U. S. PAT. OFF.
10¢
15¢ in Canada
FO

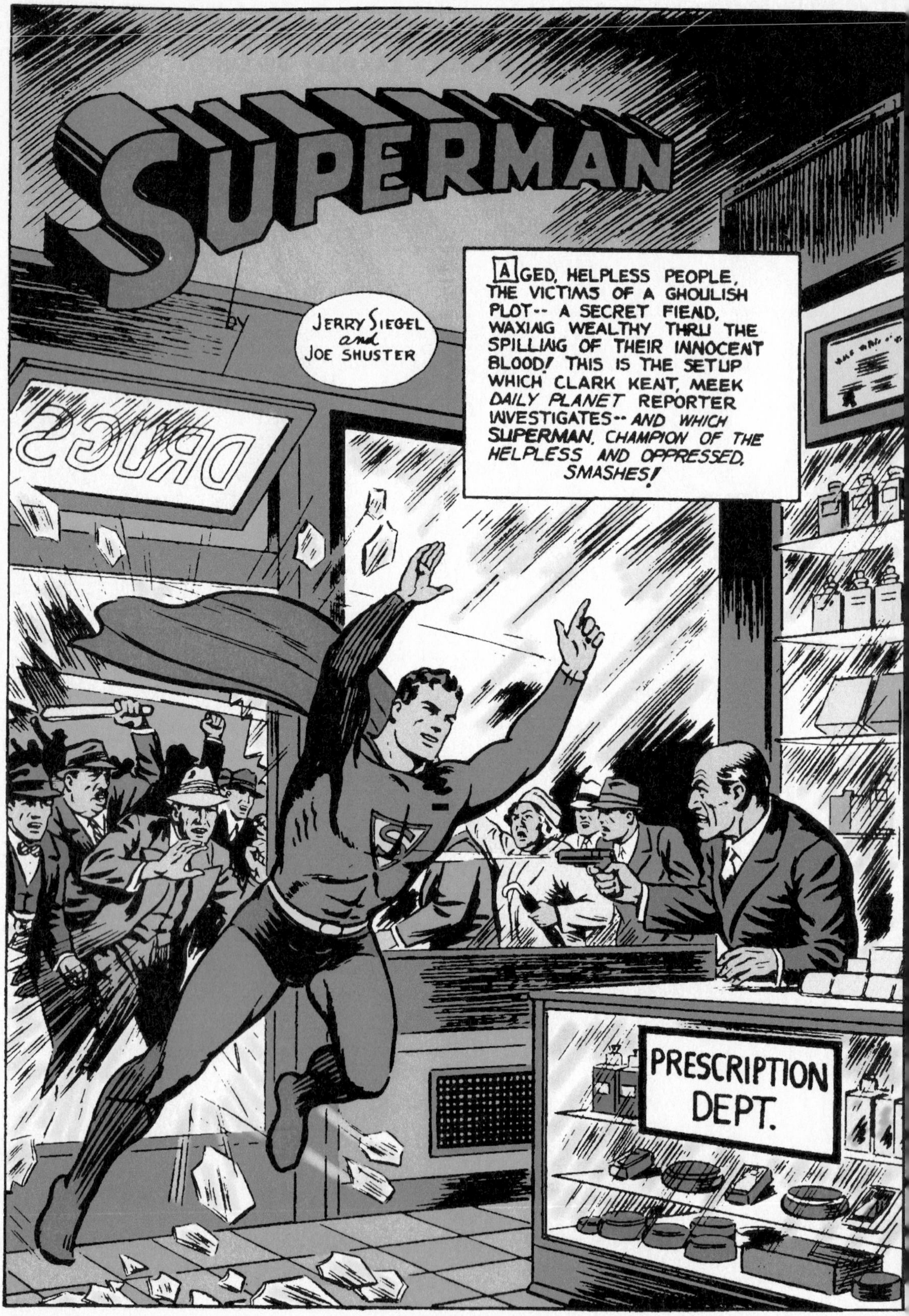
SUPERMAN
BY
JERRY SIEGEL and JOE SHUSTER
AGED, HELPLESS PEOPLE, THE VICTIMS OF A GHOULISH PLOT-- A SECRET FIEND, WAXING WEALTHY THRU THE SPILLING OF THEIR INNOCENT BLOOD! THIS IS THE SETUP WHICH CLARK KENT, MEEK DAILY PLANET REPORTER INVESTIGATES-- AND WHICH SUPERMAN, CHAMPION OF THE HELPLESS AND OPPRESSED, SMASHES!
DRUGS
PRESCRIPTION DEPT.

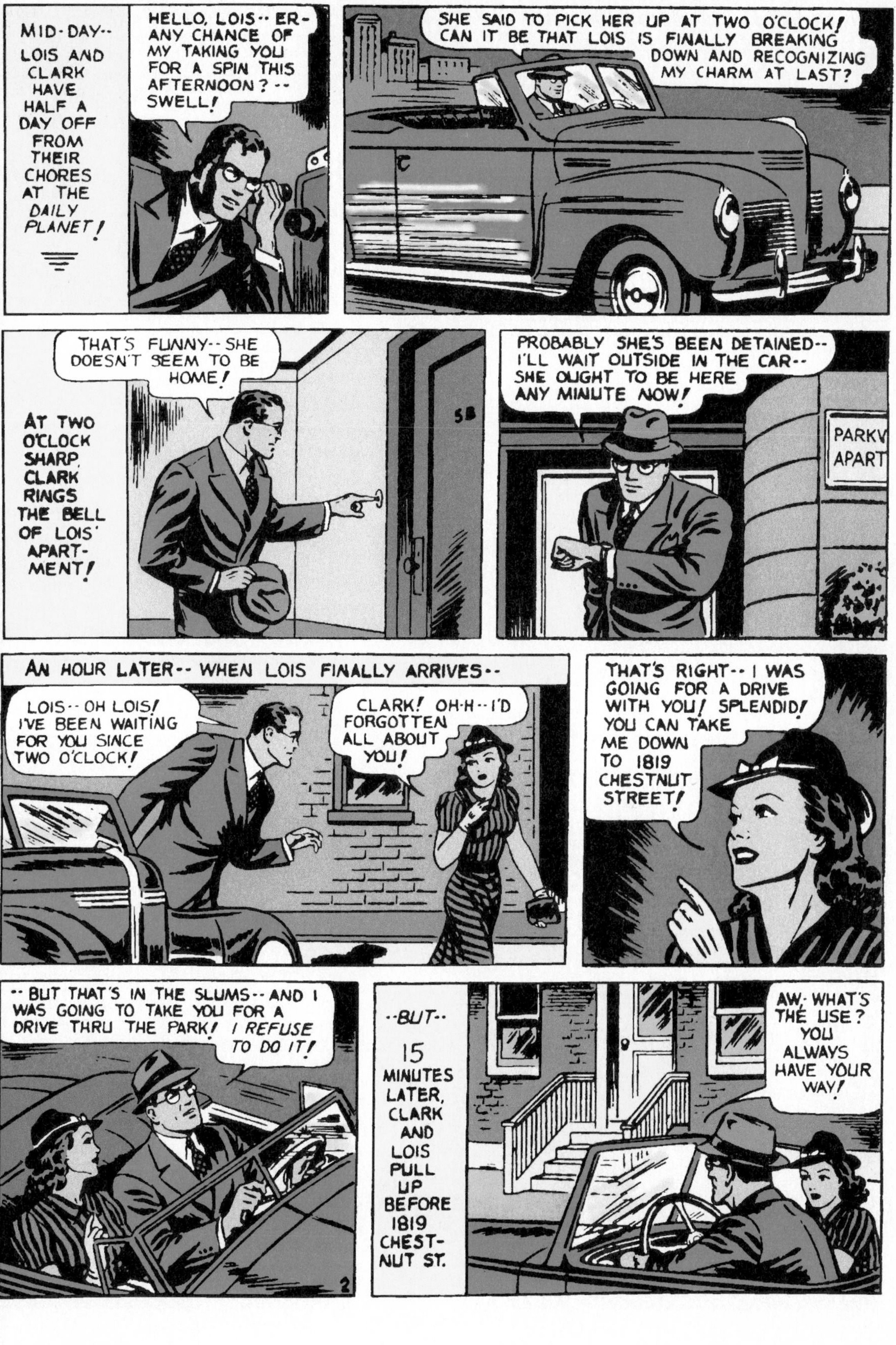
MID-DAY-- LOIS AND CLARK HAVE HALF A DAY OFF FROM THEIR CHORES AT THE DAILY PLANET!
HELLO, LOIS-- ER-- ANY CHANCE OF MY TAKING YOU FOR A SPIN THIS AFTERNOON? -- SWELL!
SHE SAID TO PICK HER UP AT TWO O'CLOCK! CAN IT BE THAT LOIS IS FINALLY BREAKING DOWN AND RECOGNIZING MY CHARM AT LAST?
AT TWO O'CLOCK SHARP, CLARK RINGS THE BELL OF LOIS' APARTMENT!
THAT'S FUNNY-- SHE DOESN'T SEEM TO BE HOME!
5B
PROBABLY SHE'S BEEN DETAINED-- I'LL WAIT OUTSIDE IN THE CAR-- SHE OUGHT TO BE HERE ANY MINUTE NOW!
PARKV
APART
AN HOUR LATER-- WHEN LOIS FINALLY ARRIVES--
LOIS-- OH LOIS! I'VE BEEN WAITING FOR YOU SINCE TWO O'CLOCK!
CLARK! OH-H-- I'D FORGOTTEN ALL ABOUT YOU!
THAT'S RIGHT-- I WAS GOING FOR A DRIVE WITH YOU! SPLENDID! YOU CAN TAKE ME DOWN TO 1819 CHESTNUT STREET!
-- BUT THAT'S IN THE SLUMS-- AND I WAS GOING TO TAKE YOU FOR A DRIVE THRU THE PARK! I REFUSE TO DO IT!
2
--BUT-- 15 MINUTES LATER, CLARK AND LOIS PULL UP BEFORE 1819 CHESTNUT ST.
AW, WHAT'S THE USE? YOU ALWAYS HAVE YOUR WAY!

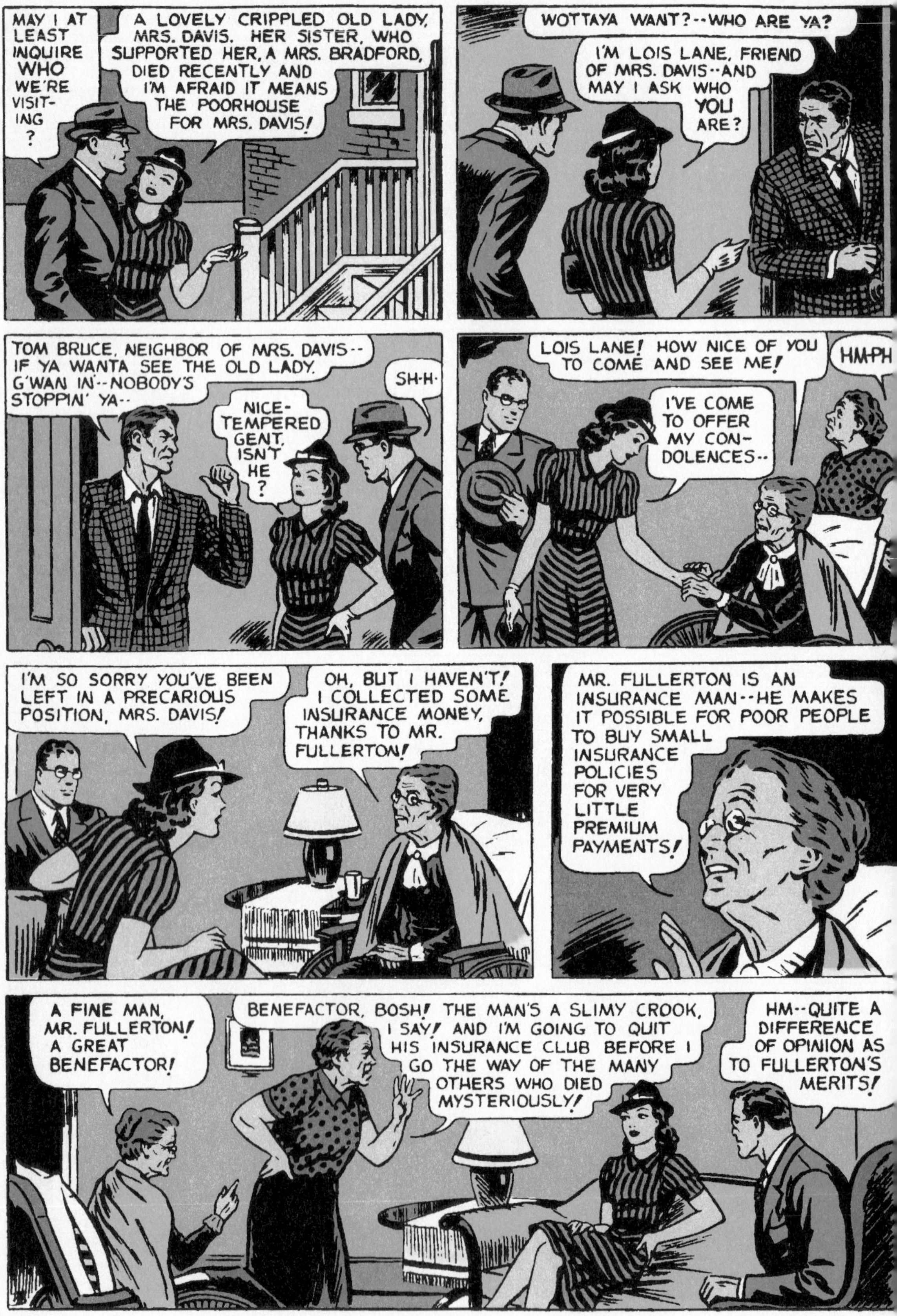
MAY I AT LEAST INQUIRE WHO WE'RE VISITING?
A LOVELY CRIPPLED OLD LADY, MRS. DAVIS. HER SISTER, WHO SUPPORTED HER, A MRS. BRADFORD, DIED RECENTLY AND I'M AFRAID IT MEANS THE POORHOUSE FOR MRS. DAVIS!
WOTTAYA WANT?--WHO ARE YA?
I'M LOIS LANE, FRIEND OF MRS. DAVIS--AND MAY I ASK WHO YOU ARE?
TOM BRUCE, NEIGHBOR OF MRS. DAVIS--IF YA WANTA SEE THE OLD LADY, G'WAN IN--NOBODY'S STOPPIN' YA--
NICE-TEMPERED GENT, ISN'T HE?
SH-H-
LOIS LANE! HOW NICE OF YOU TO COME AND SEE ME!
HM-PH
I'VE COME TO OFFER MY CONDOLENCES--
I'M SO SORRY YOU'VE BEEN LEFT IN A PRECARIOUS POSITION, MRS. DAVIS!
OH, BUT I HAVEN'T! I COLLECTED SOME INSURANCE MONEY, THANKS TO MR. FULLERTON!
MR. FULLERTON IS AN INSURANCE MAN--HE MAKES IT POSSIBLE FOR POOR PEOPLE TO BUY SMALL INSURANCE POLICIES FOR VERY LITTLE PREMIUM PAYMENTS!
A FINE MAN, MR. FULLERTON! A GREAT BENEFACTOR!
BENEFACTOR, BOSH! THE MAN'S A SLIMY CROOK, I SAY! AND I'M GOING TO QUIT HIS INSURANCE CLUB BEFORE I GO THE WAY OF THE MANY OTHERS WHO DIED MYSTERIOUSLY!
HM--QUITE A DIFFERENCE OF OPINION AS TO FULLERTON'S MERITS!

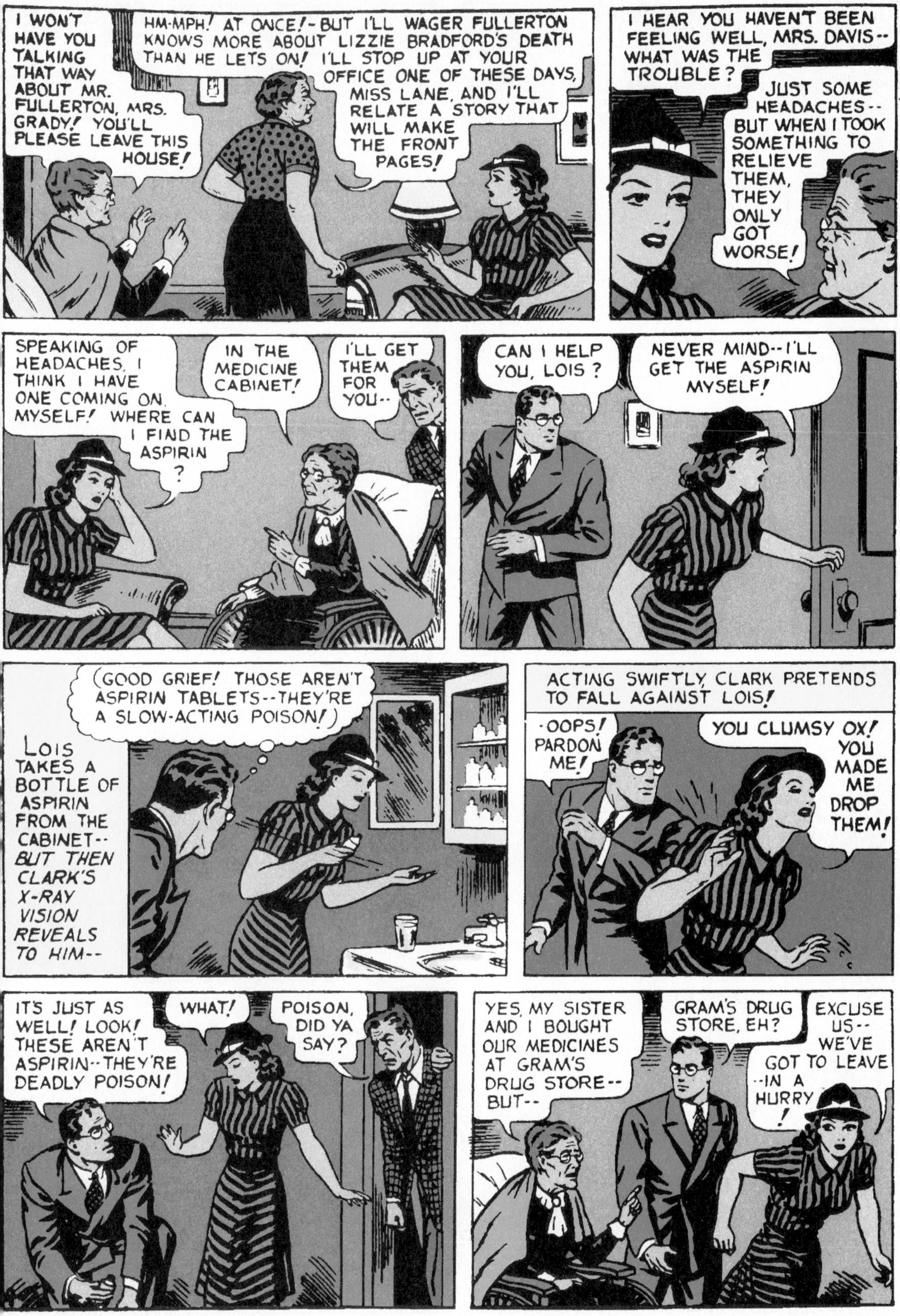
I WON'T HAVE YOU TALKING THAT WAY ABOUT MR. FULLERTON, MRS. GRADY! YOU'LL PLEASE LEAVE THIS HOUSE!
HM-MPH! AT ONCE! - BUT I'LL WAGER FULLERTON KNOWS MORE ABOUT LIZZIE BRADFORD'S DEATH THAN HE LETS ON! I'LL STOP UP AT YOUR OFFICE ONE OF THESE DAYS, MISS LANE, AND I'LL RELATE A STORY THAT WILL MAKE THE FRONT PAGES!
I HEAR YOU HAVEN'T BEEN FEELING WELL, MRS. DAVIS -- WHAT WAS THE TROUBLE?
JUST SOME HEADACHES -- BUT WHEN I TOOK SOMETHING TO RELIEVE THEM, THEY ONLY GOT WORSE!
SPEAKING OF HEADACHES, I THINK I HAVE ONE COMING ON, MYSELF! WHERE CAN I FIND THE ASPIRIN?
IN THE MEDICINE CABINET!
I'LL GET THEM FOR YOU --
CAN I HELP YOU, LOIS?
NEVER MIND -- I'LL GET THE ASPIRIN MYSELF!
(GOOD GRIEF! THOSE AREN'T ASPIRIN TABLETS -- THEY'RE A SLOW-ACTING POISON!)
LOIS TAKES A BOTTLE OF ASPIRIN FROM THE CABINET -- *BUT THEN CLARK'S X-RAY VISION REVEALS TO HIM --*
ACTING SWIFTLY, CLARK PRETENDS TO FALL AGAINST LOIS!
- OOPS! PARDON ME!
YOU CLUMSY OX! YOU MADE ME DROP THEM!
IT'S JUST AS WELL! LOOK! THESE AREN'T ASPIRIN -- THEY'RE DEADLY POISON!
WHAT!
POISON, DID YA SAY?
YES, MY SISTER AND I BOUGHT OUR MEDICINES AT GRAM'S DRUG STORE -- BUT --
GRAM'S DRUG STORE, EH?
EXCUSE US -- WE'VE GOT TO LEAVE -- IN A HURRY!

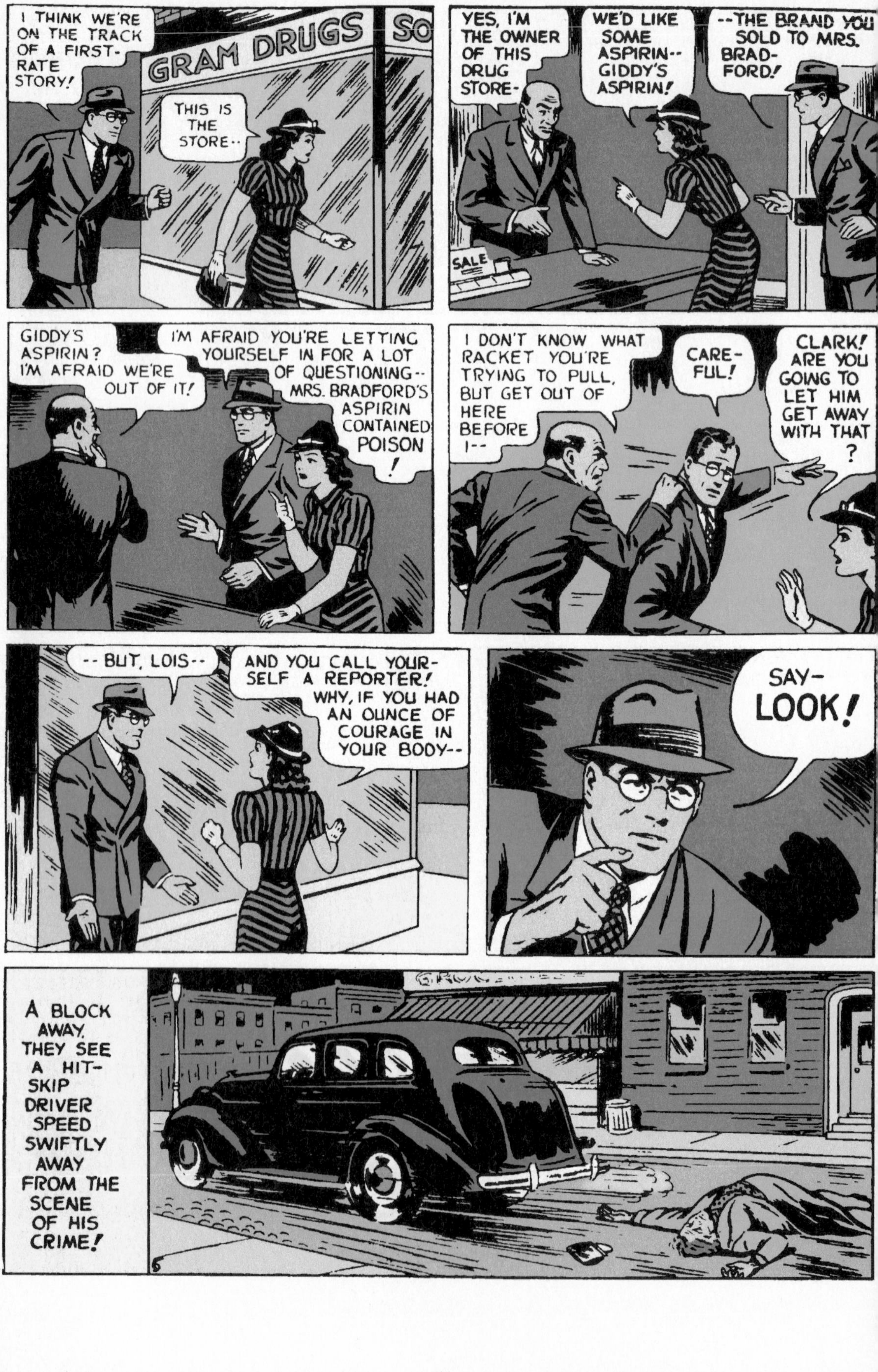
I THINK WE'RE ON THE TRACK OF A FIRST-RATE STORY!
GRAM DRUGS
THIS IS THE STORE--
YES, I'M THE OWNER OF THIS DRUG STORE-
WE'D LIKE SOME ASPIRIN--GIDDY'S ASPIRIN!
--THE BRAND YOU SOLD TO MRS. BRADFORD!
SALE
GIDDY'S ASPIRIN? I'M AFRAID WE'RE OUT OF IT!
I'M AFRAID YOU'RE LETTING YOURSELF IN FOR A LOT OF QUESTIONING--MRS. BRADFORD'S ASPIRIN CONTAINED POISON!
I DON'T KNOW WHAT RACKET YOU'RE TRYING TO PULL, BUT GET OUT OF HERE BEFORE I--
CARE-FUL!
CLARK! ARE YOU GOING TO LET HIM GET AWAY WITH THAT?
--BUT, LOIS--
AND YOU CALL YOURSELF A REPORTER! WHY, IF YOU HAD AN OUNCE OF COURAGE IN YOUR BODY--
SAY-LOOK!
A BLOCK AWAY, THEY SEE A HIT-SKIP DRIVER SPEED SWIFTLY AWAY FROM THE SCENE OF HIS CRIME!

As Clark and Lois rush to the scene, they find that the victim of the hit-skip car is none other than Mrs. Grady!

IT'S MRS. GRADY! SHE WAS GOING TO TELL ME SOMETHING ABOUT FULLERTON! PERHAPS HER DEATH ISN'T AS ACCIDENTAL AS IT SEEMS!

SHE DIDN'T HAVE TIME TO QUIT THE FULLERTON INSURANCE CLUB!

CITY HOSPITAL

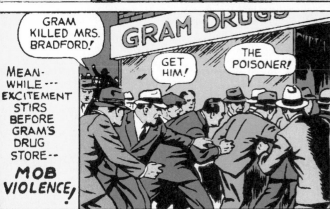

Meanwhile--- excitement stirs before Gram's drug store-- MOB VIOLENCE!

GRAM KILLED MRS. BRADFORD!

GET HIM!

THE POISONER!

KEEP BACK, I SAY!

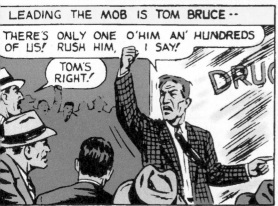

LEADING THE MOB IS TOM BRUCE--

THERE'S ONLY ONE O'HIM AN' HUNDREDS OF US! RUSH HIM, I SAY!

TOM'S RIGHT!

WE'VE GOT TO PREVENT A RIOT! STOP THEM, CLARK-- SOME WAY, SOME- HOW!

I'D BETTER RUN FOR THE POLICE!

LOIS! COME BACK!

YOU CAN RUN OFF AND HIDE, BUT I'M GOING TO TRY AND STOP THIS BEFORE IT'S TOO LATE!

LITTLE TIME TO ACT!--THAT MOB'S ABOUT TO GO WILD--AND LOIS IS IN THE THICK OF IT!

MOMENTS LATER-- IN A SECLUDED ALLEY!

6

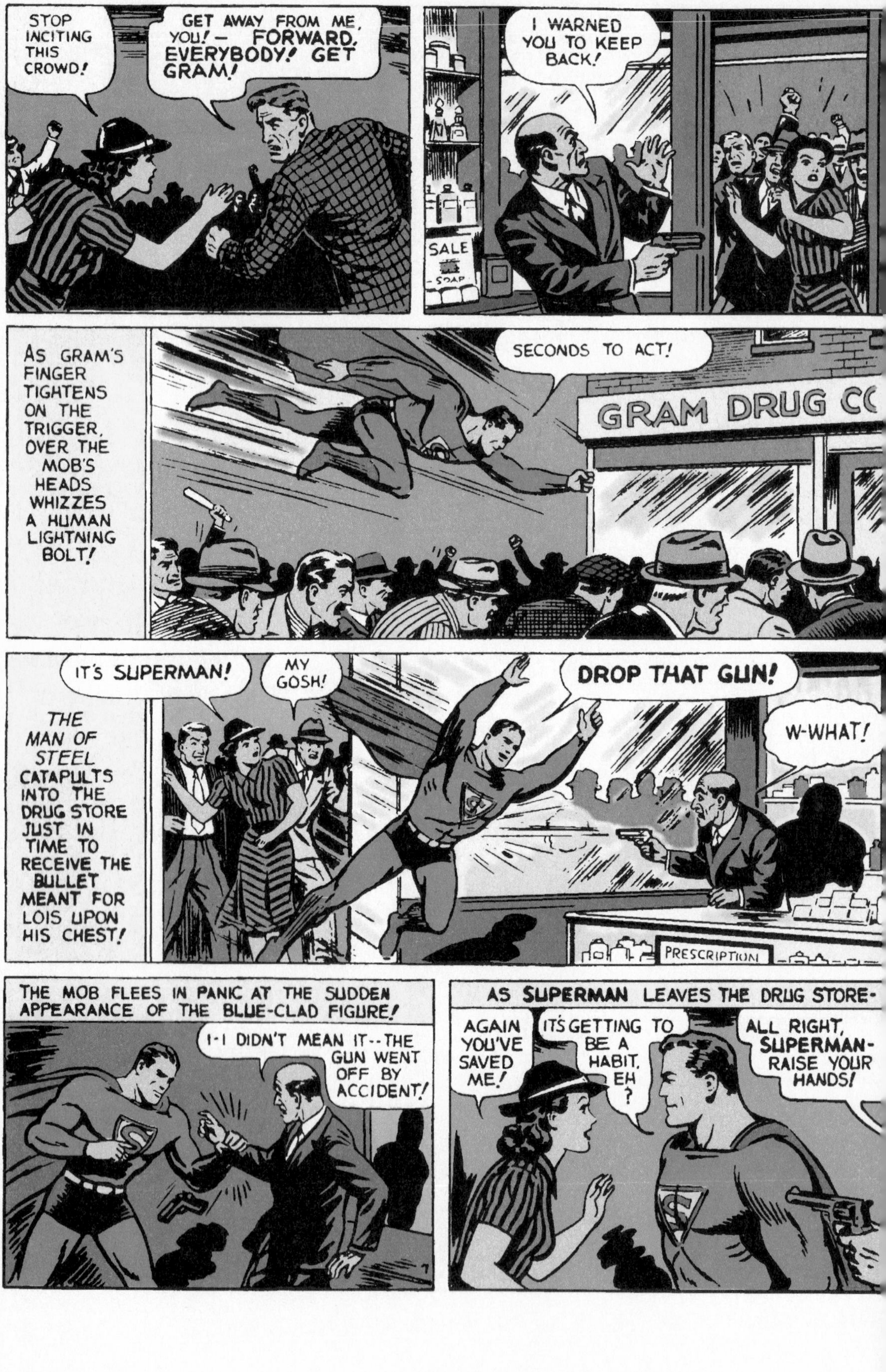
STOP INCITING THIS CROWD!
GET AWAY FROM ME, YOU! — FORWARD, EVERYBODY! GET GRAM!
I WARNED YOU TO KEEP BACK!
SALE
SOAP
AS GRAM'S FINGER TIGHTENS ON THE TRIGGER, OVER THE MOB'S HEADS WHIZZES A HUMAN LIGHTNING BOLT!
SECONDS TO ACT!
GRAM DRUG CO
IT'S SUPERMAN!
MY GOSH!
DROP THAT GUN!
W-WHAT!
THE MAN OF STEEL CATAPULTS INTO THE DRUG STORE JUST IN TIME TO RECEIVE THE BULLET MEANT FOR LOIS UPON HIS CHEST!
PRESCRIPTION
THE MOB FLEES IN PANIC AT THE SUDDEN APPEARANCE OF THE BLUE-CLAD FIGURE!
I-I DIDN'T MEAN IT--THE GUN WENT OFF BY ACCIDENT!
AS SUPERMAN LEAVES THE DRUG STORE-
AGAIN YOU'VE SAVED ME!
IT'S GETTING TO BE A HABIT, EH?
ALL RIGHT, SUPERMAN- RAISE YOUR HANDS!

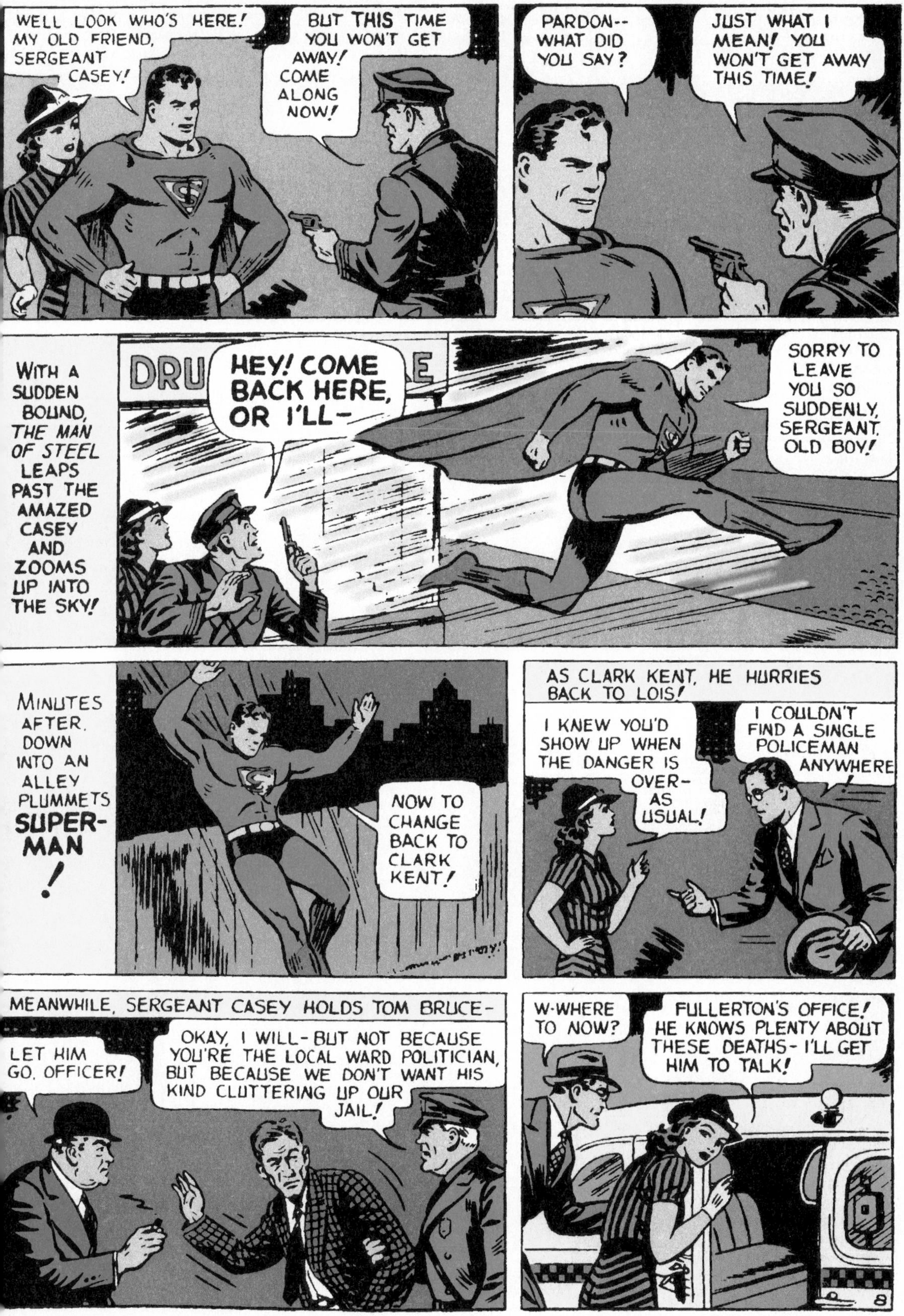
WELL LOOK WHO'S HERE! MY OLD FRIEND, SERGEANT CASEY!
BUT THIS TIME YOU WON'T GET AWAY! COME ALONG NOW!
PARDON-- WHAT DID YOU SAY?
JUST WHAT I MEAN! YOU WON'T GET AWAY THIS TIME!
WITH A SUDDEN BOUND, THE MAN OF STEEL LEAPS PAST THE AMAZED CASEY AND ZOOMS UP INTO THE SKY!
DRU
E
HEY! COME BACK HERE, OR I'LL-
SORRY TO LEAVE YOU SO SUDDENLY, SERGEANT, OLD BOY!
MINUTES AFTER, DOWN INTO AN ALLEY PLUMMETS SUPER-MAN!
NOW TO CHANGE BACK TO CLARK KENT!
AS CLARK KENT, HE HURRIES BACK TO LOIS!
I KNEW YOU'D SHOW UP WHEN THE DANGER IS OVER-AS USUAL!
I COULDN'T FIND A SINGLE POLICEMAN ANYWHERE!
MEANWHILE, SERGEANT CASEY HOLDS TOM BRUCE-
LET HIM GO, OFFICER!
OKAY, I WILL-BUT NOT BECAUSE YOU'RE THE LOCAL WARD POLITICIAN, BUT BECAUSE WE DON'T WANT HIS KIND CLUTTERING UP OUR JAIL!
W-WHERE TO NOW?
FULLERTON'S OFFICE! HE KNOWS PLENTY ABOUT THESE DEATHS-I'LL GET HIM TO TALK!
8

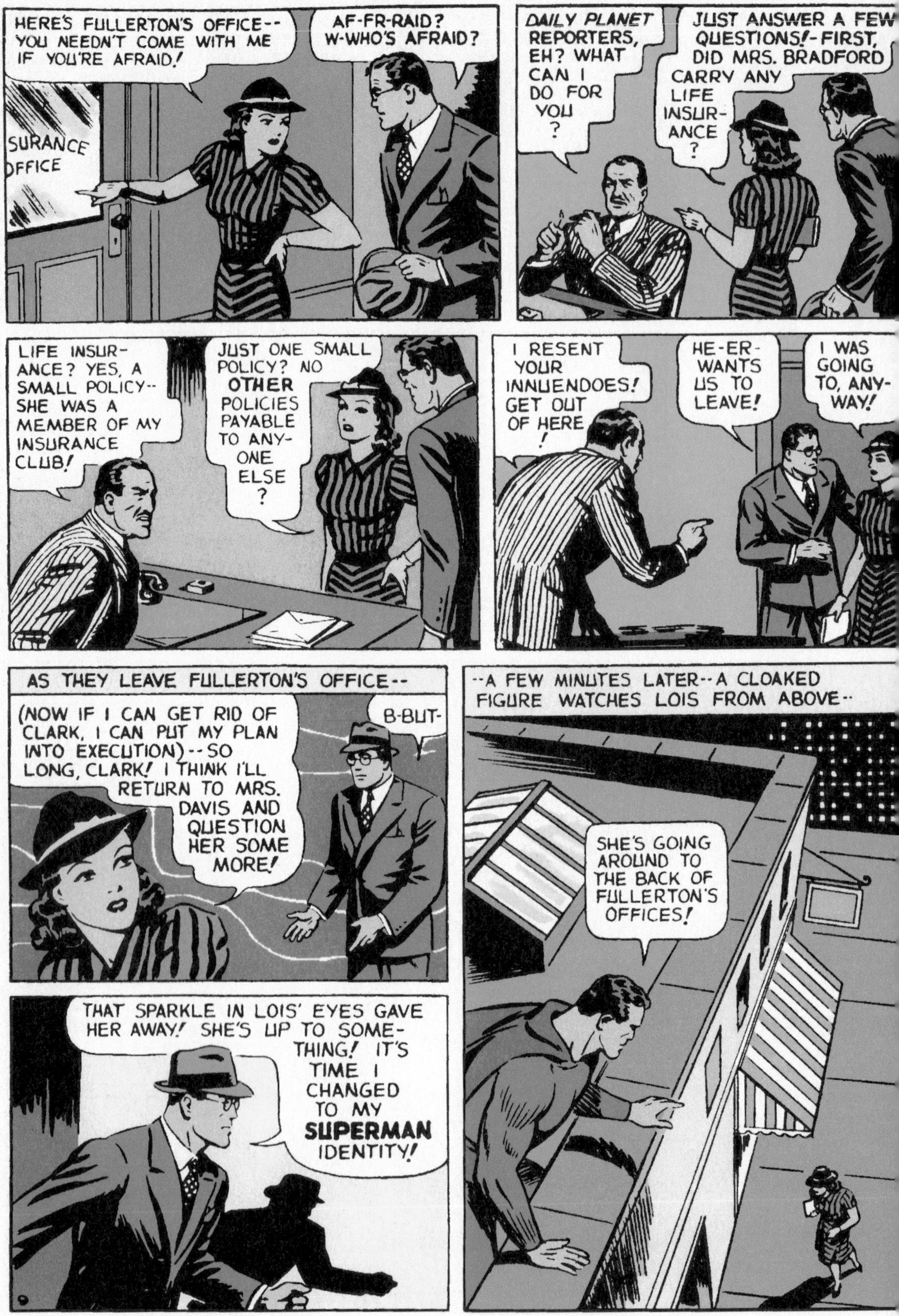
HERE'S FULLERTON'S OFFICE-- YOU NEEDN'T COME WITH ME IF YOU'RE AFRAID!
AF-FR-RAID? W-WHO'S AFRAID?
SURANCE OFFICE
DAILY PLANET REPORTERS, EH? WHAT CAN I DO FOR YOU?
JUST ANSWER A FEW QUESTIONS!-FIRST, DID MRS. BRADFORD CARRY ANY LIFE INSURANCE?
LIFE INSURANCE? YES, A SMALL POLICY-- SHE WAS A MEMBER OF MY INSURANCE CLUB!
JUST ONE SMALL POLICY? NO OTHER POLICIES PAYABLE TO ANYONE ELSE?
I RESENT YOUR INNUENDOES! GET OUT OF HERE!
HE-ER-WANTS US TO LEAVE!
I WAS GOING TO, ANYWAY!
AS THEY LEAVE FULLERTON'S OFFICE--
(NOW IF I CAN GET RID OF CLARK, I CAN PUT MY PLAN INTO EXECUTION)--SO LONG, CLARK! I THINK I'LL RETURN TO MRS. DAVIS AND QUESTION HER SOME MORE!
B-BUT-
THAT SPARKLE IN LOIS' EYES GAVE HER AWAY! SHE'S UP TO SOMETHING! IT'S TIME I CHANGED TO MY SUPERMAN IDENTITY!
--A FEW MINUTES LATER--A CLOAKED FIGURE WATCHES LOIS FROM ABOVE--
SHE'S GOING AROUND TO THE BACK OF FULLERTON'S OFFICES!

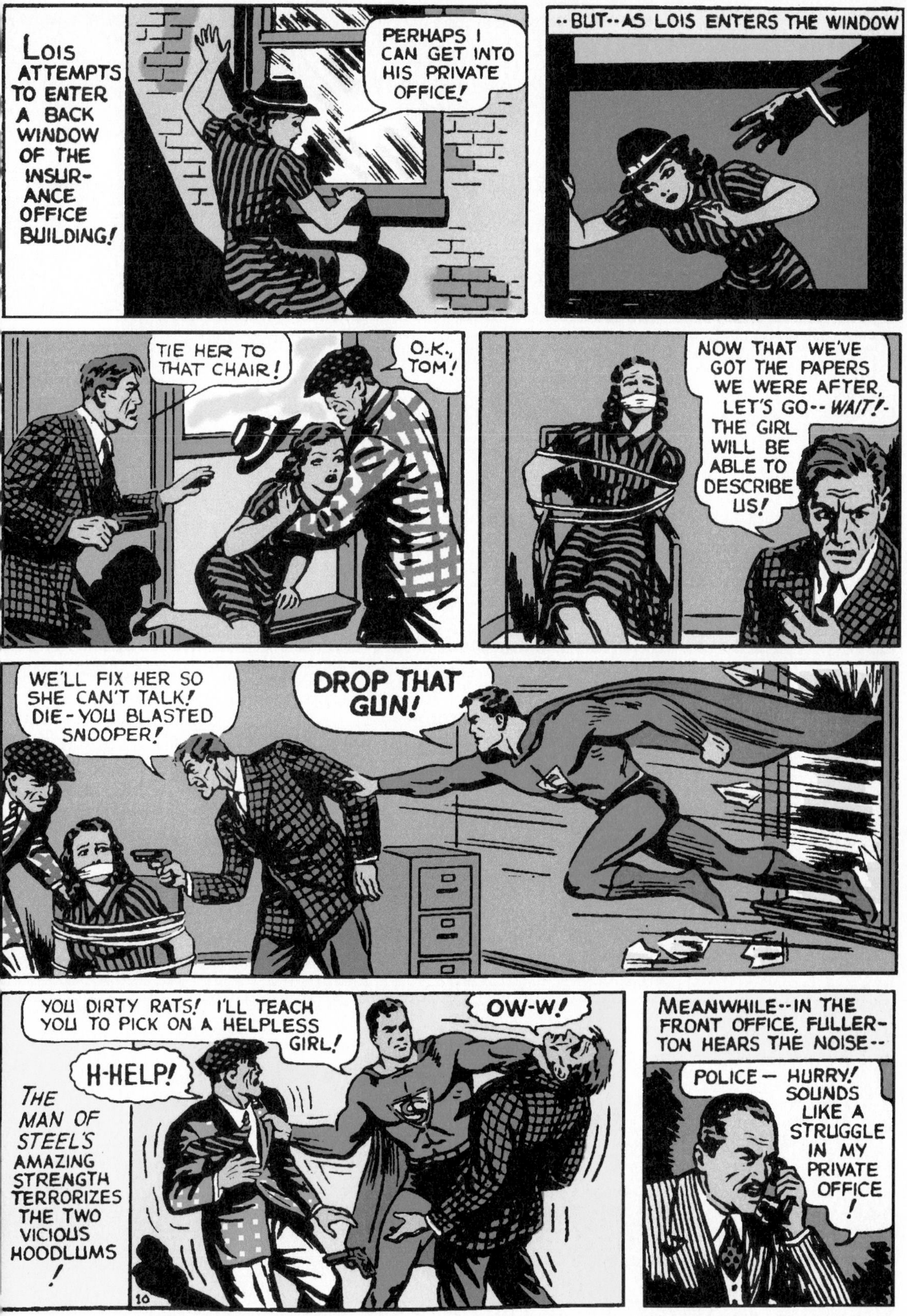
LOIS ATTEMPTS TO ENTER A BACK WINDOW OF THE INSURANCE OFFICE BUILDING!
PERHAPS I CAN GET INTO HIS PRIVATE OFFICE!
--BUT--AS LOIS ENTERS THE WINDOW
TIE HER TO THAT CHAIR!
O.K., TOM!
NOW THAT WE'VE GOT THE PAPERS WE WERE AFTER, LET'S GO-- WAIT!- THE GIRL WILL BE ABLE TO DESCRIBE US!
WE'LL FIX HER SO SHE CAN'T TALK! DIE- YOU BLASTED SNOOPER!
DROP THAT GUN!
YOU DIRTY RATS! I'LL TEACH YOU TO PICK ON A HELPLESS GIRL!
OW-W!
H-HELP!
THE MAN OF STEEL'S AMAZING STRENGTH TERRORIZES THE TWO VICIOUS HOODLUMS!
10
MEANWHILE--IN THE FRONT OFFICE, FULLERTON HEARS THE NOISE--
POLICE — HURRY! SOUNDS LIKE A STRUGGLE IN MY PRIVATE OFFICE!

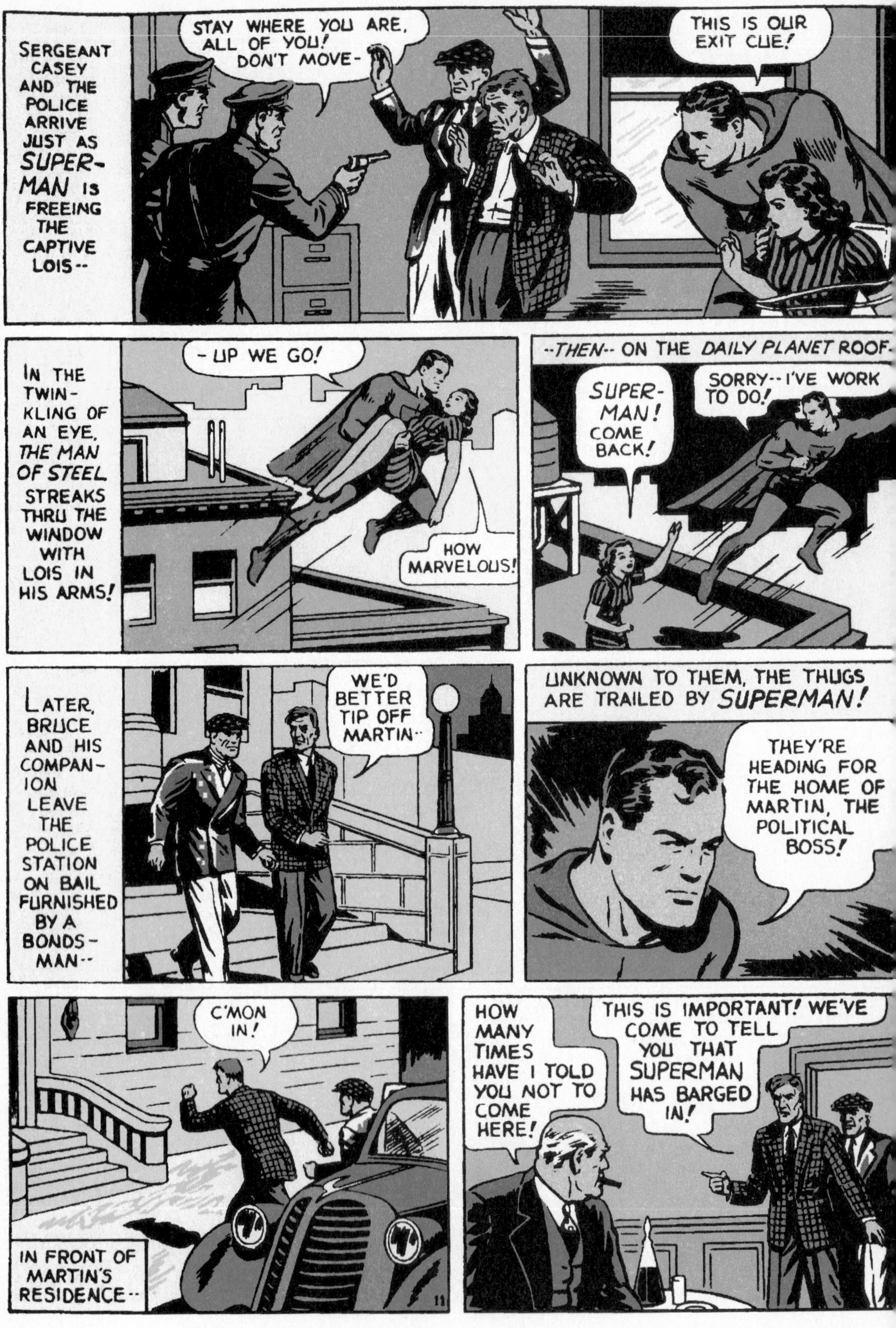
SERGEANT CASEY AND THE POLICE ARRIVE JUST AS SUPERMAN IS FREEING THE CAPTIVE LOIS--
STAY WHERE YOU ARE, ALL OF YOU! DON'T MOVE-
THIS IS OUR EXIT CUE!
IN THE TWINKLING OF AN EYE, THE MAN OF STEEL STREAKS THRU THE WINDOW WITH LOIS IN HIS ARMS!
-UP WE GO!
HOW MARVELOUS!
--THEN-- ON THE DAILY PLANET ROOF-
SUPERMAN! COME BACK!
SORRY--I'VE WORK TO DO!
LATER, BRUCE AND HIS COMPANION LEAVE THE POLICE STATION ON BAIL FURNISHED BY A BONDSMAN--
WE'D BETTER TIP OFF MARTIN--
UNKNOWN TO THEM, THE THUGS ARE TRAILED BY SUPERMAN!
THEY'RE HEADING FOR THE HOME OF MARTIN, THE POLITICAL BOSS!
C'MON IN!
IN FRONT OF MARTIN'S RESIDENCE--
HOW MANY TIMES HAVE I TOLD YOU NOT TO COME HERE!
THIS IS IMPORTANT! WE'VE COME TO TELL YOU THAT SUPERMAN HAS BARGED IN!

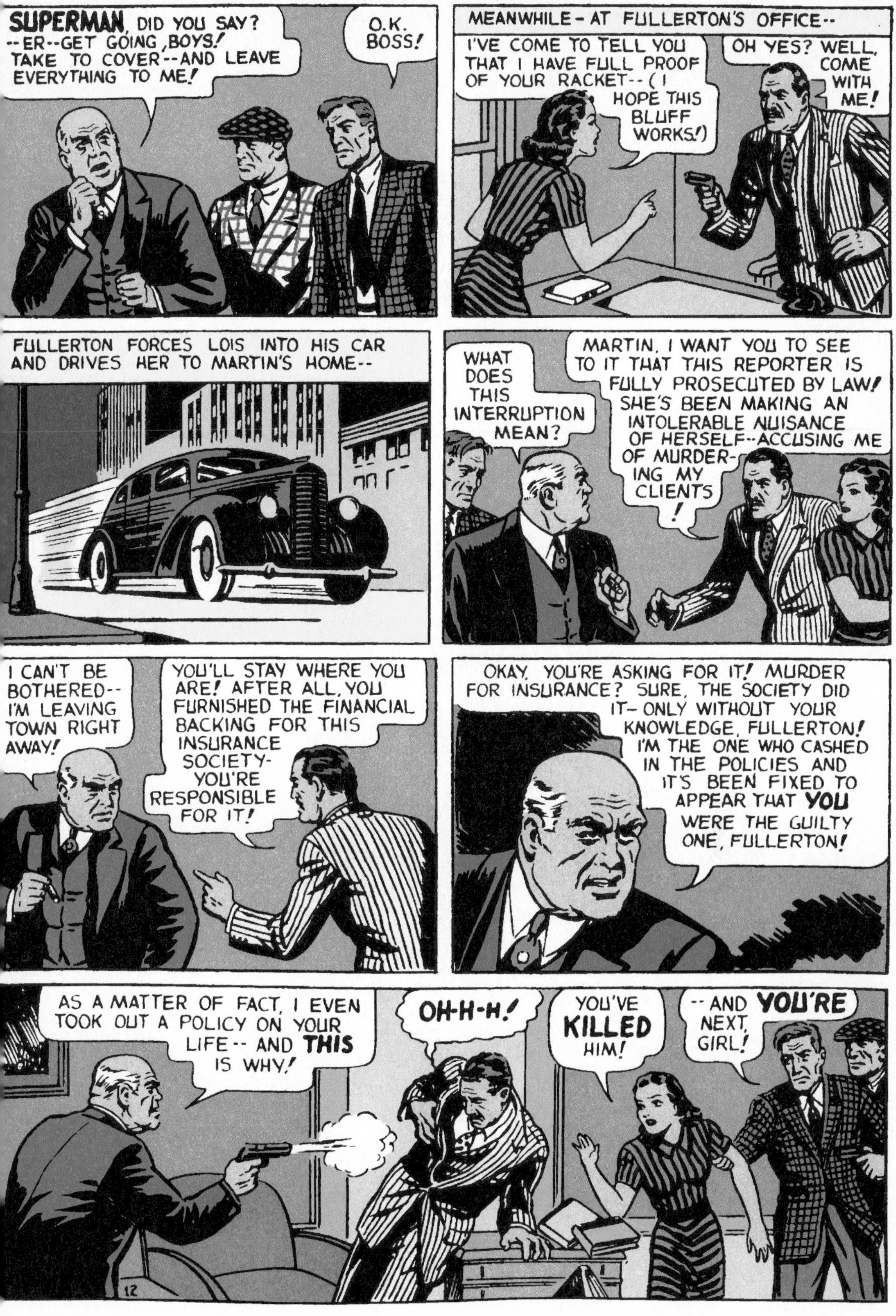
SUPERMAN, DID YOU SAY? --ER--GET GOING, BOYS! TAKE TO COVER--AND LEAVE EVERYTHING TO ME!
O.K. BOSS!
MEANWHILE - AT FULLERTON'S OFFICE--
I'VE COME TO TELL YOU THAT I HAVE FULL PROOF OF YOUR RACKET--(I HOPE THIS BLUFF WORKS!)
OH YES? WELL, COME WITH ME!
FULLERTON FORCES LOIS INTO HIS CAR AND DRIVES HER TO MARTIN'S HOME--
WHAT DOES THIS INTERRUPTION MEAN?
MARTIN, I WANT YOU TO SEE TO IT THAT THIS REPORTER IS FULLY PROSECUTED BY LAW! SHE'S BEEN MAKING AN INTOLERABLE NUISANCE OF HERSELF--ACCUSING ME OF MURDER-ING MY CLIENTS!
I CAN'T BE BOTHERED-- I'M LEAVING TOWN RIGHT AWAY!
YOU'LL STAY WHERE YOU ARE! AFTER ALL, YOU FURNISHED THE FINANCIAL BACKING FOR THIS INSURANCE SOCIETY- YOU'RE RESPONSIBLE FOR IT!
OKAY, YOU'RE ASKING FOR IT! MURDER FOR INSURANCE? SURE, THE SOCIETY DID IT- ONLY WITHOUT YOUR KNOWLEDGE, FULLERTON! I'M THE ONE WHO CASHED IN THE POLICIES AND IT'S BEEN FIXED TO APPEAR THAT YOU WERE THE GUILTY ONE, FULLERTON!
AS A MATTER OF FACT, I EVEN TOOK OUT A POLICY ON YOUR LIFE-- AND THIS IS WHY!
OH-H-H!
YOU'VE KILLED HIM!
--AND YOU'RE NEXT, GIRL!
12

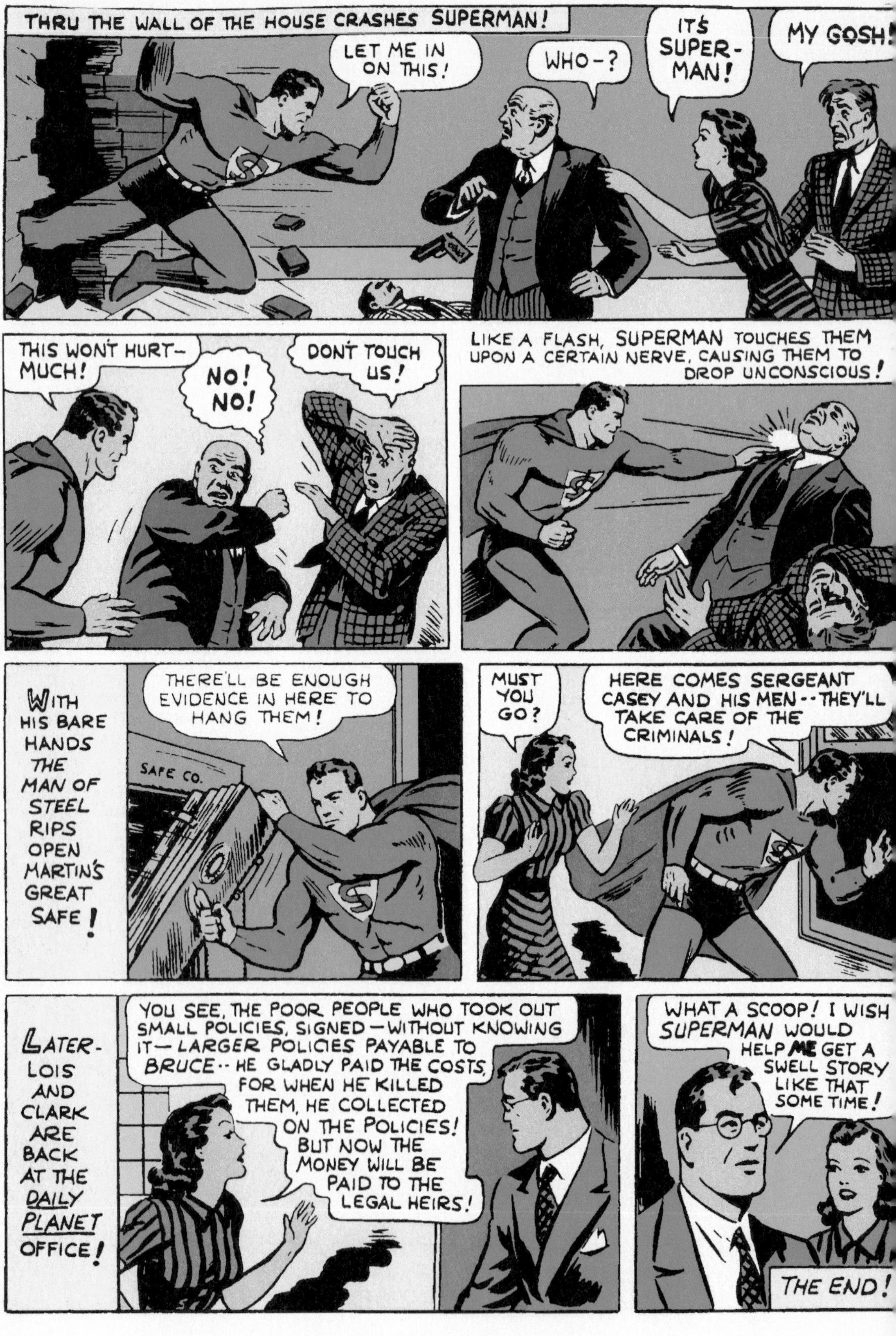
THRU THE WALL OF THE HOUSE CRASHES SUPERMAN!
LET ME IN ON THIS!
WHO-?
IT'S SUPER-MAN!
MY GOSH!
THIS WON'T HURT-MUCH!
NO! NO!
DON'T TOUCH US!
LIKE A FLASH, SUPERMAN TOUCHES THEM UPON A CERTAIN NERVE, CAUSING THEM TO DROP UNCONSCIOUS!
WITH HIS BARE HANDS THE MAN OF STEEL RIPS OPEN MARTIN'S GREAT SAFE!
THERE'LL BE ENOUGH EVIDENCE IN HERE TO HANG THEM!
SAFE CO.
MUST YOU GO?
HERE COMES SERGEANT CASEY AND HIS MEN--THEY'LL TAKE CARE OF THE CRIMINALS!
LATER-LOIS AND CLARK ARE BACK AT THE DAILY PLANET OFFICE!
YOU SEE, THE POOR PEOPLE WHO TOOK OUT SMALL POLICIES, SIGNED—WITHOUT KNOWING IT—LARGER POLICIES PAYABLE TO BRUCE-- HE GLADLY PAID THE COSTS, FOR WHEN HE KILLED THEM, HE COLLECTED ON THE POLICIES! BUT NOW THE MONEY WILL BE PAID TO THE LEGAL HEIRS!
WHAT A SCOOP! I WISH SUPERMAN WOULD HELP ME GET A SWELL STORY LIKE THAT SOME TIME!
THE END!

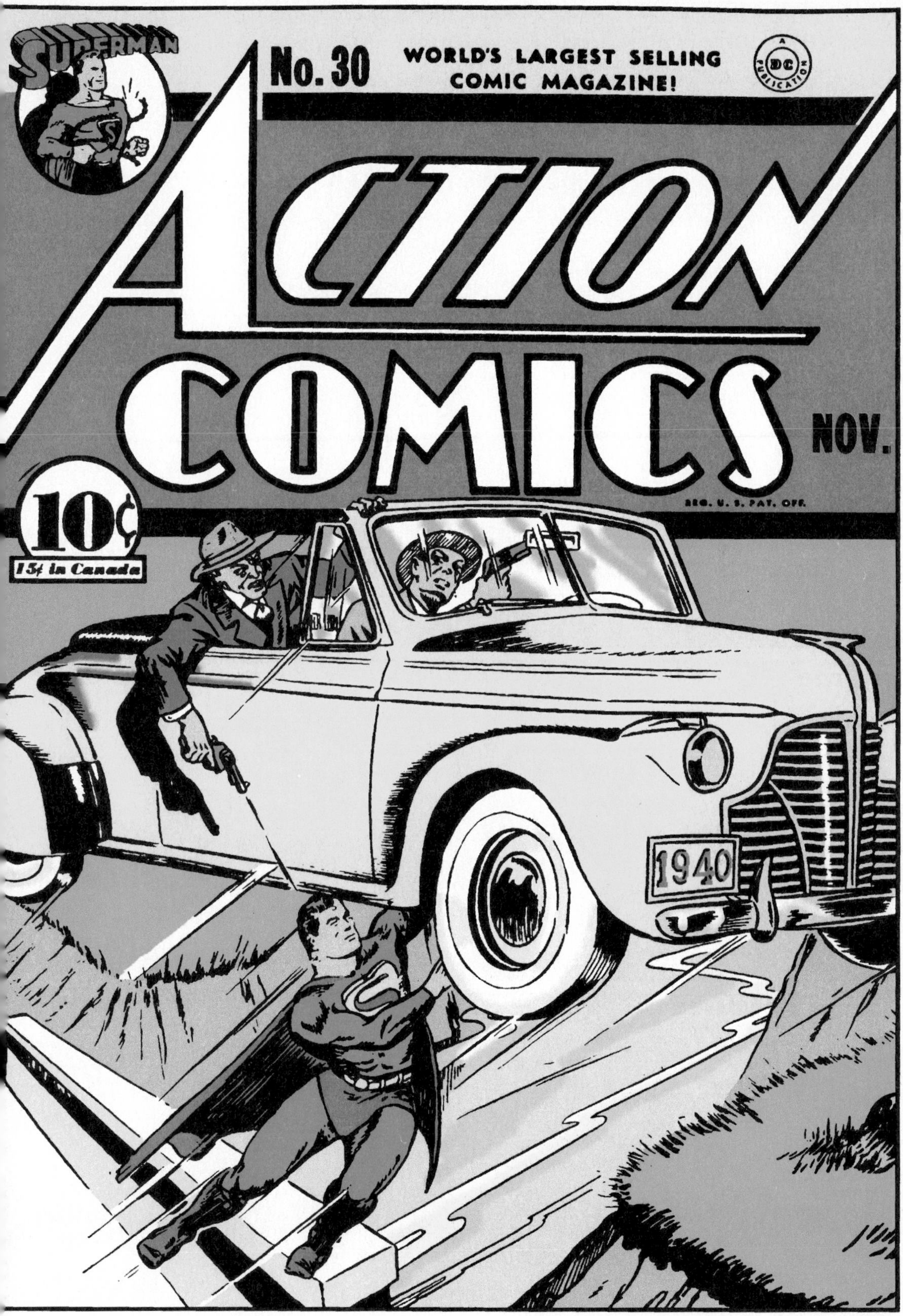
SUPERMAN
No. 30
WORLD'S LARGEST SELLING
COMIC MAGAZINE!
A DC PUBLICATION
ACTION COMICS
NOV.
REG. U. S. PAT. OFF.
10¢
15¢ in Canada
1940

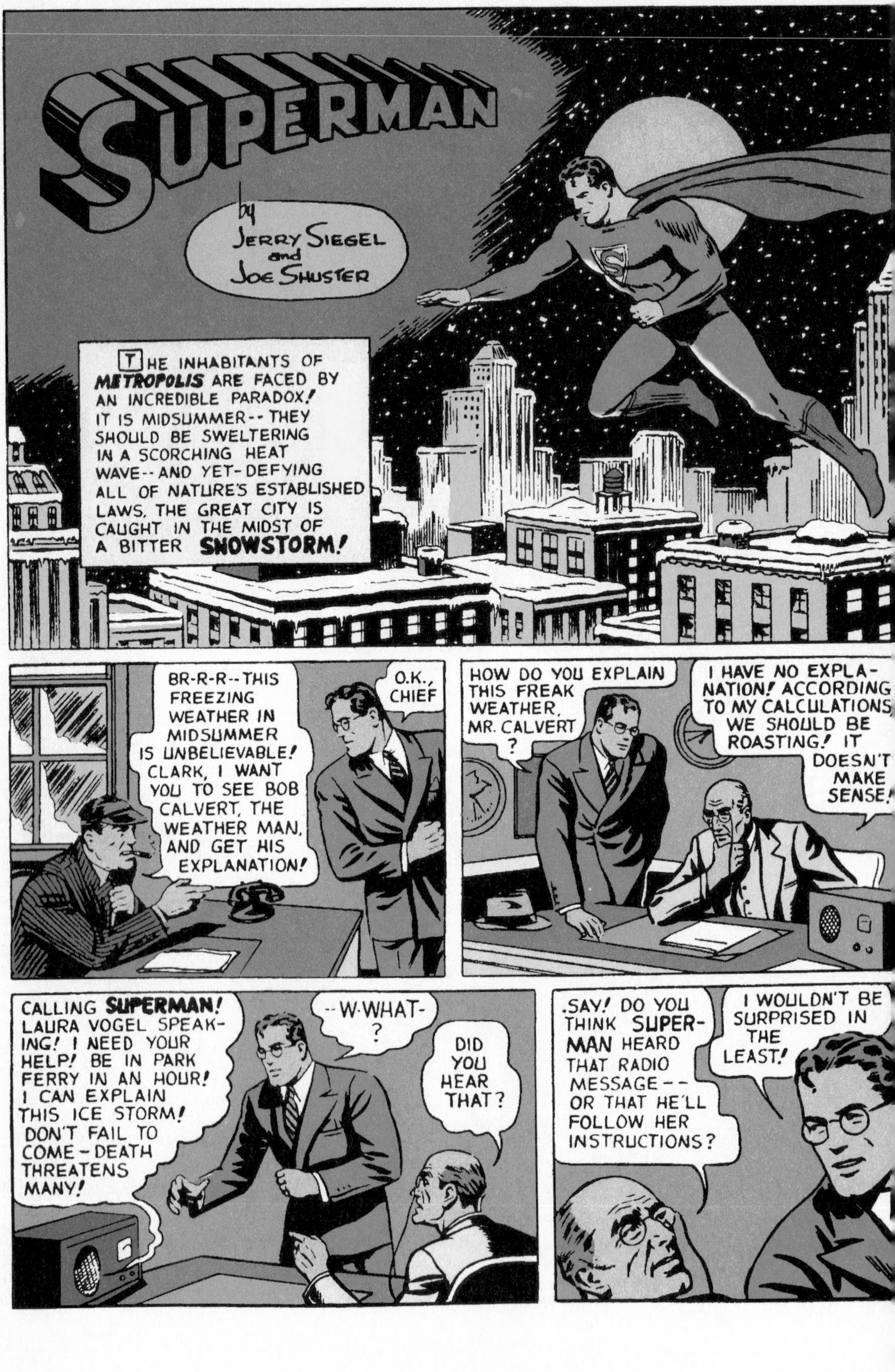
SUPERMAN
by
JERRY SIEGEL
and
JOE SHUSTER
THE INHABITANTS OF METROPOLIS ARE FACED BY AN INCREDIBLE PARADOX! IT IS MIDSUMMER-- THEY SHOULD BE SWELTERING IN A SCORCHING HEAT WAVE-- AND YET- DEFYING ALL OF NATURE'S ESTABLISHED LAWS, THE GREAT CITY IS CAUGHT IN THE MIDST OF A BITTER SNOWSTORM!
BR-R-R-- THIS FREEZING WEATHER IN MIDSUMMER IS UNBELIEVABLE! CLARK, I WANT YOU TO SEE BOB CALVERT, THE WEATHER MAN, AND GET HIS EXPLANATION!
O.K., CHIEF
HOW DO YOU EXPLAIN THIS FREAK WEATHER, MR. CALVERT ?
I HAVE NO EXPLANATION! ACCORDING TO MY CALCULATIONS WE SHOULD BE ROASTING! IT DOESN'T MAKE SENSE!
CALLING SUPERMAN! LAURA VOGEL SPEAKING! I NEED YOUR HELP! BE IN PARK FERRY IN AN HOUR! I CAN EXPLAIN THIS ICE STORM! DON'T FAIL TO COME - DEATH THREATENS MANY!
-- W-WHAT- ?
DID YOU HEAR THAT ?
SAY! DO YOU THINK SUPERMAN HEARD THAT RADIO MESSAGE -- OR THAT HE'LL FOLLOW HER INSTRUCTIONS?
I WOULDN'T BE SURPRISED IN THE LEAST!

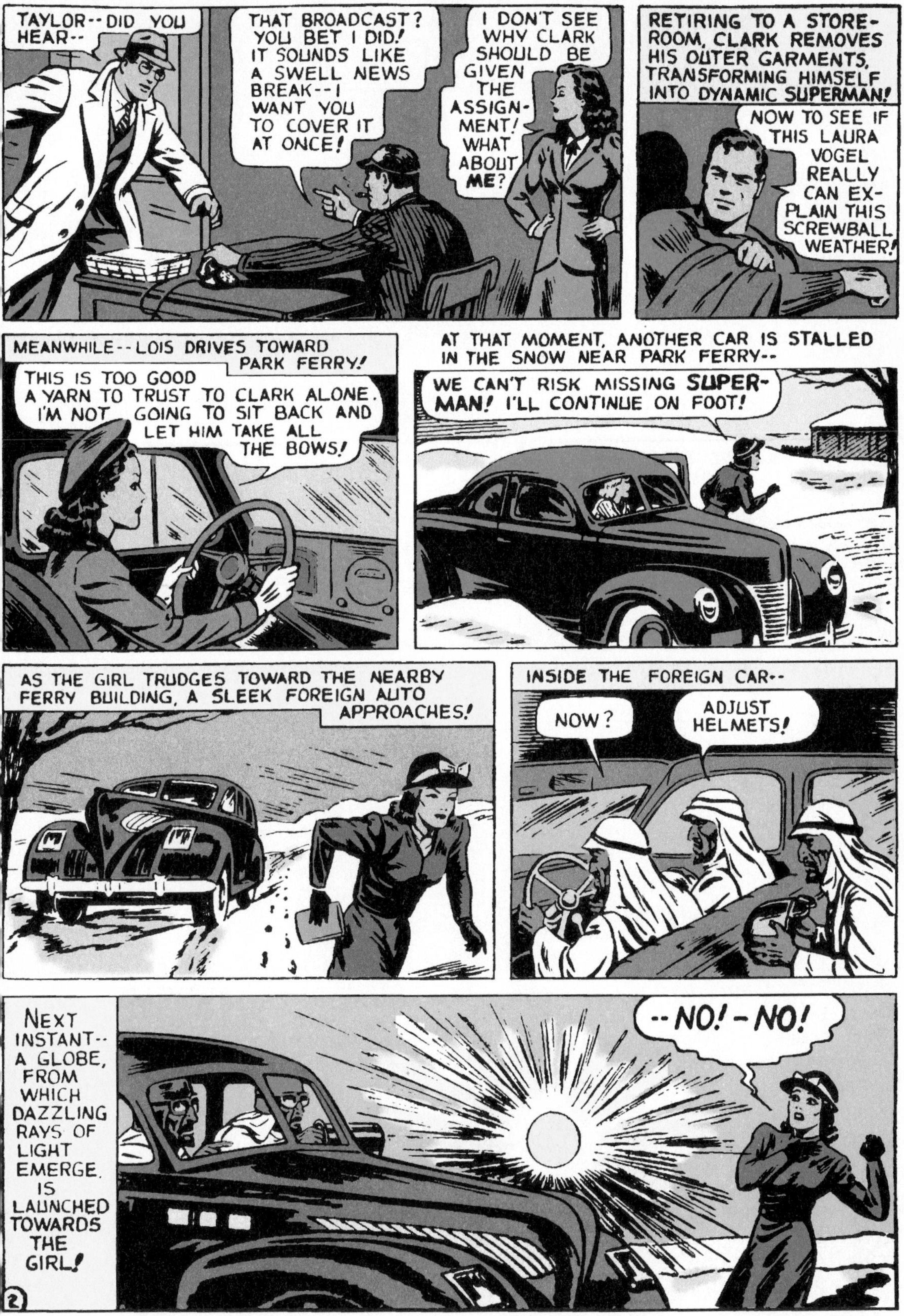
TAYLOR--DID YOU HEAR--
THAT BROADCAST? YOU BET I DID! IT SOUNDS LIKE A SWELL NEWS BREAK--I WANT YOU TO COVER IT AT ONCE!
I DON'T SEE WHY CLARK SHOULD BE GIVEN THE ASSIGNMENT! WHAT ABOUT ME?
RETIRING TO A STOREROOM, CLARK REMOVES HIS OUTER GARMENTS, TRANSFORMING HIMSELF INTO DYNAMIC SUPERMAN!
NOW TO SEE IF THIS LAURA VOGEL REALLY CAN EXPLAIN THIS SCREWBALL WEATHER!
MEANWHILE--LOIS DRIVES TOWARD PARK FERRY!
THIS IS TOO GOOD A YARN TO TRUST TO CLARK ALONE. I'M NOT GOING TO SIT BACK AND LET HIM TAKE ALL THE BOWS!
AT THAT MOMENT, ANOTHER CAR IS STALLED IN THE SNOW NEAR PARK FERRY--
WE CAN'T RISK MISSING SUPERMAN! I'LL CONTINUE ON FOOT!
AS THE GIRL TRUDGES TOWARD THE NEARBY FERRY BUILDING, A SLEEK FOREIGN AUTO APPROACHES!
INSIDE THE FOREIGN CAR--
NOW?
ADJUST HELMETS!
NEXT INSTANT--A GLOBE, FROM WHICH DAZZLING RAYS OF LIGHT EMERGE, IS LAUNCHED TOWARDS THE GIRL!
--NO!-NO!
2

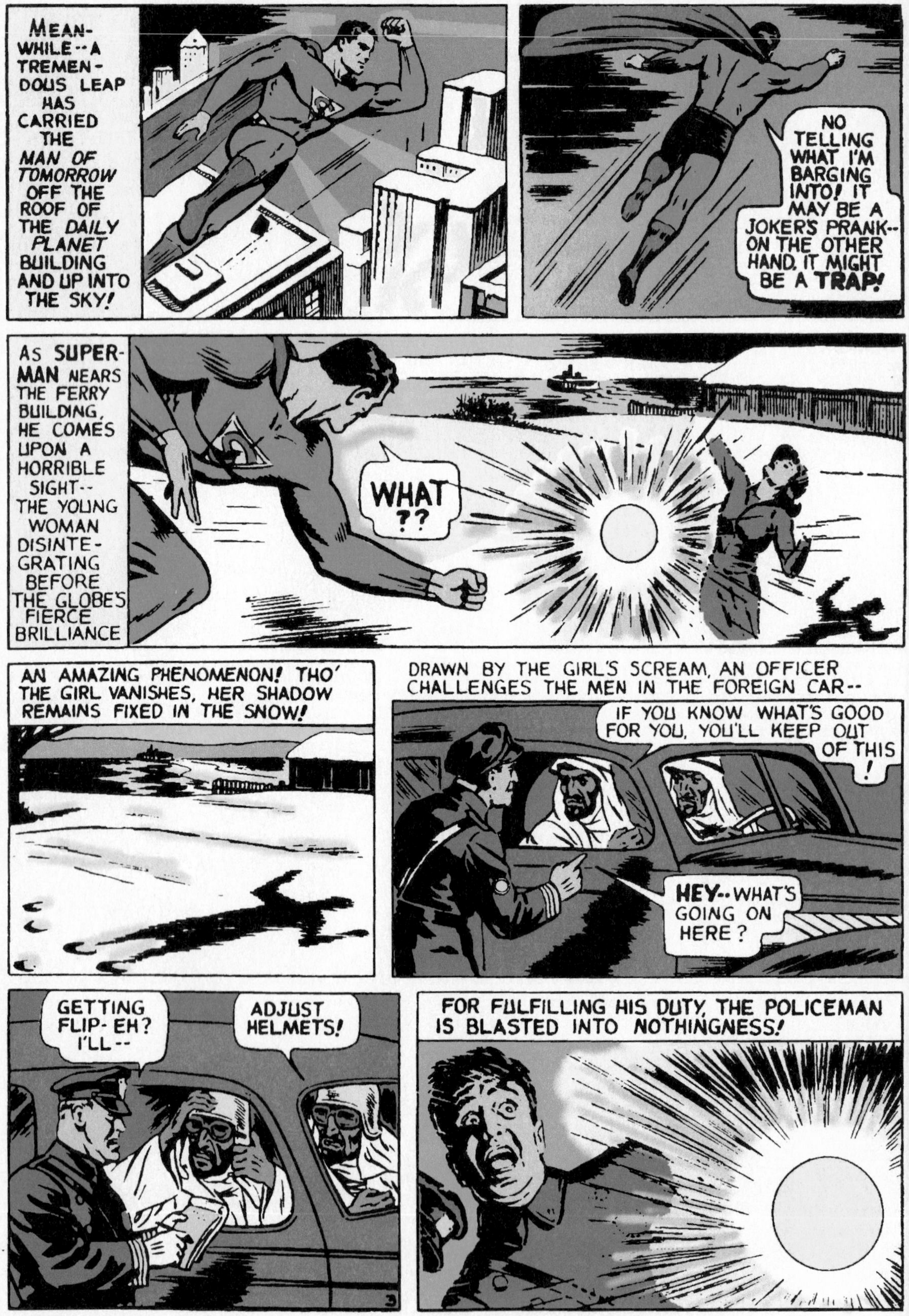
MEAN-WHILE--A TREMENDOUS LEAP HAS CARRIED THE *MAN OF TOMORROW* OFF THE ROOF OF THE *DAILY PLANET* BUILDING AND UP INTO THE SKY!
NO TELLING WHAT I'M BARGING INTO! IT MAY BE A JOKER'S PRANK--ON THE OTHER HAND, IT MIGHT BE A **TRAP!**
AS **SUPERMAN** NEARS THE FERRY BUILDING, HE COMES UPON A HORRIBLE SIGHT--THE YOUNG WOMAN DISINTEGRATING BEFORE THE GLOBE'S FIERCE BRILLIANCE
WHAT ??
AN AMAZING PHENOMENON! THO' THE GIRL VANISHES, HER SHADOW REMAINS FIXED IN THE SNOW!
DRAWN BY THE GIRL'S SCREAM, AN OFFICER CHALLENGES THE MEN IN THE FOREIGN CAR--
IF YOU KNOW WHAT'S GOOD FOR YOU, YOU'LL KEEP OUT OF THIS!
HEY--WHAT'S GOING ON HERE?
GETTING FLIP- EH? I'LL--
ADJUST HELMETS!
FOR FULFILLING HIS DUTY, THE POLICEMAN IS BLASTED INTO NOTHINGNESS!

PEERING DOWN FROM THE BUILDING ATOP WHICH HE HAD ALIGHTED, **SUPERMAN** SEES ONLY THE POLICEMAN'S SHADOW LEFT IN THE SNOW!

THAT BLAZING GLOBE DISINTEGRATED A MAN -- LEAVING NOTHING BUT HIS SHADOW? IF I HADN'T SEEN IT WITH MY OWN EYES --

BUT THE *MAN OF STEEL* IS NOT THE ONLY WITNESS -- FOR LOIS HAD APPROACHED IN TIME TO SEE THE INCREDIBLE DRAMA!

THE MEN IN THAT FOREIGN CAR -- THEY'RE RESPONSIBLE!

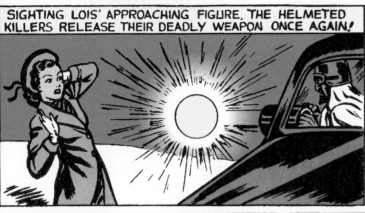

SIGHTING LOIS' APPROACHING FIGURE, THE HELMETED KILLERS RELEASE THEIR DEADLY WEAPON ONCE AGAIN!

DOWN STREAKS **SUPERMAN!**

LOIS IN THE THICK OF THIS! I MIGHT HAVE EXPECTED IT!

IF I HAD ANY SENSE, I'D LET YOU PLAY CATCH WITH THAT BALL!

SUPERMAN!

THE MAN OF STEEL SWOOPS DOWN IN TIME TO SAVE LOIS FROM THE GLOBE!

AS THEY STRIKE THE GROUND A SHORT DISTANCE AWAY --

I OWE MY LIFE TO YOU!

SAVE YOUR THANKS! I HAVEN'T TIME TO ACKNOWLEDGE THEM!

SUPERMAN HAS SIGHTED THE WIELDERS OF THE SHADOW DEATH PULLING THE BLONDE GIRL FROM HER AUTO --

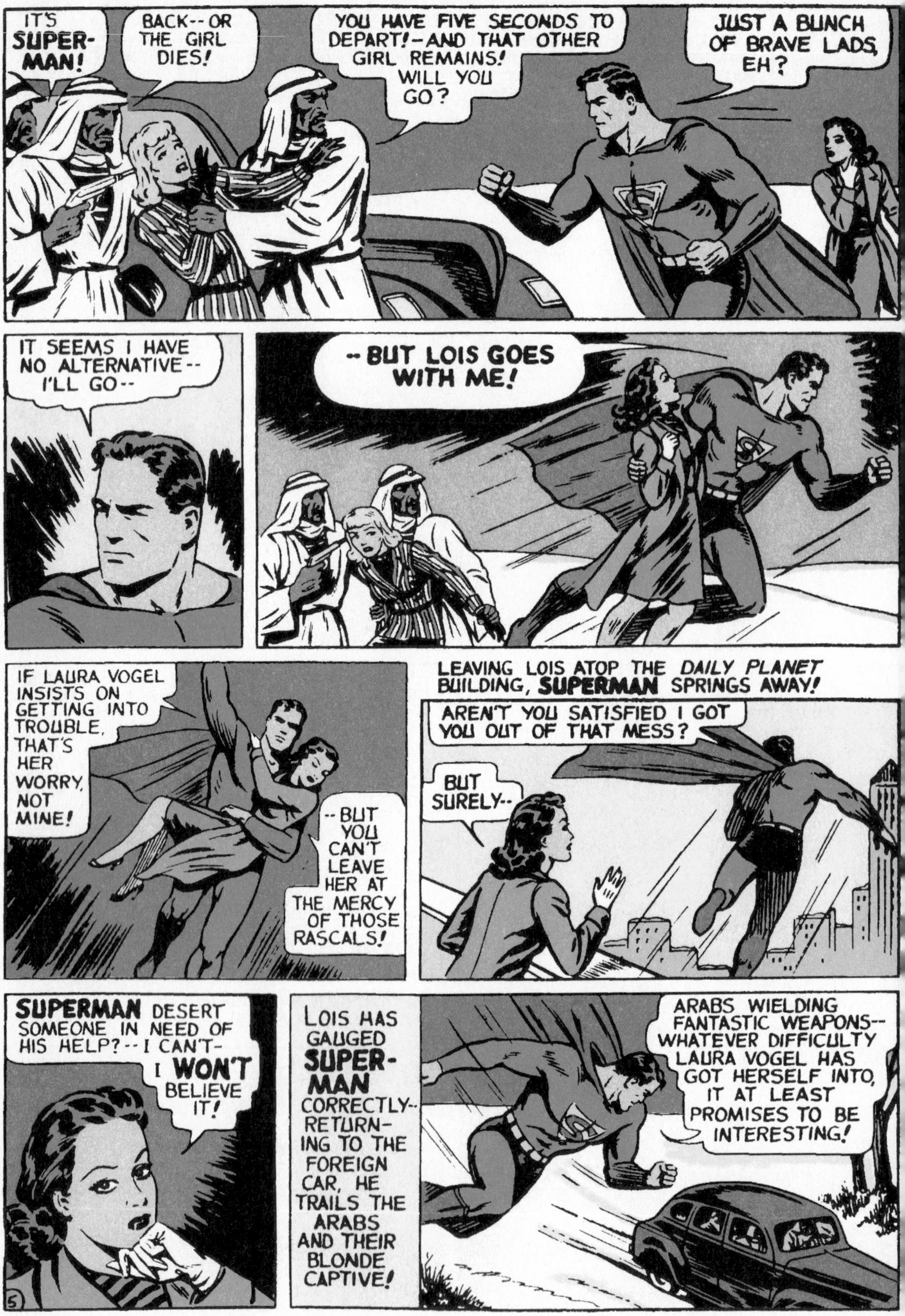
IT'S SUPERMAN!
BACK--OR THE GIRL DIES!
YOU HAVE FIVE SECONDS TO DEPART!--AND THAT OTHER GIRL REMAINS! WILL YOU GO?
JUST A BUNCH OF BRAVE LADS, EH?
IT SEEMS I HAVE NO ALTERNATIVE-- I'LL GO--
--BUT LOIS GOES WITH ME!
IF LAURA VOGEL INSISTS ON GETTING INTO TROUBLE, THAT'S HER WORRY, NOT MINE!
--BUT YOU CAN'T LEAVE HER AT THE MERCY OF THOSE RASCALS!
LEAVING LOIS ATOP THE DAILY PLANET BUILDING, SUPERMAN SPRINGS AWAY!
AREN'T YOU SATISFIED I GOT YOU OUT OF THAT MESS?
BUT SURELY--
SUPERMAN DESERT SOMEONE IN NEED OF HIS HELP?--I CAN'T-- I WON'T BELIEVE IT!
5
LOIS HAS GAUGED SUPERMAN CORRECTLY--RETURNING TO THE FOREIGN CAR, HE TRAILS THE ARABS AND THEIR BLONDE CAPTIVE!
ARABS WIELDING FANTASTIC WEAPONS--WHATEVER DIFFICULTY LAURA VOGEL HAS GOT HERSELF INTO, IT AT LEAST PROMISES TO BE INTERESTING!

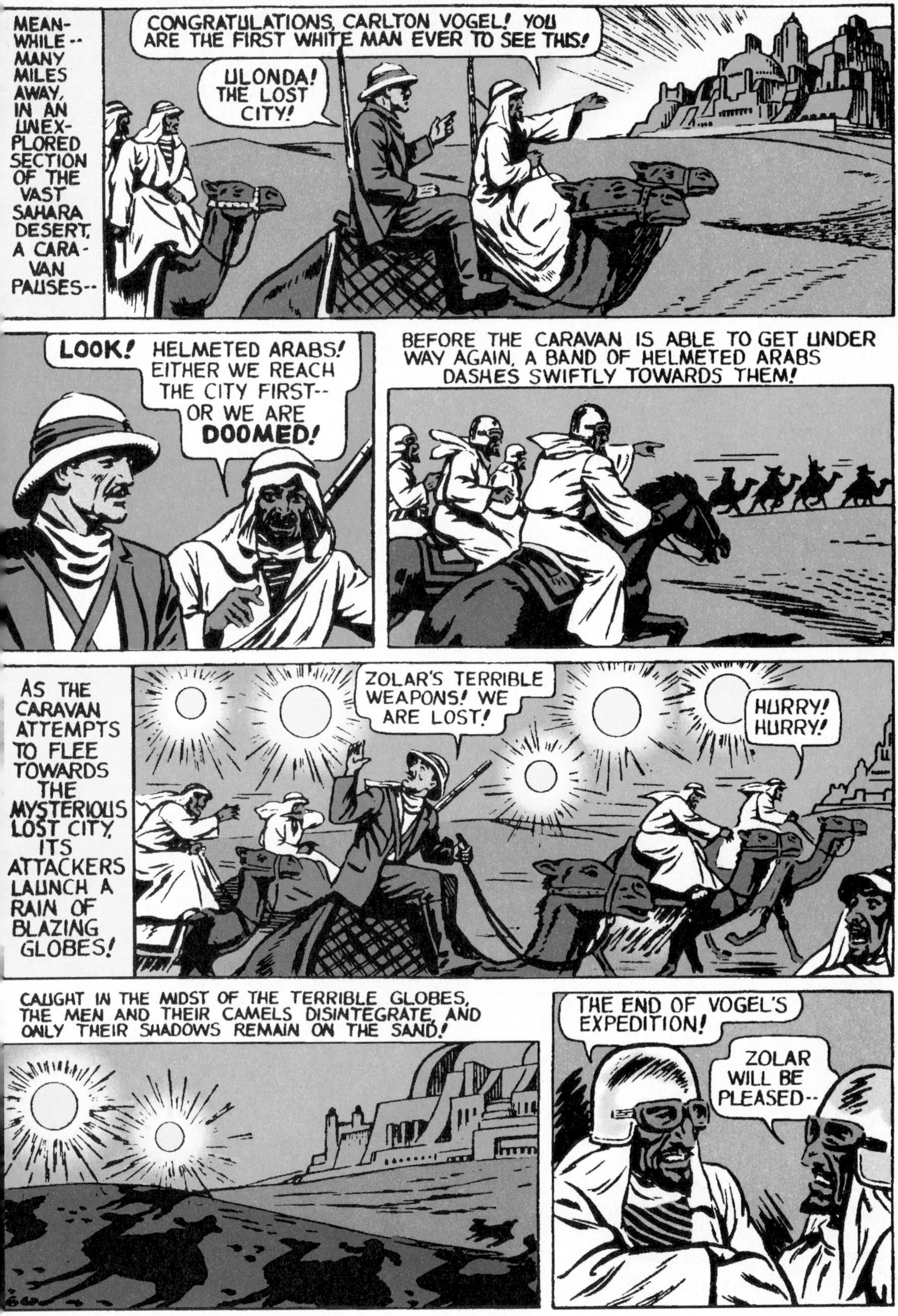
MEAN-WHILE--MANY MILES AWAY, IN AN UNEXPLORED SECTION OF THE VAST SAHARA DESERT, A CARA-VAN PAUSES--
CONGRATULATIONS, CARLTON VOGEL! YOU ARE THE FIRST WHITE MAN EVER TO SEE THIS!
ULONDA! THE LOST CITY!
LOOK! HELMETED ARABS! EITHER WE REACH THE CITY FIRST--OR WE ARE DOOMED!
BEFORE THE CARAVAN IS ABLE TO GET UNDER WAY AGAIN, A BAND OF HELMETED ARABS DASHES SWIFTLY TOWARDS THEM!
AS THE CARAVAN ATTEMPTS TO FLEE TOWARDS THE MYSTERIOUS LOST CITY, ITS ATTACKERS LAUNCH A RAIN OF BLAZING GLOBES!
ZOLAR'S TERRIBLE WEAPONS! WE ARE LOST!
HURRY! HURRY!
CAUGHT IN THE MIDST OF THE TERRIBLE GLOBES, THE MEN AND THEIR CAMELS DISINTEGRATE, AND ONLY THEIR SHADOWS REMAIN ON THE SAND!
THE END OF VOGEL'S EXPEDITION!
ZOLAR WILL BE PLEASED--

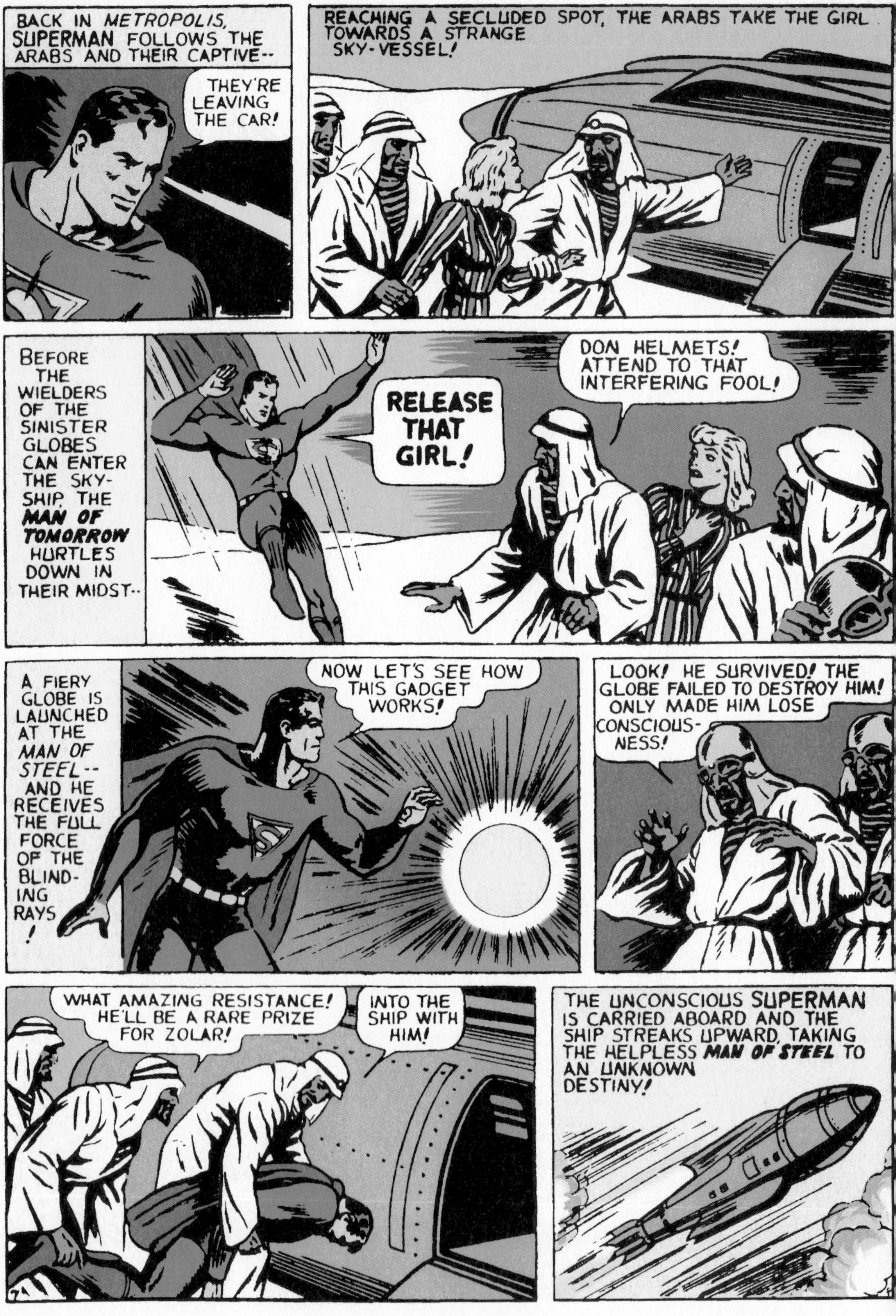
BACK IN METROPOLIS, SUPERMAN FOLLOWS THE ARABS AND THEIR CAPTIVE--
THEY'RE LEAVING THE CAR!
REACHING A SECLUDED SPOT, THE ARABS TAKE THE GIRL TOWARDS A STRANGE SKY-VESSEL!
BEFORE THE WIELDERS OF THE SINISTER GLOBES CAN ENTER THE SKY-SHIP, THE MAN OF TOMORROW HURTLES DOWN IN THEIR MIDST--
RELEASE THAT GIRL!
DON HELMETS! ATTEND TO THAT INTERFERING FOOL!
A FIERY GLOBE IS LAUNCHED AT THE MAN OF STEEL-- AND HE RECEIVES THE FULL FORCE OF THE BLINDING RAYS!
NOW LET'S SEE HOW THIS GADGET WORKS!
LOOK! HE SURVIVED! THE GLOBE FAILED TO DESTROY HIM! ONLY MADE HIM LOSE CONSCIOUSNESS!
WHAT AMAZING RESISTANCE! HE'LL BE A RARE PRIZE FOR ZOLAR!
INTO THE SHIP WITH HIM!
THE UNCONSCIOUS SUPERMAN IS CARRIED ABOARD AND THE SHIP STREAKS UPWARD, TAKING THE HELPLESS MAN OF STEEL TO AN UNKNOWN DESTINY!

ABOARD THE SKY SHIP, THE STILL GROGGY **SUPERMAN** REVIVES AND FINDS HIMSELF CHAINED AND HANDCUFFED!

W-WHERE-- I'M IN CHAINS!

FORGIVE ME! I'M SORRY I GOT YOU INTO THIS!

JUST WHAT IS THIS ALL ABOUT, ANYWAY?

I AM LAURA VOGEL, SISTER OF CARLTON VOGEL, THE ARCHAEOLOGIST. AT PRESENT, HE IS IN AN UNEXPLORED PORTION OF THE SAHARA DESERT-- HE WROTE TELLING ME STRANGE THINGS ABOUT A SINISTER INDIVIDUAL NAMED ZOLAR!

WHAT HAS THAT TO DO WITH THE ICY WEATHER-- AND THE SHADOW DEATHS?

ZOLAR POSSESSES GREAT STORES OF RADIUM--AND WITH IT IS ABLE TO PERFORM SUCH MIRACLES AS TOTAL DISINTEGRATION, AND CONTROLLING THE WEATHER!

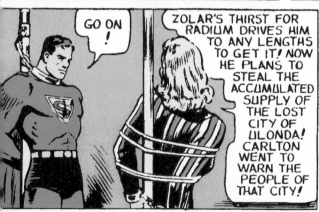

GO ON!

ZOLAR'S THIRST FOR RADIUM DRIVES HIM TO ANY LENGTHS TO GET IT! NOW HE PLANS TO STEAL THE ACCUMULATED SUPPLY OF THE LOST CITY OF ULONDA! CARLTON WENT TO WARN THE PEOPLE OF THAT CITY!

AND HOW DOES THAT INVOLVE METROPOLIS AND THE CHANGE IN THE WEATHER?

ZOLAR LEARNED OF THE LETTER SENT TO ME--HIS EMISSARIES CAME TO WARN ME TO SILENCE

THEY GAVE ME UNTIL THE FIRST SNOWFALL TO MAKE MY DECISION-- THINKING THAT WOULD BE A LONG TIME OFF, I ACCEPTED-- THEY TRICKED ME BY ARTIFICIALLY CAUSING A SNOWSTORM-- THEN I BROADCAST MY APPEAL TO YOU!

YOU'LL BE INTERESTED TO LEARN THAT CARLTON VOGEL HAS SUCCUMBED TO THE SHADOW DEATH! THUS PERISH THOSE WHO OPPOSE ZOLAR!

CARLTON DEAD? NO! NO!

(WHAT WOULDN'T I GIVE TO MEET THIS ZOLAR!)

AT THAT MOMENT A SCREEN FLICKERS-- AN EVIL FACE MATERIALIZES UPON IT-- THE FACE OF **ZOLAR!**

O ZOLAR, BEHOLD WHOM WE HAVE CAPTURED-- THE MIGHTY **SUPERMAN**, NOW RENDERED POWERLESS BY YOUR MAGIC!

SPLENDID! BRING THE **MAN OF STEEL** TO ME!

YOU MAY NOT BE SO GLAD TO SEE ME WHEN WE COME FACE TO FACE!

I KNOW HOW TO DEAL WITH DOGS SUCH AS YOU! YOU FORGET, ARROGANT **SUPERMAN** THAT YOUR TREMENDOUS STRENGTH HAS DESERTED YOU!

BUT **SUPERMAN** HAS A SECRET THAT WOULD HAVE COST ZOLAR SOME OF HIS ASSURANCE, IF IT HAD BEEN REVEALED!

HE DOESN'T KNOW THAT THE EFFECTS OF THE GLOBE HAVE WORN OFF AND I'M AGAIN IN COMPLETE CONTROL OF MY STRENGTH!

AVAILING HIMSELF OF HIS X-RAY VISION, **SUPERMAN** SEES THAT THEY ARE NOW ABOVE ZOLAR'S DESERT STRONGHOLD!

BREAKING HIS THICK STEEL BONDS AS IF THEY WERE THREAD, **THE MAN OF STEEL** FREES HIMSELF!

THE TIME HAS COME FOR ACTION!

SPEEDILY HE FREES THE GIRL-- BUT THE ARAB GUARD GIVES THE ALARM!

HE'S LOOSE! GET THE GLOBE GUN!

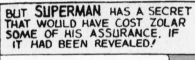

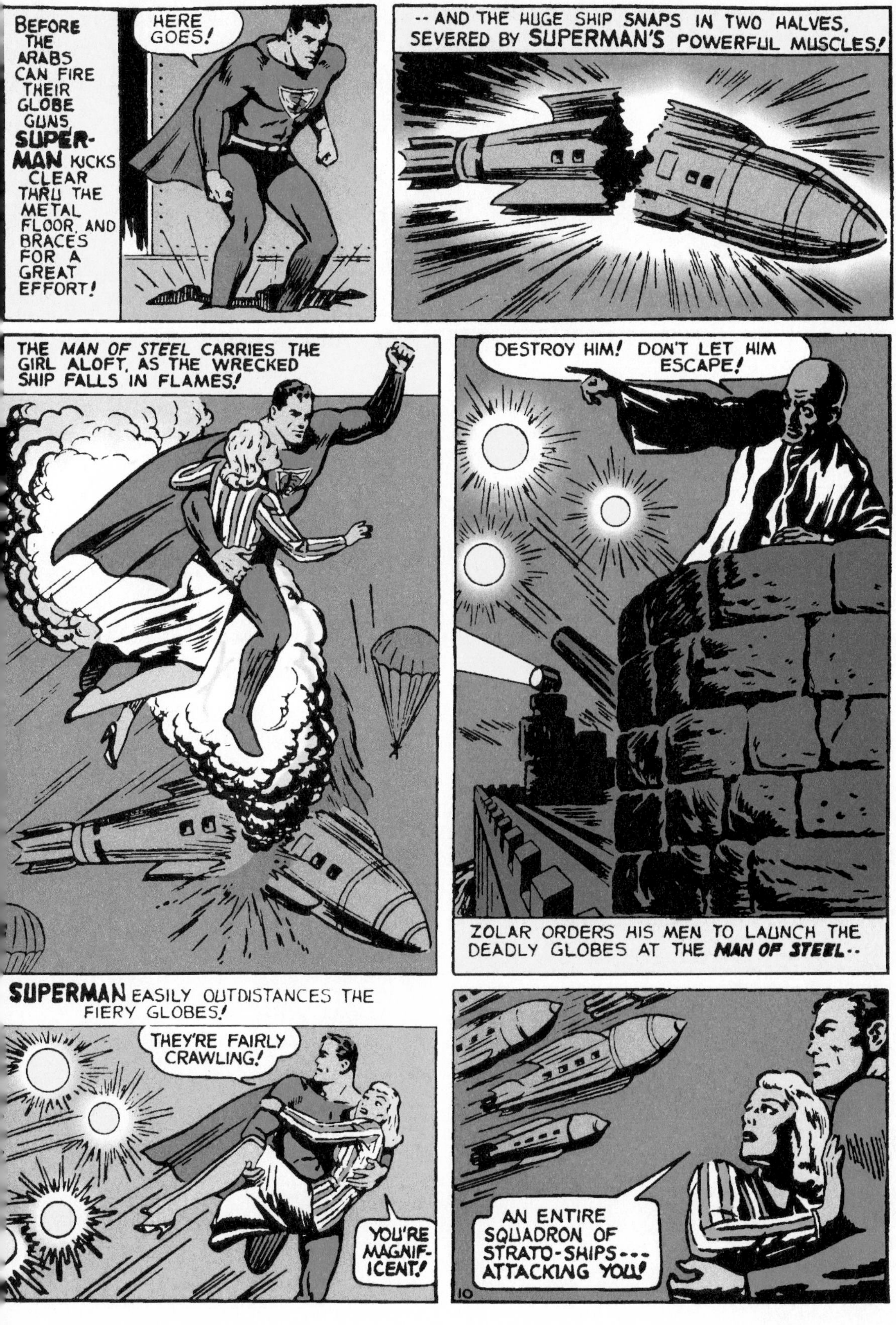
BEFORE THE ARABS CAN FIRE THEIR GLOBE GUNS, SUPERMAN KICKS CLEAR THRU THE METAL FLOOR, AND BRACES FOR A GREAT EFFORT!
HERE GOES!
-- AND THE HUGE SHIP SNAPS IN TWO HALVES, SEVERED BY SUPERMAN'S POWERFUL MUSCLES!
THE MAN OF STEEL CARRIES THE GIRL ALOFT, AS THE WRECKED SHIP FALLS IN FLAMES!
DESTROY HIM! DON'T LET HIM ESCAPE!
ZOLAR ORDERS HIS MEN TO LAUNCH THE DEADLY GLOBES AT THE MAN OF STEEL--
SUPERMAN EASILY OUTDISTANCES THE FIERY GLOBES!
THEY'RE FAIRLY CRAWLING!
YOU'RE MAGNIF-ICENT!
AN ENTIRE SQUADRON OF STRATO-SHIPS--- ATTACKING YOU!
10

LEAPING UPWARD, **SUPERMAN** SEIZES THE LEADING SKY-VESSEL--

YOU'LL DO!

--AND HURLS IT AT THE OTHERS, MASSED IN ATTACKING FORMATION!

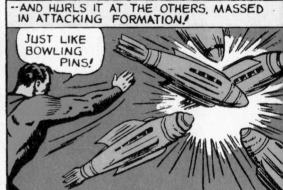

JUST LIKE BOWLING PINS!

MEAN-WHILE, ZOLAR BOARDS A STRATO-SHIP AND SHOUTS ORDERS INTO A MICRO-PHONE!

DISREGARD **SUPERMAN!**--ON TO ULONDA! DESTROY THE LOST CITY!

WE'VE GOT TO PREVENT ZOLAR FROM DEMOLISH-ING THAT CITY!

AS ZOLAR'S SHIPS SWOOP OVER ULONDA!

FLEE!

RUN FOR YOUR LIVES!

DOWN PLUNGE BLAZING GLOBES, EN-GULFING ULONDA IN AWFUL DESTRUCTION!

RELEASE THE METEOR DEATH!

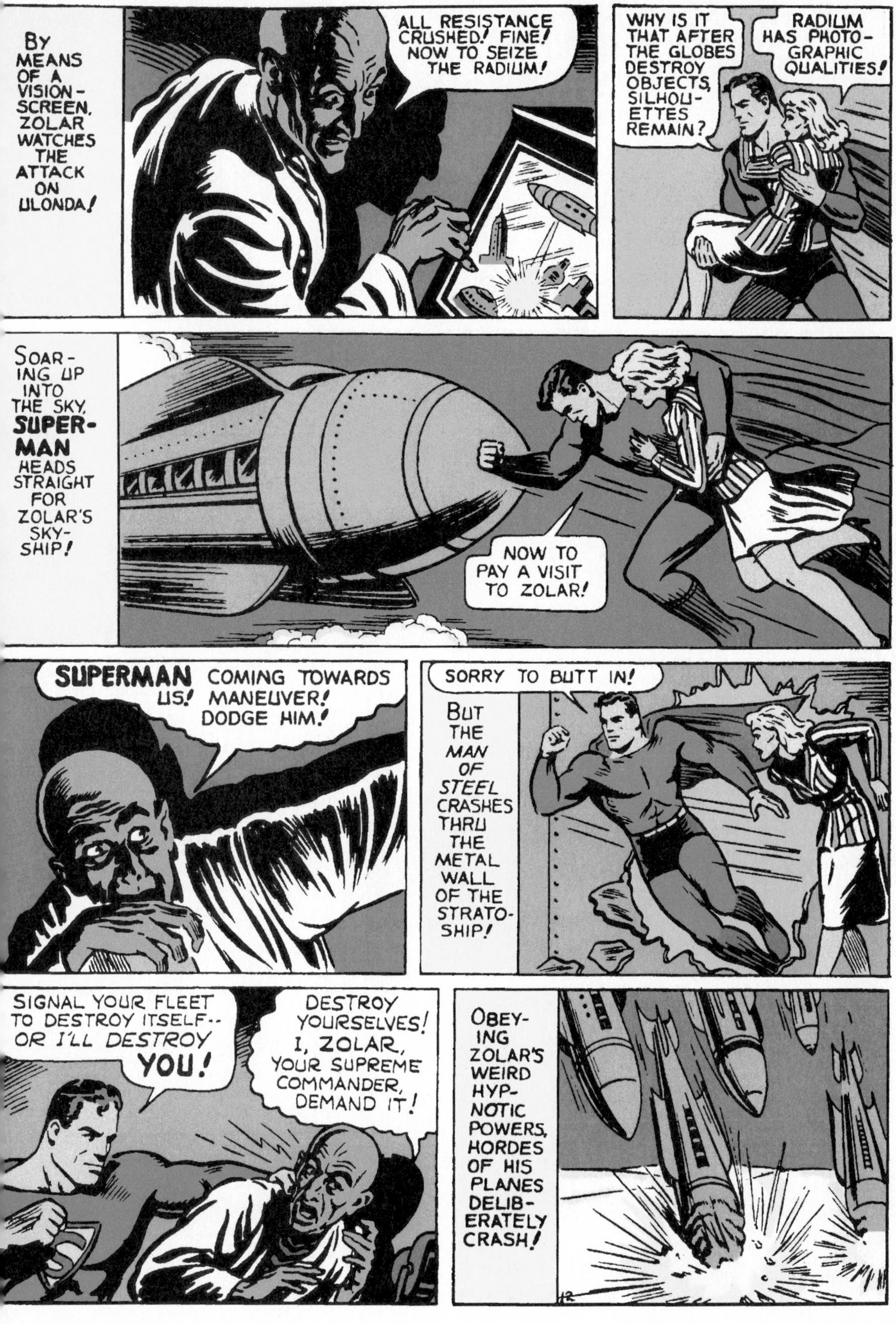

BY MEANS OF A VISION-SCREEN, ZOLAR WATCHES THE ATTACK ON ULONDA!
ALL RESISTANCE CRUSHED! FINE! NOW TO SEIZE THE RADIUM!
WHY IS IT THAT AFTER THE GLOBES DESTROY OBJECTS, SILHOUETTES REMAIN?
RADIUM HAS PHOTOGRAPHIC QUALITIES!
SOARING UP INTO THE SKY, SUPERMAN HEADS STRAIGHT FOR ZOLAR'S SKY-SHIP!
NOW TO PAY A VISIT TO ZOLAR!
SUPERMAN COMING TOWARDS US! MANEUVER! DODGE HIM!
SORRY TO BUTT IN!
BUT THE MAN OF STEEL CRASHES THRU THE METAL WALL OF THE STRATO-SHIP!
SIGNAL YOUR FLEET TO DESTROY ITSELF-- OR I'LL DESTROY YOU!
DESTROY YOURSELVES! I, ZOLAR, YOUR SUPREME COMMANDER, DEMAND IT!
OBEYING ZOLAR'S WEIRD HYPNOTIC POWERS, HORDES OF HIS PLANES DELIBERATELY CRASH!

AN AMAZING TURN OF EVENTS--THE GIRL AIMS A GLOBE GUN AT **SUPERMAN!**

LAURA! ARE YOU MAD?

I'M NOT LAURA VOGEL!

LAURA WAS SLAIN WHEN SHE EMERGED FROM THE CAR! I'M ONE OF ZOLAR'S AGENTS! --AND THIS IS YOUR FINISH. **SUPER-MAN!**

THE GIRL FIRES THE GLOBE-GUN-- BUT THE FIERY SPHERE BOUNCES OFF THE MAN OF STEEL'S CHEST!

-- AND REBOUNDS BACK TOWARDS ZOLAR AND HIS FEMININE HIRELING!

ZOLAR AND THE GIRL VANISH, LEAVING SILHOUETTES AND AN UNCONSCIOUS **SUPERMAN!**

DOWN CRASH-ES THE SHIP TO TOTAL DES-TRUCTION!

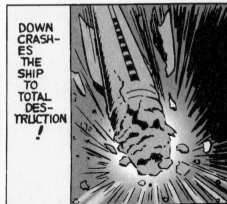

BUT THE FORCE OF THE SHOCK REVIVES **SUPER-MAN!** EMERG-ING FROM THE WRECK-AGE, OFF HE LEAPS!

THE SURVIVING ULONDIANS WILL NO LONGER BE MENACED BY ZOLAR!

LATER-- OFFICE OF THE *DAILY PLANET*--

IT'S OBVIOUS **SUPER-MAN** FUMBLED HIS ATTEMPT TO SAVE LAURA VOGEL -- BUT AT LEAST THE WEATH-ER IS BACK TO NORMAL!

SO YOUR IDOL HAS FUMBLED, EH? PARDON ME WHILE I LAUGH!

THE END.

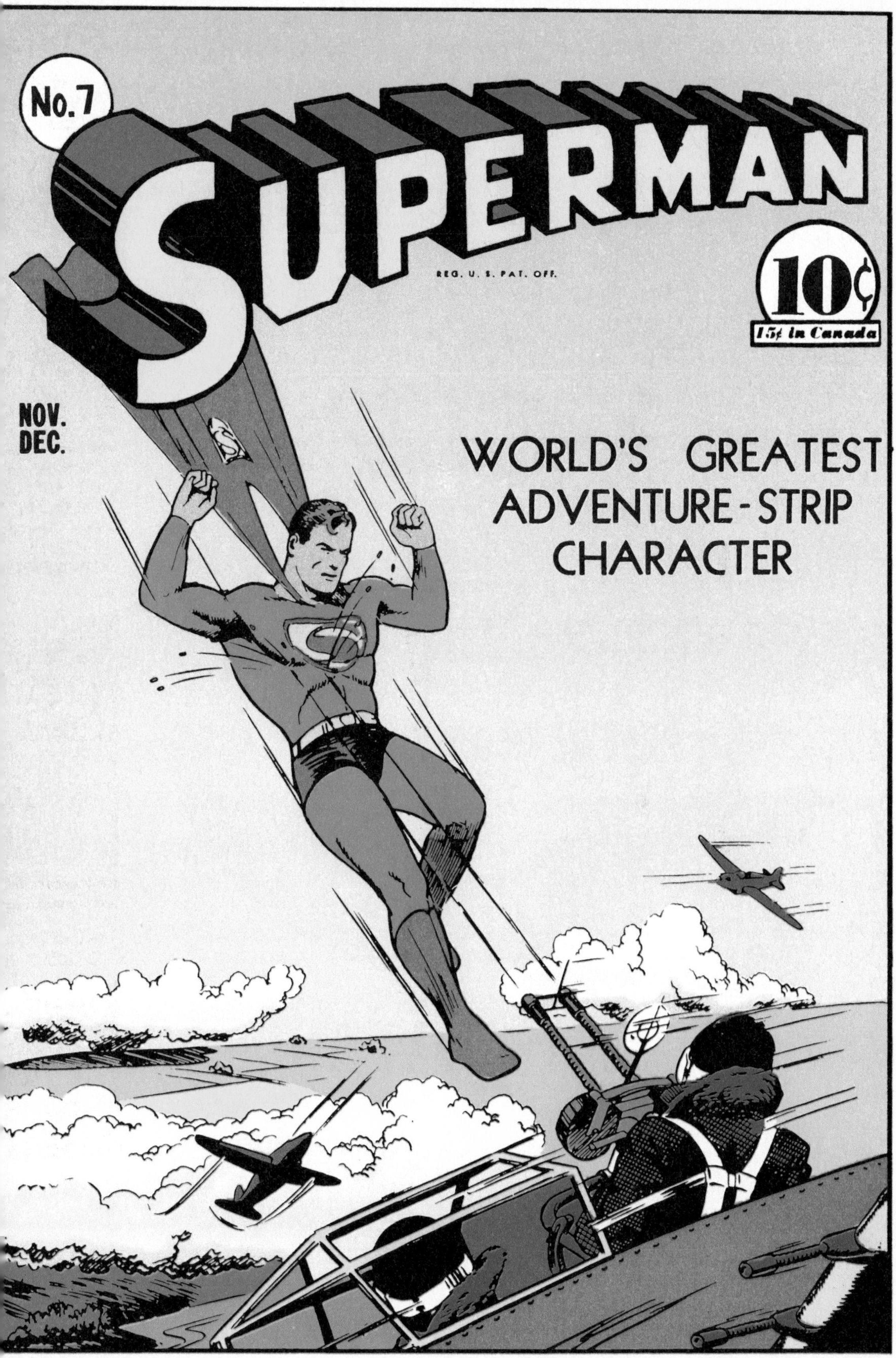
No. 7
SUPERMAN
REG. U. S. PAT. OFF.
10¢
15¢ in Canada
NOV.
DEC.
WORLD'S GREATEST
ADVENTURE-STRIP
CHARACTER

THE GOLDEN AGE

SUPERMAN

VOLUME TWO

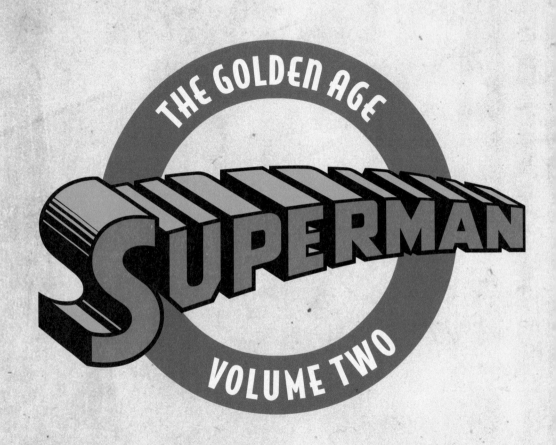

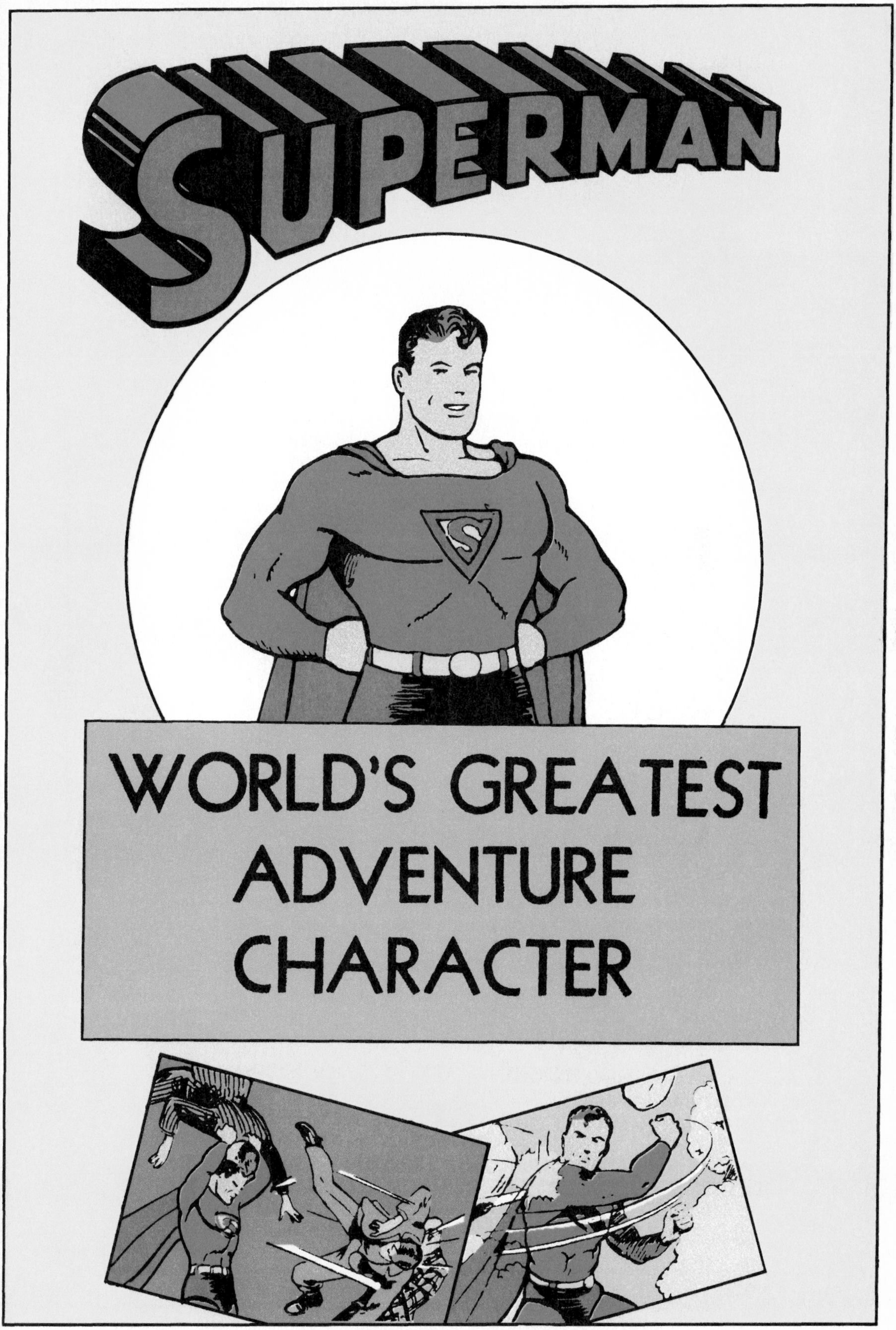
SUPERMAN
WORLD'S GREATEST ADVENTURE CHARACTER

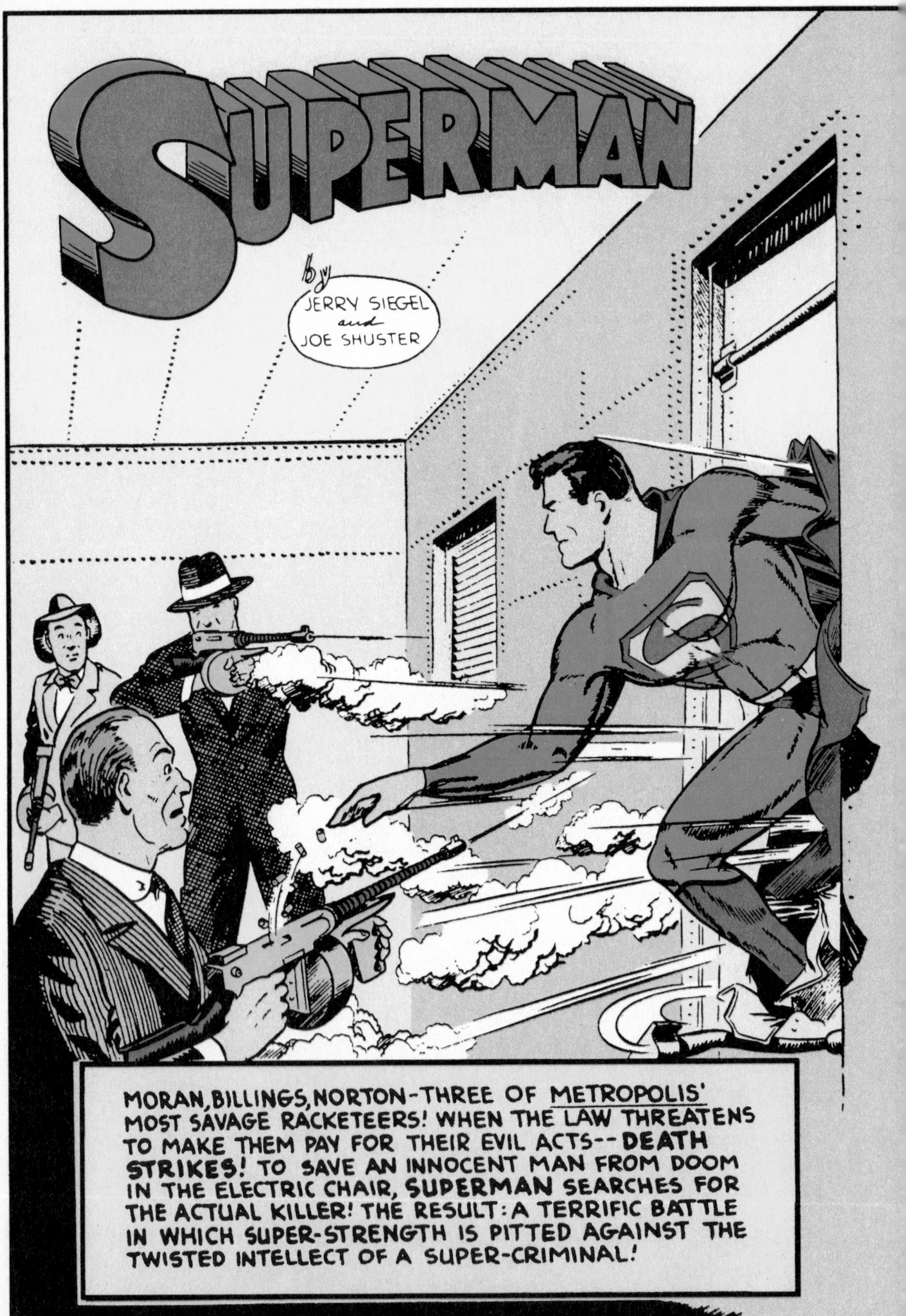
SUPERMAN
by
JERRY SIEGEL
and
JOE SHUSTER
MORAN, BILLINGS, NORTON-THREE OF METROPOLIS' MOST SAVAGE RACKETEERS! WHEN THE LAW THREATENS TO MAKE THEM PAY FOR THEIR EVIL ACTS--DEATH STRIKES! TO SAVE AN INNOCENT MAN FROM DOOM IN THE ELECTRIC CHAIR, SUPERMAN SEARCHES FOR THE ACTUAL KILLER! THE RESULT: A TERRIFIC BATTLE IN WHICH SUPER-STRENGTH IS PITTED AGAINST THE TWISTED INTELLECT OF A SUPER-CRIMINAL!

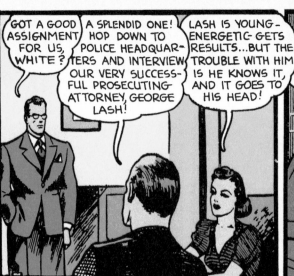

GOT A GOOD ASSIGNMENT FOR US, WHITE?

A SPLENDID ONE! HOP DOWN TO POLICE HEADQUARTERS AND INTERVIEW OUR VERY SUCCESSFUL PROSECUTING ATTORNEY, GEORGE LASH!

LASH IS YOUNG-ENERGETIC-GETS RESULTS...BUT THE TROUBLE WITH HIM IS HE KNOWS IT, AND IT GOES TO HIS HEAD!

SPLENDID ASSIGNMENT, EH? WHITE WOULDN'T THINK SO IF **HE** HAD TO LISTEN TO THAT WINDBAG BLOW OFF STEAM!

IT MUST BE FUN TO BE AN EDITOR AND PASS OUT SOUR ASSIGNMENTS LIKE THIS TO UNSUSPECTING REPORTERS LIKE US!

WE'RE FROM THE DAILY PLANET, MR. LASH. WE'D LIKE TO QUOTE YOU ON YOUR FUTURE PLANS!

SOMETHING SENSATIONAL, EH - LIKE MY PAST RECORD?

THEY ALL TOLD ME YOU WERE LIKE THIS-BUT I COULDN'T BELIEVE IT!

THAT I'M SO SUCCESSFUL?

NO---SO SMUG! I THOUGHT THEY WERE EXAGGERATING, BUT NOW I CAN SEE THEY WERE **UNDERRATING** YOUR CONCEIT!

PLEASE, LOIS! WE'VE COME HERE TO GET A STATEMENT FROM THE PROSECUTOR.. NOT TO START AN ARGUMENT!

WELL, HERE'S A STATEMENT THAT OUGHT TO PLEASE YOU!-MORAN, BILLINGS, AND NORTON HAVE BEEN KING-PINS IN THE UNDERWORLD UP TO NOW! BUT I'VE GOT THE GOODS ON THOSE UNSAVORY GENTS, AND THEY'RE OUT ON BAIL NOW AWAITING TRIAL ON CONSPIRACY CHARGES!

YOU'RE GOING TO DO WHAT EVERY OTHER PROSECUTOR HAS FAILED TO DO! NOW WON'T THAT BE DANDY-FOR YOUR SCRAPBOOK!

YOU'VE HAD YOUR INTERVIEW. YOU CAN GO NOW!

THANK YOU, SIR! YOU'VE BEEN VERY KIND!

AS CLARK DEPARTS, HIS KEEN, OBSERVANT EYES NOTE LASH NERVOUSLY CRUSH HIS CIGARETTE INTO AN ASHTRAY SO THAT IT IS BENT TWICE...

LATER-AT A RESTAURANT...

S'MATTER? SEEN A GHOST?

SEATING THEMSELVES AT THAT TABLE --MORAN, BILLINGS, AND NORTON!

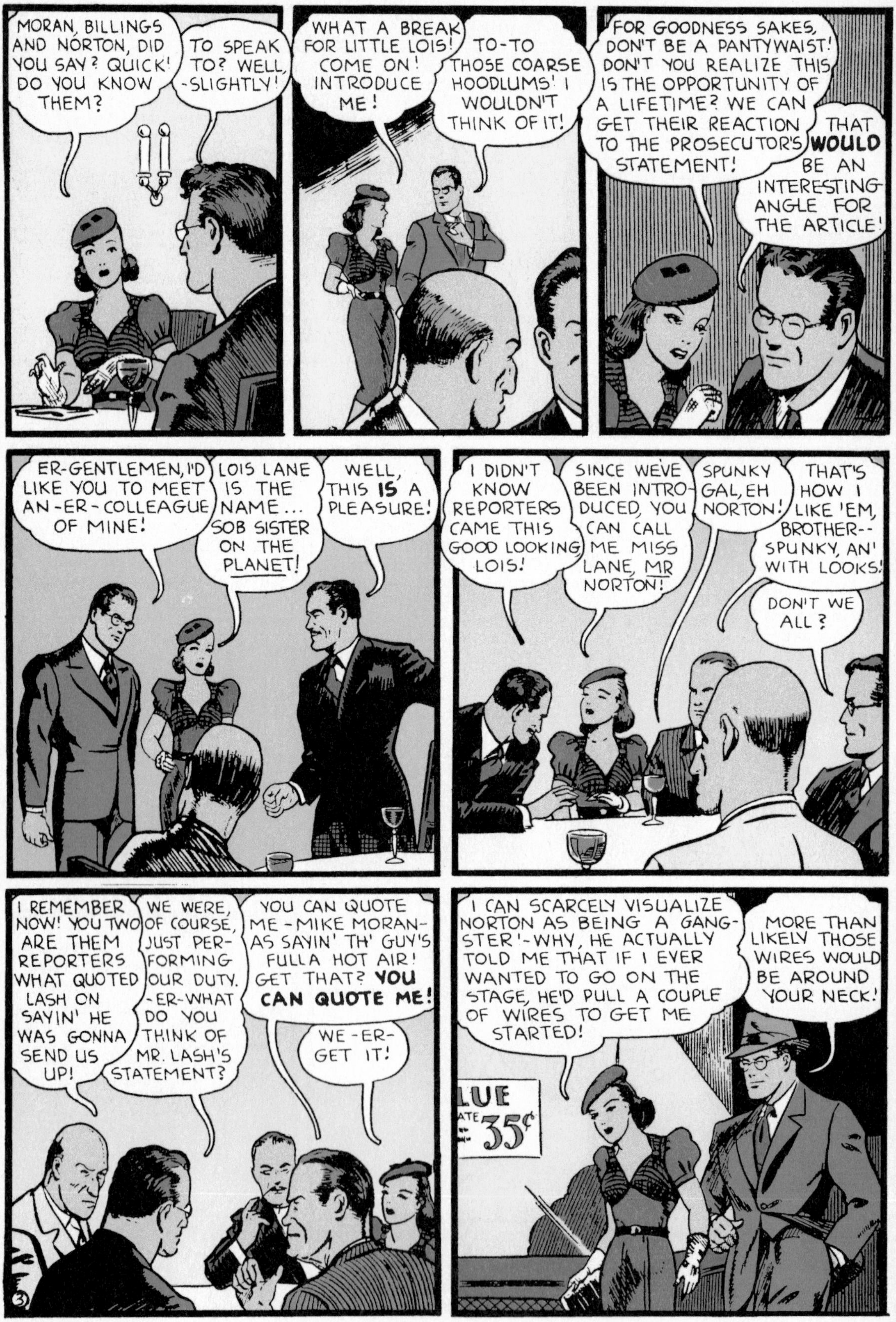
MORAN, BILLINGS AND NORTON, DID YOU SAY? QUICK! DO YOU KNOW THEM?
TO SPEAK TO? WELL, -SLIGHTLY!
WHAT A BREAK FOR LITTLE LOIS! COME ON! INTRODUCE ME!
TO-TO THOSE COARSE HOODLUMS! I WOULDN'T THINK OF IT!
FOR GOODNESS SAKES, DON'T BE A PANTYWAIST! DON'T YOU REALIZE THIS IS THE OPPORTUNITY OF A LIFETIME? WE CAN GET THEIR REACTION TO THE PROSECUTOR'S STATEMENT!
THAT WOULD BE AN INTERESTING ANGLE FOR THE ARTICLE!
ER-GENTLEMEN, I'D LIKE YOU TO MEET AN-ER-COLLEAGUE OF MINE!
LOIS LANE IS THE NAME... SOB SISTER ON THE PLANET!
WELL, THIS IS A PLEASURE!
I DIDN'T KNOW REPORTERS CAME THIS GOOD LOOKING LOIS!
SINCE WE'VE BEEN INTRODUCED, YOU CAN CALL ME MISS LANE, MR NORTON!
SPUNKY GAL, EH NORTON!
THAT'S HOW I LIKE 'EM, BROTHER-- SPUNKY, AN' WITH LOOKS!
DON'T WE ALL?
I REMEMBER NOW! YOU TWO ARE THEM REPORTERS WHAT QUOTED LASH ON SAYIN' HE WAS GONNA SEND US UP!
WE WERE, OF COURSE, JUST PERFORMING OUR DUTY. -ER-WHAT DO YOU THINK OF MR. LASH'S STATEMENT?
YOU CAN QUOTE ME-MIKE MORAN-AS SAYIN' TH' GUY'S FULLA HOT AIR! GET THAT? YOU CAN QUOTE ME!
WE-ER-GET IT!
3
I CAN SCARCELY VISUALIZE NORTON AS BEING A GANGSTER!-WHY, HE ACTUALLY TOLD ME THAT IF I EVER WANTED TO GO ON THE STAGE, HE'D PULL A COUPLE OF WIRES TO GET ME STARTED!
MORE THAN LIKELY THOSE WIRES WOULD BE AROUND YOUR NECK!
LUE
35¢

LATER-WITH NO PARTICULARLY
IMPORTANT DUTIES TO OCCUPY
HIS TIME, CLARK KENT, MEEK
REPORTER, SURREPTITIOUSLY
REMOVES HIS OUTER GARMENTS
SO THAT HE STANDS REVEALED
AS **SUPERMAN**...

NO ONE
LOOKING!

I'VE A HUNCH THE PROSECUTOR
MAY NEED PROTECTION FROM
THOSE CORNERED THUGS!

SUPERMAN SIGHTS A FIGURE
HURLED FROM AN AUTO BEFORE
THE METROPOLIS HOTEL ...THEN
THE CAR DRIVES OFF...

WHAT-??

IT'S THE
PROSECUTOR-
GEORGE LASH!

SHORTLY AFTER.. **SUPERMAN**
HURTLES INTO THE PROSECU-
TOR'S ROOM IN THE HOTEL...

- AND DOES
HE **REEK**
WITH ALCOHOL!

THE PUPILS OF HIS EYES-
CONTRACTED! HE'S NOT
DRUNK! SOMEONE GAVE
HIM DOPE SO THAT HE
WOULD APPEAR TO BE!

HIS POCKET'S RIPPED, AND
A BUTTON IS MISSING FROM
HIS COAT! THERE'S SOME-
THING ODD AFOOT, HERE.
AND I THINK LASH'S
FRIEND, POLICE CHIEF
WATSON, OUGHT TO
KNOW ABOUT THIS!

DOWN
TO THE
WINDOW-
LEDGE
OF
CHIEF
WATSON'S
OFFICE
STREAKS
THE MAN
OF
STEEL

I'LL SIMPLY CONFRONT
WATSON AND LET HIM KNOW
WHAT HAPPENED TO LASH!

NEXT
INSTANT,
SOMETHING
OCCURS
WHICH
CAUSES
SUPERMAN
TO
CHANGE
HIS MIND...!

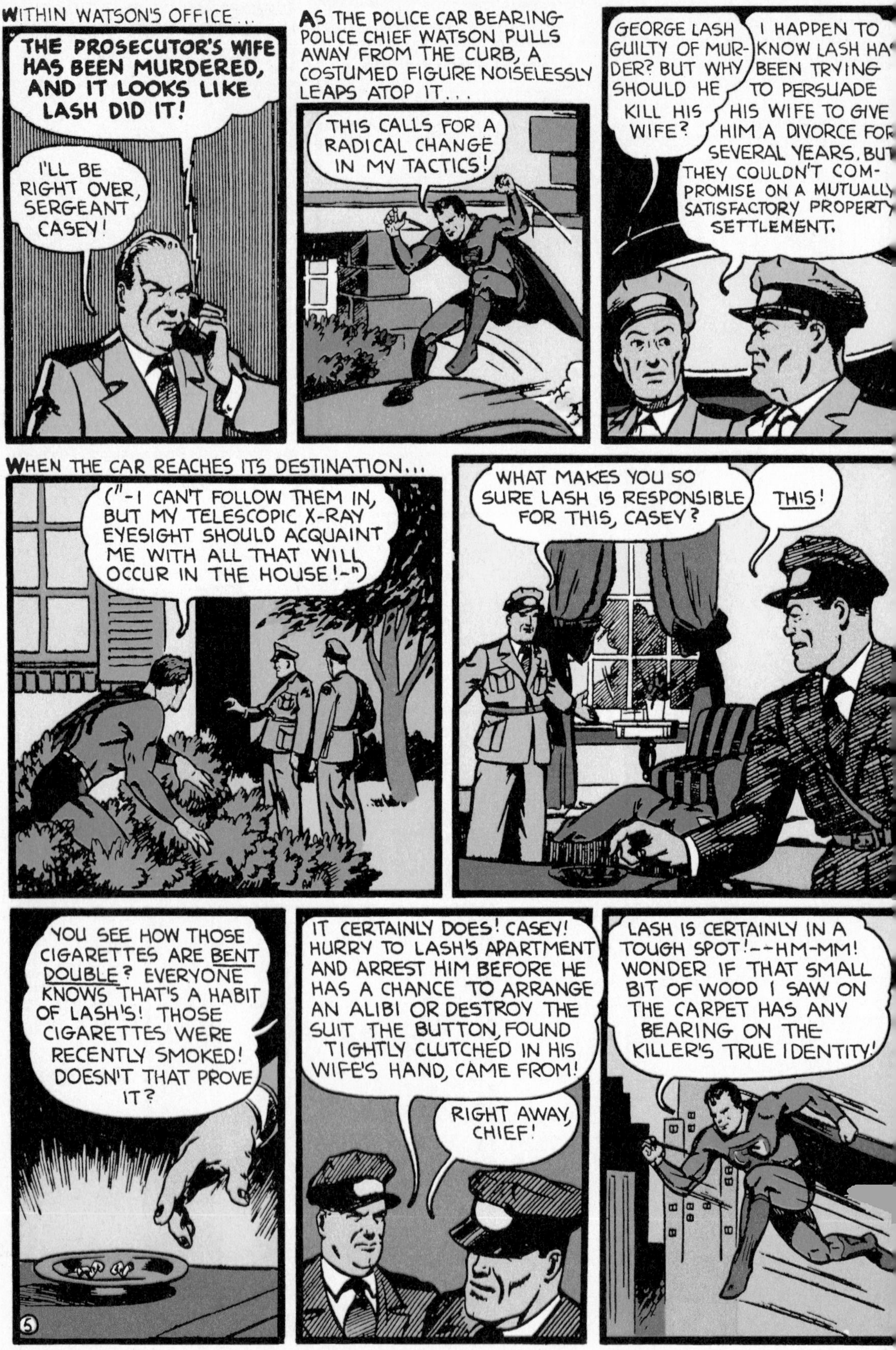
WITHIN WATSON'S OFFICE...
THE PROSECUTOR'S WIFE HAS BEEN MURDERED, AND IT LOOKS LIKE LASH DID IT!
I'LL BE RIGHT OVER, SERGEANT CASEY!
AS THE POLICE CAR BEARING POLICE CHIEF WATSON PULLS AWAY FROM THE CURB, A COSTUMED FIGURE NOISELESSLY LEAPS ATOP IT...
THIS CALLS FOR A RADICAL CHANGE IN MY TACTICS!
GEORGE LASH GUILTY OF MURDER? BUT WHY SHOULD HE KILL HIS WIFE?
I HAPPEN TO KNOW LASH HAS BEEN TRYING TO PERSUADE HIS WIFE TO GIVE HIM A DIVORCE FOR SEVERAL YEARS. BUT THEY COULDN'T COMPROMISE ON A MUTUALLY SATISFACTORY PROPERTY SETTLEMENT.
WHEN THE CAR REACHES ITS DESTINATION...
("-I CAN'T FOLLOW THEM IN, BUT MY TELESCOPIC X-RAY EYESIGHT SHOULD ACQUAINT ME WITH ALL THAT WILL OCCUR IN THE HOUSE!-")
WHAT MAKES YOU SO SURE LASH IS RESPONSIBLE FOR THIS, CASEY?
THIS!
YOU SEE HOW THOSE CIGARETTES ARE BENT DOUBLE? EVERYONE KNOWS THAT'S A HABIT OF LASH'S! THOSE CIGARETTES WERE RECENTLY SMOKED! DOESN'T THAT PROVE IT?
5
IT CERTAINLY DOES! CASEY! HURRY TO LASH'S APARTMENT AND ARREST HIM BEFORE HE HAS A CHANCE TO ARRANGE AN ALIBI OR DESTROY THE SUIT THE BUTTON, FOUND TIGHTLY CLUTCHED IN HIS WIFE'S HAND, CAME FROM!
RIGHT AWAY, CHIEF!
LASH IS CERTAINLY IN A TOUGH SPOT!--HM-MM! WONDER IF THAT SMALL BIT OF WOOD I SAW ON THE CARPET HAS ANY BEARING ON THE KILLER'S TRUE IDENTITY!

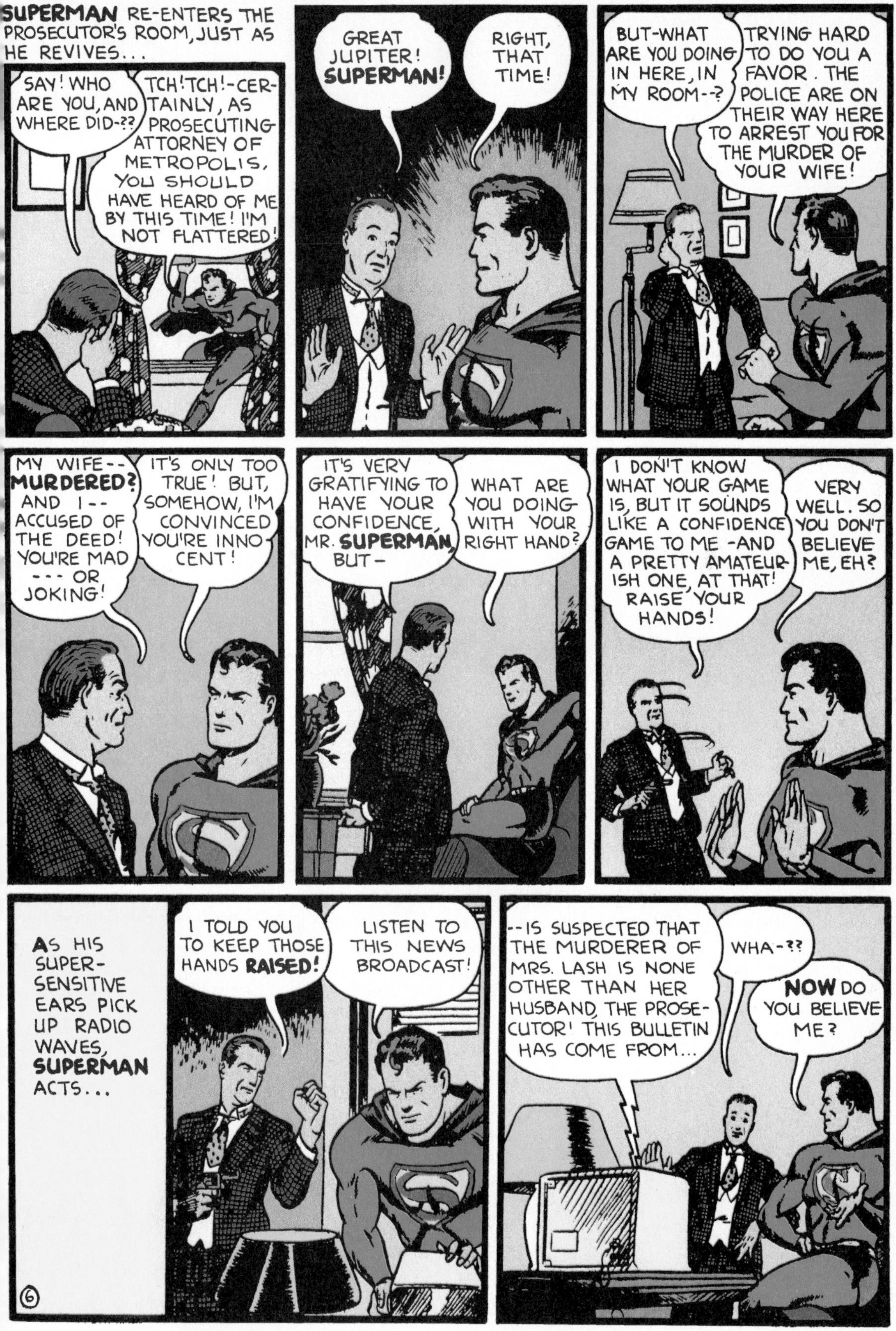
SUPERMAN RE-ENTERS THE PROSECUTOR'S ROOM, JUST AS HE REVIVES...
SAY! WHO ARE YOU, AND WHERE DID-??
TCH! TCH! - CERTAINLY, AS PROSECUTING ATTORNEY OF METROPOLIS, YOU SHOULD HAVE HEARD OF ME BY THIS TIME! I'M NOT FLATTERED!
GREAT JUPITER! SUPERMAN!
RIGHT, THAT TIME!
BUT-WHAT ARE YOU DOING IN HERE, IN MY ROOM--?
TRYING HARD TO DO YOU A FAVOR. THE POLICE ARE ON THEIR WAY HERE TO ARREST YOU FOR THE MURDER OF YOUR WIFE!
MY WIFE--MURDERED? AND I--ACCUSED OF THE DEED! YOU'RE MAD --- OR JOKING!
IT'S ONLY TOO TRUE! BUT, SOMEHOW, I'M CONVINCED YOU'RE INNOCENT!
IT'S VERY GRATIFYING TO HAVE YOUR CONFIDENCE, MR. SUPERMAN, BUT-
WHAT ARE YOU DOING WITH YOUR RIGHT HAND?
I DON'T KNOW WHAT YOUR GAME IS, BUT IT SOUNDS LIKE A CONFIDENCE GAME TO ME -AND A PRETTY AMATEURISH ONE, AT THAT! RAISE YOUR HANDS!
VERY WELL. SO YOU DON'T BELIEVE ME, EH?
AS HIS SUPER-SENSITIVE EARS PICK UP RADIO WAVES, SUPERMAN ACTS...
6
I TOLD YOU TO KEEP THOSE HANDS RAISED!
LISTEN TO THIS NEWS BROADCAST!
--IS SUSPECTED THAT THE MURDERER OF MRS. LASH IS NONE OTHER THAN HER HUSBAND, THE PROSECUTOR! THIS BULLETIN HAS COME FROM...
WHA-??
NOW DO YOU BELIEVE ME?

MY WIFE SLAIN... MYSELF ACCUSED— THIS MUST BE A NIGHTMARE — IT MUST!

IT'S REALITY, I ASSURE YOU! TELL ME! EXACTLY WHAT HAPPENED AT YOUR WIFE'S HOME? YOU WERE THERE, WERE YOU NOT?

YES—YES, I RECALL THAT I WAS. GRACE HAD FINALLY CONSENTED TO SIGN THE PROPERTY SETTLEMENT. AS I LEFT WITH IT, SOMEONE HIT ME OVER THE HEAD. AFTER THAT, A COMPLETE BLANK UNTIL I AWOKE HERE!

SHE SIGNED A SETTLEMENT PAPER? THEN THAT WILL PROVE YOU HAD NO MOTIVE · FOR KILLING HER! LET'S SEE IT!

THE PAPER... -- I CAN'T FIND IT!

WELL— THERE GOES THAT HOPE!

QUIETLY NOW! WE MUST GIVE HIM NO CHANCE TO ESCAPE!

SH-HH!

BUT THE POLICE ARE UNAWARE THAT THEIR SILENT STEPS SOUND AS LOUD AS THUNDER-CLAPS TO THE MAN OF TOMORROW'S SUPER-SENSITIVE HEARING...

SOMEONE COMING — THE POLICE!

POLICE! THEY'LL ARREST ME! I'LL BE RAILROADED TO THE CHAIR! I'VE GOT TO GET AWAY—FAST!

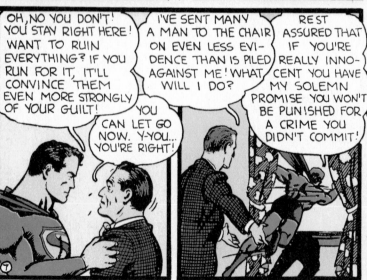

OH, NO YOU DON'T! YOU STAY RIGHT HERE! WANT TO RUIN EVERYTHING? IF YOU RUN FOR IT, IT'LL CONVINCE THEM EVEN MORE STRONGLY OF YOUR GUILT!

YOU CAN LET GO NOW. Y-YOU... YOU'RE RIGHT!

I'VE SENT MANY A MAN TO THE CHAIR ON EVEN LESS EVI-DENCE THAN IS PILED AGAINST ME! WHAT WILL I DO?

REST ASSURED THAT IF YOU'RE REALLY INNO-CENT YOU HAVE MY SOLEMN PROMISE YOU WON'T BE PUNISHED FOR A CRIME YOU DIDN'T COMMIT!

LATER—AT THE DAILY PLANET OFFICE

NICE WORK, CLARK-- NICE! THAT SCOOP ON LASH'S ARREST WAS A HUM-DINGER! YOU MUST BE TICKLED PINK!

TICKLED?—OH YEAH... SURE! ("PLEASED WITH MYSELF? HARDLY! I'VE BUT LITTLE TIME TO PROVE LASH'S INNOCENCE, AND HAVE MADE NO HEADWAY!--")

⑦

...GAIN, CLARK MEETS MORAN, BILLINGS, AND NORTON..

WELL, WELL, IF IT AIN'T OUR PAL, TH' PLANET REPORTER! WOTTAYA SAY **NOW** ABOUT LASH?

HE'S GONNA BE TOO BUSY TRYING TO DODGE THE HOT SEAT TO PAY MUCH ATTENTION TO US HARD WORKING BUSINESS MEN!

CONVENIENT, EH - FOR **YOU**!

LATER-- AND ONCE AGAIN HE DONS THE UNIFORM OF **SUPERMAN**..

SO LASH'S FRAME-UP MAKES THE GOING EASIER FOR THOSE CROOKS? HM-MM! THAT'S JUST A LITTLE TOO NEAT A SET-UP FOR MERE COINCIDENCE!

THE MAN OF STEEL SCALES THE SHEER WALL OF THE RACKETEERS' HEADQUARTERS UNTIL HE REMAINS SUSPENDED BENEATH THE WINDOW OF THEIR PRIVATE OFFICE...

NOW TO GET AN EARFUL.. I HOPE!

HO! HO! - IT HANDS ME A LAUGH TO THINK OF TH' PROSECUTOR BEIN' A PRISONER IN ONE O' HIS OWN CELLS!

YEAH? DOESN'T IT--UH-HH--?? ("-FINGERTIPS! ON THE WINDOWSILL!-")

("-SH-HH!-")

...OWN SMASHES THE HAMMER!

HUH? NO EFFECT!

CONCEALMENT NO LONGER POSSIBLE, I MIGHT AS WELL JOIN YOUR COMPANY!

IT'S **SUPERMAN**!

C'MERE, YOU LUGS - ON TH' RUN!

GET THAT GUY!

OKAY, BOSS!

FIRE AWAY, BOYS!

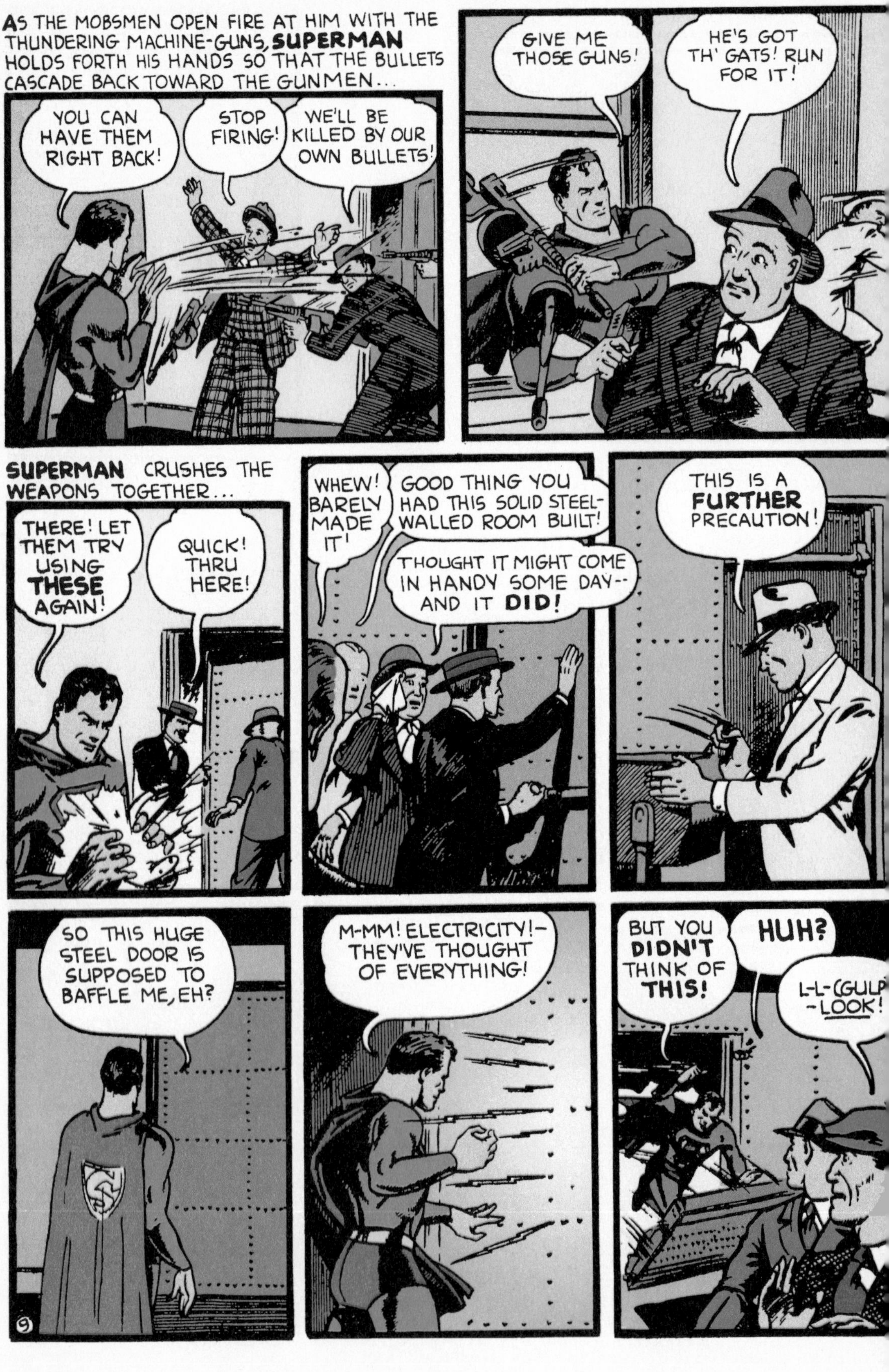
AS THE MOBSMEN OPEN FIRE AT HIM WITH THE THUNDERING MACHINE-GUNS, SUPERMAN HOLDS FORTH HIS HANDS SO THAT THE BULLETS CASCADE BACK TOWARD THE GUNMEN...
YOU CAN HAVE THEM RIGHT BACK!
STOP FIRING!
WE'LL BE KILLED BY OUR OWN BULLETS!
GIVE ME THOSE GUNS!
HE'S GOT TH' GATS! RUN FOR IT!
SUPERMAN CRUSHES THE WEAPONS TOGETHER...
THERE! LET THEM TRY USING THESE AGAIN!
QUICK! THRU HERE!
WHEW! BARELY MADE IT!
GOOD THING YOU HAD THIS SOLID STEEL-WALLED ROOM BUILT!
THOUGHT IT MIGHT COME IN HANDY SOME DAY-- AND IT DID!
THIS IS A FURTHER PRECAUTION!
SO THIS HUGE STEEL DOOR IS SUPPOSED TO BAFFLE ME, EH?
9
M-MM! ELECTRICITY!- THEY'VE THOUGHT OF EVERYTHING!
BUT YOU DIDN'T THINK OF THIS!
HUH?
L-L-(GULP -LOOK!

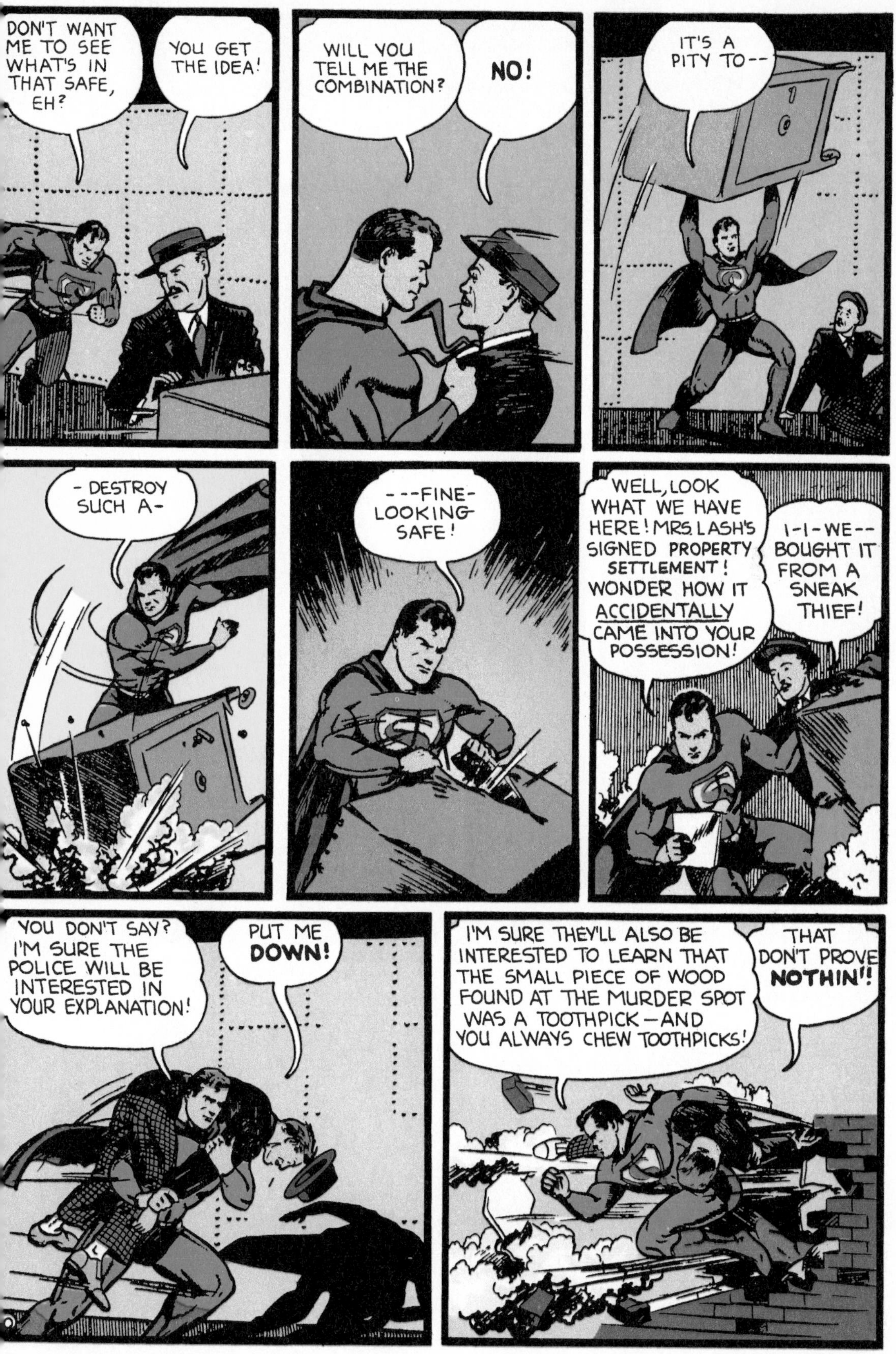
DON'T WANT ME TO SEE WHAT'S IN THAT SAFE, EH?
YOU GET THE IDEA!
WILL YOU TELL ME THE COMBINATION?
NO!
IT'S A PITY TO--
- DESTROY SUCH A-
---FINE-LOOKING SAFE!
WELL, LOOK WHAT WE HAVE HERE! MRS. LASH'S SIGNED PROPERTY SETTLEMENT! WONDER HOW IT ACCIDENTALLY CAME INTO YOUR POSSESSION!
I-I-WE-- BOUGHT IT FROM A SNEAK THIEF!
YOU DON'T SAY? I'M SURE THE POLICE WILL BE INTERESTED IN YOUR EXPLANATION!
PUT ME DOWN!
I'M SURE THEY'LL ALSO BE INTERESTED TO LEARN THAT THE SMALL PIECE OF WOOD FOUND AT THE MURDER SPOT WAS A TOOTHPICK—AND YOU ALWAYS CHEW TOOTHPICKS!
THAT DON'T PROVE NOTHIN'!

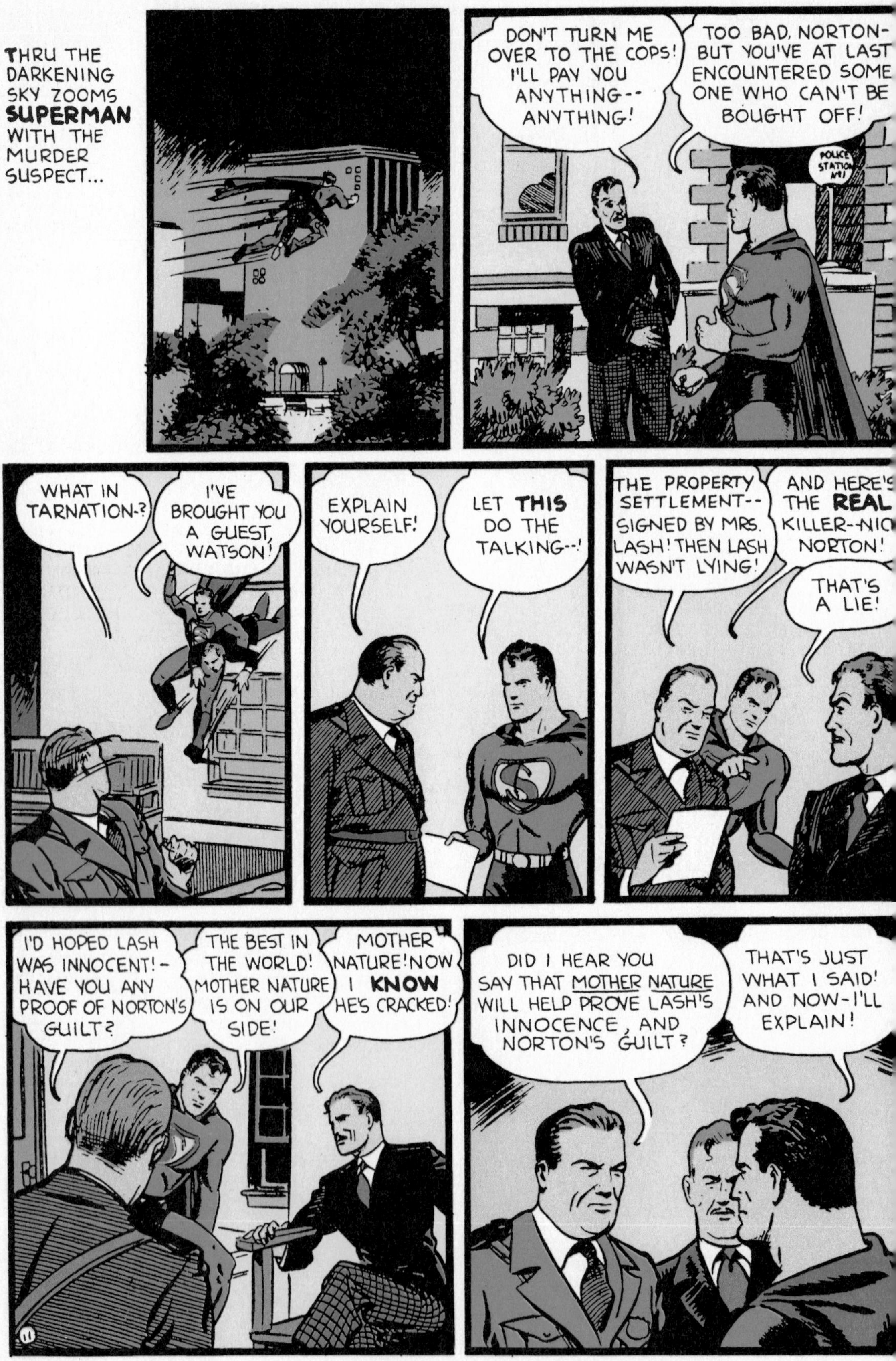
THRU THE DARKENING SKY ZOOMS **SUPERMAN** WITH THE MURDER SUSPECT...
DON'T TURN ME OVER TO THE COPS! I'LL PAY YOU ANYTHING-- ANYTHING!
TOO BAD, NORTON- BUT YOU'VE AT LAST ENCOUNTERED SOME ONE WHO CAN'T BE BOUGHT OFF!
POLICE STATION No1
WHAT IN TARNATION-?
I'VE BROUGHT YOU A GUEST, WATSON!
EXPLAIN YOURSELF!
LET **THIS** DO THE TALKING--!
THE PROPERTY SETTLEMENT-- SIGNED BY MRS. LASH! THEN LASH WASN'T LYING!
AND HERE'S THE **REAL** KILLER--NIC NORTON!
THAT'S A LIE!
I'D HOPED LASH WAS INNOCENT! - HAVE YOU ANY PROOF OF NORTON'S GUILT?
THE BEST IN THE WORLD! MOTHER NATURE IS ON OUR SIDE!
MOTHER NATURE! NOW I **KNOW** HE'S CRACKED!
DID I HEAR YOU SAY THAT MOTHER NATURE WILL HELP PROVE LASH'S INNOCENCE, AND NORTON'S GUILT?
THAT'S JUST WHAT I SAID! AND NOW-I'LL EXPLAIN!
11

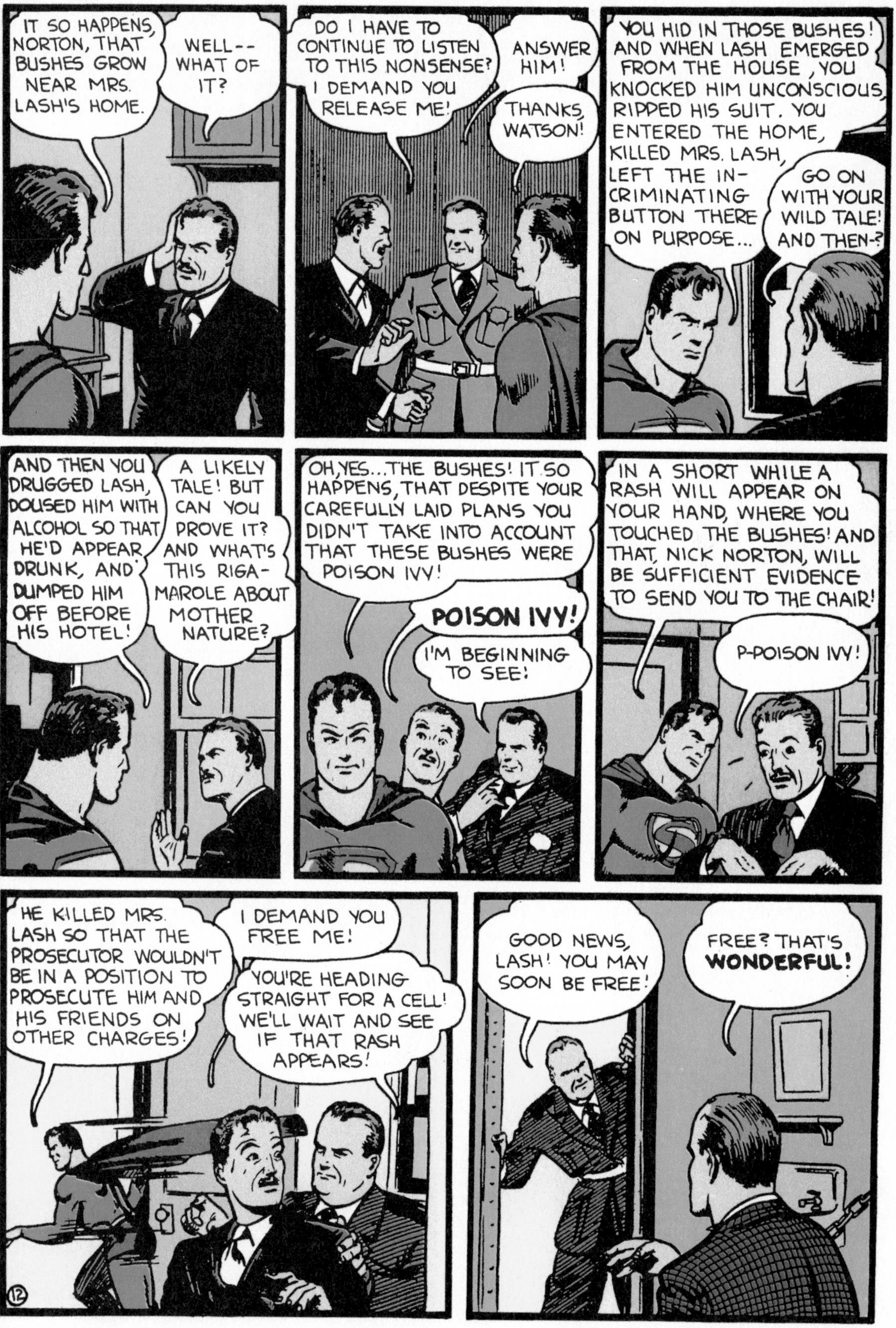
IT SO HAPPENS, NORTON, THAT BUSHES GROW NEAR MRS. LASH'S HOME.
WELL-- WHAT OF IT?
DO I HAVE TO CONTINUE TO LISTEN TO THIS NONSENSE? I DEMAND YOU RELEASE ME!
ANSWER HIM!
THANKS, WATSON!
YOU HID IN THOSE BUSHES! AND WHEN LASH EMERGED FROM THE HOUSE, YOU KNOCKED HIM UNCONSCIOUS, RIPPED HIS SUIT. YOU ENTERED THE HOME, KILLED MRS. LASH, LEFT THE IN-CRIMINATING BUTTON THERE ON PURPOSE...
GO ON WITH YOUR WILD TALE! AND THEN-?
AND THEN YOU DRUGGED LASH, DOUSED HIM WITH ALCOHOL SO THAT HE'D APPEAR DRUNK, AND DUMPED HIM OFF BEFORE HIS HOTEL!
A LIKELY TALE! BUT CAN YOU PROVE IT? AND WHAT'S THIS RIGA-MAROLE ABOUT MOTHER NATURE?
OH, YES...THE BUSHES! IT SO HAPPENS, THAT DESPITE YOUR CAREFULLY LAID PLANS YOU DIDN'T TAKE INTO ACCOUNT THAT THESE BUSHES WERE POISON IVY!
POISON IVY!
I'M BEGINNING TO SEE!
IN A SHORT WHILE A RASH WILL APPEAR ON YOUR HAND, WHERE YOU TOUCHED THE BUSHES! AND THAT, NICK NORTON, WILL BE SUFFICIENT EVIDENCE TO SEND YOU TO THE CHAIR!
P-POISON IVY!
HE KILLED MRS. LASH SO THAT THE PROSECUTOR WOULDN'T BE IN A POSITION TO PROSECUTE HIM AND HIS FRIENDS ON OTHER CHARGES!
I DEMAND YOU FREE ME!
YOU'RE HEADING STRAIGHT FOR A CELL! WE'LL WAIT AND SEE IF THAT RASH APPEARS!
12
GOOD NEWS, LASH! YOU MAY SOON BE FREE!
FREE? THAT'S WONDERFUL!

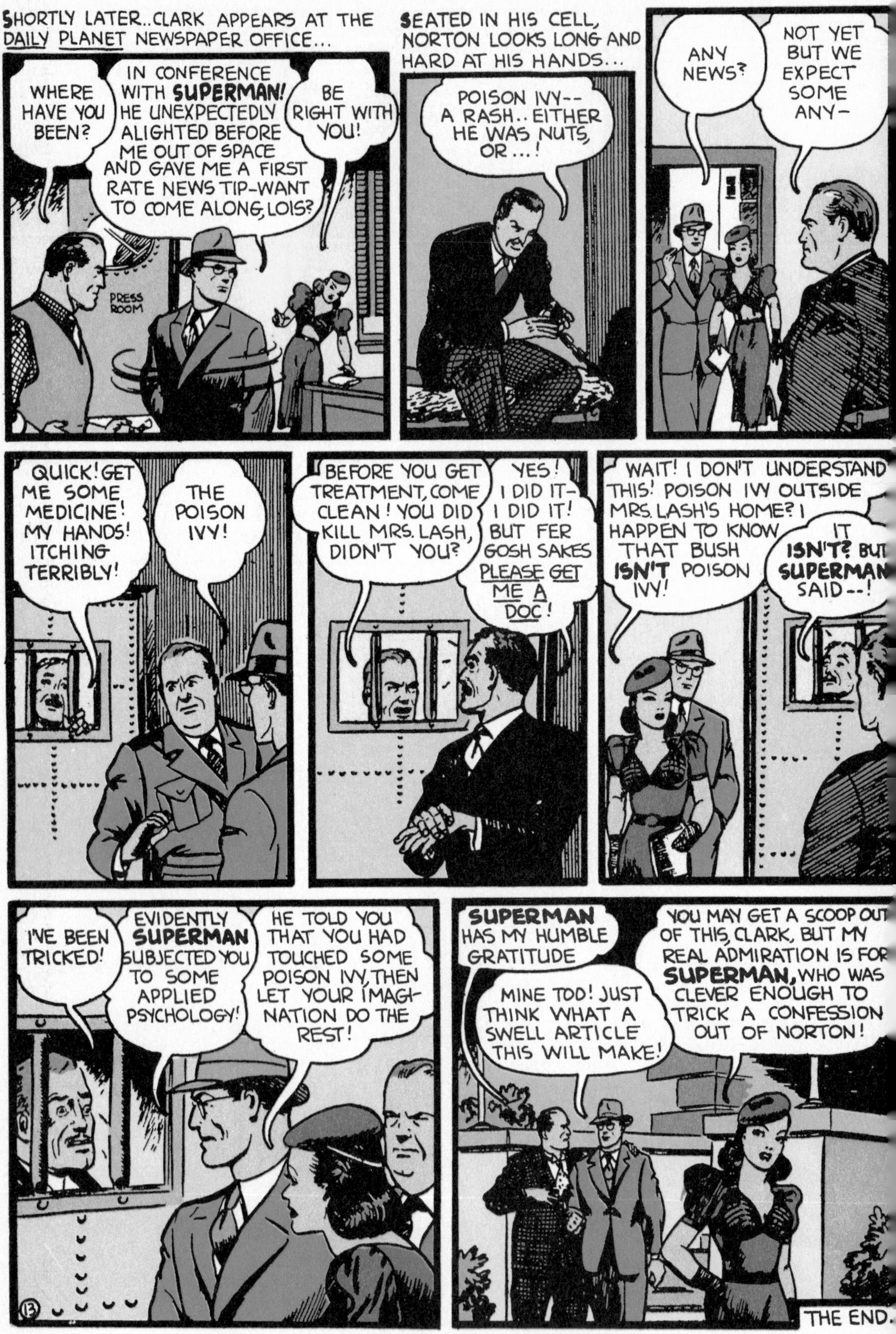
SHORTLY LATER..CLARK APPEARS AT THE DAILY PLANET NEWSPAPER OFFICE...
WHERE HAVE YOU BEEN?
IN CONFERENCE WITH SUPERMAN! HE UNEXPECTEDLY ALIGHTED BEFORE ME OUT OF SPACE AND GAVE ME A FIRST RATE NEWS TIP-WANT TO COME ALONG, LOIS?
BE RIGHT WITH YOU!
PRESS ROOM
SEATED IN HIS CELL, NORTON LOOKS LONG AND HARD AT HIS HANDS...
POISON IVY-- A RASH.. EITHER HE WAS NUTS, OR...!
ANY NEWS?
NOT YET BUT WE EXPECT SOME ANY-
QUICK! GET ME SOME MEDICINE! MY HANDS! ITCHING TERRIBLY!
THE POISON IVY!
BEFORE YOU GET TREATMENT, COME CLEAN! YOU DID KILL MRS. LASH, DIDN'T YOU?
YES! I DID IT-I DID IT! BUT FER GOSH SAKES PLEASE GET ME A DOC!
WAIT! I DON'T UNDERSTAND THIS! POISON IVY OUTSIDE MRS. LASH'S HOME? I HAPPEN TO KNOW THAT BUSH ISN'T POISON IVY!
IT ISN'T? BUT SUPERMAN SAID--!
I'VE BEEN TRICKED!
EVIDENTLY SUPERMAN SUBJECTED YOU TO SOME APPLIED PSYCHOLOGY!
HE TOLD YOU THAT YOU HAD TOUCHED SOME POISON IVY, THEN LET YOUR IMAGINATION DO THE REST!
13
SUPERMAN HAS MY HUMBLE GRATITUDE
MINE TOO! JUST THINK WHAT A SWELL ARTICLE THIS WILL MAKE!
YOU MAY GET A SCOOP OUT OF THIS, CLARK, BUT MY REAL ADMIRATION IS FOR SUPERMAN, WHO WAS CLEVER ENOUGH TO TRICK A CONFESSION OUT OF NORTON!
THE END.

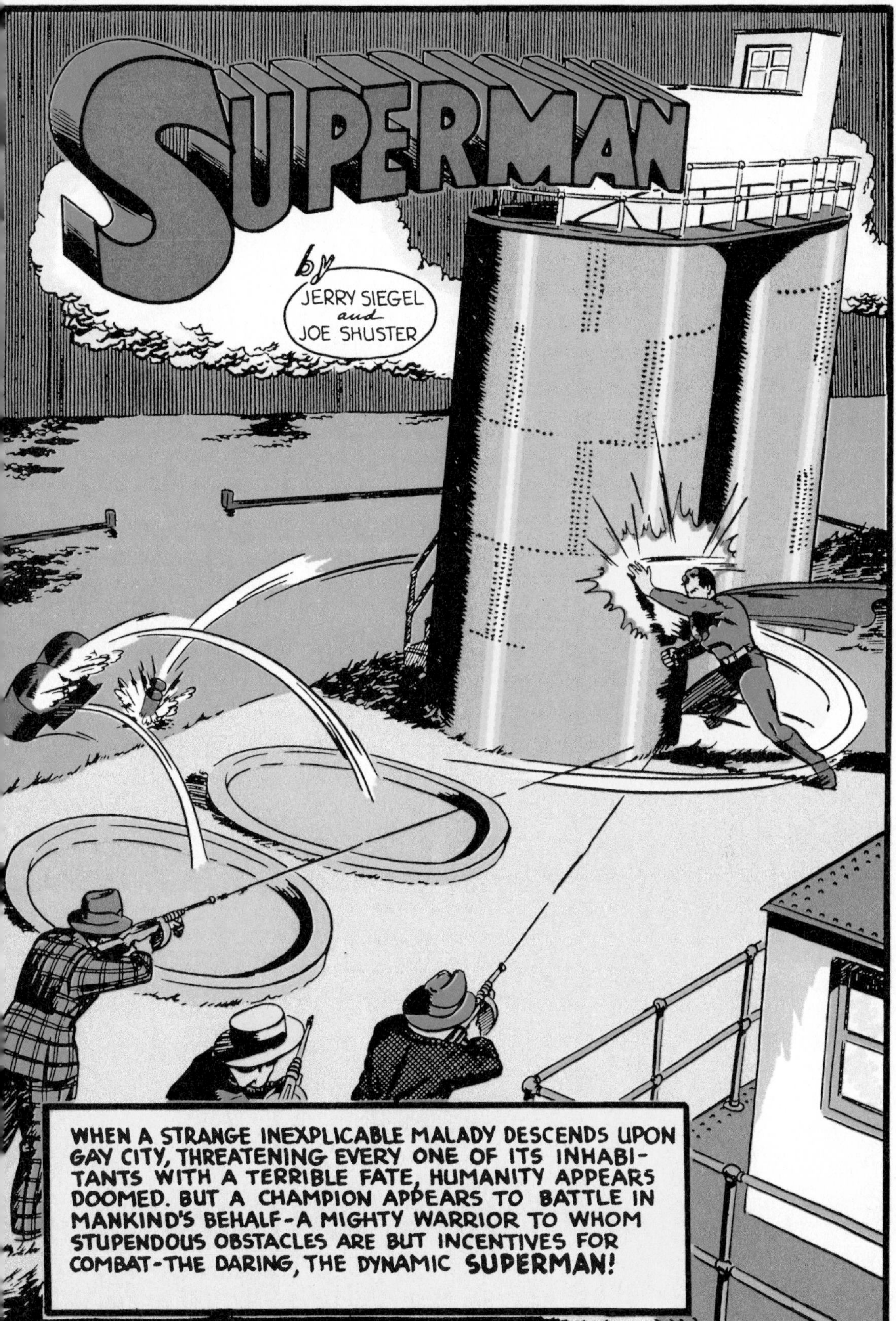
SUPERMAN
by
JERRY SIEGEL
and
JOE SHUSTER
WHEN A STRANGE INEXPLICABLE MALADY DESCENDS UPON GAY CITY, THREATENING EVERY ONE OF ITS INHABITANTS WITH A TERRIBLE FATE, HUMANITY APPEARS DOOMED. BUT A CHAMPION APPEARS TO BATTLE IN MANKIND'S BEHALF-A MIGHTY WARRIOR TO WHOM STUPENDOUS OBSTACLES ARE BUT INCENTIVES FOR COMBAT-THE DARING, THE DYNAMIC SUPERMAN!

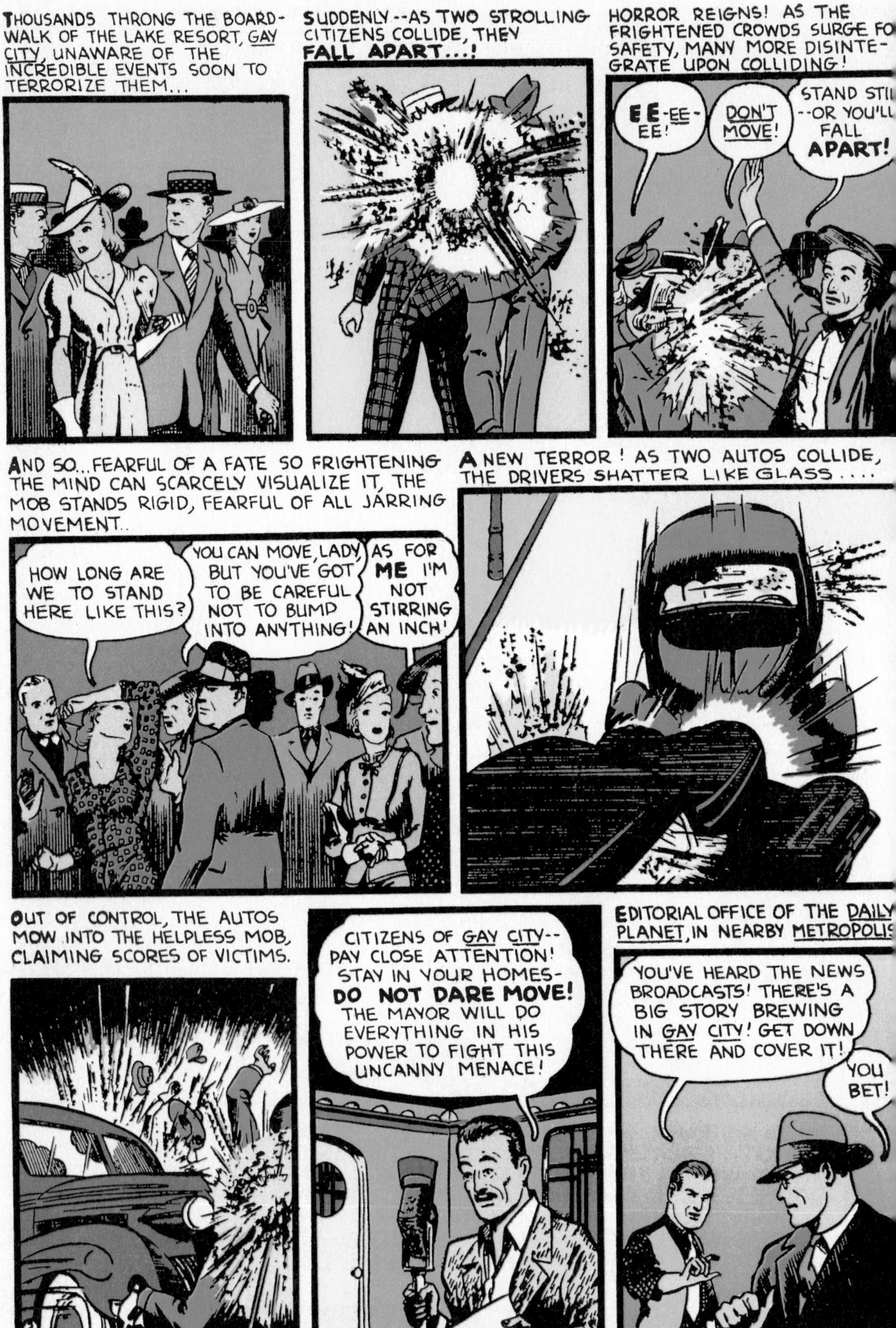
THOUSANDS THRONG THE BOARD-WALK OF THE LAKE RESORT, GAY CITY, UNAWARE OF THE INCREDIBLE EVENTS SOON TO TERRORIZE THEM...
SUDDENLY--AS TWO STROLLING CITIZENS COLLIDE, THEY FALL APART...!
HORROR REIGNS! AS THE FRIGHTENED CROWDS SURGE FO SAFETY, MANY MORE DISINTE-GRATE UPON COLLIDING!
EE-EE-EE!
DON'T MOVE!
STAND STI --OR YOU'LL FALL APART!
AND SO... FEARFUL OF A FATE SO FRIGHTENING THE MIND CAN SCARCELY VISUALIZE IT, THE MOB STANDS RIGID, FEARFUL OF ALL JARRING MOVEMENT..
HOW LONG ARE WE TO STAND HERE LIKE THIS?
YOU CAN MOVE, LADY, BUT YOU'VE GOT TO BE CAREFUL NOT TO BUMP INTO ANYTHING!
AS FOR ME I'M NOT STIRRING AN INCH!
A NEW TERROR! AS TWO AUTOS COLLIDE, THE DRIVERS SHATTER LIKE GLASS....
OUT OF CONTROL, THE AUTOS MOW INTO THE HELPLESS MOB, CLAIMING SCORES OF VICTIMS.
CITIZENS OF GAY CITY--PAY CLOSE ATTENTION! STAY IN YOUR HOMES-DO NOT DARE MOVE! THE MAYOR WILL DO EVERYTHING IN HIS POWER TO FIGHT THIS UNCANNY MENACE!
EDITORIAL OFFICE OF THE DAILY PLANET, IN NEARBY METROPOLIS
YOU'VE HEARD THE NEWS BROADCASTS! THERE'S A BIG STORY BREWING IN GAY CITY! GET DOWN THERE AND COVER IT!
YOU BET!

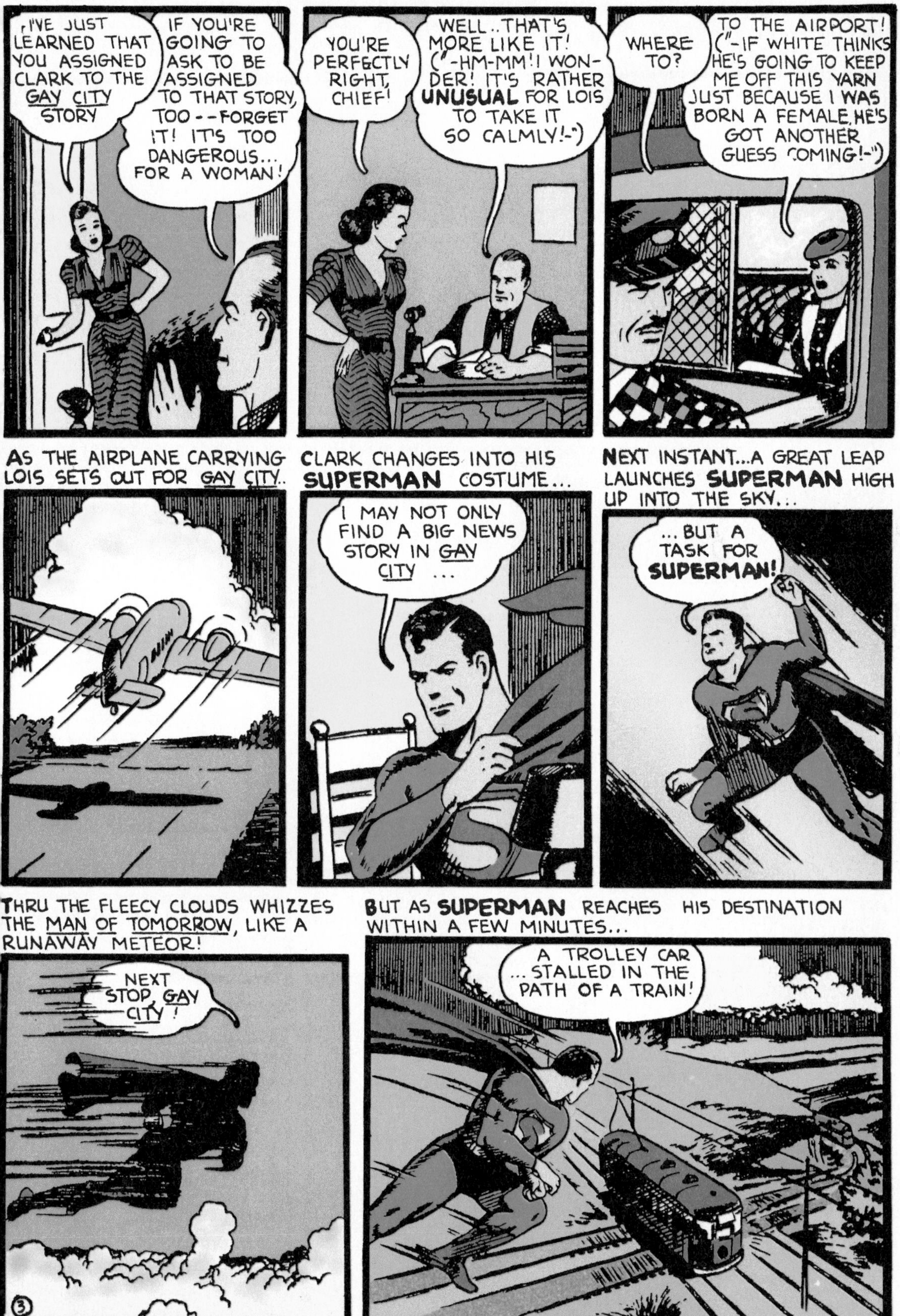
I'VE JUST LEARNED THAT YOU ASSIGNED CLARK TO THE GAY CITY STORY
IF YOU'RE GOING TO ASK TO BE ASSIGNED TO THAT STORY, TOO -- FORGET IT! IT'S TOO DANGEROUS... FOR A WOMAN!
YOU'RE PERFECTLY RIGHT, CHIEF!
WELL.. THAT'S MORE LIKE IT! ("-HM-MM! I WONDER! IT'S RATHER UNUSUAL FOR LOIS TO TAKE IT SO CALMLY!-")
WHERE TO?
TO THE AIRPORT! ("-IF WHITE THINKS HE'S GOING TO KEEP ME OFF THIS YARN JUST BECAUSE I WAS BORN A FEMALE, HE'S GOT ANOTHER GUESS COMING!-")
AS THE AIRPLANE CARRYING LOIS SETS OUT FOR GAY CITY..
CLARK CHANGES INTO HIS SUPERMAN COSTUME...
I MAY NOT ONLY FIND A BIG NEWS STORY IN GAY CITY ...
NEXT INSTANT...A GREAT LEAP LAUNCHES SUPERMAN HIGH UP INTO THE SKY...
... BUT A TASK FOR SUPERMAN!
THRU THE FLEECY CLOUDS WHIZZES THE MAN OF TOMORROW, LIKE A RUNAWAY METEOR!
NEXT STOP, GAY CITY!
3
BUT AS SUPERMAN REACHES HIS DESTINATION WITHIN A FEW MINUTES...
A TROLLEY CAR ... STALLED IN THE PATH OF A TRAIN!

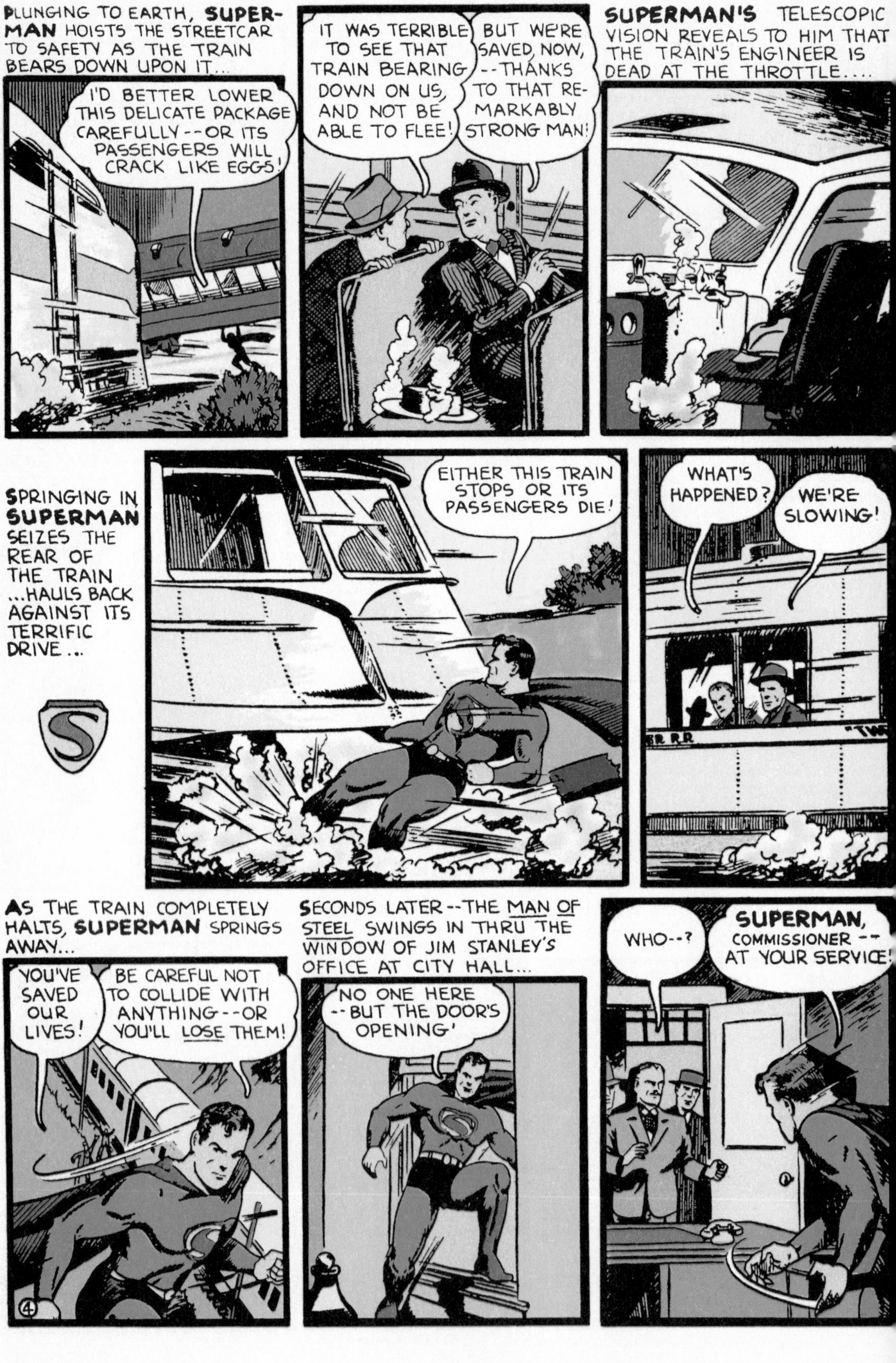
PLUNGING TO EARTH, SUPERMAN HOISTS THE STREETCAR TO SAFETY AS THE TRAIN BEARS DOWN UPON IT...
I'D BETTER LOWER THIS DELICATE PACKAGE CAREFULLY--OR ITS PASSENGERS WILL CRACK LIKE EGGS!
IT WAS TERRIBLE TO SEE THAT TRAIN BEARING DOWN ON US, AND NOT BE ABLE TO FLEE!
BUT WE'RE SAVED, NOW, --THANKS TO THAT REMARKABLY STRONG MAN!
SUPERMAN'S TELESCOPIC VISION REVEALS TO HIM THAT THE TRAIN'S ENGINEER IS DEAD AT THE THROTTLE....
SPRINGING IN, SUPERMAN SEIZES THE REAR OF THE TRAIN ...HAULS BACK AGAINST ITS TERRIFIC DRIVE...
EITHER THIS TRAIN STOPS OR ITS PASSENGERS DIE!
WHAT'S HAPPENED?
WE'RE SLOWING!
AS THE TRAIN COMPLETELY HALTS, SUPERMAN SPRINGS AWAY...
YOU'VE SAVED OUR LIVES!
BE CAREFUL NOT TO COLLIDE WITH ANYTHING--OR YOU'LL LOSE THEM!
4
SECONDS LATER--THE MAN OF STEEL SWINGS IN THRU THE WINDOW OF JIM STANLEY'S OFFICE AT CITY HALL...
NO ONE HERE --BUT THE DOOR'S OPENING!
WHO--?
SUPERMAN, COMMISSIONER --AT YOUR SERVICE!

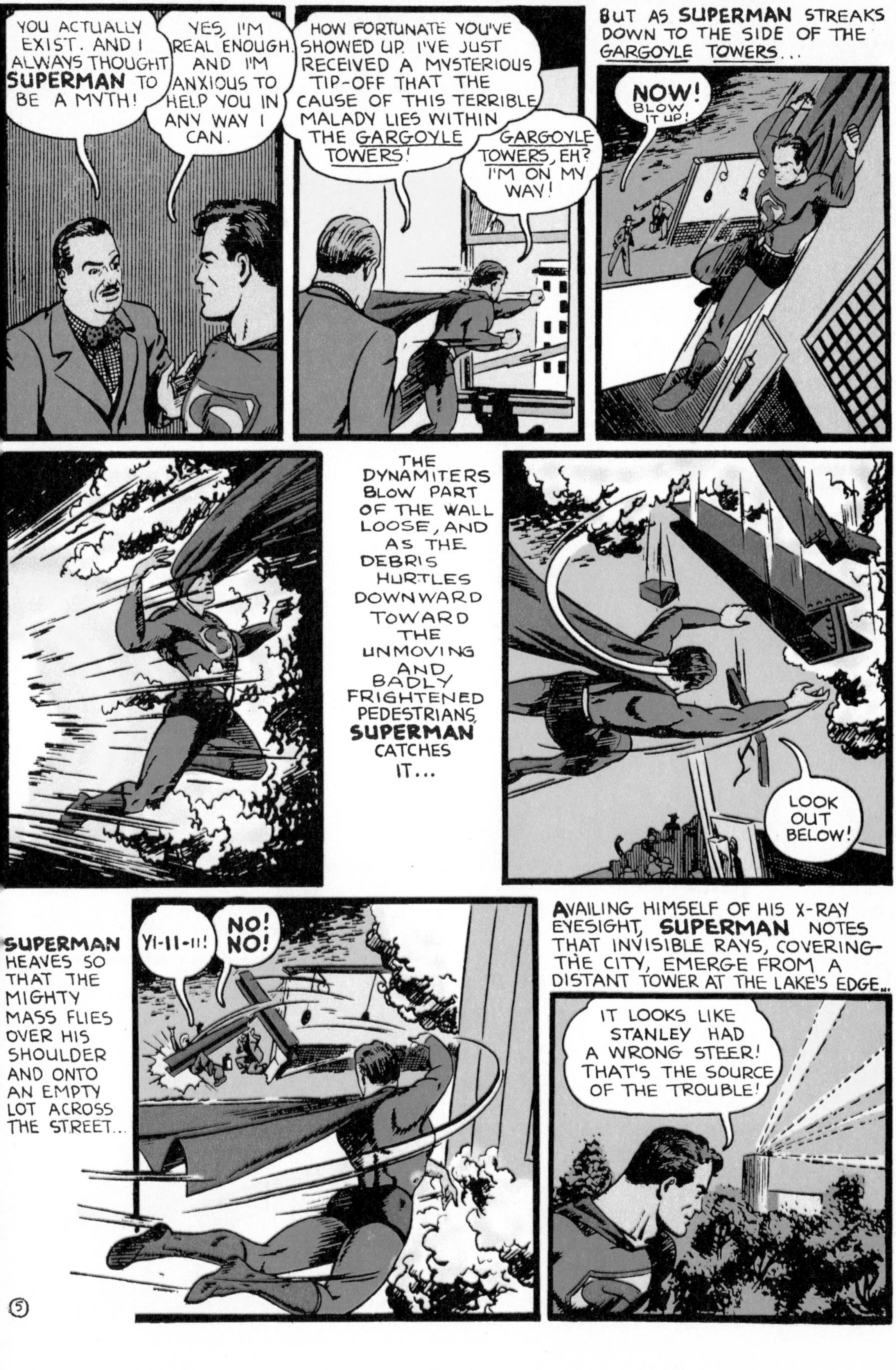

YOU ACTUALLY EXIST. AND I ALWAYS THOUGHT SUPERMAN TO BE A MYTH!
YES, I'M REAL ENOUGH. AND I'M ANXIOUS TO HELP YOU IN ANY WAY I CAN.
HOW FORTUNATE YOU'VE SHOWED UP. I'VE JUST RECEIVED A MYSTERIOUS TIP-OFF THAT THE CAUSE OF THIS TERRIBLE MALADY LIES WITHIN THE GARGOYLE TOWERS!
GARGOYLE TOWERS, EH? I'M ON MY WAY!
BUT AS SUPERMAN STREAKS DOWN TO THE SIDE OF THE GARGOYLE TOWERS...
NOW! BLOW IT UP!
THE DYNAMITERS BLOW PART OF THE WALL LOOSE, AND AS THE DEBRIS HURTLES DOWNWARD TOWARD THE UNMOVING AND BADLY FRIGHTENED PEDESTRIANS, SUPERMAN CATCHES IT...
LOOK OUT BELOW!
SUPERMAN HEAVES SO THAT THE MIGHTY MASS FLIES OVER HIS SHOULDER AND ONTO AN EMPTY LOT ACROSS THE STREET...
YI-II-II!
NO! NO!
5
AVAILING HIMSELF OF HIS X-RAY EYESIGHT, SUPERMAN NOTES THAT INVISIBLE RAYS, COVERING THE CITY, EMERGE FROM A DISTANT TOWER AT THE LAKE'S EDGE...
IT LOOKS LIKE STANLEY HAD A WRONG STEER! THAT'S THE SOURCE OF THE TROUBLE!

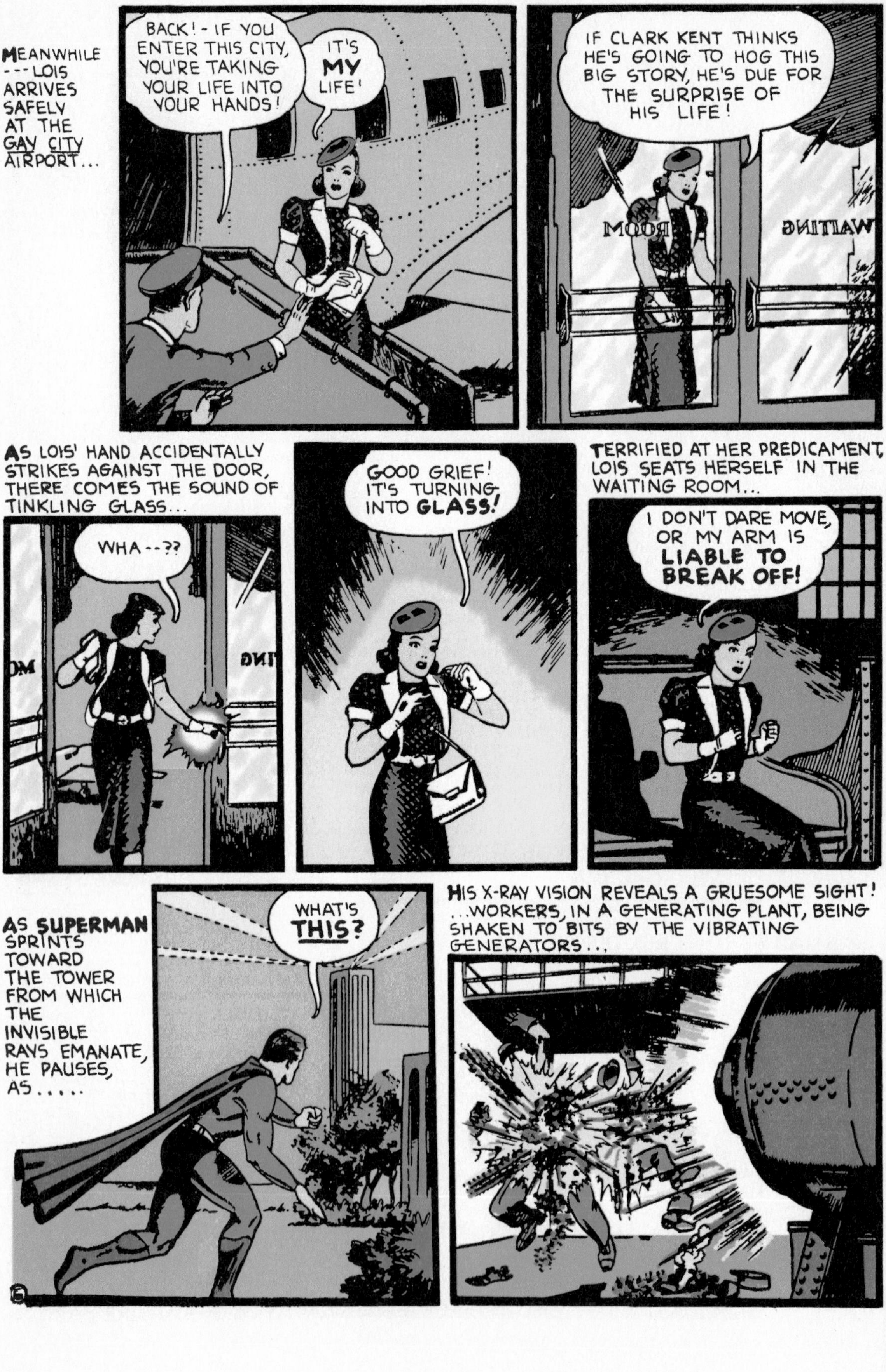
MEANWHILE ---LOIS ARRIVES SAFELY AT THE GAY CITY AIRPORT...
BACK! - IF YOU ENTER THIS CITY, YOU'RE TAKING YOUR LIFE INTO YOUR HANDS!
IT'S MY LIFE!
IF CLARK KENT THINKS HE'S GOING TO HOG THIS BIG STORY, HE'S DUE FOR THE SURPRISE OF HIS LIFE!
AS LOIS' HAND ACCIDENTALLY STRIKES AGAINST THE DOOR, THERE COMES THE SOUND OF TINKLING GLASS...
WHA--??
GOOD GRIEF! IT'S TURNING INTO GLASS!
TERRIFIED AT HER PREDICAMENT, LOIS SEATS HERSELF IN THE WAITING ROOM...
I DON'T DARE MOVE, OR MY ARM IS LIABLE TO BREAK OFF!
AS SUPERMAN SPRINTS TOWARD THE TOWER FROM WHICH THE INVISIBLE RAYS EMANATE, HE PAUSES, AS.....
WHAT'S THIS?
HIS X-RAY VISION REVEALS A GRUESOME SIGHT! ...WORKERS, IN A GENERATING PLANT, BEING SHAKEN TO BITS BY THE VIBRATING GENERATORS...

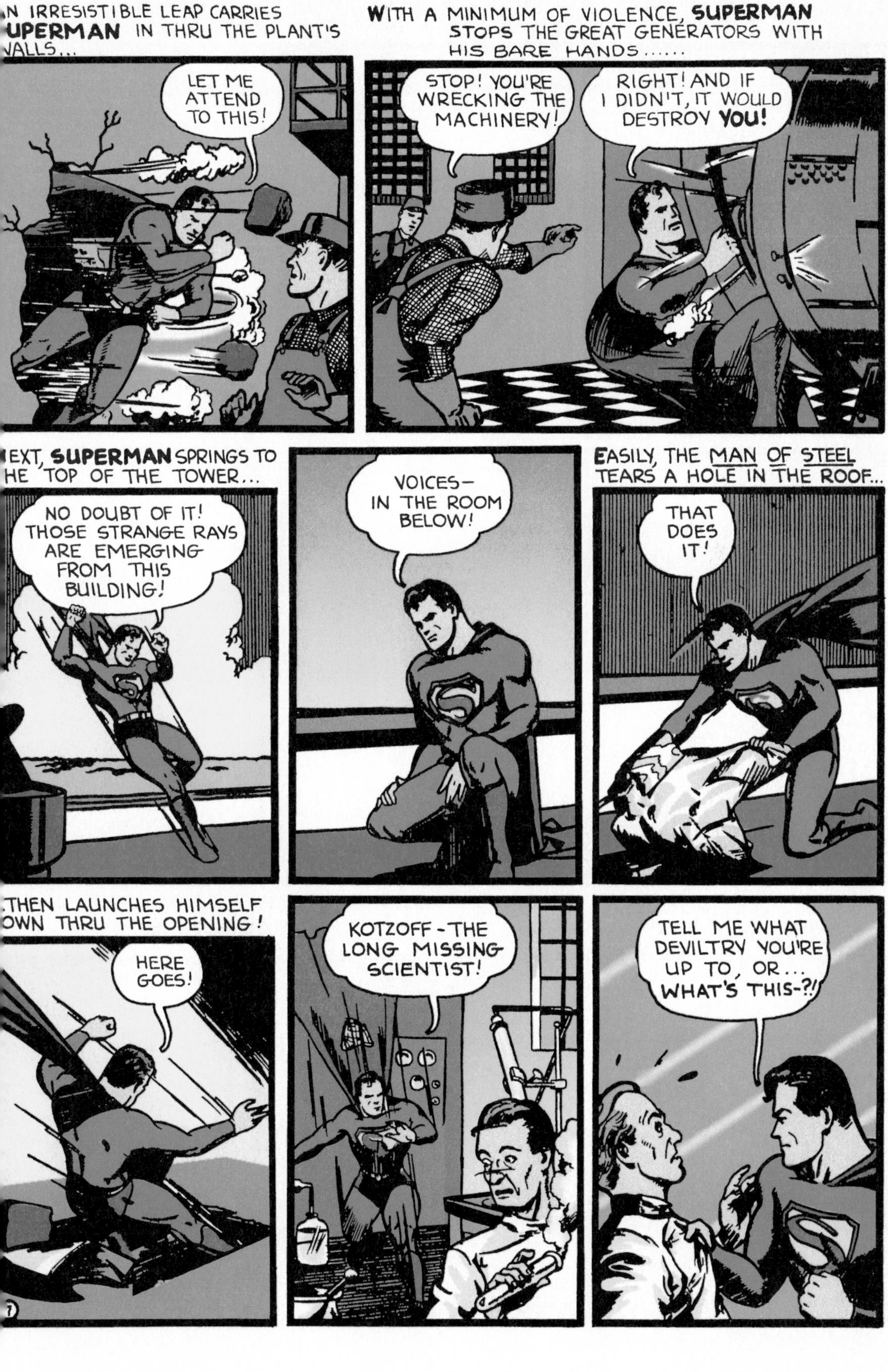
N IRRESISTIBLE LEAP CARRIES SUPERMAN IN THRU THE PLANT'S WALLS...
LET ME ATTEND TO THIS!
WITH A MINIMUM OF VIOLENCE, SUPERMAN STOPS THE GREAT GENERATORS WITH HIS BARE HANDS......
STOP! YOU'RE WRECKING THE MACHINERY!
RIGHT! AND IF I DIDN'T, IT WOULD DESTROY YOU!
EXT, SUPERMAN SPRINGS TO HE TOP OF THE TOWER...
NO DOUBT OF IT! THOSE STRANGE RAYS ARE EMERGING FROM THIS BUILDING!
VOICES— IN THE ROOM BELOW!
EASILY, THE MAN OF STEEL TEARS A HOLE IN THE ROOF...
THAT DOES IT!
.THEN LAUNCHES HIMSELF OWN THRU THE OPENING!
HERE GOES!
KOTZOFF - THE LONG MISSING SCIENTIST!
TELL ME WHAT DEVILTRY YOU'RE UP TO, OR... WHAT'S THIS-?!

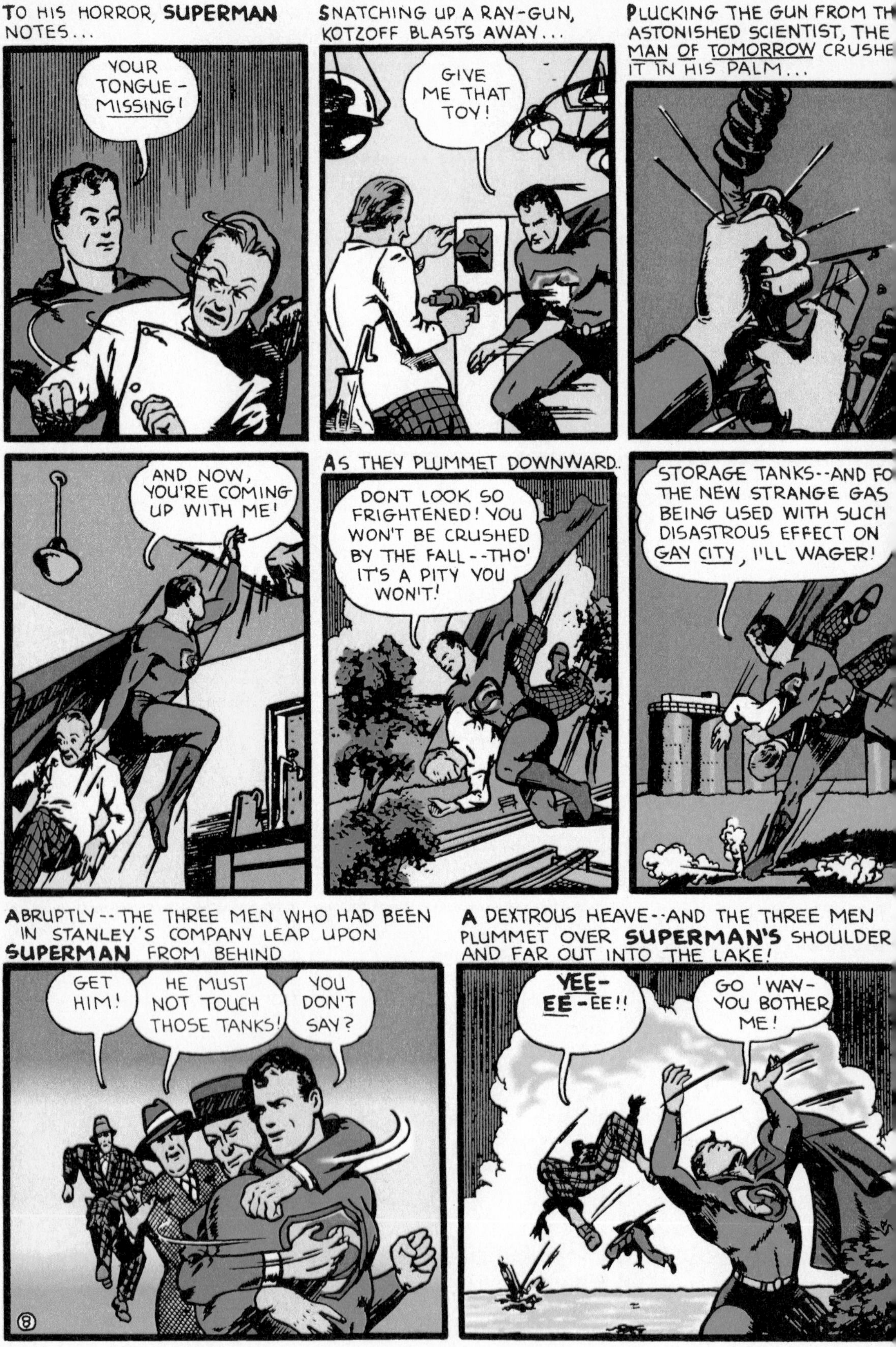
TO HIS HORROR, SUPERMAN NOTES...
YOUR TONGUE - MISSING!
SNATCHING UP A RAY-GUN, KOTZOFF BLASTS AWAY...
GIVE ME THAT TOY!
PLUCKING THE GUN FROM TH ASTONISHED SCIENTIST, THE MAN OF TOMORROW CRUSHE IT IN HIS PALM...
AND NOW, YOU'RE COMING UP WITH ME!
AS THEY PLUMMET DOWNWARD..
DONT LOOK SO FRIGHTENED! YOU WON'T BE CRUSHED BY THE FALL--THO' IT'S A PITY YOU WON'T!
STORAGE TANKS--AND FO THE NEW STRANGE GAS BEING USED WITH SUCH DISASTROUS EFFECT ON GAY CITY, I'LL WAGER!
ABRUPTLY--THE THREE MEN WHO HAD BEEN IN STANLEY'S COMPANY LEAP UPON SUPERMAN FROM BEHIND
GET HIM!
HE MUST NOT TOUCH THOSE TANKS!
YOU DON'T SAY?
8
A DEXTROUS HEAVE--AND THE THREE MEN PLUMMET OVER SUPERMAN'S SHOULDER AND FAR OUT INTO THE LAKE!
YEE-EE-EE!!
GO 'WAY- YOU BOTHER ME!

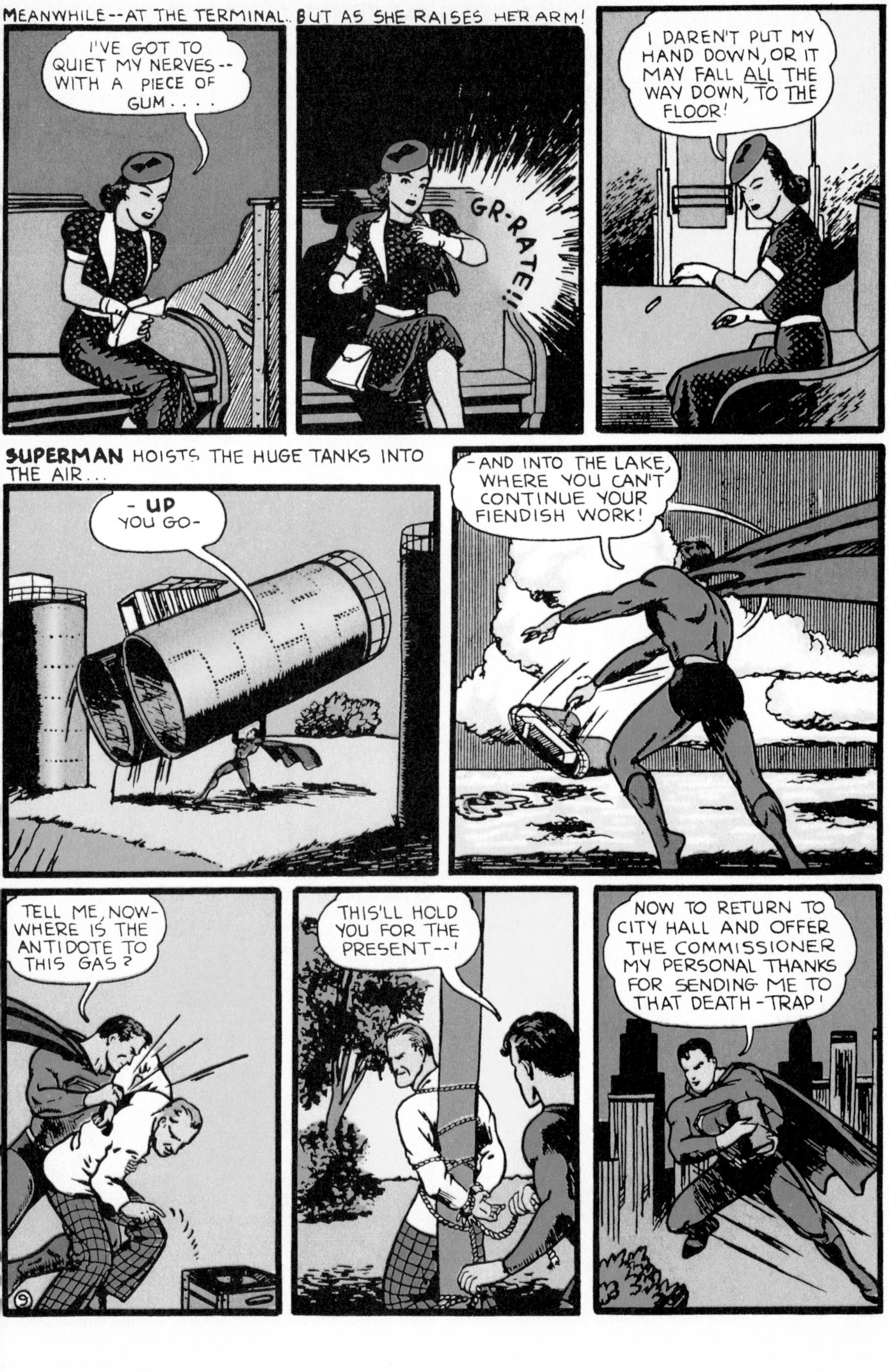
MEANWHILE--AT THE TERMINAL..
I'VE GOT TO QUIET MY NERVES-- WITH A PIECE OF GUM....
BUT AS SHE RAISES HER ARM!
GR-RATE!!
I DAREN'T PUT MY HAND DOWN, OR IT MAY FALL ALL THE WAY DOWN, TO THE FLOOR!
SUPERMAN HOISTS THE HUGE TANKS INTO THE AIR...
- UP YOU GO-
-AND INTO THE LAKE, WHERE YOU CAN'T CONTINUE YOUR FIENDISH WORK!
TELL ME, NOW- WHERE IS THE ANTIDOTE TO THIS GAS?
THIS'LL HOLD YOU FOR THE PRESENT--!
NOW TO RETURN TO CITY HALL AND OFFER THE COMMISSIONER MY PERSONAL THANKS FOR SENDING ME TO THAT DEATH-TRAP!
9

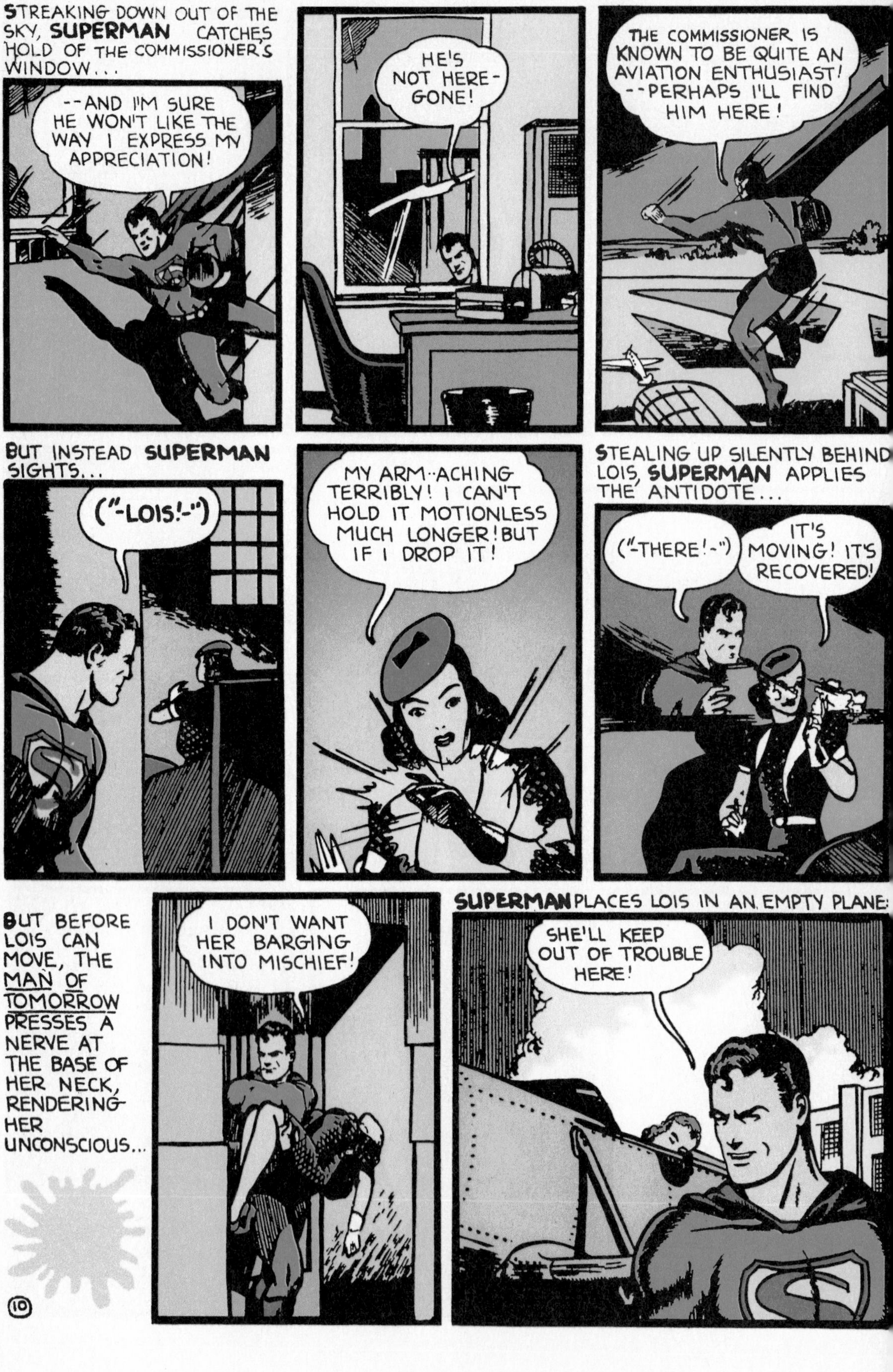
STREAKING DOWN OUT OF THE SKY, SUPERMAN CATCHES HOLD OF THE COMMISSIONER'S WINDOW...
--AND I'M SURE HE WON'T LIKE THE WAY I EXPRESS MY APPRECIATION!
HE'S NOT HERE-GONE!
THE COMMISSIONER IS KNOWN TO BE QUITE AN AVIATION ENTHUSIAST! --PERHAPS I'LL FIND HIM HERE!
BUT INSTEAD SUPERMAN SIGHTS...
("-LOIS!-")
MY ARM--ACHING TERRIBLY! I CAN'T HOLD IT MOTIONLESS MUCH LONGER! BUT IF I DROP IT!
STEALING UP SILENTLY BEHIND LOIS, SUPERMAN APPLIES THE ANTIDOTE...
("-THERE!-")
IT'S MOVING! IT'S RECOVERED!
BUT BEFORE LOIS CAN MOVE, THE MAN OF TOMORROW PRESSES A NERVE AT THE BASE OF HER NECK, RENDERING HER UNCONSCIOUS...
10
I DON'T WANT HER BARGING INTO MISCHIEF!
SUPERMAN PLACES LOIS IN AN EMPTY PLANE:
SHE'LL KEEP OUT OF TROUBLE HERE!

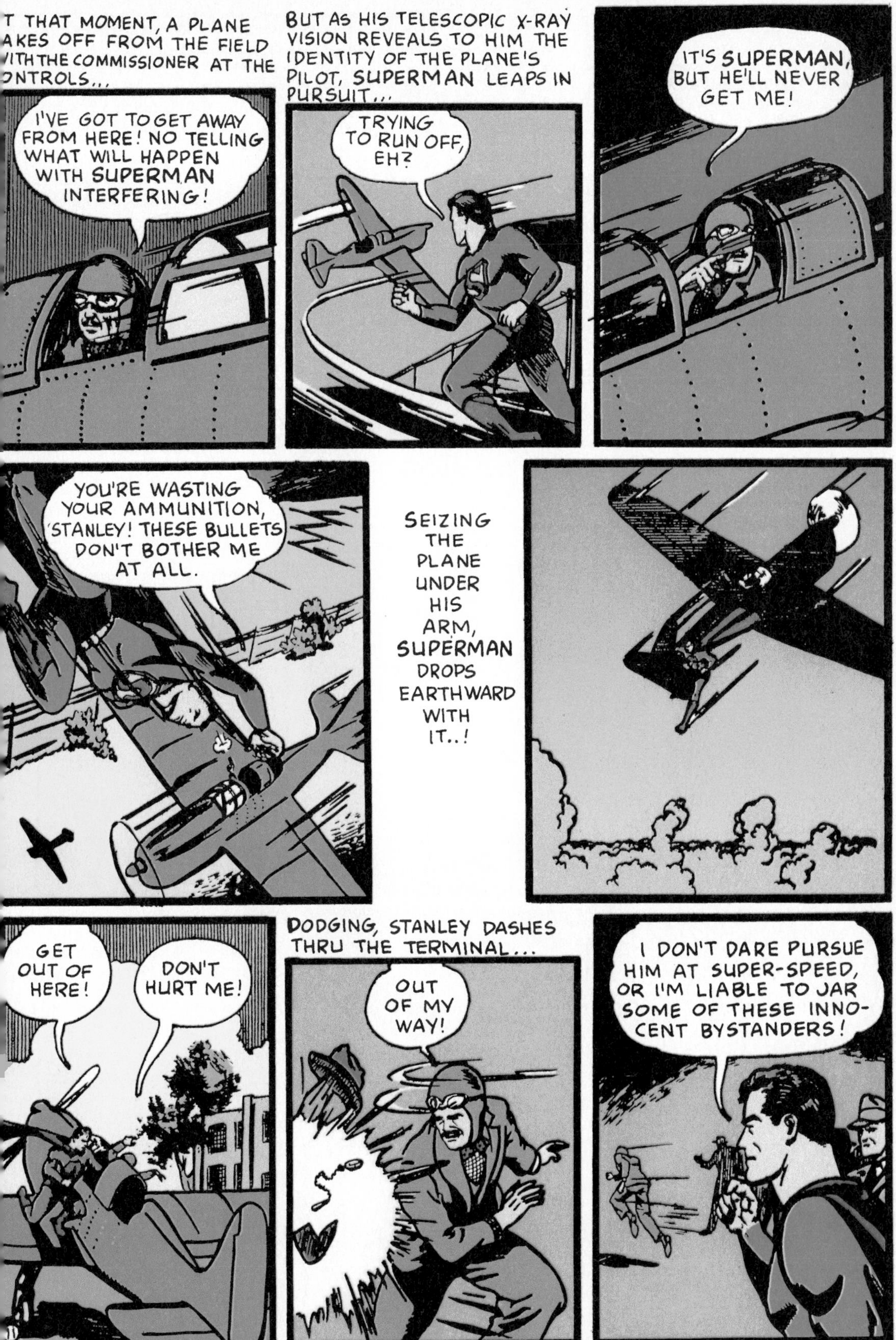
T THAT MOMENT, A PLANE AKES OFF FROM THE FIELD VITH THE COMMISSIONER AT THE ONTROLS...
I'VE GOT TO GET AWAY FROM HERE! NO TELLING WHAT WILL HAPPEN WITH SUPERMAN INTERFERING!
BUT AS HIS TELESCOPIC X-RAY VISION REVEALS TO HIM THE IDENTITY OF THE PLANE'S PILOT, SUPERMAN LEAPS IN PURSUIT...
TRYING TO RUN OFF, EH?
IT'S SUPERMAN, BUT HE'LL NEVER GET ME!
YOU'RE WASTING YOUR AMMUNITION, STANLEY! THESE BULLETS DON'T BOTHER ME AT ALL.
SEIZING THE PLANE UNDER HIS ARM, SUPERMAN DROPS EARTHWARD WITH IT..!
GET OUT OF HERE!
DON'T HURT ME!
DODGING, STANLEY DASHES THRU THE TERMINAL...
OUT OF MY WAY!
I DON'T DARE PURSUE HIM AT SUPER-SPEED, OR I'M LIABLE TO JAR SOME OF THESE INNO-CENT BYSTANDERS!

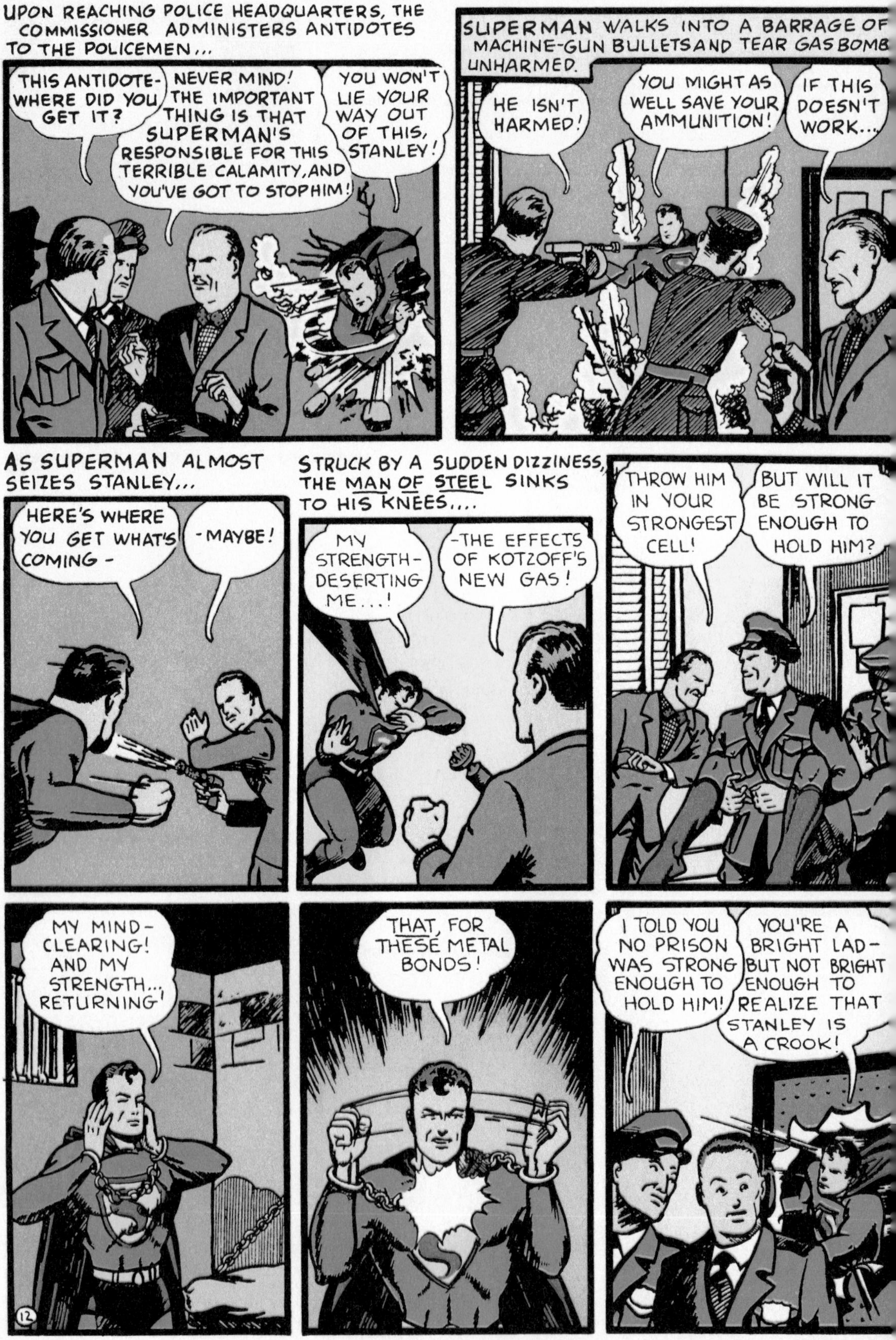
UPON REACHING POLICE HEADQUARTERS, THE COMMISSIONER ADMINISTERS ANTIDOTES TO THE POLICEMEN...
THIS ANTIDOTE- WHERE DID YOU GET IT?
NEVER MIND! THE IMPORTANT THING IS THAT SUPERMAN'S RESPONSIBLE FOR THIS TERRIBLE CALAMITY, AND YOU'VE GOT TO STOP HIM!
YOU WON'T LIE YOUR WAY OUT OF THIS, STANLEY!
SUPERMAN WALKS INTO A BARRAGE OF MACHINE-GUN BULLETS AND TEAR GAS BOMB UNHARMED.
HE ISN'T HARMED!
YOU MIGHT AS WELL SAVE YOUR AMMUNITION!
IF THIS DOESN'T WORK...
AS SUPERMAN ALMOST SEIZES STANLEY...
HERE'S WHERE YOU GET WHAT'S COMING -
-MAYBE!
STRUCK BY A SUDDEN DIZZINESS, THE MAN OF STEEL SINKS TO HIS KNEES....
MY STRENGTH- DESERTING ME...!
-THE EFFECTS OF KOTZOFF'S NEW GAS!
THROW HIM IN YOUR STRONGEST CELL!
BUT WILL IT BE STRONG ENOUGH TO HOLD HIM?
MY MIND- CLEARING! AND MY STRENGTH... RETURNING!
12
THAT, FOR THESE METAL BONDS!
I TOLD YOU NO PRISON WAS STRONG ENOUGH TO HOLD HIM!
YOU'RE A BRIGHT LAD- BUT NOT BRIGHT ENOUGH TO REALIZE THAT STANLEY IS A CROOK!

SUPERMAN STREAKS TO OTZOFF'S LABORATORY TO FIND THE CONSPIRATORS PREPARING TO FLEE...

WE'VE GOT TO LOSE NO TIME IN FLEEING!

SORRY--BUT YOU'RE A LITTLE TOO LATE!

IT'S HIM!

IF IT'S FIGHT YOU WANT, HERE IT IS!

CLEAR THE AIR OF YOUR INVISIBLE AND ODORLESS GAS, AND SPREAD THE ANTIDOTE OVER THE TOWN!

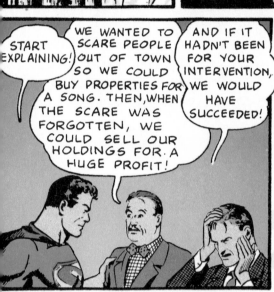

START EXPLAINING!

WE WANTED TO SCARE PEOPLE OUT OF TOWN SO WE COULD BUY PROPERTIES FOR A SONG. THEN, WHEN THE SCARE WAS FORGOTTEN, WE COULD SELL OUR HOLDINGS FOR A HUGE PROFIT!

AND IF IT HADN'T BEEN FOR YOUR INTERVENTION, WE WOULD HAVE SUCCEEDED!

AFTER THE CITY'S AIR HAS BEEN CLEARED OF THE DREAD GAS, SUPERMAN LEAPS OFF WITH HIS CAPTIVES...

WHERE ARE YOU TAKING US?

TO THE STATE CAPITOL!

AT THE CAPITOL... AFTER THE CAPTIVES HAVE CONFESSED TO STATE POLICE...

AND THAT'S THE STORY OF OUR GUILT!

YOU'LL ALL BE DEALT WITH SEVERELY FOR THIS!

THAT'S ALL I WANTED TO HEAR!

REVERTING TO HIS IDENTITY AS CLARK KENT, THE MAN OF TOMORROW RETURNS TO LOIS AS SHE REVIVES...

WH-WHAT HAPPENED?

PLENTY! SUPERMAN HAS FREED THE CITY OF ITS CROOKED OFFICIAL'S MAD DESIGNS!

LATER-- IN METROPOLIS...

A GRAND STORY! BOTH OF YOU SHOULD BE PROUD OF THE SPLENDID WAY YOU HANDLED IT!

THANKS, BOSS!

I'D BE EVEN PROUDER, IF I'D LEARNED SUPERMAN'S TRUE IDENTITY!

THE END.

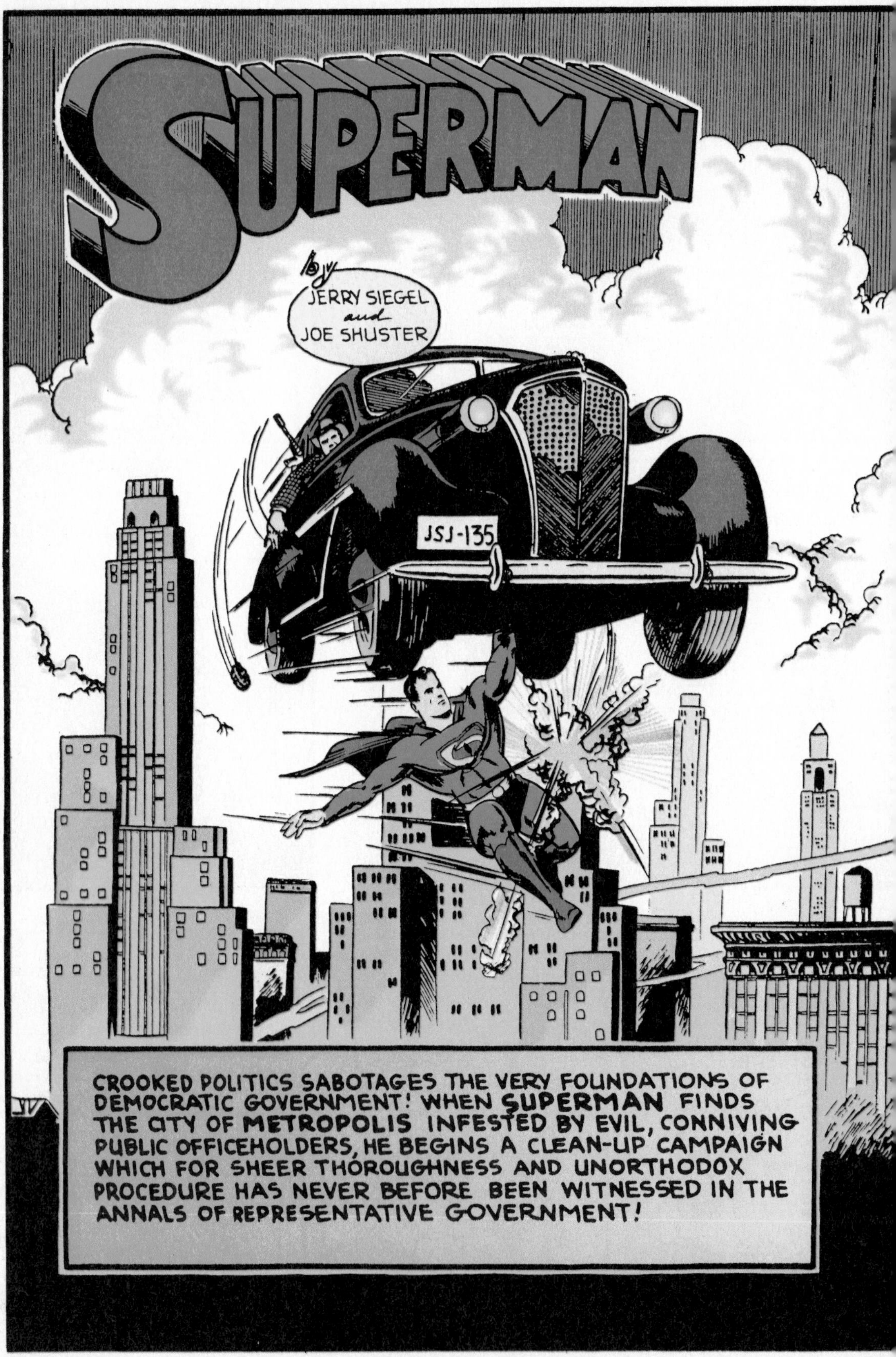
SUPERMAN
by
JERRY SIEGEL
and
JOE SHUSTER
JSJ-135
CROOKED POLITICS SABOTAGES THE VERY FOUNDATIONS OF DEMOCRATIC GOVERNMENT! WHEN SUPERMAN FINDS THE CITY OF METROPOLIS INFESTED BY EVIL, CONNIVING PUBLIC OFFICEHOLDERS, HE BEGINS A CLEAN-UP CAMPAIGN WHICH FOR SHEER THOROUGHNESS AND UNORTHODOX PROCEDURE HAS NEVER BEFORE BEEN WITNESSED IN THE ANNALS OF REPRESENTATIVE GOVERNMENT!

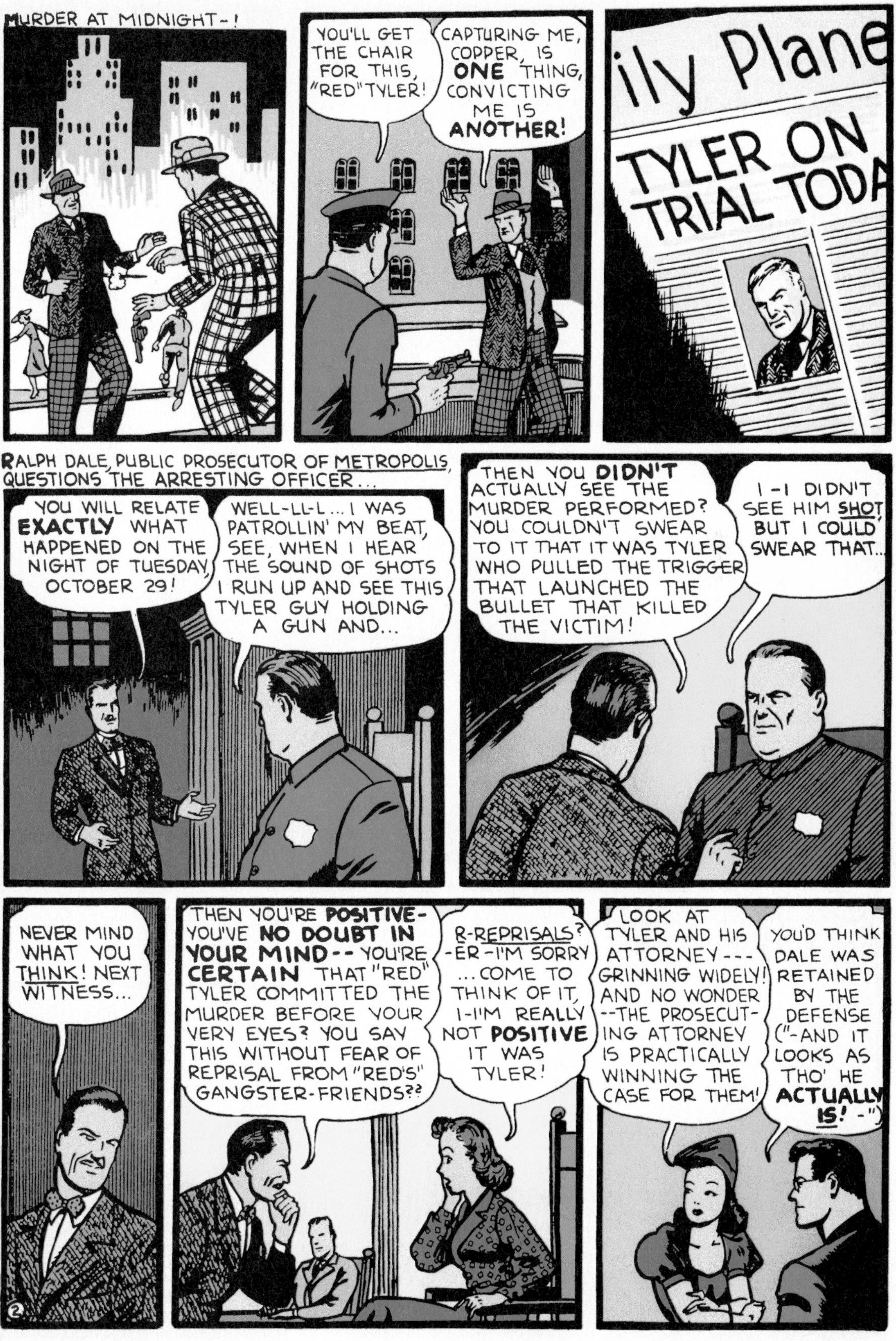
MURDER AT MIDNIGHT-!
YOU'LL GET THE CHAIR FOR THIS, "RED" TYLER!
CAPTURING ME, COPPER, IS ONE THING, CONVICTING ME IS ANOTHER!
ily Plane
TYLER ON TRIAL TODA
RALPH DALE, PUBLIC PROSECUTOR OF METROPOLIS, QUESTIONS THE ARRESTING OFFICER...
YOU WILL RELATE EXACTLY WHAT HAPPENED ON THE NIGHT OF TUESDAY, OCTOBER 29!
WELL-LL-L... I WAS PATROLLIN' MY BEAT, SEE, WHEN I HEAR THE SOUND OF SHOTS I RUN UP AND SEE THIS TYLER GUY HOLDING A GUN AND...
THEN YOU DIDN'T ACTUALLY SEE THE MURDER PERFORMED? YOU COULDN'T SWEAR TO IT THAT IT WAS TYLER WHO PULLED THE TRIGGER THAT LAUNCHED THE BULLET THAT KILLED THE VICTIM!
I-I DIDN'T SEE HIM SHOT, BUT I COULD SWEAR THAT...
NEVER MIND WHAT YOU THINK! NEXT WITNESS...
THEN YOU'RE POSITIVE-YOU'VE NO DOUBT IN YOUR MIND-- YOU'RE CERTAIN THAT "RED" TYLER COMMITTED THE MURDER BEFORE YOUR VERY EYES? YOU SAY THIS WITHOUT FEAR OF REPRISAL FROM "RED'S" GANGSTER-FRIENDS??
R-REPRISALS? -ER-I'M SORRY ...COME TO THINK OF IT, I-I'M REALLY NOT POSITIVE IT WAS TYLER!
LOOK AT TYLER AND HIS ATTORNEY--- GRINNING WIDELY! AND NO WONDER --THE PROSECUTING ATTORNEY IS PRACTICALLY WINNING THE CASE FOR THEM!
YOU'D THINK DALE WAS RETAINED BY THE DEFENSE ("-AND IT LOOKS AS THO' HE ACTUALLY IS! -")
2

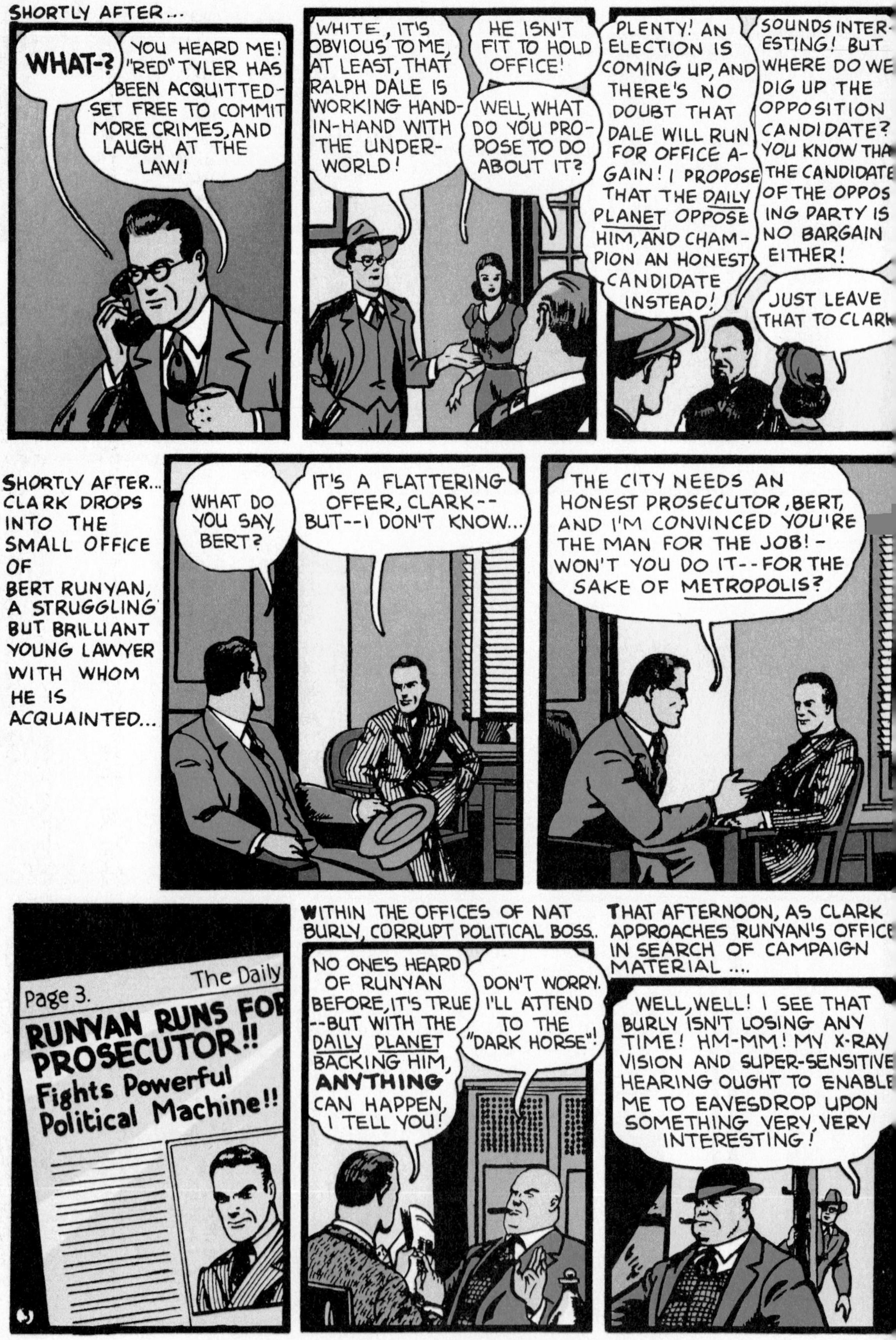
SHORTLY AFTER...
WHAT-?
YOU HEARD ME! "RED" TYLER HAS BEEN ACQUITTED-SET FREE TO COMMIT MORE CRIMES, AND LAUGH AT THE LAW!
WHITE, IT'S OBVIOUS TO ME, AT LEAST, THAT RALPH DALE IS WORKING HAND-IN-HAND WITH THE UNDER-WORLD!
HE ISN'T FIT TO HOLD OFFICE!
WELL, WHAT DO YOU PRO-POSE TO DO ABOUT IT?
PLENTY! AN ELECTION IS COMING UP, AND THERE'S NO DOUBT THAT DALE WILL RUN FOR OFFICE A-GAIN! I PROPOSE THAT THE DAILY PLANET OPPOSE HIM, AND CHAM-PION AN HONEST CANDIDATE INSTEAD!
SOUNDS INTER-ESTING! BUT WHERE DO WE DIG UP THE OPPOSITION CANDIDATE? YOU KNOW THA THE CANDIDATE OF THE OPPOS ING PARTY IS NO BARGAIN EITHER!
JUST LEAVE THAT TO CLARK
SHORTLY AFTER... CLARK DROPS INTO THE SMALL OFFICE OF BERT RUNYAN, A STRUGGLING BUT BRILLIANT YOUNG LAWYER WITH WHOM HE IS ACQUAINTED...
WHAT DO YOU SAY, BERT?
IT'S A FLATTERING OFFER, CLARK-- BUT--I DON'T KNOW...
THE CITY NEEDS AN HONEST PROSECUTOR, BERT, AND I'M CONVINCED YOU'RE THE MAN FOR THE JOB! - WON'T YOU DO IT--FOR THE SAKE OF METROPOLIS?
The Daily
Page 3.
RUNYAN RUNS FOR PROSECUTOR!!
Fights Powerful Political Machine!!
WITHIN THE OFFICES OF NAT BURLY, CORRUPT POLITICAL BOSS..
NO ONE'S HEARD OF RUNYAN BEFORE, IT'S TRUE --BUT WITH THE DAILY PLANET BACKING HIM, ANYTHING CAN HAPPEN, I TELL YOU!
DON'T WORRY. I'LL ATTEND TO THE "DARK HORSE"!
THAT AFTERNOON, AS CLARK APPROACHES RUNYAN'S OFFICE IN SEARCH OF CAMPAIGN MATERIAL ....
WELL, WELL! I SEE THAT BURLY ISN'T LOSING ANY TIME! HM-MM! MY X-RAY VISION AND SUPER-SENSITIVE HEARING OUGHT TO ENABLE ME TO EAVESDROP UPON SOMETHING VERY, VERY INTERESTING!

YOU'RE RUNYAN! ME, I'M NAT BURLY--YOU'VE HEARD OF ME, NO DOUBT!

YES - I'VE HEARD OF YOU! I'VE HEARD A GREAT DEAL ABOUT YOU!

THEN YOU KNOW I ALWAYS GET WHAT I WANT...ONE WAY OR ANOTHER. I LIKE TO WORK THINGS OUT IN A NICE FRIENDLY WAY. BUT WHEN A STUBBORN CUSS INSISTS ON GETTING TOUGH, WHY...

CUT OUT THE TRIMMINGS. WHAT HAVE YOU COME TO TELL ME?

WITHDRAW FROM THE RACE!-DO SO, AND I GUARANTEE YOU THAT YOU'LL GET SO MUCH BUSINESS YOU'LL HAVE TO EXPAND THIS OFFICE TO TAKE UP THE ENTIRE FLOOR!

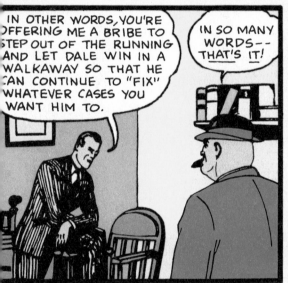

IN OTHER WORDS, YOU'RE OFFERING ME A BRIBE TO STEP OUT OF THE RUNNING AND LET DALE WIN IN A WALKAWAY SO THAT HE CAN CONTINUE TO "FIX" WHATEVER CASES YOU WANT HIM TO.

IN SO MANY WORDS-- THAT'S IT!

WELL, HERE'S A FEW WORDS YOU WON'T LIKE! I CAN'T BE BRIBED! I'M NOT INTERESTED IN YOUR FILTHY MONEY!-- GET YOUR FAT CARCASS OUT OF THAT CHAIR AND OUT OF THE DOOR, BEFORE...

SO IT'S TROUBLE YOU WANT, EH?- WELL, MY FINE YOUNG IDEALIST, I'LL SEE TO IT THAT YOU GET PLENTY!

OUTA MY WAY!

ER-- EXCUSE ME!

SHORTLY AFTER, BURLY ENTERS AN APARTMENT IN THE TOUGHEST PART OF TOWN...

THOUGHT I WAS FOOLING, EH? YOUNG WHIPPERSNAPPER! I'LL MAKE HIM REGRET THE DAY HE EVER TALKED BACK TO NAT BURLY!

WATCHING BURLY'S MOVEMENTS FROM ATOP A HIGH NEARBY SKYSCRAPER--THE FOE OF ALL EVIL-SUPERMAN!

WONDER WHAT UNSAVORY BUSINESS THAT SCOUNDREL IS UP TO NOW?

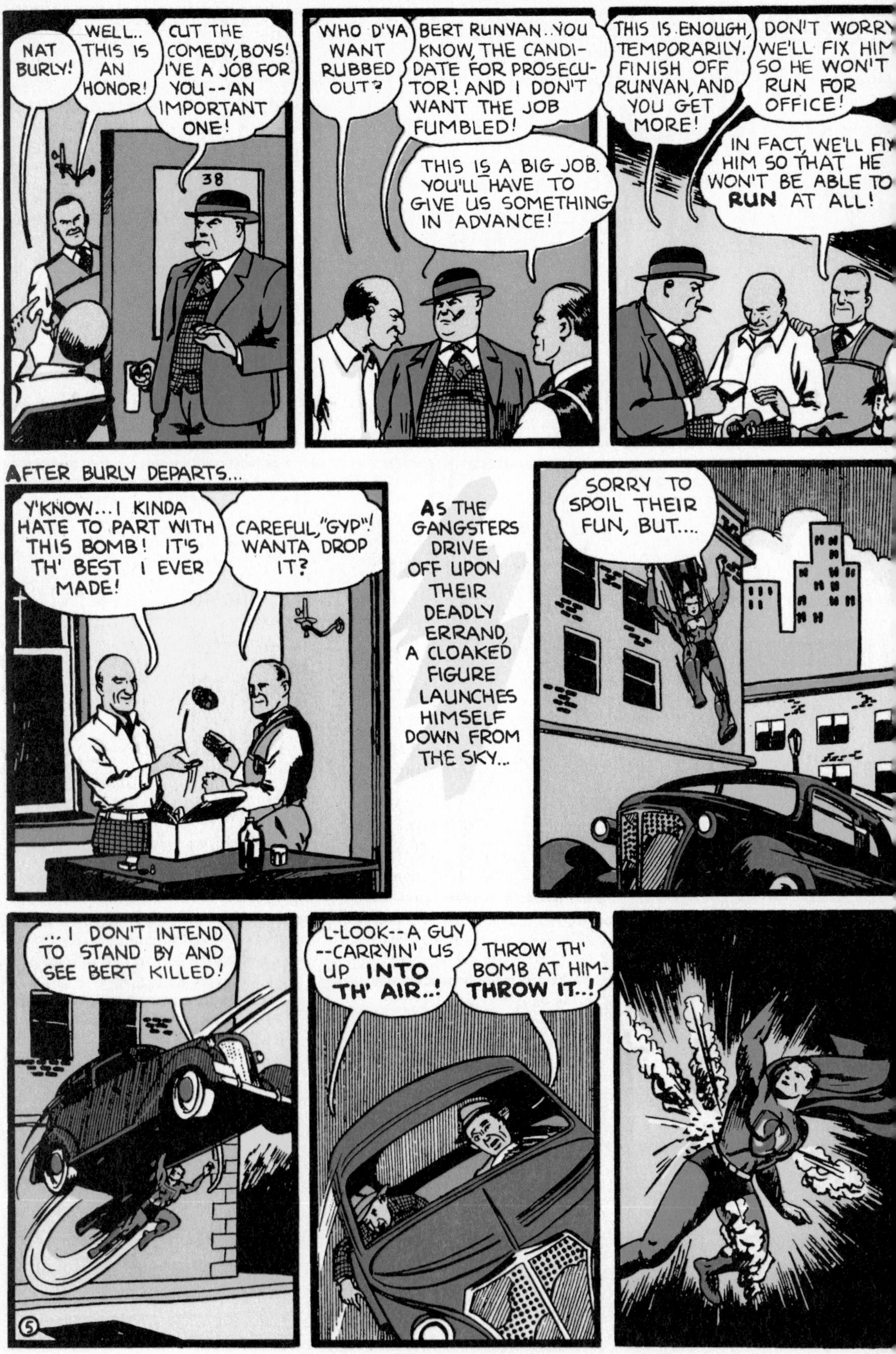
NAT BURLY!
WELL.. THIS IS AN HONOR!
CUT THE COMEDY, BOYS! I'VE A JOB FOR YOU--AN IMPORTANT ONE!
38
WHO D'YA WANT RUBBED OUT?
BERT RUNYAN..YOU KNOW, THE CANDIDATE FOR PROSECUTOR! AND I DON'T WANT THE JOB FUMBLED!
THIS IS A BIG JOB. YOU'LL HAVE TO GIVE US SOMETHING IN ADVANCE!
THIS IS ENOUGH, TEMPORARILY. FINISH OFF RUNYAN, AND YOU GET MORE!
DON'T WORRY WE'LL FIX HIM SO HE WON'T RUN FOR OFFICE!
IN FACT, WE'LL FIX HIM SO THAT HE WON'T BE ABLE TO RUN AT ALL!
AFTER BURLY DEPARTS...
Y'KNOW...I KINDA HATE TO PART WITH THIS BOMB! IT'S TH' BEST I EVER MADE!
CAREFUL, "GYP"! WANTA DROP IT?
AS THE GANGSTERS DRIVE OFF UPON THEIR DEADLY ERRAND, A CLOAKED FIGURE LAUNCHES HIMSELF DOWN FROM THE SKY...
SORRY TO SPOIL THEIR FUN, BUT....
...I DON'T INTEND TO STAND BY AND SEE BERT KILLED!
5
L-LOOK--A GUY--CARRYIN' US UP INTO TH' AIR..!
THROW TH' BOMB AT HIM-THROW IT..!

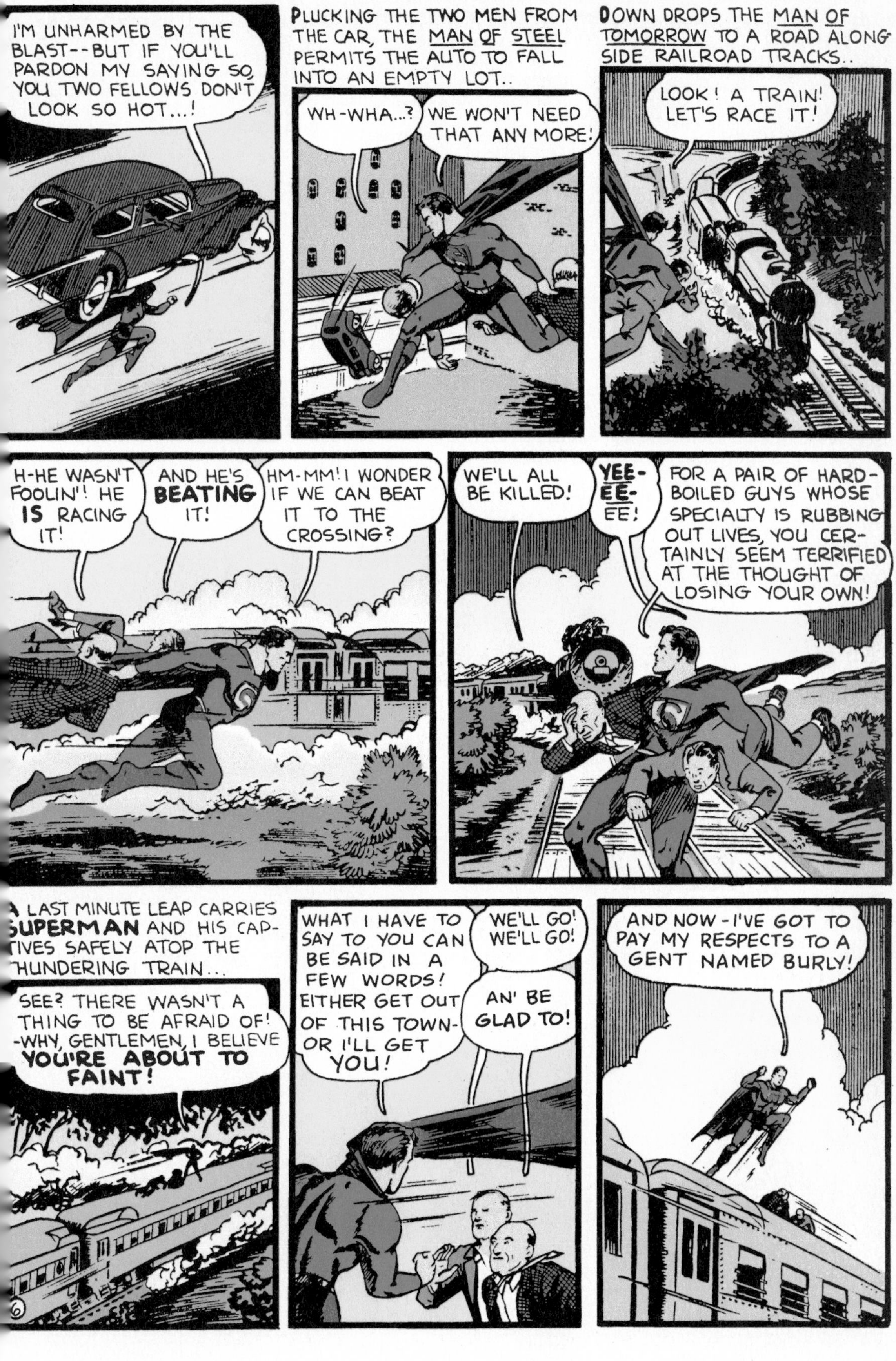
I'M UNHARMED BY THE BLAST--BUT IF YOU'LL PARDON MY SAYING SO, YOU TWO FELLOWS DON'T LOOK SO HOT...!
PLUCKING THE TWO MEN FROM THE CAR, THE MAN OF STEEL PERMITS THE AUTO TO FALL INTO AN EMPTY LOT..
WH-WHA...?
WE WON'T NEED THAT ANY MORE!
DOWN DROPS THE MAN OF TOMORROW TO A ROAD ALONGSIDE RAILROAD TRACKS..
LOOK! A TRAIN! LET'S RACE IT!
H-HE WASN'T FOOLIN'! HE IS RACING IT!
AND HE'S BEATING IT!
HM-MM! I WONDER IF WE CAN BEAT IT TO THE CROSSING?
WE'LL ALL BE KILLED!
YEE-EE-EE!
FOR A PAIR OF HARD-BOILED GUYS WHOSE SPECIALTY IS RUBBING OUT LIVES, YOU CERTAINLY SEEM TERRIFIED AT THE THOUGHT OF LOSING YOUR OWN!
A LAST MINUTE LEAP CARRIES SUPERMAN AND HIS CAPTIVES SAFELY ATOP THE THUNDERING TRAIN...
SEE? THERE WASN'T A THING TO BE AFRAID OF! -WHY, GENTLEMEN, I BELIEVE YOU'RE ABOUT TO FAINT!
WHAT I HAVE TO SAY TO YOU CAN BE SAID IN A FEW WORDS! EITHER GET OUT OF THIS TOWN- OR I'LL GET YOU!
WE'LL GO! WE'LL GO!
AN' BE GLAD TO!
AND NOW - I'VE GOT TO PAY MY RESPECTS TO A GENT NAMED BURLY!

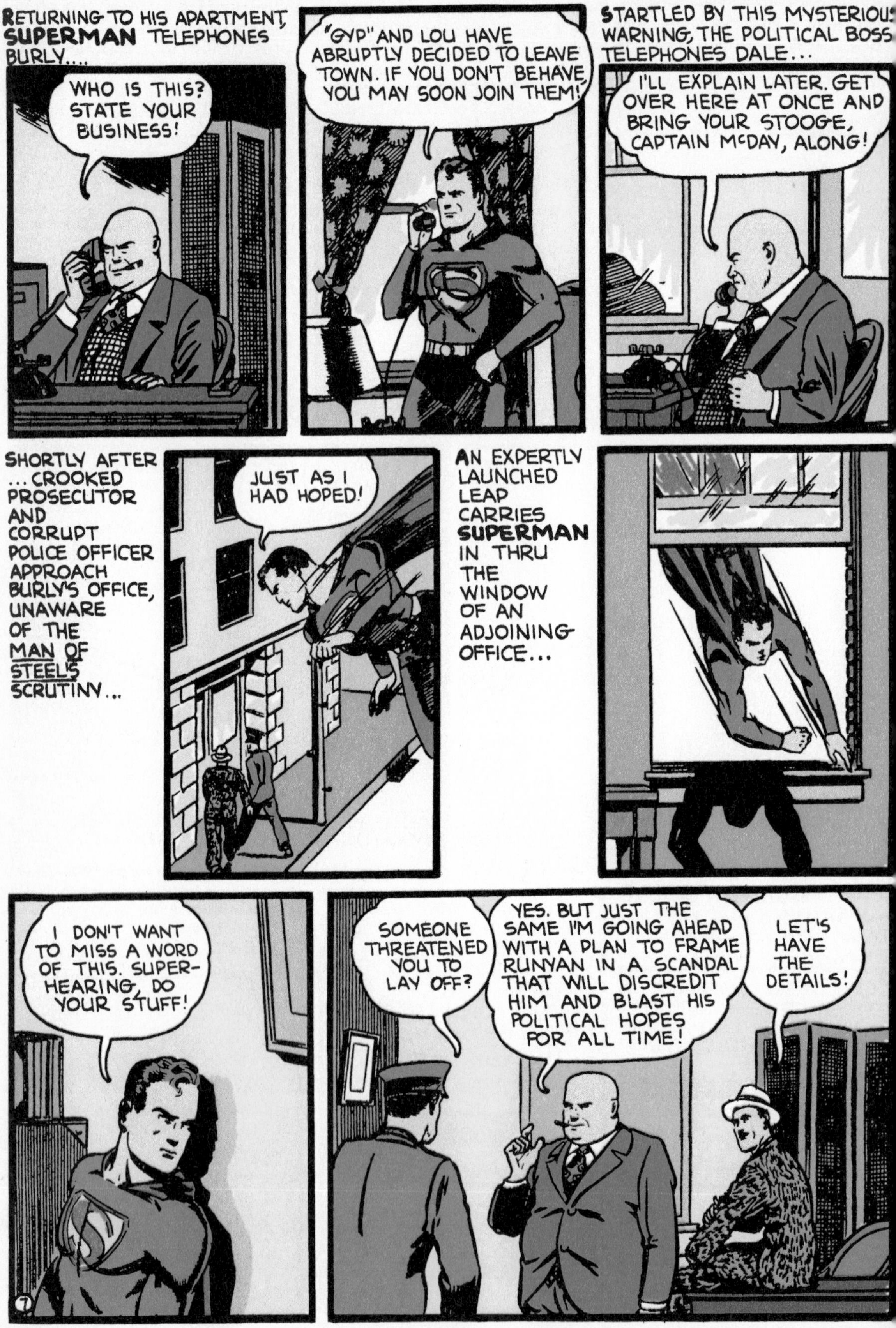
RETURNING TO HIS APARTMENT, SUPERMAN TELEPHONES BURLY....
WHO IS THIS? STATE YOUR BUSINESS!
"GYP" AND LOU HAVE ABRUPTLY DECIDED TO LEAVE TOWN. IF YOU DON'T BEHAVE, YOU MAY SOON JOIN THEM!
STARTLED BY THIS MYSTERIOUS WARNING, THE POLITICAL BOSS TELEPHONES DALE...
I'LL EXPLAIN LATER. GET OVER HERE AT ONCE AND BRING YOUR STOOGE, CAPTAIN McDAY, ALONG!
SHORTLY AFTER ...CROOKED PROSECUTOR AND CORRUPT POLICE OFFICER APPROACH BURLY'S OFFICE, UNAWARE OF THE MAN OF STEEL'S SCRUTINY...
JUST AS I HAD HOPED!
AN EXPERTLY LAUNCHED LEAP CARRIES SUPERMAN IN THRU THE WINDOW OF AN ADJOINING OFFICE...
I DON'T WANT TO MISS A WORD OF THIS. SUPER-HEARING, DO YOUR STUFF!
SOMEONE THREATENED YOU TO LAY OFF?
YES. BUT JUST THE SAME I'M GOING AHEAD WITH A PLAN TO FRAME RUNYAN IN A SCANDAL THAT WILL DISCREDIT HIM AND BLAST HIS POLITICAL HOPES FOR ALL TIME!
LET'S HAVE THE DETAILS!
7

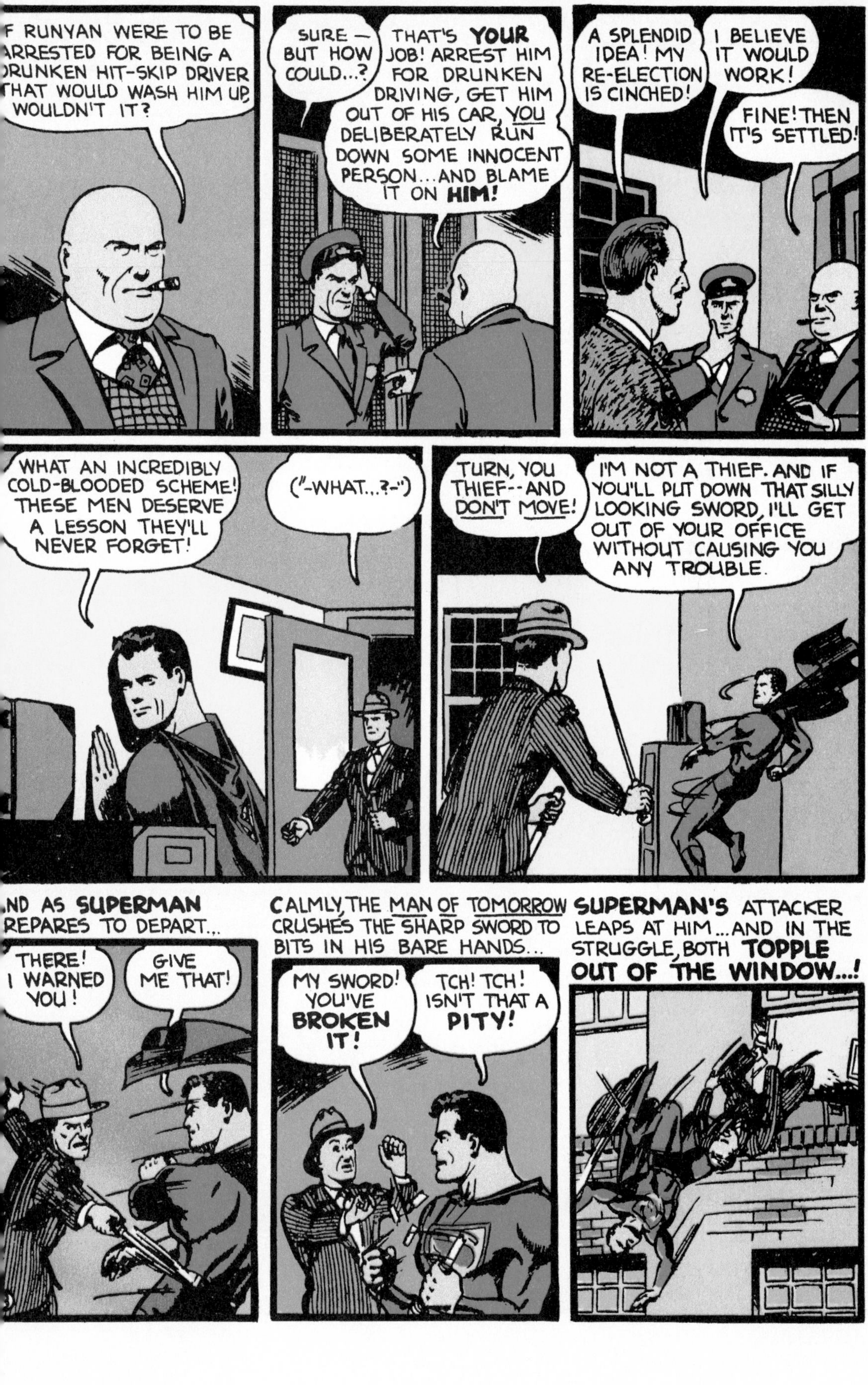
F RUNYAN WERE TO BE ARRESTED FOR BEING A DRUNKEN HIT-SKIP DRIVER THAT WOULD WASH HIM UP, WOULDN'T IT?
SURE — BUT HOW COULD...?
THAT'S YOUR JOB! ARREST HIM FOR DRUNKEN DRIVING, GET HIM OUT OF HIS CAR, YOU DELIBERATELY RUN DOWN SOME INNOCENT PERSON... AND BLAME IT ON HIM!
A SPLENDID IDEA! MY RE-ELECTION IS CINCHED!
I BELIEVE IT WOULD WORK!
FINE! THEN IT'S SETTLED!
WHAT AN INCREDIBLY COLD-BLOODED SCHEME! THESE MEN DESERVE A LESSON THEY'LL NEVER FORGET!
("-WHAT...?-")
TURN, YOU THIEF--AND DON'T MOVE!
I'M NOT A THIEF. AND IF YOU'LL PUT DOWN THAT SILLY LOOKING SWORD, I'LL GET OUT OF YOUR OFFICE WITHOUT CAUSING YOU ANY TROUBLE.
ND AS SUPERMAN REPARES TO DEPART...
THERE! I WARNED YOU!
GIVE ME THAT!
CALMLY, THE MAN OF TOMORROW CRUSHES THE SHARP SWORD TO BITS IN HIS BARE HANDS...
MY SWORD! YOU'VE BROKEN IT!
TCH! TCH! ISN'T THAT A PITY!
SUPERMAN'S ATTACKER LEAPS AT HIM... AND IN THE STRUGGLE, BOTH TOPPLE OUT OF THE WINDOW...!

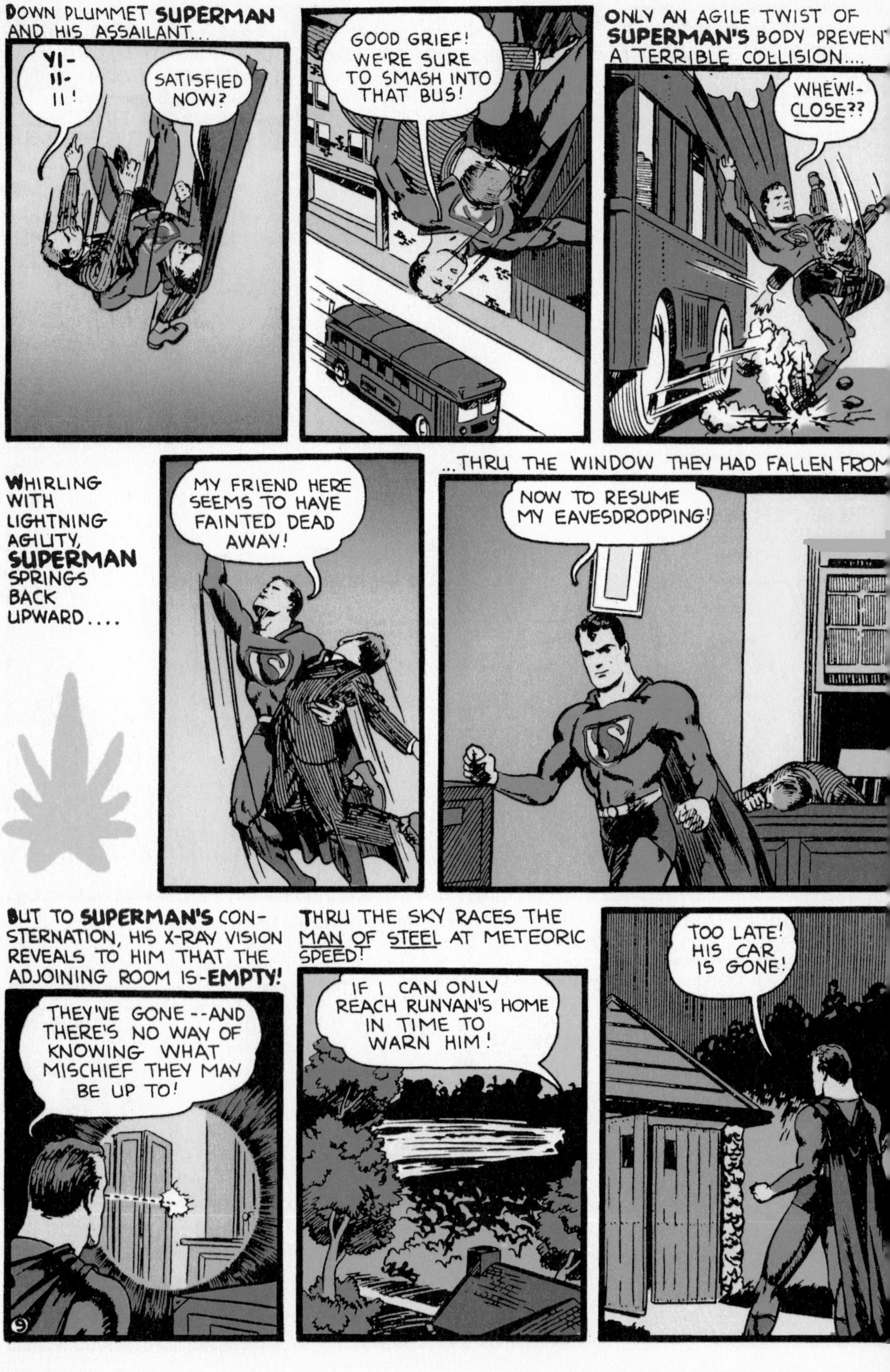
DOWN PLUMMET SUPERMAN AND HIS ASSAILANT...
YI-II-II!
SATISFIED NOW?
GOOD GRIEF! WE'RE SURE TO SMASH INTO THAT BUS!
ONLY AN AGILE TWIST OF SUPERMAN'S BODY PREVEN
A TERRIBLE COLLISION....
WHEW!- CLOSE??
WHIRLING WITH LIGHTNING AGILITY, SUPERMAN SPRINGS BACK UPWARD....
MY FRIEND HERE SEEMS TO HAVE FAINTED DEAD AWAY!
...THRU THE WINDOW THEY HAD FALLEN FROM
NOW TO RESUME MY EAVESDROPPING!
BUT TO SUPERMAN'S CONSTERNATION, HIS X-RAY VISION REVEALS TO HIM THAT THE ADJOINING ROOM IS-EMPTY!
THEY'VE GONE--AND THERE'S NO WAY OF KNOWING WHAT MISCHIEF THEY MAY BE UP TO!
9
THRU THE SKY RACES THE MAN OF STEEL AT METEORIC SPEED!
IF I CAN ONLY REACH RUNYAN'S HOME IN TIME TO WARN HIM!
TOO LATE! HIS CAR IS GONE!

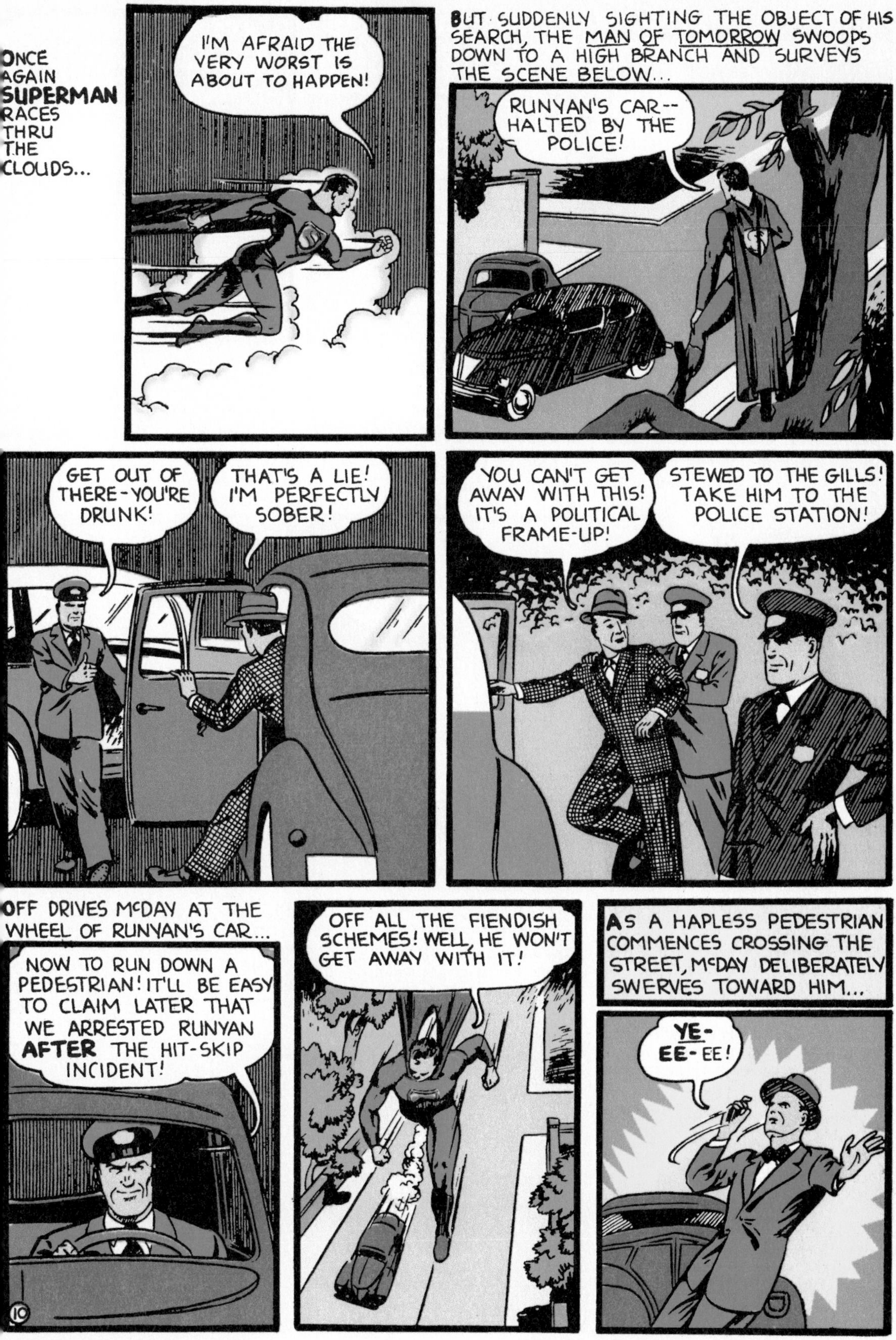
ONCE AGAIN SUPERMAN RACES THRU THE CLOUDS...
I'M AFRAID THE VERY WORST IS ABOUT TO HAPPEN!
BUT SUDDENLY SIGHTING THE OBJECT OF HIS SEARCH, THE MAN OF TOMORROW SWOOPS DOWN TO A HIGH BRANCH AND SURVEYS THE SCENE BELOW...
RUNYAN'S CAR-- HALTED BY THE POLICE!
GET OUT OF THERE-YOU'RE DRUNK!
THAT'S A LIE! I'M PERFECTLY SOBER!
YOU CAN'T GET AWAY WITH THIS! IT'S A POLITICAL FRAME-UP!
STEWED TO THE GILLS! TAKE HIM TO THE POLICE STATION!
OFF DRIVES McDAY AT THE WHEEL OF RUNYAN'S CAR...
NOW TO RUN DOWN A PEDESTRIAN! IT'LL BE EASY TO CLAIM LATER THAT WE ARRESTED RUNYAN AFTER THE HIT-SKIP INCIDENT!
10
OFF ALL THE FIENDISH SCHEMES! WELL, HE WON'T GET AWAY WITH IT!
AS A HAPLESS PEDESTRIAN COMMENCES CROSSING THE STREET, McDAY DELIBERATELY SWERVES TOWARD HIM...
YE-EE-EE!

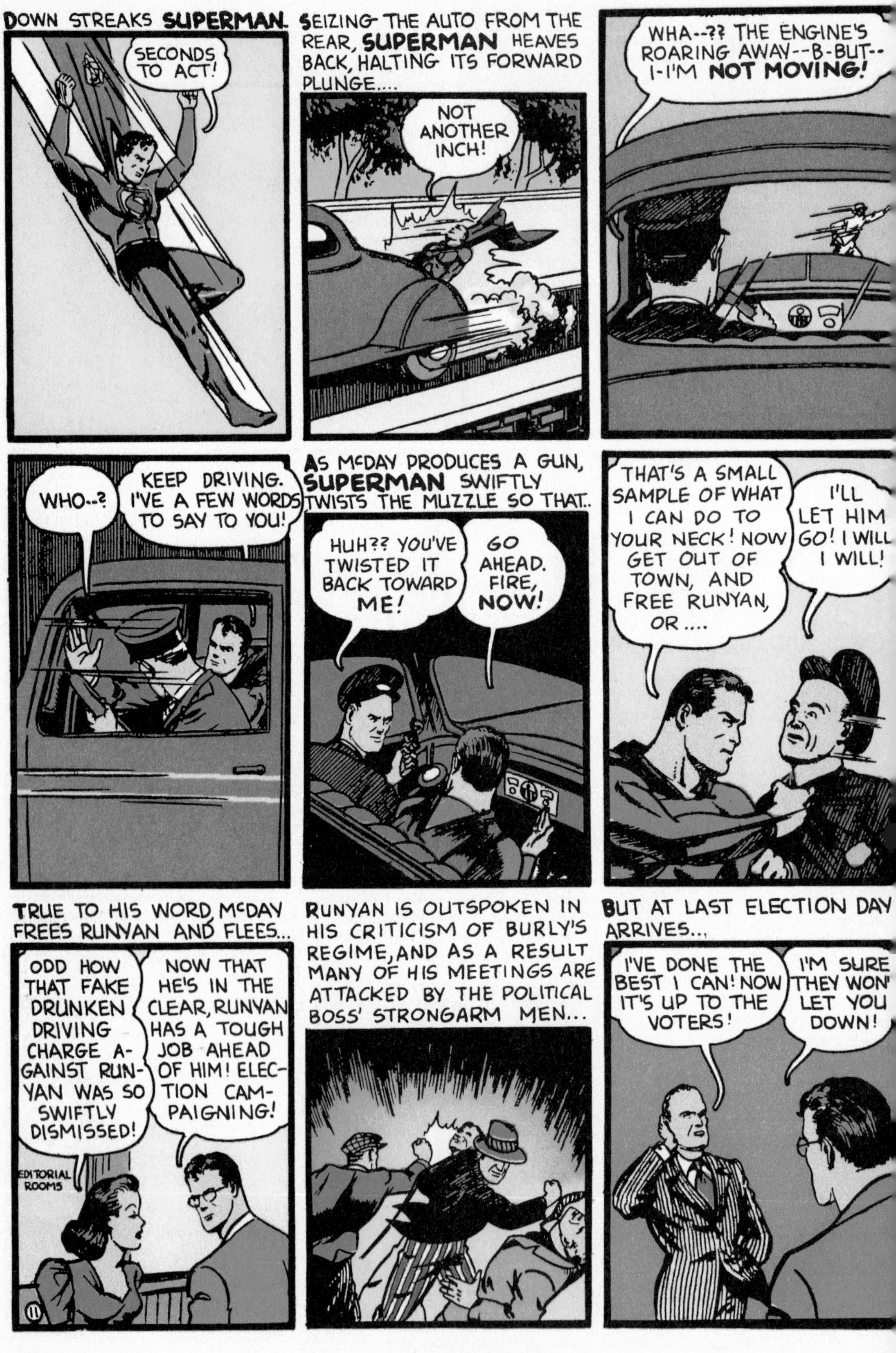
DOWN STREAKS SUPERMAN.
SECONDS TO ACT!
SEIZING THE AUTO FROM THE REAR, SUPERMAN HEAVES BACK, HALTING ITS FORWARD PLUNGE....
NOT ANOTHER INCH!
WHA--?? THE ENGINE'S ROARING AWAY--B-BUT--I-I'M NOT MOVING!
WHO--?
KEEP DRIVING. I'VE A FEW WORDS TO SAY TO YOU!
AS McDAY PRODUCES A GUN, SUPERMAN SWIFTLY TWISTS THE MUZZLE SO THAT..
HUH?? YOU'VE TWISTED IT BACK TOWARD ME!
GO AHEAD. FIRE, NOW!
THAT'S A SMALL SAMPLE OF WHAT I CAN DO TO YOUR NECK! NOW GET OUT OF TOWN, AND FREE RUNYAN, OR ....
I'LL LET HIM GO! I WILL I WILL!
TRUE TO HIS WORD, McDAY FREES RUNYAN AND FLEES...
ODD HOW THAT FAKE DRUNKEN DRIVING CHARGE AGAINST RUNYAN WAS SO SWIFTLY DISMISSED!
NOW THAT HE'S IN THE CLEAR, RUNYAN HAS A TOUGH JOB AHEAD OF HIM! ELECTION CAMPAIGNING!
EDITORIAL ROOMS
11
RUNYAN IS OUTSPOKEN IN HIS CRITICISM OF BURLY'S REGIME, AND AS A RESULT MANY OF HIS MEETINGS ARE ATTACKED BY THE POLITICAL BOSS' STRONGARM MEN...
BUT AT LAST ELECTION DAY ARRIVES...
I'VE DONE THE BEST I CAN! NOW IT'S UP TO THE VOTERS!
I'M SURE THEY WON' LET YOU DOWN!

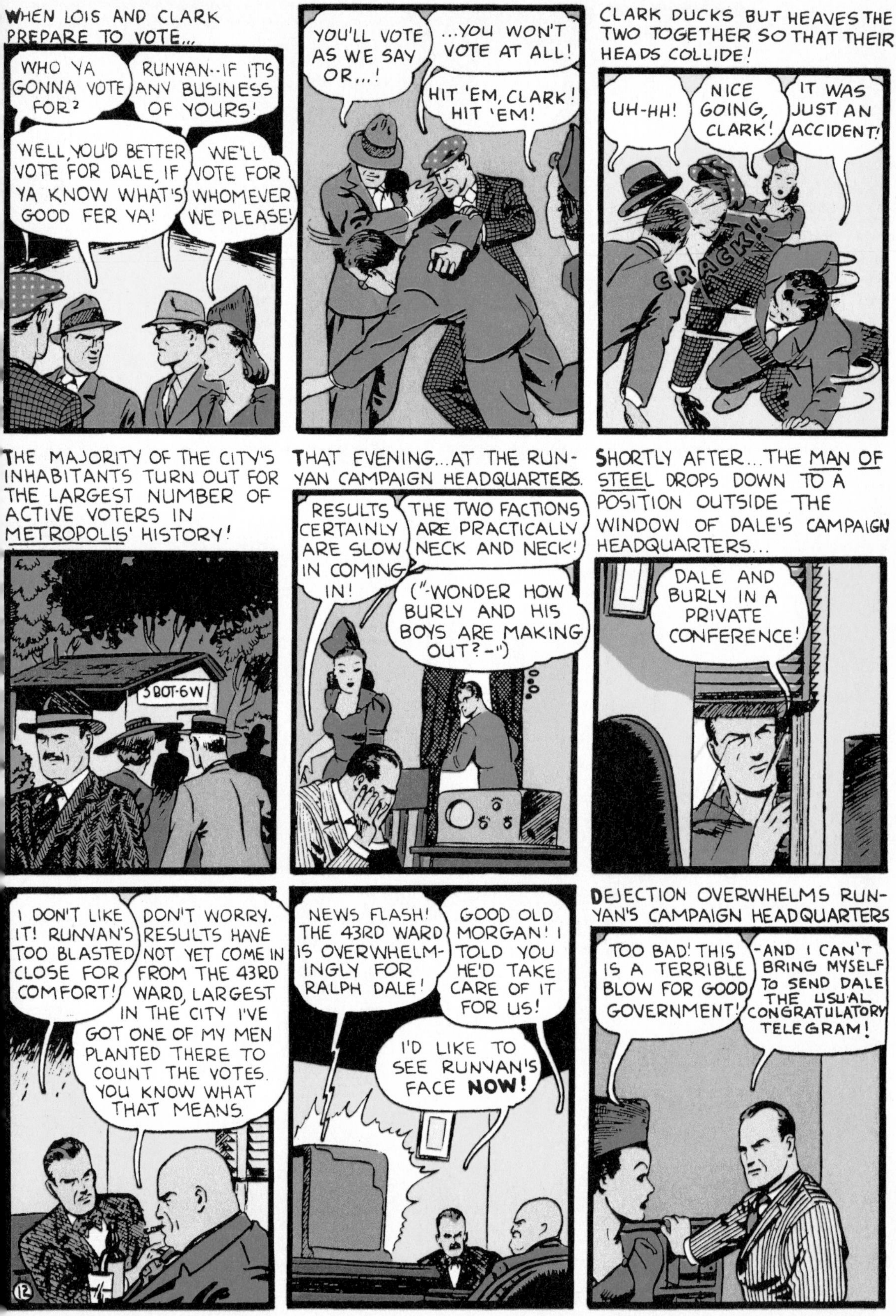
WHEN LOIS AND CLARK PREPARE TO VOTE...
WHO YA GONNA VOTE FOR?
RUNYAN--IF IT'S ANY BUSINESS OF YOURS!
WELL, YOU'D BETTER VOTE FOR DALE, IF YA KNOW WHAT'S GOOD FER YA!
WE'LL VOTE FOR WHOMEVER WE PLEASE!
YOU'LL VOTE AS WE SAY OR...!
...YOU WON'T VOTE AT ALL!
HIT 'EM, CLARK! HIT 'EM!
CLARK DUCKS BUT HEAVES THE TWO TOGETHER SO THAT THEIR HEADS COLLIDE!
UH-HH!
NICE GOING, CLARK!
IT WAS JUST AN ACCIDENT!
CRACK!!
THE MAJORITY OF THE CITY'S INHABITANTS TURN OUT FOR THE LARGEST NUMBER OF ACTIVE VOTERS IN METROPOLIS' HISTORY!
3 BOT-6 W
THAT EVENING... AT THE RUNYAN CAMPAIGN HEADQUARTERS.
RESULTS CERTAINLY ARE SLOW IN COMING IN!
THE TWO FACTIONS ARE PRACTICALLY NECK AND NECK!
("-WONDER HOW BURLY AND HIS BOYS ARE MAKING OUT? -")
SHORTLY AFTER... THE MAN OF STEEL DROPS DOWN TO A POSITION OUTSIDE THE WINDOW OF DALE'S CAMPAIGN HEADQUARTERS...
DALE AND BURLY IN A PRIVATE CONFERENCE!
I DON'T LIKE IT! RUNYAN'S TOO BLASTED CLOSE FOR COMFORT!
DON'T WORRY. RESULTS HAVE NOT YET COME IN FROM THE 43RD WARD, LARGEST IN THE CITY. I'VE GOT ONE OF MY MEN PLANTED THERE TO COUNT THE VOTES. YOU KNOW WHAT THAT MEANS.
12
NEWS FLASH! THE 43RD WARD IS OVERWHELMINGLY FOR RALPH DALE!
GOOD OLD MORGAN! I TOLD YOU HE'D TAKE CARE OF IT FOR US!
I'D LIKE TO SEE RUNYAN'S FACE NOW!
DEJECTION OVERWHELMS RUNYAN'S CAMPAIGN HEADQUARTERS
TOO BAD! THIS IS A TERRIBLE BLOW FOR GOOD GOVERNMENT!
-AND I CAN'T BRING MYSELF TO SEND DALE THE USUAL CONGRATULATORY TELEGRAM!

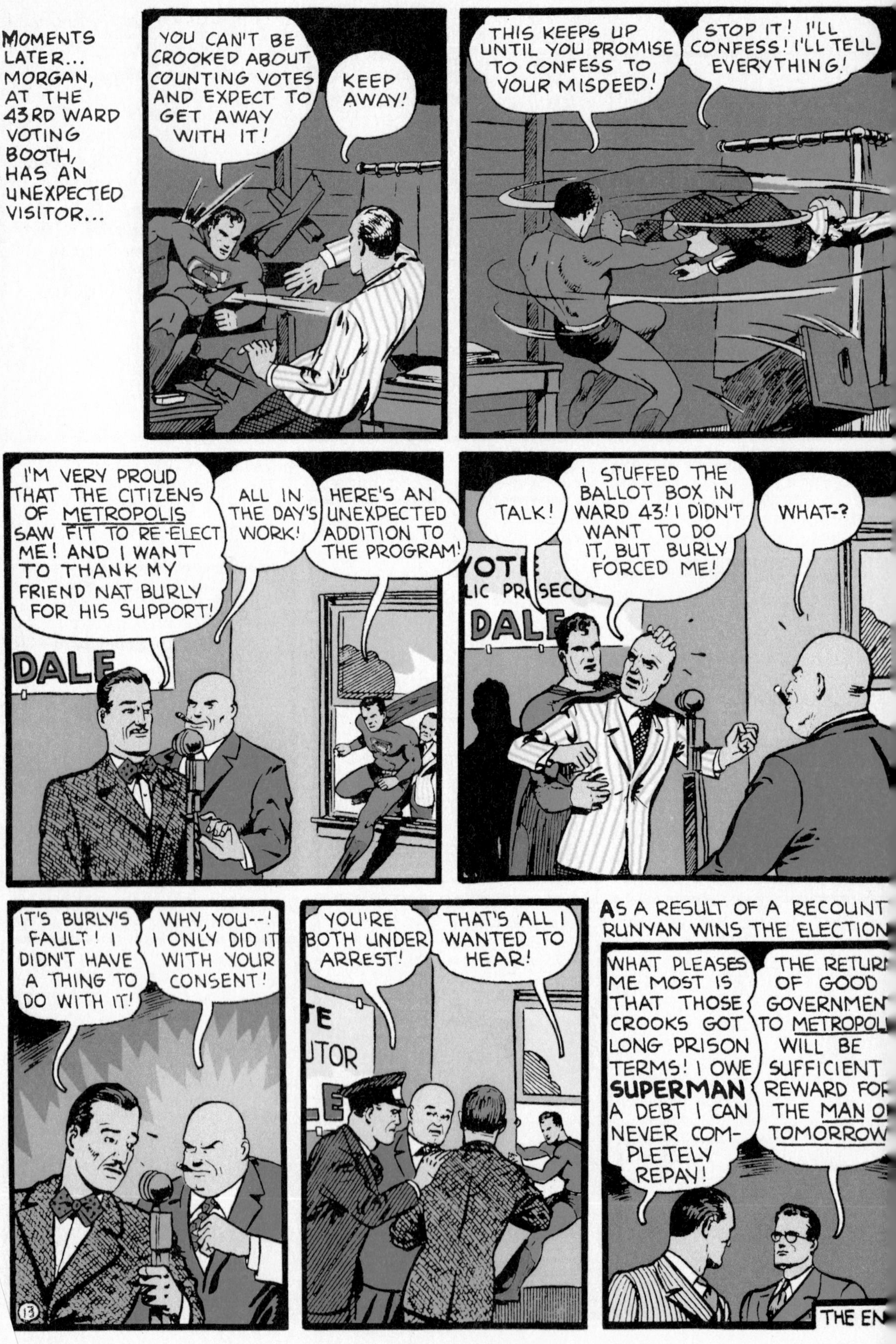
MOMENTS LATER... MORGAN, AT THE 43RD WARD VOTING BOOTH, HAS AN UNEXPECTED VISITOR...
YOU CAN'T BE CROOKED ABOUT COUNTING VOTES AND EXPECT TO GET AWAY WITH IT!
KEEP AWAY!
THIS KEEPS UP UNTIL YOU PROMISE TO CONFESS TO YOUR MISDEED!
STOP IT! I'LL CONFESS! I'LL TELL EVERYTHING!
I'M VERY PROUD THAT THE CITIZENS OF METROPOLIS SAW FIT TO RE-ELECT ME! AND I WANT TO THANK MY FRIEND NAT BURLY FOR HIS SUPPORT!
ALL IN THE DAY'S WORK!
HERE'S AN UNEXPECTED ADDITION TO THE PROGRAM!
DALE
TALK!
I STUFFED THE BALLOT BOX IN WARD 43! I DIDN'T WANT TO DO IT, BUT BURLY FORCED ME!
WHAT-?
IT'S BURLY'S FAULT! I DIDN'T HAVE A THING TO DO WITH IT!
WHY, YOU--! I ONLY DID IT WITH YOUR CONSENT!
13
YOU'RE BOTH UNDER ARREST!
THAT'S ALL I WANTED TO HEAR!
AS A RESULT OF A RECOUNT RUNYAN WINS THE ELECTION
WHAT PLEASES ME MOST IS THAT THOSE CROOKS GOT LONG PRISON TERMS! I OWE SUPERMAN A DEBT I CAN NEVER COMPLETELY REPAY!
THE RETURN OF GOOD GOVERNMENT TO METROPOLIS WILL BE SUFFICIENT REWARD FOR THE MAN OF TOMORROW
THE END

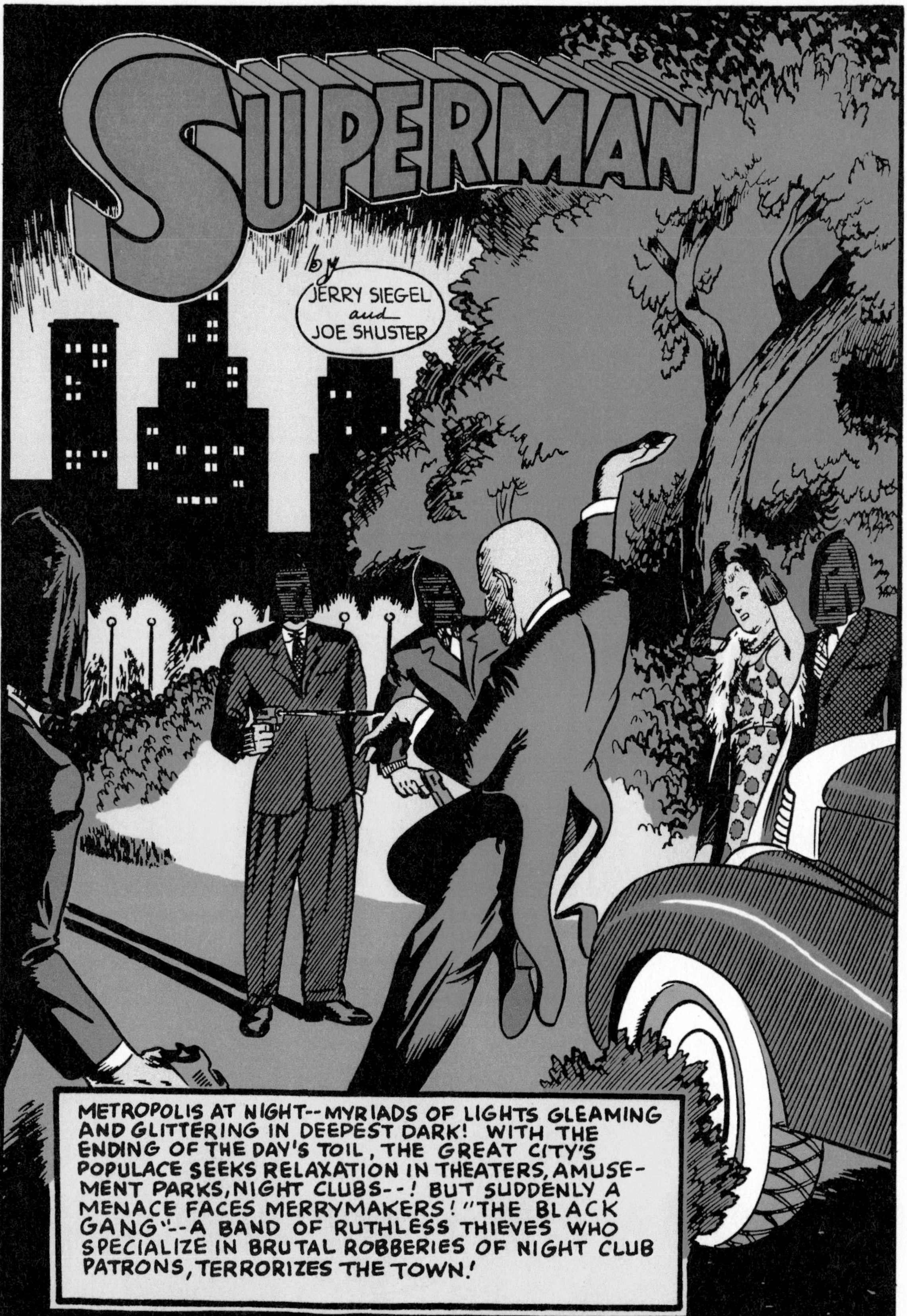
SUPERMAN
by
JERRY SIEGEL
and
JOE SHUSTER
METROPOLIS AT NIGHT--MYRIADS OF LIGHTS GLEAMING AND GLITTERING IN DEEPEST DARK! WITH THE ENDING OF THE DAY'S TOIL, THE GREAT CITY'S POPULACE SEEKS RELAXATION IN THEATERS, AMUSEMENT PARKS, NIGHT CLUBS--! BUT SUDDENLY A MENACE FACES MERRYMAKERS! "THE BLACK GANG"--A BAND OF RUTHLESS THIEVES WHO SPECIALIZE IN BRUTAL ROBBERIES OF NIGHT CLUB PATRONS, TERRORIZES THE TOWN!

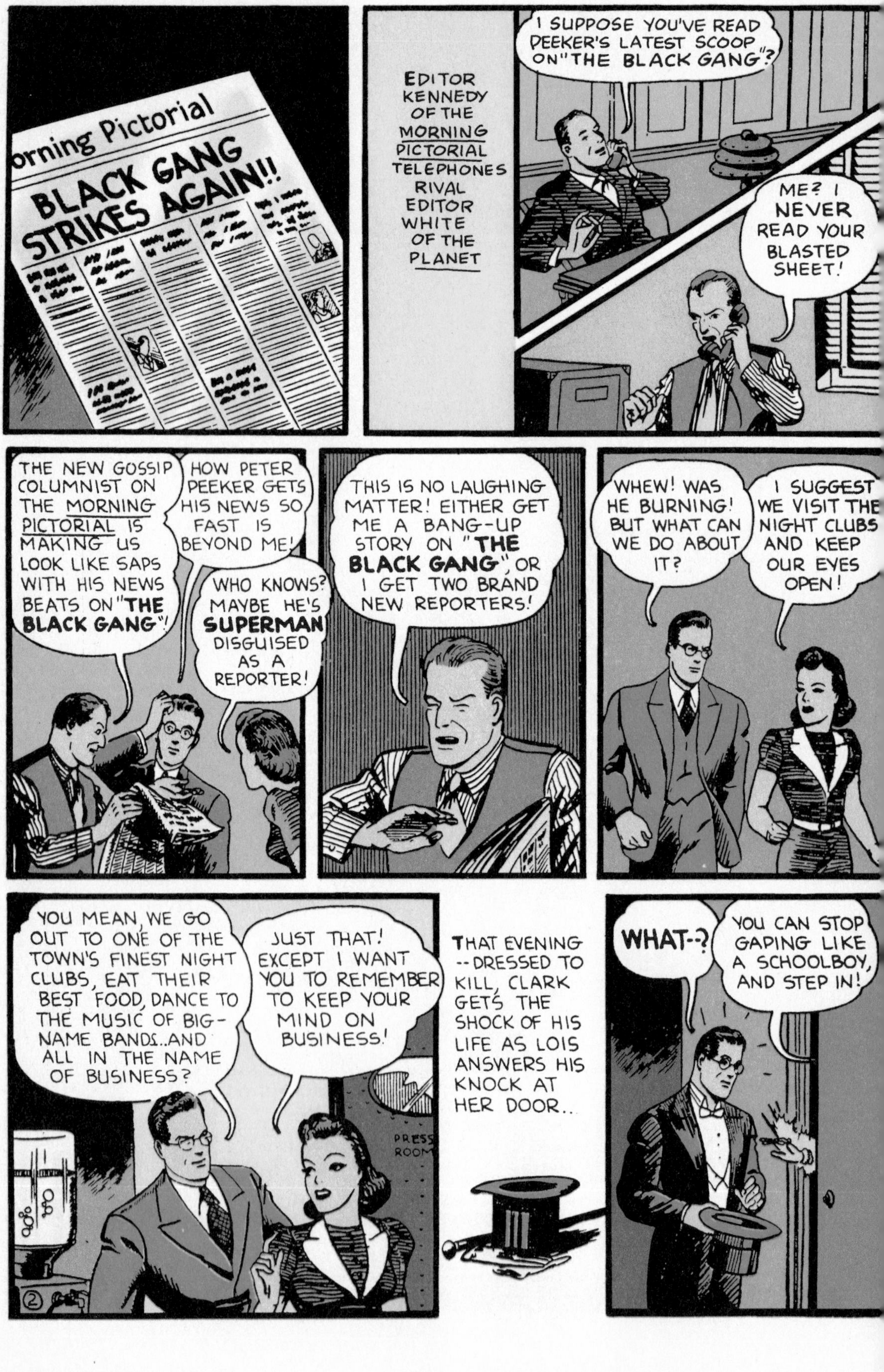

orning Pictorial
BLACK GANG STRIKES AGAIN!!
EDITOR KENNEDY OF THE MORNING PICTORIAL TELEPHONES RIVAL EDITOR WHITE OF THE PLANET
I SUPPOSE YOU'VE READ PEEKER'S LATEST SCOOP ON "THE BLACK GANG"?
ME? I NEVER READ YOUR BLASTED SHEET!
THE NEW GOSSIP COLUMNIST ON THE MORNING PICTORIAL IS MAKING US LOOK LIKE SAPS WITH HIS NEWS BEATS ON "THE BLACK GANG"!
HOW PETER PEEKER GETS HIS NEWS SO FAST IS BEYOND ME!
WHO KNOWS? MAYBE HE'S SUPERMAN DISGUISED AS A REPORTER!
THIS IS NO LAUGHING MATTER! EITHER GET ME A BANG-UP STORY ON "THE BLACK GANG", OR I GET TWO BRAND NEW REPORTERS!
WHEW! WAS HE BURNING! BUT WHAT CAN WE DO ABOUT IT?
I SUGGEST WE VISIT THE NIGHT CLUBS AND KEEP OUR EYES OPEN!
YOU MEAN, WE GO OUT TO ONE OF THE TOWN'S FINEST NIGHT CLUBS, EAT THEIR BEST FOOD, DANCE TO THE MUSIC OF BIG-NAME BANDS...AND ALL IN THE NAME OF BUSINESS?
JUST THAT! EXCEPT I WANT YOU TO REMEMBER TO KEEP YOUR MIND ON BUSINESS!
PRESS ROOM
2
THAT EVENING --DRESSED TO KILL, CLARK GETS THE SHOCK OF HIS LIFE AS LOIS ANSWERS HIS KNOCK AT HER DOOR...
WHAT--?
YOU CAN STOP GAPING LIKE A SCHOOLBOY, AND STEP IN!

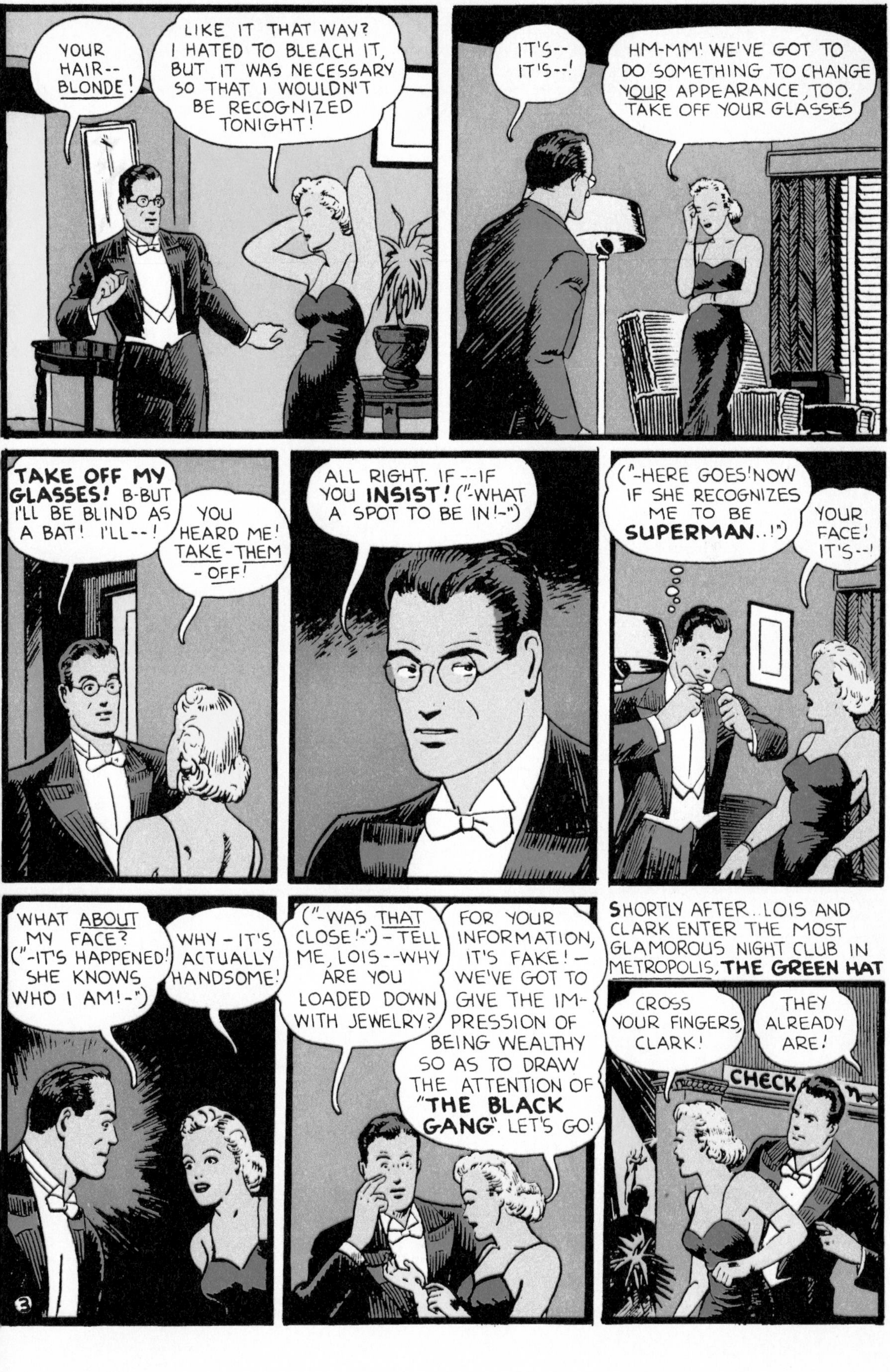
YOUR HAIR-- BLONDE!
LIKE IT THAT WAY? I HATED TO BLEACH IT, BUT IT WAS NECESSARY SO THAT I WOULDN'T BE RECOGNIZED TONIGHT!
IT'S-- IT'S--!
HM-MM! WE'VE GOT TO DO SOMETHING TO CHANGE YOUR APPEARANCE, TOO. TAKE OFF YOUR GLASSES
TAKE OFF MY GLASSES! B-BUT I'LL BE BLIND AS A BAT! I'LL--!
YOU HEARD ME! TAKE-THEM-OFF!
ALL RIGHT. IF--IF YOU INSIST! ("-WHAT A SPOT TO BE IN!-")
("-HERE GOES! NOW IF SHE RECOGNIZES ME TO BE SUPERMAN..!")
YOUR FACE! IT'S--!
WHAT ABOUT MY FACE? ("-IT'S HAPPENED! SHE KNOWS WHO I AM!-")
WHY - IT'S ACTUALLY HANDSOME!
("-WAS THAT CLOSE!-") - TELL ME, LOIS--WHY ARE YOU LOADED DOWN WITH JEWELRY?
FOR YOUR INFORMATION, IT'S FAKE! — WE'VE GOT TO GIVE THE IM-PRESSION OF BEING WEALTHY SO AS TO DRAW THE ATTENTION OF "THE BLACK GANG". LET'S GO!
SHORTLY AFTER.. LOIS AND CLARK ENTER THE MOST GLAMOROUS NIGHT CLUB IN METROPOLIS, THE GREEN HAT
CROSS YOUR FINGERS, CLARK!
THEY ALREADY ARE!
CHECK

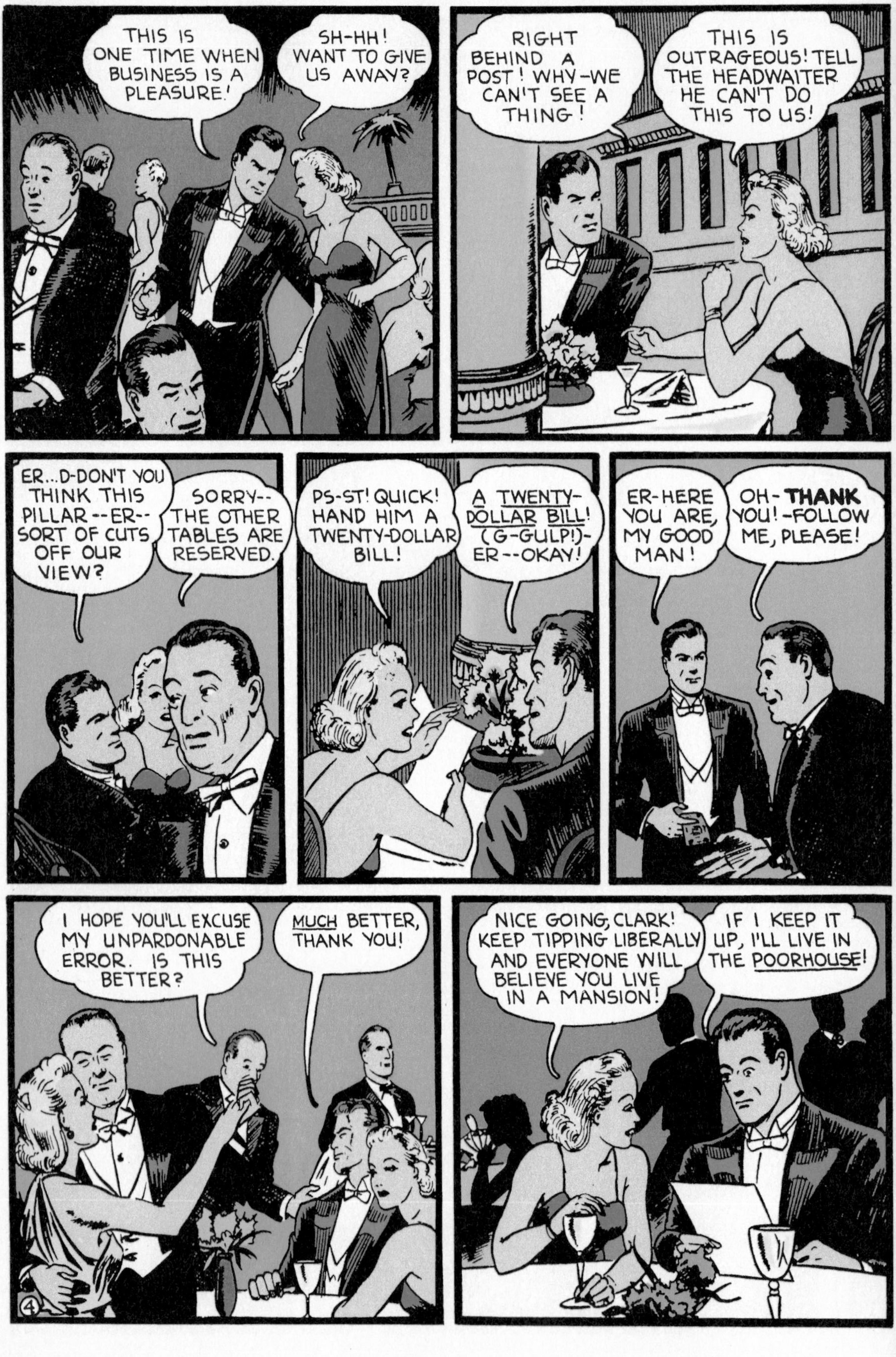
THIS IS ONE TIME WHEN BUSINESS IS A PLEASURE!
SH-HH! WANT TO GIVE US AWAY?
RIGHT BEHIND A POST! WHY-WE CAN'T SEE A THING!
THIS IS OUTRAGEOUS! TELL THE HEADWAITER HE CAN'T DO THIS TO US!
ER...D-DON'T YOU THINK THIS PILLAR--ER--SORT OF CUTS OFF OUR VIEW?
SORRY--THE OTHER TABLES ARE RESERVED.
PS-ST! QUICK! HAND HIM A TWENTY-DOLLAR BILL!
A TWENTY-DOLLAR BILL! (G-GULP!)-ER--OKAY!
ER-HERE YOU ARE, MY GOOD MAN!
OH-THANK YOU!-FOLLOW ME, PLEASE!
I HOPE YOU'LL EXCUSE MY UNPARDONABLE ERROR. IS THIS BETTER?
MUCH BETTER, THANK YOU!
4
NICE GOING, CLARK! KEEP TIPPING LIBERALLY AND EVERYONE WILL BELIEVE YOU LIVE IN A MANSION!
IF I KEEP IT UP, I'LL LIVE IN THE POORHOUSE!

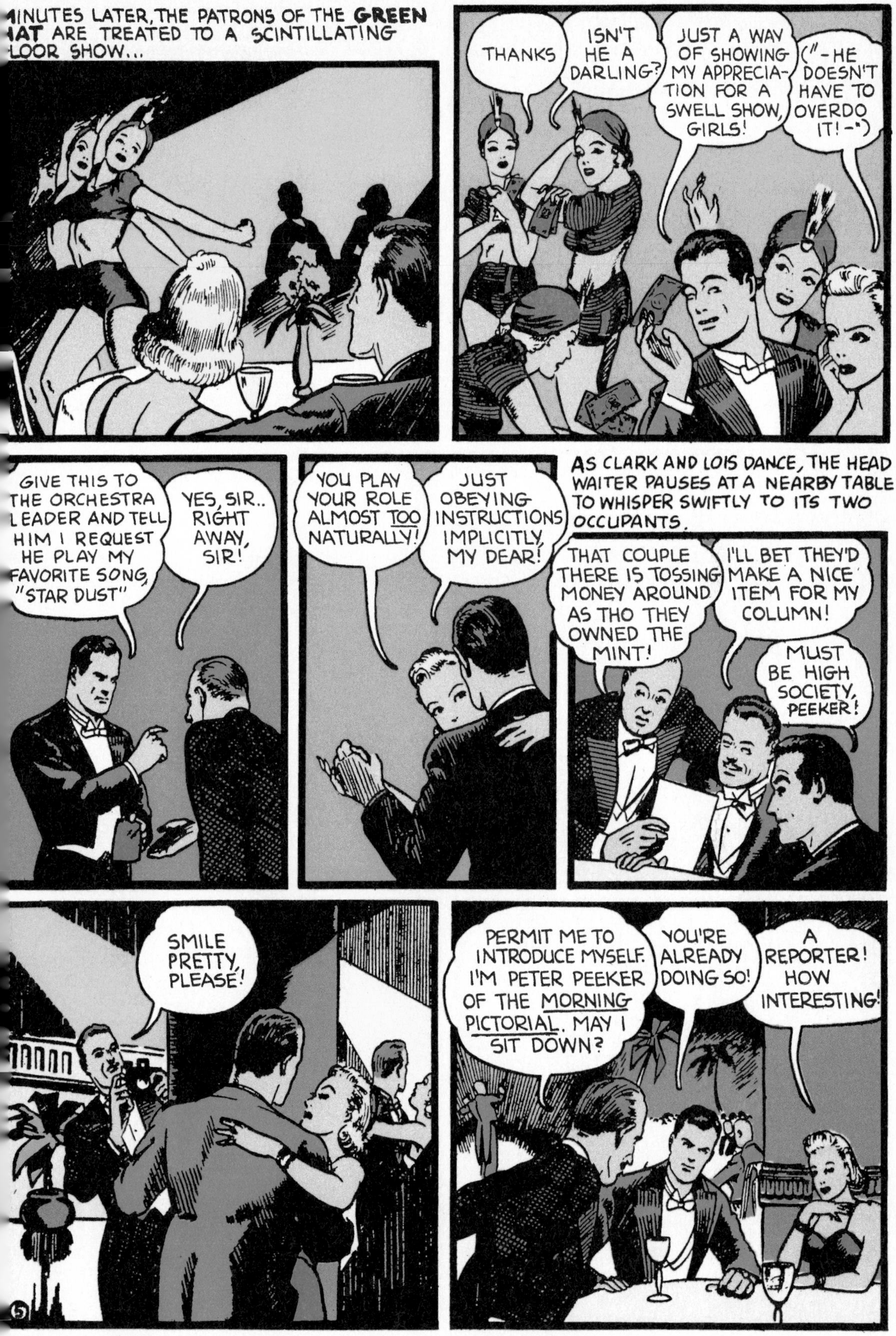
MINUTES LATER, THE PATRONS OF THE GREEN HAT ARE TREATED TO A SCINTILLATING LOOR SHOW...
THANKS
ISN'T HE A DARLING?
JUST A WAY OF SHOWING MY APPRECIATION FOR A SWELL SHOW, GIRLS!
("-HE DOESN'T HAVE TO OVERDO IT!-")
GIVE THIS TO THE ORCHESTRA LEADER AND TELL HIM I REQUEST HE PLAY MY FAVORITE SONG, "STAR DUST"
YES, SIR.. RIGHT AWAY, SIR!
YOU PLAY YOUR ROLE ALMOST TOO NATURALLY!
JUST OBEYING INSTRUCTIONS IMPLICITLY, MY DEAR!
AS CLARK AND LOIS DANCE, THE HEAD WAITER PAUSES AT A NEARBY TABLE TO WHISPER SWIFTLY TO ITS TWO OCCUPANTS.
THAT COUPLE THERE IS TOSSING MONEY AROUND AS THO THEY OWNED THE MINT!
I'LL BET THEY'D MAKE A NICE ITEM FOR MY COLUMN!
MUST BE HIGH SOCIETY, PEEKER!
SMILE PRETTY, PLEASE!
PERMIT ME TO INTRODUCE MYSELF. I'M PETER PEEKER OF THE MORNING PICTORIAL. MAY I SIT DOWN?
YOU'RE ALREADY DOING SO!
A REPORTER! HOW INTERESTING!

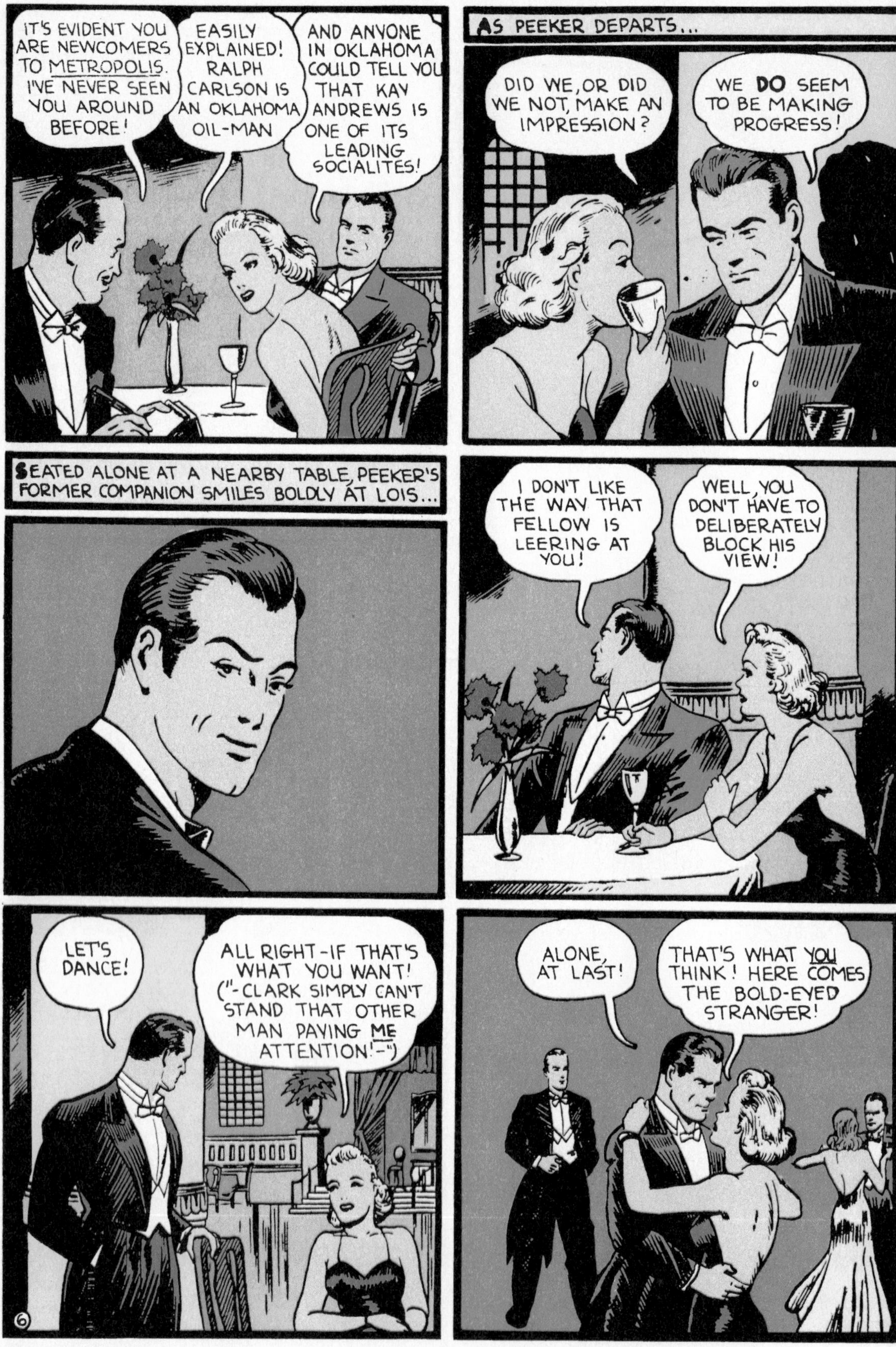
IT'S EVIDENT YOU ARE NEWCOMERS TO METROPOLIS. I'VE NEVER SEEN YOU AROUND BEFORE!
EASILY EXPLAINED! RALPH CARLSON IS AN OKLAHOMA OIL-MAN
AND ANYONE IN OKLAHOMA COULD TELL YOU THAT KAY ANDREWS IS ONE OF ITS LEADING SOCIALITES!
AS PEEKER DEPARTS...
DID WE, OR DID WE NOT, MAKE AN IMPRESSION?
WE DO SEEM TO BE MAKING PROGRESS!
SEATED ALONE AT A NEARBY TABLE, PEEKER'S FORMER COMPANION SMILES BOLDLY AT LOIS...
I DON'T LIKE THE WAY THAT FELLOW IS LEERING AT YOU!
WELL, YOU DON'T HAVE TO DELIBERATELY BLOCK HIS VIEW!
LET'S DANCE!
ALL RIGHT-IF THAT'S WHAT YOU WANT! ("-CLARK SIMPLY CAN'T STAND THAT OTHER MAN PAYING ME ATTENTION!-")
6
ALONE, AT LAST!
THAT'S WHAT YOU THINK! HERE COMES THE BOLD-EYED STRANGER!

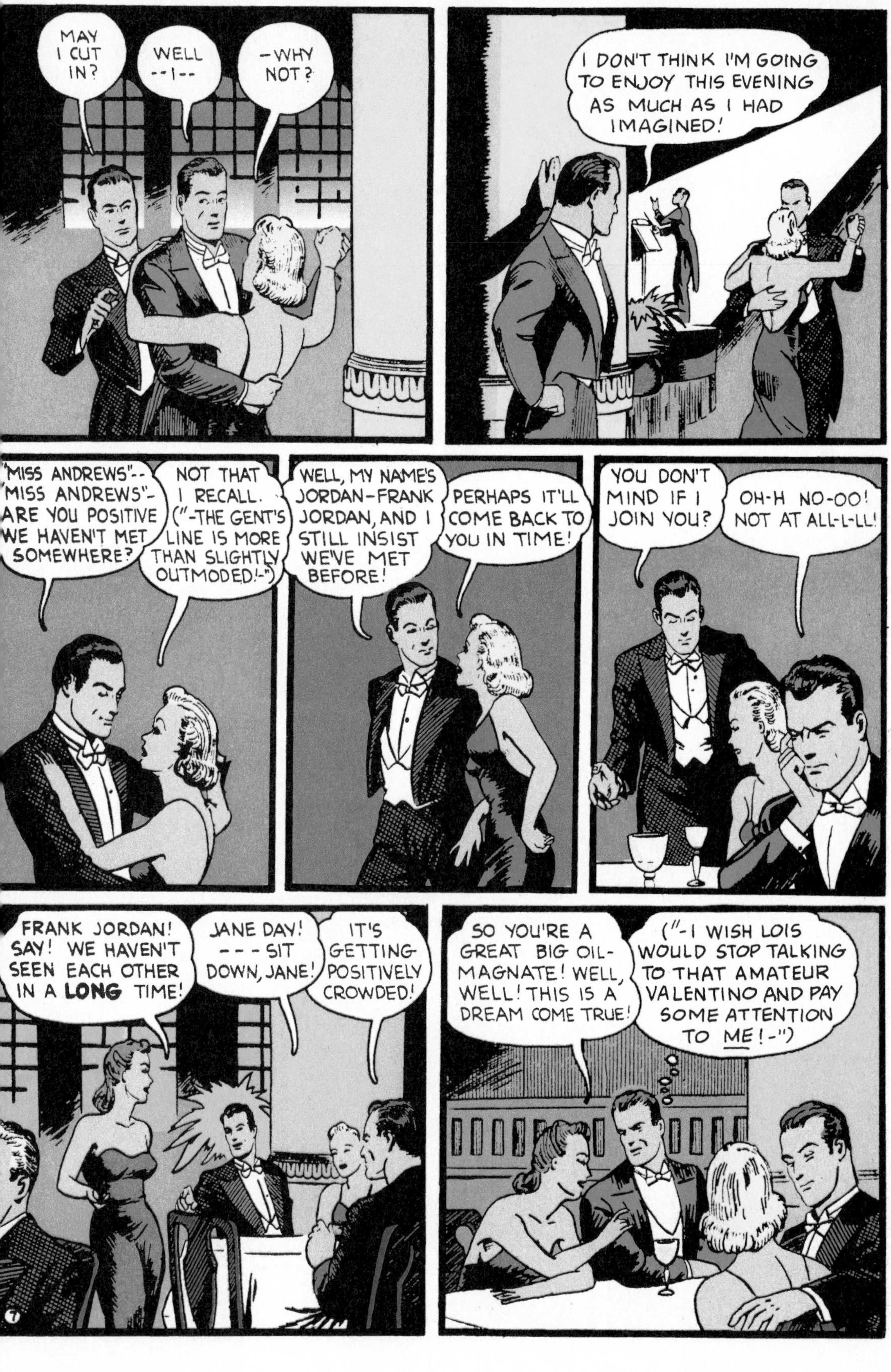
MAY I CUT IN?
WELL --I--
-WHY NOT?
I DON'T THINK I'M GOING TO ENJOY THIS EVENING AS MUCH AS I HAD IMAGINED!
"MISS ANDREWS"-- "MISS ANDREWS"- ARE YOU POSITIVE WE HAVEN'T MET SOMEWHERE?
NOT THAT I RECALL. ("-THE GENT'S LINE IS MORE THAN SLIGHTLY OUTMODED!-")
WELL, MY NAME'S JORDAN-FRANK JORDAN, AND I STILL INSIST WE'VE MET BEFORE!
PERHAPS IT'LL COME BACK TO YOU IN TIME!
YOU DON'T MIND IF I JOIN YOU?
OH-H NO-OO! NOT AT ALL-L-LL!
FRANK JORDAN! SAY! WE HAVEN'T SEEN EACH OTHER IN A **LONG** TIME!
JANE DAY! --- SIT DOWN, JANE!
IT'S GETTING POSITIVELY CROWDED!
SO YOU'RE A GREAT BIG OIL-MAGNATE! WELL, WELL! THIS IS A DREAM COME TRUE!
("-I WISH LOIS WOULD STOP TALKING TO THAT AMATEUR VALENTINO AND PAY SOME ATTENTION TO ME!-")
7

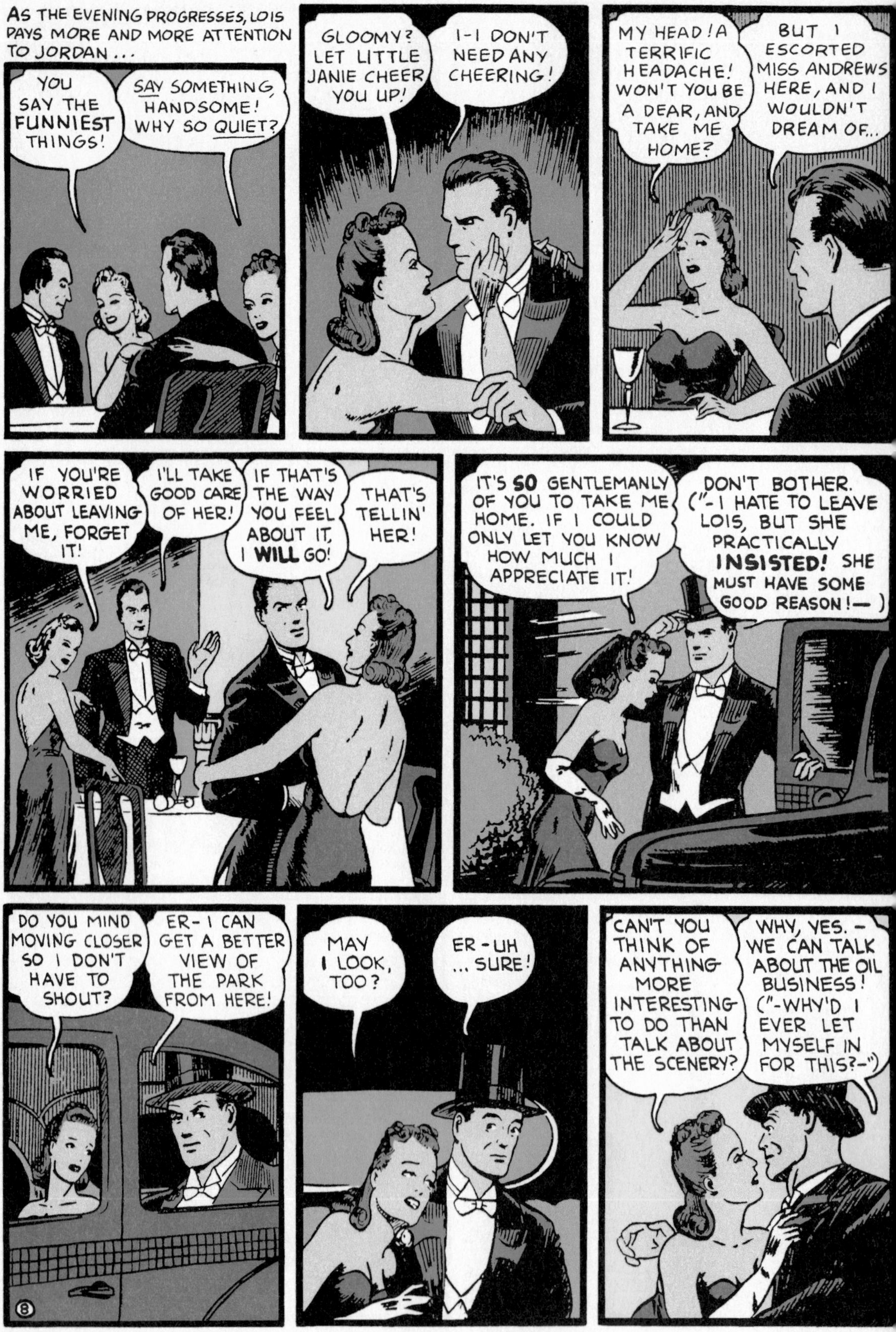
AS THE EVENING PROGRESSES, LOIS PAYS MORE AND MORE ATTENTION TO JORDAN...
YOU SAY THE FUNNIEST THINGS!
SAY SOMETHING, HANDSOME! WHY SO QUIET?
GLOOMY? LET LITTLE JANIE CHEER YOU UP!
I-I DON'T NEED ANY CHEERING!
MY HEAD! A TERRIFIC HEADACHE! WON'T YOU BE A DEAR, AND TAKE ME HOME?
BUT I ESCORTED MISS ANDREWS HERE, AND I WOULDN'T DREAM OF...
IF YOU'RE WORRIED ABOUT LEAVING ME, FORGET IT!
I'LL TAKE GOOD CARE OF HER!
IF THAT'S THE WAY YOU FEEL ABOUT IT, I WILL GO!
THAT'S TELLIN' HER!
IT'S SO GENTLEMANLY OF YOU TO TAKE ME HOME. IF I COULD ONLY LET YOU KNOW HOW MUCH I APPRECIATE IT!
DON'T BOTHER. ("-I HATE TO LEAVE LOIS, BUT SHE PRACTICALLY INSISTED! SHE MUST HAVE SOME GOOD REASON!—)
DO YOU MIND MOVING CLOSER SO I DON'T HAVE TO SHOUT?
ER- I CAN GET A BETTER VIEW OF THE PARK FROM HERE!
8
MAY I LOOK, TOO?
ER-UH ... SURE!
CAN'T YOU THINK OF ANYTHING MORE INTERESTING TO DO THAN TALK ABOUT THE SCENERY?
WHY, YES. - WE CAN TALK ABOUT THE OIL BUSINESS! ("-WHY'D I EVER LET MYSELF IN FOR THIS?-")

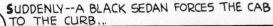

THE OIL BUSINESS! I WOULDN'T BE SURPRISED IF OIL INSTEAD OF BLOOD FLOWS THROUGH YOUR VEINS. HAVEN'T YOU EVER HAD THE URGE TO HOLD A GIRL IN YOUR ARMS, CRUSH HER TIGHT..?

("-INASMUCH AS I'M **SUPERMAN**, I'M AFRAID I MIGHT FORGET MYSELF AND CRACK HER RIBS!-")

SUDDENLY--A BLACK SEDAN FORCES THE CAB TO THE CURB...

PULL OVER!

OUT OF THERE--ALL OF YOU!

A FALSE MOVE FROM ANYONE, AND WE SHOOT!

"THE BLACK GANG"!

THEY'LL SHOOT ME! DON'T RESIST THEM! PLEASE DON'T!

YOUR WALLET!

AND IF I DON'T HAND IT OVER?

MAYBE THIS'LL KNOCK A LITTLE OF TH' BACKTALK OUTA YA!

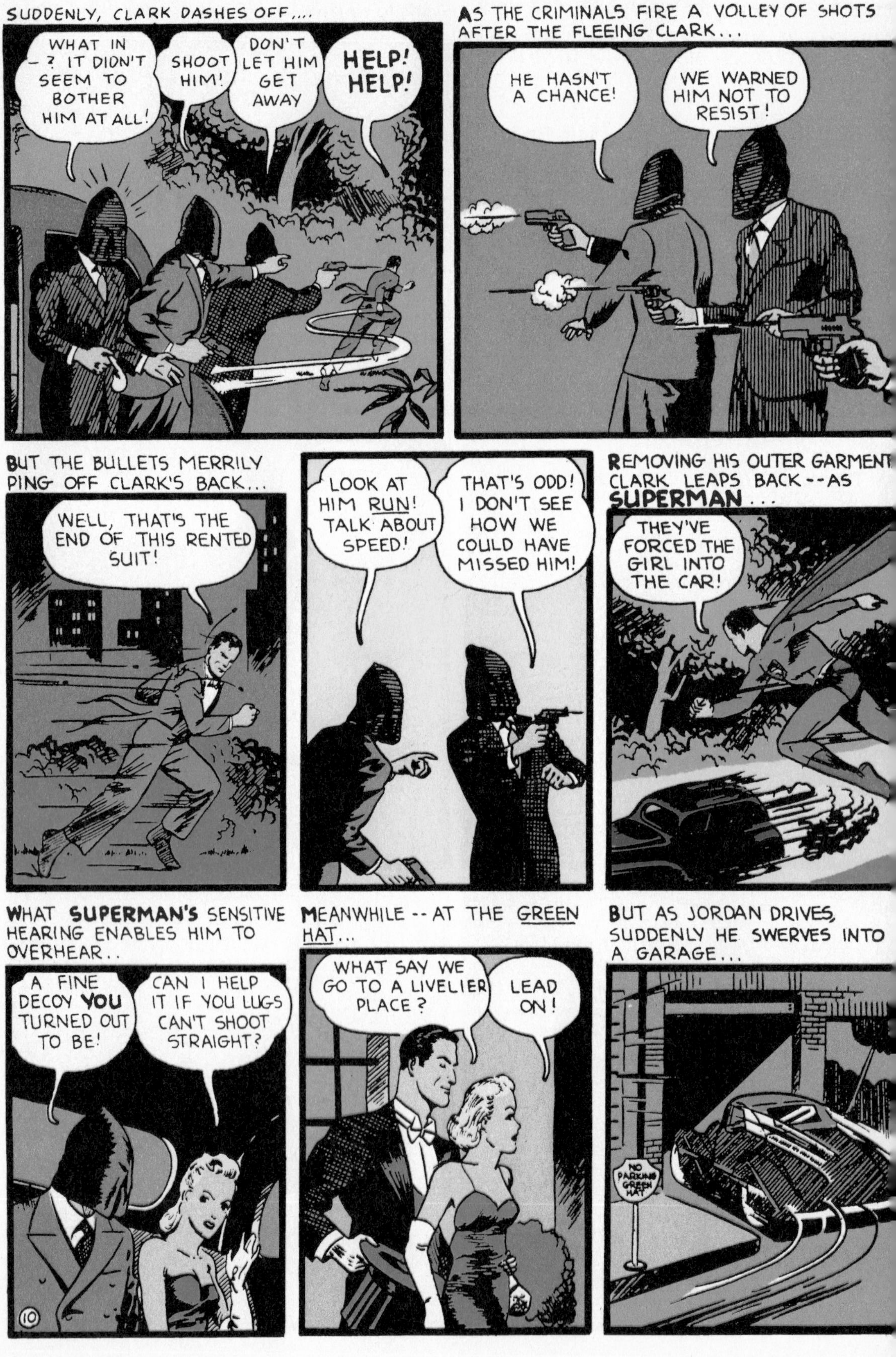
SUDDENLY, CLARK DASHES OFF,....
WHAT IN —? IT DIDN'T SEEM TO BOTHER HIM AT ALL!
SHOOT HIM!
DON'T LET HIM GET AWAY
HELP! HELP!
AS THE CRIMINALS FIRE A VOLLEY OF SHOTS AFTER THE FLEEING CLARK...
HE HASN'T A CHANCE!
WE WARNED HIM NOT TO RESIST!
BUT THE BULLETS MERRILY PING OFF CLARK'S BACK...
WELL, THAT'S THE END OF THIS RENTED SUIT!
LOOK AT HIM RUN! TALK ABOUT SPEED!
THAT'S ODD! I DON'T SEE HOW WE COULD HAVE MISSED HIM!
REMOVING HIS OUTER GARMENT CLARK LEAPS BACK--AS SUPERMAN ...
THEY'VE FORCED THE GIRL INTO THE CAR!
WHAT SUPERMAN'S SENSITIVE HEARING ENABLES HIM TO OVERHEAR..
A FINE DECOY YOU TURNED OUT TO BE!
CAN I HELP IT IF YOU LUGS CAN'T SHOOT STRAIGHT?
10
MEANWHILE -- AT THE GREEN HAT...
WHAT SAY WE GO TO A LIVELIER PLACE?
LEAD ON!
BUT AS JORDAN DRIVES, SUDDENLY HE SWERVES INTO A GARAGE...
NO PARKING GREEN HAT

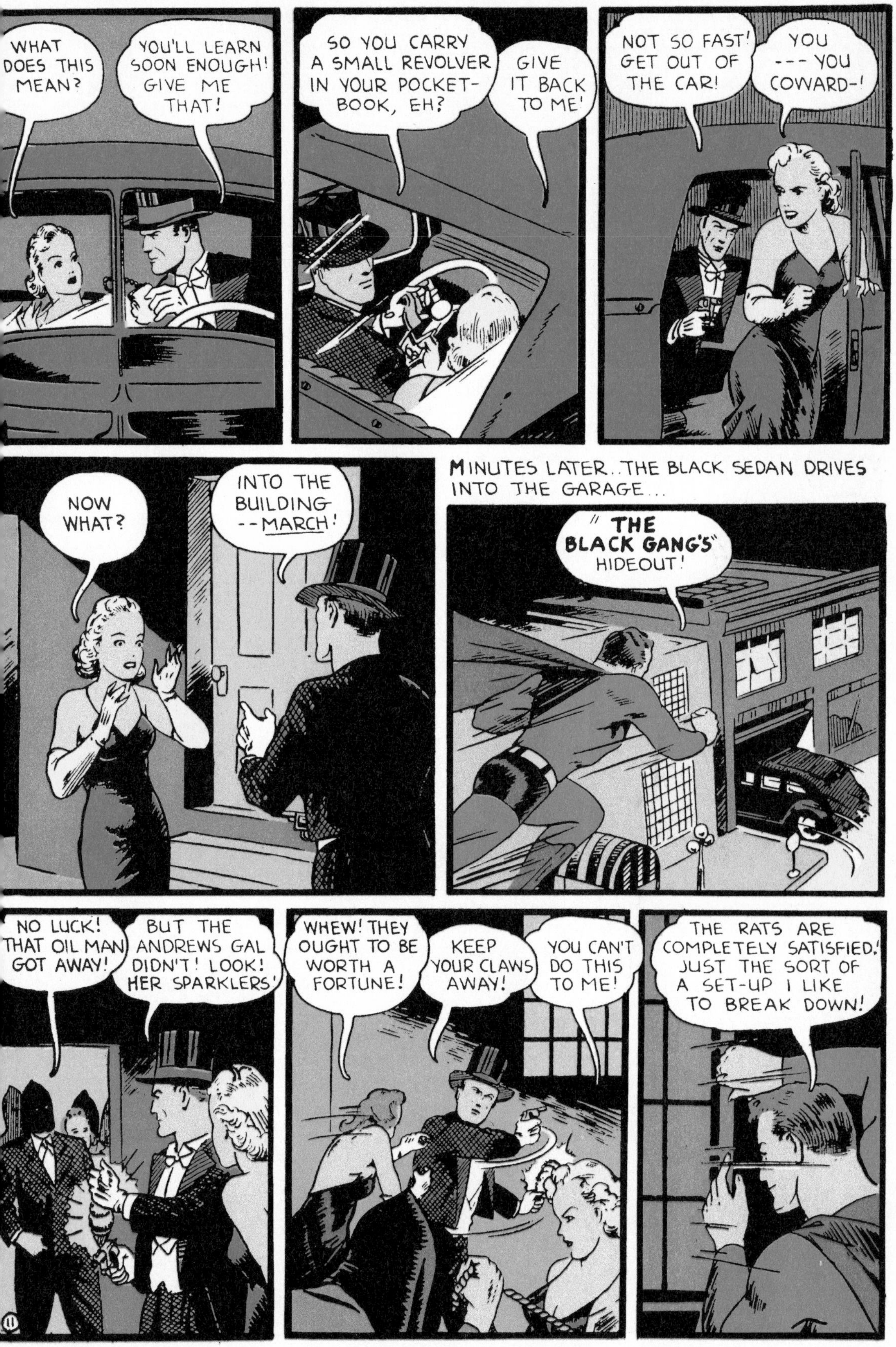
WHAT DOES THIS MEAN?
YOU'LL LEARN SOON ENOUGH! GIVE ME THAT!
SO YOU CARRY A SMALL REVOLVER IN YOUR POCKET-BOOK, EH?
GIVE IT BACK TO ME!
NOT SO FAST! GET OUT OF THE CAR!
YOU --- YOU COWARD-!
NOW WHAT?
INTO THE BUILDING --MARCH!
MINUTES LATER.. THE BLACK SEDAN DRIVES INTO THE GARAGE...
"THE BLACK GANG'S" HIDEOUT!
NO LUCK! THAT OIL MAN GOT AWAY!
BUT THE ANDREWS GAL DIDN'T! LOOK! HER SPARKLERS!
WHEW! THEY OUGHT TO BE WORTH A FORTUNE!
KEEP YOUR CLAWS AWAY!
YOU CAN'T DO THIS TO ME!
THE RATS ARE COMPLETELY SATISFIED! JUST THE SORT OF A SET-UP I LIKE TO BREAK DOWN!
11

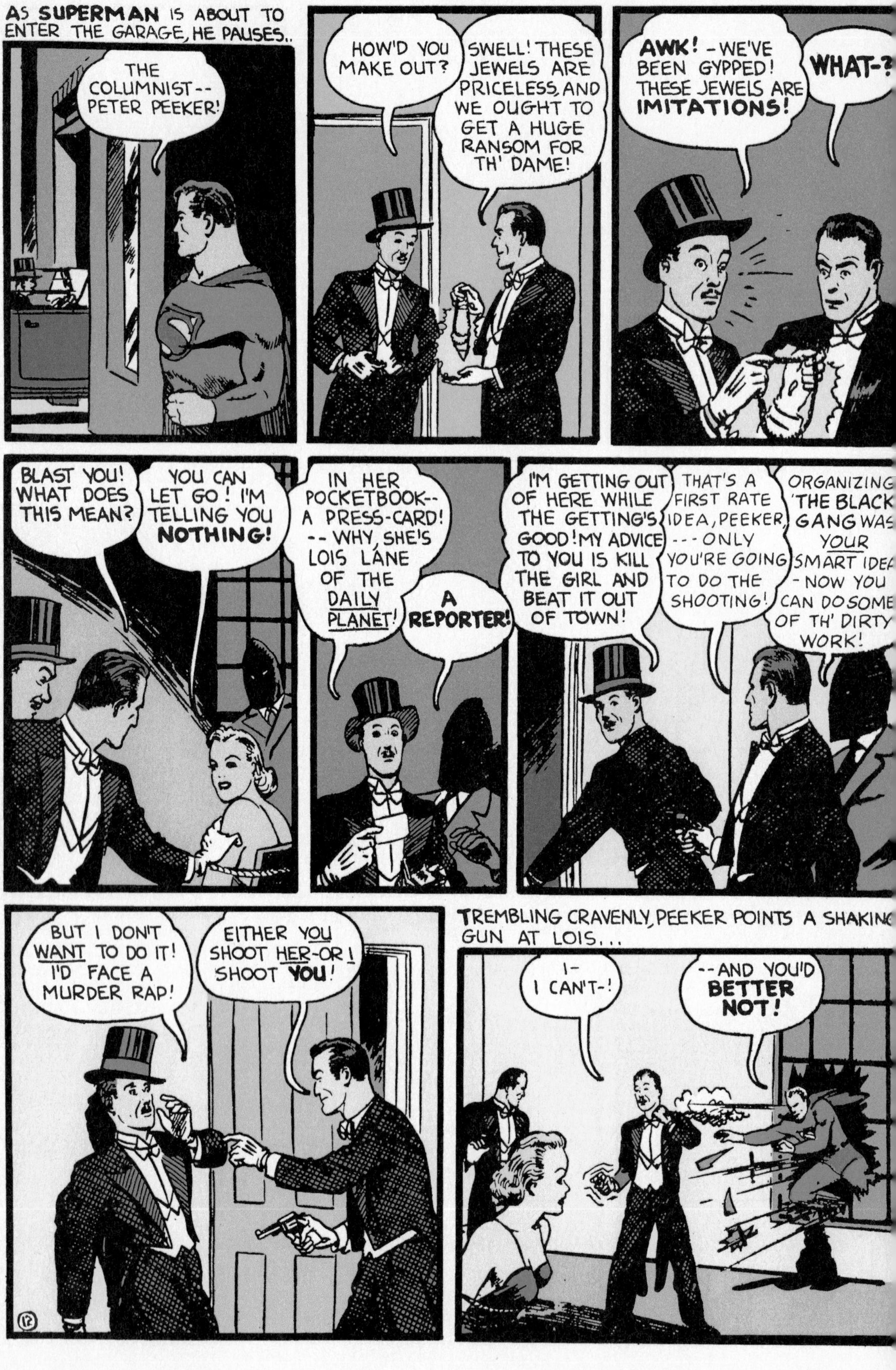

AS SUPERMAN IS ABOUT TO ENTER THE GARAGE, HE PAUSES..
THE COLUMNIST-- PETER PEEKER!
HOW'D YOU MAKE OUT?
SWELL! THESE JEWELS ARE PRICELESS, AND WE OUGHT TO GET A HUGE RANSOM FOR TH' DAME!
AWK! - WE'VE BEEN GYPPED! THESE JEWELS ARE IMITATIONS!
WHAT-?
BLAST YOU! WHAT DOES THIS MEAN?
YOU CAN LET GO! I'M TELLING YOU NOTHING!
IN HER POCKETBOOK-- A PRESS-CARD! -- WHY, SHE'S LOIS LANE OF THE DAILY PLANET!
A REPORTER!
I'M GETTING OUT OF HERE WHILE THE GETTING'S GOOD! MY ADVICE TO YOU IS KILL THE GIRL AND BEAT IT OUT OF TOWN!
THAT'S A FIRST RATE IDEA, PEEKER, --- ONLY YOU'RE GOING TO DO THE SHOOTING!
ORGANIZING 'THE BLACK GANG WAS YOUR SMART IDEA - NOW YOU CAN DO SOME OF TH' DIRTY WORK!
BUT I DON'T WANT TO DO IT! I'D FACE A MURDER RAP!
EITHER YOU SHOOT HER-OR I SHOOT YOU!
12
TREMBLING CRAVENLY, PEEKER POINTS A SHAKING GUN AT LOIS...
I- I CAN'T-!
--AND YOU'D BETTER NOT!

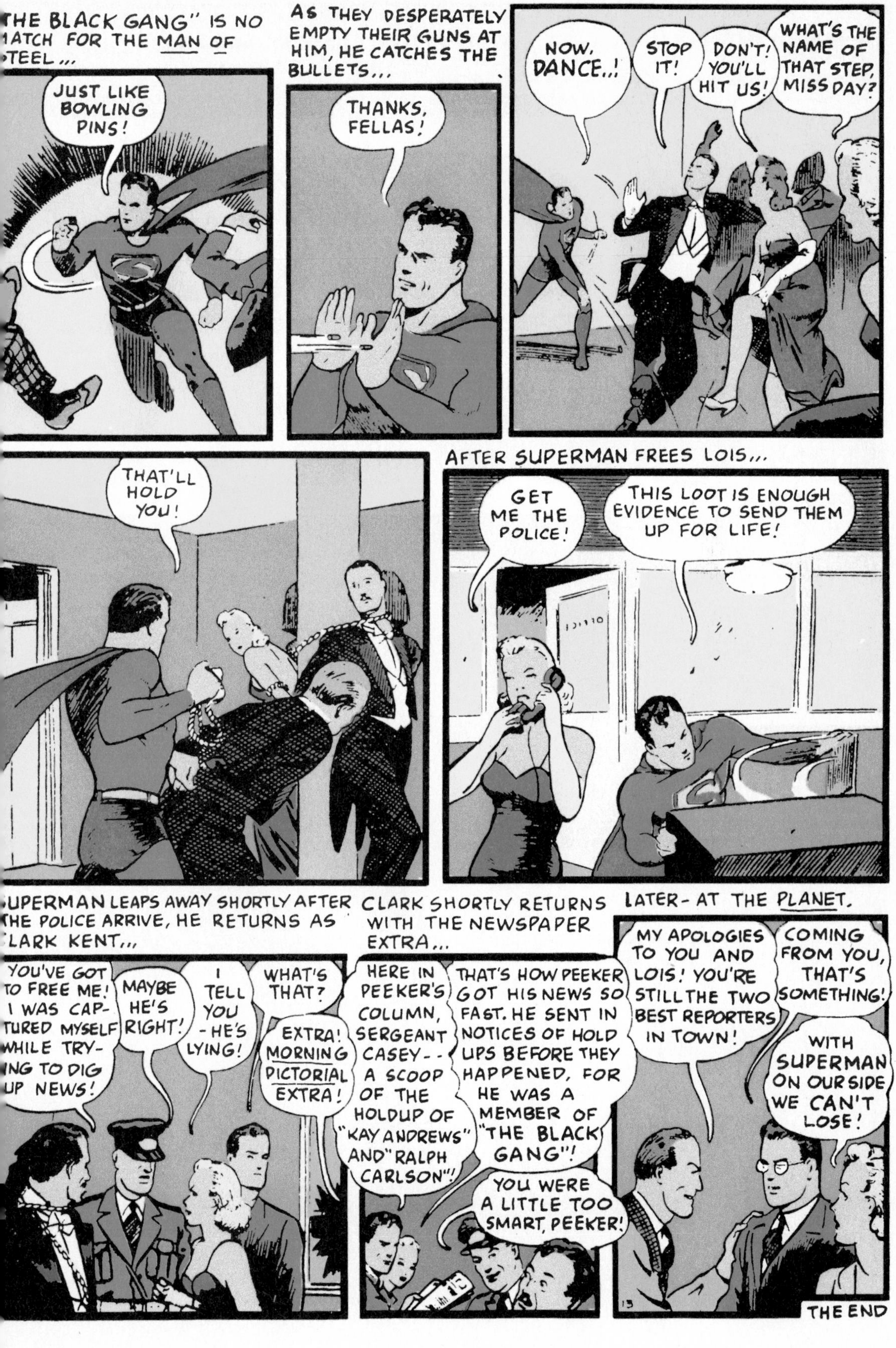

"THE BLACK GANG" IS NO MATCH FOR THE MAN OF STEEL...
JUST LIKE BOWLING PINS!
AS THEY DESPERATELY EMPTY THEIR GUNS AT HIM, HE CATCHES THE BULLETS...
THANKS, FELLAS!
NOW, DANCE..!
STOP IT!
DON'T! YOU'LL HIT US!
WHAT'S THE NAME OF THAT STEP, MISS DAY?
THAT'LL HOLD YOU!
AFTER SUPERMAN FREES LOIS...
GET ME THE POLICE!
THIS LOOT IS ENOUGH EVIDENCE TO SEND THEM UP FOR LIFE!
SUPERMAN LEAPS AWAY SHORTLY AFTER THE POLICE ARRIVE, HE RETURNS AS CLARK KENT...
YOU'VE GOT TO FREE ME! I WAS CAPTURED MYSELF WHILE TRYING TO DIG UP NEWS!
MAYBE HE'S RIGHT!
I TELL YOU - HE'S LYING!
WHAT'S THAT?
EXTRA! MORNING PICTORIAL EXTRA!
CLARK SHORTLY RETURNS WITH THE NEWSPAPER EXTRA...
HERE IN PEEKER'S COLUMN, SERGEANT CASEY- - A SCOOP OF THE HOLDUP OF "KAY ANDREWS" AND "RALPH CARLSON"!
THAT'S HOW PEEKER GOT HIS NEWS SO FAST. HE SENT IN NOTICES OF HOLD UPS BEFORE THEY HAPPENED, FOR HE WAS A MEMBER OF "THE BLACK GANG"!
YOU WERE A LITTLE TOO SMART, PEEKER!
LATER- AT THE PLANET.
MY APOLOGIES TO YOU AND LOIS! YOU'RE STILL THE TWO BEST REPORTERS IN TOWN!
COMING FROM YOU, THAT'S SOMETHING!
WITH SUPERMAN ON OUR SIDE WE CAN'T LOSE!
13
THE END

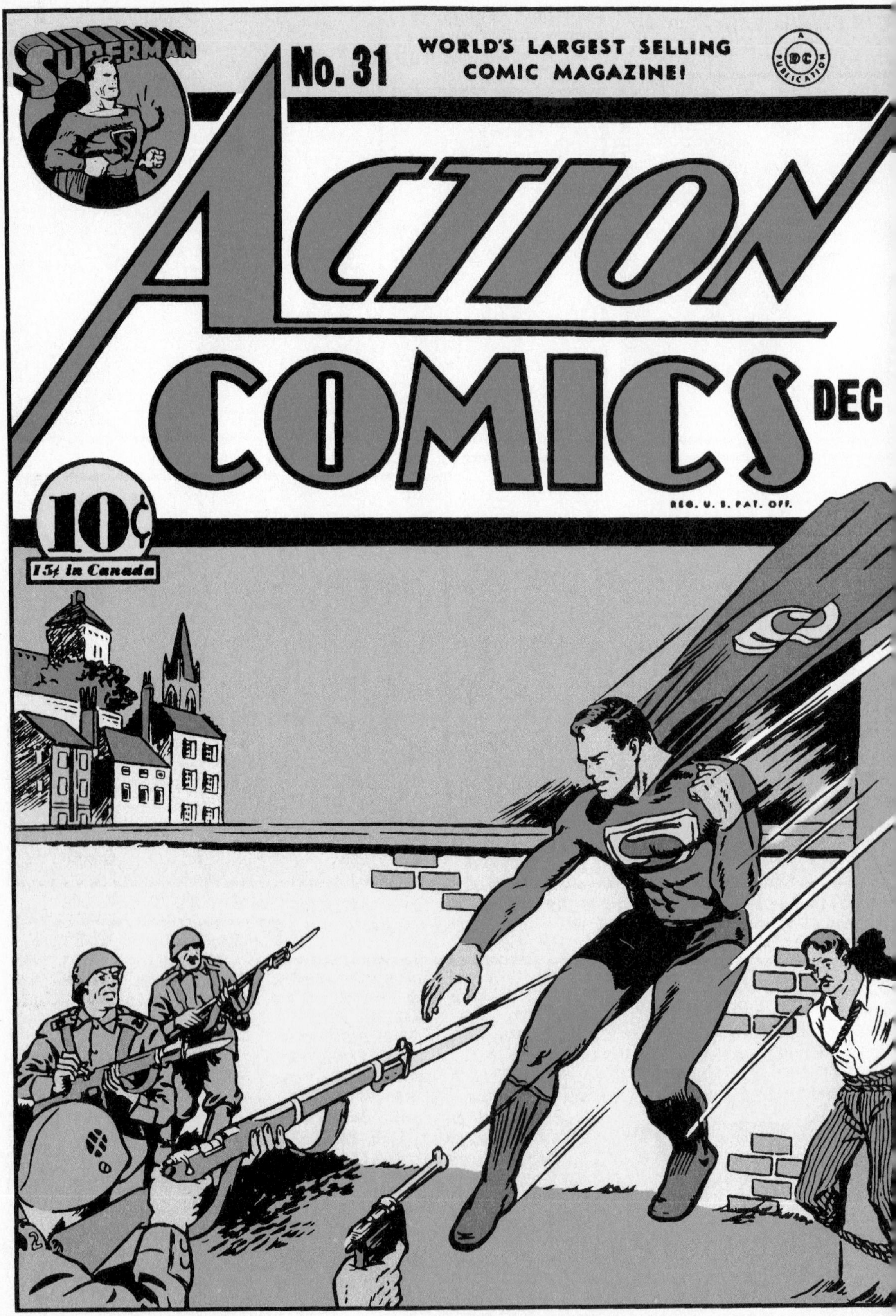
SUPERMAN
No. 31
WORLD'S LARGEST SELLING
COMIC MAGAZINE!
A DC PUBLICATION
ACTION COMICS
DEC
REG. U. S. PAT. OFF.
10¢
15¢ in Canada

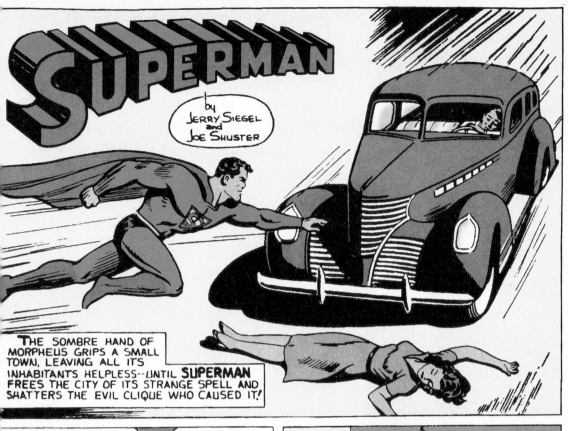

SUPERMAN

by Jerry Siegel and Joe Shuster

THE SOMBRE HAND OF MORPHEUS GRIPS A SMALL TOWN, LEAVING ALL ITS INHABITANTS HELPLESS--UNTIL **SUPERMAN** FREES THE CITY OF ITS STRANGE SPELL AND SHATTERS THE EVIL CLIQUE WHO CAUSED IT!

IT CERTAINLY WAS NICE OF YOU TO DRIVE ME UP TO BRENTVILLE, CLARK! I'M SURE I'LL ENJOY MY VACATION IN THIS LITTLE TOWN--

IT WILL DO YOU GOOD TO RELAX FOR A WHILE IN A SLEEPY COUNTRY VILLAGE!

AS CLARK AND LOIS ENTER THE TOWN OF BRENTVILLE, THEY SEE NO ACTIVITY ANYWHERE!

SLEEPY TOWN IS RIGHT! EVERYONE SEEMS TO BE TAKING A SNOOZE AROUND HERE!

CLARK IS AMUSED TO SEE THE VILLAGERS ASLEEP EVEN IN FRONT OF THE GENERAL STORE!

SAY--LOIS HAS DROPPED OFF TO SLEEP, TOO!

TO HIS AMAZEMENT, CLARK NOTES A CAR SMASHED THRU A BRIDGE'S RAIL, HANGING SUSPENDED — ITS DRIVER SNORING!

WHAT—! THIS IS MORE THAN MERE COINCIDENCE!

THERE'S SOMETHING VERY STRANGE GOING ON HERE! EVERYONE ASLEEP EXCEPT MYSELF—AND I, NO DOUBT, IMMUNE BECAUSE OF MY SUPERHUMAN POWERS!

CLARK TAKES TIME OUT TO HAUL THE AUTO TO SAFETY—

I HOPE HE DOESN'T MAKE A HABIT OF THIS!

CLARK HELPS HIMSELF TO TWO GAS MASKS AT A FIRE STATION—PLACING ONE MASK ON LOIS, HE DONS THE OTHER HIMSELF AND DRIVES TOWARD A HOUSE ON THE TOWN'S OUTSKIRTS—

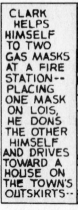

PERHAPS THE STRANGE SOPORIFIC INFLUENCE DOESN'T EXTEND AS FAR AS THAT HOUSE!

WELL?

MAY I USE YOUR PHONE? IT'S URGENT!

CLARK PHONES THE SHERIFF OF A NEARBY TOWN—

HURRY, SHERIFF! SOMETHING INEXPLICABLE HAS HAPPENED HERE AT BRENTVILLE! EVERYONE HAS FALLEN ASLEEP!

WHAT?

HE'S INSANE, PROFESSOR!

WHAT'S COME OVER YOU?

GIVE ME THAT PHONE, YOU CRAZY LIAR! GET OUT OF HERE!

PLEASE, KOLB! NO VIOLENCE!

--*BUT* AS CLARK DEPARTS, KOLB STEALS UP BEHIND, --A WRENCH RAISED HIGH--

BEHIND ME-- KOLB--

TURNING AS THOUGH BY CHANCE, CLARK ALLOWS HIS SHOULDER TO HIT KOLB'S JAW

OOPS! SORRY!

IN THE SHERIFF'S OFFICE IN THE ADJOINING TOWN--

FELLER ON THE PHONE SAID FOLKS AT BRENTVILLE ARE ALL SNOOZIN'! MAY BE A WASTE OF TIME, BUT YOU BOYS TAKE A LOOK-SEE!

WE'LL LOOK-- FOR THE LUNATIC WHO MADE THAT CALL!

--AS CLARK RETURNS TO THE CAR--

LOIS! WAKE UP!

W-WHAT IS IT? I SEEM TO HAVE FALLEN ASLEEP! THE MASK! WHAT DOES IT MEAN?

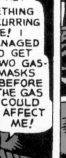

T'S INCREDIBLE, BUT-- THE WHOLE TOWN OF BRENTVILLE IS FAST ASLEEP! SOMETHING UNCANNY IS OCCURRING HERE! I MANAGED TO GET TWO GAS-MASKS BEFORE THE GAS COULD AFFECT ME!

--BUT AS THEY ARE ABOUT TO DRIVE BACK ONTO THE MAIN ROAD, CLARK STOPS AS A CARLOAD OF MEN IN GAS-MASKS SPEED BY!

MEN IN GAS-MASKS! WE'LL TRAIL THEM!

WITHIN THE MYSTERY-CAR ARE FOUR THUGS-- CLARK'S ULTRA-KEEN SENSE OF HEARING ENABLES HIM TO OVERHEAR THEIR REMARKS!

KEEP YOUR EYES PEELED FOR THE GUY KOLB WARNED US ABOUT!

HE WON'T GET AWAY!

AS THE POLICEMEN FROM THE OTHER TOWN ENTER BRENTVILLE--

SAY, LOOK! PEOPLE *DO* SEEM TO BE ASLEEP!

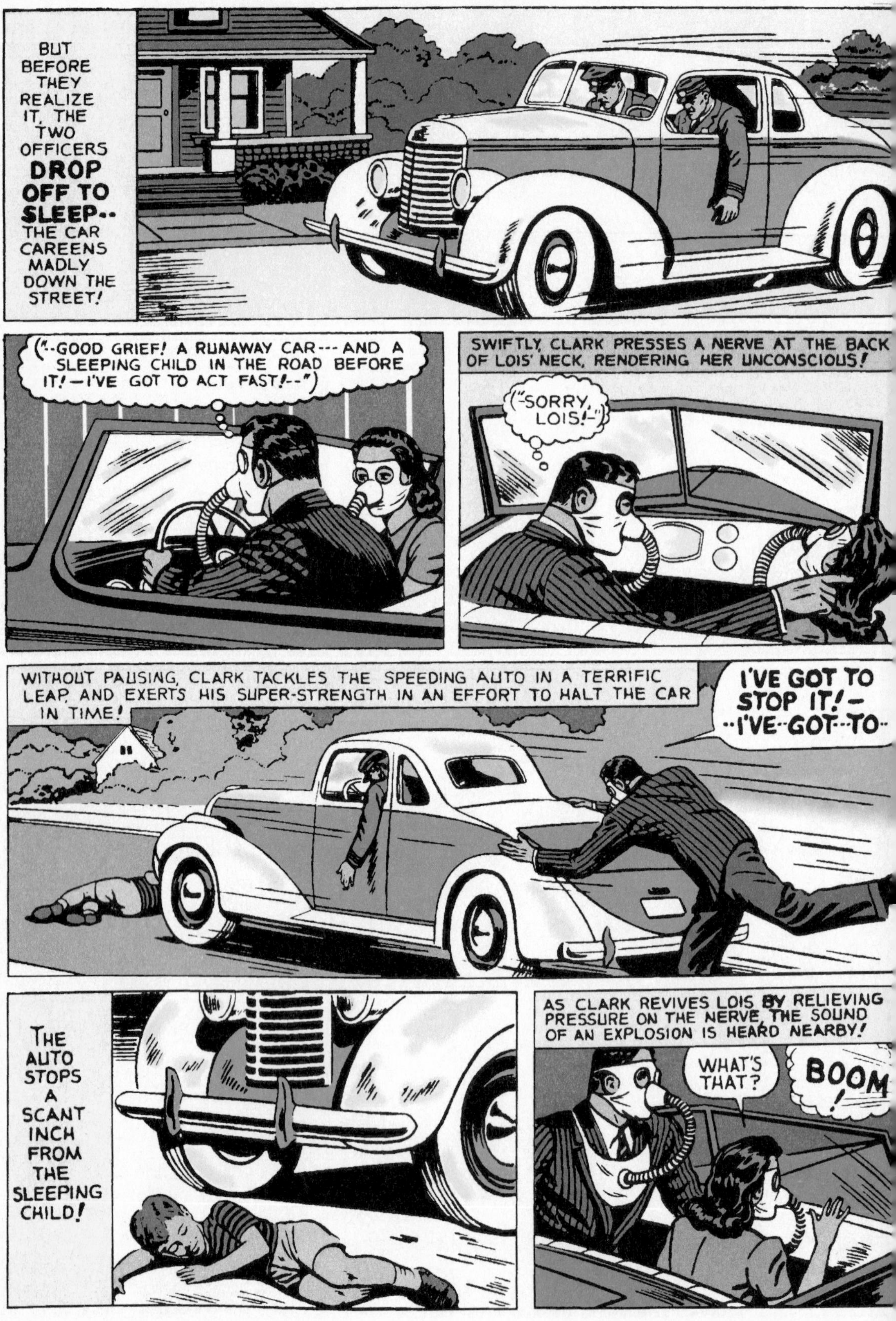
BUT BEFORE THEY REALIZE IT, THE TWO OFFICERS DROP OFF TO SLEEP.. THE CAR CAREENS MADLY DOWN THE STREET!
("-GOOD GRIEF! A RUNAWAY CAR---AND A SLEEPING CHILD IN THE ROAD BEFORE IT!—I'VE GOT TO ACT FAST!--")
SWIFTLY, CLARK PRESSES A NERVE AT THE BACK OF LOIS' NECK, RENDERING HER UNCONSCIOUS!
("SORRY, LOIS!-")
WITHOUT PAUSING, CLARK TACKLES THE SPEEDING AUTO IN A TERRIFIC LEAP, AND EXERTS HIS SUPER-STRENGTH IN AN EFFORT TO HALT THE CAR IN TIME!
I'VE GOT TO STOP IT!— --I'VE--GOT--TO--
THE AUTO STOPS A SCANT INCH FROM THE SLEEPING CHILD!
AS CLARK REVIVES LOIS BY RELIEVING PRESSURE ON THE NERVE, THE SOUND OF AN EXPLOSION IS HEARD NEARBY!
WHAT'S THAT?
BOOM!

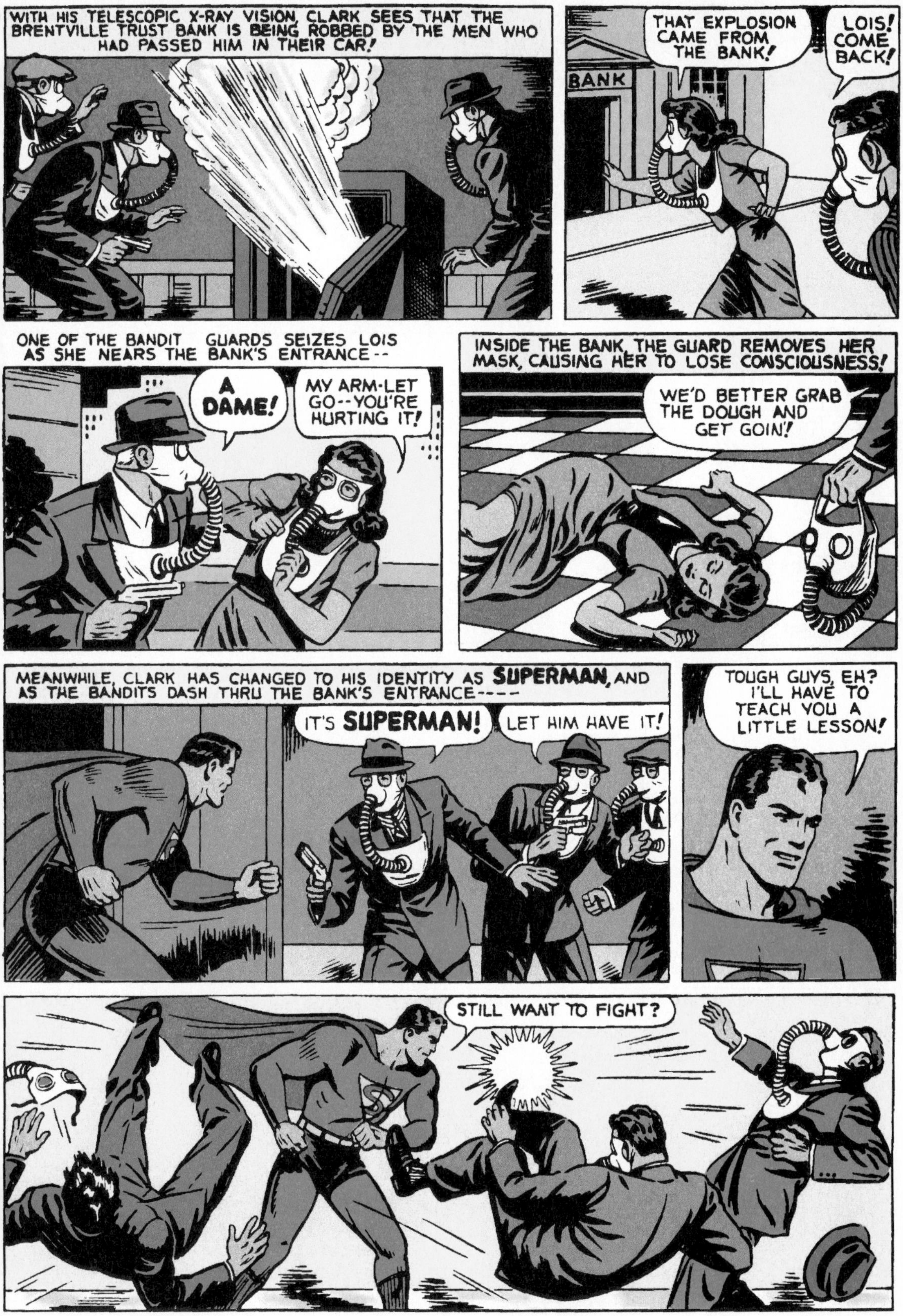
WITH HIS TELESCOPIC X-RAY VISION, CLARK SEES THAT THE BRENTVILLE TRUST BANK IS BEING ROBBED BY THE MEN WHO HAD PASSED HIM IN THEIR CAR!
THAT EXPLOSION CAME FROM THE BANK!
LOIS! COME BACK!
BANK
ONE OF THE BANDIT GUARDS SEIZES LOIS AS SHE NEARS THE BANK'S ENTRANCE--
A DAME!
MY ARM-LET GO--YOU'RE HURTING IT!
INSIDE THE BANK, THE GUARD REMOVES HER MASK, CAUSING HER TO LOSE CONSCIOUSNESS!
WE'D BETTER GRAB THE DOUGH AND GET GOIN'!
MEANWHILE, CLARK HAS CHANGED TO HIS IDENTITY AS SUPERMAN, AND AS THE BANDITS DASH THRU THE BANK'S ENTRANCE----
IT'S SUPERMAN!
LET HIM HAVE IT!
TOUGH GUYS, EH? I'LL HAVE TO TEACH YOU A LITTLE LESSON!
STILL WANT TO FIGHT?

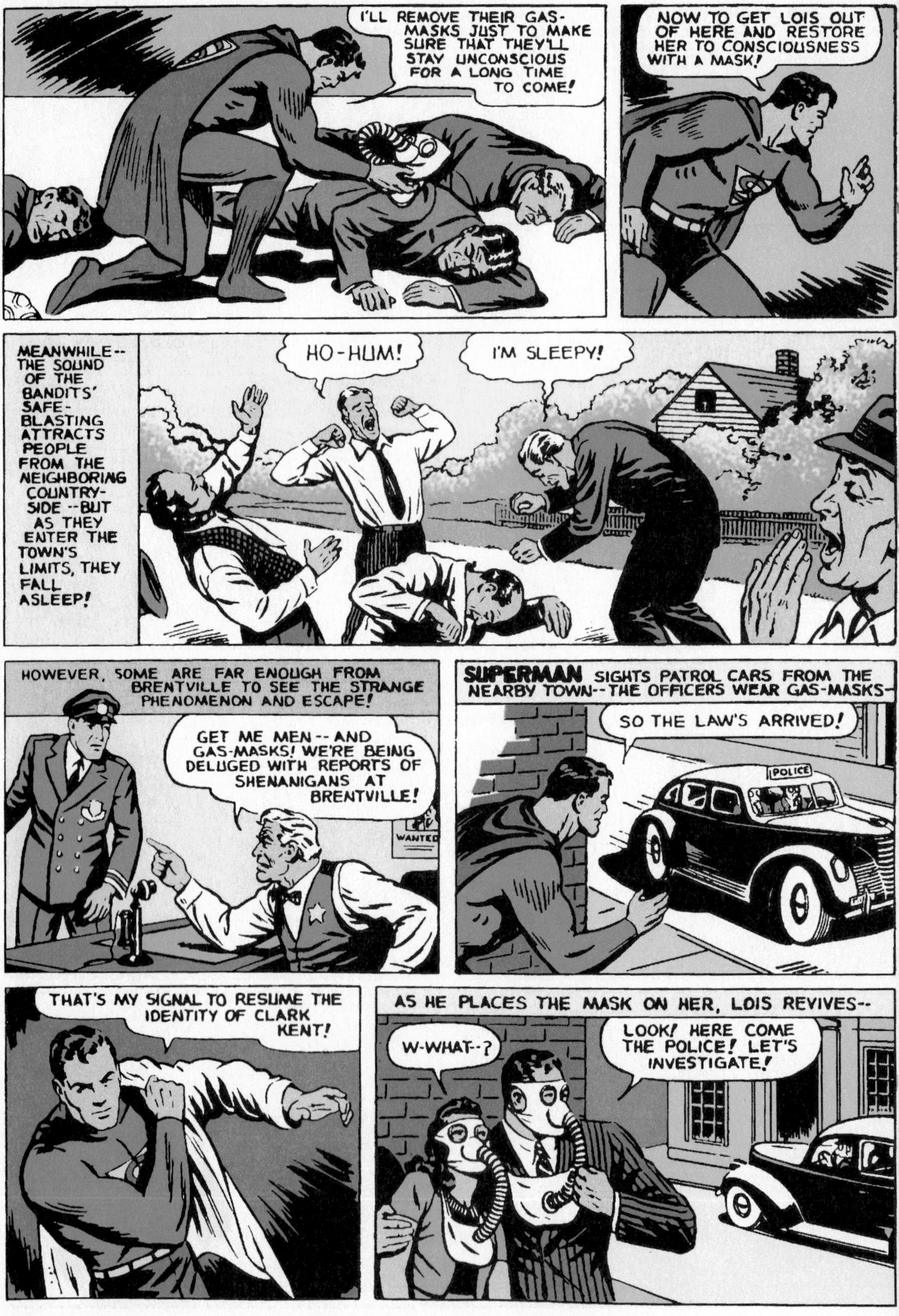
I'LL REMOVE THEIR GAS-MASKS JUST TO MAKE SURE THAT THEY'LL STAY UNCONSCIOUS FOR A LONG TIME TO COME!
NOW TO GET LOIS OUT OF HERE AND RESTORE HER TO CONSCIOUSNESS WITH A MASK!
MEANWHILE -- THE SOUND OF THE BANDITS' SAFE-BLASTING ATTRACTS PEOPLE FROM THE NEIGHBORING COUNTRY-SIDE -- BUT AS THEY ENTER THE TOWN'S LIMITS, THEY FALL ASLEEP!
HO-HUM!
I'M SLEEPY!
HOWEVER, SOME ARE FAR ENOUGH FROM BRENTVILLE TO SEE THE STRANGE PHENOMENON AND ESCAPE!
GET ME MEN -- AND GAS-MASKS! WE'RE BEING DELUGED WITH REPORTS OF SHENANIGANS AT BRENTVILLE!
WANTED
SUPERMAN SIGHTS PATROL CARS FROM THE NEARBY TOWN -- THE OFFICERS WEAR GAS-MASKS --
SO THE LAW'S ARRIVED!
POLICE
THAT'S MY SIGNAL TO RESUME THE IDENTITY OF CLARK KENT!
AS HE PLACES THE MASK ON HER, LOIS REVIVES --
W-WHAT--?
LOOK! HERE COME THE POLICE! LET'S INVESTIGATE!

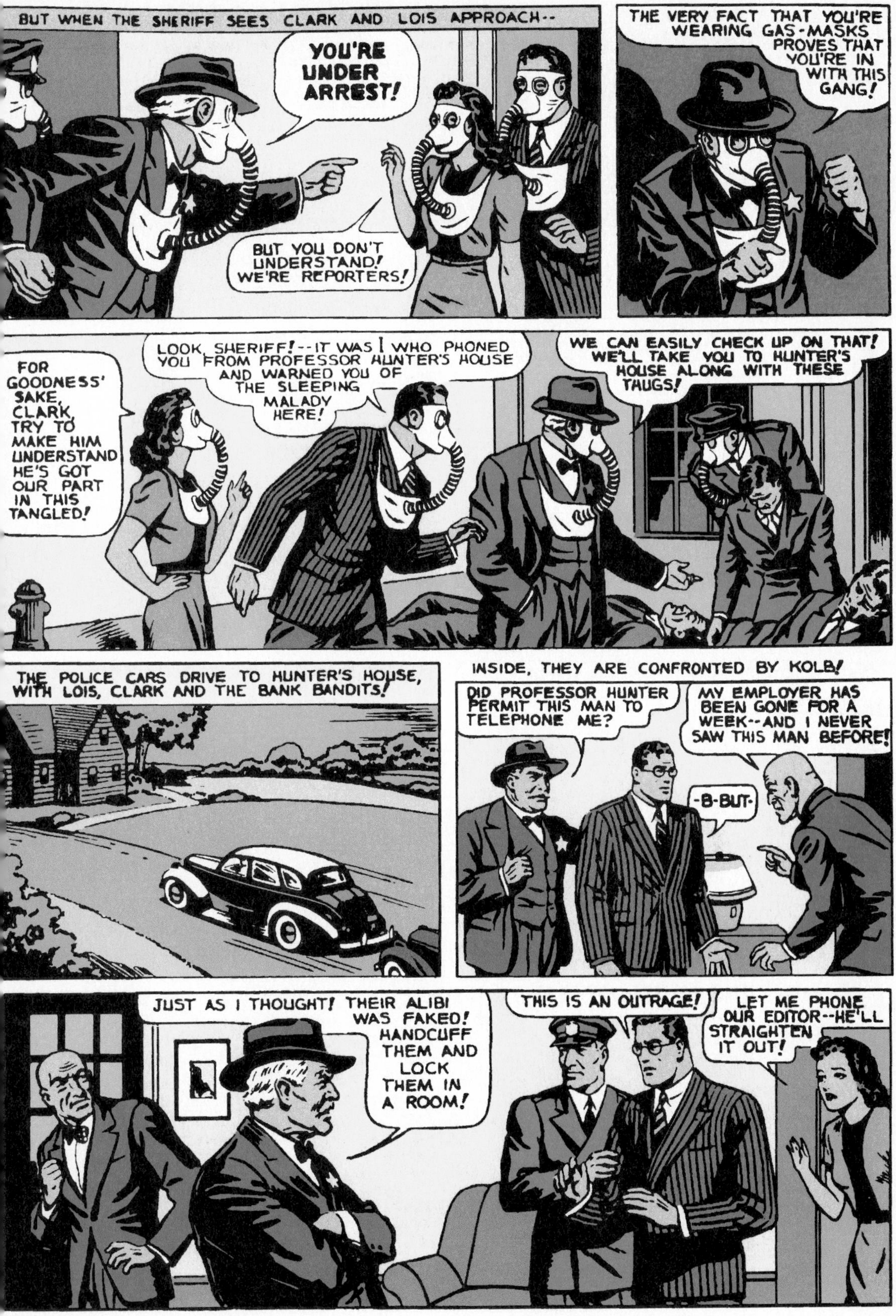
BUT WHEN THE SHERIFF SEES CLARK AND LOIS APPROACH--
YOU'RE UNDER ARREST!
BUT YOU DON'T UNDERSTAND! WE'RE REPORTERS!
THE VERY FACT THAT YOU'RE WEARING GAS-MASKS PROVES THAT YOU'RE IN WITH THIS GANG!
FOR GOODNESS' SAKE, CLARK, TRY TO MAKE HIM UNDERSTAND HE'S GOT OUR PART IN THIS TANGLED!
LOOK, SHERIFF!--IT WAS I WHO PHONED YOU FROM PROFESSOR HUNTER'S HOUSE AND WARNED YOU OF THE SLEEPING MALADY HERE!
WE CAN EASILY CHECK UP ON THAT! WE'LL TAKE YOU TO HUNTER'S HOUSE ALONG WITH THESE THUGS!
THE POLICE CARS DRIVE TO HUNTER'S HOUSE, WITH LOIS, CLARK AND THE BANK BANDITS!
INSIDE, THEY ARE CONFRONTED BY KOLB!
DID PROFESSOR HUNTER PERMIT THIS MAN TO TELEPHONE ME?
MY EMPLOYER HAS BEEN GONE FOR A WEEK--AND I NEVER SAW THIS MAN BEFORE!
-B-BUT-
JUST AS I THOUGHT! THEIR ALIBI WAS FAKED! HANDCUFF THEM AND LOCK THEM IN A ROOM!
THIS IS AN OUTRAGE!
LET ME PHONE OUR EDITOR--HE'LL STRAIGHTEN IT OUT!

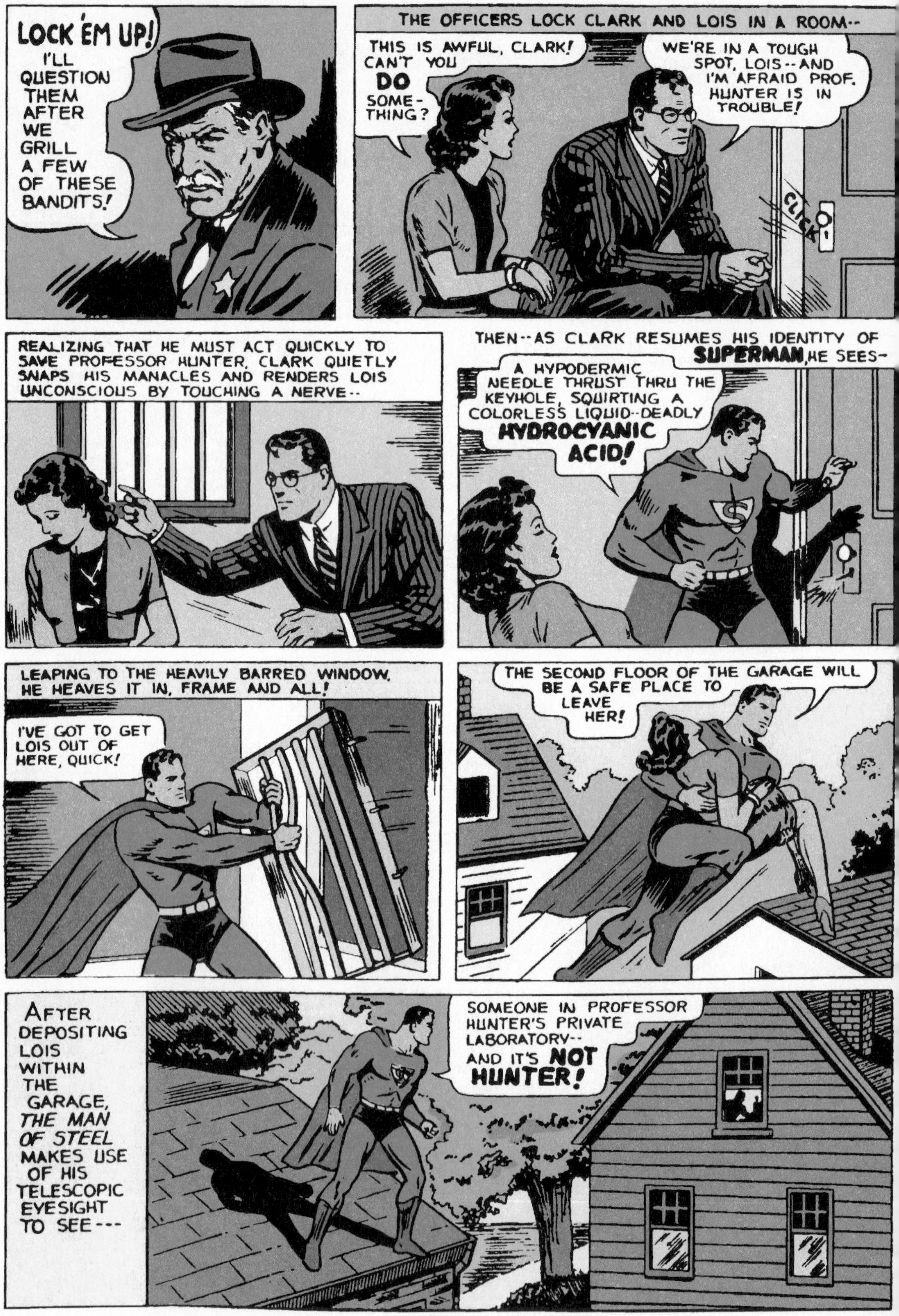
LOCK 'EM UP! I'LL QUESTION THEM AFTER WE GRILL A FEW OF THESE BANDITS!
THE OFFICERS LOCK CLARK AND LOIS IN A ROOM--
THIS IS AWFUL, CLARK! CAN'T YOU DO SOME-THING?
WE'RE IN A TOUGH SPOT, LOIS--AND I'M AFRAID PROF. HUNTER IS IN TROUBLE!
CLICK
REALIZING THAT HE MUST ACT QUICKLY TO SAVE PROFESSOR HUNTER, CLARK QUIETLY SNAPS HIS MANACLES AND RENDERS LOIS UNCONSCIOUS BY TOUCHING A NERVE--
THEN--AS CLARK RESUMES HIS IDENTITY OF SUPERMAN, HE SEES-
A HYPODERMIC NEEDLE THRUST THRU THE KEYHOLE, SQUIRTING A COLORLESS LIQUID--DEADLY HYDROCYANIC ACID!
LEAPING TO THE HEAVILY BARRED WINDOW, HE HEAVES IT IN, FRAME AND ALL!
I'VE GOT TO GET LOIS OUT OF HERE, QUICK!
THE SECOND FLOOR OF THE GARAGE WILL BE A SAFE PLACE TO LEAVE HER!
AFTER DEPOSITING LOIS WITHIN THE GARAGE, THE MAN OF STEEL MAKES USE OF HIS TELESCOPIC EYESIGHT TO SEE---
SOMEONE IN PROFESSOR HUNTER'S PRIVATE LABORATORY--AND IT'S NOT HUNTER!

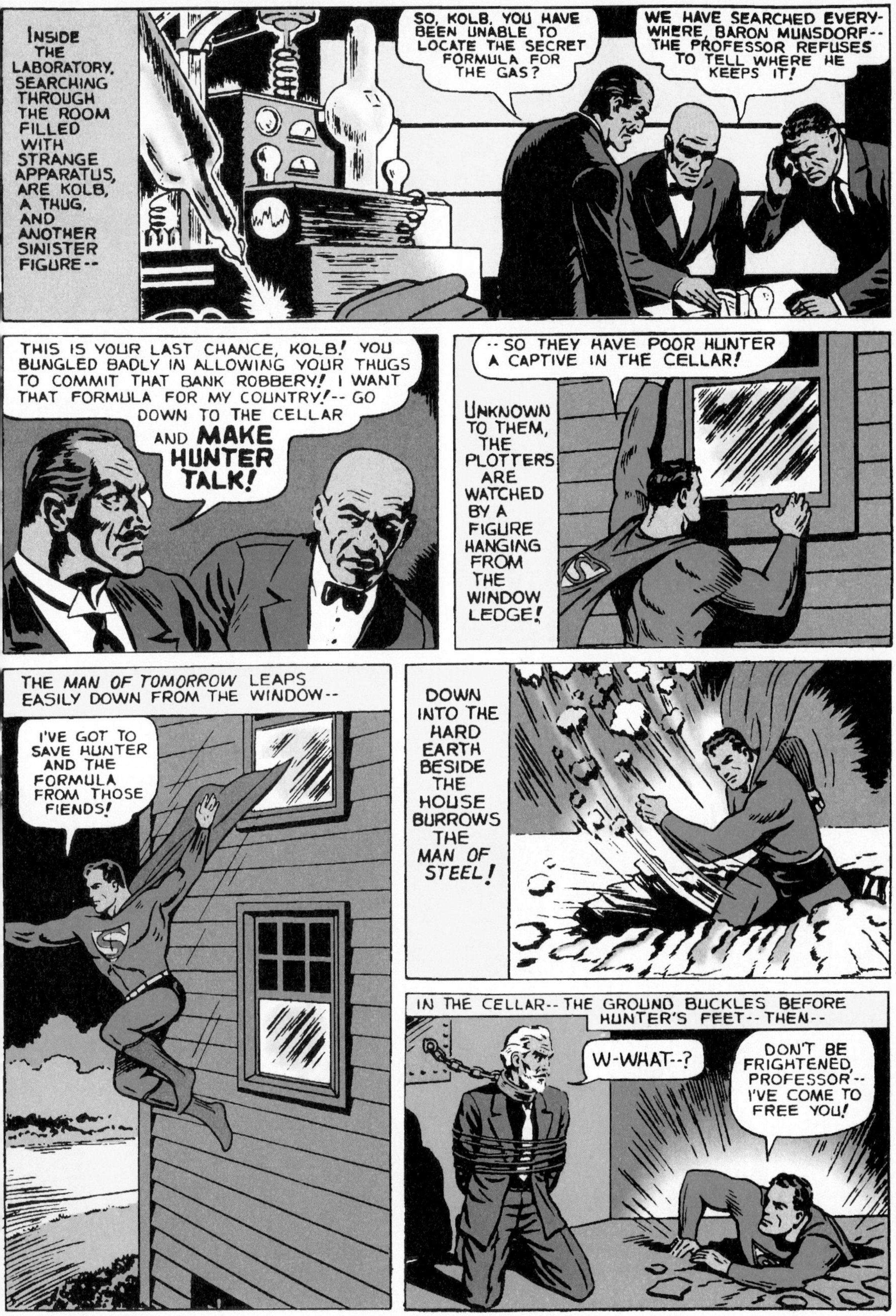
INSIDE THE LABORATORY, SEARCHING THROUGH THE ROOM FILLED WITH STRANGE APPARATUS, ARE KOLB, A THUG, AND ANOTHER SINISTER FIGURE--
SO, KOLB, YOU HAVE BEEN UNABLE TO LOCATE THE SECRET FORMULA FOR THE GAS?
WE HAVE SEARCHED EVERYWHERE, BARON MUNSDORF-- THE PROFESSOR REFUSES TO TELL WHERE HE KEEPS IT!
THIS IS YOUR LAST CHANCE, KOLB! YOU BUNGLED BADLY IN ALLOWING YOUR THUGS TO COMMIT THAT BANK ROBBERY! I WANT THAT FORMULA FOR MY COUNTRY!-- GO DOWN TO THE CELLAR AND MAKE HUNTER TALK!
--SO THEY HAVE POOR HUNTER A CAPTIVE IN THE CELLAR!
UNKNOWN TO THEM, THE PLOTTERS ARE WATCHED BY A FIGURE HANGING FROM THE WINDOW LEDGE!
THE MAN OF TOMORROW LEAPS EASILY DOWN FROM THE WINDOW--
I'VE GOT TO SAVE HUNTER AND THE FORMULA FROM THOSE FIENDS!
DOWN INTO THE HARD EARTH BESIDE THE HOUSE BURROWS THE MAN OF STEEL!
IN THE CELLAR-- THE GROUND BUCKLES BEFORE HUNTER'S FEET-- THEN--
W-WHAT--?
DON'T BE FRIGHTENED, PROFESSOR-- I'VE COME TO FREE YOU!

I HIRED KOLB AS MY ASSISTANT, NOT KNOWING THAT HE WAS THE AGENT OF A SPY RING OUT TO GET THE FORMULA OF MY NEW ANAESTHETIC GAS--

HE'S COMING DOWN NOW TO TRY TO TORTURE YOU INTO TALKING!

YES--BARON MUNSDORF, THE HEAD OF THE RING, WILL STOP AT NOTHING TO GET MY FORMULA-- BUT I TOLD THEM IT WAS FOR THE UNITED STATES-- NO FOREIGN RACKETEER NATION IS GOING TO BENEFIT FROM IT-- THEY COULDN'T FORCE THE SECRET OUT OF ME WITH RED HOT IRONS!

HOWEVER, ONE OF KOLB'S THUGS STOLE A SAMPLE OF THE GAS AND USED IT TO PUT THE PEOPLE OF BRENTVILLE ASLEEP WHILE STAGING A BANK ROBBERY!

THAT CLEARS UP THE MYSTERY-- NOW TO ATTEND TO MUNSDORF AND KOLB!

WHAM! OUT THRU THE SIDE OF THE CELLAR ZOOMS THE MAN OF STEEL, CARRYING HUNTER!

OUT WE GO!

THIS IS MOST AMAZING!

YOU'D BETTER STAY OUTSIDE WHERE YOU'LL BE SAFE, PROFESSOR-- I'M GOING BACK IN TO GET THOSE SPIES!

MUNSDORF IS DESPERATE-- HE MAY HAVE FOUND ONE OF MY NEW DEATH-RAY GUNS!

MEANWHILE, KOLB AND HIS HENCHMAN HAVE DESCENDED INTO THE CELLAR--

WE'VE GOT TO MAKE HIM TALK!

HE'S GONE! HALF THE WALL IS TORN AWAY!

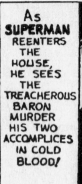

As SUPERMAN REENTERS THE HOUSE, HE SEES THE TREACHEROUS BARON MURDER HIS TWO ACCOMPLICES IN COLD BLOOD!

SO YOU LET HUNTER ESCAPE? DIE, YOU BLASTED BUNGLERS!

YA-A-A-A--

DROP THAT GUN, MUNSDORF!

THIS WILL TEACH YOU NOT TO INTERFERE IN MY AFFAIRS!

SORRY, BARON,--BUT YOUR BULLETS DON'T EVEN ANNOY ME-- **YOU'RE** THE ONE THAT'S GOING TO BE TAUGHT A LESSON!

("I MUST DESTROY THIS MEDDLER-- --PERHAPS ONE OF HUNTER'S NEW DEATH-DEALING WEAPONS--")

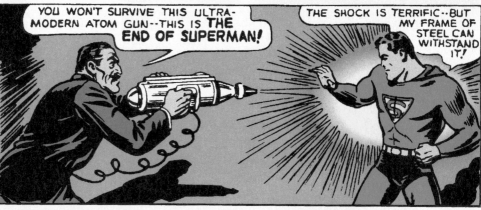

MUNSDORF MAKES A SUDDEN GRAB FOR PROFESSOR HUNTER'S DEADLY SUBATOMIC DEATH-RAY GUN, AND TURNING THE DIAL, UNLEASHES A BOLT OF INCREDIBLE VOLTAGE!

YOU WON'T SURVIVE THIS ULTRA-MODERN ATOM GUN--THIS IS **THE END OF SUPERMAN!**

THE SHOCK IS TERRIFIC--BUT MY FRAME OF STEEL CAN WITHSTAND IT!

-- A WEIRD CRACKLING SOUND, AS THE MIGHTY SUBATOMIC DISCHARGE FLARES UPON THE *MAN OF STEEL*--- LEAVING HIM UNHARMED!

("--PERHAPS I CAN DISTRACT HIS ATTENTION BY SETTING FIRE TO THE NEARBY BUILDINGS!--)

THE GARAGE IN FLAMES! LOIS IS TRAPPED IN THERE!

SMASHING THRU THE WINDOW OF THE FLAMING GARAGE, **SUPERMAN** PLUCKS LOIS AWAY FROM THE ADVANCING FLAMES!

SHE'LL NEVER KNOW HOW CLOSE DEATH WAS!

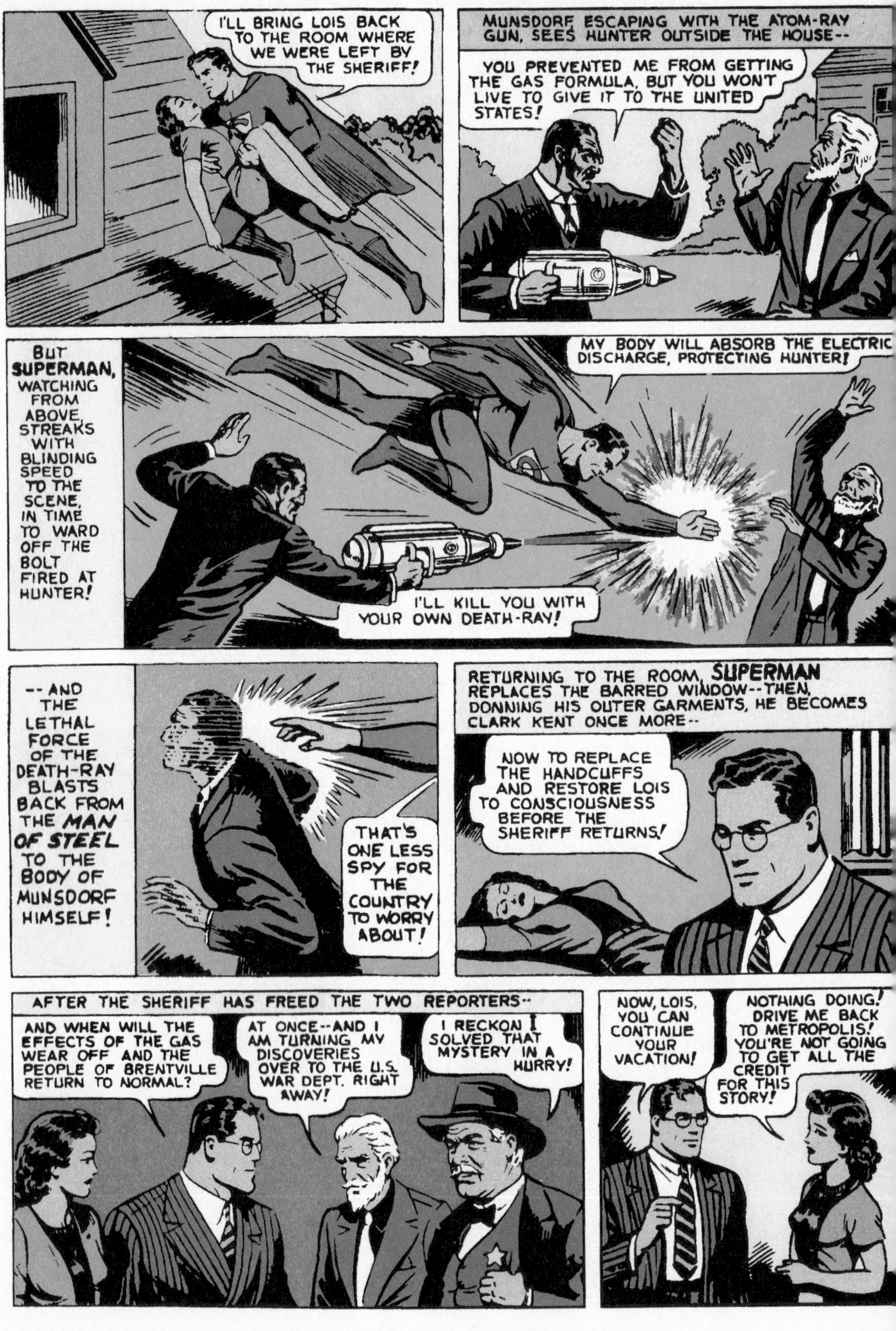
I'LL BRING LOIS BACK TO THE ROOM WHERE WE WERE LEFT BY THE SHERIFF!
MUNSDORF ESCAPING WITH THE ATOM-RAY GUN, SEES HUNTER OUTSIDE THE HOUSE--
YOU PREVENTED ME FROM GETTING THE GAS FORMULA, BUT YOU WON'T LIVE TO GIVE IT TO THE UNITED STATES!
BUT SUPERMAN, WATCHING FROM ABOVE, STREAKS WITH BLINDING SPEED TO THE SCENE, IN TIME TO WARD OFF THE BOLT FIRED AT HUNTER!
MY BODY WILL ABSORB THE ELECTRIC DISCHARGE, PROTECTING HUNTER!
I'LL KILL YOU WITH YOUR OWN DEATH-RAY!
--AND THE LETHAL FORCE OF THE DEATH-RAY BLASTS BACK FROM THE MAN OF STEEL TO THE BODY OF MUNSDORF HIMSELF!
THAT'S ONE LESS SPY FOR THE COUNTRY TO WORRY ABOUT!
RETURNING TO THE ROOM, SUPERMAN REPLACES THE BARRED WINDOW--THEN, DONNING HIS OUTER GARMENTS, HE BECOMES CLARK KENT ONCE MORE--
NOW TO REPLACE THE HANDCUFFS AND RESTORE LOIS TO CONSCIOUSNESS BEFORE THE SHERIFF RETURNS!
AFTER THE SHERIFF HAS FREED THE TWO REPORTERS--
AND WHEN WILL THE EFFECTS OF THE GAS WEAR OFF AND THE PEOPLE OF BRENTVILLE RETURN TO NORMAL?
AT ONCE--AND I AM TURNING MY DISCOVERIES OVER TO THE U.S. WAR DEPT. RIGHT AWAY!
I RECKON I SOLVED THAT MYSTERY IN A HURRY!
NOW, LOIS, YOU CAN CONTINUE YOUR VACATION!
NOTHING DOING! DRIVE ME BACK TO METROPOLIS! YOU'RE NOT GOING TO GET ALL THE CREDIT FOR THIS STORY!

THE GOLDEN AGE

SUPERMAN

VOLUME TWO

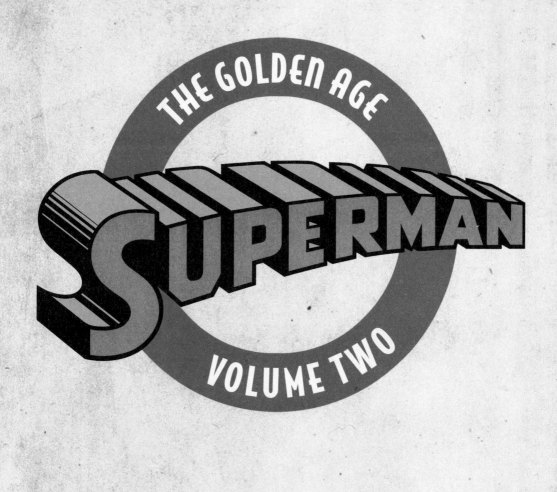

THE GOLDEN AGE

SUPERMAN

VOLUME TWO

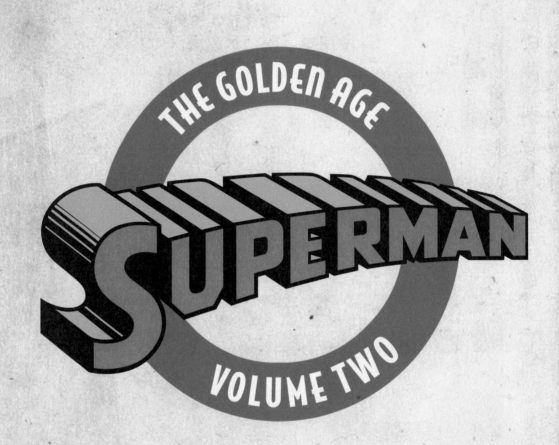